THE COMPLETE WORKS OF WILLIAM SHAKESPEARE

VOLUME III

A NOTE TO THE READER

For each work in this set the editors have provided supplementary material that will help the reader better understand the work as both a play to be performed and a literary work.

In his general Foreword, Joseph Papp brings Shakespeare alive as he has for the audiences at his productions. The reader is also acquainted with the theater in which the plays were originally performed.

More detailed information precedes the text of each work: an Introduction places the work in context and discusses its structure and action, and performance notes give a director's view of the problems presented by the characters and themes of each work as interpreted in previous productions.

Each work is followed by a brief record of what is known about the original publication and performance and an attempt to date them; textual departures from the copy text; and an extensive essay on Shakespeare's sources. There are also suggestions for further reading on each work.

THE COMPLETE WORKS OF WILLIAM SHAKESPEARE

VOLUME III

HENRY IV
PART ONE

HENRY IV
PART TWO

THE MERRY WIVES OF WINDSOR

HAMLET

AS YOU LIKE IT

HENRY V

BANTAM BOOKS
Toronto • New York • London • Sydney • Auckland

THIS EDITION CREATED BY
QUALITY PAPERBACK BOOK CLUB

A Bantam Book / published by arrangement
with Scott, Foresman and Company

PRINTING HISTORY
Scott, Foresman edition published/January 1980
Bantam edition, with newly edited text and substantially
revised, edited, and amplified notes, introductions, and
other materials, published/February 1988
Valuable advice on staging matters has been
provided by Richard Hosley.
Collations checked by Eric Rasmussen.
Additional editorial assistance by Claire McEachern

Cover and display type designed by Charlotte Staub.

Published simultaneously in the United States and Canada.

Bantam Books are published by Bantam Books,
a division of Bantam Doubleday Dell Publishing Group, Inc.
Its trademark, consisting of the words "Bantam Books"
and the portrayal of a rooster, is Registered in U.S. Patent
and Trademark Office and in other countries. Marca Registrada.
Bantam Books, 666 Fifth Avenue, New York, NY 10103.
Printed in the United States of America.

Foreword

It's hard to imagine, but Shakespeare wrote all of his plays with a quill pen, a goose feather whose hard end had to be sharpened frequently. How many times did he scrape the dull end to a point with his knife, dip it into the inkwell, and bring up, dripping wet, those wonderful words and ideas that are known all over the world?

In the age of word processors, typewriters, and ballpoint pens, we have almost forgotten the meaning of the word "blot." Yet when I went to school, in the 1930s, my classmates and I knew all too well what an inkblot from the metal-tipped pens we used would do to a nice clean page of a test paper, and we groaned whenever a splotch fell across the sheet. Most of us finished the school day with ink-stained fingers; those who were less careful also went home with ink-stained shirts, which were almost impossible to get clean.

When I think about how long it took me to write the simplest composition with a metal-tipped pen and ink, I can only marvel at how many plays Shakespeare scratched out with his goose-feather quill pen, year after year. Imagine him walking down one of the narrow cobblestoned streets of London, or perhaps drinking a pint of beer in his local alehouse. Suddenly his mind catches fire with an idea, or a sentence, or a previously elusive phrase. He is burning with impatience to write it down—but because he doesn't have a ballpoint pen or even a pencil in his pocket, he has to keep the idea in his head until he can get to his quill and parchment.

He rushes back to his lodgings on Silver Street, ignoring the vendors hawking brooms, the coaches clattering by, the piteous wails of beggars and prisoners. Bounding up the stairs, he snatches his quill and starts to write furiously, not even bothering to light a candle against the dusk. "To be, or not to be," he scrawls, "that is the—." But the quill point has gone dull, the letters have fattened out illegibly, and in the middle of writing one of the most famous passages in the history of dramatic literature, Shakespeare has to stop to sharpen his pen.

Taking a deep breath, he lights a candle now that it's dark, sits down, and begins again. By the time the candle has burned out and the noisy apprentices of his French Huguenot landlord have quieted down, Shakespeare has finished Act 3 of *Hamlet* with scarcely a blot.

Early the next morning, he hurries through the fog of a London summer morning to the rooms of his colleague Richard Burbage, the actor for whom the role of Hamlet is being written. He finds Burbage asleep and snoring loudly, sprawled across his straw mattress. Not only had the actor performed in *Henry V* the previous afternoon, but he had then gone out carousing all night with some friends who had come to the performance.

Shakespeare shakes his friend awake, until, bleary-eyed, Burbage sits up in his bed. "Dammit, Will," he grumbles, "can't you let an honest man sleep?" But the playwright, his eyes shining and the words tumbling out of his mouth, says, "Shut up and listen—tell me what you think of *this*!"

He begins to read to the still half-asleep Burbage, pacing around the room as he speaks. ". . . Whether 'tis nobler in the mind to suffer the slings and arrows of outrageous fortune—"

Burbage interrupts, suddenly wide awake, "That's excellent, very good, 'the slings and arrows of outrageous fortune,' yes, I think it will work quite well. . . ." He takes the parchment from Shakespeare and murmurs the lines to himself, slowly at first but with growing excitement.

The sun is just coming up, and the words of one of Shakespeare's most famous soliloquies are being uttered for the first time by the first actor ever to bring Hamlet to life. It must have been an exhilarating moment.

Shakespeare wrote most of his plays to be performed live by the actor Richard Burbage and the rest of the Lord Chamberlain's men (later the King's men). Today, however, our first encounter with the plays is usually in the form of the printed word. And there is no question that reading Shakespeare for the first time isn't easy. His plays aren't comic books or magazines or the dime-store detective novels I read when I was young. A lot of his sentences are complex. Many of his words are no longer used in our everyday speech. His profound thoughts are often condensed into poetry, which is not as straightforward as prose.

Yet when you hear the words spoken aloud, a lot of the language may strike you as unexpectedly modern. For Shakespeare's plays, like any dramatic work, weren't really meant to be read; they were meant to be spoken, seen, and performed. It's amazing how lines that are so troublesome in print can flow so naturally and easily when spoken.

I think it was precisely this music that first fascinated me. When I was growing up, Shakespeare was a stranger to me. I had no particular interest in him, for I was from a different cultural tradition. It never occurred to me that his plays might be more than just something to "get through" in school, like science or math or the physical education requirement we had to fulfill. My passions then were movies, radio, and vaudeville—certainly not Elizabethan drama.

I was, however, fascinated by words and language. Because I grew up in a home where Yiddish was spoken, and English was only a second language, I was acutely sensitive to the musical sounds of different languages and had an ear for lilt and cadence and rhythm in the spoken word. And so I loved reciting poems and speeches even as a very young child. In first grade I learned lots of short nature verses—"Who has seen the wind?," one of them began. My first foray into drama was playing the role of Scrooge in Charles Dickens's *A Christmas Carol* when I was eight years old. I liked summoning all the scorn and coldness I possessed and putting them into the words, "Bah, humbug!"

From there I moved on to longer and more famous poems and other works by writers of the 1930s. Then, in junior high school, I made my first acquaintance with Shakespeare through his play *Julius Caesar*. Our teacher, Miss McKay, assigned the class a passage to memorize from the opening scene of the play, the one that begins "Wherefore rejoice? What conquest brings he home?" The passage seemed so wonderfully theatrical and alive to me, and the experience of memorizing and reciting it was so much fun, that I went on to memorize another speech from the play on my own.

I chose Mark Antony's address to the crowd in Act 3,

scene 2, which struck me then as incredibly high drama. Even today, when I speak the words, I feel the same thrill I did that first time. There is the strong and athletic Antony descending from the raised pulpit where he has been speaking, right into the midst of a crowded Roman square. Holding the torn and bloody cloak of the murdered Julius Caesar in his hand, he begins to speak to the people of Rome:

> If you have tears, prepare to shed them now.
> You all do know this mantle. I remember
> The first time ever Caesar put it on;
> 'Twas on a summer's evening in his tent,
> That day he overcame the Nervii.
> Look, in this place ran Cassius' dagger through.
> See what a rent the envious Casca made.
> Through this the well-belovèd Brutus stabbed,
> And as he plucked his cursèd steel away,
> Mark how the blood of Caesar followed it,
> As rushing out of doors to be resolved
> If Brutus so unkindly knocked or no;
> For Brutus, as you know, was Caesar's angel.
> Judge, O you gods, how dearly Caesar loved him!
> This was the most unkindest cut of all . . .

I'm not sure now that I even knew Shakespeare had written a lot of other plays, or that he was considered "timeless," "universal," or "classic"—but I knew a good speech when I heard one, and I found the splendid rhythms of Antony's rhetoric as exciting as anything I'd ever come across.

Fifty years later, I still feel that way. Hearing good actors speak Shakespeare gracefully and naturally is a wonderful experience, unlike any other I know. There's a satisfying fullness to the spoken word that the printed page just can't convey. This is why seeing the plays of Shakespeare performed live in a theater is the best way to appreciate them. If you can't do that, listening to sound recordings or watching film versions of the plays is the next best thing.

But if you do start with the printed word, use the play as a script. Be an actor yourself and say the lines out loud. Don't worry too much at first about words you don't immediately understand. Look them up in the footnotes or a dictionary, but don't spend too much time on this. It is more profitable (and fun) to get the sense of a passage and sing it out. Speak naturally, almost as if you were talking to a friend, but be sure to enunciate the words properly. You'll be surprised at how much you understand simply by speaking the speech "trippingly on the tongue," as Hamlet advises the Players.

You might start, as I once did, with a speech from *Julius Caesar,* in which the tribune (city official) Marullus scolds the commoners for transferring their loyalties so quickly from the defeated and murdered general Pompey to the newly victorious Julius Caesar:

> Wherefore rejoice? What conquest brings he home?
> What tributaries follow him to Rome
> To grace in captive bonds his chariot wheels?
> You blocks, you stones, you worse than senseless
> things!
> O you hard hearts, you cruel men of Rome,
> Knew you not Pompey? Many a time and oft
> Have you climbed up to walls and battlements,
> To towers and windows, yea, to chimney tops,
> Your infants in your arms, and there have sat
> The livelong day, with patient expectation,
> To see great Pompey pass the streets of Rome.

With the exception of one or two words like "wherefore" (which means "why," not "where"), "tributaries" (which means "captives"), and "patient expectation" (which means patient waiting), the meaning and emotions of this speech can be easily understood.

From here you can go on to dialogues or other more challenging scenes. Although you may stumble over unaccustomed phrases or unfamiliar words at first, and even fall flat when you're crossing some particularly rocky passages, pick yourself up and stay with it. Remember that it takes time to feel at home with anything new. Soon you'll come to recognize Shakespeare's unique sense of humor and way of saying things as easily as you recognize a friend's laughter.

And then it will just be a matter of choosing which one of Shakespeare's plays you want to tackle next. As a true fan of his, you'll find that you're constantly learning from his plays. It's a journey of discovery that you can continue for the rest of your life. For no matter how many times you read or see a particular play, there will always be something new there that you won't have noticed before.

Why do so many thousands of people get hooked on Shakespeare and develop a habit that lasts a lifetime? What can he really say to us today, in a world filled with inventions and problems he never could have imagined? And how do you get past his special language and difficult sentence structure to understand him?

The best way to answer these questions is to go see a live production. You might not know much about Shakespeare, or much about the theater, but when you watch actors performing one of his plays on the stage, it will soon become clear to you why people get so excited about a playwright who lived hundreds of years ago.

For the story—what's happening in the play—is the most accessible part of Shakespeare. In *A Midsummer Night's Dream,* for example, you can immediately understand the situation: a girl is chasing a guy who's chasing a girl who's chasing another guy. No wonder *A Midsummer Night's Dream* is one of the most popular of Shakespeare's plays: it's about one of the world's most popular pastimes—falling in love.

But the course of true love never did run smooth, as the young suitor Lysander says. Often in Shakespeare's comedies the girl whom the guy loves doesn't love him back, or she loves him but he loves someone else. In *The Two Gentlemen of Verona,* Julia loves Proteus, Proteus loves Sylvia, and Sylvia loves Valentine, who is Proteus's best friend. In the end, of course, true love prevails, but not without lots of complications along the way.

For in all of his plays—comedies, histories, and tragedies—Shakespeare is showing you human nature. His characters act and react in the most extraordinary ways—and sometimes in the most incomprehensible ways. People are always trying to find motivations for what a character does. They ask, "Why does Iago want to destroy Othello?"

The answer, to me, is very simple—because that's the way Iago is. That's just his nature. Shakespeare doesn't explain his characters; he sets them in motion—and away they go. He doesn't worry about whether they're likable or not. He's interested in interesting people, and his most fascinating characters are those who are unpredictable. If you lean back in your chair early on in one of his plays, thinking you've figured out what Iago or Shylock (in *The Merchant of Venice*) is up to, don't be too sure—because that great judge of human nature, Shakespeare, will surprise you every time.

He is just as wily in the way he structures a play. In *Macbeth,* a comic scene is suddenly introduced just after the bloodiest and most treacherous slaughter imaginable, of a guest and king by his host and subject, when in comes a drunk porter who has to go to the bathroom. Shakespeare is tickling your emotions by bringing a stand-up comic onstage right on the heels of a savage murder.

It has taken me thirty years to understand even some of these things, and so I'm not suggesting that Shakespeare is immediately understandable. I've gotten to know him not through theory but through practice, the practice of the *living* Shakespeare—the playwright of the theater.

Of course the plays are a great achievement of dramatic literature, and they should be studied and analyzed in schools and universities. But you must always remember, when reading all the words *about* the playwright and his plays, that *Shakespeare's* words came first and that in the end there is nothing greater than a single actor on the stage speaking the lines of Shakespeare.

Everything important that I know about Shakespeare comes from the practical business of producing and directing his plays in the theater. The task of classifying, criticizing, and editing Shakespeare's printed works I happily leave to others. For me, his plays really do live on the stage, not on the page. That is what he wrote them for and that is how they are best appreciated.

Although Shakespeare lived and wrote hundreds of years ago, his name rolls off my tongue as if he were my brother. As a producer and director, I feel that there is a professional relationship between us that spans the centuries. As a human being, I feel that Shakespeare has enriched my understanding of life immeasurably. I hope you'll let him do the same for you.

Joseph Papp

Joseph Papp gratefully acknowledges the help of Elizabeth Kirkland in preparing this Foreword.

The Playhouse

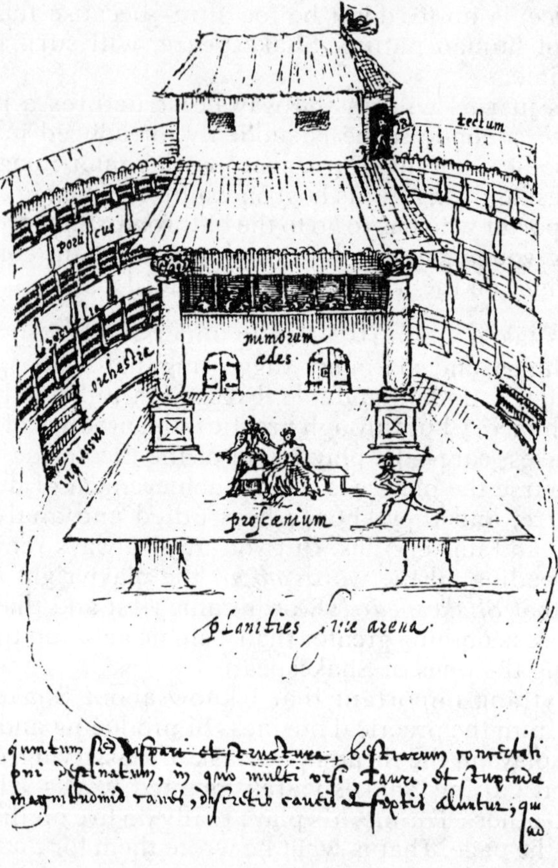

This early copy of a drawing by Johannes de Witt of the Swan Theatre in London (c. 1596), made by his friend Arend van Buchell, is the only surviving contemporary sketch of the interior of a public theater in the 1590s.

From other contemporary evidence, including the stage directions and dialogue of Elizabethan plays, we can surmise that the various public theaters where Shakespeare's plays were produced (the Theatre, the Curtain, the Globe) resembled the Swan in many important particulars, though there must have been some variations as well. The public playhouses were essentially round, or polygonal, and open to the sky, forming an acting arena approximately 70 feet in diameter; they did not have a large curtain with which to open and close a scene, such as we see today in opera and some traditional theater. A platform measuring approximately 43 feet across and 27 feet deep, referred to in the de Witt drawing as the *proscaenium*, projected into the yard, *planities sive arena*. The roof, *tectum*, above the stage and supported by two pillars, could contain machinery for ascents and descents, as were required in several of Shakespeare's late plays. Above this roof was a hut, shown in the drawing with a flag flying atop it and a trumpeter at its door announcing the performance of a play. The underside of the stage roof, called the heavens, was usually richly decorated with symbolic figures of the sun, the moon, and the constellations. The platform stage stood at a height of 5½ feet or so above the yard, providing room under the stage for underworldly effects. A trapdoor, which is not visible in this drawing, gave access to the space below.

The structure at the back of the platform (labeled *mimorum aedes*), known as the tiring-house because it was the actors' attiring (dressing) space, featured at least two doors, as shown here. Some theaters seem to have also had a discovery space, or curtained recessed alcove, perhaps between the two doors—in which Falstaff could have hidden from the sheriff (*1 Henry IV*, 2.4) or Polonius could have eavesdropped on Hamlet and his mother (*Hamlet*, 3.4). This discovery space probably gave the actors a means of access to and from the tiring-house. Curtains may also have been hung in front of the stage doors on occasion. The de Witt drawing shows a gallery above the doors that extends across the back and evidently contains spectators. On occasions when action "above" demanded the use of this space, as when Juliet appears at her "window" (*Romeo and Juliet*, 2.2 and 3.5), the gallery seems to have been used by the actors, but large scenes there were impractical.

The three-tiered auditorium is perhaps best described by Thomas Platter, a visitor to London in 1599 who saw on that occasion Shakespeare's *Julius Caesar* performed at the Globe:

> The playhouses are so constructed that they play on a raised platform, so that everyone has a good view. There are different galleries and places [*orchestra, sedilia, porticus*], however, where the seating is better and more comfortable and therefore more expensive. For whoever cares to stand below only pays one English penny, but if he wishes to sit, he enters by another door [*ingressus*] and pays another penny, while if he desires to sit in the most comfortable seats, which are cushioned, where he not only sees everything well but can also be seen, then he pays yet another English penny at another door. And during the performance food and drink are carried round the audience, so that for what one cares to pay one may also have refreshment.

Scenery was not used, though the theater building itself was handsome enough to invoke a feeling of order and hierarchy that lent itself to the splendor and pageantry onstage. Portable properties, such as thrones, stools, tables, and beds, could be carried or thrust on as needed. In the scene pictured here by de Witt, a lady on a bench, attended perhaps by her waiting-gentlewoman, receives the address of a male figure. If Shakespeare had written *Twelfth Night* by 1596 for performance at the Swan, we could imagine Malvolio appearing like this as he bows before the Countess Olivia and her gentlewoman, Maria.

Photo © George Joseph

From the 1968 New York Shakespeare Festival production of *Henry IV, Part One*, with Stacy Keach as Sir John Falstaff, directed by Gerald Freedman at the Delacorte Theater in Central Park.

HENRY IV
—PART ONE—

HENRY IV, PART ONE

Introductory Material
Foreword by Joseph Papp
Introduction
Henry IV, Part One
in Performance

THE PLAY

Supplementary Material
Date and Text
Textual Notes
Shakespeare's Sources
Further Reading

Foreword

Henry IV, Part One is a continuation of *Richard II,* and it was interesting for me to direct both in one season in 1987. If the main focus in *Richard* was the relationship between Bolingbroke and the King, *1 Henry IV* revolves around three central characters—Falstaff, Prince Hal, and Hotspur. This trio determines the tone of the entire play, and it's important to make sure that the three harmonize and complement each other as they should. The casting of the trio can be problematic, because it's not just a question of getting any three actors, but three actors who "fit" together. It's a triangle full of possibilities for both directors and actors.

Of the three, Falstaff rules—or misrules—the play, for one of the same reasons that Richard II rules his play, his command of language. This unregenerate rogue blusters his way through the play, getting himself out of every predicament with his shrewdness and wit. Unlike the Falstaff of *The Merry Wives of Windsor,* who is a victim of others' shrewdness, here Falstaff indisputably reigns in the Eastcheap setting of *1 Henry IV;* no matter what tricks are played on him, he manages to rise above them. Gradually, as the *Henry IV* saga unfolds in *Part Two* he'll become less and less capable of doing so, but for the duration of this play, he is irrepressible.

JOSEPH PAPP

JOSEPH PAPP GRATEFULLY ACKNOWLEDGES THE HELP OF ELIZABETH KIRKLAND IN PREPARING THIS FOREWORD.

Introduction

The opening of *1 Henry IV* is taut and grave in tone. England is "shaken" and "wan with care." The troubles of *Richard II,* to which this play (c. 1596–1597) is a close sequel, have not been left behind. However much King Henry would prefer to unite his countrymen against a common foreign enemy in a crusade to the holy lands, he is prevented from doing so by continuing civil war. The impassioned rhetoric of his opening speech proclaiming a new era of peace can only end in anticlimax, for the actual purpose of this meeting in council is to receive and assess reports of military action against the throne.

Henry's current troubles are in the far reaches of his kingdom: Scots in the north, Welsh in the west. Fighting for Henry on these two fronts are the nobles of the Percy family who helped him to power: Harry Percy (Hotspur), his father (Henry Percy) the Earl of Northumberland, his uncle the Earl of Worcester, and his brother-in-law Edmund Mortimer the Earl of March. Apparently they have fought bravely. Yet we soon sense that all is not well between the new king and those who rebelled with him against Richard II. A quarrel breaks out because Hotspur refuses to deliver to Henry some prisoners as required by feudal obedience. The matter of the ransom money is only a technicality; what is really at issue? In part, it is Henry's insistence on being obeyed on principle. Admiring Hotspur inordinately, the King feels he must discipline affectionately this fine young warrior as a father would discipline his son. Even more deeply, however, the issue of the prisoners galls Henry because of the proviso that he ransom Mortimer, captured by the Welsh. Henry has not forgotten that Mortimer is his chief rival for the English crown, being descended from the Duke of Clarence (elder brother to Henry's father, Gaunt), and having been proclaimed by Richard heir to the throne. Mortimer is the last person Henry would wish ransomed. Moreover, the King suspects Mortimer of having fought with something less than total zeal against the Welsh Glendower. News of Mortimer's marriage to Glendower's daughter confirms the King's worst fears.

Henry knows Northumberland and Worcester to be expert in treasonous plotting, since they conspired with him to overthrow Richard. Now, Henry believes, these Percys are extending their alliance by a series of calculated marriages in order to seize power once again. This time their claimant is Mortimer.

Shakespeare's sympathies are many-sided. The Percy clan is in fact organizing against Henry, but not without cause. As they see it, the man they helped to the throne has done little for them since. His manner of disciplining them sounds too much like hostility and ingratitude. Other counselors attend the King constantly, while Worcester is banished from court. In such an atmosphere of distrust, suspicion breeds still more suspicion. The situation has polarized, surely more than either party originally intended.

Hotspur is the most attractive of the rebels, to us as well as to King Henry. He is outspoken, courageous, witty, domineering in conversation. Above all, he is a disciple of manliness, loyalty, chivalry, bravery in battle—the attributes of an upstanding and somewhat old-fashioned sense of honor. Yet a fatal defect dwells among these attractive qualities. Hotspur is impatient, proud, unwilling to tolerate a rival—be it Glendower or Prince Hal (Henry, Prince of Wales). In his first speech, purporting to explain his refusal to deliver the prisoners, he brilliantly satirizes an effete courtier who had come to him from King Henry in the midst of a battle. The satire betrays many harsh qualities in Hotspur: the self-indulgent wrath that returns fully to him even in recollection of the encounter, the pride in his own stoical indifference to suffering, and especially the obsessive nature (revealed in the repetitive pattern of the rhetoric) of his contempt for courtiers generally. Surely his scorn for stay-at-home politicians is directed in part at King Henry himself. To Hotspur all courtiers are effeminate, perfume-wearing, affected in mannerism and speech, scarcely masculine. This preoccupation of Hotspur's makes him extraordinarily prone to one-sided judgments. Like most excessive devotees of chivalry, he divides mankind into two categories: those who are gentlemen, like himself, and those who are beneath contempt. The "vile politician" Bolingbroke and his son the "sword-and-buckler Prince of Wales" (1.3.240, 229) fall into the latter category.

Prone as he is to such an overly simple view of political behavior, Hotspur can see no good in the King's cause and no evil in his own. He is a poor listener because of his obsession and yet an easy prey for his uncle and father, who require his leadership for their cause. They need only implant the suggestion that King Henry is acting from a political motive in his refusal to ransom Mortimer, and Hotspur is ready to leap incautiously to the defense of their cause. The great irony is that Hotspur fails to see political motives in the machinations of his own relatives. While he fights for bright honor, they maneuver cautiously for position and prove uncertain allies when the hour of battle approaches. Most crucially, they betray Hotspur in the prebattle negotiations, at which he is not present. As Worcester explains to Vernon during their return to rebel headquarters (5.2.3–25), they cannot let Hotspur know of the King's offer to settle matters by a general pardon. Although, as they realize, the King could pardon Hotspur's youth, there can be no turning back for themselves. Thus the honor for which Hotspur fights is at bottom a lie, and the mutual esteem that might have grown between him and a much-reformed Prince of Wales is thwarted by the polarization of attitudes in the two camps. Hotspur's brand of honor is the victim of its own excess, and lends some credence to Falstaff's wry conclusion that honor "is a mere scutcheon" (5.1.139–140).

The contrasting of Falstaff and Hotspur on the theme of honor suggests that they are dramatic foils for each other, representing extremes between which Prince Hal must choose. Shakespeare uses this foil device structurally and consciously; for example, he has considerably reduced the age of the Hotspur he found in Raphael Holinshed's *Chronicles* (1578) in order to accentuate the similarity between Hotspur and Hal. Conversely, to emphasize the contrast between Falstaff and Hotspur, Shakespeare envisages Falstaff as old (nearly sixty, by his own admission), fat, humorous, and without honor. Falstaff's vices are Hotspur's virtues, and the reverse. Whereas Hotspur offers to Hal a model of chivalric striving and attention to duty, Falstaff is a highwayman and liar. On the other hand, Hotspur is a fanatic, unbending and self-absorbed even in the company of his sprightly wife, Kate, irritated by music and poetry; Falstaff is the epitome of merriment and joie de vivre. We excuse much in him because he lusts after life with such an appetite, and ingratiates himself to others by inviting them to laugh at his expense.

Despite the nearly irresistible attractiveness of Falstaff as a jolly companion and butt of humorous joking, his conversations with Prince Hal are, from their first moments together, involved with the issue of Hal's ultimate rejection of Falstaff. The witty raillery of their first scene (1.2) seems designed to provide diverting entertainment for the Prince and for us, and yet beneath the gay surface we perceive that Hal and Falstaff are talking about the hanging of thieves and the question of whether or not Hal should give in to sinful temptation. Can the relationship of Hal and Falstaff continue unchanged into the reign of Henry V? Will there be gallows standing and justice for highwaymen? Will "Monsieur Remorse," as Poins calls Falstaff, ever sincerely repent? Will the Prince, for that matter? To allay our fears, Hal soliloquizes at scene's end, vowing his determination to use these scapegrace companions as mere foils for his triumphal reformation at the appropriate time. But this explanation raises an opposite danger in our sympathies: Is he callously using his companions merely to create a self-serving myth of Prince Hal, the Politician with the Common Touch? Is Francis the drawer no more to Hal than a butt for his raillery? Since the rejection of Falstaff is, by Hal's own words, already determined, can we credit him with a serious friendship? Where do Shakespeare's sympathies lie, with the need for political order or with the hedonistic spirit of youth? Perhaps he recognizes the validity of both, and accordingly shows us a prince who is genuinely fond of Falstaff's exuberant company, but who also knows that he is a king's son and must sooner or later accept the consequences of that unsought role. Falstaff's gift to him is youthful irresponsibility, which must be cherished (by all of us) even though it cannot last.

In the Gad's Hill robbery, Falstaff reveals that his "cowardice" differs from the natural craven fear of Bardolph and Peto. He fights no longer than he sees "reason," that is, not against such unfair odds as two athletic young men in the dark (or later, at Shrewsbury, against the burly Scots giant, the Douglas). A man could get killed that way. Falstaff's cowardice, then, is philosophic, seen by himself in a humorous perspective. The same is true of his lying about the robbery. However much Hal exults in exposing Falstaff as a fraud, we cannot dismiss the possibility that Falstaff may see through the Prince's scheme and then feed Hal the expectedly outlandish lie (two men in buckram become eleven men) as a means of begging for affection. Falstaff's only way of pleading his cause is to tickle the Prince's fancy, in his role as a kind of court fool. What Falstaff most wants is to be loved and retained for what he is; and that, poignantly enough, is the one thing the mature Henry V cannot grant.

Throughout *1 Henry IV,* Shakespeare seems interested in the relationships between fathers and sons. These relationships help structure the comparisons and contrasts among foil characters. Falstaff is a foil not only for Hotspur, but also for Henry IV; that is, despite all his insistence on youthful irresponsibility, Falstaff acts as a kind of parental figure to Hal. In the tavern scene (2.4), Falstaff and Hal take turns playing king and crown prince, and in both roles Falstaff wittily argues his case as companion and guide to the heir to the throne. Is it better to be old and merry, fat and loved, or to be hated like Pharaoh's lean kine? Falstaff argues against the gravity of council meetings with the same amused fervor he later directs at the grinning honor of a dead hero. Hal, in his turn as king, questions the propriety of a "devil" haunting the crown prince "in the likeness of an old fat man," a "reverend Vice," a "gray Iniquity," a "father ruffian" (2.4.442–449). For all the good humor in this exchange, both men are asking whether Falstaff or King Henry serves Hal as the better model. Hal anticipates some of the very arguments his father will use against him next day at court, and indeed the insistent presence of that sober adult world makes itself felt even in the tavern. To Falstaff's moving litany, urging that Hal "banish not him thy Harry's company—banish plump Jack, and banish all the world," the Prince can only reply, "I do, I will" (ll. 472–476).

Hotspur too is regarded as a son by more than one father. King Henry only half-jokingly wishes it could be proved that some night-tripping fairy had exchanged his Harry in the cradle for Harry Percy (1.1.85–89). Paradoxically, the King admires Hotspur all the more for standing up to him, just as another imperious father figure, Owen Glendower, bestows grudging but real admiration on Hotspur for his outspokenness (3.1.1–185). Hotspur's rebellious ways are cherished because they seem to promise manliness and fame; Hal's rebellious ways are feared and despised because they seem to reject the values of duty and leadership on which King Henry bases his self-respect. In these terms, the play must resolve Hal's coming of age, his acceptance of his role as true son of the King and his proving his worth to the King. Hal must find his adult self, a self that differs greatly from that of King Henry, but must do so in a way that preserves the integrity of their relationship and the real debt he owes his father.

These conflicts reach their climax and resolution at the field of Shrewsbury in Act 5. Hal's worth must be proven at Hotspur's expense. The rivalry between the two has been intense throughout the play, as seen for example in Hal's brilliant mimicking of Hotspur's devotion to bloodshed (2.4.101–108). Aware that his tarnished reputation puts him at a disadvantage, Hal speaks nobly of his rival and impresses even the adversary camp with his regal bearing (5.1.83–100, 5.2.51–68). He rescues his father in the battle, thereby proving to King Henry that his son does not wish to supplant him as he had feared. After the battle, Hal frees his Scottish adversary the Douglas in a display of princely magnificence, doing so with a more generous motive than Hotspur had displayed in his earlier release of the Douglas as his prisoner (1.3.259–262). Meantime, Hal has put considerable distance between himself and Falstaff, though sensitive still to the warmth of old memories. When he sees Hotspur and Falstaff on the ground together, both seemingly dead, Hal views as in a tableau the contrasting models between which he has shaped his own identity. Yet Falstaff is not dead. He rises to mutilate Hotspur's body and to claim the honor due Hal for Hotspur's death. For all Falstaff's witty commentary at the expense of honor, his own opposite course is unsuited to a time of war or to Hal's new public role. Falstaff's abuse of military conscription, his carrying a bottle of sack in place of a pistol, show him at his wittiest still, but in a world that may not tolerate such pranks. The merry games are out of place, childish. With characteristic generosity and imprudence, Hal gives the credit for Hotspur's death to Falstaff who claims it so cravenly. Even so, the magic of their association has vanished. The time of manhood is upon Hal.

[illegible]

Henry IV, Part One in Performance

1 Henry IV enjoyed an instant success in the late 1590s, owing especially to the appeal of Falstaff, and has remained popular onstage ever since. Though certainly it was acted in the public theater, the first recorded performance is one in 1600 for the Flemish Ambassador, Louis Verreyken, at Essex House, and it appeared several more times at court before the Interregnum of the mid-seventeenth century when the theaters were closed. Its early popularity is confirmed by Leonard Digges's assertion in his prefatory verse for the 1640 edition of Shakespeare's *Poems:* "let but Falstaff come, / Hal, Poins, the rest, you scarce shall have a room, / All is so pestered."

A shortened version or "droll" called *The Bouncing Knight, or The Robbers Robbed* was shown surreptitiously during the Interregnum, and the play itself was soon revived on the Restoration stage. The diarist Samuel Pepys saw at least parts of *1 Henry IV* on four occasions during the 1660s. Thomas Betterton as Falstaff took London by storm in the 1699–1700 season, after earlier successes with the part of Hotspur, which he played, according to Colley Cibber, with "fierce and flashing fire." James Quin played Hotspur at the theater in Lincoln's Inn Fields, London, in 1718 and then, like Betterton, shifted to the role of Falstaff for his greatest triumphs in the play in 1721 and after. John Henderson, Thomas Ryder, and John Fawcett, Jr., were among the many popular Falstaffs of the eighteenth century. At the Haymarket Theatre in 1786, Lydia Webb chose to play the fat knight for her benefit performance, but the experiment did not meet with critical approval: "every joke was delivered with a sort of sententious dignity," the *Morning Chronicle* reported, "that destroyed its natural impression."

In the early nineteenth century, the roles of Falstaff and Hotspur continued to dominate productions of the play and attract the leading actors of the day, often in very broad interpretation. George Frederick Cooke, in 1802 at the Theatre Royal, Covent Garden, acted Falstaff "like an old lurching sharper," according to the editor of the *London Sun*. John Philip Kemble's heavyset brother, Stephen, was the most acclaimed Falstaff of the era, acting the role between 1802 and 1820, usually in tandem with his famous sibling as Hotspur, though in 1819 and 1820 he played opposite Edmund Kean. William Charles Macready played Hotspur to appreciative audiences between 1815 and 1847. When Queen Victoria requested a revival two years after Macready's last performance in the role, he politely declined, claiming that his age made him unfit for the part. For sheer spectacle, the most eye-catching production of the early nineteenth century was Charles Kemble's monumental *1 Henry IV* in 1824 at Covent Garden. With scrupulous and perhaps overly realistic attention to the accuracy of the historical reconstruction (Henry IV, for example, was dressed according to an effigy of that monarch in Canterbury Cathedral), Kemble's elaborate production gained considerable attention. Kemble's Falstaff disappointed or surprised some spectators who did not think his usual graceful and courtly style well suited to an old, fat rogue who must "lard the lean earth" as he walks along. Samuel Phelps was perhaps an equally unlikely Falstaff in his production at the Sadler's Wells Theatre in 1846 (at least one critic thought he could use "a little more stuffing"), though he managed to succeed in the role by emphasizing Falstaff's shrewdness and caustic wit.

Charles Kemble and Phelps were among the very few exceptions to the prevailing tendency in the eighteenth and nineteenth centuries to portray Falstaff through slapstick and even coarse stage business, making of him a buffoon and comic scapegoat. Productions often exploited his ungainly corpulence. The American actor James Henry Hackett, appearing often as Falstaff in a long career from 1832 to 1870, interpreted the old, fat sinner as an epitome of vanity and vice. Once, when Hackett appeared onstage in Edinburgh with his famous artificially inflated belly, he was attacked by a pin-wielding fellow actor wishing to deflate the egocentric star. During the Gad's Hill robbery (2.2), the Falstaff of this era often incongruously pranced about in wild excitement as he defied his victims. Sitting down to divide the spoils with his comrades, and being set upon by Hal and Poins, Falstaff inevitably found he was unable to get up, and so he had to crawl to safety at considerable cost to his dignity. In the long tavern scene (2.4) he was apt to throw the dregs of his sack in Francis's face and play the business of being caught out in a lie with the resourcefulness of a practiced liar. At Shrewsbury Field, before the battle (5.1), Falstaff was sometimes directed to sit on a drum next to Henry IV and then tumble off when the King suddenly got up. When Falstaff fell down in battle to avoid the might of the Douglas (5.4), he made no attempt to convince the spectators that he was really dead in order that he might surprise them by coming again to life; instead, he dodged his head about, winked, started to get up only to duck down nervously at the sound of approaching military activity, and generally played the situation for broad laughs. Falstaff's difficulty in getting the dead Hotspur on his back became so great at times that his comic crew, Bardolph, Peto, and the rest, had to help lug off the corpse. Not all these routines were included in any single performance, but cumulatively they do indicate the extent to which Falstaff was played as a comic butt, a coward, and a liar.

The demeaning nature of this comedy helps explain why Maurice Morgann, in his *Essay on the Dramatic Character of Sir John Falstaff* (1777), felt it necessary to defend Falstaff as neither a liar nor a coward, but rather a vital, fascinating, and even courageous man. Morgann's sentimental apology was part of a literary rejection of the stage for the world of books, where Falstaff's wit could be savored as that of a companion and witty table guest, one whose seemingly craven behavior is only part of a self-aware repertory of antics designed to humor the Prince. Other devotees of Shakespeare during the Romantic period joined Morgann in admiring Falstaff's joie de vivre while disapproving of Prince Henry's calculated prudence and political pragmatism. Falstaff onstage in the early nineteenth century, contrastingly, was a corrupter of Hal's innocence. Seldom have the theater and literary worlds been so far apart.

Beginning in the early twentieth century, the modern theater has moved away from both the sentimental and the moralistic responses to character expressed in nineteenth-century criticism and stagecraft, finding instead, with the assistance of a full playing text and continuous action made possible by the abandonment of Victorian scenic elaboration, a balance between Falstaff's wit and the threat he poses to civil order. Padded with extensive wickerwork, Herbert Beerbohm Tree played an immense, jovial Falstaff in his productions in 1896 at the Haymarket Theatre and in 1914 at His Majesty's Theatre. The text was essentially unaltered, in a major departure from Tree's usual freewheeling practice. Matheson Lang stammered in his playing of Hotspur in the 1914 production, using a mannerism that was to become characteristic of later Hotspurs. (Lady Percy's reference in *2 Henry IV* to Hotspur's "speaking thick," from which Lang took his cue, probably means only that he spoke quickly.) Frank Benson directed an energetic *1 Henry IV* at Stratford-upon-Avon both in 1905 and in 1909, the last brilliantly balanced in sympathy between Louis Calvert's Falstaff, Lewis Waller's Hotspur, and Hal (played by Fred G. Worlock, though Benson himself played the role in 1905). Barry Jackson's imaginative direction of the play in the first season of the Birmingham Repertory Theatre in 1913 explored the parallels between the historical action and the tavern world through the uninterrupted transitions of locale possible on his permanent set. Russell Thorndike and Charles Warburton directed the play at the Old Vic in 1920, with Thorndike as Falstaff, in a swift, economical production that, like Nugent Monck's production at the small Maddermarket Theatre in Norwich in 1922 and Ben Iden Payne's at Stratford-upon-Avon in 1935, demonstrated the play's refusal, when unabridged and unelaborated, to allow any one of its characters to dominate the action. Indeed the full text, staged with "speed and simplicity," as critic W. A. Darlington put it in behalf of the new credo, drew its energy precisely from the lines of tension established by the balance of its three main characters. Hal's father, the careworn and aging king, added his perspective to the complex debate on statecraft and maturity as *1 Henry IV* was increasingly examined from its various angles of vision.

After World War II, these subtle tensions lent themselves to a new pertinence and a new emphasis directed at a world grown weary, even suspicious, of politicians and military heroes. Productions increasingly showed Hal's father as cold and Machiavellian and Hotspur as the tragic embodiment of an archaic if rigorous code of honor. Such was the case, for example, in the 1964 production at Stratford-upon-Avon directed by Peter Hall, John Barton, and Clifford Williams, in which Hugh Griffith's vitality as Falstaff was set off against the emotionally sterile world of politics and war embodied in a cold-blooded and self-aware Prince of Wales (Ian Holm). The battle scenes were deliberately frightening, not stylized or balletic; the strain and violence were always distressingly evident. Orson Welles's 1965 film *Chimes at Midnight* (called *Falstaff* in the United States) centered on the hurt of the rejection of Falstaff; Welles's Falstaff was funny but also poignant, always aware of the blow that was sure to fall.

Many recent productions have sought a complex sense of the play as a whole by focusing less on Falstaff as the comic antagonist of scheming politicians and more on the intricacies of relationship between Hal and Falstaff, Hal and his father, Hal and Hotspur. The range of interpretation has been considerable, suggesting the versatility of Shakespeare's script. In John Burrell's Old Vic production of 1945 at London's New Theatre, Ralph Richardson's sensitive and funny portrayal of Falstaff was set off against the fire and atmospherics of Laurence Olivier's Hotspur. Richard Burton's interpretation of Hal at Stratford-upon-Avon in 1951 found little room for merriment in a young man determined from the start to break with Falstaff. Alan Howard, similarly, played Hal, under the direction of Terry Hands at Stratford-upon-Avon in 1975, as joyless in his role as future king, delighted neither by Falstaff nor the possibilities of future rule. Conversely, in Gerald Freedman's production of the play for the New York Shakespeare Festival in 1968, Sam Waterston was an awkwardly attractive Prince unsure of what was expected of him, at once fascinated and repelled by Stacy Keach's comically smug Falstaff. Gerard Murphy portrayed Hal, in the Royal Shakespeare Company's production, directed by Trevor Nunn at the Barbican Theatre in 1982, as an immature young man clinging to Falstaff in defiance of his austere father. Murphy's Hal sat in Falstaff's lap during their first scene together and even cleaned up the mess that Falstaff had made of his breakfast. The Prince's reconciliation with his father was never complete. At Shrewsbury, Hal engaged with Hotspur in an exhausting and unchivalrous duel. Hal's choice, between an oppressive and guilt-ridden father and a waggish, genial companion whose claims on Hal were nonetheless disturbing in their insinuations of a claim of power, was not an easy one.

Balanced between the extremes of an unsmiling, politic prince and an emotionally dependent son, the performance of Robert Hardy, directed by Douglas Seale at the Old Vic in 1955, caught the two sides of Hal's maturation in a different and perhaps more sympathetic way. This Hal though always aware of the call of royal duty, entered into the life of the tavern with spontaneous enjoyment and hilarity until the press of national affairs could no longer be ignored. His turning away from Falstaff (Paul Rogers) was reluctant and loving, yet firmly resolved. Michael Bogdanov's modern-dress *1 Henry IV,* at the Old Vic in 1987 after a national tour the previous year, focused on the conflict in the world with which Hal must come to terms, by evoking with theatrical brilliance a culture in awkward transition from a stable world of traditional values to one that provided more room for opportunism and conscious self-fashioning. Michael Pennington's self-effacing Prince revealed both the patience and the guile that would make his rule successful.

Any production of *1 Henry IV* must find theatrical expression for the juxtaposed realms of experience called for in the play's script and originally designed for performance on the Elizabethan stage. As the opening scenes shift back and forth from royal court to Prince Hal's life with Falstaff, from high seriousness to comedy, the stage must alternately present scenes of taut negotiation and witty repartee. Falstaff's world burlesques that of the court: he is a kind of adviser to a prince, to be sure, but in him everything is inverted. On the Elizabethan stage or on the modern stage, Falstaff's comic world is essentially the world of the tavern, conjured up in the spectators' imagination by tables and chairs, by tapsters and tavern keepers, by knocks at the door, by extemporaneous playacting, by racy and colloquial language. With or without scenery, the tavern world defines itself theatrically by its festive atmosphere and its topsy-turvy presentation of everything serious in the world of political struggle.

The contrasts between court and tavern, though requiring no shift of elaborate sets, exploit a number of opportunities for recurrent visual effects to intensify the juxtaposition of two worlds, as when, in the long tavern scene (2.4), Falstaff mockingly assumes the "throne" and is then "deposed" by Prince Hal. When Hal goes to court the next morning to see his father, the memory of his hilarious rehearsal the night before adds immeasurably to the dimensions of generational conflict. Such parallels may well have been reinforced on Shakespeare's stage by parallel gesture and blocking. When Falstaff goes to war, in Act 5, the two worlds of political responsibility and carefree pleasure are at last jarringly drawn together; Hal's various role models are all present at the conflict. Perhaps the most arresting stage image of the choice Hal must make is at the moment of Hotspur's death, when Hal beholds the prostrate bodies of Falstaff and Hotspur, both seemingly dead, the one symbolizing honor and the other a hedonistic preference for life by whatever means necessary. Yet Hotspur is really dead; Falstaff survives, breaking through the very illusion of stage convention to rise from death as actors do at the end of a play. Playacting and serious action mingle on the field of Shrewsbury, hinting at the complex ways in which theater imitates life.

HENRY IV
–PART ONE–

[*Dramatis Personae*

KING HENRY THE FOURTH
PRINCE HENRY, *Prince of Wales,* } *sons of the King*
PRINCE JOHN OF LANCASTER, }
EARL OF WESTMORLAND
SIR WALTER BLUNT

EARL OF NORTHUMBERLAND, *Henry Percy,*
HARRY PERCY (HOTSPUR), *his son,*
EARL OF WORCESTER, *Northumberland's younger brother,*
LORD MORTIMER, *Edmund Mortimer, also referred to as the Earl of March,*
OWEN GLENDOWER,
EARL OF DOUGLAS, *Archibald Douglas,*
SIR RICHARD VERNON,
ARCHBISHOP OF YORK, *Richard Scroop,*
SIR MICHAEL, *a member of the Archbishop's household,*
} *rebels against the King*

LADY PERCY, *Hotspur's wife and Mortimer's sister*
LADY MORTIMER, *Mortimer's wife and Glendower's daughter*

SIR JOHN FALSTAFF
NED POINS
BARDOLPH
PETO
GADSHILL, *arranger of the highway robbery*
HOSTESS *of the tavern, Mistress Quickly*
FRANCIS, *a drawer, or tapster*
VINTNER, *or tavern keeper*

FIRST CARRIER
SECOND CARRIER
HOSTLER
CHAMBERLAIN
FIRST TRAVELER
SHERIFF
SERVANT *to Hotspur*
MESSENGER
SECOND MESSENGER

Soldiers, Travelers, Lords, Attendants

SCENE: *England and Wales*]

1.1 *Enter the King, Lord John of Lancaster,* [*the*] *Earl of Westmorland,* [*Sir Walter Blunt,*] *with others.*

KING

So shaken as we are, so wan with care,
Find we a time for frighted peace to pant, 2
And breathe short-winded accents of new broils 3
To be commenced in strands afar remote. 4
No more the thirsty entrance of this soil 5
Shall daub her lips with her own children's blood; 6
No more shall trenching war channel her fields 7
Nor bruise her flowerets with the armèd hoofs
Of hostile paces. Those opposèd eyes, 9
Which, like the meteors of a troubled heaven,
All of one nature, of one substance bred,
Did lately meet in the intestine shock 12
And furious close of civil butchery, 13
Shall now, in mutual well-beseeming ranks,
March all one way and be no more opposed
Against acquaintance, kindred, and allies.
The edge of war, like an ill-sheathèd knife,
No more shall cut his master. Therefore, friends, 18
As far as to the sepulcher of Christ—
Whose soldier now, under whose blessèd cross
We are impressèd and engaged to fight— 21
Forthwith a power of English shall we levy, 22
Whose arms were molded in their mother's womb 23
To chase these pagans in those holy fields
Over whose acres walked those blessèd feet
Which fourteen hundred years ago were nailed
For our advantage on the bitter cross.
But this our purpose now is twelve month old,

1.1. Location: London. The royal court.
2 Find we let us find. **frighted** frightened **3 breathe short-winded accents** speak even though we are out of breath. **accents** words. **broils** battles **4 strands afar remote** far-off shores, i.e., of the Holy Land (to which, at the end of *Richard II,* Henry has pledged himself to a crusade) **5 thirsty entrance** i.e., parched mouth **6 daub** coat, smear **7 trenching** cutting **9 paces** horses' tread **12 intestine** internal **13 close** hand-to-hand encounter. **civil** (as in "civil war") **18 his** its **21 impressèd** conscripted **22 power** army **23 their mother's** i.e., England's

And bootless 'tis to tell you we will go. 29
Therefor we meet not now. Then let me hear
Of you, my gentle cousin Westmorland, 31
What yesternight our Council did decree
In forwarding this dear expedience. 33

WESTMORLAND
My liege, this haste was hot in question, 34
And many limits of the charge set down 35
But yesternight, when all athwart there came 36
A post from Wales loaden with heavy news, 37
Whose worst was that the noble Mortimer,
Leading the men of Herefordshire to fight
Against the irregular and wild Glendower,
Was by the rude hands of that Welshman taken,
A thousand of his people butcherèd—
Upon whose dead corpse there was such misuse, 43
Such beastly shameless transformation, 44
By those Welshwomen done as may not be
Without much shame retold or spoken of.

KING
It seems then that the tidings of this broil
Brake off our business for the Holy Land.

WESTMORLAND
This matched with other did, my gracious lord; 49
For more uneven and unwelcome news 50
Came from the north, and thus it did import:
On Holy Rood Day, the gallant Hotspur there, 52
Young Harry Percy, and brave Archibald,
That ever-valiant and approvèd Scot, 54
At Holmedon met, where they did spend 55
A sad and bloody hour,
As by discharge of their artillery, 57
And shape of likelihood, the news was told; 58
For he that brought them, in the very heat 59

29 bootless useless **31 Of** from. **gentle cousin** noble kinsman **33 dear expedience** urgent expedition **34 hot in question** being hotly debated **35 limits . . . charge** particulars of military responsibility **36 athwart** at cross purposes, contrarily **37 post** messenger. **loaden** heavily laden **43 corpse** corpses **44 transformation** mutilation **49 other** i.e., other news **50 uneven** disconcerting, distressing **52 Holy Rood Day** September 14 **54 approvèd** proved by experience **55 Holmedon** Humbleton in Northumberland **57 by** i.e., judging from **58 shape of likelihood** likely outcome **59 them** i.e., the news

And pride of their contention did take horse, 60
Uncertain of the issue any way.

KING

Here is a dear, a true industrious friend,
Sir Walter Blunt, new lighted from his horse,
Stained with the variation of each soil
Betwixt that Holmedon and this seat of ours;
And he hath brought us smooth and welcome news. 66
The Earl of Douglas is discomfited; 67
Ten thousand bold Scots, two-and-twenty knights,
Balked in their own blood, did Sir Walter see 69
On Holmedon's plains. Of prisoners, Hotspur took
Mordake Earl of Fife and eldest son 71
To beaten Douglas, and the Earl of Atholl,
Of Murray, Angus, and Menteith.
And is not this an honorable spoil?
A gallant prize? Ha, cousin, is it not?

WESTMORLAND

In faith, it is a conquest for a prince to boast of.

KING

Yea, there thou mak'st me sad, and mak'st me sin
In envy that my lord Northumbcrland
Should be the father to so blest a son—
A son who is the theme of honor's tongue,
Amongst a grove the very straightest plant, 81
Who is sweet Fortune's minion and her pride, 82
Whilst I, by looking on the praise of him,
See riot and dishonor stain the brow
Of my young Harry. O, that it could be proved
That some night-tripping fairy had exchanged 86
In cradle clothes our children where they lay,
And called mine Percy, his Plantagenet! 88
Then would I have his Harry, and he mine.
But let him from my thoughts. What think you, coz, 90
Of this young Percy's pride? The prisoners
Which he in this adventure hath surprised 92

60 pride height **66 smooth** pleasant **67 discomfited** defeated **69 Balked** heaped up in balks, or ridges **71 Mordake** i.e., Murdoch, son of the Earl of Albany **81 plant** i.e., tree **82 minion** favorite **86 night-tripping** i.e., moving nimbly in the night **88 Plantagenet** (Family name of English royalty since Henry II.) **90 let him** let him go. **coz** cousin, i.e., kinsman **92 surprised** ambushed, captured

To his own use he keeps, and sends me word 93
I shall have none but Mordake Earl of Fife. 94

WESTMORLAND
This is his uncle's teaching, this is Worcester,
Malevolent to you in all aspects, 96
Which makes him prune himself and bristle up 97
The crest of youth against your dignity.

KING
But I have sent for him to answer this;
And for this cause awhile we must neglect
Our holy purpose to Jerusalem.
Cousin, on Wednesday next our Council we
Will hold at Windsor. So inform the lords.
But come yourself with speed to us again,
For more is to be said and to be done
Than out of anger can be uttered.

WESTMORLAND I will, my liege. *Exeunt.*

✤

1.2 *Enter Prince of Wales and Sir John Falstaff.*

FALSTAFF Now, Hal, what time of day is it, lad?

PRINCE Thou art so fat-witted with drinking of old sack, 2
and unbuttoning thee after supper, and sleeping upon
benches after noon, that thou hast forgotten to de- 4
mand that truly which thou wouldst truly know. What
a devil hast thou to do with the time of the day? Unless 6
hours were cups of sack, and minutes capons, and
clocks the tongues of bawds, and dials the signs of 8
leaping houses, and the blessed sun himself a fair hot 9
wench in flame-colored taffeta, I see no reason why 10

93 To . . . use i.e., to collect ransom for them **94 none but Mordake** (Since Mordake was of royal blood, being grandson to Robert II of Scotland, Hotspur could not claim him as his prisoner according to the law of arms.) **96 Malevolent, aspects** (Astrological terms.) **97 Which . . . himself** i.e., which teaching makes Hotspur preen himself (as a falcon preens its feathers)

1.2. Location: London. An apartment of the Prince's.
2 sack a Spanish white wine **4 forgotten** forgotten how **6 a devil** in the devil **8 dials** clocks **9 leaping houses** houses of prostitution **10 taffeta** (Commonly worn by prostitutes.)

thou shouldst be so superfluous to demand the time of the day.

FALSTAFF Indeed, you come near me now, Hal, for we that take purses go by the moon and the seven stars, and not by Phoebus, "he, that wandering knight so fair." And I prithee, sweet wag, when thou art king, as, God save Thy Grace—Majesty I should say, for grace thou wilt have none—

PRINCE What, none?

FALSTAFF No, by my troth, not so much as will serve to be prologue to an egg and butter.

PRINCE Well, how then? Come, roundly, roundly.

FALSTAFF Marry, then, sweet wag, when thou art king, let not us that are squires of the night's body be called thieves of the day's beauty. Let us be Diana's foresters, gentlemen of the shade, minions of the moon; and let men say we be men of good government, being governed, as the sea is, by our noble and chaste mistress the moon, under whose countenance we steal.

PRINCE Thou sayest well, and it holds well too, for the fortune of us that are the moon's men doth ebb and flow like the sea, being governed, as the sea is, by the moon. As, for proof, now: a purse of gold most resolutely snatched on Monday night and most dissolutely spent on Tuesday morning, got with swearing "Lay by" and spent with crying "Bring in," now in as low

11 superfluous (1) unnecessarily concerned (2) self-indulgent **13 you . . . now** i.e., you've scored a point on me **14 go by** (1) travel by the light of (2) tell time by. **the seven stars** the Pleiades **15–16 Phoebus . . . fair** (Phoebus, god of the sun, is here equated with the wandering knight of a ballad or popular romance.) **17 Grace** royal highness (with pun on spiritual *grace* and also on the *grace* or blessing before a meal) **20 troth** faith **21 prologue . . . butter** i.e., grace before a brief meal **22 roundly** i.e., out with it **23 Marry** indeed. (Literally, "by the Virgin Mary.") **wag** joker **24–25 let . . . beauty** i.e., let not us who are attendants on the goddess of night, members of her household, be blamed for stealing daylight by sleeping in the daytime **25 Diana's foresters** (An elegant name for thieves by night; Diana is goddess of the moon and the hunt.) **26 minions** favorites **27 government** (1) conduct (2) commonwealth **29 countenance** (1) face (2) patronage, approval. **steal** (1) move stealthily (2) rob **30 it holds well** the comparison is apt **35–36 Lay by** (A cry of highwaymen, like "Hands up!") **36 Bring in** (An order given to a waiter in a tavern.)

an ebb as the foot of the ladder and by and by in as 37
high a flow as the ridge of the gallows. 38

FALSTAFF By the Lord, thou sayst true, lad. And is not
my hostess of the tavern a most sweet wench?

PRINCE As the honey of Hybla, my old lad of the castle. 41
And is not a buff jerkin a most sweet robe of durance? 42

FALSTAFF How now, how now, mad wag, what, in thy
quips and thy quiddities? What a plague have I to do 44
with a buff jerkin?

PRINCE Why, what a pox have I to do with my hostess 46
of the tavern?

FALSTAFF Well, thou hast called her to a reckoning many 48
a time and oft.

PRINCE Did I ever call for thee to pay thy part?

FALSTAFF No, I'll give thee thy due, thou hast paid all
there.

PRINCE Yea, and elsewhere, so far as my coin would
stretch, and where it would not I have used my credit.

FALSTAFF Yea, and so used it that, were it not here apparent that thou art heir apparent— But I prithee,
sweet wag, shall there be gallows standing in England
when thou art king? And resolution thus fubbed as it 58
is with the rusty curb of old Father Antic the law? Do 59
not thou, when thou art king, hang a thief.

PRINCE No, thou shalt.

FALSTAFF Shall I? O rare! By the Lord, I'll be a brave 62
judge.

PRINCE Thou judgest false already. I mean, thou shalt
have the hanging of the thieves, and so become a rare 65
hangman.

37 ladder (1) pier ladder (2) gallows ladder **38 ridge** crossbar **41 Hybla** (A town, famed for its honey, in Sicily near Syracuse.) **old . . . castle** (1) a roisterer (2) the name, Sir John Oldcastle, borne by Falstaff in the earlier version of the Henry IV plays **42 buff jerkin** a leather jacket worn by officers of the law. **durance** (1) imprisonment (2) durability, durable cloth **44 quiddities** subtleties of speech **46 pox** syphilis. (Here, *what a pox* is used as an expletive, like "what the devil.") **48 reckoning** settlement of the bill (with bawdy suggestion) **58 resolution** courage (of a highwayman). **fubbed** cheated **59 Antic** buffoon **62 brave** excellent **65 have . . . thieves** (1) be in charge of hanging thieves (or protecting them from hanging) (2) hang like other thieves. **rare** (1) rarely used (2) excellent

FALSTAFF Well, Hal, well; and in some sort it jumps with my humor as well as waiting in the court, I can tell you.

PRINCE For obtaining of suits?

FALSTAFF Yea, for obtaining of suits, whereof the hangman hath no lean wardrobe. 'Sblood, I am as melancholy as a gib cat or a lugged bear.

PRINCE Or an old lion, or a lover's lute.

FALSTAFF Yea, or the drone of a Lincolnshire bagpipe.

PRINCE What sayest thou to a hare, or the melancholy of Moorditch?

FALSTAFF Thou hast the most unsavory similes, and art indeed the most comparative, rascalliest, sweet young prince. But, Hal, I prithee, trouble me no more with vanity. I would to God thou and I knew where a commodity of good names were to be bought. An old lord of the Council rated me the other day in the street about you, sir, but I marked him not; and yet he talked very wisely, but I regarded him not; and yet he talked wisely, and in the street too.

PRINCE Thou didst well, for wisdom cries out in the streets and no man regards it.

FALSTAFF O, thou hast damnable iteration, and art indeed able to corrupt a saint. Thou hast done much harm upon me, Hal, God forgive thee for it! Before I knew thee, Hal, I knew nothing; and now am I, if a man should speak truly, little better than one of the wicked. I must give over this life, and I will give it over. By the Lord, an I do not I am a villain. I'll be damned for never a king's son in Christendom.

67–68 jumps . . . humor suits my temperament **68 waiting in the court** being in attendance at the royal court **70 suits** petitions. (But Falstaff uses the word to mean suits of clothes; clothes belonging to an executed man were given to the executioner.) **72 'Sblood** by his (Christ's) blood **73 gib cat** tomcat. **lugged bear** bear led by a chain and baited by dogs **76 hare** (A proverbially melancholy animal.) **77 Moorditch** (A foul ditch draining Moorfields, outside London walls.) **79 comparative** given to abusive comparisons **81 vanity** worldliness **81–82 commodity** supply **82 names** reputations **83 rated** chastised **87–88 wisdom . . . it** (An allusion to Proverbs 1:20–24.) **89 iteration** repetition (of biblical texts, with a neat twist) **92 nothing** i.e., no evil **95 an** if

PRINCE Where shall we take a purse tomorrow, Jack?
FALSTAFF Zounds, where thou wilt, lad, I'll make one. 98
An I do not, call me villain and baffle me. 99
PRINCE I see a good amendment of life in thee—from
praying to purse taking.
FALSTAFF Why, Hal, 'tis my vocation, Hal. 'Tis no sin
for a man to labor in his vocation.

Enter Poins.

Poins! Now shall we know if Gadshill have set a 104
match. O, if men were to be saved by merit, what 105
hole in hell were hot enough for him? This is the
most omnipotent villain that ever cried "Stand!" to a 107
true man. 108
PRINCE Good morrow, Ned.
POINS Good morrow, sweet Hal. What says Monsieur
Remorse? What says Sir John Sack and Sugar Jack?
How agrees the devil and thee about thy soul that
thou soldest him on Good Friday last for a cup of Ma-
deira and a cold capon's leg?
PRINCE Sir John stands to his word; the devil shall have 115
his bargain, for he was never yet a breaker of proverbs. He will give the devil his due.
POINS Then art thou damned for keeping thy word with
the devil.
PRINCE Else he had been damned for cozening the 120
devil.
POINS But, my lads, my lads, tomorrow morning, by
four o'clock early, at Gad's Hill, there are pilgrims 123
going to Canterbury with rich offerings and traders
riding to London with fat purses. I have vizards for 125
you all; you have horses for yourselves. Gadshill lies 126
tonight in Rochester. I have bespoke supper tomorrow 127
night in Eastcheap. We may do it as secure as sleep. If

98 Zounds by his (Christ's) wounds. **make one** be one of the party **99 baffle** publicly disgrace **104 Gadshill** (The name of one of the highwaymen.) **104–105 set a match** arranged a robbery **105 by merit** i.e., according to their deservings rather than by God's grace **107 omnipotent** i.e., unparalleled, utter **108 true** honest **115 stands to** keeps **120 Else** otherwise. **cozening** cheating **123 Gad's Hill** (Location near Rochester on the road from London to Canterbury; one of the highwaymen is called Gadshill.) **125 vizards** masks **126 lies** lodges **127 bespoke** ordered

you will go, I will stuff your purses full of crowns; if
you will not, tarry at home and be hanged.

FALSTAFF Hear ye, Yedward, if I tarry at home and go 131
not, I'll hang you for going. 132

POINS You will, chops? 133

FALSTAFF Hal, wilt thou make one?

PRINCE Who, I rob? I a thief? Not I, by my faith.

FALSTAFF There's neither honesty, manhood, nor good
fellowship in thee, nor thou cam'st not of the blood
royal, if thou darest not stand for ten shillings. 138

PRINCE Well then, once in my days I'll be a madcap.

FALSTAFF Why, that's well said.

PRINCE Well, come what will, I'll tarry at home.

FALSTAFF By the Lord, I'll be a traitor then, when thou art king.

PRINCE I care not.

POINS Sir John, I prithee leave the Prince and me alone. I will lay him down such reasons for this adventure that he shall go.

FALSTAFF Well, God give thee the spirit of persuasion
and him the ears of profiting, that what thou speakest
may move and what he hears may be believed, that
the true prince may, for recreation's sake, prove a false
thief; for the poor abuses of the time want counte- 152
nance. Farewell. You shall find me in Eastcheap. 153

PRINCE Farewell, thou latter spring! Farewell, All- 154
hallown summer! [*Exit Falstaff.*] 155

POINS Now, my good sweet honey lord, ride with us
tomorrow. I have a jest to execute that I cannot manage
alone. Falstaff, Peto, Bardolph, and Gadshill shall rob
those men that we have already waylaid; yourself and 159
I will not be there; and when they have the booty, if
you and I do not rob them, cut this head off from my
shoulders.

PRINCE How shall we part with them in setting forth?

131 Yedward (Nickname for *Edward,* Poins's first name.) **132 hang you** have you hanged **133 chops** i.e., fat jaws or cheeks **138 stand . . . shillings** (1) stand up and fight for money (2) be worth 10 shillings, the value of the *royal,* the gold coin alluded to in *blood royal* (ll. 137–138) **152–153 want countenance** lack encouragement and protection (from men of rank) **154–155 All-hallown summer** (Cf. "Indian summer"; Falstaff's summer or *latter spring,* i.e., his youth, has lasted to All Saints' Day, November 1.) **159 waylaid** set an ambush for

POINS Why, we will set forth before or after them, and
appoint them a place of meeting, wherein it is at our
pleasure to fail; and then will they adventure upon the 166
exploit themselves, which they shall have no sooner
achieved but we'll set upon them.

PRINCE Yea, but 'tis like that they will know us by our 169
horses, by our habits, and by every other appoint- 170
ment, to be ourselves. 171

POINS Tut, our horses they shall not see—I'll tie them
in the wood; our vizards we will change after we leave
them; and, sirrah, I have cases of buckram for the 174
nonce, to immask our noted outward garments. 175

PRINCE Yea, but I doubt they will be too hard for us. 176

POINS Well, for two of them, I know them to be as true-
bred cowards as ever turned back; and for the third, if 178
he fight longer than he sees reason, I'll forswear arms.
The virtue of this jest will be the incomprehensible lies 180
that this same fat rogue will tell us when we meet at
supper—how thirty at least he fought with, what
wards, what blows, what extremities he endured; and 183
in the reproof of this lives the jest. 184

PRINCE Well, I'll go with thee. Provide us all things necessary and meet me tomorrow night in Eastcheap.
There I'll sup. Farewell.

POINS Farewell, my lord. *Exit Poins.*

PRINCE
I know you all, and will awhile uphold
The unyoked humor of your idleness. 190
Yet herein will I imitate the sun,
Who doth permit the base contagious clouds 192
To smother up his beauty from the world,
That when he please again to be himself, 194
Being wanted, he may be more wondered at 195
By breaking through the foul and ugly mists

166 pleasure choice, discretion **169 like** likely **170 habits** garments **170–171 appointment** accoutrement **174 sirrah** (Usually addressed to an inferior; here, a sign of intimacy.) **174–175 cases . . . nonce** suits of buckram, a stiff-finished heavily sized fabric, for the purpose **175 immask** hide, disguise. **noted** known **176 doubt** fear. **too hard** too formidable **178 turned back** turned their backs and ran away **180 incomprehensible** boundless **183 wards** parries **184 reproof** disproof **190 unyoked** uncontrolled. **idleness** frivolity **192 contagious** noxious **194 That** so that **195 wanted** missed, lacked

Of vapors that did seem to strangle him.
If all the year were playing holidays,
To sport would be as tedious as to work;
But when they seldom come, they wished-for come,
And nothing pleaseth but rare accidents.
So when this loose behavior I throw off
And pay the debt I never promisèd,
By how much better than my word I am,
By so much shall I falsify men's hopes;
And like bright metal on a sullen ground,
My reformation, glittering o'er my fault,
Shall show more goodly and attract more eyes
Than that which hath no foil to set it off.
I'll so offend to make offense a skill,
Redeeming time when men think least I will. *Exit.*

✤

1.3 *Enter the King, Northumberland, Worcester, Hotspur, Sir Walter Blunt, with others.*

KING
My blood hath been too cold and temperate,
Unapt to stir at these indignities,
And you have found me, for accordingly
You tread upon my patience. But be sure
I will from henceforth rather be myself,
Mighty and to be feared, than my condition,
Which hath been smooth as oil, soft as young down,
And therefore lost that title of respect
Which the proud soul ne'er pays but to the proud.

WORCESTER
Our house, my sovereign liege, little deserves
The scourge of greatness to be used on it—

201 accidents events **205 hopes** expectations **206 sullen ground** dark background, like a *foil.* (See l. 209.) **209 foil** metal sheet laid contrastingly behind a jewel to set off its luster **210 to** as to. **skill** i.e., clever tactic, piece of good policy **211 Redeeming time** i.e., making amends for lost time

1.3. Location: London. The royal court.
2 Unapt not readily disposed **3 found me** i.e., found me so **5 myself** i.e., my royal self **6 my condition** my natural (mild) disposition **10 Our house** i.e., the Percy family **11 scourge** whip

And that same greatness too which our own hands
Have holp to make so portly. 13
NORTHUMBERLAND [*To the King*] My lord—
KING
Worcester, get thee gone, for I do see
Danger and disobedience in thine eye.
O, sir, your presence is too bold and peremptory,
And majesty might never yet endure
The moody frontier of a servant brow. 19
You have good leave to leave us. When we need 20
Your use and counsel, we shall send for you.
Exit Worcester.
[*To Northumberland.*] You were about to speak.
NORTHUMBERLAND Yea, my good lord.
Those prisoners in Your Highness' name demanded,
Which Harry Percy here at Holmedon took,
Were, as he says, not with such strength denied 25
As is delivered to Your Majesty. 26
Either envy, therefore, or misprision 27
Is guilty of this fault, and not my son.
HOTSPUR
My liege, I did deny no prisoners.
But I remember when the fight was done,
When I was dry with rage and extreme toil,
Breathless and faint, leaning upon my sword,
Came there a certain lord, neat and trimly dressed,
Fresh as a bridegroom, and his chin new reaped 34
Showed like a stubble land at harvest home. 35
He was perfumèd like a milliner, 36
And twixt his finger and his thumb he held
A pouncet box, which ever and anon 38
He gave his nose and took 't away again,
Who therewith angry, when it next came there, 40

13 holp helped. **portly** majestic, prosperous **19 moody frontier** i.e., angry brow, frown. (*Frontier* literally means "outwork" or "fortification.") **20 good leave** full permission **25 strength** vehemence **26 delivered** reported **27 envy** malice. **misprision** misunderstanding **34 chin new reaped** i.e., with beard newly trimmed according to the latest fashion, not like a soldier's beard **35 Showed** looked. **harvest home** end of harvest, fields being neat and bare **36 milliner** man dealing in fancy articles such as gloves and hats **38 pouncet box** perfume box with perforated lid **40 Who** i.e., his nose

Took it in snuff; and still he smiled and talked, 41
And as the soldiers bore dead bodies by
He called them untaught knaves, unmannerly,
To bring a slovenly unhandsome corpse
Betwixt the wind and his nobility.
With many holiday and lady terms 46
He questioned me, amongst the rest demanded 47
My prisoners in Your Majesty's behalf.
I then, all smarting with my wounds being cold,
To be so pestered with a popinjay, 50
Out of my grief and my impatience 51
Answered neglectingly I know not what,
He should, or he should not; for he made me mad
To see him shine so brisk, and smell so sweet,
And talk so like a waiting-gentlewoman
Of guns and drums and wounds—God save the mark!— 56
And telling me the sovereignest thing on earth 57
Was parmacety for an inward bruise, 58
And that it was great pity, so it was,
This villainous saltpeter should be digged 60
Out of the bowels of the harmless earth,
Which many a good tall fellow had destroyed 62
So cowardly, and but for these vile guns
He would himself have been a soldier.
This bald unjointed chat of his, my lord, 65
I answered indirectly, as I said, 66
And I beseech you, let not his report
Come current for an accusation 68
Betwixt my love and your high majesty.

BLUNT

The circumstance considered, good my lord,
Whate'er Lord Harry Percy then had said
To such a person and in such a place,

41 Took it in snuff (1) inhaled it (2) took offense. **still** continually **46 holiday and lady** dainty and effeminate **47 questioned** (1) conversed with (2) put questions to **50 popinjay** parrot **51 grief** pain **56 God . . . mark** (Probably originally a formula to avert evil omen; here, an expression of impatience.) **57 sovereignest** most efficacious **58 parmacety** spermaceti, a fatty substance taken from the head of the sperm whale, used as a medicinal ointment **60 saltpeter** potassium nitrate, used to make gunpowder and also used medicinally **62 tall** brave **65 bald** trivial **66 indirectly** inattentively, offhandedly **68 Come current** (1) be taken at face value (2) come rushing in

At such a time, with all the rest retold,
May reasonably die, and never rise
To do him wrong or any way impeach 75
What then he said, so he unsay it now. 76

KING

Why, yet he doth deny his prisoners, 77
But with proviso and exception, 78
That we at our own charge shall ransom straight 79
His brother-in-law, the foolish Mortimer, 80
Who, on my soul, hath willfully betrayed
The lives of those that he did lead to fight
Against that great magician, damned Glendower,
Whose daughter, as we hear, that Earl of March 84
Hath lately married. Shall our coffers then
Be emptied to redeem a traitor home?
Shall we buy treason and indent with fears 87
When they have lost and forfeited themselves?
No, on the barren mountains let him starve!
For I shall never hold that man my friend
Whose tongue shall ask me for one penny cost
To ransom home revolted Mortimer. 92

HOTSPUR Revolted Mortimer!
He never did fall off, my sovereign liege, 94
But by the chance of war. To prove that true
Needs no more but one tongue for all those wounds,
Those mouthèd wounds, which valiantly he took, 97
When on the gentle Severn's sedgy bank, 98
In single opposition, hand to hand,
He did confound the best part of an hour 100

75 impeach discredit **76 so** provided that **77 yet** (emphatic) i.e., even now. **deny** refuse to surrender **78 proviso and exception** (synonymous terms) **79 straight** straightway, at once **80, 84 Mortimer, Earl of March** (There were two Edmund Mortimers; Shakespeare confuses them and combines their stories. It was the uncle [1376–1409?] who was captured by Glendower and married Glendower's daughter; it was the nephew [1391–1425], fifth Earl of March, who was proclaimed heir presumptive to King Richard II after the death of his father, the fourth earl, whom Richard had named as his heir. The uncle was brother to the fourth earl and to Hotspur's wife, Elizabeth, called Kate in this play.) **87 indent with fears** i.e., make a bargain or come to terms with traitors whom we have reason to fear **92 revolted** rebellious **94 fall off** abandon his loyalty **97 mouthèd** gaping and eloquent **98 Severn's** (The Severn River flows from northern Wales and western England into the Bristol Channel.) **sedgy** covered with weeds **100 confound** consume

In changing hardiment with great Glendower. 101
Three times they breathed, and three times did they
  drink, 102
Upon agreement, of swift Severn's flood, 103
Who then, affrighted with their bloody looks, 104
Ran fearfully among the trembling reeds
And hid his crisp head in the hollow bank, 106
Bloodstainèd with these valiant combatants.
Never did bare and rotten policy 108
Color her working with such deadly wounds, 109
Nor never could the noble Mortimer
Receive so many, and all willingly.
Then let not him be slandered with revolt. 112

KING
Thou dost belie him, Percy, thou dost belie him!
He never did encounter with Glendower.
I tell thee,
He durst as well have met the devil alone
As Owen Glendower for an enemy.
Art thou not ashamed? But, sirrah, henceforth
Let me not hear you speak of Mortimer.
Send me your prisoners with the speediest means,
Or you shall hear in such a kind from me 121
As will displease you. My lord Northumberland,
We license your departure with your son.
Send us your prisoners, or you will hear of it.
Exit King [*with Blunt, and train*].

HOTSPUR
An if the devil come and roar for them 125
I will not send them. I will after straight 126
And tell him so, for I will ease my heart,
Albeit I make a hazard of my head.

NORTHUMBERLAND
What, drunk with choler? Stay and pause awhile. 129
Here comes your uncle.

Enter Worcester.

101 changing hardiment exchanging blows, matching valor
102 breathed paused for breath **103 flood** river **104 Who** i.e., the river **106 crisp** curly, i.e., rippled **108 bare** paltry. **policy** cunning
109 Color disguise **112 revolt** i.e., the accusation of rebellion
121 kind manner **125 An if** if **126 will after straight** will go after immediately **129 choler** anger

HOTSPUR Speak of Mortimer?
Zounds, I will speak of him, and let my soul
Want mercy if I do not join with him! 132
Yea, on his part I'll empty all these veins, 133
And shed my dear blood drop by drop in the dust,
But I will lift the downtrod Mortimer
As high in the air as this unthankful king,
As this ingrate and cankered Bolingbroke. 137

NORTHUMBERLAND
Brother, the King hath made your nephew mad.

WORCESTER
Who struck this heat up after I was gone?

HOTSPUR
He will forsooth have all my prisoners; 140
And when I urged the ransom once again
Of my wife's brother, then his cheek looked pale,
And on my face he turned an eye of death, 143
Trembling even at the name of Mortimer.

WORCESTER
I cannot blame him. Was not he proclaimed 145
By Richard, that dead is, the next of blood? 146

NORTHUMBERLAND
He was; I heard the proclamation.
And then it was when the unhappy king— 148
Whose wrongs in us God pardon!—did set forth 149
Upon his Irish expedition; 150
From whence he, intercepted, did return 151
To be deposed and shortly murderèd.

WORCESTER
And for whose death we in the world's wide mouth
Live scandalized and foully spoken of.

HOTSPUR
But, soft, I pray you; did King Richard then 155

132 Want mercy lack mercy, be damned **133 on his part** i.e., fighting on Mortimer's side **137 cankered** spoiled, malignant. **Bolingbroke** i.e., King Henry IV; Hotspur pointedly refuses to acknowledge his royalty **140 forsooth** indeed **143 an eye of death** a fearful look **145 he** i.e., Mortimer **146 next of blood** heir to the throne **148 unhappy** unfortunate **149 in us** caused by our doings **150 Irish expedition** (Richard was putting down a rebellion in Ireland when Bolingbroke returned to England from exile.) **151 intercepted** interrupted **155 soft** i.e., wait a minute

Proclaim my brother Edmund Mortimer 156
Heir to the crown?

NORTHUMBERLAND He did; myself did hear it.

HOTSPUR

Nay, then I cannot blame his cousin king, 158
That wished him on the barren mountains starve.
But shall it be that you that set the crown
Upon the head of this forgetful man,
And for his sake wear the detested blot
Of murderous subornation—shall it be 163
That you a world of curses undergo,
Being the agents, or base second means, 165
The cords, the ladder, or the hangman rather?
O, pardon me that I descend so low
To show the line and the predicament 168
Wherein you range under this subtle king! 169
Shall it for shame be spoken in these days,
Or fill up chronicles in time to come,
That men of your nobility and power
Did gage them both in an unjust behalf, 173
As both of you—God pardon it!—have done,
To put down Richard, that sweet lovely rose,
And plant this thorn, this canker, Bolingbroke? 176
And shall it in more shame be further spoken
That you are fooled, discarded, and shook off
By him for whom these shames ye underwent?
No! Yet time serves wherein you may redeem 180
Your banished honors and restore yourselves
Into the good thoughts of the world again;
Revenge the jeering and disdained contempt 183
Of this proud king, who studies day and night
To answer all the debt he owes to you 185
Even with the bloody payment of your deaths.
Therefore, I say—

156 brother i.e., brother-in-law **158 cousin** (with a pun on *cozen*, "cheat") **163 murderous subornation** the suborning of or inciting to murder **165 second means** agents **168 line** station, rank; also, hangman's rope. **predicament** category; also, dangerous situation **169 range** i.e., are classified **173 gage them** engage, pledge themselves **176 canker** (1) canker rose or dog rose, wild and unfragrant (2) ulcer **180 Yet** still **183 Revenge** i.e., wherein you may revenge yourself against. **disdained** disdainful **185 answer** satisfy, discharge

WORCESTER Peace, cousin, say no more.
And now I will unclasp a secret book,
And to your quick-conceiving discontents 189
I'll read you matter deep and dangerous,
As full of peril and adventurous spirit
As to o'erwalk a current roaring loud
On the unsteadfast footing of a spear. 193

HOTSPUR
If he fall in, good night, or sink or swim! 194
Send danger from the east unto the west,
So honor cross it from the north to south, 196
And let them grapple. O, the blood more stirs
To rouse a lion than to start a hare!

NORTHUMBERLAND
Imagination of some great exploit
Drives him beyond the bounds of patience.

HOTSPUR
By heaven, methinks it were an easy leap
To pluck bright honor from the pale-faced moon,
Or dive into the bottom of the deep,
Where fathom line could never touch the ground, 204
And pluck up drownèd honor by the locks,
So he that doth redeem her thence might wear
Without corrival all her dignities; 207
But out upon this half-faced fellowship! 208

WORCESTER
He apprehends a world of figures here, 209
But not the form of what he should attend.— 210
Good cousin, give me audience for a while.

HOTSPUR
I cry you mercy.

WORCESTER Those same noble Scots 212
That are your prisoners—

189 quick-conceiving comprehending quickly **193 spear** i.e., spear laid across a stream as a narrow bridge **194 If . . . swim** i.e., such a man, walking over a roaring stream, is doomed if he fall in, whether he sink or swim **196 So** provided that. (Also at l. 206.) **204 fathom line** a weighted line marked at fathom intervals (six feet), used for measuring the depth of water **207 corrival** rival, competitor **208 out . . . fellowship** down with this paltry business of sharing glory with others **209 figures** figures of the imagination, or figures of speech **210 form** essential nature. **attend** give attention to **212 cry you mercy** beg your pardon

HOTSPUR
I'll keep them all!
By God, he shall not have a Scot of them,
No, if a scot would save his soul, he shall not!
I'll keep them, by this hand!

WORCESTER
You start away
And lend no ear unto my purposes.
Those prisoners you shall keep.

HOTSPUR
Nay, I will, that's flat.
He said he would not ransom Mortimer,
Forbade my tongue to speak of Mortimer,
But I will find him when he lies asleep,
And in his ear I'll holler "Mortimer!"
Nay, I'll have a starling shall be taught to speak
Nothing but "Mortimer," and give it him
To keep his anger still in motion.

WORCESTER Hear you, cousin, a word.

HOTSPUR
All studies here I solemnly defy,
Save how to gall and pinch this Bolingbroke.
And that same sword-and-buckler Prince of Wales—
But that I think his father loves him not
And would be glad he met with some mischance—
I would have him poisoned with a pot of ale.

WORCESTER
Farewell, kinsman. I'll talk to you
When you are better tempered to attend.

NORTHUMBERLAND
Why, what a wasp-stung and impatient fool
Art thou to break into this woman's mood,
Tying thine ear to no tongue but thine own!

HOTSPUR
Why, look you, I am whipped and scourged with rods,
Nettled and stung with pismires, when I hear
Of this vile politician, Bolingbroke.
In Richard's time—what do you call the place?—
A plague upon it, it is in Gloucestershire;
'Twas where the madcap duke his uncle kept,

214–215 Scot . . . scot (1) Scotsman (2) trifling amount **218 that's flat** that's for sure **225 still** continually **227 defy** renounce **229 sword-and-buckler** (Arms improper for a prince, who should carry rapier and dagger.) **239 pismires** ants. (From the urinous smell of an anthill.) **240 politician** deceitful schemer **243 kept** dwelled

His uncle York; where I first bowed my knee
Unto this king of smiles, this Bolingbroke—
'Sblood, when you and he came back from Ravens-
purgh— 246
NORTHUMBERLAND At Berkeley Castle. 247
HOTSPUR You say true.
Why, what a candy deal of courtesy 249
This fawning greyhound then did proffer me!
"Look when his infant fortune came to age," 251
And "gentle Harry Percy," and "kind cousin"—
O, the devil take such cozeners!—God forgive me! 253
Good uncle, tell your tale; I have done.
WORCESTER
Nay, if you have not, to it again;
We will stay your leisure.
HOTSPUR I have done, i' faith. 256
WORCESTER
Then once more to your Scottish prisoners.
Deliver them up without their ransom straight, 258
And make the Douglas' son your only means 259
For powers in Scotland, which, for divers reasons 260
Which I shall send you written, be assured
Will easily be granted. [*To Northumberland.*] You, my
lord,
Your son in Scotland being thus employed,
Shall secretly into the bosom creep 264
Of that same noble prelate well beloved,
The Archbishop.
HOTSPUR Of York, is it not?
WORCESTER True, who bears hard 268
His brother's death at Bristol, the Lord Scroop.
I speak not this in estimation, 270
As what I think might be, but what I know

246 Ravenspurgh (A port at the mouth of the River Humber in Yorkshire, now covered by the sea, where Bolingbroke landed on his return from exile.) **247 Berkeley Castle** castle near Bristol **249 candy** sugared, flattering **251 Look when** when, as soon as **253 cozeners** cheats (with pun on *cousins*) **256 stay** await **258 Deliver them up** free them **259 the Douglas' son** i.e., Mordake. (See 1.1.71 and note.) **means** i.e., agent **260 For powers** for raising an army **264 secretly . . . creep** win the confidence **268 bears hard** resents **270 estimation** guesswork

Is ruminated, plotted, and set down,
And only stays but to behold the face
Of that occasion that shall bring it on.

HOTSPUR

I smell it. Upon my life, it will do well.

NORTHUMBERLAND

Before the game is afoot thou still lett'st slip. 276

HOTSPUR

Why, it cannot choose but be a noble plot. 277
And then the power of Scotland and of York, 278
To join with Mortimer, ha?

WORCESTER

And so they shall.

HOTSPUR

In faith, it is exceedingly well aimed. 280

WORCESTER

And 'tis no little reason bids us speed,
To save our heads by raising of a head; 282
For, bear ourselves as even as we can, 283
The King will always think him in our debt, 284
And think we think ourselves unsatisfied,
Till he hath found a time to pay us home. 286
And see already how he doth begin
To make us strangers to his looks of love.

HOTSPUR

He does, he does. We'll be revenged on him.

WORCESTER

Cousin, farewell. No further go in this
Than I by letters shall direct your course.
When time is ripe, which will be suddenly, 292
I'll steal to Glendower and Lord Mortimer,
Where you and Douglas and our powers at once, 294
As I will fashion it, shall happily meet 295
To bear our fortunes in our own strong arms,
Which now we hold at much uncertainty.

NORTHUMBERLAND

Farewell, good brother. We shall thrive, I trust.

276 still lett'st slip always let loose the dogs **277 cannot choose but be** cannot help being **278 power** army **280 aimed** designed **282 head** army **283 even** carefully **284 him** himself **286 home** fully **292 suddenly** soon **294 at once** all together **295 happily** fortunately

HOTSPUR

Uncle, adieu. O, let the hours be short
Till fields and blows and groans applaud our sport!

Exeunt.

✤

300 fields battlefields

2.1 *Enter a Carrier with a lantern in his hand.*

FIRST CARRIER Heigh-ho! An it be not four by the day, I'll be hanged. Charles's Wain is over the new chimney, and yet our horse not packed. What, hostler!

HOSTLER [*Within*] Anon, anon.

FIRST CARRIER I prithee, Tom, beat Cut's saddle, put a few flocks in the point. Poor jade is wrung in the withers out of all cess.

Enter another Carrier.

SECOND CARRIER Peas and beans are as dank here as a dog, and that is the next way to give poor jades the bots. This house is turned upside down since Robin Hostler died.

FIRST CARRIER Poor fellow never joyed since the price of oats rose. It was the death of him.

SECOND CARRIER I think this be the most villainous house in all London road for fleas. I am stung like a tench.

FIRST CARRIER Like a tench? By the Mass, there is ne'er a king Christian could be better bit than I have been since the first cock.

SECOND CARRIER Why, they will allow us ne'er a jordan, and then we leak in your chimney, and your chamber-lye breeds fleas like a loach.

2.1. Location: An innyard on the London–Canterbury road.
s.d. Carrier one whose trade was conveying goods, usually by packhorses **1 An** if. **by the day** in the morning **2 Charles's Wain** i.e., Charlemagne's wagon; the constellation Ursa Major (the Big Dipper) **3 yet** still. **horse** horses. **hostler** groom **4 Anon** right away, coming **5 beat** soften. **Cut's saddle** packsaddle of the horse named *Cut,* meaning "bobtailed" **6 flocks** tufts of wool. **point** pommel of the saddle. **jade** nag **6–7 wrung . . . withers** chafed (by his saddle) on the ridge between his shoulder bones **7 cess** measure, estimate **8 Peas and beans** i.e., horse fodder **8–9 dank . . . dog** i.e., damp as can be **9 next** nearest, quickest **10 bots** intestinal maggots **16 tench** a spotted fish, whose spots may have been likened to flea bites **18 king Christian** Christian king, accustomed to have the best of everything **19 first cock** i.e., midnight **20 jordan** chamberpot **21 chimney** fireplace **21–22 chamber-lye** urine **22 loach** a small freshwater fish thought to harbor parasites

FIRST CARRIER What, hostler! Come away and be hanged! 23
Come away.
SECOND CARRIER I have a gammon of bacon and two 25
races of ginger, to be delivered as far as Charing Cross. 26
FIRST CARRIER God's body, the turkeys in my pannier 27
are quite starved. What, hostler! A plague on thee! Hast
thou never an eye in thy head? Canst not hear? An 29
'twere not as good deed as drink to break the pate on 30
thee, I am a very villain. Come, and be hanged! Hast 31
no faith in thee?

Enter Gadshill.

GADSHILL Good morrow, carriers, what's o'clock?
FIRST CARRIER I think it be two o'clock.
GADSHILL I prithee, lend me thy lantern to see my gelding in the stable.
FIRST CARRIER Nay, by God, soft, I know a trick worth 37
two of that, i' faith.
GADSHILL I pray thee, lend me thine.
SECOND CARRIER Ay, when, canst tell? Lend me thy lan- 40
tern, quoth he! Marry, I'll see thee hanged first.
GADSHILL Sirrah carrier, what time do you mean to come to London?
SECOND CARRIER Time enough to go to bed with a can-
dle, I warrant thee. Come, neighbor Mugs, we'll call
up the gentlemen. They will along with company, for 46
they have great charge. *Exeunt* [*Carriers*]. 47
GADSHILL What, ho! Chamberlain! 48

Enter Chamberlain.

CHAMBERLAIN At hand, quoth pickpurse. 49
GADSHILL That's even as fair as—at hand, quoth the 50
chamberlain; for thou variest no more from picking of

23 Come away come along **25 gammon of bacon** ham **26 races** roots. **Charing Cross** a market town lying between London and Westminster **27 pannier** basket **29 An** if **30–31 to break . . . thee** to give you a blow on the head **31 very** true **37 soft** i.e., wait a minute **40 Ay . . . tell** i.e., never **46–47 They . . . charge** i.e., they wish to travel in company, because they have lots of valuable cargo **48 Chamberlain** (Male equivalent of a chambermaid.) **49 At . . . pickpurse** i.e., I am right beside you, as the pickpurse said **50 fair** good, apt

purses than giving direction doth from laboring; thou layest the plot how.

CHAMBERLAIN Good morrow, Master Gadshill. It holds current that I told you yesternight: there's a franklin in the Weald of Kent hath brought three hundred marks with him in gold. I heard him tell it to one of his company last night at supper—a kind of auditor, one that hath abundance of charge too, God knows what. They are up already, and call for eggs and butter. They will away presently.

GADSHILL Sirrah, if they meet not with Saint Nicholas' clerks, I'll give thee this neck.

CHAMBERLAIN No, I'll none of it. I pray thee, keep that for the hangman, for I know thou worshipest Saint Nicholas as truly as a man of falsehood may.

GADSHILL What talkest thou to me of the hangman? If I hang, I'll make a fat pair of gallows; for if I hang, old Sir John hangs with me, and thou knowest he is no starveling. Tut, there are other Trojans that thou dream'st not of, the which for sport's sake are content to do the profession some grace, that would, if matters should be looked into, for their own credit's sake make all whole. I am joined with no foot-landrakers, no long-staff sixpenny strikers, none of these mad mustachio purple-hued maltworms, but with nobility and tranquillity, burgomasters and great oneyers, such as can hold in, such as will strike sooner than speak, and speak sooner than drink, and drink sooner than pray. And yet, zounds, I lie, for they pray continually to

52–53 thou . . . how i.e., you don't actually do the stealing, but you give directions, like a master workman to his apprentices **54–55 holds current that** holds true what **55 a franklin** a farmer owning his own land **56 Weald** wooded region. **marks** coins of the value of 13 shillings 4 pence **61 presently** immediately **62–63 Saint Nicholas' clerks** highwaymen. (Saint Nicholas was popularly supposed the patron of thieves.) **64 I'll none** I want none **67 What** Why **70 Trojans** i.e., slang for "sports" or "roisterers" **72 profession** i.e., robbery. **grace** credit, favor **74 joined** associated. **foot-landrakers** thieves who travel on foot **75 long-staff sixpenny strikers** robbers with long staves who would knock down their victims for sixpence **75–76 mustachio purple-hued malt-worms** common drunkards with mustaches stained with drink **77 tranquillity** those who lead easy lives. **oneyers** ones (?) **78 hold in** keep a secret

their saint, the commonwealth, or rather not pray to
her but prey on her, for they ride up and down on
her and make her their boots. 83

CHAMBERLAIN What, the commonwealth their boots?
Will she hold out water in foul way? 85

GADSHILL She will, she will. Justice hath liquored her. 86
We steal as in a castle, cocksure. We have the receipt 87
of fern seed; we walk invisible. 88

CHAMBERLAIN Nay, by my faith, I think you are more
beholding to the night than to fern seed for your walk- 90
ing invisible.

GADSHILL Give me thy hand. Thou shalt have a share
in our purchase, as I am a true man. 93

CHAMBERLAIN Nay, rather let me have it as you are a
false thief.

GADSHILL Go to, *homo* is a common name to all men. 96
Bid the hostler bring my gelding out of the stable. Farewell, you muddy knave. [*Exeunt separately.*] 98

✤

2.2 *Enter Prince, Poins, Peto, [and Bardolph].*

POINS Come, shelter, shelter! I have removed Falstaff's
horse, and he frets like a gummed velvet. 2

PRINCE Stand close. [*They step aside.*] 3

Enter Falstaff.

FALSTAFF Poins! Poins, and be hanged! Poins!

PRINCE [*Coming forward*] Peace, ye fat-kidneyed rascal!
What a brawling dost thou keep! 6

83 boots booty (with pun on *boots,* shoes) **85 Will . . . way** will she let you go dry in muddy roads, i.e., will she protect you in tight places
86 liquored (1) made waterproof by oiling (2) bribed (3) made drunk
87 as in a castle i.e., in complete security. **receipt** recipe, formula
88 of fern seed i.e., of becoming invisible (since fern seed, almost invisible itself, was popularly supposed to render its possessor invisible)
90 beholding beholden **93 purchase** booty **96 homo . . . men** i.e., the Latin name for man applies to all types **98 muddy** stupid

2.2. Location: The highway, near Gad's Hill.
2 frets chafes (with pun on another meaning of the word applying to *gummed velvet,* velvet stiffened with gum and therefore liable to *fret,* or wear) **3 close** concealed **6 keep** keep up

FALSTAFF Where's Poins, Hal?

PRINCE He is walked up to the top of the hill. I'll go seek him. [*He steps aside.*]

FALSTAFF I am accursed to rob in that thief's company. The rascal hath removed my horse and tied him I know not where. If I travel but four foot by the square further afoot, I shall break my wind. Well, I doubt not but to die a fair death for all this, if I scape hanging for killing that rogue. I have forsworn his company hourly any time this two-and-twenty years, and yet I am bewitched with the rogue's company. If the rascal have not given me medicines to make me love him, I'll be hanged; it could not be else, I have drunk medicines. Poins! Hal! A plague upon you both! Bardolph! Peto! I'll starve ere I'll rob a foot further. An 'twere not as good a deed as drink to turn true man and to leave these rogues, I am the veriest varlet that ever chewed with a tooth. Eight yards of uneven ground is threescore-and-ten miles afoot with me, and the stony-hearted villains know it well enough. A plague upon it when thieves cannot be true one to another! (*They whistle.*) Whew! A plague upon you all! Give me my horse, you rogues, give me my horse, and be hanged!

PRINCE [*Coming forward*] Peace, ye fat-guts! Lie down. Lay thine ear close to the ground and list if thou canst hear the tread of travelers.

FALSTAFF Have you any levers to lift me up again, being down? 'Sblood, I'll not bear mine own flesh so far afoot again for all the coin in thy father's Exchequer. What a plague mean ye to colt me thus?

PRINCE Thou liest. Thou art not colted, thou art uncolted.

FALSTAFF I prithee, good Prince Hal, help me to my horse, good king's son.

12 square a measuring tool **14 fair** exemplary. **for all** despite all **16 yet** still **18 medicines** love potions **22 turn true man** turn honest; turn informer **28 Whew** (Perhaps Falstaff tries to answer the whistling he hears, or mocks it.) **31 list** listen **36 colt** trick, cheat. (In ll. 37–38 Prince Hal puns on the common meaning.) **39–40 help . . . horse** help me to find my horse. (But in l. 41, the Prince comically retorts as though having been asked to hold the stirrup while Falstaff mounted, as a hostler would do.)

PRINCE Out, ye rogue! Shall I be your hostler?

FALSTAFF Go hang thyself in thine own heir-apparent garters! If I be ta'en, I'll peach for this. An I have not ballads made on you all and sung to filthy tunes, let a cup of sack be my poison. When a jest is so forward, and afoot too! I hate it.

Enter Gadshill.

GADSHILL Stand.

FALSTAFF So I do, against my will.

POINS [*Coming forward with Bardolph and Peto*] O, 'tis our setter. I know his voice.

BARDOLPH What news?

GADSHILL Case ye, case ye, on with your vizards. There's money of the King's coming down the hill; 'tis going to the King's Exchequer.

FALSTAFF You lie, ye rogue, 'tis going to the King's Tavern.

GADSHILL There's enough to make us all.

FALSTAFF To be hanged.

PRINCE Sirs, you four shall front them in the narrow lane; Ned Poins and I will walk lower. If they scape from your encounter, then they light on us.

PETO How many be there of them?

GADSHILL Some eight or ten.

FALSTAFF Zounds, will they not rob us?

PRINCE What, a coward, Sir John Paunch?

FALSTAFF Indeed, I am not John of Gaunt, your grandfather, but yet no coward, Hal.

PRINCE Well, we leave that to the proof.

POINS Sirrah Jack, thy horse stands behind the hedge. When thou need'st him, there thou shalt find him. Farewell, and stand fast.

FALSTAFF Now cannot I strike him, if I should be hanged.

43 peach inform on you. **An** if **45 so forward** (1) so far advanced (referring to the robbery plot) (2) so presumptuous (referring to the joke played on him) **46 afoot** (1) in progress (2) on foot, i.e., not on horseback **50 setter** arranger of the robbery. (See 1.2.104–105 and note.) **52 Case ye** put on your masks **57 make us all** make our fortunes **59 front** confront **66 Gaunt** i.e., Ghent (but punning on *gaunt,* thin) **68 proof** test **72–73 Now . . . hanged** (Falstaff wishes he could hit Poins, who is too quick for him.)

PRINCE [*To Poins*] Ned, where are our disguises?
POINS [*To Prince*] Here, hard by. Stand close.
[*Exeunt Prince and Poins.*]

FALSTAFF Now, my masters, happy man be his dole, 76
say I. Every man to his business.

Enter the Travelers.

FIRST TRAVELER Come, neighbor. The boy shall lead our
horses down the hill; we'll walk afoot awhile and ease
our legs.

THIEVES Stand!

TRAVELERS Jesus bless us!

FALSTAFF Strike! Down with them! Cut the villains'
throats! Ah, whoreson caterpillars, bacon-fed knaves! 84
They hate us youth. Down with them, fleece them!

TRAVELERS O, we are undone, both we and ours forever!

FALSTAFF Hang ye, gorbellied knaves, are ye undone? 88
No, ye fat chuffs, I would your store were here! On, 89
bacons, on! What, ye knaves, young men must live. 90
You are grandjurors, are ye? We'll jure ye, 'faith. 91
Here they rob them and bind them. Exeunt.

Enter the Prince and Poins [*in buckram*].

PRINCE The thieves have bound the true men. Now
could thou and I rob the thieves and go merrily to London,
it would be argument for a week, laughter for a 94
month, and a good jest forever.

POINS Stand close. I hear them coming.
[*They stand aside.*]

Enter the thieves again.

FALSTAFF Come, my masters, let us share, and then to
horse before day. An the Prince and Poins be not two
arrant cowards, there's no equity stirring. There's no 99

76 happy . . . dole may happiness be every man's portion or lot
84 whoreson i.e., scurvy, abominable. **caterpillars** i.e., parasites.
bacon-fed i.e., well-fed **88 gorbellied** big-bellied **89 chuffs** churls, rich but miserly. **store** total wealth **90 bacons** fat men **91 grandjurors** i.e., men of wealth, able to serve on juries **94 argument** a subject for conversation **99 arrant** notorious, unmitigated. **equity** judgment, discernment

more valor in that Poins than in a wild duck.
[*The thieves begin to share the booty.*]

PRINCE Your money!

POINS Villains!

As they are sharing, the Prince and Poins set upon them. They all run away, and Falstaff, after a blow or two, runs away too, leaving the booty behind them.

PRINCE
Got with much ease. Now merrily to horse.
The thieves are all scattered and possessed with fear
So strongly that they dare not meet each other;
Each takes his fellow for an officer.
Away, good Ned. Falstaff sweats to death
And lards the lean earth as he walks along. 108
Were 't not for laughing, I should pity him.

POINS How the fat rogue roared! *Exeunt.*

✤

2.3 *Enter Hotspur, solus, reading a letter.*

HOTSPUR "But, for mine own part, my lord, I could be
well contented to be there, in respect of the love I bear
your house." He could be contented; why is he not, 3
then? In respect of the love he bears our house! He
shows in this, he loves his own barn better than he 5
loves our house. Let me see some more. "The purpose
you undertake is dangerous"—why, that's certain.
'Tis dangerous to take a cold, to sleep, to drink; but I
tell you, my lord fool, out of this nettle, danger, we
pluck this flower, safety. "The purpose you undertake
is dangerous, the friends you have named uncertain,
the time itself unsorted, and your whole plot too light 12
for the counterpoise of so great an opposition." Say 13
you so, say you so? I say unto you again, you are a

108 lards drips fat, bastes

2.3. Location: Hotspur's estate (identified historically as Warkworth Castle in Northumberland).

s.d. solus alone **3 house** family **5 barn** (Hotspur refers derisively to the writer's residence, taking *house,* l. 3, in its literal sense.) **12 unsorted** unsuitable **13 for . . . of** to counterbalance

shallow, cowardly hind, and you lie. What a lack-brain is this! By the Lord, our plot is a good plot as ever was laid, our friends true and constant; a good plot, good friends, and full of expectation; an excellent plot, very good friends. What a frosty-spirited rogue is this! Why, my lord of York commends the plot and the general course of the action. Zounds, an I were now by this rascal, I could brain him with his lady's fan. Is there not my father, my uncle, and myself? Lord Edmund Mortimer, my lord of York, and Owen Glendower? Is there not besides the Douglas? Have I not all their letters to meet me in arms by the ninth of the next month, and are they not some of them set forward already? What a pagan rascal is this, an infidel! Ha, you shall see now in very sincerity of fear and cold heart will he to the King and lay open all our proceedings. O, I could divide myself and go to buffets for moving such a dish of skim milk with so honorable an action! Hang him, let him tell the King, we are prepared. I will set forward tonight.

Enter his Lady.

How now, Kate? I must leave you within these two hours.

LADY PERCY

O, my good lord, why are you thus alone?
For what offense have I this fortnight been
A banished woman from my Harry's bed?
Tell me, sweet lord, what is 't that takes from thee
Thy stomach, pleasure, and thy golden sleep?
Why dost thou bend thine eyes upon the earth
And start so often when thou sitt'st alone?
Why hast thou lost the fresh blood in thy cheeks
And given my treasures and my rights of thee
To thick-eyed musing and curst melancholy?

15 hind menial, peasant **18 expectation** promise **20 lord of York** i.e., Archbishop Scroop. (Also in l. 24.) **21 an** if **28 pagan** unbelieving **31–32 divide . . . buffets** i.e., fight with myself **32 moving** urging **41 stomach** appetite **45 And . . . thee** i.e., and given what I treasure in you and have a right, as wife, to share **46 thick-eyed** dull-sighted, vacant, abstracted. **curst** ill-tempered

In thy faint slumbers I by thee have watched 47
And heard thee murmur tales of iron wars,
Speak terms of manage to thy bounding steed, 49
Cry, "Courage! To the field!" And thou hast talked
Of sallies and retires, of trenches, tents, 51
Of palisadoes, frontiers, parapets, 52
Of basilisks, of cannon, culverin, 53
Of prisoners' ransom, and of soldiers slain,
And all the currents of a heady fight. 55
Thy spirit within thee hath been so at war,
And thus hath so bestirred thee in thy sleep,
That beads of sweat have stood upon thy brow
Like bubbles in a late-disturbèd stream, 59
And in thy face strange motions have appeared,
Such as we see when men restrain their breath
On some great sudden hest. O, what portents are these? 62
Some heavy business hath my lord in hand, 63
And I must know it, else he loves me not.

HOTSPUR
What, ho!

[*Enter a Servant.*]

Is Gilliams with the packet gone?

SERVANT He is, my lord, an hour ago.

HOTSPUR
Hath Butler brought those horses from the sheriff?

SERVANT
One horse, my lord, he brought even now. 68

HOTSPUR
What horse? Roan, a crop-ear, is it not?

SERVANT
It is, my lord.

HOTSPUR That roan shall be my throne.
Well, I will back him straight. O, *Esperance*! 71
Bid Butler lead him forth into the park.

[*Exit Servant.*]

47 faint i.e., restless. **watched** lain awake **49 manage** horsemanship **51 retires** retreats **52 palisadoes** stakes set in the ground for defense. **frontiers** outworks, ramparts **53 basilisks** large cannon. **culverin** long cannon **55 heady** headlong **59 late-disturbèd** recently stirred up **62 hest** command **63 heavy** weighty; sorrowful **68 even** just **71 back** mount. **Esperance** hope. (The motto of the Percy family.)

LADY PERCY But hear you, my lord.
HOTSPUR What sayst thou, my lady?
LADY PERCY What is it carries you away?
HOTSPUR Why, my horse, my love, my horse.
LADY PERCY Out, you mad-headed ape!
A weasel hath not such a deal of spleen 78
As you are tossed with. In faith, 79
I'll know your business, Harry, that I will.
I fear my brother Mortimer doth stir
About his title, and hath sent for you 82
To line his enterprise; but if you go— 83
HOTSPUR
So far afoot, I shall be weary, love.
LADY PERCY
Come, come, you paraquito, answer me 85
Directly unto this question that I ask.
In faith, I'll break thy little finger, Harry,
An if thou wilt not tell me all things true. 88
HOTSPUR Away,
Away, you trifler! Love? I love thee not;
I care not for thee, Kate. This is no world
To play with mammets and to tilt with lips. 91
We must have bloody noses and cracked crowns, 92
And pass them current too. Gods me, my horse! 93
What sayst thou, Kate? What wouldst thou have with me?
LADY PERCY
Do you not love me? Do you not, indeed?
Well, do not then, for since you love me not
I will not love myself. Do you not love me?
Nay, tell me if you speak in jest or no.
HOTSPUR Come, wilt thou see me ride?
And when I am a-horseback I will swear
I love thee infinitely. But hark you, Kate,
I must not have you henceforth question me

78 spleen (The spleen was thought to be the source of impulsive and irritable behavior.) **79 tossed** tossed about, agitated **82 title** claim to the throne **83 line** strengthen **85 paraquito** little parrot. (A term of endearment.) **88 An if** if **91 mammets** dolls (with a quibble on the Latin *mamma* meaning "breast") **92 crowns** (1) heads (2) coins worth 5 shillings. (Cracked coins would not "pass current," as Hotspur jokes in the next line.) **93 Gods me** God save me

Whither I go, nor reason whereabout. 103
Whither I must, I must; and, to conclude,
This evening must I leave you, gentle Kate.
I know you wise, but yet no farther wise
Than Harry Percy's wife; constant you are,
But yet a woman; and for secrecy,
No lady closer, for I well believe 109
Thou wilt not utter what thou dost not know,
And so far will I trust thee, gentle Kate.

LADY PERCY How, so far?

HOTSPUR
Not an inch further. But hark you, Kate:
Whither I go, thither shall you go too.
Today will I set forth, tomorrow you.
Will this content you, Kate?

LADY PERCY It must of force. *Exeunt.* 116

✣

2.4 *Enter Prince and Poins.*

PRINCE Ned, prithee, come out of that fat room, and 1
lend me thy hand to laugh a little.

POINS Where hast been, Hal?

PRINCE With three or four loggerheads amongst three 4
or four score hogsheads. I have sounded the very bass 5
string of humility. Sirrah, I am sworn brother to a
leash of drawers, and can call them all by their Christian 7
names, as Tom, Dick, and Francis. They take it already 8
upon their salvation that, though I be but Prince of 9
Wales, yet I am the king of courtesy, and tell me flatly
I am no proud Jack like Falstaff, but a Corinthian, a lad 11
of mettle, a good boy—by the Lord, so they call me!—

103 reason whereabout discuss about what **109 closer** more close-mouthed **116 of force** perforce, of necessity

2.4. Location: A tavern in Eastcheap, London, usually identified as the Boar's Head. Some tavern furniture, including stools, is provided onstage.

1 fat stuffy; or, a vat room **4 loggerheads** blockheads **5 bass** (with a pun on *base*) **7 leash of drawers** i.e., three waiters **8–9 take . . . salvation** already maintain it as they hope to be saved **11 Jack** (1) Jack Falstaff (2) fellow. **Corinthian** i.e., gay blade, good sport. (Corinth was reputed to be licentious.)

and when I am King of England I shall command all
the good lads in Eastcheap. They call drinking deep, 14
"dyeing scarlet"; and when you breathe in your water- 15
ing they cry "hem!" and bid you "play it off." To con- 16
clude, I am so good a proficient in one quarter of an
hour that I can drink with any tinker in his own language during my life. I tell thee, Ned, thou hast lost
much honor that thou wert not with me in this action.
But, sweet Ned—to sweeten which name of Ned, I
give thee this pennyworth of sugar, clapped even now 22
into my hand by an underskinker, one that never 23
spake other English in his life than "Eight shillings
and sixpence," and "You are welcome," with this
shrill addition, "Anon, anon, sir! Score a pint of bas- 26
tard in the Half-Moon," or so. But, Ned, to drive away 27
the time till Falstaff come, I prithee do thou stand in
some by-room while I question my puny drawer to 29
what end he gave me the sugar; and do thou never
leave calling "Francis," that his tale to me may be
nothing but "Anon." Step aside, and I'll show thee a
precedent. [*Exit Poins.*] 33

POINS [*Within*] Francis!

PRINCE Thou art perfect.

POINS [*Within*] Francis!

Enter [*Francis, a*] *drawer.*

FRANCIS Anon, anon, sir.—Look down into the Pomgar- 37
net, Ralph. 38

PRINCE Come hither, Francis.

FRANCIS My lord?

PRINCE How long hast thou to serve, Francis? 41

FRANCIS Forsooth, five years, and as much as to—

POINS [*Within*] Francis!

14–15 They . . . scarlet (Either because excessive drinking causes a red complexion or because urine, produced by *drinking deep,* was sometimes used for fixing dyes.) **15–16 breathe . . . watering** pause for breath in your drinking **16 play it off** drink it up **22 sugar** (Used to sweeten wine.) **23 underskinker** assistant to a waiter or bartender **26 Anon** right away, coming. **Score** charge **26–27 bastard** (A sweet Spanish wine.) **27 Half-Moon** (The name of a room in the inn.) **29 by-room** side-room. **puny** inexperienced, raw. **drawer** tapster, one who draws liquor **33 precedent** example **37–38 Pomgarnet** Pomegranate. (Another room in the inn.) **41 serve** i.e., serve out your apprenticeship

FRANCIS Anon, anon, sir.

PRINCE Five year! By 'r Lady, a long lease for the clinking of pewter. But Francis, darest thou be so valiant as to play the coward with thy indenture and show it a fair pair of heels and run from it?

FRANCIS O Lord, sir, I'll be sworn upon all the books in England, I could find in my heart—

POINS [*Within*] Francis!

FRANCIS Anon, sir.

PRINCE How old art thou, Francis?

FRANCIS Let me see, about Michaelmas next I shall be—

POINS [*Within*] Francis!

FRANCIS Anon, sir. Pray, stay a little, my lord.

PRINCE Nay, but hark you, Francis: for the sugar thou gavest me, 'twas a pennyworth, was 't not?

FRANCIS O Lord, I would it had been two!

PRINCE I will give thee for it a thousand pound. Ask me when thou wilt, and thou shalt have it.

POINS [*Within*] Francis!

FRANCIS Anon, anon.

PRINCE Anon, Francis? No, Francis; but tomorrow, Francis, or, Francis, o' Thursday, or indeed, Francis, when thou wilt. But, Francis—

FRANCIS My lord?

PRINCE Wilt thou rob this leathern-jerkin, crystal-button, not-pated, agate-ring, puke-stocking, caddis-garter, smooth-tongue, Spanish-pouch—

FRANCIS O Lord, sir, who do you mean?

PRINCE Why, then, your brown bastard is your only drink; for look you, Francis, your white canvas doublet will sully. In Barbary, sir, it cannot come to so much.

45 By 'r Lady by Our Lady **47 indenture** contract of apprenticeship **49 books** i.e., Bibles **54 Michaelmas** September 29 **69–71 Wilt . . . Spanish-pouch** i.e., will you rob your master of your services by running away, he who is characterized by a leather jacket, transparent buttons, cropped hair, a ring with small figures in an agate stone for a seal, dark woolen stockings, worsted garters, an ingratiating flattering manner of speech, a pouch of Spanish leather **73–76 Why . . . much** (The Prince talks seeming nonsense in order to bewilder Francis; but he also implies that Francis should stick to his trade, since he will not cut much of a figure in the world.) **75 it** i.e., sugar

FRANCIS What, sir?

POINS [*Within*] Francis!

PRINCE Away, you rogue! Dost thou not hear them call?

Here they both call him; the drawer stands amazed, not knowing which way to go.

Enter Vintner.

VINTNER What stand'st thou still and hear'st such a calling? Look to the guests within. [*Exit Francis.*] My lord, old Sir John, with half a dozen more, are at the door. Shall I let them in?

PRINCE Let them alone awhile, and then open the door. [*Exit Vintner.*] Poins!

Enter Poins.

POINS Anon, anon, sir.

PRINCE Sirrah, Falstaff and the rest of the thieves are at the door. Shall we be merry?

POINS As merry as crickets, my lad. But hark ye, what cunning match have you made with this jest of the drawer? Come, what's the issue?

PRINCE I am now of all humors that have showed themselves humors since the old days of Goodman Adam to the pupil age of this present twelve o'clock at midnight.

[*Enter Francis, hurrying across the stage with wine.*]

What's o'clock, Francis?

FRANCIS Anon, anon, sir. [*Exit.*]

PRINCE That ever this fellow should have fewer words than a parrot, and yet the son of a woman! His industry is upstairs and downstairs, his eloquence the parcel of a reckoning. I am not yet of Percy's mind, the Hotspur of the north, he that kills me some six or seven dozen of Scots at a breakfast, washes his hands, and says to his wife, "Fie upon this quiet life! I want

80 What why **90 match** game, contest **91 issue** outcome, point **92–95 I . . . midnight** i.e., I'm now in a mood for anything that has happened in the whole history of the world **93 Goodman** (Title for a farmer.) **94 pupil** youthful **100–101 parcel . . . reckoning** items of a bill **102 kills me** i.e., kills. (*Me* is used colloquially.)

work." "O my sweet Harry," says she, "how many hast thou killed today?" "Give my roan horse a drench," says he, and answers, "Some fourteen," an hour after, "a trifle, a trifle." I prithee, call in Falstaff. I'll play Percy, and that damned brawn shall play Dame Mortimer his wife. "Rivo!" says the drunkard. Call in ribs, call in tallow.

Enter Falstaff, [*Gadshill, Bardolph, and Peto; Francis following with wine*].

POINS Welcome, Jack. Where hast thou been?

FALSTAFF A plague of all cowards, I say, and a vengeance too! Marry and amen! Give me a cup of sack, boy. Ere I lead this life long, I'll sew netherstocks, and mend them and foot them too. A plague of all cowards! Give me a cup of sack, rogue. Is there no virtue extant? *He drinketh.*

PRINCE Didst thou never see Titan kiss a dish of butter, pitiful-hearted Titan, that melted at the sweet tale of the sun's? If thou didst, then behold that compound.

FALSTAFF You rogue, here's lime in this sack too. There is nothing but roguery to be found in villainous man, yet a coward is worse than a cup of sack with lime in it. A villainous coward! Go thy ways, old Jack, die when thou wilt; if manhood, good manhood, be not forgot upon the face of the earth, then am I a shotten herring. There lives not three good men unhanged in England, and one of them is fat and grows old, God help the while! A bad world, I say. I would I were a weaver; I could sing psalms or anything. A plague of all cowards, I say still.

PRINCE How now, woolsack, what mutter you?

107 drench dose of medicine. **says he** i.e., he tells a servant **109 brawn** fat boar **110 Rivo** (An exclamation of uncertain meaning, but related to drinking.) **111 ribs** rib roast. **tallow** fat drippings **113 of** on **115 netherstocks** stockings (the sewing or mending of which is a menial occupation) **116 foot** make a new foot for **119 Titan** i.e., the sun **120 that** i.e., the butter **121 compound** melting butter, i.e., Falstaff **122 lime in this sack** i.e., lime added to make the wine sparkle **127–128 shotten herring** a herring that has cast its roe and is consequently thin **130 the while** i.e., in these bad times **131 weaver** (Many psalm-singing Protestant immigrants from the Low Countries were weavers.) **133 woolsack** bale of wool

FALSTAFF A king's son! If I do not beat thee out of thy kingdom with a dagger of lath, and drive all thy subjects afore thee like a flock of wild geese, I'll never wear hair on my face more. You, Prince of Wales!

PRINCE Why, you whoreson round man, what's the matter?

FALSTAFF Are not you a coward? Answer me to that. And Poins there?

POINS Zounds, ye fat paunch, an ye call me coward, by the Lord, I'll stab thee.

FALSTAFF I call thee coward? I'll see thee damned ere I call thee coward, but I would give a thousand pound I could run as fast as thou canst. You are straight enough in the shoulders; you care not who sees your back. Call you that backing of your friends? A plague upon such backing! Give me them that will face me. Give me a cup of sack. I am a rogue if I drunk today.

PRINCE O villain, thy lips are scarce wiped since thou drunk'st last.

FALSTAFF All is one for that. (*He drinketh.*) A plague of all cowards, still say I.

PRINCE What's the matter?

FALSTAFF What's the matter? There be four of us here have ta'en a thousand pound this day morning.

PRINCE Where is it, Jack, where is it?

FALSTAFF Where is it? Taken from us it is. A hundred upon poor four of us.

PRINCE What, a hundred, man?

FALSTAFF I am a rogue if I were not at half-sword with a dozen of them two hours together. I have scaped by miracle. I am eight times thrust through the doublet, four through the hose, my buckler cut through and through, my sword hacked like a handsaw—*ecce signum!* I never dealt better since I was a man. All would not do. A plague of all cowards! Let them speak. If

135 dagger of lath (The Vice, a stock comic figure in morality plays, was so armed.) **142 an** if **153 All . . . that** i.e., no matter **162 at half-sword** fighting at close quarters **163 scaped** escaped **164 doublet** Elizabethan upper garment like a jacket **165 hose** close-fitting breeches. **buckler** shield **166–167 ecce signum** behold the proof. (Familiar words from the Mass.) **167–168 All . . . do** i.e., all that I did was of no use

they speak more or less than truth, they are villains
and the sons of darkness.

PRINCE Speak, sirs, how was it?

GADSHILL We four set upon some dozen—

FALSTAFF Sixteen at least, my lord.

GADSHILL And bound them.

PETO No, no, they were not bound.

FALSTAFF You rogue, they were bound, every man of
them, or I am a Jew else, an Hebrew Jew.

GADSHILL As we were sharing, some six or seven fresh
men set upon us—

FALSTAFF And unbound the rest, and then come in the
other. 181

PRINCE What, fought you with them all?

FALSTAFF All? I know not what you call all, but if I
fought not with fifty of them I am a bunch of radish.
If there were not two- or three-and-fifty upon poor old
Jack, then am I no two-legged creature.

PRINCE Pray God you have not murdered some of them.

FALSTAFF Nay, that's past praying for. I have peppered 188
two of them. Two I am sure I have paid, two rogues
in buckram suits. I tell thee what, Hal, if I tell thee a
lie, spit in my face, call me horse. Thou knowest my
old ward. Here I lay, and thus I bore my point. [*He* 192
demonstrates his stance.] Four rogues in buckram let
drive at me—

PRINCE What, four? Thou saidst but two even now. 195

FALSTAFF Four, Hal, I told thee four.

POINS Ay, ay, he said four.

FALSTAFF These four came all afront and mainly thrust 198
at me. I made me no more ado but took all their seven 199
points in my target, thus. 200

PRINCE Seven? Why, there were but four even now.

FALSTAFF In buckram?

POINS Ay, four, in buckram suits.

FALSTAFF Seven, by these hilts, or I am a villain else. 204

181 other others **188 peppered** i.e., killed **192 ward** defensive stance, parry. **lay** stood **195 even** just **198 afront** abreast. **mainly** powerfully **199 made me** i.e., made. (*Me* is used colloquially.) **200 target** shield **204 by these hilts** by my sword hilt. **villain** i.e., no gentleman

PRINCE [*Aside to Poins*] Prithee, let him alone. We shall have more anon.

FALSTAFF Dost thou hear me, Hal?

PRINCE Ay, and mark thee too, Jack.

FALSTAFF Do so, for it is worth the listening to. These nine in buckram that I told thee of—

PRINCE So, two more already.

FALSTAFF Their points being broken—

POINS Down fell their hose.

FALSTAFF Began to give me ground; but I followed me close, came in foot and hand; and with a thought seven of the eleven I paid.

PRINCE O monstrous! Eleven buckram men grown out of two!

FALSTAFF But, as the devil would have it, three misbegotten knaves in Kendal green came at my back and let drive at me, for it was so dark, Hal, that thou couldst not see thy hand.

PRINCE These lies are like their father that begets them, gross as a mountain, open, palpable. Why, thou clay-brained guts, thou knotty-pated fool, thou whoreson, obscene, greasy tallow-keech—

FALSTAFF What, art thou mad? Art thou mad? Is not the truth the truth?

PRINCE Why, how couldst thou know these men in Kendal green when it was so dark thou couldst not see thy hand? Come, tell us your reason. What sayest thou to this?

POINS Come, your reason, Jack, your reason.

FALSTAFF What, upon compulsion? Zounds, an I were at the strappado, or all the racks in the world, I would not tell you on compulsion. Give you a reason on compulsion? If reasons were as plentiful as blackberries, I would give no man a reason upon compulsion, I.

PRINCE I'll be no longer guilty of this sin. This sanguine

208 mark (1) pay heed (2) keep count **212 points** sword points. (But Poins puns on the sense of laces by which the hose were attached to the doublet.) **214 followed me** i.e., followed **215 with a thought** quick as a thought **220 Kendal** a town known for its textiles **225 knotty-pated** thickheaded **226 tallow-keech** lump of tallow **235 strappado** a kind of torture **237 reasons . . . blackberries** (Falstaff puns on *raisins,* pronounced nearly like *reasons.*) **239 sanguine** ruddy

coward, this bed-presser, this horse-backbreaker, this huge hill of flesh—

FALSTAFF 'Sblood, you starveling, you eelskin, you
dried neat's tongue, you bull's pizzle, you stockfish! 243
O, for breath to utter what is like thee! You tailor's
yard, you sheath, you bowcase, you vile standing 245
tuck— 246

PRINCE Well, breathe awhile, and then to it again, and when thou hast tired thyself in base comparisons, hear me speak but this.

POINS Mark, Jack.

PRINCE We two saw you four set on four and bound
them, and were masters of their wealth. Mark now
how a plain tale shall put you down. Then did we two
set on you four, and, with a word, outfaced you from 254
your prize, and have it, yea, and can show it you here
in the house. And, Falstaff, you carried your guts
away as nimbly, with as quick dexterity, and roared
for mercy, and still run and roared, as ever I heard bull
calf. What a slave art thou, to hack thy sword as thou
hast done, and then say it was in fight! What trick,
what device, what starting-hole canst thou now find 261
out to hide thee from this open and apparent shame?

POINS Come, let's hear, Jack. What trick hast thou now?

FALSTAFF By the Lord, I knew ye as well as he that
made ye. Why, hear you, my masters, was it for me to
kill the heir apparent? Should I turn upon the true
prince? Why, thou knowest I am as valiant as Hercules, but beware instinct. The lion will not touch the
true prince. Instinct is a great matter. I was now a coward on instinct. I shall think the better of myself and
thee during my life—I for a valiant lion, and thou for
a true prince. But by the Lord, lads, I am glad you
have the money. Hostess, clap to the doors! Watch to- 273
night, pray tomorrow. Gallants, lads, boys, hearts of 274
gold, all the titles of good fellowship come to you!

243 neat's ox's. **pizzle** penis. **stockfish** dried cod **245 yard** yardstick. **standing** standing on its point, or no longer pliant **246 tuck** rapier **254 with a word** in a word. **outfaced** frightened **261 starting-hole** point of shelter (like a rabbit's hole) **273 Watch** stay awake. (See Matthew 26:41.) **274 pray** (1) pray to God (2) prey

What, shall we be merry? Shall we have a play extempore?

PRINCE Content; and the argument shall be thy running 278
away.

FALSTAFF Ah, no more of that, Hal, an thou lovest me!

Enter Hostess.

HOSTESS O Jesu, my lord the Prince!

PRINCE How now, my lady the hostess, what sayst thou to me?

HOSTESS Marry, my lord, there is a nobleman of the court at door would speak with you. He says he comes from your father.

PRINCE Give him as much as will make him a royal 287
man and send him back again to my mother. 288

FALSTAFF What manner of man is he?

HOSTESS An old man.

FALSTAFF What doth Gravity out of his bed at midnight? 291
Shall I give him his answer?

PRINCE Prithee, do, Jack.

FALSTAFF Faith, and I'll send him packing. *Exit.*

PRINCE Now, sirs. By 'r Lady, you fought fair; so did you, Peto; so did you, Bardolph. You are lions too, you ran away upon instinct, you will not touch the true prince; no, fie!

BARDOLPH Faith, I ran when I saw others run.

PRINCE Faith, tell me now in earnest, how came Falstaff's sword so hacked?

PETO Why, he hacked it with his dagger, and said he
would swear truth out of England but he would make 303
you believe it was done in fight, and persuaded us to do the like.

BARDOLPH Yea, and to tickle our noses with spear grass
to make them bleed, and then to beslubber our gar- 307
ments with it and swear it was the blood of true men.
I did that I did not this seven year before: I blushed to 309
hear his monstrous devices.

278 argument plot of the play **287–288 Give . . . man** (Hal puns on the value of coins: a *noble* was worth 6 shillings 8 pence, a *royal* 10 shillings.) **291 What doth** why is **303 but he would** if he did not **307 beslubber** smear, cover **309 that** something

PRINCE O villain, thou stolest a cup of sack eighteen years ago and wert taken with the manner, and ever since thou hast blushed extempore. Thou hadst fire and sword on thy side, and yet thou rann'st away. What instinct hadst thou for it?

BARDOLPH My lord, do you see these meteors? Do you behold these exhalations? [*Pointing to his own face.*]

PRINCE I do.

BARDOLPH What think you they portend?

PRINCE Hot livers and cold purses.

BARDOLPH Choler, my lord, if rightly taken.

PRINCE No, if rightly taken, halter.

Enter Falstaff.

Here comes lean Jack, here comes bare-bone. How now, my sweet creature of bombast? How long is 't ago, Jack, since thou sawest thine own knee?

FALSTAFF My own knee? When I was about thy years, Hal, I was not an eagle's talon in the waist; I could have crept into any alderman's thumb ring. A plague of sighing and grief! It blows a man up like a bladder. There's villainous news abroad. Here was Sir John Bracy from your father. You must to the court in the morning. That same mad fellow of the north, Percy, and he of Wales that gave Amamon the bastinado and made Lucifer cuckold and swore the devil his true liegeman upon the cross of a Welsh hook—what a plague call you him?

312 taken . . . manner caught with the goods **313 extempore** with no preparation or provocation (since drinking has left his face permanently red). **fire** i.e., a red nose and complexion caused by heavy drinking **316, 317 meteors, exhalations** i.e., the red blotches on Bardolph's face **319 portend** signify. (Continues the metaphor of astrological influence begun in *meteors* and *exhalations*.) **320 Hot . . . purses** i.e., livers inflamed by drink and purses made empty by spending **321 Choler** a choleric or combative temperament. **taken** understood. (But the Prince, in his next speech, uses the word to mean "arrested.") **322 halter** hangman's noose. (The Prince plays on Bardolph's *choler*, which he takes as *collar*.) **324 bombast** (1) cotton padding (2) fustian speech **333 Amamon** (The name of a demon.) **bastinado** beating on the soles of the feet **334 made . . . cuckold** i.e., gave Lucifer his horns, the sign of cuckoldry **334–335 and swore . . . liegeman** and made the devil take an oath of allegiance as a true subject **335 Welsh hook** curved-bladed pike lacking the cross shape of the sword on which such oaths were usually sworn

POINS Owen Glendower.

FALSTAFF Owen, Owen, the same; and his son-in-law Mortimer, and old Northumberland, and that sprightly Scot of Scots, Douglas, that runs a-horseback up a hill perpendicular—

PRINCE He that rides at high speed, and with his pistol kills a sparrow flying.

FALSTAFF You have hit it. 344

PRINCE So did he never the sparrow.

FALSTAFF Well, that rascal hath good mettle in him; he will not run.

PRINCE Why, what a rascal art thou then to praise him so for running!

FALSTAFF A-horseback, ye cuckoo; but afoot he will not budge a foot.

PRINCE Yes, Jack, upon instinct.

FALSTAFF I grant ye, upon instinct. Well, he is there too,
and one Mordake, and a thousand blue-caps more. 354
Worcester is stolen away tonight. Thy father's beard is turned white with the news. You may buy land now as cheap as stinking mackerel.

PRINCE Why, then, it is like, if there come a hot June 358
and this civil buffeting hold, we shall buy maiden- 359
heads as they buy hobnails, by the hundreds.

FALSTAFF By the Mass, lad, thou sayest true; it is like we shall have good trading that way. But tell me, Hal, art not thou horrible afeard? Thou being heir apparent, could the world pick thee out three such enemies again as that fiend Douglas, that spirit Percy, and that devil Glendower? Art thou not horribly afraid? Doth not thy blood thrill at it?

PRINCE Not a whit, i' faith. I lack some of thy instinct.

FALSTAFF Well, thou wilt be horribly chid tomorrow 369
when thou comest to thy father. If thou love me, practice an answer.

PRINCE Do thou stand for my father and examine me upon the particulars of my life.

FALSTAFF Shall I? Content. This chair shall be my state, 374

344 hit it described it exactly (though the Prince takes *hit* literally in l. 345) **354 blue-caps** Scottish soldiers **358 like** likely **359 hold** continues **369 chid** chided **374 state** chair of state, throne

this dagger my scepter, and this cushion my crown.

[Falstaff establishes himself on his "throne."]

PRINCE Thy state is taken for a joint stool, thy golden scepter for a leaden dagger, and thy precious rich crown for a pitiful bald crown!

FALSTAFF Well, an the fire of grace be not quite out of thee, now shalt thou be moved. Give me a cup of sack to make my eyes look red, that it may be thought I have wept; for I must speak in passion, and I will do it in King Cambyses' vein.

PRINCE Well, here is my leg. *[He bows.]*

FALSTAFF And here is my speech. Stand aside, nobility.

HOSTESS O Jesu, this is excellent sport, i' faith!

FALSTAFF
Weep not, sweet queen, for trickling tears are vain.

HOSTESS O, the Father, how he holds his countenance!

FALSTAFF
For God's sake, lords, convey my tristful queen,
For tears do stop the floodgates of her eyes.

HOSTESS O Jesu, he doth it as like one of these harlotry players as ever I see!

FALSTAFF
Peace, good pint pot; peace, good tickle-brain.—
Harry, I do not only marvel where thou spendest thy time, but also how thou art accompanied; for though the camomile, the more it is trodden on the faster it grows, yet youth, the more it is wasted the sooner it wears. That thou art my son I have partly thy mother's word, partly my own opinion, but chiefly a villainous

376 joint stool a stool made by a joiner or furniture maker. (To "take someone for a joint stool" is to offer an intentionally silly apology for overlooking that person, as in *King Lear,* 3.6.52. Hal suggests that Falstaff's *state* is ridiculous [punning on *state,* throne].) **377 leaden** of soft metal, hence inferior **379 an** if **383 in . . . vein** i.e., in the ranting and (by Shakespeare's time) old-fashioned style of Thomas Preston's *Cambyses,* an early Elizabethan tragedy **389 the Father** i.e., in God's name. **holds his countenance** keeps a straight face **390 convey** escort away. **tristful** sorrowing **391 stop** fill **392 harlotry** scurvy, vagabond **393 players** actors **394 tickle-brain** (A slang term for strong liquor, here applied as a nickname for the tavern hostess.)
397–399 camomile . . . wears (This parodies the style of Lyly's *Euphues* and exaggerates the balance and alliteration of the style.) **camomile** an aromatic creeping herb whose flowers and leaves are used medicinally

trick of thine eye and a foolish hanging of thy nether lip that doth warrant me. If then thou be son to me, here lies the point: why, being son to me, art thou so pointed at? Shall the blessed sun of heaven prove a micher and eat blackberries? A question not to be asked. Shall the son of England prove a thief and take purses? A question to be asked. There is a thing, Harry, which thou hast often heard of, and it is known to many in our land by the name of pitch. This pitch, as ancient writers do report, doth defile; so doth the company thou keepest. For, Harry, now I do not speak to thee in drink but in tears, not in pleasure but in passion, not in words only but in woes also. And yet there is a virtuous man whom I have often noted in thy company, but I know not his name.

PRINCE What manner of man, an it like Your Majesty?

FALSTAFF A goodly portly man, i' faith, and a corpulent; of a cheerful look, a pleasing eye, and a most noble carriage; and, as I think, his age some fifty, or, by 'r Lady, inclining to threescore; and now I remember me, his name is Falstaff. If that man should be lewdly given, he deceiveth me; for, Harry, I scc virtuc in his looks. If then the tree may be known by the fruit, as the fruit by the tree, then peremptorily I speak it, there is virtue in that Falstaff. Him keep with, the rest banish. And tell me now, thou naughty varlet, tell me, where hast thou been this month?

PRINCE Dost thou speak like a king? Do thou stand for me, and I'll play my father.

FALSTAFF Depose me? If thou dost it half so gravely, so majestically, both in word and matter, hang me up by the heels for a rabbit-sucker or a poulter's hare.

[*Hal takes Falstaff's place on the "throne."*]

PRINCE Well, here I am set.

FALSTAFF And here I stand. Judge, my masters.

401 trick trait **402 warrant** assure **405 micher** truant **409–410 This . . . defile** (An allusion to the familiar proverb from Ecclesiasticus 13:1 about the defilement of touching pitch.) **pitch** a sticky, black residue from the distillation of tar, used to seal wood from moisture **416 an it like** if it please **417 portly** (1) stately (2) corpulent **421 lewdly** wickedly **423 If . . . by the fruit** (See Matthew 12:33.) **424 peremptorily** decisively **432 rabbit-sucker** unweaned rabbit. **poulter's** poulterer's **433 set** seated

PRINCE Now, Harry, whence come you?

FALSTAFF My noble lord, from Eastcheap.

PRINCE The complaints I hear of thee are grievous.

FALSTAFF 'Sblood, my lord, they are false.—Nay, I'll tickle ye for a young prince, i' faith.

PRINCE Swearest thou, ungracious boy? Henceforth ne'er look on me. Thou art violently carried away from grace. There is a devil haunts thee in the likeness of an old fat man; a tun of man is thy companion. Why dost thou converse with that trunk of humors, that bolting-hutch of beastliness, that swollen parcel of dropsies, that huge bombard of sack, that stuffed cloak-bag of guts, that roasted Manningtree ox with the pudding in his belly, that reverend Vice, that gray Iniquity, that father ruffian, that vanity in years? Wherein is he good but to taste sack and drink it? Wherein neat and cleanly but to carve a capon and eat it? Wherein cunning but in craft? Wherein crafty but in villainy? Wherein villainous but in all things? Wherein worthy but in nothing?

FALSTAFF I would Your Grace would take me with you. Whom means Your Grace?

PRINCE That villainous abominable misleader of youth, Falstaff, that old white-bearded Satan.

FALSTAFF My lord, the man I know.

PRINCE I know thou dost.

FALSTAFF But to say I know more harm in him than in myself were to say more than I know. That he is old, the more the pity, his white hairs do witness it; but that he is, saving your reverence, a whoremaster, that I utterly deny. If sack and sugar be a fault, God help the wicked! If to be old and merry be a sin, then many

438 'Sblood i.e., by Christ's blood **439 tickle ye for** amuse you in the role of **443 tun** (1) large barrel (2) ton **444 converse** associate. **humors** body fluids, diseases **444–445 bolting-hutch** large bin **446 bombard** leathern drinking vessel **447 Manningtree ox** (Manningtree, a town in Essex, had noted fairs where, no doubt, oxen were roasted whole.) **pudding** sausage **448 Vice, Iniquity** (Allegorical names for the chief comic character and tempter in morality plays.) **449 vanity** person given to worldly desires **451 cleanly** deft **451–452 cunning** skillful **455 take me with you** i.e., let me catch up with your meaning **464 saving your reverence** i.e., with my apology for using offensive language

an old host that I know is damned. If to be fat be to be 467
hated, then Pharaoh's lean kine are to be loved. No, 468
my good lord, banish Peto, banish Bardolph, banish
Poins; but for sweet Jack Falstaff, kind Jack Falstaff,
true Jack Falstaff, valiant Jack Falstaff, and therefore
more valiant being as he is old Jack Falstaff, banish
not him thy Harry's company, banish not him thy
Harry's company—banish plump Jack, and banish all
the world.

PRINCE I do, I will. [*A knocking.*
Exeunt Hostess, Francis, and Bardolph.]

Enter Bardolph, running.

BARDOLPH O, my lord, my lord! The sheriff with a most
monstrous watch is at the door. 478

FALSTAFF Out, ye rogue! Play out the play. I have much to say in the behalf of that Falstaff.

Enter the Hostess.

HOSTESS O Jesu, my lord, my lord!

PRINCE Heigh, heigh! The devil rides upon a fiddle- 482
stick. What's the matter? 483

HOSTESS The sheriff and all the watch are at the door. They are come to search the house. Shall I let them in?

FALSTAFF Dost thou hear, Hal? Never call a true piece of 486
gold a counterfeit. Thou art essentially made without 487
seeming so. 488

PRINCE And thou a natural coward without instinct.

FALSTAFF I deny your major. If you will deny the sher- 490
iff, so; if not, let him enter. If I become not a cart as 491
well as another man, a plague on my bringing up! I 492
hope I shall as soon be strangled with a halter as another.

467 host innkeeper **468 Pharaoh's lean kine** (See Genesis 41:3–4, 18–21.) **478 watch** posse of constables **482–483 The . . . fiddlestick** i.e., here's much ado about nothing **486–488 Dost . . . seeming so** (In this difficult passage, Falstaff seems to suggest that he is true gold, not counterfeit, and so should not be betrayed to the watch by the Prince, who, he hopes, is not merely playacting at the tavern but is truly one of its madcap members.) **490 deny your major** reject your major premise. **deny the** refuse entrance to the **491 become** befit, adorn. **cart** i.e., hangman's cart **492 bringing up** (1) upbringing (2) being brought before the authorities to be hanged

PRINCE Go hide thee behind the arras. The rest walk up above. Now, my masters, for a true face and good conscience.

FALSTAFF Both which I have had, but their date is out, and therefore I'll hide me.

[*He hides behind the arras.*]

PRINCE Call in the sheriff.

[*Exeunt all except the Prince and Peto.*]

Enter Sheriff and the Carrier.

Now, Master Sheriff, what is your will with me?

SHERIFF

First, pardon me, my lord. A hue and cry
Hath followed certain men unto this house.

PRINCE What men?

SHERIFF

One of them is well known, my gracious lord,
A gross fat man.

CARRIER As fat as butter.

PRINCE

The man, I do assure you, is not here,
For I myself at this time have employed him.
And, Sheriff, I will engage my word to thee
That I will, by tomorrow dinnertime,
Send him to answer thee, or any man,
For anything he shall be charged withal;
And so let me entreat you leave the house.

SHERIFF

I will, my lord. There are two gentlemen
Have in this robbery lost three hundred marks.

PRINCE

It may be so. If he have robbed these men,
He shall be answerable; and so farewell.

SHERIFF Good night, my noble lord.

PRINCE

I think it is good morrow, is it not?

SHERIFF

Indeed, my lord, I think it be two o'clock.

Exit [*with Carrier*].

495 arras wall hanging of tapestry **496 up above** upstairs **498 date is out** time is past **509 engage** pledge **510 dinnertime** i.e., about noon **519 morrow** morning

PRINCE This oily rascal is known as well as Paul's. Go call him forth.

PETO [*Discovering Falstaff*] Falstaff!—Fast asleep behind the arras, and snorting like a horse.

PRINCE Hark, how hard he fetches breath. Search his pockets. (*He searcheth his pockets, and findeth certain papers.*) What hast thou found?

PETO Nothing but papers, my lord.

PRINCE Let's see what they be. Read them.

PETO [*Reads*]

Item, A capon, ...2s. 2d.
Item, Sauce, ... 4d.
Item, Sack, two gallons, ...5s. 8d.
Item, Anchovies and sack after supper. . .2s. 6d.
Item, Bread, ... ob.

PRINCE O, monstrous! But one halfpennyworth of bread to this intolerable deal of sack? What there is else, keep close; we'll read it at more advantage. There let him sleep till day. I'll to the court in the morning. We must all to the wars, and thy place shall be honorable. I'll procure this fat rogue a charge of foot, and I know his death will be a march of twelve score. The money shall be paid back again with advantage. Be with me betimes in the morning; and so, good morrow, Peto.

PETO Good morrow, good my lord.

Exeunt [*separately. Falstaff is concealed once more behind the arras*].

✤

521 Paul's Saint Paul's Cathedral **534 ob.** obolus, i.e., halfpenny **537 close** hidden. **advantage** favorable opportunity **540 charge of foot** command of a company of infantry **541 twelve score** i.e., 240 yards **542 advantage** interest **543 betimes** early **545 s.d. Exeunt . . . arras** (Onstage, the arras is evidently arranged so that Falstaff can exit behind it once the scene is over.)

3.1 *Enter Hotspur, Worcester, Lord Mortimer,* [*and*] *Owen Glendower.*

MORTIMER
These promises are fair, the parties sure,
And our induction full of prosperous hope. 2

HOTSPUR
Lord Mortimer, and cousin Glendower,
Will you sit down? And uncle Worcester—
[*They sit.*]
A plague upon it, I have forgot the map.

GLENDOWER [*Producing a map*]
No, here it is. Sit, cousin Percy,
Sit, good cousin Hotspur—for by that name
As oft as Lancaster doth speak of you 8
His cheek looks pale, and with a rising sigh
He wisheth you in heaven.

HOTSPUR And you in hell,
As oft as he hears Owen Glendower spoke of.

GLENDOWER
I cannot blame him. At my nativity
The front of heaven was full of fiery shapes, 13
Of burning cressets, and at my birth 14
The frame and huge foundation of the earth
Shaked like a coward.

HOTSPUR Why, so it would have done
At the same season if your mother's cat
Had but kittened, though yourself had never been born.

GLENDOWER
I say the earth did shake when I was born.

HOTSPUR
And I say the earth was not of my mind,
If you suppose as fearing you it shook.

3.1. Location: Wales. Glendower's residence. (Holinshed places a meeting of the rebel deputies at Bangor in the Archdeacon's house, but in this present "unhistorical" scene as invented by Shakespeare, Glendower is host throughout.) Seats are provided onstage.
2 induction beginning. **prosperous hope** hope of prospering
8 Lancaster i.e., King Henry, here demoted to Duke of Lancaster
13 front brow, face (as also at l. 36) **14 cressets** lights burning in baskets atop long poles; hence, meteors

GLENDOWER
The heavens were all on fire; the earth did tremble.
HOTSPUR
O, then the earth shook to see the heavens on fire,
And not in fear of your nativity.
Diseasèd nature oftentimes breaks forth
In strange eruptions; oft the teeming earth
Is with a kind of colic pinched and vexed
By the imprisoning of unruly wind
Within her womb, which, for enlargement striving, 29
Shakes the old beldam earth and topples down 30
Steeples and moss-grown towers. At your birth
Our grandam earth, having this distemp'rature,
In passion shook.
GLENDOWER Cousin, of many men 33
I do not bear these crossings. Give me leave 34
To tell you once again that at my birth
The front of heaven was full of fiery shapes,
The goats ran from the mountains, and the herds
Were strangely clamorous to the frighted fields. 38
These signs have marked me extraordinary,
And all the courses of my life do show
I am not in the roll of common men.
Where is he living, clipped in with the sea 42
That chides the banks of England, Scotland, Wales,
Which calls me pupil, or hath read to me? 44
And bring him out that is but woman's son 45
Can trace me in the tedious ways of art 46
And hold me pace in deep experiments. 47
HOTSPUR
I think there's no man speaks better Welsh. 48
I'll to dinner.
MORTIMER
Peace, cousin Percy; you will make him mad.

29 enlargement release **30 beldam** grandmother **33 passion** suffering. **of** from **34 crossings** contradictions **38 clamorous** noisy **42 he** anyone. **clipped in with** enclosed by **44 Which** who. **read to** instructed **45 bring him out** produce any man **46 Can . . . art** who can follow me in the laborious ways of magic **47 hold me pace** keep up with me. **deep** occult **48 speaks better Welsh** (Hotspur hides an insult behind the literal meaning, since "to speak Welsh" meant colloquially both "to boast" and "to speak nonsense.")

GLENDOWER
I can call spirits from the vasty deep. 51
HOTSPUR
Why, so can I, or so can any man;
But will they come when you do call for them?
GLENDOWER
Why, I can teach you, cousin, to command the devil.
HOTSPUR
And I can teach thee, coz, to shame the devil
By telling truth. Tell truth and shame the devil.
If thou have power to raise him, bring him hither,
And I'll be sworn I have power to shame him hence.
O, while you live, tell truth and shame the devil!
MORTIMER
Come, come, no more of this unprofitable chat.
GLENDOWER
Three times hath Henry Bolingbroke made head 61
Against my power; thrice from the banks of Wye 62
And sandy-bottomed Severn have I sent him
Bootless home and weather-beaten back. 64
HOTSPUR
Home without boots, and in foul weather too!
How scapes he agues, in the devil's name? 66
GLENDOWER
Come, here is the map. Shall we divide our right
According to our threefold order ta'en? 68
MORTIMER
The Archdeacon hath divided it 69
Into three limits very equally: 70
England, from Trent and Severn hitherto, 71
By south and east is to my part assigned;
All westward, Wales beyond the Severn shore,
And all the fertile land within that bound,
To Owen Glendower; and, dear coz, to you
The remnant northward, lying off from Trent.

51 call summon. (But Hotspur sardonically replies in the sense of "call out to," whether or not there is any response.) **vasty deep** lower world **61 made head** raised a force **62 power** army **64 Bootless** without advantage (but Hotspur quibbles on the sense of "barefoot") **66 agues** fevers **68 order ta'en** arrangements made **69 Archdeacon** i.e., the Archdeacon of Bangor, in whose house, according to Holinshed, a meeting took place between deputies of the rebel leaders **70 limits** regions **71 hitherto** to this point

And our indentures tripartite are drawn, 77
Which being sealèd interchangeably—
A business that this night may execute— 79
Tomorrow, cousin Percy, you and I
And my good lord of Worcester will set forth
To meet your father and the Scottish power,
As is appointed us, at Shrewsbury.
My father Glendower is not ready yet, 84
Nor shall we need his help these fourteen days.
[*To Glendower.*] Within that space you may have
drawn together 86
Your tenants, friends, and neighboring gentlemen.

GLENDOWER
A shorter time shall send me to you, lords;
And in my conduct shall your ladies come, 89
From whom you now must steal and take no leave,
For there will be a world of water shed
Upon the parting of your wives and you.

HOTSPUR [*Consulting the map*]
Methinks my moiety, north from Burton here, 93
In quantity equals not one of yours.
See how this river comes me cranking in 95
And cuts me from the best of all my land
A huge half-moon, a monstrous cantle out. 97
I'll have the current in this place dammed up,
And here the smug and silver Trent shall run 99
In a new channel, fair and evenly.
It shall not wind with such a deep indent
To rob me of so rich a bottom here. 102

GLENDOWER
Not wind? It shall, it must! You see it doth.

MORTIMER
Yea, but mark how he bears his course and runs me up 104
With like advantage on the other side,

77 tripartite i.e., drawn up in triplicate, each document sealed *interchangeably* (l. 78) with the seal of all signatories. **drawn** drawn up **79 this night may execute** may be carried out tonight **84 father** i.e., father-in-law **86 may** will be able to **89 conduct** escort **93 moiety** share **95 comes me cranking in** comes bending in on my share. (The Trent, by turning northward instead of continuing eastward into the Wash, cuts Hotspur off from rich land in Lincolnshire and vicinity.) **97 cantle** piece **99 smug** smooth **102 bottom** valley **104 runs me** runs. (*Me* is used colloquially.)

Gelding the opposèd continent as much 106
As on the other side it takes from you.

WORCESTER
Yea, but a little charge will trench him here 108
And on this north side win this cape of land;
And then he runs straight and even.

HOTSPUR
I'll have it so. A little charge will do it.

GLENDOWER I'll not have it altered.

HOTSPUR Will not you?

GLENDOWER No, nor you shall not.

HOTSPUR Who shall say me nay?

GLENDOWER Why, that will I.

HOTSPUR
Let me not understand you, then; speak it in Welsh.

GLENDOWER
I can speak English, lord, as well as you;
For I was trained up in the English court,
Where, being but young, I framèd to the harp 120
Many an English ditty lovely well,
And gave the tongue a helpful ornament— 122
A virtue that was never seen in you.

HOTSPUR
Marry, and I am glad of it with all my heart!
I had rather be a kitten and cry "mew"
Than one of these same meter balladmongers.
I had rather hear a brazen can'stick turned 127
Or a dry wheel grate on the axletree, 128
And that would set my teeth nothing on edge, 129
Nothing so much as mincing poetry.
'Tis like the forced gait of a shuffling nag. 131

GLENDOWER Come, you shall have Trent turned.

HOTSPUR
I do not care. I'll give thrice so much land

106 Gelding . . . continent cutting off from the land which it bounds on the opposite side. (The Trent's southerly loop from Stoke to Burton deprives Mortimer of a piece of land, just as its later northerly course deprives Hotspur.) **108 charge** expenditure. **trench** provide a new channel **120 framèd to the harp** set to harp accompaniment **122 gave . . . ornament** i.e., added to the words a pleasing ornament of music; also, gave to the English tongue the ornament of music and poetry **127 can'stick turned** candlestick turned on a lathe **128 axletree** axle **129 nothing** not at all **131 shuffling** hobbled

To any well-deserving friend;
But in the way of bargain, mark ye me,
I'll cavil on the ninth part of a hair. 136
Are the indentures drawn? Shall we be gone? 137

GLENDOWER
The moon shines fair; you may away by night.
I'll haste the writer and withal 139
Break with your wives of your departure hence. 140
I am afraid my daughter will run mad,
So much she doteth on her Mortimer. *Exit.*

MORTIMER
Fie, cousin Percy, how you cross my father!

HOTSPUR
I cannot choose. Sometimes he angers me
With telling me of the moldwarp and the ant, 145
Of the dreamer Merlin and his prophecies, 146
And of a dragon and a finless fish,
A clip-winged griffin and a moulten raven, 148
A couching lion and a ramping cat, 149
And such a deal of skimble-skamble stuff 150
As puts me from my faith. I tell you what: 151
He held me last night at least nine hours
In reckoning up the several devils' names 153
That were his lackeys. I cried "Hum," and "Well, go to,"
But marked him not a word. O, he is as tedious
As a tirèd horse, a railing wife,
Worse than a smoky house. I had rather live
With cheese and garlic in a windmill, far,
Than feed on cates and have him talk to me 159
In any summer house in Christendom.

136 cavil . . . hair i.e., argue about the most trivial detail **137 drawn** drawn up **139 haste** hurry. **writer** i.e., scrivener who would be drawing the indentures. **withal** also **140 Break with** inform **145 moldwarp** mole. (Holinshed tells us that the division was arranged because of a prophecy that represented King Henry as the mole and the others as the dragon, the lion, and the wolf, who should divide the land among them.) **146 Merlin** the bard, prophet, and magician of Arthurian story, Welsh in origin **148 griffin** a fabulous beast, half lion, half eagle. **moulten** having molted **149 couching** couchant, crouching. (Heraldic term.) **ramping** rampant, advancing on its hind legs. (Hotspur is ridiculing the heraldic emblems that Glendower holds so dear.) **150 skimble-skamble** foolish, nonsensical **151 puts . . . faith** drives me from my (Christian) faith **153 several** various **159 cates** delicacies

MORTIMER
In faith, he is a worthy gentleman,
Exceedingly well read, and profited 162
In strange concealments, valiant as a lion 163
And wondrous affable, and as bountiful
As mines of India. Shall I tell you, cousin?
He holds your temper in a high respect 166
And curbs himself even of his natural scope 167
When you come 'cross his humor. Faith, he does. 168
I warrant you that man is not alive
Might so have tempted him as you have done 170
Without the taste of danger and reproof.
But do not use it oft, let me entreat you.

WORCESTER
In faith, my lord, you are too willful-blame, 173
And since your coming hither have done enough
To put him quite beside his patience. 175
You must needs learn, lord, to amend this fault.
Though sometimes it show greatness, courage, blood— 177
And that's the dearest grace it renders you— 178
Yet oftentimes it doth present harsh rage, 179
Defect of manners, want of government, 180
Pride, haughtiness, opinion, and disdain, 181
The least of which haunting a nobleman
Loseth men's hearts and leaves behind a stain
Upon the beauty of all parts besides, 184
Beguiling them of commendation. 185

HOTSPUR
Well, I am schooled. Good manners be your speed! 186
Here comes our wives, and let us take our leave.

Enter Glendower with the ladies.

MORTIMER
This is the deadly spite that angers me: 188
My wife can speak no English, I no Welsh.

162 profited proficient **163 concealments** occult practices **166 temper** temperament **167 scope** freedom of speech **168 come 'cross** contradict **170 Might** who could **173 willful-blame** blameworthy for too much self-will **175 beside** out of **177 blood** spirit **178 dearest grace** best credit **179 present** represent **180 want of government** lack of self-control **181 opinion** vanity, arrogance **184 all parts besides** all other abilities **185 Beguiling** depriving **186 be your speed** give you good fortune **188 spite** vexation

GLENDOWER

My daughter weeps. She'll not part with you;
She'll be a soldier too, she'll to the wars.

MORTIMER

Good Father, tell her that she and my aunt Percy 192
Shall follow in your conduct speedily.

Glendower speaks to her in Welsh, and she answers him in the same.

GLENDOWER

She is desperate here; a peevish self-willed harlotry, 194
One that no persuasion can do good upon.

The lady speaks in Welsh.

MORTIMER

I understand thy looks. That pretty Welsh 196
Which thou pourest down from these swelling heavens 197
I am too perfect in; and, but for shame, 198
In such a parley should I answer thee. 199

The lady again in Welsh.

I understand thy kisses and thou mine,
And that's a feeling disputation. 201
But I will never be a truant, love,
Till I have learned thy language; for thy tongue
Makes Welsh as sweet as ditties highly penned, 204
Sung by a fair queen in a summer's bower,
With ravishing division, to her lute. 206

GLENDOWER

Nay, if you melt, then will she run mad. 207

The lady speaks again in Welsh.

MORTIMER

O, I am ignorance itself in this!

GLENDOWER

She bids you on the wanton rushes lay you down 209
And rest your gentle head upon her lap,

192 aunt (Percy's wife, here called Kate, was aunt of Edmund Mortimer, the fifth Earl of March, but was sister-in-law to the Sir Edward Mortimer who married Glendower's daughter.) **194 desperate here** adamant on this point (i.e., her decision to accompany Mortimer). **peevish self-willed harlotry** childish, willful, silly wench **196 That pretty Welsh** i.e., your eloquent tears **197 heavens** i.e., eyes **198 perfect** proficient **199 such a parley** i.e., the same language (of weeping) **201 disputation** conversation, debate **204 highly** eloquently, nobly **206 division** variation (in music) **207 melt** i.e., weep **209 wanton** soft, luxurious. **rushes** (Used as floor covering.)

And she will sing the song that pleaseth you
And on your eyelids crown the god of sleep, 212
Charming your blood with pleasing heaviness, 213
Making such difference twixt wake and sleep
As is the difference betwixt day and night
The hour before the heavenly-harnessed team 216
Begins his golden progress in the east.

MORTIMER
With all my heart I'll sit and hear her sing.
By that time will our book, I think, be drawn. 219

GLENDOWER Do so;
And those musicians that shall play to you
Hang in the air a thousand leagues from hence,
And straight they shall be here. Sit, and attend.
[*Mortimer reclines with his head in his wife's lap.*]

HOTSPUR Come, Kate, thou art perfect in lying down; come, quick, quick, that I may lay my head in thy lap.

LADY PERCY Go, ye giddy goose.
[*Hotspur lies with his head in Kate's lap.*] *The music plays.*

HOTSPUR
Now I perceive the devil understands Welsh;
And 'tis no marvel he is so humorous. 228
By 'r Lady, he is a good musician.

LADY PERCY Then should you be nothing but musical, for you are altogether governed by humors. Lie still, ye thief, and hear the lady sing in Welsh.

HOTSPUR I had rather hear Lady, my brach, howl in 233
Irish.

LADY PERCY Wouldst thou have thy head broken? 235

HOTSPUR No.

LADY PERCY Then be still.

HOTSPUR Neither, 'tis a woman's fault. 238

LADY PERCY Now God help thee!

HOTSPUR To the Welsh lady's bed.

LADY PERCY What's that?

212 crown give sway to **213 heaviness** drowsiness **216 the heavenly-harnessed team** i.e., the team of horses drawing the chariot of the sun **219 book** document, indentures **228 humorous** whimsical, capricious **233 brach** bitch hound **235 broken** i.e., struck so as to break the skin **238 Neither** i.e., I won't do that either

HOTSPUR Peace, she sings.
Here the lady sings a Welsh song.
Come, Kate, I'll have your song too.
LADY PERCY Not mine, in good sooth.
HOTSPUR Not yours, in good sooth! Heart, you swear 245
like a comfit maker's wife. "Not you, in good sooth," 246
and "as true as I live," and "as God shall mend me,"
and "as sure as day,"
And givest such sarcenet surety for thy oaths 249
As if thou never walk'st further than Finsbury. 250
Swear me, Kate, like a lady as thou art,
A good mouth-filling oath, and leave "in sooth,"
And such protest of pepper-gingerbread, 253
To velvet-guards and Sunday citizens. 254
Come, sing.
LADY PERCY I will not sing.
HOTSPUR 'Tis the next way to turn tailor, or be redbreast 257
teacher. An the indentures be drawn, I'll away within 258
these two hours; and so, come in when ye will. *Exit.*
GLENDOWER
Come, come, Lord Mortimer. You are as slow
As hot Lord Percy is on fire to go.
By this our book is drawn; we'll but seal, 262
And then to horse immediately.
MORTIMER With all my heart. *Exeunt.*

✤

3.2 *Enter the King, Prince of Wales, and others.*

KING
Lords, give us leave. The Prince of Wales and I
Must have some private conference; but be near at hand,

245 Heart i.e., by Christ's heart **246 comfit maker's** confectioner's **249 sarcenet** soft, flimsy (from the soft silken material known as *sarcenet*) **250 Finsbury** a field just outside London frequented by the London citizenry. (Hotspur jokes with Kate as though she were a citizen's wife, using the pious and modest oaths of such people.) **253 protest . . . gingerbread** i.e., mealy-mouthed protestations **254 velvet-guards** i.e., wives who wear velvet trimming **257 next** nearest, quickest. **turn tailor** (Tailors were noted for singing and effeminacy.) **257–258 be redbreast teacher** i.e., teach birds to sing. (Hotspur is expressing his contempt for music.) **262 By this** by this time. **but** just

3.2. Location: London. The royal court.

For we shall presently have need of you.
Exeunt Lords.
I know not whether God will have it so
For some displeasing service I have done,
That in his secret doom out of my blood
He'll breed revengement and a scourge for me;
But thou dost in thy passages of life
Make me believe that thou art only marked
For the hot vengeance and the rod of heaven
To punish my mistreadings. Tell me else,
Could such inordinate and low desires,
Such poor, such bare, such lewd, such mean attempts,
Such barren pleasures, rude society,
As thou art matched withal and grafted to,
Accompany the greatness of thy blood
And hold their level with thy princely heart?

PRINCE
So please Your Majesty, I would I could
Quit all offenses with as clear excuse
As well as I am doubtless I can purge
Myself of many I am charged withal.
Yet such extenuation let me beg
As, in reproof of many tales devised,
Which oft the ear of greatness needs must hear
By smiling pickthanks and base newsmongers,
I may, for some things true, wherein my youth
Hath faulty wandered and irregular,
Find pardon on my true submission.

KING
God pardon thee! Yet let me wonder, Harry,
At thy affections, which do hold a wing
Quite from the flight of all thy ancestors.

6 doom judgment. **blood** offspring **8 passages** course, conduct **9–11 thou . . . mistreadings** (1) you are marked as the means of heaven's vengeance against me, or (2) you are marked to suffer heaven's vengeance because of my sins **11 else** how otherwise **12 inordinate** (1) immoderate (2) unworthy of your rank **13 lewd** low, base. **attempts** undertakings **15 withal** with **17 hold their level** claim equality **19 Quit** acquit myself of **20 doubtless** certain **23 in reproof** upon disproof **25 By** from. **pickthanks** flatterers. **newsmongers** talebearers **28 submission** admission of fault **30 affections** inclinations. **hold a wing** fly a course **31 from** at variance with

Thy place in Council thou hast rudely lost,
Which by thy younger brother is supplied,
And art almost an alien to the hearts
Of all the court and princes of my blood.
The hope and expectation of thy time
Is ruined, and the soul of every man
Prophetically do forethink thy fall.
Had I so lavish of my presence been,
So common-hackneyed in the eyes of men,
So stale and cheap to vulgar company,
Opinion, that did help me to the crown,
Had still kept loyal to possession
And left me in reputeless banishment,
A fellow of no mark nor likelihood.
By being seldom seen, I could not stir
But like a comet I was wondered at,
That men would tell their children, "This is he!"
Others would say, "Where, which is Bolingbroke?"
And then I stole all courtesy from heaven,
And dressed myself in such humility
That I did pluck allegiance from men's hearts,
Loud shouts and salutations from their mouths,
Even in the presence of the crownèd King.
Thus did I keep my person fresh and new,
My presence, like a robe pontifical,
Ne'er seen but wondered at; and so my state,
Seldom but sumptuous, showed like a feast
And won by rareness such solemnity.
The skipping King, he ambled up and down
With shallow jesters and rash bavin wits,
Soon kindled and soon burnt; carded his state,

32 rudely by violence. (According to an apocryphal story, Hal boxed the ears of the Lord Chief Justice and was sent to prison for it; see *2 Henry IV*, 1.2.54–55, 192, and 5.2.70–71.) **36 time** time of life, youth **40 common-hackneyed** cheapened, vulgarized **42 Opinion** i.e., public opinion **43 to possession** i.e., to Richard II's sovereignty **45 mark** importance. **likelihood** likelihood of success **50 I . . . heaven** i.e., I assumed a bearing of the utmost graciousness **56 pontifical** like that of a pope or archbishop **57 state** magnificence in public appearances **58 Seldom** infrequent **59 such solemnity** i.e., the solemnity appropriate to a festival **60 skipping** flighty **61 bavin** brushwood, soon burnt out **62 carded** debased. (A term applied to the adulteration or combing of wool.) **state** royal status

Mingled his royalty with capering fools,
Had his great name profanèd with their scorns, 64
And gave his countenance, against his name, 65
To laugh at gibing boys and stand the push 66
Of every beardless vain comparative; 67
Grew a companion to the common streets,
Enfeoffed himself to popularity, 69
That, being daily swallowed by men's eyes,
They surfeited with honey and began
To loathe the taste of sweetness, whereof a little
More than a little is by much too much.
So when he had occasion to be seen,
He was but as the cuckoo is in June,
Heard, not regarded—seen, but with such eyes
As, sick and blunted with community, 77
Afford no extraordinary gaze,
Such as is bent on sunlike majesty
When it shines seldom in admiring eyes;
But rather drowsed and hung their eyelids down,
Slept in his face, and rendered such aspect 82
As cloudy men use to their adversaries, 83
Being with his presence glutted, gorged, and full.
And in that very line, Harry, standest thou;
For thou hast lost thy princely privilege
With vile participation. Not an eye 87
But is aweary of thy common sight,
Save mine, which hath desired to see thee more—
Which now doth that I would not have it do, 90
Make blind itself with foolish tenderness. 91

PRINCE
I shall hereafter, my thrice gracious lord,
Be more myself.

KING For all the world

64 their scorns i.e., the scornful opinion people had of these favorites **65 gave . . . name** lent his authority, to the detriment of his royal dignity and reputation **66 stand the push** put up with the impudence **67 comparative** maker of comparisons, wisecracker **69 Enfeoffed himself** gave himself up **77 community** commonness **82 in his face** right before his eyes. **aspect** look **83 cloudy** sullen. (Also refers to the image of the sun.) **87 vile participation** base association or companionship **90 that** that which **91 tenderness** i.e., tears

As thou art to this hour was Richard then
When I from France set foot at Ravenspurgh,
And even as I was then is Percy now.
Now, by my scepter, and my soul to boot, 97
He hath more worthy interest to the state 98
Than thou the shadow of succession. 99
For of no right, nor color like to right, 100
He doth fill fields with harness in the realm, 101
Turns head against the lion's armèd jaws, 102
And, being no more in debt to years than thou, 103
Leads ancient lords and reverend bishops on
To bloody battles and to bruising arms.
What never-dying honor hath he got
Against renownèd Douglas! Whose high deeds, 107
Whose hot incursions and great name in arms
Holds from all soldiers chief majority 109
And military title capital 110
Through all the kingdoms that acknowledge Christ.
Thrice hath this Hotspur, Mars in swaddling clothes,
This infant warrior, in his enterprises
Discomfited great Douglas, ta'en him once, 114
Enlargèd him and made a friend of him, 115
To fill the mouth of deep defiance up 116
And shake the peace and safety of our throne.
And what say you to this? Percy, Northumberland,
The Archbishop's Grace of York, Douglas, Mortimer, 119
Capitulate against us and are up. 120
But wherefore do I tell these news to thee?
Why, Harry, do I tell thee of my foes,
Which art my nearest and dearest enemy? 123

97 to boot in addition **98–99 He . . . succession** i.e., even this rebel Hotspur has a better claim to the throne than you, the mere shadow of an heir **100 of no right** having no rightful claim. **color** pretext **101 harness** armor, i.e., men in armor **102 Turns head** leads an armed insurrection. **lion's** i.e., King's **103 being . . . thou** i.e., being no older than you (though historically Hotspur was twenty-three years older than the Prince) **107 Whose** i.e., Hotspur's **109 majority** preeminence **110 capital** chief, principal **114 Discomfited** defeated **115 Enlargèd** freed **116 To . . . up** i.e., to swell the roar of deep defiance **119 The Archbishop's Grace** i.e., His Grace the Archbishop **120 Capitulate** form a league, draw up articles. **up** up in arms **123 dearest** (1) most precious (2) direst

Thou that art like enough, through vassal fear, 124
Base inclination, and the start of spleen, 125
To fight against me under Percy's pay,
To dog his heels and curtsy at his frowns,
To show how much thou art degenerate.

PRINCE

Do not think so. You shall not find it so.
And God forgive them that so much have swayed
Your Majesty's good thoughts away from me!
I will redeem all this on Percy's head
And in the closing of some glorious day
Be bold to tell you that I am your son,
When I will wear a garment all of blood
And stain my favors in a bloody mask, 136
Which, washed away, shall scour my shame with it.
And that shall be the day, whene'er it lights, 138
That this same child of honor and renown,
This gallant Hotspur, this all-praisèd knight,
And your unthought-of Harry chance to meet. 141
For every honor sitting on his helm,
Would they were multitudes, and on my head
My shames redoubled! For the time will come
That I shall make this northern youth exchange
His glorious deeds for my indignities.
Percy is but my factor, good my lord, 147
To engross up glorious deeds on my behalf; 148
And I will call him to so strict account
That he shall render every glory up,
Yea, even the slightest worship of his time, 151
Or I will tear the reckoning from his heart.
This in the name of God I promise here,
The which if He be pleased I shall perform,
I do beseech Your Majesty may salve 155
The long-grown wounds of my intemperance. 156
If not, the end of life cancels all bonds,

124 like likely. **vassal** slavish **125 Base inclination** inclination for baseness. **start of spleen** fit of ill temper **136 favors** features **138 lights** dawns **141 unthought-of** ignored, disregarded **147 factor** agent **148 engross** amass, buy up **151 worship of his time** honor of his youthful lifetime **155 salve** soothe, heal **156 intemperance** dissolute living, sickness

And I will die a hundred thousand deaths
Ere break the smallest parcel of this vow.

KING
A hundred thousand rebels die in this!
Thou shalt have charge and sovereign trust herein. 161

Enter Blunt.

How now, good Blunt? Thy looks are full of speed.

BLUNT
So hath the business that I come to speak of.
Lord Mortimer of Scotland hath sent word 164
That Douglas and the English rebels met
The eleventh of this month at Shrewsbury.
A mighty and a fearful head they are, 167
If promises be kept on every hand,
As ever offered foul play in a state.

KING
The Earl of Westmorland set forth today,
With him my son, Lord John of Lancaster;
For this advertisement is five days old. 172
On Wednesday next, Harry, you shall set forward;
On Thursday we ourselves will march. Our meeting 174
Is Bridgnorth. And, Harry, you shall march 175
Through Gloucestershire; by which account,
Our business valuèd, some twelve days hence 177
Our general forces at Bridgnorth shall meet.
Our hands are full of business. Let's away!
Advantage feeds him fat while men delay. *Exeunt.* 180

✤

3.3 *Enter Falstaff and Bardolph.*

FALSTAFF Bardolph, am I not fallen away vilely since this 1

161 charge command (of troops) **164 Lord Mortimer of Scotland** (A Scottish nobleman, unrelated to Glendower's son-in-law.) **167 A** i.e., as. **head** armed force **172 advertisement** tidings, news **174 meeting** place of rendezvous **175 Bridgnorth** a town near Shrewsbury **177 Our business valuèd** estimating how long our business will take **180 Advantage . . . fat** opportunity (for rebellion) prospers

3.3. Location: A tavern in Eastcheap, as in 2.4.
1 fallen away shrunk

last action? Do I not bate? Do I not dwindle? Why, my skin hangs about me like an old lady's loose gown; I am withered like an old applejohn. Well, I'll repent, and that suddenly, while I am in some liking. I shall be out of heart shortly, and then I shall have no strength to repent. An I have not forgotten what the inside of a church is made of, I am a peppercorn, a brewer's horse. The inside of a church! Company, villainous company, hath been the spoil of me.

BARDOLPH Sir John, you are so fretful you cannot live long.

FALSTAFF Why, there is it. Come sing me a bawdy song; make me merry. I was as virtuously given as a gentleman need to be, virtuous enough: swore little, diced not above seven times—a week, went to a bawdy house not above once in a quarter—of an hour, paid money that I borrowed—three or four times, lived well and in good compass; and now I live out of all order, out of all compass.

BARDOLPH Why, you are so fat, Sir John, that you must needs be out of all compass, out of all reasonable compass, Sir John.

FALSTAFF Do thou amend thy face, and I'll amend my life. Thou art our admiral, thou bearest the lantern in the poop, but 'tis in the nose of thee. Thou art the Knight of the Burning Lamp.

BARDOLPH Why, Sir John, my face does you no harm.

FALSTAFF No, I'll be sworn, I make as good use of it as many a man doth of a death's-head or a *memento mori*. I never see thy face but I think upon hellfire and Dives that lived in purple; for there he is in his robes,

2 action i.e., the robbery at Gad's Hill. **bate** lose weight **4 applejohn** a kind of apple still in good eating condition when shriveled **5 liking** (1) good bodily condition (2) inclination **6 out of heart** (1) disinclined, disheartened (2) out of condition **7 An** if **8 peppercorn** unground dried pepper berry **9 brewer's horse** i.e., one that is old, withered, and decrepit **11 fretful** (1) anxious (2) fretted, frayed **14 given** inclined **19 good compass** reasonable limits; also, in Bardolph's speech, girth, circumference **25 admiral** flagship. **lantern** i.e., a light for the rest of the fleet to follow; here applied to Bardolph's inflamed nose, red from overdrinking **30–31 memento mori** reminder of death, such as a death's head or a skull engraved on a seal ring **32 Dives** the rich man who went to hell, referred to in Luke 16:19–31

burning, burning. If thou wert any way given to virtue, I would swear by thy face; my oath should be "By this fire, that's God's angel." But thou art altogether given over, and wert indeed, but for the light in thy face, the son of utter darkness. When thou rann'st up Gad's Hill in the night to catch my horse, if I did not think thou hadst been an *ignis fatuus* or a ball of wildfire, there's no purchase in money. O, thou art a perpetual triumph, an everlasting bonfire light! Thou hast saved me a thousand marks in links and torches, walking with thee in the night betwixt tavern and tavern; but the sack that thou hast drunk me would have bought me lights as good cheap at the dearest chandler's in Europe. I have maintained that salamander of yours with fire any time this two-and-thirty years. God reward me for it!

BARDOLPH 'Sblood, I would my face were in your belly!

FALSTAFF God-a-mercy! So should I be sure to be heartburned.

Enter Hostess.

How now, Dame Partlet the hen? Have you inquired yet who picked my pocket?

HOSTESS Why, Sir John, what do you think, Sir John? Do you think I keep thieves in my house? I have searched, I have inquired, so has my husband, man by man, boy by boy, servant by servant. The tithe of a hair was never lost in my house before.

FALSTAFF Ye lie, hostess. Bardolph was shaved and lost many a hair; and I'll be sworn my pocket was picked. Go to, you are a woman, go.

34–35 By . . . angel (A biblical echo, perhaps to Psalms 104:4, Hebrews 1:7, or Exodus 3:2.) **36 given over** abandoned to wickedness **39 ignis fatuus** will-o'-the-wisp **39–40 wildfire** fireworks; lightning; will-o'-the-wisp **41 triumph** procession led by torches **42 links** torches, flares **45 good cheap** cheap. **dearest** most expensive **45–46 chandler's** candle maker's **46 salamander** lizard reputed to be able to live in fire **49 I . . . belly** (A proverb meaning "I wish I were rid of this irritation"; stock response to an insult based on physical deformity.) **52 Partlet** (Traditional name of a hen.) **57 tithe** tenth part **59 was shaved** (1) had his beard cut (2) was cheated and robbed **59–60 lost many a hair** (1) was shaved (2) was made bald by syphilis

HOSTESS Who, I? No, I defy thee! God's light, I was 62
never called so in mine own house before.

FALSTAFF Go to, I know you well enough.

HOSTESS No, Sir John, you do not know me, Sir John. I
know you, Sir John. You owe me money, Sir John,
and now you pick a quarrel to beguile me of it. I
bought you a dozen of shirts to your back.

FALSTAFF Dowlas, filthy dowlas. I have given them 69
away to bakers' wives; they have made bolters of 70
them.

HOSTESS Now, as I am a true woman, holland of eight 72
shillings an ell. You owe money here besides, Sir 73
John, for your diet and by-drinkings, and money lent 74
you, four-and-twenty pound.

FALSTAFF He had his part of it. Let him pay. 76

HOSTESS He? Alas, he is poor, he hath nothing.

FALSTAFF How, poor? Look upon his face. What call
you rich? Let them coin his nose, let them coin his
cheeks. I'll not pay a denier. What, will you make a 80
younker of me? Shall I not take mine ease in mine inn 81
but I shall have my pocket picked? I have lost a seal
ring of my grandfather's worth forty mark.

HOSTESS O Jesu, I have heard the Prince tell him, I
know not how oft, that that ring was copper!

FALSTAFF How? The Prince is a Jack, a sneak-up. 86
'Sblood, an he were here, I would cudgel him like a
dog if he would say so. 88

Enter the Prince [*with Peto*], *marching, and Falstaff meets him playing upon his truncheon like a fife.*

How now, lad, is the wind in that door, i' faith? Must 89
we all march?

BARDOLPH Yea, two and two, Newgate fashion. 91

HOSTESS My lord, I pray you, hear me.

62 God's light (A mild oath.) **69 Dowlas** a coarse kind of linen **70 bolters** cloths for sifting flour **72 holland** fine linen **73 an ell** a measure of 45 inches **74 diet** meals. **by-drinkings** drinks between meals **76 He** i.e., Bardolph **80 denier** one-twelfth of a French sou; type of very small coin **81 younker** i.e., greenhorn **86 Jack** knave, rascal. **sneak-up** sneak **88 s.d. truncheon** officer's staff **89 is . . . door** i.e., is that the way the wind is blowing **91 Newgate** (A famous city prison in London. Prisoners marched two by two.)

PRINCE What sayst thou, Mistress Quickly? How doth thy husband? I love him well; he is an honest man.

HOSTESS Good my lord, hear me.

FALSTAFF Prithee, let her alone and list to me.

PRINCE What sayst thou, Jack?

FALSTAFF The other night I fell asleep here behind the arras and had my pocket picked. This house is turned bawdy house; they pick pockets.

PRINCE What didst thou lose, Jack?

FALSTAFF Wilt thou believe me, Hal? Three or four bonds of forty pound apiece, and a seal ring of my grandfather's.

PRINCE A trifle, some eightpenny matter.

HOSTESS So I told him, my lord, and I said I heard Your Grace say so; and, my lord, he speaks most vilely of you, like a foulmouthed man as he is, and said he would cudgel you.

PRINCE What, he did not!

HOSTESS There's neither faith, truth, nor womanhood in me else.

FALSTAFF There's no more faith in thee than in a stewed prune, nor no more truth in thee than in a drawn fox; and for womanhood, Maid Marian may be the deputy's wife of the ward to thee. Go, you thing, go.

HOSTESS Say, what thing, what thing?

FALSTAFF What thing? Why, a thing to thank God on.

HOSTESS I am no thing to thank God on, I would thou shouldst know it! I am an honest man's wife, and, setting thy knighthood aside, thou art a knave to call me so.

FALSTAFF Setting thy womanhood aside, thou art a beast to say otherwise.

HOSTESS Say, what beast, thou knave, thou?

FALSTAFF What beast? Why, an otter.

113–114 stewed prune (Customarily associated with bawdy houses.)
114 drawn fox fox driven from cover and wily in getting back
115–116 Maid . . . thee i.e., Maid Marian, disreputable woman in Robin Hood ballads, morris dances, and the like, was a model of respectability compared with you **118, 119 What thing . . . no thing** (with sexual quibbles) **120–121, 123 setting . . . aside** (Mistress Quickly means, "without wishing to offend your rank of knighthood," but Falstaff replies in l. 123 with the meaning, "setting aside your womanhood as of no value or pertinence.")

PRINCE An otter, Sir John! Why an otter?
FALSTAFF Why? She's neither fish nor flesh; a man
knows not where to have her. 129
HOSTESS Thou art an unjust man in saying so. Thou or
any man knows where to have me, thou knave, thou!
PRINCE Thou sayst true, hostess, and he slanders thee
most grossly.
HOSTESS So he doth you, my lord, and said this other
day you ought him a thousand pound. 135
PRINCE Sirrah, do I owe you a thousand pound?
FALSTAFF A thousand pound, Hal? A million. Thy love
is worth a million; thou owest me thy love.
HOSTESS Nay, my lord, he called you Jack and said he
would cudgel you.
FALSTAFF Did I, Bardolph?
BARDOLPH Indeed, Sir John, you said so.
FALSTAFF Yea, if he said my ring was copper.
PRINCE I say 'tis copper. Darest thou be as good as thy
word now?
FALSTAFF Why, Hal, thou knowest, as thou art but
man, I dare; but as thou art prince, I fear thee as I fear
the roaring of the lion's whelp. 148
PRINCE And why not as the lion?
FALSTAFF The King himself is to be feared as the lion.
Dost thou think I'll fear thee as I fear thy father? Nay,
an I do, I pray God my girdle break.
PRINCE O, if it should, how would thy guts fall about
thy knees! But, sirrah, there's no room for faith, truth,
nor honesty in this bosom of thine; it is all filled up
with guts and midriff. Charge an honest woman with
picking thy pocket! Why, thou whoreson, impudent,
embossed rascal, if there were anything in thy pocket 158
but tavern reckonings, memorandums of bawdy 159
houses, and one poor pennyworth of sugar candy to
make thee long-winded, if thy pocket were enriched
with any other injuries but these, I am a villain. And 162

129 have understand (with suggestion of enjoying sexually) **135 ought** owed **148 whelp** cub **158 embossed** (1) swollen with fat (2) foaming at the mouth and exhausted, like a hunted animal. **rascal** (1) scoundrel (2) immature and inferior deer **159 memorandums** souvenirs **162 injuries** i.e., those things you claim to have lost, thereby suffering harm

yet you will stand to it; you will not pocket up wrong! Art thou not ashamed?

FALSTAFF Dost thou hear, Hal? Thou knowest in the state of innocency Adam fell; and what should poor Jack Falstaff do in the days of villainy? Thou seest I have more flesh than another man, and therefore more frailty. You confess then you picked my pocket?

PRINCE It appears so by the story.

FALSTAFF Hostess, I forgive thee. Go make ready breakfast. Love thy husband, look to thy servants, cherish thy guests. Thou shalt find me tractable to any honest reason; thou seest I am pacified still. Nay, prithee, begone. (*Exit Hostess.*) Now, Hal, to the news at court: for the robbery, lad, how is that answered?

PRINCE O my sweet beef, I must still be good angel to thee. The money is paid back again.

FALSTAFF O, I do not like that paying back. 'Tis a double labor.

PRINCE I am good friends with my father and may do anything.

FALSTAFF Rob me the exchequer the first thing thou dost, and do it with unwashed hands too.

BARDOLPH Do, my lord.

PRINCE I have procured thee, Jack, a charge of foot.

FALSTAFF I would it had been of horse. Where shall I find one that can steal well? O, for a fine thief of the age of two-and-twenty or thereabouts! I am heinously unprovided. Well, God be thanked for these rebels; they offend none but the virtuous. I laud them, I praise them.

PRINCE Bardolph!

BARDOLPH My lord?

PRINCE
Go bear this letter to Lord John of Lancaster,

163 stand to it make a stand, insist on your supposed rights. **pocket up** endure silently **170 by** according to **174 still** always **179–180 double labor** i.e., the taking and the returning **184 with unwashed hands** i.e., at once **186 charge of foot** command of a company of infantry **188 one** i.e., a companion in thievery. (Falstaff sees war as the opportunity for stealing and conning.) **190 unprovided** ill-equipped **191 they . . . virtuous** i.e., the rebels, by providing the occasion of war, give dishonest men a chance to profiteer and hence offend only those who are honest

To my brother John; this to my lord of Westmorland.
[*He gives letters. Exit Bardolph.*]
Go, Peto, to horse, to horse, for thou and I
Have thirty miles to ride yet ere dinnertime.
[*Exit Peto.*]
Jack, meet me tomorrow in the Temple Hall 199
At two o'clock in the afternoon.
There shalt thou know thy charge, and there receive
Money and order for their furniture. 202
The land is burning. Percy stands on high,
And either we or they must lower lie. [*Exit.*]

FALSTAFF
Rare words, brave world! Hostess, my breakfast, come! 205
O, I could wish this tavern were my drum! [*Exit.*] 206

✤

199 Temple Hall i.e., at the Inner Temple, one of the Inns of Court **202 furniture** equipment, furnishing **205 brave** splendid **206 drum** (Possibly Falstaff means that he wishes he could continue to enjoy this tavern instead of risking his life in battle. He may also be punning on *tavern/taborn,* i.e., *taborin,* a kind of drum.)

4.1 [*Enter Hotspur, Worcester, and Douglas.*]

HOTSPUR
Well said, my noble Scot. If speaking truth
In this fine age were not thought flattery,
Such attribution should the Douglas have 3
As not a soldier of this season's stamp 4
Should go so general current through the world. 5
By God, I cannot flatter; I do defy 6
The tongues of soothers! But a braver place 7
In my heart's love hath no man than yourself.
Nay, task me to my word; approve me, lord. 9

DOUGLAS Thou art the king of honor.
No man so potent breathes upon the ground
But I will beard him.

Enter one [a Messenger] with letters.

HOTSPUR Do so, and 'tis well.— 12
What letters hast thou there?—I can but thank you.

MESSENGER
These letters come from your father.

HOTSPUR
Letters from him? Why comes he not himself?

MESSENGER
He cannot come, my lord. He is grievous sick.

HOTSPUR
Zounds, how has he the leisure to be sick
In such a jostling time? Who leads his power? 18
Under whose government come they along? 19

MESSENGER
His letters bears his mind, not I, my lord.
[*Hotspur reads the letter.*]

4.1. Location: The rebel camp near Shrewsbury.
3 attribution praise, tribute **4 stamp** coinage **5 go . . . current** be so widely accepted and acclaimed. (Continues the metaphor of coinage.) **6 defy** proclaim against **7 soothers** flatterers. **braver** better, dearer **9 task . . . word** challenge me to make good my word. **approve** test **12 But . . . him** but that I will defy him **18 jostling** contending, clashing **19 government** command

WORCESTER
I prithee, tell me, doth he keep his bed? 21
MESSENGER
He did, my lord, four days ere I set forth,
And at the time of my departure thence
He was much feared by his physicians. 24
WORCESTER
I would the state of time had first been whole 25
Ere he by sickness had been visited.
His health was never better worth than now.
HOTSPUR
Sick now? Droop now? This sickness doth infect
The very life-blood of our enterprise;
'Tis catching hither, even to our camp.
He writes me here that inward sickness—
And that his friends by deputation 32
Could not so soon be drawn, nor did he think it meet 33
To lay so dangerous and dear a trust
On any soul removed but on his own. 35
Yet doth he give us bold advertisement 36
That with our small conjunction we should on, 37
To see how fortune is disposed to us;
For, as he writes, there is no quailing now, 39
Because the King is certainly possessed 40
Of all our purposes. What say you to it?
WORCESTER
Your father's sickness is a maim to us. 42
HOTSPUR
A perilous gash, a very limb lopped off.
And yet, in faith, it is not! His present want 44
Seems more than we shall find it. Were it good 45
To set the exact wealth of all our states 46
All at one cast? To set so rich a main 47
On the nice hazard of one doubtful hour? 48

21 keep keep to, stay in **24 feared** feared for **25 time** the times **32 by deputation** through deputies **33 drawn** assembled. **meet** appropriate **35 On . . . own** on anyone other than himself **36 advertisement** counsel, advice **37 conjunction** joint force. **on** go on **39 quailing** losing heart **40 possessed** informed **42 maim** injury **44 want** absence **45 more** more serious **46 To . . . states** to stake the absolute total of our resources **47 cast** throw of the dice. **main** stake in gambling; also, an army **48 nice** precarious, delicate. **hazard** (1) game at dice (2) venture

It were not good, for therein should we read
The very bottom and the soul of hope,
The very list, the very utmost bound
Of all our fortunes.

DOUGLAS Faith, and so we should;
Where now remains a sweet reversion,
We may boldly spend upon the hope
Of what is to come in.
A comfort of retirement lives in this.

HOTSPUR
A rendezvous, a home to fly unto,
If that the devil and mischance look big
Upon the maidenhead of our affairs.

WORCESTER
But yet I would your father had been here.
The quality and hair of our attempt
Brooks no division. It will be thought
By some that know not why he is away
That wisdom, loyalty, and mere dislike
Of our proceedings kept the Earl from hence.
And think how such an apprehension
May turn the tide of fearful faction
And breed a kind of question in our cause.
For well you know we of the offering side
Must keep aloof from strict arbitrament,
And stop all sight holes, every loop from whence
The eye of reason may pry in upon us.
This absence of your father's draws a curtain
That shows the ignorant a kind of fear
Before not dreamt of.

HOTSPUR You strain too far.
I rather of his absence make this use:
It lends a luster and more great opinion,

49–50 should . . . hope we should discover the utmost foundation and basis of our hopes, the most we could rely on **51 list** limit
53 reversion (Literally, part of an estate yet to be inherited.)
56 retirement something to fall back on **58 big** threatening
59 maidenhead i.e., commencement **61 hair** kind, nature **62 Brooks** tolerates **64 loyalty** i.e., to the crown. **mere** absolute
66 apprehension (1) perception (2) apprehensiveness **67 fearful faction** timid support **69 offering side** side that attacks **70 strict arbitrament** just inquiry or investigation **71 loop** loophole **73 draws** draws aside, opens **75 strain too far** exaggerate **77 opinion** renown

A larger dare to our great enterprise,
Than if the Earl were here; for men must think,
If we without his help can make a head
To push against a kingdom, with his help
We shall o'erturn it topsy-turvy down.
Yet all goes well, yet all our joints are whole.

DOUGLAS

As heart can think. There is not such a word
Spoke of in Scotland as this term of fear.

Enter Sir Richard Vernon.

HOTSPUR

My cousin Vernon, welcome, by my soul.

VERNON

Pray God my news be worth a welcome, lord.
The Earl of Westmorland, seven thousand strong,
Is marching hitherwards; with him Prince John.

HOTSPUR

No harm. What more?

VERNON

And further I have learned
The King himself in person is set forth,
Or hitherwards intended speedily,
With strong and mighty preparation.

HOTSPUR

He shall be welcome too. Where is his son,
The nimble-footed madcap Prince of Wales,
And his comrades, that doffed the world aside
And bid it pass?

VERNON

All furnished, all in arms;
All plumed like estridges, that with the wind
Bated like eagles having lately bathed,
Glittering in golden coats, like images,
As full of spirit as the month of May
And gorgeous as the sun at midsummer,
Wanton as youthful goats, wild as young bulls.
I saw young Harry, with his beaver on,

80 make a head raise an armed force **83 Yet** still. **joints** limbs **92 intended** on the verge of departure **96 doffed** put aside with a gesture **97 furnished** equipped **98 estridges** ostriches. (Refers to ostrich plumes on crests.) **99 Bated** flapped their wings. (From falconry.) **100 coats** (1) coats of mail (2) heraldic coats of arms. **images** gilded statues **103 Wanton** sportive, frolicsome **104 beaver** visor; hence, helmet

His cuisses on his thighs, gallantly armed, 105
Rise from the ground like feathered Mercury,
And vaulted with such ease into his seat 107
As if an angel dropped down from the clouds
To turn and wind a fiery Pegasus 109
And witch the world with noble horsemanship. 110

HOTSPUR
No more, no more! Worse than the sun in March 111
This praise doth nourish agues. Let them come. 112
They come like sacrifices in their trim, 113
And to the fire-eyed maid of smoky war 114
All hot and bleeding will we offer them.
The mailèd Mars shall on his altar sit 116
Up to the ears in blood. I am on fire
To hear this rich reprisal is so nigh, 118
And yet not ours. Come, let me taste my horse,
Who is to bear me like a thunderbolt
Against the bosom of the Prince of Wales.
Harry to Harry shall, hot horse to horse,
Meet and ne'er part till one drop down a corse.
O, that Glendower were come!

VERNON
There is more news:
I learned in Worcester, as I rode along,
He cannot draw his power this fourteen days. 126

DOUGLAS
That's the worst tidings that I hear of yet.

WORCESTER
Ay, by my faith, that bears a frosty sound.

HOTSPUR
What may the King's whole battle reach unto? 129

VERNON
To thirty thousand.

HOTSPUR
Forty let it be!
My father and Glendower being both away,
The powers of us may serve so great a day. 132

105 cuisses armor for the thighs **107 seat** i.e., saddle **109 wind** wheel. **Pegasus** winged horse of Greek mythology **110 witch** bewitch
111–112 Worse . . . agues (The spring sun was believed to give impetus to chills and fevers, by drawing up vapors.) **113 sacrifices** beasts for sacrifice. **trim** fine apparel, trappings **114 maid** i.e., Bellona, goddess of war
116 mailèd dressed in mail, armor **118 reprisal** prize **126 draw his power** muster his army **129 battle** army **132 The . . . us** our forces

Come, let us take a muster speedily.
Doomsday is near; die all, die merrily.

DOUGLAS
Talk not of dying. I am out of fear 135
Of death or death's hand for this one half year.
Exeunt.

✤

4.2 *Enter Falstaff,* [*and*] *Bardolph.*

FALSTAFF Bardolph, get thee before to Coventry; fill me
a bottle of sack. Our soldiers shall march through; we'll
to Sutton Coldfield tonight. 3
BARDOLPH Will you give me money, Captain?
FALSTAFF Lay out, lay out. 5
BARDOLPH This bottle makes an angel. 6
FALSTAFF An if it do, take it for thy labor; an if it make 7
twenty, take them all; I'll answer the coinage. Bid my 8
lieutenant Peto meet me at town's end.
BARDOLPH I will, Captain. Farewell. *Exit.*
FALSTAFF If I be not ashamed of my soldiers, I am a
soused gurnet. I have misused the King's press dam- 12
nably. I have got, in exchange of a hundred and fifty
soldiers, three hundred and odd pounds. I press me 14
none but good householders, yeomen's sons, inquire 15
me out contracted bachelors, such as had been asked 16
twice on the banns—such a commodity of warm 17
slaves as had as lief hear the devil as a drum, such as 18
fear the report of a caliver worse than a struck fowl or 19

135 out of free from

4.2. Location: A public road near Coventry.
3 Sutton Coldfield (In Warwickshire near Coventry.) **5 Lay out** i.e., pay for it yourself **6 makes an angel** i.e., makes 10 shillings I've spent for you. (But Falstaff answers as though *makes* means "produces," implying that Bardolph has profited from the transaction.) **7 An if** if
8 answer be responsible for. **the coinage** i.e., the money produced
12 soused gurnet a kind of pickled fish. **King's press** royal warrant for the impressment of troops **14 press me** draft, conscript **15 good** i.e., wealthy. **yeomen's** small freeholders' **16 contracted** engaged to be married **17 banns** public announcements, declared on three Sundays in succession, of an intent to marry. **warm** i.e., loving their comfort
18 lief willingly **19 caliver** musket. **struck** wounded

a hurt wild duck. I pressed me none but such toasts-and-butter, with hearts in their bellies no bigger than pins' heads, and they have bought out their services; and now my whole charge consists of ancients, corporals, lieutenants, gentlemen of companies—slaves as ragged as Lazarus in the painted cloth, where the glutton's dogs licked his sores, and such as indeed were never soldiers, but discarded unjust servingmen, younger sons to younger brothers, revolted tapsters, and hostlers trade-fallen, the cankers of a calm world and a long peace, ten times more dishonorable-ragged than an old feazed ancient. And such have I, to fill up the rooms of them as have bought out their services, that you would think that I had a hundred and fifty tattered prodigals lately come from swine keeping, from eating draff and husks. A mad fellow met me on the way and told me I had unloaded all the gibbets and pressed the dead bodies. No eye hath seen such scarecrows. I'll not march through Coventry with them, that's flat. Nay, and the villains march wide betwixt the legs as if they had gyves on, for indeed I had the most of them out of prison. There's not a shirt and a half in all my company, and the half shirt is two napkins tacked together and thrown over the shoulders like a herald's coat without sleeves; and the shirt, to say the truth, stolen from my host at Saint Albans, or the red-nose innkeeper of Daventry. But that's all one; they'll find linen enough on every hedge.

Enter the Prince [*and the*] *Lord of Westmorland.*

20–21 toasts-and-butter weaklings **22 bought . . . services** i.e., paid, bribed, to be released from military duty **23 charge** company, troop. **ancients** ensigns, standard-bearers. (By appointing a disproportionate number of junior officers, Falstaff has made it possible to collect for himself their more substantial pay.) **24 gentlemen of companies** a kind of junior officer **25 painted cloth** cheap hangings for a room. (For the story of Lazarus the beggar and Dives the rich man, see Luke 16:19–31.) **27 unjust** dishonest **28 younger . . . brothers** (i.e., with no possibility of inheritance). **revolted** runaway **29 trade-fallen** whose business has fallen away. **cankers** cankerworms that destroy leaves and buds. (Used figuratively.) **31 feazed ancient** frayed flag **34 prodigals** (See Luke 15:15–16.) **35 draff** hogwash **36 gibbets** gallows **38 that's flat** that's for sure **40 gyves** fetters **45, 46 Saint Albans, Daventry** (Towns north and west of London, on the road to Coventry.) **46 that's all one** no matter **47 hedge** (Where wet linen was spread out to dry.)

PRINCE How now, blown Jack? How now, quilt? 48
FALSTAFF What, Hal? How now, mad wag? What a
devil dost thou in Warwickshire? My good lord of
Westmorland, I cry you mercy. I thought your honor 51
had already been at Shrewsbury.
WESTMORLAND Faith, Sir John, 'tis more than time that
I were there, and you too; but my powers are there 54
already. The King, I can tell you, looks for us all. We
must away all night. 56
FALSTAFF Tut, never fear me. I am as vigilant as a cat to 57
steal cream.
PRINCE I think, to steal cream indeed, for thy theft hath 59
already made thee butter. But tell me, Jack, whose fel- 60
lows are these that come after?
FALSTAFF Mine, Hal, mine.
PRINCE I did never see such pitiful rascals.
FALSTAFF Tut, tut, good enough to toss; food for pow- 64
der, food for powder. They'll fill a pit as well as better. 65
Tush, man, mortal men, mortal men.
WESTMORLAND Ay, but, Sir John, methinks they are exceeding poor and bare, too beggarly.
FALSTAFF Faith, for their poverty, I know not where 69
they had that, and for their bareness, I am sure they
never learned that of me.
PRINCE No, I'll be sworn, unless you call three fingers 72
in the ribs bare. But, sirrah, make haste. Percy is al- 73
ready in the field. *Exit.*
FALSTAFF What, is the King encamped?
WESTMORLAND He is, Sir John. I fear we shall stay too long. [*Exit.*]
FALSTAFF Well,
To the latter end of a fray and the beginning of a feast
Fits a dull fighter and a keen guest. *Exit.* 81

✤

48 blown swollen, inflated; also, short of wind **51 cry you mercy** beg your pardon **54 powers** soldiers **56 must away** must march **57 fear** worry about **59–60 thy . . . butter** i.e., all the cream (rich things) you have stolen has been churned into butterfat in your barrel-like belly **64 toss** i.e., on a pike **64–65 food for powder** cannon fodder **69 for** as for **72–73 three . . . ribs** i.e., Falstaff's fat-covered ribs. (A *finger* was a measure of three-fourths of an inch.) **81 keen** with keen appetite

4.3

Enter Hotspur, Worcester, Douglas, [*and*] *Vernon.*

HOTSPUR
We'll fight with him tonight.
WORCESTER
It may not be.
DOUGLAS
You give him then advantage.
VERNON
Not a whit.
HOTSPUR
Why say you so? Looks he not for supply?
VERNON
So do we.
HOTSPUR His is certain; ours is doubtful.
WORCESTER
Good cousin, be advised, stir not tonight.
VERNON
Do not, my lord.
DOUGLAS You do not counsel well.
You speak it out of fear and cold heart.
VERNON
Do me no slander, Douglas. By my life,
And I dare well maintain it with my life,
If well-respected honor bid me on,
I hold as little counsel with weak fear
As you, my lord, or any Scot that this day lives.
Let it be seen tomorrow in the battle
Which of us fears.
DOUGLAS Yea, or tonight.
VERNON Content.
HOTSPUR Tonight, say I.
VERNON
Come, come, it may not be. I wonder much,
Being men of such great leading as you are,
That you foresee not what impediments
Drag back our expedition. Certain horse
Of my cousin Vernon's are not yet come up.

4.3. Location: The rebel camp near Shrewsbury.
2 then i.e., if you wait. (Addressed to Worcester, not Hotspur.) **3 supply** reinforcements **10 well-respected** well weighed or considered **19 leading** leadership **21 expedition** speedy progress. **horse** cavalry (as also in l. 23)

Your uncle Worcester's horse came but today,
And now their pride and mettle is asleep, 24
Their courage with hard labor tame and dull,
That not a horse is half the half of himself.

HOTSPUR

So are the horses of the enemy
In general journey-bated and brought low. 28
The better part of ours are full of rest.

WORCESTER

The number of the King exceedeth ours.
For God's sake, cousin, stay till all come in. 31
The trumpet sounds a parley.

Enter Sir Walter Blunt.

BLUNT

I come with gracious offers from the King,
If you vouchsafe me hearing and respect. 33

HOTSPUR

Welcome, Sir Walter Blunt; and would to God
You were of our determination! 35
Some of us love you well; and even those some 36
Envy your great deservings and good name
Because you are not of our quality 38
But stand against us like an enemy.

BLUNT

And God defend but still I should stand so, 40
So long as out of limit and true rule 41
You stand against anointed majesty.
But to my charge. The King hath sent to know
The nature of your griefs and whereupon 44
You conjure from the breast of civil peace
Such bold hostility, teaching his duteous land
Audacious cruelty. If that the King
Have any way your good deserts forgot,
Which he confesseth to be manifold,
He bids you name your griefs, and with all speed

24 pride and mettle spirit **28 journey-bated** tired from the journey **31 s.d. parley** trumpet summons to a conference **33 respect** attention **35 determination** persuasion (in the fight) **36 even those some** i.e., those same persons among us who love you **38 quality** party **40 defend** forbid. **still** always **41 limit** bounds of allegiance **44 griefs** grievances

You shall have your desires with interest
And pardon absolute for yourself and these
Herein misled by your suggestion. 53

HOTSPUR

The King is kind; and well we know the King
Knows at what time to promise, when to pay.
My father and my uncle and myself
Did give him that same royalty he wears,
And when he was not six-and-twenty strong,
Sick in the world's regard, wretched and low,
A poor unminded outlaw sneaking home,
My father gave him welcome to the shore;
And when he heard him swear and vow to God
He came but to be Duke of Lancaster,
To sue his livery and beg his peace 64
With tears of innocency and terms of zeal,
My father, in kind heart and pity moved,
Swore him assistance, and performed it too.
Now when the lords and barons of the realm
Perceived Northumberland did lean to him,
The more and less came in with cap and knee, 70
Met him in boroughs, cities, villages,
Attended him on bridges, stood in lanes, 72
Laid gifts before him, proffered him their oaths,
Gave him their heirs as pages, followed him 74
Even at the heels in golden multitudes. 75
He presently, as greatness knows itself, 76
Steps me a little higher than his vow 77
Made to my father while his blood was poor 78
Upon the naked shore at Ravenspurgh,
And now, forsooth, takes on him to reform
Some certain edicts and some strait decrees 81
That lie too heavy on the commonwealth,

53 suggestion instigation **64 sue his livery** sue as an heir come of age for the delivery of his lands. **beg his peace** i.e., request to be reconciled to King Richard **70 more and less** persons of all ranks. **with . . . knee** i.e., with cap in hand and with bended knee **72 Attended** waited for. **stood in lanes** stood row-deep along the roads **74 Gave . . . heirs** i.e., to serve him **75 golden** (1) auspicious, celebrating (2) majestically attired **76 knows itself** perceives its own strength **77 Steps me** i.e., steps. (*Me* is used colloquially.) **vow** i.e., Henry's vow to seek no more than his inheritance **78 blood** spirit, temper. **poor** i.e., unambitious **81 strait** strict

Cries out upon abuses, seems to weep
Over his country's wrongs; and by this face, 84
This seeming brow of justice, did he win
The hearts of all that he did angle for;
Proceeded further—cut me off the heads 87
Of all the favorites that the absent King
In deputation left behind him here,
When he was personal in the Irish war. 90

BLUNT
Tut, I came not to hear this.

HOTSPUR
                    Then to the point.
In short time after, he deposed the King,
Soon after that, deprived him of his life,
And in the neck of that tasked the whole state; 94
To make that worse, suffered his kinsman March—
Who is, if every owner were well placed, 96
Indeed his king—to be engaged in Wales, 97
There without ransom to lie forfeited; 98
Disgraced me in my happy victories, 99
Sought to entrap me by intelligence; 100
Rated mine uncle from the Council board; 101
In rage dismissed my father from the court;
Broke oath on oath, committed wrong on wrong,
And in conclusion drove us to seek out
This head of safety, and withal to pry 105
Into his title, the which we find
Too indirect for long continuance.

BLUNT
Shall I return this answer to the King?

HOTSPUR
Not so, Sir Walter. We'll withdraw awhile.
Go to the King; and let there be impawned 110
Some surety for a safe return again,
And in the morning early shall mine uncle
Bring him our purposes. And so farewell. 113

84 face show, pretense **87 cut me** i.e., cut **90 personal** physically, in person **94 in . . . that** next, immediately after. **tasked** laid taxes upon **96 if . . . placed** if every claimant were given his proper place **97 engaged** held as hostage **98 lie forfeited** remain prisoner, unreclaimed **99 Disgraced me** (by demanding the prisoners; see 1.3.23 ff.) **happy** fortunate **100 intelligence** secret information, i.e., from spies **101 Rated** scolded **105 head of safety** armed force for our protection. **withal** also **110 impawned** pledged **113 purposes** proposals

BLUNT
I would you would accept of grace and love.
HOTSPUR
And maybe so we shall.
BLUNT
Pray God you do. [*Exeunt.*]

✤

4.4 *Enter* [*the*] *Archbishop of York,* [*and*] *Sir Michael.*

ARCHBISHOP [*Giving letters*]
Hie, good Sir Michael, bear this sealèd brief
With wingèd haste to the Lord Marshal,
This to my cousin Scroop, and all the rest
To whom they are directed. If you knew
How much they do import, you would make haste.
SIR MICHAEL My good lord, I guess their tenor.
ARCHBISHOP Like enough you do.
Tomorrow, good Sir Michael, is a day
Wherein the fortune of ten thousand men
Must bide the touch; for, sir, at Shrewsbury,
As I am truly given to understand,
The King with mighty and quick-raisèd power
Meets with Lord Harry. And I fear, Sir Michael,
What with the sickness of Northumberland,
Whose power was in the first proportion,
And what with Owen Glendower's absence thence,
Who with them was a rated sinew too
And comes not in, o'erruled by prophecies,
I fear the power of Percy is too weak
To wage an instant trial with the King.
SIR MICHAEL
Why, my good lord, you need not fear;
There is Douglas and Lord Mortimer.

4.4. Location: York. The Archbishop's palace.
1 brief letter, dispatch **2 Lord Marshal** i.e., Thomas Mowbray, son of the Duke of Norfolk who is exiled in *Richard II,* and a longtime enemy of the new King **3 Scroop** i.e., perhaps Sir Stephen Scroop of *Richard II,* 3.2.91–218, or Lord Scroop of Masham of *Henry V,* 2.2 **10 bide the touch** be put to the test (like gold) **15 in . . . proportion** of the largest size **17 rated sinew** main strength or support reckoned upon **20 instant** immediate

ARCHBISHOP No, Mortimer is not there.

SIR MICHAEL
But there is Mordake, Vernon, Lord Harry Percy,
And there is my lord of Worcester, and a head 25
Of gallant warriors, noble gentlemen.

ARCHBISHOP
And so there is. But yet the King hath drawn
The special head of all the land together: 28
The Prince of Wales, Lord John of Lancaster,
The noble Westmorland, and warlike Blunt,
And many more corrivals and dear men 31
Of estimation and command in arms. 32

SIR MICHAEL
Doubt not, my lord, they shall be well opposed.

ARCHBISHOP
I hope no less, yet needful 'tis to fear;
And, to prevent the worst, Sir Michael, speed.
For if Lord Percy thrive not, ere the King
Dismiss his power he means to visit us, 37
For he hath heard of our confederacy,
And 'tis but wisdom to make strong against him.
Therefore make haste. I must go write again
To other friends; and so farewell, Sir Michael.

Exeunt.

✤

25 head troop **28 special head** notable leaders **31 corrivals** partners in the enterprise **32 estimation** reputation, importance **37 he** i.e., the King

5.1 *Enter the King, Prince of Wales, Lord John of Lancaster, Sir Walter Blunt,* [*and*] *Falstaff.*

KING
How bloodily the sun begins to peer
Above yon bosky hill! The day looks pale 2
At his distemperature.
PRINCE The southern wind 3
Doth play the trumpet to his purposes, 4
And by his hollow whistling in the leaves
Foretells a tempest and a blustering day.
KING
Then with the losers let it sympathize,
For nothing can seem foul to those that win.
The trumpet sounds.

Enter Worcester [*and Vernon*].

How now, my lord of Worcester? 'Tis not well
That you and I should meet upon such terms
As now we meet. You have deceived our trust
And made us doff our easy robes of peace 12
To crush our old limbs in ungentle steel.
This is not well, my lord, this is not well.
What say you to it? Will you again unknit
This churlish knot of all-abhorrèd war
And move in that obedient orb again 17
Where you did give a fair and natural light,
And be no more an exhaled meteor, 19
A prodigy of fear, and a portent 20
Of broachèd mischief to the unborn times? 21
WORCESTER Hear me, my liege:
For mine own part, I could be well content

5.1. Location: The King's camp near Shrewsbury.
2 bosky bushy **3 his distemperature** i.e., the sun's unhealthy appearance **4 trumpet** trumpeter. **his** its, the sun's **12 easy** comfortable **17 orb** orbit, sphere of action. (The King's subjects, like planets and stars in the Ptolemaic cosmos, were supposed to revolve around the kingly center, comparable to the earth, in fixed courses.) **19 exhaled meteor** (Meteors were believed to be vapors drawn up or *exhaled* by the sun and visible as streaks of light; they were regarded as ill omens.) **20 prodigy of fear** fearful omen **21 broachèd** set flowing, already begun

To entertain the lag end of my life
With quiet hours, for I protest
I have not sought the day of this dislike.

KING
You have not sought it? How comes it, then?

FALSTAFF Rebellion lay in his way, and he found it.

PRINCE Peace, chewet, peace!

WORCESTER
It pleased Your Majesty to turn your looks
Of favor from myself and all our house;
And yet I must remember you, my lord,
We were the first and dearest of your friends.
For you my staff of office did I break
In Richard's time, and posted day and night
To meet you on the way, and kiss your hand,
When yet you were in place and in account
Nothing so strong and fortunate as I.
It was myself, my brother, and his son
That brought you home and boldly did outdare
The dangers of the time. You swore to us,
And you did swear that oath at Doncaster,
That you did nothing purpose 'gainst the state,
Nor claim no further than your new-fall'n right,
The seat of Gaunt, dukedom of Lancaster.
To this we swore our aid. But in short space
It rained down fortune showering on your head,
And such a flood of greatness fell on you—
What with our help, what with the absent King,
What with the injuries of a wanton time,
The seeming sufferances that you had borne,
And the contrarious winds that held the King
So long in his unlucky Irish wars
That all in England did repute him dead—
And from this swarm of fair advantages
You took occasion to be quickly wooed

24 entertain occupy **26 the . . . dislike** this time of discord **29 chewet** chough, jackdaw. (Here, a chatterer.) **32 remember** remind **35 posted** rode swiftly **38 Nothing** not at all **40 brought** escorted **44 new-fall'n** recently inherited (by the death of John of Gaunt) **50 injuries** abuses, evils. **wanton** lawless **51 sufferances** suffering, distress **56 occasion** the opportunity

To grip the general sway into your hand;
Forgot your oath to us at Doncaster;
And being fed by us, you used us so
As that ungentle gull, the cuckoo's bird, 60
Useth the sparrow; did oppress our nest,
Grew by our feeding to so great a bulk
That even our love durst not come near your sight 63
For fear of swallowing; but with nimble wing
We were enforced, for safety's sake, to fly
Out of your sight and raise this present head, 66
Whereby we stand opposèd by such means 67
As you yourself have forged against yourself
By unkind usage, dangerous countenance, 69
And violation of all faith and troth
Sworn to us in your younger enterprise.

KING
These things indeed you have articulate, 72
Proclaimed at market crosses, read in churches,
To face the garment of rebellion 74
With some fine color that may please the eye 75
Of fickle changelings and poor discontents, 76
Which gape and rub the elbow at the news 77
Of hurly-burly innovation. 78
And never yet did insurrection want 79
Such water-colors to impaint his cause, 80
Nor moody beggars, starving for a time 81
Of pell-mell havoc and confusion. 82

PRINCE
In both your armies there is many a soul 83
Shall pay full dearly for this encounter,
If once they join in trial. Tell your nephew
The Prince of Wales doth join with all the world

60 ungentle gull rude young bird, still unfledged. **cuckoo's bird** cuckoo's young offspring. (The cuckoo lays its eggs in other birds' nests.)
63 our love we in our love **66 head** armed force **67 opposèd . . . means** goaded into opposition by such factors **69 dangerous countenance** threatening behavior **72 articulate** set forth, specified **74 face** trim, adorn **75 color** (1) hue (2) specious appearance **76 changelings** turncoats **77 rub the elbow** i.e., hug themselves with delight
78 innovation rebellion **79 want** lack **80 water-colors** i.e., thin excuses. (See *color,* l. 75.) **his** its **81 moody** sullen, angry **82 havoc** plundering **83 both your** i.e., your and our

In praise of Henry Percy. By my hopes— 87
This present enterprise set off his head— 88
I do not think a braver gentleman,
More active-valiant or more valiant-young,
More daring or more bold, is now alive
To grace this latter age with noble deeds.
For my part, I may speak it to my shame,
I have a truant been to chivalry;
And so I hear he doth account me too.
Yet this before my father's majesty:
I am content that he shall take the odds
Of his great name and estimation, 98
And will, to save the blood on either side,
Try fortune with him in a single fight.

KING
And, Prince of Wales, so dare we venture thee, 101
Albeit considerations infinite 102
Do make against it. No, good Worcester, no,
We love our people well; even those we love
That are misled upon your cousin's part.
And, will they take the offer of our grace, 106
Both he and they and you, yea, every man
Shall be my friend again, and I'll be his.
So tell your cousin, and bring me word
What he will do. But if he will not yield,
Rebuke and dread correction wait on us, 111
And they shall do their office. So, begone.
We will not now be troubled with reply.
We offer fair; take it advisedly.
Exeunt Worcester [*and Vernon*].

PRINCE
It will not be accepted, on my life.
The Douglas and the Hotspur both together
Are confident against the world in arms.

KING
Hence, therefore, every leader to his charge;
For on their answer will we set on them,

87 hopes i.e., hopes of salvation **88 This . . . head** i.e., if this present rebellion is taken from his account, not held against him **98 estimation** reputation **101 venture** hazard, risk **102 Albeit** although it be that. (The subjunctive has the force of "were it not that.") **106 grace** pardon **111 wait on us** are in attendance upon us

And God befriend us as our cause is just!
Exeunt. Manent Prince, Falstaff.

FALSTAFF Hal, if thou see me down in the battle and bestride me, so; 'tis a point of friendship.

PRINCE Nothing but a colossus can do thee that friendship. Say thy prayers, and farewell.

FALSTAFF I would 'twere bedtime, Hal, and all well.

PRINCE Why, thou owest God a death. [*Exit.*]

FALSTAFF 'Tis not due yet; I would be loath to pay him before his day. What need I be so forward with him that calls not on me? Well, 'tis no matter; honor pricks me on. Yea, but how if honor prick me off when I come on? How then? Can honor set to a leg? No. Or an arm? No. Or take away the grief of a wound? No. Honor hath no skill in surgery, then? No. What is honor? A word. What is in that word "honor"? What is that "honor"? Air. A trim reckoning! Who hath it? He that died o' Wednesday. Doth he feel it? No. Doth he hear it? No. 'Tis insensible, then? Yea, to the dead. But will it not live with the living? No. Why? Detraction will not suffer it. Therefore I'll none of it. Honor is a mere scutcheon. And so ends my catechism.
Exit.

✤

5.2 *Enter Worcester,* [*and*] *Sir Richard Vernon.*

WORCESTER
O, no, my nephew must not know, Sir Richard,
The liberal and kind offer of the King.

VERNON
'Twere best he did.

WORCESTER Then are we all undone.
It is not possible, it cannot be,

120 s.d. Manent they remain onstage **122 so** well and good **126 thou . . . death** (Proverbial, with a pun on *debt.*) **129 pricks** spurs **130 prick me off** mark me off (as one dead) **131 set to** rejoin or set **132 grief** pain **138 Detraction** slander **139 suffer** allow **140 scutcheon** heraldic emblem carried in funerals, displayed on coaches, etc.; it was the lowest form of symbol, having no pennon or other insignia. **catechism** the principles of faith given in the form of question and answer

5.2 Location: Near the rebel camp.

The King should keep his word in loving us;
He will suspect us still and find a time
To punish this offense in other faults. 7
Suspicion all our lives shall be stuck full of eyes; 8
For treason is but trusted like the fox,
Who, never so tame, so cherished, and locked up, 10
Will have a wild trick of his ancestors. 11
Look how we can, or sad or merrily, 12
Interpretation will misquote our looks,
And we shall feed like oxen at a stall,
The better cherished still the nearer death.
My nephew's trespass may be well forgot;
It hath the excuse of youth and heat of blood,
And an adopted name of privilege, 18
A harebrained Hotspur, governed by a spleen. 19
All his offenses live upon my head
And on his father's. We did train him on, 21
And, his corruption being ta'en from us, 22
We as the spring of all shall pay for all. 23
Therefore, good cousin, let not Harry know
In any case the offer of the King.

Enter Hotspur [*and Douglas, with soldiers*].

VERNON
Deliver what you will; I'll say 'tis so. 26
Here comes your cousin.
HOTSPUR My uncle is returned.
Deliver up my lord of Westmorland. 28
Uncle, what news?
WORCESTER
The King will bid you battle presently.
DOUGLAS
Defy him by the lord of Westmorland. 31
HOTSPUR
Lord Douglas, go you and tell him so.

7 in in punishing **8 stuck . . . eyes** i.e., provided with many eyes, suspiciously inquisitive **10 never so** be he never so **11 trick** trait **12 or sad** either sad **18 adopted . . . privilege** i.e., a nickname, "hotspur," to justify his rashness **19 spleen** intemperate impulse **21 train** incite, draw **22 his . . . us** i.e., since his guilt originated in us **23 spring** source **26 Deliver** report **28 Deliver up** release (as hostage; see 4.3.110–111) **31 Defy him by** send back your defiance with

DOUGLAS
Marry, and shall, and very willingly. *Exit Douglas.*
WORCESTER
There is no seeming mercy in the King.
HOTSPUR
Did you beg any? God forbid!
WORCESTER
I told him gently of our grievances,
Of his oath breaking, which he mended thus,
By now forswearing that he is forsworn.
He calls us rebels, traitors, and will scourge
With haughty arms this hateful name in us.

Enter Douglas.

DOUGLAS
Arm, gentlemen, to arms! For I have thrown
A brave defiance in King Henry's teeth, 42
And Westmorland, that was engaged, did bear it; 43
Which cannot choose but bring him quickly on.
WORCESTER
The Prince of Wales stepped forth before the King,
And, nephew, challenged you to single fight.
HOTSPUR
O, would the quarrel lay upon our heads,
And that no man might draw short breath today
But I and Harry Monmouth! Tell me, tell me, 49
How showed his tasking? Seemed it in contempt? 50
VERNON
No, by my soul. I never in my life
Did hear a challenge urged more modestly, 52
Unless a brother should a brother dare
To gentle exercise and proof of arms. 54
He gave you all the duties of a man, 55
Trimmed up your praises with a princely tongue, 56
Spoke your deservings like a chronicle,
Making you ever better than his praise
By still dispraising praise valued with you; 59

42 brave proud **43 engaged** held as hostage **49 Monmouth** (A name for the Prince taken from the Welsh town where he was born.) **50 showed his tasking** appeared his giving the challenge **52 urged** put forward **54 proof** test **55 duties** due merits **56 Trimmed . . . praises** adorned his praise of you **59 dispraising** disparaging. **valued** compared

And, which became him like a prince indeed,
He made a blushing cital of himself, 61
And chid his truant youth with such a grace 62
As if he mastered there a double spirit
Of teaching and of learning instantly. 64
There did he pause. But let me tell the world,
If he outlive the envy of this day, 66
England did never owe so sweet a hope, 67
So much misconstrued in his wantonness. 68

HOTSPUR

Cousin, I think thou art enamorèd
On his follies. Never did I hear
Of any prince so wild a liberty. 71
But be he as he will, yet once ere night
I will embrace him with a soldier's arm,
That he shall shrink under my courtesy. 74
Arm, arm with speed! And, fellows, soldiers, friends,
Better consider what you have to do
Than I, that have not well the gift of tongue,
Can lift your blood up with persuasion.

Enter a Messenger.

FIRST MESSENGER My lord, here are letters for you.

HOTSPUR I cannot read them now.
O gentlemen, the time of life is short!
To spend that shortness basely were too long
If life did ride upon a dial's point, 83
Still ending at the arrival of an hour. 84
An if we live, we live to tread on kings;
If die, brave death, when princes die with us! 86
Now, for our consciences, the arms are fair 87
When the intent of bearing them is just.

Enter another [*Messenger*].

SECOND MESSENGER

My lord, prepare. The King comes on apace.

61 cital account, citation **62 chid** chided **64 instantly** simultaneously **66 envy** hostility **67 owe** own **68 wantonness** playful sportiveness **71 liberty** licentiousness **74 shrink under my courtesy** (1) be daunted by my greater courtesy (2) fall back before my attack **83 If** even if. **dial's point** hand of a watch **84 Still . . . hour** ineluctably concluding within an hour's time **86 brave** glorious **87 for** as for. **fair** just

HOTSPUR
I thank him that he cuts me from my tale,
For I profess not talking. Only this—
Let each man do his best. And here draw I
A sword, whose temper I intend to stain
With the best blood that I can meet withal
In the adventure of this perilous day.
Now, *Esperance*! Percy! And set on.
Sound all the lofty instruments of war,
And by that music let us all embrace;
For, heaven to earth, some of us never shall
A second time do such a courtesy.
Here they embrace. [*Exeunt.*]

5.3

The trumpets sound. The King enters with his power [*and passes over the stage*]. *Alarum to the battle. Then enter Douglas, and Sir Walter Blunt* [*dressed like King Henry*].

BLUNT
What is thy name, that in the battle thus
Thou crossest me? What honor dost thou seek
Upon my head?
DOUGLAS Know then my name is Douglas,
And I do haunt thee in the battle thus
Because some tell me that thou art a king.
BLUNT They tell thee true.
DOUGLAS
The lord of Stafford dear today hath bought
Thy likeness, for instead of thee, King Harry,
This sword hath ended him. So shall it thee,
Unless thou yield thee as my prisoner.
BLUNT
I was not born a yielder, thou proud Scot,
And thou shalt find a king that will revenge

96 Esperance (The motto of the Percy family.) **99 heaven to earth** i.e., I'll wager heaven against earth

5.3. Location: Shrewsbury field. The scene is virtually continuous.
s.d. power army. **Alarum** trumpet signal to advance **7 dear** dearly
7–8 bought Thy likeness paid for his resemblance to you

Lord Stafford's death. *They fight. Douglas kills Blunt.*

Then enter Hotspur.

HOTSPUR
O Douglas, hadst thou fought at Holmedon thus,
I never had triumphed upon a Scot.

DOUGLAS
All's done, all's won; here breathless lies the King. 16

HOTSPUR Where?

DOUGLAS Here.

HOTSPUR
This, Douglas? No. I know this face full well.
A gallant knight he was; his name was Blunt,
Semblably furnished like the King himself. 21

DOUGLAS
A fool go with thy soul, whither it goes! 22
A borrowed title hast thou bought too dear.
Why didst thou tell me that thou wert a king?

HOTSPUR
The King hath many marching in his coats. 25

DOUGLAS
Now, by my sword, I will kill all his coats!
I'll murder all his wardrobe, piece by piece,
Until I meet the King.

HOTSPUR Up and away!
Our soldiers stand full fairly for the day. [*Exeunt.*] 29

Alarum. Enter Falstaff, solus.

FALSTAFF Though I could scape shot-free at London, I 30
fear the shot here; here's no scoring but upon the pate. 31
Soft, who are you? Sir Walter Blunt. There's honor for
you. Here's no vanity! I am as hot as molten lead, and 33
as heavy too. God keep lead out of me! I need no more

16 breathless i.e., dead **21 Semblably furnished** similarly accoutered **22 A . . . soul** i.e., may the stigma of "fool" accompany your soul (for having dressed as a decoy of King Henry) **25 coats** vests worn over armor embroidered with a coat of arms **29 stand . . . day** i.e., seem in an auspicious position, likely to win the victory **30 shot-free** without paying the tavern bill **31 scoring** (1) cutting (2) marking up of charges, by notches on a stick or on the inn door **33 Here's no vanity** i.e. (ironically), if this doesn't show what I was saying about honor, then nothing does

weight than mine own bowels. I have led my raga-
muffins where they are peppered. There's not three of
my hundred and fifty left alive, and they are for the
town's end, to beg during life. But who comes here? 38

Enter the Prince.

PRINCE
What, stands thou idle here? Lend me thy sword.
Many a nobleman lies stark and stiff
Under the hoofs of vaunting enemies,
Whose deaths are yet unrevenged. I prithee,
Lend me thy sword.

FALSTAFF O Hal, I prithee, give me leave to breathe
awhile. Turk Gregory never did such deeds in arms as 45
I have done this day. I have paid Percy, I have made 46
him sure. 47

PRINCE
He is, indeed, and living to kill thee.
I prithee, lend me thy sword.

FALSTAFF Nay, before God, Hal, if Percy be alive, thou
gets not my sword; but take my pistol, if thou wilt.

PRINCE
Give it me. What, is it in the case?

FALSTAFF Ay, Hal, 'tis hot, 'tis hot. There's that will sack 53
a city. *The Prince draws it out, and finds it to be a bottle of sack.*

PRINCE What, is it a time to jest and dally now?
He throws the bottle at him. Exit.

FALSTAFF Well, if Percy be alive, I'll pierce him. If he do 56
come in my way, so; if he do not, if I come in his 57
willingly, let him make a carbonado of me. I like not 58
such grinning honor as Sir Walter hath. Give me life,

38 town's end i.e., city gate, frequented by beggars **45 Turk Gregory** (*Turk* is an abusive term signifying a tyrant, and *Gregory* refers probably to Pope Gregory XIII, who was assumed to have encouraged the Massacre of Saint Bartholomew [1572] in which many French Protestants were slain, and to have encouraged plots against Elizabeth.)
46–47 made him sure made sure of him. (But Hal takes *sure* in a different sense, meaning "safe.") **53 hot** (Falstaff implies he has been firing at the enemy.) **56 Percy . . . pierce** (Elizabethan pronunciation rendered the pun more obvious than it is now.) **57 so** well and good
58 carbonado meat scored across for broiling

which if I can save, so; if not, honor comes unlooked for, and there's an end. [*Exit.*]

5.4

Alarum. Excursions. Enter the King, the Prince, Lord John of Lancaster, [*and the*] *Earl of Westmorland.*

KING I prithee,
Harry, withdraw thyself; thou bleedest too much.
Lord John of Lancaster, go you with him.

LANCASTER
Not I, my lord, unless I did bleed too.

PRINCE
I beseech Your Majesty make up,
Lest your retirement do amaze your friends.

KING
I will do so. My lord of Westmorland,
Lead him to his tent.

WESTMORLAND
Come, my lord, I'll lead you to your tent.

PRINCE
Lead me, my lord? I do not need your help.
And God forbid a shallow scratch should drive
The Prince of Wales from such a field as this,
Where stained nobility lies trodden on
And rebels' arms triumph in massacres!

LANCASTER
We breathe too long. Come, cousin Westmorland,
Our duty this way lies. For God's sake, come.
[*Exeunt Prince John and Westmorland.*]

PRINCE
By God, thou hast deceived me, Lancaster!
I did not think thee lord of such a spirit.

61 there's an end (1) that concludes the subject of my catechism (2) thus life ends

5.4. Location: Scene continues at Shrewsbury field.
s.d. Excursions sorties. (The fallen body of Blunt may be removed at some point or may be onstage still at 5.4.77 when Hal kills Hotspur.)
5 make up go forward **6 retirement** retreat. **amaze** alarm **15 breathe** rest, pause for breath (as also at l. 47)

Before, I loved thee as a brother, John,
But now I do respect thee as my soul.

KING

I saw him hold Lord Percy at the point 21
With lustier maintenance than I did look for 22
Of such an ungrown warrior.

PRINCE

O, this boy lends mettle to us all! *Exit.* 24

[*Enter Douglas.*]

DOUGLAS

Another king? They grow like Hydra's heads. 25
I am the Douglas, fatal to all those
That wear those colors on them. What art thou 27
That counterfeit'st the person of a king?

KING

The King himself, who, Douglas, grieves at heart
So many of his shadows thou hast met 30
And not the very King. I have two boys
Seek Percy and thyself about the field; 32
But, seeing thou fall'st on me so luckily,
I will assay thee, and defend thyself. 34

DOUGLAS

I fear thou art another counterfeit;
And yet, in faith, thou bearest thee like a king.
But mine I am sure thou art, whoe'er thou be,
And thus I win thee.

They fight; the King being in danger, enter Prince of Wales.

PRINCE

Hold up thy head, vile Scot, or thou art like 39
Never to hold it up again! The spirits
Of valiant Shirley, Stafford, Blunt, are in my arms.
It is the Prince of Wales that threatens thee,
Who never promiseth but he means to pay. 43

They fight. Douglas flieth.

21 at the point at sword's point **22 lustier maintenance** more vigorous bearing **24 mettle** spirit **25 Hydra's heads** (The heads of the Lernaean Hydra grew again as fast as they were cut off.) **27 colors** i.e., the colors of the King's insignia **30 shadows** having form without substance **32 Seek** who seek **34 assay** put to the test **39 like** likely **43 pay** (1) settle a debt (2) kill

Cheerly, my lord. How fares Your Grace?
Sir Nicholas Gawsey hath for succor sent,
And so hath Clifton. I'll to Clifton straight.

KING Stay and breathe awhile.
Thou hast redeemed thy lost opinion, 48
And showed thou mak'st some tender of my life 49
In this fair rescue thou hast brought to me.

PRINCE
O God, they did me too much injury
That ever said I hearkened for your death. 52
If it were so, I might have let alone
The insulting hand of Douglas over you, 54
Which would have been as speedy in your end
As all the poisonous potions in the world,
And saved the treacherous labor of your son.

KING
Make up to Clifton; I'll to Sir Nicholas Gawsey. 58
Exit King.

Enter Hotspur.

HOTSPUR
If I mistake not, thou art Harry Monmouth.

PRINCE
Thou speak'st as if I would deny my name.

HOTSPUR
My name is Harry Percy.

PRINCE Why then I see
A very valiant rebel of the name.
I am the Prince of Wales; and think not, Percy,
To share with me in glory any more.
Two stars keep not their motion in one sphere,
Nor can one England brook a double reign 66
Of Harry Percy and the Prince of Wales.

HOTSPUR
Nor shall it, Harry, for the hour is come
To end the one of us; and would to God
Thy name in arms were now as great as mine!

PRINCE
I'll make it greater ere I part from thee,

48 opinion reputation **49 mak'st . . . of** have some care for
52 hearkened listened (as for welcome news) **54 insulting** exulting
58 Make up advance **66 brook** endure

And all the budding honors on thy crest
I'll crop to make a garland for my head. 73

HOTSPUR
I can no longer brook thy vanities. *They fight.* 74

Enter Falstaff.

FALSTAFF Well said, Hal! To it, Hal! Nay, you shall find 75
no boy's play here, I can tell you. 76

Enter Douglas. He fighteth with Falstaff, who falls down as if he were dead. [*Exit Douglas.*] *The Prince killeth Percy.*

HOTSPUR
O Harry, thou hast robbed me of my youth!
I better brook the loss of brittle life
Than those proud titles thou hast won of me;
They wound my thoughts worse than thy sword my flesh.
But thoughts, the slaves of life, and life, time's fool, 81
And time, that takes survey of all the world,
Must have a stop. O, I could prophesy,
But that the earthy and cold hand of death
Lies on my tongue. No, Percy, thou art dust,
And food for— [*He dies.*]

PRINCE
For worms, brave Percy. Fare thee well, great heart!
Ill-weaved ambition, how much art thou shrunk!
When that this body did contain a spirit,
A kingdom for it was too small a bound;
But now two paces of the vilest earth
Is room enough. This earth that bears thee dead
Bears not alive so stout a gentleman. 93
If thou wert sensible of courtesy, 94
I should not make so dear a show of zeal; 95
But let my favors hide thy mangled face, 96
And, even in thy behalf, I'll thank myself

73 crop pluck **74 vanities** empty boasts **75 Well said** well done **76 s.d. killeth** mortally wounds **81 thoughts . . . fool** i.e., our mental consciousness, which is dependent on physical existence, and our life itself, which is subject to time **93 stout** valiant **94 sensible of courtesy** i.e., able to hear my praise **95 dear** handsome, heartfelt. **zeal** admiration **96 favors** plume, scarf, glove, or similar article

For doing these fair rites of tenderness.
[*He covers Hotspur's face with a scarf or other favor.*]
Adieu, and take thy praise with thee to heaven!
Thy ignominy sleep with thee in the grave,
But not remembered in thy epitaph!
He spieth Falstaff on the ground.
What, old acquaintance, could not all this flesh
Keep in a little life? Poor Jack, farewell!
I could have better spared a better man.
O, I should have a heavy miss of thee 105
If I were much in love with vanity! 106
Death hath not struck so fat a deer today,
Though many dearer, in this bloody fray.
Emboweled will I see thee by and by. 109
Till then in blood by noble Percy lie. *Exit.*
Falstaff riseth up.

FALSTAFF Emboweled? If thou embowel me today, I'll
give you leave to powder me and eat me too tomor- 112
row. 'Sblood, 'twas time to counterfeit, or that hot ter- 113
magant Scot had paid me, scot and lot too. Counterfeit? 114
I lie, I am no counterfeit. To die is to be a counterfeit,
for he is but the counterfeit of a man who hath not the
life of a man; but to counterfeit dying, when a man
thereby liveth, is to be no counterfeit but the true and
perfect image of life indeed. The better part of valor is 119
discretion, in the which better part I have saved my
life. Zounds, I am afraid of this gunpowder Percy,
though he be dead. How if he should counterfeit too
and rise? By my faith, I am afraid he would prove the
better counterfeit. Therefore I'll make him sure; yea,
and I'll swear I killed him. Why may not he rise as well
as I? Nothing confutes me but eyes, and nobody sees 126
me. Therefore, sirrah [*Stabbing him*], with a new

105 heavy (1) serious (2) corpulent **106 vanity** frivolity **109 Emboweled** disemboweled, i.e., for embalming and burial **112 powder** salt **113–114 termagant** violent and blustering, like the heathen god of the Saracens in medieval and Renaissance lore **114 paid** i.e., killed. **scot and lot** i.e., completely. (Originally the phrase was the term for a parish tax.) **119 part** constituent part, quality, role **126 Nothing . . . eyes** i.e., nothing can contradict me but an eyewitness

wound in your thigh, come you along with me.
He takes up Hotspur on his back.

Enter Prince [*and*] *John of Lancaster.*

PRINCE
Come, brother John; full bravely hast thou fleshed 129
Thy maiden sword.
LANCASTER But soft, whom have we here?
Did you not tell me this fat man was dead?
PRINCE I did; I saw him dead,
Breathless and bleeding on the ground.—Art thou alive?
Or is it fantasy that plays upon our eyesight?
I prithee, speak. We will not trust our eyes
Without our ears. Thou art not what thou seem'st.
FALSTAFF No, that's certain, I am not a double man; but 137
if I be not Jack Falstaff, then am I a Jack. There is Percy 138
[*Throwing the body down*]. If your father will do me
any honor, so; if not, let him kill the next Percy him-
self. I look to be either earl or duke, I can assure you.
PRINCE
Why, Percy I killed myself and saw thee dead.
FALSTAFF Didst thou? Lord, Lord, how this world is
given to lying! I grant you I was down and out of
breath, and so was he; but we rose both at an instant 145
and fought a long hour by Shrewsbury clock. If I may
be believed, so; if not, let them that should reward
valor bear the sin upon their own heads. I'll take it 148
upon my death, I gave him this wound in the thigh. 149
If the man were alive and would deny it, zounds, I
would make him eat a piece of my sword.
LANCASTER
This is the strangest tale that ever I heard.
PRINCE
This is the strangest fellow, brother John.—
Come, bring your luggage nobly on your back.
For my part, if a lie may do thee grace, 155

129 fleshed initiated (in battle) **137 double man** (1) specter (2) two men **138 Jack** knave **145 at an instant** simultaneously **148–149 take . . . death** i.e., swear with my eternal soul at risk **155 a lie** i.e., this lie of yours. **grace** credit

I'll gild it with the happiest terms I have.
A retreat is sounded.
The trumpet sounds retreat; the day is ours.
Come, brother, let us to the highest of the field,
To see what friends are living, who are dead.
Exeunt [Prince of Wales and Lancaster].

FALSTAFF I'll follow, as they say, for reward. He that rewards me, God reward him! If I do grow great, I'll grow less; for I'll purge, and leave sack, and live cleanly as a nobleman should do.
Exit [bearing off the body].

✤

5.5

The trumpets sound. Enter the King, Prince of Wales, Lord John of Lancaster, Earl of Westmorland, with Worcester and Vernon prisoners.

KING
Thus ever did rebellion find rebuke.
Ill-spirited Worcester! Did not we send grace,
Pardon, and terms of love to all of you?
And wouldst thou turn our offers contrary?
Misuse the tenor of thy kinsman's trust?
Three knights upon our party slain today,
A noble earl, and many a creature else
Had been alive this hour,
If like a Christian thou hadst truly borne
Betwixt our armies true intelligence.

WORCESTER
What I have done my safety urged me to;
And I embrace this fortune patiently,
Since not to be avoided it falls on me.

156 happiest most felicitous **158 highest** highest vantage point
162 purge (1) reduce in weight, using laxatives (2) repent

5.5. Location: The battlefield.
4 turn . . . contrary reverse the intention of our offers **5 Misuse . . . trust** i.e., abuse Hotspur's confidence (by concealing the generosity of my offer, in your role as emissary) **10 intelligence** information, report

KING
Bear Worcester to the death and Vernon too.
Other offenders we will pause upon.
[*Exeunt Worcester and Vernon, guarded.*]
How goest the field?

PRINCE
The noble Scot, Lord Douglas, when he saw
The fortune of the day quite turned from him,
The noble Percy slain, and all his men
Upon the foot of fear, fled with the rest; 20
And falling from a hill, he was so bruised
That the pursuers took him. At my tent
The Douglas is; and I beseech Your Grace
I may dispose of him.

KING With all my heart.

PRINCE
Then, brother John of Lancaster,
To you this honorable bounty shall belong. 26
Go to the Douglas and deliver him
Up to his pleasure, ransomless and free.
His valors shown upon our crests today 29
Have taught us how to cherish such high deeds
Even in the bosom of our adversaries.

LANCASTER
I thank Your Grace for this high courtesy,
Which I shall give away immediately. 33

KING
Then this remains, that we divide our power.
You, son John, and my cousin Westmorland
Towards York shall bend you with your dearest speed 36
To meet Northumberland and the prelate Scroop,
Who, as we hear, are busily in arms.
Myself and you, son Harry, will towards Wales,
To fight with Glendower and the Earl of March.
Rebellion in this land shall lose his sway, 41
Meeting the check of such another day;
And since this business so fair is done, 43
Let us not leave till all our own be won. *Exeunt.* 44

20 Upon . . . fear fleeing in panic **26 bounty** assignment, act of benevolence **29 crests** i.e., helmets **33 give away** pass along, confer on Douglas **36 bend you** direct your course. **dearest** most urgent **41 his** its **43 fair** successfully **44 leave** leave off

Date and Text

On February 25, 1598, "The historye of Henry the IIIJ[th] with his battaile of Shrewsburye against Henry Hottspurre of the Northe with the conceipted mirthe of Sir John Ffalstoff" was entered in the Stationers' Register, the official record book of the London Company of Stationers (booksellers and printers), by Andrew Wise. Later that year appeared the following quarto:

> THE HISTORY OF HENRIE THE FOVRTH; With the battell at Shrewsburie, *betweene the King and Lord* Henry Percy, surnamed Henrie Hotspur of the North. *With the humorous conceits of Sir* Iohn Falstalffe. AT LONDON, Printed by *P. S.* [Peter Short] for *Andrew Wise,* dwelling in Paules Churchyard, at the signe of the Angell. 1598.

Actually this was not the first quarto, for an earlier fragment of eight pages has survived, part of a text that served as copy for the first complete extant quarto. Together these quartos make up an excellent authoritative text, based seemingly on the author's papers or, more probably, a scribal transcript of them. Four more quartos appeared before the First Folio of 1623, each based on the previous quarto. The Folio itself was based on the last of these, perhaps with reference also to some kind of manuscript, although the number of authoritative readings that can be claimed for the Folio is small.

1 Henry IV shows signs of revision in the use of characters' names, most notably that of Falstaff. Plainly the original version of the play called him Sir John Oldcastle, after one of the prince's companions in the anonymous *Famous Victories of Henry the Fifth* (c. 1588). The name "Oldcastle" was originally intended for *2 Henry IV* as well. The speech prefix "Old." is left standing at 1.2.138 in the quarto of *2 Henry IV,* one or two lines of verse in *1 Henry IV* are one syllable short evidently because "Oldcastle" has been altered to "Falstaff," and Falstaff is jokingly referred to as "my old lad of the castle" (*1 Henry IV,* 1.2.41). Moreover, there are several contemporary allusions to a play about a fat knight named Oldcastle. Apparently Henry Brooke,

Lord Cobham, a living descendant of the Lollard martyr Oldcastle of Henry V's reign, took umbrage at the profane use Shakespeare had made of this revered name, whereupon Shakespeare's acting company shifted to another less controversial name from the chronicles, Sir John Fastolfe or Falstaff (called "Falstaffe" in the Folio text of Shakespeare's *1 Henry VI* and assigned a cowardly role in the French wars of that play). The revision also changed the names of Oldcastle's cronies from Harvey and Russell to Peto and Bardolph. This edition retains the name "Falstaff" since Shakespeare clearly accepted it as the new name of the character in all his "Falstaff" plays.

Cobham was Lord Chamberlain from July 1596 until his death in March 1597, during which interval Shakespeare's company bore the name of Lord Hunsdon's men. Quite possibly the difficulty over the name Oldcastle erupted during that period, for *1 Henry IV* seems to have been written and performed in late 1596 and early 1597 not long after Shakespeare had finished *Richard II* (c. 1595–1596).

Francis Meres, in his *Palladis Tamia: Wit's Treasury* (a slender volume on contemporary literature and art; valuable because it lists most of the plays of Shakespeare's that existed at that time), refers in 1598 to "*Henry the* 4" without specifying one or two parts. Publication of *1 Henry IV* in 1598 confirmed to the Elizabethan public that the changes in names to Falstaff, Peto, and Bardolph had taken place.

Textual Notes

These textual notes are not a historical collation, either of the early quartos and the early folios or of more recent editions; they are simply a record of departures in this edition from the copy text. The reading adopted in this edition appears in boldface, followed by the rejected reading from the copy text, i.e., the first quarto of 1598. Only major alterations in punctuation are noted. Changes in lineation are not indicated, nor are some minor and obvious typographical errors.

Abbreviations used:
F the First Folio
Q quarto
s.d. stage direction
s.p. speech prefix

Copy text: the first complete quarto of 1598 [Q1]; and, for 1.3.201 through 2.2.110, the fragment of an earlier quarto (Q0).

1.1. 22 levy leauy **39 Herefordshire** Herdforshire **62 a dear** deere **76 In faith, it is** [assigned in Q1 to King]

1.2. 16 king a king **78 similes** smiles **154 thou** the **158 Peto, Bardolph** Haruey, Rossill

1.3. 194 good night god-night **201 s.p. Hotspur** [missing in Q0–Q4] **238 whipped** [Q1] whip [Q0]

2.1. 34 s.p. First Carrier Car **48 s.d.** [at l. 47 in Q0]

2.2. s.d. Poins, Peto Poines, and Peto &c **20 Bardolph** Bardol [and thus, or "Bardoll," throughout the play] **34 mine** [Q1] my [Q0] **42 Go hang** [F] Hang [Q0] **51 s.p. and text BARDOLPH What news** [all assigned as continuation of Poins's speech in l. 50] **52 s.p. Gadshill** Bar **78 s.p. First Traveler** Trauel **82 s.p. Travelers** Trauel **86 s.p. Travelers** Tra

2.3. 1 s.p. Hotspur [not in Q1] **4 In** In the **48 thee** the

2.4. 33 precedent present **36 s.p. Poins** Prin **171 s.p. Prince** Gad **172 s.p. Gadshill** Ross [also at ll. 174 and 178] **226 keech** catch **242 eelskin** ellskin **322 s.d.** [at l. 321 in Q1] **337 Owen** O **390 tristful** trustfull **398 yet** so **468 lean** lane **518 Good** God [also at l. 519] **526 s.d. pockets** pocket **530 s.p. Peto** [not in Q1] **535 s.p. Prince** [not in Q1]

3.1. 97 cantle scantle **126 meter** miter

3.2. 84 gorged gordge **145 northern** Northren **161 s.d.** [at. l. 162 in Q1]

3.3. 35 that's that **57 tithe** tight **173 guests** ghesse **200 o' clock** of clocke

4.1. 1 s.p. [and elsewhere] Hotspur Per **20 lord** mind **55 is** tis **108 dropped** drop **116 altar** altars **123 ne'er** neare **126 cannot** can **127 yet** it

4.2. 3 Coldfield cophill **15 yeomen's** Yeomans **31 feazed** fazd **81 s.d. Exit** Exeunt

4.3. 23 horse horses **74 heirs . . . followed** heires, as Pages followed **84 country's** Countrey

4.4. 18 o'erruled ouerrulde

5.1. s.d. Lancaster Lancaster, Earle of Westmerland **3 southern** Southren **88 off** of **114 s.d. Exeunt** Exit **138 will it** will

5.2. 3 undone vnder one **8 Suspicion** Supposition **12 merrily** merely **25 s.d. Hotspur** Percy **79 s.p. First Messenger** Mes **89 s.p. Second Messenger** Mes

5.3. 22 A Ah

5.4. 4 s.p. [and elsewhere] Lancaster P. Iohn **68 Nor** Now **76 s.d. who** he **92 thee** the

Shakespeare's Sources

Shakespeare's chief historical source for *1 Henry IV* was the 1587 edition of Raphael Holinshed's *Chronicles,* but he also took some important ideas from Samuel Daniel's *The First Four Books of the Civil Wars* (1595). Relevant passages from both sources appear in the following pages. Following Daniel, Shakespeare readjusts the age of Hotspur (who was historically older than Henry IV) to match that of Prince Hal. Daniel's Hotspur is, like Shakespeare's, dauntless and stubborn, a turbulent yet noble spirit. The theme of a nemesis of rebellion afflicting Henry IV for his usurpation, only touched upon in Shakespeare's play, owes something to Daniel's presentation, although the idea of nemesis is to be found also in Holinshed. Both Holinshed and Daniel err in confusing the Edmund Mortimer whom Glendower captured with his nephew Edmund Mortimer, claimant to the throne; Shakespeare perpetuates this error. Hal's killing of Hotspur is unhistorical, since both Holinshed and Daniel report only that Hal bravely helped rescue his father from attack and that Hotspur was killed in the melee. Daniel does give prominence to Prince Henry in the battle, however, and implies that he and Hotspur will meet face-to-face. Shakespeare invents the scenes in which we see Mortimer as a devoted husband and Hotspur as a fond combatant in wit with his wife, Kate; Holinshed merely informs us that both these men were married. Shakespeare greatly expands Glendower's fascination with magic and poetry, changing him from a ruthless barbarian (in Holinshed) into a cranky but charismatic Welshman. Hotspur, despite hints from Daniel and Holinshed, is chiefly Shakespeare's creation.

The most impressive transformations are those of Hal and Falstaff. Shakespeare knew many legends of Hal's wild youth, some from John Stow's *The Chronicles of England* (1580) and *The Annals of England* (1592), others from oral tradition. Many of these stories were also available in Holinshed. Shakespeare's readiest source, however, was a rowdy and chauvinistic play called *The Famous Victories of Henry the Fifth,* registered 1594 but usually ascribed to

Richard Tarleton or Samuel Rowley around 1587 or 1588. A brief selection follows. This play covers all the events of the *Henry IV* plays and *Henry V* in one chaotic sequence. Prince Hal has three companions, Sir John Oldcastle, Tom, and Ned (cf. Ned Poins), in whose company he robs the King's receivers of £1,000, visits the old tavern in Eastcheap, vexes his father, and strikes the Lord Chief Justice. A crucial difference is that this Hal is truly unregenerate. He not only chases after women and robs, but encourages his companions to look forward to unrestricted license when he is King. Hal seems consciously to desire his father's death. Yet he does reform, and banishes his companions beyond a ten-mile limit with a promise to assist them if they amend their conduct. Although Hal's reform is crude and sudden, his popularity aids him when he goes to war against the French. He is followed by a comic crew of London artisans and thieves, who prove invincible against the effete enemy.

Shakespeare owes much to this unsophisticated, vibrant account of Hal's riotous youth, but he has transformed it to his own use. He limits himself in *1 Henry IV* to the action leading up to the Battle of Shrewsbury in order to focus on the coming of age of Prince Henry and the pairing and contrasting of Hotspur, Falstaff, and King Henry IV as alternative models for Hal's behavior. He invents unforgettable comic characters such as Mistress Quickly, Francis, and Bardolph. Most of all, Shakespeare's portrayal of Falstaff is essentially his own. Sir John Oldcastle of the anonymous play is a minor character, not Hal's closest companion. Falstaff owes something to the tradition of the guileful and inventive Vice of the Tudor morality play (especially when Falstaff is called jestingly "that reverend Vice, that gray Iniquity"; 2.4.448), but the influence of the morality play is general rather than specific. To label Falstaff a "Vice" is to reduce him to comic tempter and villain. Falstaff is in part an allowed fool, a parasite, and a *miles gloriosus* or braggart soldier, but he transcends all these conventionalized types with his own unique vitality.

1 Henry IV suggests some acquaintance with the anonymous play *Thomas of Woodstock* (c. 1591–1595), which Shakespeare may also have used in *Richard II,* and with the complaints of Owen Glendower and Northumberland in *A Mirror for Magistrates* (1559). In neither case is the debt extensive. More suggestive as possible sources are events and social conditions in Shakespeare's England: the Northern Rebellion of 1569 against Queen Elizabeth's government, abuses of military authority by unscrupulous officers, the dangerous state of the highways, the raucous vitality of tavern life in Eastcheap, and the like.

The Third Volume of Chronicles (1587 edition)

Compiled by Raphael Holinshed

Henry the Fourth

[From the beginning of his reign, King Henry IV encounters opposition, especially in the north and along the Welsh border. Henry leads an expedition against Scotland in 1402.]

In the King's absence, whilst he was forth of the realm in Scotland against his enemies, the Welshmen took occasion to rebel under the conduct of their captain Owen Glendower, doing what mischief they could devise unto their English neighbors. This Owen Glendower was son to an esquire of Wales named Griffith Vichan. He dwelled in the parish of Conway, within the county of Merioneth in North Wales, in a place called Glindourwie, which is as much to say in English as "the valley by the side of the water of Dee"; by occasion whereof he was surnamed Glindour Dew.

He was first set to study the laws of the realm, and became an utter barrister[1] or an apprentice of the law (as they term him) and served King Richard at Flint Castle when he was taken by Henry, Duke of Lancaster, though other have written that he served this King Henry the Fourth, before he came to attain the crown, in room[2] of an esquire.

[One sign of civil unrest is an attempt made on the life of King Henry IV, from which he manages to escape unharmed.]

1 utter barrister one called to the bar and having the privilege of practicing as advocate; utter barristers sit uttermost or outermost on the forms that are called the bar, this being the most senior place in the house next to the benchers **2 room** position

Howbeit, he was not so soon delivered from fear, for he might well have his life in suspicion and provide for the preservation of the same, sith[3] perils of death crept into his secret chamber and lay lurking in the bed of down where his body was to be reposed and to take rest. O, what a suspected[4] state therefore is that of a king holding his regiment[5] with the hatred of his people, the heartgrudgings of his courtiers, and the peremptory practices[6] of both together! Could he confidently compose or settle himself to sleep for fear of strangling? Durst he boldly eat and drink without dread of poisoning? Might he adventure to show himself in great meetings or solemn[7] assemblies without mistrust of mischief against his person intended? What pleasure or what felicity could he take in his princely pomp, which he knew by manifest and fearful experience to be envied and maligned to the very death?

[Other prodigies attest to the unquiet times of Henry IV.]

Owen Glendower, according to his accustomed manner robbing and spoiling[8] within the English borders, caused all the forces of the shire of Hereford to assemble together against them under the conduct of Edmund Mortimer, Earl of March. But coming to try the matter by battle, whether by treason or otherwise, so it fortuned that the English power was discomfited,[9] the Earl taken prisoner, and above a thousand of his people slain in the place. The shameful villainy used by the Welshwomen towards the dead carcasses was such as honest ears would be ashamed to hear and continent[10] tongues to speak thereof. The dead bodies might not be buried without great sums of money given for liberty[11] to convey them away.

The King was not hasty to purchase the deliverance of the Earl of March, because his title to the crown was well enough known, and therefore suffered him to remain in miserable prison, wishing both the said Earl and all other of his lineage out of this life with God and his saints in

3 sith since **4 suspected** regarded with suspicion **5 holding his regiment** ruling **6 heartgrudgings . . . peremptory practices** heartfelt discontent . . . obstinate conspirings **7 solemn** ceremonial **8 spoiling** plundering **9 discomfited** routed, defeated **10 continent** temperate **11 liberty** permission

heaven so they had been out of the way,[12] for then all had been well enough as he thought. But to let these things pass, the King this year sent his eldest daughter, Blanche, accompanied with the Earl of Somerset, the Bishop of Worcester, the Lord Clifford, and others, into Almaine,[13] which brought her to Cologne, and there with great triumph she was married to William, Duke of Bavaria, son and heir to Lewis, the Emperor. About mid of August, the King, to chastise the presumptuous attempts of the Welshmen, went with a great power of men into Wales to pursue the Captain of the Welsh rebel, Owen Glendower, but in effect he lost his labor; for Owen conveyed himself out of the way into his known lurking places, and (as was thought) through art magic he caused such foul weather of winds, tempest, rain, snow, and hail to be raised for the annoyance of the King's army that the like had not been heard of; in such sort that the King was constrained to return home, having caused his people yet to spoil and burn first a great part of the country. The same time, the Lord Edmund of Langley, Duke of York, departed this life and was buried at Langley with his brethren. The Scots, under the leading of Patrick Hepborne of the Hales the younger, entering into England were overthrown at Nesbit in the marches,[14] as in the Scottish chronicle ye may find more at large. This battle was fought the two-and-twentieth of June, in this year of our Lord, 1402.

Archibald, Earl Douglas, sore displeased in his mind for this overthrow, procured a commission to invade England, and that to his cost, as ye may likewise read in the Scottish histories. For at a place called Homeldon they were so fiercely assailed by the Englishmen, under the leading of the Lord Percy, surnamed Henry Hotspur, and George, Earl of March, that with violence of the English shot they were quite vanquished and put to flight on the Rood Day[15] in harvest, with a great slaughter made by the Englishmen. . . .

12 so . . . way i.e., so long as they were no longer a source of trouble to King Henry. (Holinshed confuses two Mortimers: [1] Sir Edmund Mortimer, son-in-law of Glendower and Hotspur's brother-in-law, and [2] Sir Edmund's nephew, also named Edmund, the fifth Earl of March, who was proclaimed heir to the throne by Richard II in 1398 but who was never captured by Glendower. Shakespeare follows Holinshed's error.) **13 Almaine** Germany **14 marches** frontiers, borders **15 the Rood Day** Holy Rood Day, September 14. (See *1 Henry IV,* 1.1.52.)

There were slain of men of estimation[16] Sir John Swinton, Sir Adam Gordon, Sir John Leviston, Sir Alexander Ramsey of Dalhousie, and three-and-twenty knights, besides ten thousand of the commons; and of prisoners among other were these: Mordake, Earl of Fife, son to the Governor; Archibald, Earl Douglas,[17] which in the fight lost one of his eyes; Thomas, Earl of Murray; Robert, Earl of Angus; and, as some writers have, the Earls of Atholl and Menteith, with five hundred other of meaner degrees.[18] . . .

Edmund Mortimer, Earl of March, prisoner with Owen Glendower, whether for irksomeness of cruel captivity or fear of death or for what other cause it is uncertain, agreed to take part with Owen against the King of England and took to wife the daughter of the said Owen.

Strange wonders happened, as men reported, at the nativity of this man,[19] for the same night he was born, all his father's horses in the stable were found to stand in blood up to the bellies.

[The Percy clan, although they supported Henry in his rebellion against Richard II in 1399, grow increasingly restive during the latter months of 1402.]

Henry, Earl of Northumberland, with his brother Thomas, Earl of Worcester, and his son, the Lord Henry Percy, surnamed Hotspur, which were to King Henry in the beginning of his reign both faithful friends and earnest aiders, began now to envy his wealth and felicity; and especially they were grieved because the King demanded of the Earl and his son such Scottish prisoners as were taken at Homeldon and Nesbit. For of all the captives which were taken in the conflicts foughten in those two places, there was delivered to the King's possession only Mordake, Earl of Fife, the Duke of Albany's son, though the King did

16 estimation noble and gentle rank **17 Mordake . . . Douglas** (In Holinshed, this reads with an error in punctuation: "Mordacke earle of Fife, son to the gouernour archembald earle Dowglas," from which Shakespeare erroneously gathered that Mordake was the son of Archibald; see *1 Henry IV*, 1.1.71–72.) **18 meaner degrees** lower station
19 this man (Grammatically this seems to refer to Glendower, and so Shakespeare appears to have understood it at 3.1.12 ff., but Holinshed probably is talking here about the birth of Mortimer.)

divers and sundry times require deliverance of the residue, and that with great threatening. Wherewith the Percys, being sore offended, for that they claimed them as their own proper prisoners and their peculiar prize,[20] by the counsel of the Lord Thomas Percy, Earl of Worcester, whose study was ever, as some write, to procure malice and set things in a broil, came to the King unto Windsor upon a purpose to prove[21] him and there required[22] of him that, either by ransom or otherwise, he would cause to be delivered out of prison Edmund Mortimer, Earl of March, their cousin-german,[23] whom, as they reported, Owen Glendower kept in filthy prison, shackled with irons, only for that he took his part[24] and was to him faithful and true.

The King began not a little to muse at this request, and not without cause; for indeed it touched him somewhat near, sith this Edmund was son to Roger, Earl of March, son to the Lady Philip, daughter of Lionel, Duke of Clarence, the third son of King Edward the Third; which Edmund,[25] at King Richard's going into Ireland, was proclaimed heir apparent to the crown and realm; whose aunt called Eleanor[26] the Lord Henry Percy had married; and therefore King Henry could not well hear that any man should be earnest about the advancement of that lineage. The King, when he had studied on the matter, made answer that the Earl of March was not taken prisoner for his cause nor in his service[27] but willingly suffered himself to be taken, because he would not withstand the attempts of Owen Glendower and his complices,[28] and therefore he would neither ransom him nor relieve him.

The Percys with this answer and fraudulent excuse were not a little fumed,[29] insomuch that Henry Hotspur said openly: "Behold, the heir of the realm is robbed of his right,

20 prize booty **21 prove** test **22 required** requested **23 cousin-german** first cousin **24 only for that he took his part** i.e., the Percys requested Henry to ransom the Earl of March because Mortimer was loyal to Henry **25 which Edmund** (In fact, the Earl first named as heir to the Crown was the fourth Earl of March, Roger Mortimer, though his son Edmund was later designated heir when the fourth Earl died.) **26 Eleanor** (Actually, the sister of Sir Edmund Mortimer and of the fourth Earl of March was named Elizabeth. Shakespeare calls her Kate.) **27 his cause . . . his service** i.e., King Henry's cause and service **28 complices** accomplices **29 fumed** incensed

and yet the robber with his own will not redeem him." So in this fury the Percys departed, minding[30] nothing more than to depose King Henry from the high type[31] of his royalty and to place in his seat their cousin Edmund, Earl of March, whom they did not only deliver out of captivity but also, to the high displeasure of King Henry, entered in league with the foresaid Owen Glendower. Herewith they, by their deputies in the house of the Archdeacon of Bangor, divided the realm amongst them, causing a tripartite indenture to be made and sealed with their seals, by the covenants whereof all England from Severn and Trent south and eastward was assigned to the Earl of March, all Wales and the lands beyond Severn westward were appointed to Owen Glendower, and all the remnant from Trent northward to the Lord Percy.

This was done, as some have said, through a foolish credit given to a vain prophecy, as though King Henry was the moldwarp,[32] cursed of God's own mouth, and they three were the dragon, the lion, and the wolf which should divide this realm between them. Such is the deviation (saith Hall)[33] and not divination of those blind and fantastical dreams of the Welsh prophesiers. King Henry, not knowing of this new confederacy, and nothing less minding than that which after happened,[34] gathered a great army to go again into Wales, whereof the Earl of Northumberland and his son were advertised[35] by the Earl of Worcester, and with all diligence raised all the power they could make and sent to the Scots which before were taken prisoners at Homeldon for aid of men, promising to the Earl of Douglas the town of Berwick and a part of Northumberland and to other Scottish lords great lordships and seigniories if they obtained the upper hand. The Scots, in hope of gain and desirous to be revenged of their old griefs,[36] came to the Earl with a great company well appointed.[37]

The Percys, to make their part seem good, devised certain articles by the advice of Richard Scroop, Archbishop of

30 minding intending **31 type** summit **32 moldwarp** mole **33 Hall** Edward Hall, author of *The Union of the Two Noble and Illustre Families of Lancaster and York* (1542) **34 nothing . . . happened** not at all anticipating what eventually took place **35 advertised** advised, informed **36 griefs** complaints **37 appointed** equipped

York, brother to the Lord Scroop, whom King Henry had caused to be beheaded at Bristol. These articles, being showed to divers noblemen and other states[38] of the realm, moved them to favor their purpose, insomuch that many of them did not only promise to the Percys aid and succor by words but also by their writings and seals confirmed the same. Howbeit, when the matter came to trial, the most part of the confederates abandoned them and at the day of the conflict left them alone. Thus, after that the conspirators had discovered themselves,[39] the Lord Henry Percy, desirous to proceed in the enterprise, upon trust to be assisted by Owen Glendower, the Earl of March, and other, assembled an army of men-of-arms and archers forth of Cheshire and Wales. Incontinently[40] his uncle Thomas Percy, Earl of Worcester, that had the government[41] of the Prince of Wales, who as then lay[42] at London in secret manner, conveyed himself out of the Prince's house, and coming to Stafford, where he met his nephew, they increased their power by all ways and means they could devise. The Earl of Northumberland himself was not with them but, being sick, had promised upon his amendment to repair unto them, as some write, with all convenient speed.

These noblemen, to make their conspiracy to seem excusable, besides the articles above-mentioned sent letters abroad,[43] wherein was contained that their gathering of an army tended to none other end but only for the safeguard of their own persons and to put some better government in the commonwealth. For whereas taxes and tallages[44] were daily levied under pretense to be employed in defense of the realm, the same were vainly wasted and unprofitably consumed; and where through the slanderous reports of their enemies the King had taken a grievous displeasure with them, they durst not appear personally in the King's presence until the prelates and barons of the realm had obtained of the King license for them to come and purge themselves before him by lawful trial of their peers, whose judgment, as they pretended, they would in no wise refuse.

38 states noblemen **39 after that . . . themselves** after the conspirators had revealed their purposes **40 Incontinently** immediately **41 government** guardianship **42 lay** resided **43 abroad** round about **44 tallages** arbitrary taxes

Many that saw and heard these letters did commend their diligence and highly praised their assured fidelity and trustiness towards the commonwealth. . . .

And to speak a truth, no marvel it was if many envied the prosperous state of King Henry, sith it was evident enough to the world that he had with wrong usurped the crown, and not only violently deposed King Richard but also cruelly procured his death, for the which undoubtedly both he and his posterity tasted such troubles as put them still in danger of their states, till their direct succeeding line was quite rooted out by the contrary faction, as in Henry the Sixth and Edward the Fourth it may appear.

But now to return where we left. King Henry, advertised of the proceedings of the Percys, forthwith gathered about him such power as he might make, and being earnestly called upon by the Scot, the Earl of March,[45] to make haste and give battle to his enemies before their power by delaying of time should still too much increase, he passed forward with such speed that he was in sight of his enemies, lying in camp near to Shrewsbury, before they were in doubt of[46] any such thing; for the Percys thought that he would have stayed at Burton-upon-Trent till his council had come thither to him to give their advice what he were best to do. But herein the enemy was deceived of his expectation, sith the King had great regard of expedition and making speed for the safety of his own person whereunto the Earl of March incited him, considering that in delay is danger and loss in lingering, as the poet in the like case saith:

Dum trepidant nullo firmatae robore partes,
Tolle moras; semper nocuit differre paratis.[47]

By reason of the King's sudden coming in this sort, they stayed[48] from assaulting the town of Shrewsbury, which enterprise they were ready at that instant to have taken in hand; and forthwith the Lord Percy, as a captain of high

45 Scot . . . March i.e., George Dunbar, Earl of March of Scotland, not to be confused with Edmund Mortimer, the Earl of March in England **46 were in doubt of** feared, anticipated **47 Dum . . . partes** (An often-quoted maxim from Lucan's *Pharsalia,* 1:280–281, to the effect that it is folly to allow one's enemies to consolidate power, and that delay is always harmful once you are prepared. Holinshed prints the lines in reverse order.) **48 stayed** refrained, withheld

courage, began to exhort the captains and soldiers to prepare themselves to battle, sith the matter was grown to that point that by no means it could be avoided. "So that," said he, "this day shall either bring us all to advancement and honor, or else, if it shall chance us to be overcome, shall deliver us from the King's spiteful malice and cruel disdain; for playing the men, as we ought to do, better it is to die in battle for the commonwealth's cause than through cowardlike fear to prolong life which after shall be taken from us by sentence of the enemy."

Hereupon the whole army, being in number about fourteen thousand chosen men, promised to stand with him so long as life lasted. There were with the Percys as chieftains of this army the Earl of Douglas, a Scottish man; the Baron of Kinderton; Sir Hugh Browne and Sir Richard Vernon, knights; with divers other stout and right valiant captains. Now when the two armies were encamped, the one against the other, the Earl of Worcester and the Lord Percy with their complices sent the articles (whereof I spake before) by Thomas Caton and Thomas Salvain, esquires, to King Henry, under their hands and seals, which articles in effect charged him with manifest perjury, in that, contrary to his oath received upon the evangelists at Doncaster when he first entered the realm after his exile, he had taken upon him the crown and royal dignity, imprisoned King Richard, caused him to resign his title and finally to be murdered. Divers other matters they laid to his charge, as levying of taxes and tallages contrary to his promise, infringing of laws and customs of the realm, and suffering the Earl of March to remain in prison without travailing[49] to have him delivered. All which things they, as procurers and protectors of the commonwealth, took upon them to prove against him, as they protested unto the whole world.

King Henry, after he had read their articles, with the defiance which they annexed to the same, answered the esquires that he was ready with dint of sword and fierce battle to prove their quarrel false and nothing else than a forged matter, not doubting but that God would aid and assist him in his righteous cause against the disloyal and false

49 travailing laboring

forsworn traitors. The next day in the morning early, being the even of Mary Magdalene,[50] they set their battles[51] in order on both sides, and now, whilst the warriors looked when the token of battle should be given, the Abbot of Shrewsbury and one of the clerks of the Privy Seal were sent from the King unto the Percys to offer them pardon if they would come to any reasonable agreement. By their persuasions, the Lord Henry Percy began to give ear unto the King's offer and so sent with them his uncle, the Earl of Worcester, to declare unto the King the causes of those troubles and to require some effectual reformation in the same.

It was reported for a truth that now, when the King had condescended unto all that was reasonable at his hands to be required and seemed to humble himself more than was meet for his estate, the Earl of Worcester, upon his return to his nephew, made relation clean contrary to that[52] the King had said in such sort that he set his nephew's heart more in displeasure towards the King than ever it was before, driving him by that means to fight whether he would or not. Then suddenly blew the trumpets, the King's part[53] crying "Saint George! Upon them!" The adversaries cried "Esperance! Percy!" and so the two armies furiously joined. The archers on both sides shot for the best game, laying on such load with arrows that many died and were driven down that never rose again.

The Scots, as some write, which had the foreward[54] on the Percys' side, intending to be revenged of their old displeasures done to them by the English nation, set so fiercely on the King's foreward, led by the Earl of Stafford, that they made the same draw back and had almost broken their adversaries' array. The Welshmen also, which before had lain lurking in the woods, mountains, and marshes, hearing of this battle toward,[55] came to the aid of the Percys and refreshed the wearied people with new succors. The King, perceiving that his men were thus put to distress what with the violent impression[56] of the Scots and the tempestuous

50 the even of Mary Magdalene the eve before the Feast of Mary Magdalene on July 22 (1403) **51 battles** battalions, armed forces **52 that** that which **53 part** supporters **54 foreward** vanguard **55 toward** impending, at hand **56 impression** assault, attack

storms of arrows that his adversaries discharged freely against him and his people, it was no need to will him to stir; for suddenly, with his fresh battle,[57] he approached and relieved his men, so that the battle began more fierce than before. Here the Lord Henry Percy and the Earl Douglas, a right stout and hardy captain, not regarding the shot of the King's battle nor the close order of the ranks, pressing forward together bent their whole forces towards the King's person, coming upon him with spears and swords so fiercely that the Earl of March the Scot, perceiving their purpose, withdrew the King from that side of the field, as some write, for his great benefit and safeguard, as it appeared. For they gave such a violent onset upon them that stood about the King's standard that, slaying his standard-bearer, Sir Walter Blunt, and overthrowing the standard, they made slaughter of all those that stood about it, as[58] the Earl of Stafford, that day made by the King Constable of the realm, and divers other.

The Prince that day holp his father like a lusty young gentleman; for although he was hurt in the face with an arrow, so that divers noblemen that were about him would have conveyed him forth of the field, yet he would not suffer them so to do, lest his departure from amongst his men might haply have stricken some fear into their hearts. And so, without regard of his hurt, he continued with his men and never ceased either to fight where the battle was most hot or to encourage his men where it seemed most need. This battle lasted three long hours with indifferent fortune on both parts till at length the King, crying "Saint George! Victory!" brake the array of his enemies and adventured so far that, as some write, the Earl Douglas strake him down and at that instant slew Sir Walter Blunt and three other appareled in the King's suit and clothing, saying: "I marvel to see so many kings thus suddenly arise one in the neck of[59] another." The King indeed was raised and did that day many a noble feat of arms, for as it is written, he slew that day with his own hands six-and-thirty persons of his enemies. The other on his part,[60] encouraged by his doings,

57 battle battalion **58 as** such as, including **59 in the neck of** immediately following **60 The other on his part** others in his army. (Not, as it might be interpreted, a reference to Prince Henry.)

fought valiantly and slew the Lord Percy, called Sir Henry Hotspur. To conclude, the King's enemies were vanquished and put to flight, in which flight the Earl of Douglas, for haste, falling from the crag of an high mountain, brake one of his cullions[61] and was taken, and, for his valiantness, of the King frankly[62] and freely delivered.

There was also taken the Earl of Worcester, the procurer and setter-forth of all this mischief, Sir Richard Vernon, and the Baron of Kinderton, with divers other. There were slain upon the King's part, besides the Earl of Stafford, to the number of ten knights: Sir Hugh Shirley, Sir John Clifton, Sir John Cokayne, Sir Nicholas Gawsey, Sir Walter Blunt, Sir John Calverley, Sir John Massey of Podington, Sir Hugh Mortimer, and Sir Robert Gawsey, all the which received the same morning the order of knighthood; Sir Thomas Wensley was wounded to death and so passed out of this life shortly after. There died in all upon the King's side sixteen hundred, and four thousand were grievously wounded. On the contrary side were slain, besides the Lord Percy, the most part of the knights and esquires of the county of Chester, to the number of two hundred, besides yeomen and footmen; in all there died of those that fought on the Percys' side about five thousand. This battle was fought on Mary Magdalene Even, being Saturday. Upon the Monday following, the Earl of Worcester, the Baron of Kinderton, and Sir Richard Vernon, knights, were condemned and beheaded. The Earl's head was sent to London, there to be set on the Bridge.

[Holinshed gives an account of friction between King Henry and his son, although from a considerably later date, 1412, and having no connection with the Percy rebellion and the Battle of Shrewsbury.]

The Lord Henry, Prince of Wales, eldest son to King Henry, got knowledge that certain of his father's servants were busy to give informations against him, whereby discord might arise betwixt him and his father; for they put into the King's head not only what evil rule (according to the course of youth) the Prince kept, to the offense of many,

61 cullions testicles **62 frankly** generously

but also what great resort of people came to his house, so that the court was nothing[63] furnished with such a train as daily followed the Prince. These tales brought no small suspicion into the King's head, lest his son would presume to usurp the Crown, he being yet alive, through which suspicious jealousy it was perceived that he favored not his son as in times past he had done.

The Prince, sore offended with such persons as, by slanderous reports, sought not only to spot his good name abroad in the realm but to sow discord also betwixt him and his father, wrote his letters into every part of the realm to reprove[64] all such slanderous devices of those that sought his discredit. And to clear himself the better, that the world might understand what wrong he had to be slandered in such wise, about the feast of Peter and Paul, to wit the nine-and-twentieth day of June, he came to the court with such a number of noblemen and other his friends that wished him well as the like train had been seldom seen repairing to the court at any one time in those days. He was appareled in a gown of blue satin full of small eyelet holes, at every hole the needle hanging by a silk thread with which it was sewed. About his arm he ware an hound's collar set full of SS of gold and the terrets[65] likewise being of the same metal.

The court was then at Westminster where, he being entered into the hall, not one of his company durst once advance himself further than the fire in the same hall, notwithstanding they were earnestly requested by the lords to come higher; but they, regarding what they had in commandment of the Prince, would not presume to do in any thing contrary thereunto. He himself, only accompanied with those of the King's house, was straight admitted to the presence of the King his father, who, being at that time grievously diseased, yet caused himself in his chair to be borne into his privy chamber, where in the presence of three or four persons in whom he had most confidence he commanded the Prince to show what he had to say concerning the cause of his coming.

The Prince, kneeling down before his father, said: "Most

63 nothing not at all **64 reprove** disprove, confute **65 terrets** rings by which objects can be attached to a chain

redoubted[66] and sovereign lord and Father, I am at this time come to your presence as your liege man and as your natural son, in all things to be at your commandment. And where I understand you have in suspicion my demeanor against Your Grace, you know very well that if I knew any man within this realm of whom you should stand in fear, my duty were to punish that person, thereby to remove that grief from your heart. Then how much more ought I to suffer death, to ease Your Grace of that grief which you have of me, being your natural son and liege man, and to that end I have this day made myself ready by confession and receiving of the Sacrament. And therefore I beseech you, most redoubted lord and dear Father, for the honor of God, to ease your heart of all such suspicion as you have of me and to dispatch me here before your knees with this same dagger"—and withal he delivered unto the King his dagger, in all humble reverence, adding further that his life was not so dear to him that he wished to live one day with his displeasure—"and therefore in thus ridding me out of life and yourself from all suspicion, here in presence of these lords and before God at the day of the General Judgment, I faithfully protest clearly to forgive you."[67]

The King, moved herewith, cast from him the dagger and, embracing the Prince, kissed him and with shedding tears confessed that indeed he had him partly in suspicion, though now, as he perceived, not with just cause, and therefore from thenceforth no misreport should cause him to have him in mistrust, and this he promised of his honor. So by his great wisdom was the wrongful suspicion which his father had conceived against him removed and he restored to his favor. And further, where he could not but grievously complain of them that had slandered him so greatly, to the defacing not only of his honor but also putting him in danger of his life, he humbly besought the King that they might answer their unjust accusation, and in case they were found to have forged such matters upon a malicious purpose that then they might suffer some punishment for their faults, though not to the full of that they had deserved. The King, seeming to grant his reasonable desire, yet told him

66 redoubted reverenced, feared **67 forgive you** i.e., forgive you for killing me, if you choose to do so

that he must tarry[68] a parliament, that such offenders might be punished by judgment of their peers; and so for that time he was dismissed with great love and signs of fatherly affection.

Thus, were the father and the son reconciled, betwixt whom the said pickthanks[69] had sown division, insomuch that the son, upon a vehement conceit of unkindness sprung in the father, was in the way to be worn out of favor. Which was the more likely to come to pass by their informations that privily charged him with riot and other uncivil demeanor unseemly for a prince. Indeed, he was youthfully given, grown to audacity,[70] and had chosen him companions agreeable to his age, with whom he spent the time in such recreations, exercises, and delights as he fancied. But yet it should seem by the report of some writers that his behavior was not offensive or at least tending to the damage of anybody, sith he had a care to avoid doing of wrong and to tether his affections within the tract[71] of virtue, whereby he opened unto himself a ready passage of good liking among the prudent sort and was beloved of such as could discern his disposition, which was in no degree so excessive as that he deserved in such vehement manner to be suspected. In whose dispraise I find little but, to his praise very much.

The second edition of Raphael Holinshed's *Chronicles* was published in 1587. This selection is based on that edition, Volume 3, folios 518–539. Some proper names have been modernized or regularized, including Glendower (Glendouer), Almaine (Almane or Almanie), Cologne (Colin), Bavaria (Bauier), Archibald (Archembald), Mordake (Mordacke), Murray (Murrey), Shirley (Shorlie), Gawsey (Gausell), and Wensley (Wendesleie).

68 tarry await **69 pickthanks** sycophants, talebearers **70 audacity** boldness, confidence **71 tract** path, territory

The First Four Books of the Civil Wars Between the Two Houses of Lancaster and York (1595)

By Samuel Daniel

Book 3

[Bolingbroke, having become Henry IV, encounters military difficulties, especially with the Scots and Welsh.]

86

And yet new Hydras, lo, new heads appear
T'afflict that peace reputed then so sure,
And gave him much to do and much to fear,
And long and dangerous tumults did procure;
And those even of his chiefest followers were
Of whom he might presume him most secure,
Who, whether not so graced or so preferred
As they expected, these new factions stirred.

87

The Percys were the men, men of great might,
Strong in alliance and in courage strong,
That thus conspire under pretense to right
The crookèd courses they had suffered long;
Whether their conscience urged them or despite,
Or that they saw the part they took was wrong,
Or that ambition hereto did them call,
Or others envied grace, or rather all.

88

What cause soever were, strong was their plot,
Their parties great, means good, th' occasion fit;

86 • 1 Hydras (The Hydra was a mythical monster with many heads that grew again as soon as they were cut off.) **7 whether** i.e., whether it was because they were

87 • 6 the part they took i.e., that their role in supporting Bolingbroke against Richard II, the legitimate king

Their practice close, their faith suspected not,
Their states far off and they of wary wit;
Who with large promises draw in the Scot
To aid their cause. He likes and yields to it,
Not for the love of them or for their good,
But glad hereby of means to shed our blood.

89

Then join they with the Welsh, who, fitly trained
And all in arms under a mighty head,
Great Glendower, who long warred and much attained,
Sharp conflicts made and many vanquishèd;
With whom was Edmund, Earl of March, retained,
Being first his prisoner, now confederèd,
A man the King much feared, and well he might
Lest he should look whether his crown stood right.

90

For Richard, for the quiet of the state,
Before he took those Irish wars in hand,
About succession doth deliberate,
And finding how the certain right did stand,
With full consent this man did ordinate
The heir apparent to the Crown and land.
Then judge if this the King might nearly touch,
Although his might were small, his right being much.

91

With these the Percys them confederate,
And as three heads they league in one intent,
And, instituting a triumvirate,

88 • 3 Their practice close their plotting secret **4 Their states far off** i.e., their estates far to the north in Northumberland **8 our** i.e., English

89 • 6 confederèd allied, in league

90 • 5 this man i.e., Edmund, Earl of March. (But Daniel, like Holinshed, and Shakespeare after them, conflates the fifth Earl of March, claimant to the throne, with his uncle, Sir Edmund Mortimer, who was captured by Glendower and married his daughter.) **ordinate** name **7 touch** concern

91 • 1 them confederate ally themselves

Do part the land in triple government,
Dividing thus among themselves the state:
The Percys should rule all the North from Trent,
And Glendower Wales; the Earl of March should be
Lord of the South from Trent; and thus they 'gree.

92

Then those two helps which still such actors find—
Pretense of common good, the King's disgrace—
Doth fit their course and draw the vulgar mind
To further them and aid them in this case.
The King they accused for cruel and unkind,
That did the state, and Crown, and all deface—
A perjured man that held all faith in scorn,
Whose trusted oaths had others made forsworn.

93

Besides, the odious detestable act
Of that late murdered king they aggravate,
Making it his that so had willed the fact
That he the doers did remunerate,
And then such taxes daily doth exact
That were against the orders of the state;
And with all these, or worse, they him assailed
Who late of others with the like prevailed.

94

Thus doth contentious proud mortality
Afflict each other and itself torment.
And thus O thou, mind-torturing misery,
Restless Ambition, born in discontent,
Turn'st and retossest with iniquity
The unconstant courses frailty did invent,

92 • 1 still always **3 vulgar** popular **5 for** of being

93 • 3 his i.e., Bolingbroke's **8 Who . . . prevailed** i.e., who himself only recently succeeded in urging, along with others, similar complaints against Richard II

94 • 1 mortality humankind

And foul'st fair order and defil'st the earth,
Fost'ring up War, father of blood and dearth.

95

Great seemed the cause, and greatly, too, did add
The peoples' love thereto, these crimes rehearsed,
That many gathered to the troops they had,
And many more do flock from coasts dispersed.
But when the King had heard these news so bad,
Th' unlooked-for dangerous toil more nearly pierced;
For, bent towards Wales t'appease those tumults there,
He's forced divert his course, and them forbear.

96

Not to give time unto th' increasing rage
And gathering fury, forth he hastes with speed,
Lest more delay, or giving longer age
To th' evil grown, it might the cure exceed.
All his best men at arms and leaders sage
All he prepared he could, and all did need;
For to a mighty work thou goest, O King,
To such a field that power to power shall bring.

97

There shall young Hotspur with a fury led
Meet with thy forward son as fierce as he;
There warlike Worcester, long experiencèd
In foreign arms, shall come t' encounter thee;
There Douglas to thy Stafford shall make head;

94 • 7 And foul'st and you befoul

95 • 4 from coasts dispersed i.e., from far and near **8 them forbear** i.e., forbear fighting the Welsh

96 • 3–4 Lest . . . exceed i.e., lest further delay, giving rebellion time to ripen still more, might allow the disease to grow beyond the ability of means to cure it **8 field** battlefield. **power to power** army against army

97 • 2 forward ardent, eager **4 In foreign arms** in fighting abroad **5 make head** advance

There Vernon for thy valiant Blunt shall be.
There shalt thou find a doubtful bloody day,
Though sickness keep Northumberland away,

98

Who yet reserved, though after quit for this,
Another tempest on thy head to raise,
As if still-wrong revenging Nemesis
Did mean t' afflict all thy continual days.
And yet this field he happily might miss
For thy great good, and therefore well he stays.
What might his force have done, being joined thereto,
When that already gave so much to do?

99

The swift approach and unexpected speed
The King had made upon this new-raised force
In th' unconfirmèd troops much fear did breed,
Untimely hindering their intended course;
The joining with the Welsh they had decreed
Was hereby stopped, which made their part the worse;
Northumberland, with forces from the North
Expected to be there, was not set forth.

100

And yet undaunted Hotspur, seeing the King
So near approached, leaving the work in hand,
With forward speed his forces marshaling,
Sets forth his farther coming to withstand
And, with a cheerful voice encouraging
By his great spirit his well-emboldened band,
Brings a strong host of firm-resolvèd might
And placed his troops before the King in sight.

98 • 1 after quit subsequently requited **5 field** battlefield. **happily** haply, perchance **6 For thy great good** i.e., a thing of great good fortune to you **8 When . . . do** i.e., when the rebel force, even without Northumberland, gave so much trouble to Henry

99 • 3 unconfirmèd not knowing the rumor to be true for certain

101

"This day," saith he, "O faithful valiant friends,
Whatever it doth give, shall glory give.
This day with honor frees our state or ends
Our misery with fame, that still shall live.
And do but think how well this day he spends
That spends his blood his country to relieve!
Our holy cause, our freedom, and our right
Sufficient are to move good minds to fight.

102

"Besides, th' assurèd hope of victory
That we may even promise on our side
Against this weak constrainèd company
Whom force and fear, not will and love, doth guide,
Against a prince whose foul impiety
The heavens do hate, the earth cannot abide,
Our number being no less, our courage more,
What need we doubt if we but work therefor?"

103

This said, and thus resolved, even bent to charge
Upon the King, who well their order viewed
And careful noted all the form at large
Of their proceeding and their multitude;
And, deeming better if he could discharge
The day with safety and some peace conclude,
Great proffers sends of pardon and of grace
If they would yield and quietness embrace.

104

But this refused, the King, with wrath incensed,
Rage against fury doth with speed prepare.
And "O," saith he, "though I could have dispensed
With this day's blood, which I have sought to spare

101 • 5 he i.e., that person

102 • 3 constrainèd i.e., forced to fight on Henry's side, not willingly

103 • 1 even bent fully ready **3 careful** carefully

That greater glory might have recompensed
The forward worth of these that so much dare,
That we might honor had by th' overthrown,
That th' wounds we make might not have been our own,

105

"Yet since that other men's iniquity
Calls on the sword of wrath against my will,
And that themselves exact this cruelty,
And I constrainèd am this blood to spill,
Then on, my masters! On courageously,
True-hearted subjects, against traitors ill,
And spare them not who seek to spoil us all,
Whose foul confusèd end soon see you shall!"

106

Straight moves with equal motion equal rage
The like incensèd armies unto blood,
One to defend, another side to wage
Foul civil war. Both vows their quarrel good.
Ah, too much heat to blood doth now enrage
Both who the deed provokes and who withstood,
That valor here is vice, here manhood sin.
The forward'st hands doth, O, least honor win.

107

But now begin these fury-moving sounds,
The notes of wrath that music brought from hell—
The rattling drums which trumpets' voice confounds,
The cries, th' encouragements, the shouting shrill—
That all about the beaten air rebounds,
Thund'ring confusèd, murmurs horrible,

104 • 7 had have had **8 our own** i.e., English

105 • 1 since that since

106 • 1–2 Straight . . . blood immediately, with equal motion, an equal rage moves these two armies, alike incensed, to bloodshed **6 Both . . . provokes** both those who provoke the deed **7–8 That . . . win** i.e., in civil war, valor and bravery prove dishonorable

To rob all sense except the sense to fight.
Well hands may work; the mind hath lost his sight.

108

O War! Begot in pride and luxury,
The child of wrath and of dissension,
Horrible good, mischief necessary,
The foul reformer of confusion,
Unjust-just scourge of our iniquity,
Cruel recurrer of corruption!
O that these sin-sick states in need should stand
To be let blood with such a boisterous hand!

109

And O, how well thou hadst been spared this day
Had not wrong-counseled Percy been perverse,
Whose young undangered hand now rash makes way
Upon the sharpest fronts of the most fierce;
Where now an equal fury thrusts to stay
And rebeat back that force and his disperse,
Then these assail, then those chase back again,
Till stayed with new-made hills of bodies slain.

110

There, lo! That new-appearing glorious star,
Wonder of arms, the terror of the field,
Young Henry, laboring where the stoutest are,
And even the stoutest forces back to yield;
There is that hand, boldened to blood and war,
That must the sword in woundrous actions wield.
But better hadst thou learned with others' blood,
A less expense to us, to thee more good.

107 • 8 his its

108 • 6 recurrer curer

109 • 1 thou i.e., War. **spared** avoided, done without **3 young undangered hand** i.e., young arm not yet tested in battle **4 fronts** points **5 stay** halt **6 rebeat back** beat back. **his disperse** disperse his (Percy's) troops

110 • 3 stoutest bravest **6 woundrous** wondrous (punning on *wound*)

111

Hadst thou not there lent present speedy aid
To thy endangered father, nearly tired,
Whom fierce encountering Douglas overlaid,
That day had there his troublous life expired.
Heroical courageous Blunt, arrayed
In habit like as was the King attired,
And deemed for him, excused that fate with his,
For he had what his lord did hardly miss.

112

For thought a king he would not now disgrace
The person then supposed, but princelike shows
Glorious effects of worth that fit his place,
And fighting dies, and dying overthrows.
Another of that forward name and race
In that hot work his valiant life bestows,
Who bare the standard of the King that day,
Whose colors overthrown did much dismay.

113

And dear it cost, and O, much blood is shed
To purchase thee this losing victory,
O travailed King. Yet hast thou conquerèd
A doubtful day, a mighty enemy.
But O, what wounds, what famous worth lies dead
That makes the winner look with sorrowing eye!
Magnanimous Stafford lost, that much had wrought,
And valiant Shirley, who great glory got.

111 • 1 present immediate **7 excused . . . his** i.e., deflected King Henry's destined death onto his own **8 For . . . miss** i.e., for he received what the King scarcely avoided, a death thrust

112 • 1–3 For . . . place i.e., buoyed up with the thought that he would not disgrace the royal person whom he impersonated, but instead in princelike fashion do glorious warlike deeds fitting a royal role **5–6 Another . . . bestows** i.e., another Blunt also gives up his life in the heat of battle **8 Whose . . . dismay** on which occasion the throwing down of the King's standard caused widespread dismay

113 • 3 travailed hard-pressed

114

Such wrack of others' blood thou didst behold,
O furious Hotspur, ere thou lost thine own!
Which now, once lost, that heat in thine waxed cold,
And soon became thy army overthrown;
And O, that this great spirit, this courage bold,
Had in some good cause been rightly shown!
So had not we thus violently then
Have termed that "rage" which "valor" should have been.

This selection is based on Samuel Daniel's *The First Four Books of the Civil Wars Between the Two Houses of Lancaster and York,* London, 1595.

The Famous Victories of Henry the Fifth, Containing the Honorable Battle of Agincourt

Any departures from the original text are noted with an asterisk and appear at the bottom of the page in boldface; original readings are in roman.

[Scene 1] *Enter the young Prince, Ned, and Tom* [*with stolen money*].

PRINCE Come away, Ned and Tom.
BOTH Here, my lord.
PRINCE Come away, my lads. Tell me, sirs, how much gold have you got?
NED Faith, my lord, I have got five hundred pound.
PRINCE But tell me, Tom, how much hast thou got?
TOM Faith, my lord, some four hundred pound.
PRINCE Four hundred pounds! Bravely spoken, lads. But tell me, sirs, think you not that it was a villainous part of me to rob my father's receivers?[1]
NED Why, no, my lord. It was but a trick of youth.

114 • 1 wrack devastation

Scene 1. Location: The highway south of London, about a mile from the city.
1 receivers treasury officials who receive or collect taxes

PRINCE Faith, Ned, thou sayest true. But tell me, sirs, whereabouts are we?

TOM My lord, we are now about a mile off London.

PRINCE But, sirs, I marvel that Sir John Oldcastle comes not away. Zounds,[2] see where he comes.

Enter Jockey[3] [*i.e., Sir John Oldcastle, with money*].

How now, Jockey, what news with thee?

SIR JOHN OLDCASTLE Faith, my lord, such news as passeth.[4] For the town of Deptford is risen with hue and cry after your man, which parted from us the last night and has set upon and hath robbed a poor carrier.[5]

PRINCE Zounds, the villain that was wont to spy out our booties?[6]

SIR JOHN OLDCASTLE Ay, my lord, even the very same.

PRINCE Now base-minded rascal, to rob a poor carrier! Well, it skills not.[7] I'll save the base villain's life. Ay, I may. But tell me, Jockey, whereabout be the receivers?

SIR JOHN OLDCASTLE Faith, my lord, they are hard by. But the best is we are ahorseback and they be afoot, so we may escape them.

PRINCE Well, if* the villains come, let me alone with them.[8] But tell me, Jockey, how much gots thou from the knaves? For I am sure I got something, for one of the villains so belammed[9] me about the shoulders as I shall feel it this month.

SIR JOHN OLDCASTLE Faith, my lord, I have got a hundred pound.

PRINCE A hundred pound! Now bravely spoken, Jockey. But come, sirs, lay all your money before me. [*They lay out the stolen money.*] Now, by heaven, here is a brave show! But, as I am true gentleman, I will have the half of this spent tonight. But, sirs, take up your bags. Here comes the receivers. [*They gather up the money.*] Let me alone.

Enters two Receivers.

FIRST RECEIVER [*To his companion*] Alas, good fellow, what

*if I [Q]

2 Zounds by his (God's) wounds **3 Jockey** Jack **4 passeth** surpasses **5 carrier** one who hauls produce, a teamster **6 spy out our booties** act as spy on our intended victims, our prizes **7 it skills not** it makes no difference **8 let . . . them** let me handle them **9 belammed** beat

shall we do? I dare never go home to the court, for I shall be hanged. But look, here is the young Prince. What shall we do?

PRINCE How now, you villains, what are you?

FIRST RECEIVER [*To his companion*] Speak you to him.

SECOND RECEIVER No, I pray, speak you to him.

PRINCE Why, how now, you rascals, why speak you not?

FIRST RECEIVER Forsooth, we be—pray, speak you to him.

PRINCE Zounds, villains, speak, or I'll cut off your heads!

SECOND RECEIVER Forsooth, he can tell the tale better than I.

FIRST RECEIVER Forsooth, we be your father's receivers.

PRINCE Are you my father's receivers? Then I hope ye have brought me some money.

FIRST RECEIVER Money? Alas, sir, we be robbed!

PRINCE Robbed! How many were there of them?

FIRST RECEIVER Marry, sir, there were four of them. And one of them had Sir John Oldcastle's bay hobby[10] and your black nag.

PRINCE Gog's wounds![11] How like you this, Jockey? Blood,[12] you villains, my father robbed of his money abroad, and we robbed in our stables! But tell me, how many were of them?

FIRST RECEIVER If it please you, there were four of them. And there was one about the bigness of you, but I am sure I so belammed him about the shoulders that he will feel it this month.

PRINCE Gog's wounds! You lammed them fairly, so that they have carried away your money. [*To his companions.*] But come, sirs, what shall we do with the villains?

BOTH RECEIVERS [*Kneeling*] I beseech Your Grace, be good to us.

NED I pray you, my lord, forgive them this once.

PRINCE* Well, stand up and get you gone. And look that you speak not a word of it, for, if there be, zounds! I'll hang you and all your kin. *Exit* [*Receivers*].*
Now, sirs, how like you this? Was not this bravely done? For now the villains dare not speak a word of it, I have so feared them with words. Now, whither shall we go?

ALL Why, my lord, you know our old host's at Faversham.

PRINCE Our host's at Faversham? Blood, what shall we do

***Prince** [not in Q] ***Exit [Receivers]** Exit Purseuant [Q]

10 hobby pony **11 Gog's wounds** by God's wounds **12 Blood** by God's blood

there? We have a thousand pound about us, and we shall go to a petty alehouse? No, no. You know the old tavern in Eastcheap. There is good wine. Besides, there is a pretty wench that can talk well, for I delight as much in their tongues as any part[13] about them.

ALL We are ready to wait upon[14] Your Grace.

PRINCE Gog's wounds, "Wait"? We will go altogether; we are all fellows. I tell you, sirs, an[15] the King my father were dead, we would be all kings. Therefore, come away.

NED Gog's wounds, bravely spoken, Harry! [*Exeunt.*]

[Scene 2] *Enter John Cobbler, Robin Pewterer, Lawrence Costermonger.*

JOHN All is well here. All is well, masters.

LAWRENCE* How say you, neighbor John Cobbler? I think it best that my neighbor, Robin Pewterer, went to Pudding Lane End, and we will watch here at Billingsgate Ward.[1] How say you, neighbor Robin? How like you this?

ROBIN Marry, well, neighbors. I care not much if I go to Pudding Lane's End. But, neighbors, an you hear any ado about me, make haste; and if I hear any ado about you, I will come to you. *Exit Robin.*

LAWRENCE Neighbor, what news hear you of the young Prince?

JOHN Marry, neighbor, I hear say he is a toward[2] young prince; for, if he meet any by the highway, he will not let[3] to talk with[4] him. I dare not call him thief, but sure he is one of these taking fellows.[5]

LAWRENCE Indeed, neighbor, I hear say he is as lively a young prince as ever was.

JOHN Ay, and I hear say if he use it long, his father will cut him off from the Crown. But, neighbor, say nothing of that!

***Lawrence** Robin [Q]

13 part (with bawdy suggestion) **14 wait upon** attend **15 an** if

Scene 2. Location: London, near Eastcheap, at night.
1 Pudding Lane End, Billingsgate Ward (Places between Eastcheap and the Thames River. The men here are part of the night watch.) **2 toward** (1) promising (2) quick to learn tricks **3 let** hesitate, pass up the opportunity **4 talk with** (1) converse with (2) rob **5 taking fellows** (1) engaging chaps (2) robbers

LAWRENCE No, no, neighbor, I warrant you.

JOHN Neighbor, methinks you begin to sleep. If you will, we will sit down, for I think it is about midnight.

LAWRENCE Marry, content, neighbor. Let us sleep.

Enter Derick, roving.[6]

DERICK Who? Who there, who there?[7] *Exit Derick.*

Enter Robin.

ROBIN O neighbors, what mean you to sleep, and such ado in the streets?

BOTH How now, neighbor, what's the matter?

Enter Derick again.

DERICK Who there? Who there? Who there?

JOHN Why, what ailst thou? Here is no horses.[8]

DERICK O, alas, man, I am robbed! Who there? Who there?

ROBIN Hold him, neighbor Cobbler. Why, I see thou art a plain clown.[9]

DERICK Am I a clown? Zounds, masters, do clowns go in silk apparel? I am sure all we gentlemen-clowns in Kent scant go so well. Zounds, you know clowns very well. Hear you, are you Master Constable? An[10] you be, speak, for I will not take it at his hands.[11]

JOHN Faith, I am not Master Constable, but I am one of his bad[12] officers, for he is not here.

DERICK Is not Master Constable here? Well, it is no matter. I'll have the law at his hands.[13]

JOHN Nay, I pray you, do not take the law of us.[14]

DERICK Well, you are one of his beastly[15] officers.

JOHN I am one of his bad officers.

DERICK Why, then, I charge thee, look to him![16]

6 roving wandering about **7 who there** i.e., is anybody there? (Derick, a poor carrier who has been robbed, is looking for help.) **8 Here is no horses** (John Cobbler evidently thinks Derick is calling out for someone from whom he can hire horses.) **9 clown** rustic countryman, bumpkin **10 An** if **11 take it at his hands** take it from him, believe his word **12 bad** (1) poor, unworthy, humble (2) *bade,* bidden to serve **13 at his hands** from him (the Constable) directly **14 take the law of** invoke the law on (playing on the meaning in the previous speech) **15 beastly** (playing on the normal meaning of *bad*) **16 look to him** i.e., look to the thief (?)

JOHN Nay, but hear ye, sir. You seem to be an honest fellow, and we are poor men; and now 'tis night, and we would be loath to have anything ado.[17] Therefore, I pray thee, put it up.[18]

DERICK First, thou sayest true. I am an honest fellow, and a proper,[19] handsome fellow, too. And you seem to be poor men; therefore I care not greatly. Nay, I am quickly pacified. But, an you chance to spy the thief, I pray you lay hold on him.

ROBIN Yes, that we will, I warrant you.

DERICK 'Tis a wonderful thing to see how glad the knave is, now I have forgiven him.

JOHN Neighbors, do ye look about you.[20] How now, who's there?

Enter the Thief.

THIEF Here is a good fellow. I pray you, which is the way to the old tavern in Eastcheap?

DERICK Whoop halloo! Now, Gad's Hill,[21] knowest thou me?

THIEF I know thee for an ass.

DERICK And I know thee for a taking fellow upon Gad's Hill in Kent. A bots[22] light upon ye.

THIEF The whoreson villain would be knocked.[23]

DERICK Masters, villain! An ye be men, stand to him and take his weapon from him. Let him not pass you!

JOHN My friend, what make you abroad[24] now? It is too late to walk now.

THIEF It is not too late for true men to walk.

LAWRENCE We know thee not to be a true man.

[*They seize the Thief.*]

THIEF Why, what do you mean to do with me? Zounds! I am one of the King's liege people.[25]

DERICK Hear you, sir, are you one of the King's liege people?

THIEF Ay, marry am I, sir. What say you to it?

17 ado amiss **18 put it up** i.e., pocket up your complaint **19 proper** good-looking **20 look about you** look sharp **21 Gad's Hill** (The name of a place in Kent notorious for highway robberies, here applied to the Thief, as also in Shakespeare's play.) **22 bots** (Literally, a disease in horses caused by parasites; here, an expression of execration.) **23 The whoreson . . . knocked** i.e., the rascally knave (Derick) is asking for a blow **24 make you abroad** are you doing out and around **25 liege people** loyal subjects

DERICK Marry, sir, I say you are one of the King's filching people.

JOHN Come, come. Let's have him away.

THIEF Why, what have I done?

ROBIN Thou hast robbed a poor fellow and taken away his goods from him.

THIEF I never saw him before.

DERICK Masters, who comes here?

Enter the Vintner's Boy.

BOY How now, goodman Cobbler?

JOHN How now, Robin, what makes thou abroad at this time of night?

BOY Marry, I have been at the Counter.[26] I can tell such news as never you have heard the like.

JOHN What is that, Robin? What is the matter?

BOY Why, this night, about two hours ago, there came the young Prince and three or four more of his companions, and called for wine good store,[27] and then they sent for a noise[28] of musicians and were very merry for the space of an hour. Then, whether their music liked them not,[29] or whether they had drunk too much wine or no, I cannot tell, but our pots flew against the walls. And then they drew their swords and went into the street and fought, and some took one part and some took another, but for the space of half an hour there was such a bloody fray as passeth![30] And none could part them until such time as the Mayor and Sheriff were sent for. And then at the last with much ado they took them, and so the young Prince was carried to the Counter. And then about one hour after there came a messenger from the court in all haste from the King for my Lord Mayor and the Sheriff, but for what cause I know not.

JOHN Here is news, indeed, Robert!

LAWRENCE Marry, neighbor, this news is strange indeed. I think it best, neighbor, to rid our hands of this fellow first.

THIEF What mean you to do with me?

JOHN We mean to carry you to the prison, and there to remain[31] till the sessions day.

26 the Counter a London prison **27 good store** in abundant quantity **28 noise** consort, band **29 liked them not** displeased them **30 passeth** surpasses belief **31 and there to remain** and you to remain there

THIEF Then, I pray you, let me go to the prison where my master[32] is.

JOHN Nay, thou must go to the country prison,[33] to Newgate. Therefore, come away.

THIEF [*To Derick*] I prithee, be good to me, honest fellow.

DERICK Ay, marry, will I. I'll be very charitable to thee, for I will never leave thee till I see thee on the gallows.

[*Exeunt.*]

[The subsequent scenes, in which Prince Henry boxes the ear of the Lord Chief Justice, is imprisoned by him, and is at last reconciled with his dying father, are materials for *2 Henry IV* and are printed as sources for that play.]

This selection is based on the first edition of *The Famous Victories of Henry the Fifth, Containing the Honorable Battle of Agincourt; As It Was Played by the Queen's Majesty's Players. London: Printed by Thomas Creede, 1598.* [Designated in the textual notes as Q.]

32 my master i.e., Prince Henry **33 the country prison** i.e., the prison not under the jurisdiction of the city of London as was the Counter. (The Thief has been apprehended in Kent.)

Further Reading

Auden, W. H. "The Prince's Dog." *The Dyer's Hand and Other Essays*. New York: Random House, 1948. Auden inventively examines Falstaff's character, motives, and function within the play, and concludes that "sober reflection in the study may tell us that Falstaff is not, after all, a very admirable person, but Falstaff on the stage gives us no time for sober reflection." Auden denies the damaging irresponsibility many critics have found in Falstaff, declaring him to be "a comic symbol for the supernatural order of charity."

Barber, C. L. "Rule and Misrule in *Henry IV*." *Shakespeare's Festive Comedy*. Princeton, N.J.: Princeton Univ. Press, 1959. In his seminal study of the relation of social and artistic forms, Barber sees Falstaff as a Lord of Misrule burlesquing the sanctities of the historical world. Barber finds, however, that misrule does not threaten the social order, since "it depends utterly on what it mocks." Ultimately "misrule works . . . to consolidate rule," though Falstaff's saturnalian energy always threatens to turn from a "dependent holiday skepticism" to a "dangerously self-sufficient everyday skepticism."

Barish, Jonas A. "The Turning Away of Prince Hal." *Shakespeare Studies* 1 (1965): 9–17. Barish sees Falstaff's rejection as the moment that reveals to us whether we are "moralists or sentimentalists"; we also sense at this moment the antithetical pressures of history and comedy. In rejecting Falstaff, Hal is, in effect, rejecting himself: "to banish plump Jack is to banish what is free and vital and pleasurable in life."

Bradley, A. C. "The Rejection of Falstaff." *Oxford Lectures on Poetry*, 1909. Rpt. New York: St. Martin's Press, 1959. Bradley's influential essay explores the inevitability of Hal's rejection of Falstaff. He recognizes both Falstaff's dangerous attractiveness and Hal's Lancastrian "hardness" that qualifies him for political success but limits his personal appeal. If we enjoy the Falstaff scenes "as surely Shakespeare meant for them to be enjoyed," Bradley argues, we must feel in Falstaff's rejection "a good deal of pain and some resentment."

Brooks, Cleanth, and Robert B. Heilman. "Shakespeare, *Henry IV, Part I.*" *Understanding Drama*. New York: Holt, Rinehart, and Winston, 1945. For Brooks and Heilman, the play is a "study in the nature of kingship" in which Hal must choose a course of action from among the models offered him by his father, Falstaff, and Hotspur. Brooks and Heilman explore the careful balance of sympathies established by the play that lead an audience "to contemplate, with understanding and some irony, a world very much like the world we know."

Burckhardt, Sigurd. "'Swoll'n with Some Other Grief': Shakespeare's Prince Hal Trilogy." *Shakespearean Meanings*. Princeton, N.J.: Princeton Univ. Press, 1968. Burckhardt argues that the structure of Shakespeare's plays "undercuts Tudor doctrine," exposing its contradictions and inadequacies. The apparently satisfying resolution of *1 Henry IV* dissolves as Falstaff rises from the battlefield, "reminding us that disorder is not slain so neatly and inexpensively as the calculated symmetries of dialectics would have us believe."

Calderwood, James L. "*1 Henry IV:* Art's Gilded Lie." *Metadrama in Shakespeare's Henriad: "Richard II" to "Henry V."* Berkeley and Los Angeles: Univ. of California Press, 1979. Calderwood ingeniously explores the metadramatic implications of Hal's lie supporting Falstaff's claim to have killed Hotspur. What is at stake, Calderwood argues, is "theatrical illusion itself." Hal, who historically must unify a country torn by dissension, must reunite a play threatening to split into competing dramatic modes. Falstaff, in his outrageous theatricality, threatens to withdraw from the play's mimesis of history, and Hal's lie is necessary to persuade him to remain within the historical action.

Campbell, Lily B. "The Unquiet Time of Henry IV." *Shakespeare's "Histories": Mirrors of Elizabethan Policy*. San Marino, Calif.: Huntington Library, 1947. Campbell considers the historical action of the play in the context of Elizabethan political theory and anxieties about succession. She argues that "the problem of rebellion" is central to the design of *Henry IV* and reflects the realities of sixteenth-century politics as much as the medieval history overtly represented.

Council, Norman. "*1 Henry IV:* The Mirror up to Nature." *When Honour's at the Stake: Ideas of Honour in Shakespeare's Plays.* London: George Allen and Unwin; New York: Barnes and Noble, 1973. Council argues that the theme of honor is central to the play, but denies that Hotspur and Falstaff represent moral extremes for Hal to mediate. Council's reading of both the play and sixteenth-century ethical treatises and courtesy books reveals Hotspur to be the "true and perfect image of honor," Falstaff the embodiment of "the nature and consequences of a reasoned rejection of the pervasive code of honor," and Hal one who neither simply accepts nor rejects the code but successfully "exploits it for his pragmatic purposes."

Dessen, Alan C. "Dual Protagonists in *1 Henry IV.*" *Shakespeare and the Late Moral Plays.* Lincoln, Nebr., and London: Univ. of Nebraska Press, 1986. Dessen finds in the dramaturgy of the late morality plays of the 1560s and 1570s a structural model for *1 Henry IV*. In the dual protagonists of plays such as *The Trial of Treasure* (1567), Shakespeare finds a prototype for his pairing of Hal and Hotspur, who enact "far more complex versions" of the morality action.

Greenblatt, Stephen. "Invisible Bullets: Renaissance Authority and Its Subversion." *Glyph* 8 (1981): 40–61. Rev. and rpt. in *Political Shakespeare: New Essays in Cultural Materialism,* ed. Jonathan Dollimore and Alan Sinfield. Ithaca and London: Cornell Univ. Press, 1985. Greenblatt considers the *Henry IV* plays in a provocative account of the operations of Renaissance power. He argues that the subversive challenge to the principles of authority in the play is never really dangerous; indeed, it is not merely contained but actually encouraged by the power structure, since its presence works paradoxically to ratify and reinforce the existing order.

Hunter, G. K. "*Henry IV* and the Elizabethan Two-Part Play." *Review of English Studies* n. s. 5 (1954): 236–248. Rpt. in *Dramatic Identities and Cultural Tradition: Stud-*

ies in Shakespeare and His Contemporaries. New York: Barnes and Noble, 1978. Entering into the debate about the relationship of the two parts of *Henry IV,* Hunter argues not that the two plays are continuous but that they have the unity, found also in plays by Christopher Marlowe, John Marston, and George Chapman, "of a dyptich, in which repetition of shape and design focuses attention on what is common to the two parts."

Kelly, Henry Ansgar. *Divine Providence in the England of Shakespeare's Histories,* pp. 214–222. Cambridge: Harvard Univ. Press, 1970. Examining the play's often noted "providentialism," Kelly finds that the "moral and providential judgments of the sources" are not normative but are distributed in the play according to the partisan uses that can be made of them. He denies there is any evidence that the play enacts "the providential punishment of Henry IV" for the deposition of Richard II. Henry "regards himself as the rightful king," and if the play suggests divine support for anyone, "that person is Henry IV."

Kernan, Alvin B. "The Henriad: Shakespeare's Major History Plays." In *Modern Shakespearean Criticism: Essays on Style, Dramaturgy, and the Major Plays,* ed. Alvin B. Kernan. New York: Harcourt, Brace and World, 1970. Kernan traces the movement of the second tetralogy from a sacred, providential conception of history to a secular, pragmatic view, "in which any identity is only a temporary role." Richard II, Henry IV, and Prince Hal mark stages in this transition, and the latter emerges as the modern prince who "never seems to lose sight of the fact he is preparing to be king of England."

Morgann, Maurice. "An Essay on the Dramatic Character of Sir John Falstaff" (1777). In *Eighteenth Century Essays on Shakespeare,* 2nd edition, ed. D. Nichol Smith. Oxford: Clarendon Press, 1963. In an essay that is the earliest sustained account of a Shakespearean character, Morgann sees the complexity of Falstaff's nature as it is presented in the play. He is not the "constitutional coward" that many have seen but a man "of much natural courage and resolution." Morgann, however, recognizes that if Falstaff is endowed with "great natural vigour and alacrity of mind," he also engages "in every debauchery." He has "a mind free of malice or any evil principle; but he never took the trouble of acquiring any good one."

Ornstein, Robert. *"Henry IV Part I." A Kingdom for a Stage: The Achievement of Shakespeare's History Plays.* Cambridge: Harvard Univ. Press, 1972. Examining the "illogic of human motive" that lies "behind the logic of events" in the play, Ornstein sensitively examines the roles "which personality and circumstance dictate" to its characters. At the center of the analysis is Hal, and Ornstein finds him "fascinating but not endearing," incapable of intimacy, shrewd, and pragmatic: "he studies other men so that he may learn to master them."

Porter, Joseph A. *"1 Henry IV." The Drama of Speech Acts: Shakespeare's Lancastrian Tetralogy.* Berkeley, Calif.: Univ. of California Press, 1979. Porter examines the various "ways of conceiving and using language" in the play: King Henry's "inexplicitness," Hotspur's "energetic noncommunication," Falstaff's "refusal to converse responsibly," and Prince Hal's efforts to master "the variety of languages" of the realm, a mastery necessary for his eventual rule.

Reese, M. M. *"Henry IV." The Cease of Majesty: A Study of Shakespeare's History Plays.* London: Edward Arnold, 1961; New York: St. Martin's Press, 1962. Reese argues that Shakespeare in the two parts of *Henry IV* dramatizes "the education of a prince" and "considers in personal and political terms the sacrifices and disciplines [Hal] will have to accept." Reese considers Falstaff, Hotspur, and Henry IV to be "three tempters" whose defective examples Hal must reject as his youthful impulses are "steeled into disciplined courage and dedicated to honourable ends."

Saccio, Peter. "Henry IV: The King Embattled." *Shakespeare's English Kings: History, Chronicle, and Drama.* New York: Oxford Univ. Press, 1977. Focusing especially on the political challenges to Henry's rule, the military encounters at Shrewsbury and Gaultree Forest, and the relations between Henry IV and his son, Saccio examines the historical background of the two parts of *Henry IV,* and traces Shakespeare's transformation of this history into drama.

Tillyard, E. M. W. "The Second Tetralogy." *Shakespeare's History Plays*, 1944. Rpt., New York: Barnes and Noble, 1964. In an enormously influential study of Shakespeare's histories, Tillyard argues that the two parts of *Henry IV* form a single sequence of ten acts in which Hal is tested, "Morality-fashion," to prove his worthiness to rule. *Part One* demonstrates Hal's education in military virtues, as he tries to mediate between "the excess and the defect of the military spirit" as they are embodied in Hotspur and Falstaff; *Part Two* displays his education in the "civil virtues," as he must choose between Falstaff and the Lord Chief Justice.

Photo © George Joseph

From the 1968 New York Shakespeare Festival production of *Henry IV, Part Two,* with Sam Waterston as Prince Hal (l.) and James Ray as Henry IV, directed by Gerald Freedman at the Delacorte Theater in Central Park.

HENRY IV
—PART TWO—

HENRY IV, PART TWO

Introductory Material

Foreword by Joseph Papp

Introduction

Henry IV, Part Two
in Performance

THE PLAY

Supplementary Material

Date and Text

Textual Notes

Shakespeare's Sources

Further Reading

Foreword

In *Henry IV, Part Two,* Shakespeare begins putting distance between us and the Falstaff we knew and loved in *Part One,* preparing us for Hal's rejection of the fat man at the end of the play:

> I know thee not, old man. Fall to thy prayers.
> How ill white hairs becomes a fool and jester!
> I have long dreamt of such a kind of man,
> So surfeit-swelled, so old, and so profane,
> But being awaked, I do despise my dream. . . .
> Presume not that I am the thing I was,
> For God doth know, so shall the world perceive,
> That I have turned away my former self;
> So will I those that kept me company.

In a sense this rejection comes as no surprise, for throughout the play there has been a subtle and gradual shift in how we perceive Falstaff—we don't like him as much, especially when he's not with Hal. The old geniality seems a little sharper now, and a tone of bitterness or cynicism has crept in with it. Falstaff has lost some of the humorous spontaneity and improvisational ability he entertained us with in *Part One*. For example, in the first part, Shakespeare let him conduct his money-making impressment of soldiers offstage; here we see it directly onstage, where it shows a side of Falstaff that's not entirely attractive. Shakespeare is deliberately drawing away from his popular creation, and taking the audience with him.

To buffer us against the blow of losing Falstaff, he introduces a new character—Master Shallow, country justice. Shallow is so gentle, warm, and human that he immediately endears himself to us. We like him; his friends and servants like him; even the late *New York Times* critic Brooks Atkinson, when asked what Shakespearean role he'd most like to play, smiled and said, "Justice Shallow." But Shakespeare has Falstaff speak derogatorily of Shallow and pick him out as the victim of his next swindling operation. We don't want to see Falstaff cheat Shallow or abuse his friendship—and it gives us mixed feelings when he does. And that's exactly what Shakespeare is after.

Shakespeare doesn't stop there; he's determined to turn our sympathies away from Falstaff. He gives the fat knight a cynical soliloquy at the end of Act 3 that is in striking contrast to the friendliness of Shallow's farewell: "Sir John, the Lord bless you! God prosper your affairs! God send us peace! At your return, visit our house; let our old acquaintance be renewed. Peradventure I will with ye to the court." The ensuing speech shows a very tough Falstaff, openly contemptuous of someone he thinks beneath him, someone whose prosperity he seems to resent—"And now is this Vice's dagger become a squire. . . . And now has he land and beefs." He concludes, "I see no reason in the law of nature but I may snap at him. Let time shape, and there an end." The bitter language and the blatant opportunism shock us—is this the Falstaff that is not only witty in himself, but "the cause that wit is in other men"? What has happened?

Yet we still have a place in our hearts for Falstaff, and Shakespeare knows it. The playwright shows how sensitive he is to the audience in his Epilogue, in which he apologizes should the play have proved to be displeasing. He promises more Falstaff, and plugs his next play, *Henry V:* "If you be not too much cloyed with fat meat, our humble author will continue the story, with Sir John in it, and make you merry with fair Katharine of France. Where, for anything I know, Falstaff shall die of a sweat, unless already 'a be killed with your hard opinions." Shakespeare barely keeps his promise, since Falstaff doesn't appear in person in *Henry V,* but only in the words of Mistress Quickly, who describes his death: "his nose was as sharp as a pen, and 'a babbled of green fields."

JOSEPH PAPP

JOSEPH PAPP GRATEFULLY ACKNOWLEDGES THE HELP OF ELIZABETH KIRKLAND IN PREPARING THIS FOREWORD.

Introduction

Shakespeare wrote *2 Henry IV* quite soon after *1 Henry IV,* perhaps in 1597, partly no doubt to capitalize on the enormous theatrical success of Falstaff, partly to finish the story of Falstaff's rejection. In writing *2 Henry IV,* Shakespeare drew on materials similar to those used for *I Henry IV,* notably Raphael Holinshed's *Chronicles* (1587) and the anonymous play *The Famous Victories of Henry V* (1583–1588). Moreover, he undertook to write a play that structurally is much like its predecessor, revealing more similarity between these plays than one can find elsewhere in Shakespeare. Even the three *Henry VI* plays do not reiterate structural patterns to the same degree. Is Shakespeare repeating himself, rewriting the earlier play, and if so why? Is *2 Henry IV* essentially a way of giving audiences more of what they had found so entertaining in the earlier play, or is it a way of reflecting on new and troublesome issues only partially raised in *1 Henry IV*?

The structural pattern runs as follows. In both plays, Shakespeare alternates between scenes of political seriousness and scenes of comic irresponsibility, juxtaposing a rebellion in the land with a rebellion in the King's own family. In *1 Henry IV* we move from a council of war (1.1) to a planning of the robbery at Gad's Hill (1.2). The scenes comment on each other by their nearness and by their mutual concern with lawlessness. Similarly in *2 Henry IV* we are at first introduced to a political rebellion in the north of England, after which we encounter Falstaff and Prince Hal's page. In both plays Act 2 scene 2 shows us Hal with Poins, setting up a future meeting to embarrass Falstaff by means of a plot, and in both plays Act 2 scene 4 is a long, centrally located scene at the tavern involving Hal and Falstaff in a contest of wits devised to expose Falstaff as a resourceful liar. The festivities in both scenes are brought to an end by a knocking at the door. (The act-scene divisions are probably not Shakespeare's, for they do not appear in the early quartos of either play; nevertheless, the structural location of these scenes is similar.) Between these linked scenes of comic action, we turn in both plays to the rebel camp of the Percys for a discussion of military planning against King Henry (2.3). In both plays Falstaff goes off supposedly to fight against the rebels but instead manages to abuse his authority as recruiting officer and to garner undeserved honors, either through wounding the dead Hotspur in the leg or through capturing Coleville of the Dale with the aid of an inflated reputation. The battle scenes are punctuated by Falstaff's wry soliloquies; his disputation on wine in *2 Henry IV* (4.3.88–123) serves a function like that of his better-known catechism on honor in *1 Henry IV* (5.1.129–140). Both plays introduce a confrontation between Hal and his father: the son is penitent for his waywardness, the father lectures on statecraft, and the prodigal son is recovered into kingly grace. Prince Hal goes on thereafter to win public honor and to prove himself his father's true son. Even the rejection of Falstaff, with which the second play ends, finds its counterpart in *1 Henry IV* in Hal's impatience with Falstaff during the battle of Shrewsbury, his elegy over the seemingly dead body of his onetime companion, and his resolve to be henceforth a prince.

These resemblances, and still others, are further highlighted when we realize that Shakespeare continues to use in his second play the structural device of foils, or paired characters around Hal who help define alternative models of conduct. The father is, as before, an awesome figure of authority, one whose sternness Hal never fully adopts and yet one whose public role as king Hal must inherit. Falstaff, as before, offers himself as a companion in revelry, dissipation, and joie de vivre, and must be rejected even though much of what he says offers insight into the coldness of King Henry and especially of Hal's dutiful brother Prince John. Yet the chief purpose of these recapitulations is to suggest profound differences. *2 Henry IV* does not simply go over familiar material. Repeatedly, the similarities of situation reveal how much Hal has still to learn, how much Falstaff has changed, and how much more complicated the political process is than it first appeared. The foil relationships in this play focus less on honor, as in *1 Henry IV*, than on two related matters: rumor or reputation, and justice.

Rumor begins the play—quite literally, since Rumor is presented to us in allegorized form as portrayed by Virgil, painted full of tongues, spreading false information about the battle of Shrewsbury just ended. Rumor takes particular delight in its most cruel trick of all, raising false hopes and then dashing them. In the scene following at the Percys' household, we see rumor as it manifests itself in the real world of men, beguiling Northumberland with the "news" of his son Hotspur's triumph only to disappoint him afterward with the stark truth of defeat and death. What is the function of the uncharacteristic allegory at the start of this play? It serves first to establish a new dispiriting tone. The rebels are in disarray, their cause in jeopardy. Hotspur is dead, and with him has died the bright honor of his cause. His kinsmen, always more Machiavellian than he, are now warier than ever. Northumberland is persuaded, in a later scene, to prevaricate to his allies and withdraw to Scotland when they most need his support, waiting to come in on their side only when he can be sure of success. The atmosphere of realpolitik and of dealing in false appearances is a consequence of a world governed by rumor. The rebels' case is never as attractive in this play as in *1 Henry IV;* Hotspur's idealism and chivalry are sorely missed.

Rumor has profound consequences for the King's side as well, and for Falstaff and Prince Hal. Falstaff rides on false reputation through the early scenes of *2 Henry IV*. He evades arrest at the hands of the Lord Chief Justice because of his presumed deeds at Shrewsbury, deeds that we know to be illusory. His day's service at Shrewsbury "hath a little gilded over" his "night's exploit on Gad's Hill," as the Lord Chief Justice reluctantly concedes (1.2.147–148). His reputation makes possible his capture of Coleville of the Dale at Gaultree Forest, even though by this time Falstaff's reputation is clearly beginning to wear thin.

Conversely, Hal discovers that his reputation for prodigality will not leave him. Hal begins to realize that despite the fact that the King has severed Falstaff from him (1.2.201–202), so that Hal scarcely knows of Falstaff's whereabouts until he agrees to a kind of reunion for old times' sake at the tavern, everyone assumes the worst of Hal and expects his future reign to be one of continual riot. He himself characterizes his visit to the tavern, in order to see Falstaff again, as a base "transformation" like those Ovidian portrayals of Jove in lowly human disguise. Talking with Poins in 2.2.1–44, Hal professes to be "exceeding weary" of the "disgrace" it is in him to remember all his vile companions, including Poins, and he sardonically congratulates his companion on thinking like everyone else when Poins assumes that any weeping on Hal's part for his father's death would be no more than princely hypocrisy. "Let the end try the man," says Hal, in what should be a plain notice of his reformation, but no one credits him with sincerity. When his father does take to his deathbed, surrounded by hushed courtiers, Hal, until now notably absent from court, enters with exaggerated offhandedness as though eschewing the show of mourning he knows cannot be believed in him. His taking the crown from the pillow of his seemingly dead father strikes King Henry and his courtiers as one last confirmation of Hal's desire to supplant his father, and indeed we too are forced to wonder at Hal's imprudence. (The patricidal overtones in one of Shakespeare's sources, *The Famous Victories of Henry V,* are much more overt than those in Shakespeare's play.)

The structural recapitulations of *2 Henry IV,* then, in which Hal first jests with Falstaff at the tavern and afterward confronts his father at court, are no mere repetitions; they stress the dreary fact that a reputation for riotous conduct persists, that the father's embracing of his son has lapsed into renewed distrust, that "reformation" is not the simple process Hal once supposed. Reformation is first a matter of improving one's own conduct, but it is also a matter of improving one's image. This is not a happy revelation to a young man impatient of ceremony and public display, but it is the way of the world and an integral part of any successful kingship. King Henry's last advice to Hal, in fact, once they have been reconciled anew, concerns the manipulation of appearances in the name of statecraft; the father urges the son to resolve civil strife by going to war against some foreign enemy. He must "busy giddy minds / With foreign quarrels" (4.5.213–214). Hal will adopt this stratagem in *Henry V* by warring against the French. Meantime, in *2 Henry IV,* he must overcome his reputation not only with his father but with the Lord Chief Justice, the nobles of the court, and his brother John. Not until the play's end do they believe other than that Hal will turn riot loose in his kingdom. The intransigent nature of false "rumor" or reputation does much to explain why the new king must reject Falstaff so publicly and so sharply. He has in fact already rejected Falstaff in the sense of leaving him, but no one has taken the point—least of all Falstaff, who now presses in upon the new king with hopes of reward and license to act as he pleases. "The laws of England are at my commandment," he exults (5.3.138–139). Only a public repudiation can meet the demands of kingship by making full use of the act's symbolic value. Hal must reject Falstaff not only in his heart but in the view of his nation. It is a distasteful act, perhaps to him as to us, but is made necessary by the political exigencies of the moment.

The play's concern with justice emerges in the first confrontation between the Lord Chief Justice and Falstaff (1.2.54–226). The one represents law, the other license. Who is to represent and administer the law in Henry V's reign? The Lord Chief Justice is a firm and austere figure, a deputy or substitute for the father-king, one who has presumed to imprison Hal for resisting his authority. This Lord Chief Justice does not expect to remain in office once the new king is crowned; like other serious characters in the play, and ourselves as well, he longs for reassurance in the troubled times of civil war and change of administration under a monarchy. In contrast to this somewhat awesome parental figure, Falstaff offers hedonism and irresponsibility. His wit is in a sense no less engaging than in *1 Henry IV*. His scenes with Shallow and Silence, as they choose soldiers for the upcoming campaign or prepare for the golden time they anticipate, are as funny as the best of Falstaff. The pairing of the Lord Chief Justice and Falstaff as foils might suggest at first that one is lacking where the other is strong, and that Hal must steer between extremes.

Yet this play does not give us a genuine debate on justice like that on honor in *1 Henry IV,* where Falstaff's comments on honor strike home because of Hotspur's fanaticism. The Lord Chief Justice of this play is essentially in the right, however austere, and Falstaff is essentially in the wrong, however funny. The Lord Chief Justice sees through Falstaff and patiently bides his time. Falstaff's excesses are more pronounced than in the earlier play. We see him with Doll Tearsheet, a whore, in maudlin, drunken conversation. He is associated with images of disease—gout, the pox or syphilis, consumption, lameness—and of purging. His lying is not as consistently clever as before. Hal recalls the brilliant lie about the Gad's Hill robbery and credits Falstaff with having seen through the Prince's trick on that occasion (2.4.305–307), but in the second tavern scene Falstaff can only mutter incoherently that he had no idea that Hal was behind him in disguise listening to his foulmouthed reproaches. Falstaff's rioting with Pistol disturbs the peace, and in such brawls homicides occur necessitating arrest and punishment (5.4). When Falstaff appears with the diminutive page, as in scene 2, we are forcefully reminded of the grossness of his body, though he too laughs at this. His mooching off Mistress Quickly and his breach of promise of marriage to her, though hinted at in the earlier play, are much more open here; the humor is keen, but we cannot forget that Falstaff is victimizing a woman. Lawsuits and arrests are more prominent in this play than in its predecessor. Falstaff's abuse of authority to recruit soldiers, about which he discourses wittily in the earlier play, is here fully shown both in its hilarity and in its lawless consequences.

Falstaff's new companions, Pistol, Doll, and then Justice Shallow and Justice Silence, sharpen our perception of Falstaff's increasingly flagrant lawlessness. Shallow and Silence are, by their very profession, counterparts to the Lord Chief Justice. In their complacent interest in their own prosperity ("How a good yoke of bullocks at Stamford fair?" 3.2.39), in their countenancing of influence peddling by their subordinates (5.1.37–52), and in Shallow's foxy aspirations to deceive Falstaff before Falstaff can deceive him, these pillars of rural respectability reveal how far injustice has permeated the English countryside. They are fit companions for Falstaff when he hears the news of his rejection and are suitably victimized by Falstaff's inability to repay a loan that Justice Shallow has advanced to him from motives of self-interest. These old men, myopically recollecting the jolly days of their youth, accentuate Falstaff's physical frailty and aging. Falstaff mocks the stories of their escapades, but he too, as he confesses to Doll over his drink, is old. The necessary course of justice is made plain by the structural configurations of the play. Falstaff and his companions seek lawlessness and must be rebuked; the Lord Chief Justice, who fears rejection, must instead be embraced by Hal explicitly as a father figure ("You shall be as a father to my youth," 5.2.118) in order to reaffirm public decency. The Lord Chief Justice is to bear "the balance and the sword" (l. 103) as emblems of justice and its stern role in maintaining order; Falstaff is dismissed as "The tutor and the feeder of my riots" (5.5.62). These necessities are plain, even though they do not answer the emotionally complicated issue of Hal's (and our) fondness for the companion of his youth.

Hal's brother Prince John of Lancaster is another opposite to Falstaff. Here the contrast is less prejudicial to Falstaff. Prince John takes charge of his ailing father's wars, and engineers a surrender of the rebels at Gaultree Forest that is a triumph of equivocation and double-dealing. It also saves the nation from further civil conflict, at least for the time being, and establishes the peace that Hal inherits and turns to his advantage against France. What are we to make of what has been called (by Paul Jorgensen, *PMLA*, 1961) John's "dastardly treachery"? It seems all too much in keeping with the realpolitik that has characterized the conduct of both sides heretofore, and may thus be said to be a suitable conclusion. The dismaying "revolution of the times" (3.1.46) brings with it the cooling of friendships and the recollection of dire prophecies from the days of Richard II. The only justification possible for what John does is that it succeeds. It surely lacks the glory and honor attendant on the conflict of Hal and Hotspur in *1 Henry IV*. Not coincidentally, Hal is far away from Gaultree Forest when this dismal surrender is brought about. Prince John is a master at knowing how to "construe the times to their necessities" (4.1.104). His acts scarcely represent justice any more than honor. "Is this proceeding just and honorable?" ask the betrayed rebels, and are answered merely "Is your assembly so?" (4.2.110–111). The end justifies the means. Falstaff's observations at Prince John's expense therefore have a point. John is, as Falstaff characterizes him, "sober-blooded"; he drinks no wine and relies not on valor but on sagacity. Falstaff hopes that Hal will prove more valiant, tempering "the cold blood he did naturally inherit of his father" (4.3.88–117) with the imbibing of sherry and other pleasures learned from Falstaff. Whatever the merits of drinking as an inducement to courage, we do perceive that

Prince John is too much his father's son, and that Hal will avoid this cold extreme in his quest for a kingly identity that is both symbol and substance.

Hal has thus learned something from Falstaff, if only as a caution against extremes, and partly for this reason his rejection of Falstaff must come as a shock no matter how inevitable. Hal may well appear to dwindle in the process, for he has given up a good deal of his private self to adopt the public role thrust upon him. He accepts that public role not unwillingly but may also perceive that he does so at some cost to himself—and to Falstaff. His terms of rejection are not wholly ungenerous—he allows the possibility of Falstaff's returning to court if he reforms, and makes financial allowance so that Falstaff will have no need to continue in crime—but the finality of the action remains stunning. We are left with a broken Falstaff, on his way to the Fleet prison by order of the Lord Chief Justice, trying to deceive himself into believing that all will be well. Hal and England have turned in a new direction; a war against the French is clearly in prospect already, one that will absorb the energies of the new king and his father's erstwhile political enemies as well. The emergence of Hal into his public role is complete.

Henry IV, Part Two in Performance

2 Henry IV has not enjoyed the popularity onstage of *1 Henry IV,* despite the continuing presence of Falstaff. Perhaps audiences have felt uncomfortable with a Falstaff who is visibly older, more disreputable, surrounded by such companions as Pistol, Doll Tearsheet, and Justice Shallow, and at last rejected by King Henry V; or perhaps producers have been unwilling to offer a play with no dignified women's roles; or perhaps (especially in the eighteenth and nineteenth centuries) audiences have been reluctant to see their heroic Henry do such a mean-spirited thing as rejecting his old companion. No doubt it is a darker and more disillusioned play than *1 Henry IV.*

Still, *2 Henry IV* has had significant stage successes. Thomas Betterton, playing Falstaff, apparently did well with a revival about 1704 at the theater in Lincoln's Inn Fields, London, albeit in a much-changed version that cut Rumor's prologue and thc Northumberland–Lady Percy scenes, and ended with material added from the early part of *Henry V* to provide a less dispiriting conclusion than that found in Shakespeare's *2 Henry IV*. In similarly rearranged form the play was again well received in 1720 at the Theatre Royal, Drury Lane, with Barton Booth as Henry IV, John Mills as Falstaff, and Robert Wilks as Hal; and the play was revived with some regularity through the rest of the eighteenth and early nineteenth centuries. A production at Drury Lane in 1736 advertised itself as "Written by Shakespeare, in which will be restored scenes, soliloquies, and other circumstances, originally in the part of Falstaff, which have been for many years omitted." Two years later the rival theater at Covent Garden also produced "the genuine play of Shakespeare, and not that altered by Mr. Betterton." Nonetheless, Betterton's version was not entirely displaced from the stage, and clearly the success of productions of *2 Henry IV* depended less on the acting text than on the skill of the actor playing Falstaff. James Quin, John Henderson, and George Frederick Cooke were among those who ensured that the play, in whatever version, continued in the repertory.

Though David Garrick produced *2 Henry IV* and acted the King, first in 1758, during the period of his management at Drury Lane, he had no great success with the play, in large part because he lacked an actor to play Falstaff with the ebullience the role demands. Perhaps for the same reason, John Philip Kemble's production of *2 Henry IV* at Covent Garden in 1804 introduced new pageantry and spectacle to refocus attention on the King. An essay of that year admired this strategy, claiming that Kemble "in giving the scene all the splendor the chamber of a monarch requires, and his person all the elegance of costume, shows a desire to render stage exhibitions as perfect as possible for public gratification." The final scene introduced the arrest of Falstaff before the reconciliation of Henry V with the Lord Chief Justice so that the play could end with a triumphant restoration of order.

Covent Garden's production of *2 Henry IV* in 1821 illustrates the extent to which the play could be rewritten to accommodate audiences' desire to see King Henry and the English monarchy in an attractive light. The show was designed, in fact, as a way of celebrating the accession to the throne in that year of King George IV. To that end the theater managers, who included Charles Kemble, staged a spectacular coronation procession for Henry V in a stage replica of Westminster Abbey, its galleries and aisles filled with noble spectators. The procession led off with the King's herb-woman, six strewers of flowers, the Dean's Beadle of Westminster, the High Constable of Westminster, drums and trumpets, chaplains, sheriffs and aldermen of London, Masters in Chancery, the King's Sergeant and Attorney General, judges, the Lord Chief Justice, a choir singing the coronation anthem, and many more. The King then followed under the royal canopy, escorted by two bishops, train bearers, mace bearers, and halberdiers. The critic for *John Bull* objected to the inclusion of the Yeomen of the Guard, on the grounds that they had not in fact been established until the reign of Henry VII, but admitted that "a more splendid pageant never graced a theatre." The production, extravagant and unwieldy by today's standards, merely amplified the realistic attention to detail and glorification of English royalty of Kemble's version seventeen years earlier.

The production also cut and rearranged scenes to minimize the unpleasantness of Shakespeare's conclusion. A reordering of events enabled audiences to hear the reassuring news of Henry V's accession even before his appearance as king. Gone were the arrests of Mistress Quickly and Doll Tearsheet (5.4), with their reminder of the disreputable past that Prince Hal had once known in the company of Falstaff. The rejection of Falstaff could scarcely be left out, but any negative effect it might have had on the spectators' view of King Henry was, as in Kemble's text of 1804, neutralized by a subsequent upbeat ending: the King was reconciled to his Lord Chief Justice and no mention was made of the Lord Chief Justice's imprisonment of Falstaff and Shallow (5.5.99 ff.). Clearly the actor-managers of this age were intent on presenting Henry as the future king, no longer encumbered by his association with a thoroughly dissipated Falstaff. Predictably, the spectacular production, starring William Charles Macready as the King and Charles Kemble as Hal, was a great success, and for its performance on July 19, the coronation day itself, the theater was opened free to the public.

Royalty obviously approved of *2 Henry IV* as it was acted in the nineteenth century, and when Samuel Phelps was asked to give a command performance before Queen Victoria at Windsor Castle in January of 1853, he chose *2 Henry IV*. This was his first production of the play; his own theater at Sadler's Wells had to wait until March for a performance. Phelps revived the play at Sadler's Wells in 1861. His unusually versatile doubling of the parts of King Henry IV and Shallow earned him warm praise. The *Morning Advertiser* spoke for others when it congratulated Phelps on his "plasticity of imagination" that was able to "conceive and represent mankind in all its varied and varying phases."

Although the two parts of *Henry IV* were performed on consecutive nights on at least eight occasions prior to 1750, only rarely during the later eighteenth and the nineteenth centuries were the two parts of *Henry IV* produced within a week of one another. The twentieth century, then, has discovered anew the value of exploring the emotional and political transformations of these and other historical plays when they are played in sequence. Frank Benson was the first to present a "cycle" of history plays, in 1901 and then again in 1906, at Stratford-upon-Avon. He omitted *1 Henry IV,* sad to say, but included *2 Henry IV* as a necessary link to *Henry V*. And in 1905 he did produce both *Henry IV* plays as part of a season that included all four plays of the second tetralogy—that is, *Richard II* through *Henry V*. Barry Jackson seems to have been the first to present *1* and *2 Henry IV* on a single day, April 23 (Shakespeare's birthday), in 1921, at the Birmingham Repertory Theatre. The two parts were paired again on Shakespeare's birthday at Stratford-upon-Avon in 1932; Edward, the Prince of Wales, flew over from Windsor in his private plane for the occasion. Orson Welles put together parts of *Henry IV* and *Henry V* into a single dramatic presentation, *Five Kings,* at Philadelphia in 1939; and Welles's 1965 film, called *Chimes at Midnight* (in England) or *Falstaff* (in the United States), with Welles himself as Falstaff and Jeanne Moreau implausibly cast as Doll Tearsheet, included parts of both plays down through the rejection of Falstaff. More recent productions in sequence include Terry Hands's direction of all three "Hal" plays, *1* and *2 Henry IV* and *Henry V,* at Stratford-upon-Avon in 1975 and Michael Bogdanov's three-play "Hal" series at the Old Vic in 1987.

Inevitably, the rejection of Falstaff is the touchstone of every version of the play. To fulfill his destiny as Henry V, Hal must repudiate his dissolute friend, but it is in how he does it that productions reveal their moral center. John Burrell's Old Vic *2 Henry IV* in 1945 at London's New Theatre, with Ralph Richardson as Falstaff and Laurence Olivier as Shallow, tried to subordinate the pressures of history to the humanity of the play's comic energies. Nevertheless, when in Act 5 the newly crowned Henry V arrogantly cut off Falstaff's last attempted joke with his curt "Reply not to me with a fool-born jest," Falstaff was crushed by the betrayal. In Gerald Freedman's 1968 New York Shakespeare Festival production, both Hal and Falstaff were distraught by the event, however inevitable it must have seemed to them both: Sam Waterston as Hal turned away from his erstwhile companion in pain, while Stacy Keach as Falstaff knelt before the new King, in the words of *The New York Times,* "as though he would never rise again." Conversely, in 1951 at Stratford-upon-Avon, Michael Redgrave directed a production that made Hal's rejection of Anthony Quayle's opportunistic Falstaff seem necessary and right, while in Douglas Seale's *2 Henry IV* in 1955 at the Old Vic, the rejection of a coarse and self-serving Falstaff was even less lamentable. The range of theatrical possibilities arising from the complex mixture of love and rejection give the play an intensity of vision that no single production can exhaust.

Theatrical explorations of the complexities of *2 Henry IV* have been enhanced in recent years by a search for balance and multiplicity of points of view, qualities that can only be increased by the staging of the *Henry* plays in sequence. When Terry Hands directed the three "Hal" plays in 1975 at Stratford-upon-Avon, he focused on the development of Hal from Prince to King. Alan Howard's Hal revealed how fully he had learned the lessons of kingship as he stood in golden armor before a ragged Falstaff and pronounced the inevitable verdict. He spoke dispassionately, almost charitably; as critic Robert Speaight wrote, what the king said was "spoken *about* Falstaff rather than *at* him." A dead tree stood in the background of the dazzling vision of Henry's kingship as mute commentary on what lay in the future. In Trevor Nunn's production at London's Barbican Theatre in 1982, Hal stepped out of the coronation procession to address Falstaff with obvious strain, and then resumed his emotionless, public persona, revealing the terrible human cost of his crown. In Michael Bogdanov's modern-dress "Hal" trilogy, the opening offering of the new English Shakespeare Company (at the Old Vic, 1987, after a fall 1986 national tour), Michael Pennington played a shrewd and secure Hal who coolly snubbed Falstaff (John Woodvine) in his mature awareness of Falstaff's irrelevance to the historical world Hal had just inherited.

Any production of *2 Henry IV* that does not willfully cut and rearrange its scenes in the manner of Betterton or Kemble must take account of the play's dark humor and disillusionment. The alternations back and forth between court and tavern, as in *1 Henry IV,* provide contrasting theatrical worlds of political manipulation and festive dissipation; but whereas in *1 Henry IV* the tavern world is (for a time at least) one of release and nearly magical inversion, the corresponding world in *2 Henry IV* is more disillusioned from the start. No longer is there any joyous playacting and exchanging of roles between Hal and Falstaff, and virtually no badinage. Falstaff presides over a kingdom populated by swaggerers, cheats, and whores, or venal country justices and their cunning servants. The political world, too, is largely governed (until the very last) by the likes of Prince John, maker of deceitful promises at Gaultree Forest. The Royal Shakespeare Company's production at Stratford-upon-Avon in 1964, directed by Peter Hall, John Barton, and Clifford Williams, was well attuned to the iconoclastic vision called for in the play's contrasts: Hugh Griffith as Falstaff reveled in his debauchery in a way that vividly offset the coldly political behavior of Prince John. Such a Brechtian interpretation necessarily found less patriotic inspiration in the final emergence of Henry V than, for example, did the lavish triumphal processions of the Covent Garden production in 1821. But productions will always in some way respond to their historical moment, and the wide variance of successful interpretations in the stage history of this complex and unsettling play reveals its ability to speak powerfully to different needs and times.

HENRY IV
–PART TWO–

The Actors' Names

RUMOR, *the Presenter*

KING HENRY THE FOURTH
PRINCE HENRY, *afterwards crowned* KING HENRY THE FIFTH

PRINCE JOHN OF LANCASTER,
HUMPHREY, [DUKE] OF GLOUCESTER,
THOMAS, [DUKE] OF CLARENCE,
} *sons to Henry IV and brethren to Henry V*

[EARL OF] NORTHUMBERLAND,
[SCROOP,] THE ARCHBISHOP OF YORK,
[LORD] MOWBRAY,
[LORD] HASTING,
LORD BARDOLPH,
TRAVERS,
MORTON,
[SIR JOHN] COLEVILLE,
} *opposites against King Henry IV*

[EARL OF] WARWICK,
[EARL OF] WESTMORLAND,
[EARL OF] SURREY,
GOWER,
HARCOURT,
[BLUNT],
LORD CHIEF JUSTICE,
[*His* SERVANT],
} *of the King's party*

POINS,
[SIR JOHN] FALSTAFF,
BARDOLPH,
PISTOL,
PETO,
[FALSTAFF'S] PAGE,
} *irregular humorists*

SHALLOW,
SILENCE,
} *both country justices*

DAVY, *servant to Shallow*

FANG *and* SNARE, *two sergeants*
MOLDY, SHADOW, WART, FEEBLE, [*and*] BULLCALF, *country soldiers*
[FRANCIS, *a drawer*]

NORTHUMBERLAND'S WIFE
PERCY'S WIDOW [LADY PERCY]
HOSTESS QUICKLY
DOLL TEARSHEET

DRAWERS
BEADLES
GROOMS
[PORTER]

EPILOGUE

[*Lords, Attendants, Messengers, Pages, Musicians, Officers, etc.*]

[SCENE: *England*]

Induction *Enter Rumor, painted full of tongues.*

RUMOR

Open your ears, for which of you will stop
The vent of hearing when loud Rumor speaks?
I, from the orient to the drooping west,
Making the wind my post-horse, still unfold 4
The acts commencèd on this ball of earth.
Upon my tongues continual slanders ride,
The which in every language I pronounce,
Stuffing the ears of men with false reports.
I speak of peace while covert enmity,
Under the smile of safety, wounds the world.
And who but Rumor, who but only I,
Make fearful musters and prepared defense, 12
Whiles the big year, swoll'n with some other grief, 13
Is thought with child by the stern tyrant War,
And no such matter? Rumor is a pipe 15
Blown by surmises, jealousies, conjectures, 16
And of so easy and so plain a stop 17
That the blunt monster with uncounted heads, 18
The still-discordant wavering multitude,
Can play upon it. But what need I thus 20
My well-known body to anatomize 21
Among my household? Why is Rumor here? 22
I run before King Harry's victory,

Induction. Location: Although the allegory of Rumor, based ultimately on Virgil's depiction of Fama as full of eyes, ears, and tongues, in the *Aeneid* (4.179–190), is timeless, Rumor is here represented as standing in front of Northumberland's castle, Warkworth. The play is supposed to open immediately after the battle of Shrewsbury, in which Henry Percy, or Hotspur, and the Scottish Earl of Douglas have been overthrown. We are concerned first of all with the news of the battle, with which *1 Henry IV* ended.

4 post-horse horse kept at an inn or post-house for the use of travelers. **still** continually **12 musters** assemblies of soldiers **13 big** swollen, pregnant with disaster **15 And no such matter** and yet there is no substance in such rumors. **pipe** recorder (a wind instrument) **16 jealousies** suspicions **17 of . . . stop** i.e., whose stops or openings are so easily played on **18 blunt** stupid, dull-witted **20 what** why **21 anatomize** lay open minutely, explain **22 household** retinue, i.e., the audience

Who in a bloody field by Shrewsbury
Hath beaten down young Hotspur and his troops,
Quenching the flame of bold rebellion
Even with the rebels' blood. But what mean I
To speak so true at first? My office is
To noise abroad that Harry Monmouth fell 29
Under the wrath of noble Hotspur's sword,
And that the King before the Douglas' rage
Stooped his anointed head as low as death.
This have I rumored through the peasant towns 33
Between that royal field of Shrewsbury
And this worm-eaten hold of ragged stone, 35
Where Hotspur's father, old Northumberland,
Lies crafty-sick. The posts come tiring on, 37
And not a man of them brings other news
Than they have learned of me. From Rumor's tongues
They bring smooth comforts false, worse than true
wrongs. *Exit Rumor.* 40

29 Harry Monmouth Prince Hal (who was born at Monmouth in Wales) **33 peasant** rural, provincial **35 hold** stronghold, fortress **37 crafty-sick** feigning sickness. **The . . . on** the messengers gallop hard, exhausted by their effort **40 worse . . . wrongs** i.e., false good news is ultimately worse than hurtful truth

1.1 *Enter the Lord Bardolph at one door.*

LORD BARDOLPH
Who keeps the gate here, ho?

[*Enter the Porter.*]

Where is the Earl?

PORTER
What shall I say you are?

LORD BARDOLPH
Tell thou the Earl
That the Lord Bardolph doth attend him here.

PORTER
His lordship is walked forth into the orchard.
Please it your honor knock but at the gate,
And he himself will answer.

Enter the Earl [*of*] *Northumberland* [*in a nightcap, supporting himself with a crutch*].

LORD BARDOLPH
Here comes the Earl.

[*Exit Porter.*]

NORTHUMBERLAND
What news, Lord Bardolph? Every minute now
Should be the father of some stratagem.
The times are wild. Contention, like a horse
Full of high feeding, madly hath broke loose
And bears down all before him.

LORD BARDOLPH
Noble Earl,
I bring you certain news from Shrewsbury.

NORTHUMBERLAND
Good, an God will!

LORD BARDOLPH
As good as heart can wish.
The King is almost wounded to the death,
And, in the fortune of my lord your son,
Prince Harry slain outright; and both the Blunts
Killed by the hand of Douglas. Young Prince John
And Westmorland and Stafford fled the field,

1.1. Location: Warkworth. Before Northumberland's castle.
s.d. Lord Bardolph (An ally of the Percys; not to be confused with Bardolph, Falstaff's red-faced companion.) **1 keeps** guards **3 attend** await **8 stratagem** violence **10 high feeding** too-rich fodder **12 certain** reliable **13 an** if **15 in the fortune of** by the good fortune of, or, for what has befallen

And Harry Monmouth's brawn, the hulk Sir John, 19
Is prisoner to your son. O, such a day,
So fought, so followed, and so fairly won, 21
Came not till now to dignify the times
Since Caesar's fortunes!

NORTHUMBERLAND How is this derived? 23
Saw you the field? Came you from Shrewsbury?

LORD BARDOLPH
I spake with one, my lord, that came from thence,
A gentleman well bred and of good name,
That freely rendered me these news for true.

Enter Travers.

NORTHUMBERLAND
Here comes my servant Travers, who I sent
On Tuesday last to listen after news.

LORD BARDOLPH
My lord, I overrode him on the way, 30
And he is furnished with no certainties
More than he haply may retail from me. 32

NORTHUMBERLAND
Now, Travers, what good tidings comes with you?

TRAVERS
My lord, Sir John Umfrevile turned me back 34
With joyful tidings and, being better horsed,
Outrode me. After him came spurring hard
A gentleman almost forspent with speed 37
That stopped by me to breathe his bloodied horse. 38
He asked the way to Chester, and of him
I did demand what news from Shrewsbury.
He told me that rebellion had ill luck
And that young Harry Percy's spur was cold.
With that, he gave his able horse the head,
And bending forward struck his armèd heels
Against the panting sides of his poor jade 45
Up to the rowel head, and starting so 46

19 brawn fat boar **21 followed** carried through **23 fortunes** successes. **derived** learned, obtained **30 overrode** outrode **32 haply** perhaps. **retail** relate **34 Sir John Umfrevile** (Perhaps the name of Lord Bardolph in an earlier version of this scene.) **37 forspent** exhausted **38 bloodied** i.e., with spurring **45 jade** nag **46 rowel head** the end of the spur, in which the barbed wheel turns. **starting** springing forward

He seemed in running to devour the way,
Staying no longer question.

NORTHUMBERLAND Ha? Again. 48
Said he young Harry Percy's spur was cold?
Of Hotspur, Coldspur? That rebellion
Had met ill luck?

LORD BARDOLPH My lord, I'll tell you what:
If my young lord your son have not the day, 52
Upon mine honor, for a silken point 53
I'll give my barony. Never talk of it.

NORTHUMBERLAND
Why should that gentleman that rode by Travers
Give then such instances of loss?

LORD BARDOLPH Who, he?
He was some hilding fellow that had stol'n 57
The horse he rode on and, upon my life,
Spoke at a venture. Look, here comes more news. 59

Enter Morton.

NORTHUMBERLAND
Yea, this man's brow, like to a title leaf, 60
Foretells the nature of a tragic volume.
So looks the strand whereon the imperious flood 62
Hath left a witnessed usurpation. 63
Say, Morton, didst thou come from Shrewsbury?

MORTON
I ran from Shrewsbury, my noble lord,
Where hateful death put on his ugliest mask
To fright our party.

NORTHUMBERLAND How doth my son and brother?
Thou tremblest, and the whiteness in thy cheek
Is apter than thy tongue to tell thy errand.
Even such a man, so faint, so spiritless,
So dull, so dead in look, so woebegone,
Drew Priam's curtain in the dead of night 72
And would have told him half his Troy was burnt;

48 Staying waiting for **52 day** victory **53 point** tag for fastening clothes (i.e., something of very small value) **57 hilding** good-for-nothing **59 at a venture** at random, recklessly **60 title leaf** title page **62 strand** shore **63 witnessed usurpation** evidence of its (the sea's) invasion, encroachment. (Morton's brow is furrowed like wrinkled sand.) **72 Priam** King of Troy. **curtain** bedcurtain

But Priam found the fire ere he his tongue,
And I my Percy's death ere thou report'st it.
This thou wouldst say, "Your son did thus and thus;
Your brother thus; so fought the noble Douglas"—
Stopping my greedy ear with their bold deeds. 78
But in the end, to stop my ear indeed, 79
Thou hast a sigh to blow away this praise,
Ending with "Brother, son, and all are dead."

MORTON
Douglas is living, and your brother, yet;
But for my lord your son—

NORTHUMBERLAND Why, he is dead.
See what a ready tongue suspicion hath!
He that but fears the thing he would not know
Hath by instinct knowledge from others' eyes
That what he feared is chancèd. Yet speak, Morton. 87
Tell thou an earl his divination lies, 88
And I will take it as a sweet disgrace
And make thee rich for doing me such wrong.

MORTON
You are too great to be by me gainsaid. 91
Your spirit is too true, your fears too certain. 92

NORTHUMBERLAND
Yet, for all this, say not that Percy's dead. 93
I see a strange confession in thine eye.
Thou shak'st thy head and hold'st it fear or sin
To speak a truth. If he be slain, say so.
The tongue offends not that reports his death;
And he doth sin that doth belie the dead, 98
Not he which says the dead is not alive.
Yet the first bringer of unwelcome news
Hath but a losing office, and his tongue 101
Sounds ever after as a sullen bell 102
Remembered tolling a departing friend. 103

LORD BARDOLPH
I cannot think, my lord, your son is dead.

78 Stopping filling **79 stop . . . indeed** i.e., prevent my ever hearing again **87 is chancèd** has occurred **88 divination** prophecy **91 gainsaid** contradicted **92 spirit** intuition, powers of perception **93 for** in spite of **98 belie** slander **101 losing office** i.e., thankless task **102 sullen** mournful **103 tolling** ringing the funeral bell for

MORTON

I am sorry I should force you to believe
That which I would to God I had not seen;
But these mine eyes saw him in bloody state,
Rend'ring faint quittance, wearied and outbreathed, 108
To Harry Monmouth, whose swift wrath beat down
The never-daunted Percy to the earth,
From whence with life he never more sprung up.
In few, his death, whose spirit lent a fire 112
Even to the dullest peasant in his camp,
Being bruited once, took fire and heat away 114
From the best-tempered courage in his troops; 115
For from his metal was his party steeled, 116
Which once in him abated, all the rest 117
Turned on themselves, like dull and heavy lead. 118
And as the thing that's heavy in itself
Upon enforcement flies with greatest speed, 120
So did our men, heavy in Hotspur's loss,
Lend to this weight such lightness with their fear
That arrows fled not swifter toward their aim
Than did our soldiers, aiming at their safety,
Fly from the field. Then was that noble Worcester
So soon ta'en prisoner; and that furious Scot,
The bloody Douglas, whose well-laboring sword
Had three times slain th' appearance of the King, 128
'Gan vail his stomach and did grace the shame 129
Of those that turned their backs, and in his flight,
Stumbling in fear, was took. The sum of all
Is that the King hath won and hath sent out
A speedy power to encounter you, my lord, 133
Under the conduct of young Lancaster 134
And Westmorland. This is the news at full. 135

108 quittance requital, i.e., resistance. **outbreathed** out of breath **112 In few** in few words **114 bruited** rumored, reported **115 best-tempered** i.e., like the highest quality steel **116 metal** (1) steel, continuing the metaphor of l. 115 (2) mettle, courage **117 abated** (1) blunted (2) slackened **118 Turned on themselves** (1) bent backwards (2) turned and ran **120 Upon enforcement** when set forcibly in motion **128 appearance of the King** i.e., warriors dressed like the King. (See *1 Henry IV*, 5.3 and 5.4.25–38.) **129 'Gan . . . stomach** began to abate or lower his courage. **grace** sanction (by his own running away) **133 power** armed force **134 conduct** command **135 at** in

NORTHUMBERLAND

For this I shall have time enough to mourn.
In poison there is physic; and these news, 137
Having been well, that would have made me sick, 138
Being sick, have in some measure made me well. 139
And as the wretch whose fever-weakened joints
Like strengthless hinges buckle under life, 141
Impatient of his fit, breaks like a fire 142
Out of his keeper's arms, even so my limbs, 143
Weakened with grief, being now enraged with grief, 144
Are thrice themselves. Hence, therefore, thou nice
crutch! [*He throws away his crutch.*] 145
A scaly gauntlet now with joints of steel 146
Must glove this hand. And hence, thou sickly coif! 147
[*He takes off his nightcap.*]
Thou art a guard too wanton for the head 148
Which princes, fleshed with conquest, aim to hit. 149
Now bind my brows with iron, and approach
The ragged'st hour that time and spite dare bring 151
To frown upon th' enraged Northumberland!
Let heaven kiss earth! Now let not Nature's hand
Keep the wild flood confined! Let order die, 154
And let this world no longer be a stage
To feed contention in a lingering act; 156
But let one spirit of the firstborn Cain 157
Reign in all bosoms, that, each heart being set 158
On bloody courses, the rude scene may end,
And darkness be the burier of the dead!

LORD BARDOLPH

This strainèd passion doth you wrong, my lord. 161

MORTON

Sweet Earl, divorce not wisdom from your honor.

137 physic medicine **138 Having . . . sick** that would have made me sick if I had been well **139 Being sick, have** I being sick, this same news has **141 buckle under life** bend under the weight of the living man **142 fit** attack of illness **143 keeper's** nurse's **144 grief . . . grief** pain and sickness . . . sorrow **145 nice** delicate, effeminate **146 scaly** i.e., mailed **147 sickly coif** close-fitting cap worn by an invalid
148 wanton effeminate, luxurious **149 fleshed** inflamed by foretaste of blood and success **151 ragged'st** roughest **154 flood** river **156 in . . . act** in a drawn-out act (as of a play). (Northumberland wishes for an end to the lingering dissolution of a world in conflict.) **157 of . . . Cain** i.e., of murder **158 that** so that **161 strainèd** excessive

The lives of all your loving complices 163
Lean on your health, the which, if you give o'er
To stormy passion, must perforce decay. 165
You cast th' event of war, my noble lord, 166
And summed the account of chance, before you said
"Let us make head." It was your presurmise 168
That, in the dole of blows, your son might drop. 169
You knew he walked o'er perils, on an edge,
More likely to fall in than to get o'er;
You were advised his flesh was capable 172
Of wounds and scars, and that his forward spirit 173
Would lift him where most trade of danger ranged. 174
Yet did you say, "Go forth." And none of this,
Though strongly apprehended, could restrain
The stiff-borne action. What hath then befallen, 177
Or what hath this bold enterprise brought forth,
More than that being which was like to be? 179

LORD BARDOLPH

We all that are engagèd to this loss 180
Knew that we ventured on such dangerous seas
That if we wrought out life 'twas ten to one. 182
And yet we ventured, for the gain proposed
Choked the respect of likely peril feared; 184
And since we are o'erset, venture again. 185
Come, we will all put forth, body and goods. 186

MORTON

'Tis more than time. And, my most noble lord,
I hear for certain, and dare speak the truth,
The gentle Archbishop of York is up 189
With well-appointed powers. He is a man 190
Who with a double surety binds his followers. 191

163 complices allies **165 perforce** necessarily **166 cast th' event** calculated the outcome **168 make head** raise an army **169 dole** dealing out, distribution **172 advised** aware **173 Of** of receiving. **forward** eager, ardent **174 trade** trafficking **177 stiff-borne** obstinately carried out **179 being** event; having occurred. **like** likely **180 engagèd to** involved in **182 if . . . one** if we came out alive we survived ten-to-one odds **184 Choked the respect** suppressed the consideration **185 o'erset** defeated, overthrown **186 all put forth** (1) all set out, as though putting out to sea (2) stake everything **189 gentle** wellborn. **Archbishop of York** i.e., Archbishop Scroop. **up** in arms **190 well-appointed powers** well-equipped armed forces **191 double surety** i.e., a bond of allegiance in terms of body and soul

My lord your son had only but the corpse, 192
But shadows and the shows of men, to fight; 193
For that same word "rebellion" did divide
The action of their bodies from their souls,
And they did fight with queasiness, constrained,
As men drink potions, that their weapons only 197
Seemed on our side. But, for their spirits and souls, 198
This word "rebellion," it had froze them up
As fish are in a pond. But now the Bishop
Turns insurrection to religion. 201
Supposed sincere and holy in his thoughts, 202
He's followed both with body and with mind,
And doth enlarge his rising with the blood 204
Of fair King Richard, scraped from Pomfret stones; 205
Derives from heaven his quarrel and his cause;
Tells them he doth bestride a bleeding land,
Gasping for life under great Bolingbroke; 208
And more and less do flock to follow him. 209

NORTHUMBERLAND
I knew of this before, but to speak truth
This present grief had wiped it from my mind.
Go in with me, and counsel every man 212
The aptest way for safety and revenge.
Get posts and letters, and make friends with speed— 214
Never so few, and never yet more need. *Exeunt.*

✤

1.2 *Enter Sir John [Falstaff] alone, with his Page bearing his sword and buckler.*

FALSTAFF Sirrah, you giant, what says the doctor to my 1
water? 2

192 only but only. **corpse** i.e., corpses, living bodies without their souls **193 But** only. **to fight** to use for fighting **197 potions** medicine, poison **198 for** as for **201 to religion** into a sacred cause **202 Supposed** i.e., rightly thought to be **204 enlarge his rising** enhance the merit of his insurrection **205 Pomfret** i.e., Pontefract Castle in Yorkshire, where Richard II was murdered **208 Bolingbroke** i.e., King Henry IV, here deprived of his title by the Archbishop **209 more and less** all classes **212 counsel every man** let every man give advice as to **214 posts** messengers. **make** collect

1.2. Location: London. A street.
s.d. buckler shield **1 Sirrah** (Form of address to a social inferior.)
1–2 to my water about my urine sample

PAGE He said, sir, the water itself was a good healthy water, but for the party that owed it, he might have more diseases than he knew for.

FALSTAFF Men of all sorts take a pride to gird at me. The brain of this foolish-compounded clay, man, is not able to invent anything that intends to laughter more than I invent or is invented on me. I am not only witty in myself, but the cause that wit is in other men. I do here walk before thee like a sow that hath overwhelmed all her litter but one. If the Prince put thee into my service for any other reason than to set me off, why then I have no judgment. Thou whoreson mandrake, thou art fitter to be worn in my cap than to wait at my heels. I was never manned with an agate till now; but I will inset you neither in gold nor silver, but in vile apparel, and send you back again to your master, for a jewel—the juvenal, the Prince your master, whose chin is not yet fledge. I will sooner have a beard grow in the palm of my hand than he shall get one of his cheek, and yet he will not stick to say his face is a face royal. God may finish it when he will, 'tis not a hair amiss yet. He may keep it still at a face royal, for a barber shall never earn sixpence out of it; and yet he'll be crowing as if he had writ man ever since his father was a bachelor. He may keep his own grace, but he's almost out of mine, I can assure him. What said Master Dommelton about the satin for my short cloak and my slops?

4 owed owned **5 knew for** was aware of **6 gird** jeer **7 foolish-compounded** composed of folly **8 intends** tends **13 set me off** show me to the best advantage **14 whoreson** (A generalized term of abuse meaning "vile" or "detestable.") **14–15 mandrake** plant with a forked, man-shaped root **15 fitter . . . cap** i.e., as small and decorous as a brooch worn in my hat **15–16 wait at my heels** i.e., wait in attendance on me, follow me about **16 manned . . . agate** i.e., provided with a servant as small as the little figures cut in agate stone for jewelry and seal rings **19 juvenal** youth **20 fledge** covered with down **22 stick** hesitate **23 face royal** (punning on the *royal,* a coin with the King's face stamped on it) **23–24 a hair** (1) a single hair of the beard (2) a jot **24 at** at the value of **26 writ man** i.e., attained manhood **27 grace** (1) title suited to his royal rank (2) favor **30 slops** loose breeches

PAGE He said, sir, you should procure him better assurance than Bardolph. He would not take his bond and yours; he liked not the security.

FALSTAFF Let him be damned like the glutton! Pray God his tongue be hotter! A whoreson Achitophel! A rascally yea-forsooth knave, to bear a gentleman in hand and then stand upon security! The whoreson smoothy-pates do now wear nothing but high shoes and bunches of keys at their girdles; and if a man is through with them in honest taking up, then they must stand upon security. I had as lief they would put ratsbane in my mouth as offer to stop it with security. I looked 'a should have sent me two-and-twenty yards of satin, as I am a true knight, and he sends me "security"! Well he may sleep in security, for he hath the horn of abundance, and the lightness of his wife shines through it. And yet cannot he see, though he have his own lantern to light him. Where's Bardolph?

PAGE He's gone into Smithfield to buy your worship a horse.

FALSTAFF I bought him in Paul's, and he'll buy me a

31–32 assurance guarantee **32 Bardolph** (One of Falstaff's followers, not the Lord Bardolph of scene 1.) **34 the glutton** (A reference to the parable of Dives the rich man, Luke 16:19–31.) **35 hotter** i.e., than Dives' tongue in hell. Achitophel abettor of Absalom's treason against David. (2 Samuel 15–17.) **36 yea-forsooth** i.e., yes-man
36–37 bear . . . in hand delude one with false hopes **37 stand upon security** insist upon guarantee of payment (as also in l. 41)
38 smoothy-pates (Alludes to the short hair of tradesmen.) **38–39 high shoes . . . keys** (Indications of their financial prosperity and pride.)
39–40 is through . . . taking up has agreed with them on an honest bargain **41 lief** willingly **42 ratsbane** rat poison **43 looked 'a** expected that he **45 security** i.e., a false and complacent sense of security **46 horn of abundance** (1) cornucopia (2) cuckold's horn, a sign of his wife's infidelity. **lightness** (1) wantonness (2) light showing through a lantern (which would have windows of *horn,* thereby giving the cuckold a lantern in his own forehead) **47 cannot he see** i.e., he cannot see his own wife's infidelity **48 lantern** (The old spelling "lanthorn" preserves Falstaff's continued joke about cuckold's horns.) **49 Smithfield** district near Saint Paul's Cathedral, famous as a livestock market **51 Paul's** i.e., Saint Paul's Cathedral nave, resort of servingmen seeking employment

horse in Smithfield. An I could get me but a wife in the stews, I were manned, horsed, and wived.

Enter [*the*] *Lord Chief Justice* [*and Servant*].

PAGE Sir, here comes the nobleman that committed the Prince for striking him about Bardolph.

FALSTAFF Wait close; I will not see him.

[*He tries to slip away.*]

CHIEF JUSTICE What's he that goes there?

SERVANT Falstaff, an 't please your lordship.

CHIEF JUSTICE He that was in question for the robbery?

SERVANT He, my lord. But he hath since done good service at Shrewsbury, and, as I hear, is now going with some charge to the Lord John of Lancaster.

CHIEF JUSTICE What, to York? Call him back again.

SERVANT Sir John Falstaff!

FALSTAFF Boy, tell him I am deaf.

PAGE You must speak louder; my master is deaf.

CHIEF JUSTICE I am sure he is, to the hearing of anything good. Go pluck him by the elbow; I must speak with him.

SERVANT Sir John!

FALSTAFF What, a young knave, and begging? Is there not wars? Is there not employment? Doth not the King lack subjects? Do not the rebels need soldiers? Though it be a shame to be on any side but one, it is worse shame to beg than to be on the worst side, were it worse than the name of rebellion can tell how to make it.

SERVANT You mistake me, sir.

FALSTAFF Why, sir, did I say you were an honest man? Setting my knighthood and my soldiership aside, I had lied in my throat if I had said so.

SERVANT I pray you, sir, then set your knighthood and

52 An if **53 stews** brothels. **I . . . wived** (Proverbially, to be thus manned, horsed, and wived at Saint Paul's, Smithfield, and the stews respectively, was to be taken for a sucker.) **54 committed** i.e., to prison. (According to an apocryphal story, Hal boxed the ears of the Lord Chief Justice; see *1 Henry IV,* 3.2.32–33 and note, and *2 Henry IV,* 5.2.70–71 and notes.) **56 close** concealed **59 in question** under judicial examination **62 charge** command of soldiers **77 make** regard your soldiership aside and give me leave to tell you you lie in your throat if you say I am any other than an honest man.

FALSTAFF I give thee leave to tell me so? I lay aside that which grows to me? If thou gett'st any leave of me, hang me; if thou tak'st leave, thou wert better be hanged. You hunt counter. Hence! Avaunt!

SERVANT Sir, my lord would speak with you.

CHIEF JUSTICE Sir John Falstaff, a word with you.

FALSTAFF My good lord! God give your lordship good time of day. I am glad to see your lordship abroad. I heard say your lordship was sick. I hope your lordship goes abroad by advice. Your lordship, though not clean past your youth, have yet some smack of age in you, some relish of the saltness of time in you, and I most humbly beseech your lordship to have a reverent care of your health.

CHIEF JUSTICE Sir John, I sent for you before your expedition to Shrewsbury.

FALSTAFF An 't please your lordship, I hear His Majesty is returned with some discomfort from Wales.

CHIEF JUSTICE I talk not of His Majesty. You would not come when I sent for you.

FALSTAFF And I hear, moreover, His Highness is fallen into this same whoreson apoplexy.

CHIEF JUSTICE Well, God mend him! I pray you, let me speak with you.

FALSTAFF This apoplexy, as I take it, is a kind of lethargy, an 't please your lordship, a kind of sleeping in the blood, a whoreson tingling.

CHIEF JUSTICE What tell you me of it? Be it as it is.

FALSTAFF It hath its original from much grief, from study, and perturbation of the brain. I have read the cause of his effects in Galen. It is a kind of deafness.

CHIEF JUSTICE I think you are fallen into the disease, for you hear not what I say to you.

FALSTAFF Very well, my lord, very well. Rather, an 't

83 leave permission **84 in your throat** i.e., outrageously **87 grows to** is an integral part of **89 hunt counter** i.e., run backward on the trail. (A hunting term.) **93 abroad** out of doors **95 by advice** by medical advice **113 What** why **114 its original** its origin **116 his** its. **Galen** the famous Greek authority on medicine

please you, it is the disease of not listening, the malady
of not marking, that I am troubled withal.

CHIEF JUSTICE To punish you by the heels would 122
amend the attention of your ears, and I care not if I do
become your physician.

FALSTAFF I am as poor as Job, my lord, but not so patient. Your lordship may minister the potion of imprisonment to me in respect of poverty; but how I 127
should be your patient to follow your prescriptions,
the wise may make some dram of a scruple, or indeed 129
a scruple itself.

CHIEF JUSTICE I sent for you, when there were matters
against you for your life, to come speak with me. 132

FALSTAFF As I was then advised by my learned counsel
in the laws of this land service, I did not come. 134

CHIEF JUSTICE Well, the truth is, Sir John, you live in great infamy.

FALSTAFF He that buckles himself in my belt cannot live in less.

CHIEF JUSTICE Your means are very slender, and your 139
waste is great.

FALSTAFF I would it were otherwise; I would my means were greater, and my waist slenderer.

CHIEF JUSTICE You have misled the youthful Prince.

FALSTAFF The young Prince hath misled me. I am the fellow with the great belly, and he my dog.

CHIEF JUSTICE Well, I am loath to gall a new-healed
wound. Your day's service at Shrewsbury hath a little
gilded over your night's exploit on Gad's Hill. You may 148
thank th' unquiet time for your quiet o'erposting that 149
action.

FALSTAFF My lord?

CHIEF JUSTICE But since all is well, keep it so. Wake not a sleeping wolf.

122 punish . . . heels i.e., by setting you in the stocks or fetters **127 in . . . poverty** i.e., by reason of my being too poor to pay a fine **129 make . . . scruple** entertain some small portion of doubt. (*Dram* and *scruple* are small apothecaries' weights.) **132 for your life** i.e., carrying the death penalty **134 land service** military service (with a pun on avoiding the "service" of a legal summons) **139 means** financial resources **148 exploit** i.e., the famous robbery in *1 Henry IV*, 2.2 **149 o'erposting** escaping the consequences of

FALSTAFF To wake a wolf is as bad as smell a fox.

CHIEF JUSTICE What, you are as a candle, the better part burnt out.

FALSTAFF A wassail candle, my lord, all tallow. If I did say of wax, my growth would approve the truth.

CHIEF JUSTICE There is not a white hair on your face but should have his effect of gravity.

FALSTAFF His effect of gravy, gravy, gravy.

CHIEF JUSTICE You follow the young Prince up and down, like his ill angel.

FALSTAFF Not so, my lord. Your ill angel is light, but I hope he that looks upon me will take me without weighing. And yet in some respects I grant I cannot go. I cannot tell. Virtue is of so little regard in these costermongers' times that true valor is turned bearward; pregnancy is made a tapster, and his quick wit wasted in giving reckonings. All the other gifts appurtenant to man, as the malice of this age shapes them, are not worth a gooseberry. You that are old consider not the capacities of us that are young; you do measure the heat of our livers with the bitterness of your galls. And we that are in the vaward of our youth, I must confess, are wags too.

CHIEF JUSTICE Do you set down your name in the scroll

154 smell a fox suspect something. (Cf. "smell a rat.") **157 wassail candle** large candle lighted up at a feast. **tallow** a mixture of animal fats (which Falstaff thinks is more appropriate for him than a candle made of bees' *wax*) **158 wax** beeswax (with a pun on "growth"). **approve** prove **160 his effect** its sign **161 gravy** (Sweat was thought to be fat exuded from the flesh, like gravy from meat.) **163 ill angel** evil attendant spirit. (But Falstaff quibbles on the meaning "a clipped angel," a coin worth 6 shillings 8 pence.) **164 light** i.e., underweight (because the coin is "clipped"). (Refers also to Satan, "an angel of light," 2 Corinthians 11.14.) **165 take me** accept me at face value **166 weighing** (1) putting me on the scales (2) considering further, interpreting **167 go** (1) walk (2) pass current. **cannot tell** (1) don't know what to think (2) don't count as good money **168 costermongers'** i.e., commercial. (A costermonger is a hawker of fruits or vegetables.) **168–169 bearward** one who handles tame bears **169 pregnancy** quickness (of wit), intellectual capacity **170 reckonings** tavern bills **170–171 appurtenant** belonging **174 heat . . . galls** (The liver was thought to be the source of passion and to be active in youth; the gall was thought the seat of melancholy and rancor, and to be prevalent in age.) **175 vaward** vanguard, forefront

of youth, that are written down old with all the characters of age? Have you not a moist eye, a dry hand, a yellow cheek, a white beard, a decreasing leg, an increasing belly? Is not your voice broken, your wind short, your chin double, your wit single, and every part about you blasted with antiquity? And will you yet call yourself young? Fie, fie, fie, Sir John!

FALSTAFF My lord, I was born about three of the clock in the afternoon, with a white head and something a round belly. For my voice, I have lost it with halloing and singing of anthems. To approve my youth further, I will not. The truth is, I am only old in judgment and understanding; and he that will caper with me for a thousand marks, let him lend me the money, and have at him! For the box of the ear that the Prince gave you, he gave it like a rude prince, and you took it like a sensible lord. I have checked him for it, and the young lion repents—[*Aside*] marry, not in ashes and sackcloth, but in new silk and old sack.

CHIEF JUSTICE Well, God send the Prince a better companion!

FALSTAFF God send the companion a better prince! I cannot rid my hands of him.

CHIEF JUSTICE Well, the King hath severed you and Prince Harry. I hear you are going with Lord John of Lancaster against the Archbishop and the Earl of Northumberland.

FALSTAFF Yea, I thank your pretty sweet wit for it. But look you pray, all you that kiss my lady Peace at home, that our armies join not in a hot day; for, by the Lord, I take but two shirts out with me, and I mean not to sweat extraordinarily. If it be a hot day, and I brandish anything but a bottle, I would I might never spit white

178–179 characters (1) characteristics (2) letters **182 single** i.e., feeble **183 blasted** withered, blighted **186 something a** a somewhat **187 halloing** shouting to hounds **188 approve** prove **190 caper with me** compete with me in dancing **191 marks** coins worth 13 shillings 4 pence **192 For** as for. **box of the ear** (See note to l. 54, above.) **194 sensible** (1) intelligent (2) capable of receiving physical sensations. **checked** rebuked **195 marry** indeed. (Literally, "by the Virgin Mary.") **196 sack** a white Spanish wine **206 look** be sure, take care **210 spit white** i.e., from thirst

again. There is not a dangerous action can peep
out his head but I am thrust upon it. Well, I cannot last
ever. But it was alway yet the trick of our English na- 213
tion, if they have a good thing, to make it too common. If ye will needs say I am an old man, you should
give me rest. I would to God my name were not so
terrible to the enemy as it is. I were better to be eaten
to death with a rust than to be scoured to nothing with
perpetual motion.

CHIEF JUSTICE Well, be honest, be honest; and God
bless your expedition!

FALSTAFF Will your lordship lend me a thousand pound
to furnish me forth? 223

CHIEF JUSTICE Not a penny, not a penny. You are too
impatient to bear crosses. Fare you well. Commend 225
me to my cousin Westmorland.

[*Exeunt Chief Justice and Servant.*]

FALSTAFF If I do, fillip me with a three-man beetle. A 227
man can no more separate age and covetousness than
'a can part young limbs and lechery; but the gout galls
the one, and the pox pinches the other, and so both 230
the degrees prevent my curses. Boy! 231

PAGE Sir?

FALSTAFF What money is in my purse?

PAGE Seven groats and two pence. 234

FALSTAFF I can get no remedy against this consumption
of the purse; borrowing only lingers and lingers it out, 236
but the disease is incurable. [*He gives letters.*] Go bear
this letter to my lord of Lancaster, this to the Prince,
this to the Earl of Westmorland, and this to old Mistress Ursula, whom I have weekly sworn to marry
since I perceived the first white hair of my chin. About
it. You know where to find me. [*Exit Page.*] A pox of
this gout! Or, a gout of this pox! For the one or the
other plays the rogue with my great toe. 'Tis no matter

213 alway yet always. **trick** habit **223 furnish** equip **225 crosses** (1) afflictions (2) silver coins stamped with the figure of the cross
227 fillip knock. **three-man beetle** a huge pile-driving mallet requiring three men to wield it **230–231 both the degrees** i.e., age and youth, the one afflicted with gout and the other with *pox* or syphilis **231 prevent** anticipate **234 groats** coins worth 4 pence **236 lingers** prolongs, draws

if I do halt; I have the wars for my color, and my pen- 245
sion shall seem the more reasonable. A good wit will
make use of anything. I will turn diseases to com- 247
modity. [*Exit.*] 248

✤

1.3

Enter the Archbishop [*of York*], *Thomas Mowbray* (*Earl Marshal*), *the Lord Hastings, and* [*Lord*] *Bardolph.*

ARCHBISHOP
Thus have you heard our cause and known our means;
And, my most noble friends, I pray you all,
Speak plainly your opinions of our hopes.
And first, Lord Marshal, what say you to it?

MOWBRAY
I well allow the occasion of our arms, 5
But gladly would be better satisfied
How in our means we should advance ourselves 7
To look with forehead bold and big enough 8
Upon the power and puissance of the King. 9

HASTINGS
Our present musters grow upon the file 10
To five-and-twenty thousand men of choice; 11
And our supplies live largely in the hope 12
Of great Northumberland, whose bosom burns
With an incensèd fire of injuries.

LORD BARDOLPH
The question then, Lord Hastings, standeth thus:
Whether our present five-and-twenty thousand
May hold up head without Northumberland? 17

HASTINGS
With him, we may.

LORD BARDOLPH Yea, marry, there's the point.

245 halt limp. **color** excuse **247–248 commodity** profit

1.3. Location: York. The Archbishop's palace.
s.d. Thomas Mowbray son of Thomas Mowbray, Duke of Norfolk, who was banished by Richard II **5 allow . . . arms** concede the justice of our arming **7 in** with **8 forehead** i.e., assurance, defiant gaze **9 puissance** strength **10 file** roll **11 men of choice** choice men **12 supplies** reinforcements. **largely** abundantly **17 hold up head** i.e., succeed, be confident

But if without him we be thought too feeble,
My judgment is we should not step too far
Till we had his assistance by the hand;
For in a theme so bloody-faced as this 22
Conjecture, expectation, and surmise
Of aids incertain should not be admitted.

ARCHBISHOP

'Tis very true, Lord Bardolph, for indeed
It was young Hotspur's case at Shrewsbury.

LORD BARDOLPH

It was, my lord; who lined himself with hope, 27
Eating the air on promise of supply, 28
Flattering himself in project of a power 29
Much smaller than the smallest of his thoughts,
And so, with great imagination
Proper to madmen, led his powers to death 32
And winking leapt into destruction. 33

HASTINGS

But, by your leave, it never yet did hurt
To lay down likelihoods and forms of hope.

LORD BARDOLPH

Yes, if this present quality of war— 36
Indeed the instant action, a cause on foot— 37
Lives so in hope, as in an early spring 38
We see th' appearing buds, which to prove fruit 39
Hope gives not so much warrant as despair 40
That frosts will bite them. When we mean to build, 41
We first survey the plot, then draw the model; 42
And when we see the figure of the house, 43
Then must we rate the cost of the erection, 44
Which if we find outweighs ability, 45

22 theme business **27 lined** strengthened **28 Eating . . . supply** i.e., living in false hopes of reinforcement **29 project . . . power** anticipation of the arrival of an armed force **32 powers** forces **33 winking** shutting his eyes **36–41 Yes . . . them** i.e., Yes (replying to Lord Hastings), it can do hurt to be too hopeful about war; if, for example, this present business of war—indeed, the very campaign we anticipate, the matter that is now afoot—depends merely on such desperate hopes as we experience about buds appearing too early in the spring, since in reality hope gives us not so much warrant to expect their maturing into fruit as despair that frosts will bite them. (The text may be corrupt here.) **42 model** plan **43 figure** design **44 rate** estimate **45 ability** i.e., ability to pay

What do we then but draw anew the model
In fewer offices, or at least desist 47
To build at all? Much more, in this great work,
Which is almost to pluck a kingdom down
And set another up, should we survey
The plot of situation and the model,
Consent upon a sure foundation, 52
Question surveyors, know our own estate, 53
How able such a work to undergo,
To weigh against his opposite; or else 55
We fortify in paper and in figures, 56
Using the names of men instead of men,
Like one that draws the model of an house
Beyond his power to build it, who, half through,
Gives o'er and leaves his part-created cost 60
A naked subject to the weeping clouds 61
And waste for churlish winter's tyranny.

HASTINGS
Grant that our hopes, yet likely of fair birth, 63
Should be stillborn, and that we now possessed
The utmost man of expectation, 65
I think we are a body strong enough,
Even as we are, to equal with the King. 67

LORD BARDOLPH
What, is the King but five-and-twenty thousand?

HASTINGS
To us no more, nay, not so much, Lord Bardolph.
For his divisions, as the times do brawl, 70
Are in three heads: one power against the French, 71
And one against Glendower; perforce a third 72
Must take up us. So is the unfirm King 73
In three divided, and his coffers sound 74
With hollow poverty and emptiness.

47 offices rooms. **at least** at the worst **52 Consent** agree **53 surveyors** architects. **estate** wealth **55 his opposite** adverse conditions **56 in paper** merely on paper **60 part-created cost** partly finished splendor **61 naked subject** exposed (i.e., helpless) victim **63 yet** still **65 The . . . expectation** i.e., all the men that we might hope to have **67 equal** match **70 as . . . brawl** in accordance with the discordant necessity of the time **71 heads** armies **72 perforce** necessarily **73 take up** encounter, oppose **74 sound** resound, echo

ARCHBISHOP
That he should draw his several strengths together
And come against us in full puissance
Need not to be dreaded.

HASTINGS If he should do so,
To French and Welsh he leaves his back unarmed,
They baying him at the heels. Never fear that.

LORD BARDOLPH
Who is it like should lead his forces hither?

HASTINGS
The Duke of Lancaster and Westmorland;
Against the Welsh, himself and Harry Monmouth.
But who is substituted 'gainst the French
I have no certain notice.

ARCHBISHOP Let us on,
And publish the occasion of our arms.
The commonwealth is sick of their own choice;
Their overgreedy love hath surfeited.
An habitation giddy and unsure
Hath he that buildeth on the vulgar heart.
O thou fond many, with what loud applause
Didst thou beat heaven with blessing Bolingbroke,
Before he was what thou wouldst have him be!
And being now trimmed in thine own desires,
Thou, beastly feeder, art so full of him
That thou provok'st thyself to cast him up.
So, so, thou common dog, didst thou disgorge
Thy glutton bosom of the royal Richard;
And now thou wouldst eat thy dead vomit up,
And howl'st to find it. What trust is in these times?
They that, when Richard lived, would have him die,
Are now become enamored on his grave.
Thou, that threw'st dust upon his goodly head
When through proud London he came sighing on
After th' admirèd heels of Bolingbroke,
Criest now "O earth, yield us that king again,

76 several strengths various armies **80 baying** pursuing (like hunting dogs) **81 Who . . . should** who is likely to **84 substituted** delegated **86 arms** hostilities **90 vulgar** common, plebeian **91 fond many** foolish multitude **92 beat heaven** assail heaven with prayers **94 trimmed in** furnished with, dressed in **97 disgorge** vomit

And take thou this!" O thoughts of men accurst!
Past and to come seems best; things present worst.

MOWBRAY
Shall we go draw our numbers and set on? 109

HASTINGS
We are time's subjects, and time bids begone.

Exeunt.

✤

109 draw our numbers assemble or muster our forces. **set on** march

2.1 *Enter Hostess* [*Quickly*] *of the tavern and two officers:* [*Fang, followed by Snare*].

HOSTESS Master Fang, have you entered the action? 1
FANG It is entered.
HOSTESS Where's your yeoman? Is 't a lusty yeoman? 3
Will 'a stand to 't? 4
FANG [*Looking around him*] Sirrah—where's Snare?
HOSTESS O Lord, ay, good Master Snare.
SNARE [*From behind them*] Here, here.
FANG Snare, we must arrest Sir John Falstaff.
HOSTESS Yea, good Master Snare, I have entered him 9
and all.
SNARE It may chance cost some of us our lives, for he 11
will stab.
HOSTESS Alas the day, take heed of him! He stabbed me
in mine own house, most beastly, in good faith. 'A
cares not what mischief he does, if his weapon be out.
He will foin like any devil; he will spare neither man, 16
woman, nor child.
FANG If I can close with him, I care not for his thrust. 18
HOSTESS No, nor I neither. I'll be at your elbow.
FANG An I but fist him once, and 'a come but within 20
my vice— 21
HOSTESS I am undone by his going. I warrant you, he's 22
an infinitive thing upon my score. Good Master Fang, 23
hold him sure. Good Master Snare, let him not scape.
'A comes continuantly to Pie Corner—saving your 25
manhoods—to buy a saddle; and he is indited to din- 26

2.1. Location: London. A street.
1 entered the action begun the lawsuit **3 yeoman** sheriff's man **4 Will . . . to 't** will he fight boldly **9 entered** brought action against in court **11 chance** possibly **16 foin** thrust in fencing; with unintended sexual double meaning, as also in *stabbed, weapon, thrust, entered, undone, saddle* (suggesting a prostitute), *case* (female pudendum), *openly known to the world, brought in, long one, borne, fubbed off* (meaning also to be put off with excuses), *do me, stand to me,* etc. **18 close** grapple **20 fist** i.e., seize **21 vice** vise, grip **22 going** i.e., going without paying **23 infinitive** (Hostess Quickly's malapropism for *infinite,* endless.) **score** accounts **25 continuantly** (Perhaps a mixup of *continually* and *incontinently,* immediately.) **Pie Corner** a corner in the Smithfield district of London known for its cooks' shops **25–26 saving your manhoods** i.e., with apologies for mentioning anything so indelicate **26 indited** i.e., invited

ner to the Lubber's Head in Lumbert Street, to Master Smooth's the silkman. I pray you, since my exion is entered and my case so openly known to the world, let him be brought in to his answer. A hundred mark is a long one for a poor lone woman to bear; and I have borne, and borne, and borne, and have been fubbed off, and fubbed off, and fubbed off, from this day to that day, that it is a shame to be thought on. There is no honesty in such dealing, unless a woman should be made an ass and a beast, to bear every knave's wrong. Yonder he comes, and that arrant malmsey-nose knave, Bardolph, with him. Do your offices, do your offices. Master Fang and Master Snare, do me, do me, do me your offices.

Enter Sir John [*Falstaff*], *and Bardolph, and the Boy* [*Page*].

FALSTAFF How now, whose mare's dead? What's the matter?

FANG Sir John, I arrest you at the suit of Mistress Quickly.

FALSTAFF Away, varlets! Draw, Bardolph. Cut me off the villain's head. Throw the quean in the channel.

[*They draw.*]

HOSTESS Throw me in the channel? I'll throw thee in the channel. Wilt thou? Wilt thou? Thou bastardly rogue! Murder, murder! Ah, thou honeysuckle villain! Wilt thou kill God's officers and the King's? Ah, thou honeyseed rogue! Thou art a honeyseed, a man-queller, and a woman-queller.

FALSTAFF Keep them off, Bardolph.

OFFICERS A rescue! A rescue!

27 Lubber's Head i.e., Libbard's Head, Leopard's Head Inn. **Lumbert** i.e., Lombard **28 exion** action, lawsuit **30 mark** (Worth 13 shillings 4 pence.) **31 long one** huge reckoning (with unconscious sexual suggestion) **37–38 malmsey-nose** red-nosed (from drinking malmsey, a sweet red wine) **39 do me** i.e., do your duty for me (with unintended sexual suggestion) **41 whose mare's dead** i.e., what's all the fuss about **46 quean** slut, hussy. **channel** street gutter **49 honeysuckle** (For *homicidal.*) **50–51 honeyseed** (For *homicide.*) **51 man-queller** murderer **52 woman-queller** destroyer of women (but with suggestion also of "seducer") **54 A rescue** i.e., come help the officers in their rescue of the hostess. (Said to anyone within earshot.)

HOSTESS Good people, bring a rescue or two. Thou woo't, woo't thou? Thou woo't, woo't ta? Do, do, thou rogue! Do, thou hempseed!

PAGE Away, you scullion, you rampallian, you fustilarian! I'll tickle your catastrophe.

Enter [*the*] *Lord Chief Justice and his men.*

CHIEF JUSTICE
What is the matter? Keep the peace here, ho!

HOSTESS Good my lord, be good to me. I beseech you, stand to me.

CHIEF JUSTICE
How now, Sir John? What are you brawling here?
Doth this become your place, your time, and business?
You should have been well on your way to York.
[*To an officer.*] Stand from him, fellow. Wherefore
hang'st thou upon him?

HOSTESS O my most worshipful lord, an 't please Your Grace, I am a poor widow of Eastcheap, and he is arrested at my suit.

CHIEF JUSTICE For what sum?

HOSTESS It is more than for some, my lord, it is for all, all I have. He hath eaten me out of house and home; he hath put all my substance into that fat belly of his. But I will have some of it out again, [*To Falstaff*] or I will ride thee o' nights like the mare.

FALSTAFF I think I am as like to ride the mare, if I have any vantage of ground to get up.

CHIEF JUSTICE How comes this, Sir John? What man of good temper would endure this tempest of exclamation? Are you not ashamed to enforce a poor widow to so rough a course to come by her own?

FALSTAFF What is the gross sum that I owe thee?

HOSTESS Marry, if thou wert an honest man, thyself and

56 woo't thou wilt thou. **ta** thou **57 hempseed** (Alludes to the hangman's rope; Mistress Quickly probably means *homicide*.) **58 scullion** kitchen wench. **rampallian** scoundrel, ruffian **58–59 fustilarian** fat, frowsy woman **59 catastrophe** backside **62 stand to** help (with bawdy suggestion) **63 What** why **75 o' nights** by night. **mare** nightmare **77 vantage of ground** superior position. **get up** mount (with intended sexual suggestion, continued from *ride the mare* in l. 76) **79 temper** disposition **81 come by her own** get what is hers **82 gross** whole

the money too. Thou didst swear to me upon a parcel-gilt goblet, sitting in my Dolphin chamber, at the round table, by a seacoal fire, upon Wednesday in Wheeson week, when the Prince broke thy head for liking his father to a singing-man of Windsor, thou didst swear to me then, as I was washing thy wound, to marry me and make me my lady thy wife. Canst thou deny it? Did not goodwife Keech, the butcher's wife, come in then and call me gossip Quickly? Coming in to borrow a mess of vinegar, telling us she had a good dish of prawns, whereby thou didst desire to eat some, whereby I told thee they were ill for a green wound? And didst thou not, when she was gone downstairs, desire me to be no more so familiarity with such poor people, saying that ere long they should call me madam? And didst thou not kiss me and bid me fetch thee thirty shillings? I put thee now to thy book oath. Deny it if thou canst.

FALSTAFF My lord, this is a poor mad soul, and she says up and down the town that her eldest son is like you. She hath been in good case, and the truth is, poverty hath distracted her. But for these foolish officers, I beseech you I may have redress against them.

CHIEF JUSTICE Sir John, Sir John, I am well acquainted with your manner of wrenching the true cause the false way. It is not a confident brow, nor the throng of words that come with such more than impudent sauciness from you, can thrust me from a level consideration. You have, as it appears to me, practiced upon the easy-yielding spirit of this woman and made her serve your uses both in purse and in person.

HOSTESS Yea, in truth, my lord.

84–85 parcel-gilt partly gilded **85 Dolphin chamber** (The name of a room in her inn; *Dolphin* means "Dauphin.") **86 seacoal** bituminous coal, brought in by sea **87 Wheeson** Whitsun (Pentecost). **broke** hit, made a cut on
88 liking comparing. **singing-man** chorister **91 goodwife** (Title of a married woman.) **Keech** (Literally, "a lump of tallow.") **92 gossip** (Literally, a fellow godparent; hence, a female friend.) **93 mess** small quantity
94 prawns shrimps. **whereby** whereupon **95 green** raw **97 familiarity** (The hostess's word for "familiar.") **101 book oath** oath on a Bible **104 in good case** well to do (perhaps with bawdy suggestion) **105 distracted her** driven her mad **111 level** fair-minded, evenhanded **114 serve your uses** (with erotic suggestion)

CHIEF JUSTICE Pray thee, peace.—Pay her the debt you owe her, and unpay the villainy you have done her. The one you may do with sterling money, and the other with current repentance.

FALSTAFF My lord, I will not undergo this sneap without reply. You call honorable boldness impudent sauciness. If a man will make curtsy and say nothing, he is virtuous. No, my lord, my humble duty remembered, I will not be your suitor. I say to you, I do desire deliverance from these officers, being upon hasty employment in the King's affairs.

CHIEF JUSTICE You speak as having power to do wrong. But answer in th' effect of your reputation, and satisfy the poor woman.

FALSTAFF Come hither, hostess. [*He takes her aside.*]

Enter a messenger [*Gower*].

CHIEF JUSTICE Now, Master Gower, what news?

GOWER

The King, my lord, and Harry Prince of Wales
Are near at hand. The rest the paper tells.
[*He gives a letter. The Chief Justice reads.*]

FALSTAFF [*To Mistress Quickly*] As I am a gentleman.

HOSTESS Faith, you said so before.

FALSTAFF As I am a gentleman. Come, no more words of it.

HOSTESS By this heavenly ground I tread on, I must be fain to pawn both my plate and the tapestry of my dining chambers.

FALSTAFF Glasses, glasses, is the only drinking. And for thy walls, a pretty slight drollery, or the story of the Prodigal, or the German hunting in water work, is

119 current genuine (with an allusion to current, or lawful, coin, the *sterling* of l. 118) **120 sneap** reproof **122 curtsy** bow **123–124 my . . . remembered** i.e., with all due consideration of the respect I owe to your position **128 in . . . reputation** i.e., in a manner becoming a man of your reputation **139 fain** obliged, content **141 Glasses . . . drinking** i.e., glasses are all the fashion now for drinking, instead of metal tankards **142 drollery** comic picture **142–143 the Prodigal** the Prodigal Son. (See Luke 15.11–32.) **143 German hunting** hunting scene painted by a German or Dutch artist. **water work** watercolor

worth a thousand of these bed-hangers and these fly- 144
bitten tapestries. Let it be ten pound, if thou canst.
Come, an 'twere not for thy humors, there's not a 146
better wench in England. Go wash thy face, and draw 147
the action. Come, thou must not be in this humor
with me. Dost not know me? Come, come, I know
thou wast set on to this.

HOSTESS Pray thee, Sir John, let it be but twenty nobles. 151
I' faith, I am loath to pawn my plate, so God save 152
me, la!

FALSTAFF Let it alone; I'll make other shift. You'll be a 154
fool still.

HOSTESS Well, you shall have it, though I pawn my
gown. I hope you'll come to supper. You'll pay me all
together?

FALSTAFF Will I live? [*To Bardolph.*] Go, with her, with 159
her; hook on, hook on. 160

HOSTESS Will you have Doll Tearsheet meet you at
supper?

FALSTAFF No more words. Let's have her.

Exeunt Hostess and Sergeant [*Fang, Bardolph, and others*].

CHIEF JUSTICE I have heard better news.

FALSTAFF What's the news, my lord?

CHIEF JUSTICE Where lay the King tonight? 166

GOWER At Basingstoke, my lord. 167

FALSTAFF I hope, my lord, all's well. What is the news,
my lord?

CHIEF JUSTICE Come all his forces back?

GOWER
No, fifteen hundred foot, five hundred horse 171
Are marched up to my lord of Lancaster, 172
Against Northumberland and the Archbishop.

FALSTAFF Comes the King back from Wales, my noble
lord?

144 bed-hangers curtains around a four-poster bed **146 an 'twere** if it were. **humors** whims, vagaries **147 draw** withdraw **151 nobles** coins current at 6 shillings 8 pence **152 loath** reluctant **154 shift** expedient **159 Will I live** i.e., as sure as I live **160 hook on** i.e., follow her **166 tonight** this past night **167 Basingstoke** a town in Hampshire **171 foot** foot soldiers. **horse** cavalry troops **172 to** i.e., led by

CHIEF JUSTICE
You shall have letters of me presently.
Come, go along with me, good Master Gower.
[*He starts to go.*]

FALSTAFF My lord!

CHIEF JUSTICE What's the matter?

FALSTAFF Master Gower, shall I entreat you with me to dinner?

GOWER I must wait upon my good lord here, I thank you, good Sir John.

CHIEF JUSTICE Sir John, you loiter here too long, being you are to take soldiers up in counties as you go.

FALSTAFF Will you sup with me, Master Gower?

CHIEF JUSTICE What foolish master taught you these manners, Sir John?

FALSTAFF Master Gower, if they become me not, he was a fool that taught them me. This is the right fencing grace, my lord—tap for tap, and so part fair.

CHIEF JUSTICE Now the Lord lighten thee! Thou art a great fool. [*Exeunt separately.*]

✤

2.2 *Enter the Prince* [*Henry*], *Poins, with others.*

PRINCE Before God, I am exceeding weary.

POINS Is 't come to that? I had thought weariness durst not have attached one of so high blood.

PRINCE Faith, it does me, though it discolors the complexion of my greatness to acknowledge it. Doth it not show vilely in me to desire small beer?

POINS Why, a prince should not be so loosely studied

176 presently immediately **182 wait upon** accompany **184–185 being . . . up** seeing that you are to levy soldiers **191 grace** form, style. (Falstaff is saying that by refusing to answer the Chief Justice's questions in ll. 180 ff., Falstaff is only paying him back tit for tat for ignoring Falstaff's questions, ll. 165–177.) **fair** on good terms **192 lighten** (1) enlighten (2) reduce in weight

2.2. Location: London. Prince Henry's dwelling.
3 attached seized **4–5 discolors . . . greatness** i.e., makes me blush or look pale with weariness, and casts a shadow over my princely greatness **6 show** appear. **small beer** weak kind of beer, hence inferior **7 studied** versed, inclined

as to remember so weak a composition.

PRINCE Belike then my appetite was not princely got, for, by my troth, I do now remember the poor creature, small beer. But indeed these humble considerations make me out of love with my greatness. What a disgrace is it to me to remember thy name! Or to know thy face tomorrow! Or to take note how many pair of silk stockings thou hast, viz., these, and those that were thy peach-colored ones! Or to bear the inventory of thy shirts, as, one for superfluity, and another for use! But that the tennis-court keeper knows better than I; for it is a low ebb of linen with thee when thou keepest not racket there, as thou hast not done a great while, because the rest of the low countries have made a shift to eat up thy holland. And God knows whether those that bawl out the ruins of thy linen shall inherit His kingdom. But the midwives say the children are not in the fault, whereupon the world increases and kindreds are mightily strengthened.

POINS How ill it follows, after you have labored so hard, you should talk so idly! Tell me, how many good young princes would do so, their fathers being so sick as yours at this time is?

PRINCE Shall I tell thee one thing, Poins?

POINS Yes, faith, and let it be an excellent good thing.

PRINCE It shall serve among wits of no higher breeding than thine.

8 so . . . composition i.e., weak beer, trifles **9 Belike** probably. **got** begotten **15 viz.** namely. (An abbreviation of the Latin *videlicet.*) **16 bear** bear in mind **17 for superfluity** as a clean change (of shirt) **18–21 But . . . while** i.e., the keeper of the tennis court knows that Poins's inventory of shirts is at a low ebb, that he does not have a spare clean shirt to shift into, because he has not been seen at the tennis court lately **21 the low countries** i.e., the brothels where Poins spends his money (with a pun on "the Netherlands") **21–22 made a shift** contrived (with a pun on *shift,* shirt) **22 eat . . . holland** i.e., used up all the money you would spend on a linen shirt (with a pun on *Holland* as one of the Low Countries) **23 those . . . linen** i.e., your bastards, who wear your cast-off shirts made into swaddling clothes. **bawl out** cry out from **23–24 inherit His kingdom** i.e., go to heaven. (See Matthew 5.10, 25.34, or 19.14: "Suffer the little children . . . to come to me, for of such is the kingdom of heaven.") **25 in the fault** to be blamed (for being illegitimate) **26 kindreds** families. (The Prince's point is that this is how families are increased in size.)

POINS Go to. I stand the push of your one thing that you will tell.

PRINCE Marry, I tell thee it is not meet that I should be sad, now my father is sick. Albeit I could tell to thee, as to one it pleases me, for fault of a better, to call my friend, I could be sad, and sad indeed too.

POINS Very hardly upon such a subject.

PRINCE By this hand, thou thinkest me as far in the devil's book as thou and Falstaff for obduracy and persistency. Let the end try the man. But I tell thee, my heart bleeds inwardly that my father is so sick. And keeping such vile company as thou art hath in reason taken from me all ostentation of sorrow.

POINS The reason?

PRINCE What wouldst thou think of me if I should weep?

POINS I would think thee a most princely hypocrite.

PRINCE It would be every man's thought, and thou art a blessed fellow to think as every man thinks. Never a man's thought in the world keeps the roadway better than thine. Every man would think me an hypocrite indeed. And what accites your most worshipful thought to think so?

POINS Why, because you have been so lewd and so much engraffed to Falstaff.

PRINCE And to thee.

POINS By this light, I am well spoke on; I can hear it with mine own ears. The worst that they can say of me is that I am a second brother and that I am a proper fellow of my hands, and those two things I confess I cannot help. By the Mass, here comes Bardolph.

Enter Bardolph and Boy [*Page*].

PRINCE And the boy that I gave Falstaff. 'A had him

35 push attack, thrust **37 meet** fitting, appropriate **41 Very hardly** scarcely, with difficulty **47 ostentation** outward indication **54 keeps the roadway** i.e., follows the common way of thinking **56 accites** induces (with a quibble on "summons") **58 lewd** base **59 engraffed** closely attached **63 second brother** i.e., a younger son, without inheritance **63–64 proper . . . hands** i.e., good fighter

from me Christian, and look if the fat villain have not transformed him ape.

BARDOLPH God save Your Grace!

PRINCE And yours, most noble Bardolph!

POINS [*To Bardolph*] Come, you virtuous ass, you bashful fool, must you be blushing? Wherefore blush you now? What a maidenly man-at-arms are you become! Is 't such a matter to get a pottle pot's maidenhead?

PAGE 'A calls me e'en now, my lord, through a red lattice, and I could discern no part of his face from the window. At last I spied his eyes, and methought he had made two holes in the alewife's petticoat and so peeped through.

PRINCE Has not the boy profited?

BARDOLPH Away, you whoreson upright rabbit, away!

PAGE Away, you rascally Althaea's dream, away!

PRINCE Instruct us, boy. What dream, boy?

PAGE Marry, my lord, Althaea dreamt she was delivered of a firebrand, and therefore I call him her dream.

PRINCE A crown's worth of good interpretation. There 'tis, boy. [*He gives money.*]

POINS O, that this blossom could be kept from cankers! Well, there is sixpence to preserve thee.

[*He gives money.*]

BARDOLPH An you do not make him be hanged among you, the gallows shall have wrong.

PRINCE And how doth thy master, Bardolph?

BARDOLPH Well, my lord. He heard of Your Grace's coming to town. There's a letter for you.

[*He gives a letter.*]

67–68 have . . . ape i.e., has not dressed him fantastically **72 blushing** i.e., red-faced (from drink). **Wherefore** why **74 get . . . maidenhead** i.e., knock off a two-quart tankard of ale **75 e'en now** just now, a moment ago **75–76 red lattice** (Red lattices identified taverns.) **76 discern** distinguish **82 Althaea's dream** (Althaea dreamed that her newborn son would live only so long as a brand on the fire lasted. The Page mistakenly relates Hecuba's dream: when pregnant with Paris, Hecuba dreamed she would be delivered of a firebrand that would destroy Troy.) **86 crown** i.e., 5 shillings **88 cankers** cankerworms, worms that destroy buds and leaves **89 to preserve thee** (Allusion to the cross on the sixpence.) **90 An** if

POINS Delivered with good respect. And how doth the martlemas, your master?

BARDOLPH In bodily health, sir.

POINS Marry, the immortal part needs a physician, but that moves not him. Though that be sick, it dies not.

PRINCE I do allow this wen to be as familiar with me as my dog, and he holds his place, for look you how he writes. [*He shows a letter to Poins.*]

POINS [*Reading the superscription*] "John Falstaff, knight."—Every man must know that as oft as he has occasion to name himself, even like those that are kin to the King, for they never prick their finger but they say, "There's some of the King's blood spilt." "How comes that?" says he that takes upon him not to conceive. The answer is as ready as a borrower's cap: "I am the King's poor cousin, sir."

PRINCE Nay, they will be kin to us, or they will fetch it from Japheth. But the letter. [*He reads.*] "Sir John Falstaff, knight, to the son of the King nearest his father, Harry Prince of Wales, greeting."

POINS Why, this is a certificate.

PRINCE Peace! [*He reads.*] "I will imitate the honorable Romans in brevity."

POINS He sure means brevity in breath, short-winded.

PRINCE [*Reads*] "I commend me to thee, I commend thee, and I leave thee. Be not too familiar with Poins, for he misuses thy favors so much that he swears thou art to marry his sister Nell. Repent at idle times as thou mayst, and so farewell.

"Thine, by yea and no, which is as much as to say, as thou usest him, Jack Falstaff with my familiars, John with my brothers and sisters, and Sir John with all Europe."

95 good respect proper ceremony. (Said ironically.) **96 martlemas** i.e., Martinmas beef, beef slaughtered on November 11 (and fattened beforehand) **100 wen** swelling, tumor **104 Every . . . that** i.e., Falstaff wants to make sure that everyone is aware of his knightly rank **108–109 takes . . . conceive** pretends not to understand **109 as ready . . . cap** i.e., as quick in coming forth as a cap is doffed by one seeking aid **111–112 fetch . . . Japheth** i.e., trace their ancestry back to Japheth, one of the sons of Noah. (Genesis 10.2–5.) **115 certificate** legal document **124 by yea and no** (A Puritan oath.) **125 familiars** intimate friends

POINS My lord, I'll steep this letter in sack and make 128
him eat it.

PRINCE That's to make him eat twenty of his words. But 130
do you use me thus, Ned? Must I marry your sister?

POINS God send the wench no worse fortune! But I never said so.

PRINCE Well, thus we play the fools with the time, and the spirits of the wise sit in the clouds and mock us.—Is your master here in London?

BARDOLPH Yea, my lord.

PRINCE Where sups he? Doth the old boar feed in the
old frank? 139

BARDOLPH At the old place, my lord, in Eastcheap.

PRINCE What company?

PAGE Ephesians, my lord, of the old church. 142

PRINCE Sup any women with him?

PAGE None, my lord, but old Mistress Quickly and Mistress Doll Tearsheet.

PRINCE What pagan may that be? 146

PAGE A proper gentlewoman, sir, and a kinswoman of my master's.

PRINCE Even such kin as the parish heifers are to the
town bull. Shall we steal upon them, Ned, at supper? 150

POINS I am your shadow, my lord; I'll follow you.

PRINCE Sirrah, you boy, and Bardolph, no word to your master that I am yet come to town. There's for your silence. [*He gives money.*]

BARDOLPH I have no tongue, sir.

PAGE And for mine, sir, I will govern it.

PRINCE Fare you well; go. [*Exeunt Bardolph and Page.*]
This Doll Tearsheet should be some road. 158

POINS I warrant you, as common as the way between Saint Albans and London.

PRINCE How might we see Falstaff bestow himself to- 161
night in his true colors, and not ourselves be seen?

128 steep soak **130 twenty** i.e., a considerable number **139 frank** sty, pen. (Often thought to refer to the Boar's Head Tavern.) **142 Ephesians . . . church** i.e., good fellows of the usual, disreputable fellowship **146 pagan** i.e., harlot **150 town bull** a communally owned bull that local farmers could mate with their heifers **158 should** must. **road** i.e., common whore **161 bestow** behave

POINS Put on two leathern jerkins and aprons, and wait 163
upon him at his table as drawers. 164
PRINCE From a god to a bull? A heavy descension! It 165
was Jove's case. From a prince to a prentice? A low 166
transformation! That shall be mine, for in everything
the purpose must weigh with the folly. Follow me, 168
Ned. *Exeunt.*

✤

2.3 *Enter Northumberland, his wife* [*Lady Northumberland*], *and the wife to Harry Percy* [*Lady Percy*].

NORTHUMBERLAND
I pray thee, loving wife and gentle daughter, 1
Give even way unto my rough affairs. 2
Put not you on the visage of the times 3
And be like them to Percy troublesome.
LADY NORTHUMBERLAND
I have given over; I will speak no more.
Do what you will; your wisdom be your guide.
NORTHUMBERLAND
Alas, sweet wife, my honor is at pawn,
And, but my going, nothing can redeem it. 8
LADY PERCY
O, yet for God's sake, go not to these wars!
The time was, Father, that you broke your word,
When you were more endeared to it than now, 11
When your own Percy, when my heart's dear Harry,
Threw many a northward look to see his father
Bring up his powers; but he did long in vain. 14
Who then persuaded you to stay at home?
There were two honors lost, yours and your son's.

163 jerkins jackets **164 drawers** tapsters, tavern waiters **165 heavy descension** grievous descent **166 Jove's case** (Jupiter, for the love of Europa, transformed himself into a bull.) **168 weigh with** match, balance

2.3. Location: Warkworth. Before Northumberland's castle.
1 daughter i.e., daughter-in-law **2 even way** free scope **3 Put . . . times** i.e., don't look as bleak or troubled as are the times **8 but** except for **11 endeared** pledged, bound by affection **14 powers** armed forces

For yours, the God of heaven brighten it! 17
For his, it stuck upon him as the sun
In the gray vault of heaven, and by his light 19
Did all the chivalry of England move 20
To do brave acts. He was indeed the glass 21
Wherein the noble youth did dress themselves.
He had no legs that practiced not his gait; 23
And speaking thick, which nature made his blemish, 24
Became the accents of the valiant,
For those that could speak low and tardily
Would turn their own perfection to abuse 27
To seem like him. So that in speech, in gait,
In diet, in affections of delight, 29
In military rules, humors of blood, 30
He was the mark and glass, copy and book, 31
That fashioned others. And him, O, wondrous him!
O, miracle of men! Him did you leave,
Second to none, unseconded by you, 34
To look upon the hideous god of war
In disadvantage, to abide a field 36
Where nothing but the sound of Hotspur's name
Did seem defensible. So you left him. 38
Never, O, never do his ghost the wrong
To hold your honor more precise and nice 40
With others than with him! Let them alone.
The Marshal and the Archbishop are strong.
Had my sweet Harry had but half their numbers,
Today might I, hanging on Hotspur's neck,
Have talked of Monmouth's grave.

NORTHUMBERLAND Beshrew your heart, 45
Fair daughter, you do draw my spirits from me
With new lamenting ancient oversights. 47

17 For as for **19 gray** sky-blue **20 chivalry** men-at-arms **21 glass** mirror **23 He . . . gait** i.e., there was no man alive and able to walk who did not imitate Hotspur's stride **24 thick** impulsively, impetuously **27 turn . . . abuse** i.e., debase their own manner of speech and adopt his **29 affections of delight** choice of pleasurable occupations **30 humors of blood** temperament **31 mark** pattern, guiding object **34 unseconded** unsupported **36 In disadvantage** i.e., outnumbered. **abide a field** face a battle **38 defensible** able to make defense **40 nice** punctilious **45 Monmouth's** i.e., Prince Hal's (since he was born at Monmouth). **Beshrew your heart** (A reproachful oath.) **47 new lamenting** lamenting anew

But I must go and meet with danger there,
Or it will seek me in another place
And find me worse provided.
LADY NORTHUMBERLAND O, fly to Scotland, 50
Till that the nobles and the armèd commons
Have of their puissance made a little taste. 52

LADY PERCY
If they get ground and vantage of the King, 53
Then join you with them like a rib of steel,
To make strength stronger; but, for all our loves,
First let them try themselves. So did your son; 56
He was so suffered. So came I a widow, 57
And never shall have length of life enough
To rain upon remembrance with mine eyes, 59
That it may grow and sprout as high as heaven
For recordation to my noble husband. 61

NORTHUMBERLAND
Come, come, go in with me. 'Tis with my mind
As with the tide swelled up unto his height,
That makes a still-stand, running neither way. 64
Fain would I go to meet the Archbishop, 65
But many thousand reasons hold me back.
I will resolve for Scotland. There am I, 67
Till time and vantage crave my company. *Exeunt.* 68

✤

2.4 *Enter a Drawer, [Francis, and another].*

FRANCIS What the devil hast thou brought there?
Applejohns? Thou knowest Sir John cannot endure 2
an applejohn.

50 provided prepared **52 taste** trial **53 get . . . of** achieve a military advantage over **56 try** test **57 suffered** allowed to proceed. **came** became **59 rain . . . eyes** water remembrance with my tears, as though it were a plant like rosemary **61 recordation** remembrance, memorial **64 still-stand** point of balance, standstill **65 Fain** gladly **67 resolve for** decide to go to **68 vantage** opportunity

2.4. Location: London. A tavern in Eastcheap, usually identified as the Boar's Head. Some tavern furniture is provided.
2 Applejohns a kind of apple eaten when shriveled and withered

SECOND DRAWER Mass, thou sayst true. The Prince 4
once set a dish of applejohns before him, and told
him there were five more Sir Johns, and, putting off
his hat, said, "I will now take my leave of these six dry,
round, old, withered knights." It angered him to the
heart. But he hath forgot that.

FRANCIS Why, then, cover, and set them down. And 10
see if thou canst find out Sneak's noise; Mistress Tear- 11
sheet would fain hear some music.

Enter Will [a third Drawer].

THIRD DRAWER Dispatch! The room where they supped 13
is too hot; they'll come in straight. 14

FRANCIS Sirrah, here will be the Prince and Master
Poins anon, and they will put on two of our jerkins
and aprons, and Sir John must not know of it. Bardolph hath brought word.

THIRD DRAWER By the Mass, here will be old utas. It 19
will be an excellent stratagem.

SECOND DRAWER I'll see if I can find out Sneak. *Exit.*

Enter Mistress Quickly [the hostess] and Doll Tearsheet.

HOSTESS I' faith, sweetheart, methinks now you are in
an excellent good temperality. Your pulsidge beats as 23
extraordinarily as heart would desire, and your color, 24
I warrant you, is as red as any rose, in good truth, la!
But, i' faith, you have drunk too much canaries, and 26
that's a marvelous searching wine, and it perfumes 27
the blood ere one can say, "What's this?" How do
you now?

DOLL Better than I was. Hem!

HOSTESS Why, that's well said. A good heart's worth gold. Lo, here comes Sir John.

Enter Sir John [Falstaff].

4 Mass i.e., by the Mass **10 cover** spread the cloth, set the table **11 noise** band of musicians **13 Dispatch** hurry up **14 straight** very soon **19 old utas** i.e., rare fun **23 temperality** i.e., temper. **pulsidge** i.e., pulse **24 extraordinarily** i.e., ordinarily **26 canaries** (A light, sweet wine from the Canary Islands.) **27 searching** potent

FALSTAFF [*Singing*] "When Arthur first in court"— 33
Empty the jordan. [*Exit a Drawer.*]—[*Singing.*] "And 34
was a worthy king." How now, Mistress Doll?
HOSTESS Sick of a calm, yea, good faith. 36
FALSTAFF So is all her sect. An they be once in a calm, 37
they are sick.
DOLL A pox damn you, you muddy rascal, is that all
the comfort you give me?
FALSTAFF You make fat rascals, Mistress Doll. 41
DOLL I make them? Gluttony and diseases make them;
I make them not.
FALSTAFF If the cook help to make the gluttony, you
help to make the diseases, Doll. We catch of you, Doll,
we catch of you. Grant that, my poor virtue, grant that.
DOLL Yea, joy, our chains and our jewels. 47
FALSTAFF "Your brooches, pearls, and ouches." For to 48
serve bravely is to come halting off, you know; to
come off the breach with his pike bent bravely, and to
surgery bravely; to venture upon the charged cham- 51
bers bravely— 52
DOLL Hang yourself, you muddy conger, hang yourself!
HOSTESS By my troth, this is the old fashion. You two
never meet but you fall to some discord. You are both,
i' good truth, as rheumatic as two dry toasts; you can- 57
not one bear with another's confirmities. What the 58
goodyear! One must bear, and that [*To Doll*] must be 59
you. You are the weaker vessel, as they say,
the emptier vessel.
DOLL Can a weak empty vessel bear such a huge full

33 When . . . court (A fragment from the ballad "Sir Launcelot du Lake.") **34 jordan** chamber pot **36 calm** i.e., qualm **37 sect** sex **41 rascals** (1) lean deer (2) good-for-nothings **47 Yea . . . jewels** i.e., yes, indeed, you *catch* or steal our valuables **48 ouches** jewels. (The line is from a ballad.) **51–52 charged chambers** small cannon; with bawdy double meaning, as also in *breach, pike, surgery* (venereal treatment), *conger* (eel, with sexual connotation), *bear* **57 rheumatic** (Blunder for *choleric* or *splenetic*?) **58 confirmities** (For *infirmities.*) **58–59 What the goodyear** (An expletive, meaning something like "what the devil.") **59 bear** (1) put up with another's infirmities (2) bear the weight of a lover (3) bear children

hogshead? There's a whole merchant's venture of Bor- 63
deaux stuff in him; you have not seen a hulk better 64
stuffed in the hold.—Come, I'll be friends with thee,
Jack. Thou art going to the wars, and whether I shall
ever see thee again or no there is nobody cares.

Enter Drawer.

DRAWER Sir, Ancient Pistol's below, and would speak 68
with you.

DOLL Hang him, swaggering rascal! Let him not come hither. It is the foul-mouthed'st rogue in England.

HOSTESS If he swagger, let him not come here. No, by
my faith, I must live among my neighbors. I'll no 73
swaggerers. I am in good name and fame with the
very best. Shut the door; there comes no swaggerers
here. I have not lived all this while to have swaggering
now. Shut the door, I pray you.

FALSTAFF Dost thou hear, Hostess?

HOSTESS Pray ye, pacify yourself, Sir John. There comes no swaggerers here.

FALSTAFF Dost thou hear? It is mine ancient.

HOSTESS Tilly-fally, Sir John, ne'er tell me. An your an- 82
cient swagger, 'a comes not in my doors. I was before 83
Master Tisick, the debuty, t'other day, and, as he said 84
to me, 'twas no longer ago than Wednesday last, i' good
faith, "Neighbor Quickly," says he—Master Dumbe,
our minister, was by then—"Neighbor Quickly," says
he, "receive those that are civil, for," said he, "you are 88
in an ill name." Now 'a said so, I can tell where- 89
upon. "For," says he, "you are an honest woman, and 90
well thought on; therefore take heed what guests you
receive. Receive," says he, "no swaggering compan- 92
ions." There comes none here. You would bless you 93
to hear what he said. No, I'll no swaggerers.

63 hogshead large cask. **venture** cargo **63–64 Bordeaux stuff** i.e., wine **64 hulk** large, unwieldy cargo ship **68 Ancient** ensign, standard-bearer **73 I'll no** I'll have no **82 Tilly-fally** i.e., fiddlesticks **82–83 An your ancient swagger, 'a** if your ensign is going to swagger, he **84 Tisick** (Literally, phthisic, a cough or consumption.) **debuty** deputy, deputy alderman **88–89 are . . . name** have a bad reputation **89–90 where-upon** upon what grounds **92–93 companions** ruffians **93 bless you** i.e., feel yourself fortunate

FALSTAFF He's no swaggerer, hostess; a tame cheater, i' faith; you may stroke him as gently as a puppy greyhound. He'll not swagger with a Barbary hen, if her feathers turn back in any show of resistance. Call him up, drawer. [*Exit Drawer.*]

HOSTESS Cheater, call you him? I will bar no honest man my house, nor no cheater, but I do not love swaggering, by my troth. I am the worse when one says "swagger." Feel, masters, how I shake; look you, I warrant you.

DOLL So you do, Hostess.

HOSTESS Do I? Yea, in very truth, do I, an 'twere an aspen leaf. I cannot abide swaggerers.

Enter Ancient Pistol, [*Bardolph,*] *and Boy* [*Page*].

PISTOL God save you, Sir John!

FALSTAFF Welcome, Ancient Pistol. Here, Pistol, I charge you with a cup of sack. Do you discharge upon mine hostess.

PISTOL I will discharge upon her, Sir John, with two bullets.

FALSTAFF She is pistol-proof, sir; you shall not hardly offend her.

HOSTESS Come, I'll drink no proofs nor no bullets. I'll drink no more than will do me good, for no man's pleasure, I.

PISTOL Then to you, Mistress Dorothy; I will charge you.

DOLL Charge me? I scorn you, scurvy companion. What, you poor, base, rascally, cheating, lack-linen mate? Away, you moldy rogue, away! I am meat for your master.

PISTOL I know you, Mistress Dorothy.

95 cheater decoy in a team of confidence men **97 Barbary hen** guinea hen. (Slang term for a prostitute.) **100 Cheater** (Mistress Quickly may understand the word as *escheator,* an officer of the King's exchequer.) **106 an 'twere** i.e., as if I were **110 charge** pledge, drink to. **discharge upon** toast; with bawdy double meaning; see also *charge, Pistol, bullets* (testicles), *meat* (slang for "whore"), etc. **114 shall not** i.e., shall. (A colloquial expression.) **115 offend** wound **122 lack-linen** i.e., without a shirt to your name **123 mate** low fellow. **meat** (with a pun on *mate;* pronounced alike)

DOLL Away, you cutpurse rascal! You filthy bung, away! By this wine, I'll thrust my knife in your moldy chops, an you play the saucy cuttle with me. Away, you bottle-ale rascal! You basket-hilt stale juggler, you! Since when, I pray you, sir? God's light, with two points on your shoulders? Much!

PISTOL God let me not live, but I will murder your ruff for this.

FALSTAFF No more, Pistol, I would not have you go off here. Discharge yourself of our company, Pistol.

HOSTESS No, good Captain Pistol, not here, sweet Captain.

DOLL Captain? Thou abominable damned cheater, art thou not ashamed to be called captain? An captains were of my mind, they would truncheon you out for taking their names upon you before you have earned them. You a captain? You slave, for what? For tearing a poor whore's ruff in a bawdy house? He a captain? Hang him, rogue! He lives upon moldy stewed prunes and dried cakes. A captain? God's light, these villains will make the word as odious as the word "occupy," which was an excellent good word before it was ill sorted. Therefore captains had need look to 't.

BARDOLPH Pray thee, go down, good Ancient.

FALSTAFF Hark thee hither, Mistress Doll.

PISTOL Not I. I tell thee what, Corporal Bardolph, I could tear her. I'll be revenged of her.

PAGE Pray thee, go down.

PISTOL I'll see her damned first, to Pluto's damned lake,
by this hand, to th' infernal deep,
With Erebus and tortures vile also.

126 bung (1) pickpocket (2) something that fills a hole **128 chops** cheeks. **cuttle** cutthroat or cutpurse **129 basket-hilt** basketlike hilt or handguard for a practice weapon only; see 3.2.65, note. (Doll scornfully accuses Pistol of avoiding danger by not using a real sword.) **juggler** imposter **130 Since when** i.e., since when do you claim to be so brave and military? **131 points** lace tags (for securing armor to the shoulders). **Much** (An exclamation of scornful incredulity.) **132 murder** i.e., tear. **ruff** pleated, starched collar **140 truncheon** cudgel **144 stewed prunes** (Associated with brothels.) **146 occupy** fornicate **147–148 ill sorted** corrupted, put in such bad company **148 had need** would do well to **149 go down** calm down, or, go downstairs and leave
154 Pluto's damned lake the river of the underworld **156 Erebus** the underworld

Hold hook and line, say I.
Down, down, dogs! Down, faitors! 158
Have we not Hiren here? 159

HOSTESS Good Captain Peesel, be quiet; 'tis very late, i' faith. I beseek you now, aggravate your choler. 161

PISTOL
These be good humors, indeed! Shall packhorses 162
And hollow pampered jades of Asia,
Which cannot go but thirty mile a day,
Compare with Caesars, and with Cannibals, 165
And Troiant Greeks? Nay, rather damn them with 166
King Cerberus, and let the welkin roar. 167
Shall we fall foul for toys? 168

HOSTESS By my troth, Captain, these are very bitter words.

BARDOLPH Begone, good Ancient. This will grow to a brawl anon.

PISTOL
Die men like dogs! Give crowns like pins! Have we not
Hiren here? 173

HOSTESS O' my word, Captain, there's none such here. 174
What the goodyear, do you think I would deny her? 175
For God's sake, be quiet.

PISTOL
Then feed, and be fat, my fair Calipolis. 177
Come, give 's some sack.

158 faitors imposters, cheats **159 Hiren** i.e., Pistol's fanciful name for his sword, with a seeming allusion to a lost play by Peele, *The Turkish Mahomet and Hiren the Fair Greek*. *Hiren* means Irene. (Throughout, Pistol's colorful speech is full of echoes from the contemporary theater.) **161 beseek** beseech. **aggravate** (For *moderate*.) **162 humors** whimsies of conduct **162–166 Shall . . . Greeks** (Misquotation from Marlowe's *Second Part of Tamburlaine*, 4.4.1–2.) **165 Cannibals** (The association here with Caesar would seem to suggest *Hannibals*, but *Cannibals* appears in the apparent source for this passage, John Eliot's *Ortho-epia Gallica*, 1593. Pistol is ready to take on Cannibals, Trojan Greeks, or anybody.) **166 Troiant** Trojan **167 Cerberus** three-headed dog guarding the entrance to Hades. **welkin** heavens **168 fall . . . toys** fall out over trifles **173 Give crowns like pins** pass out kingdoms as if they were of the value of a pin (as Tamburlaine does to his followers) **174 there's none such here** (The hostess seems to think that Pistol is asking after Hiren or Irene as though she were a boarder or habitué of the tavern.) **175 deny her** deny that she was here, if she were **177 Then . . . Calipolis** (Garbled version of a line in Peele's *The Battle of Alcazar*, 2.3.70.)

Si fortune me tormente, sperato me contento.
Fear we broadsides? No, let the fiend give fire.
Give me some sack, and, sweetheart, lie thou there.
[*He lays down his sword.*]
Come we to full points here, and are etceteras nothings?

FALSTAFF Pistol, I would be quiet.

PISTOL
Sweet knight, I kiss thy neaf.
What, we have seen the seven stars.

DOLL For God's sake, thrust him downstairs. I cannot endure such a fustian rascal.

PISTOL
Thrust him downstairs? Know we not Galloway nags?

FALSTAFF Quoit him down, Bardolph, like a shove-groat shilling. Nay, an 'a do nothing but speak nothing, 'a shall be nothing here.

BARDOLPH Come, get you downstairs.

PISTOL [*Snatching up his sword*]
What, shall we have incision? Shall we imbrue?
Then death rock me asleep, abridge my doleful days!
Why then, let grievous, ghastly, gaping wounds
Untwine the Sisters Three! Come, Atropos, I say!

HOSTESS Here's goodly stuff toward!

FALSTAFF Give me my rapier, boy.

DOLL I pray thee, Jack, I pray thee, do not draw.

FALSTAFF Get you downstairs. [*They fight.*]

HOSTESS Here's a goodly tumult! I'll forswear keeping house afore I'll be in these tirrits and frights. So, mur-

179 Si . . . contento if fortune torments me, hope contents me. (An ignorant medley of Spanish and Italian.) **180 broadsides** volleys fired from one side of a ship. **give fire** shoot **182 full points** full stops, periods; also, swords' points. **etceteras** (Probably with bawdy suggestion.) **184 neaf** fist **185 the seven stars** the Pleiades. (Pistol means they have enjoyed themselves at night.) **187 fustian** bombast, worthless **188 Galloway nags** a Scottish breed of small but swift horses (here used abusively to mean "harlots") **189 Quoit** throw **189–190 shove-groat shilling** an Edward VI shilling used in shove-groat, a game in which the coins were shoved toward a mark **190 an 'a** if he **190–191 speak nothing** speak nonsense **191 nothing here** gone from here **193 incision** bloodshed. **imbrue** shed blood **194 death . . . asleep** (Quotation from a current poem about Anne Boleyn and her brother as they awaited execution.) **196 Sisters Three** i.e., the three Fates, Clotho, Lachesis, and Atropos. Atropos severed the thread of life. **197 toward** forthcoming **202 tirrits** fits of temper

der, I warrant now. Alas, alas, put up your naked weapons, put up your naked weapons.

[*Exit Bardolph, driving Pistol out.*]

DOLL I pray thee, Jack, be quiet; the rascal's gone. Ah, you whoreson little valiant villain, you!

HOSTESS Are you not hurt i' the groin? Methought 'a made a shrewd thrust at your belly.

[*Enter Bardolph.*]

FALSTAFF Have you turned him out o' doors?

BARDOLPH Yea, sir. The rascal's drunk. You have hurt him, sir, i' the shoulder.

FALSTAFF A rascal! To brave me?

DOLL Ah, you sweet little rogue, you! Alas, poor ape, how thou sweat'st! Come, let me wipe thy face. Come on, you whoreson chops. Ah, rogue, i' faith, I love thee. Thou art as valorous as Hector of Troy, worth five of Agamemnon, and ten times better than the Nine Worthies. Ah, villain!

FALSTAFF A rascally slave! I will toss the rogue in a blanket.

DOLL Do, an thou dar'st for thy heart. An thou dost, I'll canvass thee between a pair of sheets.

Enter Music.

PAGE The music is come, sir.

FALSTAFF Let them play. Play, sirs. Sit on my knee, Doll. A rascal bragging slave! The rogue fled from me like quicksilver.

DOLL [*Sitting on his knee*] I' faith, and thou followedst him like a church. Thou whoreson little tidy Bartholomew boar-pig, when wilt thou leave fighting o' days

208 shrewd vicious **215 chops** fat jaws **216 Hector of Troy** leader of the Trojans; the type of valor **217 Agamemnon** leader of the Greeks at Troy **218 Nine Worthies** Arthur, Charlemagne, Godfrey of Boulogne; Hector, Alexander, Julius Caesar; Joshua, David, Judas Maccabaeus
221 for thy heart to save your life **222 canvass** toss. (Doll gives a sexual interpretation to Falstaff's phrase, *toss . . . in a blanket,* which means to subject a coward to ignominious treatment.) **s.d. Music** musicians
228 a church i.e., a ponderous structure (?) **tidy** plump, tender
228–229 Bartholomew boar-pig (Allusion to the serving of roast pig at Bartholomew Fair, August 24, in Smithfield.)

and foining o' nights, and begin to patch up thine old body for heaven?

Enter [*behind*] *Prince and Poins* [*disguised as drawers*].

FALSTAFF Peace, good Doll, do not speak like a death's-head; do not bid me remember mine end.

DOLL Sirrah, what humor's the Prince of?

FALSTAFF A good shallow young fellow. 'A would have made a good pantler, 'a would ha' chipped bread well.

DOLL They say Poins has a good wit.

FALSTAFF He a good wit? Hang him, baboon! His wit's as thick as Tewkesbury mustard. There's no more conceit in him than is in a mallet.

DOLL Why does the Prince love him so, then?

FALSTAFF Because their legs are both of a bigness, and 'a plays at quoits well, and eats conger and fennel, and drinks off candles' ends for flapdragons, and rides the wild mare with the boys, and jumps upon joint stools, and swears with a good grace, and wears his boots very smooth like unto the sign of the Leg, and breeds no bate with telling of discreet stories; and such other gambol faculties 'a has that show a weak mind and an able body, for the which the Prince admits him. For the Prince himself is such another; the weight of a hair will turn the scales between their avoirdupois.

230 foining thrusting, fornicating **232–233 death's-head** skull, used emblematically as a reminder of the inevitability of death **234 what . . . of** what is the Prince's disposition, temperament, mood
236 pantler pantry worker. **chipped bread** cut off the hard bread crusts **239 Tewkesbury mustard** (Tewkesbury in Gloucestershire was famous for mustard balls.) **239–240 conceit** wit **240 mallet** wooden hammer, heavy and not at all sharp **242 of a bigness** of equal size
243 conger and fennel conger eel seasoned with a yellow-flowered herb. (Rich fare, likely to dull the wits.) **244 drinks . . . flapdragons** i.e., drinks liquor with a lighted candle floating in it. (An act of bravado.)
245 wild mare seesaw, or a game in which boys pile on top of one another until the *mare* collapses **245–246 joint stools** stools made by a joiner or craftsman in furniture, etc. **247 smooth** i.e., well-fitting. **sign . . . Leg** sign over a bootmaker's shop **248 breeds no bate** causes no strife. (Falstaff may be saying sardonically that Poins is not one to make his listeners impatient by limiting himself to discreet stories.)
249 gambol sportive **253 avoirdupois** weight

PRINCE [*To Poins*] Would not this nave of a wheel have his ears cut off?

POINS Let's beat him before his whore.

PRINCE Look whe'er the withered elder hath not his poll clawed like a parrot.

POINS Is it not strange that desire should so many years outlive performance?

FALSTAFF Kiss me, Doll.

PRINCE [*To Poins*] Saturn and Venus this year in conjunction? What says th' almanac to that?

POINS And look whether the fiery Trigon, his man, be not lisping to his master's old tables, his notebook, his counsel keeper.

FALSTAFF Thou dost give me flattering busses.

DOLL By my troth, I kiss thee with a most constant heart.

FALSTAFF I am old, I am old.

DOLL I love thee better than I love e'er a scurvy young boy of them all.

FALSTAFF What stuff wilt have a kirtle of? I shall receive money o' Thursday; shalt have a cap tomorrow. A merry song, come. It grows late; we'll to bed. Thou'lt forget me when I am gone.

DOLL By my troth, thou'lt set me a-weeping an thou sayst so. Prove that ever I dress myself handsome till thy return—well, hearken a' th' end.

FALSTAFF Some sack, Francis.

254 nave hub. (Refers to Falstaff's rotundity; with a pun on *knave*.) **254–255 have . . . off** i.e., as the punishment for slandering royalty **256 before** in front of **257 elder** (1) elder tree (2) old man **257–258 poll . . . parrot** (Doll is probably rumpling the hair on Falstaff's head, his *poll*.) **262–263 Saturn . . . conjunction** i.e., will the planets that govern old age and love be near one another in the heavens **264 fiery Trigon** (The twelve signs of the zodiac were divided into four *trigons* or triangles, one of which, consisting of Aries, Leo, and Sagittarius, was characterized as fiery. These three form a triangle because they are not contiguous on the circle of the zodiac but occur at points equivalent roughly to April, August, and December, at 120-degree intervals. The other three *trigons* were characterized as watery, airy, and earthy. The joke here is directed against Bardolph's fiery face.) **265 lisping . . . notebook** whispering lovingly to Falstaff's old confidante, i.e., Mistress Quickly. **tables** notebook (for assignations) **267 busses** kisses **273 stuff** material. **kirtle** skirt **277 an** if **279 hearken a' th' end** i.e., wait to see how it turns out

PRINCE, POINS [*Coming forward*] Anon, anon, sir. 281
FALSTAFF Ha? A bastard son of the King's? And art not
thou Poins his brother?
PRINCE Why, thou globe of sinful continents, what a 284
life dost thou lead!
FALSTAFF A better than thou. I am a gentleman; thou
art a drawer.
PRINCE Very true, sir, and I come to draw you out by 288
the ears. 289
HOSTESS O, the Lord preserve Thy Grace! By my troth,
welcome to London. Now, the Lord bless that sweet
face of thine! O Jesu, are you come from Wales?
FALSTAFF Thou whoreson mad compound of majesty, 293
by this light flesh and corrupt blood, thou art wel- 294
come.
DOLL How, you fat fool! I scorn you.
POINS My lord, he will drive you out of your revenge
and turn all to a merriment, if you take not the heat. 298
PRINCE You whoreson candle-mine you, how vilely 299
did you speak of me even now before this honest, vir- 300
tuous, civil gentlewoman!
HOSTESS God's blessing of your good heart! And so she
is, by my troth.
FALSTAFF Didst thou hear me?
PRINCE Yea, and you knew me, as you did when you 305
ran away by Gad's Hill. You knew I was at your back, 306
and spoke it on purpose to try my patience.
FALSTAFF No, no, no, not so, I did not think thou wast
within hearing.
PRINCE I shall drive you then to confess the willful
abuse, and then I know how to handle you.
FALSTAFF No abuse, Hal, o' mine honor, no abuse.
PRINCE Not? To dispraise me, and call me pantler and 313
bread-chipper and I know not what?

281 Anon, anon (The cry of the drawer, or tapster, in answering his customers' demands for service, as in *1 Henry IV,* 2.4.21 ff.) **284 globe** (1) terrestrial globe (2) sphere. **continents** (1) the continents of the earth (2) contents (3) containers (of sin) **288–289 draw . . . ears** (as one might grab by the ears a naughty child caught in some mischief) **293 compound** lump, mass **294 light . . . blood** i.e., Doll **298 if . . . heat** if you don't strike while the iron is hot **299 candle-mine** magazine or storehouse of tallow **300 honest** chaste **305–306 Yea . . . Gad's Hill** (See *1 Henry IV,* 2.4.) **313 Not** i.e., you mean it's not abuse?

FALSTAFF No abuse, Hal.

POINS No abuse?

FALSTAFF No abuse, Ned, i' the world, honest Ned, none. I dispraised him before the wicked, that the wicked might not fall in love with thee [*To Hal*]; in which doing, I have done the part of a careful friend and a true subject, and thy father is to give me thanks for it. No abuse, Hal. None, Ned, none. No, faith, boys, none.

PRINCE See now whether pure fear and entire cowardice doth not make thee wrong this virtuous gentlewoman to close with us. Is she of the wicked? Is thine hostess here of the wicked? Or is thy boy of the wicked? Or honest Bardolph, whose zeal burns in his nose, of the wicked?

POINS Answer, thou dead elm, answer.

FALSTAFF The fiend hath pricked down Bardolph irrecoverable, and his face is Lucifer's privy kitchen, where he doth nothing but roast maltworms. For the boy, there is a good angel about him, but the devil blinds him too.

PRINCE For the women?

FALSTAFF For one of them, she's in hell already and burns poor souls. For th' other, I owe her money, and whether she be damned for that I know not.

HOSTESS No, I warrant you.

FALSTAFF No, I think thou art not; I think thou art quit for that. Marry, there is another indictment upon thee, for suffering flesh to be eaten in thy house, contrary to the law, for the which I think thou wilt howl.

HOSTESS All victuallers do so. What's a joint of mutton or two in a whole Lent?

PRINCE You, gentlewoman—

324 entire sheer **326 close** come to terms, agree **331 pricked down** marked, or designated **332 privy** private **333 maltworms** topers, drunkards. **For** as for **335 blinds** (A textual crux. The Folio reads *outbids;* sometimes emended to *attends* or *binds.*) **338 burns** i.e., infects with venereal disease **339 damned** (since usury was condemned by the church as well as the state) **341–342 quit for that** (1) acquitted of that charge (2) repaid (as much as you are ever likely to be)
343 flesh to be eaten (Allusion to enactments to prevent the sale of meat in Lent; with sexual double entendre on *mutton,* whore.) **344 howl** (like damned souls in hell) **345 victuallers** i.e., innkeepers

DOLL What says Your Grace?

FALSTAFF His Grace says that which his flesh rebels 349
against. *Peto knocks at door.*

HOSTESS Who knocks so loud at door? Look to the door there, Francis.

[*Francis goes to the door. Enter Peto.*]

PRINCE Peto, how now, what news?

PETO
The King your father is at Westminster,
And there are twenty weak and wearied posts 355
Come from the north. And as I came along
I met and overtook a dozen captains,
Bareheaded, sweating, knocking at the taverns,
And asking everyone for Sir John Falstaff.

PRINCE
By heaven, Poins, I feel me much to blame,
So idly to profane the precious time,
When tempest of commotion, like the south 362
Borne with black vapor, doth begin to melt 363
And drop upon our bare unarmèd heads.—
Give me my sword and cloak.—Falstaff, good night.
Exeunt Prince and Poins, [*and Peto*].

FALSTAFF Now comes in the sweetest morsel of the night, and we must hence and leave it unpicked. [*Knocking within. Bardolph goes to the door.*] More knocking at the door!

[*Bardolph returns.*]

How now, what's the matter?

BARDOLPH
You must away to court, sir, presently. 371
A dozen captains stay at door for you. 372

FALSTAFF [*To the Page*] Pay the musicians, sirrah. Farewell, hostess; farewell, Doll. You see, my good wenches, how men of merit are sought after. The un-

349 Grace (1) royal grace (2) inclination toward spiritual grace. (The Prince may call Doll "gentlewoman," says Falstaff, but the flesh is ever rebellious; the Prince as a man knows Doll to be something very different.) **355 posts** messengers **362 commotion** insurrection. **south** south wind (regarded as a breeder of tempests) **363 Borne** laden **371 presently** immediately **372 stay** wait

deserver may sleep, when the man of action is called on. Farewell, good wenches. If I be not sent away post, 377
I will see you again ere I go.

DOLL I cannot speak. If my heart be not ready to burst—well, sweet Jack, have a care of thyself.

FALSTAFF Farewell, farewell.

Exit [*with Bardolph and Page*].

HOSTESS Well, fare thee well. I have known thee these twenty-nine years, come peascod time, but an honest- 383
er and truer-hearted man—well, fare thee well.

BARDOLPH [*At the door*] Mistress Tearsheet!

HOSTESS What's the matter?

BARDOLPH Bid Mistress Tearsheet come to my master.

HOSTESS O, run, Doll, run; run, good Doll. Come.—
She comes blubbered.—Yea, will you come, Doll? 389

Exeunt.

✤

377 post immediately **383 peascod time** i.e., early summer, when peas are still unripe **389 blubbered** disfigured with weeping

3.1 *Enter the King in his nightgown, alone* [*with a Page*].

KING

Go call the Earls of Surrey and of Warwick;
But ere they come, bid them o'erread these letters 2
And well consider of them. Make good speed.
[*He gives letters. Exit Page.*]
How many thousand of my poorest subjects
Are at this hour asleep! O sleep, O gentle sleep,
Nature's soft nurse, how have I frighted thee,
That thou no more wilt weigh my eyelids down
And steep my senses in forgetfulness?
Why rather, sleep, liest thou in smoky cribs, 9
Upon uneasy pallets stretching thee, 10
And hushed with buzzing night-flies to thy slumber,
Than in the perfumed chambers of the great,
Under the canopies of costly state, 13
And lulled with sound of sweetest melody?
O thou dull god, why liest thou with the vile 15
In loathsome beds, and leavest the kingly couch
A watch-case or a common 'larum bell? 17
Wilt thou upon the high and giddy mast
Seal up the shipboy's eyes, and rock his brains
In cradle of the rude imperious surge 20
And in the visitation of the winds, 21
Who take the ruffian billows by the top, 22
Curling their monstrous heads and hanging them
With deafing clamor in the slippery clouds, 24
That, with the hurly, death itself awakes? 25
Canst thou, O partial sleep, give thy repose
To the wet sea-boy in an hour so rude,
And, in the calmest and most stillest night,
With all appliances and means to boot, 29

3.1. Location: Westminster. The royal court.
s.d. nightgown dressing gown **2 o'erread** read over **9 cribs** hovels **10 uneasy** uncomfortable. **thee** thyself **13 state** magnificence **15 dull** drowsy. **vile** low in rank **17 watch-case** sentry box, or a space in which the occupant is restlessly aware of the passage of time **20 rude** turbulent **21 visitation** violent onset **22 Who** which, i.e., the winds **24 deafing** deafening. **slippery** quickly slipping by **25 That** so that. **hurly** tumult **29 appliances** devices. **to boot** as well, besides

Deny it to a king? Then happy low, lie down!
Uneasy lies the head that wears a crown.

Enter Warwick, Surrey, and Sir John Blunt.

WARWICK
Many good morrows to Your Majesty!
KING Is it good morrow, lords?
WARWICK 'Tis one o'clock, and past.
KING
Why, then, good morrow to you all, my lords.
Have you read o'er the letters that I sent you?
WARWICK We have, my liege.
KING
Then you perceive the body of our kingdom
How foul it is, what rank diseases grow,
And with what danger, near the heart of it.
WARWICK
It is but as a body yet distempered,
Which to his former strength may be restored
With good advice and little medicine.
My Lord Northumberland will soon be cooled.
KING
O God, that one might read the book of fate,
And see the revolution of the times
Make mountains level, and the continent,
Weary of solid firmness, melt itself
Into the sea, and other times to see
The beachy girdle of the ocean
Too wide for Neptune's hips, how chance's mocks
And changes fill the cup of alteration
With divers liquors! O, if this were seen,
The happiest youth, viewing his progress through,
What perils past, what crosses to ensue,
Would shut the book, and sit him down and die.

30 low humble persons **31 s.d. Sir John Blunt** (Since he says nothing and is omitted from the Folio, his presence may be unnecessary, but see l. 35, "to you all.") **39 rank** festering **41 distempered** sick **42 his** its **43 little** a little **46 revolution of** changes brought by **47 continent** dry land **51 Too wide** i.e., vast in expanse, when the ocean recedes. **chance's mocks** (A textual crux. The quarto and Folio read *chances mocks;* sometimes emended to *chances mock.*) **54 progress through** life's progress from beginning to end **55 crosses** afflictions

'Tis not ten years gone
Since Richard and Northumberland, great friends,
Did feast together, and in two years after
Were they at wars. It is but eight years since
This Percy was the man nearest my soul, 61
Who like a brother toiled in my affairs
And laid his love and life under my foot, 63
Yea, for my sake, even to the eyes of Richard 64
Gave him defiance. But which of you was by—
[*To Warwick*] You, cousin Nevil, as I may remember— 66
When Richard, with his eye brimful of tears,
Then checked and rated by Northumberland, 68
Did speak these words, now proved a prophecy?
"Northumberland, thou ladder by the which 70
My cousin Bolingbroke ascends my throne"—
Though then, God knows, I had no such intent,
But that necessity so bowed the state
That I and greatness were compelled to kiss—
"The time shall come," thus did he follow it,
"The time will come, that foul sin, gathering head,
Shall break into corruption"—so went on, 77
Foretelling this same time's condition 78
And the division of our amity.

WARWICK
There is a history in all men's lives,
Figuring the nature of the times deceased, 81
The which observed, a man may prophesy,
With a near aim, of the main chance of things 83
As yet not come to life, who in their seeds 84
And weak beginnings lie intreasurèd. 85
Such things become the hatch and brood of time, 86
And by the necessary form of this 87
King Richard might create a perfect guess
That great Northumberland, then false to him,
Would of that seed grow to a greater falseness,

61 This Percy i.e., Northumberland **63 under my foot** i.e., under my control **64 to the eyes** i.e., face to face **66 Nevil** (An error; this Earl of Warwick's surname is Beauchamp.) **68 checked and rated** rebuked **70–77 Northumberland . . . corruption** (See *Richard II,* 5.1.55 ff.) **78 same** present **81 Figuring** depicting. **deceased** past **83 main chance** general probability **84 who** which **85 intreasurèd** stored up **86 hatch and brood** offspring **87 necessary . . . this** logical consequence of this principle

Which should not find a ground to root upon
Unless on you.

KING Are these things then necessities?
Then let us meet them like necessities;
And that same word even now cries out on us. 94
They say the Bishop and Northumberland
Are fifty thousand strong.

WARWICK It cannot be, my lord.
Rumor doth double, like the voice and echo,
The numbers of the feared. Please it Your Grace
To go to bed. Upon my soul, my lord,
The powers that you already have sent forth
Shall bring this prize in very easily.
To comfort you the more, I have received
A certain instance that Glendower is dead. 103
Your Majesty hath been this fortnight ill,
And these unseasoned hours perforce must add 105
Unto your sickness.

KING I will take your counsel.
And were these inward wars once out of hand, 107
We would, dear lords, unto the Holy Land. *Exeunt.*

✤

3.2 *Enter Justice Shallow and Justice Silence.*

SHALLOW Come on, come on, come on, give me your hand, sir, give me your hand, sir. An early stirrer, by the rood! And how doth my good cousin Silence? 3

SILENCE Good morrow, good cousin Shallow.

SHALLOW And how doth my cousin your bedfellow? And your fairest daughter and mine, my goddaughter Ellen?

SILENCE Alas, a black ouzel, cousin Shallow! 8

SHALLOW By yea and no, sir. I dare say my cousin Wil-

94 cries out on denounces **103 certain instance** unquestionable proof **105 unseasoned** unseasonable, late **107 inward** civil. **out of hand** done with

3.2. Location: Gloucestershire. Before Justice Shallow's house. A table and chairs must be provided onstage.
3 rood cross. **cousin** kinsman (as also in ll. 4, 5, and 9) **8 ouzel** blackbird. (Ellen is *black* or dark-complexioned, not fair.)

liam is become a good scholar. He is at Oxford still, is he not?

SILENCE Indeed, sir, to my cost.

SHALLOW 'A must then to the Inns o' Court shortly. I was once of Clement's Inn, where I think they will talk of mad Shallow yet.

SILENCE You were called "lusty Shallow" then, cousin.

SHALLOW By the Mass, I was called anything, and I would have done anything indeed too, and roundly too. There was I, and Little John Doit of Staffordshire, and black George Barnes, and Francis Pickbone, and Will Squele, a Cotswold man. You had not four such swinge-bucklers in all the Inns o' Court again. And I may say to you, we knew where the bona-robas were and had the best of them all at commandment. Then was Jack Falstaff, now Sir John, a boy, and page to Thomas Mowbray, Duke of Norfolk.

SILENCE This Sir John, cousin, that comes hither anon about soldiers?

SHALLOW The same Sir John, the very same. I see him break Scoggin's head at the court gate, when 'a was a crack not thus high. And the very same day did I fight with one Samson Stockfish, a fruiterer, behind Gray's Inn. Jesu, Jesu, the mad days that I have spent! And to see how many of my old acquaintance are dead!

SILENCE We shall all follow, cousin.

SHALLOW Certain, 'tis certain, very sure, very sure. Death, as the Psalmist saith, is certain to all, all shall die. How a good yoke of bullocks at Stamford fair?

13 Inns o' Court legal societies of London **14 Clement's Inn** one of the Inns of Chancery; in Shallow's time, these institutions prepared one for the Inns of Court **16 lusty** merry, lascivious **18 roundly** thoroughly, without ceremony **21 Cotswold** from the Cotswold Hills in Gloucestershire **22 swinge-bucklers** swashbucklers, roisterers **23 bona-robas** good-looking wenches, smart prostitutes **24 at commandment** at our beck and call **25–26 page to Thomas Mowbray** (Both Sir John Oldcastle, Falstaff's original, and Sir John Fastolfe, for whom Falstaff was renamed, were pages to the Duke of Norfolk, who figures in the play *Richard II*.) **29 see** saw **30 Scoggin** (Perhaps John Scogan, court jester to Edward IV and protagonist of an Elizabethan jestbook known as "Scogan's Jests.") **31 crack** pert little boy **33 Gray's Inn** one of the Inns of Court **38–39 Death . . . die** (See Psalm 89:48.) **39 How** how much (is the asking price for)

SILENCE By my troth, I was not there.

SHALLOW Death is certain. Is old Double of your town living yet?

SILENCE Dead, sir.

SHALLOW Jesu, Jesu, dead! 'A drew a good bow; and dead? 'A shot a fine shoot. John o' Gaunt loved him well, and betted much money on his head. Dead? 'A would have clapped i' the clout at twelve score, and carried you a forehand shaft a fourteen and fourteen and a half, that it would have done a man's heart good to see. How a score of ewes now?

SILENCE Thereafter as they be; a score of good ewes may be worth ten pounds.

SHALLOW And is old Double dead?

SILENCE Here come two of Sir John Falstaff's men, as I think.

Enter Bardolph and one with him.

SHALLOW Good morrow, honest gentlemen.

BARDOLPH I beseech you, which is Justice Shallow?

SHALLOW I am Robert Shallow, sir, a poor esquire of this county, and one of the King's justices of the peace. What is your good pleasure with me?

BARDOLPH My captain, sir, commends him to you, my captain, Sir John Falstaff, a tall gentleman, by heaven, and a most gallant leader.

SHALLOW He greets me well, sir. I knew him a good backsword man. How doth the good knight? May I ask how my lady his wife doth?

BARDOLPH Sir, pardon; a soldier is better accommodated than with a wife.

SHALLOW It is well said, in faith, sir, and it is well said indeed too. "Better accommodated"! It is good, yea, indeed is it. Good phrases are surely, and ever were,

45 John o' Gaunt (Father of Henry IV.) **47 clapped . . . score** hit the bull's-eye at 240 yards **48–49 carried . . . half** i.e., could shoot a heavy arrow in a straight line rather than in a curved trajectory for a distance of 280 to 290 yards **51 Thereafter . . . be** according to their quality **58 esquire** (A social rank between gentleman and knight.) **61 commends him** sends his respects **62 tall** valiant **65 backsword** stick with a basket hilt used for fencing practice. (See 2.4.129, note.) **67–68 accommodated** furnished equipped. (A bit of fine language on Bardolph's part.)

very commendable. "Accommodated"! It comes of *ac-*
commodo. Very good, a good phrase.

BARDOLPH Pardon, sir, I have heard the word. Phrase
call you it? By this day, I know not the phrase. But I
will maintain the word with my sword to be a soldierlike word, and a word of exceeding good command, 77
by heaven. Accommodated; that is, when a man is, as
they say, accommodated; or when a man is being
whereby 'a may be thought to be accommodated,
which is an excellent thing.

Enter Falstaff.

SHALLOW It is very just.—Look, here comes good Sir 82
John. Give me your good hand, give me your worship's good hand. By my troth, you like well and bear 84
your years very well. Welcome, good Sir John.

FALSTAFF I am glad to see you well, good Master Robert
Shallow. Master Surecard, as I think?

SHALLOW No, Sir John, it is my cousin Silence, in com- 88
mission with me. 89

FALSTAFF Good Master Silence, it well befits you should
be of the peace. 91

SILENCE Your good worship is welcome.

FALSTAFF Fie, this is hot weather, gentlemen. Have you
provided me here half a dozen sufficient men? 94

SHALLOW Marry, have we, sir. Will you sit?

[*They sit at a table.*]

FALSTAFF Let me see them, I beseech you.

SHALLOW Where's the roll? Where's the roll? Where's
the roll? Let me see, let me see, let me see. So, so, so,
so, so, so, so; yea, marry, sir. Ralph Moldy! Let them
appear as I call; let them do so, let them do so. Let me
see, where is Moldy?

[*Enter Moldy.*]

MOLDY Here, an 't please you. 102

77 a word . . . command a perfectly good military term **82 just** true **84 like well** are in good condition, thrive **88–89 in . . . me** a fellow justice of the peace **91 of the peace** i.e., a magistrate (with a play on the name *Silence*, peace) **94 sufficient** fit for service **102 an 't** if it (also in l. 106)

SHALLOW What think you, Sir John? A good-limbed fel-
low, young, strong, and of good friends. 104
FALSTAFF Is thy name Moldy?
MOLDY Yea, an 't please you.
FALSTAFF 'Tis the more time thou wert used.
SHALLOW Ha, ha, ha! Most excellent, i' faith! Things
that are moldy lack use. Very singular good, in faith,
well said, Sir John, very well said.
FALSTAFF Prick him. 111
[*Shallow writes on the muster roll.*]
MOLDY I was pricked well enough before, an you 112
could have let me alone. My old dame will be undone 113
now for one to do her husbandry and her drudgery. 114
You need not to have pricked me. There are other men
fitter to go out than I.
FALSTAFF Go to. Peace, Moldy, you shall go, Moldy,
it is time you were spent. 118
MOLDY Spent?
SHALLOW Peace, fellow, peace. Stand aside. Know you
where you are? For th' other, Sir John, let me see: Si- 121
mon Shadow!

[*Enter Shadow.*]

FALSTAFF Yea, marry, let me have him to sit under. He's
like to be a cold soldier. 124
SHALLOW Where's Shadow?
SHADOW Here, sir.
FALSTAFF Shadow, whose son art thou?
SHADOW My mother's son, sir.
FALSTAFF Thy mother's son! Like enough, and thy fa- 129
ther's shadow. So the son of the female is the shadow 130
of the male. It is often so, indeed; but much of the
father's substance.

104 of good friends well connected by family **111 Prick** mark him down on the list **112 pricked** i.e., (1) goaded by nagging (2) turning sour or moldy (with sexual suggestion also, continued in *undone, husbandry,* and *spent,* sexually used up) **113 dame** mother, or, more probably in view of the sexual punning, "wife" **114 husbandry** farm work. (But see note at l. 112.) **118 spent** used up (But see note at l. 112.) **121 other** others **124 like** likely. **cold** (1) cool, deliberate (2) cowardly **129 son** (with play on "sun") **130 shadow** i.e., image, copy. (But, Falstaff jests, the father is only dimly copied in a bastard son who lacks the true substance of his purported father.)

SHALLOW Do you like him, Sir John?

FALSTAFF Shadow will serve for summer. Prick him, for we have a number of shadows fill up the muster book.

SHALLOW Thomas Wart!

[*Enter Wart.*]

FALSTAFF Where's he?

WART Here, sir.

FALSTAFF Is thy name Wart?

WART Yea, sir.

FALSTAFF Thou art a very ragged wart.

SHALLOW Shall I prick him, Sir John?

FALSTAFF It were superfluous, for his apparel is built upon his back and the whole frame stands upon pins. Prick him no more.

SHALLOW Ha, ha, ha! You can do it, sir, you can do it. I commend you well. Francis Feeble!

[*Enter Feeble.*]

FEEBLE Here, sir.

SHALLOW What trade art thou, Feeble?

FEEBLE A woman's tailor, sir.

SHALLOW Shall I prick him, sir?

FALSTAFF You may. But if he had been a man's tailor, he'd a' pricked you.—Wilt thou make as many holes in an enemy's battle as thou hast done in a woman's petticoat?

FEEBLE I will do my good will, sir. You can have no more.

FALSTAFF Well said, good woman's tailor! Well said, courageous Feeble! Thou wilt be as valiant as the wrathful dove or most magnanimous mouse. Prick the

134 serve (1) suffice (2) be inducted **135 shadows** i.e., fictitious names for which the officer in charge receives pay. **fill** to fill **145 the whole . . . pins** i.e., he's pinned together, badly made physically, and therefore needs no more pinpricks. (In a carpentry metaphor, the *pins* are also pegs for joining timber.) **147 can** know how to. **do it** i.e., make a joke **151 woman's tailor** (Often regarded as an effeminate occupation.) **154 a' pricked** (1) have attired (2) have thrust you through. (The word has a sexual suggestion also.) *Tailor* could mean the male or female sex organ. **155 battle** army **161 magnanimous** stouthearted

woman's tailor. Well, Master Shallow; deep, Master Shallow.

FEEBLE I would Wart might have gone, sir.

FALSTAFF I would thou wert a man's tailor, that thou mightst mend him and make him fit to go. I cannot put him to a private soldier that is the leader of so many thousands. Let that suffice, most forcible Feeble.

FEEBLE It shall suffice, sir.

FALSTAFF I am bound to thee, reverend Feeble. Who is next?

SHALLOW Peter Bullcalf o' the green!

[*Enter Bullcalf.*]

FALSTAFF Yea, marry, let's see Bullcalf.

BULLCALF Here, sir.

FALSTAFF 'Fore God, a likely fellow! Come, prick me Bullcalf till he roar again.

BULLCALF O Lord! Good my lord Captain—

FALSTAFF What, dost thou roar before thou art pricked?

BULLCALF O Lord, sir! I am a diseased man.

FALSTAFF What disease hast thou?

BULLCALF A whoreson cold, sir, a cough, sir, which I caught with ringing in the King's affairs upon his coronation day, sir.

FALSTAFF Come, thou shalt go to the wars in a gown. We will have away thy cold, and I will take such order that thy friends shall ring for thee. Is here all?

SHALLOW Here is two more called than your number; you must have but four here, sir. And so, I pray you, go in with me to dinner.

FALSTAFF Come, I will go drink with you, but I cannot tarry dinner. I am glad to see you, by my troth, Master Shallow.

SHALLOW O, Sir John, do you remember since we lay all night in the Windmill in Saint George's Field?

167 put him to enlist him as **168 thousands** i.e., of vermin, lice **170 bound** obliged **182–183 ringing . . . day** i.e., ringing the church bells to celebrate the anniversary of the King's coronation **184 gown** dressing gown **185 have away** do away with. **take such order** provide **186 for thee** (1) in your place (2) at your death **191 tarry** wait for **193 since** when **194 the Windmill** a brothel, or an inn in a brothel district. **Saint George's Field** a popular place of resort on the south bank of the Thames

FALSTAFF No more of that, good Master Shallow, no more of that.

SHALLOW Ha! 'Twas a merry night. And is Jane Nightwork alive?

FALSTAFF She lives, Master Shallow.

SHALLOW She never could away with me.

FALSTAFF Never, never; she would always say she could not abide Master Shallow.

SHALLOW By the Mass, I could anger her to the heart. She was then a bona-roba. Doth she hold her own well?

FALSTAFF Old, old, Master Shallow.

SHALLOW Nay, she must be old. She cannot choose but be old. Certain she's old, and had Robin Nightwork by old Nightwork before I came to Clement's Inn.

SILENCE That's fifty-five year ago.

SHALLOW Ha, cousin Silence, that thou hadst seen that that this knight and I have seen! Ha, Sir John, said I well?

FALSTAFF We have heard the chimes at midnight, Master Shallow.

SHALLOW That we have, that we have, that we have, in faith, Sir John, we have. Our watchword was "Hem boys!" Come, let's to dinner, come, let's to dinner. Jesus, the days that we have seen! Come, come.

Exeunt [*Falstaff and the Justices*].

BULLCALF Good Master Corporate Bardolph, stand my friend, and here's four Harry ten shillings in French crowns for you. [*He gives money.*] In very truth, sir, I had as lief be hanged, sir, as go. And yet for mine own part, sir, I do not care, but rather because I am unwilling, and for mine own part have a desire to stay with my friends. Else, sir, I did not care, for mine own part, so much.

BARDOLPH Go to, stand aside.

200 away with tolerate **217–218 Hem boys** i.e., down the hatch
220 Corporate (For *Corporal.*) **stand** be, act as **221 Harry ten shillings** i.e., money coined in the reign of Henry VII, current in late Elizabethan times at half the face value. The reference is anachronistic. Four such coins would be worth 20 shillings, or 1 pound. Bullcalf gives his bribe in *French crowns,* worth 4 shillings each; presumably he gives five such coins **223 lief** willingly

MOLDY And, good Master Corporal Captain, for my old
dame's sake, stand my friend. She has nobody to do
anything about her when I am gone, and she is old
and cannot help herself. [*He gives money.*] You shall
have forty, sir. 233

BARDOLPH Go to, stand aside.

FEEBLE By my troth, I care not. A man can die but once.
We owe God a death. I'll ne'er bear a base mind.
An 't be my destiny, so; an 't be not, so. No man's
too good to serve 's prince. And let it go which way it
will, he that dies this year is quit for the next. 239

BARDOLPH Well said. Thou'rt a good fellow.

FEEBLE Faith, I'll bear no base mind. 241

Enter Falstaff and the Justices.

FALSTAFF Come, sir, which men shall I have?

SHALLOW Four of which you please.

BARDOLPH [*To Falstaff*] Sir, a word with you. [*Aside.*] I have three pound to free Moldy and Bullcalf.

FALSTAFF Go to, well.

SHALLOW Come, Sir John, which four will you have?

FALSTAFF Do you choose for me.

SHALLOW Marry, then, Moldy, Bullcalf, Feeble, and Shadow.

FALSTAFF Moldy and Bullcalf: for you, Moldy, stay at 251
home till you are past service; and for your part, Bull- 252
calf, grow till you come unto it. I will none of you. 253

SHALLOW Sir John, Sir John, do not yourself wrong. They are your likeliest men, and I would have you served with the best.

FALSTAFF Will you tell me, Master Shallow, how to
choose a man? Care I for the limb, the thews, the stat- 258
ure, bulk, and big assemblance of a man? Give me the 259
spirit, Master Shallow. Here's Wart; you see what a
ragged appearance it is. 'A shall charge you and dis- 261
charge you with the motion of a pewterer's hammer, 262

233 forty i.e., 40 shillings **239 quit** free, clear **241 bear** have **251 for** as for **252 past service** (1) too old to serve militarily (2) too old for sexual functioning **253 come unto it** (1) are a man old enough to fight (2) have arrived at sexual maturity **258 thews** strength **259 assemblance** appearance, frame **261–262 charge . . . discharge you** load and fire **262 motion . . . hammer** i.e., precise, quick motion

come off and on swifter than he that gibbets on the brewer's bucket. And this same half-faced fellow, Shadow; give me this man. He presents no mark to the enemy; the foeman may with as great aim level at the edge of a penknife. And for a retreat, how swiftly will this Feeble the woman's tailor run off! O, give me the spare men, and spare me the great ones. Put me a caliver into Wart's hand, Bardolph.

BARDOLPH [*Giving Wart a musket*] Hold, Wart, traverse. Thus, thus, thus.

FALSTAFF Come, manage me your caliver. So. [*Wart performs maneuvers with the musket.*] Very well. Go to. Very good, exceeding good. O, give me always a little, lean, old, chapped, bald shot. Well said, i' faith, Wart, thou'rt a good scab. Hold, there's a tester for thee.

[*He gives sixpence.*]

SHALLOW He is not his craft's master; he doth not do it right. I remember at Mile End Green, when I lay at Clement's Inn—I was then Sir Dagonet in Arthur's show—there was a little quiver fellow, and 'a would manage you his piece thus [*Shallow demonstrates*], and 'a would about and about, and come you in and come you in. "Rah, tah, tah," would 'a say, "Bounce," would 'a say, and away again would 'a go, and again would 'a come. I shall ne'er see such a fellow.

FALSTAFF These fellows will do well, Master Shallow. God keep you, Master Silence. I will not use many words with you. Fare you well, gentlemen both. I

263–264 come . . . bucket raise and lower his musket quicker than a brewer's man raises and lowers the beam (*bucket*) of the brewer's yoke across his shoulders **264 half-faced** thin-faced. (Alludes to the profile portraits on coins.) **266 as great aim** as much likelihood of hitting the target. **level** aim **270 caliver** light musket **271 traverse** march, or, perhaps, perform the manual of arms, an exercise drill with a musket **276 shot** marksman **277 scab** rascal (punning on the name *Wart*). **tester** sixpence **279 Mile End Green** a drilling ground for citizen soldiers, to the east of London. **lay** lodged **280–281 Sir . . . show** (An exhibition of archery was held annually at Mile End Green called "Arthur's show," in which each archer took the name of one of King Arthur's knights; Shallow played the part of Sir Dagonet, Arthur's fool.) **281 quiver** nimble **282 piece** firearm **283–284 'a would . . . you in** i.e., he was skillful at firing and then running around to the rear rank of musketeers to reload while the next rank fired, and so on **284 Bounce** bang

thank you. I must a dozen mile tonight. Bardolph, give the soldiers coats.

SHALLOW Sir John, the Lord bless you! God prosper your affairs! God send us peace! At your return, visit our house; let our old acquaintance be renewed. Peradventure I will with ye to the court.

FALSTAFF 'Fore God, would you would.

SHALLOW Go to; I have spoke at a word. God keep you.

FALSTAFF Fare you well, gentle gentlemen. *Exeunt* [*Justices.*] On, Bardolph; lead the men away. [*Exeunt Bardolph, recruits, etc.*] As I return, I will fetch off these justices. I do see the bottom of Justice Shallow. Lord, Lord, how subject we old men are to this vice of lying! This same starved justice hath done nothing but prate to me of the wildness of his youth and the feats he hath done about Turnbull Street, and every third word a lie, duer paid to the hearer than the Turk's tribute. I do remember him at Clement's Inn like a man made after supper of a cheese paring. When 'a was naked, he was, for all the world, like a forked radish, with a head fantastically carved upon it with a knife. 'A was so forlorn that his dimensions to any thick sight were invisible. 'A was the very genius of famine, yet lecherous as a monkey, and the whores called him mandrake. 'A came ever in the rearward of the fashion, and sung those tunes to the overscutched huswives that he heard the carmen whistle, and sware they were his fancies or his good-nights. And now is this Vice's dagger become a squire, and talks as familiarly of John o' Gaunt as if he had been sworn brother

297 I have . . . word I mean what I say **300 fetch off** get the better of **305 Turnbull Street** a street in Clerkenwell, ill-reputed **306 duer** more promptly **306–307 Turk's tribute** tribute money paid annually to the Sultan of Turkey by merchants and others **311 forlorn** meager, thin **312 thick** imperfect. **invisible** (Some editors retain the reading of the quarto and the Folio, *invincible,* as meaning "invisible.") **genius** spirit, personification **314 mandrake** root of a plant, said to resemble the body of a man **315–316 overscutched huswives** outworn and often-whipped prostitutes **316 carmen** wagoners **317 fancies . . . good-nights** fantasies and serenades (of which he claimed authorship) **318 Vice's dagger** (The Vice, or comic character of the morality plays, was armed with a wooden dagger.) **319 sworn brother** companion in arms who has taken a chivalric oath to share his fortunes

to him, and I'll be sworn 'a ne'er saw him but once in the tilt-yard, and then he burst his head for crowding among the marshal's men. I saw it, and told John o' Gaunt he beat his own name, for you might have thrust him and all his apparel into an eelskin; the case of a treble hautboy was a mansion for him, a court. And now has he land and beefs. Well, I'll be acquainted with him if I return, and 't shall go hard but I'll make him a philosopher's two stones to me. If the young dace be a bait for the old pike, I see no reason in the law of nature but I may snap at him. Let time shape, and there an end. [*Exit.*]

✤

321 tilt-yard arena for jousting at Westminster. **he burst his head** he, Shallow, had his head beaten so that he bled **323 beat his own name** i.e., was thrashing a gaunt person **324 case** instrument case
325 hautboy ancestor of the oboe. (The *treble hautboy* was the smallest and narrowest of this family of instruments.) **326 beefs** oxen **328 a philosopher's two stones** i.e., as valuable as the philosopher's stones that supposedly changed ordinary metal into gold and preserved youth and health. (*Two stones* also suggests "testicles.") **329 dace** small fish used for live bait

4.1 *Enter the Archbishop* [*of York*], *Mowbray,* [*Lord*] *Bardolph, Hastings,* [*and others,*] *within the Forest of Gaultree.*

ARCHBISHOP What is this forest called?

HASTINGS
'Tis Gaultree Forest, an 't shall please Your Grace. 2

ARCHBISHOP
Here stand, my lords, and send discoverers forth 3
To know the numbers of our enemies. 4

HASTINGS
We have sent forth already.

ARCHBISHOP 'Tis well done.
My friends and brethren in these great affairs,
I must acquaint you that I have received
New-dated letters from Northumberland, 8
Their cold intent, tenor, and substance, thus: 9
Here doth he wish his person, with such powers 10
As might hold sortance with his quality, 11
The which he could not levy. Whereupon
He is retired, to ripe his growing fortunes, 13
To Scotland, and concludes in hearty prayers
That your attempts may overlive the hazard 15
And fearful meeting of their opposite. 16

MOWBRAY
Thus do the hopes we have in him touch ground 17
And dash themselves to pieces.

Enter Messenger.

HASTINGS Now, what news?

MESSENGER
West of this forest, scarcely off a mile,
In goodly form comes on the enemy, 20
And by the ground they hide, I judge their number
Upon or near the rate of thirty thousand. 22

4.1. Location: Yorkshire. Gaultree Forest.
2 an 't if it **3 discoverers** scouts **4 know** learn **8 New** recently **9 cold** dispiriting, gloomy **10 powers** forces **11 hold sortance** accord. **quality** rank **13 ripe** make ripe **15 overlive** outlive **16 opposite** adversary **17 touch ground** hit bottom **20 form** military formation **22 rate** estimate

MOWBRAY
The just proportion that we gave them out. 23
Let us sway on and face them in the field. 24
ARCHBISHOP
What well-appointed leader fronts us here? 25

Enter Westmorland.

MOWBRAY
I think it is my lord of Westmorland.
WESTMORLAND
Health and fair greeting from our general,
The Prince, Lord John and Duke of Lancaster.
ARCHBISHOP
Say on, my lord of Westmorland, in peace,
What doth concern your coming.
WESTMORLAND Then, my lord, 30
Unto Your Grace do I in chief address
The substance of my speech. If that rebellion
Came like itself, in base and abject routs, 33
Led on by bloody youth, guarded with rags, 34
And countenanced by boys and beggary, 35
I say, if damned commotion so appeared 36
In his true, native, and most proper shape,
You, reverend father, and these noble lords
Had not been here to dress the ugly form
Of base and bloody insurrection
With your fair honors. You, Lord Archbishop,
Whose see is by a civil peace maintained, 42
Whose beard the silver hand of peace hath touched,
Whose learning and good letters peace hath tutored, 44
Whose white investments figure innocence, 45
The dove and very blessèd spirit of peace,
Wherefore do you so ill translate yourself 47
Out of the speech of peace that bears such grace
Into the harsh and boisterous tongue of war,

23 just . . . out precise number that we estimated **24 sway on** advance **25 well-appointed** well-armed. **fronts** confronts **30 What . . . coming** what your coming means **33 routs** mobs **34 bloody** passionate. **guarded** adorned, trimmed **35 countenanced** supported. **beggary** beggars **36 commotion** tumult, sedition **42 see** diocese. **civil** orderly, law-abiding **44 good letters** scholarship **45 investments** vestments. **figure** symbolize **47 translate** (1) change from one language to another (2) transform

Turning your books to graves, your ink to blood,
Your pens to lances, and your tongue divine
To a loud trumpet and a point of war? 52

ARCHBISHOP

Wherefore do I this? So the question stands.
Briefly to this end: we are all diseased,
And with our surfeiting and wanton hours 55
Have brought ourselves into a burning fever,
And we must bleed for it; of which disease 57
Our late King Richard, being infected, died.
But, my most noble lord of Westmorland,
I take not on me here as a physician, 60
Nor do I as an enemy to peace
Troop in the throngs of military men,
But rather show awhile like fearful war 63
To diet rank minds sick of happiness 64
And purge th' obstructions which begin to stop
Our very veins of life. Hear me more plainly.
I have in equal balance justly weighed 67
What wrongs our arms may do, what wrongs we suffer,
And find our griefs heavier than our offenses. 69
We see which way the stream of time doth run,
And are enforced from our most quiet there 71
By the rough torrent of occasion, 72
And have the summary of all our griefs,
When time shall serve, to show in articles; 74
Which long ere this we offered to the King,
And might by no suit gain our audience.
When we are wronged and would unfold our griefs,
We are denied access unto his person
Even by those men that most have done us wrong. 79
The dangers of the days but newly gone,
Whose memory is written on the earth
With yet-appearing blood, and the examples

52 point of war trumpet signal of war **55–79 And . . . wrong** (Omitted from the quarto probably because of censorship, since these lines plead the cause of rebellion; also ll. 103–139.) **55 wanton** self-indulgent **57 bleed** be bled (as a medical treatment) **60 take . . . as** do not now undertake the role of **63 show** appear **64 rank** swollen, bloated **67 equal balance** balanced scales. **justly** exactly **69 griefs** grievances **71 our . . . there** our greatest quiet therein, i.e., in the stream of time **72 occasion** circumstances **74 articles** specified items

Of every minute's instance, present now, 83
Hath put us in these ill-beseeming arms,
Not to break peace or any branch of it,
But to establish here a peace indeed,
Concurring both in name and quality. 87

WESTMORLAND
Whenever yet was your appeal denied?
Wherein have you been gallèd by the King? 89
What peer hath been suborned to grate on you, 90
That you should seal this lawless bloody book 91
Of forged rebellion with a seal divine 92
And consecrate commotion's bitter edge?

ARCHBISHOP
My brother general, the commonwealth, 94
To brother born an household cruelty, 95
I make my quarrel in particular. 96

WESTMORLAND
There is no need of any such redress;
Or if there were, it not belongs to you.

MOWBRAY
Why not to him in part, and to us all
That feel the bruises of the days before,
And suffer the condition of these times
To lay a heavy and unequal hand 102
Upon our honors?

WESTMORLAND O my good Lord Mowbray,
Construe the times to their necessities, 104
And you shall say indeed it is the time,
And not the King, that doth you injuries.
Yet for your part, it not appears to me
Either from the King or in the present time

83 Of . . . instance presented every minute **87 Concurring . . . quality** i.e., a peace that will be both in name and in fact **89 gallèd** injured, made sore with chafing **90 suborned . . . on** induced to annoy, harass **91–92 That . . . divine** i.e., that you should put your seal of approval on this lawless and forged rebellion, much as if a bishop were to license a troublesome book **94–96 My brother . . . particular** (The text is perhaps corrupt here, but the general sense seems to be: The grievances of my brother-Englishmen, and the cruelty shown to my blood brother Scroop [who was executed at Bristol by Henry IV; see *1 Henry IV*, 1.3.269], provoke me to make this cause my own.) **102 unequal** unjust **104 to** according to. **their necessities** i.e., that which is necessary in a time of disorder and civil strife

That you should have an inch of any ground
To build a grief on. Were you not restored
To all the Duke of Norfolk's seigniories, 111
Your noble and right well remembered father's?

MOWBRAY

What thing, in honor, had my father lost,
That need to be revived and breathed in me? 114
The King that loved him, as the state stood then, 115
Was force perforce compelled to banish him; 116
And then that Henry Bolingbroke and he,
Being mounted and both rousèd in their seats, 118
Their neighing coursers daring of the spur, 119
Their armèd staves in charge, their beavers down, 120
Their eyes of fire sparkling through sights of steel, 121
And the loud trumpet blowing them together,
Then, then, when there was nothing could have stayed
My father from the breast of Bolingbroke,
O, when the King did throw his warder down— 125
His own life hung upon the staff he threw—
Then threw he down himself and all their lives
That by indictment and by dint of sword 128
Have since miscarried under Bolingbroke. 129

WESTMORLAND

You speak, Lord Mowbray, now you know not what.
The Earl of Hereford was reputed then 131
In England the most valiant gentleman.
Who knows on whom fortune would then have smiled?
But if your father had been victor there,
He ne'er had borne it out of Coventry; 135
For all the country in a general voice
Cried hate upon him, and all their prayers and love
Were set on Hereford, whom they doted on,
And blessed, and graced, indeed more than the King.

111 seigniories properties, estates **114 breathed** given the breath of life **115 state** condition of things **116 force perforce** willy-nilly. (For the banishment of Mowbray by Richard II, see *Richard II*, 1.1 and 1.3.) **118 rousèd** raised. **seats** saddles **119 daring of the spur** i.e., eager to be urged on **120 armèd . . . charge** lances ready for the charge. **beavers** movable visors of helmets **121 sights** eye slits **125 warder** staff of command **128 dint** force **129 miscarried** died **131 Earl of Hereford** i.e., Bolingbroke, later King Henry IV **135 borne . . . Coventry** i.e., carried away the prize from the site of the intended trial by combat

But this is mere digression from my purpose.
Here come I from our princely general
To know your griefs, to tell you from His Grace
That he will give you audience; and wherein 143
It shall appear that your demands are just,
You shall enjoy them, everything set off 145
That might so much as think you enemies. 146

MOWBRAY
But he hath forced us to compel this offer,
And it proceeds from policy, not love.

WESTMORLAND
Mowbray, you overween to take it so. 149
This offer comes from mercy, not from fear.
For, lo, within a ken our army lies, 151
Upon mine honor, all too confident
To give admittance to a thought of fear.
Our battle is more full of names than yours, 154
Our men more perfect in the use of arms,
Our armor all as strong, our cause the best.
Then reason will our hearts should be as good. 157
Say you not then our offer is compelled.

MOWBRAY
Well, by my will we shall admit no parley. 159

WESTMORLAND
That argues but the shame of your offense.
A rotten case abides no handling. 161

HASTINGS
Hath the Prince John a full commission,
In very ample virtue of his father, 163
To hear and absolutely to determine
Of what conditions we shall stand upon? 165

WESTMORLAND
That is intended in the General's name. 166
I muse you make so slight a question. 167

143 wherein wherever **145 set off** put out of consideration, removed **146 think you** make you seem **149 overween** are arrogant or presumptuous **151 ken** seeing distance **154 battle** army. **names** noble names **157 reason will** i.e., it is reasonable that **159 by my will** i.e., as far as I'm concerned. **admit no parley** accept no conference **161 abides** tolerates **163 virtue** authority **165 what** whatever. **stand** insist **166 intended** understood, implied. **name** i.e., title **167 muse** wonder

ARCHBISHOP [*Giving a document*]
Then take, my lord of Westmorland, this schedule,
For this contains our general grievances.
Each several article herein redressed, 170
All members of our cause, both here and hence,
That are insinewed to this action, 172
Acquitted by a true substantial form 173
And present execution of our wills 174
To us and to our purposes confined, 175
We come within our awful banks again 176
And knit our powers to the arm of peace.

WESTMORLAND
This will I show the General. Please you, lords,
In sight of both our battles we may meet, 179
And either end in peace—which God so frame!— 180
Or to the place of difference call the swords 181
Which must decide it.

ARCHBISHOP My lord, we will do so.
Exit Westmorland.

MOWBRAY
There is a thing within my bosom tells me
That no conditions of our peace can stand.

HASTINGS
Fear you not that. If we can make our peace
Upon such large terms and so absolute 186
As our conditions shall consist upon, 187
Our peace shall stand as firm as rocky mountains.

MOWBRAY
Yea, but our valuation shall be such 189
That every slight and false-derivèd cause,
Yea, every idle, nice, and wanton reason, 191
Shall to the King taste of this action,
That, were our royal faiths martyrs in love, 193
We shall be winnowed with so rough a wind

170 Each . . . herein provided that each separate article herein is **172 insinewed** joined as by strong sinews **173 substantial form** formal agreement **174 present . . . wills** immediate fulfillment of our desires **175 To . . . confined** i.e., as regards us and our plans **176 awful banks** banks or bounds of respect **179 battles** armies **180 frame** bring about **181 difference** conflict **186 large** liberal **187 consist** insist **189 our . . . such** i.e., we shall be so considered by the King **191 idle . . . wanton** foolish, petty, and frivolous **193 That . . . love** i.e., so that even if our allegiance to the King were as strong as the devotion of martyrs

That even our corn shall seem as light as chaff 195
And good from bad find no partition. 196

ARCHBISHOP
No, no, my lord. Note this: the King is weary
Of dainty and such picking grievances; 198
For he hath found to end one doubt by death 199
Revives two greater in the heirs of life, 200
And therefore will he wipe his tables clean 201
And keep no telltale to his memory
That may repeat and history his loss 203
To new remembrance. For full well he knows
He cannot so precisely weed this land 205
As his misdoubts present occasion. 206
His foes are so enrooted with his friends
That, plucking to unfix an enemy,
He doth unfasten so and shake a friend.
So that this land, like an offensive wife
That hath enraged him on to offer strokes,
As he is striking, holds his infant up
And hangs resolved correction in the arm 213
That was upreared to execution.

HASTINGS
Besides, the King hath wasted all his rods 215
On late offenders, that he now doth lack 216
The very instruments of chastisement,
So that his power, like to a fangless lion,
May offer, but not hold.

ARCHBISHOP 'Tis very true. 219
And therefore be assured, my good Lord Marshal,
If we do now make our atonement well, 221
Our peace will, like a broken limb united,
Grow stronger for the breaking.

MOWBRAY Be it so.
Here is returned my lord of Westmorland.

195 corn grain, wheat **196 partition** distinction **198 picking** fastidious, trivial **199 doubt** danger, source of fear **200 of life** still living **201 tables** tablets, notebooks **203 history** record, chronicle **205 precisely** thoroughly **206 misdoubts** suspicions **213 hangs** suspends in midaction. **resolved correction** the punishment that was intended **215 wasted** exhausted, spent. **rods** whipping rods **216 late** (other) recent **219 offer . . . hold** offer violence, but not hold fast **221 atonement** reconciliation

Enter Westmorland.

WESTMORLAND
The Prince is here at hand. Pleaseth your lordship 225
To meet His Grace just distance 'tween our armies. 226

MOWBRAY
Your Grace of York, in God's name then set forward.

ARCHBISHOP
Before, and greet His Grace.—My lord, we come. 228

4.2 *Enter Prince John* [*of Lancaster*] *and his army.*

PRINCE JOHN
You are well encountered here, my cousin Mowbray. 1
Good day to you, gentle Lord Archbishop, 2
And so to you, Lord Hastings, and to all.
My lord of York, it better showed with you 4
When that your flock, assembled by the bell,
Encircled you to hear with reverence
Your exposition on the holy text
Than now to see you here an iron man, 8
Cheering a rout of rebels with your drum, 9
Turning the word to sword and life to death. 10
That man that sits within a monarch's heart
And ripens in the sunshine of his favor,
Would he abuse the countenance of the King, 13
Alack, what mischiefs might he set abroach 14
In shadow of such greatness! With you, Lord Bishop,
It is even so. Who hath not heard it spoken 16
How deep you were within the books of God, 17

225 Pleaseth may it please **226 just distance** i.e., halfway **228 Before** i.e., go before

4.2. Location: This scene is apparently continuous with the previous scene. In the quarto, Prince John and his army enter before the last two lines of 4.1.

1 cousin (Normal address of royal family to a duke.) **2 gentle** noble **4 it . . . you** it showed you to better advantage **8 iron man** (1) warrior clad in armor (2) merciless fighter **9 rout** mob **10 the word** i.e., the word of God, the Scripture **13 Would he** if he should choose to. **countenance** favor **14 set abroach** set aflowing, begin **16 even** just **17 within . . . God** (1) versed in works of divinity (2) in God's good graces

To us the speaker in his parliament,
To us th' imagined voice of God himself,
The very opener and intelligencer
Between the grace, the sanctities, of heaven
And our dull workings? O, who shall believe
But you misuse the reverence of your place,
Employ the countenance and grace of heaven
As a false favorite doth his prince's name,
In deeds dishonorable? You have ta'en up,
Under the counterfeited zeal of God,
The subjects of his substitute, my father,
And both against the peace of heaven and him
Have here up-swarmed them.

ARCHBISHOP Good my lord of Lancaster,
I am not here against your father's peace;
But, as I told my lord of Westmorland,
The time misordered doth, in common sense,
Crowd us and crush us to this monstrous form
To hold our safety up. I sent Your Grace
The parcels and particulars of our grief,
The which hath been with scorn shoved from the court,
Whereon this Hydra son of war is born,
Whose dangerous eyes may well be charmed asleep
With grant of our most just and right desires,
And true obedience, of this madness cured,
Stoop tamely to the foot of majesty.

MOWBRAY
If not, we ready are to try our fortunes
To the last man.

HASTINGS And though we here fall down,
We have supplies to second our attempt;
If they miscarry, theirs shall second them,

18 speaker i.e., spokesman for God, just as the Speaker of Parliament spoke in the name of the King **20 opener** revealer. **intelligencer** interpreter, agent **22 dull workings** imperfect human perceptions **26 ta'en up** enlisted **28 his substitute** God's deputy **30 up-swarmed** raised up in swarms **33 time misordered** disorders of the time. **in common sense** i.e., as anyone can see **36 parcels** items, details. **grief** grievances **38 Hydra** (The Lernaean Hydra was a fabulous monster with several heads; when one was cut off, others grew in its place.) **39 eyes** (The image here conflates Hydra with Argus, Juno's watchful guard with one hundred eyes, who was charmed asleep by Mercury's music.) **44 though** even if **45 supplies** forces in reserve

And so success of mischief shall be born 47
And heir from heir shall hold this quarrel up
Whiles England shall have generation. 49

PRINCE JOHN
You are too shallow, Hastings, much too shallow,
To sound the bottom of the aftertimes. 51

WESTMORLAND
Pleaseth Your Grace to answer them directly 52
How far forth you do like their articles.

PRINCE JOHN
I like them all, and do allow them well, 54
And swear here, by the honor of my blood,
My father's purposes have been mistook,
And some about him have too lavishly 57
Wrested his meaning and authority. 58
My lord, these griefs shall be with speed redressed,
Upon my soul, they shall. If this may please you,
Discharge your powers unto their several counties, 61
As we will ours; and here between the armies
Let's drink together friendly and embrace,
That all their eyes may bear those tokens home
Of our restorèd love and amity.

ARCHBISHOP
I take your princely word for these redresses.

PRINCE JOHN
I give it you, and will maintain my word,
And thereupon I drink unto Your Grace.
[*They drink together, and embrace.*]

HASTINGS
Go, Captain, and deliver to the army
This news of peace. Let them have pay, and part. 70
I know it will well please them. Hie thee, Captain.
[*Exit a Captain.*]

ARCHBISHOP
To you, my noble lord of Westmorland.

47 success succession **49 generation** issue, offspring **51 sound . . . aftertimes** predict what the future will bring. **sound the bottom** plumb the depths **52 Pleaseth** may it please **54 allow** approve, sanction **57 lavishly** loosely, negligently **58 Wrested** twisted **61 powers** forces. **several** respective **70 part** depart

WESTMORLAND
I pledge Your Grace; and, if you knew what pains
I have bestowed to breed this present peace,
You would drink freely. But my love to ye
Shall show itself more openly hereafter.
ARCHBISHOP
I do not doubt you.
WESTMORLAND I am glad of it.
Health to my lord and gentle cousin, Mowbray.
MOWBRAY
You wish me health in very happy season, 79
For I am on the sudden something ill. 80
ARCHBISHOP
Against ill chances men are ever merry, 81
But heaviness foreruns the good event. 82
WESTMORLAND
Therefore be merry, coz, since sudden sorrow 83
Serves to say thus, "Some good thing comes tomorrow."
ARCHBISHOP
Believe me, I am passing light in spirit. 85
MOWBRAY
So much the worse, if your own rule be true.
Shout [*within*].
PRINCE JOHN
The word of peace is rendered. Hark, how they shout! 87
MOWBRAY
This had been cheerful after victory. 88
ARCHBISHOP
A peace is of the nature of a conquest,
For then both parties nobly are subdued,
And neither party loser.
PRINCE JOHN Go, my lord,
And let our army be dischargèd too.
[*Exit Westmorland.*]
And, good my lord, so please you, let our trains 93

79 in . . . season at an opportune moment **80 something** somewhat **81 Against** when about to face **82 heaviness . . . event** sadness comes over men prior to a happy outcome **83 coz** cousin, kinsman **85 passing** surpassingly **87 rendered** proclaimed **88 had been** would have been **93 trains** followers, armies

March by us, that we may peruse the men
We should have coped withal.
ARCHBISHOP Go, good Lord Hastings,
And, ere they be dismissed, let them march by.
[*Exit Hastings.*]

PRINCE JOHN
I trust, lords, we shall lie tonight together.

Enter Westmorland.

Now, cousin, wherefore stands our army still?
WESTMORLAND
The leaders, having charge from you to stand,
Will not go off until they hear you speak.
PRINCE JOHN They know their duties.

Enter Hastings.

HASTINGS
My lord, our army is dispersed already.
Like youthful steers unyoked, they take their courses
East, west, north, south, or, like a school broke up,
Each hurries toward his home and sporting-place.
WESTMORLAND
Good tidings, my lord Hastings, for the which
I do arrest thee, traitor, of high treason.
And you, Lord Archbishop, and you, Lord Mowbray,
Of capital treason I attach you both.
MOWBRAY
Is this proceeding just and honorable?
WESTMORLAND Is your assembly so?
ARCHBISHOP
Will you thus break your faith?
PRINCE JOHN I pawned thee none.
I promised you redress of these same grievances
Whereof you did complain, which, by mine honor,
I will perform with a most Christian care.
But for you rebels, look to taste the due
Meet for rebellion.
Most shallowly did you these arms commence,

95 coped withal encountered, fought with **98 wherefore** why
105 sporting-place playground **109 capital** punishable by death.
attach arrest **112 pawned** pledged **116 for** as for. **look** expect
117 Meet fitting **118 arms** hostilities

Fondly brought here and foolishly sent hence. 119
Strike up our drums; pursue the scattered stray. 120
God, and not we, hath safely fought today.
Some guard these traitors to the block of death,
Treason's true bed and yielder-up of breath.

[*Exeunt.*]

4.3 *Alarum. Excursions. Enter Falstaff* [*and Sir John Coleville*].

FALSTAFF What's your name, sir? Of what condition are 1
you, and of what place?

COLEVILLE I am a knight, sir, and my name is Coleville of the Dale.

FALSTAFF Well, then, Coleville is your name, a knight is your degree, and your place the Dale. Coleville shall be still your name, a traitor your degree, and the dungeon your place, a place deep enough; so shall you be still Coleville of the Dale.

COLEVILLE Are not you Sir John Falstaff?

FALSTAFF As good a man as he, sir, whoe'er I am. Do
ye yield, sir, or shall I sweat for you? If I do sweat,
they are the drops of thy lovers, and they weep for thy 13
death. Therefore rouse up fear and trembling, and do
observance to my mercy. 15

COLEVILLE I think you are Sir John Falstaff, and in that thought yield me.

FALSTAFF I have a whole school of tongues in this belly 18
of mine, and not a tongue of them all speaks any other
word but my name. An I had but a belly of any indif- 20
ferency, I were simply the most active fellow in Eu- 21
rope. My womb, my womb, my womb undoes me. 22
Here comes our general.

119 Fondly foolishly **120 stray** stragglers

4.3. Location: Gaultree Forest, as before. The scene is continuous.
s.d. Alarum trumpet call to battle. **Excursions** sallies, sudden movements of troops **1 condition** rank **13 drops** tears. **lovers** friends **15 observance** reverence, homage **18 school** crowd (i.e., his belly eloquently identifies him) **20 An** if **20–21 indifferency** moderate size **22 womb** belly

Enter [*Prince*] *John* [*of Lancaster*], *Westmorland,* [*Blunt,*] *and the rest.*

PRINCE JOHN
The heat is past; follow no further now.
Call in the powers, good cousin Westmorland.
[*Exit Westmorland. Sound*] *retreat.*
Now, Falstaff, where have you been all this while?
When everything is ended, then you come.
These tardy tricks of yours will, on my life,
One time or other break some gallows' back.

FALSTAFF I would be sorry, my lord, but it should be thus. I never knew yet but rebuke and check was the reward of valor. Do you think me a swallow, an arrow, or a bullet? Have I, in my poor and old motion, the expedition of thought? I have speeded hither with the very extremest inch of possibility. I have foundered nine score and odd posts, and here, travel-tainted as I am, have in my pure and immaculate valor taken Sir John Coleville of the Dale, a most furious knight and valorous enemy. But what of that? He saw me and yielded, that I may justly say, with the hook-nosed fellow of Rome, "I came, saw, and overcame."

PRINCE JOHN It was more of his courtesy than your deserving.

FALSTAFF I know not. Here is he, and here I yield him. And I beseech Your Grace, let it be booked with the rest of this day's deeds, or, by the Lord, I will have it in a particular ballad else, with mine own picture on the top on 't, Coleville kissing my foot. To the which course if I be enforced, if you do not all show like gilt twopences to me, and I in the clear sky of fame o'ershine you as much as the full moon doth the cinders of the element, which show like pins' heads to

24 heat pursuit, race **25 powers** forces **30–31 but . . . thus** if it were not thus. (It is fitting, Falstaff wryly says, that valor is never properly recognized, because that is how the world goes.) **31 check** reprimand **34 expedition** speed **35 very extremest inch** fullest extent. **foundered** made lame **36 posts** post horses **40–41 hook-nosed . . . Rome** i.e., Julius Caesar **45 booked** recorded by the chroniclers **47 a particular ballad** a broadside ballad written and published for the particular occasion. **else** otherwise **48 on 't** of it **49 show** look **49–50 gilt twopences** coins gilded to pass for half-crowns of the same size **50 to** compared to (also in l. 52) **51–52 cinders . . . element** i.e., stars

her, believe not the word of the noble. Therefore let me have right, and let desert mount.

PRINCE JOHN Thine's too heavy to mount.

FALSTAFF Let it shine, then.

PRINCE JOHN Thine's too thick to shine.

FALSTAFF Let it do something, my good lord, that may do me good, and call it what you will.

PRINCE JOHN Is thy name Coleville?

COLEVILLE It is, my lord.

PRINCE JOHN A famous rebel art thou, Coleville.

FALSTAFF And a famous true subject took him.

COLEVILLE
I am, my lord, but as my betters are
That led me hither. Had they been ruled by me,
You should have won them dearer than you have.

FALSTAFF I know not how they sold themselves. But thou, like a kind fellow, gavest thyself away gratis, and I thank thee for thee.

Enter Westmorland.

PRINCE JOHN Now, have you left pursuit?

WESTMORLAND
Retreat is made and execution stayed.

PRINCE JOHN
Send Coleville with his confederates
To York, to present execution.
Blunt, lead him hence, and see you guard him sure.
[*Exit Blunt with Coleville.*]
And now dispatch we toward the court, my lords.
I hear the King my father is sore sick.
Our news shall go before us to His Majesty,
Which, cousin, you shall bear to comfort him,
And we with sober speed will follow you.

FALSTAFF My lord, I beseech you give me leave to go through Gloucestershire, and, when you come to court, stand my good lord in your good report.

54 desert mount merit be promoted **57 thick** (1) opaque (2) heavy **65 been ruled by me** listened to my advice **66 dearer** i.e., at greater military cost **71 Retreat . . . stayed** the order for withdrawal has been sounded and the slaughter has been stopped **73 present** immediate **75 dispatch we** let us hasten **78 cousin** i.e., Westmorland **79 sober** controlled, dignified **82 stand my good lord** act as my patron

PRINCE JOHN

Fare you well, Falstaff. I, in my condition,
Shall better speak of you than you deserve.

[*Exeunt all but Falstaff.*]

FALSTAFF I would you had but the wit; 'twere better than your dukedom. Good faith, this same young sober-blooded boy doth not love me, nor a man cannot make him laugh. But that's no marvel; he drinks no wine. There's never none of these demure boys come to any proof, for thin drink doth so overcool their blood, and making many fish meals, that they fall into a kind of male greensickness, and then, when they marry, they get wenches. They are generally fools and cowards, which some of us should be too, but for inflammation. A good sherris sack hath a twofold operation in it. It ascends me into the brain, dries me there all the foolish and dull and crudy vapors which environ it, makes it apprehensive, quick, forgetive, full of nimble, fiery, and delectable shapes, which, delivered o'er to the voice, the tongue, which is the birth, becomes excellent wit. The second property of your excellent sherris is the warming of the blood, which, before cold and settled, left the liver white and pale, which is the badge of pusillanimity and cowardice. But the sherris warms it and makes it course from the innards to the parts' extremes. It illumineth the face, which as a beacon gives warning to all the rest of this little kingdom, man, to arm; and then the vital commoners and inland petty spirits muster me all to their captain, the heart, who, great and puffed up with this retinue, doth any deed of courage; and this valor comes of sherris. So that skill in the weapon is nothing

83 condition i.e., function as commander **90 come to any proof** stand up well under testing, turn out well. **thin drink** i.e., beer **92 greensickness** a kind of anemia thought to affect young women **93 get wenches** beget girls **95 inflammation** passions excited by liquor. **sherris sack** sherry **96 ascends me** i.e., ascends. (*Me* is used colloquially, as also in l. 109.) **97 crudy** curded **98 environ** surround. **apprehensive** quick to perceive. **forgetive** inventive **101 wit** mental capacity **103 liver** (Thought to be the seat of courage.) **105 course** run **106 extremes** extremities **108–109 vital . . . spirits** vital spirits of man's internal region **109 muster me** assemble

without sack, for that sets it a-work, and learning a mere hoard of gold kept by a devil till sack commences it and sets it in act and use. Hereof comes it that Prince Harry is valiant, for the cold blood he did naturally inherit of his father, he hath, like lean, sterile, and bare land, manured, husbanded, and tilled with excellent endeavor of drinking good and good store of fertile sherris, that he is become very hot and valiant. If I had a thousand sons, the first human principle I would teach them should be to forswear thin potations and to addict themselves to sack.

Enter Bardolph.

How now, Bardolph?

BARDOLPH The army is discharged all and gone.

FALSTAFF Let them go. I'll through Gloucestershire, and there will I visit Master Robert Shallow, Esquire. I have him already tempering between my finger and my thumb, and shortly will I seal with him. Come away.

[*Exeunt.*]

✤

4.4

Enter the King; Warwick; Thomas, Duke of Clarence; Humphrey, [*Duke*] *of Gloucester;* [*and others*].

KING

Now, lords, if God doth give successful end
To this debate that bleedeth at our doors,
We will our youth lead on to higher fields

113 learning learning is **114 kept by a devil** guarded by an evil spirit, like a dragon **114–115 commences it** transforms its potential into actuality (as at a commencement) **117 lean** barren **118 husbanded** cultivated **121 human** secular **123 potations** drinks **128 tempering** softening (like a piece of wax) **129 seal with** i.e., shape him to my purposes; seal a bargain with (continuing the metaphor of sealing wax)

4.4. Location: King Henry's court at Westminster. The Jerusalem Chamber (adjoining Westminster Abbey); so called for its various inscriptions concerning Jerusalem.
2 debate strife **3 higher fields** i.e., a crusade to Palestine

And draw no swords but what are sanctified.
Our navy is addressed, our power collected,
Our substitutes in absence well invested,
And everything lies level to our wish.
Only we want a little personal strength,
And pause us till these rebels now afoot
Come underneath the yoke of government.

WARWICK
Both which we doubt not but Your Majesty
Shall soon enjoy.

KING Humphrey, my son of Gloucester,
Where is the Prince your brother?

GLOUCESTER
I think he's gone to hunt, my lord, at Windsor.

KING
And how accompanied?

GLOUCESTER I do not know, my lord.

KING
Is not his brother Thomas of Clarence with him?

GLOUCESTER
No, my good lord, he is in presence here.

CLARENCE What would my lord and father?

KING
Nothing but well to thee, Thomas of Clarence.
How chance thou art not with the Prince thy brother?
He loves thee, and thou dost neglect him, Thomas;
Thou hast a better place in his affection
Than all thy brothers. Cherish it, my boy,
And noble offices thou mayst effect
Of mediation, after I am dead,
Between his greatness and thy other brethren.
Therefore omit him not, blunt not his love,
Nor lose the good advantage of his grace
By seeming cold or careless of his will.
For he is gracious, if he be observed.
He hath a tear for pity and a hand
Open as day for melting charity.

4 what those that **5 addressed** ready, prepared **6 substitutes** deputies. **invested** empowered **7 level** conformable **8 want** lack **17 in presence** present at court **18 would** wishes **24 offices** functions. **effect** perform, accomplish **27 omit** neglect **28 grace** favor **30 observed** paid proper respect, humored **32 melting** tender, compassionate

Yet notwithstanding, being incensed, he is flint, 33
As humorous as winter, and as sudden 34
As flaws congealèd in the spring of day. 35
His temper, therefore, must be well observed. 36
Chide him for faults, and do it reverently,
When you perceive his blood inclined to mirth;
But, being moody, give him time and scope, 39
Till that his passions, like a whale on ground,
Confound themselves with working. Learn this,
  Thomas, 41
And thou shalt prove a shelter to thy friends,
A hoop of gold to bind thy brothers in,
That the united vessel of their blood,
Mingled with venom of suggestion— 45
As, force perforce, the age will pour it in—
Shall never leak, though it do work as strong
As aconitum or rash gunpowder. 48

CLARENCE
I shall observe him with all care and love.

KING
Why art thou not at Windsor with him, Thomas?

CLARENCE
He is not there today; he dines in London.

KING And how accompanied?

CLARENCE
With Poins and other his continual followers.

KING
Most subject is the fattest soil to weeds, 54
And he, the noble image of my youth,
Is overspread with them. Therefore my grief
Stretches itself beyond the hour of death.
The blood weeps from my heart when I do shape
In forms imaginary th' unguided days
And rotten times that you shall look upon

33 flint i.e., in emitting fire **34 humorous** unpredictable in mood **35 flaws congealèd** snow squalls. **spring of day** early morning **36 temper** disposition **39 moody** angry **41 Confound** exhaust, consume. **working** struggling **45 suggestion** insinuation, suspicion. (The image in ll. 43–48 is of a vessel of the brothers' combined blood, held together with golden hoops of affection and loyalty but threatened by the poison of mutual mistrust their enemies will try to foment in them.) **48 aconitum** a strong poison extracted from monkshood. **rash** quick-acting **54 fattest** richest

When I am sleeping with my ancestors.
For when his headstrong riot hath no curb,
When rage and hot blood are his counselors,
When means and lavish manners meet together, 64
O, with what wings shall his affections fly 65
Towards fronting peril and opposed decay! 66

WARWICK

My gracious lord, you look beyond him quite. 67
The Prince but studies his companions
Like a strange tongue, wherein, to gain the language, 69
'Tis needful that the most immodest word
Be looked upon and learned, which, once attained,
Your Highness knows, comes to no further use
But to be known and hated. So, like gross terms, 73
The Prince will in the perfectness of time
Cast off his followers, and their memory
Shall as a pattern or a measure live
By which His Grace must mete the lives of other, 77
Turning past evils to advantages.

KING

'Tis seldom when the bee doth leave her comb 79
In the dead carrion.

Enter Westmorland.

Who's here? Westmorland? 80

WESTMORLAND

Health to my sovereign, and new happiness
Added to that that I am to deliver!
Prince John your son doth kiss Your Grace's hand.
Mowbray, the Bishop Scroop, Hastings, and all
Are brought to the correction of your law.
There is not now a rebel's sword unsheathed,
But Peace puts forth her olive everywhere.
The manner how this action hath been borne

64 lavish unrestrained, licentious **65 affections** inclinations **66 fronting . . . decay** danger and ruin that confront him **67 look beyond** go too far in judging **69 strange** foreign **73 like gross terms** just as with coarse expressions **77 mete** measure, appraise. **other** others **79–80 'Tis . . . carrion** rarely does the bee that has placed her comb in dead carrion leave her honeycomb; i.e., the Prince will not forsake his corrupt delights

Here at more leisure may Your Highness read,
With every course in his particular. 90
[*He gives a document.*]

KING
O Westmorland, thou art a summer bird,
Which ever in the haunch of winter sings 92
The lifting up of day.

Enter Harcourt.

Look, here's more news. 93

HARCOURT
From enemies heaven keep Your Majesty,
And, when they stand against you, may they fall
As those that I am come to tell you of!
The Earl Northumberland and the Lord Bardolph,
With a great power of English and of Scots,
Are by the sheriff of Yorkshire overthrown.
The manner and true order of the fight
This packet, please it you, contains at large. 101
[*He gives letters.*]

KING
And wherefore should these good news make me sick?
Will Fortune never come with both hands full,
But write her fair words still in foulest letters? 104
She either gives a stomach and no food— 105
Such are the poor, in health; or else a feast
And takes away the stomach—such are the rich,
That have abundance and enjoy it not.
I should rejoice now at this happy news,
And now my sight fails and my brain is giddy.
O, me! Come near me. Now I am much ill.
[*The King swoons. Several come to his aid.*]

GLOUCESTER
Comfort, Your Majesty!

CLARENCE
O my royal father!

WESTMORLAND
My sovereign lord, cheer up yourself, look up.

90 course . . . particular event or phase set forth in detail **92 haunch** latter end **93 lifting up** dawn **101 at large** in full **104 still** always **105 stomach** appetite

WARWICK
Be patient, princes. You do know these fits
Are with His Highness very ordinary.
Stand from him; give him air. He'll straight be well.

CLARENCE
No, no, he cannot long hold out these pangs. 117
Th' incessant care and labor of his mind
Hath wrought the mure that should confine it in 119
So thin that life looks through.

GLOUCESTER
The people fear me, for they do observe 121
Unfathered heirs and loathly births of nature. 122
The seasons change their manners, as the year 123
Had found some months asleep and leapt them over.

CLARENCE
The river hath thrice flowed, no ebb between, 125
And the old folk, time's doting chronicles,
Say it did so a little time before
That our great-grandsire, Edward, sicked and died. 128

WARWICK
Speak lower, princes, for the King recovers.

GLOUCESTER
This apoplexy will certain be his end.

KING
I pray you, take me up and bear me hence
Into some other chamber.

4.5

[*The King is borne to another part of the stage, to bed.*]

[KING]
Let there be no noise made, my gentle friends,
Unless some dull and favorable hand 2
Will whisper music to my weary spirit.

117 hold out endure **119 wrought the mure** made the wall **121 fear** frighten **122 Unfathered heirs** persons believed to be supernaturally conceived. **loathly births** monstrous offspring **123 as** as if **125 river** i.e., Thames. (Holinshed records this event as having happened on October 12, 1412.) **128 Edward** Edward III. **sicked** fell sick

4.5. Location: The scene is continuous.
2 dull soft, soothing. **favorable** kindly

WARWICK
Call for the music in the other room.
[*Exit one or more. Soft music within.*]

KING
Set me the crown upon my pillow here.

CLARENCE
His eye is hollow, and he changes much. 6

WARWICK
Less noise, less noise!
[*The crown is placed on the King's pillow.*]

Enter [*Prince*] *Harry.*

PRINCE Who saw the Duke of Clarence?

CLARENCE
I am here, brother, full of heaviness. 8

PRINCE
How now, rain within doors, and none abroad? 9
How doth the King?

GLOUCESTER Exceeding ill.

PRINCE
Heard he the good news yet? Tell it him.

GLOUCESTER
He altered much upon the hearing it.

PRINCE If he be sick with joy, he'll recover without physic.

WARWICK
Not so much noise, my lords. Sweet Prince, speak low.
The King your father is disposed to sleep.

CLARENCE
Let us withdraw into the other room.

WARWICK
Will 't please Your Grace to go along with us?

PRINCE
No, I will sit and watch here by the King.
[*Exeunt all but the Prince.*]
Why doth the crown lie there upon his pillow,
Being so troublesome a bedfellow?
O polished perturbation! Golden care! 23
That keep'st the ports of slumber open wide 24

6 changes changes color, turns pale **8 heaviness** sadness **9 rain** i.e., tears **23 perturbation** cause of perturbation **24 ports** gates

To many a watchful night! Sleep with it now! 25
Yet not so sound and half so deeply sweet 26
As he whose brow with homely biggen bound 27
Snores out the watch of night. O majesty!
When thou dost pinch thy bearer, thou dost sit 29
Like a rich armor worn in heat of day,
That scald'st with safety. By his gates of breath 31
There lies a downy feather which stirs not.
Did he suspire, that light and weightless down 33
Perforce must move. My gracious lord! My Father!
This sleep is sound indeed. This is a sleep
That from this golden rigol hath divorced 36
So many English kings. Thy due from me
Is tears and heavy sorrows of the blood, 38
Which nature, love, and filial tenderness
Shall, O dear Father, pay thee plenteously.
My due from thee is this imperial crown,
Which, as immediate from thy place and blood, 42
Derives itself to me. [*He puts on the crown.*] Lo, where
it sits, 43
Which God shall guard. And put the world's whole
strength
Into one giant arm, it shall not force
This lineal honor from me. This from thee 46
Will I to mine leave, as 'tis left to me. *Exit.*

KING [*Awaking*] Warwick! Gloucester! Clarence!

Enter Warwick, Gloucester, Clarence, [*and others*].

CLARENCE
Doth the King call?

WARWICK What would Your Majesty?

KING
Why did you leave me here alone, my lords?

25 watchful wakeful. **Sleep with it** i.e., may you (King Henry) sleep with this symbol of care beside you **26 Yet not** i.e., yet your sleep will nonetheless not be **27 biggen** nightcap **29 pinch** torment **31 scald'st with safety** burns while providing safety. **gates of breath** lips **33 suspire** breathe **36 rigol** circle, i.e., crown **38 blood** (1) heart (2) kinship **42 as immediate from** as I am next in line to **43 Derives itself** descends **46 lineal** inherited

CLARENCE
We left the Prince my brother here, my liege,
Who undertook to sit and watch by you.

KING
The Prince of Wales? Where is he? Let me see him.
He is not here.

WARWICK
This door is open; he is gone this way.

GLOUCESTER
He came not through the chamber where we stayed.

KING
Where is the crown? Who took it from my pillow?

WARWICK
When we withdrew, my liege, we left it here.

KING
The Prince hath ta'en it hence. Go seek him out.
Is he so hasty that he doth suppose
My sleep my death?
Find him, my lord of Warwick; chide him hither.
[*Exit Warwick.*]
This part of his conjoins with my disease 63
And helps to end me. See, sons, what things you are!
How quickly Nature falls into revolt
When gold becomes her object!
For this the foolish overcareful fathers
Have broke their sleep with thoughts, 68
Their brains with care, their bones with industry;
For this they have engrossèd and piled up 70
The cankered heaps of strange-achievèd gold; 71
For this they have been thoughtful to invest 72
Their sons with arts and martial exercises—
When, like the bee, tolling from every flower 74
The virtuous sweets,
Our thighs packed with wax, our mouths with honey,
We bring it to the hive, and like the bees
Are murdered for our pains. This bitter taste 78
Yields his engrossments to the ending father. 79

63 part act. **conjoins** unites, joins **68 thoughts** cares **70 engrossèd** amassed **71 cankered** rusting and malignant. **strange-achievèd** won by unusual effort or means, or in distant lands **72 thoughtful** careful **74 tolling** taking as toll, collecting **78–79 This . . . father** his storing up of treasures yields this bitter taste to the dying father

Enter Warwick.

Now, where is he that will not stay so long
Till his friend sickness have determined me? 81

WARWICK

My lord, I found the Prince in the next room,
Washing with kindly tears his gentle cheeks, 83
With such a deep demeanor in great sorrow 84
That tyranny, which never quaffed but blood, 85
Would, by beholding him, have washed his knife
With gentle eyedrops. He is coming hither.

KING

But wherefore did he take away the crown?

Enter [*Prince*] *Harry* [*with the crown*].

Lo, where he comes. Come hither to me, Harry.—
Depart the chamber; leave us here alone.
Exeunt [*Warwick and the rest*].

PRINCE

I never thought to hear you speak again.

KING

Thy wish was father, Harry, to that thought.
I stay too long by thee; I weary thee.
Dost thou so hunger for mine empty chair 94
That thou wilt needs invest thee with my honors 95
Before thy hour be ripe? O foolish youth,
Thou seek'st the greatness that will overwhelm thee.
Stay but a little, for my cloud of dignity 98
Is held from falling with so weak a wind 99
That it will quickly drop. My day is dim.
Thou hast stol'n that which after some few hours
Were thine without offense, and at my death
Thou hast sealed up my expectation. 103
Thy life did manifest thou lovedst me not,
And thou wilt have me die assured of it.
Thou hid'st a thousand daggers in thy thoughts,

81 determined ended, put an end to **83 kindly** natural **84 deep** intense **85 tyranny** cruelty. **quaffed** drank **94 chair** throne **95 wilt needs** must **98 my cloud of dignity** the fragile substance of my high estate **99 so weak a wind** i.e., the King's failing breath, compared to the wind that was thought to hold up the clouds **103 sealed up** confirmed

Which thou hast whetted on thy stony heart, 107
To stab at half an hour of my life.
What, canst thou not forbear me half an hour? 109
Then get thee gone and dig my grave thyself,
And bid the merry bells ring to thine ear
That thou art crownèd, not that I am dead.
Let all the tears that should bedew my hearse
Be drops of balm to sanctify thy head. 114
Only compound me with forgotten dust; 115
Give that which gave thee life unto the worms.
Pluck down my officers, break my decrees,
For now a time is come to mock at form. 118
Harry the Fifth is crowned. Up, vanity! 119
Down, royal state! All you sage counselors, hence! 120
And to the English court assemble now,
From every region, apes of idleness!
Now, neighbor confines, purge you of your scum. 123
Have you a ruffian that will swear, drink, dance,
Revel the night, rob, murder, and commit
The oldest sins the newest kind of ways?
Be happy; he will trouble you no more.
England shall double gild his treble guilt;
England shall give him office, honor, might;
For the fifth Harry from curbed license plucks
The muzzle of restraint, and the wild dog
Shall flesh his tooth on every innocent. 132
O my poor kingdom, sick with civil blows!
When that my care could not withhold thy riots, 134
What wilt thou do when riot is thy care? 135
O, thou wilt be a wilderness again, 136
Peopled with wolves, thy old inhabitants!

PRINCE [*Kneeling and returning the crown*]
O, pardon me, my liege! But for my tears, 138

107 whetted sharpened **109 forbear** spare **114 balm** consecrated oil used in anointing the king at his coronation **115 compound** mix **118 form** ceremony, orderly usages **119 vanity** folly **120 state** ceremony **123 neighbor confines** territories of neighboring countries **132 flesh his tooth on** i.e., plunge his teeth into the flesh of. (To *flesh* means to initiate into bloodshed, to make an animal eager for prey by the taste of blood.) **134 When that** when. **care** careful maintenance of discipline **135 care** concern **136 thou** i.e., the Prince and his kingdom **138 But for** were it not for

The moist impediments unto my speech,
I had forestalled this dear and deep rebuke 140
Ere you with grief had spoke and I had heard
The course of it so far. There is your crown;
And He that wears the crown immortally
Long guard it yours! If I affect it more 144
Than as your honor and as your renown,
Let me no more from this obedience rise, 146
Which my most inward true and duteous spirit
Teacheth this prostrate and exterior bending.
God witness with me, when I here came in,
And found no course of breath within Your Majesty, 150
How cold it struck my heart! If I do feign,
O, let me in my present wildness die
And never live to show th' incredulous world
The noble change that I have purposèd!
Coming to look on you, thinking you dead,
And dead almost, my liege, to think you were,
I spake unto this crown as having sense, 157
And thus upbraided it: "The care on thee depending
Hath fed upon the body of my father;
Therefore, thou best of gold art worst of gold.
Other, less fine in carat, is more precious,
Preserving life in med'cine potable; 162
But thou, most fine, most honored, most renowned,
Hast eat thy bearer up." Thus, my most royal liege, 164
Accusing it, I put it on my head,
To try with it, as with an enemy 166
That had before my face murdered my father,
The quarrel of a true inheritor. 168
But if it did infect my blood with joy
Or swell my thoughts to any strain of pride, 170
If any rebel or vain spirit of mine
Did with the least affection of a welcome 172

140 had would have. **dear** severe (because deeply felt emotionally)
144 affect desire **146 obedience** obeisance **150 course** current
157 as having sense as if it were capable of sense impressions
162 med'cine potable potable gold, an elixir, thought from Galen's time to possess magical power to cure **164 eat** eaten. (Pronounced "et.")
166 try struggle **168 The quarrel . . . inheritor** (The Prince, as the son and heir of a murdered man, has a quarrel to settle with the murderer.) **170 strain** feeling, tendency **172 affection** inclination

Give entertainment to the might of it,
Let God forever keep it from my head
And make me as the poorest vassal is
That doth with awe and terror kneel to it!

KING O my son,
God put it in thy mind to take it hence,
That thou mightst win the more thy father's love,
Pleading so wisely in excuse of it!
Come hither, Harry, sit thou by my bed,
[*The Prince rises and sits by the bed*]
And hear, I think, the very latest counsel 182
That ever I shall breathe. God knows, my son,
By what bypaths and indirect crook'd ways
I met this crown, and I myself know well
How troublesome it sat upon my head.
To thee it shall descend with better quiet,
Better opinion, better confirmation, 188
For all the soil of the achievement goes 189
With me into the earth. It seemed in me
But as an honor snatched with boisterous hand, 191
And I had many living to upbraid
My gain of it by their assistances,
Which daily grew to quarrel and to bloodshed,
Wounding supposèd peace. All these bold fears 195
Thou seest with peril I have answerèd,
For all my reign hath been but as a scene
Acting that argument. And now my death 198
Changes the mood, for what in me was purchased 199
Falls upon thee in a more fairer sort; 200
So thou the garland wear'st successively. 201
Yet, though thou stand'st more sure than I could do,
Thou art not firm enough, since griefs are green. 203
And all my friends, which thou must make thy friends,
Have but their stings and teeth newly ta'en out,
By whose fell working I was first advanced 206
And by whose power I well might lodge a fear 207

182 latest last **188 opinion** public support, reputation **189 soil** stain **191 boisterous** violent **195 fears** objects of fear **198 argument** theme **199 mood** state of mind; mode, musical key. **purchased** i.e., gained by transaction **200 sort** manner, way **201 So** thus. **garland** crown. **successively** by right of succession **203 griefs are green** grievances are fresh **206 fell working** fierce effort **207 lodge** harbor

To be again displaced. Which to avoid,
I cut them off, and had a purpose now
To lead out many to the Holy Land,
Lest rest and lying still might make them look 211
Too near unto my state. Therefore, my Harry, 212
Be it thy course to busy giddy minds
With foreign quarrels, that action, hence borne out, 214
May waste the memory of the former days. 215
More would I, but my lungs are wasted so
That strength of speech is utterly denied me.
How I came by the crown, O God forgive,
And grant it may with thee in true peace live!

PRINCE My gracious liege,
You won it, wore it, kept it, gave it me.
Then plain and right must my possession be,
Which I with more than with a common pain 223
'Gainst all the world will rightfully maintain.

Enter [*Prince John of*] *Lancaster* [*and Warwick*].

KING
Look, look, here comes my John of Lancaster.

PRINCE JOHN
Health, peace, and happiness to my royal father!

KING
Thou bring'st me happiness and peace, son John;
But health, alack, with youthful wings is flown
From this bare withered trunk. Upon thy sight 229
My worldly business makes a period. 230
Where is my lord of Warwick?

PRINCE My lord of Warwick!

[*Warwick comes forward.*]

KING
Doth any name particular belong
Unto the lodging where I first did swoon? 233

WARWICK
'Tis called Jerusalem, my noble lord.

211–212 look . . . state examine too painstakingly my regal status, my claim **214 action . . . out** military action, conducted in other lands **215 waste** efface, obliterate **223 pain** effort **229 Upon thy sight** at the very moment of my seeing you **230 makes a period** comes to an end, rounds out a whole **233 lodging** room, chamber

KING

Laud be to God! Even there my life must end.
It hath been prophesied to me many years
I should not die but in Jerusalem,
Which vainly I supposed the Holy Land.
But bear me to that chamber; there I'll lie.
In that Jerusalem shall Harry die. [*Exeunt.*]

✤

5.1 *Enter Shallow, Falstaff, and Bardolph* [*and Page*].

SHALLOW By Cock and pie, sir, you shall not away to- 1
night.—What, Davy, I say!

FALSTAFF You must excuse me, Master Robert Shallow.

SHALLOW I will not excuse you, you shall not be
excused, excuses shall not be admitted, there is no excuse shall serve, you shall not be excused.—Why, Davy!

[*Enter Davy*.]

DAVY Here, sir.

SHALLOW Davy, Davy, Davy, Davy, let me see, Davy,
let me see, Davy, let me see. Yea, marry, William cook, 9
bid him come hither.—Sir John, you shall not be excused.

DAVY Marry, sir, thus, those precepts cannot be served. 12
And again, sir, shall we sow the hade land with 13
wheat?

SHALLOW With red wheat, Davy. But for William 15
cook—are there no young pigeons?

DAVY Yes, sir. Here is now the smith's note for shoeing 17
and plow irons. [*He gives a paper*.]

SHALLOW Let it be cast and paid.—Sir John, you shall not 19
be excused.

DAVY Now, sir, a new link to the bucket must needs be 21
had. And, sir, do you mean to stop any of William's
wages about the sack he lost the other day at Hinckley 23
fair?

SHALLOW 'A shall answer it. Some pigeons, Davy, a 25
couple of short-legged hens, a joint of mutton, and any
pretty little tiny kickshaws, tell William cook. 27

[*Davy and Shallow confer privately*.]

5.1. Location: Gloucestershire. Shallow's house.
1 By Cock and pie (A mild oath, meaning "By God and the ordinal or book of services for the Church.") **9 William cook** William the cook **12 precepts** writs, summonses **13 hade land** strip of unplowed land between two plowed fields **15 red wheat** a variety of red-tinged wheat planted late in the summer **17 note** bill **19 cast** added up **21 link** chain. **bucket** yoke or pail **23 Hinckley** market town not far from Coventry, famous for its fairs **25 answer** pay for **27 kickshaws** fancy dishes. (From French *quelque chose*.)

DAVY Doth the man of war stay all night, sir?

SHALLOW Yea, Davy. I will use him well. A friend i' the court is better than a penny in purse. Use his men well, Davy, for they are arrant knaves, and will backbite.

DAVY No worse than they are backbitten, sir, for they 33
have marvelous foul linen. 34

SHALLOW Well conceited, Davy. About thy business, 35
Davy.

DAVY I beseech you, sir, to countenance William Visor 37
of Woncot against Clement Perkes o' the hill.

SHALLOW There is many complaints, Davy, against that Visor. That Visor is an arrant knave, on my knowledge.

DAVY I grant your worship that he is a knave, sir; but yet, God forbid, sir, but a knave should have some countenance at his friend's request. An honest man, sir, is able to speak for himself, when a knave is not. I have served your worship truly, sir, this eight years;
an I cannot once or twice in a quarter bear out a knave 47
against an honest man, I have little credit with your worship. The knave is mine honest friend, sir; therefore, I beseech you, let him be countenanced.

SHALLOW Go to, I say he shall have no wrong. Look 51
about, Davy. [*Exit Davy.*] Where are you, Sir John? 52
Come, come, come, off with your boots. Give me your hand, Master Bardolph.

BARDOLPH I am glad to see your worship.

SHALLOW I thank thee with all my heart, kind Master
Bardolph. And welcome, my tall fellow [*To the Page*]. 57
Come, Sir John.

FALSTAFF I'll follow you, good Master Robert Shallow.
[*Exit Shallow.*] Bardolph, look to our horses. [*Exeunt
Bardolph and Page.*] If I were sawed into quantities, I 61
should make four dozen of such bearded hermits' staves as Master Shallow. It is a wonderful thing to see

33 backbitten (with pun on "bitten by vermin") **34 marvelous** marvelously **35 Well conceited** ingeniously punned **37 countenance** favor **47 bear out** support **51–52 Look about** look sharp, be on the alert **57 tall** brave (but also with an ironic witticism about the page's small stature) **61 quantities** pieces

the semblable coherence of his men's spirits and his. They, by observing of him, do bear themselves like foolish justices; he, by conversing with them, is turned into a justice-like servingman. Their spirits are so married in conjunction with the participation of society that they flock together in consent, like so many wild geese. If I had a suit to Master Shallow, I would humor his men with the imputation of being near their master; if to his men, I would curry with Master Shallow that no man could better command his servants. It is certain that either wise bearing or ignorant carriage is caught, as men take diseases, one of another. Therefore let men take heed of their company. I will devise matter enough out of this Shallow to keep Prince Harry in continual laughter the wearing out of six fashions, which is four terms, or two actions, and 'a shall laugh without intervallums. O, it is much that a lie with a slight oath and a jest with a sad brow will do with a fellow that never had the ache in his shoulders! O, you shall see him laugh till his face be like a wet cloak ill laid up.

SHALLOW [*Within*] Sir John!

FALSTAFF I come, Master Shallow, I come, Master Shallow. [*Exit*.]

5.2 *Enter Warwick* [*and the*] *Lord Chief Justice* [*meeting*].

WARWICK

How now, my Lord Chief Justice, whither away?

64 semblable coherence similar or complete agreement **66 conversing** associating **68 with . . . society** by close association **69 consent** agreement **71 with . . . near** implying that I am friendly with **72 curry with** employ flattery with **74 carriage** demeanor, behavior **79 four terms** i.e., of court, Michaelmas, Hilary, Easter, and Trinity, all in all comprising one legal year. **actions** lawsuits **80 intervallums** intervals between terms of court **81 sad** serious **82–83 a fellow . . . shoulders** i.e., someone who is inexperienced in the troubles and complexities of this world and hence gullible **84 ill laid up** carelessly put away so that it wrinkles

5.2. Location: Westminster. The royal court.
1 whither away where are you going

CHIEF JUSTICE How doth the King?

WARWICK
Exceeding well. His cares are now all ended.

CHIEF JUSTICE
I hope, not dead.

WARWICK He's walked the way of nature, 4
And to our purposes he lives no more.

CHIEF JUSTICE
I would His Majesty had called me with him.
The service that I truly did his life 7
Hath left me open to all injuries.

WARWICK
Indeed I think the young King loves you not.

CHIEF JUSTICE
I know he doth not, and do arm myself
To welcome the condition of the time,
Which cannot look more hideously upon me
Than I have drawn it in my fantasy.

Enter [*Prince*] *John* [*of Lancaster*], *Thomas* [*of Clarence*], *and Humphrey* [*of Gloucester, with*] *Westmorland,* [*and others*].

WARWICK
Here comes the heavy issue of dead Harry. 14
O, that the living Harry had the temper 15
Of he, the worst of these three gentlemen! 16
How many nobles then should hold their places
That must strike sail to spirits of vile sort! 18

CHIEF JUSTICE
O God, I fear all will be overturned.

PRINCE JOHN
Good morrow, cousin Warwick, good morrow.

GLOUCESTER, CLARENCE Good morrow, cousin.

PRINCE JOHN
We meet like men that had forgot to speak. 22

WARWICK
We do remember, but our argument 23
Is all too heavy to admit much talk.

4 walked . . . nature i.e., died **7 truly** loyally **14 heavy issue** grieving sons **15 temper** disposition **16 he, the worst** the least worthy **18 strike sail** i.e., salute as a token of submission. (A naval custom.) **22 forgot** forgotten how **23 argument** subject

PRINCE JOHN
Well, peace be with him that hath made us heavy!

CHIEF JUSTICE
Peace be with us, lest we be heavier!

GLOUCESTER
O good my lord, you have lost a friend indeed,
And I dare swear you borrow not that face
Of seeming sorrow; it is sure your own.

PRINCE JOHN
Though no man be assured what grace to find, 30
You stand in coldest expectation. 31
I am the sorrier; would 'twere otherwise. 32

CLARENCE
Well, you must now speak Sir John Falstaff fair, 33
Which swims against your stream of quality. 34

CHIEF JUSTICE
Sweet princes, what I did I did in honor,
Led by th' impartial conduct of my soul,
And never shall you see that I will beg
A ragged and forestalled remission. 38
If truth and upright innocency fail me,
I'll to the King my master that is dead
And tell him who hath sent me after him.

WARWICK Here comes the Prince.

Enter the Prince [*as King Henry the Fifth*] *and Blunt.*

CHIEF JUSTICE
Good morrow, and God save Your Majesty!

KING
This new and gorgeous garment, majesty,
Sits not so easy on me as you think.
Brothers, you mix your sadness with some fear.
This is the English, not the Turkish court;
Not Amurath an Amurath succeeds, 48

30 grace to find favor he will find **31 coldest** most comfortless **32 would** I wish **33 speak . . . fair** speak courteously to Sir John Falstaff **34 swims . . . quality** runs counter to your natural inclination and position **38 A . . . remission** a half-hearted (beggarly) pardon, which is sure to be refused, or whose effect is gone before it is granted **48 Amurath** a Turkish sultan who, upon succeeding his father, had his brothers strangled

But Harry Harry. Yet be sad, good brothers,
For, by my faith, it very well becomes you.
Sorrow so royally in you appears
That I will deeply put the fashion on
And wear it in my heart. Why then, be sad,
But entertain no more of it, good brothers,
Than a joint burden laid upon us all.
For me, by heaven, I bid you be assured, 56
I'll be your father and your brother too.
Let me but bear your love, I'll bear your cares.
Yet weep that Harry's dead, and so will I;
But Harry lives that shall convert those tears
By number into hours of happiness. 61

PRINCES
We hope no otherwise from Your Majesty.

KING
You all look strangely on me. [*To the Chief Justice.*]
And you most.
You are, I think, assured I love you not.

CHIEF JUSTICE
I am assured, if I be measured rightly,
Your Majesty hath no just cause to hate me.

KING No?
How might a prince of my great hopes forget
So great indignities you laid upon me?
What? Rate, rebuke, and roughly send to prison 70
Th' immediate heir of England? Was this easy? 71
May this be washed in Lethe and forgotten? 72

CHIEF JUSTICE
I then did use the person of your father; 73
The image of his power lay then in me.
And in th' administration of his law,
Whiles I was busy for the commonwealth,
Your Highness pleasèd to forget my place,
The majesty and power of law and justice,
The image of the King whom I presented, 79
And struck me in my very seat of judgment;

56 For as for **61 By number** i.e., for each of our many tears there will be an hour of happiness **70 Rate** chide **71 immediate heir** next heir in succession. **easy** of small importance, easily forgotten **72 Lethe** the river of forgetfulness in Hades **73 use the person** act as representative **79 presented** represented

Whereon, as an offender to your father,
I gave bold way to my authority
And did commit you. If the deed were ill, 83
Be you contented, wearing now the garland, 84
To have a son set your decrees at naught,
To pluck down justice from your awful bench, 86
To trip the course of law and blunt the sword
That guards the peace and safety of your person,
Nay, more, to spurn at your most royal image
And mock your workings in a second body? 90
Question your royal thoughts, make the case yours;
Be now the father and propose a son, 92
Hear your own dignity so much profaned,
See your most dreadful laws so loosely slighted,
Behold yourself so by a son disdained,
And then imagine me taking your part
And in your power soft silencing your son. 97
After this cold considerance sentence me, 98
And, as you are a king, speak in your state 99
What I have done that misbecame my place,
My person, or my liege's sovereignty.

KING
You are right justice, and you weigh this well. 102
Therefore still bear the balance and the sword; 103
And I do wish your honors may increase,
Till you do live to see a son of mine
Offend you and obey you, as I did.
So shall I live to speak my father's words:
"Happy am I that have a man so bold
That dares do justice on my proper son; 109
And not less happy, having such a son
That would deliver up his greatness so
Into the hands of justice." You did commit me;
For which I do commit into your hand
Th' unstainèd sword that you have used to bear, 114
With this remembrance, that you use the same 115

83 commit i.e., to prison **84 garland** crown **86 awful** inspiring awe **90 second body** representative, deputy **92 propose** imagine, suppose **97 soft** gently **98 cold considerance** calm reflection **99 state** royal capacity **102 right** true, ideal **103 balance** scale (which along with the *sword* was an emblem of justice) **109 proper** own **114 have used** were accustomed **115 remembrance** reminder, admonition

With the like bold, just, and impartial spirit
As you have done 'gainst me. There is my hand.
You shall be as a father to my youth.
My voice shall sound as you do prompt mine ear, 119
And I will stoop and humble my intents
To your well-practiced wise directions.
And, princes all, believe me, I beseech you:
My father is gone wild into his grave, 123
For in his tomb lie my affections, 124
And with his spirits sadly I survive 125
To mock the expectation of the world,
To frustrate prophecies, and to rase out 127
Rotten opinion, who hath writ me down 128
After my seeming. The tide of blood in me 129
Hath proudly flowed in vanity till now; 130
Now doth it turn and ebb back to the sea,
Where it shall mingle with the state of floods 132
And flow henceforth in formal majesty.
Now call we our high court of Parliament.
And let us choose such limbs of noble counsel
That the great body of our state may go
In equal rank with the best-governed nation;
That war, or peace, or both at once, may be
As things acquainted and familiar to us,
[*To Chief Justice*] In which you, father, shall have
  foremost hand.
Our coronation done, we will accite, 141
As I before remembered, all our state. 142
And, God consigning to my good intents, 143
No prince nor peer shall have just cause to say,
God shorten Harry's happy life one day! *Exeunt.*

✤

119 sound speak **123–124 My . . . affections** i.e., my wildness, having disappeared with my father's death, is buried along with my father **124 affections** (wild) inclinations **125 sadly** soberly **127 rase out** erase **128 who** which **129 After my seeming** according to what I appeared to be. **blood** passion **130 vanity** folly **132 state of floods** majesty of the ocean **141 accite** summon **142 remembered** mentioned. **state** peers, nobility **143 consigning to** sanctioning

5.3

Enter Sir John [*Falstaff*], *Shallow, Silence, Davy, Bardolph,* [*and the*] *Page.* [*Davy provides food and wine.*]

SHALLOW Nay, you shall see my orchard, where, in an
arbor, we will eat a last year's pippin of mine own 2
grafting, with a dish of caraways, and so forth. Come, 3
cousin Silence. And then to bed.

FALSTAFF 'Fore God, you have here a goodly dwelling
and a rich.

SHALLOW Barren, barren, barren. Beggars all, beggars
all, Sir John. Marry, good air.—Spread, Davy, spread, 8
Davy. Well said, Davy. 9

FALSTAFF This Davy serves you for good uses. He is
your servingman and your husband. 11

SHALLOW A good varlet, a good varlet, a very good var- 12
let, Sir John. By the Mass, I have drunk too much sack
at supper. A good varlet. Now sit down, now sit
down. Come, cousin. [*They sit.*]

SILENCE Ah, sirrah, quoth 'a, we shall 16
[*Sings.*] "Do nothing but eat, and make good cheer,
And praise God for the merry year,
When flesh is cheap and females dear, 19
And lusty lads roam here and there
So merrily,
And ever among so merrily." 22

FALSTAFF There's a merry heart! Good Master Silence,
I'll give you a health for that anon. 24

SHALLOW Give Master Bardolph some wine, Davy.

DAVY Sweet sir, sit, I'll be with you anon. Most sweet
sir, sit. Master page, good master page, sit. Proface! 27
What you want in meat, we'll have in drink. But you 28
must bear; the heart's all. [*Exit.*] 29

SHALLOW Be merry, Master Bardolph, and, my little
soldier there, be merry.

5.3. Location: Gloucestershire. Shallow's orchard.
2 pippin a kind of apple **3 caraways** caraway seeds (often eaten with apples) **8 Spread** spread the cloth **9 said** done **11 husband** manager of the household **12 varlet** servant **16 quoth 'a** said he **19 flesh** meat (with sexual suggestion) **22 ever among** all the while **24 give you a health** drink you a toast **27 Proface** (Formula of welcome to a meal, meaning "May it do you good.") **28 want** lack. **meat** food **29 bear** be forbearing

SILENCE [*Sings*]
"Be merry, be merry, my wife has all,
For women are shrews, both short and tall.
'Tis merry in hall when beards wags all, 34
And welcome merry Shrovetide. 35
Be merry, be merry."

FALSTAFF I did not think Master Silence had been a man
of this mettle. 38

SILENCE Who, I? I have been merry twice and once 39
ere now.

Enter Davy.

DAVY [*To Bardolph*] There's a dish of leather-coats 41
for you.

SHALLOW Davy!

DAVY Your worship? I'll be with you straight. [*To Bardolph.*] A cup of wine, sir?

SILENCE [*Sings*]
"A cup of wine that's brisk and fine,
And drink unto thee, leman mine, 47
And a merry heart lives long-a."

FALSTAFF Well said, Master Silence.

SILENCE And we shall be merry; now comes in the sweet o' the night.

FALSTAFF Health and long life to you, Master Silence.

SILENCE [*Sings*]
"Fill the cup, and let it come, 53
I'll pledge you a mile to the bottom." 54

SHALLOW Honest Bardolph, welcome. If thou want'st
anything, and wilt not call, beshrew thy heart. Welcome, my little tiny thief [*To the Page*], and welcome
indeed, too. I'll drink to Master Bardolph, and to all the
cabileros about London. 59

DAVY I hope to see London once ere I die. 60

BARDOLPH An I might see you there, Davy!

SHALLOW By the Mass, you'll crack a quart together, ha, 62
will you not, Master Bardolph?

34 beards wags all all the beards wag up and down (as men talk and laugh) **35 Shrovetide** a season of merrymaking before Lent **38 mettle** spirit **39 twice and once** i.e., now and again **41 leather-coats** russet apples **47 leman** sweetheart **53 let it come** i.e., pass it around **54 a mile** i.e., even if it were a mile **59 cabileros** cavaliers, gallants **60 once** one day **62 crack** consume

BARDOLPH Yea, sir, in a pottle pot.

SHALLOW By God's liggens, I thank thee. The knave will stick by thee, I can assure thee that. 'A will not out, 'a; 'tis true bred.

BARDOLPH And I'll stick by him, sir.

SHALLOW Why, there spoke a king. Lack nothing; be merry. (*One knocks at door.*) Look who's at door there, ho! Who knocks? [*Davy goes to the door.*]

FALSTAFF [*To Silence, seeing him drinking*] Why, now you have done me right.

SILENCE [*Sings*]

"Do me right,
And dub me knight,
Samingo."

Is 't not so?

FALSTAFF 'Tis so.

SILENCE Is 't so? Why then, say an old man can do somewhat.

DAVY [*Returning*] An 't please your worship, there's one Pistol come from the court with news.

FALSTAFF From the court? Let him come in.

Enter Pistol.

How now, Pistol?

PISTOL Sir John, God save you!

FALSTAFF What wind blew you hither, Pistol?

PISTOL Not the ill wind which blows no man to good. Sweet knight, thou art now one of the greatest men in this realm.

SILENCE By 'r Lady, I think 'a be, but goodman Puff of Barson.

PISTOL Puff?
Puff i' thy teeth, most recreant coward base!
Sir John, I am thy Pistol and thy friend,
And helter-skelter have I rode to thee,

64 pottle pot two-quart tankard **65 liggens** (Unexplained.) **66–67 'A will not out** he won't drop out of the drinking, or won't pass out (?) **73 done me right** i.e., kept up with me in drinking **76 Samingo** Sir Mingo (from the Latin *mingo,* I urinate), the hero of the song **80 somewhat** something **90 but** except. (Silence interprets *greatest* in the sense of "heaviest.") **goodman** yeoman **93 recreant** faithless

And tidings do I bring, and lucky joys,
And golden times, and happy news of price.

FALSTAFF I pray thee now, deliver them like a man of this world.

PISTOL
A foutre for the world and worldlings base!
I speak of Africa and golden joys.

FALSTAFF
O base Assyrian knight, what is thy news?
Let King Cophetua know the truth thereof.

SILENCE [*Sings*]
"And Robin Hood, Scarlet, and John."

PISTOL
Shall dunghill curs confront the Helicons?
And shall good news be baffled?
Then, Pistol, lay thy head in Furies' lap.

SHALLOW Honest gentleman, I know not your breeding.

PISTOL Why then, lament therefor.

SHALLOW Give me pardon, sir. If, sir, you come with news from the court, I take it there's but two ways, either to utter them or conceal them. I am, sir, under the King, in some authority.

PISTOL
Under which king, Besonian? Speak, or die.

SHALLOW
Under King Harry.

PISTOL Harry the Fourth, or Fifth?

SHALLOW
Harry the Fourth.

PISTOL A foutre for thine office!
Sir John, thy tender lambkin now is king;
Harry the Fifth's the man. I speak the truth.

97 price great value **98–99 man of this world** ordinary man **100 foutre** (From the French *foutre,* fornicate; a very insulting phrase.) **101 Africa** (Fabled for wealth.) **102 Assyrian** (Falstaff adopts Pistol's highflown style and metrics.) **103 Cophetua** (King Cophetua married a beggar maid, according to the popular ballad "King Cophetua and the Beggar Maid.") **104 And . . . John** (A scrap from another ballad.) **105 Helicons** i.e., poets. (Mount Helicon was the abode of the Muses.) **106 baffled** disgraced **108–109 breeding** parentage, rank **110 therefor** for that **115 Besonian** low, beggarly rascal. (From Italian *bisogno,* need.)

When Pistol lies, do this, and fig me like
The bragging Spaniard. [*Pistol makes a fig.*]

FALSTAFF What, is the old King dead?

PISTOL
As nail in door. The things I speak are just.

FALSTAFF Away, Bardolph! Saddle my horse. Master Robert Shallow, choose what office thou wilt in the land, 'tis thine. Pistol, I will double-charge thee with dignities.

BARDOLPH O joyful day! I would not take a knighthood for my fortune.

PISTOL What, I do bring good news?

FALSTAFF Carry Master Silence to bed. [*Exit Davy, carrying Silence.*] Master Shallow, my lord Shallow—be what thou wilt, I am fortune's steward—get on thy boots. We'll ride all night. O sweet Pistol! Away, Bardolph! [*Exit Bardolph.*] Come, Pistol, utter more to me, and withal devise something to do thyself good. Boot, boot, Master Shallow! I know the young King is sick for me. Let us take any man's horses; the laws of England are at my commandment. Blessed are they that have been my friends, and woe to my Lord Chief Justice!

PISTOL
Let vultures vile seize on his lungs also!
"Where is the life that late I led?" say they.
Why, here it is. Welcome these pleasant days!
Exeunt.

✤

5.4 *Enter Beadle and three or four officers [dragging in Hostess Quickly and Doll Tearsheet].*

HOSTESS No, thou arrant knave! I would to God that I

120 fig insult with a vulgar gesture consisting in thrusting the thumb between the index and middle fingers. (The gesture originated in Spain, as l. 121 suggests. It means much the same as *foutre,* ll. 100 and 117.)
123 just true **126 double-charge** (with a play on Pistol's name)
143 Where . . . led (Fragment of a ballad.)

5.4. Location: London. A street.

might die, that I might have thee hanged. Thou hast drawn my shoulder out of joint.

BEADLE The constables have delivered her over to me, and she shall have whipping cheer, I warrant her. There hath been a man or two lately killed about her.

DOLL Nuthook, nuthook, you lie! Come on, I'll tell thee what, thou damned tripe-visaged rascal, an the child I go with do miscarry, thou wert better thou hadst struck thy mother, thou paper-faced villain!

HOSTESS O the Lord, that Sir John were come! He would make this a bloody day to somebody. But I pray God the fruit of her womb miscarry!

BEADLE If it do, you shall have a dozen of cushions again; you have but eleven now. Come, I charge you both, go with me, for the man is dead that you and Pistol beat amongst you.

DOLL I'll tell you what, you thin man in a censer, I will have you as soundly swinged for this—you bluebottle rogue, you filthy famished correctioner, if you be not swinged, I'll forswear half-kirtles.

BEADLE Come, come, you she knight-errant, come.

HOSTESS O God, that right should thus overcome might! Well, of sufferance comes ease.

DOLL Come, you rogue, come, bring me to a justice.

HOSTESS Ay, come, you starved bloodhound.

DOLL Goodman death, goodman bones!

HOSTESS Thou atomy, thou!

DOLL Come, you thin thing, come, you rascal!

BEADLE Very well. [*Exeunt.*]

5 whipping cheer i.e., a whipping for supper **6 about her** (1) in her company (2) on her account **7 Nuthook** hook for pulling down branches in nutting; here, a constable **8, 10 tripe-visaged, paper-faced** (Allusions to the pockmarked and sallow complexion of the Beadle.) **15 eleven now** (The Beadle accuses Doll of using one of the cushions to make her appear pregnant; pregnant women were spared execution.) **18 thin . . . censer** i.e., figure of a man on the lid of a censer or incense burner, embossed in low relief **19 swinged** thrashed. **bluebottle** (An allusion to the Beadle's blue coat.) **21 half-kirtles** skirts **22 she knight-errant** i.e., a woman who wanders about and sins at night **23–24 right . . . might** (The hostess gets this backward.) **24 sufferance** suffering. (Suffering now promises a better future, since one's luck is bound to change.) **28 atomy** (For *anatomy,* skeleton; an *atomy* is an atom, speck.) **29 rascal** lean deer

5.5 *Enter [Grooms as] strewers of rushes.*

FIRST GROOM More rushes, more rushes! 1
SECOND GROOM The trumpets have sounded twice.
THIRD GROOM 'Twill be two o'clock ere they come from
the coronation. Dispatch, dispatch. [*Exeunt.*] 4

Trumpets sound, and the King and his train pass over the stage. After them enter Falstaff, Shallow, Pistol, Bardolph, and the Boy [*Page*].

FALSTAFF Stand here by me, Master Shallow; I will
make the King do you grace. I will leer upon him as 6
'a comes by, and do but mark the countenance that he
will give me.
PISTOL God bless thy lungs, good knight!
FALSTAFF Come here, Pistol, stand behind me.—O, if I
had had time to have made new liveries, I would have 11
bestowed the thousand pound I borrowed of you. But 12
'tis no matter; this poor show doth better. This doth 13
infer the zeal I had to see him. 14
SHALLOW It doth so.
FALSTAFF It shows my earnestness of affection—
SHALLOW It doth so.
FALSTAFF My devotion—
SHALLOW It doth, it doth, it doth.
FALSTAFF As it were, to ride day and night, and not to
deliberate, not to remember, not to have patience to
shift me— 22
SHALLOW It is best, certain.
FALSTAFF But to stand stained with travel, and sweating
with desire to see him, thinking of nothing else, putting all affairs else in oblivion, as if there were nothing else to be done but to see him.

5.5. Location: A public place near Westminster Abbey.
1 rushes floor coverings, here used for strewing the streets in the King's path **4 Dispatch** hurry **6 grace** honor. **leer** glance sideways and invitingly **11 liveries** uniforms of a noble or royal household
12 bestowed spent. **you** i.e., Justice Shallow **13 poor show** appearing in inferior garments **14 infer** imply **22 shift me** change my apparel

PISTOL 'Tis *semper idem,* for *obsque hoc nihil est.* 28
'Tis all in every part. 29
SHALLOW 'Tis so, indeed.
PISTOL
My knight, I will inflame thy noble liver 31
And make thee rage.
Thy Doll, and Helen of thy noble thoughts, 33
Is in base durance and contagious prison, 34
Haled thither 35
By most mechanical and dirty hand. 36
Rouse up revenge from ebon den with fell Alecto's snake, 37
For Doll is in. Pistol speaks naught but truth. 38
FALSTAFF I will deliver her.
[*Shouts within, and the trumpets sound.*]
PISTOL
There roared the sea, and trumpet-clangor sounds.

Enter the King and his train, [*the Lord Chief Justice among them*].

FALSTAFF
God save Thy Grace, King Hal, my royal Hal!
PISTOL
The heavens thee guard and keep, most royal imp of fame! 42
FALSTAFF God save thee, my sweet boy!
KING
My Lord Chief Justice, speak to that vain man. 44
CHIEF JUSTICE [*To Falstaff*]
Have you your wits? Know you what 'tis you speak?
FALSTAFF
My King! My Jove! I speak to thee, my heart!
KING
I know thee not, old man. Fall to thy prayers.

28 semper . . . est "always the same," for "without this there is nothing." (Pistol approvingly rephrases Falstaff's dedication to put his loyalty to the Prince above all else.) *Obsque* is an error for *absque.*
29 'Tis . . . part (Perhaps a very free translation of the Latin.) **31 liver** (The seat of the passions.) **33 Helen** i.e., Helen of Troy, the type of womanly beauty **34 durance** imprisonment. **contagious** pestilential **35 Haled** dragged **36 mechanical** menial, base **37 ebon** black. **Alecto** one of the Furies, who were depicted with snakes twined in their hair **38 in** i.e., in prison **42 imp** scion **44 vain** foolish

How ill white hairs becomes a fool and jester!
I have long dreamt of such a kind of man,
So surfeit-swelled, so old, and so profane, 50
But being awaked I do despise my dream.
Make less thy body hence, and more thy grace; 52
Leave gormandizing. Know the grave doth gape 53
For thee thrice wider than for other men.
Reply not to me with a fool-born jest.
Presume not that I am the thing I was,
For God doth know, so shall the world perceive,
That I have turned away my former self;
So will I those that kept me company.
When thou dost hear I am as I have been,
Approach me, and thou shalt be as thou wast,
The tutor and the feeder of my riots.
Till then I banish thee, on pain of death,
As I have done the rest of my misleaders,
Not to come near our person by ten mile.
For competence of life I will allow you, 66
That lack of means enforce you not to evils.
And, as we hear you do reform yourselves,
We will, according to your strengths and qualities,
Give you advancement.—Be it your charge, my lord,
To see performed the tenor of our word.
Set on. [*Exeunt King and his train.*]

FALSTAFF Master Shallow, I owe you a thousand pound.

SHALLOW Yea, marry, Sir John, which I beseech you to let me have home with me.

FALSTAFF That can hardly be, Master Shallow. Do not you grieve at this. I shall be sent for in private to him. Look you, he must seem thus to the world. Fear not your advancements; I will be the man yet that shall make you great.

SHALLOW I cannot well perceive how, unless you should give me your doublet and stuff me out with straw. I beseech you, good Sir John, let me have five hundred of my thousand.

50 surfeit-swelled swollen from gluttony **52 hence** henceforth **53 gormandizing** gluttonous eating **66 competence of life** modest allowance

FALSTAFF Sir, I will be as good as my word. This that
you heard was but a color. 87
SHALLOW A color that I fear you will die in, Sir John. 88
FALSTAFF Fear no colors. Go with me to dinner. Come, 89
Lieutenant Pistol, come, Bardolph. I shall be sent for
soon at night. 91

Enter [*the Lord Chief*] *Justice and Prince John* [*of Lancaster, with officers*].

CHIEF JUSTICE
Go, carry Sir John Falstaff to the Fleet. 92
Take all his company along with him.
FALSTAFF My lord, my lord—
CHIEF JUSTICE
I cannot now speak. I will hear you soon.
Take them away.
PISTOL
Si fortuna me tormenta, spero me contenta. 97
Exeunt [*all but Prince John and the Chief Justice*].

PRINCE JOHN
I like this fair proceeding of the King's.
He hath intent his wonted followers
Shall all be very well provided for,
But all are banished till their conversations 101
Appear more wise and modest to the world.
CHIEF JUSTICE And so they are.
PRINCE JOHN
The King hath called his Parliament, my lord.
CHIEF JUSTICE He hath.
PRINCE JOHN
I will lay odds that, ere this year expire,
We bear our civil swords and native fire 107
As far as France. I heard a bird so sing,

87 color pretense. (But Shallow uses the word to mean *collar,* hangman's noose.) **88 die** (1) be hanged (2) be dyed **89 colors** standards or flags (of the enemy) **91 soon at night** early in the evening **92 Fleet** a famous London prison **97 Si . . . contenta** (See note on 2.4.179, above.) **101 conversations** conduct **107 civil . . . fire** i.e., our weapons used recently in civil war

Whose music, to my thinking, pleased the King.
Come, will you hence? [*Exeunt*.]

✤

Epilogue [*Enter Epilogue.*]

EPILOGUE
First, my fear; then, my curtsy; last, my speech. My 1
fear is your displeasure; my curtsy, my duty; and my
speech, to beg your pardons. If you look for a good
speech now, you undo me, for what I have to say is of
mine own making, and what indeed I should say will,
I doubt, prove mine own marring. But to the purpose, 6
and so to the venture. Be it known to you, as it is very
well, I was lately here in the end of a displeasing play, 8
to pray your patience for it and to promise you a better. I meant indeed to pay you with this, which, if like
an ill venture it come unluckily home, I break, and 11
you, my gentle creditors, lose. Here I promised you I
would be, and here I commit my body to your mer-
cies. Bate me some and I will pay you some and, as 14
most debtors do, promise you infinitely. And so I
kneel down before you—but, indeed, to pray for the
Queen.

If my tongue cannot entreat you to acquit me, will you command me to use my legs? And yet that were but light payment, to dance out of your debt. But a good conscience will make any possible satisfaction, and so would I. All the gentlewomen here have forgiven me. If the gentlemen will not, then the gentlemen do not agree with the gentlewomen, which was never seen in such an assembly.

One word more, I beseech you. If you be not too
much cloyed with fat meat, our humble author will
continue the story, with Sir John in it, and make you 28
merry with fair Katharine of France. Where, for anything I know, Falstaff shall die of a sweat, unless al- 30

Epilogue
1 curtsy bow, obeisance **6 doubt** fear **8 displeasing play** (No satisfactory identification has ever been made.) **11 ill venture** unlucky sending out of merchant vessels. **break** (1) break my promise (2) become bankrupt **14 Bate me some** let me off from some portion of the debt
28 Sir John in it (Shakespeare evidently originally intended to introduce Falstaff into *Henry V;* instead, only his death is reported there in 2.1 and 2.3.) **30 sweat** i.e., plague, fever, or venereal disease

ready 'a be killed with your hard opinions; for Oldcastle died a martyr, and this is not the man. My tongue is weary; when my legs are too, I will bid you good night. [*Dance, and exit Epilogue.*]

31–32 Oldcastle . . . man i.e., Falstaff was not intended to resemble Sir John Oldcastle, the Lollard venerated by sixteenth-century Puritans as a martyr for their beliefs. (This statement may have been intended to placate Lord Cobham, descendant of Oldcastle, whose resentment of Shakespeare's use of the Oldcastle name in an earlier version of the *Henry IV* plays may have led to the change of the name to Falstaff.)

Date and Text

"The second parte of the history of Kinge Henry the IIIJth with the humours of Sir John Fallstaff: Wrytten by master Shakespere" was entered in the Stationers' Register, the official record book of the London Company of Stationers (booksellers and printers), by Andrew Wise and William Aspley on August 23, 1600. (This is the first time Shakespeare's name appeared in the Stationers' Register.) The quarto was published later that year as

> THE Second part of Henrie the fourth, continuing to his death, *and coronation of Henrie* the fift. With the humours of sir Iohn Fal*staffe, and swaggering* Pistoll. *As it hath been sundrie times publikely* acted by the right honourable, the Lord Chamberlaine his seruants. *Written by William Shakespeare.* LONDON Printed by V. S. [Valentine Sims] for Andrew Wise, and William Aspley. 1600.

One scene, 3.1, was omitted from Sims's first printing [Qa] of this quarto, whereupon Sims reset two leaves as four new leaves [Qb] including not only the omitted 3.1, but 2.4.340–389 and 3.2.1–104. Qb is therefore the best copy text for 3.1 and Qa for those portions that were reset. In addition, still other passages were omitted from both versions of the 1600 quarto; they were later restored in or added to the First Folio. No further quartos appeared prior to the First Folio of 1623—an odd fact in view of *1 Henry IV*'s continued popularity, but perhaps the result of a large printing of *2 Henry IV* in anticipation of heavy sales. At any rate, this quarto text seems to have been based on Shakespeare's papers and was a reliable one except for some substantial omissions and for some misreadings owing to the compositors' difficulty in reading an authorial manuscript that may have been unfinished. Speech prefixes are at times quite irregular, indicative of author's papers before they have received the attentions of the prompter. Of the omitted passages, some may have been the result of shortening for performance, but some suggest political censorship. Others suggest authorial revision. The Folio text restores or adds the omitted readings.

The relationship of Folio to quarto text is extraordinarily

difficult to determine. Perhaps the Folio compositors were using a manuscript that had been transcribed either from an extensively annotated copy of the quarto or from a quarto and a manuscript source jointly compared. Another hypothesis is that the copy for the Folio was made up from actors' parts. The Folio copy was in any case a strange transcript, showing perhaps some stage influence and possibly used as a promptbook but less adequately provided with stage directions than most promptbooks; perhaps the scribe imposed certain literary features. It seems to have been a special case. George Walton Williams (*Shakespeare Studies* 9:173) speculates that it was an edited transcript of a promptbook prepared for Lord Cobham. Whatever its identity, it embodied tendencies toward sophistication and regularization that frequently render the Folio readings less authoritative than those of the quarto. The Folio text does restore the passages excised from the quarto, however, and on other occasions as well it provides what appear to be authentic corrections of and authorial additions to the quarto. The quarto text is generally the most authoritative when it is not manifestly in error or lacking material found in the Folio, but the Folio corrections and additions have to be regarded with close attention.

Like *1 Henry IV*, *Part Two* shows signs of revision in the use of characters' names, most notably that of Falstaff. Plainly the original version of both plays called him Sir John Oldcastle, after one of the prince's companions in the anonymous *Famous Victories of Henry the Fifth* (c. 1588). The speech prefix "Old." is left standing at 1.2.119 in the quarto of *2 Henry IV*, and in *1 Henry IV* Falstaff is jokingly referred to as "my old lad of the castle" (1.2.41). Moreover, there are several contemporary allusions to a play about a fat knight named Oldcastle. Apparently Henry Brooke, Lord Cobham, a living descendant of the Lollard martyr Oldcastle of Henry V's reign, took umbrage at the profane use Shakespeare had made of this revered name, whereupon Shakespeare's company shifted to another less controversial name from the chronicles, Sir John Fastolfe (called "Falstaffe" in the Folio text of Shakespeare's *1 Henry VI* and assigned a cowardly role in the French wars of that play). The revision also changed the names of Oldcastle's cronies from Harvey and Russell to Peto and Bardolph.

Cobham was Lord Chamberlain from July 1596 until his death in March 1597, during which interval Shakespeare's company bore the name of Lord Hunsdon's men. Quite possibly the difficulty over the name Oldcastle erupted during that period, for *1 Henry IV* seems to have been written and performed in late 1596 and early 1597, not long after Shakespeare had finished *Richard II* (c. 1595–1596). *2 Henry IV* must have been written before the end of 1598, so that Shakespeare could then begin *Henry V* in early 1599. Since *2 Henry IV* was originally written using the names Oldcastle, Harvey, and Russell, however, there is reason to date it somewhat earlier, in 1597, before the squabble over the names broke out. Scholars who prefer a date in 1597 for *The Merry Wives* also date *2 Henry IV* early in 1597, since it appears to have introduced Shallow and Pistol before they appeared in *The Merry Wives*. Francis Meres refers in 1598 to "*Henry the* 4" without specifying one or two parts. Publication of *1 Henry IV* in 1598 assured the Elizabethan public that the changes in names to Falstaff, Peto, and Bardolph had taken place; a revised epilogue to the 1600 quarto of *2 Henry IV* protests that "Oldcastle died a martyr, and this [Falstaff] is not the man," as though by way of apology or disclaimer. A play defending the reputation of the Lollard Oldcastle and attacking Falstaff, called *The History of the Life of Sir John Oldcastle, Lord Cobham, with his Martyrdom,* had been performed by the rival Admiral's men in 1599.

Textual Notes

These textual notes are not a historical collation, either of the early quarto and the early folios or of more recent editions; they are simply a record of departures in this edition from the copy text. The reading adopted in this edition appears in boldface, followed by the rejected reading from the copy text, i.e., the quarto of 1600. Only major alterations in punctuation are noted. Changes in lineation are not indicated, nor are some minor and obvious typographical errors.

Abbreviations used:
F the First Folio
Q the quarto of 1600
s.d. stage direction
s.p. speech prefix

Copy text: the quarto of 1600, of which 2.4.340 through 3.2.104 exists in two states: the original printing by Valentine Sims [Qa], and a second version with six reset pages [Qb] that had been expanded to include 3.1, inadvertently omitted from Qa. Qa is the copy text for those portions that were reset, Qb for 3.1 itself. In addition, the First Folio is copy text for certain passages excised from Q, as indicated below.

The Actors' Names [taken from F, at the end of the play]

Induction.1. s.p. Rumor [not in Q] **35 hold** hole **36 Where** [F] When **40 s.d. Rumor** Rumours

1.1. 7 s.d. [and elsewhere] Northumberland Earle **27 s.d.** [at l. 25 in Q] **41 ill** [F] bad **96 slain, say so** [F] slain **161 s.p. Lord Bardolph** Vmfr **162** [assigned to Bard. in Q and F] **164 Lean on your** [F] Leaue on you **166–179; 189–209** [F; not in Q] **178 brought** bring [F] **183 ventured, for . . . proposed** ventured for . . . proposed,

1.2. 1 s.p. [and elsewhere] Falstaff Iohn [or sir Iohn] **21 one of** [F] one off **31 s.p. [and elsewhere] Page** Boy **36 rascally** [F] rascall **48 Where's Bardolph** [F; in Q, follows "through it" in l. 47] **49 into** [F] in **96 age** [F] an ague **119 s.p. Falstaff** [F] Old **142 slenderer** [F] slender **159 on** [F] in **171 this** [F] his **171–172 them, are** [F] the one **177 s.p. [and elsewhere] Chief Justice** Lo **192 ear** yeere **201–202 you and Prince Harry** [F] you

1.3. s.d. Hastings Hastings, Fauconbridge **1 s.p. [and elsewhere] Archbishop** Bishop **5 s.p. Mowbray** Marsh **21–24, 36–55, 85–108** [F; not in Q] **26 case** [F] cause **28 on** [F] and **58 one** [F] on **59 through** [F] thorough **66 a** [F] so **71 Are** [F] And **79 To French** French **84 'gainst** [F] against **109 s.p. Mowbray** [F] Bish

2.1. 21 vice [F] view **25 continuantly** [F] continually **43 Sir John, I** [F] I **71–72 all, all** [F] all **102 mad** [F] made **117 done** [F] done with **143 German** Iarman **145 tapestries** [F] tapestrie **163 s.d. Exeunt** exit [at l. 160 in Q] **167, 171 s.p. Gower** Mess **167 Basingstoke** [F] Billingsgate

2.2. s.d. Poins Poynes, sir Iohn Russel **others** other **15 viz.** [F] with **16 ones** [F] once **21–22 made a shift to eat** [F] eate **75 e'en now** enow

81 rabbit rabble **90 him be** [F] him **109 borrower's** borrowed **119 s.p. Prince [Reads]** [not in Q or F] **125 familiars** [F] family

2.3. 5 s.p. [and elsewhere] Lady Northumberland Wife **9 s.p. [and elsewhere] Lady Percy** Kate **11 endeared** [F] endeere **23–45 He . . . grave** [F; not in Q]

2.4. 4 s.p. Second Drawer Draw **12 s.d.** [at l. 18 in Q] **13 s.p. Third Drawer** Dra [also at l. 19] **21 s.p. Second Drawer** [F] Francis **22 s.p. [and elsewhere] Hostess** Quickly **30 s.p. [and elsewhere] Doll** Tere **42–43 them; I** [F] I **49 know; to** know to **62 s.p. Doll** Dorothy **83 swagger, 'a** swaggrer **107 s.d. Boy** Bardolfes boy **172 Die men** [F] Men **189 Quoit** Quaite **196 Untwine** vntwinde **215 Ah, rogue** a rogue **219 A rascally** Ah rascally **252 the scales** [F] scales **253 avoirdupois** haber de poiz **257 poll** poule **265 master's** [F] master **275 It** [F] a **278 so** [F] to **300 even now** [F] now **313 Not? To** Not to **340–389** [copy text for this passage is Qa] **381 s.d. Exit** [Qb; not in Qa]

3.1 [this scene appears in Qb, not in Qa] **18 mast** [F] masse **22 billows** [F] pillowes **26 thy** [F] them **27 sea-boy** [F] season **36 letters** letter **59 years** [F] yeare **81 nature of** [F] natures or **85 beginnings** [F] beginning **87 of** [F] or

3.2. 1–104 [copy text for this passage is Qa] **23 bona-robas** [F] bona robes **39 Stamford** [F] Samforth **45 fine** [Qb, F] fiue **56 s.p. Shallow** [F] Bardolfe [Qa uncorr.; not in Qa corr. or Qb] **67–68 accommodated** [F] accommodate **82 s.p. Shallow** Iust [Qa] **87 Surecard** [F] Soccard **111 s.p. and text Falstaff Prick him** [Q prints as s.d.: "Iohn prickes him"] **144 for his** [F] for **175 prick me** [F] prick **195–196 good . . . that** [F] master Shallow **209 Clement's Inn** [F] Clemham **229–230 old dame's** [F] dames **250 Shadow** Sadow **271 traverse** trauers **272 Thus, thus, thus** thas, thas, thas **287 will** wooll **298 s.d. Exeunt** Exit **299–331 On . . . end** [this speech assigned in Q to Shallow] **312 invisible** inuincible **genius** gemies **314 ever** [F] ouer **324 eelskin** [F, Q corr.] eele-shin [Q uncorr.] **326 be** [F] he

4.1. 1 s.p. [and elsewhere] Archbishop Bish **9 tenor** tenure **12 could** [F, Q corr.] would [Q uncorr.] **30 Then, my lord** [F, Q corr.; not in Q uncorr.] **34 rags** rage **36 appeared** appeare **45 figure** [F, Q corr.] figures [Q uncorr.] **55–79** [F; not in Q] **103–139 O my . . . King** [F; not in Q] **93, 95 And . . . edge, To . . . cruelty** [Q uncorr.; not in Q corr. or F] **116 force** forc'd [F] **139 indeed** and did [F] **175 to our** [F] our **180 And** At

4.2. s.d. [appears at 4.1.226 in Q] **8 Than** [F] That **man** [F] man talking **19 imagined** imagine **24 Employ** [F] Imply **48 this** [F] his **67 s.p. Prince John** [F; not in Q] **69 s.p. Hastings** [F] Prince **97 s.d.** [at l. 96 in Q] **122 these traitors** [F] this traitour

4.3. s.d. [Q: "Alarum. Enter Falstaffe. excursions"] **25 s.d. retreat** [at l. 23 in Q] **41 I came** [F] there cosin, I came **85 had but** had

4.4. s.d. Warwick Warwike, Kent **32 melting** [F] meeting **51 s.p. [and elsewhere] Clarence** Tho **80 s.d. Enter Westmorland** [after l. 80 in Q] **94 heaven** [F] heauens **104 write** [F] wet **letters** [F] termes **112 s.p. [and elsewhere] Gloucester** Hum

4.5. 13 altered [F, Q corr.] vttred [Q uncorr.] **75 The virtuous sweets** [F; not in Q] **76 thighs** [F] thigh **79 s.d.** [at l. 81 in Q] **81 have** hands [Q] hath [F] **88 s.d.** [at l. 87 in Q] **91 s.p. Prince** Harry **107 Which** [F] Whom **160 worst of** [F] worse then **161 carat, is** [F] karrat **177 O my son** [F; not in Q] **178 it in** [F] in **204 my** thy **220 My gracious liege** [F; not in Q] **226 s.p. [and elsewhere] Prince John** Lanc

5.1. 23 lost the other day [F] lost **Hinckley** [F] Hunkly **56 all my** [F] my **65 of him** [F] him

5.2. s.d. [Q: "Enter Warwike, duke Humphrey, L. chiefe Iustice, Thomas Clarence, Prince, Iohn Westmerland"] **13 s.d. Westmorland** [at o.s.d. in Q] **21 s.p. Gloucester, Clarence** Prin. ambo **44 s.p. [and elsewhere] King** Prince **46 mix** mixt **62 s.p. Princes** Bro **127 rase** race **145 s.d. Exeunt** exit

5.3. 5–6 a goodly . . . a rich goodly . . . rich **47 thee** the **70 s.d.** [at l. 68 in Q] **83 s.d.** [after l. 82 in Q] **93 i' thy** ith thy **103 Cophetua** Couetua **128 knighthood** [F] Knight **144 s.d. Exeunt** exit

5.4. s.d. Beadle Sincklo **4 s.p. [and throughout scene] Beadle** Sincklo **6 lately killed** [F] kild **7 s.p. [and throughout scene] Doll** [F] Whoore **11 He** [F] I

5.5. 1 s.p. First Groom 1 [and similarly in ll. 2 and 3] **15 s.p. Shallow** [F] Pist **17, 19 s.p. Shallow** Pist [Q, F] **24 s.p. Falstaff** [F; not in Q] **29 all in** in **71 our** [F] my **82 cannot well** [F] cannot **83 should give** [F] giue **97 me** [F; not in Q]

Epilogue 32 died a [F] died

Shakespeare's Sources

As in the case of *1 Henry IV,* Shakespeare's chief historical source for *2 Henry IV* is the 1587 edition of Raphael Holinshed's *Chronicles.* Samuel Daniel's *Civil Wars* provides less pertinent material here than for *1 Henry IV,* so that Shakespeare is particularly indebted to Holinshed for historical information about the rebels' grievances, negotiations with the rebel leaders, King Henry IV's illness and death, and the Prince's succession to the throne. Changes are nonetheless prominent and telling. Shakespeare condenses time, giving an impression of failing health on the part of King Henry IV almost immediately after Shrewsbury, whereas historically the King reigned vigorously for ten years after that battle. The Earl of Northumberland is presented as more "crafty-sick" than in Holinshed, and Prince John, too, is shown in a disagreeable light by his cold-blooded handling of negotiations that in Holinshed are the responsibility of the Earl of Westmorland; Shakespeare thus tarnishes the integrity of both sides, accentuating (as he does also in the Induction spoken by Rumor) a mood of cynicism and world-weariness. The theme of nemesis for Henry IV's usurpation is touched upon in *2 Henry IV,* as in Daniel, and Henry is accordingly plagued by sleeplessness and mournful reflection.

Like Shakespeare's first play about Prince Hal, *2 Henry IV* makes extensive use of legends of Hal's wild youth. Some are from John Stow's *Chronicles of England* (1588) and *Annals of England* (1592). Sir Thomas Elyot's *The Governor* (1531) is the ultimate source of an account of Hal's boxing the ear of the Lord Chief Justice. Shakespeare evidently knew *The Governor* at first hand, though he could also have found the story reproduced almost verbatim in Stow; by the 1590s it was widely circulated. Shakespeare certainly used the anonymous play (usually attributed to Richard Tarleton or Samuel Rowley) called *The Famous Victories of Henry the Fifth,* usually dated around 1587–1588, a selection of which follows. He had already used parts of this play for *1 Henry IV.* In *Famous Victories* Shakespeare found a dramatization of the famous blow to the Lord Chief Justice's ear, interpreted there as a blow for freedom and against authority. He found also a vivid account of Hal's entry into his father's death chamber and the final reconciliation of father and son, followed by the coronation and the young king's rejection of his disreputable companions, Sir John Oldcastle, Tom, and Ned; they are banished beyond a ten-mile limit, though the new king will assist them if they behave. The anonymous play then goes on to King Henry's successful campaign against the French, as dramatized in *Henry V*.

Shakespeare's changes are as significant as his extensive borrowings. He mutes the parricidal suggestions of Hal's interview with his dying father; in the anonymous play Hal can hardly wait to see his father in the grave. Shakespeare greatly expands the tavern scenes, with an added emphasis on Falstaff's age and dissipation; new characters such as Pistol and Doll Tearsheet, with their rowdiness and colorful vituperation, surround Falstaff with signs of his increasing isolation from Hal. The venal country justices, Shallow and Silence, have no counterparts in *Famous Victories,* though that play does show a scene of farcical recruitment. Most of all, Shakespeare has immeasurably added to the humor and pathos of his chief comic character. Sir John Oldcastle of the anonymous play is a minor figure whose banishment at King Henry V's coronation is simply an appropriate gesture of the new king's reform. The characterization of Falstaff owes something to many traditional stage types, including the Vice of the morality play and the cowardly braggart soldier of classical comedy, but the richness and complexity are Shakespeare's own.

The Third Volume of Chronicles (1587 edition)

Compiled by Raphael Holinshed

Henry the Fourth

[After the defeat of the rebel forces and the death of Hotspur at the Battle of Shrewsbury in 1403, the Earl of Northumberland withdraws to Warkworth Castle to consider his next moves. A new conspiracy against King Henry surfaces in 1405.]

But at the same time, to his further disquieting, there was a conspiracy put in practice against him at home by the Earl of Northumberland, who had conspired with Richard Scroop, Archbishop of York; Thomas Mowbray, Earl Marshal, son to Thomas, Duke of Norfolk, who for the quarrel betwixt him and King Henry had been banished, as ye have heard; the Lords Hastings, Faulconbridge, Bardolph, and divers others. It was appointed that they should meet all together with their whole power upon Yorkswold, at a day assigned, and that the Earl of Northumberland should be chieftain, promising to bring with him a great number of Scots. The Archbishop, accompanied with the Earl Marshal, devised certain articles of such matters as it was supposed that not only the commonalty of the realm but also the nobility found themselves grieved with, which articles they showed first unto such of their adherents as were near about them and after sent them abroad to their friends further off, assuring them that for redress of such oppressions they would shed the last drop of blood in their bodies, if need were.

The Archbishop, not meaning to stay after he saw himself accompanied with a great number of men that came flocking to York to take his part in this quarrel, forthwith discovered[1] his enterprise, causing the articles aforesaid to be set up in the public streets of the city of York and upon the gates of the monasteries, that each man might understand the cause that moved him to rise in arms against the King,

1 **discovered** made public

the reforming whereof did not yet appertain unto him. Hereupon knights, esquires, gentlemen, yeomen, and other of the commons as well of the city, towns, and countries about, being allured either for desire of change or else for desire to see a reformation in such things as were mentioned in the articles, assembled together in great numbers. And the Archbishop, coming forth amongst them clad in armor, encouraged, exhorted, and by all means he could pricked them forth to take the enterprise in hand and manfully to continue in their begun purpose, promising forgiveness of sins to all them whose hap it was to die in the quarrel. And thus not only all the citizens of York but all other in the countries about that were able to bear weapon came to the Archbishop and the Earl Marshal. Indeed, the respect that men had to the Archbishop caused them to like the better of the cause, since the gravity of his age, his integrity of life and incomparable learning, with the reverent aspect of his amiable personage, moved all men to have him in no small estimation.

The King, advertised[2] of these matters, meaning to prevent them, left his journey into Wales and marched with all speed towards the north parts. Also, Ralph Neville, Earl of Westmorland, that was not far off, together with the Lord John of Lancaster, the King's son, being informed of this rebellious attempt, assembled together such power as they might make and, together with those which were appointed to attend on the said Lord John to defend the borders against the Scots (as the Lord Henry Fitzhugh, the Lord Ralph Evers, the Lord Robert Umfrevile, and others), made forward against the rebels and, coming into a plain within the forest of Gaultree, caused their standards to be pitched down in like sort as the Archbishop had pitched his, over against them,[3] being far stronger in number of people than the other, for, as some write, there were of the rebels at the least twenty thousand men.

When the Earl of Westmorland perceived the force of the adversaries, and that they lay still and attempted not to

2 advertised advised, informed **3 caused . . . them** had their ensigns or banners erected on flagpoles stuck in the ground in the same manner as the Archbishop had erected his, facing opposite

come forward upon him, he subtly devised how to quail[4] their purpose and forthwith dispatched messengers unto the Archbishop to understand the cause, as it were, of that great assembly and for what cause, contrary to the King's peace, they came so in armor. The Archbishop answered that he took nothing in hand against the King's peace,[5] but that whatsoever he did tended rather to advance the peace and quiet of the commonwealth than otherwise. And where he and his company were in arms, it was for fear of the King, to whom he could have no free access by reason of such a multitude of flatterers as were about him. And therefore he maintained that his purpose[6] to be good and profitable, as well for the King himself as for the realm, if men were willing to understand a truth. And herewith he showed forth a scroll in which the articles were written whereof before ye have heard.

The messengers, returning to the Earl of Westmorland, showed him[7] what they had heard and brought from the Archbishop. When he had read the articles, he showed in word and countenance outwardly that he liked of[8] the Archbishop's holy and virtuous intent and purpose, promising that he and his would prosecute[9] the same in assisting the Archbishop, who, rejoicing hereat, gave credit to[10] the Earl and persuaded the Earl Marshal (against his will, as it were) to go with him to a place appointed for them to commune[11] together. Here, when they were met with like number on either part,[12] the articles were read over, and without any more ado, the Earl of Westmorland and those that were with him agreed to do their best to see that a reformation might be had according to the same.

The Earl of Westmorland, using more policy[13] than the rest,[14] "Well," said he, "then our travail is come to the wished end; and where[15] our people have been long in armor, let them depart home to their wonted trades and occu-

4 quail destroy, frustrate. (Possibly *quell,* crush, though the text reads "quaile.") **5 took . . . peace** had no business in hand inimical to the peace of the realm **6 that his purpose** that purpose of his **7 showed him** revealed to him **8 liked of** liked **9 prosecute** pursue, follow up **10 gave credit to** believed **11 commune** talk **12 part** side **13 policy** cunning **14 the rest** i.e., the others who were there **15 where** whereas

pations. In the meantime, let us drink together in sign of agreement, that the people on both sides may see it and know that it is true that we be light at a point."[16] They had no sooner shaken hands together but that a knight was sent straightways from the Archbishop to bring word to the people that there was peace concluded, commanding each man to lay aside his arms and to resort home to their houses. The people, beholding such tokens of peace as shaking of hands, and drinking together of the lords in loving manner, they, being already wearied with the unaccustomed travail of war, brake up their field[17] and returned homewards. But in the meantime, whilst the people of the Archbishop's side withdrew away, the number of the contrary part increased, according to order given by the Earl of Westmorland. And yet the Archbishop perceived not that he was deceived until the Earl of Westmorland arrested both him and the Earl Marshal with divers other. Thus saith Walsingham.[18]

But others write somewhat otherwise of this matter, affirming that the Earl of Westmorland, indeed, and the Lord Ralph Evers procured[19] the Archbishop and the Earl Marshal to come to a communication with them upon a ground just in the midway betwixt both the armies, where the Earl of Westmorland in talk declared to them how perilous[20] an enterprise they had taken in hand so to raise the people and to move[21] war against the King, advising them therefore to submit themselves without further delay unto the King's mercy and his son the Lord John, who was present there in the field with banners spread, ready to try the matter by dint of sword if they refused this counsel. And therefore he willed them to remember themselves well, and, if they would not yield and crave the King's pardon, he bade them do their best to defend themselves.

Hereupon as well the Archbishop as[22] the Earl Marshal submitted themselves unto the King and to his son the Lord John that was there present and returned not to their army. Whereupon their troops skailed[23] and fled their ways, but

16 be light at a point have come to an agreement **17 field** order of battle **18 Walsingham** Thomas Walsingham, historian, author of *Historia Anglicana,* 1418 **19 procured** induced **20 perilous** (with the suggestion also of *parlous,* harmful and mischievous as well as dangerous) **21 move** urge **22 as well . . . as** both . . . and **23 skailed** scattered, dispersed

being pursued, many were taken, many slain, and many spoiled[24] of that that they had about them and so permitted to go their ways. Howsoever the matter was handled, true it is that the Archbishop and the Earl Marshal were brought to Pomfret to the King, who in this meanwhile was advanced thither with his power, and from thence he went to York, whither the prisoners were also brought, and there beheaded the morrow after Whitsunday[25] in a place without[26] the city; that is to understand, the Archbishop himself, the Earl Marshal, Sir John Lampley, and Sir Robert Plumpton. Unto all which persons though indemnity were promised, yet was the same to none of them at any hand performed. By the issue hereof,[27] I mean the death of the foresaid, but specially of the Archbishop, the prophecy of a sickly canon[28] of Bridlington in Yorkshire fell out to be true, who darkly enough foretold this matter and the infortunate event thereof in these words hereafter following, saying:

Pacem tractabunt, sed fraudem subter arabunt,
Pro nulla marca, salvabitur ille hierarcha.[29]

The Archbishop suffered death very constantly,[30] insomuch as the common people took it he died a martyr, affirming that certain miracles were wrought as well in the field where he was executed as also in the place where he was buried. And immediately upon such bruits,[31] both men and women began to worship his dead carcass, whom they loved so much when he was alive, till they were forbidden by the King's friends and for fear gave over to visit the place of his sepulture. The Earl Marshal's body, by the King's leave, was buried in the cathedral church, many lamenting his destiny. But his head was set on a pole aloft on the walls for a certain space, till by the King's permission (after the same had suffered many a hot, sunny day and many a wet shower of rain) it was taken down and buried together with the body.

24 spoiled plundered **25 Whitsunday** the seventh Sunday after Easter **26 without** outside of **27 issue hereof** consequence of this **28 canon** a clergyman living in a clergy house and abiding by the canons of the Church **29 Pacem . . . hierarcha** they will sue for peace but foster secret deceit; that bishop will not be saved for all his distinction **30 constantly** resolutely **31 bruits** rumors

After the King, accordingly as seemed to him good, had ransomed and punished by grievous fines the citizens of York which had borne armor on their Archbishop's side against him, he departed from York with an army of thirty-and-seven thousand fighting men furnished with all provision necessary, marching northwards against the Earl of Northumberland. At his coming to Durham, the Lord Hastings, the Lord Falconbridge, Sir John Coleville of the Dale, and Sir John Griffith, being convicted of the conspiracy, were there beheaded.

[The Earl of Northumberland and the Lord Bardolph rise against King Henry again in 1408. Northumberland is slain in battle and Bardolph is so wounded that he dies shortly thereafter. Glendower dies in 1409. King Henry and his son are reconciled in 1412, in a scene that Shakespeare uses primarily for *1 Henry IV* rather than for *2 Henry IV*. That same year, troubled and in ill health, Henry unsuccessfully plans a crusade to the Holy Land.]

In this fourteenth and last year of King Henry's reign, a council was holden in the Whitefriars in London, at the which, among other things, order was taken for ships and galleys to be builded and made ready and all other things necessary to be provided for a voyage which he meant to make into the Holy Land, there to recover the city of Jerusalem from the infidels. For it grieved him to consider the great malice of Christian princes that were bent upon a mischievous purpose to destroy one another, to the peril of their own souls, rather than to make war against the enemies of the Christian faith, as in conscience (it seemed to him) they were bound. He held his Christmas this year at Eltham, being sore vexed with sickness, so that it was thought sometimes that he had been dead. Notwithstanding, it pleased God that he somewhat recovered his strength again and so passed that Christmas with as much joy as he might.

The morrow after Candlemas Day[32] began a Parliament, which he had called at London, but he departed this life be-

32 Candlemas Day February 2 (1413)

fore the same Parliament was ended, for now that his provisions were ready and that he was furnished with sufficient treasure, soldiers, captains, victuals, munitions, tall ships, strong galleys, and all things necessary for such a royal journey as he pretended[33] to take into the Holy Land, he was eftsoons[34] taken with a sore sickness, which was not a leprosy stricken[35] by the hand of God (saith Master Hall),[36] as foolish friars imagined, but a very apoplexy of the which he languished till his appointed hour and had none other grief nor malady; so that what man ordaineth, God altereth at his good will and pleasure, not giving place more to the prince than to the poorest creature living, when He seeth His time to dispose of him this way or that, as to His omnipotent power and divine providence seemeth expedient. During this his last sickness, he caused his crown, as some write, to be set on a pillow at his bed's head, and suddenly his pangs so sore troubled him that he lay as though all his vital spirits had been from him departed. Such as were about him, thinking verily that he had been departed, covered his face with a linen cloth.

The Prince, his son, being hereof advertised, entered into the chamber, took away the crown, and departed. The father, being suddenly revived out of that trance, quickly perceived the lack of his crown and, having knowledge that the Prince his son had taken it away, caused him to come before his presence, requiring of him what he meant, so to misuse himself. The Prince with a good audacity answered, "Sir, to mine and all men's judgments you seemed dead in this world, wherefore I, as your next heir apparent, took that as mine own and not as yours." "Well, fair son," said the King with a great sigh, "what right I had to it, God knoweth." "Well," said the Prince, "if you die king, I will have the garland and trust to keep it with the sword against all mine enemies, as you have done." "Then," said the King, "I commit all to God, and remember you to do well." With that he turned himself in his bed and shortly after departed to God in a chamber of the Abbot's of Westminster

33 pretended intended **34 eftsoons** again **35 stricken** inflicted
36 Master Hall Edward Hall, author of *The Union of the Two Noble and Illustre Families of Lancaster and York* (1542)

called "Jerusalem." . . . He was so suddenly and grievously taken that such as were about him feared lest he would have died presently,[37] wherefore to relieve him (if it were possible) they bare him into a chamber that was next at hand, belonging to the Abbot of Westminster, where they laid him on a pallet before the fire and used all remedies to revive him. At length he recovered his speech, and understanding and perceiving himself in a strange place which he knew not, he willed to know if the chamber had any particular name, whereunto answer was made that it was called "Jerusalem." "Then," said the King, "lauds be given to the Father of Heaven, for now I know that I shall die here in this chamber, according to the prophecy of me declared that I should depart this life in Jerusalem."

Whether this was true that so he spake, as one that gave too much credit to foolish prophecies and vain tales, or whether it was feigned, as in such cases it commonly happeneth, we leave it to the advised reader to judge.

[King Henry's son and heir, Henry V, receives the homage of his new subjects.]

He was crowned the ninth of April, being Passion Sunday, which was a sore, ruggy,[38] and tempestuous day, with wind, snow, and sleet, that men greatly marveled thereat, making divers interpretations what the same might signify. But this King, even at first appointing with himself to show that in his person princely honors should change public manners, he determined to put on him the shape of a new man. For whereas aforetime he had made himself a companion unto misruly mates of dissolute order and life, he now banished them all from his presence (but not unrewarded or else unpreferred), inhibiting[39] them upon a great pain not once to approach, lodge, or sojourn within ten miles of his court or presence; and in their places he chose men of gravity, wit, and high policy, by whose wise counsel he might at all times rule to his honor and dignity, calling to mind how once, to

37 presently immediately **38 ruggy** stormy, wild **39 inhibiting** prohibiting

high offense of the King his father, he had with his fist stricken the Chief Justice for sending one of his minions (upon desert) to prison, when the Justice stoutly commanded himself also straight to ward, and he (then Prince) obeyed.

The second edition of Raphael Holinshed's *Chronicles* was published in 1587. This selection is based on that edition, Volume 3, folios 529–543.

The Famous Victories of Henry the Fifth, Containing the Honorable Battle of Agincourt

Any departures from the original text are noted with an asterisk and appear at the bottom of the page in boldface; original readings are in roman.

[The play's first two scenes, in which Prince Henry takes part in a robbery and carouses with Sir John Oldcastle and other tavern mates, are materials for *1 Henry IV* and are printed as sources for that play.]

[Scene 3] *Enter Henry the Fourth, with the Earl of Exeter and the Lord of Oxford.*

OXFORD An[1] please Your Majesty, here is my Lord Mayor and the Sheriff of London to speak with Your Majesty.

KING Admit them to our presence.

Enter the Mayor and the Sheriff.

Now, my good Lord Mayor of London, the cause of my sending for you at this time is to tell you of a matter which I have learned of my Council. Herein I understand that you have committed my son to prison without our leave and license. What? Although he be a rude youth and likely to give occasion, yet you might have considered that he is a prince, and my son, and not to be haled[2] to prison by every subject.

MAYOR May it please Your Majesty to give us leave to tell our tale?

KING Or else God forbid! Otherwise, you might think me an unequal judge, having more affection to my son than to any rightful judgment.

MAYOR Then I do not doubt but we shall rather deserve commendations at Your Majesty's hands than any anger.

KING Go to. Say on.

MAYOR Then, if it please Your Majesty, this night betwixt two and three of the clock in the morning my lord the young Prince, with a very disordered company, came to the old tavern in Eastcheap. And whether it was that their music

Scene 3. Location: The royal court of England.
1 An if it **2 haled** dragged

liked[3] them not, or whether they were overcome with wine, I know not, but they drew their swords, and into the street they went; and some took my lord the young Prince's part, and some took the other, but betwixt them there was such a bloody fray for the space of half an hour that neither watchmen nor any other could stay[4] them, till my brother, the Sheriff of London, and I were sent for. And at the last, with much ado, we stayed them. But it was long first, which was a great disquieting to all your loving subjects thereabouts. And then, my good lord, we knew not whether Your Grace had sent them to try us whether we would do justice, or whether it were of their own voluntary will or not, we cannot tell. And therefore, in such a case, we knew not what to do; but for our own safeguard, we sent him to ward,[5] where he wanteth[6] nothing that is fit for His Grace and Your Majesty's son. And thus, most humbly beseeching Your Majesty to think of our answer—

KING Stand aside until we have further deliberated on your answer. *Exit Mayor* [*with Sheriff*].
Ah, Harry, Harry, now thrice-accursed Harry, that hath gotten a son which with grief will end his father's days! Oh, my son, a prince thou art, ay, a prince indeed—and to deserve imprisonment! And well have they done, and like faithful subjects.—Discharge them and let them go.

EXETER I beseech Your Grace, be good to my lord the young Prince.

KING Nay, nay, 'tis no matter. Let him alone.

OXFORD Perchance the Mayor and the Sheriff have been too precise[7] in this matter.

KING No, they have done like faithful subjects. I will go myself to discharge them and let them go. *Exit omnes.*[8]

[Scene 4] *Enter Lord Chief Justice, Clerk of the Office, Jailer, John Cobbler, Derick, and the Thief.* [*The Chief Justice sits.*]

CHIEF JUSTICE Jailer, bring the prisoner to the bar.

3 liked pleased **4 stay** stop **5 ward** prison **6 wanteth** lacks
7 precise strict in the observance of rule **8 omnes** all

Scene 4. Location: A court of justice.

DERICK Hear you, my lord: I pray you, bring the bar[1] to the prisoner.

CHIEF JUSTICE Hold thy hand up at the bar.

THIEF Here it is, my lord.

CHIEF JUSTICE Clerk of the Office, read his indictment.

CLERK What is thy name?

THIEF My name was known before I came here and shall be when I am gone, I warrant you.

CHIEF JUSTICE Ay, I think so, but we will know it better before thou go.

DERICK Zounds, an[2] you do but send to the next jail, we are sure to know his name, for this is not the first prison he hath been in, I'll warrant you.

CLERK What is thy name?

THIEF What need you to ask, and have it in writing?

CLERK Is not thy name Cutbert Cutter?

THIEF What the devil need you ask, and know it so well?

CLERK Why then, Cutbert Cutter, I indict thee, by the name of Cutbert Cutter, for robbing a poor carrier the twentieth day of May last past, in the fourteen year of the reign of our sovereign lord King Henry the Fourth, for setting upon a poor carrier upon Gad's Hill, in Kent, and having beaten and wounded the said carrier, and taken his goods from him—

DERICK Oh, masters, stay there! Nay, let's never belie the man, for he hath not beaten and wounded me also, but he hath beaten and wounded my pack, and hath taken the great race[3] of ginger that Bouncing Bess with the jolly buttocks should have had. That grieves me most.

CHIEF JUSTICE Well, what sayest thou? Art thou guilty, or not guilty?

THIEF Not guilty, my lord.

CHIEF JUSTICE By whom wilt thou be tried?

THIEF By my lord the young Prince, or by myself, whether[4] you will.

Enter the young Prince, with Ned and Tom.

PRINCE Come away, my lads.—Gog's wounds,[5] ye villain,

1 bar (Derick may understand *bar* to mean an iron bar used in breaking criminals on the wheel, or some such instrument of punishment.)
2 Zounds, an by His (God's) wounds, if **3 race** root **4 whether** whichever **5 Gog's wounds** by God's wounds

what make you here? I must go about my business myself, and you must stand loitering here?

THIEF Why, my lord, they have bound me and will not let me go.

PRINCE Have they bound thee, villain?—Why, how now, my lord?

CHIEF JUSTICE I am glad to see Your Grace in good health.

PRINCE Why, my lord, this is my man. 'Tis marvel you knew him not long before this. I tell you he is a man of his hands.[6]

THIEF Ay, Gog's wounds, that I am! Try me who dare.

CHIEF JUSTICE Your Grace shall find small credit by acknowledging him to be your man.

PRINCE Why, my lord, what hath he done?

CHIEF JUSTICE An it please Your Majesty, he hath robbed a poor carrier.

DERICK Hear you, sir: marry, it was one Derick, goodman Hobling's man, of Kent.

PRINCE What? Was 't you, buttonbreech?[7] Of[8] my word, my lord, he did it but in jest.

DERICK Hear you, sir, is it your man's quality[9] to rob folks in jest? In faith, he shall be hanged in earnest.

PRINCE Well, my lord, what do you mean to do with my man?

CHIEF JUSTICE An please Your Grace, the law must pass on him according to justice. Then he must be executed.*

PRINCE Why, then, belike you mean to hang my man?

CHIEF JUSTICE I am sorry that it falls out so.

PRINCE Why, my lord, I pray ye, who am I?

CHIEF JUSTICE An please Your Grace, you are my lord the young Prince, our king that shall be after the decease of our sovereign lord King Henry the Fourth, whom God grant long to reign!

PRINCE You say true, my lord. And you will hang my man?

CHIEF JUSTICE An like Your Grace, I must needs do justice.

PRINCE Tell me, my lord, shall I have my man?

CHIEF JUSTICE I cannot, my lord.

PRINCE But will you not let him go?

CHIEF JUSTICE I am sorry that his case is so ill.

PRINCE Tush, case me no casings! Shall I have my man?

***executed** [Q follows with a slightly varied repetition of the previous five lines beginning with Derick's speech.]

6 man of his hands man of valor **7 buttonbreech** (A condescending term for one who dresses in rustic fashion as Derick does.) **8 Of** on
9 quality nature, disposition

CHIEF JUSTICE I cannot nor I may not, my lord.

PRINCE Nay, and "I shall not," say—and then I am answered?

CHIEF JUSTICE No.

PRINCE No? Then I will have him.

He giveth him a box on the ear.

NED Gog's wounds, my lord, shall I cut off his head?

PRINCE No, I charge you, draw not your swords, but get you hence. Provide a noise of musicians. Away, begone!

*Exeunt Ned and Tom.**

CHIEF JUSTICE Well, my lord, I am content to take it at your hands.

PRINCE Nay, an you be not, you shall have more.

CHIEF JUSTICE Why, I pray you, my lord, who am I?

PRINCE You, who knows not you? Why, man, you are Lord Chief Justice of England.

CHIEF JUSTICE Your Grace hath said truth. Therefore, in striking me in this place you greatly abuse me, and not me only but also your father, whose lively person here in this place I do represent. And therefore, to teach you what prerogatives mean, I commit you to the Fleet[10] until we have spoken with your father.

PRINCE Why, then, belike you mean to send me to the Fleet?

CHIEF JUSTICE Ay, indeed, and therefore carry him away.

Exeunt Henry V with the officers.

Jailer, carry the prisoner to Newgate again until the next 'sizes.[11]

JAILER At your commandment, my lord, it shall be done.

[*Exeunt all except*] *Derick and John Cobbler.**

[Scene 5]

DERICK Zounds, masters, here's ado when princes must go to prison! Why, John, didst ever see the like?

JOHN O Derick, trust me, I never saw the like.

DERICK Why, John, thou mayst see what princes be in choler. A judge a box on the ear! I'll tell thee, John, O John, I would not have done it for twenty shillings.

***s.d. Exeunt Ned and Tom** Exeunt the Theefe [Q] ***s.d. [Exeunt all except] Derick and John Cobbler** Enter Dericke and John Cobler [Q]

10 the Fleet a London prison **11 'sizes** assizes, court sessions

Scene 5. Location: The scene continues at the court of justice.

JOHN No, nor I. There had been no way but one with us—we should have been hanged.

DERICK Faith, John, I'll tell thee what: thou shalt be my Lord Chief Justice, and thou shalt sit in the chair, and I'll be the young Prince and hit thee a box on the ear. And then thou shalt say, "To teach you what prerogatives mean, I commit you to the Fleet."

JOHN Come on, I'll be your judge. But thou shalt not hit me hard?

DERICK No, no.

[*John Cobbler takes the Chief Justice's seat.*]

JOHN What hath he done?

DERICK Marry, he hath robbed Derick.

JOHN Why, then, I cannot let him go.

DERICK I must needs have my man.

JOHN You shall not have him.

DERICK Shall I not have my man? Say no, an you dare! How say you? Shall I not have my man?

JOHN No, marry, shall you not.

DERICK Shall I not, John?

JOHN No, Derick.

DERICK Why, then, take you that [*boxing his ear*] till more come! Zounds, shall I not have him?

JOHN Well, I am content to take this at your hand. But, I pray you, who am I?

DERICK Who art thou? Zounds, dost not know thyself?

JOHN No.

DERICK Now away, simple fellow. Why, man, thou art John the Cobbler.

JOHN No, I am my Lord Chief Justice of England.

DERICK Oh, John, Mass,[1] thou sayst true, thou art indeed.

JOHN Why, then, to teach you what prerogatives mean, I commit you to the Fleet.

DERICK Well, I will go. But i'faith, you graybeard knave, I'll course[2] you. *Exit. And straight enters again.* Oh, John, come, come out of thy chair. Why, what a clown wert thou to let me hit thee a box on the ear! And now thou seest they will not take me to the Fleet. I think that thou art one of these worenday[3] clowns.

1 Mass by the Mass **2 course** chase or drive with blows, thrash
3 worenday ordained (often spelled *wordeyned*), destined (? Derick may mean that John Cobbler is a born clown.)

JOHN But I marvel what will become of thee.

DERICK Faith, I'll be no more a carrier.

JOHN What wilt thou do, then?

DERICK I'll dwell with thee and be a cobbler.

JOHN With me? Alas, I am not able to keep thee. Why, thou wilt eat me out of doors.

DERICK Oh, John! No, John, I am none of these great slouching fellows that devour these great pieces of beef and brewis.[4] Alas, a trifle serves me—a woodcock, a chicken, or a capon's leg, or any such little thing serves me.

JOHN A capon! Why, man, I cannot get a capon once a year, except it be at Christmas, at some other man's house; for we cobblers be glad of a dish of roots.

DERICK Roots? Why, are you so good at rooting? Nay, cobbler, we'll have you ringed.[5]

JOHN But Derick,

Though we be so poor,
Yet will we have in store
A crab[6] in the fire,
With nut-brown ale
That is full stale,[7]
Which will a man quail
And lay in the mire.

DERICK A bots[8] on you! An be but for[9] your ale, I'll dwell with you. Come, let's away as fast as we can. *Exeunt.*

[Scene 6] *Enter the young Prince, with Ned and Tom.*

PRINCE Come away, sirs. Gog's wounds, Ned, didst thou not see what a box on the ear I took[1] my Lord Chief Justice?

4 brewis beef broth **5 ringed** i.e., ringed through the nose, like a pig (since pigs *root* or dig with their snouts in search of food) **6 crab** crabapple **7 stale** old and strong **8 bots** (Literally, an intestinal maggot disease affecting horses; here, used as an execration.) **9 An be but for** if only for the sake of

Scene 6. Location: somewhere in London. At one point the Prince and his companions proceed to the court.

1 took gave

TOM By Gog's blood, it did me good to see it. It made his teeth jar in his head!

Enter Sir John Oldcastle.

PRINCE How now, Sir John Oldcastle, what news with you?

SIR JOHN OLDCASTLE I am glad to see Your Grace at liberty. I was come, I, to visit you in prison.

PRINCE To visit me? Didst thou not know that I am a prince's son? Why, 'tis enough for me to look into a prison, though I come not in myself. But here's such ado nowadays—here's prisoning, here's hanging, whipping, and the devil and all. But I tell you, sirs, when I am king we will have no such things. But, my lads, if the old King, my father, were dead, we would be all kings.

SIR JOHN OLDCASTLE He is a good old man. God take him to his mercy the sooner!

PRINCE But, Ned, so soon as I am king, the first thing I will do shall be to put my Lord Chief Justice out of office, and thou shalt be my Lord Chief Justice of England.

NED Shall I be Lord Chief Justice? By Gog's wounds, I'll be the bravest[2] Lord Chief Justice that ever was in England!

PRINCE Then, Ned, I'll turn all these prisons into fence schools, and I will endue[3] thee with them, with lands to maintain them withal. Then I will have a bout with my Lord Chief Justice. Thou shalt hang none but pickpurses, and horse stealers, and such base-minded villains; but that fellow that will stand by the highway side courageously with his sword and buckler and take a purse—that fellow, give him commendations! Beside that, send him to me and I will give him an annual pension out of my exchequer to maintain him all the days of his life.

SIR JOHN OLDCASTLE Nobly spoken, Harry! We shall never have a merry world till the old King be dead.

NED But whither are you going now?

PRINCE To the court, for I hear say my father lies very sick.

TOM But I doubt[4] he will not die.

PRINCE Yet will I go thither. For the breath shall be no sooner out of his mouth but I will clap the crown on my head.

2 bravest most splendid **3 endue** invest, bestow **4 doubt** fear

SIR JOHN OLDCASTLE Will you go to the court with that cloak so full of needles?

PRINCE Cloak, eyelet holes, needles,[5] and all was of mine own devising; and therefore I will wear it.

TOM I pray you, my lord, what may be the meaning thereof?

PRINCE Why, man, 'tis a sign that I stand upon thorns till the crown be on my head.

SIR JOHN OLDCASTLE Or that every needle might be a prick to their hearts that repine at your doings?

PRINCE Thou sayst true, Jockey. But there's some will say the young Prince will be "a well toward[6] young man," and all this gear,[7] that I had as lief[8] they would break my head with a pot as to say any such thing. But we stand prating here too long. I must needs speak with my father. Therefore, come away! [*They cross the stage, and knock.*]

[*Enter a Porter.*]

PORTER What a rapping keep you at the King's court-gate?

PRINCE Here's one that must speak with the King.

PORTER The King is very sick, and none must speak with him.

PRINCE No? You rascal, do you not know me?

PORTER You are my lord the young Prince.

PRINCE Then go and tell my father that I must and will speak with him. [*Exit Porter.*]

NED [*To Prince*] Shall I cut off his head?

PRINCE No, no. Though I would help you in other places, yet I have nothing to do here.[9] What, you are in my father's court.

NED I will write him in my tables,[10] for so soon as I am made Lord Chief Justice I will put him out of his office.

The trumpet sounds.

PRINCE Gog's wounds, sirs, the King comes. Let's all stand aside. [*They stand aside.*]

Enter the King, with the Lord of Exeter.

5 eyelet holes, needles (Holinshed reports that Prince Henry went to court in 1412 in a gown of blue satin "full of small eyelet holes, at every hole the needle hanging by a silk thread with which it was sewed.")
6 well toward promising **7 and all this gear** and suchlike nonsense
8 had as lief would just as soon **9 Though I would . . . here** i.e., though I could get you off on a charge of assault or murder elsewhere, I have no authority of that kind here at my father's court **10 tables** notebook

KING And is it true, my lord, that my son is already sent to the Fleet? Now, truly, that man[11] is more fitter to rule the realm than I, for by no means could I rule my son, and he, by one word, hath caused him to be ruled. Oh, my son, my son, no sooner out of one prison but into another?[12] I had thought once whiles I had lived to have seen this noble realm of England flourish by thee, my son, but now I see it goes to ruin and decay. *He weepeth.*

Enters Lord of Oxford.

OXFORD An please Your Grace, here is my lord your son that cometh to speak with you. He saith he must and will speak with you.

KING Who? My son Harry?

OXFORD Ay, an please Your Majesty.

KING I know wherefore he cometh. But look that none come with him.

OXFORD A very disordered company, and such as make very ill rule in Your Majesty's house.

KING Well, let him come, but look that none come with him. *He* [*Oxford*] *goeth* [*to the Prince*].

OXFORD An please Your Grace, my lord the King sends for you.

PRINCE Come away, sirs, let's go all together.

OXFORD An please Your Grace, none must go with you.

PRINCE Why, I must needs have them with me; otherwise I can do my father no countenance.[13] Therefore, come away.

OXFORD The King your father commands there should none come.

PRINCE Well, sirs, then begone. And provide me three noise[14] of musicians. *Exeunt Knights.*[15]

Enters[16] *the Prince, with a dagger in his hand* [*to the King, attended*].

KING Come, my son, come on, i' God's name! I know

11 that man i.e., the Lord Chief Justice **12 one prison . . . another** (The Prince was sent to the Counter for his earlier offense, now to the Fleet.) **13 can do . . . countenance** i.e., will not be able to make a proper show before my father **14 noise** bands **15 Knights** i.e., Sir John Oldcastle, Ned, and Tom. (Ned is presumably Ned Poins.) **16 Enters** (The Prince approaches the King, who is still onstage.)

wherefore thy coming is. Oh, my son, my son, what cause hath ever been that thou shouldst forsake me and follow this vile and reprobate company which abuseth youth so manifestly? Oh, my son, thou knowest that these thy doings will end thy father's days. *He weeps.*
Ay, so, so, my son, thou fearest not to approach the presence of thy sick father in that disguised sort. I tell thee, my son, that there is never a needle in thy cloak but it is a prick to my heart, and never an eyelet hole but it is a hole to my soul; and wherefore thou bringest that dagger in thy hand I know not but by conjecture. *He weeps.*

PRINCE My conscience accuseth me. Most sovereign lord and well-beloved Father, to answer first to the last point, that is, whereas you conjecture that this hand and this dagger shall be armed against your life: no! Know, my beloved Father, far be the thoughts of your son—"son," said I? an unworthy son for so good a father!—but far be the thoughts of any such pretended[17] mischief. And I most humbly render it to Your Majesty's hand. [*He gives the King the dagger.*] And live, my lord and sovereign, forever! And with your dagger-arm show like vengeance upon the body of—"that your son," I was about to say, and dare not; ah, woe is me therefore!—that your vile* slave. 'Tis not the crown that I come for, sweet Father, because I am unworthy. And those vile and reprobate companions*—I abandon and utterly abolish their company forever! Pardon, sweet Father, pardon, the least thing and most desire.[18] And this ruffianly cloak I here tear from my back and sacrifice it to the devil, which is master of all mischief. [*He tears off his cloak.*] Pardon me, sweet Father, pardon me! Good my Lord of Exeter, speak for me. Pardon me, pardon, good Father! Not a word? Ah, he will not speak one word! Ah, Harry, now thrice-unhappy Harry! But what shall I do? I will go take me into some solitary place and there lament my sinful life, and when I have done, I will lay me down and die. *Exit.*

KING Call him again. Call my son again.

[*The Prince is summoned.*]

[*Enter the Prince.*]

*__vile__ wilde *__companions__ company

17 pretended intended **18 the least . . . desire** i.e., my least offense as well as the thing I have most desired (?)

PRINCE And doth my father call me again? Now, Harry, happy be the time that thy father calleth thee again! [*He kneels.*]

KING Stand up, my son, and do not think thy father but at the request of thee, my son, I will pardon thee.[19] And God bless thee and make thee his servant!

PRINCE Thanks, good my lord. And no doubt but this day, even this day, I am born new again.

KING Come, my son and lords, take me by the hands.

Exeunt omnes, [*the King being led*].

[Scene 7] *Enter Derick* [*shouting at Mistress Cobbler within*].

DERICK Thou art a stinking whore, and a whoreson stinking whore! Dost think I'll take it at thy hands?[1]

Enter John Cobbler, running.

JOHN Derick, Derick, Derick,* hearest 'a?[2] Do, Derick, never while thou livest use[3] that! Why, what will my neighbors say an thou go away so?

DERICK She's an arrant whore, and I'll have the law on you, John.

JOHN Why, what hath she done?

DERICK Marry, mark thou, John. I will prove it, that I will!

JOHN What wilt thou prove?

DERICK That she called me in to dinner—John, mark the tale well, John—and when I was set, she brought me a dish of roots and a piece of barrel-butter[4] therein. And she is a very knave, and thou a drab if* thou take her part.

JOHN Hearest 'a, Derick? Is this the matter? Nay, an it be no worse, we will go home again, and all shall be amended.

***Derick, Derick, Derick** Derick, D. D. [Q] ***if** it [Q]

19 and do not . . . thee (The text is seemingly corrupt, but the King is probably saying, do not think but that at your request I will surely pardon you.)

Scene 7. Location: John Cobbler's house, evidently a public house.
1 take . . . hands take such behavior from you **2 hearest 'a** do you hear **3 use** use such language as **4 barrel-butter** butter heavily salted for preservation and hence not of the quality that Derick evidently expects

DERICK Oh, John, hearest 'a, John? Is all well?

JOHN Ay, all is well.

DERICK Then I'll go home before, and break all the glass windows. [*Exeunt.*]

[Scene 8] *Enter the King* [*in his chair*] *with his Lords* [*Exeter and Oxford*].

KING Come, my lords. I see it boots[1] me not to take any physic,[2] for all the physicians in the world cannot cure me; no, not one. But, good my lords, remember my last will and testament concerning my son, for truly, my lords, I do not think but he will prove as valiant and victorious a king as ever reigned in England.

BOTH Let heaven and earth be witness between us if we accomplish not thy will to the uttermost!

KING I give you most unfeigned thanks, good my lords. Draw the curtains and depart my chamber awhile, and cause some music to rock me asleep.

[*The curtains are drawn around his throne.*]
He sleepeth. Exeunt Lords.

Enter the Prince.

PRINCE Ah, Harry, thrice unhappy, that hath neglect[3] so long from visiting of thy sick father! I will go. Nay, but why do I not go to the chamber of my sick father to comfort the melancholy soul of his body? His soul, said I? Here is his body, indeed, but his soul is whereas it needs no body. Now, thrice-accursed Harry, that hath offended thy father so much! And could not I crave pardon for all? O my dying Father! Cursed be the day wherein I was born, and accursed be the hour wherein I was begotten! But what shall I do? If weeping tears, which come too late, may suffice the negligence neglected too soon,* I will weep day and night until the fountain be dry with weeping.

Exit [*taking the crown*].

Enter Lord[*s*] *of Exeter and Oxford.*

***too soon** to some [Q]

Scene 8. Location: The royal court.

1 boots avails **2 physic** medicine **3 neglect** neglected

EXETER Come easily,[4] my lord, for waking of[5] the King.

KING [*Waking*] Now, my lords?

OXFORD How doth Your Grace feel yourself?

KING Somewhat better after my sleep. But, good my lords, take off my crown. Remove my chair a little back and set me right.

BOTH An please Your Grace, the crown is taken away.

KING The crown taken away! Good my Lord of Oxford, go see who hath done this deed. [*Exit Oxford.*]
No doubt 'tis some vile traitor that hath done it to deprive my son. They that would do it now would seek to scrape and scrawl[6] for it after my death.

Enter Lord of Oxford with the Prince [*with the crown*].

OXFORD Here, an please Your Grace, is my lord the young Prince with the crown.

KING Why, how now, my son? I had thought the last time I had you in schooling[7] I had given you a lesson for all,[8] and do you now begin again? Why, tell me, my son, dost thou think the time so long that thou wouldst have it before the breath be out of my mouth?

PRINCE [*Kneeling*] Most sovereign lord and well-beloved Father, I came into your chamber to comfort the melancholy soul of your body, and finding you at that time past all recovery and dead, to my thinking—God is my witness! And what should I do but with weeping tears lament the death of you, my Father? And after that, seeing the crown, I took it. And tell me, my Father, who might better take it than I, after your death? But, seeing you live, I most humbly render it into Your Majesty's hands; and the happiest man alive that my father live. [*He gives back the crown.*] And live, my lord and father, forever!

KING Stand up, my son. [*The Prince arises.*] Thine answer hath sounded well in mine ears, for I must need confess that I was in a very sound sleep and altogether unmindful of thy coming. But come near, my son, and let me put thee in

4 easily gently, quietly **5 for waking of** for fear of waking **6 scrape and scrawl** claw and scramble **7 in schooling** as a pupil **8 for all** for all time

possession whilst I live, that none deprive thee of it after my death.

PRINCE Well may I take it at Your Majesty's hands, but it shall never touch my head so long as my father lives.

He taketh the crown.

KING God give thee joy, my son. God bless thee, and make thee his servant, and send thee a prosperous reign! For God knows, my son, how hardly[9] I came by it and how hardly I have maintained it.

PRINCE Howsoever you came by it I know not; but now I have it from you, and from you I will keep it. And he that seeks to take the crown from my head, let him look that his armor be thicker than mine, or I will pierce him to the heart, were it harder than brass or bullion.

KING Nobly spoken, and like a king! Now trust me, my lords, I fear not but my son will be as warlike and victorious a prince as ever reigned in England.

BOTH LORDS His former life shows no less.

KING Well, my lords, I know not whether it be for sleep, or drawing near of drowsy summer of death, but I am very much given to sleep. Therefore, good my lords and my son, draw the curtains. Depart my chamber and cause some music to rock me asleep.

[*The curtains are drawn. Music sounds.*]
Exeunt omnes. The King dieth.[10]

[Scene 9] *Enter the Thief.*

THIEF Ah, God, I am now much like to a bird which hath escaped out of the cage! For so soon as my Lord Chief Justice heard that the old King was dead, he was glad to let me go for fear of my lord the young Prince. But here comes some of his companions. I will see an I can get anything of them for old acquaintance.[1]

9 hardly with difficulty **10 dieth** (The curtains presumably make it possible for the King to exit after the scene is over without being seen.)

Scene 9. Location: A street where the coronation procession will pass.
1 for old acquaintance for the sake of old acquaintance

Enter Knights, ranging.[2]

TOM Gog's wounds, the King is dead!

SIR JOHN OLDCASTLE Dead? Then, Gog's blood, we shall be all kings!

NED Gog's wounds, I shall be Lord Chief Justice of England.

TOM [*To the Thief*] Why, how![3] Are you broken out of prison?

NED Gog's wounds, how the villain stinks!

SIR JOHN OLDCASTLE Why, what will become of thee now? Fie upon him, how the rascal stinks!

THIEF Marry, I will go and serve my master[4] again.

TOM Gog's blood, dost think that he will have any such scabbed knave as thou art? What, man, he is a king now.

NED [*Giving him money*] Hold thee. Here's a couple of angels[5] for thee. And get thee gone, for the King will not be long before he come this way. And hereafter I will tell the King of thee. *Exit Thief.*

SIR JOHN OLDCASTLE Oh, how it did me good to see the King when he was crowned! Methought his seat was like the figure of heaven and his person like unto a god.

NED But who would have thought that the King would have changed his countenance so?

SIR JOHN OLDCASTLE Did you not scc with what gracc hc scnt his embassage into France to tell the French King that Harry of England hath sent for the crown, and Harry of England will have it?

TOM But 'twas but a little[6] to make the people believe that he was sorry for his father's death. *The trumpet sounds.*

NED Gog's wounds, the King comes! Let's all stand aside.

Enter the King with the Archbishop [*of Canterbury*] *and the Lord of Oxford.*

SIR JOHN OLDCASTLE How do you, my lord?

NED How now, Harry? Tut, my lord, put away these dumps. You are a king, and all the realm is yours. What, man, do you not remember the old sayings? You know I must be Lord Chief Justice of England. Trust me, my lord, methinks you

2 ranging roaming about **3 how** how now, what's the news **4 my master** i.e., Prince Henry, now King **5 angels** gold coins **6 'twas but a little** i.e., it was only a little device

are very much changed. And 'tis but with a little sorrowing, to make folks believe the death of your father grieves you—and 'tis nothing so.

KING HENRY V I prithee, Ned, mend thy manners, and be more modester in thy terms, for my unfeigned grief is not to be ruled by thy flattering and dissembling talk. Thou sayst I am changed. So I am, indeed, and so must thou be, and that quickly, or else I must cause thee to be changed.

SIR JOHN OLDCASTLE Gog's wounds, how like you this? Zounds, 'tis not so sweet as music.

TOM I trust we have not offended Your Grace no way.

KING HENRY V Ah, Tom, your former life grieves me and makes me to abandon and abolish your company forever. And therefore, not upon pain of death to approach my presence by ten miles' space. Then, if I hear well of you, it may be I will do somewhat for you. Otherwise, look for no more favor at my hands than at any other man's. And, therefore, begone! We have other matters to talk on.

Exeunt Knights.

[The rest of *Famous Victories* is chiefly concerned with King Henry's exploits in France and his famous victory at Agincourt.]

This selection is based on the first edition of *The Famous Victories of Henry the Fifth, Containing the Honorable Battle of Agincourt; As It Was Played by the Queen's Majesty's Players. London: Printed by Thomas Creede, 1598.* [Designated in textual notes as Q.]

Further Reading

Auden, W. H. "The Prince's Dog." *The Dyer's Hand and Other Essays*. New York: Random House, 1948. Auden inventively examines Falstaff's character, motives, and function within the play, and concludes that "sober reflection in the study may tell us that Falstaff is not, after all, a very admirable person, but Falstaff on the stage gives us no time for sober reflection." Auden denies the damaging irresponsibility many critics have found in Falstaff, declaring him to be "a comic symbol for the supernatural order of charity."

Barber, C. L. "Rule and Misrule in *Henry IV*." *Shakespeare's Festive Comedy*. Princeton, N.J.: Princeton Univ. Press, 1959. In his seminal study of the relation of social and artistic forms, Barber sees Falstaff as a Lord of Misrule burlesquing the sanctities of the historical world. Barber finds, however, that misrule does not threaten the social order, since "it depends utterly on what it mocks." Ultimately "misrule works . . . to consolidate rule," though Falstaff's saturnalian energy always threatens to turn from a "dependent holiday skepticism" to a "dangerously self-sufficient everyday skepticism."

Barish, Jonas A. "The Turning Away of Prince Hal." *Shakespeare Studies* 1 (1965): 18–28. Barish sees Falstaff's rejection as the moment that reveals to us whether we are "moralists or sentimentalists"; we also sense at this moment the antithetical pressures of history and comedy. In rejecting Falstaff, Hal is, in effect, rejecting himself: "to banish plump Jack is to banish what is free and vital and pleasurable in life."

Berger, Harry, Jr. "Sneak's Noise, or Rumor and Detextualization in *2 Henry IV*." *Kenyon Review* n.s. 6.4 (1984): 58–78. Berger explores the tension between "stage-centered" readings, which fix meaning, "detextualizing" language by visualizing it in character and action, and "text-centered" readings, which oppose this fixing, "retextualizing" the language "to recuperate what has been repressed." Focusing on the figure of Rumor, Berger explores the ways in which *2 Henry IV* builds the problematic relationship of text and performance into the play itself as part of "a critical thesis about theater in particular and theatricality in general."

Bradley, A. C. "The Rejection of Falstaff." *Oxford Lectures on Poetry,* 1909. Rpt. New York: St. Martin's Press, 1959. Bradley's influential essay explores the inevitability of Hal's rejection of Falstaff. He recognizes both Falstaff's dangerous attractiveness and Hal's Lancastrian "hardness" that qualifies him for political success but limits his personal appeal. If we enjoy the Falstaff scenes "as surely Shakespeare meant for them to be enjoyed," Bradley argues, we must feel in Falstaff's rejection "a good deal of pain and some resentment."

Burckhardt, Sigurd. " 'Swoll'n with Some Other Grief': Shakespeare's Prince Hal Trilogy." *Shakespearean Meanings.* Princeton, N.J.: Princeton Univ. Press, 1968. Burckhardt argues that the structure of Shakespeare's plays "undercuts Tudor doctrine," exposing its contradictions and inadequacies. The apparently satisfying resolution of *1 Henry IV* dissolves as Falstaff rises from the battlefield, "reminding us that disorder is not slain so neatly and inexpensively as the calculated symmetries of dialectics would have us believe." *2 Henry IV,* even more disillusioned, reveals that the political order of England "has become *secular.* The sanctions it rests on are not divine or cosmic but at best pragmatic."

Calderwood, James L. "*2 Henry IV:* The Embodied Name and the Rejected Mask." *Metadrama in Shakespeare's Henriad: "Richard II" to "Henry V."* Berkeley and Los Angeles: Univ. of California Press, 1979. In *2 Henry IV,* Calderwood sees Falstaff, with his newly gained reputation, entering into "the illusion of historical reality." He abandons the "comic invulnerability" of his former outrageously theatrical existence for a commitment to the historical fiction that ultimately must reveal him to be a disease-ridden old man who must (and can) be repudiated.

Campbell, Lily B. "The Unquiet Time of Henry IV." *Shakespeare's "Histories": Mirrors of Elizabethan Policy.* San Marino, Calif.: Huntington Library, 1947. Campbell considers the historical action of the play in the context of Elizabethan political theory and anxieties about succession. She argues that "the problem of rebellion" is central to the design of *Henry IV* and reflects the realities of sixteenth-century politics as much as the medieval history overtly represented.

Dessen, Alan C. "The Two Phased Structure of *2 Henry IV.*" *Shakespeare and the Late Moral Plays.* Lincoln, Nebr., and London: Univ. of Nebraska Press, 1986. Dessen finds in the dramaturgy of the late morality plays of the 1560s and 1570s a structural model for *2 Henry IV*. In plays such as *The Tide Tarrieth No Man* (1576), with a two-phased action in which the public Vice initially controls the action until finally he is superseded by allegorical figures embodying the play's moral norms, Shakespeare finds a prototype for his drama of the "reordering of England."

Greenblatt, Stephen. "Invisible Bullets: Renaissance Authority and Its Subversion." *Glyph* 8 (1981): 40–61. Rev. and rpt. in *Political Shakespeare: New Essays in Cultural Materialism,* ed. Jonathan Dollimore and Alan Sinfield. Ithaca and London: Cornell Univ. Press, 1985. Greenblatt considers the *Henry IV* plays in a provocative account of the operations of Renaissance power. He argues that the subversive challenge to the principles of authority in the play is never really dangerous; indeed, it is not merely contained but actually encouraged by the power structure, since its presence works paradoxically to ratify and reinforce the existing order.

Hunter, G. K. "*Henry IV* and the Elizabethan Two-Part Play." *Review of English Studies* n.s. 5 (1954): 236–248. Rpt. in *Dramatic Identities and Cultural Tradition: Studies in Shakespeare and His Contemporaries.* New York: Barnes and Noble, 1978. Entering into the debate about the relationship of the two parts of *Henry IV,* Hunter argues not that the two plays are continuous but that they have the unity, found also in plays by Christopher Marlowe, John Marston, and George Chapman, "of a dyptich, in which repetition of shape and design focuses attention on what is common to the two parts."

Johnson, Samuel. *"2 Henry IV." Johnson on Shakespeare,* ed. Arthur Sherbo. *The Yale Edition of the Works of Samuel Johnson,* vol. 7. New Haven and London: Yale Univ. Press, 1968. Johnson sees Falstaff as dangerous and despicable: "He is a thief, and a glutton, and a coward, and a boaster, always ready to cheat the weak, and prey upon the poor." He is able, however, to endear himself to the Prince "by the most pleasing of all qualities, perpetual gaiety."

Jorgensen, Paul A. "The 'Dastardly Treachery' of Prince John of Lancaster." *PMLA* 76 (1961): 488–492. Jorgensen finds a relationship between the scene of John of Lancaster's arrest of the rebels and the demoralizing war Elizabeth waged against the Irish. Revealing how far the world has fallen from "the happy warriors and outmoded warfare of Agincourt," Prince's John's cynical actions reflect the dispiriting realities of anxious governmental policy in the 1590s.

Kelly, Henry Ansgar. *Divine Providence in the England of Shakespeare's Histories*, pp. 222–232. Cambridge: Harvard Univ. Press, 1970. Examining the play's often noted "providentialism," Kelly finds that the "moral and spiritual sentiments" of Shakespeare's sources are not normative but are distributed in the play according to the partisan uses that can be made of them. He denies that the play presents Henry's difficulties during his reign as "in any way a punishment from God for his sins in acquiring the throne," and concludes that "the crown in *2 Henry IV* is definitely regarded as the rightful possession of the Henrys."

Kernan, Alvin B. "The Henriad: Shakespeare's Major History Plays." In *Modern Shakespearean Criticism: Essays on Style, Dramaturgy, and the Major Plays*, ed. Alvin B. Kernan. New York: Harcourt, Brace, and World, 1970. Kernan traces the movement of the second tetralogy from a sacred, providential conception of history to a secular, pragmatic view, "in which any identity is only a temporary role." Richard II, Henry IV, and Prince Hal mark stages in this transition, and the latter emerges as the modern prince who "never seems to lose sight of the fact he is preparing to be king of England."

Morgann, Maurice. "An Essay on the Dramatic Character of Sir John Falstaff" (1777). In *Eighteenth Century Essays on Shakespeare*, ed. D. Nichol Smith. 2nd edition. Oxford: Clarendon Press, 1963. In an essay that is the earliest sustained account of a Shakespearean character, Morgann sees the complexity of Falstaff's nature as it is presented in the play. He is not the "constitutional coward" that many have seen but a man "of much natural courage and resolution." Morgann, however, recognizes that if Falstaff is endowed with "great natural vigour and alacrity of mind," he also engages "in every debauchery." He has "a mind free of malice or any evil principle; but he never took the trouble of acquiring any good one."

Ornstein, Robert. *"Henry IV Part II." A Kingdom for a Stage: The Achievement of Shakespeare's History Plays.* Cambridge: Harvard Univ. Press, 1972. Ornstein defends the artistic independence and integrity of *2 Henry IV,* finding it a study of dispiriting political realities achieved in a "somber and shadowed monochrome." The play reveals the fragility of human relationships and man's helplessness before the "relentless movement of time." It presents a world of "anti-heroes" for whom "gallantry exists only in memory."

Porter, Joseph A. *"2 Henry IV." The Drama of Speech Acts: Shakespeare's Lancastrian Tetralogy.* Berkeley, Calif.: Univ. of California Press, 1979. Porter examines "the topic of language in the play." Rumor introduces a world of proliferating, private speech that inhibits communication and "eliminates community." In Hal, however, the newly crowned Henry V, "we have a many-tongued monarch who, using a wide range of language purposefully and responsibly, initiates a reign of 'high . . . parliament.'"

Reese, M. M. *"Henry IV." The Cease of Majesty: A Study of Shakespeare's History Plays.* London: Edward Arnold, 1961; New York: St. Martin's Press, 1962. Reese argues that Shakespeare in the two parts of *Henry IV* dramatizes "the education of a prince" and "considers in personal and political terms the sacrifices and disciplines [Hal] will have to accept." Reese considers Falstaff, Hotspur, and Henry IV to be "three tempters" whose defective examples Hal must reject as his youthful impulses are "steeled into disciplined courage and dedicated to honourable ends."

Saccio, Peter. "Henry IV: The King Embattled." *Shakespeare's English Kings: History, Chronicle, and Drama.*

New York: Oxford Univ. Press, 1977. Focusing especially on the political challenges to Henry's rule, the military encounters at Shrewsbury and Gaultree Forest, and the relations between Henry IV and his son, Saccio examines the historical background of the two parts of *Henry IV* and traces Shakespeare's transformation of this history into drama.

Tillyard, E. M. W. "The Second Tetralogy." *Shakespeare's History Plays,* 1944. Rpt., New York: Barnes and Noble, 1964. In an enormously influential study of Shakespeare's histories, Tillyard argues that the two parts of *Henry IV* form a single sequence of ten acts in which Hal is tested, "Morality-fashion," to prove his worthiness to rule. *Part One* demonstrates Hal's education in military virtues, as he tries to mediate between "the excess and the defect of the military spirit" as they are embodied in Hotspur and Falstaff; *Part Two* displays his education in the "civil virtues," as he must choose between Falstaff and the Lord Chief Justice.

Photo © George Joseph

The Merry Wives of Windsor, with Danny DeVito as John Rugby and Marilyn Sokol as Mistress Quickly, directed by David Margulies in 1974.

THE MERRY WIVES OF WINDSOR

THE MERRY WIVES OF WINDSOR

Introductory Material
Foreword by Joseph Papp
Introduction
The Merry Wives of Windsor in Performance

THE PLAY

Supplementary Material
Date and Text
Textual Notes
Shakespeare's Sources
Further Reading

Foreword

The Merry Wives of Windsor is interesting because it shows Falstaff in a whole new light—and not exactly a flattering one. In fact, it was a long time before the New York Shakespeare Festival produced the play, mainly because it was difficult to find an actor to play this new and undignified Falstaff. By the end of the *Henry IV* plays, he is momentarily touched with tragedy; in *The Merry Wives of Windsor,* he's just plain absurd. As the story goes, Queen Elizabeth herself insisted that Falstaff come back, after Shakespeare had let him die in the beginning of *Henry V*.

Whether or not this is true, *The Merry Wives of Windsor* was born with a Falstaff who is nothing but a slightly foolish womanizer eventually humiliated by the tricks of two housewives. Even he himself has a hard time accepting this demotion; after the wives have played their first trick on him and dumped him from a laundry basket into the muddy river, he exclaims, "Have I lived to be carried in a basket, like a barrow of butcher's offal, and to be thrown in the Thamcs?"

Despite the downturn in the fat knight's fortunes, *The Merry Wives* is an intriguing play, because it gives a sense of the middle class in Shakespeare's day—their values, their customs, and their preoccupations. Shakespeare takes us away from the grand sweep of the histories and the imposing edifices and personages of the court and plants us in the households of Mistress Ford and Mistress Page, with their laundry baskets, matchmaking schemes, and homey country fires. These two women are delightfully shrewd and daring, carrying out their tricks with real panache. They succeed in exposing Falstaff as the lecherous womanizer he appears to be and command him to reform his ways. For in the end virtue triumphs—as it usually does in Shakespeare's comedies.

JOSEPH PAPP

JOSEPH PAPP GRATEFULLY ACKNOWLEDGES THE HELP OF ELIZABETH KIRKLAND IN PREPARING THIS FOREWORD.

Introduction

According to an early eighteenth-century tradition, Shakespeare composed *The Merry Wives of Windsor* at the behest of Queen Elizabeth. John Dennis, a critic and dramatist, asserted in 1702 that the Queen "was so eager to see it acted, that she commanded it to be finished in fourteen days." The editor Nicholas Rowe added in 1709 that the Queen, having been so pleased with Falstaff in the *Henry IV* plays, wished to see him in love. Such legends, emerging more than a century after the event, must be regarded with caution. Whether true or not, however, they do point to a passage of courtly flattery in the play that strongly suggests the presence of the court at some performance. The fairy blessing bestowed on Windsor Castle in Act 5 is unquestionably intended to celebrate the famous Order of the Garter. Mistress Quickly, disguised as leader of the fairies, orders her charges to sing nightly "Like to the Garter's compass, in a ring," to write *"Honi soit qui mal y pense,"* the motto of the Garter, and to tend carefully the "several chairs of order"—those decorated stalls in the Chapel of St. George belonging to the illustrious lords who made up the Order of the Garter. Every such "installment" receives her blessing, along with each knight's "coat," "crest," and "blazon" (5.5.54–75). The topical nature of this passage is stressed by its apparent lack of relevance to the plot.

Other extraneous bits of action may allude to courtly matters or to Windsor gossip. The business about the three German horse thieves and their Duke (4.3, 5), which makes little sense in the play as it stands, can perhaps be explained as an in-group joke on Frederick of Würtemburg, Count Mompelgard, a German nobleman obsessively intent on joining the Garter. He was the object of much anti-German scorn. His name, Mompelgard, is possibly scrambled into "garmombles" in the corrupt 1602 quarto text where the Folio text reads "Iermans" (4.5.74). Also, the geography of Windsor is rendered with loving and accurate attention to detail, as though for an audience familiar with its environs.

Such topical flourishes do not rob the drama of its general

appeal; it has had great success, both as a stage play and in Verdi's and Nicolai's operatic versions, and was presumably popular with Shakespeare's London audience. Shakespeare never composed exclusively for special audiences, so far as we know, and indeed the blessing of Windsor Castle could have been added to a commercial play in order to render it particularly suitable for royal performance. The allusion to "the fat woman of Brentford," a notorious tavern keeper of Brentford (halfway between London and Windsor) would have been as meaningful to Shakespeare's London audience as to the court. The same may be true of the "luces" in the coat of arms of Justice Shallow (1.1.14), sometimes thought to ridicule Shakespeare's Stratford neighbor Sir Thomas Lucy, but believed by Leslie Hotson to be a dig at William Gardiner, a Justice of the Peace in Surrey near London. The dig at the Brooke family, the lords of Cobham, in the disguise name (Brook) of the jealous Ford (as recorded in the bad quarto of 1602), must have amused knowledgeable Londoners; indeed, the satirical hit was evidently so offensive that the name had to be changed to "Broome" (as in the Folio text). Nevertheless, *The Merry Wives* could have been originally planned as entertainment to please Queen Elizabeth. A Feast of St. George in honor of the Garter was held at Westminster on April 23, 1597, in the Queen's presence. Among those elected to the Order was George Carey, Lord Hunsdon, the patron of Shakespeare's company and the new Lord Chamberlain. He was actually installed in the Order at Windsor in May. This date is early for a play that appears to borrow several comic figures from the *Henry IV* plays and perhaps from *Henry V* (usually dated 1599) as well. Recently, however, it has been argued persuasively that *The Merry Wives* may have been written while *2 Henry IV* was in the process of composition, making use of its comic types but before they had actually appeared on the London stage. According to this theory, Nym was created first for *The Merry Wives* and was then reintroduced into *Henry V*. The dating and order of composition of these plays is still controversial, however, so that the dating of *The Merry Wives* must remain uncertain from 1597 to 1601.

Despite this uncertainty, Shakespeare's comic strategy in *The Merry Wives* seems reasonably clear: to translate highly popular comic figures such as Falstaff, Bardolph, Pistol, and Slender from the history plays into a ludicrously different kind of situation. Falstaff, the once resourceful and self-aware companion of Prince Hal, becomes the buffoonish wooer of two virtuously married women who thoroughly best him and subject him to a series of amusingly humiliating punishments. Hal too, of course, treats Falstaff as a scapegoat in the *Henry IV* plays and ultimately rejects him, but the farcical nature of the action in *The Merry Wives* exposes Falstaff to more openly satirical laughter and discomfiture than in the history plays. Some admirers of Falstaff have been dismayed by the falling off, and dismiss the play as an insult to his greatness, but surely to view the play thus is to create false expectations and thereby miss the point of Shakespeare's comic intent. Falstaff and his companions should not be judged against their counterparts in the history plays, even though an awareness of their existence in that different context is an essential part of the jest. To see Falstaff in love! This tour de force required that Shakespeare devise a multiple plot as unlike that of the history plays as possible, in order to stress the comic discrepancy.

The result is a structurally complex comic plot that appropriately bears more resemblance to Shakespeare's other comedies than to the history plays. At the center of *The Merry Wives* is a familiar plot of romantic intrigue, featuring a young heroine (Anne Page) whose parents object to her attachment to young Fenton. They pester her with unwelcome rival wooers (Slender and Dr. Caius), obliging her finally to dupe her parents by a cleverly engineered elopement. This plot to outwit parents and rivals in the name of young love has an ancestry in the classical comedy of Plautus and in neoclassical comedy, though Shakespeare uses no particular recognizable source. To this plot he adds a second and parallel story of a lover (Falstaff) caught in the act of wooing two women. Italian *novelle* provide many situations of this sort, including that in which the husband is deceived by concealment of the lover in a clothes-basket; see especially "Of Two Brethren and Their Wives" from *Riche His Farewell to Military Profession,* 1581, "Two Lovers of Pisa" from *Tarleton's News Out of Purgatory,* 1590, and the second story of the first day from Ser Giovanni

Fiorentino's *Il Pecorone,* 1558. The effect of the combined plots is often farcelike, especially in the emphasis on swift, hilarious action and comic physical abuse at the expense of consistency in character. For example, we must accept as a given the preference of wise Master Page for Slender as his son-in-law, and the inexplicable preference of Mistress Page for the suit of Dr. Caius. Reasons are stated, but symmetry of the design is paramount.

In addition, Shakespeare enriches these two plot situations with minor characters, such as the rival wooers, go-betweens, and informers, who inevitably come in conflict with one another and thereby reveal their "humors" or idiosyncrasies. Only tangentially connected with the plot, these characters are prized for their eccentricity. The Welsh Parson Evans and the French Dr. Caius nearly come to blows over Caius's courtship of Anne Page. They are safely kept apart by the genial Host of the Garter Inn and are reconciled to the extent of plotting against the Host for having deceived them both. (Perhaps they carry out their threat as the mysterious Germans who steal the Host's horses, though the text is murky on this point.) Justice Shallow, a humors character in *2 Henry IV,* is given nominal justification in this play as cousin of Anne's second unwanted suitor, Slender; but Shallow's essential function is to quarrel with Falstaff about the latter's poaching and riotous behavior. This plot goes nowhere and indeed is little more than a means for the revelation of humorous characters. Shallow's is a cameo role, like many others, enabling him to assume the fatuous postures we also encounter in *2 Henry IV*. Pistol and Nym, similarly requiring some pretext for being on hand, revenge their dismissal from Falstaff's service by informing the two husbands of Falstaff's designs on the two merry wives. Bardolph finds suitable employment as a bartender. Mistress Quickly's transformation is perhaps the most gloriously improbable of all: she becomes confidante of all three wooers of Anne Page (offering equal encouragement to each and receiving payment from each), as well as go-between for Falstaff and the two wives. She is no longer a married and then widowed hostess of a London tavern, but an unmarried housekeeper of Windsor. She triumphs over Falstaff in a way not possible in the history plays, joining the entire cast as they jeer at the discomfited horn-browed knight.

By providing occasion for the exhibition of idiosyncratic character for its own sake, side by side with his fast-moving farcical action, Shakespeare seems to have been responding to the newest dramatic genre of the late 1590s: the humors comedy. George Chapman's *The Blind Beggar of Alexandria* (1596) had done much to establish the new fashion. Ben Jonson's *Every Man in His Humor* (1598) either influenced Shakespeare or was influenced by him, depending upon the dates. Jonson's plot, like Shakespeare's, is chiefly a vehicle for displaying various humors or comically obsessed types: the overly watchful father, the jealous husband, the braggart soldier, the country simpleton intent on learning to quarrel like a gentleman, the waspishly impatient man. Similar types appear in *The Merry Wives,* although Shakespeare characteristically does not satirize affectation so much as cherish it.

Shakespeare's comic types endear themselves chiefly through their verbal traits: Nym with his use of the word "humor"; Pistol with his anachronistic terms, recondite allusions, stilted poetic inversions, and hyperboles ("O base Hungarian wight! Wilt thou the spigot wield?"; 1.3.19–20); Mistress Quickly with her pungent homely metaphors (comparing a beard to "a glover's paring knife," 1.4.19–20) and her pat phrases ("But let that pass," l. 14); Shallow with his legal jargon; and the French Caius and the Welsh Evans with their ability to "keep their limbs whole and hack our English" (3.1.73). Shakespeare also caricatures these humorous types by distinctive physical traits, such as Bardolph's "tinderbox" nose (1.3.23), or Slender's unappealing face and little yellow beard that so aptly suit his passion for bearbaiting and his idiotic deference to his superiors. We laugh at these deformities, and yet see that no one is incorrigible. The characters amiably poke fun at one another, and every discomfiture leads ultimately to a reconciliation. Few escape laughter, even those we might regard as normative characters if this were a satire; the Host, for example, loses his horses, and Mistress Page is tricked at last by her daughter's elopement.

Nevertheless, the merry wives of the play's title come as

close as any to representing the normative vision of the play, functioning as witty manipulators in a plot to expose hypocrisy and lechery. The devices they invent for Falstaff are rather like Maria's schemes for Malvolio in *Twelfth Night,* since all depend upon the complicity of the self-blinded victim. Falstaff is the dominant humors character of the play, obsessed both with lust and greed, amusing to us because the greed is predominant. His hypocritical reasons for wooing deserve comic reprisal, or "vengeance." His greed and his fatuous belief in his own charm overwhelm his natural sagacity and leave him vulnerable. He credulously accepts the bribes of the jealous Ford, disguised as Brook, and is deceived by the wives on no less than three occasions. For their part, the wives are delighted with their "sport," for they must devise increasingly clever schemes to offset Falstaff's growing suspicions. The more unlikely he is to return for more punishment, the greater must be their ingenuity in order to fool him once again. Mistress Ford enjoys the added pleasure of teaching her husband a lesson about jealousy. The cleverness of their sport is justified by its moral intent, and conversely the moral point is deprived of any tedious didacticism by the good humor of the jest. In his final humiliation, plagued by virtually all the play's characters, reduced to an absurd belief in fairies, Falstaff becomes a scapegoat in the truest sense of that term: a horned figure who embodies the faults of an entire society, and whose chastisement brings about purification. Yet as Mistress Quickly observes, "nobody but has his fault" (1.4.13–14), and this comic rejection of Falstaff leads not to banishment but to a reconciling feast at the Pages' house. Without intending it, Falstaff has cured Ford's jealousy and has helped show that "Wives may be merry, and yet honest too" (4.2.97).

The Merry Wives is a remarkable play in terms of the relation between comedy and history, the two genres most evident in Shakespeare's dramatic writing of the 1590s. The romantic plot of love's triumph, though nominally at the center of the plot, is decidedly secondary in importance. The more dominant motif of scapegoating and renewal concerns not young lovers but married women who claim the dominant position of wit. Falstaff's claim to wit and vitality in *1* and *2 Henry IV* gives place here to the ascendancy of domestic women; the comic principle shifts to them. Mistress Quickly, translated like Falstaff and his crew from the history plays into comedy, shares in this vindication of women's wit and virtue; no longer a tavern keeper or widow enduring Falstaff's broken promises or patiently supplying him with women, Quickly becomes a go-between in a comic plot of exposure of male philandering. Women are no longer on the periphery of a male-dominated world, as in the history plays, but in their element. At the same time, the women of this play embody married virtues for the most part rather than the youthful companionship (Portia, Beatrice, Rosalind, Viola) of the romantic comedies. The location of the play in a part of England not far from where Shakespeare grew up, the inclusion of place names familiar from his youth, the fond portrait of a schoolboy's terror in coping with Latin paradigms, all suggest a kind of tribute to the world in which Shakespeare's own family affairs remained while he sought professional advancement in London.

The Merry Wives of Windsor in Performance

The Merry Wives of Windsor has always attracted the attention of theatrical producers with its rich humor, especially its comical portrayal of Falstaff as a wooer, but it has also often invited extensive revision or adaptation. The usual criticisms of it are that it contains too many episodes, too many whimsical characters involved in little plots of their own, too little love interest, and, hence, not enough of the kind of unity a comedy ought to have. Shakespeare has been regarded, in other words, as a writer of incomparable comic genius whose work needs discipline.

Presumably the original performances in 1597 to 1601 or thereabouts (see the Introduction) by Shakespeare's company, the Lord Chamberlain's men, whether at the Globe Theatre or at the court of Queen Elizabeth or, probably, both, used Shakespeare's script as he wrote it. Nothing is known about such possible performances, though the 1602 quarto edition of the play reports that it was "divers times acted" by the Lord Chamberlain's men, and the play was revived for King James I at court in 1604 and for Charles I in 1638 at the Cockpit Theatre.

Nor do we know what sort of play emerged in the 1660s after the reopening of the theaters, when *The Merry Wives* was selected by Thomas Killigrew for the repertory of the King's company and acted "now and then," according to John Downes, into the 1670s. Diarist Samuel Pepys saw it three times, in 1660, 1661, and 1667, commenting sourly, on the first of these occasions, that "the humors of the country gentleman and the French doctor" were very well done but that the rest went "but very poorly, and Sir J. Falstaff as bad as any." Pepys was no better pleased on his second and third tries. Whatever version he may have seen, and whatever the reasons for his disappointment, *The Merry Wives* was obviously ripe for adaptation. The result was John Dennis's *The Comical Gallant, or The Amours of Sir John Falstaff*, at the Theatre Royal in Drury Lane, 1702.

Dennis's recasting of Shakespeare's play aptly illustrates

the kind of unity that Shakespeare's play was perceived to lack. Dennis gathers his plot around young Fenton, the gentlemanly wooer of Anne Page, thereby centering on the love interest and providing a rationale for virtually everything else that occurs. Mistress Ford becomes Fenton's aunt and go-between in his affair with Anne, eliminating the need for Mistress Quickly. Fenton is responsible for encouraging Falstaff to believe that the merry wives are responsive to his charms. In the interests of his own pursuit of Anne, Fenton urges the Host of the Garter Inn to foment a quarrel between Sir Hugh Evans and Doctor Caius; the quarrel will, Fenton hopes, upset the plans both of Anne's father to marry her to Slender and of Anne's mother to marry her to Doctor Caius. All the plots, going their separate ways it seems in Shakespeare's play, now depend on Fenton's romantic motivations. In one of his extended love scenes with Anne, he instructs her in what to wear in Windsor Forest in order to deceive her father and mother.

The episodes of Falstaff's wooing, meantime, are reduced in number by the elimination of Falstaff's disguising himself as the fat woman of Brentford. In another relationship devised by Dennis to unify the plot, Mistress Ford's brother turns out to be the Host of the Bull Inn, where Falstaff dwells and where he receives Mistress Ford in the longed-for assignation. Mistress Page interrupts this rendezvous disguised as one Captain Dingboy, frightening Falstaff with her pistol and leaving him to the jealousies of Ford. Falstaff escapes the wrath of the husband by means of the buck basket, as in Shakespeare, while in another room of the inn the merry wives, in order to teach their husbands a lesson, pretend to be having affairs. Everyone ends up at Herne's Oak, where Ford, having meanwhile outfitted himself in Falstaff's wet clothes (wet from the immersion in the Thames), must fight a duel with Falstaff. Assorted business such as the horse-stealing episode (4.3, 4.5) and young William Page's struggles with Latin (4.1) are of course excised. Dennis's adaptation reflects his view, in short, that Shakespeare's play is "by no means a despicable comedy" and yet "not so admirable but that it might receive improvement."

The theater in Lincoln's Inn Fields, London, revived something closer to Shakespeare's play in 1721, and it enjoyed considerable success in its own right for a time thereafter. The play was popular at Drury Lane in mid century and afterward under David Garrick. Hannah Pritchard regularly took the role of Mistress Ford, while Peg Woffington had great success with the role at the Theatre Royal, Covent Garden. The eighteenth century seemed to be comfortable with Shakespeare's text; Bell's acting version of 1773 omits the Latin grammar lesson, much of the fourth act, and parts of the fifth, but what remains is essentially Shakespeare's. John Philip Kemble acted the play essentially in this form around the turn of the century.

In the nineteenth century, however, *The Merry Wives* had its greatest success as an opera. The first such, by Frederic Reynolds and H. R. Bishop, opened at Drury Lane in 1824 and could still occasionally be seen in the 1890s. John Braham sang Fenton, and Madame Vestris (Lucia Elizabeth Mathews) excelled in the role of Mistress Page. The songs were, for the most part, taken from other plays and poems: "When it is the time of night" from Act 5 of *A Midsummer Night's Dream,* "Crabbed age and youth" (a poem doubtfully ascribed to Shakespeare in *The Passionate Pilgrim,* 1599, and for some reason very popular in the eighteenth century), "Love like a shadow flies" (a bit of poetry from *The Merry Wives,* but here converted from a wry remark offered by Ford to Falstaff into a throbbing love duet for Fenton and Anne), "All that glitters is not gold" from the casket scene in *The Merchant of Venice,* "When daisies pied" from the finale of *Love's Labor's Lost,* and still others, including "Trip, trip away" from Act 5 of *The Merry Wives.* Madame Vestris kept much of Bishop's operatic music when she staged the play in 1839 at Covent Garden, then under the joint management of herself and her husband, Charles Mathews. Benjamin Webster cast Madame Vestris and Louisa Cranstoun Nisbett as the merry wives in his production at the Haymarket Theatre in 1844. The American actor James Henry Hackett played Falstaff in *The Merry Wives* in 1851, and also at the Haymarket, after having great success with the role in the United States. "The real Falstaff died with Hackett," one theatergoer lamented in 1862.

Charles Kean finally got rid of Bishop's music for his opening production at the Princess's Theatre in late 1851, with a strong cast and an essentially Shakespearean text, but his production too was typical of its age in its splendid and costly sets. When John Hollingshead produced *The Merry Wives* at the Gaiety Theatre in 1874 with another stellar cast that included Samuel Phelps as Falstaff and Johnston Forbes-Robertson as Fenton, the Windsor Forest scenes, so inviting to nineteenth-century theater managers interested in lavish scenic beauty onstage, were a delight to the eye. The music was once again a notable feature: Arthur Sullivan wrote the score, including a setting for a lyric by Algernon Swinburne, and singing boys performed Sullivan's music for a concluding revel at Herne's Oak. In America, Augustin Daly produced the play, with Ada Rehan as Mistress Ford and Otis Skinner as Page, in 1886 as the first of his Shakespearean revivals at Daly's Theatre in New York, having earlier directed it at the small Fifth Avenue Theatre in 1872. Like Daly, Herbert Beerbohm Tree, at London's Haymarket Theatre in 1889, did nothing to interrupt the tradition of musical and scenic splendor: he contributed a song, "Love laid his weary head," for his wife, Maud Tree, in the role of Anne, and made much of the scenery and costuming. In 1902 Tree reshaped *The Merry Wives* into three acts, as he had done with *Julius Caesar* in 1898, in order to accommodate the spectacle. Ellen Terry and Madge Kendal played Mistresses Ford and Page.

The major musical adaptations of the nineteenth century were not British, however, but German and Italian. The operas of Carl Otto Ehrenfried Nicolai (1849, with libretto by Salomon Herman von Mosenthal) and Giuseppe Verdi (1893, with libretto by Arrigo Boito) supremely illustrate the aesthetic concerns that had motivated Dennis, Reynolds, and the rest. The devices that are used in Nicolai's *Die lustigen Weiber von Windsor* (*The Merry Wives of Windsor*) and Verdi's *Falstaff* are not unlike those of the English adapters. Both composers use libretti that amplify the love attachment between Fenton and Anne. Both willingly forgo the Latin lesson for William Page, Doctor Caius's arguing with Jack Rugby, much of the strife between Caius and Evans, the business of the horse stealing, and the like. Both reduce the number of episodes in which Falstaff evades the jealous Ford, though Nicolai does keep a version of the fat woman of Brentford. Nicolai's delightfully bourgeois opera expresses well the particular kind of German temperament for which it was written. Verdi's masterful last opera includes some material from the *Henry IV* plays, including Falstaff's catechism on honor, and centers the opera, as its title implies, on the fat knight. Mistress Quickly, sacrificed by Dennis, is a triumph of subservient cunning in Verdi's work. Verdi's opening quarrel between Falstaff and Justice Shallow offers deft musical characterization in the bit parts for Pistol, Bardolph, and Nym. Nicolai's Slender is endearingly idiotic with his one-line refrain, *"O süßer Anna!"* ("O sweet Anne!"). Shakespeare's comedy of humors survives so well in these adaptations that opera lovers the world over are ready to assert that Verdi's version in particular is better than Shakespeare's original. Whether true or not, this claim attests to the play's ability to speak to succeeding generations.

The Merry Wives has not been an important vehicle of theatrical reform or revolution in the twentieth century, but it has had some memorable productions. The play was one of Frank Benson's regularly produced comedies, along with *The Taming of the Shrew* and *The Merchant of Venice,* so much so that people joked about his *Merry Shrews of Venice*. He played Dr. Caius and his wife, Constance, played Mistress Ford in high-spirited productions, such as that at the Lyceum Theatre in 1901. Oscar Asche produced the play at the Garrick Theatre in 1911, "as a snowy Christmas card," in critic J. C. Trewin's phrase, with characters dressed in mufflers and mittens and the stage covered in four inches of salt to represent snow. In 1929 Asche returned to the play, directing and playing Falstaff in a modern-dress production that opened at the Haymarket Theatre and then switched to the Apollo for a short run. William Bridges-Adams's production, starring Edith Evans as Mistress Page, in 1923 at the Lyric Theatre, Hammersmith, was hailed by critic James Agate as "a gorgeous success." Theodore Komisarjevsky directed the play, as he said, "as farce or musical comedy" at Stratford-upon-Avon in 1935, abandoning the traditional timbered houses and trees of Windsor for a set he described as "a highly decorated birthday cake of many tiers." Tudor dress gave way to heterogeneous costuming generally reminiscent of the mid-nineteenth century, with Falstaff in a scarlet hunting coat and *jaeger* hat with feathers. William Poel's disciple, Robert Atkins, striving for the swift pace and flexible staging of the Elizabethan theater, directed the play several times, most notably in 1922 at the Old Vic; in 1937 at the Ring, a converted boxing stadium in Blackfriars; and in 1945 at Stratford-upon-Avon. In 1940 Donald Wolfit directed a shortened version of the play, starring Irene and Violet Vanbrugh, then in their seventies, as the merry wives, at the Strand Theatre. Forty-four years after Oscar Asche, Glen Byam Shaw produced a robust but wintery *Merry Wives* with icicles and wood fires in 1955 at Stratford-upon-Avon, and, like Asche, was roundly criticized for the setting (even though the text occasionally supports such an idea in Page's remark that it is a "raw rheumatic day," at 3.1.44, and Mistress Page's invitation to "laugh this sport o'er by a country fire," at 5.5.236).

More recently, Terry Hands directed the play in 1968 at Stratford-upon-Avon as a feverishly inventive farce on a timbered set with twittering sparrows, and revived the production in 1975, again with Ian Richardson as an insanely jealous Ford humorously inviting the audience to share his obsession. In 1979 Trevor Nunn and John Caird directed the play at Stratford-upon-Avon with Ben Kingsley as Ford and John Woodvine as a Falstaff who seemed to the reviewer of the *New Statesman* to be "Santa on the skids." Bill Alexander's *Merry Wives* in 1985 at Stratford-upon-Avon set the play in the late 1950s. The wives compared their identical love letters while sitting under driers at the hairdresser's; small-town Windsor turned into suburbia, in a witty portrayal (according to *The Times*) of a "new, powerful bourgeois class that was emerging in a time of upward mobility." Here was an instance where period transposition worked especially well to engage something essential in the text of the play. Even in its more usual Tudor costume and timber-framed set, however, the play's energy is almost irresistible on the stage.

THE MERRY WIVES OF WINDSOR

[*Dramatis Personae*

MISTRESS MARGARET PAGE, *a wife of Windsor*
MASTER GEORGE PAGE, *her husband*
ANNE PAGE, *their daughter*
WILLIAM PAGE, *a schoolboy, their son*

MISTRESS ALICE FORD, *a wife of Windsor*
MASTER FRANK FORD, *her husband*
JOHN, } *their servants*
ROBERT, }

SIR JOHN FALSTAFF
ROBIN, *his page*
BARDOLPH, }
PISTOL, } *his followers*
NYM, }

SIR HUGH EVANS, *a Welsh parson*

DOCTOR CAIUS, *a French physician*
MISTRESS QUICKLY, *his housekeeper*
JOHN RUGBY, *his servant*

ROBERT SHALLOW, *a country justice of the peace*
ABRAHAM SLENDER, *his nephew*
PETER SIMPLE, *Slender's servant*

HOST *of the Garter Inn*
FENTON, *a gentleman in love with Anne Page*

Children of Windsor, disguised as fairies

SCENE: *Windsor, and the neighborhood*]

1.1 *Enter Justice Shallow, Slender,* [*and*] *Sir Hugh Evans.*

SHALLOW Sir Hugh, persuade me not. I will make a Star Chamber matter of it. If he were twenty Sir John Falstaffs, he shall not abuse Robert Shallow, Esquire.

SLENDER In the county of Gloucester, Justice of Peace and Coram.

SHALLOW Ay, cousin Slender, and Custalorum.

SLENDER Ay, and Ratolorum too. And a gentleman born, Master Parson, who writes himself "Armigero" in any bill, warrant, quittance, or obligation: "Armigero."

SHALLOW Ay, that I do, and have done any time these three hundred years.

SLENDER All his successors gone before him hath done 't; and all his ancestors that come after him may. They may give the dozen white luces in their coat.

SHALLOW It is an old coat.

EVANS The dozen white louses do become an old coat well. It agrees well, passant. It is a familiar beast to man and signifies love.

SHALLOW The luce is the fresh fish. The salt fish is an old coat.

SLENDER I may quarter, coz.

SHALLOW You may, by marrying.

EVANS It is marring indeed, if he quarter it.

1.1. Location: Windsor. Before Master Page's house.
s.d. Sir (Courtesy title for a priest.) **1 persuade** argue with **2 Star Chamber matter** (The court of Star Chamber, composed chiefly of the King's Privy Council, was the highest and most powerful court in the realm.) **5 Coram** i.e., quorum, a title of certain justices whose presence was necessary to constitute a bench **6 cousin** kinsman. **Custalorum** (A corruption of Latin *custos rotulorum,* keeper of the rolls.)
7 Ratolorum (For *rotulorum.*) **8 Armigero** Esquire, one entitled to bear arms. (A heraldic term.) **9 bill** bill of financial exchange. **quittance** discharge from legal agreement. **obligation** contract **14 give** display heraldically. **luces** pikes, freshwater fish. **coat** coat of arms
17 passant (1) walking (in heraldic language) (2) passing, exceeding. **familiar** (1) well known and part of the family (2) overfamiliar (taking *louse* in the sense of a tiny biting insect) **19–20 The luce . . . coat** (Meaning unclear, though Shallow is seemingly joking about Evans's pronunciation of *coat* as "cod.") **21 quarter** combine the arms of two families by adding to one's own coat the arms of another family in one quarter of the escutcheon. **coz** cousin, kinsman

SHALLOW Not a whit.

EVANS Yes, py'r Lady. If he has a quarter of your coat, there is but three skirts for yourself, in my simple conjectures. But that is all one. If Sir John Falstaff have committed disparagements unto you, I am of the Church, and will be glad to do my benevolence to make atonements and compromises between you.

SHALLOW The Council shall hear it. It is a riot.

EVANS It is not meet the Council hear a riot. There is no fear of Got in a riot. The Council, look you, shall desire to hear the fear of Got, and not to hear a riot. Take your visaments in that.

SHALLOW Ha! O' my life, if I were young again, the sword should end it.

EVANS It is petter that friends is the sword and end it. And there is also another device in my prain, which peradventure prings goot discretions with it: there is Anne Page, which is daughter to Master George Page, which is pretty virginity.

SLENDER Mistress Anne Page? She has brown hair and speaks small like a woman?

EVANS It is that fery person for all the 'orld, as just as you will desire. And seven hundred pounds of moneys, and gold, and silver, is her grandsire upon his death's-bed—Got deliver to a joyful resurrections!—give, when she is able to overtake seventeen years old. It were a goot motion if we leave our pribbles and prabbles, and desire a marriage between Master Abraham and Mistress Anne Page.

25 py'r Lady by Our Lady. (Evans's Welsh dialect often substitutes "p" for "b" at the start of words, as in *petter, prain,* and *prings,* ll. 38–40, substitutes, "f" for "v" and "t" for "d," as in *Fery goot,* l. 133, leaves out initial "w," as in *'orld* and *'oman,* ll. 45, 210, etc.) **26 skirts** the tails of a long doublet or coat. (Evans is still thinking of a literal coat that would be marred by quartering, i.e., cutting into quarters.)
30 compromises i.e., settlement by arbitration **31 The Council . . . riot** (The King's Privy Council, sitting in Star Chamber, frequently concerned itself with riots. Evans, however, understands *Council* to refer to an ecclesiastical council.) **32 meet** fitting **35 visaments** (For *advisements,* deliberations.) **38 that friends is the sword** i.e., that the quarrel be ended by friendly motions **43 Mistress** (Used of married or unmarried women.) **44 small** with a gentle, high voice **45 just** exactly
50 motion plan **50–51 pribbles and prabbles** i.e., petty disputes

SLENDER Did her grandsire leave her seven hundred pound?

EVANS Ay, and her father is make her a petter penny.

SHALLOW I know the young gentlewoman. She has good gifts.

EVANS Seven hundred pounds and possibilities is goot gifts.

SHALLOW Well, let us see honest Master Page. Is Falstaff there?

EVANS Shall I tell you a lie? I do despise a liar as I do despise one that is false, or as I despise one that is not true. The knight Sir John is there, and I beseech you be ruled by your well-willers. I will peat the door for Master Page. [*He knocks.*] What ho! Got pless your house here!

PAGE [*Within*] Who's there?

EVANS Here is Got's plessing, and your friend, and Justice Shallow, and here young Master Slender, that peradventures shall tell you another tale, if matters grow to your likings.

[*Enter*] *Master Page.*

PAGE I am glad to see your worships well. I thank you for my venison, Master Shallow.

SHALLOW Master Page, I am glad to see you. Much good do it your good heart! I wished your venison better; it was ill killed. How doth good Mistress Page?—And I thank you always with my heart, la, with my heart.

PAGE Sir, I thank you.

SHALLOW Sir, I thank you. By yea and no, I do.

PAGE I am glad to see you, good Master Slender.

SLENDER How does your fallow greyhound, sir? I heard say he was outrun on Cotswold.

PAGE It could not be judged, sir.

SLENDER You'll not confess, you'll not confess.

55 is make . . . penny will provide her a pretty penny more **57 gifts** natural endowments **58 possibilities** pecuniary prospects **60 honest** worthy **65 well-willers** well-wishers. **peat** beat, knock **71 tell . . . tale** i.e., have something more to say to you **77 ill** i.e., illegally, by Falstaff. (See below, ll. 105–106.) **83 fallow** fawn-colored **84 on Cotswold** in the Cotswold hills in Gloucestershire

SHALLOW That he will not. 'Tis your fault, 'tis your fault. 'Tis a good dog.

PAGE A cur, sir.

SHALLOW Sir, he's a good dog, and a fair dog. Can there be more said? He is good and fair. Is Sir John Falstaff here?

PAGE Sir, he is within; and I would I could do a good office between you.

EVANS It is spoke as a Christians ought to speak.

SHALLOW He hath wronged me, Master Page.

PAGE Sir, he doth in some sort confess it.

SHALLOW If it be confessed, it is not redressed. Is not that so, Master Page? He hath wronged me, indeed he hath; at a word, he hath. Believe me, Robert Shallow, Esquire, saith he is wronged.

[*Enter Sir John*] *Falstaff, Bardolph, Nym,* [*and*] *Pistol.*

PAGE Here comes Sir John.

FALSTAFF Now, Master Shallow, you'll complain of me to the King?

SHALLOW Knight, you have beaten my men, killed my deer, and broke open my lodge.

FALSTAFF But not kissed your keeper's daughter?

SHALLOW Tut, a pin! This shall be answered.

FALSTAFF I will answer it straight: I have done all this. That is now answered.

SHALLOW The Council shall know this.

FALSTAFF 'Twere better for you if it were known in counsel. You'll be laughed at.

EVANS *Pauca verba,* Sir John, good worts.

FALSTAFF Good worts? Good cabbage!—Slender, I broke your head. What matter have you against me?

SLENDER Marry, sir, I have matter in my head against

87 fault misfortune (with a suggestion also of "loss of scent") **97 in some sort** to some extent **100 at a word** in a word **103 of** about **106 lodge** forest keeper's dwelling **108 pin** trifle. **answered** accounted for. (But Falstaff plays on the meaning "replied to.") **109 straight** (1) at once (2) strictly **112–113 in counsel** secretly (playing on *King's Privy Council*) **114 Pauca verba** few words **115 worts** vegetables, cabbages. (A quibble on Sir Hugh's pronunciation of *words.*) **115–116 broke your head** made a slight bleeding wound on your head **116, 117 matter** (1) cause of complaint (2) matter of consequence; pus

you, and against your coney-catching rascals, Bardolph, 118
Nym, and Pistol.

BARDOLPH You Banbury cheese! 120

SLENDER Ay, it is no matter.

PISTOL How now, Mephistopheles? 122

SLENDER Ay, it is no matter.

NYM Slice, I say! *Pauca, pauca.* Slice, that's my humor. 124

SLENDER Where's Simple, my man? Can you tell,
cousin?

EVANS Peace, I pray you. Now let us understand. There
is three umpires in this matter, as I understand; that
is, Master Page, fidelicet Master Page, and there is my- 129
self, fidelicet myself, and the three party is, lastly and
finally, mine Host of the Garter. 131

PAGE We three to hear it, and end it between them.

EVANS Fery goot. I will make a prief of it in my note- 133
book, and we will afterwards 'ork upon the cause with
as great discreetly as we can.

FALSTAFF Pistol!

PISTOL He hears with ears.

EVANS The tevil and his tam! What phrase is this, "He 138
hears with ear"? Why, it is affectations.

FALSTAFF Pistol, did you pick Master Slender's purse?

SLENDER Ay, by these gloves, did he—or I would I
might never come in mine own great chamber again 142
else—of seven groats in mill-sixpences, and two Ed- 143
ward shovelboards, that cost me two shilling and two 144
pence apiece of Yed Miller, by these gloves. 145

FALSTAFF Is this true, Pistol?

EVANS No, it is false, if it is a pickpurse. 147

118 coney-catching cheating. (A *coney* is literally a rabbit.) **120 Banbury cheese** (Banbury cheeses were noted for their thinness; a reference to Slender's name and physique.) **122 Mephistopheles** name of the devil in Marlowe's *Doctor Faustus* **124 Slice** (1) speak briefly (2) I will slice with my sword (3) a reference to Bardolph's calling Slender a cheese (?) **humor** mood **129 fidelicet** i.e., *videlicet,* namely **131 Garter** the name of an inn in Windsor **133 prief** brief, summary **138 tam** dam, mother **142 great chamber** hall **143 groats** coins equal to four pence. **mill-sixpences** coins stamped by means of the mill and press **143–144 Edward shovelboards** shillings coined in the reign of Edward VI (so called from their use in the gambling game of shovelboard) **145 Yed** Ed, Edward **147 it is false** i.e., Pistol is false, not *true* (honest). **if it** if he

PISTOL
Ha, thou mountain-foreigner! Sir John and master mine,
I combat challenge of this latten bilbo.
Word of denial in thy *labras* here!
Word of denial! Froth and scum, thou liest!

SLENDER [*Indicating Nym*] By these gloves, then 'twas he.

NYM Be advised, sir, and pass good humors. I will say "marry, trap with you," if you run the nuthook's humor on me. That is the very note of it.

SLENDER By this hat, then, he in the red face had it. For though I cannot remember what I did when you made me drunk, yet I am not altogether an ass.

FALSTAFF What say you, Scarlet and John?

BARDOLPH Why, sir, for my part, I say the gentleman had drunk himself out of his five sentences.

EVANS It is his five "senses." Fie, what the ignorance is!

BARDOLPH And being fap, sir, was, as they say, cashiered. And so conclusions passed the careers.

SLENDER Ay, you spake in Latin then too. But 'tis no matter. I'll ne'er be drunk whilst I live again but in honest, civil, godly company, for this trick. If I be drunk, I'll be drunk with those that have the fear of God, and not with drunken knaves.

EVANS So Got 'udge me, that is a virtuous mind.

148 mountain-foreigner i.e., Welshman **149 combat challenge** challenge to trial by combat. (A flowery way of issuing a challenge to a duel.) **latten** mixed metal of yellow color, resembling brass. **bilbo** finely tempered sword of Bilbao in Spain. (Here alludes to Slender's thinness.) **150 labras** lips, i.e., face **153 advised** on your guard. **pass good humors** do nothing ill-natured **154 marry, trap with you** (An insulting phrase meaning something like "run off," "beat it.")
154–155 run . . . me threaten me with a constable, or behave like one. (A *nuthook* literally is a hooked stick used to pull nuts from trees; applied to a constable.) **155 very note** true observation **156 he . . . face** i.e., Bardolph **159 Scarlet and John** (Names of Robin Hood's companions, Will Scarlet and Little John; *Scarlet* is humorously applied to Bardolph's color.) **163 fap** drunk **163–164 cashiered** deprived (of his senses; but perhaps suggesting too that he was fleeced) **164 conclusions . . . careers** i.e., his conclusions about matters made a wild gallop, went wide of the mark; or, what happened to him got out of control. (*Careers:* a short gallop at full speed, a feat of horsemanship.)
170 'udge (For *judge.*) **mind** intent

FALSTAFF You hear all these matters denied, gentlemen. You hear it.

[Enter] Anne Page [with wine]; Mistress Ford [and] Mistress Page [following].

PAGE Nay, daughter, carry the wine in. We'll drink within. *[Exit Anne Page.]*

SLENDER O heaven! This is Mistress Anne Page.

PAGE How now, Mistress Ford?

FALSTAFF Mistress Ford, by my troth, you are very well met. By your leave, good mistress. *[He kisses her.]*

PAGE Wife, bid these gentlemen welcome.—Come, we have a hot venison pasty to dinner. Come, gentlemen, I hope we shall drink down all unkindness.

[Exeunt all except Shallow, Slender, and Evans.]

SLENDER I had rather than forty shillings I had my book of songs and sonnets here.

[Enter] Simple.

How now, Simple, where have you been? I must wait on myself, must I? You have not the book of riddles about you, have you?

SIMPLE Book of riddles? Why, did you not lend it to Alice Shortcake upon Allhallowmas last, a fortnight afore Michaelmas?

SHALLOW Come, coz, come, coz, we stay for you. A word with you, coz—marry, this, coz: there is as 'twere a tender, a kind of tender, made afar off by Sir Hugh here. Do you understand me?

SLENDER Ay, sir, you shall find me reasonable. If it be so, I shall do that that is reason.

SHALLOW Nay, but understand me.

180 to for **182–183 book of songs and sonnets** (Probably refers to Tottel's *Miscellany,* published 1557 and quite old-fashioned by the late 1590s.) **185 book of riddles** (Such a book is mentioned as in the library of Captain Cox in *Laneham's Letter,* 1575. No copy is extant earlier than 1629.) **188–189 Allhallowmas . . . Michaelmas** (Simple's blunder. Michaelmas occurs on September 29, Allhallowmas or All Saints' Day on November 1.) **190 stay** wait **192 tender** offer. **afar off** indirectly

SLENDER So I do, sir.
EVANS Give ear to his motions. Master Slender, I will 198
description the matter to you, if you be capacity of it.
SLENDER Nay, I will do as my cousin Shallow says. I
pray you, pardon me. He's a Justice of Peace in his
country, simple though I stand here. 202
EVANS But that is not the question. The question is
concerning your marriage.
SHALLOW Ay, there's the point, sir.
EVANS Marry, is it, the very point of it—to Mistress
Anne Page.
SLENDER Why, if it be so, I will marry her upon any
reasonable demands. 209
EVANS But can you affection the 'oman? Let us command to know that of your mouth or of your lips; for
divers philosophers hold that the lips is parcel of the 212
mouth. Therefore, precisely, can you carry your good
will to the maid?
SHALLOW Cousin Abraham Slender, can you love her?
SLENDER I hope, sir, I will do as it shall become one that
would do reason.
EVANS Nay, Got's lords and his ladies! You must speak
positable, if you can carry her your desires towards 219
her.
SHALLOW That you must. Will you, upon good dowry, 221
marry her?
SLENDER I will do a greater thing than that, upon your
request, cousin, in any reason.
SHALLOW Nay, conceive me, conceive me, sweet coz. 225
What I do is to pleasure you, coz. Can you love the 226
maid?
SLENDER I will marry her, sir, at your request. But if
there be no great love in the beginning, yet heaven
may decrease it upon better acquaintance, when we 230
are married and have more occasion to know one an-

198 motions proposals **202 country** district. **simple though** as sure as (but also suggesting "however humble I, his kinsman, may appear to be") **209 demands** requests **212 parcel** part **219 positable** (For *positively.*) **221 upon good dowry** on the strength of a prospect of a good dowry **225 conceive** understand **226 pleasure** please **230 decrease** (For *increase.*)

other. I hope upon familiarity will grow more content. But if you say, "Marry her," I will marry her. That I am freely dissolved, and dissolutely.

EVANS It is a fery discretion answer, save the faul is in the 'ort "dissolutely." The 'ort is, according to our meaning, "resolutely." His meaning is good.

SHALLOW Ay, I think my cousin meant well.

SLENDER Ay, or else I would I might be hanged, la!

[*Enter Anne Page.*]

SHALLOW Here comes fair Mistress Anne.—Would I were young for your sake, Mistress Anne!

ANNE The dinner is on the table. My father desires your worships' company.

SHALLOW I will wait on him, fair Mistress Anne.

EVANS 'Od's plessed will! I will not be absence at the grace. [*Exeunt Shallow and Evans.*]

ANNE Will 't please your worship to come in, sir?

SLENDER No, I thank you, forsooth, heartily. I am very well.

ANNE The dinner attends you, sir.

SLENDER I am not ahungry, I thank you, forsooth. [*To Simple.*] Go, sirrah, for all you are my man, go wait upon my cousin Shallow. [*Exit Simple.*] A Justice of Peace sometimes may be beholding to his friend for a man. I keep but three men and a boy yet, till my mother be dead. But what though? Yet I live like a poor gentleman born.

ANNE I may not go in without your worship. They will not sit till you come.

SLENDER I' faith, I'll eat nothing. I thank you as much as though I did.

ANNE I pray you, sir, walk in.

SLENDER I had rather walk here, I thank you. I bruised

232 hope hope that. **content** (Suggesting *contempt,* as in the proverb "Familiarity breeds contempt.") **234 dissolved** (For *resolved.*) **dissolutely** (For *resolutely.*) **235 faul** i.e., fault **236 'ort** word **244 wait on him** keep him company **245 'Od's** God's **250 attends** waits for **252 sirrah** (Usual form of address to a social inferior.) **for all** even though **252–253 wait upon** attend **254 beholding** beholden **256 what though** what of it

my shin th' other day with playing at sword and dagger with a master of fence—three veneys for a dish of stewed prunes—and, by my troth, I cannot abide the smell of hot meat since. Why do your dogs bark so? Be there bears i' the town?

ANNE I think there are, sir. I heard them talked of.

SLENDER I love the sport well, but I shall as soon quarrel at it as any man in England. You are afraid if you see the bear loose, are you not?

ANNE Ay, indeed, sir.

SLENDER That's meat and drink to me, now. I have seen Sackerson loose twenty times, and have taken him by the chain. But, I warrant you, the women have so cried and shrieked at it that it passed. But women, indeed, cannot abide 'em—they are very ill-favored, rough things.

[*Enter Page.*]

PAGE Come, gentle Master Slender, come. We stay for you.

SLENDER I'll eat nothing, I thank you, sir.

PAGE By Cock and pie, you shall not choose, sir! Come, come.

SLENDER Nay, pray you, lead the way.

PAGE Come on, sir.

SLENDER Mistress Anne, yourself shall go first.

ANNE Not I, sir. Pray you, keep on.

SLENDER Truly, I will not go first, truly, la! I will not do you that wrong.

ANNE I pray you, sir.

SLENDER I'll rather be unmannerly than troublesome. You do yourself wrong, indeed, la! *Exeunt.*

265 fence fencing. **veneys** bouts in fencing **266 stewed prunes** (A favorite dish at the "stews" or brothel houses; hence an indelicate remark to address to Anne.) **270 the sport** i.e., bearbaiting **275 Sackerson** a famous bear at the Paris Garden near the theaters on the Bankside **277 passed** i.e., surpassed description **278 ill-favored** ugly **283 Cock** (A perversion of *God.*) **pie** service book of the pre-Reformation church. **shall not choose** must **288 keep on** go ahead

1.2 *Enter Evans and Simple* [*from dinner*].

EVANS Go your ways, and ask of Doctor Caius' house which is the way. And there dwells one Mistress Quickly, which is in the manner of his nurse, or his dry nurse, or his cook, or his laundry, his washer, and his wringer.

SIMPLE Well, sir.

EVANS Nay, it is petter yet. Give her this letter. [*He gives a letter.*] For it is a 'oman that altogether's acquaintance with Mistress Anne Page. And the letter is to desire and require her to solicit your master's desires to Mistress Anne Page. I pray you, begone. I will make an end of my dinner; there's pippins and cheese to come.

Exeunt [*separately*].

✣

1.3 *Enter Falstaff, Host, Bardolph, Nym, Pistol,* [*and Robin, Falstaff's*] *Page.*

FALSTAFF Mine Host of the Garter!

HOST What says my bullyrook? Speak scholarly and wisely.

FALSTAFF Truly, mine Host, I must turn away some of my followers.

HOST Discard, bully Hercules, cashier. Let them wag; trot, trot.

FALSTAFF I sit at ten pounds a week.

HOST Thou'rt an emperor—Caesar, Kaiser, and Pheezer. I will entertain Bardolph; he shall draw, he shall tap. Said I well, bully Hector?

FALSTAFF Do so, good mine Host.

1.2. Location: The same scene, a short time later, essentially continuous.
1 ask of inquire concerning **4 dry nurse** i.e., attendant to an adult, not a child; a housekeeper **8 altogether's acquaintance** is well acquainted **12 pippins** a kind of apple

1.3. Location: The Garter Inn.
2 bullyrook fine fellow **6 cashier** dismiss. **wag** move on **8 I sit at** my expenses are **9 Kaiser** emperor **9–10 Pheezer** i.e., Vizier (?) or, one who beats or frightens, "does for" someone (?) **10 entertain** employ. **draw** draw liquor **11 tap** serve as tapster. **Hector** (The hero of Troy, and a type of manliness.)

HOST I have spoke; let him follow. [*To Bardolph.*] Let me
see thee froth and lime. I am at a word. Follow. [*Exit.*] 14
FALSTAFF Bardolph, follow him. A tapster is a good
trade. An old cloak makes a new jerkin; a withered 16
servingman a fresh tapster. Go; adieu.

BARDOLPH It is a life that I have desired. I will thrive.
[*Exit Bardolph.*]

PISTOL O base Hungarian wight! Wilt thou the spigot 19
wield?

NYM He was gotten in drink. Is not the humor con- 21
ceited? 22

FALSTAFF I am glad I am so acquit of this tinderbox. His 23
thefts were too open. His filching was like an unskillful singer: he kept not time.

NYM The good humor is to steal at a minute's rest. 26

PISTOL "Convey," the wise it call. "Steal"? Foh! A fico 27
for the phrase!

FALSTAFF Well, sirs, I am almost out at heels. 29

PISTOL Why then, let kibes ensue. 30

FALSTAFF There is no remedy. I must coney-catch, I must 31
shift. 32

PISTOL Young ravens must have food.

FALSTAFF Which of you know Ford of this town?

PISTOL I ken the wight. He is of substance good. 35

FALSTAFF My honest lads, I will tell you what I am 36
about. 37

PISTOL Two yards, and more.

14 froth draw liquor in such a way as to make it frothy, filling the glass with less beer. **lime** adulterate wine by putting lime into it to mask the sour taste. **at a word** a man of few words **16 jerkin** jacket **19 Hungarian wight** i.e., beggarly person **21 gotten** begotten **21–22 conceited** ingenious **23 acquit** rid. **tinderbox** (alluding to Bardolph's fiery complexion) **26 good humor** i.e., smart way to do it. **at a minute's rest** i.e., within a minute's time. (Or possibly an error for *minim rest,* the shortest rest in music.) **27 Convey . . . call** i.e., those in the know use the cant phrase for stealing, "convey." **fico** Italian for *fig,* an insulting phrase and obscene gesture of putting the thumb between the second and third fingers **29 out at heels** i.e., out of money. (Literally, with stockings or shoes worn through at the heel.) **30 kibes** chilblains. (Pistol interprets *out at heels* literally.) **31 coney-catch** catch rabbits, i.e., cheat victims in a con game **32 shift** devise a stratagem **35 ken the wight** know the person. **of substance good** a person of means **36–37 what I am about** what I am up to. (But Pistol plays with the meaning "what I measure round about.")

FALSTAFF No quips now, Pistol. Indeed, I am in the
waist two yards about. But I am now about no waste;
I am about thrift. Briefly, I do mean to make love to
Ford's wife. I spy entertainment in her. She dis- 42
courses, she carves, she gives the leer of invitation. I 43
can construe the action of her familiar style; and the 44
hardest voice of her behavior, to be Englished rightly, 45
is, "I am Sir John Falstaff's."

PISTOL He hath studied her well and translated her
will—out of honesty into English. 48

NYM The anchor is deep. Will that humor pass? 49

FALSTAFF Now, the report goes she has all the rule of
her husband's purse. He hath a legion of angels. 51

PISTOL As many devils entertain; and "To her, boy!" 52
say I.

NYM The humor rises; it is good. Humor me the an- 54
gels. 55

FALSTAFF [*Showing letters*] I have writ me here a letter 56
to her; and here another to Page's wife, who even now
gave me good eyes too, examined my parts with most
judicious oeillades. Sometimes the beam of her view 59
gilded my foot, sometimes my portly belly.

PISTOL [*To Nym*] Then did the sun on dunghill shine.

NYM [*To Pistol*] I thank thee for that humor.

FALSTAFF O, she did so course o'er my exteriors, with 63
such a greedy intention, that the appetite of her eye 64

42 entertainment (1) readiness to receive me (2) a source of supply **43 carves** shows courtesy and affability, or speaks affectedly. **leer** come-hither glance **44 construe** interpret (introducing an extended grammatical pun, continued in *style, voice,* and *Englished*) **45 hardest voice** (1) severest judgment (2) most difficult construction. **Englished** expressed in English **48 honesty** chastity **49 The . . . deep** i.e., the plan is fixed firmly, or is a deep one (?) **Will . . . pass** i.e., will my expression pass muster **51 angels** coins stamped with the figure of the archangel Michael, worth about ten shillings **52 As . . . entertain** (Pistol, taking *legion of angels* in the sense of "heavenly host," plays on the idea of a battle between them and a legion of devils. Falstaff with his devilish devices is to take on the angels and *entertain* them to his own use.) **To her, boy** (A cry of encouragement to a hunting hound.) **54–55 Humor me the angels** i.e., yes, take the money by this device. (Nym is seconding Pistol's advice; the *humor* of the enterprise takes shape.) **56 writ me** written. (*Me* is used colloquially.) **59 oeillades** amorous glances **63 course o'er** run her eyes over **64 intention** intentness of gaze

did seem to scorch me up like a burning glass! Here's 65
another letter to her. She bears the purse too; she is a
region in Guiana, all gold and bounty. I will be cheat- 67
ers to them both, and they shall be exchequers to me. 68
They shall be my East and West Indies, and I will trade
to them both. [*To Pistol.*] Go bear thou this letter to
Mistress Page; [*To Nym*] and thou this to Mistress
Ford. We will thrive, lads, we will thrive.

PISTOL [*Giving the letter back*]
Shall I Sir Pandarus of Troy become, 73
And by my side wear steel? Then Lucifer take all! 74

NYM I will run no base humor. Here, take the humor-
letter. [*Giving the letter back.*] I will keep the havior of 76
reputation. 77

FALSTAFF [*To Robin*]
Hold, sirrah, bear you these letters tightly. 78
[*He gives the letters.*]
Sail like my pinnace to these golden shores. 79
Rogues, hence, avaunt! Vanish like hailstones, go!
Trudge, plod away o' the hoof! Seek shelter, pack! 81
Falstaff will learn the humor of the age: 82
French thrift, you rogues—myself and skirted page. 83
[*Exeunt Falstaff and Robin.*]

PISTOL
Let vultures gripe thy guts! For gourd and fullam holds, 84
And high and low beguiles the rich and poor. 85
Tester I'll have in pouch when thou shalt lack, 86

65 burning glass magnifying glass to focus rays of the sun **67 region in Guiana** (A possible reference to Sir Walter Ralegh's *Discovery of the Large, Rich, and Beautiful Empire of Guiana,* published 1596.) **67–68 cheaters** escheaters, officers appointed to look after the King's escheats, i.e., land reverted to the crown (with a quibble on the ordinary sense of "those who cheat") **68 exchequers** treasuries **73 Sir Pandarus** uncle of Cressida, and go-between in the story of Troilus and Cressida. (From his name originated the word "pander.") **74 And . . . steel** i.e., even though I am a soldier **76–77 keep . . . reputation** keep up good appearances **78 tightly** deftly, securely **79 pinnace** a small, swift sailing vessel **81 pack** be off **82 humor** fashion **83 French thrift** (Alludes to the current practice in France of economizing with one page instead of a more numerous retinue.) **skirted** wearing a doublet with long skirts or tails **84 gourd and fullam** two kinds of false dice. **holds** hold good, can still be used as a means of livelihood **85 high and low** i.e., false dice weighted so as to produce high and low numbers **86 Tester** sixpence. **pouch** purse

Base Phrygian Turk!
NYM I have operations which be humors of revenge.
PISTOL Wilt thou revenge?
NYM By welkin and her star!
PISTOL With wit or steel?
NYM
With both the humors, I.
I will discuss the humor of this love to Page.
PISTOL
And I to Ford shall eke unfold
How Falstaff, varlet vile,
His dove will prove, his gold will hold,
And his soft couch defile.

NYM My humor shall not cool. I will incense Page to deal with poison; I will possess him with yellowness, for the revolt of mine is dangerous. That is my true humor.

PISTOL Thou art the Mars of malcontents. I second thee. Troop on. *Exeunt.*

✤

1.4 *Enter Mistress Quickly* [*and*] *Simple.*

QUICKLY [*Calling*] What, John Rugby!

[*Enter Rugby.*]

I pray thee, go to the casement and see if you can see my master, Master Doctor Caius, coming. If he do, i' faith, and find anybody in the house, here will be an old abusing of God's patience and the King's English.

RUGBY I'll go watch.

87 Phrygian Turk (A term of opprobrium.) **88 operations** plans **90 welkin** sky **91 wit or steel** i.e., cunning or violence **92 humors** i.e., methods **93 discuss** declare **94 eke** also **96 prove** test **99 possess** fill. **yellowness** i.e., jealousy. (In the Folio text, Nym plans to incense *Ford* with jealousy, which seems more appropriate to Ford's jealous temperament, while in line 94 Pistol plans to speak to Page; but in 2.1.104 ff. Nym speaks to Page, trying to make him jealous, and Pistol to Ford, and so it seems best to follow the quarto assignments here in ll. 93–94 and 98.) **100 revolt . . . dangerous** i.e., my turning against Falstaff will harm him **102 the Mars** i.e., the most warlike and mighty

1.4. Location: Doctor Caius's house.
5 old plentiful, great

QUICKLY Go; and we'll have a posset for 't soon at 7
night, in faith, at the latter end of a sea-coal fire. 8
[*Rugby goes to look out the window*.] An honest, will- 9
ing, kind fellow as ever servant shall come in house
withal, and, I warrant you, no telltale nor no breed- 11
bate. His worst fault is that he is given to prayer. He 12
is something peevish that way, but nobody but has 13
his fault. But let that pass. Peter Simple you say your
name is?

SIMPLE Ay, for fault of a better. 16

QUICKLY And Master Slender's your master?

SIMPLE Ay, forsooth.

QUICKLY Does he not wear a great round beard, like a glover's paring knife?

SIMPLE No, forsooth. He hath but a little whey face, 21
with a little yellow beard, a Cain-colored beard. 22

QUICKLY A softly spirited man, is he not? 23

SIMPLE Ay, forsooth. But he is as tall a man of his hands 24
as any is between this and his head. He hath fought 25
with a warrener. 26

QUICKLY How say you? O, I should remember him. Does he not hold up his head, as it were, and strut in his gait?

SIMPLE Yes indeed does he.

QUICKLY Well, heaven send Anne Page no worse fortune! Tell Master Parson Evans I will do what I can for your master. Anne is a good girl, and I wish—

[*Rugby returns*.]

RUGBY Out, alas! Here comes my master.

QUICKLY We shall all be shent. Run in here, good 34
young man; go into this closet. He will not stay long. 35
[*She shuts Simple in the closet*.] What, John Rugby!

7 a posset a drink of hot milk curdled with ale or wine **7–8 soon at night** as soon as night comes **8 sea-coal** mineral coal brought by sea (as distinguished from charcoal) **9 s.d. window** (Rugby perhaps looks offstage.) **11 withal** with **11–12 breedbate** mischief-maker **13 something peevish** somewhat foolish **16 for fault of** in default of **21 whey** i.e., pallid **22 Cain-colored** (Cain is often pictured in old tapestries with a yellow or reddish beard.) **23 softly spirited** gentle **24 as tall . . . hands** as valiant a man, as stout of arms **25 between . . . head** i.e., in these parts. (Proverbial.) **26 warrener** gamekeeper **34 shent** blamed, disgraced **35 closet** closet or private room

John! What, John, I say! Go, John, go inquire for my
master. I doubt he be not well, that he comes not home. 38
[*Exit Rugby.*]
[*Singing*] And down, down, adown-a, etc.

[*Enter*] *Doctor Caius.*

CAIUS Vat is you sing? I do not like dese toys. Pray you, 40
go and vetch me in my closet *un boîtier vert,* a box, a 41
green-a box. Do intend vat I speak? A green-a box. 42

QUICKLY Ay, forsooth, I'll fetch it you. [*Aside.*] I am
glad he went not in himself. If he had found the young
man, he would have been horn-mad. 45
[*She goes to the door.*]

CAIUS *Fe, fe, fe, fe! Ma foi, il fait fort chaud. Je m'en* 46
vais à la cour—la grande affaire. 47

QUICKLY Is it this, sir? [*She offers him a box.*]

CAIUS *Oui; mets-le à ma* pocket. *Dépêche,* quickly. 49
Vere is dat knave Rugby?

QUICKLY What, John Rugby! John!

[*Enter Rugby.*]

RUGBY Here, sir.

CAIUS You are John Rugby, and you are Jack Rugby.
Come, take-a your rapier, and come after my heel to 54
the court.

RUGBY 'Tis ready, sir, here in the porch.

CAIUS By my trot, I tarry too long. 'Od's me, *qu'ai-* 57
j'oublié? Dere is some simples in my closet dat I vill 58
not for the varld I shall leave behind.

QUICKLY [*Aside*] Ay me, he'll find the young man there,
and be mad!

CAIUS [*Going to the closet*] O *diable, diable!* Vat is in my 62
closet? Villainy! *Larron*! [*Pulling Simple out.*] Rugby, 63
my rapier!

38 doubt fear **40 toys** trifles, i.e., songs **41 un boîtier vert** a green box **42 Do intend** do you understand. (French *entendre.*) **45 horn-mad** (1) enraged, like a horned beast (2) enraged like a jealous cuckold **46–47 Ma foi . . . affaire** by my faith, it is very hot; I am going to court—the great affair **49 Oui . . . Dépêche** yes, put it in my pocket; be quick **54 your rapier** i.e., your master's rapier **57 trot** truth. **'Od's me** God save me **57–58 qu'ai-j'oublié** what have I forgotten **58 simples** medicinal herbs **62 diable** devil **63 Larron** robber

QUICKLY Good master, be content.

CAIUS Wherefore shall I be content-a?

QUICKLY The young man is an honest man.

CAIUS What shall de honest man do in my closet? Dere is no honest man dat shall come in my closet.

QUICKLY I beseech you, be not so phlegmatic. Hear the truth of it: he came of an errand to me from Parson Hugh.

CAIUS Vell?

SIMPLE Ay, forsooth, to desire her to—

QUICKLY Peace, I pray you.

CAIUS Peace-a your tongue. [*To Simple.*] Speak-a your tale.

SIMPLE To desire this honest gentlewoman, your maid, to speak a good word to Mistress Anne Page for my master in the way of marriage.

QUICKLY This is all, indeed, la! But I'll ne'er put my finger in the fire, and need not.

CAIUS Sir Hugh send-a you? Rugby, *baille* me some paper. [*To Simple.*] Tarry you a little-a while. [*Rugby fetches paper, and Dr. Caius writes.*]

QUICKLY [*Aside to Simple*] I am glad he is so quiet. If he had been throughly moved, you should have heard him so loud and so melancholy. But notwithstanding, man, I'll do you your master what good I can. And the very yea and the no is, the French doctor, my master—I may call him my master, look you, for I keep his house, and I wash, wring, brew, bake, scour, dress meat and drink, make the beds, and do all myself—

SIMPLE [*Aside to Quickly*] 'Tis a great charge to come under one body's hand.

QUICKLY [*Aside to Simple*] Are you advised o' that? You shall find it a great charge. And to be up early and down late. But notwithstanding—to tell you in your ear; I would have no words of it—my master himself is in love with Mistress Anne Page. But notwithstand-

65 content calm **70 phlegmatic** (Probably a blunder for *choleric,* hot-tempered; phlegmatic is the very opposite in the physiology of humors.) **71 of an** on an **81 and need not** if I don't need to **82 baille** fetch **85 throughly moved** thoroughly angered **86 melancholy** (Perhaps a blunder again, like *phlegmatic,* above.) **87–88 the very yea and the no** what is certain **90–91 dress meat** prepare food **92 charge** responsibility **94 Are . . . that** i.e., you may well say so

ing that, I know Anne's mind: that's neither here nor
there.

CAIUS You jack'nape, give-a this letter to Sir Hugh. 101
[*He gives Simple the letter.*] By gar, it is a shallenge. I 102
will cut his troat in de park, and I will teach a scurvy
jackanape priest to meddle or make. You may be 104
gone; it is not good you tarry here. [*Exit Simple.*] By gar,
I will cut all his two stones. By gar, he shall not have a 106
stone to throw at his dog.

QUICKLY Alas, he speaks but for his friend.

CAIUS It is no matter-a ver dat. Do not you tell-a me dat 109
I shall have Anne Page for myself? By gar, I vill kill de
jack priest; and I have appointed mine Host of de Jar- 111
teer to measure our weapon. By gar, I will myself have 112
Anne Page.

QUICKLY Sir, the maid loves you, and all shall be well.
We must give folks leave to prate. What the goodyear! 115

CAIUS Rugby, come to the court with me. [*To Mistress Quickly.*] By gar, if I have not Anne Page, I shall turn your head out of my door. Follow my heels, Rugby.

[*Exeunt Caius and Rugby.*]

QUICKLY You shall have An fool's head of your own. 119
No, I know Anne's mind for that. Never a woman in
Windsor knows more of Anne's mind than I do, nor
can do more than I do with her, I thank heaven.

FENTON [*Within*] Who's within there, ho?

QUICKLY Who's there, I trow? Come near the house, I 124
pray you.

[*Enter*] *Fenton.*

FENTON How now, good woman, how dost thou?

QUICKLY The better that it pleases your good worship to ask.

101 jack'nape ape, tame monkey; i.e., fop, worthless fellow **102 gar** i.e., God **104 meddle or make** meddle **106 cut. . . stones** castrate him **109 ver** for **111 jack** (A contemptuous epithet.) **111–112 Jarteer** Garter **112 measure our weapon** i.e., act as second or referee. (Literally, to make sure that the swords are of equal length.) **115 What the goodyear** i.e., what the deuce (?) **119 An** (The Folio uses the same spelling, *An,* for *Anne,* in ll. 120 and 121, suggesting a pun on *Anne Page;* Caius is to have a fool's head for wooing Anne.) **124 trow** wonder. **Come near** enter

FENTON What news? How does pretty Mistress Anne?

QUICKLY In truth, sir, and she is pretty, and honest, and gentle; and one that is your friend, I can tell you that by the way, I praise heaven for it.

FENTON Shall I do any good, think'st thou? Shall I not lose my suit?

QUICKLY Troth, sir, all is in His hands above. But notwithstanding, Master Fenton, I'll be sworn on a book she loves you. Have not your worship a wart above your eye?

FENTON Yes, marry, have I. What of that?

QUICKLY Well, thereby hangs a tale. Good faith, it is such another Nan! But, I detest, an honest maid as ever broke bread. We had an hour's talk of that wart. I shall never laugh but in that maid's company! But indeed she is given too much to allicholy and musing. But for you—well, go to.

FENTON Well, I shall see her today. Hold, there's money for thee. [*He gives money.*] Let me have thy voice in my behalf. If thou seest her before me, commend me.

QUICKLY Will I? I' faith, that I will. And I will tell your worship more of the wart the next time we have confidence, and of other wooers.

FENTON Well, farewell. I am in great haste now.

QUICKLY Farewell to your worship. [*Exit Fenton.*] Truly, an honest gentleman. But Anne loves him not, for I know Anne's mind as well as another does.—Out upon 't! What have I forgot? *Exit.*

✤

130 honest chaste **131 gentle** well-bred. **your friend** friendly disposed toward you **136 a book** i.e., a Bible **140–141 it . . . Nan** i.e., Anne is so remarkable a girl, so lively and merry **141 detest** (For *protest.*) **143 but** except **144 allicholy** (For *melancholy.*) **145 go to** i.e., enough, come, come **147 voice** word of support **150–151 confidence** (For *conference.*) **156 Out upon 't** i.e., dear me

2.1 *Enter Mistress Page [with a letter].*

MRS. PAGE What, have I scaped love letters in the holiday time of my beauty, and am I now a subject for them? Let me see. [*She reads.*]

"Ask me no reason why I love you, for though Love use Reason for his precisian, he admits him not for his counselor. You are not young; no more am I. Go to then, there's sympathy. You are merry; so am I. Ha, ha! Then there's more sympathy. You love sack, and so do I. Would you desire better sympathy? Let it suffice thee, Mistress Page—at the least, if the love of soldier can suffice—that I love thee. I will not say, pity me—'tis not a soldierlike phrase—but I say, love me. By me,

Thine own true knight,
By day or night,
Or any kind of light,
With all his might
For thee to fight,

John Falstaff."

What a Herod of Jewry is this! O wicked, wicked world! One that is well-nigh worn to pieces with age, to show himself a young gallant! What an unweighed behavior hath this Flemish drunkard picked, i' the devil's name, out of my conversation, that he dares in this manner assay me? Why, he hath not been thrice in my company. What should I say to him? I was then frugal of my mirth. Heaven forgive me! Why, I'll exhibit a bill in the Parliament for the putting down of men. How shall I be revenged on him? For revenged I will be, as sure as his guts are made of puddings.

[Enter] Mistress Ford.

2.1. Location: Before Page's house.
5 precisian strict adviser **6 counselor** practical guide **7 sympathy** congeniality, agreement **8 sack** a Spanish wine **20 Herod of Jewry** bombastic ranter, like the comic villain of the Corpus Christi plays **22 unweighed** ill-considered **23 Flemish drunkard** (The Flemish were proverbially heavy drinkers.) **24 conversation** conduct **25 assay** accost, address (with proposals of love) **26 should I say** could I have said **27 exhibit** introduce **28 putting down** suppression (but with bawdy suggestion) **30 puddings** mixture of meat, herbs, etc., stuffed into intestines of animals, as sausage

MRS. FORD Mistress Page! Trust me, I was going to your house.

MRS. PAGE And, trust me, I was coming to you. You look very ill.

MRS. FORD Nay, I'll ne'er believe that. I have to show to the contrary.

MRS. PAGE Faith, but you do, in my mind.

MRS. FORD Well, I do then. Yet I say I could show you to the contrary. O Mistress Page, give me some counsel!

MRS. PAGE What's the matter, woman?

MRS. FORD O woman, if it were not for one trifling respect, I could come to such honor!

MRS. PAGE Hang the trifle, woman, take the honor. What is it? Dispense with trifles. What is it?

MRS. FORD If I would but go to hell for an eternal moment or so, I could be knighted.

MRS. PAGE What? Thou liest! Sir Alice Ford? These knights will hack, and so thou shouldst not alter the article of thy gentry.

MRS. FORD We burn daylight. Here, read, read. Perceive how I might be knighted. [*She gives a letter.*] I shall think the worse of fat men as long as I have an eye to make difference of men's liking. And yet he would not swear; praised women's modesty; and gave such orderly and well-behaved reproof to all uncomeliness that I would have sworn his disposition would have gone to the truth of his words. But they do no more adhere and keep place together than the Hundredth Psalm to the tune of "Greensleeves." What tempest, I

31 Trust me believe me **34 ill** unhappy, out of sorts. (But Mistress Ford, in replying, plays on the sense of "ugly.") **35 have** have something, i.e., the letter **42–43 respect** matter, consideration **49 hack** (Of uncertain meaning; perhaps "fight with swords," together with a play on the idea of sexual intercourse; see also *to hick and to hack*, 4.1.61. Mrs. Page suggests that knights are likely to behave promiscuously.) **50 article of thy gentry** character of your rank **51 burn daylight** i.e., waste time **53–54 make . . . liking** discriminate among men's looks and physiques **54–55 would not swear** i.e., decorously avoided all profanity in my presence **56 uncomeliness** unseemly behavior **58 gone . . . of** supported **60 Greensleeves** (A popular tune to which many sets of words have been sung, some of them erotic; cf. 5.5.19.)

trow, threw this whale, with so many tuns of oil in his belly, ashore at Windsor? How shall I be revenged on him? I think the best way were to entertain him with hope, till the wicked fire of lust have melted him in his own grease. Did you ever hear the like?

MRS. PAGE Letter for letter, but that the name of Page and Ford differs! To thy great comfort in this mystery of ill opinions, here's the twin brother of thy letter. [*She shows her letter.*] But let thine inherit first, for I protest mine never shall. I warrant he hath a thousand of these letters, writ with blank space for different names—sure, more—and these are of the second edition. He will print them, out of doubt; for he cares not what he puts into the press, when he would put us two. I had rather be a giantess and lie under Mount Pelion. Well, I will find you twenty lascivious turtles ere one chaste man.

MRS. FORD [*Comparing the letters*] Why, this is the very same; the very hand, the very words. What doth he think of us?

MRS. PAGE Nay, I know not. It makes me almost ready to wrangle with mine own honesty. I'll entertain myself like one that I am not acquainted withal; for, sure, unless he know some strain in me that I know not myself, he would never have boarded me in this fury.

MRS. FORD "Boarding," call you it? I'll be sure to keep him above deck.

MRS. PAGE So will I. If he come under my hatches, I'll never to sea again. Let's be revenged on him. Let's appoint him a meeting, give him a show of comfort in

61 trow wonder. **tuns** (1) large casks (2) tons **63–64 entertain . . . hope** lead him on **67–68 mystery of ill opinions** i.e., situation in which Falstaff seems to have formed a bad opinion of her virtue for no apparent reason **69 inherit** come into possession, as of a legacy (since it is the "older" letter) **73 out of** without **74 into the press** (1) into the printing press (2) under his weight **76 Pelion** mountain in Thessaly. (The giants, according to Greek mythology, heaped it on a neighboring mountain, Ossa, and Ossa on Olympus, in their attempts to overthrow the gods.) **turtles** turtledoves, proverbially chaste, i.e., faithful to their mates **82 wrangle** quarrel. **honesty** chastity. **entertain** treat **83 withal** with **84 strain** quality **85 boarded** accosted, made advances to. (A term of naval warfare.)

his suit, and lead him on with a fine-baited delay till 91
he hath pawned his horses to mine Host of the Garter.
MRS. FORD Nay, I will consent to act any villainy against 93
him that may not sully the chariness of our honesty. 94
O, that my husband saw this letter! It would give eternal food to his jealousy.
MRS. PAGE Why, look where he comes, and my good- 97
man too. He's as far from jealousy as I am from giving 98
him cause, and that, I hope, is an unmeasurable distance.

MRS. FORD You are the happier woman.

MRS. PAGE Let's consult together against this greasy knight. Come hither. [*They retire.*]

[*Enter*] *Master Page* [*with*] *Nym, Master Ford* [*with*] *Pistol.*

FORD Well, I hope it be not so.

PISTOL
Hope is a curtal dog in some affairs. 105
Sir John affects thy wife. 106

FORD Why, sir, my wife is not young.

PISTOL
He woos both high and low, both rich and poor,
Both young and old, one with another, Ford.
He loves the gallimaufry. Ford, perpend. 110

FORD Love my wife?

PISTOL
With liver burning hot. Prevent, or go thou, 112
Like Sir Actaeon he, with Ringwood at thy heels.— 113
O, odious is the name! 114

FORD What name, sir?

91 fine-baited i.e., subtly alluring **93 Nay** i.e., indeed, what's more **94 chariness** scrupulous integrity **97–98 goodman** husband **105 curtal** having the tail docked. (A term of opprobrium or condescension.) **106 affects** loves **110 gallimaufry** a dish of miscellaneous ingredients; hence, the whole lot. **perpend** consider **112 liver burning hot** (Allusion to the liver as the seat of the passions.) **113 Actaeon** huntsman who was changed into a stag by Diana as punishment for watching her and her nymphs at their bath and was torn to pieces by his own hounds. (The comparison here is to a horned beast, like a cuckold, being pursued.) **Ringwood** one of Actaeon's hounds (mentioned in Golding's translation of Ovid) **114 the name** i.e., the name of cuckold

PISTOL The horn, I say. Farewell.
Take heed, have open eye, for thieves do foot by night. 117
Take heed, ere summer comes or cuckoo birds do sing. 118
Away, Sir Corporal Nym! 119
Believe it, Page, he speaks sense. [*Exit*.]
FORD [*Aside*] I will be patient. I will find out this. 121
NYM [*To Page*] And this is true. I like not the humor of
lying. He hath wronged me in some humors. I should 123
have borne the humored letter to her; but I have a 124
sword, and it shall bite upon my necessity. He loves 125
your wife; there's the short and the long. My name is
Corporal Nym. I speak and I avouch 'tis true. My
name is Nym, and Falstaff loves your wife. Adieu. I
love not the humor of bread and cheese, and there's 129
the humor of it. Adieu.
PAGE [*Aside*] "The humor of it," quoth 'a! Here's a fellow 131
frights English out of his wits. 132
FORD [*Aside*] I will seek out Falstaff.
PAGE [*Aside*] I never heard such a drawling, affecting 134
rogue.
FORD [*Aside*] If I do find it—well. 136
PAGE [*Aside*] I will not believe such a Cathayan, though 137
the priest o' the town commended him for a true man.
FORD [*Aside*] 'Twas a good sensible fellow. Well.

[*Mistress Page and Mistress Ford come forward*.]

PAGE How now, Meg?
MRS. PAGE Whither go you, George? Hark you.
[*They converse apart*.]
MRS. FORD How now, sweet Frank, why art thou melancholy?
FORD I melancholy? I am not melancholy. Get you home, go.

117 foot walk **118 cuckoo birds** (Associated with cuckoldry because of their call, "cuckoo," and because they lay eggs in other birds' nests.) **119 Away** come away **121 find out** make inquiry into **123–124 I . . . borne** i.e., he wanted me to carry **125 upon my necessity** when I have need **129 humor . . . cheese** (Alludes to the scant rations Nym received as Falstaff's retainer.) **131 'a** he **132 his** its **134 affecting** affected **136 If . . . well** if I find it's true, well, I'll take steps **137 Cathayan** person from Cathay, i.e., China; hence, sharper, scoundrel

MRS. FORD Faith, thou hast some crotchets in thy head now.—Will you go, Mistress Page?

MRS. PAGE Have with you.—You'll come to dinner, George?

[*Enter Mistress*] *Quickly.*

[*Aside to Mistress Ford*] Look who comes yonder. She shall be our messenger to this paltry knight.

MRS. FORD [*Aside to Mistress Page*] Trust me, I thought on her. She'll fit it.

MRS. PAGE [*To Mistress Quickly*] You are come to see my daughter Anne?

QUICKLY Ay, forsooth; and, I pray, how does good Mistress Anne?

MRS. PAGE Go in with us and see. We have an hour's talk with you.

[*Exeunt Mistress Page, Mistress Ford, and Mistress Quickly.*]

PAGE How now, Master Ford?

FORD You heard what this knave told me, did you not?

PAGE Yes, and you heard what the other told me?

FORD Do you think there is truth in them?

PAGE Hang 'em, slaves! I do not think the knight would offer it. But these that accuse him in his intent towards our wives are a yoke of his discarded men—very rogues, now they be out of service.

FORD Were they his men?

PAGE Marry, were they.

FORD I like it never the better for that. Does he lie at the Garter?

PAGE Ay, marry, does he. If he should intend this voyage toward my wife, I would turn her loose to him; and what he gets more of her than sharp words, let it lie on my head.

FORD I do not misdoubt my wife, but I would be loath to turn them together. A man may be too confident. I

146 crotchets whims, fancies **148 Have with you** I'll go along with you **152 She'll fit it** she is just the person for the part **164 offer** venture **165 yoke** pair **169 lie** lodge **171 intend** propose making **174 lie on my head** be my responsibility. (But Ford, in his reply, sees a joke on cuckold's horns.) **175 misdoubt** mistrust **176 turn them together** i.e., let them loose together in the same pasture, as in l. 172 above

would have nothing lie on my head. I cannot be thus
satisfied.

[*Enter*] *Host*.

PAGE Look where my ranting Host of the Garter comes. 179
There is either liquor in his pate or money in his purse
when he looks so merrily.—How now, mine Host?

HOST How now, bullyrook? Thou'rt a gentleman.
[*He turns and calls*.] Cavaleiro Justice, I say! 183

[*Enter*] *Shallow*.

SHALLOW I follow, mine Host, I follow.—Good even and 184
twenty, good Master Page! Master Page, will you go 185
with us? We have sport in hand.

HOST Tell him, Cavaleiro Justice. Tell him, bullyrook.

SHALLOW Sir, there is a fray to be fought between Sir
Hugh, the Welsh priest, and Caius, the French doctor.

FORD Good mine Host o' the Garter, a word with you.

HOST What say'st thou, my bullyrook?

[*They converse apart*.]

SHALLOW [*To Page*] Will you go with us to behold it?
My merry Host hath had the measuring of their weap- 193
ons and, I think, hath appointed them contrary 194
places; for, believe me, I hear the parson is no jester. 195
Hark, I will tell you what our sport shall be.

[*They converse apart*.]

HOST [*To Ford*] Hast thou no suit against my knight, my
guest cavalier?

FORD None, I protest. But I'll give you a pottle of burnt 199
sack to give me recourse to him and tell him my name 200
is Brook—only for a jest. 201

HOST My hand, bully. Thou shalt have egress and re-
gress—said I well?—and thy name shall be Brook. It
is a merry knight.—Will you go, mynheers? 204

179 ranting speaking in a high-flown, bombastic style **183 Cavaleiro Justice** gallant justice. (Put here in the form of an honorific title. A Spanish *caballero* is a gentleman trained in arms.) **184–185 Good . . . twenty** i.e., good afternoon, many times over **193–194 hath had . . . weapons** i.e., has been appointed referee **194–195 contrary places** different meeting places **199 pottle** two-quart measure. **burnt** heated **200 recourse** access **201 Brook** (Ford's alias, usually spelled *Brooke* in the second quarto, was changed to *Broom*—as it is spelled in the Folio—because Brooke was the family name of Lord Cobham. See Introduction.) **204 mynheers** gentlemen. (Dutch.)

SHALLOW Have with you, mine Host.

PAGE I have heard the Frenchman hath good skill in his rapier.

SHALLOW Tut, sir, I could have told you more. In these times you stand on distance—your passes, stoccados, and I know not what. 'Tis the heart, Master Page; 'tis here, 'tis here. I have seen the time, with my long sword I would have made you four tall fellows skip like rats.

HOST Here, boys, here, here! Shall we wag?

PAGE Have with you. I had rather hear them scold than fight. *Exeunt* [*Host, Shallow, and Page*].

FORD Though Page be a secure fool, and stands so firmly on his wife's frailty, yet I cannot put off my opinion so easily. She was in his company at Page's house; and what they made there, I know not. Well, I will look further into 't, and I have a disguise to sound Falstaff. If I find her honest, I lose not my labor; if she be otherwise, 'tis labor well bestowed. [*Exit*.]

✤

2.2 *Enter Falstaff* [*and*] *Pistol.*

FALSTAFF I will not lend thee a penny.

PISTOL

Why, then the world's mine oyster,
Which I with sword will open.
I will retort the sum in equipage.

FALSTAFF Not a penny. I have been content, sir, you should lay my countenance to pawn. I have grated upon my good friends for three reprieves for you and

205 Have with you I'll come with you. (Also in l. 215.) **209 you stand on distance** one relies on and attaches great importance to prescribed space between fencers. **passes** lunges. **stoccados** thrusts
210–211 'Tis . . . 'tis here i.e., real fencing, Master Page, is a matter of the heart, not of this affected modern etiquette. (Shallow perhaps taps his chest as he says, "'Tis here.") **211–212 long sword** an old-fashioned heavy weapon **212 tall** valiant **214 wag** go. (See 1.3.6.) **217 secure** overconfident **219 She** i.e., Mrs. Ford. **his** i.e., Falstaff's **220 made** did **221 sound** plumb

2.2. Location: The Garter Inn.
4 retort . . . equipage i.e., pay back the whole amount in military equipment **6 lay . . . pawn** i.e., borrow money on the strength of my patronage **6–7 grated upon** i.e., persistently and irritatingly begged

your coach-fellow Nym, or else you had looked through the grate like a gemini of baboons. I am damned in hell for swearing to gentlemen my friends you were good soldiers and tall fellows. And when Mistress Bridget lost the handle of her fan, I took 't upon mine honor thou hadst it not.

PISTOL

Didst not thou share? Hadst thou not fifteen pence?

FALSTAFF Reason, you rogue, reason. Think'st thou I'll endanger my soul gratis? At a word, hang no more about me. I am no gibbet for you. Go. A short knife and a throng! To your manor of Pickt-hatch, go. You'll not bear a letter for me, you rogue? You stand upon your honor! Why, thou unconfinable baseness, it is as much as I can do to keep the terms of my honor precise. Ay, ay, I myself sometimes, leaving the fear of God on the left hand and hiding mine honor in my necessity, am fain to shuffle, to hedge, and to lurch; and yet you, you rogue, will ensconce your rags, your cat-a-mountain looks, your red-lattice phrases, and your bold-beating oaths, under the shelter of your honor! You will not do it? You?

PISTOL

I do relent. What would thou more of man?

[*Enter*] *Robin.*

ROBIN Sir, here's a woman would speak with you.

FALSTAFF Let her approach.

[*Enter Mistress*] *Quickly.*

8 coach-fellow partner (like a fellow horse in harness) **9 grate** i.e., of a debtor's prison window. **gemini** pair **10 gentlemen my friends** my gentlemen friends **12–13 took 't upon** swore by **15 Reason** with good reason **17–18 A short . . . throng** i.e., with a short knife you might cut purses in a crowd **18 Pickt-hatch** (A quarter in London notorious in Elizabethan times for criminal types and prostitutes, the houses having hatches, or half doors, guarded with spikes.) **20 unconfinable** infinite **21 terms** condition **21–22 precise** pure. (A term often associated with puritanism.) **22–23 leaving . . . hand** i.e., disregarding a proper fear of God **24 fain** obliged. **to shuffle . . . lurch** to practice trickery, to dodge, and to steal **25–26 cat-a-mountain** catamount, leopard or panther, wildcat **26 red-lattice phrases** alehouse talk. (Lattices painted red identified an alehouse.) **27 bold-beating** (Perhaps a conflation of "bold-faced" and "brow-beating.")

QUICKLY Give your worship good morrow.
FALSTAFF Good morrow, goodwife.
QUICKLY Not so, an 't please your worship. 34
FALSTAFF Good maid, then.
QUICKLY I'll be sworn, as my mother was, the first hour 36
I was born. 37
FALSTAFF I do believe the swearer. What with me?
QUICKLY Shall I vouchsafe your worship a word or two? 39
FALSTAFF Two thousand, fair woman, and I'll vouchsafe
thee the hearing.
QUICKLY There is one Mistress Ford, sir—I pray, come
a little nearer this ways. I myself dwell with Master
Doctor Caius—
FALSTAFF Well, on. Mistress Ford, you say—
QUICKLY Your worship says very true. I pray your worship, come a little nearer this ways.
FALSTAFF I warrant thee, nobody hears. Mine own
people, mine own people.
QUICKLY Are they so? God bless them and make them
His servants!
FALSTAFF Well, Mistress Ford: what of her?
QUICKLY Why, sir, she's a good creature. Lord, Lord,
your worship's a wanton! Well, heaven forgive you
and all of us, I pray!
FALSTAFF Mistress Ford; come, Mistress Ford—
QUICKLY Marry, this is the short and the long of it: you
have brought her into such a canaries as 'tis wonder- 58
ful. The best courtier of them all, when the court lay at 59
Windsor, could never have brought her to such a canary. Yet there has been knights, and lords, and gentlemen, with their coaches, I warrant you, coach after
coach, letter after letter, gift after gift, smelling so
sweetly, all musk, and so rushling, I warrant you, in 64
silk and gold, and in such alligant terms, and in such 65
wine and sugar of the best and the fairest, that would

34 Not so i.e., I am not a wife. **an 't** if it **36–37 as . . . born** (Mistress Quickly probably means "as much a maid as when I was born, just like my mother before me," but what she says is quite the opposite.)
39 vouchsafe deign to grant. (Used with comical incorrectness here.)
58 canaries state of excitement. (Confusing *quandary* with the dance called the canary?) **59 lay** resided **64 rushling** i.e., rustling **65 alligant** i.e., elegant, or eloquent (?)

have won any woman's heart; and, I warrant you, they could never get an eye-wink of her. I had myself twenty angels given me this morning; but I defy all angels, in any such sort, as they say, but in the way of honesty; and, I warrant you, they could never get her so much as sip on a cup with the proudest of them all. And yet there has been earls, nay, which is more, pensioners, but I warrant you all is one with her.

FALSTAFF But what says she to me? Be brief, my good she-Mercury.

QUICKLY Marry, she hath received your letter, for the which she thanks you a thousand times, and she gives you to notify that her husband will be absence from his house between ten and eleven.

FALSTAFF Ten and eleven?

QUICKLY Ay, forsooth; and then you may come and see the picture, she says, that you wot of. Master Ford, her husband, will be from home. Alas, the sweet woman leads an ill life with him. He's a very jealousy man. She leads a very frampold life with him, good heart.

FALSTAFF Ten and eleven. Woman, commend me to her. I will not fail her.

QUICKLY Why, you say well. But I have another messenger to your worship. Mistress Page hath her hearty commendations to you too; and let me tell you in your ear, she's as fartuous a civil modest wife, and one, I tell you, that will not miss you morning nor evening prayer, as any is in Windsor, whoe'er be the other. And she bade me tell your worship that her husband is seldom from home, but she hopes there will come a time. I never knew a woman so dote upon a man. Surely I think you have charms, la! Yes, in truth.

FALSTAFF Not I, I assure thee. Setting the attraction of my good parts aside, I have no other charms.

69 twenty angels i.e., as a bribe to act as go-between. *Angels* are gold coins. **defy** reject, spurn **70 sort** manner **73–74 pensioners** gentlemen bodyguards to a sovereign in the royal palace **76 she-Mercury** woman messenger **78–79 gives you to notify** bids you take notice **79 absence** (For *absent*.) **83 wot** know **86 frampold** disagreeable **89–90 messenger** (For *message*.) **92 fartuous** (For *virtuous*.) **modest** decent, proper **93 miss you** miss. (*You* is used colloquially.) **98 have charms** use magic **100 parts** qualities

QUICKLY Blessing on your heart for 't!

FALSTAFF But, I pray thee, tell me this: has Ford's wife and Page's wife acquainted each other how they love me?

QUICKLY That were a jest indeed! They have not so little grace, I hope. That were a trick indeed! But Mistress Page would desire you to send her your little page, of all loves. Her husband has a marvelous infection to the little page; and truly Master Page is an honest man. Never a wife in Windsor leads a better life than she does. Do what she will, say what she will, take all, pay all, go to bed when she list, rise when she list—all is as she will. And truly she deserves it, for if there be a kind woman in Windsor, she is one. You must send her your page, no remedy.

FALSTAFF Why, I will.

QUICKLY Nay, but do so, then. And, look you, he may come and go between you both. And in any case have a nayword, that you may know one another's mind, and the boy never need to understand anything; for 'tis not good that children should know any wickedness. Old folks, you know, have discretion, as they say, and know the world.

FALSTAFF Fare thee well. Commend me to them both. There's my purse; I am yet thy debtor. [*He gives money.*] Boy, go along with this woman. [*Exeunt Mistress Quickly and Robin.*] This news distracts me!

PISTOL [*Aside*]
This punk is one of Cupid's carriers.
Clap on more sails; pursue; up with your fights;
Give fire! She is my prize, or ocean whelm them all!
[*Exit.*]

FALSTAFF Sayst thou so, old Jack? Go thy ways. I'll make more of thy old body than I have done. Will they

107–108 of all loves for love's sake **108 infection to** (For *affection for.*) **109 an honest** a worthy **112 list** wishes **115 no remedy** undoubtedly **119 nayword** watchword **127 distracts** bewilders (with ecstasy) **128 punk** whore. **carriers** messengers **129 Clap** put. **fights** fighting sails, i.e., screens raised during naval engagements to conceal and protect the crew **130 prize** booty. **ocean whelm** let the ocean overwhelm. (Pistol evidently has designs on Mistress Quickly, though they do not materialize in this play.)

yet look after thee? Wilt thou, after the expense of so much money, be now a gainer? Good body, I thank thee. Let them say 'tis grossly done; so it be fairly done, no matter.

[*Enter*] *Bardolph* [*with wine*].

BARDOLPH Sir John, there's one Master Brook below would fain speak with you and be acquainted with you, and hath sent your worship a morning's draft of sack.

FALSTAFF Brook is his name?

BARDOLPH Ay, sir.

FALSTAFF Call him in. Such Brooks are welcome to me, that o'erflows such liquor. [*Exit Bardolph.*] Aha! Mistress Ford and Mistress Page, have I encompassed you? Go to. *Via!*

[*Enter Bardolph, with*] *Ford* [*disguised*].

FORD Bless you, sir.

FALSTAFF And you, sir. Would you speak with me?

FORD I make bold to press with so little preparation upon you.

FALSTAFF You're welcome. What's your will? [*To Bardolph.*] Give us leave, drawer. [*Exit Bardolph.*]

FORD Sir, I am a gentleman that have spent much. My name is Brook.

FALSTAFF Good Master Brook, I desire more acquaintance of you.

FORD Good Sir John, I sue for yours—not to charge you, for I must let you understand I think myself in better plight for a lender than you are, the which hath something emboldened me to this unseasoned intrusion; for they say if money go before, all ways do lie open.

FALLSTAFF Money is a good soldier, sir, and will on.

FORD Troth, and I have a bag of money here troubles

135 grossly badly (with pun on "fat"). **fairly** handsomely, fortunately **145–146 encompassed you** taken you in **146 Via** go on. (A shout of encouragement.) **149 preparation** advance notice **152 Give us leave** i.e., leave us alone. **drawer** tapster **157–158 charge you** put you to expense **160 unseasoned** unseasonable

me. If you will help to bear it, Sir John, take all, or half, for easing me of the carriage.

FALSTAFF Sir, I know not how I may deserve to be your porter.

FORD I will tell you, sir, if you will give me the hearing.

FALSTAFF Speak, good Master Brook. I shall be glad to be your servant.

FORD Sir, I hear you are a scholar—I will be brief with you—and you have been a man long known to me, though I had never so good means as desire to make myself acquainted with you. I shall discover a thing to you wherein I must very much lay open mine own imperfection. But, good Sir John, as you have one eye upon my follies, as you hear them unfolded, turn another into the register of your own, that I may pass with a reproof the easier, sith you yourself know how easy it is to be such an offender.

FALSTAFF Very well, sir. Proceed.

FORD There is a gentlewoman in this town; her husband's name is Ford.

FALSTAFF Well, sir.

FORD I have long loved her, and, I protest to you, bestowed much on her, followed her with a doting observance, engrossed opportunities to meet her, fee'd every slight occasion that could but niggardly give me sight of her, not only bought many presents to give her but have given largely to many to know what she would have given. Briefly, I have pursued her as love hath pursued me, which hath been on the wing of all occasions. But whatsoever I have merited—either in my mind or in my means—meed I am sure I have received none, unless experience be a jewel. That I have purchased at an infinite rate, and that hath taught me to say this:

"Love like a shadow flies when substance love pursues,
Pursuing that that flies, and flying what pursues."

166 carriage burden **175 discover** reveal **179 register** record **180 sith** since **187–188 observance** attentiveness **188 engrossed** seized. **fee'd** employed **191 largely** generously **191–192 what . . . given** what she would like to have given to her **195 meed** reward **199–200 Love . . . pursues** i.e., love runs away when pursued but pursues when run away from. (Proverbial.) **substance** (1) the person desired (2) wealth

FALSTAFF Have you received no promise of satisfaction at her hands?

FORD Never.

FALSTAFF Have you importuned her to such a purpose?

FORD Never.

FALSTAFF Of what quality was your love, then?

FORD Like a fair house built on another man's ground, so that I have lost my edifice by mistaking the place where I erected it.

FALSTAFF To what purpose have you unfolded this to me?

FORD When I have told you that, I have told you all. Some say that though she appear honest to me, yet in other places she enlargeth her mirth so far that there is shrewd construction made of her. Now, Sir John, here is the heart of my purpose. You are a gentleman of excellent breeding, admirable discourse, of great admittance, authentic in your place and person, generally allowed for your many warlike, courtlike, and learned preparations.

FALSTAFF O, sir!

FORD Believe it, for you know it. There is money. Spend it, spend it; spend more; spend all I have. [*He offers money.*] Only give me so much of your time in exchange of it as to lay an amiable siege to the honesty of this Ford's wife. Use your art of wooing; win her to consent to you. If any man may, you may as soon as any.

FALSTAFF Would it apply well to the vehemency of your affection that I should win what you would enjoy? Methinks you prescribe to yourself very preposterously.

FORD O, understand my drift. She dwells so securely on the excellency of her honor that the folly of my soul dares not present itself; she is too bright to be looked against. Now, could I come to her with any detection

213 honest chaste **214 enlargeth** gives free scope to **215 shrewd construction** malicious interpretation **217–218 of great admittance** i.e., readily received in society **218 authentic** recognized **219 allowed** acknowledged **220 preparations** accomplishments **225 amiable** amorous **236 against** directly toward (like looking at the sun)

in my hand, my desires had instance and argument to 237
commend themselves. I could drive her then from the
ward of her purity, her reputation, her marriage vow, 239
and a thousand other her defenses, which now are too 240
too strongly embattled against me. What say you to 't,
Sir John?

FALSTAFF Master Brook, I will first make bold with your money; next, give me your hand; and last, as I am a gentleman, you shall, if you will, enjoy Ford's wife.

[*He accepts the money and takes Ford's hand.*]

FORD O, good sir!

FALSTAFF I say you shall.

FORD Want no money, Sir John, you shall want none. 248

FALSTAFF Want no Mistress Ford, Master Brook, you
shall want none. I shall be with her, I may tell you, by
her own appointment. Even as you came in to me, her
assistant or go-between parted from me. I say I shall
be with her between ten and eleven, for at that time
the jealous rascally knave her husband will be forth. 254
Come you to me at night; you shall know how I
speed. 256

FORD I am blest in your acquaintance. Do you know Ford, sir?

FALSTAFF Hang him, poor cuckoldly knave! I know him
not. Yet I wrong him to call him poor. They say the
jealous wittolly knave hath masses of money, for the 261
which his wife seems to me well-favored. I will use her 262
as the key of the cuckoldly rogue's coffer, and there's
my harvest home. 264

FORD I would you knew Ford, sir, that you might avoid him if you saw him.

FALSTAFF Hang him, mechanical salt-butter rogue! I 267
will stare him out of his wits. I will awe him with my

237 had instance would have proof and precedent **239 ward** defensive posture in fencing **240 other her defenses** other defenses of hers
248 Want lack **254 forth** away from home **256 speed** succeed
261 wittolly one willingly cheated on by his wife, a complacent cuckold
261–262 for the which for which reason **262 well-favored** attractive
264 harvest home occasion for reaping a profit **267 mechanical** (Literally, one engaged in manual occupation, hence, base.) **salt-butter** i.e., cheap, coarse. (*Salt butter* is butter preserved with salt, often old and of inferior quality.)

cudgel; it shall hang like a meteor o'er the cuckold's 269
horns. Master Brook, thou shalt know I will predomi- 270
nate over the peasant, and thou shalt lie with his wife. 271
Come to me soon at night. Ford's a knave, and I will
aggravate his style: thou, Master Brook, shalt know 273
him for knave and cuckold. Come to me soon at night.
[*Exit.*]

FORD What a damned Epicurean rascal is this! My heart 275
is ready to crack with impatience. Who says this is
improvident jealousy? My wife hath sent to him, the
hour is fixed, the match is made. Would any man have
thought this? See the hell of having a false woman! My
bed shall be abused, my coffers ransacked, my reputation gnawn at; and I shall not only receive this villainous wrong but stand under the adoption of abomi- 282
nable terms, and by him that does me this wrong. 283
Terms! Names! "Amaimon" sounds well, "Lucifer" well, 284
"Barbason" well; yet they are devils' additions, the 285
names of fiends. But "Cuckold!" "Wittol!" "Cuckold!"
The devil himself hath not such a name. Page is an ass,
a secure ass. He will trust his wife; he will not be jeal- 288
ous. I will rather trust a Fleming with my butter, Parson Hugh the Welshman with my cheese, an Irishman
with my aqua vitae bottle, or a thief to walk my am- 291
bling gelding, than my wife with herself. Then she
plots, then she ruminates, then she devises; and what
they think in their hearts they may effect, they will
break their hearts but they will effect. Heaven be praised
for my jealousy! Eleven o'clock the hour. I will prevent 296
this, detect my wife, be revenged on Falstaff, and laugh
at Page. I will about it; better three hours too soon
than a minute too late. Fie, fie, fie! Cuckold, cuckold,
cuckold! *Exit.*

269 meteor (An ominous sign.) **270–271 predominate** be in the ascendancy. (An astrological term.) **273 aggravate his style** increase or add to his title (by adding *cuckold*) **275 Epicurean** sensual **282–283 stand . . . terms** have to put up with being called names **284, 285 Amaimon, Lucifer, Barbason** (Names of devils; they occur in Scot's *Discovery of Witchcraft,* 1584.) **285 additions** titles **288 secure** overconfident **291 aqua vitae** any strong spirit like brandy. (Irish were known for their drinking, just as Welshmen for eating of cheese and Flemish for love of butter.) **walk** exercise **296 prevent** come there before

2.3 *Enter Caius* [*and*] *Rugby.*

CAIUS Jack Rugby!

RUGBY Sir?

CAIUS Vat is de clock, Jack?

RUGBY 'Tis past the hour, sir, that Sir Hugh promised to meet.

CAIUS By gar, he has save his soul dat he is no come; he has pray his Pible well dat he is no come. By gar, Jack Rugby, he is dead already if he be come.

RUGBY He is wise, sir. He knew your worship would kill him if he came.

CAIUS By gar, de herring is no dead so as I vill kill him. Take your rapier, Jack. I vill tell you how I vill kill him.

RUGBY Alas, sir, I cannot fence.

CAIUS Villainy, take your rapier.

RUGBY Forbear. Here's company.

[*Enter*] *Page, Shallow, Slender,* [*and*] *Host.*

HOST Bless thee, bully Doctor!

SHALLOW Save you, Master Doctor Caius!

PAGE Now, good Master Doctor!

SLENDER Give you good morrow, sir.

CAIUS Vat be all you, one, two, tree, four, come for?

HOST To see thee fight, to see thee foin, to see thee traverse; to see thee here, to see thee there; to see thee pass thy punto, thy stock, thy reverse, thy distance, thy montant. Is he dead, my Ethiopian? Is he dead, my Francisco? Ha, bully? What says my Aesculapius, my Galen, my heart of elder, ha? Is he dead, bully stale? Is he dead?

2.3. Location: A field near Windsor.
11 no dead so not so dead. (Cf. "dead as a herring.") **17 Save** God save **21 foin** thrust **21–22 traverse** march back and forth, or from side to side **23 pass** employ **23–24 thy punto . . . montant** your stroke or thrust with the point of the sword, your stoccado or thrust, your backhand stroke, your keeping of the prescribed distance between contestants, your upright thrust **24 Ethiopian** i.e., one of dark complexion (?) **25 Francisco** i.e., Frenchman. **Aesculapius** i.e., doctor. (Literally, Greek god of medicine.) **26 Galen** famous Greek physician. **heart of elder** i.e., opposite of "heart of oak"; the elder has no heart (though Caius, with his halting English, presumably is unaware of the insult). **27 stale** i.e., Doctor. (Literally, "urine," which is used to make medical diagnosis; see also *urinal* in Host's next speech, and *Mockwater,* ll. 51–52. A *stale* is also a dupe.)

CAIUS By gar, he is de coward jack priest of de vorld. He is not show his face.

HOST Thou art a Castilian King-Urinal. Hector of Greece, my boy!

CAIUS I pray you, bear witness that me have stay six or seven, two, tree hours for him, and he is no come.

SHALLOW He is the wiser man, Master Doctor. He is a curer of souls, and you a curer of bodies. If you should fight, you go against the hair of your professions. Is it not true, Master Page?

PAGE Master Shallow, you have yourself been a great fighter, though now a man of peace.

SHALLOW Bodykins, Master Page, though I now be old and of the peace, if I see a sword out, my finger itches to make one. Though we are justices and doctors and churchmen, Master Page, we have some salt of our youth in us. We are the sons of women, Master Page.

PAGE 'Tis true, Master Shallow.

SHALLOW It will be found so, Master Page.—Master Doctor Caius, I am come to fetch you home. I am sworn of the peace. You have showed yourself a wise physician, and Sir Hugh hath shown himself a wise and patient churchman. You must go with me, Master Doctor.

HOST Pardon, guest justice. A word, Monsieur Mockwater.

CAIUS Mockvater? Vat is dat?

HOST "Mockwater," in our English tongue, is "valor," bully.

CAIUS By gar, den, I have as mush mockvater as de Englishman. Scurvy jack-dog priest! By gar, me vill cut his ears.

HOST He will clapper-claw thee tightly, bully.

CAIUS Clapper-de-claw? Vat is dat?

30 Castilian i.e., Spanish. (An insulting term in a time of war with Spain, though Caius, with his imperfect English, is presumably oblivious of this. The term also suggests *Castalian* [Folio: Castalion], relating to the sacred spring on Mount Parnassus.) **Urinal** (Comically appropriate to a doctor, who uses urine for diagnosis.) **Hector** chief warrior of ancient Troy (not Greece) **36 go . . . of** i.e., act contrary to. (Literally, rub hair the wrong way.) **40 Bodykins** i.e., by God's little body **42 make one** join in **43 salt** savor **51–52 Mockwater** (See note to l. 27, above.) **57 jack-dog** mongrel **59 clapper-claw** thrash. **tightly** soundly

HOST That is, he will make thee amends.

CAIUS By gar, me do look he shall clapper-de-claw me, for, by gar, me vill have it.

HOST And I will provoke him to 't, or let him wag.

CAIUS Me tank you for dat.

HOST And, moreover, bully—[*Aside to the others*] but first, master guest and Master Page, and eke Cavaleiro Slender, go you through the town to Frogmore.

PAGE Sir Hugh is there, is he?

HOST He is there. See what humor he is in, and I will bring the doctor about by the fields. Will it do well?

SHALLOW We will do it.

PAGE, SHALLOW, AND SLENDER Adieu, good Master Doctor. [*Exeunt Page, Shallow, and Slender.*]

CAIUS [*Drawing his rapier*] By gar, me vill kill de priest, for he speak for a jackanape to Anne Page.

HOST Let him die. But first, sheathe thy impatience; throw cold water on thy choler. Go about the fields with me through Frogmore. I will bring thee where Mistress Anne Page is, at a farmhouse a-feasting, and thou shalt woo her. Cried game? Said I well?

CAIUS [*Sheathing his rapier*] By gar, me dank you vor dat. By gar, I love you; and I shall procure-a you de good guest: de earl, de knight, de lords, de gentlemen, my patients.

HOST For the which I will be thy adversary toward Anne Page. Said I well?

CAIUS By gar, 'tis good. Vell said.

HOST Let us wag, then.

CAIUS Come at my heels, Jack Rugby. *Exeunt.*

✤

64 wag go on his way, run for his life **68 Frogmore** small village near Windsor **76 for a jackanape** on behalf of an ape, i.e., Slender **81 Cried game** have I announced good sport. (A hunting cry.) **86 adversary** (The Host again takes advantage of Caius's poor English; the expected word is *emissary*.)

3.1 *Enter Evans [and] Simple.*

EVANS I pray you now, good Master Slender's serving-man, and friend Simple by your name, which way have you looked for Master Caius, that calls himself doctor of physic?

SIMPLE Marry, sir, the Petty-ward, the Park-ward, every way; Old Windsor way, and every way but the town way.

EVANS I most fehemently desire you you will also look that way.

SIMPLE I will, sir. *[Going aside.]*

EVANS Pless my soul, how full of cholers I am, and trempling of mind! I shall be glad if he have deceived
me. How melancholies I am! I will knog his urinals 13
about his knave's costard when I have good opportu- 14
nities for the 'ork. Pless my soul! *[He sings.]*

"To shallow rivers, to whose falls 16
Melodious birds sings madrigals;
There will we make our peds of roses,
And a thousand fragrant posies.
To shallow—"

Mercy on me! I have a great dispositions to cry. *[He sings.]*

"Melodious birds sing madrigals—
Whenas I sat in Pabylon— 23
And a thousand vagram posies. 24
To shallow," etc.

[Simple returns.]

SIMPLE Yonder he is, coming this way, Sir Hugh.

EVANS He's welcome. *[He sings.]*

"To shallow rivers, to whose falls—"

God prosper the right! What weapons is he?

SIMPLE No weapons, sir. There comes my master, Mas-

3.1. Location: A field near Frogmore.
5 the Petty-ward toward Windsor Petty (or Little) Park. **the Park-ward** toward Windsor Great Park **13 knog** knock **14 costard** i.e., head. (Literally, apple.) **16 To shallow rivers,** etc. (Lines from Marlowe's "Come live with me and be my love.") **23 Whenas . . . Pabylon** (An insertion of a line from the metrical Psalms, number 137.) **24 vagram** i.e., vagrant. (But Evans means *fragrant.*)

ter Shallow, and another gentleman, from Frogmore, over the stile, this way.

EVANS Pray you, give me my gown; or else keep it in your arms. [*He reads in a book.*]

[*Enter*] *Page, Shallow,* [*and*] *Slender.*

SHALLOW How now, Master Parson? Good morrow, good Sir Hugh. Keep a gamester from the dice and a good student from his book, and it is wonderful.

SLENDER [*Aside*] Ah, sweet Anne Page!

PAGE God save you, good Sir Hugh!

EVANS God pless you from His mercy sake, all of you!

SHALLOW What, the sword and the Word? Do you study them both, Master Parson?

PAGE And youthful still—in your doublet and hose this raw rheumatic day?

EVANS There is reasons and causes for it.

PAGE We are come to you to do a good office, Master Parson.

EVANS Fery well. What is it?

PAGE Yonder is a most reverend gentleman, who, belike having received wrong by some person, is at most odds with his own gravity and patience that ever you saw.

SHALLOW I have lived fourscore years and upward; I never heard a man of his place, gravity, and learning so wide of his own respect.

EVANS What is he?

PAGE I think you know him: Master Doctor Caius, the renowned French physician.

EVANS Got's will and His passion of my heart! I had as lief you would tell me of a mess of porridge.

PAGE Why?

EVANS He has no more knowledge in Hibbocrates and

36–37 Keep . . . wonderful i.e., it's as hard to keep a true student from his book as to keep a gamester from dice **40 from His mercy sake** (The correct phrase is "for His mercy's sake.") **41 the Word** i.e., the Bible **43 in . . . hose** i.e., without a cloak, in close-fitting jacket and breeches **49–50 belike** it would seem **51 odds** strife. **gravity** dignity **55 wide . . . respect** at variance with or indifferent to his own reputation **59–60 had as lief** would just as soon **62 Hibbocrates** Hippocrates, ancient Greek physician

Galen—and he is a knave besides, a cowardly knave as you would desires to be acquainted withal.

PAGE [*To Shallow*] I warrant you, he's the man should 65
fight with him.

SLENDER [*Aside*] O sweet Anne Page!

SHALLOW It appears so by his weapons. Keep them
asunder. Here comes Doctor Caius. 69

[*Enter*] *Host, Caius,* [*and*] *Rugby.* [*Evans and Caius offer to fight.*]

PAGE Nay, good Master Parson, keep in your weapon.

SHALLOW So do you, good Master Doctor.

HOST Disarm them and let them question. Let them 72
keep their limbs whole and hack our English.

[*Caius and Evans are disarmed.*]

CAIUS [*To Evans*] I pray you, let-a me speak a word with your ear. Vherefore vill you not meet-a me?

EVANS [*Aside to Caius*] Pray you, use your patience. [*Aloud.*] In good time.

CAIUS By gar, you are de coward, de jack dog, john ape.

EVANS [*Aside to Caius*] Pray you, let us not be laughing-stocks to other men's humors; I desire you in friendship, and I will one way or other make you amends. [*Aloud.*] I will knog your urinals about your knave's cogscomb for missing your meetings and appointments.

CAIUS *Diable!* Jack Rugby—mine Host de Jarteer—
have I not stay for him to kill him? Have I not, at de 87
place I did appoint?

EVANS As I am a Christians soul now, look you, this is
the place appointed. I'll be judgment by mine Host of 90
the Garter.

HOST Peace, I say, Gallia and Gaul, French and Welsh, 92
soul curer and body curer!

CAIUS Ay, dat is very good, *excellent*.

HOST Peace, I say! Hear mine Host of the Garter. Am I

65 he's i.e., Evans is. **should** who is supposed to **69 s.d. offer** make as if, prepare. (The stage direction is substantially from the quarto.)
72 question talk, discuss **87 stay** waited **90 judgment by** ruled by the judgment of **92 Gallia and Gaul** Wales and France

politic? Am I subtle? Am I a Machiavel? Shall I lose my 96
doctor? No, he gives me the potions and the motions. 97
Shall I lose my parson, my priest, my Sir Hugh? No,
he gives me the proverbs and the no-verbs. Give me 99
thy hand, terrestrial; so. Give me thy hand, celestial; 100
so. [*He joins their hands.*] Boys of art, I have deceived 101
you both; I have directed you to wrong places. Your
hearts are mighty, your skins are whole, and let burnt 103
sack be the issue.—Come, lay their swords to pawn. 104
Follow me, lads of peace, follow, follow, follow.

SHALLOW Trust me, a mad host. Follow, gentlemen, 106
follow.

SLENDER [*Aside*] O sweet Anne Page!

[*Exeunt Shallow, Slender, Page, and Host.*]

CAIUS Ha, do I perceive dat? Have you make-a de sot 109
of us, ha, ha?

EVANS This is well! He has made us his vloutingstog. 111
I desire you that we may be friends; and let us knog
our prains together to be revenge on this same scall, 113
scurvy, cogging companion, the Host of the Garter. 114

CAIUS By gar, with all my heart. He promise to bring
me where is Anne Page. By gar, he deceive me too.

EVANS Well, I will smite his noddles. Pray you, follow. 117

[*Exeunt.*]

✣

3.2 [*Enter*] *Mistress Page* [*and*] *Robin.*

MRS. PAGE Nay, keep your way, little gallant. You were 1
wont to be a follower, but now you are a leader.

96 Machiavel Niccolò Machiavelli, an Italian political philosopher who symbolized crafty and ruthless ambition to Elizabethans; an intriguer **97 motions** purges **99 proverbs . . . no-verbs** i.e., wisdom and some Welsh colorful speech **100 terrestrial** i.e., the Doctor, who treats the body **101 art** learning **103–104 burnt sack** heated and mulled wine, as at 2.1.199–200 **104 issue** outcome. **to pawn** as a pledge or surety **106 Trust me** believe me **109 sot** fool **111 vloutingstog** floutingstock, i.e., laughingstock **113 scall** scald, i.e., scurvy **114 cogging companion** cheating rascal **117 noddles** head

3.2. Location: A street in Windsor.
1 keep your way keep on your way (in front of me)

Whether had you rather, lead mine eyes or eye your 3
master's heels?

ROBIN I had rather, forsooth, go before you like a man
than follow him like a dwarf.

MRS. PAGE O, you are a flattering boy. Now I see you'll
be a courtier.

[*Enter*] *Ford.*

FORD Well met, Mistress Page. Whither go you?

MRS. PAGE Truly, sir, to see your wife. Is she at home?

FORD Ay, and as idle as she may hang together, for 11
want of company. I think if your husbands were 12
dead you two would marry.

MRS. PAGE Be sure of that—two other husbands.

FORD Where had you this pretty weathercock? 15

MRS. PAGE I cannot tell what the dickens his name is my
husband had him of.—What do you call your knight's 17
name, sirrah?

ROBIN Sir John Falstaff.

FORD Sir John Falstaff!

MRS. PAGE He, he. I can never hit on 's name. There is
such a league between my goodman and he! Is your 22
wife at home indeed?

FORD Indeed she is.

MRS. PAGE By your leave, sir. I am sick till I see her.
[*Exeunt Mistress Page and Robin.*]

FORD Has Page any brains? Hath he any eyes? Hath he
any thinking? Sure they sleep; he hath no use of
them. Why, this boy will carry a letter twenty mile as
easy as a cannon will shoot point-blank twelve score. 29
He pieces out his wife's inclination; he gives her folly 30
motion and advantage. And now she's going to my 31

3 Whether which of the two **11 as idle . . . together** i.e., as idle as she can be without going to pieces; or, persons as idle as she (and you) are may keep company **12 want** lack **15 had you** did you find. **pretty weathercock** i.e., sprucely dressed little fellow. (A *weathercock* changes quickly, here in matters of fashion of dress. Robin may have a feather in his hat.) **17 had him of** got him from **22 league** friendship. **goodman** husband **29 point-blank** in a straight trajectory. **twelve score** i.e., 240 paces **30 pieces out** augments, encourages. **folly** wantonness **31 motion** instigation. **advantage** opportunity

wife, and Falstaff's boy with her. A man may hear this 32
shower sing in the wind. And Falstaff's boy with her! 33
Good plots! They are laid; and our revolted wives share
damnation together. Well, I will take him, then torture 35
my wife, pluck the borrowed veil of modesty from the
so-seeming Mistress Page, divulge Page himself for a 37
secure and willful Actaeon; and to these violent pro- 38
ceedings all my neighbors shall cry aim. [*A clock strikes.*] 39
The clock gives me my cue, and my assurance bids me 40
search. There I shall find Falstaff. I shall be rather
praised for this than mocked, for it is as positive as the
earth is firm that Falstaff is there. I will go.

[*Enter*] *Page, Shallow, Slender, Host, Evans, Caius,* [*and Rugby*].

SHALLOW, PAGE, ETC. Well met, Master Ford.

FORD [*Aside*] Trust me, a good knot. [*To them.*] I have 45
good cheer at home, and I pray you all go with me. 46

SHALLOW I must excuse myself, Master Ford.

SLENDER And so must I, sir. We have appointed to dine
with Mistress Anne, and I would not break with her 49
for more money than I'll speak of.

SHALLOW We have lingered about a match between Anne Page and my cousin Slender, and this day we shall have our answer.

SLENDER I hope I have your good will, father Page.

PAGE You have, Master Slender; I stand wholly for you.—But my wife, Master Doctor, is for you altogether.

CAIUS Ay, by gar, and de maid is love-a me. My nursh-a Quickly tell me so mush.

HOST What say you to young Master Fenton? He capers, he dances, he has eyes of youth, he writes
verses, he speaks holiday, he smells April and May. 61
He will carry 't, he will carry 't. 'Tis in his buttons he 62
will carry 't. 63

32–33 hear . . . wind tell from the rising wind that a storm is coming up, i.e., that trouble is brewing **35 take him** take him by surprise **37 divulge** reveal **38 secure** overconfident. **Actaeon** i.e., horned man, cuckold. (See 2.1.113, note.) **39 cry aim** applaud. (A term from archery.) **40 assurance** foreknowledge **45 knot** group, company. **46 cheer** fare **49 break with** break my promise to **61 speaks holiday** speaks in a fashion appropriate to a holiday **62 carry 't** win the day **62–63 'Tis . . . carry 't** i.e., he's sure to succeed

PAGE Not by my consent, I promise you. The gentleman is of no having. He kept company with the wild 65
Prince and Poins. He is of too high a region; he knows 66
too much. No, he shall not knit a knot in his fortunes 67
with the finger of my substance. If he take her, let him
take her simply. The wealth I have waits on my con- 69
sent, and my consent goes not that way.

FORD I beseech you heartily, some of you go home with
me to dinner. Besides your cheer, you shall have sport:
I will show you a monster. Master Doctor, you shall 73
go. So shall you, Master Page, and you, Sir Hugh.

SHALLOW Well, fare you well. We shall have the freer woo- 75
ing at Master Page's. [*Exeunt Shallow and Slender.*] 76

CAIUS Go home, John Rugby. I come anon. [*Exit Rugby.*] 77

HOST Farewell, my hearts. I will to my honest knight
Falstaff, and drink canary with him. [*Exit.*] 79

FORD [*Aside*] I think I shall drink in pipe-wine first 80
with him; I'll make him dance.—Will you go, gentles? 81

ALL Have with you to see this monster. *Exeunt.*

3.3 *Enter Mistress Ford* [*and*] *Mistress Page.*

MRS. FORD What, John! What, Robert! 1

MRS. PAGE Quickly, quickly! Is the buck basket— 2

MRS. FORD I warrant. What, Robert, I say!

[*Enter*] *Servants* [*with a great basket.*]

MRS. PAGE Come, come, come.

65 having estate **65–66 wild . . . Poins** i.e., Prince Hal and Poins of *1* and *2 Henry IV* **66 region** social status **67 knit a knot in** mend **69 simply** i.e., by herself. **waits on** is subject to **73 monster** (As if Falstaff were a freak to be exhibited at a fair.) **75–76 We shall . . . Page's** i.e., the wooing of Anne will be less constrained if Caius, Evans, and Anne's father are not there **77 anon** at once **79 canary** a sweet wine from the Canaries. (But Ford plays on *canary* in the sense of "a lively dance" in his reply.) **80 pipe-wine** wine from the cask, or wood (with a pun on *pipe* as a musical instrument played for the *dance,* l. 81. Ford means that he'll make Falstaff jump, make it hot for him.) **81 gentles** gentlemen

3.3. Location: Ford's house.
1 What i.e., move quickly **2 buck basket** basket for soiled clothes. (*Bucking* means "washing.")

MRS. FORD Here, set it down.

MRS. PAGE Give your men the charge. We must be brief.

MRS. FORD Marry, as I told you before, John and Robert, be ready here hard by in the brewhouse; and when I suddenly call you, come forth, and without any pause or staggering take this basket on your shoulders. That done, trudge with it in all haste, and carry it among the whitsters in Datchet Mead, and there empty it in the muddy ditch close by the Thames side.

MRS. PAGE You will do it?

MRS. FORD I ha' told them over and over; they lack no direction.—Begone, and come when you are called. [*Exeunt Servants.*]

MRS. PAGE Here comes little Robin.

[*Enter*] *Robin.*

MRS. FORD How now, my eyas musket, what news with you?

ROBIN My master, Sir John, is come in at your back door, Mistress Ford, and requests your company.

MRS. PAGE You little Jack-a-Lent, have you been true to us?

ROBIN Ay, I'll be sworn. My master knows not of your being here and hath threatened to put me into everlasting liberty if I tell you of it; for he swears he'll turn me away.

MRS. PAGE Thou'rt a good boy. This secrecy of thine shall be a tailor to thee and shall make thee a new doublet and hose. I'll go hide me.

MRS. FORD Do so.—Go tell thy master I am alone. [*Exit Robin.*] Mistress Page, remember you your cue.

MRS. PAGE I warrant thee. If I do not act it, hiss me. [*Exit.*]

MRS. FORD Go to, then. We'll use this unwholesome humidity, this gross watery pumpkin. We'll teach him to know turtles from jays.

[*Enter*] *Falstaff.*

6 charge instructions **12 whitsters** bleachers of linen. **Datchet Mead** a meadow along the Thames, near Windsor Park **18 eyas musket** young sparrow hawk **22 Jack-a-Lent** figure of a man set up to be pelted, a puppet **26 liberty** i.e., unemployment **26–27 turn me away** dismiss me **36 turtles** turtledoves, a type of constancy in love. **jays** i.e., loose women

FALSTAFF "Have I caught thee, my heavenly jewel?" Why, now let me die, for I have lived long enough. This is the period of my ambition. O, this blessed hour!

MRS. FORD O sweet Sir John!

FALSTAFF Mistress Ford, I cannot cog, I cannot prate, Mistress Ford. Now shall I sin in my wish: I would thy husband were dead. I'll speak it before the best lord: I would make thee my lady.

MRS. FORD I your lady, Sir John? Alas, I should be a pitiful lady!

FALSTAFF Let the court of France show me such another. I see how thine eye would emulate the diamond. Thou hast the right arched beauty of the brow that becomes the ship-tire, the tire-valiant, or any tire of Venetian admittance.

MRS. FORD A plain kerchief, Sir John. My brows become nothing else, nor that well neither.

FALSTAFF By the Lord, thou art a tyrant to say so. Thou wouldst make an absolute courtier, and the firm fixture of thy foot would give an excellent motion to thy gait in a semicircled farthingale. I see what thou wert, if Fortune thy foe were not, Nature thy friend. Come, thou canst not hide it.

MRS. FORD Believe me, there's no such thing in me.

FALSTAFF What made me love thee? Let that persuade thee there's something extraordinary in thee. Come, I cannot cog and say thou art this and that, like a many of these lisping hawthorn buds, that come like women in men's apparel and smell like Bucklersbury in simple time. I cannot. But I love thee, none but thee; and thou deserv'st it.

37 Have . . . jewel (From Sir Philip Sidney's *Astrophel and Stella*.) **39 period** goal **41 cog** cheat, flatter **50 ship-tire** woman's headdress resembling a ship. **tire-valiant** fanciful headdress **51 admittance** fashion **52 become** suit **55 absolute** perfect **55–56 fixture** setting, placing **57 semicircled farthingale** petticoat with hoops at the sides and back but not meeting in front **57–58 I see . . . friend** i.e., I can imagine how impressive you would be at court if Fortune had not cast you in a lowly lot with only your natural beauty to assist you. ("Fortune My Foe" is the name of a popular ballad tune.) **63 cog** use deceiving language in sport **64 hawthorn buds** i.e., young fops **65 Bucklersbury** a London street inhabited by herbalists **65–66 simple time** midsummer, the time when apothecaries were supplied with simples or herbs

MRS. FORD Do not betray me, sir. I fear you love Mistress Page.

FALSTAFF Thou mightst as well say I love to walk by the Counter gate, which is as hateful to me as the reek of a limekiln.

MRS. FORD Well, heaven knows how I love you, and you shall one day find it.

FALSTAFF Keep in that mind. I'll deserve it.

MRS. FORD Nay, I must tell you, so you do, or else I could not be in that mind.

[*Enter Robin.*]

ROBIN Mistress Ford, Mistress Ford! Here's Mistress Page at the door, sweating and blowing and looking wildly, and would needs speak with you presently.

FALSTAFF She shall not see me. I will ensconce me behind the arras.

MRS. FORD Pray you, do so. She's a very tattling woman. [*Falstaff hides himself behind the arras.*]

[*Enter Mistress Page.*]

What's the matter? How now?

MRS. PAGE O Mistress Ford, what have you done? You're shamed, you're overthrown, you're undone forever!

MRS. FORD What's the matter, good Mistress Page?

MRS. PAGE O welladay, Mistress Ford, having an honest man to your husband, to give him such cause of suspicion!

MRS. FORD What cause of suspicion?

MRS. PAGE What cause of suspicion? Out upon you! How am I mistook in you!

MRS. FORD Why, alas, what's the matter?

MRS. PAGE Your husband's coming hither, woman, with all the officers in Windsor, to search for a gentleman that he says is here now in the house, by your consent, to take an ill advantage of his absence. You are undone.

68 betray deceive **71 Counter gate** gate of the Counter or debtors' prison in London **79 blowing** puffing **80 presently** at once **81 ensconce me** hide myself **82 arras** tapestry wall hanging **87 overthrown** ruined **90 welladay** alas **91 to your** as your **94 Out upon you** i.e., for shame

MRS. FORD 'Tis not so, I hope.

MRS. PAGE Pray heaven it be not so, that you have such
a man here! But 'tis most certain your husband's coming, with half Windsor at his heels, to search for such
a one. I come before to tell you. If you know yourself
clear, why, I am glad of it. But if you have a friend 107
here, convey, convey him out. Be not amazed! Call all 108
your senses to you; defend your reputation, or bid
farewell to your good life forever. 110

MRS. FORD What shall I do? There is a gentleman, my dear friend; and I fear not mine own shame so much as his peril. I had rather than a thousand pound he were out of the house.

MRS. PAGE For shame! Never stand "you had rather" 115
and "you had rather." Your husband's here at hand!
Bethink you of some conveyance. In the house you 117
cannot hide him. O, how have you deceived me! Look,
here is a basket. If he be of any reasonable stature, he
may creep in here; and throw foul linen upon him, as
if it were going to bucking. Or—it is whiting time— 121
send him by your two men to Datchet Mead.

MRS. FORD He's too big to go in there. What shall I do?

FALSTAFF [*Coming forward*] Let me see 't, let me see 't, O, let me see 't! I'll in, I'll in. Follow your friend's counsel. I'll in.

MRS. PAGE What, Sir John Falstaff? [*Aside to him.*] Are these your letters, knight?

FALSTAFF [*Aside to her*] I love thee. Help me away. Let me creep in here. I'll never—

[*He gets into the basket; they cover him with foul linen.*]

MRS. PAGE Help to cover your master, boy.—Call your men, Mistress Ford.—You dissembling knight!

MRS. FORD What, John! Robert! John!

[*Enter Servants.*]

Go take up these clothes here quickly. Where's the

107 clear clear of blame. **friend** lover **108 amazed** stunned, bewildered **110 your good life** your respectability **115 stand** lose time over **117 conveyance** stratagem **121 bucking** washing. **whiting time** bleaching time

cowlstaff? Look how you drumble! Carry them to the laundress in Datchet Mead. Quickly! Come.

[*The Servants lift the basket and start to leave.*]

[*Enter*] *Ford, Page, Caius,* [*and*] *Evans.*

FORD Pray you, come near. If I suspect without cause, why then make sport at me. Then let me be your jest; I deserve it.—How now? Whither bear you this?

SERVANT To the laundress, forsooth.

MRS. FORD Why, what have you to do whither they bear it? You were best meddle with buck washing.

FORD Buck? I would I could wash myself of the buck! Buck, buck, buck! Ay, buck! I warrant you, buck—and of the season too, it shall appear. [*Exeunt Servants with the basket.*] Gentlemen, I have dreamed tonight; I'll tell you my dream. Here, here, here be my keys. Ascend my chambers. Search, seek, find out. I'll warrant we'll unkennel the fox. Let me stop this way first. [*He locks the door.*] So, now uncape.

PAGE Good Master Ford, be contented. You wrong yourself too much.

FORD True, Master Page. Up, gentlemen, you shall see sport anon. Follow me, gentlemen. [*Exit.*]

EVANS This is fery fantastical humors and jealousies.

CAIUS By gar, 'tis no the fashion of France. It is not jealous in France.

PAGE Nay, follow him, gentlemen. See the issue of his search. [*Exeunt Page, Caius, and Evans.*]

MRS. PAGE Is there not a double excellency in this?

MRS. FORD I know not which pleases me better, that my husband is deceived, or Sir John.

MRS. PAGE What a taking was he in when your husband asked who was in the basket!

135 cowlstaff pole on which a "cowl" or basket is carried between two persons. **drumble** are sluggish **142 buck washing** washing clothes. (But Ford puns on *buck* in the sense of "horned male deer," resembling the cuckold, and also of "copulating.") **145 of the season** in the rutting season **146 tonight** last night **149 unkennel** reveal, unearth **150 uncape** i.e., unleash, unloose (?) **151 be contented** be calm **151–152 wrong yourself** put yourself in the wrong **153 True** (Ford may mean that he is indeed too much wronged, or else placates Page by seeming to agree with him.) **158 issue** outcome **163 taking** fright

MRS. FORD I am half afraid he will have need of washing, so throwing him into the water will do him a benefit.

MRS. PAGE Hang him, dishonest rascal! I would all of the same strain were in the same distress.

MRS. FORD I think my husband hath some special suspicion of Falstaff's being here, for I never saw him so gross in his jealousy till now.

MRS. PAGE I will lay a plot to try that, and we will yet have more tricks with Falstaff. His dissolute disease will scarce obey this medicine.

MRS. FORD Shall we send that foolish carrion Mistress Quickly to him, and excuse his throwing into the water, and give him another hope, to betray him to another punishment?

MRS. PAGE We will do it. Let him be sent for tomorrow eight o'clock, to have amends.

[*Enter Ford, Page, Caius, and Evans.*]

FORD I cannot find him. Maybe the knave bragged of that he could not compass.

MRS. PAGE [*Aside to Mrs. Ford*] Heard you that?

MRS. FORD You use me well, Master Ford, do you?

FORD Ay, I do so.

MRS. FORD Heaven make you better than your thoughts!

FORD Amen!

MRS. PAGE You do yourself mighty wrong, Master Ford.

FORD Ay, ay, I must bear it.

EVANS If there be anypody in the house, and in the chambers, and in the coffers, and in the presses, heaven forgive my sins at the day of judgment!

CAIUS By gar, nor I too. There is nobodies.

PAGE Fie, fie, Master Ford, are you not ashamed? What spirit, what devil suggests this imagination? I would not ha' your distemper in this kind for the wealth of Windsor Castle.

165–166 will . . . washing i.e., will have befouled himself in fright **169 strain** character, kind **173 try** test **175 obey this medicine** i.e., yield to this first dose **176 carrion** rotten old flesh, bawd (?) **177 excuse** make excuses for **183 that** that which. **compass** accomplish **192 presses** cupboards, clothes presses **196 suggests** incites, prompts you to. **imagination** wild suspicion **197 distemper** disorder of mind. **in this kind** of this sort

FORD 'Tis my fault, Master Page. I suffer for it.

EVANS You suffer for a pad conscience. Your wife is as
honest a 'omans as I will desires among five thousand,
and five hundred too.

CAIUS By gar, I see 'tis an honest woman.

FORD Well, I promised you a dinner. Come, come, walk 204
in the park. I pray you, pardon me. I will hereafter 205
make known to you why I have done this.—Come,
wife, come, Mistress Page, I pray you, pardon me.
Pray, heartily, pardon me.

PAGE Let's go in, gentlemen; but trust me, we'll mock 209
him. I do invite you tomorrow morning to my house
to breakfast. After, we'll a-birding together. I have a 211
fine hawk for the bush. Shall it be so? 212

FORD Anything.

EVANS If there is one, I shall make two in the company.

CAIUS If there be one or two, I shall make-a the turd.

FORD Pray you, go, Master Page.

[*Exeunt Ford and Page.*]

EVANS [*To Caius*] I pray you now, remembrance to- 217
morrow on the lousy knave, mine Host. 218

CAIUS Dat is good, by gar; with all my heart!

EVANS A lousy knave, to have his gibes and his mockeries! *Exeunt.*

✤

3.4 *Enter Fenton* [*and*] *Anne Page.*

FENTON

I see I cannot get thy father's love; 1
Therefore no more turn me to him, sweet Nan. 2

ANNE

Alas, how then?

204–205 walk . . . park i.e., stroll till dinnertime **209 go in** i.e., go in to dinner at the proper time **211 a-birding** hunting small birds of the bush with a hawk and guns **212 for the bush** for driving the small birds into the bush (where they can be shot) **217–218 remembrance . . . Host** (A seeming allusion to the conversation at the end of 3.1 and to the plot carried out in 4.5.)

3.4. Location: Before Page's house.
1 love good will **2 turn** direct

FENTON Why, thou must be thyself.
He doth object I am too great of birth,
And that, my state being galled with my expense,
I seek to heal it only by his wealth.
Besides these, other bars he lays before me—
My riots past, my wild societies;
And tells me 'tis a thing impossible
I should love thee but as a property.

ANNE Maybe he tells you true.

FENTON
No, heaven so speed me in my time to come!
Albeit I will confess thy father's wealth
Was the first motive that I wooed thee, Anne,
Yet, wooing thee, I found thee of more value
Than stamps in gold or sums in sealèd bags;
And 'tis the very riches of thyself
That now I aim at.

ANNE Gentle Master Fenton,
Yet seek my father's love; still seek it, sir.
If opportunity and humblest suit
Cannot attain it, why, then—hark you hither.
[*They converse apart.*]

[*Enter*] *Shallow, Slender,* [*and Mistress*] *Quickly.*

SHALLOW Break their talk, Mistress Quickly. My kinsman shall speak for himself.

SLENDER I'll make a shaft or a bolt on 't. 'Slid, 'tis but venturing.

SHALLOW Be not dismayed.

SLENDER No, she shall not dismay me. I care not for that, but that I am afeard.

QUICKLY [*To Anne*] Hark ye, Master Slender would speak a word with you.

3 be thyself be your own mistress **5 state . . . expense** estate being hurt by my extravagance **8 societies** companionships **10 property** possession and means to an end **12 speed** prosper **13 Albeit** although **16 stamps in gold** gold coins **22 Break** interrupt **24 I'll . . . on 't** i.e., whether I make a good or bad job of it, I'll give it a try. (A *shaft* is a slender arrow, a *bolt* a thick and blunt one.) **'Slid** by his (God's) eyelid **28 but . . . afeard** if I weren't so scared. (Slender evidently doesn't understand what *dismay* means.)

ANNE
I come to him. [*Aside.*] This is my father's choice.
O, what a world of vile ill-favored faults
Looks handsome in three hundred pounds a year!

QUICKLY And how does good Master Fenton? Pray you, a word with you. [*She draws him aside.*]

SHALLOW She 's coming. To her, coz! O boy, thou hadst a father!

SLENDER I had a father, Mistress Anne; my uncle can tell you good jests of him.—Pray you, uncle, tell Mistress Anne the jest how my father stole two geese out of a pen, good uncle.

SHALLOW Mistress Anne, my cousin loves you.

SLENDER Ay, that I do, as well as I love any woman in Gloucestershire.

SHALLOW He will maintain you like a gentlewoman.

SLENDER Ay, that I will, come cut and longtail, under the degree of a squire.

SHALLOW He will make you a hundred and fifty pounds jointure.

ANNE Good Master Shallow, let him woo for himself.

SHALLOW Marry, I thank you for it; I thank you for that good comfort.—She calls you, coz. I'll leave you. [*He moves aside.*]

ANNE Now, Master Slender—

SLENDER Now, good Mistress Anne—

ANNE What is your will?

SLENDER My will? 'Od's heartlings, that's a pretty jest indeed! I ne'er made my will yet, I thank heaven; I am not such a sickly creature, I give heaven praise.

ANNE I mean, Master Slender, what would you with me?

SLENDER Truly, for mine own part, I would little or nothing with you. Your father and my uncle hath

32 ill-favored ugly **36–37 thou hadst a father** i.e., remember that your father wooed a woman; be like him. (But Slender misses the point.)
42 cousin i.e., kinsman **46 come . . . longtail** i.e., come what may. (Literally, horses or dogs with docked and long tails, i.e., all sorts.)
46–47 under the degree of in the rank of **48 make** give **49 jointure** settlement in the marriage contract providing for the wife's widowhood
56 'Od's heartlings by God's little heart

made motions. If it be my luck, so; if not, happy man 63
be his dole! They can tell you how things go better 64
than I can. You may ask your father. Here he comes.

[*Enter*] *Page* [*and*] *Mistress Page.*

PAGE
Now, Master Slender. Love him, daughter Anne.—
Why, how now? What does Master Fenton here?
You wrong me, sir, thus still to haunt my house.
I told you, sir, my daughter is disposed of.

FENTON
Nay, Master Page, be not impatient.

MRS. PAGE
Good Master Fenton, come not to my child.

PAGE She is no match for you.

FENTON Sir, will you hear me?

PAGE No, good Master Fenton.
Come, Master Shallow; come, son Slender, in.—
Knowing my mind, you wrong me, Master Fenton.
[*Exeunt Page, Shallow, and Slender.*]

QUICKLY [*To Fenton*] Speak to Mistress Page.

FENTON
Good Mistress Page, for that I love your daughter 78
In such a righteous fashion as I do,
Perforce, against all checks, rebukes, and manners, 80
I must advance the colors of my love 81
And not retire. Let me have your good will.

ANNE Good Mother, do not marry me to yond fool.

MRS. PAGE I mean it not; I seek you a better husband. 84

QUICKLY [*Aside to Anne*] That's my master, Master Doctor.

ANNE
Alas, I had rather be set quick i' the earth 86
And bowled to death with turnips! 87

MRS. PAGE
Come, trouble not yourself. Good Master Fenton,

63 motions offers. **so** well and good **63–64 happy . . . dole** i.e., may whoever succeeds with you be happy. (Literally, may his lot in life be that of a happy man.) **78 for that** because **80 checks** reproofs
81 advance the colors raise high the standard (as in anticipation of battle) **84 mean** intend **86 quick** alive **87 bowled** pelted

I will not be your friend nor enemy.
My daughter will I question how she loves you,
And, as I find her, so am I affected. 91
Till then farewell, sir. She must needs go in;
Her father will be angry.

FENTON
Farewell, gentle mistress. Farewell, Nan.
[*Exeunt Mistress Page and Anne.*]

QUICKLY This is my doing, now. "Nay," said I, "will you cast away your child on a fool, and a physician? Look on Master Fenton." This is my doing.

FENTON
I thank thee; and I pray thee, once tonight 98
Give my sweet Nan this ring. There's for thy pains.
[*He gives a ring and money.*]

QUICKLY Now heaven send thee good fortune! [*Exit Fenton.*] A kind heart he hath. A woman would run through fire and water for such a kind heart. But yet I would my master had Mistress Anne; or I would Master Slender had her; or, in sooth, I would Master Fenton had her. I will do what I can for them all three; for so I have promised, and I'll be as good as my word—
but speciously for Master Fenton. Well, I must of an- 107
other errand to Sir John Falstaff from my two mistresses. What a beast am I to slack it! *Exit.* 109

✤

3.5 *Enter Falstaff.*

FALSTAFF Bardolph, I say!

[*Enter*] *Bardolph.*

BARDOLPH Here, sir.

FALSTAFF Go fetch me a quart of sack; put a toast in 't. 3
[*Exit Bardolph.*] Have I lived to be carried in a basket,
like a barrow of butcher's offal, and to be thrown in 5

91 affected inclined **98 once** sometime **107 speciously** (For *specially.*) **must of** must undertake **109 slack** be remiss about

3.5. Location: The Garter Inn.
3 toast piece of toast **5 barrow** wheelbarrowful

the Thames? Well, if I be served such another trick, I'll
have my brains ta'en out and buttered, and give them
to a dog for a New Year's gift. The rogues slighted me 8
into the river with as little remorse as they would have 9
drowned a blind bitch's puppies, fifteen i' the litter! 10
And you may know by my size that I have a kind of
alacrity in sinking; if the bottom were as deep as hell,
I should down. I had been drowned, but that the shore 13
was shelvy and shallow—a death that I abhor; for the 14
water swells a man, and what a thing should I have
been when I had been swelled! I should have been a
mountain of mummy. 17

[*Enter Bardolph with sack.*]

BARDOLPH Here's Mistress Quickly, sir, to speak with you.

FALSTAFF Come, let me pour in some sack to the
Thames water, for my belly's as cold as if I had swal-
lowed snowballs for pills to cool the reins. [*He drinks.*] 22
Call her in.

BARDOLPH Come in, woman!

[*Enter Mistress*] *Quickly.*

QUICKLY By your leave; I cry you mercy. Give your 25
worship good morrow.

FALSTAFF [*To Bardolph*] Take away these chalices. Go 27
brew me a pottle of sack finely. 28

BARDOLPH With eggs, sir?

FALSTAFF Simple of itself. I'll no pullet sperm in my 30
brewage. [*Exit Bardolph.*] How now?

QUICKLY Marry, sir, I come to your worship from Mistress Ford.

FALSTAFF Mistress Ford? I have had ford enough. I was 34
thrown into the ford. I have my belly full of ford.

8 slighted me dumped me heedlessly **9 remorse** pity, compassion **10 a blind bitch's** a bitch's blind (at birth) **13 down** sink. **shore** bottom near the edge **14 shelvy** shelving, sloping **17 mummy** dead flesh **22 reins** kidneys **25 cry you mercy** beg your pardon **27 chalices** (A lofty name for drinking cups.) **28 brew** prepare, concoct. **pottle** two-quart measure. **finely** tastefully **30 Simple of itself** unadulterated. **I'll** I'll have **34 ford** i.e., river, stream. (Literally, a shallow place in the river where one may cross.)

QUICKLY Alas the day, good heart, that was not her
fault. She does so take on with her men; they mistook 37
their erection. 38
FALSTAFF So did I mine, to build upon a foolish
woman's promise.
QUICKLY Well, she laments, sir, for it, that it would 41
yearn your heart to see it. Her husband goes this 42
morning a-birding; she desires you once more to come
to her between eight and nine. I must carry her word
quickly. She'll make you amends, I warrant you.
FALSTAFF Well, I will visit her; tell her so. And bid her
think what a man is. Let her consider his frailty, and 47
then judge of my merit.
QUICKLY I will tell her.
FALSTAFF Do so. Between nine and ten, sayst thou?
QUICKLY Eight and nine, sir.
FALSTAFF Well, begone. I will not miss her. 52
QUICKLY Peace be with you, sir. [*Exit.*]
FALSTAFF I marvel I hear not of Master Brook; he sent
me word to stay within. I like his money well. O, here
he comes.

[*Enter*] *Ford* [*disguised*].

FORD Bless you, sir!
FALSTAFF Now, Master Brook, you come to know what
hath passed between me and Ford's wife?
FORD That, indeed, Sir John, is my business.
FALSTAFF Master Brook, I will not lie to you. I was at
her house the hour she appointed me.
FORD And sped you, sir?
FALSTAFF Very ill-favoredly, Master Brook. 64
FORD How so, sir? Did she change her determination? 65
FALSTAFF No, Master Brook, but the peaking cornuto 66
her husband, Master Brook, dwelling in a continual 67
'larum of jealousy, comes me in the instant of our en- 68
counter, after we had embraced, kissed, protested, and,

37 take on with berate, scold **38 erection** (Blunder for *direction;* Falstaff plays bawdily on her malapropism.) **41 that** so that **42 yearn** grieve **47 his** i.e., man's **52 miss** fail **64 ill-favoredly** badly **65 determination** decision **66 peaking cornuto** sneaking cuckold **67 dwelling** remaining, being **68 'larum** i.e., state of surprise and fear. **comes me** comes. (*Me* is used colloquially.)

as it were, spoke the prologue of our comedy; and at his heels a rabble of his companions, thither provoked and instigated by his distemper, and, forsooth, to search his house for his wife's love.

FORD What, while you were there?

FALSTAFF While I was there.

FORD And did he search for you, and could not find you?

FALSTAFF You shall hear. As good luck would have it, comes in one Mistress Page, gives intelligence of Ford's approach, and, in her invention and Ford's wife's distraction, they conveyed me into a buck basket.

FORD A buck basket?

FALSTAFF By the Lord, a buck basket! Rammed me in with foul shirts and smocks, socks, foul stockings, greasy napkins, that, Master Brook, there was the rankest compound of villainous smell that ever offended nostril.

FORD And how long lay you there?

FALSTAFF Nay, you shall hear, Master Brook, what I have suffered to bring this woman to evil for your good. Being thus crammed in the basket, a couple of Ford's knaves, his hinds, were called forth by their mistress to carry me in the name of foul clothes to Datchet Lane. They took me on their shoulders, met the jealous knave their master in the door, who asked them once or twice what they had in their basket. I quaked for fear, lest the lunatic knave would have searched it; but fate, ordaining he should be a cuckold, held his hand. Well, on went he for a search, and away went I for foul clothes. But mark the sequel, Master Brook. I suffered the pangs of three several deaths: first, an intolerable fright to be detected with a jealous rotten bellwether; next, to be compassed, like a good bilbo, in the circumference of a peck, hilt to point, heel

71 rabble pack **83 smocks** slips **84 that** so that **91 hinds** servants **100 several** distinct **101 with** by **102 bellwether** castrated or old ram, leader of a flock (provided with a noisy bell and horned like a cuckold). **compassed** (1) encompassed, surrounded (2) bent into a circle **103 bilbo** finely tempered and flexible sword of Bilbao in Spain. **peck** container holding a quarter of a bushel; i.e., a very small space. **hilt to point** (Falstaff is bent over, head to toes, like a fine Spanish sword that could be bent thus without breaking.)

to head; and then, to be stopped in, like a strong dis- 104
tillation, with stinking clothes that fretted in their own 105
grease. Think of that—a man of my kidney. Think of 106
that—that am as subject to heat as butter; a man of
continual dissolution and thaw. It was a miracle to 108
scape suffocation. And in the height of this bath,
when I was more than half stewed in grease, like a
Dutch dish, to be thrown into the Thames and cooled,
glowing hot, in that surge, like a horseshoe! Think of
that—hissing hot—think of that, Master Brook!

FORD In good sadness, sir, I am sorry that for my sake 114
you have suffered all this. My suit then is desperate;
you'll undertake her no more?

FALSTAFF Master Brook, I will be thrown into Etna, as I 117
have been into Thames, ere I will leave her thus. Her
husband is this morning gone a-birding. I have received from her another embassy of meeting. Twixt 120
eight and nine is the hour, Master Brook.

FORD 'Tis past eight already, sir.

FALSTAFF Is it? I will then address me to my appoint- 123
ment. Come to me at your convenient leisure, and you
shall know how I speed; and the conclusion shall be
crowned with your enjoying her. Adieu. You shall
have her, Master Brook; Master Brook, you shall cuckold Ford. [*Exit*.]

FORD Hum, ha! Is this a vision? Is this a dream? Do I
sleep? Master Ford, awake! Awake, Master Ford!
There's a hole made in your best coat, Master Ford. 131
This 'tis to be married! This 'tis to have linen and
buck baskets! Well, I will proclaim myself what I am.
I will now take the lecher. He is at my house. He cannot scape me. 'Tis impossible he should. He cannot
creep into a halfpenny purse, nor into a pepperbox. 136
But, lest the devil that guides him should aid him, I

104 stopped shut, stoppered **105 fretted** decayed **106 kidney** temperament, constitution **108 dissolution** liquefaction **114 good sadness** all seriousness **117 Etna** volcano in Sicily **120 embassy** message **123 address me to** prepare myself for, betake myself to **131 There's . . . coat** (A proverb suggesting that a reputation can easily be ruined.) **136 halfpenny purse** small purse for small coins

will search impossible places. Though what I am I cannot avoid, yet to be what I would not shall not make me tame. If I have horns to make one mad, let the proverb go with me: I'll be horn-mad. *Exit.*

141 horn-mad frenzied like a horned animal in rutting season (as at 1.4.45)

4.1 *Enter Mistress Page, [Mistress] Quickly, [and] William.*

MRS. PAGE Is he at Master Ford's already, think'st thou?
QUICKLY Sure he is by this, or will be presently. But
truly he is very courageous mad about his throwing 3
into the water. Mistress Ford desires you to come sud- 4
denly. 5

MRS. PAGE I'll be with her by and by. I'll but bring my young man here to school.

[Enter Sir Hugh] Evans.

Look where his master comes. 'Tis a playing day, I see.— 8
How now, Sir Hugh, no school today?

EVANS No. Master Slender is let the boys leave to play. 10

QUICKLY Blessing of his heart! 11

MRS. PAGE Sir Hugh, my husband says my son profits 12
nothing in the world at his book. I pray you, ask him 13
some questions in his accidence. 14

EVANS Come hither, William. Hold up your head. Come.

MRS. PAGE Come on, sirrah, hold up your head. Answer your master. Be not afraid.

EVANS William, how many numbers is in nouns? 19

WILLIAM Two.

QUICKLY Truly, I thought there had been one number
more, because they say, "'Od's nouns." 22

EVANS Peace your tattlings!—What is "fair," William? 23

WILLIAM *Pulcher.*

QUICKLY Polecats? There are fairer things than polecats, 25
sure.

4.1. Location: A street in Windsor.
3 courageous (For *outrageous*?) **4–5 suddenly** at once **8 playing day** holiday **10 is let . . . play** i.e., has asked, as a visitor of rank, that the boys be given a holiday **11 of** on **12–13 profits . . . book** isn't making any progress in his studies **14 accidence** rudiments of Latin grammar **19 numbers** i.e., singular and plural **22 'Od's nouns** by God's wounds (confused with *odd* numbers, i.e., three) **23 Peace your tattlings** cease your prattle **25 Polecats** (Many of Quickly's misconstruings are bawdy: *polecats* [prostitutes], *horum* [whores], *harum* [hare, prostitute], *Jenny's case* [a whore's pudendum], etc.)

EVANS You are a very simplicity 'oman. I pray you, peace.—What is *lapis,* William?

WILLIAM A stone.

EVANS And what is "a stone," William?

WILLIAM A pebble.

EVANS No, it is *lapis.* I pray you, remember in your prain.

WILLIAM *Lapis.*

EVANS That is a good William. What is he, William, that does lend articles?

WILLIAM Articles are borrowed of the pronoun, and be 37
thus declined, *singulariter, nominativo, hic, haec,* 38
hoc.

EVANS *Nominativo, hig, hag, hog.* Pray you, mark: *genitivo, huius.* Well, what is your accusative case?

WILLIAM *Accusativo, hinc—*

EVANS I pray you, have your remembrance, child. *Accusativo, hung, hang, hog.*

QUICKLY "Hang-hog" is Latin for bacon, I warrant you. 45

EVANS Leave your prabbles, 'oman.—What is the focative case, William?

WILLIAM O—*vocativo,* O.

EVANS Remember, William, focative is *caret.* 49

QUICKLY And that's a good root.

EVANS 'Oman, forbear.

MRS. PAGE [*To Mistress Quickly*] Peace!

EVANS What is your genitive case plural, William?

WILLIAM Genitive case?

EVANS Ay.

WILLIAM *Genitivo—horum, harum, horum.*

QUICKLY Vengeance of Jenny's case! Fie on her! Never name her, child, if she be a whore.

EVANS For shame, 'oman!

QUICKLY You do ill to teach the child such words. He

37 Articles . . . pronoun (William is reciting uncomprehendingly from William Lilly's widely used Latin grammar, which followed the ancient stoic grammarians in regarding demonstrative pronouns—*hic, haec, hoc*—as a sort of article like *the.*) **38 singulariter** in the singular. **nominativo** in the nominative. (Similarly with *genitivo, accusativo,* and *vocativo.*) **45 Hang-hog** (Bacon is made by hanging up a hog.) **49 caret** is lacking. (But Quickly interprets it as *carrot.*)

teaches him to hick and to hack, which they'll do fast 61
enough of themselves, and to call "whorum." Fie upon
you!

EVANS 'Oman, art thou lunatics? Hast thou no under-
standings for thy cases and the numbers of the gen-
ders? Thou art as foolish Christian creatures as I would
desires.

MRS. PAGE [*To Mistress Quickly*] Prithee, hold thy peace.

EVANS Show me now, William, some declensions of your pronouns.

WILLIAM Forsooth, I have forgot.

EVANS It is *qui, quae, quod*. If you forget your
qui's, your *quae*'s, and your *quod*'s, you must
be preeches. Go your ways and play, go. 74

MRS. PAGE He is a better scholar than I thought he was.

EVANS He is a good sprag memory. Farewell, Mistress 76
Page.

MRS. PAGE Adieu, good Sir Hugh. [*Exit Sir Hugh.*] Get you home, boy. [*Exit William.*] Come, we stay too long.

Exeunt.

✣

4.2 *Enter Falstaff* [*and*] *Mistress Ford.*

FALSTAFF Mistress Ford, your sorrow hath eaten up
my sufferance. I see you are obsequious in your love, 2
and I profess requital to a hair's breadth, not only,
Mistress Ford, in the simple office of love, but in all
the accoutrement, complement, and ceremony of it. 5
But are you sure of your husband now?

MRS. FORD He's a-birding, sweet Sir John.

MRS. PAGE [*Within*] What ho, gossip Ford! What ho! 8

61 to hick and to hack i.e., to drink and engage in sex; see 2.1.49
74 preeches breeched, i.e., whipped on the bare buttocks **76 sprag** sprack, lively, alert

4.2. Location: Ford's house.
2 sufferance suffering, pain. **obsequious** zealously devoted **5 complement** that which completes the whole, ceremoniousness **8 gossip** i.e., friend, neighbor. (Literally, fellow godparent.)

MRS. FORD Step into the chamber, Sir John.
[*Exit Falstaff.*]

[*Enter*] *Mistress Page.*

MRS. PAGE How now, sweetheart, who's at home besides yourself?
MRS. FORD Why, none but mine own people. 12
MRS. PAGE Indeed?
MRS. FORD No, certainly. [*Aside to her.*] Speak louder.
MRS. PAGE Truly, I am so glad you have nobody here.
MRS. FORD Why?
MRS. PAGE Why, woman, your husband is in his old
lines again. He so takes on yonder with my husband, 18
so rails against all married mankind, so curses all Eve's
daughters, of what complexion soever, and so buffets
himself on the forehead, crying, "Peer out, peer out!", 21
that any madness I ever yet beheld seemed but tameness, civility, and patience to this his distemper he is in now. I am glad the fat knight is not here.
MRS. FORD Why, does he talk of him?
MRS. PAGE Of none but him, and swears he was carried out, the last time he searched for him, in a basket; protests to my husband he is now here, and hath drawn
him and the rest of their company from their sport to
make another experiment of his suspicion. But I am 30
glad the knight is not here. Now he shall see his own foolery.
MRS. FORD How near is he, Mistress Page?
MRS. PAGE Hard by, at street end. He will be here anon.
MRS. FORD I am undone! The knight is here.
MRS. PAGE Why, then, you are utterly shamed, and he's
but a dead man. What a woman are you! Away with 37
him, away with him! Better shame than murder.
MRS. FORD Which way should he go? How should I be- 39
stow him? Shall I put him into the basket again?

[*Enter Falstaff.*]

12 people household servants **18 lines** vein, role **21 Peer out** i.e., let my cuckold's horns come forth and be visible **30 experiment** trial **37 What a** what kind of **39 should** can

FALSTAFF No, I'll come no more i' the basket. May I not go out ere he come?

MRS. PAGE Alas, three of Master Ford's brothers watch the door with pistols, that none shall issue out; otherwise you might slip away ere he came. But what make you here?

FALSTAFF What shall I do? I'll creep up into the chimney.

MRS. FORD There they always use to discharge their birding pieces.

MRS. PAGE Creep into the kilnhole.

FALSTAFF Where is it?

MRS. FORD He will seek there, on my word. Neither press, coffer, chest, trunk, well, vault, but he hath an abstract for the remembrance of such places, and goes to them by his note. There is no hiding you in the house.

FALSTAFF I'll go out, then.

MRS. PAGE If you go out in your own semblance, you die, Sir John—unless you go out disguised.

MRS. FORD How might we disguise him?

MRS. PAGE Alas the day, I know not! There is no woman's gown big enough for him; otherwise he might put on a hat, a muffler, and a kerchief, and so escape.

FALSTAFF Good hearts, devise something. Any extremity rather than a mischief.

MRS. FORD My maid's aunt, the fat woman of Brentford, has a gown above.

MRS. PAGE On my word, it will serve him; she's as big as he is. And there's her thrummed hat and her muffler too. Run up, Sir John.

MRS. FORD Go, go, sweet Sir John. Mistress Page and I will look some linen for your head.

MRS. PAGE Quick, quick! We'll come dress you straight. Put on the gown the while. [*Exit Falstaff.*]

45 make do **49 use** make it a practice **50 birding pieces** guns for bird hunting **51 kilnhole** oven **54 press** clothes cupboard **55 abstract** inventory **64 muffler** kerchief or scarf worn by women over part of the face and neck **67 mischief** calamity **68 Brentford** a nearby village **69 above** upstairs **71 thrummed** made of coarse yarn **74 look** look for **75 straight** at once

MRS. FORD I would my husband would meet him in this shape. He cannot abide the old woman of Brentford. He swears she's a witch, forbade her my house, and hath threatened to beat her.

MRS. PAGE Heaven guide him to thy husband's cudgel, and the devil guide his cudgel afterwards!

MRS. FORD But is my husband coming?

MRS. PAGE Ay, in good sadness, is he, and talks of the 84
basket too, howsoever he hath had intelligence.

MRS. FORD We'll try that; for I'll appoint my men to carry 86
the basket again, to meet him at the door with it, as they did last time.

MRS. PAGE Nay, but he'll be here presently. Let's go 89
dress him like the witch of Brentford.

MRS. FORD I'll first direct my men what they shall do with the basket. Go up. I'll bring linen for him straight. [*Exit.*]

MRS. PAGE Hang him, dishonest varlet! We cannot mis- 94
use him enough.
We'll leave a proof, by that which we will do,
Wives may be merry, and yet honest too. 97
We do not act that often jest and laugh; 98
'Tis old, but true, "Still swine eats all the draff." [*Exit.*] 99

[*Enter Mistress Ford with two*] *Servants.*

MRS. FORD Go, sirs, take the basket again on your shoulders. Your master is hard at door. If he bid you set it
down, obey him. Quickly, dispatch! [*Exit.*] 102

FIRST SERVANT Come, come, take it up.

SECOND SERVANT Pray heaven it be not full of knight again.

FIRST SERVANT I hope not. I had as lief bear so much lead. [*They take up the basket.*]

[*Enter*] *Ford, Page, Caius, Evans,* [*and*] *Shallow.*

FORD Ay, but if it prove true, Master Page, have you

84 in good sadness in all seriousness **86 try** test **89 presently** right away **94 dishonest** lecherous **97 honest** chaste **98 act** i.e., act unchastely **99 Still** quiet. **draff** pigwash. (The proverb reinforces Mistress Page's point that merry talk does not ensure wantonness; adulterous women are usually quiet about it.) **102 dispatch** hurry

any way then to unfool me again?—Set down the basket, villain! Somebody call my wife. Youth in a basket! O, you panderly rascals! There's a knot, a ging, a pack, a conspiracy against me. Now shall the devil be shamed.—What, wife, I say! Come, come forth! Behold what honest clothes you send forth to bleaching!

PAGE Why, this passes, Master Ford. You are not to go loose any longer; you must be pinioned.

EVANS Why, this is lunatics. This is mad as a mad dog.

SHALLOW Indeed, Master Ford, this is not well, indeed.

FORD So say I too, sir.

[*Enter Mistress Ford.*]

Come hither, Mistress Ford—Mistress Ford, the honest woman, the modest wife, the virtuous creature, that hath the jealous fool to her husband! I suspect without cause, mistress, do I?

MRS. FORD Heaven be my witness you do, if you suspect me in any dishonesty.

FORD Well said, brazenface! Hold it out.—Come forth, sirrah! [*He pulls clothes out of the basket.*]

PAGE This passes!

MRS. FORD Are you not ashamed? Let the clothes alone.

FORD I shall find you anon.

EVANS 'Tis unreasonable. Will you take up your wife's clothes? Come, away.

FORD Empty the basket, I say!

MRS. FORD Why, man, why?

FORD Master Page, as I am a man, there was one conveyed out of my house yesterday in this basket. Why may not he be there again? In my house I am sure he is. My intelligence is true; my jealousy is reasonable. Pluck me out all the linen.

109 unfool me disburden me of a reputation for folly **111 a knot . . . pack** a company, a gang, a confederacy **112–113 Now . . . shamed** i.e., now truth will out. (From the proverb "Tell the truth and shame the devil.") **115 passes** surpasses, goes beyond all bounds **119 So say I too** (Ford means that something is amiss, not, as Shallow intended to say, that Ford's behavior is deplorable.) **126 Hold it out** i.e., continue to maintain your falsehood **131 take up** pick up (but with unintended bawdy suggestion of lifting his wife's dress) **138 intelligence** information **139 Pluck me out** pluck out for me

MRS. FORD If you find a man there, he shall die a flea's death.

PAGE Here's no man.

SHALLOW By my fidelity, this is not well, Master Ford. This wrongs you.

EVANS Master Ford, you must pray, and not follow the imaginations of your own heart. This is jealousies.

FORD Well, he's not here I seek for.

PAGE No, nor nowhere else but in your brain.

FORD Help to search my house this one time. If I find not what I seek, show no color for my extremity; let me forever be your table sport. Let them say of me, "As jealous as Ford, that searched a hollow walnut for his wife's leman." Satisfy me once more; once more search with me. [*Exeunt Servants with basket.*]

MRS. FORD [*Calling upstairs*] What ho, Mistress Page! Come you and the old woman down. My husband will come into the chamber.

FORD Old woman? What old woman's that?

MRS. FORD Why, it is my maid's aunt of Brentford.

FORD A witch, a quean, an old cozening quean! Have I not forbid her my house? She comes of errands, does she? We are simple men; we do not know what's brought to pass under the profession of fortune-telling. She works by charms, by spells, by the figure, and such daubery as this is, beyond our element. We know nothing.—Come down, you witch, you hag, you! Come down, I say!

MRS. FORD Nay, good sweet husband!—Good gentlemen, let him not strike the old woman.

[*Enter Falstaff in woman's clothes, and Mistress Page.*]

144 wrongs you does you dishonor **145 you must pray** i.e., you must seek spiritual grace in combatting the devil who possesses you
150 show . . . extremity make no attempt to excuse my extreme behavior
151 your table sport butt or laughingstock of the company **153 leman** paramour **160 quean** jade, hussy. **cozening** deceiving **161 of** on
164 by the figure i.e., by making wax figures and sticking pins in them, or, by astrological charts **165 daubery** false show. **beyond our element** beyond our comprehension, belonging to another world

MRS. PAGE Come, Mother Prat, come, give me your hand.

FORD I'll prat her. [*Beating him.*] Out of my door, you 172
witch, you rag, you baggage, you polecat, you ronyon! 173
Out, out! I'll conjure you, I'll fortune-tell you.

[*Exit Falstaff.*]

MRS. PAGE Are you not ashamed? I think you have killed the poor woman.

MRS. FORD Nay, he will do it.—'Tis a goodly credit for 177
you. 178

FORD Hang her, witch!

EVANS By Jeshu, I think the 'oman is a witch indeed. I like not when a 'oman has a great peard. I spy a great peard under his muffler.

FORD Will you follow, gentlemen? I beseech you, follow. See but the issue of my jealousy. If I cry out thus 184
upon no trail, never trust me when I open again. 185

PAGE Let's obey his humor a little further. Come, gentlemen. [*Exeunt Ford, Page, Shallow, Caius, and Evans.*]

MRS. PAGE Trust me, he beat him most pitifully.

MRS. FORD Nay, by the Mass, that he did not; he beat him most unpitifully, methought.

MRS. PAGE I'll have the cudgel hallowed and hung o'er the altar. It hath done meritorious service.

MRS. FORD What think you? May we, with the warrant of womanhood and the witness of a good conscience, pursue him with any further revenge?

MRS. PAGE The spirit of wantonness is, sure, scared out
of him. If the devil have him not in fee simple, with 197
fine and recovery, he will never, I think, in the way of 198
waste, attempt us again. 199

172 prat beat, teach a lesson, practice tricks on (?) **173 rag** worthless person. **baggage** hussy. **polecat** whore. **ronyon** disreputable woman
177–178 'Tis . . . you it does you great credit. (Said ironically.)
184 issue conclusion **184–185 cry . . . trail** bay like a hunting dog despite the absence of a scent **185 open** give voice (like a hunting dog)
197 fee simple estate belonging to an owner and his heirs forever; hence, absolute possession **198 fine and recovery** procedures by which an entailed estate was converted into fee simple **199 waste** spoliation, despoiling

MRS. FORD Shall we tell our husbands how we have served him?

MRS. PAGE Yes, by all means, if it be but to scrape the
figures out of your husband's brains. If they can find 203
in their hearts the poor unvirtuous fat knight shall be
any further afflicted, we two will still be the ministers. 205

MRS. FORD I'll warrant they'll have him publicly shamed,
and methinks there would be no period to the jest 207
should he not be publicly shamed.

MRS. PAGE Come, to the forge with it, then shape it. I would not have things cool. *Exeunt.*

4.3 *Enter Host and Bardolph.*

BARDOLPH Sir, the Germans desire to have three of your horses. The Duke himself will be tomorrow at court, and they are going to meet him.

HOST What duke should that be comes so secretly? I hear not of him in the court. Let me speak with the gentlemen. They speak English?

BARDOLPH Ay, sir. I'll call them to you.

HOST They shall have my horses, but I'll make them
pay; I'll sauce them. They have had my house a week 9
at command. I have turned away my other guests. 10
They must come off. I'll sauce them. Come. *Exeunt.* 11

4.4 *Enter Page, Ford, Mistress Page, Mistress Ford, and Evans.*

EVANS 'Tis one of the best discretions of a 'oman as 1
ever I did look upon.

203 figures fantasies, conceits **205 ministers** agents **207 period** suitable conclusion

4.3. Location: The Garter Inn.
9 sauce them i.e., make them pay dearly **10 at command** retained for their use upon their expected arrival **11 come off** pay, disburse handsomely

4.4. Location: Ford's house.
1 'Tis i.e., she is. **best . . . 'oman** i.e., most discreet women

PAGE And did he send you both these letters at an instant?

MRS. PAGE Within a quarter of an hour.

FORD
Pardon me, wife. Henceforth do what thou wilt;
I rather will suspect the sun with cold
Than thee with wantonness. Now doth thy honor stand,
In him that was of late an heretic,
As firm as faith.

PAGE 'Tis well, 'tis well. No more.
Be not as extreme in submission as in offense.
But let our plot go forward. Let our wives
Yet once again, to make us public sport,
Appoint a meeting with this old fat fellow,
Where we may take him and disgrace him for it.

FORD
There is no better way than that they spoke of.

PAGE How? To send him word they'll meet him in the park at midnight? Fie, fie, he'll never come.

EVANS You say he has been thrown in the rivers and has been grievously peaten as an old 'oman. Methinks there should be terrors in him that he should not come. Methinks his flesh is punished; he shall have no desires.

PAGE So think I too.

MRS. FORD
Devise but how you'll use him when he comes,
And let us two devise to bring him thither.

MRS. PAGE
There is an old tale goes that Herne the hunter,
Sometime a keeper here in Windsor Forest,
Doth all the wintertime, at still midnight,
Walk round about an oak, with great ragg'd horns;
And there he blasts the tree, and takes the cattle,
And makes milch kine yield blood, and shakes a chain
In a most hideous and dreadful manner.
You have heard of such a spirit, and well you know
The superstitious idle-headed eld

3–4 at an instant at the same time **7 with** of **25 use** treat **28 Sometime** formerly **30 ragg'd** shaggy, pronged **31 blasts** blights, or blasts with lightning. **takes** bewitches **32 milch kine** dairy cattle **35 eld** old age, i.e., elders, an earlier generation

Received and did deliver to our age
This tale of Herne the hunter for a truth.

PAGE
Why, yet there want not many that do fear
In deep of night to walk by this Herne's Oak.
But what of this?

MRS. FORD Marry, this is our device:
That Falstaff at that oak shall meet with us,
Disguised like Herne, with huge horns on his head.

PAGE
Well, let it not be doubted but he'll come.
And in this shape when you have brought him thither,
What shall be done with him? What is your plot?

MRS. PAGE
That likewise have we thought upon, and thus:
Nan Page my daughter, and my little son,
And three or four more of their growth, we'll dress
Like urchins, aufs, and fairies, green and white,
With rounds of waxen tapers on their heads
And rattles in their hands. Upon a sudden,
As Falstaff, she, and I are newly met,
Let them from forth a sawpit rush at once
With some diffusèd song. Upon their sight,
We two in great amazedness will fly.
Then let them all encircle him about,
And, fairylike, to pinch the unclean knight,
And ask him why, that hour of fairy revel,
In their so sacred paths he dares to tread
In shape profane.

MRS. FORD And till he tell the truth,
Let the supposèd fairies pinch him sound
And burn him with their tapers.

MRS. PAGE The truth being known,
We'll all present ourselves, dis-horn the spirit,
And mock him home to Windsor.

FORD The children must
Be practiced well to this, or they'll ne'er do 't.

EVANS I will teach the children their behaviors, and I

38 want lack **40 device** plan **44 shape** disguise **48 growth** size, age
49 urchins, aufs (Terms for goblins or elves.) **50 rounds** circlets
53 sawpit a pit over which wood was sawed **54 diffusèd** confused, disorderly **61 sound** soundly

will be like a jackanapes also, to burn the knight with 67
my taber. 68

FORD
That will be excellent. I'll go buy them vizards. 69

MRS. PAGE
My Nan shall be the queen of all the fairies,
Finely attirèd in a robe of white.

PAGE
That silk will I go buy. [*Aside*.] And in that tire 72
Shall Master Slender steal my Nan away
And marry her at Eton. [*To Mrs. Page*.] Go, send to
Falstaff straight. 74

FORD
Nay, I'll to him again in name of Brook.
He'll tell me all his purpose. Sure he'll come.

MRS. PAGE
Fear not you that. Go get us properties
And tricking for our fairies. 78

EVANS Let us about it. It is admirable pleasures and fery honest knaveries. [*Exeunt Page, Ford, and Evans*.]

MRS. PAGE Go, Mistress Ford,
Send quickly to Sir John, to know his mind.
[*Exit Mistress Ford*.]
I'll to the Doctor. He hath my good will,
And none but he, to marry with Nan Page.
That Slender, though well landed, is an idiot;
And he my husband best of all affects. 86
The Doctor is well moneyed, and his friends
Potent at court. He, none but he, shall have her,
Though twenty thousand worthier come to crave her.
[*Exit*.]

✣

67 like a jackanapes disguised as an ape or monkey. (Evans actually disguises himself as a satyr.) **68 taber** taper, candle **69 vizards** visors, masks **72 tire** attire **74 Eton** town across the Thames from Windsor **78 tricking** adornment, costumes **86 he** i.e., him. **affects** prefers

4.5 *Enter Host* [*and*] *Simple.*

HOST What wouldst thou have, boor? What, thickskin? Speak, breathe, discuss; brief, short, quick, snap.

SIMPLE Marry, sir, I come to speak with Sir John Falstaff from Master Slender.

HOST There's his chamber, his house, his castle, his standing bed and truckle bed. 'Tis painted about with the story of the Prodigal, fresh and new. Go, knock and call. He'll speak like an Anthropophaginian unto thee. Knock, I say.

SIMPLE There's an old woman, a fat woman, gone up into his chamber. I'll be so bold as stay, sir, till she come down. I come to speak with her, indeed.

HOST Ha, a fat woman? The knight may be robbed. I'll call.—Bully knight! Bully Sir John! Speak from thy lungs military. Art thou there? It is thine Host, thine Ephesian, calls.

FALSTAFF [*Within*] How now, mine Host?

HOST Here's a Bohemian Tartar tarries the coming down of thy fat woman. Let her descend, bully, let her descend. My chambers are honorable. Fie, privacy? Fie!

[*Enter*] *Falstaff.*

FALSTAFF There was, mine Host, an old fat woman even now with me, but she's gone.

SIMPLE Pray you, sir, was 't not the wise woman of Brentford?

FALSTAFF Ay, marry, was it, mussel shell. What would you with her?

SIMPLE My master, sir, Master Slender, sent to her, seeing her go through the streets, to know, sir,

4.5. Location: The Garter Inn.
1 thickskin one slow or dull of feeling **2 discuss** declare **6 truckle bed** trundle bed, low bed stored under the *standing bed* or regular bed **7 the Prodigal** (Cf. *1 Henry IV,* 4.2.34 and *2 Henry IV,* 2.1.143, where this story from Luke 15:11–32 is again associated with Falstaff.) **8 Anthropophaginian** i.e., cannibal **15–16 Ephesian** i.e., boon companion **18 Bohemian Tartar** i.e., barbarian, wild man. **tarries** (who) awaits **24 wise woman** i.e., fortune-teller **26 mussel shell** i.e., one who gapes

whether one Nym, sir, that beguiled him of a chain,
had the chain or no.

FALSTAFF I spake with the old woman about it.

SIMPLE And what says she, I pray, sir?

FALSTAFF Marry, she says that the very same man that
beguiled Master Slender of his chain cozened him of it.

SIMPLE I would I could have spoken with the woman
herself. I had other things to have spoken with her too
from him.

FALSTAFF What are they? Let us know.

HOST Ay, come. Quick.

SIMPLE I may not conceal them, sir. 41

HOST Conceal them or thou diest.

SIMPLE Why, sir, they were nothing but about Mistress
Anne Page, to know if it were my master's fortune to
have her or no.

FALSTAFF 'Tis, 'tis his fortune.

SIMPLE What, sir?

FALSTAFF To have her or no. Go, say the woman told
me so.

SIMPLE May I be bold to say so, sir?

FALSTAFF Ay, sir; like who more bold. 51

SIMPLE I thank your worship. I shall make my master
glad with these tidings. [*Exit.*]

HOST Thou art clerkly, thou art clerkly, Sir John. Was 54
there a wise woman with thee?

FALSTAFF Ay, that there was, mine Host, one that hath
taught me more wit than ever I learned before in my
life. And I paid nothing for it neither, but was paid for 58
my learning.

[*Enter*] *Bardolph.*

BARDOLPH Out, alas, sir! Cozenage, mere cozenage! 60

HOST Where be my horses? Speak well of them, var- 61
letto. 62

BARDOLPH Run away with the cozeners. For so soon as
I came beyond Eton, they threw me off from behind

41 conceal (For *reveal*. The Host answers ironically with the same misused word.) **51 like who more bold** as bold as the boldest
54 clerkly scholarly, wise **58 was paid** (i.e., with a beating)
60 Cozenage double-dealing. **mere** absolute **61 Speak well of them** i.e., tell me good news of them **61–62 varletto** varlet, rascal

one of them, in a slough of mire, and set spurs and away, like three German devils, three Doctor Faustuses.

HOST They are gone but to meet the Duke, villain. Do not say they be fled. Germans are honest men.

[*Enter*] *Evans.*

EVANS Where is mine Host?

HOST What is the matter, sir?

EVANS Have a care of your entertainments. There is a friend of mine come to town tells me there is three cozen-germans that has cozened all the hosts of Reading, of Maidenhead, of Colnbrook, of horses and money. I tell you for good will, look you. You are wise, and full of gibes and vloutingstocks, and 'tis not convenient you should be cozened. Fare you well. [*Exit.*]

[*Enter*] *Caius.*

CAIUS Vere is mine Host de Jarteer?

HOST Here, Master Doctor, in perplexity and doubtful dilemma.

CAIUS I cannot tell vat is dat. But it is tell-a me dat you make grand preparation for a duke de Jamany. By my trot, dere is no duke that the court is know to come. I tell you for good will. Adieu. [*Exit.*]

HOST Hue and cry, villain, go!—Assist me, knight. I am undone!—Fly, run, hue and cry, villain! I am undone!

[*Exeunt Host and Bardolph.*]

FALSTAFF I would all the world might be cozened, for I have been cozened and beaten too. If it should come to the ear of the court how I have been transformed, and how my transformation hath been washed and cudgeled, they would melt me out of my fat drop by drop and liquor fishermen's boots with me. I warrant they

66–67 Doctor Faustuses (Named for the scholar-magician of Marlowe's play.) **72 your entertainments** i.e., your guests **74 cozen-germans** (1) cousins-german, close relatives (2) cozening or cheating Germans **74–75 Reading** a town not far from Windsor. (Also true of *Maidenhead* and *Colnbrook*.) **77 vloutingstocks** i.e., taunts **77–78 convenient** fitting **80 doubtful** full of doubts **83 Jamany** Germany **84 trot** troth **86 Hue and cry** (The shout raised for pursuit of a felon.) **93 liquor** saturate with oil to make waterproof

would whip me with their fine wits till I were as crestfallen as a dried pear. I never prospered since I forswore myself at primero. Well, if my wind were but long enough to say my prayers, I would repent.

[*Enter Mistress*] *Quickly.*

Now, whence come you?

QUICKLY From the two parties, forsooth.

FALSTAFF The devil take one party and his dam the other! And so they shall be both bestowed. I have suffered more for their sakes, more than the villainous inconstancy of man's disposition is able to bear.

QUICKLY And have not they suffered? Yes, I warrant, speciously one of them. Mistress Ford, good heart, is beaten black and blue, that you cannot see a white spot about her.

FALSTAFF What tell'st thou me of black and blue? I was beaten myself into all the colors of the rainbow, and I was like to be apprehended for the witch of Brentford. But that my admirable dexterity of wit, my counterfeiting the action of an old woman, delivered me, the knave constable had set me i' the stocks, i' the common stocks, for a witch.

QUICKLY Sir, let me speak with you in your chamber. You shall hear how things go, and, I warrant, to your content. Here is a letter will say somewhat. [*She gives a letter.*] Good hearts, what ado here is to bring you together! Sure, one of you does not serve heaven well, that you are so crossed.

FALSTAFF Come up into my chamber. *Exeunt.*

✤

4.6 *Enter Fenton* [*and*] *Host.*

HOST Master Fenton, talk not to me. My mind is heavy. I will give over all.

94–95 crestfallen i.e., shriveled **95–96 forswore . . . primero** cheated in a gambling card game **105 speciously** (For *specially.*) **110 like** likely, about **120 crossed** thwarted

4.6. Location: The Garter Inn, as before.
2 give over abandon

FENTON
Yet hear me speak. Assist me in my purpose,
And, as I am a gentleman, I'll give thee
A hundred pound in gold more than your loss.

HOST I will hear you, Master Fenton, and I will at the least keep your counsel. 7

FENTON
From time to time I have acquainted you
With the dear love I bear to fair Anne Page,
Who mutually hath answered my affection,
So far forth as herself might be her chooser, 11
Even to my wish. I have a letter from her 12
Of such contents as you will wonder at,
The mirth whereof so larded with my matter 14
That neither singly can be manifested
Without the show of both. Fat Falstaff
Hath a great scene; the image of the jest 17
I'll show you here at large. [*He shows a letter.*] Hark,
good mine Host. 18
Tonight at Herne's Oak, just twixt twelve and one,
Must my sweet Nan present the Fairy Queen— 20
The purpose why, is here—in which disguise,
While other jests are something rank on foot, 22
Her father hath commanded her to slip
Away with Slender, and with him at Eton
Immediately to marry. She hath consented.
Now, sir,
Her mother, even strong against that match 27
And firm for Doctor Caius, hath appointed
That he shall likewise shuffle her away, 29
While other sports are tasking of their minds, 30
And at the deanery, where a priest attends,
Straight marry her. To this her mother's plot
She, seemingly obedient, likewise hath
Made promise to the Doctor. Now, thus it rests: 34
Her father means she shall be all in white,

7 keep your counsel keep your secret **11 So far forth** insofar **12 to** according to **14 larded . . . matter** intermingled with what concerns me **17 image** form, idea **18 at large** at length **20 present** represent **22 something rank** rather abundantly. **on foot** afoot, being devised **27 even** equally **29 shuffle** smuggle, steal **30 tasking of** busily occupying **34 it rests** matters stand

And in that habit, when Slender sees his time 36
To take her by the hand and bid her go,
She shall go with him. Her mother hath intended, 38
The better to denote her to the Doctor—
For they must all be masked and vizarded—
That quaint in green she shall be loose enrobed, 41
With ribbons pendent flaring 'bout her head;
And when the Doctor spies his vantage ripe,
To pinch her by the hand, and on that token
The maid hath given consent to go with him.

HOST
Which means she to deceive, father or mother?

FENTON
Both, my good Host, to go along with me.
And here it rests: that you'll procure the vicar
To stay for me at church twixt twelve and one,
And, in the lawful name of marrying,
To give our hearts united ceremony.

HOST
Well, husband your device. I'll to the vicar. 52
Bring you the maid, you shall not lack a priest. 53

FENTON
So shall I evermore be bound to thee.
Besides, I'll make a present recompense. *Exeunt.* 55

✤

36 habit dress **38 intended** arranged **41 quaint** decorously
52 husband manage prudently **53 Bring you** if you bring **55 present** immediate

5.1 *Enter Falstaff* [*and Mistress*] *Quickly.*

FALSTAFF Prithee, no more prattling; go. I'll hold. This 1
is the third time; I hope good luck lies in odd numbers. Away, go. They say there is divinity in odd 3
numbers, either in nativity, chance, or death. Away!

QUICKLY I'll provide you a chain, and I'll do what I can to get you a pair of horns.

FALSTAFF Away, I say! Time wears. Hold up your head, 7
and mince. [*Exit Mistress Quickly.*] 8

[*Enter*] *Ford* [*disguised*].

How now, Master Brook? Master Brook, the matter will be known tonight or never. Be you in the park about midnight, at Herne's Oak, and you shall see wonders.

FORD Went you not to her yesterday, sir, as you told 13
me you had appointed?

FALSTAFF I went to her, Master Brook, as you see, like
a poor old man, but I came from her, Master Brook,
like a poor old woman. That same knave Ford, her
husband, hath the finest mad devil of jealousy in him,
Master Brook, that ever governed frenzy. I will tell you:
he beat me grievously, in the shape of a woman; for
in the shape of man, Master Brook, I fear not Goliath 21
with a weaver's beam, because I know also life is a 22
shuttle. I am in haste. Go along with me; I'll tell you 23
all, Master Brook. Since I plucked geese, played truant, 24
and whipped top, I knew not what 'twas to be beaten 25
till lately. Follow me. I'll tell you strange things of this
knave Ford, on whom tonight I will be revenged, and
I will deliver his wife into your hand. Follow. Strange
things in hand, Master Brook! Follow. *Exeunt.*

✤

5.1. Location: The Garter Inn, as before.
1 hold persevere, keep the appointment **3 divinity** mysterious power
7 Hold up your head i.e., keep up your spirits **8 mince** trip off **13 yesterday** (Actually, the meeting appears to have been earlier this same day.) **21–22 Goliath . . . beam** (See 1 Samuel 17:7: "The staff of his [Goliath's] spear was like a weaver's beam." See also 2 Samuel 21:19. A weaver's beam is a wooden cylinder in a loom.) **22–23 life is a shuttle** (See Job 7:6: "My days are swifter than a weaver's shuttle.")
24–25 plucked . . . top i.e., committed various boyhood pranks. To whip a top is to set it spinning.

5.2 *Enter Page, Shallow,* [*and*] *Slender.*

PAGE Come, come. We'll couch i' the castle ditch till we see the light of our fairies. Remember, son Slender, my daughter.

SLENDER Ay, forsooth. I have spoke with her and we have a nayword how to know one another. I come to her in white and cry "mum," she cries "budget," and by that we know one another.

SHALLOW That's good too. But what needs either your "mum" or her "budget"? The white will decipher her well enough. It hath struck ten o'clock.

PAGE The night is dark; light and spirits will become it well. Heaven prosper our sport! No man means evil but the devil, and we shall know him by his horns. Let's away. Follow me. *Exeunt.*

✤

5.3 *Enter Mistress Page, Mistress Ford,* [*and*] *Caius.*

MRS. PAGE Master Doctor, my daughter is in green. When you see your time, take her by the hand, away with her to the deanery, and dispatch it quickly. Go before into the park. We two must go together.

CAIUS I know vat I have to do. Adieu.

MRS. PAGE Fare you well, sir. [*Exit Caius.*] My husband will not rejoice so much at the abuse of Falstaff as he will chafe at the Doctor's marrying my daughter. But 'tis no matter. Better a little chiding that a great deal of heartbreak.

MRS. FORD Where is Nan now, and her troop of fairies, and the Welsh devil Hugh?

MRS. PAGE They are all couched in a pit hard by Herne's Oak, with obscured lights, which, at the very instant of

5.2. Location: Windsor Park.
1 couch hide **5 nayword** password, watchword **6 mum, budget** (*Mum-budget* connotes silence, as in a children's game by that name.) **9 decipher** identify **11 become** suit

5.3. Location: Windsor Park, as before.
3 dispatch conclude

Falstaff's and our meeting, they will at once display to the night.

MRS. FORD That cannot choose but amaze him. 17

MRS. PAGE If he be not amazed, he will be mocked. If he be amazed, he will every way be mocked.

MRS. FORD We'll betray him finely.

MRS. PAGE
Against such lewdsters and their lechery,
Those that betray them do no treachery.

MRS. FORD The hour draws on. To the oak, to the oak!
Exeunt.

✤

5.4 *Enter Evans* [*as a satyr*] *and* [*children disguised as*] *fairies.*

EVANS Trib, trib, fairies. Come, and remember your 1
parts. Be pold, I pray you. Follow me into the pit, and when I give the watch'ords, do as I pid you. Come, come; trib, trib. *Exeunt.*

✤

5.5 *Enter Falstaff* [*disguised as Herne, wearing a buck's head*].

FALSTAFF The Windsor bell hath struck twelve; the
minute draws on. Now, the hot-blooded gods assist
me! Remember, Jove, thou wast a bull for thy Europa; 3
love set on thy horns. O powerful Love, that in some
respects makes a beast a man, in some other a man
a beast! You were also, Jupiter, a swan for the love of 6
Leda. O omnipotent Love, how near the god drew to 7
the complexion of a goose! A fault done first in the
form of a beast—O Jove, a beastly fault!—and then

17 cannot choose but is certain to. **amaze** perplex

5.4. Location: Windsor Park, as before.
1 Trib trip, move nimbly

5.5. Location: Windsor Park, as before.
3, 6–7 bull . . . Europa, swan . . . Leda (References to legends of Jupiter's disguises when engaged in various amours.)

another fault in the semblance of a fowl; think on 't, Jove, a foul fault! When gods have hot backs, what shall poor men do? For me, I am here a Windsor stag, and the fattest, I think, i' the forest. Send me a cool rut-time, Jove, or who can blame me to piss my tallow? Who comes here? My doe?

[Enter] Mistress Page [and] Mistress Ford.

MRS. FORD Sir John? Art thou there, my deer, my male deer?

FALSTAFF My doe with the black scut! Let the sky rain potatoes; let it thunder to the tune of "Greensleeves," hail kissing-comfits, and snow eringoes; let there come a tempest of provocation, I will shelter me here. *[He embraces her.]*

MRS. FORD Mistress Page is come with me, sweetheart.

FALSTAFF Divide me like a bribed buck, each a haunch. I will keep my sides to myself, my shoulders for the fellow of this walk, and my horns I bequeath your husbands. Am I a woodman, ha? Speak I like Herne the hunter? Why, now is Cupid a child of conscience; he makes restitution. As I am a true spirit, welcome! *[A noise within.]*

MRS. PAGE Alas, what noise?

MRS. FORD Heaven forgive our sins!

FALSTAFF What should this be?

MRS. FORD, MRS. PAGE Away, away! *[They run off.]*

FALSTAFF I think the devil will not have me damned, lest the oil that's in me should set hell on fire. He would never else cross me thus.

13–14 rut-time mating season **14 piss my tallow** i.e., sweat off and excrete excess fat during mating season, like a stag **18 scut** tail, pudendum **19 potatoes** i.e., sweet potatoes. (Regarded by Elizabethans as aphrodisiac.) **Greensleeves** (A popular tune; see 2.1.60, note.) **20 kissing-comfits** perfumed sweetmeats for sweetening the breath. **eringoes** candied root of a plant called sea holly. (Regarded as aphrodisiac.) **20–21 let there come** if there come **21 provocation** i.e., sexual stimulation **23 bribed** stolen (and then quickly cut up and divided by the poachers) **25 fellow of this walk** i.e., keeper of this forest, perhaps Herne himself. (Falstaff punningly suggests he will "shoulder off" or repel the forester if he makes trouble.) **26 woodman** (1) hunter (2) woman-chaser **27 is Cupid . . . conscience** i.e., Cupid is keeping faith with me **35 cross** thwart

[*Enter*] *Evans,* [*disguised as a satyr, Mistress*] *Quickly* [*as the Fairy Queen*], *Anne Page* [*and children as*] *fairies,* [*with tapers, and*] *Pistol* [*as Hobgoblin*].

QUICKLY [*as Fairy Queen*]
Fairies black, gray, green, and white,
You moonshine revelers, and shades of night, 37
You orphan heirs of fixèd destiny, 38
Attend your office and your quality. 39
Crier Hobgoblin, make the fairy oyes. 40

PISTOL [*as Hobgoblin*]
Elves, list your names. Silence, you airy toys! 41
Cricket, to Windsor chimneys shalt thou leap.
Where fires thou find'st unraked and hearths unswept, 43
There pinch the maids as blue as bilberry. 44
Our radiant Queen hates sluts and sluttery. 45

FALSTAFF
They are fairies. He that speaks to them shall die. 46
I'll wink and couch; no man their works must eye. 47
[*He lies face downward.*]

EVANS [*as a Satyr*]
Where's Bead? Go you, and where you find a maid
That, ere she sleep, has thrice her prayers said,
Raise up the organs of her fantasy; 50
Sleep she as sound as careless infancy. 51
But those as sleep and think not on their sins, 52
Pinch them, arms, legs, backs, shoulders, sides, and shins.

QUICKLY About, about!
Search Windsor Castle, elves, within and out.
Strew good luck, aufs, on every sacred room, 56

37 shades spirits **38 orphan** i.e., fatherless. (Fairies were thought to be the result of spontaneous birth.) **heirs . . . destiny** i.e., those endowed with power to fulfill destiny (?) **39 office** duty. **quality** business, particular function **40 oyes** hear ye. (The call of the public crier.) **41 list** listen for. **toys** substanceless beings **43 unraked** not raked together to last through the night **44 bilberry** a kind of blueberry **45 sluttery** sluttishness **46 He . . . die** (A widespread tradition about fairies.) **47 wink** close my eyes. **couch** lie hidden **50 Raise . . . fantasy** i.e., give her elevating and pleasant dreams **51 Sleep she** let her sleep. **careless** free of care **52 as** who **56 aufs** elves

That it may stand till the perpetual doom 57
In state as wholesome as in state 'tis fit, 58
Worthy the owner, and the owner it.
The several chairs of order look you scour 60
With juice of balm and every precious flower.
Each fair installment, coat, and several crest 62
With loyal blazon evermore be blest! 63
And nightly, meadow fairies, look you sing,
Like to the Garter's compass, in a ring. 65
Th' expressure that it bears, green let it be, 66
More fertile-fresh than all the field to see;
And *"Honi soit qui mal y pense"* write 68
In emerald tufts, flowers purple, blue, and white,
Like sapphire, pearl, and rich embroidery,
Buckled below fair knighthood's bending knee;
Fairies use flowers for their charactery. 72
Away, disperse! But till 'tis one o'clock,
Our dance of custom round about the oak
Of Herne the hunter let us not forget.

EVANS Pray you,
Lock hand in hand. Yourselves in order set;
And twenty glowworms shall our lanterns be
To guide our measure round about the tree. 79
But, stay! I smell a man of middle-earth. 80

FALSTAFF Heavens defend me from that Welsh fairy, lest he transform me to a piece of cheese! 82

[*They discover Falstaff hiding.*]

PISTOL
Vile worm, thou wast o'erlooked even in thy birth. 83

57 perpetual doom Day of Judgment **58 In state . . . fit** i.e., as healthy in condition as it is fitting in dignity **60 several . . . order** i.e., the individual stalls of the Garter knights (in Saint George's chapel at Windsor) **62 installment** stall, place or seat in which a knight is installed. **coat** coat of arms. **several crest** separate heraldic device **63 blazon** coat of arms, armorial bearings **65 compass** circle. (The garter was worn below the left knee by knights of the order.) **66 expressure** image, picture **68 Honi . . . pense** Evil to him who evil thinks. (The motto of the Order of the Garter.) **72 charactery** writing **79 measure** stately dance **80 middle-earth** i.e., the earth, the center of the universe, conceived of as between the heavens and the underworld **82 cheese** (The Welshman's favorite food; cf. 2.2.290.) **83 o'erlooked** bewitched, looked on with an evil eye

QUICKLY [*To Fairies*]
With trial-fire touch me his finger end.
If he be chaste, the flame will back descend
And turn him to no pain; but if he start, 86
It is the flesh of a corrupted heart.

PISTOL
A trial, come.

EVANS Come, will this wood take fire? 88

[*They put the tapers to his fingers, and he starts.*]

FALSTAFF O, O, O!

QUICKLY
Corrupt, corrupt, and tainted in desire!
About him, fairies. Sing a scornful rhyme,
And, as you trip, still pinch him to your time. 92

The Song.

FAIRIES
Fie on sinful fantasy!
Fie on lust and luxury! 94
Lust is but a bloody fire, 95
Kindled with unchaste desire,
Fed in heart, whose flames aspire,
As thoughts do blow them, higher and higher.
Pinch him, fairies, mutually! 99
Pinch him for his villainy.
Pinch him, and burn him, and turn him about,
Till candles and starlight and moonshine be out.

[*During this song they pinch Falstaff. Doctor*] *Caius* [*enters one way, and steals away a fairy in green*]; *Slender,* [*another way, and takes off a fairy in white; and*] *Fenton* [*enters and steals away Mistress Anne Page. A noise of hunting is heard within. Mistress Quickly, Evans, Pistol, and all the Fairies run away. Falstaff pulls off his buck's head, and rises.*]

[*Enter*] *Page, Ford,* [*Mistress Page, and Mistress Ford*].

86 turn put **88 s.d. fingers** fingertips. (The stage direction is from the quarto.) **92 still** continually **94 luxury** lechery **95 bloody fire** fire in the blood **99 mutually** jointly, in common

PAGE
Nay, do not fly. I think we have watched you now.
Will none but Herne the hunter serve your turn?

MRS. PAGE
I pray you, come, hold up the jest no higher.
Now, good Sir John, how like you Windsor wives?
[*She points to Falstaff's horns.*]
See you these, husband? Do not these fair yokes
Become the forest better than the town?

FORD Now, sir, who's a cuckold now? Master Brook, Falstaff's a knave, a cuckoldly knave; here are his horns, Master Brook. And, Master Brook, he hath enjoyed nothing of Ford's but his buck basket, his cudgel, and twenty pounds of money, which must be paid to Master Brook. His horses are arrested for it, Master Brook.

MRS. FORD Sir John, we have had ill luck; we could never meet. I will never take you for my love again, but I will always count you my deer.

FALSTAFF I do begin to perceive that I am made an ass.

FORD Ay, and an ox too. Both the proofs are extant.

FALSTAFF And these are not fairies? I was three or four times in the thought they were not fairies; and yet the guiltiness of my mind, the sudden surprise of my powers, drove the grossness of the foppery into a received belief, in despite of the teeth of all rhyme and reason, that they were fairies. See now how wit may be made a Jack-a-Lent when 'tis upon ill employment!

EVANS Sir John Falstaff, serve Got and leave your desires, and fairies will not pinse you.

FORD Well said, fairy Hugh.

EVANS And leave you your jealousies too, I pray you.

FORD I will never mistrust my wife again till thou art able to woo her in good English.

FALSTAFF Have I laid my brain in the sun and dried it,

103 watched you caught you in the act **105 hold . . . higher** maintain the jest no longer **107 fair yokes** i.e., the horns **114 arrested** seized by warrant as a security for paying **117 meet** (with a pun on *mate*) **118 deer** (with a pun on *dear*) **120 ox** i.e., fool (with reference to the ox's horns, the *proofs* that are *extant*) **124 powers** faculties. **foppery** deceit **124–125 received** accepted **125 in despite of the teeth of** in the teeth of, in defiance of **127 Jack-a-Lent** butt. (See 3.3.22, note.)

that it wants matter to prevent so gross o'erreaching as this? Am I ridden with a Welsh goat too? Shall I have a coxcomb of frieze? 'Tis time I were choked with a piece of toasted cheese.

EVANS Seese is not good to give putter. Your belly is all putter.

FALSTAFF "Seese" and "putter"! Have I lived to stand at the taunt of one that makes fritters of English? This is enough to be the decay of lust and late walking through the realm.

MRS. PAGE Why, Sir John, do you think, though we would have thrust virtue out of our hearts by the head and shoulders and have given ourselves without scruple to hell, that ever the devil could have made you our delight?

FORD What, a hodge pudding? A bag of flax?

MRS. PAGE A puffed man?

PAGE Old, cold, withered, and of intolerable entrails?

FORD And one that is as slanderous as Satan?

PAGE And as poor as Job?

FORD And as wicked as his wife?

EVANS And given to fornications, and to taverns, and sack, and wine, and metheglins, and to drinkings, and swearings and starings, pribbles and prabbles?

FALSTAFF Well, I am your theme. You have the start of me. I am dejected. I am not able to answer the Welsh flannel. Ignorance itself is a plummet o'er me. Use me as you will.

FORD Marry, sir, we'll bring you to Windsor, to one

135 wants matter lacks means **136 ridden with** mastered by **137 coxcomb** fool's cap. **frieze** kind of coarse woolen cloth, common in Wales **143 decay** ruin. **late walking** keeping late hours (in pursuit of women) **150 hodge pudding** large "pudding," or sausage, made with a medley of ingredients. **bag of flax** i.e., a large, shapeless bag **151 puffed** dropsied, corpulent **152 intolerable** excessive **154 Job** (See Job 1 for Job's sudden descent into poverty.) **155 his wife** i.e., Job's wife, who advised him to curse God (Job 2:9) **157 metheglins** spiced drink made from wort and honey, Welsh in origin **158 starings** glaring, madly raving **159 theme** i.e., subject of mirth. **start** advantage **160 dejected** cast down **161 flannel** a Welsh cloth. **plummet** (A quibble on *plumbet,* a woolen fabric, suggested by *flannel,* and *plummet,* a line for fathoming; Falstaff laments that he has been fathomed even by an ignorant Welshman.)

Master Brook, that you have cozened of money, to whom you should have been a pander. Over and above that you have suffered, I think to repay that money will be a biting affliction.

PAGE Yet be cheerful, knight. Thou shalt eat a posset tonight at my house, where I will desire thee to laugh at my wife that now laughs at thee. Tell her Master Slender hath married her daughter.

MRS. PAGE [*Aside*] Doctors doubt that. If Anne Page be my daughter, she is, by this, Doctor Caius' wife.

[*Enter Slender.*]

SLENDER Whoa, ho, ho, father Page!

PAGE Son, how now? How now, son? Have you dispatched?

SLENDER Dispatched? I'll make the best in Gloucestershire know on 't. Would I were hanged, la, else!

PAGE Of what, son?

SLENDER I came yonder at Eton to marry Mistress Anne Page, and she's a great lubberly boy. If it had not been i' the church, I would have swinged him or he should have swinged me. If I did not think it had been Anne Page, would I might never stir! And 'tis a postmaster's boy.

PAGE Upon my life, then, you took the wrong.

SLENDER What need you tell me that? I think so, when I took a boy for a girl. If I had been married to him, for all he was in woman's apparel, I would not have had him.

PAGE Why, this is your own folly. Did not I tell you how you should know my daughter by her garments?

SLENDER I went to her in white and cried "mum," and she cried "budget," as Anne and I had appointed. And yet it was not Anne but a postmaster's boy.

165 should have been were to have been **166 that** that which **168 eat** imbibe. **posset** curdled ale or wine **172 Doctors doubt that** (Proverbial; i.e., the wise are skeptical. The saying particularly applies here to Doctor Caius.) **173 this** this time **175–176 dispatched** finished the business **178 on 't** of it. **else** if I don't **181 lubberly** loutish **182 swinged** thrashed **184–185 postmaster's boy** boy of the master of the post-horses

MRS. PAGE Good George, be not angry. I knew of your purpose; turned my daughter into green; and indeed she is now with the Doctor at the deanery, and there married.

[*Enter Caius.*]

CAIUS Vere is Mistress Page? By gar, I am cozened! I ha'
married *un garçon,* a boy; *un paysan,* by gar, a boy. It 201
is not Anne Page. By gar, I am cozened.

MRS. PAGE Why, did you take her in green?

CAIUS Ay, by gar, and 'tis a boy. By gar, I'll raise all Windsor.

FORD This is strange. Who hath got the right Anne?

PAGE My heart misgives me. Here comes Master Fenton.

[*Enter Fenton and Anne Page.*]

How now, Master Fenton?

ANNE
Pardon, good Father! Good my Mother, pardon!

PAGE Now, mistress, how chance you went not with Master Slender?

MRS. PAGE
Why went you not with Master Doctor, maid?

FENTON
You do amaze her. Hear the truth of it. 214
You would have married her most shamefully,
Where there was no proportion held in love. 216
The truth is, she and I, long since contracted, 217
Are now so sure that nothing can dissolve us. 218
Th' offense is holy that she hath committed,
And this deceit loses the name of craft,
Of disobedience, or unduteous title, 221
Since therein she doth evitate and shun 222
A thousand irreligious cursèd hours
Which forcèd marriage would have brought upon her.

FORD
Stand not amazed. Here is no remedy.

201 paysan peasant, i.e., yokel **214 amaze** bewilder **216 proportion** equality **217 contracted** betrothed **218 sure** fast knit **221 unduteous title** title of unduteousness **222 evitate** avoid

In love the heavens themselves do guide the state;
Money buys lands, and wives are sold by fate.

FALSTAFF I am glad, though you have ta'en a special stand to strike at me, that your arrow hath glanced.

PAGE
Well, what remedy? Fenton, heaven give thee joy!
What cannot be eschewed must be embraced.

FALSTAFF
When night dogs run, all sorts of deer are chased.

MRS. PAGE
Well, I will muse no further. Master Fenton,
Heaven give you many, many merry days!
Good husband, let us every one go home
And laugh this sport o'er by a country fire—
Sir John and all.

FORD Let it be so. Sir John,
To Master Brook you yet shall hold your word,
For he tonight shall lie with Mistress Ford. *Exeunt.*

227 Money . . . fate (A variant of the proverb, "Marriage and hanging go by destiny.") **229 stand** concealed place for shooting **233 muse** grumble, complain

Date and Text

The Stationers' Register, the official record book of the London Company of Stationers (booksellers and printers), for January 18, 1602, carries an entry for "A booke called an excellent and pleasant conceited commedie of Sir John Faulstof and the merry wyves of Windesor," by assignment from John Busby to Arthur Johnson. Later that year, Thomas Creed printed the following quarto:

> A Most pleasaunt and excellent conceited Comedie, of Syr *Iohn Falstaffe,* and the merrie Wiues of *Windsor.* Entermixed with sundrie variable and pleasing humors, of Syr *Hugh* the Welch Knight, Iustice *Shallow,* and his wise Cousin M. *Slender.* With the swaggering vaine of Auncient *Pistoll,* and Corporall *Nym.* By *William Shakespeare.* As it hath bene diuers times Acted by the right Honorable my Lord Chamberlaines seruants. Both before her Maiestie, and else-where. LONDON Printed by T. C. [Thomas Creed] for Arthur Iohnson, and are to be sold at his shop in Powles Church-yard, at the signe of the Flower de Leuse and the Crowne. 1602.

This text is now generally regarded as a bad quarto, memorially reconstructed perhaps by the actors who played the Host and Falstaff, and shortened for touring in the provinces. A second quarto in 1619, printed by William Jaggard for Thomas Pavier, was based on it. The First Folio text of 1623, however, was taken from a manuscript evidently copied by Ralph Crane (hence the "massed entries" of characters' names at the beginnings of scenes), and based perhaps on a theatrical promptbook. It is the most authoritative text. Several interesting variant readings occur in the bad quarto, despite its unreliability, and seem to indicate original readings that were altered in the Folio version for reasons of prudence. We find "garmombles" in place of the Folio "Iermans" at 4.5.74, and "Brook" in place of the Folio "Broome" throughout as the disguise name for the jealous Ford. "Garmombles" is often interpreted as an unflattering allusion to Frederick, Count Mompelgard (see Introduction). "Brook" is a seeming dig at the family name of the powerful Henry Brooke (a descendant of Sir John

Oldcastle), eighth Lord Cobham, whose intervention probably led to the similar changing of "Oldcastle" to "Falstaff" in *Henry IV*. The quarto can also be used sparingly to correct errors and omissions in the Folio text when, as seems likely in a small number of instances, the omission looks like eye-skip in the Folio text rather than actors' or reporters' interpolations in the quarto.

On dating, two irreconcilable choices are still very much alive: 1597, when the Lord Chamberlain was elected to the Order of the Garter, and 1600–1601, after *Henry V* (1599) in which Nym had been introduced. (There is more on the Order of the Garter in the Introduction.) The Stationers' Register entry in January of 1602 provides a forward limit in time.

Textual Notes

These textual notes are not a historical collation, either of the early quartos and folios or of more recent editions; they are simply a record of departures in this edition from the copy text. The reading adopted in this edition appears in boldface, followed by the rejected reading from the copy text, i.e., the First Folio. Only major alterations in punctuation are noted. Changes in lineation are not indicated, nor are some minor and obvious typographical errors.

Abbreviations used:
F the First Folio
Q the first quarto of 1602
s.d. stage direction
s.p. speech prefix

Copy text: the First Folio.

1.1. s.d. [Entering characters are grouped at the heads of scenes throughout the play.] **41 George** Thomas **56 s.p. Shallow** Slen **131 Garter** Gater **164 careers** Car-eires **235 faul** fall **236 the 'ort** the'ord [and in a few other instances dialect has been similarly regularized]

1.3. 14 lime [Q] liue **47 well** [Q] will **51 legion** [Q: legians] legend **59 oeillades** illiads **81 o' the** ith' **82 humor** [Q] honor **93, 98 Page** [Q] Ford **94 Ford** [Q] Page

1.4. 21 whey face wee-face **41 un boîtier vert** vnboyteene verd **46 Ma** mai **fort chaud** for chando **46–47 m'en vais** man voi **47 la cour** le Court **affaire** affaires **49 à ma** au mon **53 and** [Q] aad **57–58 qu'ai-j'oublié** que ay ie oublie **63 Larron** La-roone **82 baille** ballow **99 that, . . . mind:** that I know *Ans* mind, **115 goodyear** good-ier **149 that I will** that wee will

2.1. 1 have I haue **23 i' the** with The **48 What? Thou liest!** What thou liest? **55 praised** praise **59–60 Hundredth Psalm** hundred Psalms **129–130 and . . . of it** [Q; not in F] **141 Whither** Whether [and at 3.3.139, 141] **182 gentleman.** Gentleman **199 s.p. Ford** [Q] Shal **201 Brook** [Q] Broome [and at l. 203 and elsewhere] **204 mynheers** An-heires **216 s.d. Exeunt** [at l. 223 in F]

2.2. 4 I will . . . equipage [Q; not in F] **21 honor** honoror **22, 50 [and elsewhere] God** heauen **25 you, you** you **196 jewel. That** Iewell, that **224–225 exchange** enchange

2.3. 30 Castilian Castalion **34 He is a** rhe is a **51 A word** [Q] a **56 mush** much **73 s.p. Page, Shallow, and Slender** All **77 But first** [Q; not in F]

3.1. 5 Petty-ward pittie-ward **29 God** Heauen **39 God save** [Q] 'Saue **40 God pless** [Q] 'Plesse **83 urinals** [Q] Vrinal **84–85 for . . . appointments** [Q; not in F] **99–100 Give me . . . terrestrial; so** [Q; not in F] **105 lads** Lad

3.2. 7 s.p. [and elsewhere] Mrs. Page M. Pa [used previously for Page]

3.3. 3 Robert Robin **54 By the Lord** [Q; not in F] **58 not, Nature** not Nature **62 thee there's** thee. Ther's **176 foolish** foolishion **194 By** Be

3.4. 12 s.p. Fenton [not in F] **67 Fenton** Fenter **109 s.d. Exit** Exeunt

3.5. 82 By the Lord [Q] Yes **141 s.d. Exit** Exeunt

4.1. 44 hung hing **56 Genitivo** Genitiue **64 lunatics** Lunaties **73 quae's** Ques

4.2. 51 s.p. Mrs. Page [not in F] **59 s.p. Mrs. Page** [Q] Mist. Ford **68 [and elsewhere] Brentford** Brainford **91 direct** direct direct **94–95 misuse him** misuse **106 as lief** liefe as **111 ging** gin **118 this** thi **169 not strike** strike

4.3. 1 Germans desire Germane desires **7 them** [Q] him **9 house** [Q] houses

4.4. 7 cold gold **30 ragg'd horns** rag'd-hornes **32 makes** make **42** [Q, reading "Horne" for "Herne"; not in F] **60 s.p. Mrs. Ford** Ford **65 ne'er** neu'r **72 tire** time

4.5. 28 Master my master **41 s.p. Simple** Fal **54 Thou art** [Q] Thou are **74–75 Reading . . . Colnbrook** Readins, of Maidenhead; of Cole-brooke **86 Hue** Huy [also in l. 87] **97 to say my prayers** [Q; not in F]

4.6. 39 denote deuote

5.2. 3 my daughter my

5.3. 12 Hugh Herne

5.5. 2 hot-blooded hot-bloodied **3 Jove** loue **20 hail kissing-comfits** haile-kissing Comfits **67 More** Mote **70 sapphire, pearl** Saphire-pearle **93 s.p. Fairies** [not in F] **179 what, son** what sonne **193 white** green **197 green** white **201 un garçon** oon Garsoon **un paysan** oon pesant **203 green** white **204 by** bee **By** be

Shakespeare's Sources

Any departures from the original text are noted with an asterisk and appear at the bottom of the page in boldface; original readings are in roman.

The Merry Wives of Windsor is indebted to no single source that combines the various elements found in the play: the courtship of Anne Page, the hoodwinking of Falstaff by the merry wives, the horse-stealing business, and the various "humors" portraits. Nor does any one element derive from a single source. The entire play is brilliantly improvised.

Many analogues exist to the courtship of Anne Page, for it is essentially a plot in which parents and unwelcome wooers are outwitted by resourceful young people. The Bianca-Lucentio plot of Shakespeare's own *The Taming of the Shrew* is a good enough instance. Similarly, analogues have been found to the discomfiture of Falstaff. In Ser Giovanni Fiorentino's *Il Pecorone* (Day 1, Novelle 2), for example, a student twice cuckolds the very professor who is instructing him in the art of love. Comically, the student reports back to the professor at every turn and is coached in his next move. He doesn't know that the lady is the professor's wife, but the professor begins to suspect and so follows after. On the first occasion the student escapes detection by hiding under a pile of newly washed linen. The second time he slips out the door, whereupon the neighbors arrive and, finding no intruder, berate the professor for his mad suspicions. The wife's brothers even search the linen pile at the professor's suggestion but find nothing. They thrash the professor and chain him up as a madman. Next day, intending once again to report to the professor what had happened, the student discovers the truth. This version differs markedly from Shakespeare's in that the husband is the chief comic butt. Nevertheless Shakespeare may have known it. Although *Il Pecorone* (1558) is not known to have been translated into English in the sixteenth century, Shakespeare had already used it (or some now-lost manuscript translation) as his chief source for *The Merchant of Venice*.

Certainly available to Shakespeare was a similar story, "Two Lovers of Pisa," from *Tarleton's News Out of Purgatory* (1590). In this story, as we see in the following text, the husband is again the one who is duped. An old doctor, wedded to a beautiful young wife, becomes by chance the confidential adviser of a young man who has fallen in love with the wife. The young man reports to the husband his plans and successes in detail. The lover thrice escapes detection (when warned by the lady's maid of the husband's approach) by hiding in a vat of feathers, in a false ceiling, and in an old chest full of legal documents. When on the third occasion the jealous husband sets fire to his own house, the lover is saved by the husband's order to carry out the chest of documents. At last the lover reveals his knowledge of the husband's identity, and everyone laughs at the old fool. Elsewhere, Tarleton's book has suggestive references to Robin Goodfellow and other prankish spirits that may have influenced the concluding scene of *The Merry Wives of Windsor*.

The story "Of Two Brethren and Their Wives" in *Riche His Farewell to Military Profession* (1581) features two wives, one of "light disposition" and much given to adultery, the other a tedious scold. The first wife desires to rid herself of her two erstwhile lovers, a doctor and a lawyer, in order to enjoy a new liaison with a soldier. Accordingly she pretends to encourage the lawyer's advances, but when the lawyer comes to her she feigns the approach of her husband and enjoins the lawyer to hide in a large mailbag. Meanwhile, the merry wife has arranged for the doctor to come and pick up the mailbag, on the assumption that she will be hiding in it. The doctor thus carries off the lawyer, nearly suffocating from his close confinement, into the country, where the doctor expects to enjoy his rendezvous. Instead, the soldier accosts them, cudgeling first the body in the bag and then the one who has done the laborious carrying. The lawyer is no less astonished to discover where he has arrived than is the doctor to discover what he has been carrying.

For the background of Shakespeare's horse-stealing episodes and "humors" portraits, see the Introduction to the play. The explicit comparison between Falstaff's ludicrous fate in Windsor Forest and the legend of Actaeon is ultimately indebted to Ovid's *Metamorphoses* (3, 150–304 in William Golding's translation, 1567). In this account, Actaeon, grandson of Cadmus and a mighty hunter, happens to disturb Diana and her nymphs while they are bathing naked. Transformed by the vengeful Diana into a horned stag, he is hunted to death by his own hounds.

Tarleton's News Out of Purgatory

The Tale of the Two Lovers of Pisa, and Why They Were Whipped in Purgatory With Nettles

In Pisa, a famous city of Italy, there lived a gentleman of good lineage and lands, feared[1] as well for his wealth as honored for his virtue, but indeed well thought on for both, yet the better for his riches. This gentleman had one only daughter, called Margaret, who for her beauty was liked of all and desired of many. But neither might their suits nor her own* prevail about her father's resolution, who was determined not to marry her but to such a man as should be able in abundance to maintain the excellency of her beauty. Divers young gentlemen proffered large feoffments,[2] but in vain; a maid she must be still, till at last an old doctor in the town that professed physic[3] became a suitor to her, who was a welcome man to her father in that he was one of the wealthiest men in all Pisa.

A tall stripling[4] he was and a proper youth,[5] his age about fourscore, his head as white as milk, wherein for offense's sake there was left never a tooth. But it is no matter; what he wanted[6] in person he had in the purse—which the poor gentlewoman little regarded, wishing rather to tie herself to one that might fit her content, though they lived meanly, than to him with all the wealth in Italy. But she was young and forced to follow her father's direction, who, upon large covenants,[7] was content his daughter should marry with the doctor; and whether she liked him or no, the match was made up, and in short time she was married.

The poor wench was bound to the stake, and had not only

*__own__ [so in the present text, but "owne eie" in a text also of 1590 printed for T. G. and T. N.]

1 feared held in reverence **2 feoffments** endowments of money or property **3 professed physic** followed the profession of medicine **4 tall stripling** brave youth. (Said ironically.) **5 proper youth** handsome young man. (Said ironically.) **6 wanted** lacked **7 upon large covenants** in consideration of a generous marriage contract an old impotent man but one that was so jealous as[8] none might enter into his house without suspicion nor she do anything without blame. The least glance, the smallest countenance,[9] any smile was a manifest instance to him that she thought of others better than himself. Thus he himself lived in a hell and tormented his wife in as ill perplexity.

At last it chanced that a young gentleman of the city, coming by her house and seeing her look out at her window, noting her rare and excellent proportion,[10] fell in love with her and that so extremely as his passions had no means[11] till her favor might mitigate his heartsick discontent. The young man, that was ignorant in amorous matters and had never been used to court any gentlewoman, thought to reveal his passions to some one friend that might give him counsel for the winning of her love, and thinking experience was the surest master, on a day seeing the old doctor walking in the church that was Margaret's husband, little knowing who he was, he thought this the fittest man to whom he might discover[12] his passions, for that he was old and knew much and was a physician that with his drugs might help him forward in his purposes.

So that, seeing the old man walk solitary, he joined unto him and, after a courteous salute, told him that he was to impart a matter of great import unto him,[13] wherein, if he would not only be secret but endeavor to pleasure him,[14] his pains should be every way to the full considered.

"You must imagine, gentleman," quoth Mutio, for so was the doctor's name, "that men of our profession are no blabs, but hold their secrets in their hearts' bottom. And therefore reveal what you please. It shall not only be concealed but cured, if either my art or counsel may do it."

Upon this, Lionel—so was the young gentleman called—told and discoursed unto him from point to point how he was fallen in love with a gentlewoman that was married to one of his profession; discovered her dwelling and the house; and, for that[15] he was unacquainted with the woman

8 as that **9 countenance** expression **10 proportion** shape, figure **11 means** moderation **12 discover** reveal **13 him** himself **14 pleasure him** satisfy his desire **15 for that** because

and a man little experienced in love matters, he required his favor[16] to further him with his advice.

Mutio at this motion[17] was stung to the heart, knowing it was his wife he was fallen in love withal. Yet to conceal the matter and to experience[18] his wife's chastity, and that if she played false he might be revenged on them both, he dissembled the matter and answered that he knew the woman very well and commended her highly, but said she had a churl to her husband and therefore he thought she would be the more tractable. "Try her, man," quoth he. "Faint heart never won fair lady. And if she will not be brought to the bent of your bow,[19] I will provide such a potion as shall dispatch all to your own content. And to give you further instructions for opportunity, know that her husband is forth every afternoon from three till six. Thus far I have advised you, because I pity your passions as myself being once a lover. But now I charge thee reveal it to none whomsoever, lest it do disparage my credit to meddle in amorous matters."

The young gentleman not only promised all careful secrecy but gave him hearty thanks for his good counsel, promising to meet him there the next day and tell him what news. Then he left the old man, who was almost mad for fear his wife any way should play false. He saw by experience brave men came to besiege the castle, and seeing it was in a woman's custody and had so weak a governor as himself, he doubted[20] it would in time be delivered up, which fear made him almost frantic; yet he drived of[21] the time in great torment till he might hear from his rival.

Lionello he hastes him home and suits him in his bravery[22] and goes down towards the house of Mutio, where he sees her at her window, whom he courted with a passionate look with such an humble salute as she might perceive how the gentleman was affectionate. Margaretta, looking earnestly upon him and noting the perfection of his proportion, accounted him in her eye the flower of all Pisa,

16 required his favor begged his assistance **17 motion** proposal
18 experience test **19 to the bent of your bow** i.e., within range. (An archery metaphor.) **20 doubted** feared **21 drived of** passed, endured
22 suits him in his bravery dresses himself in his finery

thinking* herself fortunate if she might have him for her friend to supply those defaults that she found in Mutio. Sundry times that afternoon he passed by her window, and he cast not up more loving looks than he received gracious favors. Which did so encourage him that the next day between three and six he went to her house and, knocking at the door, desired to speak with the mistress of the house, who, hearing by her maid's description what he was, commanded him to come in, where she entertained him with all courtesy.

The youth, that never before had given the attempt to court* a lady, began his exordium[23] with a blush, and yet went forward so well that he discoursed unto her how he loved her, and that, if it might please her so to accept of his service as of a friend ever vowed in all duty to be at her command, the care of her honor should be dearer to him than his life, and he would be ready to prize her discontent[24] with his blood at all times.

The gentlewoman was a little coy, but before they passed[25] they concluded that the next day at four of the clock he should come thither and eat a pound of cherries, which was resolved on with a *succado des labres*,[26] and so with a "loath to depart" they took their leaves. Lionello, as joyful a man as might be, hied him to the church to meet his old doctor, where he found him in his old[27] walk. "What news, sir?" quoth Mutio. "How have you sped?"[28] "Even as I can wish," quoth Lionello. "For I have been with my mistress, and have found her so tractable that I hope to make the old peasant her husband look broadheaded by a pair of brow-antlers."[29] How deep this struck into Mutio's heart, let them imagine that can conjecture what jealousy is; insomuch that the old doctor asked when should be the time. "Marry," quoth Lionello, "tomorrow at four of the clock in the afternoon. And then, Master Doctor," quoth he, "will I dub the old squire knight of the forked order."[30]

***thinking** thinkte   ***court** couet

23 exordium introduction **24 prize her discontent** i.e., redeem her displeasure **25 passed** went on about their affairs, separated **26 succado des labres** kiss **27 old** accustomed **28 sped** succeeded **29 brow-antlers** antlers growing from the forehead, i.e., cuckold's horns, a sign on a husband of his wife's infidelity **30 knight of the forked order** i.e., cuckold, wearing the badge of forked horns

Thus they passed on in chat* till it grew late, and then Lionello went home to his lodging and Mutio to his house, covering all his sorrows with a merry countenance, with full resolution to revenge them both the next day with extremity. He passed the night as patiently as he could, and the next day after dinner away he went, watching when it should be four of the clock.

At the hour justly[31] came Lionello and was entertained with all courtesy. But scarce had they kissed ere the maid cried out to her mistress that her master was at the door; for he hasted, knowing that a horn was but a little while on grafting.[32] Margaret at this alarum was amazed,[33] and yet for a shift chopped[34] Lionello into a great dryfat[35] full of feathers and sat her down close[36] to her work. By that[37] came Mutio in blowing[38] and, as though he came to look somewhat in haste, called for the keys of his chambers and looked in every place, searching so narrowly[39] in every corner of the house that he left not the very privy unsearched. Seeing he could not find him, he said nothing, but, feigning himself not well at ease, stayed at home, so that poor Lionello was fain to stay in the dryfat till the old churl was in bed with his wife; and then the maid let him out at a back door, who went home with a flea in his ear[40] to his lodging.

Well, the next day he went again to meet his doctor, whom he found in his wonted walk. "What news?" quoth Mutio. "How have you sped?" "A pox of the old slave!" quoth Lionello. "I was no sooner in and had given my mistress one kiss but the jealous ass was at the door. The maid spied him and cried her master,[41] so that the poor gentlewoman for very shift was fain[42] to put me in a dry fat of feathers that stood in an old chamber, and there I was fain to tarry while[43] he was in bed and asleep; and then the maid let me out and I departed. But it is no matter. 'Twas but a chance,[44]

***chat** that

31 justly promptly **32 a horn . . . on grafting** i.e., a cuckold's horn was within a very short time of being planted in his brows **33 amazed** thrown into consternation **34 for a shift chopped** as a desperate expedient thrust **35 dryfat** vat, cask **36 close** i.e., with concentration **37 By that** by that time **38 blowing** breathing hard **39 narrowly** carefully, closely **40 with a flea in his ear** i.e., frustrated **41 cried her master** i.e., cried out that her master was approaching **42 for very shift was fain** for a desperate expedient was obliged **43 while** until **44 a chance** a freak event and I hope to cry quittance[45] with him ere it be long." "As how?" quoth Mutio. "Marry, thus," quoth Lionello. "She sent me word by her maid this day that upon Thursday next the old churl suppeth with a patient of his a mile out of Pisa, and then I fear not but to quit[46] him for all." "It is well," quoth Mutio. "Fortune be your friend!" "I thank you," quoth Lionello. And so after a little more prattle[47] they departed.

To be short, Thursday came, and about six of the clock forth goes Mutio no further than a friend's house of his from whence he might descry who went into his house. Straight[48] he saw Lionello enter in, and after goes he, insomuch that he[49] was scarcely sitten down before the maid cried out again, "My master comes!" The goodwife, that before had provided for afterclaps,[50] had found out a privy place between two ceilings of a plancher,[51] and there she thrust Lionello; and her husband came sweating. "What news," quoth she, "drives you home again so soon, husband?" "Marry, sweet wife," quoth he, "a fearful dream that I had this night which came to my remembrance, and that was this: methought there was a villain that came secretly into my house with a naked poinard in his hand and hid himself, but I could not find the place. With that mine nose bled, and I came back.[52] And by the grace of God I will seek every corner in the house for the quiet of my mind." "Marry, I pray you, do, husband," quoth she. With that he locked in all the doors and began to search every chamber, every hole, every chest, every tub, the very well. He stabbed every featherbed through and made havoc like a madman, which made him think all was in vain, and he began to blame his eyes that thought they saw that which they did not. Upon this he rest half lunatic,[53] and all night he was very wakeful, that towards the morning he fell into a dead sleep, and then was Lionello conveyed away.

In the morning, when Mutio wakened, he thought how by

45 cry quittance i.e., get even (for the time spent in the vat) **46 quit** repay **47 prattle** chat **48 Straight** at once **49 he** i.e., Lionello **50 afterclaps** unexpected strokes that would fall if they were caught **51 a plancher** a wooden inner roof or ceiling **52 came back** i.e., came back to consciousness **53 Upon this . . . lunatic** i.e., with this he nearly went out of his mind

no means he should be able to take Lionello tardy.[54] Yet he laid in his head a most dangerous plot, and that was this. "Wife," quoth he, "I must the next Monday ride to Vicenza to visit an old patient of mine. Till my return, which will be some ten days, I will have thee stay at our little grange house[55] in the country." "Marry, very well content, husband," quoth she. With that he kissed her and was very pleasant, as though he had suspected nothing, and away he flings[56] to the church, where he meets Lionello. "What, sir?" quoth he. "What news? Is your mistress yours in possession?" "No. A plague of[57] the old slave!" quoth he. "I think he is either a witch or else works by magic. For I can no sooner enter in the doors but he is at my back, and so he was again yesternight. For I was not warm in my seat before the maid cried, "My master comes!" And then was the poor soul fain to convey me between two ceilings of a chamber in a fit place for the purpose, where I laughed heartily to myself to see how he sought every corner, ransacked every tub, and stabbed every featherbed, but in vain. I was safe enough till the morning, and then when he was fast asleep I leaped out." "Fortune frowns on you," quoth Mutio. "Ay, but I hope," quoth Lionello, "this is the last time, and now she will begin to smile; for on Monday next he rides to Vicenza, and his wife lies at a grange house a little of the town,[58] and there in his absence I will revenge all forepassed misfortunes." "God send it be so," quoth Mutio, and so took his leave.

These two lovers longed for Monday, and at last it came. Early in the morning Mutio horsed himself and his wife, his maid, and a man,[59] and no more, and away he rides to his grange house, where, after he had broke his fast, he took his leave and away towards Vicenza. He rode not far ere by a false way he returned into a thicket and there with a company of country peasants lay in an ambuscado[60] to take the young gentleman. In the afternoon comes Lionello galloping, and as soon as he came within sight of the house he sent back his horse by his boy and went easily afoot and there at

54 take Lionello tardy catch Lionello unawares **55 grange house** country house **56 flings** dashes **57 A plague of** a plague on, a plague take **58 lies . . . town** resides at a country house a little outside of town **59 man** servant **60 ambuscado** ambush

the very entry was entertained[61] by Margaret, who led him up the stairs and conveyed him into her bedchamber, saying he was welcome into so mean[62] a cottage. "But," quoth she, "now I hope fortune shall not envy the purity of our loves." "Alas, alas, mistress," cried the maid, "here is my master and a hundred men with him with bills and staves!"[63] "We are betrayed!" quoth Lionello, "and I am but a dead man." "Fear not," quoth she, "but follow me." And straight she carried him down into a low parlor[64] where stood an old rotten chest full of writings.

She put him into that and covered him with old papers and evidences[65] and went to the gate to meet her husband. "Why, Signor Mutio, what means this hurly-burly?" quoth she. "Vile and shameless strumpet as thou art, thou shalt know by and by," quoth he. "Where is thy love? All we have watched him and seen him enter in. Now," quoth he, "shall neither thy tub of feathers nor thy ceiling serve, for perish he shall with fire or else fall into my hands." "Do thy worst, jealous fool," quoth she. "I ask thee no favor." With that in a rage he beset the house round and then set fire on it. O, in what a perplexity was poor Lionello, that was shut in a chest and the fire about his ears? And how was Margaret passionate,[66] that knew her lover in such danger? Yet she made light of the matter and as one in a rage called her maid to her and said, "Come on, wench, seeing thy master, mad with jealousy, hath set the house and all my living[67] on fire, I will be revenged upon him. Help me here to lift this old chest where all his writings and deeds are. Let that burn first, and as soon as I see that on* fire I will walk towards my friends; for the old fool will be beggared[68] and I will refuse him.[69] Mutio, that knew all his obligations and statutes[70] lay there, pulled her back and bade two of his men carry the chest into the field and see it were safe, himself standing by and seeing his house burned down stick and stone. Then, quieted in his mind, he went home with his

*__on__ one

61 entertained received **62 mean** humble **63 bills and staves** poleaxes and cudgels **64 low parlor** parlor on a lower floor **65 evidences** title deeds **66 passionate** i.e., possessed with anxiety **67 living** property, wealth **68 beggared** financially ruined **69 refuse** abandon, renounce **70 obligations and statutes** i.e., contracts of money owed him and other legal documents

wife and began to flatter her,[71] thinking assuredly that he had burned her paramour, causing his chest to be carried in a cart to his house at Pisa.

Margaret, impatient,[72] went to her mother's and complained to her and to her brethren of the jealousy of her husband, who[73] maintained it* to be true and desired but a day's respite to prove it. Well, he was bidden to supper the next night at her mother's, she thinking to make her daughter and him friends again.

In the meantime he to his wonted walk in the church, and there, *praeter expectationem,*[74] he found Lionello walking. Wondering at this, he straight inquires, "What news?" "What news, Master Doctor?" quoth he, and he fell in a great laughing. "In faith, yesterday I scaped a scouring.[75] For, sirrah, I went to the grange house where I was appointed to come, and I was no sooner gotten up the chamber but the magical[76] villain her husband beset the house with bills and staves, and, that he might be sure no ceiling nor corner should shroud[77] me, he set the house on fire and so burnt it down to the ground." "Why," quoth Mutio, "and how did you escape?" "Alas," quoth he, "well fare a woman's wit![78] She conveyed me into an old chestful of writings which she knew her husband durst not burn, and so was I saved and brought to Pisa and yesternight by her maid let[79] home to my lodging."

"This," quoth he, "is the pleasantest[80] jest that ever I heard! And upon this I have a suit[81] to you. I am this night bidden forth[82] to supper. You shall be my guest. Only I will crave so much favor as, after supper for a pleasant sport, to make relation what success you have had in your loves." "For that I will not stick," quoth he.[83]

And so he carried Lionello to his mother-in-law's house with him, and discovered to his wife's brethren who he was and how at supper he would disclose the whole matter.

***it** her it

71 to flatter her to try to please her and win her favor **72 impatient** unable to put up with any more of this **73 who** i.e., the husband (?) **74 praeter expectationem** contrary to expectation **75 a scouring** i.e., a severe beating **76 magical** i.e., turning up as if by magic **77 shroud** hide **78 well fare a woman's wit** good luck to a woman's wit, thanks to a woman's wit **79 let** let go **80 pleasantest** merriest **81 suit** petition **82 bidden forth** invited **83 For that . . . quoth he** I won't hesitate to do that, said Lionello

"For," quoth he, "he knows not that I am Margaret's husband." At this all the brethren bade him welcome, and so did the mother too, and Margaret—she was kept out of sight. Suppertime being come, they fell to their victuals, and Lionello was caroused unto[84] by Mutio, who was very pleasant[85] to draw him to a merry humor that he might to the full discourse the effect and fortunes of his love.

Supper being ended, Mutio requested him to tell to the gentlemen what had happened between him and his mistress. Lionello, with a smiling countenance, began to describe his mistress, the house, and street where she dwelt, how he fell in love with her, and how he used the counsel of this doctor, who in all his affairs was his secretary. Margaret heard all this with a great fear, and when he came at the last point, she caused a cup of wine to be given him by one of her sisters wherein was a ring that he had given Margaret. As he had told how he escaped burning and was ready to confirm all for a truth, the gentlewoman drunk to him,[86] who, taking the cup and seeing the ring, having a quick wit and a reaching[87] head, spied the fetch[88] and perceived that all this while this was his lover's husband to whom he had revealed these escapes.[89]

At this, drinking the wine and swallowing the ring into his mouth, he went forward: "Gentlemen," quoth he, "how like you of my loves and my fortunes?" "Well," quoth the gentlemen, "I pray you, is it true?" "As true," quoth he, "as if I would be so simple[90] as to reveal what I did to Margaret's husband; for, know you, gentlemen, that I knew this Mutio to be her husband whom I notified[91] to be my lover, and for that[92] he was generally known through Pisa to be a jealous fool; therefore[93] with these tales I brought him into this paradise, which indeed are follies of mine own brain. For, trust me by the faith of a gentleman, I never spake to the woman, was never in her company, neither do I know her if I see her." At this they all fell in a-laughing at Mutio,

84 caroused unto toasted with wine **85 pleasant** jolly **86 drunk to him** drank a toast to him, Lionello **87 reaching** having great mental reach or capacity **88 fetch** trick **89 escapes** escapades, transgressions, breaches of chastity **90 simple** simpleminded **91 notified** intimated **92 for that** because **93 therefore** for that reason

who was ashamed that Lionello had so scoffed[94] him. But all was well; they were made friends. But the jest went so to his heart that he shortly after died, and Lionello enjoyed the lady; and for that[95] they two were the death of the old man, now are they plagued in Purgatory and he whips them with nettles.

Text based on *Tarleton's News out of Purgatory. Only Such a Jest as His Jig, Fit for Gentlemen to Laugh an Hour, etc. Published by an old companion of his, Robin Goodfellow. At London, printed for Edward White.* 1590. Another quarto appeared in the same year and with the same title, but printed for T. G. and T. N. The present text appears to be the corrected one.

94 scoffed ridiculed **95 for that** because

Further Reading

Berry, Ralph. "The Revenger's Comedy." *Shakespeare's Comedies: Explorations in Form*. Princeton, N.J.: Princeton Univ. Press, 1972. Berry calls the play a "brutal farce." The plot is a revenge action directed against Falstaff that ultimately undercuts the revengers themselves. The comic ending is thus not festive but is nonetheless satisfying as it achieves an equilibrium of the contending forces.

Bryant, J. A., Jr. "Falstaff and the Renewal of Windsor." *PMLA* 89 (1974): 296–301. For Bryant the play is a comedy of renewal in which Falstaff becomes the scapegoat for a community that exhibits many of the sexual and economic obsessions it attributes solely to him. His humiliation successfully purges the anticomic values, becoming the means by which young love triumphs over and redeems the social and psychological oppressiveness of Windsor.

Carroll, William. " 'A Received Belief': Imagination in *The Merry Wives of Windsor*." *Studies in Philology* 74 (1977): 186–215. Rev. and rpt. as "Falstaff and Ford: Forming and Reforming." *The Metamorphoses of Shakespearean Comedy*. Princeton, N.J.: Princeton Univ. Press, 1985. Carroll finds in the play thematic concerns similar to those of the major comedies. He sees *Merry Wives* as a play about the "use and abuse of imagination," and, focusing mainly on Ford and Falstaff, he explores the power of the imagination to animate, deceive, and transform.

Evans, Bertrand. "For the Love of Mockery: Approach to the Summit." *Shakespeare's Comedies*. Oxford: Clarendon Press, 1960, esp. pp. 98–117. Evans discusses the play's "extraordinary multiplicity of practices," in which virtually all characters participate in a complex dance of deceiver and deceived. The excellence of the play's formal design, Evans argues, provides a model Shakespeare would return to in his more mature comedies.

Gilbert, Allan H. *"The Merry Wives of Windsor." The Principles and Practice of Criticism*. Detroit: Wayne State

Univ. Press, 1959. Assuming the play to be an early comedy written about 1592 rather than in 1597 as many others believe (see, for example, Green below), Gilbert compares Falstaff's role with his appearances in the two parts of *Henry IV* and concludes that the play is unified and successful with Falstaff as its "moving force."

Green, William. *Shakespeare's "Merry Wives of Windsor."* Princeton, N.J.: Princeton Univ. Press, 1962. Green provides a comprehensive treatment of the text, date, and occasion of the play, arguing that it was written for the April 1597 celebration of the installation of Lord Hunsdon (newly appointed Lord Chamberlain and patron of Shakespeare's company) to the Order of the Garter.

Hinely, Jan Lawson. "Comic Scapegoats and the Falstaff of *The Merry Wives of Windsor.*" *Shakespeare Studies* 15 (1982): 37–55. Hinely observes that Falstaff differs from Shakespeare's other scapegoats, such as Malvolio or Shylock, in that he is ultimately accepted into the social harmony at the end. Falstaff acknowledges his folly, just as the citizens come to recognize that they share Falstaff's human frailties. This awareness of their common if flawed humanity permits the play to achieve the integration that preserves the comic form.

Kahn, Coppélia. " 'The Savage Yoke': Cuckoldry and Marriage." *Man's Estate: Masculine Identity in Shakespeare.* Berkeley: Univ. of California Press, 1981. Kahn discusses Falstaff's anarchic desire within a broader consideration of masculine sexual anxiety and the social and psychological implications of cuckoldry in Shakespeare's plays. According to Kahn, the mockery by the faithful and ingenious wives is a therapeutic comic agent that cures Ford's jealousy and frustrates Falstaff's lust.

Nevo, Ruth. "The Case of Falstaff and the Merry Wives." *Comic Transformations in Shakespeare*. London and New York: Methuen, 1980. Nevo convincingly argues that *The Merry Wives* is best understood in relation both to *1* and *2 Henry IV* and to Shakespeare's romantic comedies. The play preserves and transfers Falstaff's comic energy to its heroines, marking a turning point in Shakespeare's comic development that leads to the vibrant heroines of the mature comedies.

Parten, Anne. "Falstaff's Horns: Masculine Inadequacy and

Feminine Mirth in *The Merry Wives of Windsor.*" *Studies in Philology* 82 (1985): 184–199. Concerned with the way the play contains the social anxieties raised by the threats of infidelity, Parten explores the implications of Falstaff's humiliation. She argues that for the wives it is a means not only of punishing Falstaff's lust but of vindicating their chastity and rehabilitating "the concept of innocent feminine mirth."

Roberts, Jeanne Addison. *Shakespeare's English Comedy: "The Merry Wives of Windsor" in Context.* Lincoln, Nebr.: Univ. of Nebraska Press, 1979. Roberts provides an extensive commentary on the play, exploring its text, date, sources, and its place in the development of Shakespeare's comic imagination. She finds the play to be not farce but "a comedy of forgiveness," dramatically experimental but socially and morally conservative.

Steadman, John M. "Falstaff as Actaeon: A Dramatic Emblem." *Shakespeare Quarterly* 14 (1963): 231–244. Steadman explores in detail the implications of the association of the horned Falstaff with the mythical figure of Actaeon. Examining the iconographic significance of the Actaeon story, Steadman finds the play to be constructed around "familiar symbols of 'unchaste desire.'"

Photo © Martha Swope

From the 1986 New York Shakespeare Festival production of *Hamlet*, with Kevin Kline as Hamlet, directed by Liviu Ciulei at the Public Theater.

—HAMLET—

HAMLET

Introductory Material

Foreword by Joseph Papp

Introduction

Hamlet in Performance

THE PLAY

Supplementary Material

Date and Text

Textual Notes

Shakespeare's Sources

Further Reading

Foreword

Hamlet has got just about all the ingredients of exciting, interesting theater—grand soliloquies, complex philosophizing, love relationships, family conflicts, ghosts, murder, revenge, swordplay, and a great death scene where bodies pile up on the stage. Young actors want to cut their teeth on the title role, and indeed, there is no more complex and challenging role for them, partly because of the weight of all the Hamlets who have gone before—among them Edwin Booth, the nineteenth-century American player, and Laurence Olivier, the great British actor of this century.

As I've been thinking about the play recently, it has struck me that *Hamlet* is a study of death and dying. Shakespeare's preoccupation is with life and death, and in his *Hamlet* he takes the popular form of the revenge tragedy and reduces it to its most basic elements. Death is the most recurrent theme in the play. From his first appearance onstage wearing the "inky cloak" of mourning and "customary suits of solemn black" that are "but the trappings and the suits of woe," Hamlet is fundamentally contemplating death. He sustains this preoccupation throughout the play, in his soliloquies—"To die, to sleep; / To sleep, perchance to dream. Ay, there's the rub, / For in that sleep of death what dreams may come, / When we have shuffled off this mortal coil, / Must give us pause."

In the end, death is the victor. Eight people die in the course of the play, the stage is littered with bodies in the last scene, and two entire families are wiped out, two bloodlines cut off forever. Yet this bloodbath at the end doesn't really solve anything, or answer the questions that plague Hamlet and perhaps plague us. To Hamlet, who has spent the entire play thinking about it and maybe even preparing for it, death comes too soon—as it always does:

> You that look pale and tremble at this chance,
> That are but mutes or audience to this act,
> Had I but time—as this fell sergeant, Death,
> Is strict in his arrest—O, I could tell you—

Yet in the midst of death, the wonder of the theater and the wonder of life persist. In his instructions to the Players, (3.2), Hamlet gives the greatest lesson in acting ever, better than anything modern theories or teachers can offer. He counsels restraint—"Nor do not saw the air too much with your hand, thus, but use all gently"—and decorum—"Suit the action to the word, the word to the action"—and reminds the Players that the purpose of acting, "both at the first and now, was and is to hold as 'twere the mirror up to nature."

Hamlet is a play *about* the theater, about the techniques of acting. In the entire middle section, beginning with the arrival of the traveling players in Act 2, scene 2, Shakespeare is reflecting on the uses and purposes of the theater by putting them inside the play itself. And Hamlet's method, like Shakespeare's, is to use theater to further his plot—"The play's the thing / Wherein I'll catch the conscience of the King"—to answer unanswerable questions, and ultimately, perhaps, to put off the death that haunts him.

Joseph Papp

Joseph Papp gratefully acknowledges the help of Elizabeth Kirkland in preparing this Foreword.

Introduction

A recurring motif in *Hamlet* is of a seemingly healthy exterior concealing an interior sickness. Mere pretense of virtue, as Hamlet warns his mother, "will but skin and film the ulcerous place, / Whiles rank corruption, mining all within, / Infects unseen" (3.4.154–156). Polonius confesses, when he is about to use his daughter as a decoy for Hamlet, that "with devotion's visage / And pious action we do sugar o'er / The devil himself"; and his observation elicits a more anguished mea culpa from Claudius in an aside: "How smart a lash that speech doth give my conscience! / The harlot's cheek, beautied with plastering art, / Is not more ugly to the thing that helps it / Than is my deed to my most painted word" (3.1.47–54).

This motif of concealed evil and disease continually reminds us that, in both a specific and a broader sense, "Something is rotten in the state of Denmark" (1.4.90). The specific source of contamination is a poison: the poison with which Claudius has killed Hamlet's father, the poison in the players' version of this same murder, and the two poisons (envenomed sword and poisoned drink) with which Claudius and Laertes plot to rid themselves of young Hamlet. More generally, the poison is an evil nature seeking to destroy humanity's better nature, as in the archetypal murder of Abel by Cain. "O, my offense is rank, it smells to heaven," laments Claudius, "It hath the primal eldest curse upon 't, / A brother's murder" (3.3.36–38). Hamlet's father and Claudius typify what is best and worst in humanity; one is the sun-god Hyperion, the other a satyr. Claudius is a "serpent" and a "mildewed ear, / Blasting his wholesome brother" (1.5.40; 3.4.65–66). Many a person, in Hamlet's view, is tragically destined to behold his or her better qualities corrupted by "some vicious mole of nature" over which the individual seems to have no control. "His virtues else, be they as pure as grace, / As infinite as man may undergo, / Shall in the general censure take corruption / From that particular fault." The "dram of evil" pollutes "all the noble substance" (1.4.24–37). Thus poison spreads outward to infect individual persons, just as bad individuals can infect an entire court or nation.

Hamlet, his mind attuned to philosophical matters, is keenly and poetically aware of humanity's fallen condition. He is, moreover, a shrewd observer of the Danish court, one familiar with its ways and at the same time newly returned from abroad, looking at Denmark with a stranger's eyes. What particularly darkens his view of humanity, however, is not the general fact of corrupted human nature but rather Hamlet's knowledge of a dreadful secret. Even before he learns of his father's murder, Hamlet senses that there is something more deeply amiss than his mother's overhasty marriage to her deceased husband's brother. This is serious enough, to be sure, for it violates a taboo (parallel to the marriage of a widower to his deceased wife's sister, long regarded as incestuous by the English) and is thus understandably referred to as "incest" by Hamlet and his father's ghost. The appalling spectacle of Gertrude's "wicked speed, to post / With such dexterity to incestuous sheets" (1.2.156–157) overwhelms Hamlet with revulsion at carnal appetite and intensifies the emotional crisis any son would go through when forced to contemplate his father's death and his mother's remarriage. Still, the Ghost's revelation is of something far worse, something Hamlet has subconsciously feared and suspected. "O my prophetic soul! My uncle!" (1.5.42). Now Hamlet has confirming evidence for his intuition that the world itself is "an unweeded garden / That grows to seed. Things rank and gross in nature / Possess it merely" (1.2.135–137).

Something is indeed rotten in the state of Denmark. The monarch on whom the health and safety of the kingdom depend is a murderer. Yet few persons know his secret: Hamlet, Horatio only belatedly, Claudius himself, and ourselves as audience. Many ironies and misunderstandings of the play cannot be understood without a proper awareness of this gap between Hamlet's knowledge and most others' ignorance of the murder. For, according to their own lights, Polonius and the rest behave as courtiers normally behave, obeying and flattering a king whom they acknowledge as their legitimate ruler. Hamlet, for his part, is so obsessed with the secret murder that he overreacts to those around him, rejecting overtures of friendship and becoming embittered, callous, brutal, and even violent. His antisocial behavior gives the others good reason to fear him as a menace to the state. Nevertheless, we share with Hamlet a knowledge of the truth and know that he is right, whereas the others are at best unhappily deceived by their own blind complicity in evil.

Rosencrantz and Guildenstern, for instance, are boyhood friends of Hamlet but are now dependent on the favor of King Claudius. Despite their seeming concern for their onetime comrade, and Hamlet's initial pleasure in receiving them, they are faceless courtiers whose very names, like their personalities, are virtually interchangeable. "Thanks, Rosencrantz and gentle Guildenstern," says the King, and "Thanks, Guildenstern and gentle Rosencrantz," echoes the Queen (2.2.33–34). They cannot understand why Hamlet increasingly mocks their overtures of friendship, whereas Hamlet cannot stomach their subservience to the King. The secret murder divides Hamlet from them, since only he knows of it. As the confrontation between Hamlet and Claudius grows more deadly, Rosencrantz and Guildenstern, not knowing the true cause, can only interpret Hamlet's behavior as dangerous madness. The wild display he puts on during the performance of "The Murder of Gonzago" and the killing of Polonius are evidence of a treasonous threat to the crown, eliciting from them staunch assertions of the divine right of kings. "Most holy and religious fear it is / To keep those many many bodies safe / That live and feed upon Your Majesty," professes Guildenstern, and Rosencrantz reiterates the theme: "The cess of majesty / Dies not alone, but like a gulf doth draw / What's near it with it" (3.3.8–17). These sentiments of Elizabethan orthodoxy, similar to ones frequently heard in Shakespeare's history plays, are here undercut by a devastating irony, since they are spoken unwittingly in defense of a murderer. This irony pursues Rosencrantz and Guildenstern to their graves, for they are killed performing what they see as their duty to convey Hamlet safely to England. They are as ignorant of Claudius's secret orders for the murder of Hamlet in England as they are of Claudius's real reason for wishing to be rid of his stepson. That Hamlet should ingeniously remove the secret commission from Rosencrantz and Guildenstern's packet and substitute an order for their execution is ironically fitting, even though they are guiltless of having plotted Hamlet's death. "Why, man, they did make love to this employment," says Hamlet to Horatio. "They are not near my conscience. Their defeat / Does by their own insinuation grow" (5.2.57–59). They have condemned themselves, in Hamlet's eyes, by interceding officiously in deadly affairs of which they had no comprehension. Hamlet's judgment of them is harsh, and he himself appears hardened and pitiless in his role as agent in their deaths, but he is right that they have courted their own destiny.

Polonius, too, dies for meddling. It seems an unfair fate, since he wishes no physical harm to Hamlet, and is only trying to ingratiate himself with Claudius. Yet Polonius's complicity in jaded court politics is deeper than his fatuous parental sententiousness might lead one to suppose. His famous advice to his son, often quoted out of context as though it were wise counsel, is in fact a worldly gospel of self-interest and concern for appearances. Like his son, Laertes, he cynically presumes that Hamlet's affection for Ophelia cannot be serious, since princes are not free to marry ladies of the court; accordingly, Polonius obliges his daughter to return the love letters she so cherishes. Polonius's spies are everywhere, seeking to entrap Polonius's own son in fleshly sin or to discover symptoms of Hamlet's presumed lovesickness. Polonius may cut a ridiculous figure as a prattling busybody, but he is wily and even menacing in his intent. He has actually helped Claudius to the throne and is an essential instrument of royal policy. His ineffectuality and ignorance of the murder do not really excuse his guilty involvement.

Ophelia is more innocent than her father and brother, and more truly affectionate toward Hamlet. She earns our sympathy because she is caught between the conflicting wills of the men who are supremely important to her—her lover, her father, her brother. Obedient by instinct and training to patriarchal instruction, she is unprepared to cope with divided authority and so takes refuge in passivity. Nevertheless her pitiable story suggests that weak-willed acquiescence is poisoned by the evil to which it surrenders. However passively, Ophelia becomes an instrument through which Claudius attempts to spy on Hamlet. She is much like Gertrude, for the Queen has yielded to Claudius's importunity without ever knowing fully what awful price Claudius has paid for her and for the throne. The resemblance between Ophelia and Gertrude confirms Hamlet's tendency to generalize about feminine weakness—"frailty, thy name is woman" (1.2.146)—and prompts his misogynistic outburst against Ophelia when he concludes she, too, is spying on him. His rejection of love and friendship (except for Horatio's) seems paranoid in character and yet is at least partially justified by the fact that so many of the court are in fact conspiring to learn what he is up to.

Their oversimplification of his dilemma and their facile analyses vex Hamlet as much as their meddling. When they presume to diagnose his malady, the courtiers actually reveal more about themselves than about Hamlet—something we as readers and viewers might well bear in mind. Rosencrantz and Guildenstern think in political terms, reflecting their own ambitious natures, and Hamlet takes mordant delight in leading them on. "Sir, I lack advancement," he mockingly answers Rosencrantz's questioning as to the cause of his distemper. Rosencrantz is immediately taken in: "How can that be, when you have the voice of the King himself for your succession in Denmark?" (3.2.338–341). Actually Hamlet does hold a grudge against Claudius for having "Popped in between th' election and my hopes" (5.2.65) by using the Danish custom of "election" by the chief lords of the realm to deprive young Hamlet of the succession that would normally have been his. Nevertheless, it is a gross oversimplification to suppose that political frustration is the key to Hamlet's sorrow, and to speculate thus is presumptuous. "Why, look you now, how unworthy a thing you make of me!" Hamlet protests to Rosencrantz and Guildenstern. "You would play upon me, you would seem to know my stops, you would pluck out the heart of my mystery" (3.2.362–365). Yet the worst offender in these distortions of complex truth is Polonius, whose diagnosis of lovesickness appears to have been inspired by recollections of Polonius's own far-off youth. ("Truly in my youth I suffered much extremity for love, very near this," 2.2.189–191.) Polonius's fatuous complacency in his own powers of analysis—"If circumstances lead me, I will find / Where truth is hid, though it were hid indeed / Within the center" (2.2.157–159)—reads like a parody of Hamlet's struggle to discover what is true and what is not.

Thus, although Hamlet may seem to react with excessive bitterness toward those who are set to watch over him, the corruption he decries in Denmark is both real and universal. "The time is out of joint," he laments. "O cursèd spite / That ever I was born to set it right!" (1.5.197–198). How is he to proceed in setting things right? Ever since the nineteenth century it has been fashionable to discover reasons for Hamlet's delaying his revenge. The basic Romantic approach is to find a defect, or tragic flaw, in Hamlet himself. In Coleridge's words, Hamlet suffers from "an overbalance in the contemplative faculty" and is "one who vacillates from sensibility and procrastinates from thought, and loses the power of action in the energy of resolve." More recent psychological critics, such as Freud's disciple Ernest Jones, still seek answers to the Romantics' question by explaining Hamlet's failure of will. In Jones's interpretation, Hamlet is the victim of an Oedipal trauma; he has longed unconsciously to possess his mother and for that very reason cannot bring himself to punish the hated uncle who has supplanted him in his incestuous and forbidden desire. Such interpretations suggest, among other things, that Hamlet continues to serve as a mirror in which analysts who would pluck out the heart of his mystery see an image of their own concerns—just as Rosencrantz and Guildenstern read politics, and Polonius lovesickness, into Hamlet's distress.

We can ask, however, not only whether the explanations for Hamlet's supposed delay are valid but whether the question they seek to answer is itself valid. Is the delay unnecessary or excessive? The question did not even arise until the nineteenth century. Earlier audiences were evidently satisfied that Hamlet must test the Ghost's credibility, since apparitions can tell half-truths to deceive men, and that once Hamlet has confirmed the Ghost's word, he proceeds as resolutely as his canny adversary allows. More recent criticism, perhaps reflecting a modern absorption in existentialist philosophy, has proposed that Hamlet's dilemma is a matter not of personal failure but of the absurdity of action itself in a corrupt world. Does what Hamlet is asked to do make any sense, given the bestial nature of man and the impossibility of knowing what is right? In part it is a matter of style: Claudius's Denmark is crassly vulgar, and to combat this vulgarity on its own terms seems to require the sort of bad histrionics Hamlet derides in actors who mouth their lines or tear a passion to tatters. Hamlet's dilemma of action can best be studied in the play by comparing him with various characters who are obliged to act in situations similar to his own and who respond in meaningfully different ways.

Three young men—Hamlet, Laertes, and Fortinbras—are called upon to avenge their fathers' violent deaths. Ophelia, too, has lost a father by violent means, and her madness and death are another kind of reaction to such a loss. The responses of Laertes and Fortinbras offer implicit lessons to Hamlet, and in both cases the lesson seems to be of the futility of positive and forceful action. Laertes thinks he has received an unambiguous mandate to revenge, since Hamlet has undoubtedly slain Polonius and helped to deprive Ophelia of her sanity. Accordingly Laertes comes back to Denmark in a fury, stirring the rabble with his demagoguery and spouting Senecan rant about dismissing conscience "to the profoundest pit" in his quest for vengeance (4.5.135). When Claudius asks what Laertes would do to Hamlet "To show yourself in deed your father's son / More than in words," Laertes fires back: "To cut his throat i' the church" (4.7.126–127). This resolution is understandable. The pity is, however, that Laertes has only superficially identified the murderer in the case. He is too easily deceived by Claudius because he has accepted easy and fallacious conclusions, and so is doomed to become a pawn in Claudius's sly maneuverings. Too late he sees his error and must die for it, begging and receiving Hamlet's forgiveness. Before we accuse Hamlet of thinking too deliberately before acting, we must consider that Laertes does not think enough.

Fortinbras of Norway, as his name implies ("strong in

arms"), is one who believes in decisive action. At the beginning of the play we learn that his father has been slain in battle by old Hamlet, and that Fortinbras has collected an army to win back by force the territory fairly won by the Danes in that encounter. Like Hamlet, young Fortinbras does not succeed his father to the throne, but must now contend with an uncle-king. When this uncle, at Claudius's instigation, forbids Fortinbras to march against the Danes, and rewards him for his restraint with a huge annual income and a commission to fight the Poles instead, Fortinbras sagaciously welcomes the new opportunity. He pockets the money, marches against Poland, and waits for occasion to deliver Denmark as well into his hands. Clearly this is more of a success story than that of Laertes, and Hamlet does after all give his blessing to the "election" of Fortinbras to the Danish throne. Fortinbras is the man of the hour, the representative of a restored political stability. Yet Hamlet's admiration for this man on horseback is qualified by a profound reservation. The spectacle of Fortinbras marching against Poland "to gain a little patch of ground / That hath in it no profit but the name" prompts Hamlet to berate himself for inaction, but he cannot ignore the absurdity of the effort. "Two thousand souls and twenty thousand ducats / Will not debate the question of this straw." The soldiers will risk their very lives "Even for an eggshell" (4.4.19–54). It is only one step from this view of the vanity of ambitious striving to the speculation that great Caesar or Alexander, dead and turned to dust, may one day produce the loam or clay with which to stop the bunghole of a beer barrel. Fortinbras epitomizes the ongoing political order after Hamlet's death, but is that order of any consequence to us after we have imagined with Hamlet the futility of most human endeavor?

To ask such a question is to seek passive or self-abnegating answers to the riddle of life, and Hamlet is attuned to such inquiries. Even before he learns of his father's murder, he contemplates suicide, wishing "that the Everlasting had not fixed / His canon 'gainst self-slaughter" (1.2.131–132). As with the alternative of action, other characters serve as foils to Hamlet, revealing both the attractions and perils of withdrawal. Ophelia is destroyed by meekly acquiescing in others' desires. Whether she commits suicide is uncertain, but the very possibility reminds us that Hamlet has considered and reluctantly rejected this despairing path as forbidden by Christian teaching. He has also playacted at the madness to which Ophelia succumbs. Gertrude identifies herself with Ophelia and, like her, has surrendered her will to male aggressiveness. We suspect she knows little of the actual murder but dares not think how deeply she may be implicated. Her death may possibly be a suicide also, one of atonement. A more attractive alternative to decisive action for Hamlet is acting in the theater, and he is full of advice to the visiting players. The play they perform before Claudius at Hamlet's request and with some lines added by him, a play consciously archaic in style, offers to the Danish court a kind of heightened reflection of itself, a homiletic artifact rendering in conventional terms the taut anxieties and terrors of murder for the sake of ignoble passion. We are not surprised when, in his conversations with the players, Hamlet openly professes his admiration for the way in which art holds "the mirror up to nature, to show virtue her feature, scorn her own image, and the very age and body of the time his form and pressure" (3.2.22–24). Hamlet admires the dramatist's ability to transmute raw human feeling into tragic art, depicting and ordering reality as Shakespeare's play of *Hamlet* does for us. Yet playacting is also, Hamlet recognizes, a self-indulgent escape for him, a way of unpacking his heart with words, of verbalizing his situation without doing something to remedy it. Acting and talking remind him too much of Polonius, who was an actor in his youth and who continues to be, like Hamlet, an inveterate punster.

Of the passive responses in the play, the stoicism of Horatio is by far the most attractive to Hamlet. "More an antique Roman than a Dane" (5.2.343), Horatio is, as Hamlet praises him, immune to flattering or to opportunities for cheap self-advancement. He is "As one, in suffering all, that suffers nothing, / A man that Fortune's buffets and rewards / Hast ta'en with equal thanks" (3.2.65–67). Such a person has a sure defense against the worst that life can offer. Hamlet can trust and love Horatio as he can no one else. Yet even here there are limits, for Horatio's skeptical and Roman philosophy cuts him off from a Christian and metaphysical overview. "There are more things in heaven and earth, Horatio, / Than are dreamt of in your philosophy" (1.5.175–176). After they have beheld together the skulls of Yorick's graveyard, Horatio seemingly does not share with Hamlet the exulting Christian perception that, although human life is indeed vain, providence will reveal a pattern transcending human sorrow.

Hamlet's path must lie somewhere between the rash suddenness of Laertes or the canny resoluteness of Fortinbras on the one hand, and the passivity of Ophelia or Gertrude and the stoic resignation of Horatio on the other, but he alternates between action and inaction, finding neither satisfactory. The Ghost has commanded Hamlet to revenge, but has not explained how this is to be done; indeed, Gertrude is to be left passively to heaven and her conscience. If this method will suffice for her (and Christian wisdom taught that such a purgation was as thorough as it was sure), why not for Claudius? If Claudius must be killed, should it be while he is at his sin rather than at his prayers? The play is full of questions, stemming chiefly from the enigmatic commands of the Ghost. "Say, why is this? Wherefore? What should we do?" (1.4.57). Hamlet is not incapable of action. He shows unusual strength and cunning on the pirate ship, or in his duel with Laertes ("I shall win at the odds"; 5.2.209–210), or especially in his slaying of Polonius—an action hardly characterized by "thinking too precisely on th' event" (4.4.42). Here is forthright action of the sort Laertes espouses. Yet when the corpse behind his mother's arras turns out to be Polonius rather than Claudius, Hamlet knows he has offended heaven. Even if Polonius deserves what he got, Hamlet has made himself into a cruel "scourge" of providence who must himself suffer retribution as well as deal it out. Swift action has not accomplished what the Ghost commanded.

The Ghost in fact does not appear to speak for providence. His message is of revenge, a pagan concept basic to all primitive societies but at odds with Christian teaching. His wish that Claudius be sent to hell and that Gertrude be more gently treated is not the judgment of an impartial deity but the emotional reaction of a murdered man's restless spirit. This is not to say that Hamlet is being tempted to perform a damnable act, as he fears is possible, but that the Ghost's command cannot readily be reconciled with a complex and balanced view of justice. If Hamlet were to spring on Claudius in the fullness of his vice and cut his throat, we would pronounce Hamlet a murderer. What Hamlet believes he has learned instead is that he must become the instrument of providence according to *its* plans, not his own. After his return from England, he senses triumphantly that all will be for the best if he allows an unseen power to decide the time and place for his final act. Under these conditions, rash action will be right. "Rashly, / And praised be rashness for it—let us know / Our indiscretion sometimes serves us well / When our deep plots do pall, and that should learn us / There's a divinity that shapes our ends, / Rough-hew them how we will" (5.2.6–11). Passivity, too, is now a proper course, for Hamlet puts himself wholly at the disposal of providence. What had seemed so impossible when Hamlet tried to formulate his own design now proves elementary once he trusts to heaven's justice. Rashness and passivity are perfectly fused. Hamlet is revenged without having to commit premeditated murder and is relieved of his painful existence without having to commit suicide.

The circumstances of *Hamlet*'s catastrophe do indeed accomplish all that Hamlet desires, by a route so circuitous that no man could ever have foreseen or devised it. Polonius's death, as it turns out, was instrumental after all, for it led to Laertes's angry return to Denmark and the challenge to a duel. Every seemingly unrelated event has its place; "There is special providence in the fall of a sparrow" (5.2.217–218). Repeatedly the characters stress the role of seeming accident leading to just retribution. Horatio sums up a pattern "Of accidental judgments, casual slaughters . . . And, in this upshot, purposes mistook / Fall'n on th' inventors' heads" (5.2.384–387). Laertes confesses himself "a woodcock to mine own springe" (l. 309). As Hamlet had said earlier, of Rosencrantz and Guildenstern, " 'tis the sport to have the enginer / Hoist with his own petard" (3.4.213–214). Thus, too, Claudius's poisoned cup, intended for Hamlet, kills the Queen for whom Claudius had done such evil in order to acquire.

In its final resolution, *Hamlet* incorporates a broader conception of justice than its revenge formula seemed at first to make possible. Yet in its origins *Hamlet* is a revenge story, and these traditions have left some residual savagery in the play. In the *Historia Danica* of Saxo Grammaticus, 1180–1208, and in the rather free translation of Saxo into French by François de Belleforest, *Histoires Tragiques* (1576), Hamlet is cunning and bloodily resolute throughout. He kills an eavesdropper without a qualm during the interview with his mother and exchanges letters on his way to England with characteristic shrewdness. Ultimately he returns to Denmark, sets fire to his uncle's hall, slays its courtly inhabitants, and claims his rightful throne from a grateful people. The Ghost, absent in this account, may well have been supplied by Thomas Kyd, author of *The Spanish Tragedy* (c. 1587) and seemingly of a lost *Hamlet* play in existence by 1589. *The Spanish Tragedy* bears many resemblances to our *Hamlet* and suggests what the lost *Hamlet* may well have contained: a sensational murder, a Senecan Ghost demanding revenge, the avenger hampered by court intrigue, his resort to a feigned madness, his difficulty in authenticating the ghostly vision. A German version of *Hamlet,* called *Der bestrafte Brudermord* (1710), based seemingly on the older *Hamlet,* includes such details as the play within the play, the sparing of the King at his prayers in order to damn his soul, Ophelia's madness, the fencing match with poisoned swords and poisoned drink, and the final catastrophe of vengeance and death. Similarly, the early pirated first quarto of *Hamlet* (1603) offers some passages seemingly based on the older play by Kyd.

Although this evidence suggests that Shakespeare received most of the material for the plot intact, his transformation of that material was nonetheless immeasurable. To be sure, Kyd's *The Spanish Tragedy* contains many rhetorical passages on the inadequacy of human justice, but the overall effect is still sensational and the outcome is a triumph for the pagan spirit of revenge. So, too, with the many revenge plays of the 1590s and 1600s that Kyd's dramatic genius had inspired, including Shakespeare's own *Titus Andronicus* (c. 1589–1591). *Hamlet,* written in about 1599–1601 (it is not mentioned by Francis Meres in his *Palladis Tamia: Wit's Treasury,* in 1598, and was entered in the Stationers'

Register, the official record book of the London Company of Stationers [booksellers and printers], in 1602), is unparalleled in its philosophical richness. Its ending is truly cathartic, for Hamlet dies not as a bloodied avenger but as one who has affirmed the tragic dignity of man. His courage and faith, maintained in the face of great odds, atone for the dismal corruption in which Denmark has festered. His resolutely honest inquiries have taken him beyond the revulsion and doubt that express so eloquently, among other matters, the fearful response of Shakespeare's own generation to a seeming breakdown of established political, theological, and cosmological beliefs. Hamlet finally perceives that "if it be not now, yet it will come," and that "The readiness is all" (5.2.219–220). This discovery, this revelation of necessity and meaning in Hamlet's great reversal of fortune, enables him to confront the tragic circumstance of his life with understanding and heroism, and to demonstrate the triumph of the human spirit even in the moment of his catastrophe.

Such an assertion of the individual will does not lessen the tragic waste with which *Hamlet* ends. Hamlet is dead, the great promise of his life forever lost. Few others have survived. Justice has seemingly been fulfilled in the deaths of Claudius, Gertrude, Rosencrantz and Guildenstern, Polonius, Laertes, and perhaps even Ophelia, but in a wild and extravagant way, as though Justice herself, more vengeful than providential, were unceasingly hungry for victims. Hamlet, the minister of that justice, has likewise grown indifferent to the spilling of blood, even if he submits himself at last to the will of a force he recognizes as providential. Denmark faces the kind of political uncertainty with which the play began. However much Hamlet may admire Fortinbras's resolution, the prince of Norway seems an alien choice for Denmark, even an ironic one. Horatio sees so little point in outliving the catastrophe of this play that he would choose death were it not that he must draw his breath in pain to ensure that Hamlet's story is truly told. Still, that truth has been rescued from oblivion. Amid the ruin of the final scene we share the artist's vision, through which we struggle to interpret and give order to the tragedy of human existence.

Hamlet in Performance

Most people who know their Shakespeare are surprised and disconcerted by the cutting of so much material when they see the otherwise admirable film of *Hamlet* by Laurence Olivier (1948): all of Fortinbras's role and the negotiations with Norway, all of Rosencrantz and Guildenstern, a good deal of Act 4, and still more. The supposed reason, that a film must cut heavily to make room for visual material and to be of an acceptable length, is of course true in the main, but it overlooks the long history of the play in production. Many of the same cuts prevailed from the Restoration until the later nineteenth century as a way not only of shortening a long play but of highlighting the role of Hamlet for the lead actor.

Even in its own day, *Hamlet* (with Richard Burbage in the title role) must have been heavily cut at times, especially in the fourth act; the so-called "bad" quarto of 1603, though garbled presumably by the actors who helped to prepare a stolen copy, appears to be the report of a shortened acting text. During the Restoration, the published edition of the version that diarist Samuel Pepys saw and enjoyed five times during the 1660s was offered to its readers with a warning: "This play being too long to be conveniently acted, such places as might be least prejudicial to the plot or sense are left out upon the stage." This *Hamlet,* prepared by William Davenant and acted by Thomas Betterton at intervals from 1661 until 1709, took out some 841 lines, including most of Fortinbras's part, Polonius's advice to Laertes and instructions to Reynaldo, much of Rosencrantz and Guildenstern, the scene between Hamlet and Fortinbras's captain (4.4), and other matters, though the appearance of Fortinbras at the end was retained. Betterton's successor, Robert Wilks (active in the part until 1732), went further by removing Fortinbras from Act 5 entirely, concluding the play instead with Horatio's farewell and eulogy to his sweet prince. This ending was the only one to be seen onstage from 1732 until 1897. An operatic version of *Ham-*

let in 1712 bore even less resemblance to Shakespeare's play, taking its inspiration chiefly from Saxo Grammaticus's *Historia Danica,* the twelfth-century narrative from which the history of Hamlet derives.

David Garrick used for a time a version of the Wilks text from which he also cut Hamlet's soliloquy in Act 3, scene 3 ("Now might I do it pat"), and all mention of Hamlet's voyage to England. Then, in 1772, Garrick ventured to remove nearly all of the fifth act. In Garrick's *Hamlet* the protagonist never embarks for England at all, having been prevented from doing so by the arrival of Fortinbras. Laertes, hindered by a shipwreck, never gets to France. Laertes is a more estimable person than in Shakespeare's play, since he is entirely freed of the taint of plotting to kill Hamlet with a poisoned sword. Hamlet and Laertes fight, but without the poisoned sword; Claudius tries to intervene in the duel of the two young men and is slain by Hamlet, who then runs on Laertes's sword and falls, exchanging forgiveness with Laertes as he dies. Horatio, after attempting to kill Laertes in revenge, is persuaded by the dying Hamlet to accept the will of Heaven and to rule jointly with Laertes. The gravediggers are not needed since Ophelia's burial is omitted. Gertrude is not poisoned but, we are told, is in a trance and on the verge of madness from remorse. We do not hear of the execution of Rosencrantz and Guildenstern. Garrick's intention in all this novelty seems to have been to ennoble Hamlet by pairing him in the last scene with a worthy opponent, by reducing the bloodthirstiness of his killing of Claudius, and by omitting all mention of his part in the deaths of Rosencrantz and Guildenstern. Classical decorum was served by excising long gaps of time and travels into other lands, and by refusing to countenance the comedy of the gravediggers in a tragic play. Garrick restored the soliloquy, "How all occasions do inform against me" (4.4), again enhancing the role of the protagonist, along with some of Polonius's advice to his son.

Garrick called his alterations of *Hamlet* "the most imprudent thing" he had ever done. Although he was "sanguine" about the results, modern audiences are more likely to feel that the Romantic era was not an auspicious time for the play. In addition to Garrick's adaptations, German actors in England at the end of the century provided the play a happy ending, with the Queen's illness warning Hamlet in time. John Philip Kemble, acting the part at various times from 1783 to 1817, cut the play back to a series of well-known theatrical vignettes, prompting critic William Hazlitt, while admiring Kemble's acting, to complain that *Hamlet* is better not acted at all.

As if to confirm Hazlitt's worry about the often empty theatricality of the nineteenth-century stage, a chief preoccupation of the time was to add pictorial splendor to stage production. Actor-manager William Charles Macready, at the Theatre Royal, Covent Garden, in 1838, won praise for "a series of glorious pictures." Charles Kean, who in 1838 had a great success acting Hamlet at the Theatre Royal, Drury Lane, lavished money and attention on the fortress of Elsinore in his own production of the play at the Princess's Theatre in 1850. With his customary passion for scenic elaboration, he showed, among other scenes, a guard platform of the castle and then another part of the platform, the royal court of Denmark and its handsome theater, the Queen's "closet" or chamber, and the ancient burying ground in the vicinity of the palace to which Ophelia was borne with impressive if maimed rites. Nineteenth-century illustrations of Shakespeare's plays testify to the age's interest in pictorially detailed reproductions of the play within the play, Ophelia's mad scenes, and other emotionally powerful moments in *Hamlet*. Ophelia became a favorite subject for the visual arts, in the theater and out of it, perhaps because she was so well suited, like the Lady of Shalott, for pre-Raphaelite interpretation. Pictorialism in the theater thus accentuated the trend, already seen among earlier actor-managers, toward highlighting the play's great iconic moments at the expense of the rest of the text. Ophelia became a leading role for actresses such as Julia Bennett, Ellen and Kate Terry, and Helena Modjeska, especially in the latter part of the century.

Charles Fechter appears to have been the first, at the Princess's Theatre in 1861 and then at the Lyceum Theatre in 1864, to garb Hamlet, not in the velvet and lace of an English aristocrat, but in Viking attire appropriate to the play's Danish setting, which was matched with surrounding sets in primitive and medieval decor. His Hamlet was flaxen-haired; Rosencrantz and Guildenstern were bearded Scandinavian warriors in coarse cross-gartered leggings. Much of the action took place in the large main hall of Elsinore. Edwin Booth in America and Henry Irving in England were the leading Hamlets of the late century. Booth appeared first in the role in 1853, in San Francisco, winning instant renown both in America and abroad. In 1861, in Manchester, England, he played Hamlet to Irving's Laertes. Three years later, Irving himself first played Hamlet, and he continued in the role until 1885. Irving chose a decor of the fifth or sixth century, though not rigorously so, and his costumes retained the attractiveness of Elizabethan dress. Hamlet's first encounter with his father's ghost was impressively set in a remote part of the battlements of the castle, amid massive rocks, with the soft light of the moon filtering onto the Ghost while hints of dawn appeared over the expanse of water to be seen in the background. The scenes on the battlements showed the illuminated windows of the palace in the distance. The funeral of Ophelia took place on a hill near the palace. Irving portrayed Hamlet as deeply affected by his love for Ophelia in a sentimental interpretation that gave prominence to Ellen Terry's Ophelia. Irving made little of Hamlet's voyage to England or his encounter with Fortinbras's captain, devoting most of Act 4 instead to Ophelia's mad scenes and ending the play with "The rest is silence." These descriptions suggest the extent to which the actor-managers of that age turned to favorite scenes for their theatrical effects, cutting much else to accommodate the ponderous scenery.

Beginning with Johnston Forbes-Robertson's restoration of the Fortinbras ending in 1897, as he was encouraged to do by George Bernard Shaw, twentieth-century directors have generally shown more respect for the play's text than did their predecessors. In 1881 at St. George's Hall, William Poel had already directed a group of amateur actors in a reading of the play based on the 1603 quarto, and in 1899 Frank Benson staged an uncut composite Folio-quarto text (something never acted in Shakespeare's day) at the Shakespeare Memorial Theatre in Stratford-upon-Avon. These were experimental performances and not rigorously followed since, though Harcourt Williams directed John Gielgud, in his first Hamlet, at the Old Vic in 1930 in a production without significant cuts. Tyrone Guthrie successfully produced the play in an uncut version, which starred Laurence Olivier, at the Old Vic in 1937, and Olivier himself directed an uncut *Hamlet* at London's National Theatre starring Peter O'Toole in 1963. At the same time, directors have turned away from the nineteenth-century sentimental focus on Hamlet's delay and love melancholy to explore ironies and conflict. *Hamlet* in modern dress, beginning with H. K. Ayliff at the Birmingham Repertory Theatre in 1925, and followed by, among others, Tyrone Guthrie in 1938, in another production at the Old Vic, explored the existential challenges of the play in the context of Europe between two world wars. Freudian interpretation played a major part in Laurence Olivier's film version of 1948, as evidenced by the camera's preoccupation with Gertrude's bedroom and by the intimate scenes between mother and son. Olivier's cutting and rearranging of scenes owed much to eighteenth- and nineteenth-century traditions, as we have seen, even while his camera work found new ways to explore the mysterious and labyrinthine corridors of Elsinore Castle. Joseph Papp's *Hamlet* (Public Theater, New York, 1968) went beyond Olivier in an iconoclastic and deliberately overstated psychological shocker, featuring a manacled Hamlet (Martin Sheen) in a coffinlike cradle at the feet of Claudius's and Gertrude's bed. Grigori Kozintsev's Russian film version of 1964, using a cut text by Boris Pasternak, found eloquent visual metaphors for Hamlet's story in the recurring images of stone, iron, fire, sea, and earth. Among the best Hamlets have been those of Richard Burton (in 1964 at New York's Lunt-Fontanne Theater, directed by John Gielgud), Nicol Williamson (in 1969 at the Roundhouse Theatre in London, directed by Tony Richardson), and Derek Jacobi (in 1979 at the Old Vic, directed by Toby Robertson) portraying the protagonist as tough and serious, capable of great tenderness in friendship and love, but faced with hard necessities and pursuing them with fierce energy. Jacobi's *Hamlet* can be seen today in the generally excellent BBC Shakespeare television version, with a strong supporting cast.

The melancholic, pale, introspective Hamlet of Kemble and the lovestruck prince of Irving have thus seldom been seen on the modern stage, though Olivier recalls the tradition of melancholy with his voice-over soliloquies, and John Gielgud's sonorously spectral voice excels in the meditations on suicide. Today the play is more apt to be satirical, even funny at times, presenting a mordant and disillusioned view of life at court, as in Peter Hall's 1965 production at Stratford-upon-Avon, or in Jonathan Miller's more austere *Hamlet* at London's Warehouse Theatre in 1982, both of which disturbingly portray a world in which, as Hall wrote, "politics are a game and a lie." Polonius, long regarded in the theater as little more than a "tedious old fool," as Hamlet calls him, can reveal in the performance of Felix Alymer or Hume Cronyn or Del Close a canniness in political survival that fits well with his matter-of-fact and philistine outlook. The scenes at court lend themselves to contemporary political analogies: Claudius can become the Great Communicator, adept at public relations gimmicks, the darling of television, while the creatures who bustle about him do their part to "sell" Claudius to a complacent court and a thoroughly skeptical Hamlet. As the outsider, Hamlet today is likely to be the rebel, a misfit, and justly so in view of what he sees in Denmark. Stacy Keach, in Gerald Freedman's *Hamlet* at New York's Delacorte Theater in 1972, was neither melancholy nor vulnerable; rather he was bitter, shrewd, and, as the drama critic of *The New York Times* wrote, "hell-bent for revenge."

As originally staged, *Hamlet* must have made good use of the handsome Globe Theatre, where it first appeared. Without scenery, the Globe offered its spectators an impressive evocation of an idea of order, with the heavens above, hell below the trapdoor, and on the main stage the ceremonial magnificence of the court of Denmark. Claudius's appearances are generally marked by ritual, by the presence of throne and crown, by an entourage of obsequious courtiers. Yet Claudius has vitiated all this seeming order by his secret murder, and Hamlet's presence is a continual reminder that all is not well in Denmark. Hamlet attires himself in black, acts strangely, insults the courtiers, makes fun of their ceremoniousness, and prefers to be alone or on the battlements with Horatio and the guard. The Ghost's appearances, too, betoken inversions of order; he reminds us of a greatness now lost to Denmark as he stalks on, usually through the stage doors, in armor and in the full light of day during an afternoon performance at the Globe. He also speaks from beneath the stage. The performance of Hamlet's "Mousetrap" play is a scene of rich panoply that is once again undercut by the secret act of murder now represented in a mimetic drama for the King who is also a murderer. The final scene of *Hamlet* is Claudius's most splendid moment of presiding over the court, until it is suddenly his last moment. The play's reflexive interest in the art of theater is everywhere evident, in Hamlet's instructions to the players and in his appraisal of himself as an actor, as he explores all that it might mean to "act." Shakespeare wrote *Hamlet* with his own theater very much in mind, and, paradoxically, precisely this has allowed it to remain so vibrantly alive in the modern theater.

—HAMLET—

[*Dramatis Personae*

GHOST *of Hamlet, the former King of Denmark*
CLAUDIUS, *King of Denmark, the former King's brother*
GERTRUDE, *Queen of Denmark, widow of the former King and now wife of Claudius*
HAMLET, *Prince of Denmark, son of the late King and of Gertrude*

POLONIUS, *councillor to the King*
LAERTES, *his son*
OPHELIA, *his daughter*
REYNALDO, *his servant*

HORATIO, *Hamlet's friend and fellow student*

VOLTIMAND, CORNELIUS, ROSENCRANTZ, GUILDENSTERN, OSRIC, A GENTLEMAN, A LORD, *members of the Danish court*

BERNARDO, FRANCISCO, MARCELLUS, *officers and soldiers on watch*

FORTINBRAS, *Prince of Norway*
CAPTAIN *in his army*

Three or Four PLAYERS, *taking the roles of* PROLOGUE, PLAYER KING, PLAYER QUEEN, *and* LUCIANUS
Two MESSENGERS
FIRST SAILOR
Two CLOWNS, *a gravedigger and his companion*
PRIEST
FIRST AMBASSADOR *from England*

Lords, Soldiers, Attendants, Guards, other Players, Followers of Laertes, other Sailors, another Ambassador or Ambassadors from England

SCENE: *Denmark*]

1.1 *Enter Bernardo and Francisco, two sentinels, [meeting].*

BERNARDO Who's there?
FRANCISCO
Nay, answer me. Stand and unfold yourself. 2
BERNARDO Long live the King!
FRANCISCO Bernardo?
BERNARDO He.
FRANCISCO
You come most carefully upon your hour.
BERNARDO
'Tis now struck twelve. Get thee to bed, Francisco.
FRANCISCO
For this relief much thanks. 'Tis bitter cold,
And I am sick at heart.
BERNARDO Have you had quiet guard?
FRANCISCO Not a mouse stirring.
BERNARDO Well, good night.
If you do meet Horatio and Marcellus,
The rivals of my watch, bid them make haste. 14

Enter Horatio and Marcellus.

FRANCISCO
I think I hear them.—Stand, ho! Who is there?
HORATIO Friends to this ground. 16
MARCELLUS And liegemen to the Dane. 17
FRANCISCO Give you good night. 18
MARCELLUS
O, farewell, honest soldier. Who hath relieved you?
FRANCISCO
Bernardo hath my place. Give you good night.
Exit Francisco.
MARCELLUS Holla! Bernardo!
BERNARDO Say, what, is Horatio there?
HORATIO A piece of him.

1.1. Location: Elsinore castle. A guard platform.
2 me (Francisco emphasizes that *he* is the sentry currently on watch.) **unfold yourself** reveal your identity **14 rivals** partners **16 ground** country, land **17 liegemen to the Dane** men sworn to serve the Danish king **18 Give** i.e., may God give

BERNARDO
Welcome, Horatio. Welcome, good Marcellus.
HORATIO
What, has this thing appeared again tonight?
BERNARDO I have seen nothing.
MARCELLUS
Horatio says 'tis but our fantasy, 27
And will not let belief take hold of him
Touching this dreaded sight twice seen of us.
Therefore I have entreated him along 30
With us to watch the minutes of this night, 31
That if again this apparition come
He may approve our eyes and speak to it. 33
HORATIO
Tush, tush, 'twill not appear.
BERNARDO Sit down awhile,
And let us once again assail your ears,
That are so fortified against our story,
What we have two nights seen.
HORATIO Well, sit we down, 37
And let us hear Bernardo speak of this.
BERNARDO Last night of all, 39
When yond same star that's westward from the pole 40
Had made his course t' illume that part of heaven 41
Where now it burns, Marcellus and myself,
The bell then beating one—

Enter Ghost.

MARCELLUS
Peace, break thee off! Look where it comes again!
BERNARDO
In the same figure like the King that's dead.
MARCELLUS
Thou art a scholar. Speak to it, Horatio. 46
BERNARDO
Looks 'a not like the King? Mark it, Horatio. 47

27 fantasy imagination **30 along** i.e., to come along **31 watch** i.e., keep watch during **33 approve** corroborate **37 What** i.e., with what **39 Last . . . all** i.e., this *very* last night. (Emphatic.) **40 pole** polestar, north star **41 his** its. **illume** illuminate **46 scholar** one learned enough to know how to question a ghost properly **47 'a** he

HORATIO
Most like. It harrows me with fear and wonder.
BERNARDO
It would be spoke to.
MARCELLUS Speak to it, Horatio. 49
HORATIO
What art thou that usurp'st this time of night, 50
Together with that fair and warlike form
In which the majesty of buried Denmark 52
Did sometime march? By heaven, I charge thee speak! 53
MARCELLUS
It is offended.
BERNARDO See, it stalks away.
HORATIO
Stay! Speak, speak! I charge thee, speak! *Exit Ghost.*
MARCELLUS 'Tis gone and will not answer.
BERNARDO
How now, Horatio? You tremble and look pale.
Is not this something more than fantasy?
What think you on 't? 59
HORATIO
Before my God, I might not this believe
Without the sensible and true avouch 61
Of mine own eyes.
MARCELLUS Is it not like the King?
HORATIO As thou art to thyself.
Such was the very armor he had on
When he the ambitious Norway combated. 65
So frowned he once when, in an angry parle, 66
He smote the sledded Polacks on the ice. 67
'Tis strange.
MARCELLUS
Thus twice before, and jump at this dead hour, 69
With martial stalk hath he gone by our watch.
HORATIO
In what particular thought to work I know not, 71

49 It . . . to (It was commonly believed that a ghost could not speak until spoken to.) **50 usurp'st** wrongfully takes over **52 buried Denmark** the buried King of Denmark **53 sometime** formerly **59 on 't** of it **61 sensible** confirmed by the senses. **avouch** warrant, evidence **65 Norway** King of Norway **66 parle** parley **67 sledded** traveling on sleds. **Polacks** Poles **69 jump** exactly **71 to work** i.e., to collect my thoughts and try to understand this

But in the gross and scope of mine opinion 72
This bodes some strange eruption to our state.

MARCELLUS
Good now, sit down, and tell me, he that knows, 74
Why this same strict and most observant watch
So nightly toils the subject of the land, 76
And why such daily cast of brazen cannon 77
And foreign mart for implements of war, 78
Why such impress of shipwrights, whose sore task 79
Does not divide the Sunday from the week.
What might be toward, that this sweaty haste 81
Doth make the night joint-laborer with the day?
Who is 't that can inform me?

HORATIO
That can I;
At least, the whisper goes so. Our last king,
Whose image even but now appeared to us,
Was, as you know, by Fortinbras of Norway,
Thereto pricked on by a most emulate pride, 87
Dared to the combat; in which our valiant Hamlet—
For so this side of our known world esteemed him— 89
Did slay this Fortinbras; who by a sealed compact 90
Well ratified by law and heraldry
Did forfeit, with his life, all those his lands
Which he stood seized of to the conqueror; 93
Against the which a moiety competent 94
Was gagèd by our king, which had returned 95
To the inheritance of Fortinbras
Had he been vanquisher, as, by the same covenant 97
And carriage of the article designed, 98
His fell to Hamlet. Now, sir, young Fortinbras,
Of unimprovèd mettle hot and full, 100

72 gross and scope general drift **74 Good now** (An expression denoting entreaty or expostulation.) **76 toils** causes to toil. **subject** subjects **77 cast** casting **78 mart** buying and selling **79 impress** impressment, conscription **81 toward** in preparation **87 Thereto . . . pride** (Refers to old Fortinbras, not the Danish King.) **pricked on** incited. **emulate** emulous, ambitious **89 this . . . world** i.e., all Europe, the Western world **90 sealed** certified, confirmed **93 seized** possessed **94 Against the** in return for. **moiety competent** sufficient portion **95 gagèd** engaged, pledged **97 covenant** i.e., the *sealed compact* of l. 90 **98 carriage** import, bearing. **article designed** article or clause drawn up or prearranged **100 unimprovèd** unrestrained, undisciplined

Hath in the skirts of Norway here and there
Sharked up a list of lawless resolutes
For food and diet to some enterprise
That hath a stomach in 't, which is no other—
As it doth well appear unto our state—
But to recover of us, by strong hand
And terms compulsatory, those foresaid lands
So by his father lost. And this, I take it,
Is the main motive of our preparations,
The source of this our watch, and the chief head
Of this posthaste and rummage in the land.

BERNARDO

I think it be no other but e'en so.
Well may it sort that this portentous figure
Comes armèd through our watch so like the King
That was and is the question of these wars.

HORATIO

A mote it is to trouble the mind's eye.
In the most high and palmy state of Rome,
A little ere the mightiest Julius fell,
The graves stood tenantless and the sheeted dead
Did squeak and gibber in the Roman streets;
As stars with trains of fire and dews of blood,
Disasters in the sun; and the moist star
Upon whose influence Neptune's empire stands
Was sick almost to doomsday with eclipse.
And even the like precurse of feared events,
As harbingers preceding still the fates
And prologue to the omen coming on,
Have heaven and earth together demonstrated
Unto our climatures and countrymen.

101 skirts outlying regions, outskirts **102 Sharked up** got together in irregular fashion. **list** i.e., troop. **resolutes** desperadoes **103 For food and diet** i.e., they are to serve as *food,* or means, *to some enterprise* **104 stomach** (1) a spirit of daring (2) an appetite that is fed by the *lawless resolutes* **110 head** source **111 rummage** bustle, commotion **113 sort** suit **115 question** focus of contention **116 mote** speck of dust **117 palmy** flourishing **119 sheeted** shrouded **121 As** (This abrupt transition suggests that matter is possibly omitted between ll. 120 and 121.) **122 Disasters** unfavorable signs or aspects. **moist star** i.e., moon, governing tides **123 Neptune** god of the sea. **stands** depends **124 sick . . . doomsday** (See Matthew 24:29 and Revelation 6:12.) **125 precurse** heralding, foreshadowing **126 harbingers** forerunners. **still** continually **127 omen** calamitous event **129 climatures** regions

Enter Ghost.

But soft, behold! Lo, where it comes again! 130
I'll cross it, though it blast me. (*It spreads his arms.*)
  Stay, illusion! 131
If thou hast any sound or use of voice,
Speak to me!
If there be any good thing to be done
That may to thee do ease and grace to me,
Speak to me!
If thou art privy to thy country's fate,
Which, happily, foreknowing may avoid, 138
O, speak!
Or if thou hast uphoarded in thy life
Extorted treasure in the womb of earth,
For which, they say, you spirits oft walk in death,
Speak of it! (*The cock crows.*) Stay and speak!—
  Stop it, Marcellus.

MARCELLUS
Shall I strike at it with my partisan? 144

HORATIO Do, if it will not stand. [*They strike at it.*]

BERNARDO 'Tis here!

HORATIO 'Tis here! [*Exit Ghost.*]

MARCELLUS 'Tis gone.
We do it wrong, being so majestical,
To offer it the show of violence,
For it is as the air invulnerable,
And our vain blows malicious mockery.

BERNARDO
It was about to speak when the cock crew.

HORATIO
And then it started like a guilty thing
Upon a fearful summons. I have heard
The cock, that is the trumpet to the morn, 156
Doth with his lofty and shrill-sounding throat
Awake the god of day, and at his warning,
Whether in sea or fire, in earth or air,
Th' extravagant and erring spirit hies 160

130 soft i.e., enough, break off **131 cross** stand in its path, confront. **blast** wither, strike with a curse **s.d. his** its **138 happily** haply, perchance **144 partisan** long-handled spear **156 trumpet** trumpeter **160 extravagant and erring** wandering beyond bounds. (The words have similar meaning.)

To his confine; and of the truth herein
This present object made probation. 162

MARCELLUS
It faded on the crowing of the cock.
Some say that ever 'gainst that season comes 164
Wherein our Savior's birth is celebrated,
This bird of dawning singeth all night long,
And then, they say, no spirit dare stir abroad;
The nights are wholesome, then no planets strike, 168
No fairy takes, nor witch hath power to charm, 169
So hallowed and so gracious is that time. 170

HORATIO
So have I heard and do in part believe it.
But, look, the morn in russet mantle clad
Walks o'er the dew of yon high eastward hill.
Break we our watch up, and by my advice
Let us impart what we have seen tonight
Unto young Hamlet; for upon my life,
This spirit, dumb to us, will speak to him.
Do you consent we shall acquaint him with it,
As needful in our loves, fitting our duty?

MARCELLUS
Let's do 't, I pray, and I this morning know
Where we shall find him most conveniently.

Exeunt.

✣

1.2

Flourish. Enter Claudius, King of Denmark, Gertrude the Queen, [*the*] *Council, as Polonius and his son Laertes, Hamlet, cum aliis* [*including Voltimand and Cornelius*].

KING
Though yet of Hamlet our dear brother's death
The memory be green, and that it us befitted
To bear our hearts in grief and our whole kingdom

162 probation proof **164 'gainst** just before **168 strike** destroy by evil influence **169 takes** bewitches **170 gracious** full of grace

1.2. Location: The castle.
s.d. as i.e., such as, including. **cum aliis** with others **1 our** my. (The royal "we"; also in the following lines.)

To be contracted in one brow of woe,
Yet so far hath discretion fought with nature
That we with wisest sorrow think on him
Together with remembrance of ourselves.
Therefore our sometime sister, now our queen, 8
Th' imperial jointress to this warlike state, 9
Have we, as 'twere with a defeated joy—
With an auspicious and a dropping eye, 11
With mirth in funeral and with dirge in marriage,
In equal scale weighing delight and dole— 13
Taken to wife. Nor have we herein barred
Your better wisdoms, which have freely gone
With this affair along. For all, our thanks.
Now follows that you know young Fortinbras, 17
Holding a weak supposal of our worth, 18
Or thinking by our late dear brother's death
Our state to be disjoint and out of frame,
Colleaguèd with this dream of his advantage, 21
He hath not failed to pester us with message
Importing the surrender of those lands 23
Lost by his father, with all bonds of law, 24
To our most valiant brother. So much for him.
Now for ourself and for this time of meeting.
Thus much the business is: we have here writ
To Norway, uncle of young Fortinbras—
Who, impotent and bedrid, scarcely hears 29
Of this his nephew's purpose—to suppress
His further gait herein, in that the levies, 31
The lists, and full proportions are all made 32
Out of his subject; and we here dispatch 33
You, good Cornelius, and you, Voltimand,
For bearers of this greeting to old Norway,
Giving to you no further personal power
To business with the King more than the scope

8 sometime former **9 jointress** woman possessing property with her husband **11 With . . . eye** with one eye smiling and the other weeping **13 dole** grief **17 know** be informed (that) **18 weak supposal** low estimate **21 Colleaguèd with** joined to, allied with. **dream . . . advantage** illusory hope of success. (His only ally is this hope.) **23 Importing** pertaining to **24 bonds** contracts **29 impotent** helpless **31 His** i.e., Fortinbras's. **gait** proceeding **31–33 in that . . . subject** since the levying of troops and supplies is drawn entirely from the King of Norway's own subjects

Of these dilated articles allow. [*He gives a paper.*]
Farewell, and let your haste commend your duty.

CORNELIUS, VOLTIMAND
In that, and all things, will we show our duty.

KING
We doubt it nothing. Heartily farewell.
[*Exeunt Voltimand and Cornelius.*]
And now, Laertes, what's the news with you?
You told us of some suit; what is 't, Laertes?
You cannot speak of reason to the Dane
And lose your voice. What wouldst thou beg, Laertes,
That shall not be my offer, not thy asking?
The head is not more native to the heart,
The hand more instrumental to the mouth,
Than is the throne of Denmark to thy father.
What wouldst thou have, Laertes?

LAERTES
My dread lord,
Your leave and favor to return to France,
From whence though willingly I came to Denmark
To show my duty in your coronation,
Yet now I must confess, that duty done,
My thoughts and wishes bend again toward France
And bow them to your gracious leave and pardon.

KING
Have you your father's leave? What says Polonius?

POLONIUS
H'ath, my lord, wrung from me my slow leave
By laborsome petition, and at last
Upon his will I sealed my hard consent.
I do beseech you, give him leave to go.

KING
Take thy fair hour, Laertes. Time be thine,
And thy best graces spend it at thy will!

38 dilated set out at length **39 commend** recommend to friendly remembrance. (Their haste will impress the King with their attention to duty.) **41 nothing** not at all **44 the Dane** the Danish king **45 lose your voice** waste your speech **47 native** closely connected, related **48 instrumental** serviceable **51 leave and favor** kind permission **56 leave and pardon** permission to depart **58 H'ath** he has **60 sealed** (as if sealing a legal document). **hard** reluctant **62 Take thy fair hour** enjoy your time of youth **63 And . . . will** and may your finest qualities guide the way you choose to spend your time

But now, my cousin Hamlet, and my son— 64
HAMLET
A little more than kin, and less than kind. 65
KING
How is it that the clouds still hang on you?
HAMLET
Not so, my lord. I am too much in the sun. 67
QUEEN
Good Hamlet, cast thy nighted color off, 68
And let thine eye look like a friend on Denmark. 69
Do not forever with thy vailèd lids 70
Seek for thy noble father in the dust.
Thou know'st 'tis common, all that lives must die, 72
Passing through nature to eternity.
HAMLET
Ay, madam, it is common.
QUEEN
If it be,
Why seems it so particular with thee? 75
HAMLET
Seems, madam? Nay, it is. I know not "seems."
'Tis not alone my inky cloak, good Mother,
Nor customary suits of solemn black, 78
Nor windy suspiration of forced breath, 79
No, nor the fruitful river in the eye, 80
Nor the dejected havior of the visage, 81
Together with all forms, moods, shapes of grief, 82
That can denote me truly. These indeed seem,
For they are actions that a man might play.
But I have that within which passes show;
These but the trappings and the suits of woe.

64 cousin any kin not of the immediate family **65 A little . . . kind** i.e., closer than an ordinary nephew (since I am stepson), and yet more separated in natural feeling (with pun on *kind* meaning "affectionate" and "natural," "lawful." This line is often read as an aside, but it need not be. The King chooses perhaps not to respond to Hamlet's cryptic and bitter remark.) **67 the sun** i.e., the sunshine of the King's royal favor (with pun on *son*) **68 nighted color** (1) mourning garments of black (2) dark melancholy **69 Denmark** the King of Denmark **70 vailèd lids** lowered eyes **72 common** of universal occurrence. (But Hamlet plays on the sense of "vulgar" in l. 74.) **75 particular** personal **78 customary** (1) socially conventional (2) habitual with me **79 suspiration** sighing **80 fruitful** abundant **81 havior** expression **82 moods** outward expressions of feeling

KING
'Tis sweet and commendable in your nature, Hamlet,
To give these mourning duties to your father.
But you must know your father lost a father,
That father lost, lost his, and the survivor bound
In filial obligation for some term
To do obsequious sorrow. But to persever 92
In obstinate condolement is a course 93
Of impious stubbornness. 'Tis unmanly grief.
It shows a will most incorrect to heaven,
A heart unfortified, a mind impatient, 96
An understanding simple and unschooled. 97
For what we know must be and is as common
As any the most vulgar thing to sense, 99
Why should we in our peevish opposition
Take it to heart? Fie, 'tis a fault to heaven,
A fault against the dead, a fault to nature,
To reason most absurd, whose common theme
Is death of fathers, and who still hath cried, 104
From the first corpse till he that died today, 105
"This must be so." We pray you, throw to earth
This unprevailing woe and think of us 107
As of a father; for let the world take note,
You are the most immediate to our throne, 109
And with no less nobility of love
Than that which dearest father bears his son
Do I impart toward you. For your intent 112
In going back to school in Wittenberg, 113
It is most retrograde to our desire, 114
And we beseech you bend you to remain 115
Here in the cheer and comfort of our eye,
Our chiefest courtier, cousin, and our son.

QUEEN
Let not thy mother lose her prayers, Hamlet.
I pray thee, stay with us, go not to Wittenberg.

92 obsequious suited to obsequies or funerals. **persever** persevere **93 condolement** sorrowing **96 unfortified** i.e., against adversity **97 simple** ignorant **99 As . . . sense** as the most ordinary experience **104 still** always **105 the first corpse** (Abel's) **107 unprevailing** unavailing **109 most immediate** next in succession **112 impart toward** i.e., bestow my affection on. **For** as for **113 to school** i.e., to your studies. **Wittenberg** famous German university founded in 1502 **114 retrograde** contrary **115 bend you** incline yourself

HAMLET

I shall in all my best obey you, madam. 120

KING

Why, 'tis a loving and a fair reply.
Be as ourself in Denmark. Madam, come.
This gentle and unforced accord of Hamlet
Sits smiling to my heart, in grace whereof 124
No jocund health that Denmark drinks today 125
But the great cannon to the clouds shall tell,
And the King's rouse the heaven shall bruit again, 127
Respeaking earthly thunder. Come away. 128

Flourish. Exeunt all but Hamlet.

HAMLET

O, that this too too sullied flesh would melt, 129
Thaw, and resolve itself into a dew!
Or that the Everlasting had not fixed
His canon 'gainst self-slaughter! O God, God, 132
How weary, stale, flat, and unprofitable
Seem to me all the uses of this world! 134
Fie on 't, ah fie! 'Tis an unweeded garden
That grows to seed. Things rank and gross in nature
Possess it merely. That it should come to this! 137
But two months dead—nay, not so much, not two.
So excellent a king, that was to this 139
Hyperion to a satyr, so loving to my mother 140
That he might not beteem the winds of heaven 141
Visit her face too roughly. Heaven and earth,
Must I remember? Why, she would hang on him
As if increase of appetite had grown
By what it fed on, and yet within a month—
Let me not think on 't; frailty, thy name is woman!—
A little month, or ere those shoes were old 147
With which she followed my poor father's body,

120 in all my best to the best of my ability **124 to** i.e., at. **grace** thanksgiving **125 jocund** merry **127 rouse** drinking of a draft of liquor. **bruit again** loudly echo **128 thunder** i.e., of trumpet and kettledrum, sounded when the King drinks; see 1.4.8–12 **129 sullied** defiled. (The early quartos read *sallied*, the Folio *solid*.) **132 canon** law **134 all the uses** the whole routine **137 merely** completely **139 to** in comparison to **140 Hyperion** Titan sun-god, father of Helios. **satyr** a lecherous creature of classical mythology, half-human but with a goat's legs, tail, ears, and horns **141 beteem** allow **147 or ere** even before

Like Niobe, all tears, why she, even she—
O God, a beast, that wants discourse of reason,
Would have mourned longer—married with my uncle,
My father's brother, but no more like my father
Than I to Hercules. Within a month,
Ere yet the salt of most unrighteous tears
Had left the flushing in her gallèd eyes,
She married. O, most wicked speed, to post
With such dexterity to incestuous sheets!
It is not, nor it cannot come to good.
But break, my heart, for I must hold my tongue.

Enter Horatio, Marcellus, and Bernardo.

HORATIO
Hail to your lordship!

HAMLET
I am glad to see you well.
Horatio!—or I do forget myself.

HORATIO
The same, my lord, and your poor servant ever.

HAMLET
Sir, my good friend; I'll change that name with you.
And what make you from Wittenberg, Horatio?
Marcellus.

MARCELLUS My good lord.

HAMLET
I am very glad to see you. [*To Bernardo.*] Good even, sir.—
But what in faith make you from Wittenberg?

HORATIO
A truant disposition, good my lord.

HAMLET
I would not hear your enemy say so,
Nor shall you do my ear that violence
To make it truster of your own report
Against yourself. I know you are no truant.

149 Niobe Tantalus' daughter, Queen of Thebes, who boasted that she had more sons and daughters than Leto; for this, Apollo and Artemis, children of Leto, slew her fourteen children. She was turned by Zeus into a stone that continually dropped tears. **150 wants . . . reason** lacks the faculty of reason **155 gallèd** irritated, inflamed **157 incestuous** (In Shakespeare's day, the marriage of a man like Claudius to his deceased brother's wife was considered incestuous.) **163 change** exchange (i.e., the name of friend) **164 make** do

But what is your affair in Elsinore?
We'll teach you to drink deep ere you depart.

HORATIO
My lord, I came to see your father's funeral.

HAMLET
I prithee, do not mock me, fellow student;
I think it was to see my mother's wedding.

HORATIO
Indeed, my lord, it followed hard upon. 179

HAMLET
Thrift, thrift, Horatio! The funeral baked meats 180
Did coldly furnish forth the marriage tables. 181
Would I had met my dearest foe in heaven 182
Or ever I had seen that day, Horatio! 183
My father!—Methinks I see my father.

HORATIO
Where, my lord?

HAMLET In my mind's eye, Horatio.

HORATIO
I saw him once. 'A was a goodly king. 186

HAMLET
'A was a man. Take him for all in all,
I shall not look upon his like again.

HORATIO
My lord, I think I saw him yesternight.

HAMLET Saw? Who?

HORATIO My lord, the King your father.

HAMLET The King my father?

HORATIO
Season your admiration for a while 193
With an attent ear till I may deliver, 194
Upon the witness of these gentlemen,
This marvel to you.

HAMLET For God's love, let me hear!

HORATIO
Two nights together had these gentlemen,
Marcellus and Bernardo, on their watch,
In the dead waste and middle of the night,

179 hard close **180 baked meats** meat pies **181 coldly** i.e., as cold leftovers **182 dearest** closest (and therefore deadliest) **183 Or ever** before **186 'A** he **193 Season your admiration** restrain your astonishment **194 attent** attentive

Been thus encountered. A figure like your father,
Armèd at point exactly, cap-à-pie, 201
Appears before them, and with solemn march
Goes slow and stately by them. Thrice he walked
By their oppressed and fear-surprisèd eyes
Within his truncheon's length, whilst they, distilled 205
Almost to jelly with the act of fear, 206
Stand dumb and speak not to him. This to me
In dreadful secrecy impart they did,
And I with them the third night kept the watch,
Where, as they had delivered, both in time,
Form of the thing, each word made true and good,
The apparition comes. I knew your father;
These hands are not more like.

HAMLET
But where was this?

MARCELLUS
My lord, upon the platform where we watch.

HAMLET
Did you not speak to it?

HORATIO
My lord, I did,
But answer made it none. Yet once methought
It lifted up its head and did address 217
Itself to motion, like as it would speak; 218
But even then the morning cock crew loud, 219
And at the sound it shrunk in haste away
And vanished from our sight.

HAMLET
'Tis very strange.

HORATIO
As I do live, my honored lord, 'tis true,
And we did think it writ down in our duty
To let you know of it.

HAMLET
Indeed, indeed, sirs. But this troubles me.
Hold you the watch tonight?

ALL
We do, my lord.

HAMLET Armed, say you?
ALL Armed, my lord.
HAMLET From top to toe?

201 at point correctly in every detail. **cap-à-pie** from head to foot **205 truncheon** officer's staff. **distilled** dissolved **206 act** action, operation **217–218 did . . . speak** began to move as though it were about to speak **219 even then** at that very instant

ALL My lord, from head to foot.
HAMLET Then saw you not his face?
HORATIO
O, yes, my lord, he wore his beaver up. 232
HAMLET What looked he, frowningly? 233
HORATIO
A countenance more in sorrow than in anger.
HAMLET Pale or red?
HORATIO Nay, very pale.
HAMLET And fixed his eyes upon you?
HORATIO Most constantly.
HAMLET I would I had been there.
HORATIO It would have much amazed you.
HAMLET Very like, very like. Stayed it long?
HORATIO
While one with moderate haste might tell a hundred. 242
MARCELLUS, BERNARDO Longer, longer.
HORATIO Not when I saw 't.
HAMLET His beard was grizzled—no? 245
HORATIO
It was, as I have seen it in his life,
A sable silvered.
HAMLET I will watch tonight. 247
Perchance 'twill walk again.
HORATIO I warrant it will.
HAMLET
If it assume my noble father's person,
I'll speak to it though hell itself should gape
And bid me hold my peace. I pray you all,
If you have hitherto concealed this sight,
Let it be tenable in your silence still, 253
And whatsoever else shall hap tonight,
Give it an understanding but no tongue.
I will requite your loves. So, fare you well.
Upon the platform twixt eleven and twelve
I'll visit you.
ALL Our duty to your honor.

232 beaver visor on the helmet **233 What** how **242 tell** count
245 grizzled gray **247 sable silvered** black mixed with white
253 tenable held tightly

HAMLET
Your loves, as mine to you. Farewell.
Exeunt [*all but Hamlet*].
My father's spirit in arms! All is not well.
I doubt some foul play. Would the night were come! 261
Till then sit still, my soul. Foul deeds will rise,
Though all the earth o'erwhelm them, to men's eyes.
Exit.

✣

1.3 *Enter Laertes and Ophelia, his sister.*

LAERTES
My necessaries are embarked. Farewell.
And, sister, as the winds give benefit
And convoy is assistant, do not sleep 3
But let me hear from you.
OPHELIA Do you doubt that?
LAERTES
For Hamlet, and the trifling of his favor,
Hold it a fashion and a toy in blood, 6
A violet in the youth of primy nature, 7
Forward, not permanent, sweet, not lasting, 8
The perfume and suppliance of a minute— 9
No more.
OPHELIA No more but so?
LAERTES Think it no more.
For nature crescent does not grow alone 11
In thews and bulk, but as this temple waxes 12
The inward service of the mind and soul
Grows wide withal. Perhaps he loves you now, 14
And now no soil nor cautel doth besmirch 15
The virtue of his will; but you must fear, 16

261 doubt suspect

1.3. Location: Polonius's chambers.
3 convoy is assistant means of conveyance are available **6 toy in blood** passing amorous fancy **7 primy** in its prime, springtime **8 Forward** precocious **9 suppliance** supply, filler **11 crescent** growing, waxing **12 thews** bodily strength. **temple** i.e., body **14 Grows wide withal** grows along with it **15 soil** blemish. **cautel** deceit **16 will** desire

His greatness weighed, his will is not his own.
For he himself is subject to his birth.
He may not, as unvalued persons do,
Carve for himself, for on his choice depends
The safety and health of this whole state,
And therefore must his choice be circumscribed
Unto the voice and yielding of that body
Whereof he is the head. Then if he says he loves you,
It fits your wisdom so far to believe it
As he in his particular act and place
May give his saying deed, which is no further
Than the main voice of Denmark goes withal.
Then weigh what loss your honor may sustain
If with too credent ear you list his songs,
Or lose your heart, or your chaste treasure open
To his unmastered importunity.
Fear it, Ophelia, fear it, my dear sister,
And keep you in the rear of your affection,
Out of the shot and danger of desire.
The chariest maid is prodigal enough
If she unmask her beauty to the moon.
Virtue itself scapes not calumnious strokes.
The canker galls the infants of the spring
Too oft before their buttons be disclosed,
And in the morn and liquid dew of youth
Contagious blastments are most imminent.
Be wary then; best safety lies in fear.
Youth to itself rebels, though none else near.

OPHELIA

I shall the effect of this good lesson keep
As watchman to my heart. But, good my brother,
Do not, as some ungracious pastors do,

17 His greatness weighed considering his high position **20 Carve** i.e., choose **23 voice and yielding** assent, approval **26 in . . . place** in his particular restricted circumstances **27 deed** effect **28 main voice** general assent. **withal** along with **30 credent** credulous. **list** listen to **34 keep . . . affection** don't advance as far as your affection might lead you. (A military metaphor.) **35 shot** range **36 chariest** most scrupulously modest **37 If she unmask** if she does no more than show her beauty. **moon** (Symbol of chastity.) **39 canker galls** cankerworm destroys **40 buttons** buds. **disclosed** opened **41 liquid dew** i.e., time when dew is fresh and bright **42 blastments** blights **44 Youth . . . rebels** youth is inherently rebellious **47 ungracious** ungodly

Show me the steep and thorny way to heaven,
Whiles like a puffed and reckless libertine 49
Himself the primrose path of dalliance treads,
And recks not his own rede.

Enter Polonius.

LAERTES O, fear me not. 51
I stay too long. But here my father comes.
A double blessing is a double grace; 53
Occasion smiles upon a second leave. 54

POLONIUS
Yet here, Laertes? Aboard, aboard, for shame!
The wind sits in the shoulder of your sail,
And you are stayed for. There—my blessing with thee!
And these few precepts in thy memory
Look thou character. Give thy thoughts no tongue, 59
Nor any unproportioned thought his act. 60
Be thou familiar, but by no means vulgar. 61
Those friends thou hast, and their adoption tried, 62
Grapple them unto thy soul with hoops of steel,
But do not dull thy palm with entertainment 64
Of each new-hatched, unfledged courage. Beware 65
Of entrance to a quarrel, but being in,
Bear 't that th' opposèd may beware of thee. 67
Give every man thy ear, but few thy voice;
Take each man's censure, but reserve thy judgment. 69
Costly thy habit as thy purse can buy, 70
But not expressed in fancy; rich, not gaudy, 71
For the apparel oft proclaims the man,
And they in France of the best rank and station
Are of a most select and generous chief in that. 74
Neither a borrower nor a lender be,

49 puffed bloated, or swollen with pride **51 recks** heeds. **rede** counsel **53 double** (Laertes has already bidden his father good-bye.) **54 Occasion . . . leave** happy is the circumstance that provides a second leave-taking. (The goddess Occasion, or Opportunity, smiles.) **59 Look** be sure that. **character** inscribe **60 unproportioned** badly calculated, intemperate. **his** its **61 familiar** sociable. **vulgar** common **62 tried** tested **64 dull thy palm** i.e., shake hands so often as to make the gesture meaningless **65 courage** young man of spirit **67 Bear 't that** manage it so that **69 censure** opinion, judgment **70 habit** clothing **71 fancy** excessive ornament, decadent fashion **74 Are . . . that** i.e., are of a most refined and well-bred preeminence in choosing what to wear

For loan oft loses both itself and friend,
And borrowing dulls the edge of husbandry. 77
This above all: to thine own self be true,
And it must follow, as the night the day,
Thou canst not then be false to any man.
Farewell. My blessing season this in thee! 81

LAERTES
Most humbly do I take my leave, my lord.

POLONIUS
The time invests you. Go, your servants tend. 83

LAERTES
Farewell, Ophelia, and remember well
What I have said to you.

OPHELIA 'Tis in my memory locked,
And you yourself shall keep the key of it.

LAERTES Farewell. *Exit Laertes.*

POLONIUS
What is 't, Ophelia, he hath said to you?

OPHELIA
So please you, something touching the Lord Hamlet.

POLONIUS Marry, well bethought. 91
'Tis told me he hath very oft of late
Given private time to you, and you yourself
Have of your audience been most free and bounteous.
If it be so—as so 'tis put on me, 95
And that in way of caution—I must tell you
You do not understand yourself so clearly
As it behooves my daughter and your honor. 98
What is between you? Give me up the truth.

OPHELIA
He hath, my lord, of late made many tenders 100
Of his affection to me.

POLONIUS
Affection? Pooh! You speak like a green girl,
Unsifted in such perilous circumstance. 103
Do you believe his tenders, as you call them?

77 husbandry thrift **81 season** mature **83 invests** besieges, presses upon. **tend** attend, wait **91 Marry** i.e., by the Virgin Mary. (A mild oath.) **95 put on** impressed on, told to **98 behooves** befits **100 tenders** offers **103 Unsifted** i.e., untried

OPHELIA

I do not know, my lord, what I should think.

POLONIUS

Marry, I will teach you. Think yourself a baby
That you have ta'en these tenders for true pay 107
Which are not sterling. Tender yourself more dearly, 108
Or—not to crack the wind of the poor phrase, 109
Running it thus—you'll tender me a fool. 110

OPHELIA

My lord, he hath importuned me with love
In honorable fashion.

POLONIUS

Ay, fashion you may call it. Go to, go to. 113

OPHELIA

And hath given countenance to his speech, my lord, 114
With almost all the holy vows of heaven.

POLONIUS

Ay, springes to catch woodcocks. I do know, 116
When the blood burns, how prodigal the soul 117
Lends the tongue vows. These blazes, daughter,
Giving more light than heat, extinct in both
Even in their promise as it is a-making, 120
You must not take for fire. From this time
Be something scanter of your maiden presence. 122
Set your entreatments at a higher rate 123
Than a command to parle. For Lord Hamlet, 124
Believe so much in him that he is young, 125
And with a larger tether may he walk
Than may be given you. In few, Ophelia, 127

107 tenders (with added meaning here of "promises to pay") **108 sterling** legal currency. **Tender** hold, look after, offer **109 crack the wind** i.e., run it until it is broken-winded **110 tender me a fool** (1) show yourself to me as a fool (2) show me up as a fool (3) present me with a grandchild. (*Fool* was a term of endearment for a child.) **113 fashion** mere form, pretense. **Go to** (An expression of impatience.) **114 countenance** credit, confirmation **116 springes** snares. **woodcocks** birds easily caught; here used to connote gullibility **117 prodigal** i.e., prodigally **120 it** i.e., the promise **122 something** somewhat **123 entreatments** negotiations for surrender. (A military term.) **124 parle** discuss terms with the enemy. (Polonius urges his daughter, in the metaphor of military language, not to meet with Hamlet and consider giving in to him merely because he requests an interview.) **125 so . . . him** this much concerning him **127 In few** briefly

Do not believe his vows, for they are brokers,
Not of that dye which their investments show,
But mere implorators of unholy suits,
Breathing like sanctified and pious bawds
The better to beguile. This is for all:
I would not, in plain terms, from this time forth
Have you so slander any moment leisure
As to give words or talk with the Lord Hamlet.
Look to 't, I charge you. Come your ways.

OPHELIA I shall obey, my lord. *Exeunt.*

✤

1.4 *Enter Hamlet, Horatio, and Marcellus.*

HAMLET
The air bites shrewdly; it is very cold.

HORATIO
It is a nipping and an eager air.

HAMLET
What hour now?

HORATIO I think it lacks of twelve.

MARCELLUS
No, it is struck.

HORATIO Indeed? I heard it not.
It then draws near the season
Wherein the spirit held his wont to walk.
A flourish of trumpets, and two pieces go off [*within*].
What does this mean, my lord?

HAMLET
The King doth wake tonight and takes his rouse,

128 brokers go-betweens, procurers **129 dye** color or sort. **investments** clothes. (The vows are not what they seem.) **130 mere implorators** out and out solicitors **131 Breathing** speaking **132 for all** once for all, in sum **134 slander** abuse, misuse. **moment** moment's **136 Come your ways** come along

1.4. Location: The guard platform.
1 shrewdly keenly, sharply **2 eager** biting **3 lacks of** is just short of **5 season** time **6 held his wont** was accustomed **s.d. pieces** i.e., of ordnance, cannon **8 wake** stay awake and hold revel. **rouse** carouse, drinking bout

Keeps wassail, and the swaggering upspring reels;
And as he drains his drafts of Rhenish down,
The kettledrum and trumpet thus bray out
The triumph of his pledge.

HORATIO Is it a custom?

HAMLET Ay, marry, is 't,
But to my mind, though I am native here
And to the manner born, it is a custom
More honored in the breach than the observance.
This heavy-headed revel east and west
Makes us traduced and taxed of other nations.
They clepe us drunkards, and with swinish phrase
Soil our addition; and indeed it takes
From our achievements, though performed at height,
The pith and marrow of our attribute.
So, oft it chances in particular men,
That for some vicious mole of nature in them,
As in their birth—wherein they are not guilty,
Since nature cannot choose his origin—
By their o'ergrowth of some complexion,
Oft breaking down the pales and forts of reason,
Or by some habit that too much o'erleavens
The form of plausive manners, that these men,
Carrying, I say, the stamp of one defect,
Being nature's livery or fortune's star,
His virtues else, be they as pure as grace,
As infinite as man may undergo,
Shall in the general censure take corruption

9 wassail carousal. **upspring** wild German dance. **reels** dances **10 Rhenish** Rhine wine **12 the triumph . . . pledge** i.e., his feat in draining the wine in a single draft **15 manner** custom (of drinking) **16 More . . . observance** better neglected than followed **17 east and west** i.e., everywhere **18 taxed of** censured by **19 clepe** call. **with swinish phrase** i.e., by calling us swine **20 addition** reputation **21 at height** outstandingly **22 The pith . . . attribute** the essence of the reputation that others attribute to us **24 for** on account of. **mole of nature** natural blemish in one's constitution **26 his** its **27 their o'ergrowth . . . complexion** the excessive growth in individuals of some natural trait **28 pales** palings, fences (as of a fortification) **29 o'erleavens** induces a change throughout (as yeast works in dough) **30 plausive** pleasing **32 nature's livery** sign of one's servitude to nature. **fortune's star** the destiny that chance brings **33 His virtues else** i.e., the other qualities of *these men* (l. 30) **34 may undergo** can sustain **35 general censure** general opinion that people have of him

From that particular fault. The dram of evil
Doth all the noble substance often dout
To his own scandal.

Enter Ghost.

HORATIO Look, my lord, it comes!

HAMLET

Angels and ministers of grace defend us!
Be thou a spirit of health or goblin damned,
Bring with thee airs from heaven or blasts from hell,
Be thy intents wicked or charitable,
Thou com'st in such a questionable shape
That I will speak to thee. I'll call thee Hamlet,
King, Father, royal Dane. O, answer me!
Let me not burst in ignorance, but tell
Why thy canonized bones, hearsèd in death,
Have burst their cerements; why the sepulcher
Wherein we saw thee quietly inurned
Hath oped his ponderous and marble jaws
To cast thee up again. What may this mean,
That thou, dead corpse, again in complete steel,
Revisits thus the glimpses of the moon,
Making night hideous, and we fools of nature
So horridly to shake our disposition
With thoughts beyond the reaches of our souls?
Say, why is this? Wherefore? What should we do?

[*The Ghost*] *beckons* [*Hamlet*].

HORATIO

It beckons you to go away with it,
As if it some impartment did desire
To you alone.

36–38 The dram . . . scandal i.e., the small drop of evil blots out or works against the noble substance of the whole and brings it into disrepute. To *dout* is to blot out. (A famous crux.) **38 To . . . scandal** i.e., with consequent ruin or disgrace to that man **40 Be thou** i.e., whether you are. **spirit of health** good angel **41 Bring** i.e., whether you bring **42 Be thy intents** i.e., whether your intents are **43 questionable** inviting question **47 canonized** buried according to the canons of the church. **hearsèd** coffined **48 cerements** grave-clothes **49 inurned** entombed **52 complete steel** full armor **53 glimpses of the moon** pale and uncertain moonlight **54 fools of nature** mere men, limited to natural knowledge and subject to the caprices of nature **55 So . . . disposition** to distress our mental composure so violently **59 impartment** communication

MARCELLUS Look with what courteous action
It wafts you to a more removèd ground.
But do not go with it.

HORATIO No, by no means.

HAMLET
It will not speak. Then I will follow it.

HORATIO
Do not, my lord!

HAMLET Why, what should be the fear?
I do not set my life at a pin's fee,
And for my soul, what can it do to that,
Being a thing immortal as itself?
It waves me forth again. I'll follow it.

HORATIO
What if it tempt you toward the flood, my lord,
Or to the dreadful summit of the cliff
That beetles o'er his base into the sea,
And there assume some other horrible form
Which might deprive your sovereignty of reason
And draw you into madness? Think of it.
The very place puts toys of desperation,
Without more motive, into every brain
That looks so many fathoms to the sea
And hears it roar beneath.

HAMLET
It wafts me still.—Go on, I'll follow thee.

MARCELLUS
You shall not go, my lord. [*They try to stop him.*]

HAMLET Hold off your hands!

HORATIO
Be ruled. You shall not go.

HAMLET My fate cries out,
And makes each petty artery in this body
As hardy as the Nemean lion's nerve.
Still am I called. Unhand me, gentlemen.

65 fee value **69 flood** sea **71 beetles o'er** overhangs threateningly (like bushy eyebrows). **his** its **73 deprive . . . reason** take away the rule of reason over your mind **75 toys of desperation** fancies of desperate acts, i.e., suicide **81 My fate cries out** my destiny summons me **82 petty** weak. **artery** (through which the vital spirits were thought to have been conveyed) **83 Nemean lion** one of the monsters slain by Hercules in his twelve labors. **nerve** sinew

By heaven, I'll make a ghost of him that lets me! 85
I say, away!—Go on, I'll follow thee.
Exeunt Ghost and Hamlet.

HORATIO
He waxes desperate with imagination.

MARCELLUS
Let's follow. 'Tis not fit thus to obey him.

HORATIO
Have after. To what issue will this come? 89

MARCELLUS
Something is rotten in the state of Denmark.

HORATIO
Heaven will direct it.

MARCELLUS Nay, let's follow him. *Exeunt.* 91

✤

1.5 *Enter Ghost and Hamlet.*

HAMLET
Whither wilt thou lead me? Speak. I'll go no further.

GHOST
Mark me.

HAMLET I will.

GHOST My hour is almost come,
When I to sulfurous and tormenting flames
Must render up myself.

HAMLET Alas, poor ghost!

GHOST
Pity me not, but lend thy serious hearing
To what I shall unfold.

HAMLET Speak. I am bound to hear. 7

GHOST
So art thou to revenge, when thou shalt hear.

HAMLET What?

GHOST I am thy father's spirit,
Doomed for a certain term to walk the night,

85 lets hinder **89 Have after** let's go after him. **issue** outcome
91 it i.e., the outcome

1.5. Location: The battlements of the castle.
7 bound (1) ready (2) obligated by duty and fate. (The Ghost, in l. 8, answers in the second sense.)

And for the day confined to fast in fires, 12
Till the foul crimes done in my days of nature 13
Are burnt and purged away. But that I am forbid 14
To tell the secrets of my prison house,
I could a tale unfold whose lightest word
Would harrow up thy soul, freeze thy young blood, 17
Make thy two eyes like stars start from their spheres, 18
Thy knotted and combinèd locks to part, 19
And each particular hair to stand on end
Like quills upon the fretful porpentine. 21
But this eternal blazon must not be 22
To ears of flesh and blood. List, list, O, list!
If thou didst ever thy dear father love—

HAMLET O God!

GHOST
Revenge his foul and most unnatural murder.

HAMLET Murder?

GHOST
Murder most foul, as in the best it is, 28
But this most foul, strange, and unnatural.

HAMLET
Haste me to know 't, that I, with wings as swift
As meditation or the thoughts of love
May sweep to my revenge.

GHOST I find thee apt;
And duller shouldst thou be than the fat weed 33
That roots itself in ease on Lethe wharf, 34
Wouldst thou not stir in this. Now, Hamlet, hear.
'Tis given out that, sleeping in my orchard, 36
A serpent stung me. So the whole ear of Denmark
Is by a forgèd process of my death 38
Rankly abused. But know, thou noble youth, 39
The serpent that did sting thy father's life
Now wears his crown.

12 fast do penance **13 crimes** sins **14 But that** were it not that **17 harrow up** lacerate, tear **18 spheres** i.e., eye-sockets, here compared to the orbits or transparent revolving spheres in which, according to Ptolemaic astronomy, the heavenly bodies were fixed **19 knotted . . . locks** i.e., hair neatly arranged and confined **21 porpentine** porcupine **22 eternal blazon** revelation of the secrets of eternity **28 in the best** even at best **33 shouldst thou be** you would have to be. **fat** torpid, lethargic **34 Lethe** the river of forgetfulness in Hades. **wharf** bank **36 orchard** garden **38 forgèd process** falsified account **39 abused** deceived

HAMLET O, my prophetic soul! My uncle!
GHOST
Ay, that incestuous, that adulterate beast, 43
With witchcraft of his wit, with traitorous gifts— 44
O wicked wit and gifts, that have the power
So to seduce!—won to his shameful lust
The will of my most seeming-virtuous queen.
O Hamlet, what a falling off was there!
From me, whose love was of that dignity
That it went hand in hand even with the vow 50
I made to her in marriage, and to decline
Upon a wretch whose natural gifts were poor
To those of mine! 53
But virtue, as it never will be moved, 54
Though lewdness court it in a shape of heaven, 55
So lust, though to a radiant angel linked,
Will sate itself in a celestial bed 57
And prey on garbage.
But soft, methinks I scent the morning air.
Brief let me be. Sleeping within my orchard,
My custom always of the afternoon,
Upon my secure hour thy uncle stole, 62
With juice of cursèd hebona in a vial, 63
And in the porches of my ears did pour 64
The leprous distillment, whose effect 65
Holds such an enmity with blood of man
That swift as quicksilver it courses through
The natural gates and alleys of the body,
And with a sudden vigor it doth posset 69
And curd, like eager droppings into milk, 70
The thin and wholesome blood. So did it mine,
And a most instant tetter barked about, 72

43 adulterate adulterous **44 gifts** (1) talents (2) presents **50 even with the vow** with the very vow **53 To** compared to **54 virtue, as it** as virtue **55 shape of heaven** heavenly form **57 sate . . . bed** i.e., cease to find sexual pleasure in a virtuously lawful marriage **62 secure** confident, unsuspicious **63 hebona** a poison. (The word seems to be a form of *ebony,* though it is thought perhaps to be related to *henbane,* a poison, or to *ebenus,* yew.) **64 porches of my ears** ears as a porch or entrance of the body **65 leprous distillment** distillation causing leprosy-like disfigurement **69 posset** coagulate, curdle **70 eager** sour, acid **72 tetter** eruption of scabs. **barked** covered with a rough covering, like bark on a tree

Most lazar-like, with vile and loathsome crust, 73
All my smooth body.
Thus was I, sleeping, by a brother's hand
Of life, of crown, of queen at once dispatched, 76
Cut off even in the blossoms of my sin,
Unhouseled, disappointed, unaneled, 78
No reckoning made, but sent to my account 79
With all my imperfections on my head.
O, horrible! O, horrible, most horrible!
If thou hast nature in thee, bear it not. 82
Let not the royal bed of Denmark be
A couch for luxury and damnèd incest. 84
But, howsoever thou pursues this act,
Taint not thy mind nor let thy soul contrive
Against thy mother aught. Leave her to heaven
And to those thorns that in her bosom lodge,
To prick and sting her. Fare thee well at once.
The glowworm shows the matin to be near, 90
And 'gins to pale his uneffectual fire. 91
Adieu, adieu, adieu! Remember me. [*Exit.*]

HAMLET

O all you host of heaven! O earth! What else?
And shall I couple hell? O, fie! Hold, hold, my heart, 94
And you, my sinews, grow not instant old, 95
But bear me stiffly up. Remember thee?
Ay, thou poor ghost, whiles memory holds a seat
In this distracted globe. Remember thee? 98
Yea, from the table of my memory 99
I'll wipe away all trivial fond records, 100
All saws of books, all forms, all pressures past 101
That youth and observation copied there,
And thy commandment all alone shall live
Within the book and volume of my brain,

73 lazar-like leper-like **76 dispatched** suddenly deprived **78 Unhouseled** without having received the Sacrament. **disappointed** unready (spiritually) for the last journey. **unaneled** without having received extreme unction **79 reckoning** settling of accounts **82 nature** i.e., the promptings of a son **84 luxury** lechery **90 matin** i.e., morning **91 uneffectual fire** light rendered ineffectual by the approach of bright day **94 couple** add. **Hold** hold together **95 instant** instantly **98 globe** (1) head (2) world **99 table** tablet, slate **100 fond** foolish **101 saws** wise sayings. **forms** shapes or images copied onto the slate; general ideas. **pressures** impressions stamped

Unmixed with baser matter. Yes, by heaven!
O most pernicious woman!
O villain, villain, smiling, damnèd villain!
My tables—meet it is I set it down 108
That one may smile, and smile, and be a villain.
At least I am sure it may be so in Denmark.
[*Writing.*]
So, uncle, there you are. Now to my word: 111
It is "Adieu, adieu! Remember me."
I have sworn 't.

Enter Horatio and Marcellus.

HORATIO My lord, my lord!
MARCELLUS Lord Hamlet!
HORATIO Heavens secure him! 116
HAMLET So be it.
MARCELLUS Hillo, ho, ho, my lord!
HAMLET Hillo, ho, ho, boy! Come, bird, come. 119
MARCELLUS How is 't, my noble lord?
HORATIO What news, my lord?
HAMLET O, wonderful!
HORATIO Good my lord, tell it.
HAMLET No, you will reveal it.
HORATIO Not I, my lord, by heaven.
MARCELLUS Nor I, my lord.
HAMLET
How say you, then, would heart of man once think it? 127
But you'll be secret?
HORATIO, MARCELLUS Ay, by heaven, my lord.
HAMLET
There's never a villain dwelling in all Denmark
But he's an arrant knave. 130
HORATIO
There needs no ghost, my lord, come from the grave
To tell us this.
HAMLET Why, right, you are in the right.

108 tables writing tablets. **meet it is** it is fitting **111 there you are** i.e., there, I've written that down against you **116 secure him** keep him safe **119 Hillo . . . come** (A falconer's call to a hawk in air. Hamlet mocks the hallooing as though it were a part of hawking.) **127 once** ever **130 arrant** thoroughgoing

And so, without more circumstance at all, 133
I hold it fit that we shake hands and part,
You as your business and desire shall point you—
For every man hath business and desire,
Such as it is—and for my own poor part,
Look you, I'll go pray.

HORATIO
These are but wild and whirling words, my lord.

HAMLET
I am sorry they offend you, heartily;
Yes, faith, heartily.

HORATIO There's no offense, my lord.

HAMLET
Yes, by Saint Patrick, but there is, Horatio, 142
And much offense too. Touching this vision here, 143
It is an honest ghost, that let me tell you. 144
For your desire to know what is between us,
O'ermaster 't as you may. And now, good friends,
As you are friends, scholars, and soldiers,
Give me one poor request.

HORATIO What is 't, my lord? We will.

HAMLET
Never make known what you have seen tonight.

HORATIO, MARCELLUS My lord, we will not.

HAMLET Nay, but swear 't.

HORATIO In faith, my lord, not I. 153

MARCELLUS Nor I, my lord, in faith.

HAMLET Upon my sword. [*He holds out his sword.*] 155

MARCELLUS We have sworn, my lord, already. 156

HAMLET Indeed, upon my sword, indeed.

GHOST (*Cries under the stage*) Swear.

HAMLET
Ha, ha, boy, sayst thou so? Art thou there, truepenny? 159

133 circumstance ceremony, elaboration **142 Saint Patrick** (The keeper of Purgatory and patron saint of all blunders and confusion.) **143 offense** (Hamlet deliberately changes Horatio's "no offense taken" to "an offense against all decency.") **144 an honest ghost** i.e., a real ghost and not an evil spirit **153 In faith . . . I** i.e., I swear not to tell what I have seen. (Horatio is not refusing to swear.) **155 sword** i.e., the hilt in the form of a cross **156 We . . . already** i.e., we swore *in faith* **159 truepenny** honest old fellow

Come on, you hear this fellow in the cellarage.
Consent to swear.

HORATIO Propose the oath, my lord.

HAMLET
Never to speak of this that you have seen,
Swear by my sword.

GHOST [*Beneath*] Swear. [*They swear.*] 164

HAMLET
Hic et ubique? Then we'll shift our ground. 165
[*He moves to another spot.*]
Come hither, gentlemen,
And lay your hands again upon my sword.
Swear by my sword
Never to speak of this that you have heard.

GHOST [*Beneath*] Swear by his sword. [*They swear.*]

HAMLET
Well said, old mole. Canst work i' th' earth so fast?
A worthy pioner! Once more remove, good friends. 172
[*He moves again.*]

HORATIO
O day and night, but this is wondrous strange!

HAMLET
And therefore as a stranger give it welcome. 174
There are more things in heaven and earth, Horatio,
Than are dreamt of in your philosophy. 176
But come;
Here, as before, never, so help you mercy, 178
How strange or odd soe'er I bear myself—
As I perchance hereafter shall think meet
To put an antic disposition on— 181
That you, at such times seeing me, never shall,
With arms encumbered thus, or this headshake, 183

164 s.d. They swear (Seemingly they swear here, and at ll. 170 and 190, as they lay their hands on Hamlet's sword. Triple oaths would have particular force; these three oaths deal with what they have seen, what they have heard, and what they promise about Hamlet's *antic disposition.*) **165 Hic et ubique** here and everywhere. (Latin.) **172 pioner** foot soldier assigned to dig tunnels and excavations **174 as a stranger** i.e., since it is a stranger and hence needing your hospitality **176 your philosophy** i.e., this subject called "natural philosophy" or "science" that people talk about **178 so help you mercy** i.e., as you hope for God's mercy when you are judged **181 antic** fantastic **183 encumbered** folded or entwined

Or by pronouncing of some doubtful phrase
As "Well, we know," or "We could, an if we would," 185
Or "If we list to speak," or "There be, an if they might," 186
Or such ambiguous giving out, to note 187
That you know aught of me—this do swear, 188
So grace and mercy at your most need help you.

GHOST [*Beneath*] Swear. [*They swear.*]

HAMLET

Rest, rest, perturbèd spirit! So, gentlemen,
With all my love I do commend me to you; 192
And what so poor a man as Hamlet is
May do t' express his love and friending to you, 194
God willing, shall not lack. Let us go in together, 195
And still your fingers on your lips, I pray. 196
The time is out of joint. O cursèd spite 197
That ever I was born to set it right!
[*They wait for him to leave first.*]
Nay, come, let's go together. *Exeunt.* 199

✤

185 an if if **186 list** wished. **There . . . might** i.e., there are people here (we, in fact) who could tell news if we were at liberty to do so **187 giving out** intimidation, promulgating. **note** draw attention to the fact **188 aught** i.e., something secret **192 do . . . you** entrust myself to you **194 friending** friendliness **195 lack** be lacking **196 still** always **197 The time** i.e., the state of affairs. **spite** i.e., the spite of Fortune **199 let's go together** (Probably they wait for him to leave first, but he refuses this ceremoniousness.)

2.1 *Enter old Polonius with his man* [*Reynaldo*].

POLONIUS
Give him this money and these notes, Reynaldo.
[*He gives money and papers.*]

REYNALDO I will, my lord.

POLONIUS
You shall do marvelous wisely, good Reynaldo, 3
Before you visit him, to make inquire 4
Of his behavior.

REYNALDO My lord, I did intend it.

POLONIUS
Marry, well said, very well said. Look you, sir,
Inquire me first what Danskers are in Paris, 7
And how, and who, what means, and where they keep, 8
What company, at what expense; and finding
By this encompassment and drift of question 10
That they do know my son, come you more nearer 11
Than your particular demands will touch it. 12
Take you, as 'twere, some distant knowledge of him, 13
As thus, "I know his father and his friends,
And in part him." Do you mark this, Reynaldo?

REYNALDO Ay, very well, my lord.

POLONIUS
"And in part him, but," you may say, "not well.
But if 't be he I mean, he's very wild,
Addicted so and so," and there put on him 19
What forgeries you please—marry, none so rank 20
As may dishonor him, take heed of that,
But, sir, such wanton, wild, and usual slips 22
As are companions noted and most known
To youth and liberty.

REYNALDO As gaming, my lord.

2.1. Location: Polonius' chambers.
3 marvelous marvelously **4 inquire** inquiry **7 Danskers** Danes **8 what means** what wealth (they have). **keep** dwell **10 encompassment** roundabout talking. **drift** gradual approach or course **11–12 come . . . it** i.e., you will find out more this way than by asking pointed questions (*particular demands*) **13 Take you** assume, pretend **19 put on** impute to **20 forgeries** invented tales. **rank** gross **22 wanton** sportive, unrestrained

POLONIUS Ay, or drinking, fencing, swearing,
Quarreling, drabbing—you may go so far.
REYNALDO My lord, that would dishonor him.
POLONIUS
Faith, no, as you may season it in the charge.
You must not put another scandal on him
That he is open to incontinency;
That's not my meaning. But breathe his faults so
quaintly
That they may seem the taints of liberty,
The flash and outbreak of a fiery mind,
A savageness in unreclaimèd blood,
Of general assault.
REYNALDO But, my good lord—
POLONIUS
Wherefore should you do this?
REYNALDO Ay, my lord, I would know that.
POLONIUS Marry, sir, here's my drift,
And I believe it is a fetch of warrant.
You laying these slight sullies on my son,
As 'twere a thing a little soiled wi' the working,
Mark you,
Your party in converse, him you would sound,
Having ever seen in the prenominate crimes
The youth you breathe of guilty, be assured
He closes with you in this consequence:
"Good sir," or so, or "friend," or "gentleman,"
According to the phrase or the addition
Of man and country.
REYNALDO Very good, my lord.
POLONIUS And then, sir, does 'a this—'a does—what was I about to say? By the Mass, I was about to say something. Where did I leave?

27 drabbing keeping company with loose women **29 season** temper, soften **31 incontinency** habitual sexual excess **32 quaintly** artfully, subtly **33 taints of liberty** faults resulting from free living **35–36 A savageness . . . assault** a wildness in untamed youth that assails all indiscriminately **41 fetch of warrant** legitimate trick **43 soiled wi' the working** soiled by handling while it is being made **45 converse** conversation. **sound** i.e., sound out **46 Having ever** if he has ever. **prenominate crimes** before-mentioned offenses **47 breathe** speak **48 closes . . . consequence** follows your lead in some fashion as follows **50 addition** title

REYNALDO At "closes in the consequence."

POLONIUS

At "closes in the consequence," ay, marry.
He closes thus: "I know the gentleman,
I saw him yesterday," or "th' other day,"
Or then, or then, with such or such, "and as you say,
There was 'a gaming," "there o'ertook in 's rouse," 60
"There falling out at tennis," or perchance 61
"I saw him enter such a house of sale,"
Videlicet a brothel, or so forth. See you now, 63
Your bait of falsehood takes this carp of truth; 64
And thus do we of wisdom and of reach, 65
With windlasses and with assays of bias, 66
By indirections find directions out. 67
So by my former lecture and advice
Shall you my son. You have me, have you not? 69

REYNALDO

My lord, I have.

POLONIUS God b' wi' ye; fare ye well. 70

REYNALDO Good my lord.

POLONIUS

Observe his inclination in yourself. 72

REYNALDO I shall, my lord.

POLONIUS And let him ply his music. 74

REYNALDO Well, my lord.

POLONIUS

Farewell. *Exit Reynaldo.*

Enter Ophelia.

How now, Ophelia, what's the matter?

OPHELIA

O my lord, my lord, I have been so affrighted!

POLONIUS With what, i' the name of God?

60 o'ertook in 's rouse overcome by drink **61 falling out** quarreling **63 Videlicet** namely **64 carp** a fish **65 reach** capacity, ability **66 windlasses** i.e., circuitous paths. (Literally, circuits made to head off the game in hunting.) **assays of bias** attempts through indirection (like the curving path of the bowling ball which is biased or weighted to one side) **67 directions** i.e., the way things really are **69 have** understand **70 b' wi'** be with **72 in yourself** in your own person (as well as by asking questions) **74 let him ply** see that he continues to study

OPHELIA

My lord, as I was sewing in my closet, 79
Lord Hamlet, with his doublet all unbraced, 80
No hat upon his head, his stockings fouled,
Ungartered, and down-gyvèd to his ankle, 82
Pale as his shirt, his knees knocking each other,
And with a look so piteous in purport 84
As if he had been loosèd out of hell
To speak of horrors—he comes before me.

POLONIUS

Mad for thy love?

OPHELIA

My lord, I do not know,
But truly I do fear it.

POLONIUS

What said he?

OPHELIA

He took me by the wrist and held me hard.
Then goes he to the length of all his arm,
And with his other hand thus o'er his brow
He falls to such perusal of my face
As 'a would draw it. Long stayed he so. 93
At last, a little shaking of mine arm
And thrice his head thus waving up and down,
He raised a sigh so piteous and profound
As it did seem to shatter all his bulk 97
And end his being. That done, he lets me go,
And with his head over his shoulder turned
He seemed to find his way without his eyes,
For out o' doors he went without their helps,
And to the last bended their light on me.

POLONIUS

Come, go with me. I will go seek the King.
This is the very ecstasy of love, 104
Whose violent property fordoes itself 105
And leads the will to desperate undertakings
As oft as any passion under heaven
That does afflict our natures. I am sorry.
What, have you given him any hard words of late?

79 closet private chamber **80 doublet** close-fitting jacket. **unbraced** unfastened **82 down-gyvèd** fallen to the ankles (like gyves or fetters) **84 in purport** in what it expressed **93 As** as if (also in l. 97) **97 bulk** body **104 ecstasy** madness **105 property** nature. **fordoes** destroys

OPHELIA
No, my good lord, but as you did command
I did repel his letters and denied
His access to me.
POLONIUS That hath made him mad.
I am sorry that with better heed and judgment
I had not quoted him. I feared he did but trifle
And meant to wrack thee. But beshrew my jealousy!
By heaven, it is as proper to our age
To cast beyond ourselves in our opinions
As it is common for the younger sort
To lack discretion. Come, go we to the King.
This must be known, which, being kept close, might
move
More grief to hide than hate to utter love.
Come. *Exeunt.*

✤

2.2 *Flourish. Enter King and Queen, Rosencrantz, and Guildenstern* [*with others*].

KING
Welcome, dear Rosencrantz and Guildenstern.
Moreover that we much did long to see you,
The need we have to use you did provoke
Our hasty sending. Something have you heard
Of Hamlet's transformation—so call it,
Sith nor th' exterior nor the inward man
Resembles that it was. What it should be,
More than his father's death, that thus hath put him
So much from th' understanding of himself,
I cannot dream of. I entreat you both

114 quoted observed **115 wrack** i.e., ruin, seduce. **beshrew my jealousy** a plague upon my suspicious nature **116 proper . . . age** characteristic of us (old) men **117 cast beyond** overshoot, miscalculate **120 close** secret **120–121 might . . . love** i.e., might cause more grief (because of what Hamlet might do) by hiding the knowledge of Hamlet's strange behavior to Ophelia than unpleasantness by telling it

2.2. Location: The castle.
2 Moreover that besides the fact that **6 Sith** since. **nor . . . nor** neither . . . nor **7 that** what

That, being of so young days brought up with him, 11
And sith so neighbored to his youth and havior, 12
That you vouchsafe your rest here in our court 13
Some little time, so by your companies
To draw him on to pleasures, and to gather
So much as from occasion you may glean, 16
Whether aught to us unknown afflicts him thus
That, opened, lies within our remedy. 18

QUEEN
Good gentlemen, he hath much talked of you,
And sure I am two men there is not living
To whom he more adheres. If it will please you
To show us so much gentry and good will 22
As to expend your time with us awhile
For the supply and profit of our hope, 24
Your visitation shall receive such thanks
As fits a king's remembrance.

ROSENCRANTZ Both Your Majesties 26
Might, by the sovereign power you have of us, 27
Put your dread pleasures more into command 28
Than to entreaty.

GUILDENSTERN But wc both obey,
And here give up ourselves in the full bent 30
To lay our service freely at your feet,
To be commanded.

KING
Thanks, Rosencrantz and gentle Guildenstern.

QUEEN
Thanks, Guildenstern and gentle Rosencrantz.
And I beseech you instantly to visit
My too much changèd son. Go, some of you,
And bring these gentlemen where Hamlet is.

GUILDENSTERN
Heavens make our presence and our practices 38
Pleasant and helpful to him!

11 of . . . days from such early youth **12 And sith so neighbored to** i.e., and since you are (or, and since that time you are) intimately acquainted with. **havior** demeanor **13 vouchsafe your rest** please to stay **16 occasion** opportunity **18 opened** being revealed **22 gentry** courtesy **24 supply . . . hope** aid and furtherance of what we hope for **26 As fits . . . remembrance** i.e., as would be a fitting gift of a king who rewards true service **27 of** over **28 dread** inspiring awe **30 in . . . bent** to the utmost degree of our capacity **38 practices** doings

QUEEN Ay, amen!

Exeunt Rosencrantz and Guildenstern [*with some attendants*].

Enter Polonius.

POLONIUS
Th' ambassadors from Norway, my good lord,
Are joyfully returned.

KING
Thou still hast been the father of good news. 42

POLONIUS
Have I, my lord? I assure my good liege
I hold my duty, as I hold my soul, 44
Both to my God and to my gracious king;
And I do think, or else this brain of mine
Hunts not the trail of policy so sure 47
As it hath used to do, that I have found
The very cause of Hamlet's lunacy.

KING
O, speak of that! That do I long to hear.

POLONIUS
Give first admittance to th' ambassadors.
My news shall be the fruit to that great feast. 52

KING
Thyself do grace to them and bring them in.

[*Exit Polonius.*]

He tells me, my dear Gertrude, he hath found
The head and source of all your son's distemper.

QUEEN
I doubt it is no other but the main, 56
His father's death and our o'erhasty marriage.

Enter Ambassadors [*Voltimand and Cornelius, with Polonius*].

KING
Well, we shall sift him.—Welcome, my good friends! 58
Say, Voltimand, what from our brother Norway? 59

42 still always **44 hold** maintain. **as** as firmly as **47 policy** statecraft **52 fruit** dessert **56 doubt** fear, suspect. **main** chief point, principal concern **58 sift him** i.e., question Polonius closely **59 brother** i.e., fellow king

VOLTIMAND
Most fair return of greetings and desires. 60
Upon our first, he sent out to suppress 61
His nephew's levies, which to him appeared
To be a preparation 'gainst the Polack,
But, better looked into, he truly found
It was against Your Highness. Whereat grieved
That so his sickness, age, and impotence 66
Was falsely borne in hand, sends out arrests 67
On Fortinbras, which he, in brief, obeys,
Receives rebuke from Norway, and in fine 69
Makes vow before his uncle never more
To give th' assay of arms against Your Majesty. 71
Whereon old Norway, overcome with joy,
Gives him three thousand crowns in annual fee
And his commission to employ those soldiers,
So levied as before, against the Polack,
With an entreaty, herein further shown,
[*Giving a paper*]
That it might please you to give quiet pass
Through your dominions for this enterprise
On such regards of safety and allowance 79
As therein are set down.

KING
It likes us well, 80
And at our more considered time we'll read, 81
Answer, and think upon this business.
Meantime we thank you for your well-took labor.
Go to your rest; at night we'll feast together.
Most welcome home! *Exeunt Ambassadors.*

POLONIUS
This business is well ended.
My liege, and madam, to expostulate 86
What majesty should be, what duty is,
Why day is day, night night, and time is time,
Were nothing but to waste night, day, and time.

60 desires good wishes **61 Upon our first** at our first words on the business **66 impotence** helplessness **67 borne in hand** deluded, taken advantage of. **arrests** orders to desist **69 in fine** in conclusion **71 give th' assay** make trial of strength, challenge **79 On . . . allowance** i.e., with such considerations or conditions for the safety of Denmark and terms of permission for Fortinbras **80 likes** pleases **81 considered** suitable for deliberation **86 expostulate** expound, inquire into

Therefore, since brevity is the soul of wit,
And tediousness the limbs and outward flourishes,
I will be brief. Your noble son is mad.
Mad call I it, for, to define true madness,
What is 't but to be nothing else but mad?
But let that go.

QUEEN More matter, with less art.

POLONIUS

Madam, I swear I use no art at all.
That he's mad, 'tis true; 'tis true 'tis pity,
And pity 'tis 'tis true—a foolish figure,
But farewell it, for I will use no art.
Mad let us grant him, then, and now remains
That we find out the cause of this effect,
Or rather say, the cause of this defect,
For this effect defective comes by cause.
Thus it remains, and the remainder thus.
Perpend.
I have a daughter—have while she is mine—
Who, in her duty and obedience, mark,
Hath given me this. Now gather and surmise.
[*He reads the letter.*] "To the celestial and my soul's idol, the most beautified Ophelia"—
That's an ill phrase, a vile phrase; "beautified" is a vile phrase. But you shall hear. Thus: [*He reads.*]
"In her excellent white bosom, these, etc."

QUEEN Came this from Hamlet to her?

POLONIUS

Good madam, stay awhile. I will be faithful.
[*He reads.*]

"Doubt thou the stars are fire,
  Doubt that the sun doth move,
Doubt truth to be a liar,
  But never doubt I love.

O dear Ophelia, I am ill at these numbers. I have not

90 wit sound sense or judgment, intellectual keenness **98 figure** figure of speech **103 For . . . cause** i.e., for this defective behavior, this madness, has a cause **105 Perpend** consider **108 gather and surmise** draw your own conclusions **113 In . . . bosom** (The letter is poetically addressed to her heart.) **these** i.e., the letter **115 stay** wait. **faithful** i.e., in reading the letter accurately **118 Doubt** suspect **120 ill . . . numbers** unskilled at writing verses

art to reckon my groans. But that I love thee best, O 121
most best, believe it. Adieu.
Thine evermore, most dear lady, whilst this
machine is to him, Hamlet." 124
This in obedience hath my daughter shown me,
And, more above, hath his solicitings, 126
As they fell out by time, by means, and place, 127
All given to mine ear.

KING
But how hath she 128
Received his love?

POLONIUS
What do you think of me?

KING
As of a man faithful and honorable.

POLONIUS
I would fain prove so. But what might you think, 131
When I had seen this hot love on the wing—
As I perceived it, I must tell you that,
Before my daughter told me—what might you,
Or my dear Majesty your queen here, think,
If I had played the desk or table book, 136
Or given my heart a winking, mute and dumb, 137
Or looked upon this love with idle sight? 138
What might you think? No, I went round to work, 139
And my young mistress thus I did bespeak: 140
"Lord Hamlet is a prince out of thy star; 141
This must not be." And then I prescripts gave her 142
That she should lock herself from his resort, 143
Admit no messengers, receive no tokens.
Which done, she took the fruits of my advice;
And he, repellèd—a short tale to make—
Fell into a sadness, then into a fast,
Thence to a watch, thence into a weakness, 148
Thence to a lightness, and by this declension 149

121 reckon (1) count (2) number metrically, scan **124 machine** i.e., body **126 more above** moreover **127 fell out** occurred. **by** according to **128 given . . . ear** i.e., told me about **131 fain** gladly **136 played . . . table book** i.e., remained shut up, concealing the information; or, acted as a go-between, provided communication **137 given . . . winking** closed the eyes of my heart to this **138 with idle sight** complacently or incomprehendingly **139 round** roundly, plainly **140 bespeak** address **141 out of thy star** above your sphere, position **142 prescripts** orders **143 his resort** his visits **148 watch** state of sleeplessness **149 lightness** lightheadedness. **declension** decline, deterioration

Into the madness wherein now he raves
And all we mourn for.
KING [*To Queen*] Do you think 'tis this? 151
QUEEN It may be, very like.
POLONIUS
Hath there been such a time—I would fain know that—
That I have positively said " 'Tis so,"
When it proved otherwise?
KING Not that I know.
POLONIUS
Take this from this, if this be otherwise. 156
If circumstances lead me, I will find
Where truth is hid, though it were hid indeed
Within the center.
KING How may we try it further? 159
POLONIUS
You know sometimes he walks four hours together
Here in the lobby.
QUEEN So he does indeed.
POLONIUS
At such a time I'll loose my daughter to him. 162
Be you and I behind an arras then. 163
Mark the encounter. If he love her not
And be not from his reason fallen thereon, 165
Let me be no assistant for a state,
But keep a farm and carters.
KING We will try it.

Enter Hamlet [*reading on a book*].

QUEEN
But look where sadly the poor wretch comes reading. 168
POLONIUS
Away, I do beseech you both, away.

151 all i.e., into everything that **156 Take this from this** (The actor gestures, indicating that he means his head from his shoulders, or his staff of office or chain from his hands or neck, or something similar.) **159 center** middle point of the earth (which is also the center of the Ptolemaic universe). **try** test, judge **162 loose** (as one might release an animal that is being mated) **163 arras** hanging, tapestry **165 thereon** on that account **168 sadly** seriously

I'll board him presently. O, give me leave. 170
Exeunt King and Queen [*with attendants*].
How does my good Lord Hamlet?
HAMLET Well, God-a-mercy. 172
POLONIUS Do you know me, my lord?
HAMLET Excellent well. You are a fishmonger. 174
POLONIUS Not I, my lord.
HAMLET Then I would you were so honest a man.
POLONIUS Honest, my lord?
HAMLET Ay, sir. To be honest, as this world goes, is to
be one man picked out of ten thousand.
POLONIUS That's very true, my lord.
HAMLET For if the sun breed maggots in a dead dog,
being a good kissing carrion—Have you a daughter? 182
POLONIUS I have, my lord.
HAMLET Let her not walk i' the sun. Conception is a 184
blessing, but as your daughter may conceive, friend,
look to 't.
POLONIUS [*Aside*] How say you by that? Still harping
on my daughter. Yet he knew me not at first; 'a said I 188
was a fishmonger. 'A is far gone. And truly in my
youth I suffered much extremity for love, very near
this. I'll speak to him again.—What do you read, my
lord?
HAMLET Words, words, words.
POLONIUS What is the matter, my lord? 194
HAMLET Between who?
POLONIUS I mean, the matter that you read, my lord.
HAMLET Slanders, sir; for the satirical rogue says here
that old men have gray beards, that their faces are wrinkled, their eyes purging thick amber and plum-tree 199
gum, and that they have a plentiful lack of wit, to- 200

170 board accost. **presently** at once. **give me leave** i.e., excuse me. (Said to those he hurries offstage, including the King and Queen.) **172 God-a-mercy** i.e., thank you **174 fishmonger** fish merchant **182 a good kissing carrion** i.e., a good piece of flesh for kissing, or for the sun to kiss **184 i' the sun** (with additional implication of the sunshine of princely favors). **Conception** (1) understanding (2) pregnancy **188 'a** he **194 matter** substance. (But Hamlet plays on the sense of "basis for a dispute.") **199 purging** discharging. **amber** i.e., resin, like the resinous *plum-tree gum* **200 wit** understanding

gether with most weak hams. All which, sir, though I most powerfully and potently believe, yet I hold it not honesty to have it thus set down, for yourself, sir, shall grow old as I am, if like a crab you could go backward.

POLONIUS [*Aside*] Though this be madness, yet there is method in 't.—Will you walk out of the air, my lord?

HAMLET Into my grave.

POLONIUS Indeed, that's out of the air. [*Aside*.] How pregnant sometimes his replies are! A happiness that often madness hits on, which reason and sanity could not so prosperously be delivered of. I will leave him and suddenly contrive the means of meeting between him and my daughter.—My honorable lord, I will most humbly take my leave of you.

HAMLET You cannot, sir, take from me anything that I will more willingly part withal—except my life, except my life, except my life.

Enter Guildenstern and Rosencrantz.

POLONIUS Fare you well, my lord.

HAMLET These tedious old fools!

POLONIUS You go to seek the Lord Hamlet. There he is.

ROSENCRANTZ [*To Polonius*] God save you, sir!

[*Exit Polonius*.]

GUILDENSTERN My honored lord!

ROSENCRANTZ My most dear lord!

HAMLET My excellent good friends! How dost thou, Guildenstern? Ah, Rosencrantz! Good lads, how do you both?

ROSENCRANTZ
As the indifferent children of the earth.

GUILDENSTERN
Happy in that we are not overhappy.
On Fortune's cap we are not the very button.

203 honesty decency, decorum **204 old** as old **206 out of the air** (The open air was considered dangerous for sick people.) **209 pregnant** quick-witted, full of meaning. **happiness** felicity of expression **211 prosperously** successfully **212 suddenly** immediately **216 withal** with **219 old fools** i.e., old men like Polonius **227 indifferent** ordinary, at neither extreme of fortune or misfortune

HAMLET Nor the soles of her shoe?

ROSENCRANTZ Neither, my lord.

HAMLET Then you live about her waist, or in the middle of her favors? 233

GUILDENSTERN Faith, her privates we. 234

HAMLET In the secret parts of Fortune? O, most true,
she is a strumpet. What news? 236

ROSENCRANTZ None, my lord, but the world's grown honest.

HAMLET Then is doomsday near. But your news is not true. Let me question more in particular. What have you, my good friends, deserved at the hands of Fortune that she sends you to prison hither?

GUILDENSTERN Prison, my lord?

HAMLET Denmark's a prison.

ROSENCRANTZ Then is the world one.

HAMLET A goodly one, in which there are many con- 246
fines, wards, and dungeons, Denmark being one o' the 247
worst.

ROSENCRANTZ We think not so, my lord.

HAMLET Why then 'tis none to you, for there is nothing either good or bad but thinking makes it so. To me it is a prison.

ROSENCRANTZ Why then, your ambition makes it one. 'Tis too narrow for your mind.

HAMLET O God, I could be bounded in a nutshell and count myself a king of infinite space, were it not that I have bad dreams.

GUILDENSTERN Which dreams indeed are ambition, for
the very substance of the ambitious is merely the 259
shadow of a dream.

HAMLET A dream itself is but a shadow.

ROSENCRANTZ Truly, and I hold ambition of so airy and light a quality that it is but a shadow's shadow.

233 favors i.e., sexual favors **234 her privates we** i.e., (1) we are sexually intimate with Fortune, the fickle goddess who bestows her favors indiscriminately (2) we are her ordinary citizens **236 strumpet** prostitute. (A common epithet for indiscriminate Fortune; see l. 493 below.) **246–247 confines** places of confinement **247 wards** cells **259 the very . . . ambitious** that seemingly very substantial thing that the ambitious pursue

HAMLET Then are our beggars bodies, and our monarchs and outstretched heroes the beggars' shadows. Shall we to the court? For, by my fay, I cannot reason.

ROSENCRANTZ, GUILDENSTERN We'll wait upon you.

HAMLET No such matter. I will not sort you with the rest of my servants, for, to speak to you like an honest man, I am most dreadfully attended. But, in the beaten way of friendship, what make you at Elsinore?

ROSENCRANTZ To visit you, my lord, no other occasion.

HAMLET Beggar that I am, I am even poor in thanks; but I thank you, and sure, dear friends, my thanks are too dear a halfpenny. Were you not sent for? Is it your own inclining? Is it a free visitation? Come, come, deal justly with me. Come, come; nay, speak.

GUILDENSTERN What should we say, my lord?

HAMLET Anything but to the purpose. You were sent for, and there is a kind of confession in your looks which your modesties have not craft enough to color. I know the good King and Queen have sent for you.

ROSENCRANTZ To what end, my lord?

HAMLET That you must teach me. But let me conjure you, by the rights of our fellowship, by the consonancy of our youth, by the obligation of our ever-preserved love, and by what more dear a better proposer could charge you withal, be even and direct with me whether you were sent for or no.

ROSENCRANTZ [*Aside to Guildenstern*] What say you?

HAMLET [*Aside*] Nay, then, I have an eye of you.—If you love me, hold not off.

264 bodies i.e., solid substances rather than shadows (since beggars are not ambitious) **265 outstretched** (1) far-reaching in their ambition (2) elongated as shadows **266 fay** faith **267 wait upon** accompany, attend. (But Hamlet uses the phrase in the sense of providing menial service.)
268 sort class, categorize **270 dreadfully attended** waited upon in slovenly fashion **271 beaten way** familiar path, tried-and-true course. **make** do **275 dear a halfpenny** expensive at the price of a halfpenny, i.e., of little worth **276 free** voluntary **279 Anything but to the purpose** anything except a straightforward answer. (Said ironically.)
281 modesties sense of shame. **color** disguise **284 conjure** adjure, entreat **285–286 the consonancy of our youth** our closeness in our younger days **287 better proposer** more skillful propounder
288 charge urge. **even** straight, honest **291 of** on **292 hold not off** don't hold back

GUILDENSTERN My lord, we were sent for.
HAMLET I will tell you why; so shall my anticipation 294
prevent your discovery, and your secrecy to the King 295
and Queen molt no feather. I have of late—but 296
wherefore I know not—lost all my mirth, forgone all
custom of exercises; and indeed it goes so heavily with
my disposition that this goodly frame, the earth,
seems to me a sterile promontory; this most excellent
canopy, the air, look you, this brave o'erhanging fir- 301
mament, this majestical roof fretted with golden fire, 302
why, it appeareth nothing to me but a foul and pestilent congregation of vapors. What a piece of work is a 304
man! How noble in reason, how infinite in faculties,
in form and moving how express and admirable, in 306
action how like an angel, in apprehension how like a 307
god! The beauty of the world, the paragon of animals!
And yet, to me, what is this quintessence of dust? 309
Man delights not me—no, nor woman neither,
though by your smiling you seem to say so.

ROSENCRANTZ My lord, there was no such stuff in my thoughts.

HAMLET Why did you laugh then, when I said man delights not me?

ROSENCRANTZ To think, my lord, if you delight not in
man, what Lenten entertainment the players shall re- 317
ceive from you. We coted them on the way, and hither 318
are they coming to offer you service.
HAMLET He that plays the king shall be welcome; His
Majesty shall have tribute of me. The adventurous 321
knight shall use his foil and target, the lover shall not 322

294–295 so . . . discovery in that way my saying it first will spare you from revealing the truth **296 molt no feather** i.e., not diminish in the least **301 brave** splendid **302 fretted** adorned (with fretwork, as in a vaulted ceiling) **304 congregation** mass. **piece of work** masterpiece **306 express** well-framed, exact, expressive (?) **307 apprehension** power of comprehending **309 quintessence** the fifth essence of ancient philosophy, beyond earth, water, air, and fire, supposed to be the substance of the heavenly bodies and to be latent in all things **317 Lenten entertainment** meager reception (appropriate to Lent) **318 coted** overtook and passed by **321 shall . . . of me** will receive my tribute of praise **322 foil and target** sword and shield

sigh gratis, the humorous man shall end his part in 323
peace, the clown shall make those laugh whose lungs 324
are tickle o' the sear, and the lady shall say her mind 325
freely, or the blank verse shall halt for 't. What players 326
are they?

ROSENCRANTZ Even those you were wont to take such
delight in, the tragedians of the city.

HAMLET How chances it they travel? Their residence, 330
both in reputation and profit, was better both ways.

ROSENCRANTZ I think their inhibition comes by the 332
means of the late innovation. 333

HAMLET Do they hold the same estimation they did
when I was in the city? Are they so followed?

ROSENCRANTZ No, indeed are they not.

HAMLET How comes it? Do they grow rusty? 337

ROSENCRANTZ Nay, their endeavor keeps in the wonted 338
pace. But there is, sir, an aerie of children, little eyases, 339
that cry out on the top of question and are most tyran- 340
nically clapped for 't. These are now the fashion, and 341
so berattle the common stages—so they call them— 342
that many wearing rapiers are afraid of goose quills 343
and dare scarce come thither.

HAMLET What, are they children? Who maintains 'em?
How are they escoted? Will they pursue the quality no 346
longer than they can sing? Will they not say after- 347

323 gratis for nothing. **humorous man** eccentric character, dominated by one trait or "humor" **323–324 in peace** i.e., with full license **325 tickle o' the sear** easy on the trigger, ready to laugh easily. (A *sear* is part of a gunlock.) **326 halt** limp **330 residence** remaining in one place, i.e., in the city **332 inhibition** formal prohibition (from acting plays in the city) **333 late** recent. **innovation** i.e., the new fashion in satirical plays performed by boy actors in the "private" theaters; or possibly a political uprising; or the strict limitations set on the theaters in London in 1600 **337–362 How . . . load too** (The passage, omitted from the early quartos, alludes to the so-called War of the Theaters, 1599–1602, the rivalry between the children's companies and the adult actors.) **338 keeps** continues. **wonted** usual **339 aerie** nest. **eyases** young hawks **340 cry . . . question** speak shrilly, dominating the controversy (in decrying the public theaters) **340–341 tyrannically** outrageously **342 berattle** berate, clamor against. **common stages** public theaters **343 many wearing rapiers** i.e., many men of fashion, afraid to patronize the common players for fear of being satirized by the poets writing for the boy actors. **goose quills** i.e., pens of satirists **346 escoted** maintained. **quality** (acting) profession **346–347 no longer . . . sing** i.e., only until their voices change

wards, if they should grow themselves to common players—as it is most like, if their means are no better—their writers do them wrong to make them exclaim against their own succession?

ROSENCRANTZ Faith, there has been much to-do on both sides, and the nation holds it no sin to tar them to controversy. There was for a while no money bid for argument unless the poet and the player went to cuffs in the question.

HAMLET Is 't possible?

GUILDENSTERN O, there has been much throwing about of brains.

HAMLET Do the boys carry it away?

ROSENCRANTZ Ay, that they do, my lord—Hercules and his load too.

HAMLET It is not very strange; for my uncle is King of Denmark, and those that would make mouths at him while my father lived give twenty, forty, fifty, a hundred ducats apiece for his picture in little. 'Sblood, there is something in this more than natural, if philosophy could find it out.

A flourish [of trumpets within].

GUILDENSTERN There are the players.

HAMLET Gentlemen, you are welcome to Elsinore. Your hands, come then. Th' appurtenance of welcome is fashion and ceremony. Let me comply with you in this garb, lest my extent to the players, which, I tell you, must show fairly outwards, should more appear like entertainment than yours. You are welcome. But my uncle-father and aunt-mother are deceived.

348 common regular, adult **349 like** likely **349–350 if . . . better** if they find no better way to support themselves **351 succession** i.e., future careers **352 to-do** ado **353 tar** set on (as dogs) **355 argument** plot for a play **355–356 went . . . question** came to blows in the play itself **360 carry it away** i.e., win the day **361–362 Hercules . . . load** (Thought to be an allusion to the sign of the Globe Theatre, which was Hercules bearing the world on his shoulder.) **364 mouths** faces **366 ducats** gold coins. **in little** in miniature. **'Sblood** by God's (Christ's) blood **367–368 philosophy** i.e., scientific inquiry **371 appurtenance** proper accompaniment **372 comply** observe the formalities of courtesy **373 garb** i.e., manner. **my extent** that which I extend, i.e., my polite behavior **374 show fairly outwards** show every evidence of cordiality **375 entertainment** a (warm) reception

GUILDENSTERN In what, my dear lord?
HAMLET I am but mad north-north-west. When the 378
wind is southerly I know a hawk from a handsaw. 379

Enter Polonius.

POLONIUS Well be with you, gentlemen!
HAMLET Hark you, Guildenstern, and you too; at each
ear a hearer. That great baby you see there is not yet
out of his swaddling clouts. 383
ROSENCRANTZ Haply he is the second time come to 384
them, for they say an old man is twice a child.
HAMLET I will prophesy he comes to tell me of the play-
ers; mark it.—You say right, sir, o' Monday morning,
'twas then indeed.
POLONIUS My lord, I have news to tell you.
HAMLET My lord, I have news to tell you. When Ros- 390
cius was an actor in Rome— 391
POLONIUS The actors are come hither, my lord.
HAMLET Buzz, buzz! 393
POLONIUS Upon my honor—
HAMLET Then came each actor on his ass.
POLONIUS The best actors in the world, either for
tragedy, comedy, history, pastoral, pastoral-comical,
historical-pastoral, tragical-historical, tragical-comical-
historical-pastoral, scene individable, or poem unlim- 399
ited. Seneca cannot be too heavy, nor Plautus too light. 400
For the law of writ and the liberty, these are the only 401
men.
HAMLET O Jephthah, judge of Israel, what a treasure 403
hadst thou!

378 north-north-west i.e., only partly, at times **379 hawk, handsaw** i.e., two very different things, though also perhaps meaning a mattock (or *hack*) and a carpenter's cutting tool respectively; also birds, with a play on *hernshaw* or heron **383 swaddling clouts** cloths in which to wrap a newborn baby **384 Haply** perhaps **390–391 Roscius** a famous Roman actor who died in 62 B.C. **393 Buzz** (An interjection used to denote stale news.) **399 scene individable** a play observing the unity of place; or perhaps one that is unclassifiable **399–400 poem unlimited** a play disregarding the unities of time and place; one that is all-inclusive **400 Seneca** writer of Latin tragedies. **Plautus** writer of Latin comedy **401 law . . . liberty** dramatic composition both according to rules and without rules, i.e., "classical" and "romantic" dramas. **these** i.e., the actors **403 Jephthah . . . Israel** (Jephthah had to sacrifice his daughter; see Judges 11. Hamlet goes on to quote from a ballad on the theme.)

POLONIUS What a treasure had he, my lord?

HAMLET Why,

"One fair daughter, and no more,
The which he lovèd passing well."

POLONIUS [*Aside*] Still on my daughter.

HAMLET Am I not i' the right, old Jephthah?

POLONIUS If you call me Jephthah, my lord, I have a daughter that I love passing well.

HAMLET Nay, that follows not.

POLONIUS What follows then, my lord?

HAMLET Why,

"As by lot, God wot,"

and then, you know,

"It came to pass, as most like it was"—

the first row of the pious chanson will show you more, for look where my abridgment comes.

Enter the Players.

You are welcome, masters; welcome, all. I am glad to see thee well. Welcome, good friends. O, old friend! Why, thy face is valanced since I saw thee last. Com'st thou to beard me in Denmark? What, my young lady and mistress! By 'r Lady, your ladyship is nearer to heaven than when I saw you last, by the altitude of a chopine. Pray God your voice, like a piece of uncurrent gold, be not cracked within the ring. Masters, you are all welcome. We'll e'en to 't like French falconers, fly at anything we see. We'll have a speech straight. Come, give us a taste of your quality. Come, a passionate speech.

FIRST PLAYER What speech, my good lord?

408 passing surpassingly **416 lot** chance. **wot** knows **418 like** likely, probable **419 row** stanza. **chanson** ballad, song **420 my abridgment** something that cuts short my conversation; also, a diversion **423 valanced** fringed (with a beard) **424 beard** confront, challenge (with obvious pun). **young lady** i.e., boy playing women's parts **425 By 'r Lady** by Our Lady **427 chopine** thick-soled shoe of Italian fashion **427–428 uncurrent** not passable as lawful coinage **428 cracked . . . ring** i.e., changed from adolescent to male voice, no longer suitable for women's roles. (Coins featured rings enclosing the sovereign's head; if the coin was cracked within this ring, it was unfit for currency.) **429 e'en to 't** go at it **430 straight** at once **431 quality** professional skill

HAMLET I heard thee speak me a speech once, but it was never acted, or if it was, not above once, for the play, I remember, pleased not the million; 'twas caviar to the general. But it was—as I received it, and others, whose judgments in such matters cried in the top of mine—an excellent play, well digested in the scenes, set down with as much modesty as cunning. I remember one said there were no sallets in the lines to make the matter savory, nor no matter in the phrase that might indict the author of affectation, but called it an honest method, as wholesome as sweet, and by very much more handsome than fine. One speech in 't I chiefly loved: 'twas Aeneas' tale to Dido, and thereabout of it especially when he speaks of Priam's slaughter. If it live in your memory, begin at this line: let me see, let me see—

"The rugged Pyrrhus, like th' Hyrcanian beast"—

'Tis not so. It begins with Pyrrhus:

"The rugged Pyrrhus, he whose sable arms,
Black as his purpose, did the night resemble
When he lay couchèd in the ominous horse,
Hath now this dread and black complexion smeared
With heraldry more dismal. Head to foot
Now is he total gules, horridly tricked
With blood of fathers, mothers, daughters, sons,
Baked and impasted with the parching streets,

436–437 caviar to the general caviar to the multitude, i.e., a choice dish too elegant for coarse tastes **438–439 cried in the top of** i.e., spoke with greater authority than **439 digested** arranged, ordered **440 modesty** moderation, restraint. **cunning** skill **441 sallets** i.e., something savory, spicy improprieties **443 indict** convict **445 fine** elaborately ornamented, showy **447–448 Priam's slaughter** the slaying of the ruler of Troy, when the Greeks finally took the city **450 Pyrrhus** a Greek hero in the Trojan War, also known as Neoptolemus, son of Achilles—another avenging son. **Hyrcanian beast** i.e., tiger. (On the death of Priam, see Virgil, *Aeneid,* 2.506–558; compare the whole speech with Marlowe's *Dido Queen of Carthage,* 2.1.214 ff. On the *Hyrcanian* tiger, see *Aeneid*, 4.366–367. Hyrcania is on the Caspian Sea.) **452 sable** black (for reasons of camouflage during the episode of the Trojan horse) **454 couchèd** concealed. **ominous horse** Trojan horse, by which the Greeks gained access to Troy **456 dismal** ill-omened **457 gules** red. (A heraldic term.) **tricked** adorned, decorated **459 impasted** crusted, like a thick paste. **with . . . streets** by the parching heat of the streets (because of the fires everywhere)

That lend a tyrannous and a damnèd light
To their lord's murder. Roasted in wrath and fire, 461
And thus o'ersizèd with coagulate gore, 462
With eyes like carbuncles, the hellish Pyrrhus 463
Old grandsire Priam seeks."
So proceed you.

POLONIUS 'Fore God, my lord, well spoken, with good accent and good discretion.

FIRST PLAYER "Anon he finds him
Striking too short at Greeks. His antique sword,
Rebellious to his arm, lies where it falls,
Repugnant to command. Unequal matched, 471
Pyrrhus at Priam drives, in rage strikes wide,
But with the whiff and wind of his fell sword 473
Th' unnervèd father falls. Then senseless Ilium, 474
Seeming to feel this blow, with flaming top
Stoops to his base, and with a hideous crash 476
Takes prisoner Pyrrhus' ear. For, lo! His sword,
Which was declining on the milky head 478
Of reverend Priam, seemed i' th' air to stick.
So as a painted tyrant Pyrrhus stood, 480
And, like a neutral to his will and matter, 481
Did nothing.
But as we often see against some storm 483
A silence in the heavens, the rack stand still, 484
The bold winds speechless, and the orb below 485
As hush as death, anon the dreadful thunder
Doth rend the region, so, after Pyrrhus' pause, 487
Arousèd vengeance sets him new a-work,
And never did the Cyclops' hammers fall 489
On Mars's armor forged for proof eterne 490
With less remorse than Pyrrhus' bleeding sword 491
Now falls on Priam.

461 their lord's i.e., Priam's **462 o'ersizèd** covered as with size or glue **463 carbuncles** large fiery-red precious stones thought to emit their own light **471 Repugnant** disobedient, resistant **473 fell** cruel **474 unnervèd** strengthless. **senseless Ilium** inanimate citadel of Troy **476 his** its **478 declining** descending. **milky** white-haired **480 painted** i.e., painted in a picture **481 like . . . matter** i.e., as though suspended between his intention and its fulfillment **483 against** just before **484 rack** mass of clouds **485 orb** globe, earth **487 region** sky **489 Cyclops** giant armor-makers in the smithy of Vulcan **490 proof eterne** eternal resistance to assault **491 remorse** pity

Out, out, thou strumpet Fortune! All you gods
In general synod take away her power! 494
Break all the spokes and fellies from her wheel, 495
And bowl the round nave down the hill of heaven 496
As low as to the fiends!"

POLONIUS This is too long.

HAMLET It shall to the barber's with your beard.—Prithee, say on. He's for a jig or a tale of bawdry, or he 500
sleeps. Say on; come to Hecuba. 501

FIRST PLAYER
"But who, ah woe! had seen the moblèd queen"— 502

HAMLET "The moblèd queen"?

POLONIUS That's good. "Moblèd queen" is good.

FIRST PLAYER
"Run barefoot up and down, threat'ning the flames
With bisson rheum, a clout upon that head 506
Where late the diadem stood, and, for a robe, 507
About her lank and all o'erteemèd loins 508
A blanket, in the alarm of fear caught up—
Who this had seen, with tongue in venom steeped,
'Gainst Fortune's state would treason have
pronounced. 511
But if the gods themselves did see her then
When she saw Pyrrhus make malicious sport
In mincing with his sword her husband's limbs,
The instant burst of clamor that she made,
Unless things mortal move them not at all,
Would have made milch the burning eyes of heaven, 517
And passion in the gods." 518

POLONIUS Look whe'er he has not turned his color and 519
has tears in 's eyes. Prithee, no more.

HAMLET 'Tis well. I'll have thee speak out the rest of
this soon.—Good my lord, will you see the players well

494 synod assembly **495 fellies** pieces of wood forming the rim of a wheel **496 nave** hub **500 jig** comic song and dance often given at the end of a play **501 Hecuba** wife of Priam **502 who . . . had** anyone who had (also in l. 510). **moblèd** muffled **506 bisson rheum** blinding tears. **clout** cloth **507 late** lately **508 o'erteemèd** worn out with bearing children **511 state** rule, managing. **pronounced** proclaimed **517 milch** milky, moist with tears **518 passion** overpowering emotion **519 whe'er** whether

bestowed? Do you hear, let them be well used, for they 523
are the abstract and brief chronicles of the time. After 524
your death you were better have a bad epitaph than
their ill report while you live.

POLONIUS My lord, I will use them according to their
desert.

HAMLET God's bodikin, man, much better. Use every 529
man after his desert, and who shall scape whipping?
Use them after your own honor and dignity. The less
they deserve, the more merit is in your bounty. Take
them in.

POLONIUS Come, sirs.

HAMLET Follow him, friends. We'll hear a play tomorrow. [*As they start to leave, Hamlet detains the First Player.*] Dost thou hear me, old friend? Can you play *The Murder of Gonzago*?

FIRST PLAYER Ay, my lord.

HAMLET We'll ha 't tomorrow night. You could, for 540
a need, study a speech of some dozen or sixteen lines 541
which I would set down and insert in 't, could you
not?

FIRST PLAYER Ay, my lord.

HAMLET Very well. Follow that lord, and look you mock 545
him not. (*Exeunt Polonius and Players.*) My good friends,
I'll leave you till night. You are welcome to Elsinore.

ROSENCRANTZ Good my lord!

Exeunt [*Rosencrantz and Guildenstern*].

HAMLET

Ay, so, goodbye to you.—Now I am alone.
O, what a rogue and peasant slave am I!
Is it not monstrous that this player here,
But in a fiction, in a dream of passion, 552
Could force his soul so to his own conceit 553
That from her working all his visage wanned, 554
Tears in his eyes, distraction in his aspect,

523 bestowed lodged **524 abstract** summary account **529 God's bodikin** by God's (Christ's) little body, *bodykin.* (Not to be confused with *bodkin,* dagger.) **540 ha 't** have it **541 study** memorize **545 mock** mimic derisively **552 But** merely **553 to** in accord with. **conceit** conception **554 from her working** as a result of, or in response to, his soul's activity. **wanned** grew pale

A broken voice, and his whole function suiting 556
With forms to his conceit? And all for nothing! 557
For Hecuba!
What's Hecuba to him, or he to Hecuba,
That he should weep for her? What would he do
Had he the motive and the cue for passion
That I have? He would drown the stage with tears
And cleave the general ear with horrid speech, 563
Make mad the guilty and appall the free, 564
Confound the ignorant, and amaze indeed
The very faculties of eyes and ears. Yet I,
A dull and muddy-mettled rascal, peak 567
Like John-a-dreams, unpregnant of my cause, 568
And can say nothing—no, not for a king
Upon whose property and most dear life 570
A damned defeat was made. Am I a coward? 571
Who calls me villain? Breaks my pate across?
Plucks off my beard and blows it in my face?
Tweaks me by the nose? Gives me the lie i' the throat 574
As deep as to the lungs? Who does me this?
Ha, 'swounds, I should take it; for it cannot be 576
But I am pigeon-livered and lack gall 577
To make oppression bitter, or ere this 578
I should ha' fatted all the region kites 579
With this slave's offal. Bloody, bawdy villain!
Remorseless, treacherous, lecherous, kindless villain! 581
O, vengeance!
Why, what an ass am I! This is most brave, 583
That I, the son of a dear father murdered,
Prompted to my revenge by heaven and hell,
Must like a whore unpack my heart with words

556–557 his whole . . . conceit all his bodily powers responding with actions to suit his thought **563 the general ear** everyone's ear. **horrid** horrible **564 appall** (Literally, make pale.) **free** innocent **567 muddy-mettled** dull-spirited. **peak** mope, pine **568 John-a-dreams** a sleepy, dreaming idler. **unpregnant of** not quickened by **570 property** i.e., the crown; perhaps also character, quality **571 defeat** destruction
574 Gives me the lie calls me a liar **576 'swounds** by his (Christ's) wounds **577 pigeon-livered** (The pigeon or dove was popularly supposed to be mild because it secreted no gall.) **578 To . . . bitter** to make tyranny bitter to itself **579 region kites** kites (birds of prey) of the air **581 Remorseless** pitiless. **kindless** unnatural **583 brave** fine, admirable. (Said ironically.)

And fall a-cursing, like a very drab, 587
A scullion! Fie upon 't, foh! About, my brain! 588
Hum, I have heard
That guilty creatures sitting at a play
Have by the very cunning of the scene 591
Been struck so to the soul that presently 592
They have proclaimed their malefactions;
For murder, though it have no tongue, will speak
With most miraculous organ. I'll have these players
Play something like the murder of my father
Before mine uncle. I'll observe his looks;
I'll tent him to the quick. If 'a do blench, 598
I know my course. The spirit that I have seen
May be the devil, and the devil hath power
T' assume a pleasing shape; yea, and perhaps,
Out of my weakness and my melancholy,
As he is very potent with such spirits, 603
Abuses me to damn me. I'll have grounds 604
More relative than this. The play's the thing 605
Wherein I'll catch the conscience of the King. *Exit.*

♣

587 drab prostitute **588 scullion** menial kitchen servant (apt to be foulmouthed). **About** about it, to work **591 cunning** art, skill. **scene** dramatic presentation **592 presently** at once **598 tent** probe. **blench** quail, flinch **603 spirits** humors (of melancholy) **604 Abuses** deludes **605 relative** cogent, pertinent

3.1 *Enter King, Queen, Polonius, Ophelia, Rosencrantz, Guildenstern, lords.*

KING
And can you by no drift of conference 1
Get from him why he puts on this confusion,
Grating so harshly all his days of quiet
With turbulent and dangerous lunacy?

ROSENCRANTZ
He does confess he feels himself distracted,
But from what cause 'a will by no means speak.

GUILDENSTERN
Nor do we find him forward to be sounded, 7
But with a crafty madness keeps aloof
When we would bring him on to some confession
Of his true state.

QUEEN Did he receive you well?

ROSENCRANTZ Most like a gentleman.

GUILDENSTERN
But with much forcing of his disposition. 12

ROSENCRANTZ
Niggard of question, but of our demands 13
Most free in his reply.

QUEEN Did you assay him 14
To any pastime?

ROSENCRANTZ
Madam, it so fell out that certain players
We o'erraught on the way. Of these we told him, 17
And there did seem in him a kind of joy
To hear of it. They are here about the court,
And, as I think, they have already order
This night to play before him.

POLONIUS 'Tis most true,
And he beseeched me to entreat Your Majesties
To hear and see the matter.

KING
With all my heart, and it doth much content me
To hear him so inclined.

3.1. Location: The castle.
1 drift of conference directing of conversation **7 forward** willing. **sounded** questioned **12 disposition** inclination **13 question** conversation **14 assay** try to win **17 o'erraught** overtook and passed

Good gentlemen, give him a further edge 26
And drive his purpose into these delights.

ROSENCRANTZ
We shall, my lord.
Exeunt Rosencrantz and Guildenstern.

KING Sweet Gertrude, leave us too,
For we have closely sent for Hamlet hither, 29
That he, as 'twere by accident, may here
Affront Ophelia. 31
Her father and myself, lawful espials, 32
Will so bestow ourselves that seeing, unseen,
We may of their encounter frankly judge,
And gather by him, as he is behaved,
If 't be th' affliction of his love or no
That thus he suffers for.

QUEEN I shall obey you.
And for your part, Ophelia, I do wish
That your good beauties be the happy cause
Of Hamlet's wildness. So shall I hope your virtues
Will bring him to his wonted way again,
To both your honors.

OPHELIA Madam, I wish it may.
[*Exit Queen.*]

POLONIUS
Ophelia, walk you here.—Gracious, so please you, 43
We will bestow ourselves. [*To Ophelia.*] Read on this book, [*Giving her a book*] 44
That show of such an exercise may color 45
Your loneliness. We are oft to blame in this— 46
'Tis too much proved—that with devotion's visage 47
And pious action we do sugar o'er
The devil himself.

KING [*Aside*] O, 'tis too true!
How smart a lash that speech doth give my conscience!
The harlot's cheek, beautied with plastering art,
Is not more ugly to the thing that helps it 53

26 edge incitement **29 closely** privately **31 Affront** confront, meet **32 espials** spies **43 Gracious** Your Grace (i.e., the King) **44 bestow** conceal **45 exercise** act of devotion. (The book she reads is one of devotion.) **color** give a plausible appearance to **46 loneliness** being alone **47 too much proved** too often shown to be true, too often practiced **53 to** compared to. **the thing** i.e., the cosmetic

Than is my deed to my most painted word.
O heavy burden!

POLONIUS

I hear him coming. Let's withdraw, my lord.
[*The King and Polonius withdraw.*]

Enter Hamlet. [*Ophelia pretends to read a book.*]

HAMLET

To be, or not to be, that is the question:
Whether 'tis nobler in the mind to suffer
The slings and arrows of outrageous fortune,
Or to take arms against a sea of troubles
And by opposing end them. To die, to sleep—
No more—and by a sleep to say we end
The heartache and the thousand natural shocks
That flesh is heir to. 'Tis a consummation
Devoutly to be wished. To die, to sleep;
To sleep, perchance to dream. Ay, there's the rub,
For in that sleep of death what dreams may come,
When we have shuffled off this mortal coil,
Must give us pause. There's the respect
That makes calamity of so long life.
For who would bear the whips and scorns of time,
Th' oppressor's wrong, the proud man's contumely,
The pangs of disprized love, the law's delay,
The insolence of office, and the spurns
That patient merit of th' unworthy takes,
When he himself might his quietus make
With a bare bodkin? Who would fardels bear,
To grunt and sweat under a weary life,
But that the dread of something after death,
The undiscovered country from whose bourn
No traveler returns, puzzles the will,

56 s.d. withdraw (The King and Polonius may retire behind an arras. The stage directions specify that they "enter" again near the end of the scene.) **59 slings** missiles **66 rub** (Literally, an obstacle in the game of bowls.) **68 shuffled** sloughed, cast. **coil** turmoil **69 respect** consideration **70 of . . . life** so long-lived (also suggesting that long life is itself a calamity) **71 time** the world we live in **72 contumely** insolent abuse **73 disprized** unvalued **74 office** officialdom. **spurns** insults **75 of . . . takes** receives from unworthy persons **76 quietus** acquittance; here, death **77 a bare** merely a. **bodkin** dagger. **fardels** burdens **80 bourn** boundary

And makes us rather bear those ills we have
Than fly to others that we know not of?
Thus conscience does make cowards of us all;
And thus the native hue of resolution
Is sicklied o'er with the pale cast of thought,
And enterprises of great pitch and moment
With this regard their currents turn awry
And lose the name of action.—Soft you now,
The fair Ophelia. Nymph, in thy orisons
Be all my sins remembered.

OPHELIA Good my lord.
How does your honor for this many a day?

HAMLET
I humbly thank you; well, well, well.

OPHELIA
My lord, I have remembrances of yours,
That I have longèd long to redeliver.
I pray you, now receive them. [*She offers tokens.*]

HAMLET
No, not I. I never gave you aught.

OPHELIA
My honored lord, you know right well you did,
And with them words of so sweet breath composed
As made the things more rich. Their perfume lost,
Take these again, for to the noble mind
Rich gifts wax poor when givers prove unkind.
There, my lord. [*She gives tokens.*]

HAMLET Ha, ha! Are you honest?

OPHELIA My lord?

HAMLET Are you fair?

OPHELIA What means your lordship?

HAMLET That if you be honest and fair, your honesty should admit no discourse to your beauty.

OPHELIA Could beauty, my lord, have better commerce than with honesty?

85 native hue natural color, complexion **86 cast** tinge, shade of color **87 pitch** height (as of a falcon's flight). **moment** importance **88 regard** respect, consideration. **currents** courses **89 Soft you** i.e., wait a minute, gently **90 orisons** prayers **104 honest** (1) truthful (2) chaste **106 fair** (1) beautiful (2) just, honorable **108 your honesty** your chastity **109 discourse to** familiar dealings with **110 commerce** dealings, intercourse

HAMLET Ay, truly, for the power of beauty will sooner transform honesty from what it is to a bawd than the force of honesty can translate beauty into his likeness. This was sometime a paradox, but now the time gives it proof. I did love you once.

OPHELIA Indeed, my lord, you made me believe so.

HAMLET You should not have believed me, for virtue cannot so inoculate our old stock but we shall relish of it. I loved you not.

OPHELIA I was the more deceived.

HAMLET Get thee to a nunnery. Why wouldst thou be a breeder of sinners? I am myself indifferent honest, but yet I could accuse me of such things that it were better my mother had not borne me: I am very proud, revengeful, ambitious, with more offenses at my beck than I have thoughts to put them in, imagination to give them shape, or time to act them in. What should such fellows as I do crawling between earth and heaven? We are arrant knaves all; believe none of us. Go thy ways to a nunnery. Where's your father?

OPHELIA At home, my lord.

HAMLET Let the doors be shut upon him, that he may play the fool nowhere but in 's own house. Farewell.

OPHELIA O, help him, you sweet heavens!

HAMLET If thou dost marry, I'll give thee this plague for thy dowry: be thou as chaste as ice, as pure as snow, thou shalt not escape calumny. Get thee to a nunnery, farewell. Or, if thou wilt needs marry, marry a fool, for wise men know well enough what monsters you make of them. To a nunnery, go, and quickly too. Farewell.

OPHELIA Heavenly powers, restore him!

HAMLET I have heard of your paintings too, well enough. God hath given you one face, and you make

114 his its **115 sometime** formerly. **a paradox** a view opposite to commonly held opinion. **the time** the present age **119 inoculate** graft, be engrafted to **119–120 but . . . it** i.e., that we do not still have about us a taste of the old stock, i.e., retain our sinfulness **122 nunnery** convent (with possibly an awareness that the word was also used derisively to denote a brothel) **123 indifferent honest** reasonably virtuous **126 beck** command **140 monsters** (An allusion to the horns of a cuckold.) **you** i.e., you women

yourselves another. You jig, you amble, and you 146
lisp, you nickname God's creatures, and make your 147
wantonness your ignorance. Go to, I'll no more on 't; 148
it hath made me mad. I say we will have no more
marriage. Those that are married already—all but
one—shall live. The rest shall keep as they are. To a
nunnery, go. *Exit.*

OPHELIA

O, what a noble mind is here o'erthrown!
The courtier's, soldier's, scholar's, eye, tongue, sword,
Th' expectancy and rose of the fair state, 155
The glass of fashion and the mold of form, 156
Th' observed of all observers, quite, quite down! 157
And I, of ladies most deject and wretched,
That sucked the honey of his music vows,
Now see that noble and most sovereign reason
Like sweet bells jangled out of tune and harsh,
That unmatched form and feature of blown youth 162
Blasted with ecstasy. O, woe is me, 163
T' have seen what I have seen, see what I see!

Enter King and Polonius.

KING

Love? His affections do not that way tend; 165
Nor what he spake, though it lacked form a little,
Was not like madness. There's something in his soul
O'er which his melancholy sits on brood, 168
And I do doubt the hatch and the disclose 169
Will be some danger; which for to prevent,
I have in quick determination
Thus set it down: he shall with speed to England 172

146 jig i.e., dance and sing affectedly and wantonly. **amble** dance, move coquettishly **147 lisp** (A wanton affectation.) **nickname** find a new name for, transform (as in using cosmetics) **147–148 make . . . ignorance** i.e., excuse your affectation on the grounds of your ignorance **148 on 't** of it **155 Th' expectancy . . . state** the hope and ornament of the kingdom made fair (by him) **156 The glass . . . form** the mirror of true self-fashioning and the pattern of courtly behavior **157 Th' observed . . . observers** i.e., the center of attention and honor in the court **162 blown** blooming **163 Blasted** withered. **ecstasy** madness **165 affections** emotions, feelings **168 sits on brood** sits like a bird on a nest, about to *hatch* mischief (l. 169) **169 doubt** fear. **disclose** disclosure, hatching **172 set it down** resolved

For the demand of our neglected tribute. 173
Haply the seas and countries different
With variable objects shall expel 175
This something settled matter in his heart, 176
Whereon his brains still beating puts him thus 177
From fashion of himself. What think you on 't? 178

POLONIUS
It shall do well. But yet do I believe
The origin and commencement of his grief
Sprung from neglected love.—How now, Ophelia?
You need not tell us what Lord Hamlet said;
We heard it all.—My lord, do as you please,
But, if you hold it fit, after the play
Let his queen-mother all alone entreat him 185
To show his grief. Let her be round with him; 186
And I'll be placed, so please you, in the ear
Of all their conference. If she find him not, 188
To England send him, or confine him where
Your wisdom best shall think.

KING
It shall be so.
Madness in great ones must not unwatched go.

Exeunt.

3.2 *Enter Hamlet and three of the Players.*

HAMLET Speak the speech, I pray you, as I pronounced it to you, trippingly on the tongue. But if you mouth
it, as many of our players do, I had as lief the town 3
crier spoke my lines. Nor do not saw the air too much with your hand, thus, but use all gently; for in the very torrent, tempest, and, as I may say, whirlwind of your

173 For . . . of to demand **175 variable objects** various sights and surroundings to divert him **176 This something . . . heart** the strange unidentified matter settled in his heart **177 still** continually
178 From . . . himself out of his natural manner **185 queen-mother** queen and mother, not widowed dowager **186 round** blunt **188 find him not** fails to discover what is troubling him

3.2. Location: The castle.
3 our players (Indefinite use; i.e., players nowadays.) **I had as lief** I would just as soon

passion, you must acquire and beget a temperance
that may give it smoothness. O, it offends me to the
soul to hear a robustious periwig-pated fellow tear a 9
passion to tatters, to very rags, to split the ears of the
groundlings, who for the most part are capable of 11
nothing but inexplicable dumb shows and noise. I
would have such a fellow whipped for o'erdoing Ter- 13
magant. It out-Herods Herod. Pray you, avoid it. 14

FIRST PLAYER I warrant your honor.

HAMLET Be not too tame neither, but let your own discretion be your tutor. Suit the action to the word, the
word to the action, with this special observance, that
you o'erstep not the modesty of nature. For anything 19
so o'erdone is from the purpose of playing, whose 20
end, both at the first and now, was and is to hold as
'twere the mirror up to nature, to show virtue her
feature, scorn her own image, and the very age and 23
body of the time his form and pressure. Now this 24
overdone or come tardy off, though it makes the un- 25
skillful laugh, cannot but make the judicious grieve, 26
the censure of the which one must in your allowance 27
o'erweigh a whole theater of others. O, there be players that I have seen play, and heard others praise, and
that highly, not to speak it profanely, that, neither 30
having th' accent of Christians nor the gait of Chris- 31
tian, pagan, nor man, have so strutted and bellowed 32
that I have thought some of nature's journeymen had 33

9 robustious violent, boisterous. **periwig-pated** wearing a wig **11 groundlings** spectators who paid least and stood in the yard of the theater. **capable of** able to understand **13–14 Termagant** a supposed deity of the Mohammedans, not found in any English medieval play but elsewhere portrayed as violent and blustering **14 Herod** Herod of Jewry. (A character in *The Slaughter of the Innocents* and other cycle plays. The part was played with great noise and fury.) **19 modesty** restraint, moderation **20 from** contrary to **23 scorn** i.e., something foolish and deserving of scorn **23–24 the very . . . time** i.e., the present state of affairs **24 his** its. **pressure** stamp, impressed character **25 come tardy off** inadequately done **25–26 the unskillful** those lacking in judgment **27 the censure . . . one** the judgment of even one of whom. **your allowance** your scale of values **30 not . . . profanely** (Hamlet anticipates his idea in ll. 33–34 that some men were not made by God at all.) **31 Christians** i.e., ordinary decent folk **32 nor man** i.e., nor any human being at all **33 journeymen** laborers not yet masters in their trade

made men and not made them well, they imitated humanity so abominably.

FIRST PLAYER I hope we have reformed that indifferently with us, sir.

HAMLET O, reform it altogether. And let those that play your clowns speak no more than is set down for them; for there be of them that will themselves laugh, to set on some quantity of barren spectators to laugh too, though in the meantime some necessary question of the play be then to be considered. That's villainous, and shows a most pitiful ambition in the fool that uses it. Go make you ready. [*Exeunt Players.*]

Enter Polonius, Guildenstern, and Rosencrantz.

How now, my lord, will the King hear this piece of work?

POLONIUS And the Queen too, and that presently.

HAMLET Bid the players make haste. [*Exit Polonius.*]
Will you two help to hasten them?

ROSENCRANTZ
Ay, my lord. *Exeunt they two.*

HAMLET What ho, Horatio!

Enter Horatio.

HORATIO Here, sweet lord, at your service.

HAMLET
Horatio, thou art e'en as just a man
As e'er my conversation coped withal.

HORATIO
O, my dear lord—

HAMLET Nay, do not think I flatter,
For what advancement may I hope from thee
That no revenue hast but thy good spirits
To feed and clothe thee? Why should the poor be
flattered?

35 abominably (Shakespeare's usual spelling, *abhominably,* suggests a literal though etymologically incorrect meaning, "removed from human nature.") **36 indifferently** tolerably **40 of them** i.e., some among them **41 barren** i.e., of wit **48 presently** at once **54 my . . . withal** my contact with people provided opportunity for encounter with

No, let the candied tongue lick absurd pomp, 59
And crook the pregnant hinges of the knee 60
Where thrift may follow fawning. Dost thou hear? 61
Since my dear soul was mistress of her choice
And could of men distinguish her election, 63
Sh' hath sealed thee for herself, for thou hast been 64
As one, in suffering all, that suffers nothing,
A man that Fortune's buffets and rewards
Hast ta'en with equal thanks; and blest are those
Whose blood and judgment are so well commeddled 68
That they are not a pipe for Fortune's finger
To sound what stop she please. Give me that man 70
That is not passion's slave, and I will wear him
In my heart's core, ay, in my heart of heart,
As I do thee.—Something too much of this.—
There is a play tonight before the King.
One scene of it comes near the circumstance
Which I have told thee of my father's death.
I prithee, when thou seest that act afoot,
Even with the very comment of thy soul 78
Observe my uncle. If his occulted guilt 79
Do not itself unkennel in one speech, 80
It is a damnèd ghost that we have seen, 81
And my imaginations are as foul
As Vulcan's stithy. Give him heedful note, 83
For I mine eyes will rivet to his face,
And after we will both our judgments join
In censure of his seeming.

HORATIO Well, my lord. 86
If 'a steal aught the whilst this play is playing 87
And scape detecting, I will pay the theft.

59 candied sugared, flattering **60 pregnant** compliant **61 thrift** profit **63 could . . . election** could make distinguishing choices among men **64 sealed thee** (Literally, as one would seal a legal document to mark possession.) **68 blood** passion. **commeddled** commingled **70 stop** hole in a wind instrument for controlling the sound **78 very . . . soul** i.e., your most penetrating observation and consideration **79 occulted** hidden **80 unkennel** (As one would say of a fox driven from its lair.) **81 damnèd** in league with Satan **83 stithy** smithy, place of stiths (anvils) **86 censure of his seeming** judgment of his appearance or behavior **87 If 'a steal aught** i.e., if he hides anything

[*Flourish.*] *Enter trumpets and kettledrums, King, Queen, Polonius, Ophelia,* [*Rosencrantz, Guildenstern, and other lords, with guards carrying torches*].

HAMLET They are coming to the play. I must be idle. 89
Get you a place. [*The King, Queen, and courtiers sit.*]

KING How fares our cousin Hamlet? 91

HAMLET Excellent, i' faith, of the chameleon's dish: I eat 92
the air, promise-crammed. You cannot feed capons so. 93

KING I have nothing with this answer, Hamlet. These 94
words are not mine. 95

HAMLET No, nor mine now. [*To Polonius.*] My lord, 96
you played once i' th' university, you say?

POLONIUS That did I, my lord, and was accounted a good actor.

HAMLET What did you enact?

POLONIUS I did enact Julius Caesar. I was killed i' the Capitol; Brutus killed me.

HAMLET It was a brute part of him to kill so capital a 103
calf there.—Be the players ready? 104

ROSENCRANTZ Ay, my lord. They stay upon your patience.

QUEEN Come hither, my dear Hamlet, sit by me.

HAMLET No, good Mother, here's metal more attractive. 108

POLONIUS [*To the King*] Oho, do you mark that?

HAMLET Lady, shall I lie in your lap?
[*Lying down at Ophelia's feet.*]

OPHELIA No, my lord.

HAMLET I mean, my head upon your lap?

OPHELIA Ay, my lord.

89 idle (1) unoccupied (2) mad **91 cousin** i.e., close relative **92 chameleon's dish** (Chameleons were supposed to feed on air. Hamlet deliberately misinterprets the King's *fares* as "feeds." By his phrase *eat the air* he also plays on the idea of feeding himself with the promise of succession, of being the *heir*.) **93 capons** roosters castrated and *crammed* with feed to make them succulent **94 have . . . with** make nothing of, or gain nothing from **95 are not mine** do not respond to what I asked **96 nor mine now** (Once spoken, words are proverbially no longer the speaker's own—and hence should be uttered warily.) **103 brute** (The Latin meaning of *brutus,* "stupid," was often used punningly with the name Brutus.) **part** (1) deed (2) role **104 calf** fool **108 metal** substance that is *attractive,* i.e., magnetic, but with suggestion also of *mettle,* disposition

HAMLET Do you think I meant country matters? 114

OPHELIA I think nothing, my lord.

HAMLET That's a fair thought to lie between maids' legs.

OPHELIA What is, my lord?

HAMLET Nothing. 119

OPHELIA You are merry, my lord.

HAMLET Who, I?

OPHELIA Ay, my lord.

HAMLET O God, your only jig maker. What should a 123
man do but be merry? For look you how cheerfully my
mother looks, and my father died within 's two hours. 125

OPHELIA Nay, 'tis twice two months, my lord.

HAMLET So long? Nay then, let the devil wear black, for
I'll have a suit of sables. O heavens! Die two months 128
ago, and not forgotten yet? Then there's hope a great
man's memory may outlive his life half a year. But,
by 'r Lady, 'a must build churches, then, or else shall
'a suffer not thinking on, with the hobbyhorse, whose 132
epitaph is "For O, for O, the hobbyhorse is forgot." 133

The trumpets sound. Dumb show follows.

Enter a King and a Queen [*very lovingly*]; *the Queen embracing him, and he her.* [*She kneels, and makes show of protestation unto him.*] *He takes her up, and declines his head upon her neck. He lies him down upon a bank of flowers. She, seeing him asleep, leaves him. Anon comes in*

114 country matters the coarse and bawdy things that country folk do (with a pun on the first syllable of *country*) **119 Nothing** the figure zero or naught, suggesting the female anatomy. (*Thing* not infrequently has a bawdy connotation of male or female anatomy, and the reference here could be male.) **123 only jig maker** very best composer of jigs (song and dance). (Hamlet replies sardonically to Ophelia's observation that he is merry by saying, "If you're looking for someone who is really merry, you've come to the right person.") **125 within 's** within this **128 suit of sables** garments trimmed with the fur of the sable, and hence suited for a wealthy person, not a mourner (but with a pun on *sable,* black, ironically suggesting mourning once again) **132 suffer . . . on** undergo oblivion **133 For . . . forgot** (Verse of a song occurring also in *Love's Labor's Lost,* 3.1.27–28. The hobbyhorse was a character made up to resemble a horse and rider, appearing in the morris dance and such May-game sports. This song laments the disappearance of such customs under pressure from the Puritans.)

another man, takes off his crown, kisses it, pours poison in the sleeper's ears, and leaves him. The Queen returns, finds the King dead, makes passionate action. The Poisoner with some three or four come in again, seem to condole with her. The dead body is carried away. The Poisoner woos the Queen with gifts; she seems harsh awhile, but in the end accepts love.

[*Exeunt players.*]

OPHELIA What means this, my lord?

HAMLET Marry, this' miching mallico; it means mischief.

OPHELIA Belike this show imports the argument of the play.

Enter Prologue.

HAMLET We shall know by this fellow. The players cannot keep counsel; they'll tell all.

OPHELIA Will 'a tell us what this show meant?

HAMLET Ay, or any show that you will show him. Be not you ashamed to show, he'll not shame to tell you what it means.

OPHELIA You are naught, you are naught. I'll mark the play.

PROLOGUE

For us, and for our tragedy,
Here stooping to your clemency,
We beg your hearing patiently. [*Exit.*]

HAMLET Is this a prologue, or the posy of a ring?

OPHELIA 'Tis brief, my lord.

HAMLET As woman's love.

Enter [*two Players as*] *King and Queen.*

PLAYER KING

Full thirty times hath Phoebus' cart gone round

135 this' miching mallico this is sneaking mischief **137 Belike** probably. **argument** plot **140 counsel** secret **142–143 Be not you** if you are not **145 naught** indecent. (Ophelia is reacting to Hamlet's pointed remarks about not being ashamed to show all.) **148 stooping** bowing **150 posy . . . ring** brief motto in verse inscribed in a ring **153 Phoebus' cart** the sun god's chariot, making its yearly cycle

Neptune's salt wash and Tellus' orbèd ground, 154
And thirty dozen moons with borrowed sheen 155
About the world have times twelve thirties been,
Since love our hearts and Hymen did our hands 157
Unite commutual in most sacred bands. 158

PLAYER QUEEN
So many journeys may the sun and moon
Make us again count o'er ere love be done!
But, woe is me, you are so sick of late,
So far from cheer and from your former state,
That I distrust you. Yet, though I distrust, 163
Discomfort you, my lord, it nothing must. 164
For women's fear and love hold quantity; 165
In neither aught, or in extremity. 166
Now, what my love is, proof hath made you know, 167
And as my love is sized, my fear is so. 168
Where love is great, the littlest doubts are fear;
Where little fears grow great, great love grows there.

PLAYER KING
Faith, I must leave thee, love, and shortly too;
My operant powers their functions leave to do. 172
And thou shalt live in this fair world behind, 173
Honored, beloved; and haply one as kind
For husband shalt thou—

PLAYER QUEEN O, confound the rest!
Such love must needs be treason in my breast.
In second husband let me be accurst!
None wed the second but who killed the first. 178

HAMLET Wormwood, wormwood.

PLAYER QUEEN
The instances that second marriage move 180
Are base respects of thrift, but none of love. 181

154 salt wash the sea. **Tellus** goddess of the earth, of the *orbèd ground* **155 borrowed** i.e., reflected **157 Hymen** god of matrimony **158 commutual** mutually. **bands** bonds **163 distrust** am anxious about **164 nothing** not at all **165 hold quantity** keep proportion with one another **166 In . . . extremity** i.e., women fear and love either too little or too much, but the two, fear and love, are equal in either case **167 proof** experience **168 sized** in size **172 operant powers** vital functions. **leave to do** cease to perform **173 behind** after I have gone **178 None** i.e., let no woman. **but who** except her who **180 instances** motives. **move** motivate **181 base . . . thrift** ignoble considerations of material prosperity

A second time I kill my husband dead
When second husband kisses me in bed.

PLAYER KING

I do believe you think what now you speak,
But what we do determine oft we break.
Purpose is but the slave to memory, 186
Of violent birth, but poor validity, 187
Which now, like fruit unripe, sticks on the tree, 188
But fall unshaken when they mellow be.
Most necessary 'tis that we forget 190
To pay ourselves what to ourselves is debt. 191
What to ourselves in passion we propose,
The passion ending, doth the purpose lose.
The violence of either grief or joy
Their own enactures with themselves destroy. 195
Where joy most revels, grief doth most lament; 196
Grief joys, joy grieves, on slender accident. 197
This world is not for aye, nor 'tis not strange 198
That even our loves should with our fortunes change;
For 'tis a question left us yet to prove,
Whether love lead fortune, or else fortune love.
The great man down, you mark his favorite flies; 202
The poor advanced makes friends of enemies. 203
And hitherto doth love on fortune tend; 204
For who not needs shall never lack a friend, 205
And who in want a hollow friend doth try 206
Directly seasons him his enemy. 207
But, orderly to end where I begun,
Our wills and fates do so contrary run 209

186 Purpose . . . memory i.e., our good intentions are subject to forgetfulness **187 validity** strength, durability **188 Which** i.e., purpose **190–191 Most . . . debt** i.e., it's inevitable that in time we forget the obligations we have imposed on ourselves **195 enactures** fulfillments **196–197 Where . . . accident** i.e., the capacity for extreme joy and grief go together, and often one extreme is instantly changed into its opposite on the slightest provocation **198 aye** ever **202 down** fallen in fortune **203 The poor . . . enemies** i.e., when one of humble station is promoted, you see his enemies suddenly becoming his friends **204 hitherto** up to this point in the argument, or, to this extent. **tend** attend **205 who not needs** he who is not in need (of wealth) **206 who in want** he who, being in need. **try** test (his generosity) **207 seasons him** ripens him into **209 Our . . . run** what we want and what we get go so contrarily

That our devices still are overthrown; 210
Our thoughts are ours, their ends none of our own. 211
So think thou wilt no second husband wed,
But die thy thoughts when thy first lord is dead.

PLAYER QUEEN
Nor earth to me give food, nor heaven light, 214
Sport and repose lock from me day and night, 215
To desperation turn my trust and hope,
An anchor's cheer in prison be my scope! 217
Each opposite that blanks the face of joy 218
Meet what I would have well and it destroy! 219
Both here and hence pursue me lasting strife 220
If, once a widow, ever I be a wife!

HAMLET If she should break it now!

PLAYER KING
'Tis deeply sworn. Sweet, leave me here awhile;
My spirits grow dull, and fain I would beguile 224
The tedious day with sleep.

PLAYER QUEEN Sleep rock thy brain,
And never come mischance between us twain!
[*He sleeps.*] *Exit* [*Player Queen*].

HAMLET Madam, how like you this play?

QUEEN The lady doth protest too much, methinks. 228

HAMLET O, but she'll keep her word.

KING Have you heard the argument? Is there no offense 230
in 't?

HAMLET No, no, they do but jest, poison in jest. No of- 232
fense i' the world. 233

KING What do you call the play?

HAMLET *The Mousetrap.* Marry, how? Tropically. 235
This play is the image of a murder done in Vienna.

210 devices still intentions continually **211 ends** results **214 Nor** let neither **215 Sport . . . night** may day deny me its pastimes and night its repose **217 anchor's cheer** anchorite's or hermit's fare. **my scope** the extent of my happiness **218–219 Each . . . destroy** may every adverse thing that causes the face of joy to turn pale meet and destroy everything that I desire to see prosper. **blanks** causes to blanch or grow pale **220 hence** in the life hereafter **224 spirits** vital spirits **228 doth . . . much** makes too many promises and protestations **230 argument** plot **230–233 offense . . . offense** cause for objection . . . crime **232 jest** make believe **235 Tropically** figuratively. (The first quarto reading, *trapically,* suggests a pun on *trap* in *Mousetrap.*)

Gonzago is the Duke's name, his wife, Baptista. You 237
shall see anon. 'Tis a knavish piece of work, but what
of that? Your Majesty, and we that have free souls, it 239
touches us not. Let the galled jade wince, our withers 240
are unwrung. 241

Enter Lucianus.

This is one Lucianus, nephew to the King.

OPHELIA You are as good as a chorus, my lord. 243

HAMLET I could interpret between you and your love,
if I could see the puppets dallying. 245

OPHELIA You are keen, my lord, you are keen. 246

HAMLET It would cost you a groaning to take off mine
edge.

OPHELIA Still better, and worse. 249

HAMLET So you mis-take your husbands.—Begin, mur- 250
derer; leave thy damnable faces and begin. Come, the
croaking raven doth bellow for revenge.

LUCIANUS

Thoughts black, hands apt, drugs fit, and time agreeing,
Confederate season, else no creature seeing, 254
Thou mixture rank, of midnight weeds collected,
With Hecate's ban thrice blasted, thrice infected, 256
Thy natural magic and dire property 257
On wholesome life usurp immediately.

[*He pours the poison into the sleeper's ear.*]

237 Duke's i.e., King's. (A slip that may be due to Shakespeare's possible source, the actual murder of the Duke of Urbino by Luigi Gonzaga in 1538.) **239 free** guiltless **240 galled jade** horse whose hide is rubbed by saddle or harness. **withers** the part between the horse's shoulder blades **241 unwrung** not rubbed sore **243 chorus** (In many Elizabethan plays the forthcoming action was explained by an actor known as the "chorus"; at a puppet show the actor who spoke the dialogue was known as an "interpreter," as indicated by the lines following.) **245 puppets dallying** (With sexual suggestion, continued in *keen,* i.e., sexually aroused, *groaning,* i.e., moaning in pregnancy, and *edge,* i.e., sexual desire or impetuosity.) **246 keen** sharp, bitter
249 Still . . . worse more keen, always *bettering* what other people say with witty wordplay, but at the same time more offensive **250 So** even thus (in marriage). **mis-take** take erringly, falseheartedly. (The marriage vows say, "for better, for worse.") **254 Confederate season** the time and occasion conspiring (to assist the murderer). **else** otherwise
256 Hecate's ban the curse of Hecate, the goddess of witchcraft
257 dire property baleful quality

HAMLET 'A poisons him i' the garden for his estate. His name's Gonzago. The story is extant, and written in very choice Italian. You shall see anon how the murderer gets the love of Gonzago's wife.

[*Claudius rises.*]

OPHELIA The King rises.

HAMLET What, frighted with false fire?

QUEEN How fares my lord?

POLONIUS Give o'er the play.

KING Give me some light. Away!

POLONIUS Lights, lights, lights!

Exeunt all but Hamlet and Horatio.

HAMLET

"Why, let the strucken deer go weep,
The hart ungallèd play.
For some must watch, while some must sleep;
Thus runs the world away."

Would not this, sir, and a forest of feathers—if the rest of my fortunes turn Turk with me—with two Provincial roses on my razed shoes, get me a fellowship in a cry of players?

HORATIO Half a share.

HAMLET A whole one, I.

"For thou dost know, O Damon dear,
This realm dismantled was
Of Jove himself, and now reigns here
A very, very—pajock."

259 estate i.e., the kingship. **His** i.e., the King's **264 false fire** the blank discharge of a gun loaded with powder but no shot **269–272 Why . . . away** (Probably from an old ballad, with allusion to the popular belief that a wounded deer retires to weep and die; cf. *As You Like It,* 2.1.66.) **270 ungallèd** unafflicted **271 watch** remain awake **272 Thus . . . away** thus the world goes **273 this** i.e., the play. **feathers** (Allusion to the plumes that Elizabethan actors were fond of wearing.) **274 turn Turk with** turn renegade against, go back on **274–275 Provincial roses** rosettes of ribbon like the roses of a part of France **275 razed** with ornamental slashing **275–276 fellowship . . . players** partnership in a theatrical company. **cry** pack (of hounds) **279 Damon** the friend of Pythias, as Horatio is friend of Hamlet; or, a traditional pastoral name **280 dismantled** stripped, divested **281 Of Jove** (Jove, like Hamlet's father, has been taken away, leaving only a peacock or an ass.) **282 pajock** peacock, a bird with a bad reputation. (Here substituted for the obvious rhyme-word "ass.") Or possibly the word is *patchock,* savage, base person.

HORATIO You might have rhymed.

HAMLET O good Horatio, I'll take the ghost's word for a thousand pound. Didst perceive?

HORATIO Very well, my lord.

HAMLET Upon the talk of the poisoning?

HORATIO I did very well note him.

Enter Rosencrantz and Guildenstern.

HAMLET Aha! Come, some music! Come, the recorders.

"For if the King like not the comedy,
Why then, belike, he likes it not, perdy."

Come, some music.

GUILDENSTERN Good my lord, vouchsafe me a word with you.

HAMLET Sir, a whole history.

GUILDENSTERN The King, sir—

HAMLET Ay, sir, what of him?

GUILDENSTERN Is in his retirement marvelous distempered.

HAMLET With drink, sir?

GUILDENSTERN No, my lord, with choler.

HAMLET Your wisdom should show itself more richer to signify this to the doctor, for for me to put him to his purgation would perhaps plunge him into more choler.

GUILDENSTERN Good my lord, put your discourse into some frame and start not so wildly from my affair.

HAMLET I am tame, sir. Pronounce.

GUILDENSTERN The Queen, your mother, in most great affliction of spirit, hath sent me to you.

HAMLET You are welcome.

289–290 recorders wind instruments of the flute kind **292 perdy** (A corruption of the French *par dieu,* "by God.") **299 retirement** withdrawal to his chambers **299–300 distempered** out of humor. (But Hamlet deliberately plays on the wider application to any illness of mind or body, as in ll. 335–336, especially to drunkenness.) **302 choler** i.e., anger. (But Hamlet takes the word in its more basic humors sense of "bilious disorder.") **305 purgation** (Hamlet hints at something going beyond medical treatment to bloodletting and the extraction of confession.) **308 frame** order. **start** shy or jump away (like a horse; the opposite of *tame* in l. 309)

GUILDENSTERN Nay, good my lord, this courtesy is not of the right breed. If it shall please you to make me a wholesome answer, I will do your mother's commandment; if not, your pardon and my return shall be the end of my business.

HAMLET Sir, I cannot.

ROSENCRANTZ What, my lord?

HAMLET Make you a wholesome answer; my wit's diseased. But, sir, such answer as I can make, you shall command, or rather, as you say, my mother. Therefore no more, but to the matter. My mother, you say—

ROSENCRANTZ Then thus she says: your behavior hath struck her into amazement and admiration.

HAMLET O wonderful son, that can so stonish a mother! But is there no sequel at the heels of this mother's admiration? Impart.

ROSENCRANTZ She desires to speak with you in her closet ere you go to bed.

HAMLET We shall obey, were she ten times our mother. Have you any further trade with us?

ROSENCRANTZ My lord, you once did love me.

HAMLET And do still, by these pickers and stealers.

ROSENCRANTZ Good my lord, what is your cause of distemper? You do surely bar the door upon your own liberty if you deny your griefs to your friend.

HAMLET Sir, I lack advancement.

ROSENCRANTZ How can that be, when you have the voice of the King himself for your succession in Denmark?

HAMLET Ay, sir, but "While the grass grows"—the proverb is something musty.

Enter the Players with recorders.

O, the recorders. Let me see one. [*He takes a recorder.*]

314 breed (1) kind (2) breeding, manners **316 pardon** permission to depart **325 admiration** wonder **330 closet** private chamber **334 pickers and stealers** i.e., hands. (So called from the catechism, "to keep my hands from picking and stealing.") **337 deny** refuse to share **342 While . . . grows** (The rest of the proverb is "the silly horse starves"; Hamlet may not live long enough to succeed to the kingdom.) **343 something** somewhat **s.d. Players** actors

To withdraw with you: why do you go about to recover the wind of me, as if you would drive me into a toil?

GUILDENSTERN O, my lord, if my duty be too bold, my love is too unmannerly.

HAMLET I do not well understand that. Will you play upon this pipe?

GUILDENSTERN My lord, I cannot.

HAMLET I pray you.

GUILDENSTERN Believe me, I cannot.

HAMLET I do beseech you.

GUILDENSTERN I know no touch of it, my lord.

HAMLET It is as easy as lying. Govern these ventages with your fingers and thumb, give it breath with your mouth, and it will discourse most eloquent music. Look you, these are the stops.

GUILDENSTERN But these cannot I command to any utterance of harmony. I have not the skill.

HAMLET Why, look you now, how unworthy a thing you make of me! You would play upon me, you would seem to know my stops, you would pluck out the heart of my mystery, you would sound me from my lowest note to the top of my compass, and there is much music, excellent voice, in this little organ, yet cannot you make it speak. 'Sblood, do you think I am easier to be played on than a pipe? Call me what instrument you will, though you can fret me, you cannot play upon me.

Enter Polonius.

God bless you, sir!

POLONIUS My lord, the Queen would speak with you, and presently.

HAMLET Do you see yonder cloud that's almost in shape of a camel?

345 withdraw speak privately **345–346 recover the wind** get to the windward side (thus driving the game into the toil, or net) **346 toil** snare **347–348 if . . . unmannerly** if I am using an unmannerly boldness, it is my love that occasions it **349 I . . . that** i.e., I don't understand how genuine love can be unmannerly **356 ventages** stops of the recorder **365 sound** (1) fathom (2) produce sound in **366 compass** range (of voice) **367 organ** musical instrument **370 fret** irritate (with a quibble on *fret* meaning the piece of wood, gut, or metal that regulates the fingering on an instrument) **374 presently** at once

POLONIUS By the Mass and 'tis, like a camel indeed.
HAMLET Methinks it is like a weasel.
POLONIUS It is backed like a weasel.
HAMLET Or like a whale?
POLONIUS Very like a whale.
HAMLET Then I will come to my mother by and by. 382
[*Aside.*] They fool me to the top of my bent.—I will 383
come by and by.
POLONIUS I will say so. [*Exit.*]
HAMLET "By and by" is easily said. Leave me, friends.
[*Exeunt all but Hamlet.*]
'Tis now the very witching time of night, 387
When churchyards yawn and hell itself breathes out
Contagion to this world. Now could I drink hot blood 389
And do such bitter business as the day
Would quake to look on. Soft, now to my mother.
O heart, lose not thy nature! Let not ever
The soul of Nero enter this firm bosom. 393
Let me be cruel, not unnatural;
I will speak daggers to her, but use none.
My tongue and soul in this be hypocrites:
How in my words soever she be shent, 397
To give them seals never my soul consent! *Exit.* 398

✤

3.3 *Enter King, Rosencrantz, and Guildenstern.*

KING
I like him not, nor stands it safe with us 1
To let his madness range. Therefore prepare you.
I your commission will forthwith dispatch, 3
And he to England shall along with you.

382 by and by quite soon **383 fool me** make me play the fool. **top of my bent** limit of my ability or endurance. (Literally, the extent to which a bow may be bent.) **387 witching time** time when spells are cast and evil is abroad **389 Now could I** i.e., now I might be tempted to **393 Nero** murderer of his mother, Agrippina **397 How . . . soever** however much by my words. **shent** rebuked **398 give them seals** i.e., confirm them with deeds

3.3. Location: The castle.
1 him i.e., his behavior **3 dispatch** prepare, cause to be drawn up

The terms of our estate may not endure
Hazard so near 's as doth hourly grow
Out of his brows.

GUILDENSTERN We will ourselves provide.
Most holy and religious fear it is
To keep those many many bodies safe
That live and feed upon Your Majesty.

ROSENCRANTZ
The single and peculiar life is bound
With all the strength and armor of the mind
To keep itself from noyance, but much more
That spirit upon whose weal depends and rests
The lives of many. The cess of majesty
Dies not alone, but like a gulf doth draw
What's near it with it; or it is a massy wheel
Fixed on the summit of the highest mount,
To whose huge spokes ten thousand lesser things
Are mortised and adjoined, which, when it falls,
Each small annexment, petty consequence,
Attends the boisterous ruin. Never alone
Did the King sigh, but with a general groan.

KING
Arm you, I pray you, to this speedy voyage,
For we will fetters put about this fear,
Which now goes too free-footed.

ROSENCRANTZ We will haste us.

Exeunt Gentlemen [*Rosencrantz and Guildenstern*].

Enter Polonius.

POLONIUS
My lord, he's going to his mother's closet.
Behind the arras I'll convey myself

5 terms condition, circumstances. **our estate** my royal position **7 brows** i.e., effronteries, threatening frowns, or contrivances **8 religious fear** sacred duty **11 single and peculiar** individual and private **13 noyance** harm **15 cess** decease, cessation **16 gulf** whirlpool **17 massy** massive **20 when it falls** i.e., when it descends, like the wheel of Fortune, bringing a king down with it **21 Each . . . consequence** i.e., every hanger-on and unimportant person or thing connected with the King **22 Attends** participates in **24 Arm** prepare **28 arras** screen of tapestry placed around the walls of household apartments. (On the Elizabethan stage, the arras was presumably over a door or discovery space in the tiring-house facade.)

To hear the process. I'll warrant she'll tax him home, 29
And, as you said—and wisely was it said—
'Tis meet that some more audience than a mother, 31
Since nature makes them partial, should o'erhear
The speech, of vantage. Fare you well, my liege. 33
I'll call upon you ere you go to bed
And tell you what I know.

KING Thanks, dear my lord.

Exit [*Polonius*].

O, my offense is rank, it smells to heaven;
It hath the primal eldest curse upon 't, 37
A brother's murder. Pray can I not,
Though inclination be as sharp as will; 39
My stronger guilt defeats my strong intent,
And like a man to double business bound 41
I stand in pause where I shall first begin,
And both neglect. What if this cursèd hand
Were thicker than itself with brother's blood,
Is there not rain enough in the sweet heavens
To wash it white as snow? Whereto serves mercy 46
But to confront the visage of offense? 47
And what's in prayer but this twofold force,
To be forestallèd ere we come to fall, 49
Or pardoned being down? Then I'll look up.
My fault is past. But, O, what form of prayer
Can serve my turn? "Forgive me my foul murder"?
That cannot be, since I am still possessed
Of those effects for which I did the murder:
My crown, mine own ambition, and my queen.
May one be pardoned and retain th' offense? 56
In the corrupted currents of this world 57
Offense's gilded hand may shove by justice, 58

29 process proceedings. **tax him home** reprove him severely **31 meet** fitting **33 of vantage** from an advantageous place, or, in addition **37 the primal eldest curse** the curse of Cain, the first murderer; he killed his brother Abel **39 Though . . . will** though my desire is as strong as my determination **41 bound** (1) destined (2) obliged. (The King wants to repent and still enjoy what he has gained.) **46–47 Whereto . . . offense** i.e., for what function does mercy serve other than to undo the effects of sin **49 forestallèd** prevented (from sinning) **56 th' offense** i.e., the thing for which one offended **57 currents** courses **58 gilded hand** hand offering gold as a bribe. **shove by** thrust aside

And oft 'tis seen the wicked prize itself 59
Buys out the law. But 'tis not so above.
There is no shuffling, there the action lies 61
In his true nature, and we ourselves compelled, 62
Even to the teeth and forehead of our faults, 63
To give in evidence. What then? What rests? 64
Try what repentance can. What can it not?
Yet what can it, when one cannot repent?
O wretched state! O bosom black as death!
O limèd soul, that, struggling to be free, 68
Art more engaged! Help, angels! Make assay. 69
Bow, stubborn knees, and heart with strings of steel,
Be soft as sinews of the newborn babe!
All may be well. [*He kneels.*]

Enter Hamlet.

HAMLET
Now might I do it pat, now 'a is a-praying; 73
And now I'll do 't. [*He draws his sword.*] And so 'a goes to heaven,
And so am I revenged. That would be scanned: 75
A villain kills my father, and for that,
I, his sole son, do this same villain send
To heaven.
Why, this is hire and salary, not revenge.
'A took my father grossly, full of bread, 80
With all his crimes broad blown, as flush as May; 81
And how his audit stands who knows save heaven? 82
But in our circumstance and course of thought 83
'Tis heavy with him. And am I then revenged,
To take him in the purging of his soul,

59 wicked prize prize won by wickedness **61 There** i.e., in heaven. **shuffling** escape by trickery. **the action lies** the accusation is made manifest, comes up for consideration. (A legal metaphor.) **62 his** its **63 to the teeth and forehead** face to face, concealing nothing **64 give in** provide. **rests** remains **68 limèd** caught as with birdlime, a sticky substance used to ensnare birds **69 engaged** embedded. **assay** trial. (Said to himself.) **73 pat** opportunely **75 would be scanned** needs to be looked into, or, would be interpreted as follows **80 grossly** i.e., not spiritually prepared. **full of bread** i.e., enjoying his worldly pleasures. (See Ezekiel 16:49.) **81 crimes broad blown** sins in full bloom. **flush** lusty **82 audit** account **83 in . . . thought** as we see it from our mortal perspective

When he is fit and seasoned for his passage? 86
No!
Up, sword, and know thou a more horrid hent. 88
[*He puts up his sword.*]
When he is drunk asleep, or in his rage,
Or in th' incestuous pleasure of his bed,
At game a-swearing, or about some act
That has no relish of salvation in 't— 92
Then trip him, that his heels may kick at heaven,
And that his soul may be as damned and black
As hell, whereto it goes. My mother stays. 95
This physic but prolongs thy sickly days. *Exit.* 96

KING
My words fly up, my thoughts remain below.
Words without thoughts never to heaven go. *Exit.*

✤

3.4 *Enter* [*Queen*] *Gertrude and Polonius.*

POLONIUS
'A will come straight. Look you lay home to him. 1
Tell him his pranks have been too broad to bear with, 2
And that Your Grace hath screened and stood between
Much heat and him. I'll shroud me even here. 4
Pray you, be round with him. 5

HAMLET (*Within*) Mother, Mother, Mother!

QUEEN I'll warrant you, fear me not.
Withdraw, I hear him coming.
[*Polonius hides behind the arras.*]

Enter Hamlet.

HAMLET Now, Mother, what's the matter?

86 seasoned matured, readied **88 know . . . hent** await to be grasped by me on a more horrid occasion **92 relish** trace, savor **95 stays** awaits (me) **96 physic** purging (by prayer), or, Hamlet's postponement of the killing

3.4. Location: The Queen's private chamber.
1 lay thrust (i.e., reprove him soundly) **2 broad** unrestrained **4 Much heat** i.e., the King's anger. **shroud** conceal (with ironic fitness to Polonius's imminent death. The word is only in the first quarto; the second quarto and the Folio read "silence.") **5 round** blunt

QUEEN
Hamlet, thou hast thy father much offended.

HAMLET
Mother, you have my father much offended.

QUEEN
Come, come, you answer with an idle tongue.

HAMLET
Go, go, you question with a wicked tongue.

QUEEN
Why, how now, Hamlet?

HAMLET
What's the matter now?

QUEEN
Have you forgot me?

HAMLET
No, by the rood, not so:
You are the Queen, your husband's brother's wife,
And—would it were not so!—you are my mother.

QUEEN
Nay, then, I'll set those to you that can speak.

HAMLET
Come, come, and sit you down; you shall not budge.
You go not till I set you up a glass
Where you may see the inmost part of you.

QUEEN
What wilt thou do? Thou wilt not murder me?
Help, ho!

POLONIUS [*Behind the arras*] What ho! Help!

HAMLET [*Drawing*]
How now? A rat? Dead for a ducat, dead!
[*He thrusts his rapier through the arras.*]

POLONIUS [*Behind the arras*]
O, I am slain! [*He falls and dies.*]

QUEEN O me, what hast thou done?

HAMLET Nay, I know not. Is it the King?

QUEEN
O, what a rash and bloody deed is this!

HAMLET
A bloody deed—almost as bad, good Mother,
As kill a king and marry with his brother.

10 thy father i.e., your stepfather, Claudius **12 idle** foolish **15 forgot me** i.e., forgotten that I am your mother. **rood** cross of Christ
25 Dead for a ducat i.e., I bet a ducat he's dead, whoever I killed; or, a ducat is his life's fee

QUEEN
As kill a king!
HAMLET Ay, lady, it was my word.
[*He parts the arras and discovers Polonius.*]
Thou wretched, rash, intruding fool, farewell!
I took thee for thy better. Take thy fortune.
Thou find'st to be too busy is some danger.— 34
Leave wringing of your hands. Peace, sit you down,
And let me wring your heart, for so I shall,
If it be made of penetrable stuff,
If damnèd custom have not brazed it so 38
That it be proof and bulwark against sense. 39
QUEEN
What have I done, that thou dar'st wag thy tongue
In noise so rude against me?
HAMLET Such an act
That blurs the grace and blush of modesty,
Calls virtue hypocrite, takes off the rose
From the fair forehead of an innocent love
And sets a blister there, makes marriage vows 45
As false as dicers' oaths. O, such a deed
As from the body of contraction plucks 47
The very soul, and sweet religion makes 48
A rhapsody of words. Heaven's face does glow 49
O'er this solidity and compound mass 50
With tristful visage, as against the doom, 51
Is thought-sick at the act.
QUEEN Ay me, what act, 52
That roars so loud and thunders in the index? 53
HAMLET [*Showing her two likenesses*]
Look here upon this picture, and on this,
The counterfeit presentment of two brothers. 55
See what a grace was seated on this brow:

34 busy playing the busybody **38 damnèd custom** habitual wickedness. **brazed** brazened, hardened **39 proof** armor. **sense** feeling **45 sets a blister** i.e., brands as a harlot **47 contraction** the marriage contract **48 sweet religion makes** i.e., makes marriage vows **49 rhapsody** senseless string **49–52 Heaven's . . . act** heaven's face looks down upon this solid world, this compound mass, with sorrowful face as though the day of doom were near, and is thought-sick at the deed (i.e., Gertrude's marriage) **53 index** table of contents, prelude or preface **55 counterfeit presentment** portrayed representation

Hyperion's curls, the front of Jove himself,
An eye like Mars to threaten and command,
A station like the herald Mercury
New-lighted on a heaven-kissing hill—
A combination and a form indeed
Where every god did seem to set his seal
To give the world assurance of a man.
This was your husband. Look you now what follows:
Here is your husband, like a mildewed ear,
Blasting his wholesome brother. Have you eyes?
Could you on this fair mountain leave to feed
And batten on this moor? Ha, have you eyes?
You cannot call it love, for at your age
The heyday in the blood is tame, it's humble,
And waits upon the judgment, and what judgment
Would step from this to this? Sense, sure, you have,
Else could you not have motion, but sure that sense
Is apoplexed, for madness would not err,
Nor sense to ecstasy was ne'er so thralled,
But it reserved some quantity of choice
To serve in such a difference. What devil was 't
That thus hath cozened you at hoodman-blind?
Eyes without feeling, feeling without sight,
Ears without hands or eyes, smelling sans all,
Or but a sickly part of one true sense
Could not so mope. O shame, where is thy blush?
Rebellious hell,
If thou canst mutine in a matron's bones,

57 Hyperion's the sun god's. **front** brow **59 station** manner of standing. **Mercury** winged messenger of the gods **60 New-lighted** newly alighted **62 set his seal** i.e., affix his approval **65 ear** i.e., of grain **66 Blasting** blighting **68 batten** gorge. **moor** barren upland (suggesting also "dark-skinned") **70 heyday** state of excitement. **blood** passion **72 Sense** perception through the five senses (the functions of the middle or sensible soul) **74 apoplexed** paralyzed. (Hamlet goes on to explain that without such a paralysis of will, mere madness would not so err, nor would the five senses so enthrall themselves to *ecstasy* or lunacy; even such deranged states of mind would be able to make the obvious choice between Hamlet Senior and Claudius.) **err** so err **76 But** but that **77 To . . . difference** to help in making choice between two such men **78 cozened** cheated. **hoodman-blind** blindman's buff. (In this game, says Hamlet, the devil must have pushed Claudius toward Gertrude while she was blindfolded.) **80 sans** without **82 mope** be dazed, act aimlessly **84 mutine** incite mutiny

To flaming youth let virtue be as wax
And melt in her own fire. Proclaim no shame
When the compulsive ardor gives the charge,
Since frost itself as actively doth burn,
And reason panders will.

QUEEN O Hamlet, speak no more!
Thou turn'st my eyes into my very soul,
And there I see such black and grainèd spots
As will not leave their tinct.

HAMLET Nay, but to live
In the rank sweat of an enseamèd bed,
Stewed in corruption, honeying and making love
Over the nasty sty!

QUEEN O, speak to me no more!
These words like daggers enter in my ears.
No more, sweet Hamlet!

HAMLET A murderer and a villain,
A slave that is not twentieth part the tithe
Of your precedent lord, a vice of kings,
A cutpurse of the empire and the rule,
That from a shelf the precious diadem stole
And put it in his pocket!

QUEEN No more!

Enter Ghost [*in his nightgown*].

HAMLET A king of shreds and patches—
Save me, and hover o'er me with your wings,
You heavenly guards! What would your gracious figure?

QUEEN Alas, he's mad!

HAMLET
Do you not come your tardy son to chide,

85–86 be as wax . . . fire i.e., melt like a candle or stick of sealing wax held over its own flame **86–89 Proclaim . . . will** call it no shameful business when the compelling ardor of youth delivers the attack, i.e., commits lechery, since the frost of advanced age burns with as active a fire of lust and reason perverts itself by fomenting lust rather than restraining it **92 grainèd** dyed in grain, indelible **93 leave their tinct** surrender their color **94 enseamèd** saturated in the grease and filth of passionate lovemaking **95 Stewed** soaked, bathed (with a suggestion of *stew,* brothel) **100 tithe** tenth part **101 precedent** former (i.e., the elder Hamlet). **vice** buffoon. (A reference to the Vice of the morality plays.) **106 shreds and patches** i.e., motley, the traditional costume of the clown or fool

That, lapsed in time and passion, lets go by 111
Th' important acting of your dread command? 112
O, say!

GHOST
Do not forget. This visitation
Is but to whet thy almost blunted purpose.
But look, amazement on thy mother sits. 116
O, step between her and her fighting soul!
Conceit in weakest bodies strongest works. 118
Speak to her, Hamlet.

HAMLET How is it with you, lady?

QUEEN Alas, how is 't with you,
That you do bend your eye on vacancy,
And with th' incorporal air do hold discourse? 122
Forth at your eyes your spirits wildly peep,
And, as the sleeping soldiers in th' alarm, 124
Your bedded hair, like life in excrements, 125
Start up and stand on end. O gentle son,
Upon the heat and flame of thy distemper
Sprinkle cool patience. Whereon do you look?

HAMLET
On him, on him! Look you how pale he glares!
His form and cause conjoined, preaching to stones, 130
Would make them capable.—Do not look upon me, 131
Lest with this piteous action you convert 132
My stern effects. Then what I have to do 133
Will want true color—tears perchance for blood. 134

QUEEN To whom do you speak this?

HAMLET Do you see nothing there?

111 lapsed in time and passion having allowed time to lapse and passion to cool, or, having lost momentum through excessive indulgence in passion **112 important** importunate, urgent **116 amazement** distraction **118 Conceit** imagination **122 incorporal** immaterial **124 as . . . alarm** like soldiers called out of sleep by an alarum **125 bedded** laid in smooth layers. **like life in excrements** i.e., as though hair, an outgrowth of the body, had a life of its own. (Hair was thought to be lifeless because it lacks sensation, and so its standing on end would be unnatural and ominous.) **130 His . . . conjoined** his appearance joined to his cause for speaking **131 capable** receptive **132–133 convert . . . effects** divert me from my stern duty **134 want . . . blood** lack plausibility so that (with a play on the normal sense of *color*) I shall shed colorless tears instead of blood

QUEEN
Nothing at all, yet all that is I see.
HAMLET Nor did you nothing hear?
QUEEN No, nothing but ourselves.
HAMLET
Why, look you there, look how it steals away!
My father, in his habit as he lived!
Look where he goes even now out at the portal!
Exit Ghost.
QUEEN
This is the very coinage of your brain.
This bodiless creation ecstasy
Is very cunning in.
HAMLET Ecstasy?
My pulse as yours doth temperately keep time,
And makes as healthful music. It is not madness
That I have uttered. Bring me to the test,
And I the matter will reword, which madness
Would gambol from. Mother, for love of grace,
Lay not that flattering unction to your soul
That not your trespass but my madness speaks.
It will but skin and film the ulcerous place,
Whiles rank corruption, mining all within,
Infects unseen. Confess yourself to heaven,
Repent what's past, avoid what is to come,
And do not spread the compost on the weeds
To make them ranker. Forgive me this my virtue;
For in the fatness of these pursy times
Virtue itself of vice must pardon beg,
Yea, curb and woo for leave to do him good.
QUEEN
O Hamlet, thou hast cleft my heart in twain.
HAMLET
O, throw away the worser part of it,

141 habit dress. **as** as when **143 very** mere **144–145 This . . . in** madness is skillful in creating this kind of hallucination **150 reword** repeat word for word **151 gambol** skip away **152 unction** ointment **154 skin** grow a skin for **155 mining** working under the surface **158 compost** manure **159 this my virtue** my virtuous talk in reproving you **160 fatness** grossness. **pursy** flabby, out of shape **162 curb** bow, bend the knee. **leave** permission

And live the purer with the other half.
Good night. But go not to my uncle's bed;
Assume a virtue, if you have it not.
That monster, custom, who all sense doth eat, 168
Of habits devil, is angel yet in this, 169
That to the use of actions fair and good
He likewise gives a frock or livery 171
That aptly is put on. Refrain tonight, 172
And that shall lend a kind of easiness
To the next abstinence; the next more easy;
For use almost can change the stamp of nature, 175
And either . . . the devil, or throw him out 176
With wondrous potency. Once more, good night;
And when you are desirous to be blest, 178
I'll blessing beg of you. For this same lord, 179
[*Pointing to Polonius*]
I do repent; but heaven hath pleased it so
To punish me with this, and this with me,
That I must be their scourge and minister. 182
I will bestow him, and will answer well 183
The death I gave him. So, again, good night.
I must be cruel only to be kind.
This bad begins, and worse remains behind. 186
One word more, good lady.

QUEEN
What shall I do?

HAMLET
Not this by no means that I bid you do:
Let the bloat king tempt you again to bed, 189
Pinch wanton on your cheek, call you his mouse, 190

168 who . . . eat which consumes all proper or natural feeling, all sensibility **169 Of habits devil** devil-like in prompting evil habits **171 livery** an outer appearance, a customary garb (and hence a predisposition easily assumed in time of stress) **172 aptly** readily **175 use** habit. **the stamp of nature** our inborn traits **176 And either** (A defective line usually emended by inserting the word *master* after *either,* following the fourth quarto and early editors.) **178–179 when . . . you** i.e., when you are ready to be penitent and seek God's blessing, I will ask your blessing as a dutiful son should (on the occasion of departure) **182 their scourge and minister** i.e., agent of heavenly retribution. (By *scourge,* Hamlet also suggests that he himself will eventually suffer punishment in the process of fulfilling heaven's will.) **183 bestow** stow, dispose of. **answer** account for **186 This** i.e., the killing of Polonius. **behind** to come **189 bloat** bloated **190 Pinch wanton** i.e., leave his love pinches on your cheeks, branding you as wanton

And let him, for a pair of reechy kisses,
Or paddling in your neck with his damned fingers,
Make you to ravel all this matter out
That I essentially am not in madness,
But mad in craft. 'Twere good you let him know,
For who that's but a queen, fair, sober, wise,
Would from a paddock, from a bat, a gib,
Such dear concernings hide? Who would do so?
No, in despite of sense and secrecy,
Unpeg the basket on the house's top,
Let the birds fly, and like the famous ape,
To try conclusions, in the basket creep
And break your own neck down.

QUEEN

Be thou assured, if words be made of breath,
And breath of life, I have no life to breathe
What thou hast said to me.

HAMLET

I must to England. You know that?

QUEEN Alack,

I had forgot. 'Tis so concluded on.

HAMLET

There's letters sealed, and my two schoolfellows,
Whom I will trust as I will adders fanged,
They bear the mandate; they must sweep my way
And marshal me to knavery. Let it work.
For 'tis the sport to have the enginer
Hoist with his own petard, and 't shall go hard
But I will delve one yard below their mines

191 reechy dirty, filthy **192 paddling** fingering amorously **193 ravel . . . out** unravel, disclose **195 in craft** by cunning. **good** (Said sarcastically; also the following 8 lines.) **197 paddock** toad. **gib** tomcat **198 dear concernings** important affairs **200 Unpeg the basket** open the cage, i.e., let out the secret **201 famous ape** (in a story now lost) **202 conclusions** experiments (in which the ape apparently enters a cage from which birds have been released and then tries to fly out of the cage as they have done, falling to his death) **203 down** in the fall; utterly **211–212 sweep . . . knavery** sweep a path before me and conduct me to some *knavery* or treachery prepared for me **212 work** proceed **213 enginer** maker of military contrivances **214 Hoist with** blown up by. **petard** an explosive used to blow in a door or make a breach **214–215 't shall . . . will** unless luck is against me, I will **215 mines** tunnels used in warfare to undermine the enemy's emplacements; Hamlet will countermine by going under their mines

And blow them at the moon. O, 'tis most sweet
When in one line two crafts directly meet. 217
This man shall set me packing. 218
I'll lug the guts into the neighbor room.
Mother, good night indeed. This counselor
Is now most still, most secret, and most grave,
Who was in life a foolish prating knave.—
Come, sir, to draw toward an end with you.— 223
Good night, Mother.

Exeunt [*separately, Hamlet dragging in Polonius*].

✤

217 in one line i.e., mines and countermines on a collision course, or the countermines directly below the mines. **crafts** acts of guile, plots **218 set me packing** set me to making schemes, and set me to lugging (him), and, also, send me off in a hurry **223 draw . . . end** finish up (with a pun on *draw*, pull)

4.1 *Enter King and Queen, with Rosencrantz and Guildenstern.*

KING
There's matter in these sighs, these profound heaves. 1
You must translate; 'tis fit we understand them.
Where is your son?

QUEEN
Bestow this place on us a little while.
[*Exeunt Rosencrantz and Guildenstern.*]
Ah, mine own lord, what have I seen tonight!

KING
What, Gertrude? How does Hamlet?

QUEEN
Mad as the sea and wind when both contend
Which is the mightier. In his lawless fit,
Behind the arras hearing something stir,
Whips out his rapier, cries, "A rat, a rat!"
And in this brainish apprehension kills 11
The unseen good old man.

KING
O heavy deed! 12
It had been so with us, had we been there. 13
His liberty is full of threats to all—
To you yourself, to us, to everyone.
Alas, how shall this bloody deed be answered? 16
It will be laid to us, whose providence 17
Should have kept short, restrained, and out of haunt 18
This mad young man. But so much was our love,
We would not understand what was most fit,
But, like the owner of a foul disease,
To keep it from divulging, let it feed 22
Even on the pith of life. Where is he gone?

4.1. Location: The castle.
s.d. Enter . . . Queen (Some editors argue that Gertrude never exits in 3.4 and that the scene is continuous here, but the second quarto marks an entrance for her and at l. 35 Claudius speaks of Gertrude's *closet* as though it were elsewhere. A short time has elapsed during which the King has become aware of her highly wrought emotional state.)
1 matter significance **11 brainish apprehension** headstrong conception **12 heavy** grievous **13 us** i.e., me. (The royal "we"; also in l. 15.) **16 answered** explained **17 providence** foresight **18 short** i.e., on a short tether. **out of haunt** secluded **22 divulging** becoming evident

QUEEN
To draw apart the body he hath killed,
O'er whom his very madness, like some ore 25
Among a mineral of metals base, 26
Shows itself pure: 'a weeps for what is done.

KING O Gertrude, come away!
The sun no sooner shall the mountains touch
But we will ship him hence, and this vile deed
We must with all our majesty and skill
Both countenance and excuse.—Ho, Guildenstern!

Enter Rosencrantz and Guildenstern.

Friends both, go join you with some further aid.
Hamlet in madness hath Polonius slain,
And from his mother's closet hath he dragged him.
Go seek him out, speak fair, and bring the body
Into the chapel. I pray you, haste in this.
[*Exeunt Rosencrantz and Guildenstern.*]
Come, Gertrude, we'll call up our wisest friends
And let them know both what we mean to do
And what's untimely done. 40
Whose whisper o'er the world's diameter, 41
As level as the cannon to his blank, 42
Transports his poisoned shot, may miss our name
And hit the woundless air. O, come away! 44
My soul is full of discord and dismay. *Exeunt.*

✤

4.2 *Enter Hamlet.*

HAMLET Safely stowed.

ROSENCRANTZ, GUILDENSTERN (*Within*) Hamlet! Lord Hamlet!

25 ore vein of gold **26 mineral** mine **40 And . . . done** (A defective line; conjectures as to the missing words include *So, haply, slander* [Capell and others]; *For, haply, slander* [Theobald and others]; and *So envious slander* [Jenkins].) **41 diameter** extent from side to side **42 As level** with as direct aim. **his blank** its target at point-blank range
44 woundless invulnerable

4.2. Location: The castle.

HAMLET But soft, what noise? Who calls on Hamlet? O, here they come.

Enter Rosencrantz and Guildenstern.

ROSENCRANTZ
What have you done, my lord, with the dead body?
HAMLET
Compounded it with dust, whereto 'tis kin.
ROSENCRANTZ
Tell us where 'tis, that we may take it thence
And bear it to the chapel.
HAMLET Do not believe it.
ROSENCRANTZ Believe what?
HAMLET That I can keep your counsel and not mine 12
own. Besides, to be demanded of a sponge, what rep- 13
lication should be made by the son of a king? 14
ROSENCRANTZ Take you me for a sponge, my lord?
HAMLET Ay, sir, that soaks up the King's countenance, 16
his rewards, his authorities. But such officers do the King best service in the end. He keeps them, like an ape, in the corner of his jaw, first mouthed to be last swallowed. When he needs what you have gleaned, it is but squeezing you, and, sponge, you shall be dry again.
ROSENCRANTZ I understand you not, my lord.
HAMLET I am glad of it. A knavish speech sleeps in a 24
foolish ear.
ROSENCRANTZ My lord, you must tell us where the body is and go with us to the King.
HAMLET The body is with the King, but the King is not 28
with the body. The King is a thing— 29
GUILDENSTERN A thing, my lord?

12–13 That . . . own (Perhaps Hamlet is suggesting that they have their secrets and he has his.) **13 demanded of** questioned by **13–14 replication** reply **16 countenance** favor **24 sleeps in** has no meaning to **28–29 The . . . body** (Perhaps alludes to the legal commonplace of "the king's two bodies," which drew a distinction between the sacred office of kingship and the particular mortal who possessed it at any given time. Hence, although Claudius's body is necessarily a part of him, true kingship is not contained in it. Similarly, Claudius will have Polonius's body when it is found, but there is no kingship in this business either.)

HAMLET Of nothing. Bring me to him. Hide fox, and all after! *Exeunt.*

✤

4.3 *Enter King, and two or three.*

KING
I have sent to seek him, and to find the body.
How dangerous is it that this man goes loose!
Yet must not we put the strong law on him.
He's loved of the distracted multitude,
Who like not in their judgment, but their eyes,
And where 'tis so, th' offender's scourge is weighed,
But never the offense. To bear all smooth and even,
This sudden sending him away must seem
Deliberate pause. Diseases desperate grown
By desperate appliance are relieved,
Or not at all.

Enter Rosencrantz, [*Guildenstern,*] *and all the rest.*

How now, what hath befall'n?

ROSENCRANTZ
Where the dead body is bestowed, my lord,
We cannot get from him.

KING
But where is he?

ROSENCRANTZ
Without, my lord; guarded, to know your pleasure.

KING
Bring him before us.

ROSENCRANTZ
Ho! Bring in the lord.

They enter [*with Hamlet*].

31 Of nothing (1) of no account (2) lacking the essence of kingship, as in ll. 28–29 and note **31–32 Hide . . . after** (An old signal cry in the game of hide-and-seek, suggesting that Hamlet now runs away from them.)

4.3. Location: The castle.
4 distracted fickle, unstable **5 Who . . . eyes** who choose not by judgment but by appearance **6 scourge** punishment. **weighed** sympathetically considered **7 To . . . even** to manage the business in an unprovocative way **9 Deliberate pause** carefully considered action **10 appliance** remedy, treatment

KING Now, Hamlet, where's Polonius?
HAMLET At supper.
KING At supper? Where?
HAMLET Not where he eats, but where 'a is eaten. A
certain convocation of politic worms are e'en at him. 20
Your worm is your only emperor for diet. We fat all 21
creatures else to fat us, and we fat ourselves for mag-
gots. Your fat king and your lean beggar is but
variable service—two dishes, but to one table. That's 24
the end.
KING Alas, alas!
HAMLET A man may fish with the worm that hath eat 27
of a king, and eat of the fish that hath fed of that
worm.
KING What dost thou mean by this?
HAMLET Nothing but to show you how a king may go
a progress through the guts of a beggar. 32
KING Where is Polonius?
HAMLET In heaven. Send thither to see. If your messenger find him not there, seek him i' th' other place yourself. But if indeed you find him not within this month, you shall nose him as you go up the stairs into the lobby.
KING [*To some attendants*] Go seek him there.
HAMLET 'A will stay till you come. [*Exeunt attendants.*]
KING
Hamlet, this deed, for thine especial safety—
Which we do tender, as we dearly grieve 42
For that which thou hast done—must send thee hence
With fiery quickness. Therefore prepare thyself.
The bark is ready, and the wind at help, 45
Th' associates tend, and everything is bent 46
For England.
HAMLET For England!
KING Ay, Hamlet.

20 politic worms crafty worms (suited to a master spy like Polonius). **e'en** even now **21 Your worm** your average worm. (On *your*, compare *your fat king and your lean beggar* in l. 23.) **diet** food, eating (with a punning reference to the Diet of Worms, a famous *convocation* held in 1521) **24 variable service** different courses of a single meal **27 eat** eaten. (Pronounced *et.*) **32 progress** royal journey of state **42 tender** regard, hold dear. **dearly** intensely **45 bark** sailing vessel **46 tend** wait. **bent** in readiness

HAMLET Good.

KING
So is it, if thou knew'st our purposes.

HAMLET I see a cherub that sees them. But come, for 52
England! Farewell, dear Mother.

KING Thy loving father, Hamlet.

HAMLET My mother. Father and mother is man and
wife, man and wife is one flesh, and so, my mother.
Come, for England! *Exit.*

KING
Follow him at foot; tempt him with speed aboard. 58
Delay it not. I'll have him hence tonight.
Away! For everything is sealed and done
That else leans on th' affair. Pray you, make haste. 61
[*Exeunt all but the King.*]
And, England, if my love thou hold'st at aught— 62
As my great power thereof may give thee sense, 63
Since yet thy cicatrice looks raw and red 64
After the Danish sword, and thy free awe 65
Pays homage to us—thou mayst not coldly set 66
Our sovereign process, which imports at full, 67
By letters congruing to that effect, 68
The present death of Hamlet. Do it, England, 69
For like the hectic in my blood he rages, 70
And thou must cure me. Till I know 'tis done,
Howe'er my haps, my joys were ne'er begun. *Exit.* 72

✤

4.4 *Enter Fortinbras with his army over the stage.*

FORTINBRAS
Go, Captain, from me greet the Danish king.

52 cherub (Cherubim are angels of knowledge. Hamlet hints that both he and heaven are onto Claudius's tricks.) **58 at foot** close behind, at heel **61 leans on** bears upon, is related to **62 England** i.e., King of England. **at aught** at any value **63 As . . . sense** for so my great power may give you a just appreciation of the importance of valuing my love **64 cicatrice** scar **65 free awe** voluntary show of respect **66 coldly set** regard with indifference **67 process** command. **imports at full** conveys specific directions for **68 congruing** agreeing **69 present** immediate **70 hectic** persistent fever **72 haps** fortunes

4.4. Location: The coast of Denmark.

Tell him that by his license Fortinbras 2
Craves the conveyance of a promised march 3
Over his kingdom. You know the rendezvous.
If that His Majesty would aught with us,
We shall express our duty in his eye; 6
And let him know so.

CAPTAIN I will do 't, my lord.

FORTINBRAS Go softly on. [*Exeunt all but the Captain.*] 9

Enter Hamlet, Rosencrantz, [*Guildenstern,*] *etc.*

HAMLET Good sir, whose powers are these? 10

CAPTAIN They are of Norway, sir.

HAMLET How purposed, sir, I pray you?

CAPTAIN Against some part of Poland.

HAMLET Who commands them, sir?

CAPTAIN
The nephew to old Norway, Fortinbras.

HAMLET
Goes it against the main of Poland, sir, 16
Or for some frontier?

CAPTAIN
Truly to speak, and with no addition, 18
We go to gain a little patch of ground
That hath in it no profit but the name.
To pay five ducats, five, I would not farm it; 21
Nor will it yield to Norway or the Pole
A ranker rate, should it be sold in fee. 23

HAMLET
Why, then the Polack never will defend it.

CAPTAIN
Yes, it is already garrisoned.

HAMLET
Two thousand souls and twenty thousand ducats
Will not debate the question of this straw. 27
This is th' impostume of much wealth and peace, 28

2 license permission **3 the conveyance of** escort during **6 duty** respect. **eye** presence **9 softly** slowly, circumspectly **10 powers** forces **16 main** main part **18 addition** exaggeration **21 To pay** i.e., for a yearly rental of. **farm it** take a lease of it **23 ranker** higher. **in fee** fee simple, outright **27 debate . . . straw** settle this trifling matter **28 impostume** abscess

That inward breaks, and shows no cause without
Why the man dies. I humbly thank you, sir.

CAPTAIN
God b' wi' you, sir. [*Exit.*]

ROSENCRANTZ Will 't please you go, my lord?

HAMLET
I'll be with you straight. Go a little before.
[*Exeunt all except Hamlet.*]
How all occasions do inform against me 33
And spur my dull revenge! What is a man,
If his chief good and market of his time 35
Be but to sleep and feed? A beast, no more.
Sure he that made us with such large discourse, 37
Looking before and after, gave us not
That capability and godlike reason
To fust in us unused. Now, whether it be 40
Bestial oblivion, or some craven scruple 41
Of thinking too precisely on th' event— 42
A thought which, quartered, hath but one part wisdom
And ever three parts coward—I do not know
Why yet I live to say "This thing's to do,"
Sith I have cause, and will, and strength, and means 46
To do 't. Examples gross as earth exhort me: 47
Witness this army of such mass and charge, 48
Led by a delicate and tender prince, 49
Whose spirit with divine ambition puffed
Makes mouths at the invisible event, 51
Exposing what is mortal and unsure
To all that fortune, death, and danger dare,
Even for an eggshell. Rightly to be great
Is not to stir without great argument,
But greatly to find quarrel in a straw
When honor's at the stake. How stand I then, 57
That have a father killed, a mother stained,
Excitements of my reason and my blood, 59

33 inform against denounce, betray; take shape against **35 market of** profit of, compensation for **37 discourse** power of reasoning **40 fust** grow moldy **41 oblivion** forgetfulness **42 precisely** scrupulously. **event** outcome **46 Sith** since **47 gross** obvious **48 charge** expense **49 delicate and tender** of fine and youthful qualities **51 Makes mouths** makes scornful faces. **invisible event** unforeseeable outcome **57 at the stake** at risk (in gambling) **59 Excitements of** promptings by

And let all sleep, while to my shame I see
The imminent death of twenty thousand men
That for a fantasy and trick of fame 62
Go to their graves like beds, fight for a plot 63
Whereon the numbers cannot try the cause, 64
Which is not tomb enough and continent 65
To hide the slain? O, from this time forth
My thoughts be bloody or be nothing worth! *Exit.*

✤

4.5 *Enter Horatio, [Queen] Gertrude, and a Gentleman.*

QUEEN
I will not speak with her.
GENTLEMAN She is importunate,
Indeed distract. Her mood will needs be pitied. 2
QUEEN What would she have?
GENTLEMAN
She speaks much of her father, says she hears
There's tricks i' the world, and hems, and beats her
heart, 5
Spurns enviously at straws, speaks things in doubt 6
That carry but half sense. Her speech is nothing,
Yet the unshapèd use of it doth move 8
The hearers to collection; they yawn at it, 9
And botch the words up fit to their own thoughts, 10
Which, as her winks and nods and gestures yield them, 11
Indeed would make one think there might be thought, 12
Though nothing sure, yet much unhappily. 13

62 fantasy fanciful caprice, illusion. **trick** trifle, deceit **63 plot** i.e., of ground **64 Whereon . . . cause** i.e., on which there is insufficient room for the soldiers needed to engage in a military contest **65 continent** receptacle, container

4.5. Location: The castle.
2 distract distracted **5 tricks** deceptions. **heart** i.e., breast **6 Spurns . . . straws** kicks spitefully, takes offense at trifles. **in doubt** obscurely **8 unshapèd use** distracted manner **9 collection** inference, a guess at some sort of meaning. **yawn** gape, wonder; grasp. (The Folio reading, *aim,* is possible.) **10 botch** patch **11 Which** i.e., the words. **yield** deliver, represent **12 thought** conjectured **13 much unhappily** very unskillfully, clumsily

HORATIO
'Twere good she were spoken with, for she may strew
Dangerous conjectures in ill-breeding minds.
QUEEN Let her come in. [*Exit Gentleman.*]
[*Aside.*] To my sick soul, as sin's true nature is,
Each toy seems prologue to some great amiss.
So full of artless jealousy is guilt,
It spills itself in fearing to be spilt.

Enter Ophelia [*distracted*].

OPHELIA
Where is the beauteous majesty of Denmark?
QUEEN How now, Ophelia?
OPHELIA (*She sings*)
"How should I your true love know
From another one?
By his cockle hat and staff,
And his sandal shoon."
QUEEN
Alas, sweet lady, what imports this song?
OPHELIA Say you? Nay, pray you, mark.
"He is dead and gone, lady, (*Song.*)
He is dead and gone;
At his head a grass-green turf,
At his heels a stone."
Oho!
QUEEN Nay, but Ophelia—
OPHELIA Pray you, mark.
[*Sings.*] "White his shroud as the mountain snow"—

Enter King.

QUEEN Alas, look here, my lord.
OPHELIA
"Larded with sweet flowers; (*Song.*)

15 ill-breeding prone to suspect the worst and to make mischief **18 toy** trifle. **amiss** calamity **19–20 So . . . spilt** guilt is so full of suspicion that it unskillfully betrays itself in fearing betrayal **20 s.d. Enter Ophelia** (In the first quarto, Ophelia enters "playing on a lute, and her hair down, singing.") **25 cockle hat** hat with cockleshell stuck in it as a sign that the wearer had been a pilgrim to the shrine of Saint James of Compostella in Spain **26 shoon** shoes **38 Larded** decorated

Which bewept to the ground did not go
With true-love showers."

KING How do you, pretty lady?

OPHELIA Well, God 'ild you! They say the owl was a baker's daughter. Lord, we know what we are, but know not what we may be. God be at your table!

KING Conceit upon her father.

OPHELIA Pray let's have no words of this; but when they ask you what it means, say you this:

"Tomorrow is Saint Valentine's day, (*Song.*)
All in the morning betime,
And I a maid at your window,
To be your Valentine.
Then up he rose, and donned his clothes,
And dupped the chamber door,
Let in the maid, that out a maid
Never departed more."

KING Pretty Ophelia—

OPHELIA Indeed, la, without an oath, I'll make an end on 't:

[*Sings.*] "By Gis and by Saint Charity,
Alack, and fie for shame!
Young men will do 't, if they come to 't;
By Cock, they are to blame.
Quoth she, 'Before you tumbled me,
You promised me to wed.'"

He answers:

"'So would I ha' done, by yonder sun,
An thou hadst not come to my bed.'"

KING How long hath she been thus?

OPHELIA I hope all will be well. We must be patient, but I cannot choose but weep to think they would lay him i' the cold ground. My brother shall know of it. And so I thank you for your good counsel. Come, my coach! Good night, ladies, good night, sweet ladies, good night, good night. [*Exit.*]

40 showers i.e., tears **42 God 'ild** God yield or reward. **owl** (Refers to a legend about a baker's daughter who was turned into an owl for refusing Jesus bread.) **45 Conceit** brooding **48 Valentine's** (This song alludes to the belief that the first girl seen by a man on the morning of this day was his valentine or truelove.) **49 betime** early **53 dupped** opened **59 Gis** Jesus **62 Cock** (A perversion of "God" in oaths.) **67 An** if

KING [*To Horatio*]
Follow her close. Give her good watch, I pray you.
[*Exit Horatio.*]
O, this is the poison of deep grief; it springs
All from her father's death—and now behold!
O Gertrude, Gertrude,
When sorrows come, they come not single spies, 79
But in battalions. First, her father slain;
Next, your son gone, and he most violent author
Of his own just remove; the people muddied, 82
Thick and unwholesome in their thoughts and whispers
For good Polonius' death—and we have done but
greenly 84
In hugger-mugger to inter him; poor Ophelia 85
Divided from herself and her fair judgment,
Without the which we are pictures or mere beasts;
Last, and as much containing as all these, 88
Her brother is in secret come from France,
Feeds on his wonder, keeps himself in clouds, 90
And wants not buzzers to infect his ear 91
With pestilent speeches of his father's death,
Wherein necessity, of matter beggared, 93
Will nothing stick our person to arraign 94
In ear and ear. O my dear Gertrude, this, 95
Like to a murdering piece, in many places 96
Gives me superfluous death. *A noise within.* 97
QUEEN Alack, what noise is this?
KING Attend! 99
Where are my Switzers? Let them guard the door. 100

Enter a Messenger.

What is the matter?
MESSENGER Save yourself, my lord!

79 spies scouts sent in advance of the main force **82 muddied** stirred up, confused **84 greenly** imprudently, foolishly **85 hugger-mugger** secret haste **88 as much containing** i.e., as full of serious matter **90 in clouds** i.e., of suspicion and rumor **91 wants** lacks. **buzzers** gossipers, informers **93 necessity** i.e., the need to invent some plausible explanation. **of matter beggared** unprovided with facts **94–95 Will . . . ear** will not hesitate to accuse my (royal) person in everybody's ears **96 murdering piece** cannon loaded so as to scatter its shot **97 Gives . . . death** kills me over and over **99 Attend** i.e., guard me **100 Switzers** Swiss guards, mercenaries

The ocean, overpeering of his list,
Eats not the flats with more impetuous haste
Than young Laertes, in a riotous head,
O'erbears your officers. The rabble call him lord,
And, as the world were now but to begin,
Antiquity forgot, custom not known,
The ratifiers and props of every word,
They cry, "Choose we! Laertes shall be king!"
Caps, hands, and tongues applaud it to the clouds,
"Laertes shall be king, Laertes king!" *A noise within.*

QUEEN
How cheerfully on the false trail they cry!
O, this is counter, you false Danish dogs!

Enter Laertes with others.

KING The doors are broke.

LAERTES
Where is this King?—Sirs, stand you all without.

ALL No, let's come in.

LAERTES I pray you, give me leave.

ALL We will, we will.

LAERTES
I thank you. Keep the door. [*Exeunt followers.*] O thou vile king,
Give me my father!

QUEEN [*Holding him*] Calmly, good Laertes.

LAERTES
That drop of blood that's calm proclaims me bastard,
Cries cuckold to my father, brands the harlot
Even here, between the chaste unsmirchèd brow
Of my true mother.

KING What is the cause, Laertes,
That thy rebellion looks so giantlike?
Let him go, Gertrude. Do not fear our person.

102 overpeering of his list overflowing its shore, boundary **103 flats** i.e., flatlands near shore. **impetuous** violent (also with the meaning of *impiteous* [*impitious,* Q2], pitiless) **104 head** armed force **106 as** as if **108 The ratifiers . . . word** i.e., *antiquity* (or tradition) and *custom* ought to confirm (*ratify*) and underprop our every word or promise **110 Caps** (The caps are thrown in the air.) **113 counter** (A hunting term meaning to follow the trail in a direction opposite to that which the game has taken.) **123 between** in the middle of **126 fear our** fear for my

There's such divinity doth hedge a king 127
That treason can but peep to what it would, 128
Acts little of his will. Tell me, Laertes, 129
Why thou art thus incensed. Let him go, Gertrude.
Speak, man.

LAERTES Where is my father?

KING Dead.

QUEEN
But not by him.

KING Let him demand his fill.

LAERTES
How came he dead? I'll not be juggled with. 133
To hell, allegiance! Vows, to the blackest devil!
Conscience and grace, to the profoundest pit!
I dare damnation. To this point I stand,
That both the worlds I give to negligence, 137
Let come what comes, only I'll be revenged
Most throughly for my father. 139

KING Who shall stay you?

LAERTES My will, not all the world's. 141
And for my means, I'll husband them so well
They shall go far with little.

KING Good Laertes,
If you desire to know the certainty
Of your dear father, is 't writ in your revenge
That, swoopstake, you will draw both friend and foe, 146
Winner and loser?

LAERTES None but his enemies.

KING Will you know them, then?

LAERTES
To his good friends thus wide I'll ope my arms,
And like the kind life-rendering pelican 151

127 hedge protect as with a surrounding barrier **128 can . . . would** can only glance, as from afar off or through a barrier, at what it would intend **129 Acts . . . will** (but) performs little of what it intends **133 juggled with** cheated, deceived **137 both . . . negligence** i.e., both this world and the next are of no consequence to me **139 throughly** thoroughly **141 My will . . . world's** i.e., I'll stop (*stay*) when my will is accomplished, not for anyone else's **146 swoopstake** (Literally, taking all stakes on the gambling table at once, i.e., indiscriminately; *draw* is also a gambling term.) **151 pelican** (Refers to the belief that the female pelican fed its young with its own blood.)

Repast them with my blood.

KING
Why, now you speak
Like a good child and a true gentleman.
That I am guiltless of your father's death,
And am most sensibly in grief for it,
It shall as level to your judgment 'pear
As day does to your eye. *A noise within.*

LAERTES
How now, what noise is that?

Enter Ophelia.

KING
Let her come in.

LAERTES
O heat, dry up my brains! Tears seven times salt
Burn out the sense and virtue of mine eye!
By heaven, thy madness shall be paid with weight
Till our scale turn the beam. O rose of May!
Dear maid, kind sister, sweet Ophelia!
O heavens, is 't possible a young maid's wits
Should be as mortal as an old man's life?
Nature is fine in love, and where 'tis fine
It sends some precious instance of itself
After the thing it loves.

OPHELIA
"They bore him barefaced on the bier, (*Song.*)
Hey non nonny, nonny, hey nonny,
And in his grave rained many a tear—"
Fare you well, my dove!

LAERTES
Hadst thou thy wits and didst persuade revenge,
It could not move thus.

OPHELIA You must sing "A-down a-down," and you "call him a-down-a." O, how the wheel becomes it! It is the false steward that stole his master's daughter.

152 Repast feed **155 sensibly** feelingly **156 level** plain **160 virtue** faculty, power **161 paid with weight** repaid, avenged equally or more **162 beam** crossbar of a balance **166 fine in** refined by **167 instance** token **168 After . . . loves** i.e., into the grave, along with Polonius **173 persuade** argue cogently for **175–176 You . . . a-down-a** (Ophelia assigns the singing of refrains, like her own "Hey non nonny," to various imaginary singers.) **176 wheel** spinning wheel as accompaniment to the song, or refrain **177 false steward** (The story is unknown.)

LAERTES This nothing's more than matter. 178
OPHELIA There's rosemary, that's for remembrance; 179
pray you, love, remember. And there is pansies; that's 180
for thoughts.
LAERTES A document in madness, thoughts and re- 182
membrance fitted.
OPHELIA There's fennel for you, and columbines. 184
There's rue for you, and here's some for me; we may 185
call it herb of grace o' Sundays. You must wear your
rue with a difference. There's a daisy. I would give 187
you some violets, but they withered all when my father 188
died. They say 'a made a good end—
[*Sings*.] "For bonny sweet Robin is all my joy."

LAERTES
Thought and affliction, passion, hell itself, 191
She turns to favor and to prettiness. 192

OPHELIA
"And will 'a not come again? (*Song*.)
And will 'a not come again?
No, no, he is dead.
Go to thy deathbed,
He never will come again.

"His beard was as white as snow,
All flaxen was his poll. 199
He is gone, he is gone.
And we cast away moan.
God ha' mercy on his soul!"
And of all Christian souls, I pray God. God b' wi' you.
[*Exit*.]

LAERTES Do you see this, O God?

178 This . . . matter this seeming nonsense is more eloquent than sane utterance **179 rosemary** (Used as a symbol of remembrance both at weddings and at funerals.) **180 pansies** (Emblems of love and courtship; perhaps from French *pensées,* thoughts.) **182 document** instruction, lesson **184 fennel** (Emblem of flattery.) **columbines** (Emblems of unchastity or ingratitude.) **185 rue** (Emblem of repentance; when mingled with holy water, it was known as *herb of grace*.) **187 with a difference** (A device used in heraldry to distinguish one family from another on the coat of arms, here suggesting that Ophelia and the Queen have different causes of sorrow and repentance; perhaps with a play on *rue* in the sense of ruth, pity.) **daisy** (Emblem of dissembling, faithlessness.) **188 violets** (Emblems of faithfulness.) **191 Thought** melancholy **192 favor** grace, beauty **199 poll** head

KING
Laertes, I must commune with your grief,
Or you deny me right. Go but apart,
Make choice of whom your wisest friends you will,
And they shall hear and judge twixt you and me.
If by direct or by collateral hand
They find us touched, we will our kingdom give,
Our crown, our life, and all that we call ours
To you in satisfaction; but if not,
Be you content to lend your patience to us,
And we shall jointly labor with your soul
To give it due content.

LAERTES Let this be so.
His means of death, his obscure funeral—
No trophy, sword, nor hatchment o'er his bones,
No noble rite, nor formal ostentation—
Cry to be heard, as 'twere from heaven to earth,
That I must call 't in question.

KING So you shall,
And where th' offense is, let the great ax fall.
I pray you, go with me. *Exeunt.*

✣

4.6 *Enter Horatio and others.*

HORATIO
What are they that would speak with me?

GENTLEMAN Seafaring men, sir. They say they have letters for you.

HORATIO Let them come in. [*Exit Gentleman.*]
I do not know from what part of the world
I should be greeted, if not from Lord Hamlet.

Enter Sailors.

FIRST SAILOR God bless you, sir.

HORATIO Let him bless thee too.

207 whom whichever of **209 collateral** indirect **210 us touched** me implicated **217 trophy** memorial. **hatchment** tablet displaying the armorial bearings of a deceased person **218 ostentation** ceremony **220 That** so that. **call 't in question** demand an explanation

4.6. Location: The castle.

FIRST SAILOR 'A shall, sir, an please him. There's a letter for you, sir—it came from th' ambassador that was bound for England—if your name be Horatio, as I am let to know it is. [*He gives a letter.*]

HORATIO [*Reads*] "Horatio, when thou shalt have overlooked this, give these fellows some means to the King; they have letters for him. Ere we were two days old at sea, a pirate of very warlike appointment gave us chase. Finding ourselves too slow of sail, we put on a compelled valor, and in the grapple I boarded them. On the instant they got clear of our ship, so I alone became their prisoner. They have dealt with me like thieves of mercy, but they knew what they did: I am to do a good turn for them. Let the King have the letters I have sent, and repair thou to me with as much speed as thou wouldest fly death. I have words to speak in thine ear will make thee dumb, yet are they much too light for the bore of the matter. These good fellows will bring thee where I am. Rosencrantz and Guildenstern hold their course for England. Of them I have much to tell thee. Farewell.

He that thou knowest thine, Hamlet."

Come, I will give you way for these your letters,
And do 't the speedier that you may direct me
To him from whom you brought them. *Exeunt.*

✤

4.7 *Enter King and Laertes.*

KING

Now must your conscience my acquittance seal,
And you must put me in your heart for friend,
Sith you have heard, and with a knowing ear,

9 an if it **10 th' ambassador** (Evidently Hamlet. The sailor is being circumspect.) **13–14 overlooked** looked over **14 means** means of access **16 appointment** equipage **21 thieves of mercy** merciful thieves **23 repair** come **26 bore** caliber, i.e., importance **31 way** means of access

4.7. Location: The castle.

1 my acquittance seal confirm or acknowledge my innocence **3 Sith** since

That he which hath your noble father slain
Pursued my life.

LAERTES It well appears. But tell me
Why you proceeded not against these feats 6
So crimeful and so capital in nature, 7
As by your safety, greatness, wisdom, all things else,
You mainly were stirred up. 9

KING O, for two special reasons,
Which may to you perhaps seem much unsinewed, 11
But yet to me they're strong. The Queen his mother
Lives almost by his looks, and for myself—
My virtue or my plague, be it either which—
She is so conjunctive to my life and soul 15
That, as the star moves not but in his sphere, 16
I could not but by her. The other motive
Why to a public count I might not go 18
Is the great love the general gender bear him, 19
Who, dipping all his faults in their affection,
Work like the spring that turneth wood to stone, 21
Convert his gyves to graces, so that my arrows, 22
Too slightly timbered for so loud a wind, 23
Would have reverted to my bow again 24
But not where I had aimed them.

LAERTES
And so have I a noble father lost,
A sister driven into desperate terms, 27
Whose worth, if praises may go back again, 28
Stood challenger on mount of all the age 29
For her perfections. But my revenge will come.

KING
Break not your sleeps for that. You must not think
That we are made of stuff so flat and dull

6 feats acts **7 capital** punishable by death **9 mainly** greatly **11 unsinewed** weak **15 conjunctive** closely united **16 his** its. **sphere** one of the hollow spheres in which, according to Ptolemaic astronomy, the planets were supposed to move **18 count** account, reckoning, indictment **19 general gender** common people **21 Work** operate, act. **spring** i.e., a spring with such a concentration of lime that it coats a piece of wood with limestone, in effect gilding it **22 gyves** fetters (which, gilded by the people's praise, would look like badges of honor) **23 slightly timbered** light. **loud** strong **24 reverted** returned **27 terms** state, condition **28 go back** i.e., recall what she was **29 on mount** set up on high

That we can let our beard be shook with danger
And think it pastime. You shortly shall hear more.
I loved your father, and we love ourself;
And that, I hope, will teach you to imagine—

Enter a Messenger with letters.

How now? What news?

MESSENGER Letters, my lord, from Hamlet:
This to Your Majesty, this to the Queen.
[*He gives letters.*]

KING From Hamlet? Who brought them?

MESSENGER
Sailors, my lord, they say. I saw them not.
They were given me by Claudio. He received them
Of him that brought them.

KING Laertes, you shall hear them.—
Leave us. [*Exit Messenger.*]
[*Reads.*] "High and mighty, you shall know I am set naked on your kingdom. Tomorrow shall I beg leave 45
to see your kingly eyes, when I shall, first asking your pardon, thereunto recount the occasion of my sudden 47
and more strange return. Hamlet."
What should this mean? Are all the rest come back?
Or is it some abuse, and no such thing? 50

LAERTES
Know you the hand?

KING 'Tis Hamlet's character. "Naked!" 51
And in a postscript here he says "alone."
Can you devise me? 53

LAERTES
I am lost in it, my lord. But let him come.
It warms the very sickness in my heart
That I shall live and tell him to his teeth,
"Thus didst thou."

KING If it be so, Laertes— 57
As how should it be so? How otherwise?— 58
Will you be ruled by me?

45 naked destitute, unarmed, without following **47 pardon** permission **50 abuse** deceit. **no such thing** no such thing has occurred **51 character** handwriting **53 devise** explain to **57 Thus didst thou** i.e., here's for what you did to my father **58 As . . . otherwise** how can this (Hamlet's return) be true? Yet how otherwise than true (since we have the evidence of his letter)

LAERTES Ay, my lord,
So you will not o'errule me to a peace.

KING
To thine own peace. If he be now returned,
As checking at his voyage, and that he means
No more to undertake it, I will work him
To an exploit, now ripe in my device,
Under the which he shall not choose but fall;
And for his death no wind of blame shall breathe,
But even his mother shall uncharge the practice
And call it accident.

LAERTES My lord, I will be ruled,
The rather if you could devise it so
That I might be the organ.

KING It falls right.
You have been talked of since your travel much,
And that in Hamlet's hearing, for a quality
Wherein they say you shine. Your sum of parts
Did not together pluck such envy from him
As did that one, and that, in my regard,
Of the unworthiest siege.

LAERTES What part is that, my lord?

KING
A very ribbon in the cap of youth,
Yet needful too, for youth no less becomes
The light and careless livery that it wears
Than settled age his sables and his weeds
Importing health and graveness. Two months since
Here was a gentleman of Normandy.
I have seen myself, and served against, the French,
And they can well on horseback, but this gallant
Had witchcraft in 't; he grew unto his seat,
And to such wondrous doing brought his horse

60 So provided that **62 checking at** i.e., turning aside from (like a falcon leaving the quarry to fly at a chance bird). **that** if **64 device** devising, invention **67 uncharge the practice** acquit the stratagem of being a plot **70 organ** agent, instrument **73 Your . . . parts** i.e., all your other virtues **76 unworthiest siege** least important rank **79 no less becomes** is no less suited by **81 sables** rich robes furred with sable. **weeds** garments **82 Importing health** signifying a concern for health and dignified prosperity; also, giving an impression of comfortable prosperity **85 can well** are skilled

As had he been incorpsed and demi-natured
With the brave beast. So far he topped my thought
That I in forgery of shapes and tricks
Come short of what he did.

LAERTES A Norman was 't?

KING A Norman.

LAERTES
Upon my life, Lamord.

KING The very same.

LAERTES
I know him well. He is the brooch indeed
And gem of all the nation.

KING He made confession of you,
And gave you such a masterly report
For art and exercise in your defense,
And for your rapier most especial,
That he cried out 'twould be a sight indeed
If one could match you. Th' escrimers of their nation,
He swore, had neither motion, guard, nor eye
If you opposed them. Sir, this report of his
Did Hamlet so envenom with his envy
That he could nothing do but wish and beg
Your sudden coming o'er, to play with you.
Now, out of this—

LAERTES What out of this, my lord?

KING
Laertes, was your father dear to you?
Or are you like the painting of a sorrow,
A face without a heart?

LAERTES Why ask you this?

KING
Not that I think you did not love your father,
But that I know love is begun by time,
And that I see, in passages of proof,
Time qualifies the spark and fire of it.

88 incorpsed and demi-natured of one body and nearly of one nature (like the centaur) **89 topped** surpassed **90 forgery** imagining **94 brooch** ornament **96 confession** testimonial, admission of superiority **98 For . . . defense** in respect to your skill and practice with your weapon **101 escrimers** fencers **106 play** fence **112 begun by time** i.e., created by the right circumstance and hence subject to change **113 passages of proof** actual instances **114 qualifies** weakens, moderates

There lives within the very flame of love
A kind of wick or snuff that will abate it, 116
And nothing is at a like goodness still, 117
For goodness, growing to a pleurisy, 118
Dies in his own too much. That we would do, 119
We should do when we would; for this "would" changes
And hath abatements and delays as many 121
As there are tongues, are hands, are accidents, 122
And then this "should" is like a spendthrift sigh, 123
That hurts by easing. But, to the quick o' th' ulcer: 124
Hamlet comes back. What would you undertake
To show yourself in deed your father's son
More than in words?

LAERTES
To cut his throat i' the church.

KING
No place, indeed, should murder sanctuarize; 128
Revenge should have no bounds. But good Laertes,
Will you do this, keep close within your chamber. 130
Hamlet returned shall know you are come home.
We'll put on those shall praise your excellence 132
And set a double varnish on the fame
The Frenchman gave you, bring you in fine together, 134
And wager on your heads. He, being remiss, 135
Most generous, and free from all contriving, 136
Will not peruse the foils, so that with ease,
Or with a little shuffling, you may choose
A sword unbated, and in a pass of practice 139
Requite him for your father.

LAERTES
I will do 't,
And for that purpose I'll anoint my sword.

116 snuff the charred part of a candlewick **117 nothing . . . still** nothing remains at a constant level of perfection **118 pleurisy** excess, plethora. (Literally, a chest inflammation.) **119 in . . . much** of its own excess. **That** that which **121 abatements** diminutions **122 accidents** occurrences, incidents **123 spendthrift sigh** (An allusion to the belief that sighs draw blood from the heart.) **124 hurts by easing** i.e., costs the heart blood even while it affords emotional relief. **quick o' th' ulcer** heart of the matter **128 sanctuarize** protect from punishment. (Alludes to the right of sanctuary with which certain religious places were invested.) **130 Will you do this** if you wish to do this **132 put on those shall** arrange for some to **134 in fine** finally **135 remiss** negligently unsuspicious **136 generous** noble-minded **139 unbated** not blunted, having no button. **pass of practice** treacherous thrust

I bought an unction of a mountebank 142
So mortal that, but dip a knife in it,
Where it draws blood no cataplasm so rare, 144
Collected from all simples that have virtue 145
Under the moon, can save the thing from death 146
That is but scratched withal. I'll touch my point
With this contagion, that if I gall him slightly, 148
It may be death.

KING Let's further think of this,
Weigh what convenience both of time and means
May fit us to our shape. If this should fail, 151
And that our drift look through our bad performance, 152
'Twere better not assayed. Therefore this project
Should have a back or second, that might hold
If this did blast in proof. Soft, let me see. 155
We'll make a solemn wager on your cunnings— 156
I ha 't!
When in your motion you are hot and dry—
As make your bouts more violent to that end— 159
And that he calls for drink, I'll have prepared him
A chalice for the nonce, whereon but sipping, 161
If he by chance escape your venomed stuck, 162
Our purpose may hold there. [*A cry within.*] But stay, what noise?

Enter Queen.

QUEEN
One woe doth tread upon another's heel,
So fast they follow. Your sister's drowned, Laertes.

LAERTES Drowned! O, where?

QUEEN
There is a willow grows askant the brook, 167
That shows his hoar leaves in the glassy stream; 168
Therewith fantastic garlands did she make

142 unction ointment. **mountebank** quack doctor **144 cataplasm** plaster or poultice **145 simples** herbs **146 Under the moon** i.e., anywhere **148 gall** graze, wound **151 shape** part we propose to act **152 drift . . . performance** i.e., intention should be made visible by our bungling **155 blast in proof** burst in the test (like a cannon) **156 cunnings** respective skills **159 As** i.e., and you should **161 nonce** occasion **162 stuck** thrust. (From *stoccado,* a fencing term.) **167 askant** aslant **168 hoar** white or gray

Of crowflowers, nettles, daisies, and long purples,
That liberal shepherds give a grosser name,
But our cold maids do dead men's fingers call them.
There on the pendent boughs her crownet weeds
Clamb'ring to hang, an envious sliver broke,
When down her weedy trophies and herself
Fell in the weeping brook. Her clothes spread wide,
And mermaidlike awhile they bore her up,
Which time she chanted snatches of old lauds,
As one incapable of her own distress,
Or like a creature native and endued
Unto that element. But long it could not be
Till that her garments, heavy with their drink,
Pulled the poor wretch from her melodious lay
To muddy death.

LAERTES Alas, then she is drowned?

QUEEN Drowned, drowned.

LAERTES
Too much of water hast thou, poor Ophelia,
And therefore I forbid my tears. But yet
It is our trick; nature her custom holds,
Let shame say what it will. [*He weeps.*] When these are gone,
The woman will be out. Adieu, my lord.
I have a speech of fire that fain would blaze,
But that this folly douts it. *Exit.*

KING Let's follow, Gertrude.
How much I had to do to calm his rage!
Now fear I this will give it start again;
Therefore let's follow. *Exeunt.*

170 long purples early purple orchids **171 liberal** free-spoken. **a grosser name** (The testicle-resembling tubers of the orchid, also in some cases resembling *dead men's fingers,* have earned various slang names like dogstones and cullions.) **172 cold** chaste **173 crownet** made into a chaplet or coronet **174 envious sliver** malicious branch **175 weedy** i.e., of plants **178 lauds** hymns **179 incapable** lacking capacity to apprehend **180 endued** adapted by nature **188 It is our trick** i.e., weeping is our natural way (when sad) **189–190 When . . . out** when my tears are all shed, the woman in me will be expended, satisfied **192 douts** extinguishes. (The second quarto reads "drowns.")

5.1 *Enter two Clowns [with spades and mattocks].*

FIRST CLOWN Is she to be buried in Christian burial,
when she willfully seeks her own salvation? 2
SECOND CLOWN I tell thee she is; therefore make her
grave straight. The crowner hath sat on her, and finds 4
it Christian burial. 5
FIRST CLOWN How can that be, unless she drowned herself in her own defense?
SECOND CLOWN Why, 'tis found so. 8
FIRST CLOWN It must be *se offendendo,* it cannot be 9
else. For here lies the point: if I drown myself wittingly,
it argues an act, and an act hath three branches—it is
to act, to do, and to perform. Argal, she drowned her- 12
self wittingly.
SECOND CLOWN Nay, but hear you, goodman delver— 14
FIRST CLOWN Give me leave. Here lies the water; good.
Here stands the man; good. If the man go to this water and drown himself, it is, will he, nill he, he goes, 17
mark you that. But if the water come to him and
drown him, he drowns not himself. Argal, he that is
not guilty of his own death shortens not his own life.
SECOND CLOWN But is this law?
FIRST CLOWN Ay, marry, is 't—crowner's quest law. 22
SECOND CLOWN Will you ha' the truth on 't? If this had
not been a gentlewoman, she should have been buried out o' Christian burial.
FIRST CLOWN Why, there thou sayst. And the more 26
pity that great folk should have countenance in this 27
world to drown or hang themselves more than their

5.1. Location: A churchyard.
s.d. Clowns rustics **2 salvation** (A blunder for "damnation," or perhaps a suggestion that Ophelia was taking her own shortcut to heaven.) **4 straight** straightway, immediately. (But with a pun on *strait,* narrow.) **crowner** coroner. **sat on her** conducted a session on her case **4–5 finds it** gives his official verdict that her means of death was consistent with **8 found so** determined so in the coroner's verdict **9 se offendendo** (A comic mistake for *se defendendo,* term used in verdicts of justifiable homicide.) **12 Argal** (Corruption of *ergo,* therefore.) **14 goodman** (An honorific title often used with the name of a profession or craft.) **17 will he, nill he** whether he will or no, willy-nilly **22 quest** inquest **26 there thou sayst** i.e., that's right **27 countenance** privilege

even-Christian. Come, my spade. There is no ancient gentlemen but gardeners, ditchers, and grave makers. They hold up Adam's profession.

SECOND CLOWN Was he a gentleman?

FIRST CLOWN 'A was the first that ever bore arms.

SECOND CLOWN Why, he had none.

FIRST CLOWN What, art a heathen? How dost thou understand the Scripture? The Scripture says Adam digged. Could he dig without arms? I'll put another question to thee. If thou answerest me not to the purpose, confess thyself—

SECOND CLOWN Go to.

FIRST CLOWN What is he that builds stronger than either the mason, the shipwright, or the carpenter?

SECOND CLOWN The gallows maker, for that frame outlives a thousand tenants.

FIRST CLOWN I like thy wit well, in good faith. The gallows does well. But how does it well? It does well to those that do ill. Now thou dost ill to say the gallows is built stronger than the church. Argal, the gallows may do well to thee. To 't again, come.

SECOND CLOWN "Who builds stronger than a mason. a shipwright, or a carpenter?"

FIRST CLOWN Ay, tell me that, and unyoke.

SECOND CLOWN Marry, now I can tell.

FIRST CLOWN To 't.

SECOND CLOWN Mass, I cannot tell.

Enter Hamlet and Horatio [*at a distance*].

FIRST CLOWN Cudgel thy brains no more about it, for your dull ass will not mend his pace with beating; and when you are asked this question next, say "a grave maker." The houses he makes lasts till dooms-

29 even-Christian fellow Christians. **ancient** going back to ancient times **31 hold up** maintain **33 bore arms** (To be entitled to bear a coat of arms would make Adam a gentleman, but as one who bore a spade our common ancestor was an ordinary delver in the earth.) **37 arms** i.e., the arms of the body **39 confess thyself** (The saying continues, "and be hanged.") **43 frame** (1) gallows (2) structure **46 does well** (1) is an apt answer (2) does a good turn **52 unyoke** i.e., after this great effort you may unharness the team of your wits **55 Mass** by the Mass

day. Go get thee in and fetch me a stoup of liquor. 60
[*Exit Second Clown. First Clown digs.*]

Song.

"In youth, when I did love, did love, 61
Methought it was very sweet,
To contract—O—the time for—a—my behove, 63
O, methought there—a—was nothing—a—meet." 64

HAMLET Has this fellow no feeling of his business, 'a 65
sings in grave-making?

HORATIO Custom hath made it in him a property of 67
easiness. 68

HAMLET 'Tis e'en so. The hand of little employment
hath the daintier sense. 70

FIRST CLOWN *Song.*

"But age with his stealing steps
Hath clawed me in his clutch,
And hath shipped me into the land, 73
As if I had never been such."

[*He throws up a skull.*]

HAMLET That skull had a tongue in it and could sing
once. How the knave jowls it to the ground, as if 76
'twere Cain's jawbone, that did the first murder! This
might be the pate of a politician, which this ass now 78
o'erreaches, one that would circumvent God, might 79
it not?

HORATIO It might, my lord.

HAMLET Or of a courtier, which could say, "Good morrow, sweet lord! How dost thou, sweet lord?" This might be my Lord Such-a-one, that praised my Lord Such-a-one's horse when 'a meant to beg it, might it not?

HORATIO Ay, my lord.

60 stoup two-quart measure **61 In . . . love** (This and the two following stanzas, with nonsensical variations, are from a poem attributed to Lord Vaux and printed in *Tottel's Miscellany,* 1557. The *O* and *a* [for "ah"] seemingly are the grunts of the digger.) **63 To contract . . . behove** i.e., to shorten the time for my own advantage. (Perhaps he means to *prolong* it.) **64 meet** suitable, i.e., more suitable **65 'a** that he **67–68 property of easiness** i.e., something he can do easily and indifferently **70 daintier sense** more delicate sense of feeling **73 into the land** i.e., toward my grave (?) (But note the lack of rhyme in *steps, land.*) **76 jowls** dashes **78 politician** schemer, plotter **79 o'erreaches** circumvents, gets the better of (with a quibble on the literal sense)

HAMLET Why, e'en so, and now my Lady Worm's, chapless, and knocked about the mazard with a sexton's spade. Here's fine revolution, an we had the trick to see 't. Did these bones cost no more the breeding but to play at loggets with them? Mine ache to think on 't.

FIRST CLOWN *Song.*

"A pickax and a spade, a spade,
  For and a shrouding sheet;
O, a pit of clay for to be made
  For such a guest is meet."

[*He throws up another skull.*]

HAMLET There's another. Why may not that be the skull of a lawyer? Where be his quiddities now, his quillities, his cases, his tenures, and his tricks? Why does he suffer this mad knave now to knock him about the sconce with a dirty shovel, and will not tell him of his action of battery? Hum, this fellow might be in 's time a great buyer of land, with his statutes, his recognizances, his fines, his double vouchers, his recoveries. Is this the fine of his fines and the recovery of his recoveries, to have his fine pate full of fine dirt? Will his vouchers vouch him no more of his purchases, and double ones too, than the length and breadth of a pair of indentures? The very conveyances of his lands

89 chapless having no lower jaw. **mazard** i.e., head. (Literally, a drinking vessel.) **90 revolution** turn of Fortune's wheel, change. **an** if **90–91 trick to see** knack of seeing **91–92 cost . . . but** involve so little expense and care in upbringing that we may **92 loggets** a game in which pieces of hard wood shaped like Indian clubs or bowling pins are thrown to lie as near as possible to a stake **95 For and** and moreover **99 quiddities** subtleties, quibbles. (From Latin *quid,* a thing.) **99–100 quillities** verbal niceties, subtle distinctions. (Variation of *quiddities.*) **100 tenures** the holding of a piece of property or office, or the conditions or period of such holding **102 sconce** head **103 action of battery** lawsuit about physical assault **104–105 statutes, recognizances** legal documents guaranteeing a debt by attaching land and property **105 fines, recoveries** ways of converting entailed estates into "fee simple" or freehold. **double** signed by two signatories. **vouchers** guarantees of the legality of a title to real estate **106–107 fine of his fines . . . fine pate . . . fine dirt** end of his legal maneuvers . . . elegant head . . . minutely sifted dirt **110 pair of indentures** legal document drawn up in duplicate on a single sheet and then cut apart on a zigzag line so that each pair was uniquely matched. (Hamlet may refer to two rows of teeth, or dentures.) **conveyances** deeds

will scarcely lie in this box, and must th' inheritor 111
himself have no more, ha?

HORATIO Not a jot more, my lord.

HAMLET Is not parchment made of sheepskins?

HORATIO Ay, my lord, and of calves' skins too.

HAMLET They are sheep and calves which seek out as- 116
surance in that. I will speak to this fellow.—Whose 117
grave's this, sirrah? 118

FIRST CLOWN Mine, sir.
[*Sings.*] "O, a pit of clay for to be made
For such a guest is meet."

HAMLET I think it be thine, indeed, for thou liest in 't.

FIRST CLOWN You lie out on 't, sir, and therefore 'tis not yours. For my part, I do not lie in 't, yet it is mine.

HAMLET Thou dost lie in 't, to be in 't and say it is
thine. 'Tis for the dead, not for the quick; therefore 126
thou liest.

FIRST CLOWN 'Tis a quick lie, sir; 'twill away again from me to you.

HAMLET What man dost thou dig it for?

FIRST CLOWN For no man, sir.

HAMLET What woman, then?

FIRST CLOWN For none, neither.

HAMLET Who is to be buried in 't?

FIRST CLOWN One that was a woman, sir, but, rest her soul, she's dead.

HAMLET How absolute the knave is! We must speak by 137
the card, or equivocation will undo us. By the Lord, 138
Horatio, this three years I have took note of it: the age 139
is grown so picked that the toe of the peasant comes so 140
near the heel of the courtier, he galls his kibe.—How 141
long hast thou been grave maker?

FIRST CLOWN Of all the days i' the year, I came to 't that day that our last king Hamlet overcame Fortinbras.

111 box (1) deed box (2) coffin. ("Skull" has been suggested.) **inheritor** possessor, owner **116–117 assurance in that** safety in legal parchments **118 sirrah** (A term of address to inferiors.) **126 quick** living **137 absolute** strict, precise **137–138 by the card** by the mariner's card or chart on which the points of the compass were marked, i.e., with precision **138 equivocation** ambiguity in the use of terms **139 took** taken **140 picked** refined, fastidious **141 galls his kibe** chafes the courtier's chilblain

HAMLET How long is that since?

FIRST CLOWN Cannot you tell that? Every fool can tell that. It was that very day that young Hamlet was born—he that is mad and sent into England.

HAMLET Ay, marry, why was he sent into England?

FIRST CLOWN Why, because 'a was mad. 'A shall recover his wits there, or if 'a do not, 'tis no great matter there.

HAMLET Why?

FIRST CLOWN 'Twill not be seen in him there. There the men are as mad as he.

HAMLET How came he mad?

FIRST CLOWN Very strangely, they say.

HAMLET How strangely?

FIRST CLOWN Faith, e'en with losing his wits.

HAMLET Upon what ground?

FIRST CLOWN Why, here in Denmark. I have been sexton here, man and boy, thirty years.

HAMLET How long will a man lie i' th' earth ere he rot?

FIRST CLOWN Faith, if 'a be not rotten before 'a die—as we have many pocky corpses nowadays that will scarce hold the laying in—'a will last you some eight year or nine year. A tanner will last you nine year.

HAMLET Why he more than another?

FIRST CLOWN Why, sir, his hide is so tanned with his trade that 'a will keep out water a great while, and your water is a sore decayer of your whoreson dead body. [*He picks up a skull.*] Here's a skull now hath lien you i' th' earth three-and-twenty years.

HAMLET Whose was it?

FIRST CLOWN A whoreson mad fellow's it was. Whose do you think it was?

HAMLET Nay, I know not.

FIRST CLOWN A pestilence on him for a mad rogue! 'A poured a flagon of Rhenish on my head once. This same skull, sir, was, sir, Yorick's skull, the King's jester.

160 ground cause. (But in the next line the gravedigger takes the word in the sense of "land," "country.") **165 pocky** rotten, diseased. (Literally, with the pox, or syphilis.) **166 hold the laying in** hold together long enough to be interred **171 sore** i.e., terrible, great. **whoreson** i.e., vile, scurvy **173 lien you** lain. (*You* is used colloquially.) **179 Rhenish** Rhine wine

HAMLET This?

FIRST CLOWN E'en that.

HAMLET Let me see. [*He takes the skull.*] Alas, poor Yorick! I knew him, Horatio, a fellow of infinite jest, of most excellent fancy. He hath bore me on his back a thousand times, and now how abhorred in my imagination it is! My gorge rises at it. Here hung those lips that I have kissed I know not how oft. Where be your gibes now? Your gambols, your songs, your flashes of merriment that were wont to set the table on a roar? Not one now, to mock your own grinning? Quite chopfallen? Now get you to my lady's chamber and tell her, let her paint an inch thick, to this favor she must come. Make her laugh at that. Prithee, Horatio, tell me one thing.

HORATIO What's that, my lord?

HAMLET Dost thou think Alexander looked o' this fashion i' th' earth?

HORATIO E'en so.

HAMLET And smelt so? Pah! [*He puts down the skull.*]

HORATIO E'en so, my lord.

HAMLET To what base uses we may return, Horatio! Why may not imagination trace the noble dust of Alexander till 'a find it stopping a bunghole?

HORATIO 'Twere to consider too curiously to consider so.

HAMLET No, faith, not a jot, but to follow him thither with modesty enough, and likelihood to lead it. As thus: Alexander died, Alexander was buried, Alexander returneth to dust, the dust is earth, of earth we make loam, and why of that loam whereto he was converted might they not stop a beer barrel?
Imperious Caesar, dead and turned to clay,
Might stop a hole to keep the wind away.
O, that that earth which kept the world in awe
Should patch a wall t' expel the winter's flaw!

185 bore borne **187 My gorge rises** i.e., I feel nauseated **191 mock your own grinning** i.e., laugh at the faces you make **192 chopfallen** (1) lacking the lower jaw (2) dejected **193 favor** aspect, appearance **204 bunghole** hole for filling or emptying a cask **205 curiously** minutely **208 modesty** moderation **211 loam** mortar consisting chiefly of moistened clay and straw **213 Imperious** imperial **216 flaw** gust of wind

Enter King, Queen, Laertes, and the corpse [*of Ophelia, in procession, with Priest, lords, etc.*].

But soft, but soft awhile! Here comes the King,
The Queen, the courtiers. Who is this they follow?
And with such maimèd rites? This doth betoken
The corpse they follow did with desperate hand
Fordo its own life. 'Twas of some estate.
Couch we awhile and mark.
[*He and Horatio conceal themselves. Ophelia's body is taken to the grave.*]

LAERTES What ceremony else?

HAMLET [*To Horatio*]
That is Laertes, a very noble youth. Mark.

LAERTES What ceremony else?

PRIEST
Her obsequies have been as far enlarged
As we have warranty. Her death was doubtful,
And but that great command o'ersways the order
She should in ground unsanctified been lodged
Till the last trumpet. For charitable prayers,
Shards, flints, and pebbles should be thrown on her.
Yet here she is allowed her virgin crants,
Her maiden strewments, and the bringing home
Of bell and burial.

LAERTES
Must there no more be done?

PRIEST
No more be done.
We should profane the service of the dead
To sing a requiem and such rest to her
As to peace-parted souls.

LAERTES
Lay her i' th' earth,
And from her fair and unpolluted flesh

217 soft i.e., wait, be careful **219 maimèd** mutilated, incomplete **221 Fordo** destroy. **estate** rank **222 Couch we** let's hide, lurk **227 warranty** i.e., ecclesiastical authority **228 great . . . order** orders from on high overrule the prescribed procedures **229 She should . . . lodged** i.e., she should have been buried in unsanctified ground **230 For** in place of **231 Shards** broken bits of pottery **232 crants** garlands betokening maidenhood **233 strewments** flowers strewn on a coffin **233–234 bringing . . . burial** laying to rest of the body in consecrated ground, to the sound of the bell **237 such rest** i.e., to pray for such rest **238 peace-parted souls** those who have died at peace with God

May violets spring! I tell thee, churlish priest,
A ministering angel shall my sister be
When thou liest howling.

HAMLET [*To Horatio*] What, the fair Ophelia!

QUEEN [*Scattering flowers*] Sweets to the sweet! Farewell.
I hoped thou shouldst have been my Hamlet's wife.
I thought thy bride-bed to have decked, sweet maid,
And not have strewed thy grave.

LAERTES O, treble woe
Fall ten times treble on that cursèd head
Whose wicked deed thy most ingenious sense
Deprived thee of!—Hold off the earth awhile,
Till I have caught her once more in mine arms.
[*He leaps into the grave and embraces Ophelia.*]
Now pile your dust upon the quick and dead,
Till of this flat a mountain you have made
T' o'ertop old Pelion or the skyish head
Of blue Olympus.

HAMLET [*Coming forward*] What is he whose grief
Bears such an emphasis, whose phrase of sorrow
Conjures the wandering stars and makes them stand
Like wonder-wounded hearers? This is I,
Hamlet the Dane.

LAERTES [*Grappling with him*] The devil take thy soul!

HAMLET Thou pray'st not well.
I prithee, take thy fingers from my throat,
For though I am not splenitive and rash,
Yet have I in me something dangerous,
Which let thy wisdom fear. Hold off thy hand.

KING Pluck them asunder.

QUEEN Hamlet, Hamlet!

ALL Gentlemen!

240 violets (See 4.5.188 and note.) **242 howling** i.e., in hell
248 ingenious sense a mind that is quick, alert, of fine qualities
250 Till . . . arms (Implies an open coffin.) **253–254 Pelion, Olympus** mountains in the north of Thessaly; see also *Ossa,* below, at l. 286
255 emphasis i.e., rhetorical and florid emphasis. (*Phrase* has a similar rhetorical connotation.) **256 wandering stars** planets **257 wonder-wounded** struck with amazement **258 the Dane** (This title normally signifies the King; see 1.1.17 and note.) **259 s.d. Grappling with him** (Most editors think, despite the testimony of the first quarto that *"Hamlet leaps in after Laertes,"* that Laertes jumps out of the grave to attack Hamlet.) **262 splenitive** quick-tempered

HORATIO Good my lord, be quiet.
[*Hamlet and Laertes are parted.*]

HAMLET
Why, I will fight with him upon this theme
Until my eyelids will no longer wag.

QUEEN O my son, what theme?

HAMLET
I loved Ophelia. Forty thousand brothers
Could not with all their quantity of love
Make up my sum. What wilt thou do for her?

KING O, he is mad, Laertes.

QUEEN For love of God, forbear him.

HAMLET
'Swounds, show me what thou'lt do.
Woo't weep? Woo't fight? Woo't fast? Woo't tear thyself?
Woo't drink up eisel? Eat a crocodile?
I'll do 't. Dost come here to whine?
To outface me with leaping in her grave?
Be buried quick with her, and so will I.
And if thou prate of mountains, let them throw
Millions of acres on us, till our ground,
Singeing his pate against the burning zone,
Make Ossa like a wart! Nay, an thou'lt mouth,
I'll rant as well as thou.

QUEEN This is mere madness,
And thus awhile the fit will work on him;
Anon, as patient as the female dove
When that her golden couplets are disclosed,
His silence will sit drooping.

HAMLET Hear you, sir.
What is the reason that you use me thus?

270 wag move. (A fluttering eyelid is a conventional sign that life has not yet gone.) **276 forbear him** leave him alone **277 'Swounds** by His (Christ's) wounds **278 Woo't** wilt thou **279 drink up** drink deeply. **eisel** vinegar. **crocodile** (Crocodiles were supposed to shed hypocritical tears.) **282 quick** alive **285 his pate** its head, i.e., top. **burning zone** zone in the celestial sphere containing the sun's orbit, between the tropics of Cancer and Capricorn **286 Ossa** another mountain in Thessaly. (In their war against the Olympian gods, the giants attempted to heap Ossa, Pelion, and Olympus on one another to scale heaven.) **an** if. **mouth** i.e., rant **287 mere** utter **290 golden couplets** two baby pigeons, covered with yellow down. **disclosed** hatched

I loved you ever. But it is no matter.
Let Hercules himself do what he may, 294
The cat will mew, and dog will have his day. 295

KING
I pray thee, good Horatio, wait upon him.
Exit Hamlet and Horatio.
[*To Laertes.*] Strengthen your patience in our last night's
speech; 297
We'll put the matter to the present push.— 298
Good Gertrude, set some watch over your son.—
This grave shall have a living monument. 300
An hour of quiet shortly shall we see; 301
Till then, in patience our proceeding be. *Exeunt.*

✤

5.2 *Enter Hamlet and Horatio.*

HAMLET
So much for this, sir; now shall you see the other. 1
You do remember all the circumstance?

HORATIO Remember it, my lord!

HAMLET
Sir, in my heart there was a kind of fighting
That would not let me sleep. Methought I lay
Worse than the mutines in the bilboes. Rashly, 6
And praised be rashness for it—let us know 7
Our indiscretion sometimes serves us well 8
When our deep plots do pall, and that should learn us 9
There's a divinity that shapes our ends,
Rough-hew them how we will—

HORATIO That is most certain. 11

294–295 Let . . . day i.e., (1) even Hercules couldn't stop Laertes's theatrical rant (2) I too will have my turn; i.e., despite any blustering attempts at interference, every person will sooner or later do what he must do **297 in** i.e., by recalling **298 present push** immediate test **300 living** lasting; also refers (for Laertes's benefit) to the plot against Hamlet **301 hour of quiet** time free of conflict

5.2. Location: The castle.
1 see the other i.e., hear the other news **6 mutines** mutineers. **bilboes** shackles. **Rashly** on impulse. (This adverb goes with ll. 12ff.) **7 know** acknowledge **8 indiscretion** lack of foresight and judgment (not an indiscreet act) **9 pall** fail, falter, go stale. **learn** teach **11 Rough-hew** shape roughly, botch

HAMLET Up from my cabin,
My sea-gown scarfed about me, in the dark 13
Groped I to find out them, had my desire,
Fingered their packet, and in fine withdrew 15
To mine own room again, making so bold,
My fears forgetting manners, to unseal
Their grand commission; where I found, Horatio—
Ah, royal knavery!—an exact command,
Larded with many several sorts of reasons 20
Importing Denmark's health and England's too, 21
With, ho! such bugs and goblins in my life, 22
That on the supervise, no leisure bated, 23
No, not to stay the grinding of the ax, 24
My head should be struck off.

HORATIO Is 't possible?

HAMLET [*Giving a document*]
Here's the commission. Read it at more leisure.
But wilt thou hear now how I did proceed?

HORATIO I beseech you.

HAMLET
Being thus benetted round with villainies—
Ere I could make a prologue to my brains, 30
They had begun the play—I sat me down, 31
Devised a new commission, wrote it fair. 32
I once did hold it, as our statists do, 33
A baseness to write fair, and labored much 34
How to forget that learning, but, sir, now
It did me yeoman's service. Wilt thou know 36
Th' effect of what I wrote?

HORATIO Ay, good my lord. 37

HAMLET
An earnest conjuration from the King, 38
As England was his faithful tributary,

13 sea-gown seaman's coat. **scarfed** loosely wrapped **15 Fingered** pilfered, pinched. **in fine** finally, in conclusion **20 Larded** garnished, decorated **21 Importing** relating to **22 bugs** bugbears, hobgoblins. **in my life** i.e., to be feared if I were allowed to live **23 supervise** reading. **leisure bated** delay allowed **24 stay** await **30–31 Ere . . . play** i.e., before I could consciously turn my brain to the matter, it had started working on a plan **32 fair** in a clear hand **33 statists** statesmen **34 baseness** i.e., lower-class trait **36 yeoman's** i.e., substantial, faithful, loyal. (In the British navy, the ship's yeoman is usually a scribe or clerk.) **37 effect** purport **38 conjuration** entreaty

As love between them like the palm might flourish,
As peace should still her wheaten garland wear 41
And stand a comma 'tween their amities, 42
And many suchlike "as"es of great charge, 43
That on the view and knowing of these contents,
Without debatement further more or less,
He should those bearers put to sudden death,
Not shriving time allowed.

HORATIO
How was this sealed? 47

HAMLET
Why, even in that was heaven ordinant. 48
I had my father's signet in my purse, 49
Which was the model of that Danish seal; 50
Folded the writ up in the form of th' other, 51
Subscribed it, gave 't th' impression, placed it safely, 52
The changeling never known. Now, the next day 53
Was our sea fight, and what to this was sequent
Thou knowest already.

HORATIO
So Guildenstern and Rosencrantz go to 't.

HAMLET
Why, man, they did make love to this employment.
They are not near my conscience. Their defeat 58
Does by their own insinuation grow. 59
'Tis dangerous when the baser nature comes 60
Between the pass and fell incensèd points 61
Of mighty opposites.

HORATIO
Why, what a king is this! 62

HAMLET
Does it not, think thee, stand me now upon— 63
He that hath killed my king and whored my mother,

41 still always. **wheaten garland** (Symbolic of fruitful agriculture, of peace and plenty.) **42 comma** (Indicating continuity, link.) **43 "as"es** (1) the "whereases" of a formal document (2) asses. **charge** (1) import (2) burden (appropriate to asses) **47 shriving time** time for confession and absolution **48 ordinant** directing **49 signet** small seal **50 model** replica **51 writ** writing **52 Subscribed** signed (with forged signature). **impression** i.e., with a wax seal **53 changeling** i.e., the substituted letter. (Literally, a fairy child substituted for a human one.) **58 defeat** destruction **59 insinuation** intrusive intervention, sticking their noses in my business **60 baser** of lower social station **61 pass** thrust. **fell** fierce **62 opposites** antagonists **63 stand me now upon** become incumbent on me now

Popped in between th' election and my hopes, 65
Thrown out his angle for my proper life, 66
And with such cozenage—is 't not perfect conscience 67
To quit him with this arm? And is 't not to be damned 68
To let this canker of our nature come 69
In further evil? 70

HORATIO
It must be shortly known to him from England
What is the issue of the business there.

HAMLET
It will be short. The interim is mine,
And a man's life's no more than to say "one." 74
But I am very sorry, good Horatio,
That to Laertes I forgot myself,
For by the image of my cause I see
The portraiture of his. I'll court his favors.
But, sure, the bravery of his grief did put me 79
Into a tow'ring passion.

HORATIO Peace, who comes here?

Enter a Courtier [*Osric*].

OSRIC Your lordship is right welcome back to Denmark.

HAMLET I humbly thank you, sir. [*To Horatio.*] Dost know this water fly?

HORATIO No, my good lord.

HAMLET Thy state is the more gracious, for 'tis a vice to
know him. He hath much land, and fertile. Let a beast 86
be lord of beasts, and his crib shall stand at the King's 87
mess. 'Tis a chuff, but, as I say, spacious in the pos- 88
session of dirt.

OSRIC Sweet lord, if your lordship were at leisure, I should impart a thing to you from His Majesty.

HAMLET I will receive it, sir, with all diligence of spirit.

65 election (The Danish monarch was "elected" by a small number of high-ranking electors.) **66 angle** fishing line. **proper** very
67 cozenage trickery **68 quit** requite, pay back **69 canker** ulcer
69–70 come In grow into **74 a man's . . . one** i.e., one's whole life occupies such a short time, only as long as it takes to count to one
79 bravery bravado **86–88 Let . . . mess** i.e., if a man, no matter how beastlike, is as rich in possessions as Osric, he may eat at the King's table **88 chuff** boor, churl. (The second quarto spelling, *chough,* is a variant spelling that also suggests the meaning here of "chattering jackdaw.")

Put your bonnet to his right use; 'tis for the head.

OSRIC I thank your lordship, it is very hot.

HAMLET No, believe me, 'tis very cold. The wind is northerly.

OSRIC It is indifferent cold, my lord, indeed.

HAMLET But yet methinks it is very sultry and hot for my complexion.

OSRIC Exceedingly, my lord. It is very sultry, as 'twere—I cannot tell how. My lord, His Majesty bade me signify to you that 'a has laid a great wager on your head. Sir, this is the matter—

HAMLET I beseech you, remember.

[*Hamlet moves him to put on his hat.*]

OSRIC Nay, good my lord; for my ease, in good faith. Sir, here is newly come to court Laertes—believe me, an absolute gentleman, full of most excellent differences, of very soft society and great showing. Indeed, to speak feelingly of him, he is the card or calendar of gentry, for you shall find in him the continent of what part a gentleman would see.

HAMLET Sir, his definement suffers no perdition in you, though I know to divide him inventorially would dozy th' arithmetic of memory, and yet but yaw neither in respect of his quick sail. But, in the verity of extolment, I take him to be a soul of great article and his infusion of such dearth and rareness as, to make true diction of him, his semblable is his mirror and

93 bonnet any kind of cap or hat. **his** its **97 indifferent** somewhat **99 complexion** temperament **105 for my ease** (A conventional reply declining the invitation to put his hat back on.) **107 absolute** perfect **107–108 differences** special qualities **108 soft society** agreeable manners. **great showing** distinguished appearance **109 feelingly** with just perception. **card** chart, map. **calendar** guide **110 gentry** good breeding **110–111 the continent . . . part** one who contains in him all the qualities. (A *continent* is that which contains.) **what part** whatever part, any part which **112 definement** definition. (Hamlet proceeds to mock Osric by using his lofty diction back at him.) **perdition** loss, diminution **113 divide him inventorially** i.e., enumerate his graces **114 dozy** dizzy. **yaw** swing unsteadily off course. (Said of a ship.) **115 neither** for all that. **in respect of** in comparison with **115–116 in . . . extolment** in true praise (of him) **116 of great article** one with many articles in his inventory **117 infusion** essence, character infused into him by nature. **dearth and rareness** rarity **117–118 make true diction** speak truly **118 semblable** only true likeness

who else would trace him his umbrage, nothing 119
more.

OSRIC Your lordship speaks most infallibly of him.

HAMLET The concernancy, sir? Why do we wrap the 122
gentleman in our more rawer breath? 123

OSRIC Sir?

HORATIO Is 't not possible to understand in another 125
tongue? You will do 't, sir, really. 126

HAMLET What imports the nomination of this gen- 127
tleman?

OSRIC Of Laertes?

HORATIO [*To Hamlet*] His purse is empty already; all 's golden words are spent.

HAMLET Of him, sir.

OSRIC I know you are not ignorant—

HAMLET I would you did, sir. Yet in faith if you did,
it would not much approve me. Well, sir? 135

OSRIC You are not ignorant of what excellence Laertes is—

HAMLET I dare not confess that, lest I should compare 138
with him in excellence. But to know a man well were 139
to know himself. 140

OSRIC I mean, sir, for his weapon; but in the imputa- 141
tion laid on him by them in his meed, he's unfellowed. 142

HAMLET What's his weapon?

OSRIC Rapier and dagger.

HAMLET That's two of his weapons—but well. 145

OSRIC The King, sir, hath wagered with him six Barbary

119 who . . . trace any other person who would wish to follow. **umbrage** shadow **122 concernancy** import, relevance **123 rawer breath** i.e., speech which can only come short in praising him **125–126 to understand . . . tongue** i.e., for you, Osric, to understand when someone else speaks your language. (Horatio twits Osric for not being able to understand the kind of flowery speech he himself uses, when Hamlet speaks in such a vein. Alternatively, all this could be said to Hamlet.) **126 You will do 't** i.e., you can if you try **127 nomination** naming **135 approve** commend **138–140 I dare . . . himself** i.e., I dare not boast of knowing Laertes's excellence lest I seem to compare his with my own, since to appreciate excellence in another one must possess it oneself; by the same token, it is presumptuous to claim the self-knowledge necessary to know another person well **141 for** i.e., with **141–142 imputation . . . them** reputation given him by others **142 meed** merit. **unfellowed** unmatched **145 but well** but never mind

horses, against the which he has impawned, as I take it, six French rapiers and poniards, with their assigns, as girdle, hangers, and so. Three of the carriages, in faith, are very dear to fancy, very responsive to the hilts, most delicate carriages, and of very liberal conceit.

HAMLET What call you the carriages?

HORATIO [*To Hamlet*] I knew you must be edified by the margent ere you had done.

OSRIC The carriages, sir, are the hangers.

HAMLET The phrase would be more germane to the matter if we could carry a cannon by our sides; I would it might be hangers till then. But, on: six Barbary horses against six French swords, their assigns, and three liberal-conceited carriages; that's the French bet against the Danish. Why is this impawned, as you call it?

OSRIC The King, sir, hath laid, sir, that in a dozen passes between yourself and him, he shall not exceed you three hits. He hath laid on twelve for nine, and it would come to immediate trial, if your lordship would vouchsafe the answer.

HAMLET How if I answer no?

OSRIC I mean, my lord, the opposition of your person in trial.

HAMLET Sir, I will walk here in the hall. If it please His Majesty, it is the breathing time of day with me. Let the foils be brought, the gentleman willing, and the King hold his purpose, I will win for him an I can; if not, I will gain nothing but my shame and the odd hits.

147 he i.e., Laertes. **impawned** staked, wagered **148 poniards** daggers. **assigns** appurtenances **149 hangers** straps on the sword belt (*girdle*) from which the sword hung. **and so** and so on. **carriages** (An affected way of saying *hangers;* literally, gun carriages.) **150 dear to fancy** fancifully designed, tasteful. **responsive** corresponding closely, matching or well adjusted **151 delicate** (i.e., in workmanship) **151–152 liberal conceit** elaborate design **155 margent** margin of a book, place for explanatory notes **163 laid** wagered **164 passes** bouts. (The odds of the betting are hard to explain. Possibly the King bets that Hamlet will win at least five out of twelve, at which point Laertes raises the odds against himself by betting he will win nine.) **167 vouchsafe the answer** be so good as to accept the challenge. (Hamlet deliberately takes the phrase in its literal sense.) **172 breathing time** exercise period. **Let** i.e., if

OSRIC Shall I deliver you so?

HAMLET To this effect, sir—after what flourish your nature will.

OSRIC I commend my duty to your lordship.

HAMLET Yours, yours. [*Exit Osric.*] 'A does well to commend it himself; there are no tongues else for 's turn.

HORATIO This lapwing runs away with the shell on his head.

HAMLET 'A did comply with his dug before 'a sucked it. Thus has he—and many more of the same breed that I know the drossy age dotes on—only got the tune of the time and, out of an habit of encounter, a kind of yeasty collection, which carries them through and through the most fanned and winnowed opinions; and do but blow them to their trial, the bubbles are out.

Enter a Lord.

LORD My lord, His Majesty commended him to you by young Osric, who brings back to him that you attend him in the hall. He sends to know if your pleasure hold to play with Laertes, or that you will take longer time.

HAMLET I am constant to my purposes; they follow the King's pleasure. If his fitness speaks, mine is ready; now or whensoever, provided I be so able as now.

LORD The King and Queen and all are coming down.

177 deliver report what you say **180 commend** commit to your favor. (A conventional salutation; but Hamlet wryly uses a more literal meaning, "recommend," in l. 182.) **182–183 for 's turn** for his purposes, i.e., to do it for him **184 lapwing** (A proverbial type of youthful forwardness. Also, a bird that draws intruders away from its nest and was thought to run about when newly hatched with its head in the shell; a seeming reference to Osric's hat.) **186 comply . . . dug** observe ceremonious formality toward his nurse's or mother's teat **188 drossy** laden with scum and impurities, frivolous **189 tune** temper, mood, manner of speech. **habit of encounter** demeanor of social intercourse **190 yeasty** frothy. **collection** i.e., of current phrases **191 fanned and winnowed** select and refined. (Literally, like grain separated from its chaff. Osric is both the chaff and the bubbly froth on the surface of the liquor that is soon blown away.) **192–193 blow . . . out** i.e., put them to the test, and their ignorance is exposed **197 that** if **200 If . . . ready** if he declares his readiness, my convenience waits on his

HAMLET In happy time. 203
LORD The Queen desires you to use some gentle enter- 204
tainment to Laertes before you fall to play. 205
HAMLET She well instructs me. *[Exit Lord.]*
HORATIO You will lose, my lord.
HAMLET I do not think so. Since he went into France, I
have been in continual practice; I shall win at the
odds. But thou wouldst not think how ill all's here
about my heart; but it is no matter.
HORATIO Nay, good my lord—
HAMLET It is but foolery, but it is such a kind of gain- 213
giving as would perhaps trouble a woman. 214
HORATIO If your mind dislike anything, obey it. I will
forestall their repair hither and say you are not fit. 216
HAMLET Not a whit, we defy augury. There is special
providence in the fall of a sparrow. If it be now, 'tis
not to come; if it be not to come, it will be now; if it
be not now, yet it will come. The readiness is all. Since 220
no man of aught he leaves knows, what is 't to leave 221
betimes? Let be. 222

A table prepared. [*Enter*] *trumpets, drums, and officers with cushions; King, Queen,* [*Osric,*] *and all the state; foils, daggers,* [*and wine borne in;*] *and Laertes.*

KING
Come, Hamlet, come and take this hand from me.
[*The King puts Laertes's hand into Hamlet's.*]

HAMLET
Give me your pardon, sir. I have done you wrong,
But pardon 't as you are a gentleman.
This presence knows, 226
And you must needs have heard, how I am punished
With a sore distraction. What I have done
That might your nature, honor, and exception 229

203 In happy time (A phrase of courtesy indicating acceptance.)
204–205 entertainment greeting **213–214 gaingiving** misgiving
216 repair coming **220–222 Since . . . Let be** since no one has knowledge of what he is leaving behind, what does an early death matter after all? Enough; don't struggle against it. **226 presence** royal assembly
229 exception disapproval

Roughly awake, I here proclaim was madness.
Was 't Hamlet wronged Laertes? Never Hamlet.
If Hamlet from himself be ta'en away,
And when he's not himself does wrong Laertes,
Then Hamlet does it not, Hamlet denies it.
Who does it, then? His madness. If 't be so,
Hamlet is of the faction that is wronged; 236
His madness is poor Hamlet's enemy.
Sir, in this audience,
Let my disclaiming from a purposed evil
Free me so far in your most generous thoughts
That I have shot my arrow o'er the house 241
And hurt my brother.

LAERTES I am satisfied in nature, 242
Whose motive in this case should stir me most 243
To my revenge. But in my terms of honor
I stand aloof, and will no reconcilement
Till by some elder masters of known honor
I have a voice and precedent of peace 247
To keep my name ungored. But till that time, 248
I do receive your offered love like love,
And will not wrong it.

HAMLET I embrace it freely,
And will this brothers' wager frankly play.— 251
Give us the foils. Come on.

LAERTES Come, one for me.

HAMLET
I'll be your foil, Laertes. In mine ignorance 253
Your skill shall, like a star i' the darkest night,
Stick fiery off indeed.

LAERTES You mock me, sir. 255

HAMLET No, by this hand.

KING
Give them the foils, young Osric. Cousin Hamlet,
You know the wager?

236 faction party **241 That I have** as if I had **242 in nature** i.e., as to my personal feelings **243 motive** prompting **247 voice** authoritative pronouncement. **of peace** for reconciliation **248 name ungored** reputation unwounded **251 frankly** without ill feeling or the burden of rancor **253 foil** thin metal background which sets a jewel off (with pun on the blunted rapier for fencing) **255 Stick fiery off** stand out brilliantly

HAMLET Very well, my lord.
Your Grace has laid the odds o' the weaker side. 259

KING
I do not fear it; I have seen you both.
But since he is bettered, we have therefore odds. 261

LAERTES
This is too heavy. Let me see another.
[*He exchanges his foil for another.*]

HAMLET
This likes me well. These foils have all a length? 263
[*They prepare to play.*]

OSRIC Ay, my good lord.

KING
Set me the stoups of wine upon that table.
If Hamlet give the first or second hit,
Or quit in answer of the third exchange, 267
Let all the battlements their ordnance fire.
The King shall drink to Hamlet's better breath, 269
And in the cup an union shall he throw 270
Richer than that which four successive kings
In Denmark's crown have worn. Give me the cups,
And let the kettle to the trumpet speak, 273
The trumpet to the cannoneer without,
The cannons to the heavens, the heaven to earth,
"Now the King drinks to Hamlet." Come, begin.
Trumpets the while.
And you, the judges, bear a wary eye.

HAMLET Come on, sir.

LAERTES Come, my lord. [*They play. Hamlet scores a hit.*]

HAMLET One.

LAERTES No.

HAMLET Judgment.

OSRIC A hit, a very palpable hit.
Drum, trumpets, and shot. Flourish.
A piece goes off.

259 laid the odds o' bet on, backed **261 is bettered** has improved; is the odds-on favorite. (Laertes's handicap is the "three hits" specified in l. 165.) **263 likes me** pleases me **267 Or . . . exchange** i.e., or requites Laertes in the third bout for having won the first two **269 better breath** improved vigor **270 union** pearl. (So called, according to Pliny's *Natural History*, 9, because pearls are *unique*, never identical.) **273 kettle** kettledrum

LAERTES Well, again.

KING
Stay, give me drink. Hamlet, this pearl is thine.
[*He throws a pearl in Hamlet's cup, and drinks.*]
Here's to thy health. Give him the cup.

HAMLET
I'll play this bout first. Set it by awhile.
Come. [*They play.*] Another hit; what say you?

LAERTES A touch, a touch, I do confess 't.

KING
Our son shall win.

QUEEN He's fat and scant of breath. 289
Here, Hamlet, take my napkin, rub thy brows. 290
The Queen carouses to thy fortune, Hamlet. 291

HAMLET Good madam!

KING Gertrude, do not drink.

QUEEN
I will, my lord, I pray you pardon me. [*She drinks.*]

KING [*Aside*]
It is the poisoned cup. It is too late.

HAMLET
I dare not drink yet, madam; by and by.

QUEEN Come, let me wipe thy face.

LAERTES [*To the King*]
My lord, I'll hit him now.

KING I do not think 't.

LAERTES [*Aside*]
And yet it is almost against my conscience.

HAMLET
Come, for the third, Laertes. You do but dally.
I pray you, pass with your best violence; 301
I am afeard you make a wanton of me. 302

LAERTES Say you so? Come on. [*They play.*]

OSRIC Nothing neither way.

LAERTES
Have at you now!

289 fat not physically fit, out of training **290 napkin** handkerchief **291 carouses** drinks a toast **301 pass** thrust **302 make . . . me** i.e., treat me like a spoiled child, holding back to give me an advantage

[*Laertes wounds Hamlet; then, in scuffling, they change rapiers, and Hamlet wounds Laertes.*]

KING Part them! They are incensed.

HAMLET
Nay, come, again. [*The Queen falls.*]

OSRIC Look to the Queen there, ho!

HORATIO
They bleed on both sides. How is it, my lord?

OSRIC How is 't, Laertes?

LAERTES
Why, as a woodcock to mine own springe, Osric;
I am justly killed with mine own treachery.

HAMLET
How does the Queen?

KING She swoons to see them bleed.

QUEEN
No, no, the drink, the drink—O my dear Hamlet—
The drink, the drink! I am poisoned. [*She dies.*]

HAMLET
O villainy! Ho, let the door be locked!
Treachery! Seek it out. [*Laertes falls. Exit Osric.*]

LAERTES
It is here, Hamlet. Hamlet, thou art slain.
No med'cine in the world can do thee good;
In thee there is not half an hour's life.
The treacherous instrument is in thy hand,
Unbated and envenomed. The foul practice
Hath turned itself on me. Lo, here I lie,
Never to rise again. Thy mother's poisoned.
I can no more. The King, the King's to blame.

HAMLET
The point envenomed too? Then, venom, to thy work.
[*He stabs the King.*]

ALL Treason! Treason!

KING
O, yet defend me, friends! I am but hurt.

305 s.d. in scuffling, they change rapiers (This stage direction occurs in the Folio. According to a widespread stage tradition, Hamlet receives a scratch, realizes that Laertes's sword is unbated, and accordingly forces an exchange.) **309 woodcock** a bird, a type of stupidity or as a decoy. **springe** trap, snare **320 Unbated** not blunted with a button. **practice** plot

HAMLET [*Forcing the King to drink*]
Here, thou incestuous, murderous, damnèd Dane,
Drink off this potion. Is thy union here? 328
Follow my mother. [*The King dies.*]
LAERTES He is justly served.
It is a poison tempered by himself. 330
Exchange forgiveness with me, noble Hamlet.
Mine and my father's death come not upon thee,
Nor thine on me! [*He dies.*]
HAMLET
Heaven make thee free of it! I follow thee.
I am dead, Horatio. Wretched Queen, adieu!
You that look pale and tremble at this chance, 336
That are but mutes or audience to this act, 337
Had I but time—as this fell sergeant, Death, 338
Is strict in his arrest—O, I could tell you— 339
But let it be. Horatio, I am dead;
Thou livest. Report me and my cause aright
To the unsatisfied.
HORATIO Never believe it.
I am more an antique Roman than a Dane. 343
Here's yet some liquor left.
[*He attempts to drink from the poisoned cup. Hamlet prevents him.*]
HAMLET As thou'rt a man,
Give me the cup! Let go! By heaven, I'll ha 't.
O God, Horatio, what a wounded name,
Things standing thus unknown, shall I leave behind me!
If thou didst ever hold me in thy heart,
Absent thee from felicity awhile,
And in this harsh world draw thy breath in pain
To tell my story. (*A march afar off* [*and a volley within*].)
What warlike noise is this?

Enter Osric.

OSRIC
Young Fortinbras, with conquest come from Poland,

328 union pearl. (See l. 270; with grim puns on the word's other meanings: marriage, shared death.) **330 tempered** mixed **336 chance** mischance **337 mutes** silent observers **338 fell** cruel. **sergeant** sheriff's officer **339 strict** (1) severely just (2) unavoidable. **arrest** (1) taking into custody (2) stopping my speech **343 Roman** (It was the Roman custom to follow masters in death.)

To th' ambassadors of England gives
This warlike volley.

HAMLET
O, I die, Horatio!
The potent poison quite o'ercrows my spirit. 355
I cannot live to hear the news from England,
But I do prophesy th' election lights
On Fortinbras. He has my dying voice. 358
So tell him, with th' occurrents more and less 359
Which have solicited—the rest is silence. [*He dies.*] 360

HORATIO
Now cracks a noble heart. Good night, sweet prince,
And flights of angels sing thee to thy rest!
[*March within.*]
Why does the drum come hither?

Enter Fortinbras, with the [*English*] *Ambassadors* [*with drum, colors, and attendants*].

FORTINBRAS
Where is this sight?

HORATIO
What is it you would see?
If aught of woe or wonder, cease your search.

FORTINBRAS
This quarry cries on havoc. O proud Death, 366
What feast is toward in thine eternal cell, 367
That thou so many princes at a shot
So bloodily hast struck?

FIRST AMBASSADOR
The sight is dismal,
And our affairs from England come too late.
The ears are senseless that should give us hearing,
To tell him his commandment is fulfilled,
That Rosencrantz and Guildenstern are dead.
Where should we have our thanks?

HORATIO
Not from his mouth, 374
Had it th' ability of life to thank you.

355 o'ercrows triumphs over (like the winner in a cockfight) **358 voice** vote **359 occurrents** events, incidents **360 solicited** moved, urged. (Hamlet doesn't finish saying what the events have prompted; presumably his acts of vengeance, or his reporting those events to Fortinbras.) **366 quarry** heap of dead. **cries on havoc** proclaims a general slaughter **367 feast** i.e., Death feasting on those who have fallen. **toward** in preparation **374 his** i.e., Claudius's

He never gave commandment for their death.
But since, so jump upon this bloody question,
You from the Polack wars, and you from England,
Are here arrived, give order that these bodies
High on a stage be placèd to the view,
And let me speak to th' yet unknowing world
How these things came about. So shall you hear
Of carnal, bloody, and unnatural acts,
Of accidental judgments, casual slaughters,
Of deaths put on by cunning and forced cause,
And, in this upshot, purposes mistook
Fall'n on th' inventors' heads. All this can I
Truly deliver.

FORTINBRAS Let us haste to hear it,
And call the noblest to the audience.
For me, with sorrow I embrace my fortune.
I have some rights of memory in this kingdom,
Which now to claim my vantage doth invite me.

HORATIO
Of that I shall have also cause to speak,
And from his mouth whose voice will draw on more.
But let this same be presently performed,
Even while men's minds are wild, lest more mischance
On plots and errors happen.

FORTINBRAS Let four captains
Bear Hamlet, like a soldier, to the stage,
For he was likely, had he been put on,
To have proved most royal; and for his passage,
The soldiers' music and the rite of war
Speak loudly for him.
Take up the bodies. Such a sight as this
Becomes the field, but here shows much amiss.
Go bid the soldiers shoot.

Exeunt [*marching, bearing off the dead bodies; a peal of ordnance is shot off*].

377 jump precisely, immediately. **question** dispute **380 stage** platform **384 judgments** retributions. **casual** occurring by chance **385 put on** instigated **391 of memory** traditional, remembered, unforgotten **392 vantage** i.e., presence at this opportune moment **394 voice . . . more** vote will influence still others **395 presently** immediately **397 On** on the basis of, on top of **399 put on** i.e., invested in royal office, and so put to the test **400 passage** death **404 field** i.e., of battle

Date and Text

Like everything else about *Hamlet,* the textual problem is complicated. On July 26, 1602, James Roberts entered in the Stationers' Register, the official record book of the London Company of Stationers (booksellers and printers), "A booke called the Revenge of Hamlett Prince Denmarke as yt was latelie Acted by the Lord Chamberleyn his servantes." For some reason, however, Roberts did not print his copy of *Hamlet* until 1604, by which time had appeared the following unauthorized edition:

> THE Tragicall Historie of HAMLET *Prince of Denmarke*[.] By William Shake-speare. As it hath beene diuerse times acted by his Highnesse seruants in the Cittie of London: as also in the two Vniuersities of Cambridge and Oxford, and elsewhere At London printed for N. L. [Nicholas Ling] and Iohn Trundell. 1603.

This edition, the bad quarto of *Hamlet,* seems to have been memorially reconstructed by actors who toured the provinces (note the references to Cambridge, Oxford, etc.), with some recollection of an earlier *Hamlet* play (the *Ur-Hamlet*) written before 1589 and acted during the 1590s. The piratical actors had no recourse to an authoritative manuscript. One may have played Marcellus and possibly Lucianus and Voltimand. Their version seems to have been based on an adaptation of the company's original promptbook, which itself stood at one remove from Shakespeare's foul papers by way of an intermediate manuscript. The resulting text is very corrupt, and yet it seems to have affected the more authentic text because the compositors of the second quarto made use of it, especially when they typeset the first act.

The authorized quarto of *Hamlet* appeared in 1604. Roberts, the printer, seems to have reached some agreement with Ling, one of the publishers of the bad quarto, for their initials are now paired on the title page:

> *THE* Tragicall Historie of HAMLET, *Prince of Denmarke*. By William Shakespeare. Newly imprinted and enlarged to almost as much againe as it was, according to the true and perfect Coppie. AT LONDON, Printed by I. R. [James Roberts]

for N. L. [Nicholas Ling] and are to be sold at his shoppe vnder Saint Dunstons Church in Fleetstreet. 1604.

Some copies of this edition are dated 1605. This text was based seemingly on Shakespeare's own papers with the bookkeeper's annotations, but is marred by printing errors and is at times contaminated by the bad quarto—presumably when the printers found Shakespeare's manuscript unreadable. This second quarto served as copy for a third quarto in 1611, Ling having meanwhile transferred his rights in the play to John Smethwick. A fourth quarto, undated but before 1623, was based on the third.

The First Folio text of 1623 omits more than two hundred lines found in the second quarto. Yet it supplies some clearly authentic passages. It seems to derive from a transcript of Shakespeare's draft in which cuts made by the author were observed—cuts made by Shakespeare quite possibly because he knew the draft to be too long for performance, and which had either not been marked in the second quarto copy or had been ignored there by the compositors. The Folio also incorporates other alterations seemingly made for clarity or in anticipation of performance. To this theatrically motivated transcript Shakespeare apparently contributed some revisions. Subsequently, this version evidently was copied again by a careless scribe who took many liberties with the text. Typesetting from this inferior manuscript, the Folio compositors occasionally consulted the second quarto, but not often enough. Thus, even though the Folio supplies some genuine readings, as does the first quarto when both the Folio and the second quarto are wrong, the second quarto remains the most authentic version of the text.

Since the text of the second quarto is too long to be accommodated in the two hours' traffic of the stage and it becomes even longer when the words found only in the Folio are added, Shakespeare must have known it would have to be cut for performance and probably marked at least some omissions himself. Since he may have consented to such cuts primarily because of the constraints of time, however, this present edition holds to the view that the passages in question should not be excised from the text we read. The *Hamlet* presented here is doubtless longer than any version ever acted in Shakespeare's day, and thus does not represent a script for any actual performance, but it may well represent the play as Shakespeare wrote it and then somewhat expanded it; it also includes passages that he may reluctantly have consented to cut for performance. It is also possible that some cuts were artistically intended, but, in the face of real uncertainty in this matter, an editorial policy of inclusion gives to the reader those passages that would otherwise have to be excised or put in an appendix on questionable grounds of authorial "intent."

Hamlet must have been produced before the Stationers' Register entry of July 26, 1602. Francis Meres does not mention the play in 1598 in his *Palladis Tamia: Wit's Treasury* (a slender volume on contemporary literature and art; valuable because it lists most of the plays of Shakespeare that existed at that time). Gabriel Harvey attributes the "tragedy of Hamlet, Prince of Denmark" to Shakespeare in a marginal note in Harvey's copy of Speght's Chaucer; Harvey acquired the book in 1598, but could have written the note any time between then and 1601 or even 1603. More helpful in dating is Hamlet's clear reference to the so-called "War of the Theaters," the rivalry between the adult actors and the boy actors whose companies had newly revived in 1598–1599 after nearly a decade of inactivity. The Children of the Chapel Royal began acting at Blackfriars in 1598 and provided such keen competition in 1599–1601 that the adult actors were at times forced to tour the provinces (see *Hamlet*, 2.2.332–362). Revenge tragedy was also in fashion during these years: John Marston's *Antonio's Revenge*, for example, dates from 1599–1601, and *The Malcontent* is from about the same time or slightly later.

Textual Notes

These textual notes are not a historical collation, either of the early quartos and the early folios or of more recent editions; they are simply a record of departures in this edition from the copy text. The reading adopted in this edition appears in boldface, followed by the rejected reading from the copy text, i.e., the second quarto of 1604. Only major alterations in punctuation are noted. Changes in lineation are not indicated, nor are some minor and obvious typographical errors.

Abbreviations used:
F the First Folio
Q quarto
s.d. stage direction
s.p. speech prefix

Copy text: the second quarto of 1604–1605 [Q2]. The First Folio text also represents an independently authoritative text; although seemingly not the correct choice for copy text, the Folio text is considerably less marred by typographical errors than is Q2. The adopted readings in these notes are from F unless otherwise indicated; [eds.] means that the adopted reading was first proposed by some editor since the time of F. Some readings are also supplied from the pirated first quarto of 1603 [Q1].

1.1. 1 Who's Whose **19 soldier** [F, Q1] souldiers **44 off** [Q1] of **48 harrows** horrowes **67 sledded Polacks** [eds.] sleaded pollax **77 why** [F, Q1] with **cast** cost **91 heraldry** [F, Q1] heraldy **92 those** [F, Q1] these **95 returned** returne **97 covenant** comart **98 designed** [eds.] desseigne **112 e'en so** [eds.] enso **119 tenantless** tennatlesse **125 feared** [eds.] feare **142 you** [F, Q1] your **144 at it** it **181 conveniently** [F, Q1] conuenient

1.2. s.d. Gertrude Gertradt (and elsewhere; also Gertrad) **1 s.p. King** Claud **67 so** so much **77 good** coold **82 shapes** [Q3] chapes **83 denote** deuote **96 a** or **105 corpse** [eds.] course **112 you. For** you for **129 sullied** [eds.] sallied [Q2] solid [F] **132 self** seale **133 weary** wary **137 to this** thus **140 satyr** [F4] satire **143 would** [F, Q1] should **149 even she** [F; not in Q2] **175 to drink deep** [F, Q1] for to drinke **178 to see** [F, Q1] to **199 waste** [F2] wast [Q2, F] **210 Where, as** [Q5] Whereas **225 Indeed, indeed** [F, Q1] Indeede **241 Very like, very like** [F, Q1] Very like **242 hundred** hundreth **243 s.p. Marcellus, Bernardo** [eds.] Both **247 tonight** to nigh **256 fare** farre **257 eleven** a leaven **259 Exeunt** [at l. 258 in Q2] **262 Foul** [F, Q1] fonde

1.3. 3 convoy is conuay, in **12 bulk** bulkes **18** [F; not in Q2] **29 weigh** way **49 like a** a **74 Are** Or **75 be** boy **76 loan** loue **77 dulls the** dulleth **110 Running** [eds.] Wrong [Q2] Roaming [F] **116 springes** springs **126 tether** tider **130 implorators** imploratotors **131 bawds** [eds.] bonds **132 beguile** beguide

1.4. 2 is a is **6 s.d. go off** [eds.] goes of **17 revel** [Q3] reueale **36 evil** [eds.] eale [Q2] ease [Q3] **37 often dout** [eds.] of a doubt **49 inurned** interr'd [Q2, Q1] **61, 79 wafts** waues **80 off** of **82 artery** arture **86 s.d. Exeunt** Exit **87 imagination** [F, Q1] imagion

1.5. 1 Whither [eds.] Whether **21 fretful** [F, Q1] fearfull **44 wit** [eds.] wits **48 what a** what **56 lust** [F, Q1] but **57 sate** [F] sort **59 scent** [eds.] sent **68 alleys** [eds.] allies **69 posset** possesse **96 stiffly** swiftly **119 bird** and **128 s.p. Horatio, Marcellus** Booth [also at l. 151] **heaven, my lord** heauen **138 Look you, I'll** I will **179 soe'er** so mere **185 Well** well, well [Q1, Q2]

2.1. s.d. man [eds.] man or two **29 Faith, no** Fayth **41 warrant** wit **42 sullies** sallies **43 wi' the** with **60 o'ertook** or tooke **64 takes** take **76 s.d. Exit Reynaldo** [at l. 75 in Q2] **107 passion** passions

2.2. 57 o'erhasty hastie **73 three** [F, Q1] threescore **90 since brevity** breuitie **125 This** [Q2 has a speech prefix: *Pol.* This] **126 above** about **137 winking** working **143 his** her **148 watch** wath **149 to a** to **151 'tis** [F, Q1; not in Q2] **170 s.d. Exeunt** [eds.] Exit **210 sanity** sanctity **212–213 and suddenly . . . him** [F; not in Q2] **213 honorable lord** lord **214 most humbly take** take **215 cannot, sir** cannot **216 more** not more **224 excellent** extent **228–229 overhappy. On** euer happy on **229 cap** lap **240–270 Let . . . attended** [F; not in Q2] **267 s.p. Rosencrantz, Guildenstern** Both [F] **273 even** euer **288 could** can **292 off** of **304 What a** What **306–307 admirable, in action how . . . angel, in** [F, subst.] admirable in action, how . . . Angell in **310 no, nor** nor **314 you** yee **321 of** on **324–325 the clown . . . sear** [F; not in Q2] **tickle** [eds.] tickled [F] **326 blank** black **337–362 How . . . too** [F; not in Q2] **342 berattle** [eds.] be-ratled [F] **349 most like** [eds.] like most [F] **373 lest my** let me **381 too** to **398–399 tragical-historical, tragical-comical-historical-pastoral** [F; not in Q2] **400–401 light . . . these** [eds.] light for the lawe of writ, and the liberty: these **425 By 'r** by **429 e'en to 't** ento 't **French falconers** friendly Fankners **433 s.p. [and elsewhere] First Player** Player **443 affectation** affection **446 tale** [F, Q1] talke **454 the** th' **456 heraldry** [F, Q1] heraldy **dismal. Head** dismall head **474 Then senseless Ilium** [F; not in Q2] **481 And, like** Like **495 fellies** [F4] follies [Q2] Fallies [F] **504 "Mobled queen" is good** [F; not in Q2; F reads "Inobled"] **506 bisson** Bison **514 husband's** [F, Q1] husband **541 or** [F, Q1] lines, or **547 till** tell **548 s.d. Exeunt** [F; Q2 has "Exeunt Pol. and Players" at l. 547] **554 his** the **556 and** an **559 to Hecuba** [F, Q1] to her **561 the cue** that **582 O, vengeance** [F; not in Q2] **584 father** [Q1, Q3, Q4; not in Q2, F] **588 scullion** [F] stallyon [Q2] scalion [Q1] **600 the devil** a deale **the devil** the deale

3.1. 1 And An **28 too** two **32 lawful espials** [F; not in Q2] **33 Will** Wee'le **46 loneliness** lowlines **56 Let's withdraw** withdraw **56 s.d. Enter Hamlet** [at l. 55 in Q2] **65 wished. To** wisht to **73 disprized** despiz'd **84 of us all** [F, Q1; not in Q2] **86 sicklied** sickled **93 well, well, well** well **100 the** these **108 your honesty** you **119 inoculate** euocutat **122 to a** a **130 knaves all** knaues **144 paintings too** [Q1] paintings **146 jig, you amble** gig & amble **147 lisp** list **148 your ignorance** [F, Q1] ignorance **155 Th' expectancy** Th' expectation **159 music** musickt **160 that** what **161 tune** time **162 feature** stature **164** [Q2 has "Exit" at the end of this line] **191 unwatched** vnmatcht

3.2. 10 tatters totters **split** [F, Q1] spleet **27 of the** of **29 praise** praysd **37 sir** [F; not in Q2] **45 s.d. Enter . . . Rosencrantz** [at l. 47 in Q2] **88 detecting** detected **107 s.p. [and elsewhere] Queen** Ger **112–113** [F; not in Q2] **127 devil** deule [Q2] Diuel [F] **133 s.d. sound** [eds.] sounds **Anon**

comes Anon come **135 miching** [F, Q1] munching **140 keep counsel** [F, Q1] keepe **153 s.p. [and throughout scene] Player King** King **154 orbèd** orb'd the **159 s.p. [and throughout scene] Player Queen** Quee **162 your** our **164** [Q2 follows here with an extraneous unrhymed line: "For women feare too much, euen as they loue"] **165 For** And **166 In** Eyther none in **167 love** Lord **179 Wormwood, wormwood** That's wormwood **180 s.p. Player Queen** [not in Q2] **188 like** the **197 joys** ioy **217 An** And **221 a widow** [F, Q1] I be a widow **be** be a **226 s.d. Exit** [F, Q1] Exeunt **240 wince** [Q1] winch [Q2, F] **241 s.d.** [at l. 242 in Q2] **254 Confederate** [F, Q1] Considerat **256 infected** [F, Q1, Q4] inuected **258 usurp** vsurps **264** [F; not in Q2] **274 with two** with **288 s.d.** [F; at l. 293 in Q2] **308 start** stare **317 of my** of **343 s.d.** [at l. 341 in Q2] **357 thumb** the vmber **366 to the top of** to **370 can fret me** [F] fret me not [Q2] can fret me, yet [Q1] **371 s.d.** [at l. 372 in Q2] **385 s.p. Polonius** [F; not in Q2] **386 Leave me, friends** [so F; Q2 places before "I will say so," and assigns both to Hamlet] **388 breathes** breakes **390 bitter . . . day** busines as the bitter day **395 daggers** [F, Q1] dagger

3.3. 19 huge hough **22 ruin** raine **23 but with** but **50 pardoned** pardon **58 Offense's** [eds.] Offences **shove** showe **73 pat . . . a-praying** but now a is a praying **75 revenged** reuendge **79 hire and salary** base and silly

3.4. 4 shroud [Q1] [eds.] silence [Q2, F] **5–6 with him . . . Mother** [F; not in Q2] **7 warrant** wait **8 s.d. Enter Hamlet** [at l. 5 in Q2] **21 inmost** most **43 off** of **51 tristful** heated **53** [assigned in Q2 to Hamlet] **60 heaven-kissing** heaue, a kissing **89 panders** pardons **91 my . . . soul** [eds.] my very eyes into my soule [Q2] mine eyes into my very soul [F] **92 grainèd** greeued **93 not leave** leaue there **100 tithe** kyth **146 Ecstasy** [F; not in Q2] **150 I the** the **165 live** leaue **172 Refrain tonight** to refraine night **193 ravel** rouell **205 to breathe** [eds.] to breath **222 a** [F, Q1] a most **224 s.d. Exeunt** [eds.] Exit

4.2. s.d. [Q2: "Enter Hamlet, Rosencraus, and others."] **2** [F; not in Q2] **3 s.p. Hamlet** [not in Q2] **4 s.d.** [F; not in Q2] **7 Compounded** Compound **19 ape** apple **31–32 Hide . . . after** [F; not in Q2]

4.3. 44 With fiery quickness [F; not in Q2] **56 and so** so **72 were** will **begun** begin

4.4. 20–21 name. To name To

4.5. 16 Let . . . in [assigned in Q2 to Horatio] **20 s.d.** [at l. 16 in Q2] **38 with** all with **57 Indeed, la** Indeede **83 in their** in **90 his** this **98** [F; not in Q2] **100 are** is **100 s.d.** [at l. 97 in Q2] **103 impetuous** [Q3, F2] impitious [Q2] impittious [F] **109 They** The **146 swoopstake** [eds.] soopstake [Q1 reads "Swoop-stake-like"] **158 Let her come in** [assigned in Q2 to Laertes and placed before "How now, what noyse is that?"] **s.d. Enter Ophelia** [after l. 157 in Q2] **162 Till** Tell **165 an old** [F, Q1] a poore **166–168, 170** [F; not in Q2] **186 must** [F, Q1] may **191 affliction** [F, Q1] afflictions **199 All flaxen** Flaxen **203 Christian** [F] Christians **souls, I pray God** [F, Q1] souls **204 you see** you **217 trophy, sword** trophe sword

4.6. 7, 9 s.p. First Sailor Say **22 good turn** turn **26 bore** bord **30 He** So **31 will give** will

4.7. 6 proceeded proceede **7 crimeful** criminall **15 conjunctive** concliue

22 gyves Giues **23 loud a wind** loued Arm'd **25 had** haue **37 How . . . Hamlet** [F; not in Q2] **38 This** These **46–47 your pardon** you pardon **48 and more strange** [F; not in Q2] **Hamlet** [F; not in Q2] **56 shall live** [F, Q1] liue **62 checking** the King **78 ribbon** [eds.] ribaud **89 my** me **116 wick** [eds.] weeke **123 spendthrift** [Q5] spend thirfts **126 yourself in deed** indeede your fathers sonne **135 on** ore **139 pass** pace **141 for that** for **157 ha 't** hate **160 prepared** prefard **168 hoar** horry **172 cold** cull-cold **192 douts** [F "doubts"] drownes

5.1. 1 s.p [and throughout] First Clown Clowne **3 s.p. [and throughout] Second Clown** Other **9 se offendendo** so offended **12 and to** to **Argal** or all **34–37 Why . . . arms** [F; not in Q2] **43 that frame** that **55 s.d.** [at l. 65 in Q2] **60 stoup** soope **85 meant** [F, Q1, Q3] went **89 mazard** massene **106–107 Is . . . recoveries** [F; not in Q2] **107–108 Will his** will **109 double ones too** doubles **120 O** or **121** [F; not in Q2] **143 Of all** Of **165 nowadays** [F; not in Q2] **183 Let me see** [F; not in Q] **192 chamber** [F, Q1] table **208–209 As thus** [F; not in Q2] **216 winter's** waters **226, 235 s.p. Priest** Doct **231 Shards, flints** Flints **247 treble** double **262 and rash** rash **288 thus** this **301 shortly** thereby **302 Till** Tell

5.2. 5 Methought my thought **6 bilboes** bilbo **9 pall** fall **17 unseal** vnfold **19 Ah** [eds.] A **29 villainies** villaines **30 Ere** Or **43 "as"es** as sir **52 Subscribed** Subscribe **57, 68–80** [F; not in Q2] **73 interim is** [eds.] interim's [F] **78 court** [eds.] count [F] **81 s.p. [and throughout] Osric** Cour **82 humbly** humble **93 Put your** your **98 sultry** sully **for** or **107 gentleman** [eds.] gentlemen **109 feelingly** [Q4] fellingly **114 dozy** [eds.] dazzie **yaw** [eds.] raw **141 his** [eds.] this **149 hangers** hanger **156 carriages** carriage **159 might be** be might **162 impawned, as** [eds.] all [Q2] impon'd, as [F] **181 Yours, yours. 'A does** Yours doo's **186 comply** so **190 yeasty** histy **191 fanned** [eds.] prophane [Q2] fond [F] **winnowed** trennowed **210 But thou** thou **218 be now** be **220 will come** well come **238** [F; not in Q2] **248 To keep** To **till** all **252 foils. Come on** foils **255 off** of **261 bettered** better **270 union** Vnice ["Onixe" in some copies] **288 A touch, a touch, I** I **302 afeard** sure **316 Hamlet. Hamlet** Hamlet **319 thy** [F, Q1] my **327 murderous** [F; not in Q2] **328 off** of **thy union** [F, Q1] the Onixe **345 ha 't** [eds.] hate [Q2] have 't [F] **366 proud** prou'd **369 s.p. First Ambassador** Embas **373 [and some other places] Rosencrantz** Rosencraus **381 th' yet** yet **385 forced** for no **394 on** no

Passages contained only in F and omitted from Q2 are noted in the textual notes above. It might be useful here to list the more important instances in which Q2 contains words, lines, and passages omitted in F.

1.1. 112–129 BERNARDO I think . . . countrymen

1.2. 58–60 wrung . . . consent

1.3. 9 perfume and

1.4. 17–38 This heavy-headed . . . scandal **75–78** The very . . . beneath

2.1. 122 Come

2.2. 17 Whether . . . thus **217** except my life **363** very **366** 'Sblood (and some other profanity passim) **371** then **444–445** as wholesome . . . fine **521–522** of this **589** Hum

3.2. 169–170 Where . . . there **216–217** To . . . scope

3.4. 72–77 Sense . . . difference **79–82** Eyes . . . mope **168–172** That monster . . . put on **174–177** the next . . . potency **187** One word . . . lady **209–217** There's . . . meet

4.1. 4 Bestow . . . while **41–44** Whose . . . air

4.2. 4 But soft

4.3. 26–29 KING Alas . . . worm

4.4. 9–67 *Enter Hamlet* . . . worth

4.5. 33 Oho

4.7. 68–82 LAERTES My lord . . . graveness **101–103** Th' escrimers . . . them **115–124** There . . . ulcer

5.1. 154 There

5.2. 106–142 here is . . . unfellowed (replaced in F by "you are not ignorant of what excellence Laertes is at his weapon") **154–155** HORATIO [*To Hamlet*] I knew . . . done **193–207** *Enter a Lord* . . . lose, my lord (replaced in F by "You will lose this wager, my lord") **222** Let be

Shakespeare's Sources

The ultimate source of the *Hamlet* story is Saxo Grammaticus's *Historia Danica* (1180–1208), the saga of one Amlothi or (as Saxo calls him) Amlethus. The outline of the story is essentially that of Shakespeare's play, even though the emphasis of the Danish saga is overwhelmingly on cunning, brutality, and bloody revenge. Amlethus' father is Horwendil, a Governor of Jutland, who bravely kills the King of Norway in single combat and thereby wins the hand in marriage of Gerutha, daughter of the King of Denmark. This good fortune goads the envious Feng into slaying his brother Horwendil and marrying Gerutha, "capping unnatural murder with incest." Though the deed is known to everyone, Feng invents excuses and soon wins the approbation of the fawning courtiers. Young Amlethus vows revenge, but, perceiving his uncle's cunning, he feigns madness. His mingled words of craft and candor awaken suspicions that he may be playing a game of deception.

Two attempts are made to lure Amlethus into revealing that he is actually sane. The first plan is to tempt him into lechery, on the theory that one who lusts for women cannot be truly insane. Feng causes an attractive woman to be placed in a forest where Amlethus will meet her as though by chance; but Amlethus, secretly warned of the trap by a kindly foster brother, spirits the young lady off to a hideaway where they can make love unobserved by Feng's agents. She confesses the plot to Amlethus. In a second stratagem, a courtier who is reported to be "gifted with more assurance than judgment" hides himself under some straw in the Queen's chamber in order to overhear her private conversations with Amlethus. The hero, suspecting just such a trap, feigns madness and begins crowing like a noisy rooster, bouncing up and down on the straw until he finds the eavesdropper. Amlethus stabs the man to death, drags him forth, cuts the body into morsels, boils them, and flings the bits "through the mouth of an open sewer for the swine to eat." Thereupon he returns to his mother to accuse her of being an infamous harlot. He wins her over to repentant virtue and even cooperation. When Feng, returning from a journey, looks around for his counselor, Amlethus jestingly (but in part truly) suggests that the man went to the sewer and fell in.

Feng now sends Amlethus to the King of Britain with secret orders for his execution. However, Amlethus finds the letter to the British King in the coffers of the two unnamed retainers accompanying him on the journey, and substitutes a new letter ordering their execution instead. The new letter, purportedly written and signed by Feng, goes on to urge that the King of Britain marry his daughter to a young Dane being sent from the Danish court. By this means Amlethus gains an English wife and rids himself of the escorts. A year later Amlethus returns to Jutland, gets the entire court drunk, flings a tapestry (knitted for him by his mother) over the prostrate courtiers, secures the tapestry with stakes, and then sets fire to the palace. Feng escapes this holocaust, but Amlethus cuts him down with the King's own sword. (Amlethus exchanges swords because his own has been nailed fast into its scabbard by his enemies.) Subsequently, Amlethus convinces the people of the justice of his cause and is chosen King of Jutland. After ruling for several years, he returns to Britain, bigamously marries a Scottish queen, fights a battle with his first father-in-law, is betrayed by his second wife, and is finally killed in battle.

In Saxo's account we thus find the prototypes of Hamlet, Claudius, Gertrude, Polonius, Ophelia, Rosencrantz, and Guildenstern. Several episodes are close in narrative detail to Shakespeare's play: the original murder and incestuous marriage, the feigned madness, the woman used as a decoy, the eavesdropping counselor, and especially the trip to England. A translation of Saxo into French by François de Belleforest, in *Histoires Tragiques* (1576 edition), adds a few details, such as Gertrude's adultery before the murder and Hamlet's melancholy. Belleforest's version is longer than Saxo's, with more psychological and moral observation and more dialogue. Shakespeare probably consulted it.

Shakespeare need not have depended extensively on these older versions of his story, however. His main source was almost certainly an old play of *Hamlet*. Much evidence testifies to the existence of such a play. The *Diary* of Philip

Henslowe, a theater owner and manager, records a performance, not marked as "new," of a *Hamlet* at Newington Butts on June 11, 1594, by "my Lord Admiral's men" or "my Lord Chamberlain's men," probably the latter. Thomas Lodge's pamphlet *Wit's Misery and the World's Madness* (1596) refers to "the vizard of the ghost which cried so miserably at the theater, like an oyster wife, 'Hamlet, revenge!'" And Thomas Nashe, in his *Epistle* prefixed to Robert Greene's romance *Menaphon* (1589), offers the following observation:

> It is a common practice nowadays amongst a sort of shifting companions, that run through every art and thrive by none, to leave the trade of noverint, whereto they were born, and busy themselves with the endeavors of art, that could scarcely Latinize their neck verse if they should have need; yet English Seneca read by candlelight yields many good sentences, as "Blood is a beggar" and so forth; and if you entreat him fair in a frosty morning, he will afford you whole *Hamlets,* I should say handfuls, of tragical speeches. But O grief! *Tempus edax rerum,* what's that will last always? The sea exhaled by drops will in continuance be dry, and Seneca, let blood line by line and page by page, at length must needs die to our stage; which makes his famished followers to imitate the Kid in Aesop, who, enamored with the Fox's newfangles, forsook all hopes of life to leap into a new occupation; and these men, renouncing all possibilities of credit or estimation, to intermeddle with Italian translations . . .

Nashe's testimonial describes a *Hamlet* play, written in the Senecan style by some person born to the trade of "noverint," or scrivener, who has turned to hack writing and translation. The description has often been fitted to Thomas Kyd, though this identification is not certain. (Nashe could be punning on Kyd's name when he refers to "the Kid in Aesop.") Certainly Thomas Kyd's *The Spanish Tragedy* (c. 1587) shows many affinities with Shakespeare's play, and provides many Senecan ingredients missing from Saxo and Belleforest: the ghost, the difficulty in ascertaining whether the ghost's words are believable, the resulting need for delay and a feigning of madness, the moral perplexities afflicting a sensitive man called upon to revenge, the play within the play, the clever reversals and ironically caused deaths in the catastrophe, the rhetoric of tragical passion. Whether or not Kyd in fact wrote the *Ur-Hamlet*, his extant play enables us to see more clearly what that lost play must have contained. The pirated first quarto of *Hamlet* (1603) also offers a few seemingly authentic details that are not found in the authoritative second quarto but are found in the earlier sources and may have been a part of the *Ur-Hamlet*. For example, after Hamlet has killed Corambis (corresponding to Polonius), the Queen vows to assist Hamlet in his strategies against the King; and later, when Hamlet has returned to England, the Queen sends him a message by Horatio warning him to be careful.

One last document sheds light on the *Ur-Hamlet*. A German play, *Der bestrafte Brudermord* (*Fratricide Punished*), from a now-lost manuscript dated 1710, seems to have been based on a text used by English actors traveling in Germany in 1586 and afterward. Though changed by translation and manuscript transmission, and too entirely different from Shakespeare's play to have been based on it, this German version may well have been based on Shakespeare's source-play. Polonius's name in this text, Corambus, is the Corambis of the first quarto of 1603. (The name may mean "cabbage cooked twice," for *coramble-bis,* a proverbially dull dish.)

Der bestrafte Brudermord begins with a prologue in the Senecan manner, followed by the appearance of the ghost to Francisco, Horatio, and sentinels of the watch. Within the palace, meanwhile, the King carouses. Hamlet joins the watch, confiding to Horatio that he is "sick at heart" over his father's death and mother's hasty remarriage. The ghost appears to Hamlet, tells him how the juice of hebona was poured into his ear, and urges revenge. When Hamlet swears Horatio and Francisco to silence, the ghost (now invisible) says several times "We swear," his voice following the men as they move from place to place. Hamlet reveals to Horatio the entire circumstance of the murder. Later, in a formal session of the court, the new King speaks hypocritically of his brother's death and explains the reasons for his marriage to the Queen. Hamlet is forbidden to return to Wittenberg, though Corambus's son Leonhardus has already set out for France.

Some time afterward, Corambus reports the news of Hamlet's madness to the King and Queen, and presumes on the basis of his own youthful passions to diagnose Hamlet's malady as lovesickness. Concealed, he and the King overhear Hamlet tell Ophelia to "go to a nunnery." When players arrive from Germany, Hamlet instructs them in the natural style of acting, and then requests them to perform a play before the King about the murder of King Pyrrus by his brother. (Death is again inflicted by hebona poured in the ear.) After the King's guilty reaction to the play, Hamlet finds him alone at prayers but postpones the killing lest the King's soul be sent to heaven. Hamlet kills Corambus behind the tapestry in the Queen's chamber, and is visited again by the ghost (who says nothing, however). Ophelia, her mind deranged, thinks herself in love with a court butterfly named Phantasmo. (This creature is also involved in a comic action to help the clown Jens with a tax problem.)

The King sends Hamlet to England with two unnamed courtiers who are instructed to kill Hamlet after their arrival. A contrary wind takes them instead to an island near Dover, where Hamlet foils his two enemies by kneeling between them and asking them to shoot him on signal; at the proper moment, he ducks and they shoot each other. He finishes them off with their own swords, and discovers letters on their persons ordering Hamlet's execution by the English King if the original plot should fail. When Hamlet returns to Denmark, the King arranges a duel between him and Corambus's son Leonhardus. If Leonhardus's poisoned dagger misses its mark, a beaker of wine containing finely ground oriental diamond dust is to do the rest. Hamlet is informed of the impending duel by Phantasmo (compare Osric), whom Hamlet taunts condescendingly and calls "Signora Phantasmo." Shortly before the duel takes place, Ophelia is reported to have thrown herself off a hill to her death. The other deaths occur much as in Shakespeare's play. The dying Hamlet bids that the crown be conveyed to his cousin, Duke Fortempras of Norway, of whom we have not heard earlier.

From the extensive similarities between *Hamlet* and this German play, we can see that Shakespeare inherited his narrative material almost intact, though in a jumble and so pitifully mangled that the modern reader can only laugh at the contrast. No source study in Shakespeare reveals so clearly the extent of Shakespeare's wholesale borrowing of plot, and the incredible transformation he achieved in re-ordering his materials.

The following excerpt is from the English *The History of Hamlet,* 1608, an unacknowledged translation of Belleforest that in one or two places seems to have been influenced by Shakespeare's play—as when Hamlet beats his arms on the hangings of the Queen's apartment instead of jumping on the quilt or bed, as in Belleforest, and cries, "A rat! a rat!" It is otherwise a close translation and, although too late for Shakespeare to have used, provides an Elizabethan version of the account Shakespeare most likely used.

The History of Hamlet Prince of Denmark

Chapter 1

Any departures from the original text are noted with an asterisk and appear at the bottom of the page in boldface; original readings are in roman.

How Horvendil and Fengon were made Governors of the Province of Ditmarse, and how Horvendil married Geruth, the daughter to Roderick, chief King of Denmark, by whom he had Hamlet; and how after his marriage his brother Fengon slew him traitorously and married his brother's wife, and what followed.

You must understand, that long time before the kingdom of Denmark received the faith of Jesus Christ and embraced the doctrine of the Christians, that the common people in those days were barbarous and uncivil and their princes cruel, without faith or loyalty, seeking nothing but murder and deposing or at the least offending each other either in honors, goods, or lives, not caring to ransom such as they took prisoners but rather sacrificing them to the cruel vengeance naturally imprinted in their hearts; in such sort that if there were sometimes a good prince or king among them who, being adorned with the most perfect gifts of nature, would addict himself to virtue and use courtesy, although the people held him in admiration (as virtue is admirable to the most wicked) yet the envy of his neighbors was so great that they never ceased until that virtuous man were dispatched out of the world.

King Roderick, as then reigning in Denmark, after he had appeased the troubles in the country and driven the Swethlanders and Slaveans from thence, he divided the kingdom into divers provinces, placing governors therein, who after (as the like happened in France) bare the names of dukes, marquesses, and earls, giving the government of Jutie (at this present called Ditmarse), lying upon the country of the Cimbrians in the straight or narrow part of land that showeth like a point or cape of ground upon the sea which northward* bordereth upon the country of Norway, to two* valiant and warlike lords, Horvendil and Fengon,

***northward** neithward   ***to two** two

sons to Gervendil, who likewise had been governor of that province.

Now the greatest honor that men of noble birth could at that time win and obtain was in exercising the art of piracy upon the seas, assailing their neighbors and the countries bordering upon them; and how much the more they used to rob, pill,[1] and spoil other provinces and islands far adjacent, so much the more their honors and reputation increased and augmented. Wherein Horvendil obtained the highest place in his time, being the most renowned pirate that in those days scoured the seas and havens of the north parts; whose great fame so moved the heart of Collere, King of Norway, that he was much grieved to hear that Horvendil surmounted*[2] him in feats of arms, thereby obscuring the glory by him already obtained upon the seas—honor more than covetousness of riches in those days being the reason that provoked those barbarian princes to overthrow and vanquish one the other, not caring[3] to be slain by the hands of a victorious person.

This valiant and hardy king having challenged Horvendil to fight with him body to body, the combat was by him accepted, with conditions that he which should be vanquished should lose all the riches he had in his ship and that the vanquisher should cause the body of the vanquished (that should be slain in the combat) to be honorably buried, death being the prize and reward of him that should lose the battle. And to conclude, Collere, King of Norway, although a valiant, hardy, and courageous prince, was in the end vanquished and slain by Horvendil, who presently caused a tomb to be erected and therein, with all honorable obsequies fit for a prince, buried the body of King Collere, according to their ancient manner and superstitions in these days and the conditions of the combat, bereaving the King's ships of all their riches; and, having slain the King's sister, a very brave and valiant warrior, and overrun all the coast of Norway and the Northern Islands, returned home again laden with much treasure, sending the most part thereof to his sovereign, King Roderick, thereby to procure

***surmounted** surmounting

1 pill plunder **2 surmounted** excelled **3 not caring** i.e., not considering it dishonorable

his good liking and so to be accounted one of the greatest favorites about His Majesty.

The King, allured by those presents and esteeming himself happy to have so valiant a subject, sought by a great favor and courtesy to make him become bounden unto him perpetually, giving him Geruth his daughter to his wife, of whom he knew Horvendil to be already much enamored. And, the more to honor him, determined himself in person to conduct her into Jutie, where the marriage was celebrated according to the ancient manner. And, to be brief, of this marriage proceeded Hamlet, of whom I intend to speak, and for his cause have chosen to renew this present history.

Fengon, brother to this prince Horvendil, who, not only* fretting and despiting[4] in his heart at the great honor and reputation won by his brother in warlike affairs but solicited and provoked by a foolish jealousy to see him honored with royal alliance, and fearing thereby to be deposed from his part of the government—or rather desiring to be only governor, thereby to obscure the memory of the victories and conquests of his brother Horvendil—determined, whatsoever happened, to kill him; which he effected in such sort that no man once so much as suspected him, every man esteeming that from such and so firm a knot of alliance and consanguinity there could proceed no other issue than the full effects of virtue and courtesy. But, as I said before, the desire of bearing sovereign rule and authority respecteth neither blood nor amity, nor caring for virtue, as being wholly without respect of laws or majesty divine; for it is not possible that he which invadeth the country and taketh away the riches of another man without cause or reason should know or fear God. Was not this a crafty and subtle counselor? But he might have thought that the mother, knowing her husband's case, would not cast her son into the danger of death.

But Fengon, having secretly assembled certain men, and perceiving himself strong enough to execute his enterprise, Horvendil his brother being at a banquet with his friends,

***not only** onely

4 despiting entertaining a grudge

suddenly set upon him, where he slew him as traitorously as cunningly he purged himself of so detestable a murder to his subjects; for that before he had any violent or bloody hands, or once committed parricide upon his brother, he had incestuously abused his wife, whose honor he ought as well to have sought and procured as traitorously he pursued and effected his destruction. And it is most certain that the man that abandoneth himself to any notorious and wicked action whereby he becometh a great sinner, he careth not to commit much more heinous and abominable offenses; and covered his boldness and wicked practice with so great subtlety and policy, and under a veil of mere simplicity, that, being favored for the honest love that he bare to his sister-in-law—for whose sake, he affirmed, he had in that sort murdered his brother—that his sin found excuse among the common people and of the nobility was esteemed for justice. For that Geruth, being as courteous a princess as any then living in the north parts, and one that had never once so much as offended any of her subjects, either commons or courtiers, this adulterer and infamous murderer slandered his dead brother that he would have slain his wife,[5] and that he,[6] by chance finding him upon the point ready to do it, in defense of the lady had slain him, bearing off the blows which as then he[7] struck at the innocent princess without any other cause of malice whatsoever. Wherein he wanted[8] no false witnesses to approve[9] his act, which deposed[10] in like sort as the wicked calumniator himself protested, being the same persons that had borne him company and were participants of his treason. So that instead of pursuing him as a parricide and an incestuous person, all the courtiers admired and flattered him in his good fortune, making more account of false witnesses and detestable wicked reporters, and more honoring the calumniators, than they esteemed of those that, seeking to call the matter in question and admiring the virtues of the murdered prince, would have punished the massacrers and bereavers of his life.

5 slandered . . . wife i.e., made the slanderous accusation that Horvendil intended to slay his wife, Geruth **6 he** i.e., Fengon **7 he** i.e., Horvendil **8 he wanted** i.e., Fengon lacked **9 approve** confirm **10 which deposed** who testified

Which was the cause that Fengon, boldened and encouraged by such impunity, durst venture to couple himself in marriage with her whom he used as his concubine during good Horvendil's life, in that sort spotting his name with a double vice, and charging his conscience with abominable guilt and twofold impiety, as[11] incentuous adultery and parricide murder. And that[12] the unfortunate and wicked woman, that had received the honor to be the wife of one of the valiantest and wisest* princes in the north, embased[13] herself in such vile sort as to falsify her faith unto him and, which is worse, to marry him that had been the tyrannous murderer of her lawful husband; which made divers men think that she had been the causer of the murder, thereby to live in her adultery without control.

But where shall a man find a more wicked and bold woman than a great personage once having loosed the bonds of honor and honesty? This princess, who at the first for her rare virtues and courtesies was honored of all men and beloved of her husband, as soon as she once gave ear to the tyrant Fengon forgot both the rank she held among the greatest names and the duty of an honest wife on her behalf. But I will not stand to gaze and marvel at women, for that there are many which seek to blaze[14] and set them forth, in which their writings they spare not to blame them all for the faults of some one or few women. But I say that either nature ought to have bereaved[15] man of that opinion to accompany[16] with women, or else to endow them with such spirits as that they may easily support the crosses they endure without complaining so often and so strangely, seeing it is their own beastliness that overthrows them. For if it be so that a woman is so imperfect a creature as they make her to be, and that they know this beast to be so hard to be tamed as they affirm, why then are they so foolish to preserve them and so dull and brutish as to trust their deceitful and wanton embracings? But let us leave her in this extremity of lasciviousness, and proceed to show you in what sort the young Prince Hamlet behaved himself to escape the tyranny of his uncle.

***wisest** wiseth

11 as that is, to wit **12 And that** i.e., and was the cause that **13 embased** lowered, debased **14 blaze** proclaim **15 bereaved** deprived **16 accompany** keep company

CHAPTER 2

How Hamlet counterfeited the madman to escape the tyranny of his uncle, and how he was tempted by a woman through his uncle's procurement, who thereby thought to undermine the Prince and by that means to find out whether he counterfeited madness or not; and how Hamlet would by no means be brought to consent unto her, and what followed.

GERUTH having, as I said before, so much forgotten herself, the Prince Hamlet, perceiving himself to be in danger of his life, as being abandoned of his own mother and forsaken of all men, and assuring himself that Fengon would not detract[1] the time to send him the same way his father Horvendil was gone, to beguile[2] the tyrant in his subtleties (that esteemed him to be of such a mind that if he once attained to man's estate[3] he would not long delay the time to revenge the death of his father), counterfeited* the madman with such craft and subtle practices that he made show as if he had utterly lost his wits, and under that veil he covered his pretense and defended his life from the treasons and practices of the tyrant his uncle. And although[4] he had been at the school of[5] the Roman prince who, because he counterfeited himself to be a fool, was called Brutus,[6] yet he imitated his fashions and his wisdom. For, every day being in the Queen's palace (who as then was more careful to please her whoremaster than ready to revenge the cruel death of her husband or to restore her son to his inheritance), he rent and tore his clothes, wallowing and lying in the dirt and mire, his face all filthy and black, running through the streets like a man distraught, not speaking one word but such as seemed to proceed of madness and mere[7] frenzy, all his actions and gestures being no other than the right countenances[8] of a man wholly deprived of all reason and understanding, in such sort that as then he

***counterfeited** counterfeiting

1 detract lengthen **2 to beguile** in order to beguile **3 man's estate** manhood **4 although** inasmuch as **5 been at the school of** i.e., studied the method of **6 Brutus** (Lucius Junius Brutus assumed the disguise of idiocy in order to escape the fate of his brother, whom their uncle Tarquinius Superbus had put to death. *Brutus* means "stupid.") **7 mere** absolute **8 right countenances** true demeanor

seemed fit for nothing but to make sport[9] to the pages and ruffling[10] courtiers that attended in the court of his uncle and father-in-law.[11] But the young Prince noted them well enough, minding one day to be revenged in such manner that the memory thereof should remain perpetually to the world. . . .

Hamlet, in this sort counterfeiting the madman, many times did divers actions of great and deep consideration, and often made such and so fit answers that a wise man would soon have judged from what spirit so fine an invention might proceed; for that standing by the fire and sharpening sticks like poniards and pricks, one in smiling manner asked him wherefore he made those little staves so sharp at the points? "I prepare," saith he, "piercing darts and sharp arrows to revenge my father's death." Fools, as I said before, esteemed those his words as nothing; but men of quick spirits and such as had a deeper reach[12] began to suspect somewhat, esteeming that under that kind of folly there lay hidden a great and rare subtlety such as one day might be prejudicial to their prince, saying that under color of such rudeness he shadowed a crafty policy and by his devised simplicity he concealed a sharp and pregnant[13] spirit.

For which cause they counseled the King to try and know, if it were possible, how to discover the intent and meaning of the young Prince. And they could find no better nor more fit invention to entrap him than to set some fair and beautiful woman in a secret place that, with flattering speeches and all the craftiest means she could use, should purposely seek to allure his mind to have his pleasure of her. For the nature of all young men, especially such as are brought up wantonly, is so transported with the desires of the flesh, and entereth so greedily into the pleasures thereof, that it is almost impossible to cover the foul affection, neither yet to dissemble or hide the same by art or industry, much less to shun it. What cunning or subtlety soever they use to cloak their pretense, seeing occasion offered, and that in secret, especially in the most enticing sin that reigneth in man, they cannot choose,

9 make sport serve as the butt of joking **10 ruffling** swaggering **11 father-in-law** i.e., stepfather **12 reach** comprehension **13 pregnant** fertile, inventive

being constrained by voluptuousness, but fall to natural effect and working.

To this end certain courtiers were appointed to lead Hamlet into a solitary place within the woods, whither they brought the woman, inciting him to take their pleasures together and to embrace one another—but the subtle practices used in these our days,[14] not to try if men of great account be extract[15] out of their wits but rather to deprive them of strength, virtue, and wisdom by means of such devilish practitioners and infernal* spirits, their domestical servants and ministers of corruption. And surely the poor Prince at this assault had been[16] in great danger, if a gentleman (that in Horvendil's time had been nourished with him) had not shown himself more affectioned to the bringing-up he had received with Hamlet than desirous to please the tyrant who by all means sought to entangle the son in the same nets wherein the father had ended his days. This gentleman bare the courtiers (appointed as aforesaid of this treason) company, more desiring to give the Prince instruction what he should do than to entrap him, making full account that the least show of perfect sense and wisdom[17] that Hamlet should make would be sufficient to cause him to lose his life. And therefore by certain signs he gave Hamlet intelligence in what danger he was like[18] to fall, if by any means he seemed to obey or once like the wanton toys[19] and vicious provocations of the gentlewoman sent thither by his uncle. Which much abashed the Prince, as then wholly being in affection to the lady; but by her he was likewise informed of the treason, as being one that from her infancy loved and favored him and would have been exceeding sorrowful for his misfortune, and much more[20] to leave his company without enjoying the pleasure of his body, whom she loved more than herself. The Prince in this sort having both deceived the courtiers and the lady's expectation, that affirmed and swore that he never once offered to have his pleasure of the woman, although in subtlety[21] he affirmed the contrary, every man thereupon

***infernal** intefernal

14 but . . . days i.e., machinations used often enough in more recent times. **but** only **15 extract** extracted, removed **16 had been** would have been **17 the least . . . wisdom** (Hamlet's yielding to the lady's blandishments would be viewed as a proof of sanity and would thus betray him to his uncle.) **18 like** likely **19 toys** tricks **20 much more** much more sorrowful **21 in subtlety** in private

assured themselves that without all doubt he was distraught of his senses, that his brains were as then wholly void of force and incapable of reasonable apprehension, so that as then[22] Fengon's practice took no effect. But for all that he left not off, still seeking by all means to find out Hamlet's subtlety, as in the next chapter you shall perceive.

CHAPTER 3

How Fengon, uncle to Hamlet, a second time to entrap him in his politic madness, caused one of his counselors to be secretly hidden in the Queen's chamber, behind the arras, to hear what speeches passed between Hamlet and the Queen; and how Hamlet killed him and escaped that danger, and what followed.

AMONG the friends of Fengon there was one that above all the rest doubted of Hamlet's practices in counterfeiting the madman, who for that cause said that it was impossible that so crafty a gallant as Hamlet, that counterfeited the fool, should be discovered with so common and unskillful practices which might easily be perceived, and that to find out his politic pretense it were necessary to invent some subtle and crafty means more attractive whereby the gallant might not have the leisure to use his accustomed dissimulation. Which to effect he said he knew a fit way and a most convenient mean[1] to effect the King's desire and thereby to entrap Hamlet in his subtleties and cause him of his own accord to fall into the net prepared for him, and thereby evidently show his secret meaning.

His devise was thus: that King Fengon should make as though he were to go some long voyage concerning affairs of great importance, and that in the meantime Hamlet should be shut up alone in a chamber with his mother, wherein some other should secretly be hidden behind the hangings, unknown either to him or his mother, there to stand and hear their speeches and the complots[2] by them to be taken[3] con-

22 as then as of that time

1 mean means **2 complots** conspiracy **3 taken** undertaken

cerning the accomplishment of the dissembling fool's pretense; assuring the King that if there were any point of wisdom and perfect sense in the gallant's spirit, that without all doubt he would easily discover[4] it to his mother, as being devoid of all fear that she would utter or make known his secret intent, being the woman that had borne him in her body and nourished him so carefully; and withal[5] offered himself to be the man that should stand to hearken and bear witness of Hamlet's speeches with his mother, that he might not be esteemed a counselor in such a case wherein he refused to be the executioner for the behoof and service of his prince.

This invention pleased the King exceeding well, esteeming it as the only and sovereign remedy to heal the Prince of his lunacy, and to that end, making a long voyage, issued out of his palace and rode to hunt in the forest.

Meantime the counselor entered secretly into the Queen's chamber and there hid himself behind the arras not long before the Queen and Hamlet came thither, who, being crafty and politic, as soon as he was within the chamber, doubting[6] some treason and fearing if he should speak severely and wisely to his mother touching his secret practices he should be understood and by that means intercepted, used his ordinary manner of dissimulation and began to come like a cock,[7] beating with his arms (in such manner as cocks use to strike with their wings) upon the hangings of the chamber. Whereby, feeling something stirring under them, he cried, "A rat, a rat!" and presently drawing his sword thrust it into the hangings, which done, pulled the counselor (half dead) out by the heels, made an end of killing him, and, being slain, cut his body in pieces, which he caused to be boiled and then cast it into an open vault or privy that so it might serve for food to the hogs.

By which means having discovered the ambush and given the inventor thereof his just reward, he came again to his mother, who in the meantime wept and tormented herself to see all her hopes frustrate, for that what fault soever she had committed yet was she sore grieved to see her only child made a mere mockery—every man reproaching her with his

4 discover reveal **5 withal** in addition **6 doubting** suspecting, fearing
7 come like a cock crow like a rooster

folly, one point whereof she had as then seen before her eyes. Which was no small prick to her conscience, esteeming that the gods sent her that punishment for joining incestuously in marriage with the tyrannous murderer of her husband (who likewise ceased not to invent all the means he could to bring his nephew to his end), accusing her* own natural indiscretion, as being the ordinary guide of those that so much desire the pleasures of the body, who, shutting up the way to all reason, respect not what may ensue of their lightness and great inconstancy, and how a pleasure of small moment is sufficient to give them cause of repentance during their lives, and make them curse the day and time that ever any such apprehensions entered into their minds or that they closed their eyes to reject the honesty requisite in ladies of her quality. . . .

And while in this sort she sat tormenting herself, Hamlet entered into the chamber, who, having once again searched every corner of the same, distrusting his mother as well as the rest, and perceiving himself to be alone, began in sober and discreet manner to speak unto her, saying,

"What treason is this, O most infamous woman of all that ever prostrated themselves to the will of an abominable whoremonger, who, under the veil of a dissembling creature, covereth the most wicked and detestable crime that man could ever imagine or was committed! Now may I be assured to trust you that, like a vile wanton adulteress altogether impudent and given over to her pleasure, runs spreading forth her arms joyfully to embrace the traitorous villainous tyrant that murdered my father, and most incestuously receivest the villain into the lawful bed of your loyal spouse, imprudently entertaining him instead of the dear father of your miserable and discomforted son—if the gods grant him not the grace speedily to escape from a captivity so unworthy the degree he holdeth and the race and noble family of his ancestors. Is this the part of a queen and daughter to a king? To live like a brute beast and like a mare that yieldeth her body to the horse that hath beaten her companion away, to follow the pleasure of an abominable king that hath murdered a far more honester and better man than himself in massacring Horvendil, the honor and glory of the Danes? Who are now esteemed of no force nor valor at all since the shining splen-

***accusing her** accusing his

dor of knighthood was brought to an end by the most wickedest and cruelest villain living upon earth.

"I for my part will never account him for my kinsman nor once know him for mine uncle, nor you my dear mother, for not having respect to the blood that ought to have united us so straitly together, and who neither with your honor nor without suspicion of consent to the death of your husband could ever have agreed to have married with his cruel enemy. O, Queen Geruth! It is the part of a bitch to couple with many and desire acquaintance of divers mastiffs. It is licentiousness only that hath made you deface out of your mind the memory of the valor and virtues of the good king your husband and my father. It was an unbridled desire that guided the daughter of Roderick to embrace the tyrant Fengon, and not to remember Horvendil (unworthy of so strange entertainment),[8] neither that he[9] killed his brother traitorously, and that she being his[10] father's wife betrayed him, although he[11] so well favored and loved her that for her sake he utterly bereaved Norway of her riches and valiant soldiers to augment the treasures of Roderick and make Geruth wife to the hardiest[12] prince in Europe. It is not the part of a woman, much less of a princess, in whom all modesty, courtesy, compassion, and love ought to abound, thus to leave her dear child to fortune in the bloody and murderous hands of a villain and traitor. Brute beasts do not so, for lions tigers, ounces,[13] and leopards fight for the safety and defense of their whelps; and birds that have beaks, claws, and wings resist such as would ravish them of their young ones. But you, to the contrary, expose and deliver me to death, whereas ye should defend me. Is not this as much as if you should betray me, when you, knowing the perverseness of the tyrant and his intents (full of deadly counsel as touching the race and image of his brother), have not once sought nor desired to find the means to save your child and only son by sending him into Swethland,[14] Norway, or England, rather than to leave him as a prey to your infamous adulterer?

"Be not offended, I pray you, madam, if, transported with

8 entertainment treatment **9 neither that he** i.e., nor to remember that he, Fengon **10 his** i.e., Hamlet's **11 although he** i.e., although Horvendil **12 hardiest** bravest **13 ounces** lynxes, wildcats **14 Swethland** Sweden

dolor and grief, I speak so boldly unto you, and that I respect you less than duty requireth; for you, having forgotten me and wholly rejected the memory of the deceased king my father, must not be abashed if I also surpass the bounds and limits of due consideration. Behold into what distress I am now fallen, and to what mischief my fortune and your over-great lightness[15] and want of wisdom have induced me, that I am constrained to play the madman to save my life instead of using and practicing arms, following adventures, and seeking all means to make myself known to be the true and undoubted heir of the valiant and virtuous King Horvendil! It was not without cause and just occasion that my gestures, countenances, and words seem all to proceed from a madman, and that I desire to have all men esteem me wholly deprived of sense and reasonable understanding, because I am well assured that he that hath made no conscience to kill his own brother (accustomed to murders and allured with desire of government without control in his treasons) will not spare to save himself with the like cruelty in the blood and flesh of the loins of his brother by him massacred. . . .

"To conclude, weep not, madam, to see my folly, but rather sigh and lament your own offense, tormenting your conscience in regard of the infamy that hath so defiled the ancient renown and glory that in times past honored Queen Geruth; for we are not to sorrow and grieve at other men's vices but for our own misdeeds and great follies. Desiring you for the surplus[16] of my proceedings, above all things, as you love your own life and welfare, that neither the King nor any other may by any means know mine intent; and let me alone with the rest, for I hope in the end to bring my purpose to effect."

[The Queen contritely asks Hamlet's understanding for a marriage that (she insists) she entered into under duress, implores his forgiveness, and declares that her fondest hope is to see her son restored to his rights as heir and monarch of Denmark. Hamlet pledges his faith to her, beseeching her to put aside her attachment to Fengon, whom Hamlet "will surely kill, or cause to be put to death, in despite of all the devils in hell," along with the flatterers who serve him. In

15 lightness wantonness **16 surplus** what remains still to be done

doing so he will act as the true King of Denmark, he avers, killing a traitor, not a legitimate ruler, and crowning virtue with glory while punishing regicide with ignominious death.]

After this, Fengon, as if he had been out some long journey, came to the court again and asked for him that had received the charge to play the intelligencer to entrap Hamlet in his dissembled wisdom, was abashed to hear neither news nor tidings of him, and for that cause asked Hamlet what was become of him, naming the man. The Prince, that never used lying, and who in all the answers that ever he made during his counterfeit madness never strayed from the truth (as a generous[17] mind is a mortal enemy to untruth), answered and said that the counselor he sought for was gone down through the privy where, being choked by the filthiness of the place, the hogs meeting him had filled their bellies.

Chapter 4

How Fengon, the third time, devised to send Hamlet to the King of England with secret letters to have him put to death; and how Hamlet, when his companions slept, read the letters, and instead of them counterfeited others, willing the King of England to put the two messengers to death and to marry his daughter to Hamlet, which was effected; and how Hamlet escaped out of England.

A man would have judged anything rather than that Hamlet had committed that murder; nevertheless Fengon could not content himself, but still his mind gave him[1] that the fool would play him some trick of legerdemain, and willingly would have killed him; but he feared King Roderick, his grandfather, and further durst not offend the Queen, mother to the fool, whom she loved and much cherished, showing great grief and heaviness to see him so transported out of his wits. And in that conceit,[2] seeking to be rid of him, he

17 generous highborn, noble

1 gave him misgave him, made him apprehensive **2 conceit** frame of mind

determined* to find the means to do it by the aid of a stranger, making the King of England minister of his massacring resolution, choosing rather that his friend should defile his renown with so great a wickedness than himself to fall into perpetual infamy by an exploit of so great cruelty, to whom he purposed to send him and by letters desire him to put him to death.

Hamlet, understanding that he should be sent into England, presently doubted[3] the occasion of his voyage, and for that cause, speaking to the Queen, desired her not to make any show of sorrow or grief for his departure, but rather counterfeit a gladness as being rid of his presence whom, although she loved, yet she daily grieved to see him in so pitiful estate, deprived of all sense and reason; desiring her further that she should hang the hall with tapestry and make it fast with nails upon the walls and keep the brands[4] for him which he had sharpened at the points, then whenas[5] he said he made arrows to revenge the death of his father. Lastly he counseled her that, the year after his departure being accomplished, she should celebrate his funerals, assuring her that at the same instant she should see him return with great contentment and pleasure unto her from that his voyage.

Now, to bear him company were assigned two of Fengon's faithful ministers, bearing letters engraved in wood that contained Hamlet's death, in such sort as he had advertised[6] the King of England. But the subtle Danish Prince, being at sea, whilst his companions slept, having read the letters and known his uncle's great treason, with the wicked and villainous minds of the two courtiers that led him to the slaughter, rased[7] out the letters that concerned his death and instead thereof graved others with commission to the King of England to hang his two companions; and not content to turn the death they had devised against him upon their own necks, wrote further that King Fengon willed him to give his daughter to Hamlet in marriage.

And so arriving in England, the messengers presented

***he determined** determined

3 presently doubted at once suspected **4 brands** i.e., the staves or sticks that Hamlet sharpened as though in his madness; see Chapter 2. (*A brand* is usually a piece of wood that has been burning on the hearth or is to be used as a torch.) **5 then whenas** on that occasion when **6 advertised** given notice to, commanded **7 rased** erased, or possibly *razed,* scraped

themselves to the King, giving him Fengon's letters, who, having read the contents, said nothing as then, but stayed[8] convenient time to effect Fengon's desire, meantime using the Danes familiarly, doing them that honor to sit at his table (for that kings as then were not so curiously nor solemnly[9] served as in these our days, for in these days mean[10] kings and lords of small revenue are as difficult and hard to be seen as in times past the monarchs of Persia used to be, or as it is reported of the great King of Ethiopia, who will not permit any man to see his face, which ordinarily he covereth with a veil). And as the messengers sat at the table with the King, subtle Hamlet was so far from being merry with them that he would not taste one bit of meat, bread, nor cup of beer whatsoever as then set upon the table, not without great wondering of the company, abashed to see a young man and a stranger not to esteem of the delicate meats and pleasant drinks served at the banquet, rejecting them as things filthy, evil of taste, and worse prepared. The King, who for that time dissembled what he thought, caused his guests to be conveyed into their chamber, willing one of his secret servants to hide himself therein and so to certify him what speeches passed among the Danes at their going to bed.

Now they were no sooner entered into the chamber, and those that were appointed to attend upon them gone out, but Hamlet's companions asked him why he refused to eat and drink of that which he found upon the table, not honoring the banquet of so great a king, that entertained them in friendly sort, with such honor and courtesy as it deserved? Saying further that he did not well but dishonored him that sent him, as if he sent men into England that feared to be poisoned by so great a king. The Prince, that had done nothing without reason and prudent consideration, answered them and said: "What, think you that I will eat bread dipped in human blood, and defile my throat with the rust of iron, and use that meat that stinketh and savoreth of man's flesh already putrified and corrupted, and that scenteth like the savor of a dead carrion long since cast into a vault? And how would you have me to respect the King that hath the countenance of a slave, and the Queen, who instead of great maj-

8 stayed awaited **9 curiously nor solemnly** fastidiously or ceremoniously
10 mean insignificant

esty, hath done three things more like a woman of base parentage and fitter for a waiting-gentlewoman than beseeming a lady of her quality and estate?" And, having said so, used many injurious and sharp speeches as well against the King and Queen as others that had assisted at that banquet for the entertainment of the Danish ambassadors. And therein Hamlet said truth, as hereafter you shall hear, for that in those days, the north parts of the world, living as then under Satan's laws, were full of enchanters, so that there was not any young gentleman whatsoever that knew not something therein sufficient to serve his turn if need required, as yet in those days in Gotland[11] and Biarmy[12] there are many that knew not what the Christian religion permitteth, as by reading the histories of Norway and Gotland you may easily perceive. And so Hamlet, while his father lived, had been instructed in that devilish art whereby the wicked spirit abuseth mankind and advertiseth him (as he can) of things past.

[Hamlet, aided by the devilish power of magic he has learned, amazes the King of England by demonstrating the truth of the riddling and prophetic statements he has just uttered. It turns out that the King's bread is in fact defiled by human blood shed on the battlefield where the grain was grown, that his pork comes from hogs that have fed on a hanged thief, that his beer is brewed from a water supply polluted by rusty armor, and that, more distressingly, the King is the illegitimate son of a slave and the Queen of no less base parentage. The King thereupon treats Hamlet with the respect that such awesome magical powers deserve.]

The King, admiring the young Prince and beholding in him some matter of greater respect than in the common sort of men, gave him his daughter in marriage, according to the counterfeit letters by him devised, and the next day caused the two servants of Fengon to be executed, to satisfy, as he thought, the King's desire. But Hamlet, although the sport[13]

11 Gotland an area in what is now southern Sweden **12 Biarmy** a region in northern Lapland **13 the sport** i.e., the execution of his two companions. (Hamlet pretends to be offended at this so that the King will pacify him with a large gift, as he does.)

pleased him well, and that the King of England could not have done him a greater favor, made as though he had been much offended, threatening the King to be revenged; but the King, to appease him, gave him a great sum of gold, which Hamlet caused to be molten and put into two staves, made hollow for the same purpose, to serve his turn therewith as need should require. For of all the King's treasures he took nothing with him into Denmark but only those two staves, and as soon as the year began to be at an end, having somewhat before obtained license of the King his father-in-law to depart, went for Denmark, then with all the speed he could to return again into England to marry his daughter; and so set sail for Denmark.

CHAPTER 5

How Hamlet, having escaped out of England, arrived in Denmark the same day that the Danes were celebrating his funerals, supposing him to be dead in England; and how he revenged his father's death upon his uncle and the rest of the courtiers; and what followed.

HAMLET in that sort sailing into Denmark, being arrived in the country entered into the palace of his uncle the same day that they were celebrating his funerals, and, going into the hall, procured no small astonishment and wonder to them all—no man thinking other but that he had been dead. Among the which many of them rejoiced not a little for the pleasure which they knew Fengon would conceive for so pleasant a loss,[1] and some were sad, as remembering the honorable King Horvendil, whose victories they could by no means forget, much less deface out of their memories that which appertained unto him, who[2] as then greatly rejoiced to see a false report spread[3] of Hamlet's death and that the tyrant had not as yet obtained his will of the heir of Jutie,[4] but rather hoped God would restore him to his senses again for

1 rejoiced . . . loss i.e., rejoiced greatly to think how Fengon had desired the loss of Hamlet and how he would now be frustrated **2 who** i.e., the courtiers who admire Hamlet **3 rejoiced . . . spread** i.e., rejoiced to learn that the rumor was false **4 Jutie** Jutland, Denmark

the good and welfare of that province. Their amazement at the last[5] being turned into laughter, all that as then were assistant at the funeral banquet of him whom they esteemed dead mocked each at other for having been so simply deceived, and, wondering at the Prince, that in his so long a voyage he had not recovered any of his senses, asked what was become of them that had borne him company into Great Britain? To whom he made answer (showing them the two hollow staves wherein he had put his molten gold that the King of England had given him to appease his fury concerning the murder of his two companions) and said, "Here they are both." Whereat many that already knew his humors presently conjectured that he had played some trick of legerdemain, and to deliver himself out of danger had thrown them into the pit prepared for him; so that, fearing to follow after them and light upon some evil adventure, they went presently out of the court. And it was well for them that they did so, considering the tragedy acted by him the same day, being accounted his funeral but in truth their last days that as then rejoiced for his* overthrow.[6]

For when every man busied himself to make good cheer, and Hamlet's arrival provoked them more to drink and carouse, the Prince himself at that time played the butler and a gentleman attending on the tables, not suffering the pots nor goblets to be empty, whereby he gave the noblemen such store of liquor that all of them, being full laden with wine and gorged with meat, were constrained to lay themselves down in the same place where they had supped, so much their senses were dulled and overcome with the fire of overgreat drinking (a vice common and familiar among the Almains[7] and other nations inhabiting the north parts of the world). Which when Hamlet perceiving, and finding so good opportunity to effect his purpose and be revenged of his enemies, and, by the means to abandon the actions, gestures, and apparel of a madman, occasion so fitly finding his turn and as it were effecting itself, failed not to take hold thereof;[8] and, seeing those drunken bodies filled with wine, lying like

***his** their

5 at the last finally **6 but in truth . . . overthrow** i.e., a day that was supposed to have been for Hamlet's funeral but that in truth became the day of doom for those who had rejoiced in his overthrow
7 Almains Germans **8 take hold thereof** seize the opportunity

hogs upon the ground, some sleeping, others vomiting the over-great abundance of wine which without measure they had swallowed up, made the hangings about the hall to fall down and cover them all over, which he nailed to the ground, being boarded, and at the ends thereof he stuck the brands whereof I spake before, by him sharpened, which served for pricks,[9] binding and tying the hangings in such sort that, what force soever they used to loose themselves, it was unpossible to get from under them. And presently he set fire to the four corners of the hall in such sort that all that were as then therein not one escaped away, but were forced to purge their sins by fire and dry up the great abundance of liquor by them received into their bodies, all of them dying in the inevitable[10] and merciless flames of the hot and burning fire.

Which the Prince, perceiving, became wise; and knowing that his uncle, before the end of the banquet, had withdrawn himself into his chamber, which stood apart from the place where the fire burnt, went thither and, entering into the chamber, laid hand upon the sword of his father's murderer, leaving his own in the place (which, while he was at the banquet, some of the courtiers had nailed fast into the scabbard); and going to Fengon said: "I wonder, disloyal king, how thou canst sleep here at thine ease, and all thy palace is burnt, the fire thereof having burnt the greatest part of thy courtiers and ministers of thy cruelty and detestable tyrannies. And, which is more, I cannot imagine how thou shouldst well assure thyself and thy estate[11] as now to take thy ease, seeing Hamlet so near thee armed with the shafts by him prepared long since, and at this present is ready to revenge the traitorous injury by thee done to his lord and father."

Fengon, as then knowing the truth of his nephew's subtle practice, and hearing him speak with staid[12] mind, and, which is more, perceived a sword naked in his hand which he already lifted up to deprive him of his life, leaped quickly out of the bed, taking hold of Hamlet's sword that was nailed into the scabbard, which, as he sought to pull out, Hamlet gave him such a blow upon the chine[13] of the neck that he cut his head clean from his shoulders, and, as he fell to the

9 pricks skewers **10 inevitable** irresistible **11 assure . . . estate** feel confident about your situation **12 staid** steady **13 chine** back

ground, said, "This just and violent death is a just reward for such as thou art. Now go thy ways, and when thou comest in hell, see thou forget not to tell thy brother whom thou traitorously slewest that it was his son that sent thee thither with the message, to the end that, being comforted thereby, his soul may rest among the blessed spirits and quit[14] me of the obligation that bound me to pursue his vengeance upon mine own blood, that seeing it was by thee that I lost the chief thing that tied me to this alliance and consanguinity."

A man, to say the truth, hardy, courageous, and worthy of eternal commendation, who, arming himself with a crafty, dissembling, and strange show of being distract out of his wits, under that pretense deceived the wise, politic, and crafty, thereby not only preserving his life from the treasons and wicked practices of the tyrant, but, which is more, by a new and unexpected kind of punishment revenged his father's death many years after the act committed, in such* sort that, directing his courses with such prudence and effecting his purposes with so great boldness, and constancy, he left a judgment to be decided among men of wisdom, which[15] was more commendable in him, his constancy, or magnanimity, or his wisdom in ordering his affairs according to the premeditable determination he had conceived. . . .

Hamlet, having in this manner revenged himself, durst not presently declare his action to the people, but to the contrary determined to work by policy, so to give them intelligence what he had done and the reason that drew him thereunto; so that, being accompanied with such of his father's friends that then were rising,[16] he stayed to see what the people would do when they should hear of that sudden and fearful action. The next morning, the towns bordering thereabouts, desiring to know from whence the flames of fire proceeded the night before they had seen, came thither, and, perceiving the King's palace burnt to ashes and many bodies (most part consumed) lying among the ruins of the house, all of them were much abashed, nothing being left of the palace but the foundation. But they were much more amazed to behold the body of the King all bloody, and his head cut off lying hard by him; whereat some began to threaten revenge, yet not

***in such** in no such

14 quit acquit, free **15 which** as to which **16 rising** arising

knowing against whom; others, beholding so lamentable a spectacle, armed themselves; the rest rejoicing, yet not daring to make any show thereof, some detesting the cruelty, others lamenting the death of their prince, but the greatest part, calling Horvendil's murder to remembrance, acknowledging a just judgment from above that had thrown down the pride of the tyrant. And in this sort, the diversities of opinions among that multitude of people being many, yet every man ignorant what would be the issue of that tragedy, none stirred from thence, neither yet attempted to move[17] any tumult, every man fearing his own skin and distrusting his neighbor, esteeming each other to be consenting to the massacre.

[In the last three chapters of the story, Hamlet makes an oration to the Danes in defense of his conduct, wins the loyalty of one and all, and makes good his promise to return to England. There, threatened with a secret plot on the part of the King of England to avenge the death of Fengon, Hamlet slays the English king and returns to Denmark with two wives. He is betrayed by his second wife, Hermetrude, Queen of Scots, in league with his uncle Wiglerus, and is slain.]

Text based on *The History of Hamlet* [spelled *Hamblet* in the original]. *London: Imprinted by Richard Bradocke for Thomas Pavier, and are to be sold at his shop in Cornhill near to the Royal Exchange. 1608.*

17 move set in motion, instigate

Further Reading

Alexander, Nigel. *Poison, Play, and Duel: A Study in "Hamlet."* London: Routledge and Kegan Paul, 1971. Alexander argues that the play's representation of complex moral and psychological problems depends upon three dominant symbols—poison, play, and duel—that structure the play's action and language. Through these powerful images, which come together in the play's final scene, Shakespeare conveys a sense of the inescapable difficulties of moral choice and action.

Bevington, David. " 'Maimed Rites': Violated Ceremony in *Hamlet*." *Action Is Eloquence: Shakespeare's Language of Gesture*. Cambridge and London: Harvard Univ. Press, 1984. Bevington traces how Shakespeare shapes our responses to the play through visual means. *Hamlet,* he argues, is a play of "maimed rites," perversions of ceremony that reflect the moral and social disruptions in Denmark. In the final scene, the solemnity with which Hamlet is borne offstage serves to rehabilitate ceremony, restoring "some hope of perceivable meaning in the ceremonial meanings that hold together the social and moral order."

Bohannan, Laura. "Shakespeare in the Bush." *Natural History* 75 (1966): 28–33. Rpt. in *Every Man His Way: Readings in Cultural Anthropology,* ed. Alan Dundes. Englewood Cliffs, N.J.: Prentice-Hall, 1968. Bohannan, a cultural anthropologist, narrates the response of the elders of the Tiv tribe of West Africa to her retelling of the story of *Hamlet*. Her lively essay is a lesson in cultural relativity: familiar critical issues like the ghost, the incestuous marriage, Ophelia's madness, and Hamlet's revenge are freshly viewed from the perspective of a culture with non-Western ethical values and practices.

Booth, Stephen. "On the Value of *Hamlet*." In *Reinterpretations of Elizabethan Drama,* ed. Norman Rabkin. New York: Columbia Univ. Press, 1969. Booth focuses on the audience's experience of the play. His patient analysis of the opening scene sets forth the process whereby Hamlet's frustrated desire for certainty and coherence becomes the audience's own. The result for Booth is that "*Hamlet* is a tragedy of an audience that cannot make up its mind."

Bowers, Fredson. "Hamlet as Minister and Scourge." *PMLA* 70 (1955): 740–749. When Hamlet calls himself a "scourge and minister," Bowers argues, he signals his awareness of a conflict between his roles as private avenger and agent of providential design. By locating *Hamlet* within the moral and dramatic traditions of Elizabethan revenge tragedy, Bowers discovers the cause of the hero's delay in Hamlet's desire for Heaven to define and facilitate his complex responsibility.

Bradlay, A. C. *"Hamlet." Shakespearean Tragedy,* 1904. Rpt., New York: St. Martin's, 1985. Bradley explores the sources of Hamlet's delay, locating it not in a temperament characteristically resistant to action but in a "violent shock to his moral being" that produces an enervating melancholy. The Ghost's revelation and demand for revenge is "the last rivet in the melancholy which holds him bound," and the play presents "his vain efforts to fulfill this duty, his unconscious self-excuses and unavailing self-reproaches, and the tragic results of his delay."

Calderwood, James L. *To Be and Not to Be: Negation and Metadrama in "Hamlet."* New York: Columbia Univ. Press, 1983. Calderwood's metadramatic reading provocatively examines the tensions between illusion and reality, absence and presence, negation and assertion, inscribed into a play that relentlessly proliferates uncertainties and contradictions, but that, as Calderwood's title suggests, ultimately accepts and contains them.

Charney, Maurice. *Style in "Hamlet."* Princeton, N.J.: Princeton Univ. Press, 1969. Charney provides an extensive analysis of verbal and visual style in the play. He moves from an analysis of *Hamlet*'s dominant patterns of imagery to an examination of the play in performance, concluding with an extended rhetorical analysis of the characters of Polonius, Claudius, and Hamlet.

Coleridge, Samuel Taylor. *"Hamlet." Coleridge's Writings on Shakespeare,* ed. Terence Hawkes. New York: G. P. Putnam's Sons, 1959. Coleridge, along with other early nineteenth-century intellectuals, was strongly drawn to Hamlet ("I have a smack of Hamlet myself") and saw him as an agonizing intellectual, endlessly reasoning and hesitating, detached from the world of events. In Coleridge's influential psychological reading, Hamlet is a man both "amiable and excellent" who is defeated by his "aversion to action, which prevails among such as have a world in themselves."

Eliot, T. S. "Hamlet and His Problems." *Selected Essays, 1917–1932.* New York: Harcourt, Brace and Co., 1932. The "problems" Eliot identifies in his influential essay are not in Hamlet's character but in the play itself. Eliot believes that *Hamlet* is Shakespeare's revision of a lost revenge play onto which Shakespeare's main theme—the effect of a mother's guilt upon her son—is unsuccessfully grafted. Hamlet's emotions are "in excess of the facts as they appear," Eliot finds; Hamlet can neither understand nor objectify them, since Shakespeare himself is unable to find any "objective correlative" in his play for Hamlet's complex psychological state.

Ewbank, Inga-Stina. "*Hamlet* and the Power of Words." *Shakespeare Survey* 30 (1977): 85–102. Rpt. in *Aspects of "Hamlet": Articles Reprinted from "Shakespeare Survey,"* ed. Kenneth Muir and Stanley Wells. Cambridge: Cambridge Univ. Press, 1979. Examining how language functions as a major thematic concern in *Hamlet,* Ewbank explores the possibilities and limitations of verbal communication in the play. Speaking is the play's dominant mode of action, as characters stretch and shape words to the mysterious realities that they confront. For Ewbank, the play's greatness rests on its ability to express so much, even if what is finally expressed is the presence of something inexpressible at its heart.

Forker, Charles. "Shakespeare's Theatrical Symbolism and Its Function in *Hamlet.*" *Shakespeare Quarterly* 14 (1963): 215–229. Rpt. in *Essays in Shakespearean Criticism,* ed. James L. Calderwood and Harold E. Toliver. Englewood Cliffs, N.J.: Prentice-Hall, 1970. Forker examines Shakespeare's complex handling of the theatrical symbolism that pervades the play. Throughout, characters alternating between the roles of spectator and actor play to each other; Hamlet emerges as the consummate performer, whose role-playing embodies all the ambiguities and paradoxes of what it means to act.

Frye, Roland Mushat. *The Renaissance "Hamlet."* Princeton, N.J.: Princeton Univ. Press, 1984. Drawing upon a rich array of historical, literary, and pictorial evidence, Frye seeks to reconstruct the challenges and excitement that *Hamlet* offered to Shakespeare's Elizabethan audience. The rich specificity of the background that Frye reconstructs acknowledges "the complex and sophisticated concerns of Elizabethan minds" and the complexity of the play itself.

Goldman, Michael. " 'To Be or Not to Be' and the Spectrum of Action." *Acting and Action in Shakespearean Tragedy*. Princeton, N.J.: Princeton Univ. Press, 1985. Goldman argues that the challenges the role of Hamlet poses to an actor are analogous to the challenges the play poses to an audience. Each must engage in an act of interpretation that will discover unity and coherence in the multiple and often contradictory evidence of language and action.

Granville-Barker, Harley. *Preface to "Hamlet."* Princeton, N.J.: Princeton Univ. Press, 1946. This book-length "Preface" draws upon Granville-Barker's insights as a theatrical director and literary critic in its focus on the structure and tone of *Hamlet*. The first half of the study contains a detailed analysis of the three distinct movements (rather than the imposed five-act structure) that govern the play's action. Granville-Barker concludes with a discussion of the characters in this "tragedy of thwarted thought and tortured spirit."

Jones, Ernest. *Hamlet and Oepidus*. New York: Norton, 1949; published in 1910 in an earlier essay form. Jones, a student of Freud, considers the personality of Hamlet from a psychoanalytic perspective and diagnoses his delay as symptomatic of an Oepidal complex. Hamlet is incapable of revenge because of his unconscious identification with Claudius, who has enacted Hamlet's unconscious wish to kill his father and marry his mother. Jones extends his provocative argument with the suggestion that the play's Oedipal aspects have their origin in

Shakespeare's own psychology in 1601, the year the play was written and in which Shakespeare's father died.

Levin, Harry. *The Question of "Hamlet."* New York: Oxford Univ. Press, 1959. Levin's rhetorical analysis of the play's tone and action focuses on three dominant figures of speech (which are simultaneously modes of thought): interrogation, doubt, and irony. These, Levin finds, are organized dialectically, with the play's and Hamlet's own pervasive irony serving as a synthesis that permits us to face—though never to solve—the contradictions that the play's questions and unexpected answers expose.

Lewis, C. S. "Hamlet: The Prince or the Poem?" *Proceedings of the British Academy* 28 (1943 for 1942): 11–18. Rpt. in *They Asked for a Paper*. London: Bles, 1962; and in part as "Death in *Hamlet*" in *Shakespeare, the Tragedies: A Collection of Critical Essays,* ed. Alfred Harbage. Englewood Cliffs, N.J.: Prentice-Hall, 1964. Lewis takes issue with the focus on Hamlet's character that has dominated critical discussion of the play since the nineteenth century. He argues that the true subject of the play is death. The fear of being dead, born of a failure to understand human nature or the nature of the universe, is, for Lewis, the source of the play's powerful presentation of doubt and dread.

Mack, Maynard. "The World of *Hamlet.*" *Yale Review* 41 (1952): 502–523. Rpt. in *Shakespeare, the Tragedies: A Collection of Critical Essays,* ed. Alfred Harbage. Englewood Cliffs, N.J.: Prentice-Hall, 1964. Mack's sensitive account of the play's verbal texture establishes the "imaginative environment" of *Hamlet* that is dominated both by a deep and disabling inscrutability and by an overriding sense of morality. In the final act, Mack argues, Hamlet comes to understand what it means to live in such a world and to accept the mysterious condition of being human.

Nietzsche, Friedrich. "The Birth of Tragedy or: Hellenism and Pessimism" (1872). In *The Birth of Tragedy and the Case of Wagner,* trans. Walter Kaufmann. New York: Vintage, 1967. Nietzsche rejects the common nineteenth-century notion that Hamlet fails to act because he is paralyzed by excessive thought in favor of a view of Hamlet's "nausea" induced by looking "truly into the nature of things." What inhibits Hamlet is his tragic knowledge of the futility and folly of action in a world that is out of joint. "Knowledge kills action," Nietzsche asserts; "action requires the veil of illusion."

Prosser, Eleanor. *Hamlet and Revenge*. Stanford, Calif.: Stanford Univ. Press, 1967. Surveying Renaissance ethical codes and dramatic conventions, Prosser examines *Hamlet* in light of the Elizabethan understanding of revenge and ghosts. She contends that once we accept that the moral universe of the play (as well as of the audience) is Christian, we must see the Ghost as "demonic" and Hamlet's commitment to revenge as immoral and appalling.

Photo © George Joseph

From the 1973 New York Shakespeare Festival production of *As You Like It*, with Raul Julia as Orlando and Kathleen Widdoes as Rosalind, directed by Joseph Papp at the Delacorte Theater in Central Park.

AS YOU LIKE IT

AS YOU LIKE IT

Introductory Material

Foreword by Joseph Papp

Introduction

As You Like It in Performance

THE PLAY

Supplementary Material

Date and Text

Textual Notes

Shakespeare's Sources

Further Reading

Foreword

As You Like It is one of Shakespeare's best-written comedies, as full of lively speeches as the Forest of Arden is of living creatures. The one I enjoy most is not Jaques's famous speech beginning, "All the world's a stage, / And all the men and women merely players." Although this is well-deserving of its fame, I often respond to speeches that are less obviously philosophical and more actively theatrical, such as the speech Touchstone, the courtier-fool, has at the end of the play.

In this speech Touchstone delineates the several stages of a quarrel with a courtier, as follows: "the Retort Courteous," "the Quip Modest," "the Reply Churlish," "the Reproof Valiant," "the Countercheck Quarrelsome," "the Lie with Circumstance" and "the Lie Direct." Here we have a living example of the kind of brave, macho, chivalric exterior Elizabethans donned with words, doing their utmost to avoid any physical encounter that might provoke the drawing of swords. When an actor delivers this speech quickly and nimbly, it's a marvelously witty moment.

Another part of *As You Like It* that is as I like it is the deception Rosalind plays on Orlando, pretending to be a boy and telling him that she's going to teach him about love. At one point in their conversation he asks her how she can tell somebody's in love. Teasingly, she insists that Orlando couldn't possibly be in love because he doesn't have the marks of the lover: "A lean cheek, which you have not; a blue eye and sunken, which you have not; an unquestionable spirit, which you have not . . ." And on she goes, inventing an imaginary uncle who taught her all about love.

When Rosalind and Orlando first run across each other in the forest, she gives a wonderful discourse on Time, and how slowly it moves for someone in love waiting for his beloved. Within the play, this is Rosalind's way of playing the knave with Orlando. But it also has meaning for anyone who has ever been young and in love, watching the clock drag while waiting for that special person and then feeling the time fly by once you are together. Like so much else in Shakespeare, these lines that work so well within the play can also be applied to our own lives.

JOSEPH PAPP GRATEFULLY ACKNOWLEDGES THE HELP OF
ELIZABETH KIRKLAND IN PREPARING THIS FOREWORD.

Introduction

As You Like It represents, together with *Much Ado about Nothing* and *Twelfth Night,* the summation of Shakespeare's achievement in festive, happy comedy during the years 1598–1601. *As You Like It* contains several motifs found in other Shakespearean comedies: the journey from a jaded court into a transforming silvan environment and back to a revitalized court (as in *A Midsummer Night's Dream*); hence, a contrasting of two worlds in the play, one presided over by a virtuous but exiled older brother and the other by a usurping younger brother (as in *The Tempest*); the heroine disguised as a man (as in *The Merchant of Venice, The Two Gentlemen of Verona, Cymbeline,* and *Twelfth Night*); and a structure of multiple plotting in which numerous groups of characters are thematically played off against one another (as in several of Shakespeare's comedies). What chiefly distinguishes this play from the others, however, is the nature and function of its pastoral setting—the Forest of Arden.

The Forest of Arden is seen in many perspectives. As a natural wilderness, it is probably most like the real forest Shakespeare knew near Stratford-upon-Avon in Warwickshire—a place capable of producing the vulgarity of an Audrey or the gentle simplicity of a Corin. It also owes something to the forest in Shakespeare's source, *Rosalynde,* based in turn on the forest of Ardennes in France. As an abode that is associated with Robin Hood, it is a mythic folk world compensating for social injustice, offering an alternative way of life to those persons in retreat from a society seemingly beyond repair. As the "golden world" (1.1.114), the forest evokes an even deeper longing for a mythological past age of innocence and plenty, when men shared some attributes of the giants and the gods. This myth has its parallel in the biblical Garden of Eden, before the human race experienced "the penalty of Adam" (2.1.5). Finally, in another of its aspects, the forest is Arcadia, a pastoral landscape embodied in an ancient and sophisticated literary tradition.

All but the first of these Ardens, compared and contrasted with one another, involve some idealization not only of nature and the natural landscape, but also of the human condition. These various Ardens place our real life in a complex perspective and force us to a fresh appraisal of our own ordinary existence. Duke Senior, for example, describes the forest environment as a corrective for the evils of society. He addresses his followers in the forest as "my co-mates and brothers in exile" (2.1.1), suggesting a kind of social equality that he could never know in the cramped formality of his previous official existence. The banished Duke and his followers have had to leave behind their lands and revenues in the grip of the usurping Frederick. No longer rich, though adequately provided with all of life's necessities, the Duke and his "merry men" live "like the old Robin Hood of England," and "fleet the time carelessly as they did in the golden world" (1.1.111–114). In this friendly society, a strong communal sense replaces the necessity for individual proprietorship. All comers are welcome, with food for all.

There are no luxuries in the forest, to be sure, but even this spare existence affords relief from the decadence of courtly life. "Sweet are the uses of adversity" (2.1.12), insists the Duke. He welcomes the cold of winter because, instead of flattering him as courtiers do, it teaches him the true condition of mankind and of himself. The forest is serenely impartial, neither malicious nor compassionate. Death, and even killing for food, are an inevitable part of forest existence. The Duke concedes that his presence in the forest means the slaughter of deer, who were the original inhabitants; Orlando and Adam find that death through starvation in the forest is all too real a possibility. The forest never stoops to the degrading perversity of man at his worst, but it is also incapable of charity and forgiveness.

Shakespeare's sources reflect the complexity of his vision of Arden. The original of the Orlando story, which Shakespeare may not have used directly, is *The Cook's Tale of Gamelyn,* found in a number of manuscripts of *The Canterbury Tales* and wrongly attributed to Chaucer. This hearty English romance glorifies the rebellious and even violent spirit of its Robin Hood hero, the neglected youngest son Gamelyn, who, aided by faithful old Adam the Spencer, evades his wicked eldest brother in a cunning and bloody escape. As king of the outlaws in Sherwood Forest, Gamelyn eventually triumphs over his eldest brother (now the sheriff) and sees him hanged. Here then originates the motif of refuge from social injustice in Arden, even though most of the actual violence has been omitted from Shakespeare's version. (A series of Robin Hood plays on a similar theme, beginning in 1598 with Anthony Munday's *The Downfall of Robert Earl of Huntingdon after called Robin Hood,* were being performed with great success by the Admiral's company, chief rivals of the Lord Chamberlain's company to which Shakespeare belonged.)

As You Like It is clearly indebted to Thomas Lodge's version of the Gamelyn story entitled *Rosalynde: Euphues' Golden Legacy* (published 1590), a prose narrative romance in the ornate Euphuistic style of the 1580s. (Lodge's Epistle to the Gentleman Readers, casually inviting them to be pleased with this story if they are so inclined—*"If you like it,* so"—probably gave Shakespeare a hint for the name of his own play.) Lodge accentuated the love story with its courtship in masquerade, provided some charming songs, and introduced the pastoral love motif involving Corin, Silvius, Phoebe, and Ganymede. Shakespeare's ordering of episode is generally close to that of Lodge. Pastoral literature, which had become a literary rage in the 1580s and early 1590s owing particularly to Edmund Spenser's *Shepheardes Calendar* (1579) and Philip Sidney's *Arcadia* (1590), traced its ancestry through such Renaissance continental writers as Jorge de Montemayor, Jacopo Sannazaro, and Giovanni Battista Guarini to the so-called Greek romances, and finally back to the eclogues of Virgil, Theocritus, and Bion. A literary mode that had begun originally as a realistic evocation of difficult country life had become, by the Renaissance, an elegant vehicle for the loftiest and most patrician sentiments in love, for philosophic debate, and even for extensive political analysis.

Shakespeare's alterations and additions give us insight into his method of construction and his thematic focus. Whereas Lodge cheerfully accepts the pastoral conventions of his day, Shakespeare exposes those conventions to some criticism and considerable irony. Alongside the mannered and literary Silvius and Phoebe, he places William and Audrey, as peasantlike a couple as ever drew milk from a cow's teat. The juxtaposition holds up to critical perspective the rival claims of the literary and natural worlds by examining the defects of each in relation to the strengths of the other. William and Audrey are Shakespeare's own creation, based presumably on observation and also on the dramatic convention of the rustic clown and wench as exemplified earlier in his Costard and Jaquenetta *(Love's Labor's Lost).*

Equally original, and essential to the many-sided debate concerning the virtues of the court versus those of the country, are Touchstone and Jaques. Touchstone is a professional court fool, dressed in motley, a new comic type in Shakespeare, created apparently in response to the recent addition to the Lord Chamberlain's company of the brilliant actor Robert Armin. Jaques is also a new type, the malcontent satirist, reflecting the very latest literary vogue in the nondramatic poetry and drama for the private theater of George Chapman, John Marston, and Ben Jonson. (The private theaters, featuring boy actors, reopened in 1598–1599 after nearly a decade of enforced silence, and proceeded at once to specialize in satirical drama.) Touchstone and Jaques complement each other as critics and observers, one laughing at human folly with quizzical comic detachment and the other satirizing it with moralistic scorn. Once we have been exposed to this assortment of newly created characters, we can no longer view either pastoral life or pastoral love as simply as Lodge and other writers of the period portray them.

When *As You Like It* is compared with its chief source, Shakespeare can also be seen to have altered and considerably softened the characters of the wicked brothers Oliver and Frederick. Whereas Lodge's Saladyne is motivated by a greedy desire to seize his younger brother Rosader's property, Shakespeare's Oliver is envious of Orlando's natural goodness and popularity. As he confesses in soliloquy, Orlando is "so much in the heart of the world and especially of my own people . . . that I am altogether misprised" (1.1.159–161). In his warped way Oliver desires to be more like Orlando, and in the enchanted forest of Arden he eventually becomes so. Duke Frederick too is plainly envious of goodness. Trying to persuade his daughter Celia of the need for banishing Rosalind, he argues, "thou wilt show more bright and seem more virtuous / When she is gone"

(1.3.79–80). In a sense Frederick is ripe for conversion. Penitence and conciliation replace the vengeful conclusion of Lodge's novel, in which the nobles of France finally overthrow and execute the usurping king. Although Shakespeare's resolutions are sudden and inadequately explained, like all miracles they attest to the inexplicable power of goodness.

The court of Duke Frederick is "the envious court," identified by this fixed epithet. In it, brothers turn unnaturally against brothers: the younger Frederick usurps his older brother's throne, whereas the older Oliver denies the younger Orlando his birthright of education. In still another parallel, both Rosalind and Orlando find themselves mistrusted as the children of Frederick's political enemies, Duke Senior and Sir Rowland de Boys. A daughter and a son are held to be guilty by association. "Thou art thy father's daughter, there's enough" (1.3.56), Frederick curtly retorts in explaining Rosalind's exile. And to Orlando, triumphant in wrestling with Charles, Frederick asserts, "I would thou hadst been son to some man else" (1.2.214). Here again, Frederick plaintively reveals his attraction to goodness, even if at present this attraction is thwarted by tyrannous whim. Many of Frederick's entourage might also be better persons if they only knew how to escape the insincerities of their courtly life. Charles the wrestler, for example, places himself at Oliver's service, and yet he would happily avoid breaking Orlando's neck if to do so were consistent with self-interest. Even Le Beau, the giddy fop so delighted at first with the cruel sport of wrestling, takes Orlando aside at some personal risk to warn him of Duke Frederick's foul humor. Ideally, Le Beau would prefer to be a companion of Orlando's "in a better world than this" (1.2.275). The vision of a regenerative Utopia secretly abides in the heart of this courtly creature.

It is easier to anatomize the defects of a social order than to propound solutions. As have other Utopian visionaries (including Thomas More), Shakespeare uses playful debate to elicit complicated responses on the part of his audience. Which is preferable, the court or the country? Jaques and Touchstone are adept gadflies, incessantly pointing out contradictions and ironies. Jaques, the malcontent railer derived from literary satire, takes delight in being out of step with everyone. Seemingly his chief reason for having joined the others in the forest is to jibe at their motives for being there. To their song about the rejection of courtly ambition he mockingly supplies another verse, charging them with having left their wealth and ease out of mere willfulness (2.5.46–54). With ironic appropriateness, Jaques eventually decides to remain in the forest in the company of Frederick; Jaques cannot thrive on resolution and harmony. His humor is "melancholy," from which, as he observes, he draws consolation as a weasel sucks eggs (2.5.11–12). The others treat him as a sort of profane jester whose soured conceits add relish to their enjoyment of the forest life.

Despite his affectation, however, Jaques is serious and even excited in his defense of satire as a curative form of laughter (2.7.47–87). The appearance of Touchstone in the forest has reaffirmed in Jaques his profound commitment to a view of life as a meaningless process of decay governed by inexorable time. His function in such a life is to be mordant, unsparing. As literary satirist he must be free to awaken men's minds to their own folly. To the Duke's protestation that the satirist is merely self-indulgent and licentious, Jaques counters with a thoughtful and classically Horatian defense of satire as an art form devoted not to libelous attacks on individuals but to exposing types of folly. Any observer who feels himself individually portrayed merely condemns himself by confessing his resemblance to the type. This particular debate between the Duke and Jaques ends, appropriately, in a draw. The Duke's point is well taken, for Jaques's famous "Seven Ages of Man" speech, so often read out of context, occurs in a scene that also witnesses the rescue of Orlando and Adam from the forest. As though in answer to Jaques's acid depiction of covetous old age, we see old Adam's self-sacrifice and trust in Providence. Instead of "mere oblivion," we see charitable compassion prompting the Duke to aid Orlando and Orlando to aid Adam. Perhaps this vision seems of a higher spiritual order than that of Jaques. Nonetheless, without him the forest would be a dull and humorless place.

Touchstone's name suggests that he similarly offers a multiplicity of viewpoints. (A touchstone is a kind of stone used to test for gold and silver.) He shares with Jaques a skeptical view of life, but for Touchstone the inconsistency and absurdity of life are occasions for wit and humor rather than melancholy and cynicism. As a professional fool he observes that sane men are more foolish than he—as, for example, in their elaborate dueling code of the Retort Courteous and the Reply Churlish, leading finally to the Lie Circumstantial and the Lie Direct. He is fascinated by the games people make of their lives and is amused by their inability to be content with what they already have. Of the shepherd's life, he comments, "In respect that it is solitary, I like it very well; but in respect that it is private, it is a very vile life" (3.2.15–16). This paradox, though nonsensical, captures the restlessness of human striving for a life that can somehow combine the peaceful solitude of nature with the convenience and excitement of city life. Although Touchstone marries, even his marriage is a spoof of the institution rather than a serious attempt at commitment. Like all fools, who in Renaissance times were regarded as a breed apart, Touchstone exists outside the realm of ordinary human responses. There he can comment disinterestedly on human folly. He is prevented, however, from sharing fully in the human love and conciliation with which the play ends. He and Jaques are not touched by the play's regenerative magic; Jaques will remain in the forest, Touchstone will remain forever a childlike entertainer.

The regenerative power of Arden, as we have seen, is not the forest's alone. What saves Orlando is the human charity practiced by him and by the Duke, who, for all his love of the forest, longs to rejoin that human society where he has "with holy bell been knolled to church" (2.7.120). Civilization at its best is no less necessary to the human spirit than is the natural order of the forest. In love, also, perception and wisdom must be combined with nature's gifts. Orlando, when we first see him, is a young man of the finest natural qualities, but admittedly lacking experience in the nuances of complex human relationships. Nowhere does his lack of breeding betray him more unhappily than in his first encounter with Rosalind, following the wrestling match. In response to her unmistakable hints of favor he stands oxlike, tongue-tied. Later, however, in the forest, his first attempts at self-education in love lead him into an opposite danger: an excess of platitudinous manners parading in the guise of Petrarchism. (The Italian sonneteer Francis Petrarch has given to the language a name for the stereotypical literary mannerisms we associate with courtly love: the sighing and self-abasement of the young man, the chaste denial of love by the woman whom he worships, and the like.) Orlando's newfound self-abasement and idealization of his absent mistress are as unsatisfactory as his former naiveté. He must learn from Rosalind that a quest for true understanding in love avoids the extreme of pretentious mannerism as well as that of mere artlessness. Orlando as Petrarchan lover too much resembles Silvius, the lovesick young man, cowering before the imperious will of his coy mistress Phoebe. This stereotyped relationship, taken from the pages of fashionable pastoral romance, represents a posturing that Rosalind hopes to cure in Silvius and Phoebe even as she will also cure Orlando.

Rosalind is above all the realistic one, the plucky Shakespearean heroine showing her mettle in the world of men, emotionally more mature than her lover. Her concern is with a working and clear-sighted relationship in love, and to that end she daringly insists that Orlando learn something of woman's changeable mood. Above all, she must disabuse him of the dangerously misleading clichés of the Petrarchan love myth. When he protests he would die for love of Rosalind, she lectures him mockingly: "No, faith, die by attorney. The poor world is almost six thousand years old, and in all this time there was not any man died in his own person, videlicet, in a love cause." She debunks the legends of Troilus and Leander, youths supposed to have died for love who in fact met with more prosaic ends. "But these are all lies. Men have died from time to time, and worms have eaten them, but not for love" (4.1.89–102). When Orlando has been sufficiently tested as to patience, loyalty, and understanding, she unmasks herself to him and simultaneously unravels the plot of Silvius and Phoebe.

Rosalind's disguise name, Ganymede, taken from Jove's amorous cupbearer, has homosexual connotations. Shakespeare delicately exploits these overtones, both in Phoebe's pursuit of a young lady (but really a boy actor) in male attire, and in Orlando's courtship of Ganymede as though addressed to Rosalind. In this innocent titillation, found also in Shakespeare's source, there is no suggestion of deviate sexual practice. On the contrary, the point is that Orlando can speak frankly and personally to "Ganymede" as to a perfect friend, one to whom he can relate in platonically spiritual terms without the potentially distracting note of sexual attraction. Once this disinterested love has grown strong between them, the unmasking of Rosalind's sexual identity makes possible a physical union between them to confirm and express the spiritual. In these terms, the play's happy ending affirms marriage as an institution, not simply as the expected denouement. The procession to the altar is synchronous with the return to civilization's other institutions, made whole again not solely by the forest but by the power of goodness embodied in Rosalind, Orlando, Duke Senior, and the others who persevere.

As You Like It in Performance

The forest in *As You Like It* is much more than a realistic theatrical setting: it is an idea, or really a number of ideas put in debate with one another, ideas about social justice, literary conventions, the uses of satire, the relationships between the sexes, and still other matters. Any attempt in the theater to present the forest too literally, allowing naturalistic spectacle to overwhelm the interplay of characters and ideas, is apt to diminish the play significantly. During its long history onstage, directors of *As You Like It* have demonstrated this point again and again.

Although the play seems to have flourished in Shakespeare's day, having been first performed at the newly opened Globe Theatre in 1599, *As You Like It* was ignored for the rest of the seventeenth century and then reappeared in 1723 at the Theatre Royal, Drury Lane, only in an adaptation that differs sharply from Shakespeare's play. Charles Johnson evidently felt, when he compiled *Love in a Forest,* that *As You Like It* needed generous infusions of material from other Shakespeare plays. "Pyramus and Thisbe" is purloined from *A Midsummer Night's Dream* as entertainment for Duke Senior, rather literally in response to Duke Senior's observation that "This wide and universal theater / Presents more woeful pageants than the scene / Wherein we play in" (2.7.136–138). Charles and Orlando fight with rapiers instead of wrestling and quarrel in language appropriated (or misappropriated) from the confrontation of Bolingbroke and Mowbray in *Richard II.* Jaques (played by Colley Cibber, who wanted as large a part as he could get) is allowed to speak in person his speech about the sobbing deer, rather than having the scene described by the First Lord. Audrey, William, Phoebe, and Corin disappear to make room for the added material, and Silvius's role is severely reduced. Jaques falls in love with Celia and woos her with some of Benedick's wit from *Much Ado about Nothing*. Oliver dies the instructive death of a villain, leaving his lands to Orlando, while "the fencer Charles" confesses that he was suborned by Oliver to impeach Orlando as a traitor.

The play more nearly as Shakespeare wrote it, but with changes still, was revived at Drury Lane in 1740, with Hannah Pritchard as Rosalind. Thomas Arne provided music for Amiens's two songs ("Under the greenwood tree" and "Blow, blow, thou winter wind"), and Celia (Kitty Clive) sang the "cuckoo" song from *Love's Labor's Lost*. In later years the song was often given to Rosalind. Throughout the century the play was chiefly the vehicle for leading actresses in the part of Rosalind—Hannah Pritchard, Ann Barry, Peg Woffington, Sarah Siddons—and for leading actors in the parts of Jaques and Touchstone, including Colley Cibber, James Quin, and Charles Macklin. *As You Like It* appeared more often at Drury Lane from 1776 to 1817 than any other Shakespeare play, missing only three seasons out of forty-one. Sir Oliver Mar-text was usually cut, along with Jaques's comment on the first encounter of Touchstone and Audrey, and so was much of Phoebe's dialogue; Hymen disappeared, and some of the play's best songs were eliminated or shortened. Jaques continued to describe in first person the episode of the sobbing deer, the tradition being fixed in print by actor-manager John Philip Kemble's acting edition in 1820 (and not reformed until actor-manager William Charles Macready restored the lines to the First Lord at Drury Lane in 1842). The play was performed as "opera" in 1824–1825, with numerous songs added from other plays and the sonnets, including "Full many a glorious morning" (sonnet 33), "Tell me where is fancy bred?" (*The Merchant of Venice*, 3.2.63), "Where the bee sucks" (*The Tempest*, 5.1.88), and, of course, the "cuckoo" song from *Love's Labor's Lost*. A number of these songs had already been borrowed for similar operatic versions of *A Midsummer Night's Dream, Twelfth Night, The Tempest, The Comedy of Errors, The Two Gentlemen of Verona,* and *The Merry Wives of Windsor,* and they were subsequently to be used in operas based on *The Taming of the Shrew* and *All's Well that Ends Well*.

The main contribution of the nineteenth century to this dressing up of *As You Like It* was to provide lavish settings that left little to the spectators' imagination. Macready delighted the eye with sets by the painter Clarkson Stanfield, elaborating each scene with such attention to detail that, as one contemporary critic marveled of Macready, "he has not *realized,* he has done more—he has *verified* the dramatist." The wrestling match in Act 1, scene 2, featured an arena of ropes and staves around which the courtiers stood, pressing eagerly forward and responding with shouts of applause (seconded by the audience) to every triumphant moment in the match. The pastoral scenes were graced with the accompaniment of distant sheep bells. Helen Faucit, Ada Rehan, Lily Langtry, and other famous actresses (though not Ellen Terry) played Rosalind in productions that gave special prominence to star performers. Texts were rearranged to accommodate the elaborate scenery: in Augustin Daly's production at the Lyceum Theatre in 1890, with Ada Rehan, Act 2 began with scene 3, the departure of Orlando and Adam for the forest, so that the action could proceed uninterruptedly thereafter in Arden. In his American production that had opened the previous December, Daly provided a "terrace and courtyard before the Duke's palace" with an arched gateway at the left, enabling a group of lords and ladies to go up on the terrace and watch the wrestling. In a production by John Hare and the Kendals (W. H. and Madge) at the St. James's Theatre in 1885, "the brook rippling among the sedges" appears to have been real water, losing itself among the leaves and what looked like real grass onstage, all arranged, according to the *Athenaeum,* so that it "renders easier the task of the imagination and enhances the pleasure of the spectator." The setting for Duke Frederick's court, executed by Lewis Wingfield, adopted the milieu of Charles VII's France, complete with elaborate headdresses and a plausible replica of the Château d'Amboise. The tradition of scenic elaboration continued into the early twentieth century, perhaps most notoriously in Oscar Asche's 1907 production at Her Majesty's Theatre, in which the Forest of Arden was recreated weekly with two thousand pots of ferns and cartloads of leaves.

Twentieth-century performance, on the other hand, has generally sought a more iconoclastic and theatrically self-aware idiom, even though occasionally, as in the 1936 film version with Laurence Olivier as a strikingly young and beautiful Orlando, one can still savor the saccharine tittering of sheltered young ladies that must have dominated many a Victorian production. New settings have been introduced: the eighteenth century of Watteau in Esmé Church's production at the Old Vic in 1937, the surreal world of Salvador Dali for a performance in Rome in 1950, leafless trees and a general atmosphere of hardship at Stratford-upon-Avon in 1961, and early Victorian England in New York in 1973. At Stratford-upon-Avon, Buzz Goodbody, in 1973, produced a modern-dress *As You Like It,* with Touchstone sporting a loud, checked suit, and Rosalind in jeans, while, four years later, Trevor Nunn set the play in Stuart England. Duke Frederick has more than once been portrayed as a Nazi, and Jaques as effeminate. Perhaps the most striking production of recent years was one by Cliford Williams in 1967 at the National Theatre. Williams employed an all-male cast, in Elizabethan dress, offering a new view of the transvestite disguisings and the explorations of the relationships between men and women that are so essential to the play. Whatever distortions these experiments may have introduced into the play in their quest for relevance, they have succeeded at least in challenging the complacent images of naturalistic production. Today, even when *As You Like It* is done in an appropriately Elizabethan setting, the production usually employs swift pacing and a suggestive use of scenery that calls upon the spectators to imagine for themselves what the forest is like.

Perhaps the BBC television *As You Like It* in 1978 best illustrates what is wrong with using realistic scenery in this play. The television camera can, and does, provide handsome locales throughout, in the style of the BBC's successful *Masterpiece Theatre:* we see a greensward lying before a real castle, a wrestling arena, and later, of course, a forest. But, as Duke Senior's fellow exiles sit around disconsolately listening to a song or the First Lord's description of Jaques, the forest seems disappointingly ordinary. The camera fails, on this occasion at least, to make anything magical out of a tree or shrub. In such an environment, the actors playing Corin, Silvius, and the rest, however proficient, look like their routine counterparts from central casting. The actors do not have to invoke a sense of place, for it is there even before they come on camera. One telling detail is the disappearance of stage magic from the presentation of Hymen, the god of marriage. In the theater, Hymen's identity is perfectly ambiguous: is he a god, in fact, or someone dressed for the part by the stage-managing Rosalind? In a realistically photographed setting, on the other hand, the director has to state his case, and so the BBC's Hymen is, or looks like, an effete young man who wears strange garlands in his hair and is otherwise rather underdressed for the occasion. Illusion is a paradoxical thing in drama: the more detail the director provides, the less imaginative the experience may be for the viewer.

Shakespeare's original performance certainly had to rely on the audience's participation in the making of illusion. Boy actors took the parts of the women, with the result that the device of male disguise for Rosalind (really a boy actor) calls attention to the way in which illusion is produced. The play is reflexive in other ways, as when Jaques refers to all the world as a stage and to men and women as merely players; his view is a sardonic one, but the playacting he describes is certainly pertinent to the managerial role of Rosalind. The marked contrasts between the court of Duke Frederick and the communal forest society of Duke Senior, so vital to the play's impact, is conveyed in Shakespeare's original stage conception not by elaborate sets but by actors on a bare stage, evoking through costuming, gesture, and speech the nature of two disparate worlds. Subsequent generations of Shakespearean idolaters have insisted on literalizing Shakespeare's evocative images, in the pictorial arts as in drama; Alderman John Boydell's famous Shakespeare art collection (illustrating the plays) of the early nineteenth century was particularly attentive to scenes not actually staged by Shakespeare at all, including the Seven Ages of Man, Jaques lying under a tree beside a brook, and Oliver asleep while a lion and a snake wait for him to awake. The literalizing that has been so much a part of Shakespearean illustration and production is no doubt a tribute to his genius as an imaginative artist, but the better tribute is to use a theatrical language of gesture and setting that invites the kind of involvement Shakespeare demanded of his first spectators.

AS YOU LIKE IT

[*Dramatis Personae*

DUKE SENIOR, *a banished duke*
DUKE FREDERICK, *his usurping brother*
ROSALIND, *daughter of Duke Senior, later disguised as* GANYMEDE
CELIA, *daughter of Duke Frederick, later disguised as* ALIENA

OLIVER,
JAQUES,
ORLANDO, } *sons of Sir Rowland de Boys*

AMIENS,
JAQUES, } *lords attending Duke Senior*

LE BEAU, *a courtier attending Duke Frederick*
CHARLES, *a wrestler in the court of Duke Frederick*

ADAM, *an aged servant of Oliver and then Orlando*
DENNIS, *a servant of Oliver*

TOUCHSTONE, *the* CLOWN *or* FOOL

CORIN, *an old shepherd*
SILVIUS, *a young shepherd, in love with Phoebe*
PHOEBE, *a shepherdess*
WILLIAM, *a country youth, in love with Audrey*
AUDREY, *a country wench*
SIR OLIVER MAR-TEXT, *a country vicar*

HYMEN, *god of marriage*

Lords and Attendants waiting on Duke Frederick and Duke Senior

SCENE: *Oliver's house; Duke Frederick's court; and the Forest of Arden*]

1.1 *Enter Orlando and Adam.*

ORLANDO As I remember, Adam, it was upon this fashion bequeathed me by will but poor a thousand crowns and, as thou sayst, charged my brother on his blessing to breed me well; and there begins my sadness. My brother Jaques he keeps at school, and report speaks goldenly of his profit. For my part, he keeps me rustically at home or, to speak more properly, stays me here at home unkept; for call you that "keeping" for a gentleman of my birth, that differs not from the stalling of an ox? His horses are bred better, for besides that they are fair with their feeding, they are taught their manage, and to that end riders dearly hired. But I, his brother, gain nothing under him but growth, for the which his animals on his dunghills are as much bound to him as I. Besides this nothing that he so plentifully gives me, the something that nature gave me his countenance seems to take from me. He lets me feed with his hinds, bars me the place of a brother, and as much as in him lies, mines my gentility with my education. This is it, Adam, that grieves me; and the spirit of my father, which I think is within me, begins to mutiny against this servitude. I will no longer endure it, though yet I know no wise remedy how to avoid it.

Enter Oliver.

ADAM Yonder comes my master, your brother.

ORLANDO Go apart, Adam, and thou shalt hear how he will shake me up. [*Adam stands aside.*]

OLIVER Now, sir, what make you here?

1.1. Location: The garden of Oliver's house.
2 bequeathed i.e., he, my father, bequeathed. **but poor** merely **3 crowns** coins worth five shillings **3–4 on his blessing** on pain of losing his blessing **4 breed** bring up, educate **5 keeps at school** maintains at the university **6 profit** i.e., progress **8 stays** detains. **unkept** not maintained properly **11 fair** in handsome shape **12 manage** gaits and movements. **dearly** expensively **17 countenance** behavior, attitude **18 hinds** farm hands. **bars me** excludes me from **19 as in him lies** as he is able. **mines** undermines **20 education** i.e., lack of proper education **26 Go apart** stand aside **27 shake me up** insult me **28 make** do. (But Orlando takes it in the more usual sense.)

ORLANDO Nothing. I am not taught to make anything.

OLIVER What mar you then, sir?

ORLANDO Marry, sir, I am helping you to mar that which God made, a poor unworthy brother of yours, with idleness.

OLIVER Marry, sir, be better employed, and be naught awhile.

ORLANDO Shall I keep your hogs and eat husks with them? What prodigal portion have I spent, that I should come to such penury?

OLIVER Know you where you are, sir?

ORLANDO O, sir, very well: here in your orchard.

OLIVER Know you before whom, sir?

ORLANDO Ay, better than him I am before knows me. I know you are my eldest brother, and in the gentle condition of blood you should so know me. The courtesy of nations allows you my better, in that you are the firstborn, but the same tradition takes not away my blood, were there twenty brothers betwixt us. I have as much of my father in me as you, albeit I confess your coming before me is nearer to his reverence.

OLIVER What, boy! [*He strikes Orlando.*]

ORLANDO Come, come, elder brother, you are too young in this. [*He seizes Oliver by the throat.*]

OLIVER Wilt thou lay hands on me, villain?

ORLANDO I am no villain. I am the youngest son of Sir Rowland de Boys; he was my father, and he is thrice a villain that says such a father begot villains. Wert thou not my brother, I would not take this hand from

31 Marry i.e., indeed. (Originally an oath by the Virgin Mary.) **34–35 be naught awhile** (A mild malediction, like "go to the devil.") **36–38 Shall . . . penury** (Alluding to the story of the Prodigal Son, in Luke 15:11–32, who, having wasted his "portion" or inheritance, had to tend swine and eat with them.) **39 where** i.e., in whose presence. (But Orlando sarcastically takes the more literal meaning.) **40 orchard** garden **42 him** he whom **43–44 in . . . blood** i.e., acknowledging the bond of our being of gentle birth **44 know** acknowledge **44–45 courtesy of nations** recognized custom (of primogeniture, whereby the eldest son inherits all the land) **49 is nearer to his reverence** i.e., places you closer to the respect that was due him **52 young** raw, inexperienced (at fighting) **53 villain** i.e., worthless fellow. (But Orlando again plays on the literal meaning of bondman or serf.)

thy throat till this other had pulled out thy tongue for
saying so. Thou hast railed on thyself. 59

ADAM Sweet masters, be patient! For your father's re- 60
membrance, be at accord. 61

OLIVER Let me go, I say.

ORLANDO I will not till I please. You shall hear me. My
father charged you in his will to give me good education. You have trained me like a peasant, obscuring 65
and hiding from me all gentlemanlike qualities. The 66
spirit of my father grows strong in me, and I will no
longer endure it; therefore allow me such exercises as
may become a gentleman, or give me the poor allottery 69
my father left me by testament; with that I will go buy
my fortunes. [*He releases Oliver.*]

OLIVER And what wilt thou do? Beg when that is spent? Well, sir, get you in. I will not long be troubled with you; you shall have some part of your will. I pray you, leave me.

ORLANDO I will no further offend you than becomes me for my good.

OLIVER Get you with him, you old dog.

ADAM Is "old dog" my reward? Most true, I have lost my teeth in your service. God be with my old master! He would not have spoke such a word.

Exeunt Orlando [*and*] *Adam.*

OLIVER Is it even so? Begin you to grow upon me? I will 82
physic your rankness and yet give no thousand 83
crowns neither. Holla, Dennis!

Enter Dennis.

DENNIS Calls your worship?

OLIVER Was not Charles, the Duke's wrestler, here to speak with me?

DENNIS So please you, he is here at the door and im- 88
portunes access to you.

59 railed on thyself i.e., insulted your own blood **60–61 your father's remembrance** the memory of your father **65 obscuring** i.e., obscuring in me **66 qualities** accomplishments **69 allottery** share, portion **82 grow upon me** i.e., take liberties with me **83 physic** apply medicine to. **rankness** overgrowth, overweening **88 So please you** if you please

OLIVER Call him in. [*Exit Dennis.*] 'Twill be a good way; and tomorrow the wrestling is.

Enter Charles.

CHARLES Good morrow to your worship.

OLIVER Good Monsieur Charles, what's the new news at the new court?

CHARLES There's no news at the court, sir, but the old news: that is, the old Duke is banished by his younger brother the new Duke, and three or four loving lords have put themselves into voluntary exile with him, whose lands and revenues enrich the new Duke; therefore he gives them good leave to wander.

OLIVER Can you tell if Rosalind, the Duke's daughter, be banished with her father?

CHARLES O, no; for the Duke's daughter, her cousin, so loves her, being ever from their cradles bred together, that she would have followed her exile or have died to stay behind her. She is at the court and no less beloved of her uncle than his own daughter, and never two ladies loved as they do.

OLIVER Where will the old Duke live?

CHARLES They say he is already in the Forest of Arden, and a many merry men with him; and there they live like the old Robin Hood of England. They say many young gentlemen flock to him every day and fleet the time carelessly as they did in the golden world.

OLIVER What, you wrestle tomorrow before the new Duke?

CHARLES Marry, do I, sir; and I came to acquaint you with a matter. I am given, sir, secretly to understand that your younger brother Orlando hath a disposition to come in disguised against me to try a fall. Tomorrow, sir, I wrestle for my credit, and he that escapes me without some broken limb shall acquit him well. Your brother is but young and tender, and for your love I would be loath to foil him, as I must for my

92 Good morrow good morning **105–106 died to stay** died from staying **113 fleet** pass **114 carelessly** free from care. **golden world** the primal age of innocence and ease from which man was thought to have degenerated. (See Ovid, *Metamorphoses* 1.) **120 fall** bout **121 credit** reputation **122 shall** must **124 foil** overthrow

own honor if he come in. Therefore, out of my love to
you, I came hither to acquaint you withal, that either 126
you might stay him from his intendment or brook 127
such disgrace well as he shall run into, in that it is a
thing of his own search and altogether against my will. 129

OLIVER Charles, I thank thee for thy love to me, which
thou shalt find I will most kindly requite. I had myself
notice of my brother's purpose herein and have by
underhand means labored to dissuade him from it, but 133
he is resolute. I'll tell thee, Charles, it is the stubborn-
est young fellow of France, full of ambition, an envious emulator of every man's good parts, a secret and 136
villainous contriver against me his natural brother. 137
Therefore use thy discretion. I had as lief thou didst 138
break his neck as his finger. And thou wert best look
to 't; for if thou dost him any slight disgrace, or if he
do not mightily grace himself on thee, he will practice 141
against thee by poison, entrap thee by some treacherous device, and never leave thee till he hath ta'en thy
life by some indirect means or other; for I assure thee,
and almost with tears I speak it, there is not one so
young and so villainous this day living. I speak but
brotherly of him, but should I anatomize him to thee 147
as he is, I must blush and weep, and thou must look
pale and wonder.

CHARLES I am heartily glad I came hither to you. If he
come tomorrow, I'll give him his payment. If ever he
go alone again, I'll never wrestle for prize more. And 152
so God keep your worship!

OLIVER Farewell, good Charles. *Exit* [*Charles*]. Now
will I stir this gamester. I hope I shall see an end of 155
him; for my soul, yet I know not why, hates nothing
more than he. Yet he's gentle, never schooled and yet 157
learned, full of noble device, of all sorts enchantingly 158

126 withal with this **127 stay** keep, deter. **intendment** purpose, intent. **brook** endure **129 search** seeking **133 underhand** indirect **136 emulator** rival. **parts** qualities **137 contriver** plotter. **natural** by blood, legitimate **138 lief** willingly **141 grace . . . thee** distinguish himself at your expense. **practice** plot **147 brotherly** i.e., with a reserve proper to a brother. **anatomize** lay open in detail, analyze **152 go alone** walk unassisted **155 gamester** athlete, sportsman (here said sardonically) **157 gentle** gentlemanly **158 noble device** lofty aspiration. **sorts** classes of people. **enchantingly** as if by the effect of enchantment

beloved, and indeed so much in the heart of the world
and especially of my own people, who best know him,
that I am altogether misprized. But it shall not be so 161
long; this wrestler shall clear all. Nothing remains but 162
that I kindle the boy thither, which now I'll go about. 163
Exit.

✤

1.2 *Enter Rosalind and Celia.*

CELIA I pray thee, Rosalind, sweet my coz, be merry. 1
ROSALIND Dear Celia, I show more mirth than I am
mistress of, and would you yet I were merrier? Unless
you could teach me to forget a banished father, you
must not learn me how to remember any extraordi- 5
nary pleasure.
CELIA Herein I see thou lov'st me not with the full
weight that I love thee. If my uncle, thy banished father, had banished thy uncle, the Duke my father, so 9
thou hadst been still with me, I could have taught my
love to take thy father for mine. So wouldst thou, if the
truth of thy love to me were so righteously tempered 12
as mine is to thee.
ROSALIND Well, I will forget the condition of my estate, 14
to rejoice in yours.
CELIA You know my father hath no child but I, nor
none is like to have. And truly, when he dies, thou
shalt be his heir, for what he hath taken away from
thy father perforce I will render thee again in affec- 19
tion. By mine honor, I will, and when I break that
oath, let me turn monster. Therefore, my sweet Rose,
my dear Rose, be merry.
ROSALIND From henceforth I will, coz, and devise
sports. Let me see, what think you of falling in love?

161 misprized despised **162 clear all** solve everything **163 kindle** incite (to go). **thither** i.e., to the wrestling match

1.2. Location: Duke Frederick's court. A place suitable for wrestling.
1 sweet my coz my sweet cousin **5 learn** teach **9 so** provided that **12 righteously tempered** properly compounded **14 condition of my estate** state of my fortunes **19 perforce** by force

CELIA Marry, I prithee, do, to make sport withal. But love no man in good earnest, nor no further in sport neither than with safety of a pure blush thou mayst in honor come off again.

ROSALIND What shall be our sport, then?

CELIA Let us sit and mock the good huswife Fortune from her wheel, that her gifts may henceforth be bestowed equally.

ROSALIND I would we could do so, for her benefits are mightily misplaced, and the bountiful blind woman doth most mistake in her gifts to women.

CELIA 'Tis true, for those that she makes fair she scarce makes honest, and those that she makes honest she makes very ill-favoredly.

ROSALIND Nay, now thou goest from Fortune's office to Nature's. Fortune reigns in gifts of the world, not in the lineaments of Nature.

Enter [*Touchstone the*] *Clown.*

CELIA No; when Nature hath made a fair creature, may she not by Fortune fall into the fire? Though Nature hath given us wit to flout at Fortune, hath not Fortune sent in this fool to cut off the argument?

ROSALIND Indeed, there is Fortune too hard for Nature, when Fortune makes Nature's natural the cutter-off of Nature's wit.

CELIA Peradventure this is not Fortune's work neither but Nature's, who perceiveth our natural wits too dull to reason of such goddesses and hath sent this natural for our whetstone; for always the dullness of the fool

25 sport entertainment **27 pure** innocent **28 come off** retire, escape **30 huswife** one who manages household affairs, partially by spinning at a spinning wheel. (Shakespeare conflates this wheel with the commonplace wheel of Fortune.) *Huswife* is used derogatorily here, with a suggestion of "hussy." **34 bountiful blind woman** i.e., Fortune **36 scarce** rarely **37 honest** chaste **38 ill-favoredly** ugly **40 gifts of the world** e.g., riches and power **41 lineaments** characteristics. **s.d. Touchstone** a kind of stone used to test for gold and silver **44 flout** mock, scoff **47 natural** idiot, half-wit **51 to reason of** to think about **52 whetstone** sharpener

is the whetstone of the wits.—How now, wit, whither wander you?

TOUCHSTONE Mistress, you must come away to your father.

CELIA Were you made the messenger?

TOUCHSTONE No, by mine honor, but I was bid to come for you.

ROSALIND Where learned you that oath, Fool?

TOUCHSTONE Of a certain knight that swore by his honor they were good pancakes and swore by his honor the mustard was naught. Now I'll stand to it the pancakes were naught and the mustard was good, and yet was not the knight forsworn.

CELIA How prove you that in the great heap of your knowledge?

ROSALIND Ay, marry, now unmuzzle your wisdom.

TOUCHSTONE Stand you both forth now. Stroke your chins, and swear by your beards that I am a knave.

CELIA By our beards, if we had them, thou art.

TOUCHSTONE By my knavery, if I had it, then I were; but if you swear by that that is not, you are not forsworn. No more was this knight, swearing by his honor, for he never had any; or if he had, he had sworn it away before ever he saw those pancakes or that mustard.

CELIA Prithee, who is 't that thou mean'st?

TOUCHSTONE One that old Frederick, your father, loves.

CELIA My father's love is enough to honor him. Enough, speak no more of him; you'll be whipped for taxation one of these days.

TOUCHSTONE The more pity that fools may not speak wisely what wise men do foolishly.

CELIA By my troth, thou sayest true; for since the little wit that fools have was silenced, the little foolery that wise men have makes a great show. Here comes Monsieur Le Beau.

53–54 whither wander you (An allusion to the expression "wandering wits.") **62 pancakes** fritters (which might be made of meat and so require mustard) **63 naught** worthless. **stand to it** maintain, argue **65 forsworn** perjured **81 taxation** censure, slander **85–86 since . . . silenced** (Perhaps refers specifically to the Bishops' order of June 1599 banning satirical books.)

Enter Le Beau.

ROSALIND With his mouth full of news.

CELIA Which he will put on us as pigeons feed their young.

ROSALIND Then shall we be news-crammed.

CELIA All the better; we shall be the more marketable.—*Bonjour,* Monsieur Le Beau. What's the news?

LE BEAU Fair princess, you have lost much good sport.

CELIA Sport? Of what color?

LE BEAU What color, madam? How shall I answer you?

ROSALIND As wit and fortune will.

TOUCHSTONE Or as the Destinies decrees.

CELIA Well said; that was laid on with a trowel.

TOUCHSTONE Nay, if I keep not my rank—

ROSALIND Thou losest thy old smell.

LE BEAU You amaze me, ladies. I would have told you of good wrestling, which you have lost the sight of.

ROSALIND Yet tell us the manner of the wrestling.

LE BEAU I will tell you the beginning, and if it please your ladyships you may see the end, for the best is yet to do, and here, where you are, they are coming to perform it.

CELIA Well, the beginning, that is dead and buried.

LE BEAU There comes an old man and his three sons—

CELIA I could match this beginning with an old tale.

LE BEAU Three proper young men, of excellent growth and presence—

ROSALIND With bills on their necks, "Be it known unto all men by these presents."

LE BEAU The eldest of the three wrestled with Charles, the Duke's wrestler, which Charles in a moment threw him and broke three of his ribs, that there is little hope of life in him. So he served the second, and so the third. Yonder they lie, the poor old man their father

90 put on force upon **93–94 marketable** i.e., like animals that have been crammed with food before being sent to market **97 color** kind **101 with a trowel** i.e., clumsily, bluntly **102 rank** i.e., status as a wit. (But Rosalind plays on the sense of "evil-smelling.") **104 amaze** bewilder **109 yet to do** still to come **114 proper** handsome **116 bills** advertisements, proclamations **117 these presents** this document presented (with pun on *presence*) **121 So** similarly

making such pitiful dole over them that all the behold- 123
ers take his part with weeping.

ROSALIND Alas!

TOUCHSTONE But what is the sport, monsieur, that the ladies have lost?

LE BEAU Why, this that I speak of.

TOUCHSTONE Thus men may grow wiser every day. It is the first time that ever I heard breaking of ribs was sport for ladies.

CELIA Or I, I promise thee.

ROSALIND But is there any else longs to see this broken 133
music in his sides? Is there yet another dotes upon rib 134
breaking? Shall we see this wrestling, cousin?

LE BEAU You must if you stay here, for here is the place appointed for the wrestling, and they are ready to perform it.

CELIA Yonder, sure, they are coming. Let us now stay and see it.

Flourish. Enter Duke [*Frederick*], *Lords, Orlando, Charles, and attendants.*

DUKE FREDERICK Come on. Since the youth will not be
entreated, his own peril on his forwardness. 142

ROSALIND Is yonder the man?

LE BEAU Even he, madam.

CELIA Alas, he is too young! Yet he looks successfully. 145

DUKE FREDERICK How now, daughter and cousin? Are you crept hither to see the wrestling?

ROSALIND Ay, my liege, so please you give us leave. 148

DUKE FREDERICK You will take little delight in it, I can
tell you, there is such odds in the man. In pity of the 150
challenger's youth I would fain dissuade him, but he 151
will not be entreated. Speak to him, ladies; see if you
can move him.

123 dole grief, lamentation **133 any else** anyone else who
133–134 broken music (Literally, music arranged in parts for different instruments; here applied to the breaking of ribs.) **142 entreated . . . forwardness** i.e., entreated to desist, let the risk be blamed upon his own rashness **145 successfully** i.e., as if he would be successful
148 so . . . leave if you will permit us **150 odds** superiority. **the man** i.e., Charles **151 fain** willingly

CELIA Call him hither, good Monsieur Le Beau.

DUKE FREDERICK Do so. I'll not be by. [*He steps aside.*]

LE BEAU Monsieur the challenger, the princess calls for you.

ORLANDO [*Approaching the ladies*] I attend them with all respect and duty.

ROSALIND Young man, have you challenged Charles the wrestler?

ORLANDO No, fair princess; he is the general challenger. I come but in, as others do, to try with him the strength of my youth.

CELIA Young gentleman, your spirits are too bold for your years. You have seen cruel proof of this man's strength. If you saw yourself with your eyes or knew yourself with your judgment, the fear of your adventure would counsel you to a more equal enterprise. We pray you, for your own sake, to embrace your own safety and give over this attempt.

ROSALIND Do, young sir. Your reputation shall not therefore be misprized. We will make it our suit to the Duke that the wrestling might not go forward.

ORLANDO I beseech you, punish me not with your hard thoughts, wherein I confess me much guilty to deny so fair and excellent ladies anything. But let your fair eyes and gentle wishes go with me to my trial; wherein if I be foiled, there is but one shamed that was never gracious; if killed, but one dead that is willing to be so. I shall do my friends no wrong, for I have none to lament me; the world no injury, for in it I have nothing. Only in the world I fill up a place, which may be better supplied when I have made it empty.

ROSALIND The little strength that I have, I would it were with you.

CELIA And mine, to eke out hers.

ROSALIND Fare you well. Pray heaven I be deceived in you!

CELIA Your heart's desires be with you!

167–168 If . . . judgment i.e., if you saw yourself objectively, using your observation and your judgment **169 equal** i.e., where the odds are more equal **173 therefore** on that account. **misprized** despised **180 gracious** looked upon with favor **183 Only . . . I** in the world I merely **188–189 deceived in you** i.e., mistaken in fearing you will lose

CHARLES Come, where is this young gallant that is so desirous to lie with his mother earth?

ORLANDO Ready, sir, but his will hath in it a more modest working.

DUKE FREDERICK You shall try but one fall.

CHARLES No, I warrant Your Grace, you shall not entreat him to a second, that have so mightily persuaded him from a first.

ORLANDO You mean to mock me after; you should not have mocked me before. But come your ways.

ROSALIND Now Hercules be thy speed, young man!

CELIA I would I were invisible, to catch the strong fellow by the leg. [*Orlando and Charles*] *wrestle.*

ROSALIND O excellent young man!

CELIA If I had a thunderbolt in mine eye, I can tell who should down. *Shout.* [*Charles is thrown.*]

DUKE FREDERICK No more, no more.

ORLANDO Yes, I beseech Your Grace. I am not yet well breathed.

DUKE FREDERICK
How dost thou, Charles?

LE BEAU He cannot speak, my lord.

DUKE FREDERICK
Bear him away. What is thy name, young man?
[*Exeunt some with Charles.*]

ORLANDO Orlando, my liege, the youngest son of Sir Rowland de Boys.

DUKE FREDERICK
I would thou hadst been son to some man else.
The world esteemed thy father honorable,
But I did find him still mine enemy.
Thou shouldst have better pleased me with this deed
Hadst thou descended from another house.
But fare thee well; thou art a gallant youth.
I would thou hadst told me of another father.
Exit Duke [*with train, and others. Rosalind and Celia remain; Orlando stands apart from them*].

194 modest working decorous endeavor (than to lie with one's mother earth—an endeavor, Orlando implies, with sexual overtones) **200 come your ways** come on **201 Hercules be thy speed** may Hercules help you **206 down** fall **208–209 well breathed** warmed up **216 still** continually

CELIA [*To Rosalind*]
Were I my father, coz, would I do this?
ORLANDO [*To no one in particular*]
I am more proud to be Sir Rowland's son,
His youngest son, and would not change that calling 223
To be adopted heir to Frederick.
ROSALIND [*To Celia*]
My father loved Sir Rowland as his soul,
And all the world was of my father's mind.
Had I before known this young man his son,
I should have given him tears unto entreaties 228
Ere he should thus have ventured.
CELIA [*To Rosalind*] Gentle cousin,
Let us go thank him and encourage him.
My father's rough and envious disposition 231
Sticks me at heart.—Sir, you have well deserved. 232
If you do keep your promises in love
But justly as you have exceeded all promise, 234
Your mistress shall be happy.
ROSALIND Gentleman, 235
[*Giving him a chain from her neck*]
Wear this for me, one out of suits with fortune, 236
That could give more, but that her hand lacks means. 237
[*To Celia*] Shall we go, coz?
CELIA Ay. Fare you well, fair gentleman.
[*Rosalind and Celia start to leave.*]
ORLANDO [*Aside*]
Can I not say, "I thank you"? My better parts
Are all thrown down, and that which here stands up
Is but a quintain, a mere lifeless block. 241
ROSALIND
He calls us back. My pride fell with my fortunes;
I'll ask him what he would.—Did you call, sir? 243
Sir, you have wrestled well and overthrown
More than your enemies.

223 calling position, status **228 unto** in addition to **231 envious** malicious **232 Sticks** stabs **234 But justly** exactly **235 s.d. chain** (See 3.2.178, where Celia speaks of a chain given to Orlando by Rosalind.) **236 out . . . fortune** (1) whose petitions to Fortune are rejected (2) not wearing the livery of Fortune, not in her service **237 could** would be disposed to **241 quintain** wooden figure used as a target in tilting **243 would** wants

CELIA Will you go, coz?
ROSALIND Have with you.—Fare you well. 247
Exit [*with Celia*].

ORLANDO
What passion hangs these weights upon my tongue?
I cannot speak to her, yet she urged conference. 249
O poor Orlando, thou art overthrown!
Or Charles or something weaker masters thee. 251

Enter Le Beau.

LE BEAU
Good sir, I do in friendship counsel you
To leave this place. Albeit you have deserved
High commendation, true applause, and love,
Yet such is now the Duke's condition 255
That he misconsters all that you have done. 256
The Duke is humorous. What he is indeed 257
More suits you to conceive than I to speak of.

ORLANDO
I thank you, sir. And, pray you, tell me this:
Which of the two was daughter of the Duke
That here was at the wrestling?

LE BEAU
Neither his daughter, if we judge by manners,
But yet indeed the taller is his daughter. 263
The other is daughter to the banished Duke,
And here detained by her usurping uncle
To keep his daughter company, whose loves
Are dearer than the natural bond of sisters.
But I can tell you that of late this Duke
Hath ta'en displeasure 'gainst his gentle niece,
Grounded upon no other argument 270
But that the people praise her for her virtues
And pity her for her good father's sake;
And, on my life, his malice 'gainst the lady
Will suddenly break forth. Sir, fare you well. 274

247 Have with you I'll go with you **249 urged conference** invited conversation **251 Or** either **255 condition** state of mind, disposition **256 misconsters** misconstrues **257 humorous** temperamental, capricious **263 taller** (Possibly a textual error for *smaller* or *lesser,* or else an inconsistency on Shakespeare's part; at 1.3.113, Rosalind is shown to be the taller.) **270 argument** reason **274 suddenly** very soon

Hereafter, in a better world than this,
I shall desire more love and knowledge of you.

ORLANDO
I rest much bounden to you. Fare you well.
[*Exit Le Beau.*]
Thus must I from the smoke into the smother,
From tyrant Duke unto a tyrant brother.
But heavenly Rosalind! *Exit.*

✤

1.3 *Enter Celia and Rosalind.*

CELIA Why, cousin, why, Rosalind! Cupid have mercy! Not a word?

ROSALIND Not one to throw at a dog.

CELIA No, thy words are too precious to be cast away upon curs; throw some of them at me. Come, lame me with reasons.

ROSALIND Then there were two cousins laid up, when the one should be lamed with reasons and the other mad without any.

CELIA But is all this for your father?

ROSALIND No, some of it is for my child's father. O, how full of briers is this working-day world!

CELIA They are but burrs, cousin, thrown upon thee in holiday foolery. If we walk not in the trodden paths, our very petticoats will catch them.

ROSALIND I could shake them off my coat; these burrs are in my heart.

CELIA Hem them away.

ROSALIND I would try, if I could cry "hem" and have him.

CELIA Come, come, wrestle with thy affections.

275 world i.e., state of affairs **277 bounden** indebted **278 smoke into the smother** i.e., out of the frying pan into the fire. (*Smother* means "a dense suffocating smoke.")

1.3. Location: Duke Frederick's court.
5–6 lame . . . reasons i.e., throw some explanations (for your silence) at me **11 my child's father** one who might sire my children, i.e., Orlando **18 Hem** cough (since you say they are in the chest) **19 cry "hem"** clear away with a "hem" or a cough (with a play on *him*)

ROSALIND O, they take the part of a better wrestler than myself!

CELIA O, a good wish upon you! You will try in time, in despite of a fall. But, turning these jests out of service, let us talk in good earnest. Is it possible, on such a sudden, you should fall into so strong a liking with old Sir Rowland's youngest son?

ROSALIND The Duke my father loved his father dearly.

CELIA Doth it therefore ensue that you should love his son dearly? By this kind of chase, I should hate him, for my father hated his father dearly; yet I hate not Orlando.

ROSALIND No, faith, hate him not, for my sake.

CELIA Why should I not? Doth he not deserve well?

Enter Duke [*Frederick*], *with lords.*

ROSALIND Let me love him for that, and do you love him because I do.—Look, here comes the Duke.

CELIA With his eyes full of anger.

DUKE FREDERICK [*To Rosalind*]
Mistress, dispatch you with your safest haste
And get you from our court.

ROSALIND Me, uncle?

DUKE FREDERICK You, cousin.
Within these ten days if that thou be'st found
So near our public court as twenty miles,
Thou diest for it.

ROSALIND I do beseech Your Grace
Let me the knowledge of my fault bear with me.
If with myself I hold intelligence
Or have acquaintance with mine own desires,
If that I do not dream or be not frantic—
As I do trust I am not—then, dear uncle,
Never so much as in a thought unborn
Did I offend Your Highness.

24–25 You . . . fall i.e., you'll undertake to wrestle with Orlando sooner or later, despite the danger of your being thrown down. (Contains sexual suggestion.) **25–26 turning . . . service** i.e., dismissing this banter **31 chase** argument that is pursued **32 dearly** intensely **35 deserve well** i.e., well deserve to be hated. (But Rosalind interprets in the sense of "deserve favor.") **39 safest haste** speed necessary for your safety **40 cousin** i.e., kinsman **45 hold intelligence** am in communication **47 If that** if. **frantic** insane **49 so much as** even

DUKE FREDERICK Thus do all traitors.
If their purgation did consist in words,
They are as innocent as grace itself.
Let it suffice thee that I trust thee not.

ROSALIND
Yet your mistrust cannot make me a traitor.
Tell me whereon the likelihood depends.

DUKE FREDERICK
Thou art thy father's daughter, there's enough.

ROSALIND
So was I when Your Highness took his dukedom;
So was I when Your Highness banished him.
Treason is not inherited, my lord;
Or, if we did derive it from our friends,
What's that to me? My father was no traitor.
Then, good my liege, mistake me not so much
To think my poverty is treacherous.

CELIA Dear sovereign, hear me speak.

DUKE FREDERICK
Ay, Celia, we stayed her for your sake,
Else had she with her father ranged along.

CELIA
I did not then entreat to have her stay;
It was your pleasure and your own remorse.
I was too young that time to value her,
But now I know her. If she be a traitor,
Why so am I. We still have slept together,
Rose at an instant, learned, played, eat together,
And wheresoe'er we went, like Juno's swans
Still we went coupled and inseparable.

DUKE FREDERICK
She is too subtle for thee; and her smoothness,
Her very silence, and her patience
Speak to the people, and they pity her.
Thou art a fool. She robs thee of thy name,
And thou wilt show more bright and seem more virtuous

51 purgation proof of innocence **60 friends** relatives, kinsfolk **65 stayed** kept **66 ranged** roamed **68 remorse** compassion **69 that time** then **71 still** continually **72 eat** ate, or have eaten **73 Juno's swans** i.e., yoked together (though according to Ovid it was Venus, not Juno, who used swans to draw her chariot) **78 name** reputation, praise

When she is gone. Then open not thy lips.
Firm and irrevocable is my doom
Which I have passed upon her; she is banished.

CELIA
Pronounce that sentence then on me, my liege!
I cannot live out of her company.

DUKE FREDERICK
You are a fool. You, niece, provide yourself.
If you outstay the time, upon mine honor,
And in the greatness of my word, you die.
Exit Duke [*with Lords*].

CELIA
O my poor Rosalind, whither wilt thou go?
Wilt thou change fathers? I will give thee mine.
I charge thee, be not thou more grieved than I am.

ROSALIND
I have more cause.

CELIA Thou hast not, cousin.
Prithee, be cheerful. Know'st thou not the Duke
Hath banished me, his daughter?

ROSALIND That he hath not.

CELIA
No, hath not? Rosalind lacks then the love
Which teacheth thee that thou and I am one.
Shall we be sundered? Shall we part, sweet girl?
No, let my father seek another heir.
Therefore devise with me how we may fly,
Whither to go, and what to bear with us.
And do not seek to take your change upon you,
To bear your griefs yourself and leave me out;
For, by this heaven, now at our sorrows pale,
Say what thou canst, I'll go along with thee.

ROSALIND Why, whither shall we go?

CELIA
To seek my uncle in the Forest of Arden.

ROSALIND
Alas, what danger will it be to us,

81 doom sentence **85 provide yourself** get ready **87 in . . . word** i.e., upon my authority as Duke **89 change** exchange **100 change** change of fortune **102 pale** (Heaven is pale in sympathy with their plight.)

Maids as we are, to travel forth so far!
Beauty provoketh thieves sooner than gold.

CELIA
I'll put myself in poor and mean attire
And with a kind of umber smirch my face;
The like do you. So shall we pass along
And never stir assailants.

ROSALIND Were it not better,
Because that I am more than common tall,
That I did suit me all points like a man?
A gallant curtal ax upon my thigh,
A boar spear in my hand, and—in my heart
Lie there what hidden woman's fear there will—
We'll have a swashing and a martial outside,
As many other mannish cowards have
That do outface it with their semblances.

CELIA
What shall I call thee when thou art a man?

ROSALIND
I'll have no worse a name than Jove's own page,
And therefore look you call me Ganymede.
But what will you be called?

CELIA
Something that hath a reference to my state:
No longer Celia, but Aliena.

ROSALIND
But, cousin, what if we assayed to steal
The clownish fool out of your father's court?
Would he not be a comfort to our travel?

CELIA
He'll go along o'er the wide world with me;
Leave me alone to woo him. Let's away,
And get our jewels and our wealth together,
Devise the fittest time and safest way

109 mean lowly **110 umber** brown pigment (to make them appear tanned, as countrywomen would be) **114 suit** dress **115 curtal ax** broad cutting sword **118 swashing** swaggering, blustering
120 outface . . . semblances bluff their way through with mere appearances **123 Ganymede** Jupiter's cupbearer. (Used also in Lodge's *Rosalynde*.) **126 Aliena** the estranged one **127 assayed** tried **131 woo** persuade **133 fittest** most appropriate

To hide us from pursuit that will be made
After my flight. Now go we in content
To liberty, and not to banishment. *Exeunt.*

✤

135 content contentment

2.1

Enter Duke Senior, Amiens, and two or three Lords, [*dressed*] *like foresters.*

DUKE SENIOR
Now, my co-mates and brothers in exile,
Hath not old custom made this life more sweet 2
Than that of painted pomp? Are not these woods
More free from peril than the envious court? 4
Here feel we not the penalty of Adam, 5
The seasons' difference, as the icy fang 6
And churlish chiding of the winter's wind, 7
Which when it bites and blows upon my body
Even till I shrink with cold, I smile and say,
"This is no flattery; these are counselors
That feelingly persuade me what I am."
Sweet are the uses of adversity, 12
Which, like the toad, ugly and venomous, 13
Wears yet a precious jewel in his head; 14
And this our life, exempt from public haunt, 15
Finds tongues in trees, books in the running brooks,
Sermons in stones, and good in everything.

AMIENS
I would not change it. Happy is Your Grace
That can translate the stubbornness of fortune
Into so quiet and so sweet a style.

DUKE SENIOR
Come, shall we go and kill us venison?
And yet it irks me the poor dappled fools, 22
Being native burghers of this desert city, 23
Should in their own confines with forkèd heads 24
Have their round haunches gored.

FIRST LORD
Indeed, my lord,

2.1. Location: The Forest of Arden.
2 old custom long experience **4 envious** malicious **5 feel we not** we do not seriously suffer from. (*Not* is often emended to *but.*) **penalty of Adam** expulsion from Eden, bringing with it loss of innocence and *the seasons' difference,* the change of seasons from summer to winter **6 as** such as **7 churlish** rough **12 uses** profits **13–14 like . . . head** (Alludes to the widespread belief that the toad was a poisonous creature but with a jewel embedded in its head that worked as an antidote.) **15 exempt** cut off. **haunt** society **22 irks** grieves, vexes. **fools** innocent creatures **23 burghers** citizens. **desert** uninhabited **24 forkèd heads** i.e., barbed hunting arrows

The melancholy Jaques grieves at that,
And in that kind swears you do more usurp 27
Than doth your brother that hath banished you.
Today my lord of Amiens and myself
Did steal behind him as he lay along 30
Under an oak whose antique root peeps out 31
Upon the brook that brawls along this wood, 32
To the which place a poor sequestered stag 33
That from the hunter's aim had ta'en a hurt
Did come to languish. And indeed, my lord,
The wretched animal heaved forth such groans
That their discharge did stretch his leathern coat
Almost to bursting, and the big round tears
Coursed one another down his innocent nose 39
In piteous chase. And thus the hairy fool,
Much markèd of the melancholy Jaques, 41
Stood on th' extremest verge of the swift brook, 42
Augmenting it with tears.

DUKE SENIOR
But what said Jaques?
Did he not moralize this spectacle? 44

FIRST LORD
O, yes, into a thousand similes.
First, for his weeping into the needless stream: 46
"Poor deer," quoth he, "thou mak'st a testament 47
As worldings do, giving thy sum of more 48
To that which had too much." Then, being there alone,
Left and abandoned of his velvet friends: 50
"'Tis right," quoth he, "thus misery doth part 51
The flux of company." Anon a careless herd, 52
Full of the pasture, jumps along by him
And never stays to greet him. "Ay," quoth Jaques,
"Sweep on, you fat and greasy citizens;
'Tis just the fashion. Wherefore do you look

27 kind regard, vein **30 along** stretched out **31 antique** ancient **32 brawls** noisily flows **33 sequestered** separated (from the herd) **39 Coursed** followed **41 markèd of** observed by **42 extremest verge** very edge **44 moralize** draw out the hidden meaning of **46 needless** having no need (of more water) **47 testament** will **48 worldings** mortal men; worldly men. **sum of more** additional quantity **50 velvet** i.e., prosperous. (Velvet was an appropriately rich dress for a courtier; the term also alludes here to the velvet of the deers' antlers during rapid growth.) **51 'Tis right** i.e., that's how it goes. **part** depart from **52 flux of company** stream of fellow creatures. **Anon** soon. **careless** carefree

Upon that poor and broken bankrupt there?"
Thus most invectively he pierceth through
The body of the country, city, court,
Yea, and of this our life, swearing that we
Are mere usurpers, tyrants, and what's worse,
To fright the animals and to kill them up
In their assigned and native dwelling place.

DUKE SENIOR
And did you leave him in this contemplation?

SECOND LORD
We did, my lord, weeping and commenting
Upon the sobbing deer.

DUKE SENIOR Show me the place.
I love to cope him in these sullen fits,
For then he's full of matter.

FIRST LORD I'll bring you to him straight. *Exeunt.*

✤

2.2 *Enter Duke [Frederick], with Lords.*

DUKE FREDERICK
Can it be possible that no man saw them?
It cannot be. Some villains of my court
Are of consent and sufferance in this.

FIRST LORD
I cannot hear of any that did see her.
The ladies, her attendants of her chamber,
Saw her abed, and in the morning early
They found the bed untreasured of their mistress.

SECOND LORD
My lord, the roynish clown, at whom so oft
Your Grace was wont to laugh, is also missing.
Hisperia, the princess' gentlewoman,
Confesses that she secretly o'erheard
Your daughter and her cousin much commend
The parts and graces of the wrestler

58 invectively vehemently **61 what's worse** anything worse **62 up** off **67 cope** engage, encounter **68 matter** substance, sentiment

2.2. Location: Duke Frederick's court.
3 Are . . . this have conspired in and permitted this **8 roynish** scurvy, coarse **13 parts** good qualities

That did but lately foil the sinewy Charles,
And she believes wherever they are gone
That youth is surely in their company.

DUKE FREDERICK
Send to his brother; fetch that gallant hither. 17
If he be absent, bring his brother to me; 18
I'll make him find him. Do this suddenly, 19
And let not search and inquisition quail 20
To bring again these foolish runaways. *Exeunt.* 21

✤

2.3 *Enter Orlando and Adam,* [*meeting*].

ORLANDO Who's there?

ADAM
What, my young master? O my gentle master,
O my sweet master, O you memory 3
Of old Sir Rowland! Why, what make you here? 4
Why are you virtuous? Why do people love you?
And wherefore are you gentle, strong, and valiant? 6
Why would you be so fond to overcome 7
The bonny prizer of the humorous Duke? 8
Your praise is come too swiftly home before you.
Know you not, master, to some kind of men
Their graces serve them but as enemies?
No more do yours. Your virtues, gentle master, 12
Are sanctified and holy traitors to you.
O, what a world is this, when what is comely
Envenoms him that bears it!

ORLANDO
Why, what's the matter?

ADAM O unhappy youth,
Come not within these doors! Within this roof
The enemy of all your graces lives.
Your brother—no, no brother; yet the son—

17, 18 his brother i.e., Oliver **18 he** i.e., Orlando **19 suddenly** speedily **20 inquisition** inquiry. **quail** fail, slacken **21 again** back

2.3. Location: Before Oliver's house.

3 memory memorial **4 what make you** what are you doing **6 wherefore** why **7 fond to** foolish as to **8 bonny prizer** sturdy champion or prizefighter. **humorous** temperamental **12 No more** no better

Yet not the son, I will not call him son
Of him I was about to call his father—
Hath heard your praises, and this night he means
To burn the lodging where you use to lie 23
And you within it. If he fail of that,
He will have other means to cut you off.
I overheard him and his practices. 26
This is no place, this house is but a butchery; 27
Abhor it, fear it, do not enter it.

ORLANDO

Why, whither, Adam, wouldst thou have me go?

ADAM

No matter whither, so you come not here.

ORLANDO

What, wouldst thou have me go and beg my food?
Or with a base and boisterous sword enforce 32
A thievish living on the common road?
This I must do, or know not what to do;
Yet this I will not do, do how I can.
I rather will subject me to the malice
Of a diverted blood and bloody brother. 37

ADAM

But do not so. I have five hundred crowns,
The thrifty hire I saved under your father, 39
Which I did store to be my foster nurse
When service should in my old limbs lie lame 41
And unregarded age in corners thrown. 42
Take that, and He that doth the ravens feed, 43
Yea, providently caters for the sparrow, 44
Be comfort to my age! Here is the gold; [*Giving gold*]
All this I give you. Let me be your servant.
Though I look old, yet I am strong and lusty, 47
For in my youth I never did apply
Hot and rebellious liquors in my blood,
Nor did not with unbashful forehead woo 50
The means of weakness and debility;

23 use are accustomed **26 practices** plots **27 place** place for you, home. **butchery** slaughterhouse **32 boisterous** violent **37 diverted blood** kinship diverted from the natural source **39 thrifty . . . saved** wages I thriftily saved **41 lie lame** i.e., be performed only lamely **42 thrown** be thrown **43–44 He . . . sparrow** (See Luke 12:6, 22–24, Psalms 147:9, Job 38:41, etc.) **47 lusty** vigorous **50 unbashful forehead** shameless countenance

Therefore my age is as a lusty winter,
Frosty but kindly. Let me go with you.
I'll do the service of a younger man
In all your business and necessities.

ORLANDO

O good old man, how well in thee appears
The constant service of the antique world, 57
When service sweat for duty, not for meed! 58
Thou art not for the fashion of these times,
Where none will sweat but for promotion,
And having that do choke their service up 61
Even with the having. It is not so with thee. 62
But, poor old man, thou prun'st a rotten tree,
That cannot so much as a blossom yield
In lieu of all thy pains and husbandry. 65
But come thy ways; we'll go along together,
And ere we have thy youthful wages spent,
We'll light upon some settled low content. 68

ADAM

Master, go on, and I will follow thee
To the last gasp, with truth and loyalty.
From seventeen years till now almost fourscore
Here livèd I, but now live here no more.
At seventeen years many their fortunes seek,
But at fourscore it is too late a week; 74
Yet fortune cannot recompense me better
Than to die well and not my master's debtor.

Exeunt.

✤

2.4

Enter Rosalind for Ganymede, Celia for Aliena, and Clown, alias Touchstone.

ROSALIND O Jupiter, how weary are my spirits!

57 constant faithful **58 sweat** sweated. **meed** reward **61–62 do choke . . . having** i.e., cease serving once they have gained promotion **65 lieu of** return for **68 low content** lowly contented state **74 week** i.e., time

2.4. Location: The Forest of Arden.
s.d. for i.e., disguised as

TOUCHSTONE I care not for my spirits, if my legs were not weary.

ROSALIND I could find in my heart to disgrace my man's
apparel and to cry like a woman; but I must comfort
the weaker vessel, as doublet and hose ought to show 6
itself courageous to petticoat. Therefore courage, good
Aliena!

CELIA I pray you, bear with me; I cannot go no further.

TOUCHSTONE For my part, I had rather bear with you
than bear you; yet I should bear no cross if I did bear 11
you, for I think you have no money in your purse.

ROSALIND Well, this is the Forest of Arden.

TOUCHSTONE Ay, now am I in Arden, the more fool I. When I was at home I was in a better place, but travelers must be content.

Enter Corin and Silvius.

ROSALIND Ay, be so, good Touchstone.—Look you who comes here, a young man and an old in solemn talk. [*They stand aside and listen.*]

CORIN
This is the way to make her scorn you still.

SILVIUS
O Corin, that thou knew'st how I do love her!

CORIN
I partly guess, for I have loved ere now.

SILVIUS
No, Corin, being old, thou canst not guess,
Though in thy youth thou wast as true a lover
As ever sighed upon a midnight pillow.
But if thy love were ever like to mine—
As sure I think did never man love so—
How many actions most ridiculous
Hast thou been drawn to by thy fantasy? 29

CORIN
Into a thousand that I have forgotten.

SILVIUS
O, thou didst then never love so heartily!

6 weaker vessel i.e., woman. (See 1 Peter 3:7.) **doublet and hose** close-fitting jacket and breeches; typical male attire **11 cross** (1) burden (2) coin having on it a figure of a cross **29 fantasy** love imaginings

If thou rememberest not the slightest folly
That ever love did make thee run into,
Thou hast not loved.
Or if thou hast not sat as I do now,
Wearing thy hearer in thy mistress' praise, 36
Thou hast not loved.
Or if thou hast not broke from company
Abruptly, as my passion now makes me,
Thou hast not loved.
O Phoebe, Phoebe, Phoebe! *Exit.*

ROSALIND
Alas, poor shepherd! Searching of thy wound, 42
I have by hard adventure found mine own. 43

TOUCHSTONE And I mine. I remember, when I was in
love I broke my sword upon a stone and bid him take
that for coming a-night to Jane Smile; and I remember 46
the kissing of her batler and the cow's dugs that her 47
pretty chapped hands had milked; and I remember the
wooing of a peascod instead of her, from whom I took 49
two cods and, giving her them again, said with weep- 50
ing tears, "Wear these for my sake." We that are true
lovers run into strange capers; but as all is mortal in 52
nature, so is all nature in love mortal in folly. 53

ROSALIND Thou speak'st wiser than thou art ware of. 54

TOUCHSTONE Nay, I shall ne'er be ware of mine own wit till I break my shins against it.

ROSALIND
Jove, Jove! This shepherd's passion
Is much upon my fashion. 58

TOUCHSTONE
And mine, but it grows something stale with me. 59

CELIA
I pray you, one of you question yond man

36 Wearing wearing out, or wearying **42 Searching of** probing **43 hard adventure** bad luck **46 a-night** by night **47 batler** club or bat for beating clothes in process of washing. **dugs** udder **49 peascod** pea pod. (Regarded as a lucky gift by rustic lovers.) **whom** i.e., which (referring to the whole pea plant) **50 her** i.e., the pea plant **52 mortal** subject to death **53 mortal** extreme **54 ware** aware (but Touchstone plays upon the meaning "wary") **58 upon** after, according to **59 something** somewhat

If he for gold will give us any food.
I faint almost to death.

TOUCHSTONE Holla: you, clown!

ROSALIND
Peace, Fool! He's not thy kinsman.

CORIN Who calls?

TOUCHSTONE
Your betters, sir.

CORIN Else are they very wretched.

ROSALIND
Peace, I say.—Good even to you, friend.

CORIN
And to you, gentle sir, and to you all.

ROSALIND
I prithee, shepherd, if that love or gold
Can in this desert place buy entertainment,
Bring us where we may rest ourselves and feed.
Here's a young maid with travel much oppressed,
And faints for succor.

CORIN Fair sir, I pity her
And wish, for her sake more than for mine own,
My fortunes were more able to relieve her;
But I am shepherd to another man
And do not shear the fleeces that I graze.
My master is of churlish disposition,
And little recks to find the way to heaven
By doing deeds of hospitality.
Besides, his cote, his flocks, and bounds of feed
Are now on sale, and at our sheepcote now,
By reason of his absence, there is nothing
That you will feed on. But what is, come see,
And in my voice most welcome shall you be.

ROSALIND
What is he that shall buy his flock and pasture?

62 clown yokel. (But Rosalind uses the word as it applies to Touchstone.) **65 even** evening, i.e., afternoon **68 desert** uninhabited. **entertainment** hospitality, provision **71 for succor** for lack of succor, i.e., food **75 do . . . fleeces** i.e., do not obtain the profits from the flock **76 churlish** niggardly, miserly **77 recks** cares, reckons **79 cote** cottage. **bounds of feed** limits within which he has the right of pasturage **83 in my voice** insofar as I have authority to speak **84 What** who

CORIN
That young swain that you saw here but erewhile,
That little cares for buying anything.

ROSALIND
I pray thee, if it stand with honesty,
Buy thou the cottage, pasture, and the flock,
And thou shalt have to pay for it of us.

CELIA
And we will mend thy wages. I like this place
And willingly could waste my time in it.

CORIN
Assuredly the thing is to be sold.
Go with me. If you like upon report
The soil, the profit, and this kind of life,
I will your very faithful feeder be
And buy it with your gold right suddenly. *Exeunt.*

✣

2.5 *Enter Amiens, Jaques, and others.* [*A table is set out.*]

Song.

AMIENS
Under the greenwood tree
Who loves to lie with me,
And turn his merry note
Unto the sweet bird's throat,
Come hither, come hither, come hither.
Here shall he see
No enemy
But winter and rough weather.

JAQUES More, more, I prithee, more.

AMIENS It will make you melancholy, Monsieur Jaques.

JAQUES I thank it. More, I prithee, more. I can suck mel-

85 erewhile a short time since **87 stand** be consistent **89 have to pay** have the money **90 mend** improve **91 waste** spend **95 feeder** servant **96 right suddenly** without delay

2.5. Location: The forest.
2 Who anyone who **3 turn** attune, adapt **4 throat** voice

ancholy out of a song as a weasel sucks eggs. More, I
prithee, more.

AMIENS My voice is ragged. I know I cannot please you. 14

JAQUES I do not desire you to please me, I do desire you
to sing. Come, more, another stanzo. Call you 'em
"stanzos"?

AMIENS What you will, Monsieur Jaques.

JAQUES Nay, I care not for their names; they owe me 19
nothing. Will you sing? 20

AMIENS More at your request than to please myself.

JAQUES Well then, if ever I thank any man, I'll thank you;
but that they call "compliment" is like th' encounter 23
of two dog-apes, and when a man thanks me heartily, 24
methinks I have given him a penny and he renders
me the beggarly thanks. Come, sing; and you that will 26
not, hold your tongues.

AMIENS Well, I'll end the song.—Sirs, cover the while; 28
the Duke will drink under this tree.—He hath been all
this day to look you. [*Food and drink are set out.*] 30

JAQUES And I have been all this day to avoid him. He
is too disputable for my company. I think of as many 32
matters as he, but I give heaven thanks and make no
boast of them. Come, warble, come.

Song.

AMIENS [*Sings*]

Who doth ambition shun
And loves to live i' the sun, 36
Seeking the food he eats
And pleased with what he gets,
All together here.
Come hither, come hither, come hither.
Here shall he see
No enemy
But winter and rough weather.

14 ragged hoarse, rough **19–20 they owe me nothing** (Jaques speaks of names as of something valuable only when written as signatures to a bond of indebtedness.) **23 that** what. **"compliment"** formal politeness **24 dog-apes** dog-faced baboons **26 beggarly** effusive, like the thanks of a beggar **28 cover the while** set the table for a meal meanwhile **30 to look** looking for **32 disputable** inclined to dispute **36 live i' the sun** dwell in the open air, without the cares of the court

JAQUES I'll give you a verse to this note that I made yesterday in despite of my invention.

AMIENS And I'll sing it.

JAQUES Thus it goes:

If it do come to pass
That any man turn ass,
Leaving his wealth and ease,
A stubborn will to please,
Ducdame, ducdame, ducdame.
Here shall he see
Gross fools as he,
An if he will come to me.

AMIENS What's that "ducdame"?

JAQUES 'Tis a Greek invocation, to call fools into a circle. I'll go sleep, if I can; if I cannot, I'll rail against all the firstborn of Egypt.

AMIENS And I'll go seek the Duke. His banquet is prepared. *Exeunt [separately].*

2.6 *Enter Orlando and Adam.*

ADAM Dear master, I can go no further. O, I die for

43 note tune **44 in . . . invention** although I lack imagination; or, without even using my imagination **51 Ducdame** (Unexplained. One possible suggestion is that it is a corruption of the gypsy words *dukrā mē,* meaning "I foretell," "I tell fortunes or prophesy"; therefore, as the call of a gypsy fortuneteller at fairs, it is a "Greek" [or sharper's] invocation. This also renders the allusion to the firstborn of Egypt intelligible, since the firstborn Duke is banished and in the condition of a gypsy.) **58 firstborn of Egypt** (In Exodus 12:28–33, the firstborn of Egypt are slain by the Lord to achieve the release of the Jews. Perhaps Jaques ironically threatens to rail against the firstborn because of their role in the exile of Moses and his followers into the wilderness, which seems similar to the exile of Duke Senior and his men in the forest; or perhaps he intends to rail against the firstborn because of the "great cry" that was heard in Egypt following their slaughter, a cry that would prevent sleep.) **59 banquet** wine and dessert after dinner. (This repast, now prepared on stage, seemingly is to remain there during the short following scene.)

2.6. Location: The forest. The scene is continuous. By convention we understand that Adam and Orlando are in a different part of the forest and do not "see" the table left onstage.

food! Here lie I down and measure out my grave.
Farewell, kind master. [*He lies down.*]

ORLANDO Why, how now, Adam? No greater heart in
thee? Live a little, comfort a little, cheer thyself a little. 5
If this uncouth forest yield anything savage, I will ei- 6
ther be food for it or bring it for food to thee. Thy
conceit is nearer death than thy powers. For my sake 8
be comfortable; hold death awhile at the arm's end. I 9
will here be with thee presently, and if I bring thee not
something to eat, I will give thee leave to die; but if
thou diest before I come, thou art a mocker of my labor. Well said! Thou look'st cheerly, and I'll be with 13
thee quickly. Yet thou liest in the bleak air. Come, I 14
will bear thee to some shelter; and thou shalt not die
for lack of a dinner, if there live anything in this desert. [*He picks up Adam.*] Cheerly, good Adam! *Exeunt.*

2.7 *Enter Duke Senior and Lords, like outlaws.*

DUKE SENIOR
I think he be transformed into a beast,
For I can nowhere find him like a man.

FIRST LORD
My lord, he is but even now gone hence.
Here was he merry, hearing of a song.

DUKE SENIOR
If he, compact of jars, grow musical, 5
We shall have shortly discord in the spheres. 6
Go, seek him, tell him I would speak with him.

Enter Jaques.

FIRST LORD
He saves my labor by his own approach.

5 comfort comfort yourself **6 uncouth** strange, wild **8 conceit** thought, imagination **9 comfortable** comforted **13 Well said** well done **14 Yet** still

2.7. Location: The forest; the scene is continuous. (A light repast, set out for the Duke in 2.5, has remained onstage during 2.6.)
5 compact of jars composed of discords **6 the spheres** the concentric spheres of the Ptolemaic solar system (which, by their movement, were thought to produce harmonious music)

DUKE SENIOR
Why, how now, monsieur, what a life is this,
That your poor friends must woo your company?
What, you look merrily!

JAQUES
A fool, a fool! I met a fool i' the forest,
A motley fool. A miserable world! 13
As I do live by food, I met a fool,
Who laid him down and basked him in the sun,
And railed on Lady Fortune in good terms,
In good set terms, and yet a motley fool. 17
"Good morrow, Fool," quoth I. "No, sir," quoth he,
"Call me not fool till heaven hath sent me fortune." 19
And then he drew a dial from his poke 20
And, looking on it with lackluster eye,
Says very wisely, "It is ten o'clock.
Thus we may see," quoth he, "how the world wags. 23
'Tis but an hour ago since it was nine,
And after one hour more 'twill be eleven;
And so from hour to hour we ripe and ripe,
And then from hour to hour we rot and rot,
And thereby hangs a tale." When I did hear
The motley fool thus moral on the time, 29
My lungs began to crow like Chanticleer 30
That fools should be so deep-contemplative,
And I did laugh sans intermission 32
An hour by his dial. O noble fool!
A worthy fool! Motley's the only wear. 34

DUKE SENIOR What fool is this?

JAQUES
O worthy fool! One that hath been a courtier
And says if ladies be but young and fair
They have the gift to know it. And in his brain,
Which is as dry as the remainder biscuit 39

13 motley wearing motley, the parti-colored dress of the clown or professional jester **17 set** carefully composed **19 Call . . . fortune** (An allusion to the proverb "Fortune favors fools.") **20 dial** portable sundial. **poke** pouch or pocket **23 wags** goes **29 moral** moralize **30 crow** i.e., laugh merrily. **Chanticleer** a rooster **32 sans** without **34 only wear** only thing worth wearing **39 dry** (According to Elizabethan physiology, a dry brain was marked by a strong memory but a slow wit.) **remainder** remaining

After a voyage, he hath strange places crammed
With observation, the which he vents
In mangled forms. O, that I were a fool!
I am ambitious for a motley coat.

DUKE SENIOR
Thou shalt have one.

JAQUES
It is my only suit,
Provided that you weed your better judgments
Of all opinion that grows rank in them
That I am wise. I must have liberty
Withal, as large a charter as the wind,
To blow on whom I please, for so fools have.
And they that are most gallèd with my folly,
They most must laugh. And why, sir, must they so?
The "why" is plain as way to parish church:
He that a fool doth very wisely hit
Doth very foolishly, although he smart,
Not to seem senseless of the bob. If not,
The wise man's folly is anatomized
Even by the squandering glances of the fool.
Invest me in my motley; give me leave
To speak my mind, and I will through and through
Cleanse the foul body of th' infected world,
If they will patiently receive my medicine.

DUKE SENIOR
Fie on thee! I can tell what thou wouldst do.

JAQUES
What, for a counter, would I do but good?

DUKE SENIOR
Most mischievous foul sin, in chiding sin.
For thou thyself hast been a libertine,
As sensual as the brutish sting itself;

40 places (1) storage places (2) commonplaces, i.e., familiar ideas and quotations **44 suit** (1) request (2) suit of clothes **46 rank** wild **48 charter** license, privilege **50 gallèd** chafed, rubbed on a sore spot **53 He . . . hit** he whom a fool wittily attacks **54 Doth** acts. **smart** feels the sting **55 senseless of the bob** unaware of the jibe, taunt. **If not** otherwise **56 anatomized** dissected, revealed openly **57 squandering glances** random hits **58 Invest** dress **63 counter** (Type of a thing of no intrinsic value, a metal disk used in counting.) **65 libertine** one lacking moral restraint **66 brutish sting** carnal impulse, appetite

And all th' embossèd sores and headed evils 67
That thou with license of free foot hast caught 68
Wouldst thou disgorge into the general world. 69
JAQUES Why, who cries out on pride 70
That can therein tax any private party? 71
Doth it not flow as hugely as the sea,
Till that the weary very means do ebb? 73
What woman in the city do I name,
When that I say the city woman bears 75
The cost of princes on unworthy shoulders? 76
Who can come in and say that I mean her,
When such a one as she, such is her neighbor?
Or what is he of basest function 79
That says his bravery is not on my cost, 80
Thinking that I mean him, but therein suits 81
His folly to the mettle of my speech? 82
There then, how then? What then? Let me see wherein
My tongue hath wronged him. If it do him right, 84
Then he hath wronged himself. If he be free, 85
Why then my taxing like a wild goose flies,
Unclaimed of any man.—But who comes here?

Enter Orlando [*with his sword drawn*].

ORLANDO
Forbear, and eat no more.
JAQUES Why, I have eat none yet. 88
ORLANDO
Nor shalt not, till necessity be served.
JAQUES
Of what kind should this cock come of? 90

67 embossèd swollen, tumid. **headed evils** diseases and sores that have come to a head **68 license . . . foot** the licentious freedom of a libertine **69 disgorge** discharge, vomit **70 pride** i.e., extravagance **71 tax** blame, accuse. **any private party** i.e., only some individual **73 Till . . . ebb** until the ostentation finally subsides, having exhausted what fed it (?). (There are many conjectures, such as *wearer's very means*.) **75 the city woman** the typical citizen's wife **76 The cost of princes** i.e., clothes rich enough to adorn a prince **79 basest function** lowest position in society **80 That . . . cost** who says his finery is not bought at my expense (and is therefore none of my business) **81 suits** (1) fits (2) dresses **82 mettle** substance, contents **84 right** justice (i.e., if I have described him accurately) **85 wronged himself** (by calling attention to the accuracy of my description). **free** i.e., blameless **88 eat** eaten. (Pronounced "et.") **90 cock** fighting cock (i.e., aggressive person)

DUKE SENIOR
Art thou thus boldened, man, by thy distress,
Or else a rude despiser of good manners,
That in civility thou seem'st so empty?
ORLANDO
You touched my vein at first. The thorny point 94
Of bare distress hath ta'en from me the show
Of smooth civility; yet am I inland bred 96
And know some nurture. But forbear, I say. 97
He dies that touches any of this fruit
Till I and my affairs are answerèd. 99
JAQUES
An you will not be answered with reason, I must die. 100
DUKE SENIOR
What would you have? Your gentleness shall force
More than your force move us to gentleness.
ORLANDO
I almost die for food, and let me have it!
DUKE SENIOR
Sit down and feed, and welcome to our table.
ORLANDO
Speak you so gently? Pardon me, I pray you.
I thought that all things had been savage here,
And therefore put I on the countenance
Of stern commandment. But whate'er you are
That in this desert inaccessible,
Under the shade of melancholy boughs,
Lose and neglect the creeping hours of time;
If ever you have looked on better days,
If ever been where bells have knolled to church, 113
If ever sat at any good man's feast,
If ever from your eyelids wiped a tear
And know what 'tis to pity and be pitied,
Let gentleness my strong enforcement be,
In the which hope I blush and hide my sword.
[*He sheathes his sword.*]
DUKE SENIOR
True is it that we have seen better days,

94 vein condition, situation. **at first** i.e., in what you first suggested **96 inland bred** i.e., raised in civilized society, in the center of civilization rather than on the outskirts **97 nurture** education, training **99 answerèd** satisfied **100 An** if **113 knolled** rung

And have with holy bell been knolled to church,
And sat at good men's feasts, and wiped our eyes
Of drops that sacred pity hath engendered;
And therefore sit you down in gentleness,
And take upon command what help we have 124
That to your wanting may be ministered. 125

ORLANDO
Then but forbear your food a little while,
Whiles, like a doe, I go to find my fawn
And give it food. There is an old poor man
Who after me hath many a weary step
Limped in pure love. Till he be first sufficed,
Oppressed with two weak evils, age and hunger, 131
I will not touch a bit.

DUKE SENIOR Go find him out,
And we will nothing waste till you return. 133

ORLANDO
I thank ye; and be blest for your good comfort!
[*Exit*.]

DUKE SENIOR
Thou seest we are not all alone unhappy.
This wide and universal theater
Presents more woeful pageants than the scene
Wherein we play in.

JAQUES All the world's a stage,
And all the men and women merely players.
They have their exits and their entrances,
And one man in his time plays many parts,
His acts being seven ages. At first the infant,
Mewling and puking in the nurse's arms. 143
Then the whining schoolboy, with his satchel
And shining morning face, creeping like snail
Unwillingly to school. And then the lover,
Sighing like furnace, with a woeful ballad
Made to his mistress' eyebrow. Then a soldier,
Full of strange oaths and bearded like the pard, 149
Jealous in honor, sudden, and quick in quarrel, 150

124 upon command for the asking **125 wanting** need **131 weak** causing weakness **133 waste** consume **143 Mewling** crying **149 bearded . . . pard** having bristling mustaches like the panther's or leopard's whiskers **150 Jealous in honor** quick to anger in matters of honor. **sudden** rash

Seeking the bubble reputation
Even in the cannon's mouth. And then the justice,
In fair round belly with good capon lined,
With eyes severe and beard of formal cut,
Full of wise saws and modern instances;
And so he plays his part. The sixth age shifts
Into the lean and slippered pantaloon,
With spectacles on nose and pouch on side,
His youthful hose, well saved, a world too wide
For his shrunk shank; and his big manly voice,
Turning again toward childish treble, pipes
And whistles in his sound. Last scene of all,
That ends this strange eventful history,
Is second childishness and mere oblivion,
Sans teeth, sans eyes, sans taste, sans everything.

Enter Orlando, with Adam.

DUKE SENIOR
Welcome. Set down your venerable burden
And let him feed.
ORLANDO I thank you most for him. [*He sets down Adam.*]
ADAM So had you need.
I scarce can speak to thank you for myself.
DUKE SENIOR
Welcome, fall to. I will not trouble you
As yet to question you about your fortunes.
Give us some music, and, good cousin, sing.
[*They eat, while Orlando and Duke Senior converse apart.*]

Song.

AMIENS
Blow, blow, thou winter wind,
Thou art not so unkind
As man's ingratitude;
Thy tooth is not so keen,

153 capon a rooster castrated to make the flesh more tender for eating (and often presented to judges as a bribe) **155 saws** sayings. **modern instances** commonplace illustrations **157 pantaloon** ridiculous, enfeebled old man. (A stock type in Italian comedy.) **160 shank** lower leg **162 his** its **164 mere oblivion** total forgetfulness

Because thou art not seen,
Although thy breath be rude. 179
Heigh-ho, sing heigh-ho, unto the green holly. 180
Most friendship is feigning, most loving mere folly.
Then heigh-ho, the holly!
This life is most jolly.

Freeze, freeze, thou bitter sky,
That dost not bite so nigh 185
As benefits forgot;
Though thou the waters warp, 187
Thy sting is not so sharp
As friend remembered not.
Heigh-ho, sing heigh-ho, unto the green holly.
Most friendship is feigning, most loving mere folly.
Then heigh-ho, the holly!
This life is most jolly.

DUKE SENIOR
If that you were the good Sir Rowland's son,
As you have whispered faithfully you were
And as mine eye doth his effigies witness 196
Most truly limned and living in your face, 197
Be truly welcome hither. I am the duke
That loved your father. The residue of your fortune, 199
Go to my cave and tell me.—Good old man,
Thou art right welcome as thy master is.—
Support him by the arm. Give me your hand,
And let me all your fortunes understand. *Exeunt.* 203

179 rude rough **180 holly** (An emblem of mirth.) **185 nigh** near (to the heart) **187 warp** freeze **196 effigies** likeness, portrait **197 limned** painted, portrayed **199 The . . . fortune** the rest of your adventure **203 s.d. Exeunt** (The table must be removed at this point.)

3.1 *Enter Duke* [*Frederick*], *Lords, and Oliver.*

DUKE FREDERICK

Not see him since? Sir, sir, that cannot be.
But were I not the better part made mercy, 2
I should not seek an absent argument 3
Of my revenge, thou present. But look to it: 4
Find out thy brother, wheresoe'er he is;
Seek him with candle; bring him dead or living 6
Within this twelvemonth, or turn thou no more 7
To seek a living in our territory.
Thy lands and all things that thou dost call thine
Worth seizure do we seize into our hands,
Till thou canst quit thee by thy brother's mouth 11
Of what we think against thee.

OLIVER

O, that Your Highness knew my heart in this!
I never loved my brother in my life.

DUKE FREDERICK

More villain thou.—Well, push him out of doors,
And let my officers of such a nature 16
Make an extent upon his housc and lands. 17
Do this expediently, and turn him going. *Exeunt.* 18

✤

3.2 *Enter Orlando* [*with a paper*].

ORLANDO

Hang there, my verse, in witness of my love;
And thou, thrice-crownèd queen of night, survey 2
With thy chaste eye, from thy pale sphere above,

3.1. Location: Duke Frederick's court.
2 better greater. **made** made of **3 argument** subject (i.e., I would not seek revenge on Orlando) **4 thou present** i.e., with you here to feed my revenge **6 Seek . . . candle** (See Luke 15:8.) **7 turn** return **11 quit** acquit. **by . . . mouth** i.e., by Orlando's direct testimony **16 of such a nature** i.e., who attend to such duties **17 extent** writ of seizure
18 expediently expeditiously. **turn him going** send him packing

3.2. Location: The forest.
2 thrice-crownèd queen i.e., Diana in the three aspects of her divinity: as Luna or Cynthia, goddess of the moon; as Diana, goddess on earth; and as Hecate or Proserpina, goddess in the lower world

Thy huntress' name that my full life doth sway.
O Rosalind! These trees shall be my books,
And in their barks my thoughts I'll character,
That every eye which in this forest looks
Shall see thy virtue witnessed everywhere.
Run, run, Orlando, carve on every tree
The fair, the chaste, and unexpressive she. *Exit.*

Enter Corin and [*Touchstone the*] *Clown.*

CORIN And how like you this shepherd's life, Master Touchstone?

TOUCHSTONE Truly, shepherd, in respect of itself, it is a good life; but in respect that it is a shepherd's life, it is naught. In respect that it is solitary, I like it very well; but in respect that it is private, it is a very vile life. Now in respect it is in the fields, it pleaseth me well; but in respect it is not in the court, it is tedious. As it is a spare life, look you, it fits my humor well; but as there is no more plenty in it, it goes much against my stomach. Hast any philosophy in thee, shepherd?

CORIN No more but that I know the more one sickens the worse at ease he is; and that he that wants money, means, and content is without three good friends; that the property of rain is to wet and fire to burn; that good pasture makes fat sheep and that a great cause of the night is lack of the sun; that he that hath learned no wit by nature nor art may complain of good breeding or comes of a very dull kindred.

TOUCHSTONE Such a one is a natural philosopher. Wast ever in court, shepherd?

CORIN No, truly.

TOUCHSTONE Then thou art damned.

CORIN Nay, I hope.

TOUCHSTONE Truly, thou art damned, like an ill-roasted egg, all on one side.

CORIN For not being at court? Your reason.

4 Thy huntress' i.e., Rosalind's, who is here thought of as a chaste huntress accompanying Diana, patroness of the hunt. **sway** control **6 character** inscribe **10 unexpressive** inexpressible **13 in respect of itself** considered in and for itself **15 naught** vile, wicked **19 spare** frugal. **humor** temperament **28 wit** wisdom. **art** study **28–29 complain . . . breeding** lament the lack of good breeding

TOUCHSTONE Why, if thou never wast at court, thou never sawst good manners; if thou never sawst good manners, then thy manners must be wicked; and wickedness is sin, and sin is damnation. Thou art in a parlous state, shepherd.

CORIN Not a whit, Touchstone. Those that are good manners at the court are as ridiculous in the country as the behavior of the country is most mockable at the court. You told me you salute not at the court but you kiss your hands; that courtesy would be uncleanly, if courtiers were shepherds.

TOUCHSTONE Instance, briefly; come, instance.

CORIN Why, we are still handling our ewes, and their fells you know are greasy.

TOUCHSTONE Why, do not your courtier's hands sweat? And is not the grease of a mutton as wholesome as the sweat of a man? Shallow, shallow. A better instance, I say; come.

CORIN Besides, our hands are hard.

TOUCHSTONE Your lips will feel them the sooner. Shallow again. A more sounder instance, come.

CORIN And they are often tarred over with the surgery of our sheep; and would you have us kiss tar? The courtier's hands are perfumed with civet.

TOUCHSTONE Most shallow man! Thou worms' meat, in respect of a good piece of flesh indeed! Learn of the wise, and perpend: civet is of a baser birth than tar, the very uncleanly flux of a cat. Mend the instance, shepherd.

CORIN You have too courtly a wit for me. I'll rest.

TOUCHSTONE Wilt thou rest damned? God help thee, shallow man! God make incision in thee! Thou art raw.

39, 40 manners (1) etiquette (2) morals **42 parlous** perilous **46–47 but you kiss** without kissing **49 Instance** proof **50 still** always **51 fells** skins with the wool, or fleeces **59 tarred over** anointed with tar on their cuts and sores **61 civet** (A perfume derived from the civet cat, as Touchstone points out.) **62 worms' meat** food for worms, i.e., subject to decay of the flesh **63 respect of** comparison with **64 perpend** reflect, consider **65 flux** secretion. **Mend** improve **69 incision** a cut, perhaps for the purpose of letting blood (here, to let out folly); or for seasoning as raw meat is scored and salted before cooking **70 raw** inexperienced (with a play on "sore," requiring surgery)

CORIN Sir, I am a true laborer: I earn that I eat, get that 71
I wear, owe no man hate, envy no man's happiness,
glad of other men's good, content with my harm, and 73
the greatest of my pride is to see my ewes graze and
my lambs suck.

TOUCHSTONE That is another simple sin in you, to bring
the ewes and the rams together and to offer to get your 77
living by the copulation of cattle; to be bawd to a bell- 78
wether, and to betray a she-lamb of a twelvemonth to
a crooked-pated old cuckoldly ram, out of all reason- 80
able match. If thou beest not damned for this, the devil
himself will have no shepherds; I cannot see else how
thou shouldst scape. 83

CORIN Here comes young Master Ganymede, my new
mistress's brother.

Enter Rosalind [*with a paper, reading*].

ROSALIND

"From the east to western Ind, 86
No jewel is like Rosalind.
Her worth, being mounted on the wind,
Through all the world bears Rosalind.
All the pictures fairest lined 90
Are but black to Rosalind. 91
Let no face be kept in mind
But the fair of Rosalind."

TOUCHSTONE I'll rhyme you so eight years together, 94
dinners and suppers and sleeping hours excepted. It 95
is the right butter-women's rank to market. 96

ROSALIND Out, Fool!

TOUCHSTONE For a taste:
If a hart do lack a hind,
Let him seek out Rosalind.
If the cat will after kind, 101

71 that what **73 content . . . harm** patient with my ill fortune **77 offer** undertake **78 cattle** livestock **80 crooked-pated** with crooked horns. **cuckoldly** i.e., horned like a cuckold, or husband of an unfaithful wife. **out of** contrary to **83 scape** escape **86 Ind** Indies **90 lined** drawn **91 black** dark-complexioned. (Thought to be ugly.) **94 together** without stop **95–96 It is . . . market** i.e., the rhymes, all alike, follow each other precisely like a line of butter-women or dairywomen jogging along to market **101 after kind** follow its natural instinct

So be sure will Rosalind.
Wintered garments must be lined,
So must slender Rosalind.
They that reap must sheaf and bind;
Then to cart with Rosalind.
Sweetest nut hath sourest rind;
Such a nut is Rosalind.
He that sweetest rose will find
Must find love's prick and Rosalind.

This is the very false gallop of verses. Why do you infect yourself with them?

ROSALIND Peace, you dull fool! I found them on a tree.

TOUCHSTONE Truly, the tree yields bad fruit.

ROSALIND I'll graft it with you, and then I shall graft it with a medlar. Then it will be the earliest fruit i' the country; for you'll be rotten ere you be half ripe, and that's the right virtue of the medlar.

TOUCHSTONE You have said; but whether wisely or no, let the forest judge.

Enter Celia, with a writing.

ROSALIND Peace, here comes my sister, reading. Stand aside.

CELIA [*Reads*]

"Why should this a desert be?
  For it is unpeopled? No!
Tongues I'll hang on every tree,
  That shall civil sayings show:
Some, how brief the life of man
  Runs his erring pilgrimage,
That the stretching of a span
  Buckles in his sum of age;

103 Wintered prepared for winter **105 sheaf and bind** tie in a bundle **106 to cart** (1) onto the harvest cart (2) onto the cart used to carry delinquent women through the streets, exposing them to public ridicule **110 prick** thorn. (With bawdy suggestion, as elsewhere in Touchstone's verses: *will after kind,* etc.) **111 false gallop** canter **115 you** (with a pun on *yew*) **116 medlar** a fruit like a small brown-skinned apple that is eaten when it starts to decay (with a pun on *meddler*) **118 right virtue** true quality **126 civil sayings** maxims of civilized life **128 his erring** its wandering **129 That . . . span** so that the distance across an open-spread hand **130 Buckles in** encompasses

Some, of violated vows
  Twixt the souls of friend and friend;
But upon the fairest boughs,
  Or at every sentence end,
Will I 'Rosalinda' write,
  Teaching all that read to know
The quintessence of every sprite 137
  Heaven would in little show. 138
Therefore heaven Nature charged
  That one body should be filled
With all graces wide-enlarged. 141
  Nature presently distilled
Helen's cheek, but not her heart, 143
  Cleopatra's majesty,
Atalanta's better part, 145
  Sad Lucretia's modesty. 146
Thus Rosalind of many parts
  By heavenly synod was devised, 148
Of many faces, eyes, and hearts,
  To have the touches dearest prized. 150
Heaven would that she these gifts should have,
And I to live and die her slave."

ROSALIND O most gentle Jupiter, what tedious homily 153
of love have you wearied your parishioners withal,
and never cried, "Have patience, good people!"
CELIA How now? Back, friends. Shepherd, go off a lit- 156
tle. Go with him, sirrah. 157

137 quintessence highest perfection. (Literally, the fifth essence or element of the medieval alchemists, purer even than fire.) **sprite** spirit
138 in little in small space, i.e., in one person, Rosalind. (Alludes probably to the idea of man as the microcosm; the heavenly bodies would be composed of quintessence, which is here thought of as the supreme quality of a person.) **141 wide-enlarged** widely distributed (i.e., that had been spread through the world but now are concentrated in Rosalind)
143 Helen's . . . heart i.e., the beauty of Helen of Troy but not her false heart **145 Atalanta's better part** i.e., her fleetness of foot, not her scornfulness and greed. (She refused to marry any man who was unable to defeat her in a foot race and, when challenged by Hippomenes, lost to him because Hippomenes dropped in her way three apples of the Hesperides.) **146 Lucretia** honorable Roman lady raped by Tarquin (whose story Shakespeare tells in *The Rape of Lucrece*) **148 synod** assembly
150 touches traits **153 Jupiter** (Often emended to *pulpiter*.) **156 Back** i.e., move back, away. (Addressed to Corin and Touchstone.) **157 sirrah** (Form of address to inferiors; here, Touchstone.)

TOUCHSTONE Come, shepherd, let us make an honorable retreat, though not with bag and baggage, yet 159
with scrip and scrippage. *Exit* [*with Corin*]. 160

CELIA Didst thou hear these verses?

ROSALIND O, yes, I heard them all, and more too, for some of them had in them more feet than the verses would bear.

CELIA That's no matter. The feet might bear the verses.

ROSALIND Ay, but the feet were lame and could not
bear themselves without the verse and therefore stood 167
lamely in the verse.

CELIA But didst thou hear without wondering how thy name should be hanged and carved upon these trees?

ROSALIND I was seven of the nine days out of the won- 171
der before you came; for look here what I found on a 172
palm tree. I was never so berhymed since Pythagoras' 173
time, that I was an Irish rat, which I can hardly re- 174
member.

CELIA Trow you who hath done this? 176

ROSALIND Is it a man?

CELIA And a chain that you once wore about his neck. 178
Change you color?

ROSALIND I prithee, who?

CELIA O Lord, Lord, it is a hard matter for friends to 181
meet; but mountains may be removed with earth- 182
quakes and so encounter. 183

ROSALIND Nay, but who is it?

CELIA Is it possible?

ROSALIND Nay, I prithee now with most petitionary vehemence, tell me who it is.

CELIA O wonderful, wonderful, and most wonderful wonderful! And yet again wonderful, and after that,

159 bag and baggage i.e., equipment appropriate to a retreating army **160 scrip and scrippage** shepherd's pouch and its contents **167 without** (1) without the help of (2) outside **171–172 seven . . . wonder** (A reference to the common phrase "a nine days' wonder.") **173 Pythagoras** Greek philosopher credited with the doctrine of the transmigration of souls **174 that** when. **Irish rat** (Refers to a current belief that Irish enchanters could rhyme rats and other animals to death.) **176 Trow you** have you any idea **178 And a chain** i.e., and with a chain **181–183 friends . . . encounter** (A playful inversion of the proverb, "Friends may meet, but mountains never greet." Celia appears to be teasing Rosalind's eagerness to meet Orlando.) **removed with** moved by out of all whooping!

ROSALIND Good my complexion! Dost thou think, though I am caparisoned like a man, I have a doublet and hose in my disposition? One inch of delay more is a South Sea of discovery. I prithee, tell me who is it quickly, and speak apace. I would thou couldst stammer, that thou mightst pour this concealed man out of thy mouth, as wine comes out of a narrow-mouthed bottle, either too much at once or none at all. I prithee, take the cork out of thy mouth that I may drink thy tidings.

CELIA So you may put a man in your belly.

ROSALIND Is he of God's making? What manner of man? Is his head worth a hat, or his chin worth a beard?

CELIA Nay, he hath but a little beard.

ROSALIND Why, God will send more, if the man will be thankful. Let me stay the growth of his beard, if thou delay me not the knowledge of his chin.

CELIA It is young Orlando, that tripped up the wrestler's heels and your heart both in an instant.

ROSALIND Nay, but the devil take mocking. Speak sad brow and true maid.

CELIA I' faith, coz, 'tis he.

ROSALIND Orlando?

CELIA Orlando.

ROSALIND Alas the day, what shall I do with my doublet and hose? What did he when thou sawst him? What said he? How looked he? Wherein went he? What makes he here? Did he ask for me? Where remains he? How parted he with thee? And when shalt thou see him again? Answer me in one word.

CELIA You must borrow me Gargantua's mouth first;

190 out . . . whooping beyond all whooping, i.e., power to utter **191 Good my complexion** O my (feminine) temperament, my woman's curiosity **192 caparisoned** bedecked. (Usually said of a horse.) **194 a South Sea of discovery** i.e., as tedious as the long delays on exploratory voyages to the South Seas **201 belly** (1) stomach (2) womb **202 of God's making** i.e., a real man, not of his tailor's making **207 stay** wait for **211–212 sad . . . maid** seriously and truthfully **218 Wherein went he** in what clothes was he dressed **219 makes** does **222 Gargantua's mouth** (Gargantua is the giant of popular literature who, in Rabelais's novel, swallowed five pilgrims in a salad.)

'tis a word too great for any mouth of this age's size. To say ay and no to these particulars is more than to answer in a catechism.

ROSALIND But doth he know that I am in this forest and in man's apparel? Looks he as freshly as he did the day he wrestled?

CELIA It is as easy to count atomies as to resolve the propositions of a lover. But take a taste of my finding him, and relish it with good observance. I found him under a tree, like a dropped acorn.

ROSALIND It may well be called Jove's tree, when it drops forth such fruit.

CELIA Give me audience, good madam.

ROSALIND Proceed.

CELIA There lay he, stretched along, like a wounded knight.

ROSALIND Though it be pity to see such a sight, it well becomes the ground.

CELIA Cry "holla" to thy tongue, I prithee; it curvets unseasonably. He was furnished like a hunter.

ROSALIND O, ominous! He comes to kill my heart.

CELIA I would sing my song without a burden. Thou bring'st me out of tune.

ROSALIND Do you not know I am a woman? When I think, I must speak. Sweet, say on.

Enter Orlando and Jaques.

CELIA You bring me out.—Soft, comes he not here?

ROSALIND 'Tis he. Slink by, and note him.

[*They stand aside and listen.*]

JAQUES I thank you for your company, but, good faith, I had as lief have been myself alone.

ORLANDO And so had I; but yet, for fashion's sake, I thank you too for your society.

224–225 To . . . catechism to give even yes and no answers to these questions would take longer than to go through the catechism (i.e., the formal questioning used in the Church to teach the principles of faith)
229 atomies motes, specks of dirt **230 propositions** questions **231 relish it** heighten its pleasant taste. **observance** attention **233 Jove's tree** the oak **240 becomes** adorns **241 holla** stop. **curvets** prances
242 furnished equipped, dressed **243 heart** (with pun on *hart*)
244 burden undersong, bass part **244–245 Thou bring'st** you put

JAQUES God b' wi' you. Let's meet as little as we can.

ORLANDO I do desire we may be better strangers.

JAQUES I pray you, mar no more trees with writing love songs in their barks.

ORLANDO I pray you, mar no more of my verses with reading them ill-favoredly.

JAQUES Rosalind is your love's name?

ORLANDO Yes, just.

JAQUES I do not like her name.

ORLANDO There was no thought of pleasing you when she was christened.

JAQUES What stature is she of?

ORLANDO Just as high as my heart.

JAQUES You are full of pretty answers. Have you not been acquainted with goldsmiths' wives, and conned them out of rings?

ORLANDO Not so; but I answer you right painted cloth, from whence you have studied your questions.

JAQUES You have a nimble wit; I think 'twas made of Atalanta's heels. Will you sit down with me? And we two will rail against our mistress the world and all our misery.

ORLANDO I will chide no breather in the world but myself, against whom I know most faults.

JAQUES The worst fault you have is to be in love.

ORLANDO 'Tis a fault I will not change for your best virtue. I am weary of you.

JAQUES By my troth, I was seeking for a fool when I found you.

ORLANDO He is drowned in the brook. Look but in, and you shall see him.

JAQUES There I shall see mine own figure.

ORLANDO Which I take to be either a fool or a cipher.

JAQUES I'll tarry no longer with you. Farewell, good Seigneur Love.

254 God b' wi' you God be with you, i.e., good-bye **259 ill-favoredly** unsympathetically **261 just** just so **268 conned** memorized **269 rings** (Verses or "posies" were often inscribed in rings.) **270 right** true, perfect. **painted cloth** canvas painted with pictures and mottoes (frequently scriptural), hence a ready source of commonplaces **273 Atalanta's heels** (See above, l. 145, note.) **276 breather** living being **286 cipher** (1) nonentity (2) figure

ORLANDO I am glad of your departure. Adieu, good Monsieur Melancholy. [*Exit Jaques.*]

ROSALIND [*Aside to Celia*] I will speak to him like a saucy lackey and under that habit play the knave with him.—Do you hear, forester?

ORLANDO Very well. What would you?

ROSALIND I pray you, what is 't o'clock?

ORLANDO You should ask me what time o' day. There's no clock in the forest.

ROSALIND Then there is no true lover in the forest, else sighing every minute and groaning every hour would detect the lazy foot of Time as well as a clock.

ORLANDO And why not the swift foot of Time? Had not that been as proper?

ROSALIND By no means, sir. Time travels in divers paces with divers persons. I'll tell you who Time ambles withal, who Time trots withal, who Time gallops withal, and who he stands still withal.

ORLANDO I prithee, who doth he trot withal?

ROSALIND Marry, he trots hard with a young maid between the contract of her marriage and the day it is solemnized. If the interim be but a se'nnight, Time's pace is so hard that it seems the length of seven year.

ORLANDO Who ambles Time withal?

ROSALIND With a priest that lacks Latin and a rich man that hath not the gout, for the one sleeps easily because he cannot study and the other lives merrily because he feels no pain, the one lacking the burden of lean and wasteful learning, the other knowing no burden of heavy tedious penury. These Time ambles withal.

ORLANDO Who doth he gallop withal?

ROSALIND With a thief to the gallows, for though he go as softly as foot can fall, he thinks himself too soon there.

ORLANDO Who stays it still withal?

ROSALIND With lawyers in the vacation; for they sleep between term and term, and then they perceive not how Time moves.

292 habit guise **300 detect** reveal **305 withal** with **308 hard** slowly, with uneven pace **310 se'nnight** week **317 wasteful** making one waste away **321–322 go as softly** walk as slowly **326 term** court session

ORLANDO Where dwell you, pretty youth?

ROSALIND With this shepherdess, my sister; here in the skirts of the forest, like fringe upon a petticoat.

ORLANDO Are you native of this place?

ROSALIND As the coney that you see dwell where she is kindled.

ORLANDO Your accent is something finer than you could purchase in so removed a dwelling.

ROSALIND I have been told so of many. But indeed an old religious uncle of mine taught me to speak, who was in his youth an inland man, one that knew courtship too well, for there he fell in love. I have heard him read many lectures against it, and I thank God I am not a woman, to be touched with so many giddy offences as he hath generally taxed their whole sex withal.

ORLANDO Can you remember any of the principal evils that he laid to the charge of women?

ROSALIND There were none principal; they were all like one another as halfpence are, every one fault seeming monstrous till his fellow fault came to match it.

ORLANDO I prithee, recount some of them.

ROSALIND No, I will not cast away my physic but on those that are sick. There is a man haunts the forest that abuses our young plants with carving "Rosalind" on their barks, hangs odes upon hawthorns, and elegies on brambles, all, forsooth, deifying the name of Rosalind. If I could meet that fancymonger, I would give him some good counsel, for he seems to have the quotidian of love upon him.

ORLANDO I am he that is so love-shaked. I pray you, tell me your remedy.

ROSALIND There is none of my uncle's marks upon you. He taught me how to know a man in love, in which cage of rushes I am sure you are not prisoner.

ORLANDO What were his marks?

332 coney rabbit **333 kindled** littered, born **335 purchase** acquire. **removed** remote **337 religious** i.e., member of a religious order **338 inland** from a center of civilization **338–339 courtship** (1) wooing (2) knowledge of courtly manners **341 touched** tainted **355 fancymonger** dealer or advertiser of love **357 quotidian** fever recurring daily. (See *love-shaked,* l. 358). **362 cage of rushes** i.e., flimsy prison

ROSALIND A lean cheek, which you have not; a blue eye and sunken, which you have not; an unquestionable spirit, which you have not; a beard neglected, which you have not—but I pardon you for that, for simply your having in beard is a younger brother's revenue. Then your hose should be ungartered, your bonnet unbanded, your sleeve unbuttoned, your shoe untied, and everything about you demonstrating a careless desolation. But you are no such man; you are rather point-device in your accoutrements, as loving yourself, than seeming the lover of any other.

ORLANDO Fair youth, I would I could make thee believe I love.

ROSALIND Me believe it? You may as soon make her that you love believe it, which I warrant she is apter to do than to confess she does. That is one of the points in the which women still give the lie to their consciences. But in good sooth, are you he that hangs the verses on the trees wherein Rosalind is so admired?

ORLANDO I swear to thee, youth, by the white hand of Rosalind, I am that he, that unfortunate he.

ROSALIND But are you so much in love as your rhymes speak?

ORLANDO Neither rhyme nor reason can express how much.

ROSALIND Love is merely a madness and, I tell you, deserves as well a dark house and a whip as madmen do; and the reason why they are not so punished and cured is that the lunacy is so ordinary that the whippers are in love too. Yet I profess curing it by counsel.

ORLANDO Did you ever cure any so?

ROSALIND Yes, one, and in this manner. He was to imagine me his love, his mistress; and I set him every day to woo me. At which time would I, being but a

364 blue eye i.e., having dark circles **365 unquestionable** unwilling to converse **367–368 simply . . . revenue** what beard you have is like a younger brother's inheritance (i.e., small) **369–370 bonnet unbanded** hat lacking a band around the crown **373 point-device** faultless, correct **380 still** continually **381 good sooth** honest truth **390 merely** utterly **391 dark . . . whip** (The common treatment of lunatics.)

moonish youth, grieve, be effeminate, changeable, longing and liking, proud, fantastical, apish, shallow, inconstant, full of tears, full of smiles; for every passion something and for no passion truly anything, as boys and women are for the most part cattle of this color; would now like him, now loathe him; then entertain him, then forswear him; now weep for him, then spit at him; that I drave my suitor from his mad humor of love to a living humor of madness, which was to forswear the full stream of the world and to live in a nook merely monastic. And thus I cured him; and this way will I take upon me to wash your liver as clean as a sound sheep's heart, that there shall not be one spot of love in 't.

ORLANDO I would not be cured, youth.

ROSALIND I would cure you, if you would but call me Rosalind and come every day to my cote and woo me.

ORLANDO Now by the faith of my love, I will. Tell me where it is.

ROSALIND Go with me to it, and I'll show it you; and by the way you shall tell me where in the forest you live. Will you go?

ORLANDO With all my heart, good youth.

ROSALIND Nay, you must call me Rosalind.—Come, sister, will you go? *Exeunt.*

✤

3.3 *Enter* [*Touchstone the*] *Clown, Audrey; and Jaques* [*apart*].

TOUCHSTONE Come apace, good Audrey. I will fetch up your goats, Audrey. And how, Audrey, am I the man yet? Doth my simple feature content you?

AUDREY Your features, Lord warrant us! What features?

399 moonish changeable **406 drave** drove **406–407 mad . . . madness** mad fancy of love to a real madness **409 merely** utterly **410 liver** (Supposed seat of the emotions, especially love.) **415 cote** cottage **419 by** on

3.3. Location: The forest.
1 apace quickly **2 And how** i.e., what do you say **3 simple feature** plain appearance. (But Audrey does not understand.)

TOUCHSTONE I am here with thee and thy goats, as the most capricious poet, honest Ovid, was among the Goths.

JAQUES [*Aside*] O knowledge ill-inhabited, worse than Jove in a thatched house!

TOUCHSTONE When a man's verses cannot be understood, nor a man's good wit seconded with the forward child, understanding, it strikes a man more dead than a great reckoning in a little room. Truly, I would the gods had made thee poetical.

AUDREY I do not know what "poetical" is. Is it honest in deed and word? Is it a true thing?

TOUCHSTONE No, truly; for the truest poetry is the most feigning, and lovers are given to poetry, and what they swear in poetry may be said as lovers they do feign.

AUDREY Do you wish then that the gods had made me poetical?

TOUCHSTONE I do, truly; for thou swear'st to me thou art honest. Now, if thou wert a poet, I might have some hope thou didst feign.

AUDREY Would you not have me honest?

TOUCHSTONE No, truly, unless thou wert hard-favored; for honesty coupled to beauty is to have honey a sauce to sugar.

JAQUES [*Aside*] A material fool!

AUDREY Well, I am not fair, and therefore I pray the gods make me honest.

6 capricious witty, fanciful. (Derived from Latin *caper,* male goat; hence, "goatish, lascivious.") **7 Goths** (with pun on *goats;* the two words were pronounced alike) **8 ill-inhabited** ill-lodged **9 Jove . . . house** (An allusion to Ovid's *Metamorphoses* 8, containing the story of Jupiter and Mercury lodging disguised in the humble cottage of Baucis and Philemon.) **10–11 verses . . . understood** (Ovid's verses were misunderstood by the barbaric Goths among whom he lived in exile, just as Touchstone's wit is misunderstood by Audrey.) **11 seconded with** supported by **11–12 forward** precocious **13 great . . . room** exorbitant charge for refreshment or lodging in a cramped tavern room. (Some scholars see in this passage an allusion to the death of Christopher Marlowe, who was stabbed by Ingram Frysar at an inn in Deptford in a quarrel over a tavern reckoning, May 30, 1593.) **18 feigning** inventive, imaginative. (But Touchstone plays on the sense of "false, lying.") **19 may be said** i.e., it may be said **24 honest** chaste **25 feign** (1) pretend (2) desire **27 hard-favored** ugly **28 honesty** chastity **30 material** full of sense

TOUCHSTONE Truly, and to cast away honesty upon a foul slut were to put good meat into an unclean dish.

AUDREY I am not a slut, though I thank the gods I am foul.

TOUCHSTONE Well, praised be the gods for thy foulness! Sluttishness may come hereafter. But be it as it may be, I will marry thee, and to that end I have been with Sir Oliver Mar-text, the vicar of the next village, who hath promised to meet me in this place of the forest and to couple us.

JAQUES [*Aside*] I would fain see this meeting.

AUDREY Well, the gods give us joy!

TOUCHSTONE Amen. A man may, if he were of a fearful heart, stagger in this attempt; for here we have no temple but the wood, no assembly but horn-beasts. But what though? Courage! As horns are odious, they are necessary. It is said, "Many a man knows no end of his goods." Right! Many a man has good horns and knows no end of them. Well, that is the dowry of his wife; 'tis none of his own getting. Horns? Even so. Poor men alone? No, no, the noblest deer hath them as huge as the rascal. Is the single man therefore blessed? No; as a walled town is more worthier than a village, so is the forehead of a married man more honorable than the bare brow of a bachelor; and by how much defense is better than no skill, by so much is a horn more precious than to want.

Enter Sir Oliver Mar-text.

Here comes Sir Oliver. Sir Oliver Mar-text, you are well met. Will you dispatch us here under this tree, or shall we go with you to your chapel?

SIR OLIVER Is there none here to give the woman?

34 foul ugly **40 Sir** (Courtesy title for a clergyman.) **43 fain** gladly **46 stagger** hesitate **47 horn-beasts** (Alludes to the joke about cuckolds having horns.) **48 what though** what though it be so. **As** though **49 necessary** unavoidable **49–50 knows . . . goods** thinks there will be no end to his wealth **51 knows . . . them** i.e., doesn't realize he has pointed horns on his brow. **dowry** marriage gift **52 getting** (1) obtaining (2) begetting (since his wife's children will not be his) **54 rascal** deer that are lean and out of season **58 defense** the art of self-defense **59 than to want** i.e., than to be without a horn **61 dispatch us** finish off our business

TOUCHSTONE I will not take her on gift of any man.
SIR OLIVER Truly, she must be given, or the marriage is
not lawful.
JAQUES [*Advancing*] Proceed, proceed. I'll give her.
TOUCHSTONE Good even, good Master What-ye-call-'t.
How do you, sir? You are very well met. God 'ild you 69
for your last company. I am very glad to see you. Even
a toy in hand here, sir.—Nay, pray be covered. 71
JAQUES Will you be married, motley?
TOUCHSTONE As the ox hath his bow, sir, the horse his 73
curb, and the falcon her bells, so man hath his desires; 74
and as pigeons bill, so wedlock would be nibbling. 75
JAQUES And will you, being a man of your breeding,
be married under a bush like a beggar? Get you to 77
church, and have a good priest that can tell you what 78
marriage is. This fellow will but join you together as 79
they join wainscot; then one of you will prove a
shrunk panel and, like green timber, warp, warp.
TOUCHSTONE [*Aside*] I am not in the mind but I were 82
better to be married of him than of another, for he is 83
not like to marry me well; and not being well married,
it will be a good excuse for me hereafter to leave my
wife.
JAQUES Go thou with me, and let me counsel thee.
TOUCHSTONE Come, sweet Audrey. We must be married, or we must live in bawdry. Farewell, good Master Oliver; not

"O sweet Oliver, 91
O brave Oliver,
Leave me not behind thee";

but

"Wind away, 95
Begone, I say,

69 'ild you yield you, reward you **71 a toy in hand** a trifle to be attended to. **be covered** put on your hat, i.e., no need to show respect. (Perhaps said to Audrey, or perhaps to Jaques, who may have removed his hat in deference to the ceremony.) **73 bow** yoke **74 curb** chain or strap under the horse's jaw used to control it. **bells** (attached to a falcon's leg to warn its prey) **75 bill** peck **77 under a bush** i.e., by a "hedge-priest," an uneducated clergyman **78–79 tell . . . is** expound the obligations of marriage **82–83 I am . . . better** I do not know but that it would be better for me **83 of** by **91–97 O . . . thee** (Phrases from a current ballad.) **95 Wind** wander

I will not to wedding with thee."

[*Exeunt Jaques, Touchstone, and Audrey.*]

SIR OLIVER 'Tis no matter. Ne'er a fantastical knave of 98
them all shall flout me out of my calling. *Exit.*

✣

3.4 *Enter Rosalind and Celia.*

ROSALIND Never talk to me; I will weep.

CELIA Do, I prithee, but yet have the grace to consider that tears do not become a man.

ROSALIND But have I not cause to weep?

CELIA As good cause as one would desire; therefore weep.

ROSALIND His very hair is of the dissembling color. 7

CELIA Something browner than Judas's. Marry, his 8
kisses are Judas's own children. 9

ROSALIND I' faith, his hair is of a good color.

CELIA An excellent color. Your chestnut was ever the 11
only color.

ROSALIND And his kissing is as full of sanctity as the
touch of holy bread. 14

CELIA He hath bought a pair of cast lips of Diana. A 15
nun of winter's sisterhood kisses not more religiously; 16
the very ice of chastity is in them.

ROSALIND But why did he swear he would come this morning, and comes not?

CELIA Nay, certainly, there is no truth in him.

ROSALIND Do you think so?

CELIA Yes, I think he is not a pickpurse nor a horse-stealer, but for his verity in love, I do think him as

98 fantastical affected

3.4. Location: The forest.
7 the dissembling color i.e., reddish, traditionally the color of Judas's hair **8 Something** somewhat **9 Judas's own children** i.e., false, betraying **11 Your chestnut** i.e., this chestnut color that people talk about **14 holy bread** ordinary leavened bread which was blessed after the Eucharist and distributed to those who had not communed **15 cast** cast off, discarded, once belonging to; or, cast, molded. **Diana** goddess of chastity **16 of winter's sisterhood** i.e., devoted to barrenness and cold

concave as a covered goblet or a worm-eaten nut. 24
ROSALIND Not true in love?
CELIA Yes, when he is in, but I think he is not in.
ROSALIND You have heard him swear downright he
was.
CELIA "Was" is not "is." Besides, the oath of a lover is
no stronger than the word of a tapster; they are both
the confirmer of false reckonings. He attends here in 31
the forest on the Duke your father.
ROSALIND I met the Duke yesterday and had much
question with him. He asked me of what parentage I 34
was. I told him, of as good as he; so he laughed and let
me go. But what talk we of fathers, when there is such 36
a man as Orlando?
CELIA O, that's a brave man! He writes brave verses, 38
speaks brave words, swears brave oaths, and breaks
them bravely, quite traverse, athwart the heart of his 40
lover, as a puny tilter, that spurs his horse but on 41
one side, breaks his staff like a noble goose. But all's 42
brave that youth mounts and folly guides. Who comes
here?

Enter Corin.

CORIN
Mistress and master, you have oft inquired
After the shepherd that complained of love
Who you saw sitting by me on the turf,
Praising the proud disdainful shepherdess
That was his mistress.
CELIA Well, and what of him?
CORIN
If you will see a pageant truly played
Between the pale complexion of true love 51
And the red glow of scorn and proud disdain,

24 concave hollow. **covered goblet** i.e., an empty goblet. (The cover is on only when the goblet is empty.) **31 false reckonings** (Tapsters, or barkeeps, were notorious for inflating bills.) **34 question** conversation **36 what** why **38 brave** fine, excellent **40 traverse** across, awry. (A term from tilting, indicating a poorly aimed thrust.) **41 puny** inexperienced. (Literally, junior.) **but** only **42 noble goose** i.e., a goose-headed young nobleman **51 pale complexion** (Sighing was believed to draw the blood from the heart.)

Go hence a little, and I shall conduct you,
If you will mark it.

ROSALIND O, come, let us remove! 54
The sight of lovers feedeth those in love.
Bring us to this sight, and you shall say
I'll prove a busy actor in their play. *Exeunt.*

✣

3.5 *Enter Silvius and Phoebe.*

SILVIUS
Sweet Phoebe, do not scorn me, do not, Phoebe!
Say that you love me not, but say not so
In bitterness. The common executioner,
Whose heart th' accustomed sight of death makes hard,
Falls not the ax upon the humbled neck 5
But first begs pardon. Will you sterner be 6
Than he that dies and lives by bloody drops? 7

Enter Rosalind, Celia, and Corin [*behind*].

PHOEBE
I would not be thy executioner;
I fly thee, for I would not injure thee.
Thou tell'st me there is murder in mine eye.
'Tis pretty, sure, and very probable, 11
That eyes, that are the frail'st and softest things,
Who shut their coward gates on atomies, 13
Should be called tyrants, butchers, murderers!
Now I do frown on thee with all my heart,
And if mine eyes can wound, now let them kill thee.
Now counterfeit to swoon; why now fall down,
Or if thou canst not, O, for shame, for shame,
Lie not, to say mine eyes are murderers!
Now show the wound mine eye hath made in thee.
Scratch thee but with a pin, and there remains

54 will mark wish to see

3.5. Location: The forest.
5 Falls lets fall **6 But first begs** without first begging **7 dies and lives** i.e., makes his living his life long **11 sure** surely **13 gates on atomies** i.e., eyelids to protect against specks of dirt

SILVIUS
Sweet Phoebe—
PHOEBE Ha, what sayst thou, Silvius?
SILVIUS Sweet Phoebe, pity me.
PHOEBE
Why, I am sorry for thee, gentle Silvius.
SILVIUS
Wherever sorrow is, relief would be.
If you do sorrow at my grief in love,
By giving love, your sorrow and my grief
Were both extermined.
PHOEBE
Thou hast my love. Is not that neighborly?
SILVIUS
I would have you.
PHOEBE Why, that were covetousness.
Silvius, the time was that I hated thee,
And yet it is not that I bear thee love;
But since that thou canst talk of love so well,
Thy company, which erst was irksome to me,
I will endure, and I'll employ thee too.
But do not look for further recompense
Than thine own gladness that thou art employed.
SILVIUS
So holy and so perfect is my love,
And I in such a poverty of grace,
That I shall think it a most plenteous crop
To glean the broken ears after the man
That the main harvest reaps. Loose now and then
A scattered smile, and that I'll live upon.
PHOEBE
Know'st thou the youth that spoke to me erewhile?
SILVIUS
Not very well, but I have met him oft,
And he hath bought the cottage and the bounds

86 Wherever . . . be i.e., whenever one experiences sorrow, one ought to wish to offer relief **89 Were both extermined** would both be banished, ended **90 Is . . . neighborly** i.e., I love you as one is supposed to love one's neighbor or fellow Christian (as distinguished from conjugal love) **91 covetousness** (The tenth commandment forbids coveting anything that is your neighbor's.) **93 yet it is not** it (the time) is not yet come **95 erst** formerly **100 poverty of grace** (i.e., love, his divinity, has been ungracious to him) **105 erewhile** before **107 bounds** pastures

That the old carlot once was master of. 108

PHOEBE

Think not I love him, though I ask for him;
'Tis but a peevish boy—yet he talks well—
But what care I for words? Yet words do well
When he that speaks them pleases those that hear.
It is a pretty youth—not very pretty—
But sure he's proud—and yet his pride becomes him.
He'll make a proper man. The best thing in him
Is his complexion; and faster than his tongue
Did make offense, his eye did heal it up.
He is not very tall—yet for his years he's tall.
His leg is but so-so—and yet 'tis well.
There was a pretty redness in his lip,
A little riper and more lusty red
Than that mixed in his cheek; 'twas just the difference
Betwixt the constant red and mingled damask. 123
There be some women, Silvius, had they marked him
In parcels as I did, would have gone near 125
To fall in love with him; but for my part 126
I love him not nor hate him not; and yet
I have more cause to hate him than to love him.
For what had he to do to chide at me? 129
He said mine eyes were black and my hair black
And, now I am remembered, scorned at me. 131
I marvel why I answered not again. 132
But that's all one; omittance is no quittance. 133
I'll write to him a very taunting letter,
And thou shalt bear it. Wilt thou, Silvius?

SILVIUS

Phoebe, with all my heart.

PHOEBE

I'll write it straight; 136
The matter's in my head and in my heart.
I will be bitter with him and passing short. 138
Go with me, Silvius. *Exeunt.*

✤

108 carlot churl, countryman **123 mingled damask** mingled red and white, i.e., the color of the damask rose **125 In parcels** piece by piece, in detail. **gone near** come close **126 fall** falling **129 what . . . do** what business had he **131 am remembered** remember, recollect **132 again** back **133 But . . . quittance** i.e., but just the same, my failure to answer him doesn't mean I won't do so later **136 straight** immediately **138 passing short** exceedingly curt

4.1 *Enter Rosalind and Celia, and Jaques.*

JAQUES I prithee, pretty youth, let me be better acquainted with thee.

ROSALIND They say you are a melancholy fellow.

JAQUES I am so; I do love it better than laughing.

ROSALIND Those that are in extremity of either are abominable fellows and betray themselves to every modern censure worse than drunkards.

JAQUES Why, 'tis good to be sad and say nothing.

ROSALIND Why then 'tis good to be a post.

JAQUES I have neither the scholar's melancholy, which is emulation, nor the musician's, which is fantastical, nor the courtier's, which is proud, nor the soldier's, which is ambitious, nor the lawyer's, which is politic, nor the lady's, which is nice, nor the lover's, which is all these; but it is a melancholy of mine own, compounded of many simples, extracted from many objects, and indeed the sundry contemplation of my travels, in which my often rumination wraps me in a most humorous sadness.

ROSALIND A traveler! By my faith, you have great reason to be sad. I fear you have sold your own lands to see other men's. Then to have seen much and to have nothing is to have rich eyes and poor hands.

JAQUES Yes, I have gained my experience.

Enter Orlando.

ROSALIND And your experience makes you sad. I had rather have a fool to make me merry than experience to make me sad—and to travel for it too!

ORLANDO Good day and happiness, dear Rosalind!

JAQUES Nay, then, God b' wi' you, an you talk in blank verse.

ROSALIND Farewell, Monsieur Traveler. Look you lisp

4.1. Location: The forest.
5 are . . . of go to extremes in **7 modern censure** common judgment **11 emulation** envy. **fantastical** extravagantly fanciful **13 politic** calculated **14 nice** fastidious **16 simples** ingredients (usually herbs) of a drug **16–17 objects** i.e., objects of my observation **17 sundry** various, collected **19 humorous** moody **27 travel** (with a pun on *travail,* labor) **29 an** if **31 Look** be sure. (Said ironically.)

and wear strange suits, disable all the benefits of your own country, be out of love with your nativity, and almost chide God for making you that countenance you are, or I will scarce think you have swam in a gondola. [*Exit Jaques.*]

Why, how now, Orlando, where have you been all this while? You a lover? An you serve me such another trick, never come in my sight more.

ORLANDO My fair Rosalind, I come within an hour of my promise.

ROSALIND Break an hour's promise in love? He that will divide a minute into a thousand parts and break but a part of the thousandth part of a minute in the affairs of love, it may be said of him that Cupid hath clapped him o' the shoulder, but I'll warrant him heart-whole.

ORLANDO Pardon me, dear Rosalind.

ROSALIND Nay, an you be so tardy, come no more in my sight. I had as lief be wooed of a snail.

ORLANDO Of a snail?

ROSALIND Ay, of a snail; for though he comes slowly, he carries his house on his head—a better jointure, I think, than you make a woman. Besides, he brings his destiny with him.

ORLANDO What's that?

ROSALIND Why, horns, which such as you are fain to be beholding to your wives for. But he comes armed in his fortune and prevents the slander of his wife.

ORLANDO Virtue is no horn maker, and my Rosalind is virtuous.

ROSALIND And I am your Rosalind.

CELIA It pleases him to call you so; but he hath a Rosalind of a better leer than you.

ROSALIND Come, woo me, woo me, for now I am in a holiday humor and like enough to consent. What

32 disable depreciate, disparage **33 nativity** i.e., place of birth **35–36 swam . . . gondola** ridden in a gondola, i.e., been in Venice, where almost all travelers go **45–46 clapped . . . shoulder** i.e., accosted or arrested him **49 lief** willingly **52 jointure** marriage settlement **56 horns** (1) snails' horns (2) cuckold's horns, signs of an unfaithful wife. **fain** willing **57 beholding** beholden, indebted **57–58 armed . . . fortune** i.e., with the horns of a cuckold, which it was his fate to earn **58 prevents** forestalls, anticipates **63 of . . . leer** better-looking

would you say to me now, an I were your very, very Rosalind?

ORLANDO I would kiss before I spoke.

ROSALIND Nay, you were better speak first, and when you were graveled for lack of matter, you might take occasion to kiss. Very good orators, when they are out, they will spit; and for lovers lacking—God warrant us!—matter, the cleanliest shift is to kiss.

ORLANDO How if the kiss be denied?

ROSALIND Then she puts you to entreaty, and there begins new matter.

ORLANDO Who could be out, being before his beloved mistress?

ROSALIND Marry, that should you, if I were your mistress, or I should think my honesty ranker than my wit.

ORLANDO What, of my suit?

ROSALIND Not out of your apparel, and yet out of your suit. Am not I your Rosalind?

ORLANDO I take some joy to say you are, because I would be talking of her.

ROSALIND Well, in her person I say I will not have you.

ORLANDO Then in mine own person I die.

ROSALIND No, faith, die by attorney. The poor world is almost six thousand years old, and in all this time there was not any man died in his own person, videlicet, in a love cause. Troilus had his brains dashed out with a Grecian club, yet he did what he could to die

70 graveled stuck, at a standstill. (Literally, run aground on a shoal.) **71 out** i.e., at a loss through forgetfulness or confusion **72 warrant** defend **73 cleanliest shift** cleverest device **80 honesty** chastity. **ranker** even more corrupt. (Rosalind playfully interprets *being out before one's mistress,* l. 77–78, as not being inside her, not having sex with her; she says her lover will have to stay out, and thus will not obtain his suit, l. 84.) **82 of my suit** (Orlando means "out of my suit," at a loss for words in my wooing; but Rosalind puns on the meaning "suit of clothes"; to be out of apparel would be to be undressed.) **89 attorney** proxy **90 six . . . old** (A common figure in biblical calculation.) **91–92 videlicet** namely **92 Troilus** hero of the story of Troilus and Cressida in which he remains faithful to her but she is faithless in love **92–93 had . . . club** (Troilus was slain by Achilles; Rosalind's account of his death is calculatedly unromantic.)

before, and he is one of the patterns of love. Leander, 94
he would have lived many a fair year though Hero
had turned nun, if it had not been for a hot midsummer night; for, good youth, he went but forth to
wash him in the Hellespont and being taken with the
cramp was drowned; and the foolish chroniclers of that
age found it was—Hero of Sestos. But these are all 100
lies. Men have died from time to time, and worms
have eaten them, but not for love.

ORLANDO I would not have my right Rosalind of this 103
mind, for I protest her frown might kill me.

ROSALIND By this hand, it will not kill a fly. But come,
now I will be your Rosalind in a more coming-on dis- 106
position, and ask me what you will, I will grant it.

ORLANDO Then love me, Rosalind.

ROSALIND Yes, faith, will I, Fridays and Saturdays and all.

ORLANDO And wilt thou have me?

ROSALIND Ay, and twenty such.

ORLANDO What sayest thou?

ROSALIND Are you not good?

ORLANDO I hope so.

ROSALIND Why then, can one desire too much of a good thing? Come, sister, you shall be the priest and marry us. Give me your hand, Orlando. What do you say, sister?

ORLANDO Pray thee, marry us.

CELIA I cannot say the words.

ROSALIND You must begin, "Will you, Orlando—"

CELIA Go to. Will you, Orlando, have to wife this Rosa- 123
lind?

ORLANDO I will.

ROSALIND Ay, but when?

ORLANDO Why now, as fast as she can marry us.

ROSALIND Then you must say, "I take thee, Rosalind, for wife."

94 Leander hero of the story of Hero and Leander, who lost his life swimming the Hellespont to visit his sweetheart. (Rosalind's account of the cramp is more undercutting of romantic idealism.) **100 found it was** arrived at the verdict that the cause (of his death) was **103 right** real **106 coming-on** compliant **123 Go to** (An exclamation of mild impatience.)

ORLANDO I take thee, Rosalind, for wife.

ROSALIND I might ask you for your commission; but I 131
do take thee, Orlando, for my husband. There's a girl
goes before the priest, and certainly a woman's 133
thought runs before her actions.

ORLANDO So do all thoughts; they are winged.

ROSALIND Now tell me how long you would have her after you have possessed her.

ORLANDO For ever and a day.

ROSALIND Say "a day," without the "ever." No, no, Orlando, men are April when they woo, December when
they wed. Maids are May when they are maids, but
the sky changes when they are wives. I will be more
jealous of thee than a Barbary cock-pigeon over his 143
hen, more clamorous than a parrot against rain, more 144
newfangled than an ape, more giddy in my desires 145
than a monkey. I will weep for nothing, like Diana in 146
the fountain, and I will do that when you are disposed 147
to be merry; I will laugh like a hyena, and that when
thou art inclined to sleep.

ORLANDO But will my Rosalind do so?

ROSALIND By my life, she will do as I do.

ORLANDO O, but she is wise.

ROSALIND Or else she could not have the wit to do this;
the wiser, the waywarder. Make the doors upon a 154
woman's wit, and it will out at the casement; shut
that, and 'twill out at the keyhole; stop that, 'twill fly
with the smoke out at the chimney.

ORLANDO A man that had a wife with such a wit, he
might say, "Wit, whither wilt?" 159

131 ask . . . commission ask you what authority you have for taking her (since no one is here to give the bride away) **133 goes before** (who) anticipates **143 Barbary cock-pigeon** an ornamental pigeon originally from the Barbary (north) coast of Africa. (Following Pliny, the cock-pigeon's jealousy was often contrasted with the mildness of the hen.) **144 against** before, in expectation of **145 newfangled** infatuated with novelty **146 for nothing** for no apparent reason **146–147 Diana in the fountain** (Diana frequently appeared as the centerpiece of fountains. Stow's *Survey of London* describes the setting up of a fountain with a Diana in green marble in the year 1596.) **154 Make** make fast, shut **159 Wit, whither wilt** wit, where are you going. (A common Elizabethan expression implying that one is talking fantastically, with a wildly wandering wit.)

ROSALIND Nay, you might keep that check for it till you 160
met your wife's wit going to your neighbor's bed.

ORLANDO And what wit could wit have to excuse that?

ROSALIND Marry, to say she came to seek you there.
You shall never take her without her answer, unless
you take her without her tongue. O, that woman that
cannot make her fault her husband's occasion, let her 166
never nurse her child herself, for she will breed it like
a fool!

ORLANDO For these two hours, Rosalind, I will leave
thee.

ROSALIND Alas, dear love, I cannot lack thee two hours!

ORLANDO I must attend the Duke at dinner. By two
o'clock I will be with thee again.

ROSALIND Ay, go your ways, go your ways; I knew
what you would prove. My friends told me as much,
and I thought no less. That flattering tongue of yours
won me. 'Tis but one cast away, and so, come, death! 177
Two o'clock is your hour?

ORLANDO Ay, sweet Rosalind.

ROSALIND By my troth, and in good earnest, and so
God mend me, and by all pretty oaths that are not
dangerous, if you break one jot of your promise or
come one minute behind your hour, I will think you
the most pathetical break-promise, and the most hol- 184
low lover, and the most unworthy of her you call Rosalind, that may be chosen out of the gross band of the 186
unfaithful. Therefore beware my censure and keep
your promise.

ORLANDO With no less religion than if thou wert indeed 189
my Rosalind. So adieu.

ROSALIND Well, Time is the old justice that examines all
such offenders, and let Time try. Adieu. 192

Exit [*Orlando*].

CELIA You have simply misused our sex in your love 193

160 check retort **166 make . . . occasion** i.e., turn a defense of her own conduct into an accusation against her husband **177 but one cast away** only one woman jilted **184 pathetical** pitiable, miserable **186 gross band** whole troop **189 religion** strict fidelity **192 try** determine **193 simply misused** absolutely slandered

prate. We must have your doublet and hose plucked over your head and show the world what the bird hath done to her own nest.

ROSALIND O coz, coz, coz, my pretty little coz, that thou didst know how many fathom deep I am in love! But it cannot be sounded; my affection hath an unknown bottom, like the Bay of Portugal.

CELIA Or rather, bottomless, that as fast as you pour affection in, it runs out.

ROSALIND No, that same wicked bastard of Venus, that was begot of thought, conceived of spleen, and born of madness, that blind rascally boy that abuses everyone's eyes because his own are out, let him be judge how deep I am in love. I'll tell thee, Aliena, I cannot be out of the sight of Orlando. I'll go find a shadow and sigh till he come.

CELIA And I'll sleep. *Exeunt.*

✤

4.2 *Enter Jaques and Lords* [*dressed as*] *Foresters.*

JAQUES Which is he that killed the deer?

FIRST LORD Sir, it was I.

JAQUES Let's present him to the Duke, like a Roman conqueror, and it would do well to set the deer's horns upon his head for a branch of victory. Have you no song, Forester, for this purpose?

SECOND LORD Yes, sir.

JAQUES Sing it. 'Tis no matter how it be in tune, so it make noise enough. *Music.*

Song.

SECOND LORD

What shall he have that killed the deer?

194–196 We . . . nest i.e., we must expose you for what you are, a woman, and show everyone how a woman has defamed her own kind just as a foul bird proverbially fouls its own nest **199 sounded** measured for depth **203 bastard of Venus** i.e., Cupid, son of Venus and Mercury rather than Vulcan, Venus' husband **204 thought** fancy. **spleen** i.e., impulse **205 abuses** deceives **208 shadow** shady spot

4.2. Location: The forest.
5 branch wreath

His leather skin and horns to wear.
Then sing him home; the rest shall bear 12
        This burden. 13
Take thou no scorn to wear the horn; 14
It was a crest ere thou wast born.
        Thy father's father wore it,
        And thy father bore it.
The horn, the horn, the lusty horn
Is not a thing to laugh to scorn. *Exeunt.*

✣

4.3 *Enter Rosalind and Celia.*

ROSALIND How say you now? Is it not past two o'clock?
And here much Orlando! 2
CELIA I warrant you, with pure love and troubled 3
brain, he hath ta'en his bow and arrows and is gone
forth—to sleep.

Enter Silvius [*with a letter*].

Look who comes here.

SILVIUS
My errand is to you, fair youth.
My gentle Phoebe bid me give you this.
[*He gives the letter.*]
I know not the contents, but as I guess
By the stern brow and waspish action
Which she did use as she was writing of it,
It bears an angry tenor. Pardon me,
I am but as a guiltless messenger.

ROSALIND [*Examining the letter*]
Patience herself would startle at this letter
And play the swaggerer. Bear this, bear all!
She says I am not fair, that I lack manners;
She calls me proud, and that she could not love me

12–13 bear This burden (1) sing this refrain (2) wear the horns that all cuckolds must wear **14 Take . . . scorn** be not ashamed. (Alludes to joke about cuckold's horns.)

4.3. Location: The forest.
2 much (Said ironically: A fat lot we see of Orlando!) **3 warrant** assure

Were man as rare as phoenix. 'Od's my will! 18
Her love is not the hare that I do hunt.
Why writes she so to me? Well, shepherd, well,
This is a letter of your own device.

SILVIUS
No, I protest, I know not the contents.
Phoebe did write it.

ROSALIND Come, come, you are a fool,
And turned into the extremity of love. 24
I saw her hand; she has a leathern hand, 25
A freestone-colored hand. I verily did think 26
That her old gloves were on, but 'twas her hands;
She has a huswife's hand—but that's no matter. 28
I say she never did invent this letter;
This is a man's invention and his hand.

SILVIUS Sure it is hers.

ROSALIND
Why, 'tis a boisterous and a cruel style,
A style for challengers. Why, she defies me,
Like Turk to Christian. Women's gentle brain
Could not drop forth such giant-rude invention,
Such Ethiop words, blacker in their effect 36
Than in their countenance. Will you hear the letter?

SILVIUS
So please you, for I never heard it yet;
Yet, heard too much of Phoebe's cruelty.

ROSALIND
She Phoebes me. Mark how the tyrant writes. *Read.* 40
"Art thou god to shepherd turned,
That a maiden's heart hath burned?"
Can a woman rail thus?

SILVIUS Call you this railing?

ROSALIND *Read.*
"Why, thy godhead laid apart, 45
Warr'st thou with a woman's heart?"

18 phoenix a fabulous bird of Arabia, the only one of its kind, which lived five hundred years, died in flames, and was reborn of its own ashes. **'Od's my will** God's is my will, or, may God save my will **24 turned** brought **25 leathern** leathery **26 freestone-colored** sandstone-colored, brownish-yellow **28 hand** handwriting (with play on the ordinary meaning) **36 Ethiop** i.e., black **40 Phoebes** i.e., treats cruelly **45 thy . . . apart** having laid aside your godhead (for human shape)

Did you ever hear such railing?
"Whiles the eye of man did woo me,
That could do no vengeance to me." 49
Meaning me a beast. 50
"If the scorn of your bright eyne
Have power to raise such love in mine,
Alack, in me what strange effect
Would they work in mild aspect! 54
Whiles you chid me, I did love; 55
How then might your prayers move!
He that brings this love to thee
Little knows this love in me;
And by him seal up thy mind, 59
Whether that thy youth and kind 60
Will the faithful offer take
Of me and all that I can make,
Or else by him my love deny,
And then I'll study how to die."

SILVIUS Call you this chiding?

CELIA Alas, poor shepherd!

ROSALIND Do you pity him? No, he deserves no pity.—
Wilt thou love such a woman? What, to make thee an
instrument and play false strains upon thee? Not to be 69
endured! Well, go your way to her, for I see love hath
made thee a tame snake, and say this to her: that if she 71
love me, I charge her to love thee; if she will not, I will
never have her unless thou entreat for her. If you be a
true lover, hence, and not a word; for here comes more
company. *Exit Silvius.*

Enter Oliver.

OLIVER
Good morrow, fair ones. Pray you, if you know,
Where in the purlieus of this forest stands 77
A sheepcote fenced about with olive trees?

49 vengeance mischief, harm **50 Meaning me** i.e., implying that I am **54 in mild aspect** i.e., if they looked on me mildly. (Suggests also astrological influence.) **55 chid** chided **59 by . . . mind** i.e., send your thoughts in a letter via Silvius **60 youth and kind** youthful nature **69 instrument** (1) tool (2) musical instrument **71 tame snake** i.e., pathetic wretch **77 purlieus** tracts of land on the border of a forest

CELIA

West of this place, down in the neighbor bottom; 79
The rank of osiers by the murmuring stream 80
Left on your right hand brings you to the place. 81
But at this hour the house doth keep itself;
There's none within.

OLIVER

If that an eye may profit by a tongue,
Then should I know you by description,
Such garments and such years: "The boy is fair,
Of female favor, and bestows himself 87
Like a ripe sister; the woman, low 88
And browner than her brother." Are not you
The owner of the house I did inquire for?

CELIA

It is no boast, being asked, to say we are.

OLIVER

Orlando doth commend him to you both,
And to that youth he calls his Rosalind
He sends this bloody napkin. Are you he? 94
[*He produces a bloody handkerchief.*]

ROSALIND

I am. What must we understand by this?

OLIVER

Some of my shame, if you will know of me
What man I am, and how, and why, and where
This handkerchief was stained.

CELIA

I pray you, tell it.

OLIVER

When last the young Orlando parted from you
He left a promise to return again
Within an hour, and, pacing through the forest,
Chewing the food of sweet and bitter fancy, 102
Lo, what befell! He threw his eye aside,
And mark what object did present itself:
Under an old oak, whose boughs were mossed with age
And high top bald with dry antiquity,
A wretched ragged man, o'ergrown with hair,
Lay sleeping on his back. About his neck

79 neighbor bottom neighboring dell **80 rank of osiers** row of willows **81 Left** left behind, passed **87 favor** features. **bestows** behaves **88 ripe** mature or elder **94 napkin** handkerchief **102 fancy** love

A green and gilded snake had wreathed itself,
Who with her head nimble in threats approached
The opening of his mouth; but suddenly,
Seeing Orlando, it unlinked itself 112
And with indented glides did slip away 113
Into a bush, under which bush's shade
A lioness, with udders all drawn dry, 115
Lay couching, head on ground, with catlike watch,
When that the sleeping man should stir; for 'tis 117
The royal disposition of that beast
To prey on nothing that doth seem as dead.
This seen, Orlando did approach the man
And found it was his brother, his elder brother.

CELIA
O, I have heard him speak of that same brother,
And he did render him the most unnatural 123
That lived amongst men.

OLIVER
And well he might so do,
For well I know he was unnatural.

ROSALIND
But to Orlando: did he leave him there,
Food to the sucked and hungry lioness?

OLIVER
Twice did he turn his back and purposed so;
But kindness, nobler ever than revenge,
And nature, stronger than his just occasion, 130
Made him give battle to the lioness,
Who quickly fell before him; in which hurtling 132
From miserable slumber I awaked.

CELIA
Are you his brother?

ROSALIND
Was 't you he rescued?

CELIA
Was 't you that did so oft contrive to kill him?

OLIVER
'Twas I; but 'tis not I. I do not shame 136
To tell you what I was, since my conversion
So sweetly tastes, being the thing I am.

112 unlinked uncoiled **113 indented** zigzag **115 udders . . . dry** (It would therefore be fierce with hunger.) **117 When** for the moment **123 render him** describe him as **130 just occasion** fair chance (of revenge) **132 hurtling** clatter, tumult **136 do not shame** am not ashamed

ROSALIND
But for the bloody napkin?
OLIVER By and by. 139
When from the first to last betwixt us two
Tears our recountments had most kindly bathed, 141
As how I came into that desert place,
In brief, he led me to the gentle Duke,
Who gave me fresh array and entertainment, 144
Committing me unto my brother's love;
Who led me instantly unto his cave,
There stripped himself, and here upon his arm
The lioness had torn some flesh away,
Which all this while had bled; and now he fainted
And cried, in fainting, upon Rosalind.
Brief, I recovered him, bound up his wound, 151
And, after some small space, being strong at heart,
He sent me hither, stranger as I am,
To tell this story, that you might excuse
His broken promise, and to give this napkin
Dyed in his blood unto the shepherd youth
That he in sport doth call his Rosalind.
[*Rosalind swoons.*]

CELIA
Why, how now, Ganymede, sweet Ganymede!
OLIVER
Many will swoon when they do look on blood.
CELIA
There is more in it.—Cousin Ganymede!
OLIVER Look, he recovers.
ROSALIND I would I were at home.
CELIA We'll lead you thither.—
I pray you, will you take him by the arm?
[*They help Rosalind up.*]

OLIVER Be of good cheer, youth. You a man? You lack a man's heart.

ROSALIND I do so, I confess it. Ah, sirrah, a body would 167
think this was well counterfeited. I pray you, tell your brother how well I counterfeited. Heigh-ho!

OLIVER This was not counterfeit. There is too great tes-

139 for as regards **141 recountments** relating of events (to one another) **144 array** attire. **entertainment** hospitality, provision **151 Brief** in brief. **recovered** revived **167 a body** anybody, one

timony in your complexion that it was a passion of earnest.

ROSALIND Counterfeit, I assure you.

OLIVER Well then, take a good heart and counterfeit to be a man.

ROSALIND So I do; but i' faith, I should have been a woman by right.

CELIA Come, you look paler and paler. Pray you, draw homewards.—Good sir, go with us.

OLIVER

That will I, for I must bear answer back
How you excuse my brother, Rosalind.

ROSALIND I shall devise something. But, I pray you, commend my counterfeiting to him. Will you go?

Exeunt.

✤

171–172 a passion of earnest a genuine swoon, genuine emotion

5.1 *Enter* [*Touchstone the*] *Clown and Audrey.*

TOUCHSTONE We shall find a time, Audrey. Patience, gentle Audrey.

AUDREY Faith, the priest was good enough, for all the old gentleman's saying.

TOUCHSTONE A most wicked Sir Oliver, Audrey, a most vile Mar-text. But Audrey, there is a youth here in the forest lays claim to you.

AUDREY Ay, I know who 'tis. He hath no interest in me in the world. Here comes the man you mean.

Enter William.

TOUCHSTONE It is meat and drink to me to see a clown. By my troth, we that have good wits have much to answer for. We shall be flouting; we cannot hold.

WILLIAM Good even, Audrey.

AUDREY God gi' good even, William.

WILLIAM And good even to you, sir.

[*He removes his hat.*]

TOUCHSTONE Good even, gentle friend. Cover thy head, cover thy head; nay, prithee, be covered. How old are you, friend?

WILLIAM Five-and-twenty, sir.

TOUCHSTONE A ripe age. Is thy name William?

WILLIAM William, sir.

TOUCHSTONE A fair name. Wast born i' the forest here?

WILLIAM Ay, sir, I thank God.

TOUCHSTONE "Thank God"—a good answer. Art rich?

WILLIAM Faith, sir, so-so.

TOUCHSTONE "So-so" is good, very good, very excellent good; and yet it is not, it is but so-so. Art thou wise?

WILLIAM Ay, sir, I have a pretty wit.

TOUCHSTONE Why, thou sayst well. I do now remember a saying, "The fool doth think he is wise, but the

5.1. Location: The forest.
3–4 the old gentleman's i.e., Jaques's **8 interest in** claim to **10 clown** i.e., country yokel **12 shall** must. **flouting** scoffing, expressing contempt. **hold** i.e., hold back, hold our tongues **14 God gi' good even** God give you good evening, i.e., afternoon

wise man knows himself to be a fool." The heathen philosopher, when he had a desire to eat a grape, would open his lips when he put it into his mouth, meaning thereby that grapes were made to eat and lips to open. You do love this maid?

WILLIAM I do, sir.

TOUCHSTONE Give me your hand. Art thou learned?

WILLIAM No, sir.

TOUCHSTONE Then learn this of me: to have is to have. For it is a figure in rhetoric that drink, being poured out of a cup into a glass, by filling the one doth empty the other. For all your writers do consent that *ipse* is he. Now, you are not *ipse,* for I am he.

WILLIAM Which he, sir?

TOUCHSTONE He, sir, that must marry this woman. Therefore, you clown, abandon—which is in the vulgar "leave"—the society—which in the boorish is "company"—of this female—which in the common is "woman"; which together is, abandon the society of this female, or, clown, thou perishest; or, to thy better understanding, diest; or, to wit, I kill thee, make thee away, translate thy life into death, thy liberty into bondage. I will deal in poison with thee, or in bastinado, or in steel; I will bandy with thee in faction, I will o'errun thee with policy; I will kill thee a hundred and fifty ways. Therefore tremble, and depart.

AUDREY Do, good William.

WILLIAM God rest you merry, sir. *Exit.*

Enter Corin.

CORIN Our master and mistress seeks you. Come, away, away!

TOUCHSTONE Trip, Audrey, trip, Audrey! I attend, I attend. *Exeunt.*

31–35 The heathen . . . open (This is probably Touchstone's way of telling William, whose mouth is no doubt gaping like a rustic's, that the grape, i.e., Audrey, is not for his lips.) **40–42 drink . . . other** i.e., both Touchstone and William cannot possess Audrey **42 your writers** i.e., the authorities. **ipse** he himself. (Latin.) **53–54 bastinado** beating with a cudgel **54 bandy** contend. **in faction** factiously **55 o'errun . . . policy** overwhelm you with craft, cunning **58 God . . . merry** (Common salutation at parting.) **61 Trip** go nimbly

5.2 *Enter Orlando [with his wounded arm in a scarf] and Oliver.*

ORLANDO Is 't possible that on so little acquaintance you should like her? That but seeing you should love her? And loving woo? And, wooing, she should grant? And will you persevere to enjoy her?

OLIVER Neither call the giddiness of it in question, the poverty of her, the small acquaintance, my sudden wooing, nor her sudden consenting; but say with me, "I love Aliena"; say with her that she loves me; consent with both that we may enjoy each other. It shall be to your good; for my father's house and all the revenue that was old Sir Rowland's will I estate upon you, and here live and die a shepherd.

Enter Rosalind.

ORLANDO You have my consent. Let your wedding be tomorrow. Thither will I invite the Duke and all 's contented followers. Go you and prepare Aliena; for look you, here comes my Rosalind.

ROSALIND God save you, brother.

OLIVER And you, fair sister. [*Exit.*]

ROSALIND O my dear Orlando, how it grieves me to see thee wear thy heart in a scarf!

ORLANDO It is my arm.

ROSALIND I thought thy heart had been wounded with the claws of a lion.

ORLANDO Wounded it is, but with the eyes of a lady.

ROSALIND Did your brother tell you how I counterfeited to swoon when he showed me your handkerchief?

ORLANDO Ay, and greater wonders than that.

ROSALIND O, I know where you are. Nay, 'tis true. There was never anything so sudden but the fight of

5.2. Location: The forest.
5 giddiness sudden speed **11 estate** settle as an estate, bestow **14 all 's** all his **17 brother** i.e., brother-in-law to be **18 sister** (Rosalind is still dressed as a man, but Oliver evidently adopts the fiction that "Ganymede" is Orlando's Rosalind.) **20 wear . . . scarf** (Perhaps she suggests that Orlando has been wearing his heart on his sleeve; literally, she refers to the scarf or bandage for his wounded arm.) **28 where you are** i.e., what you mean

two rams and Caesar's thrasonical brag of "I came, saw, and overcame." For your brother and my sister no sooner met but they looked, no sooner looked but they loved, no sooner loved but they sighed, no sooner sighed but they asked one another the reason, no sooner knew the reason but they sought the remedy; and in these degrees have they made a pair of stairs to marriage which they will climb incontinent, or else be incontinent before marriage. They are in the very wrath of love, and they will together. Clubs cannot part them.

ORLANDO They shall be married tomorrow, and I will bid the Duke to the nuptial. But O, how bitter a thing it is to look into happiness through another man's eyes! By so much the more shall I tomorrow be at the height of heart-heaviness, by how much I shall think my brother happy in having what he wishes for.

ROSALIND Why then tomorrow I cannot serve your turn for Rosalind?

ORLANDO I can live no longer by thinking.

ROSALIND I will weary you then no longer with idle talking. Know of me then, for now I speak to some purpose, that I know you are a gentleman of good conceit. I speak not this that you should bear a good opinion of my knowledge, insomuch I say I know you are; neither do I labor for a greater esteem than may in some little measure draw a belief from you, to do yourself good and not to grace me. Believe then, if you please, that I can do strange things. I have, since I was three years old, conversed with a magician, most profound in his art and yet not damnable. If you do love Rosalind so near the heart as your gesture cries it out, when your brother marries Aliena, shall you marry her. I know into what straits of fortune she is driven;

30 thrasonical boastful. (From Thraso, the boaster in Terence's *Eunuchus*.) **36 degrees** (Plays on the original meaning, "steps.") **pair** flight **37 incontinent** immediately (followed by a pun on the meaning "unchaste or sexually unrestrained") **39 wrath** impetuosity, ardor **52–53 conceit** intelligence, understanding **54 insomuch** inasmuch as **56 belief** i.e., confidence in my ability **57 grace me** bring favor on myself **59 conversed** associated **60 not damnable** not a practicer of forbidden or black magic, worthy of damnation **61 gesture** bearing. **cries it out** proclaims

and it is not impossible to me, if it appear not inconvenient to you, to set her before your eyes tomorrow, human as she is, and without any danger.

ORLANDO Speak'st thou in sober meanings?

ROSALIND By my life I do, which I tender dearly, though I say I am a magician. Therefore, put you in your best array; bid your friends; for if you will be married tomorrow, you shall, and to Rosalind, if you will.

Enter Silvius and Phoebe.

Look, here comes a lover of mine and a lover of hers.

PHOEBE

Youth, you have done me much ungentleness,
To show the letter that I writ to you.

ROSALIND

I care not if I have. It is my study
To seem despiteful and ungentle to you.
You are there followed by a faithful shepherd;
Look upon him, love him; he worships you.

PHOEBE

Good shepherd, tell this youth what 'tis to love.

SILVIUS

It is to be all made of sighs and tears;
And so am I for Phoebe.

PHOEBE And I for Ganymede.

ORLANDO And I for Rosalind.

ROSALIND And I for no woman.

SILVIUS

It is to be all made of faith and service;
And so am I for Phoebe.

PHOEBE And I for Ganymede.

ORLANDO And I for Rosalind.

ROSALIND And I for no woman.

SILVIUS

It is to be all made of fantasy,

64–65 inconvenient inappropriate **66 human** i.e., the real Rosalind. **danger** i.e., the danger to the soul from one's involvement in magic or witchcraft **67 in sober meanings** seriously **68 tender dearly** value highly **69 though . . . magician** (According to Elizabethan antiwitchcraft statutes, some forms of witchcraft were punishable by death; Rosalind thus endangers her life by what she has said.) **76 study** conscious endeavor **91 fantasy** imagination

All made of passion and all made of wishes,
All adoration, duty, and observance,
All humbleness, all patience, and impatience,
All purity, all trial, all observance;
And so am I for Phoebe.

PHOEBE And so am I for Ganymede.

ORLANDO And so am I for Rosalind.

ROSALIND And so am I for no woman.

PHOEBE [*To Rosalind*]
If this be so, why blame you me to love you?

SILVIUS [*To Phoebe*]
If this be so, why blame you me to love you?

ORLANDO
If this be so, why blame you me to love you?

ROSALIND Why do you speak too, "Why blame you me to love you?"

ORLANDO To her that is not here, nor doth not hear.

ROSALIND Pray you, no more of this; 'tis like the howling of Irish wolves against the moon. [*To Silvius.*] I will help you, if I can. [*To Phoebe.*] I would love you, if I could.—Tomorrow meet me all together. [*To Phoebe.*] I will marry you, if ever I marry woman, and I'll be married tomorrow. [*To Orlando.*] I will satisfy you, if ever I satisfied man, and you shall be married tomorrow. [*To Silvius.*] I will content you, if what pleases you contents you, and you shall be married tomorrow. [*To Orlando.*] As you love Rosalind, meet. [*To Silvius.*] As you love Phoebe, meet. And as I love no woman, I'll meet. So fare you well. I have left you commands.

SILVIUS I'll not fail, if I live.

PHOEBE Nor I.

ORLANDO Nor I. *Exeunt.*

✤

5.3 *Enter* [*Touchstone the*] *Clown and Audrey.*

TOUCHSTONE Tomorrow is the joyful day, Audrey; tomorrow will we be married.

93 observance devotion, respect **95 observance** (Perhaps a compositor's error, repeated from two lines previous; many editors emend to *obedience*.) **100 to love you** for loving you

5.3. Location: The forest.

AUDREY I do desire it with all my heart; and I hope it is
no dishonest desire to desire to be a woman of the 4
world. Here come two of the banished Duke's pages. 5

Enter two Pages.

FIRST PAGE Well met, honest gentleman.

TOUCHSTONE By my troth, well met. Come, sit, sit, and
a song. [*They sit.*]

SECOND PAGE We are for you. Sit i' the middle 9

FIRST PAGE Shall we clap into 't roundly, without hawk- 10
ing or spitting or saying we are hoarse, which are the 11
only prologues to a bad voice? 12

SECOND PAGE I' faith, i' faith, and both in a tune, like 13
two gypsies on a horse. 14

Song.

BOTH PAGES

It was a lover and his lass,
  With a hey, and a ho, and a hey-nonny-no,
That o'er the green cornfield did pass 17
  In the springtime, the only pretty ring time, 18
When birds do sing, hey ding a ding, ding,
Sweet lovers love the spring.

Between the acres of the rye, 21
  With a hey, and a ho, and a hey-nonny-no,
These pretty country folks would lie
  In the springtime, the only pretty ring time,
When birds do sing, hey ding a ding, ding,
Sweet lovers love the spring.

This carol they began that hour,
  With a hey, and a ho, and a hey-nonny-no,
How that a life was but a flower
  In the springtime, the only pretty ring time,

4 dishonest immodest **4–5 woman of the world** married woman; also, one who advances herself socially **9 We are for you** i.e., fine, we're ready **10 clap . . . roundly** begin at once and with spirit **10–11 hawking** clearing the throat **12 only** common, customary **13 in a tune** (1) in unison (2) keeping time **14 on a** on one **17 cornfield** field of grain **18 ring time** time most apt for marriage **21 Between the acres** i.e., on unplowed strips between the fields

When birds do sing, hey ding a ding, ding,
Sweet lovers love the spring.

And therefore take the present time,
With a hey, and a ho, and a hey-nonny-no,
For love is crownèd with the prime
In the springtime, the only pretty ring time,
When birds do sing, hey ding a ding, ding,
Sweet lovers love the spring.

TOUCHSTONE Truly, young gentlemen, though there was no great matter in the ditty, yet the note was very untunable.

FIRST PAGE You are deceived, sir; we kept time, we lost not our time.

TOUCHSTONE By my troth, yes; I count it but time lost to hear such a foolish song. God b' wi' you, and God mend your voices! Come, Audrey. *Exeunt.*

✤

5.4 *Enter Duke Senior, Amiens, Jaques, Orlando, Oliver,* [*and*] *Celia.*

DUKE SENIOR
Dost thou believe, Orlando, that the boy
Can do all this that he hath promisèd?

ORLANDO
I sometimes do believe and sometimes do not,
As those that fear they hope and know they fear.

Enter Rosalind, Silvius, and Phoebe.

ROSALIND
Patience once more, whiles our compact is urged.
[*To the Duke.*] You say, if I bring in your Rosalind,
You will bestow her on Orlando here?

DUKE SENIOR
That would I, had I kingdoms to give with her.

35 prime spring **40 matter** sense, meaning. **note** music
41 untunable untuneful, discordant

5.4. Location: The forest.
4 they hope i.e., that they merely hope **5 urged** put forward

ROSALIND [*To Orlando*]
And you say you will have her when I bring her?
ORLANDO
That would I, were I of all kingdoms king.
ROSALIND [*To Phoebe*]
You say you'll marry me, if I be willing?
PHOEBE
That will I, should I die the hour after.
ROSALIND
But if you do refuse to marry me,
You'll give yourself to this most faithful shepherd?
PHOEBE So is the bargain.
ROSALIND [*To Silvius*]
You say that you'll have Phoebe if she will?
SILVIUS
Though to have her and death were both one thing.
ROSALIND
I have promised to make all this matter even. 18
Keep you your word, O Duke, to give your daughter;
You yours, Orlando, to receive his daughter;
Keep you your word, Phoebe, that you'll marry me,
Or else, refusing me, to wed this shepherd;
Keep your word, Silvius, that you'll marry her
If she refuse me; and from hence I go
To make these doubts all even.
Exeunt Rosalind and Celia.
DUKE SENIOR
I do remember in this shepherd boy
Some lively touches of my daughter's favor. 27
ORLANDO
My lord, the first time that I ever saw him
Methought he was a brother to your daughter.
But, my good lord, this boy is forest-born
And hath been tutored in the rudiments
Of many desperate studies by his uncle, 32
Whom he reports to be a great magician,
Obscurèd in the circle of this forest. 34

18 even smooth **27 lively** lifelike. **favor** appearance **32 desperate** dangerous **34 Obscurèd** hidden (with a possible allusion to the magic circle that protected the magician from the devil during incantation)

Enter [*Touchstone the*] *Clown and Audrey.*

JAQUES There is, sure, another flood toward, and these 35
couples are coming to the ark. Here comes a pair of
very strange beasts, which in all tongues are called
fools.

TOUCHSTONE Salutation and greeting to you all!

JAQUES Good my lord, bid him welcome. This is the
motley-minded gentleman that I have so often met in
the forest. He hath been a courtier, he swears.

TOUCHSTONE If any man doubt that, let him put me to
my purgation. I have trod a measure; I have flattered a 44
lady; I have been politic with my friend, smooth with
mine enemy; I have undone three tailors; I have had 46
four quarrels and like to have fought one. 47

JAQUES And how was that ta'en up? 48

TOUCHSTONE Faith, we met and found the quarrel was
upon the seventh cause.

JAQUES How seventh cause?—Good my lord, like this
fellow.

DUKE SENIOR I like him very well.

TOUCHSTONE God 'ild you, sir, I desire you of the like. 54
I press in here, sir, amongst the rest of the country
copulatives, to swear and to forswear, according as 56
marriage binds and blood breaks. A poor virgin, sir, 57
an ill-favored thing, sir, but mine own; a poor humor 58
of mine, sir, to take that that no man else will. Rich
honesty dwells like a miser, sir, in a poor house, as 60
your pearl in your foul oyster. 61

DUKE SENIOR By my faith, he is very swift and senten- 62
tious. 63

TOUCHSTONE According to the fool's bolt, sir, and such 64
dulcet diseases. 65

35 toward coming on **44 purgation** proof, trial. **measure** slow, stately dance **46 undone** ruined, bankrupted (by refusing to pay massive debts owed them) **47 like** been likely, came close **48 ta'en up** settled, made up **54 'ild** yield, reward. **I . . . like** I wish the same to you. (A polite phrase used to reply to a compliment.) **56 copulatives** i.e., people about to copulate within marriage **57 blood breaks** passion drives one to violate the marriage vows (with a suggestion of breaking the maidenhead) **58 humor** whim **60 honesty** chastity **61 your pearl** i.e., the pearl that one hears about **62 swift** quick-witted **62–63 sententious** pithy **64 fool's bolt** (Alluding to the proverb "A fool's bolt [arrow] is soon shot.") **65 dulcet diseases** pleasant afflictions, entertaining yet sharp

JAQUES But for the seventh cause. How did you find the quarrel on the seventh cause?

TOUCHSTONE Upon a lie seven times removed—bear your body more seeming, Audrey—as thus, sir. I did dislike the cut of a certain courtier's beard. He sent me word, if I said his beard was not cut well, he was in the mind it was: this is called the Retort Courteous. If I sent him word again it was not well cut, he would send me word he cut it to please himself: this is called the Quip Modest. If again it was not well cut, he disabled my judgment: this is called the Reply Churlish. If again it was not well cut, he would answer I spake not true: this is called the Reproof Valiant. If again it was not well cut, he would say I lie: this is called the Countercheck Quarrelsome. And so to the Lie Circumstantial and the Lie Direct.

JAQUES And how oft did you say his beard was not well cut?

TOUCHSTONE I durst go no further than the Lie Circumstantial, nor he durst not give me the Lie Direct; and so we measured swords and parted.

JAQUES Can you nominate in order now the degrees of the lie?

TOUCHSTONE O sir, we quarrel in print, by the book, as you have books for good manners. I will name you the degrees. The first, the Retort Courteous; the second, the Quip Modest; the third, the Reply Churlish; the fourth, the Reproof Valiant; the fifth, the Countercheck Quarrelsome; the sixth, the Lie with Circumstance; the seventh, the Lie Direct. All these you may avoid but the Lie Direct; and you may avoid that too, with an If. I knew when seven justices could not take up a quarrel, but when the parties were met themselves, one of them thought but of an If, as, "If you said so, then I said so"; and they shook hands and swore brothers. Your If is the only peacemaker; much virtue in If.

69 seeming seemly **70 dislike** express dislike of **75–76 disabled** disparaged **80 Countercheck** rebuff **86 measured swords** (i.e., as in the mere preliminary to a duel) **89 quarrel . . . book** (Touchstone is travestying books on the general subject of honor and arms, which dealt with occasions and circumstances of the duel.) **97–98 take up** settle **101 swore brothers** pledged themselves to act as brothers

JAQUES Is not this a rare fellow, my lord? He's as good at anything and yet a fool.

DUKE SENIOR He uses his folly like a stalking-horse, and under the presentation of that he shoots his wit.

Enter Hymen, Rosalind, and Celia. Still music.
[*Rosalind and Celia are no longer disguised.*]

HYMEN
Then is there mirth in heaven,
When earthly things made even
Atone together.
Good Duke, receive thy daughter;
Hymen from heaven brought her,
Yea, brought her hither,
That thou mightst join her hand with his
Whose heart within his bosom is.

ROSALIND [*To the Duke*]
To you I give myself, for I am yours.
[*To Orlando.*] To you I give myself, for I am yours.

DUKE SENIOR
If there be truth in sight, you are my daughter.

ORLANDO
If there be truth in sight, you are my Rosalind.

PHOEBE
If sight and shape be true,
Why then, my love adieu!

ROSALIND [*To the Duke*]
I'll have no father, if you be not he.
[*To Orlando.*] I'll have no husband, if you be not he.
[*To Phoebe.*] Nor ne'er wed woman, if you be not she.

HYMEN
Peace, ho! I bar confusion.
'Tis I must make conclusion
Of these most strange events.
Here's eight that must take hands
To join in Hymen's bands,
If truth holds true contents.

105 stalking-horse a real or artificial horse under cover of which the hunter approached his game **106 presentation** semblance. **s.d. Hymen** Roman god of faithful marriage. **Still** soft **109 Atone** are at one **129 If . . . contents** if truth be true, i.e., if the newly revealed realities truly satisfy

[*To Orlando and Rosalind.*]
You and you no cross shall part. 130
[*To Oliver and Celia.*]
You and you are heart in heart.
[*To Phoebe.*]
You to his love must accord 132
Or have a woman to your lord. 133
[*To Touchstone and Audrey.*]
You and you are sure together, 134
As the winter to foul weather.
[*To All.*]
Whiles a wedlock hymn we sing,
Feed yourselves with questioning, 137
That reason wonder may diminish 138
How thus we met, and these things finish.

Song.

Wedding is great Juno's crown, 140
O blessèd bond of board and bed!
'Tis Hymen peoples every town;
High wedlock then be honorèd. 143
Honor, high honor, and renown,
To Hymen, god of every town!

DUKE SENIOR [*To Celia*]
O my dear niece, welcome thou art to me!
Even daughter welcome in no less degree. 147

PHOEBE [*To Silvius*]
I will not eat my word, now thou art mine;
Thy faith my fancy to thee doth combine. 149

Enter Second Brother [*Jaques de Boys*].

JAQUES DE BOYS
Let me have audience for a word or two.
I am the second son of old Sir Rowland,
That bring these tidings to this fair assembly.

130 cross disagreement **132 his** i.e., Silvius's. **accord** agree **133 to** for. **lord** i.e., husband **134 sure** closely united **137 Feed** satisfy **138 reason** understanding **140 Juno's** (Juno was Roman queen of the gods, presiding, in the Renaissance view, over faithful wedlock.) **143 High** solemn **147 Even . . . degree** i.e., you are as welcome as my daughter and to no less extent **149 combine** unite

Duke Frederick, hearing how that every day
Men of great worth resorted to this forest,
Addressed a mighty power, which were on foot
In his own conduct, purposely to take
His brother here and put him to the sword;
And to the skirts of this wild wood he came,
Where, meeting with an old religious man,
After some question with him, was converted
Both from his enterprise and from the world,
His crown bequeathing to his banished brother,
And all their lands restored to them again
That were with him exiled. This to be true
I do engage my life.

DUKE SENIOR Welcome, young man.
Thou offer'st fairly to thy brothers' wedding:
To one his lands withheld and to the other
A land itself at large, a potent dukedom.
First, in this forest let us do those ends
That here were well begun and well begot;
And after, every of this happy number
That have endured shrewd days and nights with us
Shall share the good of our returnèd fortune,
According to the measure of their states.
Meantime, forget this new-fall'n dignity
And fall into our rustic revelry.
Play, music! And you brides and bridegrooms all,
With measure heaped in joy, to the measures fall.

JAQUES
Sir, by your patience. If I heard you rightly,
The Duke hath put on a religious life
And thrown into neglect the pompous court.

JAQUES DE BOYS He hath.

155 Addressed prepared. **power** army **156 In . . . conduct** under his own command **160 question** conversation **165 engage** pledge **166 Thou offer'st fairly** you contribute handsomely **167 the other** i.e., Orlando **168 A land . . . large** i.e., an entire dukedom. (As husband of Rosalind, Orlando will eventually inherit as Duke.) **169 do those ends** accomplish those purposes **170 begot** conceived **172 shrewd** hard, trying **174 states** status, rank **175 new-fall'n** newly acquired **178 With . . . joy** (1) with joyful steps (2) with joy generously bestowed. **measures** dances **179 by your patience** by your leave, i.e., let the music wait a moment **181 pompous** ceremonious

JAQUES

To him will I. Out of these convertites 183
There is much matter to be heard and learned. 184
[*To the Duke.*] You to your former honor I bequeath;
Your patience and your virtue well deserves it.
[*To Orlando.*] You to a love that your true faith doth merit;
[*To Oliver.*] You to your land and love and great allies;
[*To Silvius.*] You to a long and well-deservèd bed;
[*To Touchstone.*] And you to wrangling, for thy loving voyage
Is but for two months victualed. So, to your pleasures. 191
I am for other than for dancing measures.

DUKE SENIOR Stay, Jaques, stay.

JAQUES

To see no pastime I. What you would have
I'll stay to know at your abandoned cave. *Exit.*

DUKE SENIOR

Proceed, proceed. We'll begin these rites,
As we do trust they'll end, in true delights.
[*They dance.*] *Exeunt* [*all but Rosalind*].

183 convertites converts **184 matter** sound sense **191 victualed** provisioned

[Epilogue]

ROSALIND It is not the fashion to see the lady the epilogue; but it is no more unhandsome than to see the 2
lord the prologue. If it be true that good wine needs 3
no bush, 'tis true that a good play needs no epilogue. 4
Yet to good wine they do use good bushes, and good
plays prove the better by the help of good epilogues.
What a case am I in then, that am neither a good epilogue nor cannot insinuate with you in the behalf of a 8
good play! I am not furnished like a beggar; therefore 9
to beg will not become me. My way is to conjure you, 10
and I'll begin with the women. I charge you, O
women, for the love you bear to men, to like as much
of this play as please you; and I charge you, O men,
for the love you bear to women—as I perceive by your
simpering, none of you hates them—that between you
and the women the play may please. If I were a 16
woman I would kiss as many of you as had beards 17
that pleased me, complexions that liked me, and 18
breaths that I defied not; and I am sure as many as 19
have good beards or good faces or sweet breaths will
for my kind offer, when I make curtsy, bid me fare- 21
well. 22

Exit.

Epilogue
2 unhandsome in bad taste **3–4 good . . . bush** (A proverb derived from the custom of displaying a piece of ivy or holly at the tavern door to denote that wine was for sale there.) **8 insinuate** ingratiate myself **9 furnished** equipped, decked out **10 conjure** adjure, earnestly charge **16–17 If . . . woman** (Women's parts on the Elizabethan stage were played by boys in feminine costume.) **18 liked** pleased **19 defied** disliked **21–22 bid me farewell** i.e., applaud me

Date and Text

"As you like yt, a booke" was entered in the Stationers' Register, the official record book of the London Company of Stationers (booksellers and printers), on August 4, 1600, along with *Much Ado about Nothing, Henry V,* and Ben Jonson's *Every Man in His Humor,* all labeled as "My lord chamberlens mens plaies" and all ordered "to be staied" from publication until further notice. Evidently the Chamberlain's men (Shakespeare's acting company) were anxious to protect their rights to these very popular plays. Despite their efforts *Henry V* was pirated that same month. *As You Like It* did not appear in print, however, until the First Folio of 1623. The Folio text is a good one, based seemingly on the theatrical promptbook or on a literary transcript either of it or of an authorial manuscript.

Francis Meres does not mention the play in September of 1598 in his *Palladis Tamia: Wit's Treasury* (a slender volume on contemporary literature and art; valuable because it lists most of Shakespeare's plays that existed at that time). The play contains an unusually clear allusion to Christopher Marlowe's *Hero and Leander* ("Who ever loved that loved not at first sight?" 3.5.82), first published in 1598. Almost certainly *As You Like It* was written between 1598 and the summer of 1600, either before or after *Much Ado about Nothing.*

Textual Notes

These textual notes are not a historical collation, either of the early folios or of more recent editions; they are simply a record of departures in this edition from the copy text. The reading adopted in this edition appears in boldface, followed by the rejected reading from the copy text, i.e., the First Folio. Only a few major alterations in punctuation are noted. Changes in lineation are not indicated, nor are some minor and obvious typographical errors.

Abbreviations used:
F the First Folio
s.d. stage direction
s.p. speech prefix

Copy text: The First Folio

1.1. 105 she hee **154 s.p. Oliver** [not in F] **154 s.d. Exit** [at l. 153 in F]

1.2. 3 I were were **51 goddesses and** goddesses **55 s.p. [and elsewhere] Touchstone** Clow **55–56 father** farher **80 s.p. Celia** Ros **88 Le** the **251 s.d.** [at l. 249 in F] **280 [and occasionally elsewhere] Rosalind** Rosaline

1.3. 55 likelihood likelihoods **76 her** per **87 s.d. with Lords** &c **124 be** by **135 we in** in we

2.1. 49 much must **50 friends** friend **59 of the** of

2.3. 10 some seeme **16 s.p. Orlando** [not in F] **29 s.p. Orlando** Ad **50 woo** woe **71 seventeen** seauentie

2.4. 1 weary merry **42 thy wound** they would **65 you** your

2.5. 1 s.p. Amiens [not in F] **38 s.d. All together here** [before l. 35 in F] **41–42 No . . . weather** &c **46 s.p. Jaques** Amy

2.7. s.d. Lords Lord **10 [and elsewhere] woo** woe **38 brain** braiue **55 Not to seem** Seeme **87 comes** come **161 treble, pipes** trebble pipes, **174 s.p. Amiens** [not in F] **182 Then** The **190–193 Heigh-ho . . . jolly** &c **201 masters** masters

3.2. 26 good pood **123 a desert** Desert **143 her** his **234 such fruit** fruite **241 thy** the **340 lectures** Lectors **354 deifying** defying

3.3. 52 so so **88 s.p. Touchstone** Ol **99 s.d. Exit** Exeunt

3.4. 29 a lover Louer

3.5. 105 erewhile yerewhile **128 I have** Haue

4.1. 1 me be me **18 my** by **44 thousandth** thousand **202 it** in

4.2. 2 s.p. First Lord Lord **7 s.p. Second Lord** Lord **10 s.p. Second Lord** [not in F]

4.3. 5 s.d. [at l. 4 in F] **8 bid** did bid **143 In** I **156 his** this

5.1. 36 sir sit **55 policy** police

5.2. 7 nor her nor **31 overcame** ouercome

5.3. 15 s.p. Both Pages [not in F] **18 ring** rang **24–26 In . . . spring** In spring time, &c [also at ll. 30–32 and 36–38] **33–38** [this stanza comes before l. 21 in F]

5.4. 25 s.d. Exeunt Exit **34 s.d.** [at l. 33 in F] **80 so to the** so ro **113 her** his **150 s.p. Jaques de Boys** 2 Bro [also at l. 182] **163 them** him **170 were** vvete **197 s.d. Exeunt** Exit

Shakespeare's Sources

Any departures from the original text are noted with an asterisk and appear at the bottom of the page in boldface; original readings are in roman.

Shakespeare's chief source for *As You Like It* was Thomas Lodge's graceful pastoral romance, *Rosalynde: Euphues' Golden Legacy* (1592). Lodge was indebted in turn to *The Tale of Gamelyn,* a fourteenth-century poem wrongly included by some medieval scribes as "The Cook's Tale" in Chaucer's *Canterbury Tales. Gamelyn* was not printed until 1721, but Lodge clearly had access to a manuscript of it. Although Shakespeare may not have known *Gamelyn* directly, his play still retains the hearty spirit of this Robin Hood legend. (In later Robin Hood ballads, Gamelyn or Gandelyn is identified with Will Scarlet, a member of Robin Hood's band.)

Even a brief account of *Gamelyn* suggests how greatly the original tale is inspired by Robin Hood legends of outlaws valiantly defying the corrupt social order presided over by the Sheriff and his henchmen. Gamelyn, the youngest of three brothers, is denied his inheritance by his churlish eldest brother, John. When Gamelyn demands his rights, John orders his men to beat Gamelyn, but the young man arms himself with a club, or truncheon, and proves a formidable fighter. Later Gamelyn defeats the champion wrestler in a local wrestling match (a lower-class sport befitting the social milieu of this story) and returns home to find himself locked out by his brother. He kills the porter, flings the man's body down a well, and feasts his companions day and night for a week. John feigns a reconciliation and slyly asks if he can bind Gamelyn hand and foot merely to satisfy an oath he has sworn over the death of the porter. Gamelyn trustingly agrees and is made prisoner. After his bonds have been secretly loosed by Adam the Spencer (the steward), Gamelyn pretends to remain bound until the propitious moment for revenge and escape. The moment arrives during a feast of monks who churlishly refuse to help Gamelyn. With Adam's help he overcomes many of them, ties up his brother, and escapes to the woods, where he and Adam are rescued from hunger by a band of merry outlaws. As their chief, Gamelyn becomes a champion of the poor and an enemy of rich churchmen. His brother, now sheriff, brands

Gamelyn an outlaw and manages to imprison him, but Gamelyn's second brother, Sir Ote, stands bail for him. On the day of the trial, Gamelyn frees Sir Ote and hangs the Sheriff and the jury. Gamelyn finally obtains his inheritance and becomes chief officer of the King's royal forests. This story is uninfluenced by the pastoral tradition and contains no love plot. Its Robin Hood traditions are very much present, nonetheless, in Shakespeare's contrasting portrayal of a tyrannical court and of a just society in banishment.

Lodge retains the primitive vigor of *Gamelyn,* but adds generous infusions of pastoral sentiment in the manner of Sir Philip Sidney's *Arcadia* (1590) and sententious moralizing in the manner of John Lyly's *Euphues* (1578). The pastoralism is presented in conventional terms, with none of the genial self-reflexive satire we find in Shakespeare. Psychological motivation is intricate, often more so than in Shakespeare's play. The style is also heavily influenced by Lyly's exquisitely balanced, antithetical, and ornamented prose. For his pastoralism Lodge was indebted not only to Sidney but to the ancient pastoral tradition that included the Greek Theocritus and the Roman Virgil, the Italian Sannazaro (*Arcadia*) and the Portuguese Jorge de Montemayor (*Diana*). Pastoralism by Lodge's time had become thoroughly imbued with artificial conventions: abject lovers writing sonnets to their disdainful mistresses, princes and princesses in shepherds' disguise, idealized landscapes, stylized debate as to the relative merits of love and friendship, youth and age, city life and country life, and so on. Some of these conventions were derived also from the vogue of sonneteering pioneered by Francis Petrarch and can thus be described as the stereotypes of "Petrarchism." Lodge accepts these conventions and gives us typical pastoral lovers even in his hero and heroine, although the elements he derived from *Gamelyn* certainly add a contrasting note of violence and danger.

Selections from Lodge's *Rosalynde* follow. Because its length precludes a printing of the entire novel, however, a summary may be useful to fill in the omitted passages and to highlight what Shakespeare has retained or altered in his play. Lodge's account begins much like that of *Gamelyn*. Saladyne, the envious eldest brother, bribes the champion wrestler to do away with Rosader (Orlando) in the wrestling match. Rosader succeeds instead in killing the wrestler and in winning the heart of Rosalynde, daughter of the banished King Gerismond. When she sends him a jewel, Rosader is not at all tongue-tied like his counterpart in Shakespeare's play; instead, he composes a Petrarchan sonnet on the spot. The usurping King Torismond (who is unrelated to Gerismond and is not, like Duke Frederick, the usurper of his banished brother's title), despite his evil nature, is impressed by Rosader's grace and martial prowess. Rosader returns home with friends, breaks open the door, and feasts his company. Saladyne overwhelms Rosader in his sleep and binds him to a post, but Rosader is untied by Adam and overwhelms his eldest brother's guests as in *Gamelyn*. In this case, however, the guests are Saladyne's kindred and allies, all of whom have refused to help Rosader. The Sheriff tries to arrest Rosader and Adam, but they escape to the Forest of Arden in France. They are saved from starvation by the kindly King Gerismond and his exiled followers. Rosalynde and King Torismond's daughter Alinda have meanwhile been banished from court and have taken up residence in the forest under the names of Ganymede and Aliena. They befriend old Corydon (Corin) and young Montanus (Silvius), who is hopelessly in love with the haughty Phoebe. "Ganymede" poses as a woman to test Rosader in his wooing, and they are joined in a mock marriage. Saladyne, now repenting of his evil deeds, comes to the forest, is saved by his brother from a lion, and falls in love with Alinda (whom he helps to rescue from ruffians). The denouement is much as in Shakespeare, although the triumphant return to society is more complete: King Torismond is slain, Gerismond is restored to his throne, Rosader is named heir apparent, and all the friends are appropriately rewarded.

Despite Shakespeare's extensive indebtedness to this charming romance, there is a crucial difference: Lodge's pastoral world is never subjected to a wry or satirical exploration. Lodge offers no equivalents for Touchstone, the fool who sees the absurdity of both country and city; Jaques, the malcontent traveler; William and Audrey, the clownishly simple peasants; or Sir Oliver Mar-text, the ridiculous hedge-priest. Nor does Lodge tell of Le Beau, the court butterfly. Hymen is a Shakespearean addition, and the conversion of Duke Frederick by a hermit instead of his being overthrown and killed is a characteristically Shakespearean softening touch. Shakespeare's added characters are virtually all foils to the conventional pastoral vision he found in his source.

Rosalynde: Euphues' Golden Legacy

By Thomas Lodge

[*Rosalynde* begins with the death of a knight, John of Bordeaux, and his bestowing a legacy on his three sons. The eldest, Saladyne, receives the manor house and estate, while Fernandyne and Rosader are given certain lands and other gifts. Rosader, his father's darling, is placed in the charge of Saladyne, since he is not yet of age. Saladyne, resentful of his youngest brother, resolves to himself to abuse his authority by oppressing Rosader with an enforced low condition: "Though he be a gentleman by nature, yet form him anew and make him a peasant by nurture. So shalt thou keep him as a slave and reign thyself sole lord over all thy father's possessions."]

In this humor was Saladyne, making his brother Rosader his footboy for the space of two or three years, keeping him in such servile subjection as if he had been the son of any country vassal. The young gentleman bare[1] all with patience, till on a day, walking in the garden by himself, he began to consider how he was the son of John of Bordeaux, a knight renowned for many victories and a gentleman famoused for his virtues; how, contrary to the testament of his father, he was not only kept from his land and entreated[2] as a servant but smothered in such secret slavery as he might not attain to any honorable actions.

"Ah," quoth he to himself, nature working these effectual[3] passions, "why should I, that am a gentleman born, pass my time in such unnatural drudgery? Were it not better either in Paris to become a scholar, or in the court a courtier, or in the field a soldier, than to live a footboy to my own brother? Nature hath lent me wit to conceive,[4] but my

1 bare bore **2 entreated** treated **3 effectual** ardent **4 wit to conceive** intelligence to understand

brother denied me art[5] to contemplate. I have strength to perform any honorable exploit but no liberty to accomplish my virtuous endeavors. Those good parts that God hath bestowed upon me, the envy of my brother doth smother in obscurity; the harder is my fortune, and the more his frowardness."[6]

With that, casting up his hand, he felt hair on his face, and perceiving his beard to bud, for choler he began to blush and swore to himself he would be no more subject to such slavery. As thus he was ruminating of his melancholy passions, in came Saladyne with his men and, seeing his brother in a brown study and to forget his wonted reverence,[7] thought to shake him out of his dumps thus:

"Sirrah," quoth he, "what, is your heart on your halfpenny,[8] or are you saying a dirge for your father's soul? What, is my dinner ready?"

At this question, Rosader, turning his head askance and bending his brows as if anger there had plowed the furrows of her wrath, with his eyes full of fire he made this reply:

"Dost thou ask me, Saladyne, for thy cates?[9] Ask some of thy churls, who are fit for such an office. I am thine equal by nature, though not by birth, and though thou hast more cards in the bunch,[10] I have as many trumps in my hands as thyself. Let me question with thee why thou hast felled my woods, spoiled my manor houses, and made havoc of such utensils[11] as my father bequeathed unto me? I tell thee, Saladyne, either answer me as a brother or I will trouble thee as an enemy."

At this reply of Rosader's Saladyne smiled, as laughing at his presumption, and frowned, as checking his folly. He therefore took him up thus shortly:

"What, sirrah! Well, I see early pricks the tree that will prove a thorn. Hath my familiar conversing with you made you coy,[12] or my good looks[13] drawn you to be thus contemptuous? I can quickly remedy such a fault, and I will bend the tree while it is a wand.[14] In faith, sir boy, I have a snaffle

5 art training, skill **6 frowardness** evil disposition **7 wonted reverence** customary show of respect (due an older brother) **8 is your . . . halfpenny** i.e., is there something special on your mind, some particular object **9 cates** delicacies, things to eat **10 bunch** pack of cards **11 utensils** useful possessions **12 coy** disdainful **13 good looks** favorable regard **14 wand** i.e., sapling

for such a headstrong colt. You, sirs, lay hold on him and bind him, and then I will give him a cooling-card[15] for his choler."

This made Rosader half mad, that, stepping to a great rake that stood in the garden, he laid such load upon his brother's men that he hurt some of them and made the rest of them run away. Saladyne, seeing Rosader so resolute and with his resolution so valiant, thought his heels his best safety and took him to a loft adjoining to the garden, whither Rosader pursued him hotly. Saladyne, afraid of his brother's fury, cried out to him thus:

"Rosader, be not so rash. I am thy brother and thine elder, and if I have done thee wrong, I'll make thee amends. Revenge not anger in blood, for so shalt thou stain the virtue of old Sir John of Bordeaux. Say wherein thou art discontent, and thou shalt be satisfied. Brothers' frowns ought not to be periods[16] of wrath. What, man, look not so sourly! I know we shall be friends, and better friends than we have been, for *Amantium irae amoris redintegratio est.*"[17]

These words appeased the choler of Rosader, for he was of a mild and courteous nature, so that he laid down his weapons and, upon the faith of a gentleman, assured his brother he would offer him no prejudice; whereupon Saladyne came down, and after a little parley they embraced each other and became friends, and Saladyne promising Rosader the restitution of all his lands "and what favor else," quoth he, "any ways my ability or the nature of a brother may perform." Upon these sugared reconciliations they went into the house arm in arm together, to the great content of all the old servants of Sir John of Bordeaux.

Thus continued the pad hidden in the straw[18] till it chanced that Torismond, King of France, had appointed for his pleasure a day of wrestling and of tournament to busy his commons' heads, lest, being idle, their thoughts should run upon more serious matters and call to remembrance their old banished king. A champion there was to stand against all comers, a Norman, a man of tall stature and of great strength, so valiant that in many such conflicts he

15 a cooling-card something to cool his ardor **16 periods** sentences
17 Amantium . . . est the quarrels of lovers are the renewal of love
18 pad . . . straw i.e., concealed danger. **pad** paddock, toad or frog

always bare[19] away the victory, not only overthrowing them which he encountered but often with the weight of his body killing them outright. Saladyne, hearing of this, thinking now not to let the ball fall to the ground but to take opportunity by the forehead, first by secret means convented[20] with the Norman and procured[21] him with rich rewards to swear that if Rosader came within his claws he should nevermore return to quarrel with Saladyne for his possessions. The Norman, desirous of pelf—as *Quis nisi mentis inops oblatum respuit aurum?*[22]—taking great gifts for little gods, took the crowns of Saladyne to perform the stratagem.

Having thus the champion tied to his villainous determination by oath, he prosecuted the intent of his purpose thus. He went to young Rosader, who in all his thoughts reached at honor and gazed no lower than virtue commanded him, and began to tell him of this tournament and wrestling, how the King should be there and all the chief peers of France, with all the beautiful damosels of the country.

"Now, brother," quoth he, "for the honor of Sir John of Bordeaux, our renowned father, to famous[23] that house that never hath been found without men approved[24] in chivalry, show thy resolution to be peremptory.[25] For myself thou knowest, though I am eldest by birth, yet, never having attempted any deeds of arms, I am youngest to perform any martial exploits, knowing better how to survey my lands than to charge my lance. My brother Fernandyne he is at Paris poring on a few papers, having more insight into sophistry and principles of philosophy than any warlike endeavors. But thou, Rosader, the youngest in years but the eldest in valor, art a man of strength and darest do what honor allows thee. Take thou my father's lance, his sword, and his horse, and hie thee to the tournament, and either there valiantly crack a spear or try with the Norman for the palm of activity."

[Rosader accepts the proposal with alacrity and hastens to the tourney. Present at the event are Torismond, the usurp-

19 bare bore **20 convented** met **21 procured** persuaded **22 Quis . . . aurum** who in his right mind refuses money that is offered. (Adapted from Terence, *Andria*, l. 555. *Pelf* means "money, riches.") **23 famous** make famous **24 approved** proved, tested **25 peremptory** unhesitating

ing King of France, his daughter Alinda, and Rosalynde, daughter of the banished King Gerismond, now living in the Forest of Arden.]

At last, when the tournament ceased, the wrestling began, and the Norman presented himself as a challenger against all comers, but he looked like Hercules when he advanced himself against Achelous,[26] so that the fury of his countenance amazed all that durst attempt to encounter with him in any deed of activity; till at last a lusty[27] franklin of the country came with two tall[28] men that were his sons, of good lineaments and comely personage. The eldest of these, doing his obeisance to the King, entered the list and presented himself to the Norman, who straight coped with him and, as a man that would triumph in the glory of his strength, roused himself with such fury that not only he gave him the fall but killed him with the weight of his corpulent personage. Which the younger brother, seeing, leaped presently into the place and, thirsty after the revenge, assailed the Norman with such valor that at the first encounter he brought him to his knees, which repulsed so the Norman that, recovering himself, fear of disgracc doubling his strength, he stepped so sternly to the young franklin that, taking him up in his arms, he threw him against the ground so violently that he broke his neck and so ended his days with his brother. At this unlooked-for massacre the people murmured and were all in a deep passion of pity; but the franklin, father unto these, never changed his countenance, but as a man of a courageous resolution took up the bodies of his sons without any show of outward discontent.

All this while stood Rosader and saw this tragedy; who, noting the undoubted virtue of the franklin's mind, alighted off from his horse and presently sat down on the grass and commanded his boy to pull off his boots, making him ready to try the strength of this champion. Being furnished as he would, he clapped the franklin on the shoulder and said thus:

"Bold yeoman, whose sons have ended the term of their years with honor, for that I see thou scornest Fortune with

26 Achelous a river god with whom Hercules wrestled in order to win Dejanira as his wife **27 lusty** vigorous **28 tall** brave

patience and thwartest* the injury of Fate with content in brooking[29] the death of thy sons, stand awhile and either see me make a third in their tragedy or else revenge their fall with an honorable triumph."

The franklin, seeing so goodly a gentleman to give him such courteous comfort, gave him hearty thanks, with promise to pray for his happy success. With that Rosader vailed bonnet[30] to the King and lightly leaped within the lists, where, noting more the company than the combatant, he cast his eye upon the troop of ladies that glistered there like the stars of heaven; but at last Love, willing to make him as amorous as he was valiant, presented him with the sight of Rosalynde, whose admirable beauty so inveigled the eye of Rosader that, forgetting himself, he stood and fed his looks on the favor of Rosalynde's face; which she perceiving blushed, which was such a doubling of her beauteous excellence that the bashful red of Aurora[31] at the sight of unacquainted Phaëthon[32] was not half so glorious.

The Norman, seeing this young gentleman fettered in the looks of the ladies, drave him out of his memento[33] with a shake by the shoulder. Rosader, looking back with an angry frown as if he had been wakened from some pleasant dream, discovered to all by the fury of his countenance that he was a man of some high thoughts; but when they all noted his youth and the sweetness of his visage, with a general applause of favors,[34] they grieved that so goodly a young man should venture in so base an action; but seeing it were to his dishonor to hinder him from his enterprise, they wished him to be graced with the palm of victory. After Rosader was thus called out of his memento by the Norman, he roughly clapped to him with so fierce an encounter that they both fell to the ground and with the violence of the fall were forced to breathe, in which space the Norman called to mind by all tokens that this was he whom Saladyne had appointed him to kill, which conjecture made him stretch every limb and try every sinew that, working his death, he might recover the gold which so bountifully was promised him. On the contrary part, Rosader while he breathed was

***thwartest** twhartest

29 brooking enduring with patience **30 vailed bonnet** took off his cap **31 Aurora** goddess of the dawn **32 Phaëthon** the sun god (whose son is also named Phaëthon) **33 memento** musing **34 applause of favors** look of approval in their faces

not idle but still cast his eye upon Rosalynde, who, to encourage him with a favor, lent him such an amorous look as might have made the most coward desperate, which glance of Rosalynde so fired the passionate desires of Rosader that, turning to the Norman, he ran upon him and braved him with a strong encounter. The Norman received him as valiantly, that there was a sore combat, hard to judge on whose side Fortune would be prodigal. At last Rosader, calling to mind the beauty of his new mistress, the fame of his father's honors, and the disgrace that should fall to his house by his misfortune, roused himself and threw the Norman against the ground, falling upon his chest with so willing a weight that the Norman yielded nature her due and Rosader the victory.

The death of this champion, as it highly contented the franklin as a man satisfied with revenge, so it drew the King and all the peers into a great admiration[35] that so young years and so beautiful a personage should contain such martial excellence; but when they knew him to be the youngest son of Sir John of Bordeaux, the King rose from his seat and embraced him, and the peers entreated[36] him with all favorable courtesy, commending both his valor and his virtues, wishing him to go forward in such haughty[37] deeds that he might attain to the glory of his father's honorable fortunes.

As the King and lords graced him with embracing, so the ladies favored him with their looks, especially Rosalynde, whom the beauty and valor of Rosader had already touched; but she accounted love a toy and fancy a momentary passion that, as it was taken in with a gaze, might be shaken off with a wink, and therefore feared not to dally in the flame; and to make Rosader know she affected him, took from her neck a jewel and sent it by a page to the young gentleman. The prize that Venus gave to Paris[38] was not half so pleasing to the Trojan as this gem was to Rosader; for if Fortune had sworn to make him sole monarch of the world, he would rather have refused such dignity than have lost the jewel sent him by Rosalynde. To return her with the like he was unfurnished, and yet, that he might more than in his

35 admiration astonishment **36 entreated** treated **37 haughty** exalted
38 prize . . . Paris (Paris awarded Venus the golden apple as the fairest of the goddesses, and receives Helen as his prize.

looks discover his affection, he stepped into a tent and, taking pen and paper, writ this fancy:

Two suns at once from one fair heaven there shined,[39]
Ten branches from two boughs, tipped all with roses,
Pure locks more golden than is gold refined,
Two pearlèd rows that nature's pride incloses;
Two mounts fair marble-white, down-soft and dainty,
A snow-dyed orb, where love increased by pleasure
Full woeful makes my heart and body fainty:
Her fair, my woe, exceeds all thought and measure.
In lines confused my luckless harm appeareth,
Whom sorrow clouds, whom pleasant smiling
  cleareth.

This sonnet he sent to Rosalynde, which when she read she blushed, but with a sweet content in that she perceived love had allotted her so amorous a servant.

[Rosader, returning home to an unfriendly greeting from Saladyne, breaks open the door and, with the help of old Adam Spencer, a loyal and trusty servant, provides a hearty welcome for all his friends. He is outwardly reconciled to Saladyne, but the latter is only biding his time to be revenged. Rosalynde, meanwhile, discovering herself to be in love with Rosader, composes a madrigal on the subject of her passion.]

Scarce had Rosalynde ended her madrigal before Torismond came in with his daughter Alinda and many of the peers of France, who were enamored of her[40] beauty; which Torismond perceiving, fearing lest her perfection might be the beginning of his prejudice[41] and the hope of his fruit end in the beginning of her blossoms, he thought to banish her from the court. "For," quoth he to himself, "her face is so full of favor that it pleads pity in the eye of every man; her beauty is so heavenly and divine that she will prove to me as Helen did to Priam;[42] some one of the peers will aim at her

39 Two . . . shined (The two suns are Rosalind's eyes, followed in this catalogue of her charms by her ten fingers and two arms, her hair, her teeth, her breasts, etc.) **40 her** i.e., Rosalynde's **41 his prejudice** a dislike of him **42 Helen . . . Priam** (Helen's beauty proved the undoing of Troy, of which Priam was King.)

love, end the marriage,[43] and then in his wife's right attempt the kingdom. To prevent therefore 'had I wist'[44] in all these actions, she tarries not about the court, but shall, as an exile, either wander to her father or else seek other fortunes." In this humor, with a stern countenance full of wrath, he breathed out this censure[45] unto her before the peers, that charged her that that night she were not seen[46] about the court. "For," quoth he, "I have heard of thy aspiring speeches and intended treasons." This doom[47] was strange unto Rosalynde, and presently, covered with the shield of her innocence, she boldly brake out in reverent terms to have cleared herself; but Torismond would admit of no reason, nor durst his lords plead for Rosalynde, although her beauty had made some of them passionate, seeing the figure of wrath portrayed in his brow. Standing thus all mute, and Rosalynde amazed, Alinda, who loved her more than herself, with grief in her heart and tears in her eyes, falling down on her knees, began to entreat her father thus:

ALINDA'S ORATION TO HER FATHER IN DEFENSE OF FAIR ROSALYNDE

"If, mighty Torismond, I offend in pleading for my friend, let the law of amity crave pardon for my boldness, for where there is depth of affection there friendship alloweth a privilege. Rosalynde and I have been fostered up from our infancies and nursed under the harbor of our conversing together with such private familiarities that custom had wrought an union of our nature, and the sympathy of our affections such a secret love that we have two bodies and one soul. Then marvel not, great Torismond, if, seeing my friend distressed, I find myself perplexed with a thousand sorrows; for her virtuous and honorable thoughts, which are the glories that maketh women excellent, they be such as may challenge love and rase[48] out suspicion. Her obedience to Your Majesty I refer to the censure of your own eye, that since her father's exile hath smothered all griefs with patience and in the absence of na-

43 end the marriage i.e., achieve her in marriage and thus end the contest as to who will marry Rosalynde **44 had I wist** if I had only known **45 censure** judgment **46 were not seen** be seen no more **47 doom** verdict **48 rase** erase

ture hath honored you with all duty as her own father by nouriture,[49] not in word uttering any discontent nor in thought, as far as conjecture may reach, hammering on revenge, only in all her actions seeking to please you and to win my favor. Her wisdom, silence, chastity, and other such rich qualities I need not decipher;[50] only it rests for me to conclude, in one word, that she is innocent. If, then, Fortune, who triumphs in variety of miseries, hath presented some envious person as minister of her intended stratagem to taint Rosalynde with any surmise of treason, let him be brought to her face and confirm his accusation by witnesses; which proved, let her die, and Alinda will execute the massacre. If none can avouch any confirmed relation of her intent, use justice, my lord—it is the glory of a king—and let her live in your wonted favor; for if you banish her, myself, as copartner of her hard fortunes, will participate[51] in exile some part of her extremities."

Torismond, at this speech of Alinda, covered his face with such a frown as[52] tyranny seemed to sit triumphant in his forehead, and checked her up[53] with such taunts as made the lords, that only were hearers, to tremble.

"Proud girl," quoth he, "hath my looks made thee so light of tongue or my favors encouraged thee to be so forward that thou darest presume to preach after[54] thy father? Hath not my years more experience than thy youth and the winter of mine age deeper insight into civil policy than the prime of thy flourishing days? The old lion avoids the toils,[55] where the young one leaps into the net; the care of age is provident and foresees much; suspicion is a virtue where a man holds his enemy in his bosom.[56] Thou, fond[57] girl, measurest all by present affection, and as thy heart loves, thy thoughts censure; but if thou knewest that in liking Rosalynde thou hatchest up a bird to peck out thine own eyes, thou wouldst entreat as much for her absence as now thou delightest in her presence. But why do I allege policy[58] to thee? Sit you down, huswife, and fall to your needle; if idleness make you so wanton, or liberty so malapert, I can quickly tie you to a sharper

49 by nouriture by nurture, by adoption **50 decipher** recount **51 participate** share **52 as** that **53 checked her up** rebuked her **54 after** to **55 flourishing . . . toils** youthful . . . nets **56 holds . . . bosom** i.e., is fearful and suspicious **57 fond** foolish **58 allege policy** cite matters of statecraft

task. And you, maid, this night be packing, either into Arden to your father or whither best it shall content your humor, but in the court you shall not abide."

This rigorous reply of Torismond nothing amazed Alinda, for still she prosecuted[59] her plea in the defense of Rosalynde, wishing her father, if his censure might not be reversed, that he would appoint her partner of her exile; which if he refused to do, either she would by some secret means steal out and follow her or else end her days with some desperate kind of death. When Torismond heard his daughter so resolute, his heart was so hardened against her that he set down a definitive and peremptory sentence that they should both be banished, which presently was done, the tyrant rather choosing to hazard the loss of his only child than anyways to put in question the state of his kingdom, so suspicious and fearful is the conscience of an usurper. Well, although his lords persuaded[60] him to retain his own daughter, yet his resolution might not be reversed, but both of them must away from the court without either more company or delay. In he went with great melancholy and left these two ladies alone. Rosalynde waxed very sad and sat down and wept. Alinda she smiled, and sitting by her friend began thus to comfort her. [Alinda promises to remain faithful always.]

At this Rosalynde began to comfort her,[61] and after she had wept a few kind tears in the bosom of her Alinda, she gave her hearty thanks, and then they sat them down to consult how they should travel. Alinda grieved at nothing but that they might have no man in their company, saying it would be their greatest prejudice in that two women went wandering without either guide or attendant.

"Tush," quoth Rosalynde, "art thou a woman and hast not a sudden shift[62] to prevent a misfortune? I, thou seest, am of a tall stature and would very well become the person and apparel of a page; thou shalt be my mistress,[63] and I will play the man so properly that, trust me, in what company soever I come I will not be discovered. I will buy me a suit and have my rapier very handsomely at my side, and if any knave offer wrong, your page will show him the point of his weapon."

59 prosecuted persisted in **60 persuaded** pleaded with **61 comfort her** take comfort **62 sudden shift** quickly devised stratagem **63 my mistress** i.e., the lady I serve

At this Alinda smiled, and upon this they agreed and presently gathered up all their jewels, which they trussed up in a casket, and Rosalynde in all haste provided her of robes, and Alinda, from[64] her royal weeds, put herself in more homely attire. Thus fitted to the purpose, away go these two friends, having now changed their names, Alinda being called Aliena, and Rosalynde Ganymede. They traveled along the vineyards and by many byways at last got to the forest side,[65] where they traveled by the space of two or three days without seeing any creature, being often in danger of wild beasts and pained with many passionate sorrows.

[In the Forest of Arden, Rosalynde and Alinda encounter old Corydon and young Mantanus—the latter hopelessly in love with Phoebe—and overhear a pleasant eclogue between them on the subject of unrequited love. Striking up a conversation with these country folk, Rosalynde and Alinda agree at length to buy a farm from Corydon's master and settle down in Arden. Saladyne meanwhile devises a craven assault on Rosader in his sleep, binds him in fetters, and leaves him for two or three days without food, from which sad condition Rosader is at last secretly rescued by Adam Spencer and assisted in a counterplot. Pretending to be fettered still, Rosader awaits a time during the evening festivities when Saladyne and his guests are fuddled with wine, throws off his chains, and lays about him with a poleax, hurting many and killing some. Now outlaws and painfully aware that the law is on Saladyne's side, Rosader and Adam make a bloody escape from the Sheriff's posse that has come to arrest them.]

But Rosader and Adam, knowing full well the secret ways that led through the vineyards, stole away privily through the province of Bordeaux and escaped safe to the Forest of Arden. Being come thither, they were glad they had so good a harbor;[66] but Fortune, who is like the chameleon, variable with every object and constant in nothing but inconstancy, thought to make them mirrors of her mutability and therefore still crossed them thus contrarily. Thinking still to pass

64 from changing from **65 forest side** edge of the forest **66 harbor** place of refuge on by the byways to get to Lyons, they chanced on a path that led into the thick of the forest, where they wandered five or six days without meat, that they were almost famished, finding neither shepherd nor cottage to relieve them; and hunger growing on so extreme, Adam Spencer, being old, began first to faint and, sitting him down on a hill and looking about him, espied where Rosader lay as feeble and as ill perplexed, which sight made him shed tears and to fall into these bitter terms:

[Adam reflects on the vicissitudes of fortune and the need for patience as the only remedy.]

"Master," quoth he, "you see we are both in one predicament, and long I cannot live without meat; seeing therefore we can find no food, let the death of the one preserve the life of the other. I am old and overworn with age; you are young and are the hope of many honors. Let me then die; I will presently cut my veins, and, master, with the warm blood relieve your fainting spirits; suck on that till I end, and you be comforted."

With that Adam Spencer was ready to pull out his knife, when Rosader, full of courage though very faint, rose up, and wished Adam Spencer to sit there till his return. "For my mind gives me,"[67] quoth he, "I shall bring thee meat." With that, like a madman, he rose up and ranged up and down the woods, seeking to encounter some wild beast with his rapier that either he might carry his friend Adam food or else pledge his life in pawn of his loyalty.

It chanced that day that Gerismond, the lawful King of France banished by Torismond, who with a lusty crew of outlaws lived in that forest, that day in honor of his birth made a feast to all his bold yeomen and frolicked it with store of wine and venison, sitting all at a long table under the shadow of lemon trees. To that place by chance Fortune conducted Rosader, who, seeing such a crew of brave[68] men having store of that for want of which he and Adam perished, he stepped boldly to the board's end and saluted the company thus:

"Whatsoe'er thou be that art master of these lusty squires, I salute thee as graciously as a man in extreme dis-

67 gives me has a foreknowledge **68 brave** gallant

tress may. Know that I and a fellow friend of mine are here famished in the forest for want of food; perish we must unless relieved by thy favors. Therefore, if thou be a gentleman, give meat to men, and to such men as are every way worthy of life. Let the proudest squire that sits at thy table rise and encounter with me in any honorable point of activity whatsoever, and if he and thou prove me not a man, send me away comfortless. If thou refuse this, as a niggard of thy cates, I will have amongst you[69] with my sword; for rather will I die valiantly than perish with so cowardly an extreme."

Gerismond, looking him earnestly in the face and seeing so proper a gentleman in so bitter a passion, was moved with so great pity that, rising from the table, he took him by the hand and bade him welcome, willing him to sit down in his place and in his room not only to eat his fill but be lord of the feast.

"Gramercy,[70] sir," quoth Rosader, "but I have a feeble friend that lies hereby famished almost for food, aged and therefore less able to abide the extremity of hunger than myself, and dishonor it were for me to taste one crumb before I made him partner of my fortunes; therefore I will run and fetch him, and then I will gratefully accept of your proffer."

Away hies Rosader to Adam Spencer and tells him the news, who was glad of so happy fortune, but so feeble he was that he could not go, whereupon Rosader got him up on his back and brought him to the place. Which when Gerismond and his men saw, they greatly applauded their league of friendship; and Rosader, having Gerismond's place assigned him, would not sit there himself, but set down Adam Spencer. Well, to be short, those hungry squires fell to their victuals and feasted themselves with good delicates and great store of wine. As soon as they had taken their repast, Gerismond, desirous to hear what hard fortune drave them into those bitter extremes, requested Rosader to discourse, if it were not any way prejudicial unto him, the cause of his travel. Rosader, desirous any way to satisfy the courtesy of his favorable host, first beginning his exordium with a volley of sighs and a few lukewarm tears, prosecuted[71] his discourse and told him from point to point all his fortunes: how he was the youngest son of Sir John of Bordeaux, his name

69 cates . . . have amongst you provisions . . . attack you **70 Gramercy** many thanks **71 prosecuted** continued

Rosader, how his brother sundry times had wronged him, and lastly how, for beating the Sheriff and hurting his men, he fled.

"And this old man," quoth he, "whom I so much love and honor, is surnamed Adam Spencer, an old servant of my father's and one that for his love never failed me in all my misfortunes."

When Gerismond heard this, he fell on the neck of Rosader, and next discoursing unto him how he was Gerismond, their lawful king exiled by Torismond, what familiarity had ever been betwixt his father, Sir John of Bordeaux, and him, how faithful a subject he[72] lived and how honorably he died, promising for his sake to give both him[73] and his friend such courteous entertainment as his present estate could minister, and upon this made him one of his foresters. Rosader, seeing it was the King, craved pardon for his boldness in that he did not do him due reverence and humbly gave him thanks for his favorable courtesy. Gerismond, not satisfied yet with news, began to inquire if he had been lately in the court of Torismond, and whether he had seen his daughter Rosalynde or no. At this Rosader fetched a deep sigh and, shedding many tears, could not answer; yet at last, gathering his spirits together, he revealed unto the King how Rosalynde was banished and how there was such a sympathy of affections between Alinda and her that she chose rather to be partaker of her exile than to part fellowship, whereupon the unnatural King banished them both. "And now they are wandered none knows whither, neither could any learn since their departure the place of their abode." This news drave* the King into a great melancholy, that presently he arose from all the company and went into his privy chamber, so secret as the harbor[74] of the woods would allow him. The company was all dashed at these tidings, and Rosader and Adam Spencer, having such opportunity, went to take their rest. Where we leave them, and return again to Torismond.

[Torismond, desirous of possessing the estate to which Saladyne has become heir, picks a quarrel with Saladyne over his treatment of Rosader and has the elder brother thrown into

*__drave__ drive

72 he i.e., Sir John of Bordeaux **73 his . . . him** i.e., Sir John's . . . Rosader **74 harbor** shelter

prison. Saladyne repents his abuse of Rosader and resolves, when free, to search for him far and wide in order to be reconciled with him.]

Rosader, being thus preferred[75] to the place of a forester by Gerismond, rooted out the remembrance of his brother's unkindness by continual exercise, traversing the groves and wild forests, partly to hear the melody of the sweet birds which recorded[76] and partly to show his diligent endeavor in his master's behalf. Yet whatsoever he did, or howsoever he walked, the lively image of Rosalynde remained in memory; on her sweet perfections he fed his thoughts, proving himself like the eagle a true-born bird, since as the one is known by beholding the sun, so was he by regarding excellent beauty. One day among the rest, finding a fit opportunity and place convenient, desirous to discover his woes to the woods, he engraved with his knife on the bark of a myrtle tree this pretty estimate of his mistress's perfection:

SONETTO

Of all chaste birds the phoenix doth excel,
Of all strong beasts the lion bears the bell,
Of all sweet flowers the rose doth sweetest smell,
Of all fair maids my Rosalynde is fairest.

Of all pure metals gold is only purest,
Of all high trees the pine hath highest crest,
Of all soft sweets I like my mistress' breast,
Of all chaste thoughts my mistress' thoughts are
rarest.

Of all proud birds the eagle pleaseth Jove,
Of pretty fowls kind Venus likes the dove,
Of trees Minerva doth the olive love,
Of all sweet nymphs I honor Rosalynde.

Of all her gifts her wisdom pleaseth most,
Of all her graces virtue she doth boast.
For all these gifts my life and joy is lost
If Rosalynde prove cruel and unkind.

In these and suchlike passions Rosader did every day eternize the name of his Rosalynde, and this day especially when Aliena and Ganymede, enforced by the heat of the sun

75 preferred promoted **76 recorded** sang

to seek for shelter, by good fortune arrived in that place where this amorous forester registered his melancholy passions. They saw the sudden change of his looks, his folded arms,[77] his passionate sighs; they heard him often abruptly call on Rosalynde, who, poor soul, was as hotly burned as himself, but that she shrouded her pains in the cinders of honorable modesty. Whereupon, guessing him to be in love and according to the nature of their sex being pitiful in that behalf, they suddenly brake off his melancholy by their approach, and Ganymede shook him out of his dumps thus:

"What news, forester? Hast thou wounded some deer and lost him in the fall? Care not, man, for so small a loss; thy fees was but the skin, the shoulder, and the horns. 'Tis hunter's luck to aim fair and miss, and a woodman's fortune to strike and yet go without the game."

"Thou art beyond the mark, Ganymede," quoth Aliena. "His passions are greater and his sighs discovers more loss; perhaps in traversing these thickets he hath seen some beautiful nymph and is grown amorous."

"It may be so," quoth Ganymede, "for here he hath newly engraven some sonnet. Come and see the discourse of the forester's poems."

Reading the sonnet over and hearing him name Rosalynde, Aliena looked on Ganymede and laughed, and Ganymede, looking back on the forester and seeing it was Rosader, blushed. Yet, thinking to shroud all under her page's apparel, she boldly returned to Rosader and began thus:

"I pray thee tell me, forester, what is this Rosalynde for whom thou pinest away in such passions? Is she some nymph that waits upon Diana's train whose chastity thou hast deciphered[78] in such epithets? Or is she some shepherdess that haunts these plains whose beauty hath so bewitched thy fancy, whose name thou shadowest in covert[79] under the figure of Rosalynde, as Ovid did Julia[80] under the name of Corinna? Or say me, forsooth, is it that Rosalynde of whom we shepherds have heard talk—she, forester, that

77 folded arms (A sign of melancholy.) **78 deciphered** written down
79 thou shadowest in covert you conceal **80 Julia** (19 B.C.–A.D. 28) granddaughter of Augustus Caesar, banished from Rome. The poet Ovid, thought to have been in love with her, was also banished, though for unknown reasons.

is the daughter of Gerismond, that once was King and now an outlaw in this forest of Arden?"

At this Rosader fetched a deep sigh and said:

"It is she, O gentle swain, it is she. That saint it is whom I serve, that goddess at whose shrine I do bend all my devotions—the most fairest of all fairs, the phoenix of all that sex, and the purity of all earthly perfection."

"And why, gentle forester, if she be so beautiful and thou so amorous, is there such a disagreement[81] in thy thoughts? Haply[82] she resembleth the rose that is sweet but full of prickles? Or the serpent regius[83] that hath scales as glorious as the sun and a breath as infectious as the aconitum[84] is deadly? So thy Rosalynde may be most amiable and yet unkind, full of favor and yet froward,[85] coy without wit, and disdainful without reason."

"O shepherd," quoth Rosader, "knewest thou her personage, graced with the excellence of all perfection, being a harbor wherein the Graces shroud their virtues, thou wouldst not breathe out such blasphemy against the beauteous Rosalynde. She is a diamond bright but not hard, yet of most chaste operation, a pearl so orient that it can be stained with no blemish, a rose without prickles, and a princess absolute as well in beauty as in virtue. But I, unhappy I, have let mine eye soar with the eagle against so bright a sun that I am quite blind; I have with Apollo enamored myself of a Daphne,[86] not, as she, disdainful, but far more chaste than Daphne; I have with Ixion[87] laid my love on Juno, and shall, I fear, embrace naught but a cloud. Ah, shepherd, I have reached at a star; my desires have mounted above my degree and my thoughts above my fortunes, I, being a peasant, having ventured to gaze on a princess whose honors are too high to vouchsafe such base loves."

"Why, forester," quoth Ganymede, "comfort thyself. Be blithe and frolic, man. Love souseth[88] as low as she soareth

81 disagreement strife **82 Haply** perhaps **83 the serpent regius** a fabulous serpent **84 aconitum** aconite or wolfsbane, a poisonous plant **85 froward** perverse **86 Daphne** chaste nymph pursued by Apollo and transformed at her own request into a laurel tree rather than lose her chastity **87 Ixion** (As punishment for his crimes, including his presumption in trying to win the love of Juno or Hera, Ixion was bound to a perpetually turning wheel in the underworld.) **88 souseth** swoops (like a hawk)

ROSADER'S MEDITATION

"Now, Rosader, Fortune that long hath whipped thee with nettles means to salve[96] thee with roses, and having crossed thee with many frowns, now she presents thee with the brightness of her favors. Thou that didst count thyself the most distressed of all men mayst account thyself now the most fortunate amongst men, if Fortune can make men happy or sweet revenge be wrapped in a pleasing content. Thou seest Saladyne, thine enemy, the worker of thy misfortunes and the efficient cause[97] of thine exile, subject to the cruelty of a merciless lion, brought into this misery by the gods, that they might seem just in revenging his rigor and thy injuries. Seest thou not how the stars are in a favorable aspect, the planets in some pleasing conjunction, the Fates agreeable to thy thoughts, and the Destinies performers of thy desires, in that Saladyne shall die and thou free of his blood, he receive meed for his amiss[98] and thou erect his tomb with innocent hands? Now, Rosader, shalt thou return to Bordeaux and enjoy thy possessions by birth and his revenues by inheritance. Now mayst thou triumph in love and hang Fortune's altars with garlands. For when Rosalynde hears of thy wealth it will make her love thee the more willingly; for women's eyes are made of chrysocoll,[99] that is ever unperfect unless tempered with gold, and Jupiter soonest enjoyed Danae[100] because he came to her in so rich a shower. Thus shall this lion, Rosader, end the life of a miserable man and from distress raise thee to be most fortunate." And with that, casting his boar spear on his neck, away he began to trudge.

But he had not stepped back two or three paces but a new motion struck him to the very heart, that,[101] resting his boar spear against his breast, he fell into this passionate humor:

"Ah, Rosader, wert thou the son of Sir John of Bordeaux, whose virtues exceeded his valor, and yet the most hardiest knight in all Europe? Should the honor of the father shine in the actions of the son, and wilt thou dishonor thy parentage

96 salve assuage **97 efficient cause** cause that makes things what they are **98 meed for his amiss** reward for his misdeeds **99 chrysocoll** chrysocolla, a name of a mineral meaning "gold solder" **100 Danae** a king's daughter, confined in a tower, whom Zeus or Jupiter contrived to visit in a shower of gold **101 that** so that

in forgetting the nature of a gentleman? Did not thy father at his last gasp breathe out this golden principle: Brothers' amity is like the drops of balsamum[102] that salveth the most dangerous sores? Did he make a large exhort unto concord,[103] and wilt thou show thyself careless?[104] O Rosader, what though Saladyne hath wronged thee and made thee live an exile in the forest, shall thy nature be so cruel, or thy nurture so crooked, or thy thoughts so savage as to suffer so dismal a revenge? What, to let him be devoured by wild beasts? *Non sapit qui non sibi sapit*[105] is fondly spoken in such bitter extremes. Lose not his life, Rosader, to win a world of treasure; for in having him thou hast a brother, and by hazarding for his life thou gettest a friend and reconcilest an enemy; and more honor shalt thou purchase by pleasuring a foe than revenging a thousand injuries."

With that his brother began to stir and the lion to rouse himself, whereupon Rosader suddenly charged him with the boar spear and wounded the lion very sore at the first stroke. The beast, feeling himself to have a mortal hurt, leaped at Rosader and with his paws gave him a sore pinch on the breast, that he had almost fallen; yet as a man most valiant, in whom the sparks of Sir John of Bordeaux remained, he recovered himself and in short combat slew the lion, who at his death roared so loud that Saladyne awaked and, starting up, was amazed at the sudden sight of so monstrous a beast lie slain by him and so sweet a gentleman wounded. He presently, as he was of a ripe conceit,[106] began to conjecture that the gentleman had slain him in his defense. Whereupon, as a man in a trance, he stood staring on them both a good while, not knowing his brother, being in that disguise. At last he burst into these terms:

[Saladyne speaks to Rosader without recognizing him, thanking him for saving his life. Rosader takes the advantage of his disguise to elicit from Saladyne his life's story, which is told with such earnest remorse that Rosader perceives a true change of heart in his oldest brother. He reveals his identity and the brothers are reconciled. Rosader shows his

102 balsamum balm **103 exhort unto concord** exhortation in behalf of concord **104 careless** heedless **105 Non . . . sapit** he knows nothing who knows not himself **106 was . . . conceit** had a ready understanding

brother the forest for two or three days, during which time Rosalynde grows increasingly restive and impatient at her Rosader's absence. When Rosader eventually shows up, Rosalynde is sharp-tongued in her rebuke but finally accepts his explanation of finding his now-banished brother. A new complication arises (in an incident not dramatized by Shakespeare) when Alinda and Rosalynde are nearly abducted by some villains hoping to present her to the lustful King Torismond. Saladyne acquits himself so bravely in fighting off this attack that he wins the love of Alinda, still disguised as the shepherdess Aliena. Saladyne is no less attracted to her. As if to demonstrate that the course of true love seldom runs smoothly, however, the lovers are invited to overhear the unhappy wooing of Montanus for his proud and disdainful Phoebe, who has now fastened her affections on Ganymede. Alinda confesses to having her own doubts about men's constancy.]

Saladyne, hearing how Aliena harped still upon one string, which was the doubt of men's constancy, he broke off her sharp invective thus: "I grant, Aliena," quoth he, "many men have done amiss in proving soon ripe and soon rotten; but particular instances infer no general conclusions, and therefore I hope what others have faulted in shall not prejudice my favors. I will not use sophistry to confirm my love, for that is subtlety,[107] nor long discourses, lest my words might be thought more than my faith; but if this will suffice, that by the honor of a gentleman I love Aliena and woo Aliena not to crop the blossoms and reject the tree but to consummate my faithful desires in the honorable end of marriage."

At this word "marriage" Aliena stood in a maze what to answer, fearing that if she were too coy, to drive him away with her disdain, and if she were too courteous, to discover the heat of her desires. In a dilemma thus what to do, at last this she said: "Saladyne, ever since I saw thee I favored thee. I cannot dissemble my desires, because I see thou dost faithfully manifest thy thoughts, and in liking thee I love thee so far as mine honor holds fancy still in suspense;[108] but if I knew thee as virtuous as thy father or as well qualified as thy

107 subtlety ingenious contrivance **108 so far . . . suspense** so far as my honor, holding passion always in check, will allow

brother Rosader, the doubt should be quickly decided. But for this time to give thee an answer, assure thyself this: I will either marry with Saladyne or still live a virgin."

And with this they strained[109] one another's hand, which Ganymede espying, thinking he had had his mistress long enough at shrift,[110] said, "What, a match or no?"

"A match," quoth Aliena, "or else it were an ill market."[111]

"I am glad," quoth Ganymede. "I would Rosader were well here to make up a mess."[112]

"Well remembered," quoth Saladyne. "I forgot I left my brother Rosader alone, and therefore, lest being solitary he should increase his sorrows, I will haste me to him. May it[113] please you, then, to command me any service to him, I am ready to be a dutiful messenger."

"Only at this time commend me to him," quoth Aliena, "and tell him though we cannot pleasure him we pray for him."

"And forget not," quoth Ganymede, "my commendations; but say to him that Rosalynde sheds as many tears from her heart as he drops of blood from his wounds for the sorrow of his misfortunes, feathering all her thoughts with disquiet[114] till his welfare procure her content. Say thus, good Saladyne, and so farewell."

He, having his message, gave a courteous adieu to them both, especially to Aliena, and so, playing "Loath to depart," went to his brother. But Aliena, she perplexed and yet joyful, passed away the day pleasantly, still praising the perfection of Saladyne, not ceasing to chat of her new love till evening drew on. And then they, folding[115] their sheep, went home to bed. Where we leave them and return to Phoebe.

[Phoebe, despairing in her love for Ganymede, composes various epistles to him and commissions Montanus to act as her messenger. Rosalynde as Ganymede undertakes to cure Montanus of his infatuation by showing him the letters, to which the faithful lover responds by wishing that Ganymede may have Phoebe in Montanus's stead; Phoebe's happiness is all

109 strained confined, held **110 he had . . . shrift** i.e., Saladyne had held Aliena long enough in private conference **111 an ill market** i.e., a bad bargain, unprofitable or dishonest dealing **112 make up a mess** make up a group of four (as at table) **113 May it** if it may **114 feathering . . . disquiet** i.e., allowing herself no contented thoughts **115 folding** putting in the sheepfold

that Montanus desires. Rosalynde and Alinda resolve to assist Montanus somehow in getting the love of Phoebe. Rosalynde does so by going directly to Phoebe and offering her stern if compassionate advice: hope no longer for Ganymede, but instead seek affection where it can be reciprocated.]

Thus, Phoebe, thou mayst see I disdain not, though I desire not, remaining indifferent till time and love makes me resolute. Therefore, Phoebe, seek not to suppress affection, and with the love of Montanus quench the remembrance of Ganymede; strive thou to hate me as I seek to like of thee, and ever have the duties of Montanus in thy mind, for I promise thee thou mayst have one more wealthy but not more loyal." These words were corrosives to the perplexed Phoebe, that, sobbing out sighs and straining out tears, she blubbered out these words:

"And shall I then have no salve of Ganymede but suspense, no hope but a doubtful hazard, no comfort, but be posted off to the will of time? Justly have the gods balanced my fortunes, who, being cruel to Montanus, found Ganymede as unkind to myself; so in forcing him perish for love, I shall die myself with overmuch love."

"I am glad," quoth Ganymede, "you look into your own faults and see where your shoe wrings[116] you, measuring now the pains of Montanus by your own passions."

"Truth," quoth Phoebe, "and so deeply I repent me of my frowardness towards the shepherd that, could I cease to love Ganymede, I would resolve to like Montanus."

"What,[117] if I can with reason persuade Phoebe to mislike of[118] Ganymede, will she then favor Montanus?"

"When reason," quoth she, "doth quench that love that I owe to thee, then will I fancy him; conditionally, that if my love can be suppressed with no reason, as being without reason, Ganymede will only wed himself to Phoebe."

"I grant it, fair shepherdess," quoth he, "and to feed thee with the sweetness of hope, this resolve on: I will never marry myself to woman but unto thyself."

And with that Ganymede gave Phoebe a fruitless kiss and such words of comfort that before Ganymede departed she

116 wrings pinches **117 What** i.e., do you mean to say **118 mislike of** dislike

arose out of her bed and made him and Montanus such cheer as could be found in such a country cottage, Ganymede in the midst of their banquet rehearsing the promises of either in Montanus's favor, which highly pleased the shepherd. Thus, all three content and soothed up in hope, Ganymede took his leave of his Phoebe and departed, leaving her a contented woman and Montanus highly pleased. But poor Ganymede, who had her thoughts on her Rosader, when she called to remembrance his wounds, filled her eyes full of tears and her heart full of sorrows, plodded to find Aliena at the folds,[119] thinking with her presence to drive away her passions. As she came on the plains she might espy where Rosader and Saladyne sat with Aliena under the shade, which sight was a salve to her grief and such a cordial unto her heart that she tripped alongst the lawns full of joy.

At last Corydon, who was with them, spied Ganymede, and with that the clown[120] rose and, running to meet him, cried: "O sirrah, a match, a match! Our mistress shall be married on Sunday."

Thus the poor peasant frolicked it before Ganymede who, coming to the crew, saluted them all, and especially Rosader, saying that he was glad to see him so well recovered of his wounds.

"I had not gone abroad[121] so soon," quoth Rosader, "but that I am bidden to a marriage which, on Sunday next, must be solemnized between my brother and Aliena. I see well where love leads delay is loathsome, and that small wooing serves where both the parties are willing."

"Truth," quoth Ganymede, "but a happy day should it be if Rosader that day might be married to Rosalynde."

"Ah, good Ganymede," quoth he, "by naming Rosalynde, renew not my sorrows, for the thought of her perfections is the thrall of my miseries."

"Tush, be of good cheer, man," quoth Ganymede. "I have a friend that is deeply experienced in necromancy and magic. What art can do shall be acted for thine advantage. I will cause him to bring in Rosalynde, if either France or any bordering nation harbor her; and upon that take the faith of a young shepherd."

119 folds sheepfolds **120 clown** rustic, bumpkin **121 abroad** out of the house

Aliena smiled to see how Rosader frowned, thinking that Ganymede had jested with him. But breaking off from those matters, the page, somewhat pleasant,[122] began to discourse unto them what had passed between him and Phoebe, which, as they laughed, so they wondered at, all confessing that there is none so chaste but love will change. Thus they passed away the day in chat, and when the sun began to set, they took their leaves and departed, Aliena providing for their marriage day such solemn[123] cheer and handsome robes as fitted their country estate and yet somewhat the better in that Rosader had promised to bring Gerismond thither as a guest. Ganymede, who then meant to discover herself before her father, had made her a gown of green and a kirtle of the finest sendal[124] in such sort that she seemed some heavenly nymph harbored in country attire.

Saladyne was not behind in care to set out the nuptials, nor Rosader unmindful to bid guests, who invited Gerismond and all his followers to the feast, who willingly granted, so that there was nothing but the day wanting to this marriage.

In the meanwhile, Phoebe, being a bidden guest, made herself as gorgeous as might be to please the eye of Ganymede; and Montanus suited[125] himself with the cost of many of his flocks to be gallant against that day, for then was Ganymede to give Phoebe an answer of her loves and Montanus either to hear the doom of his misery or the censure[126] of his happiness. But while this gear was a-brewing, Phoebe passed not one day without visiting her Ganymede, so far was she wrapped in the beauties of this lovely swain. Much prattle they had and the discourse of many passions, Phoebe wishing for the day, as she thought, of her welfare and Ganymede smiling to think what unexpected events would fall out at the wedding. In these humors the week went away, that at last Sunday came.

No sooner did Phoebus' henchman[127] appear in the sky to give warning that his master's horses should be trapped in[128] his glorious coach but Corydon, in his holiday suit, marvel-

122 pleasant merry **123 solemn** ceremonial, festive **124 kirtle . . . sendal** cloak made of a thin rich silken material **125 suited** outfitted **126 doom** judgment. **censure** verdict **127 Phoebus' henchman** i.e., the groom tending the horses of the sun **128 trapped in** adorned with trappings in the harness of

ous seemly in a russet jacket welted[129] with the same and faced[130] with red worsted, having a pair of blue camlet[131] sleeves bound at the wrists with four yellow laces, closed afore[132] very richly with a dozen of pewter buttons; his hose was of gray kersey,[133] with a large slop[134] barred overthwart[135] the pocket-holes with three fair guards[136] stitched of[137] either side with red thread; his stock was of the own,[138] sewed close to his breech, and for to beautify his hose he had trussed himself round with a dozen of new-threaden points[139] of medley color; his bonnet was green, whereon stood a copper brooch with the picture of Saint Denis; and to want[140] nothing that might make him amorous in his old days, he had a fair shirtband of fine lockram,[141] whipped over[142] with Coventry blue of no small cost. Thus attired, Corydon bestirred himself as chief stickler[143] in these actions and had strewed all the house with flowers, that it seemed rather some of Flora's[144] choice bowers than any country cottage.

Thither repaired Phoebe with all the maids of the forest to set out the bride in the most seemliest sort that might be. But howsoever she helped to prank out Aliena, yet her eye was still on Ganymede, who was so neat in a suit of gray that he seemed Endymion[145] when he won Luna with his looks or Paris when he played the swain to get the beauty of the nymph Oenone.[146] Ganymede, like a pretty page, waited on his mistress Aliena and overlooked[147] that all was in a readiness against[148] the bridegroom should come, who, attired in a forester's suit, came accompanied with Gerismond and his brother Rosader early in the morning; where arrived, they were solemnly[149] entertained by Aliena and the rest of the country swains, Gerismond very highly commending the fortunate choice of Saladyne in that he had chosen a shepherd-

129 welted edged **130 faced** covered **131 camlet** costly fabric of wool and silk **132 afore** before, in front **133 kersey** a coarse, ribbed woolen cloth **134 slop** loose breeches **135 overthwart** across **136 guards** ornaments **137 of** on **138 stock . . . own** i.e., his hose were part of the slop or breeches **139 points** tags used to fasten clothing, especially the hose to the doublet **140 want** lack **141 lockram** linen fabric **142 whipped over** bound closely with thread **143 stickler** manager **144 Flora** goddess of flowers **145 Endymion** a shepherd boy whose beauty as he slept won the love of the moon (Luna) **146 Oenone** Paris' wife when he was a shepherd; he deserted her for Helen **147 overlooked** oversaw **148 against** anticipating the time when **149 solemnly** ceremoniously, festively

ess whose virtues appeared in her outward beauties, being no less fair than seeming modest.

Ganymede, coming in and seeing her father, began to blush, nature working affects by her secret effects. Scarce could she abstain from tears to see her father in so low fortunes—he that was wont to sit in his royal palace, attended on by twelve noble peers, now to be contented with a simple cottage and a troop of reveling woodmen for his train. The consideration of his fall made Ganymede full of sorrows; yet that she might triumph over fortune with patience and not any way dash that merry day with her dumps, she smothered her melancholy with a shadow of mirth and very reverently welcomed the King not according to his former degree but to his present estate, with such diligence as Gerismond began to commend the page for his exquisite person and excellent qualities.

As thus the King with his foresters frolicked it among the shepherds, Corydon came in with a fair mazer[150] full of cider and presented it to Gerismond with such a clownish salute that he began to smile and took it of[151] the old shepherd very kindly, drinking to Aliena and the rest of her fair maids, amongst whom Phoebe was the foremost. Aliena pledged[152] the King and drunk to Rosader; so the carouse[153] went round from him to Phoebe, etc. As they were thus drinking and ready to go to church, came in Montanus, appareled all in tawny,[154] to signify that he was forsaken; on his head he wore a garland of willow, his bottle[155] hanged by his side, whereon was painted despair, and on his sheephook hung two sonnets as labels of his loves and fortunes.

[Gerismond, hearing of Montanus's unavailing passion for Phoebe, orders her to be brought before him in order that he may, like Rosalynde, lecture her on the cruelty of her behavior toward Montanus. She counters by insisting that her case is as hopeless and that Ganymede is no less cruel in his treatment of her.]

Gerismond, desirous to prosecute[156] the end of these passions, called in Ganymede, who, knowing the case, came in

150 mazer wooden drinking cup **151 of** from **152 pledged** toasted
153 carouse drinking of healths **154 tawny** cloth of tawny color
155 bottle leather drink container **156 prosecute** pursue

graced with such a blush as beautified the crystal of his face with a ruddy brightness. The King, noting well the physiognomy of Ganymede, began by his favors to call to mind the face of his Rosalynde, and with that fetched a deep sigh. Rosader, that was passing[157] familiar with Gerismond, demanded of him why he sighed so sore.

"Because, Rosader," quoth he, "the favor of Ganymede puts me in mind of Rosalynde."

At this word Rosader sighed so deeply as though his heart would have burst.

"And what's the matter," quoth Gerismond, "that you quite[158] me with such a sigh?"

"Pardon me, sir," quoth Rosader, "because I love none but Rosalynde."

"And upon that condition," quoth Gerismond, "that Rosalynde were here, I would this day make up a marriage betwixt her and thee."

At this Aliena turned her head and smiled upon Ganymede, and she could scarce keep countenance. Yet she salved[159] all with secrecy; and Gerismond, to drive away such dumps, questioned with Ganymede what the reason was he regarded not Phoebe's love, seeing she was as fair as the wanton that brought Troy to ruin.[160] Ganymede mildly answered:

"If I should affect the fair Phoebe, I should offer poor Montanus great wrong to win that from him in a moment that[161] he hath labored for so many months.* Yet have I promised to the beautiful shepherdess to wed myself never to woman except unto her, but with this promise, that if I can by reason suppress Phoebe's love towards me, she shall like of none but of Montanus."

"To that," quoth Phoebe, "I stand, for my love is so far beyond reason as it will admit no persuasion of reason."

"For justice," quoth he, "I appeal to Gerismond."

"And to his censure will I stand," quoth Phoebe.

"And in your victory," quoth Montanus, "stands the hazard of my fortunes; for if Ganymede go away with conquest,[162] Montanus is in conceit[163] love's monarch; if Phoebe win, then am I in effect most miserable."

***months** monts

157 passing surpassingly, very **158 quite** requite, repay **159 salved** soothed, healed **160 the wanton . . . ruin** i.e., Helen of Troy **161 that** which **162 go away with conquest** win **163 in conceit** in thought

"We will see this controversy," quoth Gerismond, "and then we will to church. Therefore, Ganymede, let us hear your argument."

"Nay, pardon my absence awhile," quoth she, "and you shall see one in store."

In went Ganymede and dressed herself in woman's attire, having on a gown of green with kirtle[164] of rich sendal, so quaint that she seemed Diana[165] triumphing in the forest. Upon her head she wore a chaplet of roses, which gave her such a grace that she looked like Flora perked in the pride[166] of all her flowers. Thus attired came Rosalynde in and presented herself at her father's feet, with her eyes full of tears, craving his blessing and discoursing unto him all her fortunes, how she was banished by Torismond and how ever since she lived in that country disguised.

Gerismond, seeing his daughter, rose from his seat and fell upon her neck, uttering the passions of his joy in watery plaints, driven into such an ecstasy of content that he could not utter one word. At this sight if Rosader was both amazed and joyful, I refer myself to the judgment of such as have experience in love, seeing his Rosalynde before his face whom so long and deeply he had affected. At last Gerismond recovered his spirits and in most fatherly terms entertained[167] his daughter Rosalynde, after many questions demanding of her what had passed between her and Rosader.

"So much, sir," quoth she, "as there wants nothing but Your Grace to make up the marriage."

"Why, then," quoth Gerismond, "Rosader, take her. She is thine, and let this day solemnize both thy brother's and thy nuptials." Rosader, beyond measure content, humbly thanked the King and embraced his Rosalynde, who, turning towards Phoebe, demanded if she had shown sufficient reason to suppress the force of her loves.

"Yea," quoth Phoebe, "and so great a persuasive that, please it you, madam, and Aliena to give us leave, Montanus and I will make this day the third couple in marriage."

She had no sooner spake this word but Montanus threw away his garland of willow, his bottle, where was painted de-

164 kirtle cloak **165 Diana** goddess of the hunt and of the moon **166 perked in the pride** dressed in the splendor **167 entertained** spoke with, occupied the attention of

spair, and cast his sonnets in the fire, showing himself as frolic as Paris when he handseled[168] his love with Helena. At this Gerismond and the rest smiled and concluded that Montanus and Phoebe should keep their wedding with the two brethren. Aliena, seeing Saladyne stand in a dump, to wake him from his dream began thus:

"Why, how now, my Saladyne, all amort?[169] What, melancholy, man, at the day of marriage? Perchance thou art sorrowful to think on thy brother's high fortunes and thine own base desires to choose so mean a shepherdess. Cheer up thy heart, man, for this day thou shalt be married to the daughter of a King. For know, Saladyne, I am not Aliena, but Alinda, the daughter of thy mortal enemy Torismond."

At this all the company was amazed, especially Gerismond, who, rising up, took Alinda in his arms and said to Rosalynde:

"Is this that fair Alinda, famous for so many virtues, that forsook her father's court to live with thee exiled in the country?"

"The same," quoth Rosalynde.

"Then," quoth Gerismond, turning to Saladyne, "jolly forester, be frolic, for thy fortunes are great and thy desires excellent. Thou hast got a princess as famous for her perfection as exceeding in proportion."[170]

"And she hath with her beauty won," quoth Saladyne, "an humble servant as full of faith as she of amiable favor."

While everyone was amazed with these comical events, Corydon came skipping in and told them that the priest was at church and tarried for their coming. With that Gerismond led the way, and the rest followed, where to the admiration of all the country swains in Arden their marriages were solemnly solemnized.

[In the midst of a festive dinner, complete with homely fare and a song by Corydon, the brother of Saladyne and Rosader named Fernandyne arrives with news that twelve peers of France are nearby in arms to restore Gerismond's right by doing battle with Torismond. The men rush eagerly from the

168 handseled inaugurated with gifts, first experienced **169 amort** dejected **170 proportion** portion, dowry; shape

dinner to join in the encounter, wherein they put Torismond's army to flight and slay the tyrant. Alinda thus loses her father but is comforted by her union with Saladyne.]

Well, as soon as they were come to Paris, Gerismond made a royal feast for the peers and lords of his land, which continued thirty days, in which time summoning a parliament, by the consent of his nobles he created Rosader heir apparent to the kingdom. He restored Saladyne to all his father's land and gave him the dukedom of Nameurs; he made Fernandyne principal secretary to himself; and that fortune might every way seem frolic, he made Montanus lord over all the Forest of Arden, Adam Spencer captain of the King's guard, and Corydon master of Alinda's flocks.

Thomas Lodge's *Rosalynde: Euphues' Golden Legacy* was first published in London in 1590. The present excerpted text is based on the first edition.

Further Reading

Barber, C. L. "The Alliance of Seriousness and Levity in *As You Like It.*" *Shakespeare's Festive Comedy.* Princeton, N.J.: Princeton Univ. Press, 1959. In the context of his general thesis about the relation of Shakespeare's comedies to popular holiday and festivity, Barber sees the play as an exploration of passion that at once validates the experience of romantic love and exhibits a witty "detachment from its follies." Rosalind embodies and reconciles the two attitudes, alternating between "holiday and everyday perspectives."

Barton, Anne. "*As You Like It* and *Twelfth Night:* Shakespeare's Sense of an Ending." In *Shakespearian Comedy,* ed. Malcolm Bradbury and D. J. Palmer. Stratford-upon-Avon Studies 14. London: Edward Arnold; New York: Crane, Russak, 1972. Barton considers the play the "fullest and most stable realization of Shakespearian comic form," masterfully balancing romantic and realistic views of the world. Unlike *Twelfth Night,* which reveals the instabilities of comedy, the ending of this play reveals a poise and equilibrium witnessing to Shakespeare's faith in the resolutions comedy achieves.

Berry, Edward I. "Rosalynde and Rosalind." *Shakespeare Quarterly* 31 (1980): 42–52. Patiently comparing Shakespeare's play with its source, Thomas Lodge's *Rosalynde,* Berry examines the implications of Shakespeare's alterations, focusing mainly on the figure of Rosalind/Rosalynde, who becomes in Shakespeare's hands "a figure of the playwright himself."

Berry, Ralph. "No Exit from Arden." *Shakespeare's Comedies: Explorations in Form.* Princeton, N.J.: Princeton Univ. Press, 1972. Berry resists romantic readings of the play, finding instead that the romantic ideal is "challenged by the probings of realism, common sense, and satire." In the actions of both the court and the forest, Berry finds unease and the "simple will to dominate." The play's happy ending can be therefore only provisional, relocating rather than resolving the problems that have surfaced.

Bono, Barbara J. "Mixed Gender, Mixed Genre in Shakespeare's *As You Like It.*" In *Renaissance Genres: Essays on Theory, History, and Interpretation,* ed. Barbara K. Lewalski. Cambridge: Harvard Univ. Press, 1986. Examining the play's complex emotional interactions, Bono argues that both Orlando and Rosalind are transformed, as he is led to revise his early idealization of women and she is led, through her efforts to educate Orlando, to "exorcise her own fears about love." The playfulness of these negotiations of gender difference reveals a confidence, which Shakespeare's tragedies later deny, in the possibility of escaping rigid gender definitions and destructive sexual anxieties.

Cirillo, Albert R. "*As You Like It:* Pastoralism Gone Awry." *ELH* 38 (1971): 19–39. Cirillo explores the play's pastoralism, suggesting that Shakespeare undercuts its conventions in order to clarify its heuristic role. The play rejects the idea that pastoral offers "an attainable ideal in life"; rather, the pastoral episode is merely a temporary sojourn in a "second world" that transforms the characters' understanding of their values and experiences.

Erickson, Peter. "Sexual Politics and Social Structure in *As You Like It.*" *Patriarchal Structures in Shakespeare's Drama.* Berkeley, Los Angeles, and London: Univ. of California Press, 1985. In spite of Rosalind's exercise of significant authority, Erickson argues, *As You Like It* merely seduces us into imagining that her actions transform the play's sexual politics. By focusing both upon the implications of the boy actors that played female parts in Shakespeare's theater and Rosalind's actions at the end of the play, Erickson sees that the happy ending is achieved only by reinscribing Rosalind within the structures of male power and patriarchy.

Gardner, Helen. *"As You Like It."* In *More Talking of Shakespeare,* ed. John Garrett. New York: Theatre Arts Books, 1959. Rpt. in *Shakespeare, The Comedies: A Collection of Critical Essays,* ed. Kenneth Muir. Englewood Cliffs, N.J.: Prentice-Hall, 1965. For Gardner, *As You Like It* is "Shakespeare's most Mozartian comedy," elegant and refined. Through misunderstandings and feigning, characters are led to the truth about themselves and their desires. In the comedy "the world is shown not only as a place where we may find happiness, but as a place where both happiness and sorrow may be hallowed."

Hayles, Nancy K. "Sexual Disguise in *As You Like It* and *Twelfth Night*." *Shakespeare Survey* 32 (1979): 63–72. Comparing the use of sexual disguise in the two plays, Hayles sees that disguise grants Rosalind a power that it withholds from Viola in *Twelfth Night*. Disguise enables Rosalind to escape Orlando's unrealistic fantasy of her, and, as the play's disguises are finally discarded, the play reveals and resolves the "traditional tension between the needs of the female and the needs of the male."

Jamieson, Michael. *Shakespeare: "As You Like It."* London: Edward Arnold, 1965. After a discussion of the literary traditions and conventions that inform the design of the play, Jamieson's short book contains a scene-by-scene analysis, with special attention to the play's relationship to Shakespeare's other "great comedies." Jamieson views *As You Like It* as generous and affirmative, able to embrace disparate attitudes but finally adopting a romantic view of both courtship and love.

Kuhn, Maura Slattery. "Much Virtue in *If*." *Shakespeare Quarterly* 28 (1977): 40–50. Kuhn explores the many improbabilities, uncertainties, and conditional assertions of the play, and holds that the experiences in Arden function to effect the suspension of disbelief and validate the evidence of the provisional. By accepting Arden's premises, Kuhn argues, characters "are rewarded with conclusions transcending their expectations."

Leggatt, Alexander. *"As You Like It." Shakespeare's Comedy of Love*. London: Methuen, 1974. Leggatt locates the comic effects of the play in the juxtaposition of its convincing naturalism and obvious artifice, ultimately suggesting that even the commonsense distinction "between ordinary experience and the conventionalized actions of storybook characters" may be a false one. In this play of contrasting perspectives, "no one attitude can be taken as absolute or final"; at the end the audience is invited to share in the mockery of the play's conventions while being permitted to recognize the reality of the love that underlies them.

Montrose, Louis Adrian. " 'The Place of a Brother' in *As You Like It:* Social Process and Comic Form." *Shakespeare*

Quarterly 32 (1981): 28–54, Montrose examines the ways in which the comedy recognizes and resolves social conflicts, especially the rivalry between elder and younger brothers and the tension between female power and a patriarchal culture that must control it. As the play explores these differential social relations, it contains and discharges the tensions that are released, serving not only as "a theatrical *reflection* of social conflicts" but also as "a theatrical *source* of social conciliation."

Nevo, Ruth. "Existence in Arden." *Comic Transformations in Shakespeare*. London and New York: Methuen, 1980. *As You Like It,* for Nevo, is a confident and accomplished comedy, one in which Shakespeare celebrates the principles of his comic art, making them the very material of the play. Rosalind's activities in the forest embody "comic pleasure itself." They serve as "a liberating playful fantasy" that tests her capacities for life and for love as she tests "these same potencies in others."

Park, Clara Claiborne. "As We Like It: How a Girl Can Be Smart and Still Popular." *The American Scholar* 42 (1973): 262–278. Rpt. in *The Woman's Part: Feminist Criticism of Shakespeare,* ed. Carolyn Swift Ruth Lenz, Gayle Greene, and Carol Thomas Neely. Urbana, Ill.: Univ. of Illinois Press, 1980. Park's witty title nicely encapsulates what she sees as the "extent—and the limits—of acceptable feminine activity in the Shakespearean world." She finds Rosalind the most forceful and successful of Shakespeare's women, but though she appealingly extends the possibilities of female behavior, even she keeps her activity confined to traditional domains of action and "gladly and voluntarily" relinquishes her authority.

Young, David. "Earthly Things Made Even: *As You Like It.*" *The Heart's Forest: A Study of Shakespeare's Pastoral Plays*. New Haven, Conn.: Yale Univ. Press, 1972. Young explores Shakespeare's skillful use of the conventions of the pastoral in *As You Like It*. The play not only presents traditional pastoral themes, but functions ultimately as a commentary on the pastoral itself. Neither idealism nor satire—the two poles of pastoralism—satisfies Shakespeare, who continually tests one against the other and finally seeks a reconciliation between them.

Photo © Martha Swope

From the 1984 New York Shakespeare Festival production of *Henry V*, with Kevin Kline as Henry V, directed by Wilford Leach at the Delacorte Theater in Central Park.

—HENRY V—

HENRY V

Foreword

There's no question that in *Henry V* Shakespeare eulogizes a great hero and monarch of England, calling him "this star of England" and sprinkling the play with liberal doses of praise for his achievements. But *Henry V* is interesting from another viewpoint: it is the one play where Shakespeare talks, through the Chorus, directly to the audience all the way through from the very beginning, and sets this great historical work almost entirely within his own playhouse. "Can this cockpit hold / The vasty fields of France?" he asks in the Prologue. "Or may we cram / Within this wooden O [the Globe Theatre] the very casques / That did affright the air at Agincourt?" He keeps urging the audience to think big, to let the words and the language take us beyond the limitations of time and place.

But this is only the beginning. At the start of each of the acts, the Chorus is used to give vivid descriptions. The Chorus to Act 2 tells us how people all across England were reacting to the news of the war with France: "Now all the youth of England are on fire, / And silken dalliance in the wardrobe lies, / Now thrive the armorers, and honor's thought / Reigns solely in the breast of every man."

The most beautiful of these descriptions, to my mind, is the Chorus to Act 4, which takes us to the two opposing armies encamped outside of Agincourt:

> Now entertain conjecture of a time
> When creeping murmur and the poring dark
> Fills the wide vessel of the universe.
> From camp to camp, through the foul womb of
>   night,
> The hum of either army stilly sounds,
> That the fixed sentinels almost receive
> The secret whispers of each other's watch.

This Chorus also contains some of Shakespeare's most beautiful lines about Henry, as he describes the young King walking among his troops on the eve of battle:

> For forth he goes and visits all his host,
> Bids them good morrow with a modest smile,
> And calls them brothers, friends, and
>   countrymen. . . .
> A largess universal like the sun
> His liberal eye doth give to everyone,

> Thawing cold fear, that mean and gentle all
> Behold, as may unworthiness define,
> A little touch of Harry in the night.

And then Shakespeare rapidly switches to the battle—"And so our scene must to the battle fly"—thus ending this remarkable speech.

Though here he shows Henry as a noble warrior, Shakespeare is not content with an idealized portrait, here or anywhere. In the final scenes of the play, Shakespeare reveals a victorious Henry who is cruel and calculating in pressing his victory home. He is a tough negotiator, ruthless in the conditions he demands for France's surrender, bringing that proud nation to its knees without the slightest hint of compassion. One of his conditions, of course, is that the French King's daughter, Katharine, be thrown into the bargain; in a sense, she is just another city to him.

It's in this context that we must see the wooing scene. Katharine is more than just a charming woman to Henry; she is one of the fruits of war, and a necessary bond in the alliance between England and its defeated enemy. And so Katharine's resistance to Henry is more than just cute, it is inextricably wrapped up with the politics of the situation. When Katharine asks coyly, "Is it possible dat I sould love de ennemi of France?" Henry's reply makes it clear that he is playing for high stakes and will brook no resistance: "No, it is not possible you should love the enemy of France, Kate; but in loving me you should love the friend of France, for I love France so well that I will not part with a village of it, I will have it all mine."

This aspect of Harry as a ruthless negotiator influences how this scene should be played and viewed. We mustn't be taken in by its surface charm; there is a struggle for power going on here, and by showing it, Shakespeare deepens and enriches *Henry V*.

JOSEPH PAPP

JOSEPH PAPP GRATEFULLY ACKNOWLEDGES THE HELP OF ELIZABETH KIRKLAND IN PREPARING THIS FOREWORD.

Introduction

Henry V (1599) is Shakespeare's culminating statement in the genre of the English history play. Unlike the late and atypical *Henry VIII* (1613), which is separated from the rest of Shakespeare's history plays by some fourteen years, *Henry V* sums up the historical themes with which Shakespeare had been fascinated for an entire decade. The play, first published in a "bad" quarto in 1600, must have been written not long after *2 Henry IV*. To be sure, the play does not entirely fulfill the promise made in *2 Henry IV* to "continue the story, with Sir John in it, and make you merry with fair Katharine of France." Falstaff is missing. As before, Shakespeare apparently saw a grand design to his four-play sequence (which had started with *Richard II*), but improvised when he came to the writing of each part. Despite these minor adjustments in the overall plan, however, *Henry V* is clearly intended to bring to fulfillment the education of a Christian prince and to illustrate the arts of kingship Prince Hal had derived from his experiences in the earlier plays. In a sense, too, *Henry V* sums up the achievement of the English history play not only for Shakespeare but for other popular playwrights as well. The patriotic history play, born in the excitement of the Armada era (c. 1588), had nearly run its course by 1599 and was soon to be supplanted by other dramatic genres such as satire and revenge tragedy. Dark and complex political realities were already changing the buoyant mood in which the history play had been born: the aging Queen Elizabeth was near death and without a Protestant heir, while fear of another invasion threatened.

Henry V has become a controversial play, chiefly because its heroic king can, from the viewpoint of modern history, be looked upon as a warmonger and imperialist. George Bernard Shaw is prominent among those who have deplored Henry as a priggish and complacent chauvinist. Historically-minded critics have argued, on the other hand, that Henry is a perfect model of conduct according to Renaissance notions of statecraft and military leadership. What is Shakespeare's attitude toward his war hero? Does he sympathize with Henry's condescension toward the French and his ordering every soldier to kill his French prisoners? Or is Shakespeare's admiration qualified by ironic reservations? As is usual in Shakespeare's work, the perspective is complex and balanced. The play pulls us in two directions. Although the Chorus, who interprets the play for us, approves of Henry's military posture, the grandiose rhetoric of war is consistently undercut by matter-of-fact revelations of men's self-interested motives. This contrast between rhetorical illusion and political reality extends from the justification of Henry's French campaign to his state marriage with Katharine of France. The irony never amounts to open disillusionment in this play; it is instead the acknowledgment of a special kind of morality pertaining to kingship.

Skill in rhetoric is a key to Henry's success—in defying the French Dauphin, in preparing troops for battle, or in wooing the French princess for his queen. As the Archbishop of Canterbury notes approvingly, King Henry's versatility as a rhetorician applies to all the vital disciplines of kingship: Henry can "reason in divinity," "debate of commonwealth affairs," "discourse of war," handle "any cause of policy," and in all such matters speak in "sweet and honeyed sentences" (1.1.39–51). Through the arts of language Henry displays piety, learning, administrative sagacity, political cunning, and military intrepidity. Like the contemporary play *Julius Caesar* (1599), *Henry V* is concerned with techniques of persuasion. (The earlier *Richard III* is also a highly rhetorical play, though chiefly through the negative example of tyrannical behavior.) Yet however much we may be swayed emotionally by the rhetoric, we realize that the public figure of Henry V is a mask behind which we can perceive little. Only rarely do we glimpse the affable young companion of the *Henry IV* plays. King Henry has accepted the responsibility of playing a political role. It denies him a private and separate identity, even—or especially—in choosing a wife. And it complicates our task of assessing the sincerity of his utterances. Is he genuinely pious, or has he merely learned the usefulness of pious utterance in swaying men's hearts? What especially are his motives for going to war against France?

Shakespeare could have begun this play with the stirring scene (1.2) in which Hal, urged on by his advisers, issues a defiant challenge to the French ambassadors. Instead, Shakespeare treats us to a prior glimpse beneath the patriotic surface. It seems that the Archbishop of Canterbury, threatened with a bill in Parliament designed to take away the better half of the Church's possessions, has resolved to parry with a counterproposal, whereby the Church will give Henry a very substantial sum for his French campaign, provided the offensive tax bill can be conveniently forgotten. The Archbishop has already been negotiating with Henry and surmises that the plan will work. This revelation is not shocking to us; it merely reveals the political process at work. The faint undercurrent of anticlericalism suggests that Henry is to be admired for putting pressure on his clergy with such success; they are rich and can afford to support the war. In any case, the dramatic effect is to show how men's practical motives affect their rhetoric. When, in the subsequent scene, the Archbishop delivers a public lecture on the English claim to France, we know that this learned prelate has a prior and self-interested commitment to the war. His intricate dynastic argument, which he proclaims to be "as clear as is the summer's sun" (1.2.86), gives to the war a much-needed public justification. Henry's questions indicate not only his genuine concern about the legitimacy of his claim, but also his political need for the Church's endorsement of his cause; he has already claimed certain French dukedoms and must have the Church's official approval of those claims before he can proceed. He similarly needs the backing of his nobles, who also have their own reasons for approving the campaign. Henry skillfully orchestrates the scene to produce the desired effect of unanimous and patriotic consent.

Although never directly stated, Henry's own motives for going to war must also combine sincere zeal with calculated self-interest. As King, he longs to recover the French territory that England governed in the great days of Poitiers and Crécy. As a man, he bristles at the contemptuous challenge of the Dauphin; Henry must still strive to overcome his reputation as a wastrel and must prove himself worthy of honorable comparison with his great ancestors. Politically (and this motive remains most hidden), Henry has absorbed his father's sage advice to "busy giddy minds / With foreign quarrels" (*2 Henry IV*, 4.5.213–214), to blunt political opposition at home by uniting English resentment against a foreign scapegoat.

The exigencies of war do indeed provide Henry with an opportunity for proceeding against his political enemies. He arrests the Earl of Cambridge, Lord Scroop, and Sir Thomas Grey at Southampton on charges of conspiring with France. The scene (2.4) is, for Shakespeare, uncharacteristically one-sided. We are never even told that Cambridge is the chief pretender to the English throne, son of the Duke of York, married to Anne Mortimer, and founder of the Yorkist claim in the York-Lancastrian wars—the sort of rival whom Shakespeare elsewhere portrays with understanding. Instead, the rhetoric of the Chorus to Act 2 blatantly warns us to expect "hell and treason" (l. 29). These three conspirators, like Judases, says the Chorus, have bargained away their king for gold. (In fact, Cambridge insists that his motive was not financial, though he is not permitted to say what it was.) The playwright does not give them complex motives; they are sinners, so horrified by their own intents that they are actually grateful to be caught. The scene serves, by such rhetorical devices, to strengthen Henry's claim to the English throne as well as to the territories in France. Opposition to his rule during wartime is, in the view of the Chorus, simply treasonous; all persuasive evidences of dynastic rival claims are hidden from our view.

Comedy also contributes to the rhetorical image-making of the hero in *Henry V*. The tavern crew is on hand, though deprived of Falstaff's beguiling company and more distant from Henry than in the earlier history plays. Only briefly and in disguise, on the night before the battle, does the King encounter Pistol. The name of Bardolph comes to Henry as though in recollection of a distant past, when he hears that Bardolph is about to be executed for stealing from French churches. Henry confirms the sentence: "We would have all such offenders so cut off" (3.6.107). Whatever momentary pang Henry may feel, he remains constant to his banishment of Falstaff. And, although Shakespeare pleads for our sympathies in the seriocomic account of Falstaff's death, seen through the childlike naiveté of Mistress Quickly, there is no hope of reconciliation between Henry and his former mates. Pistol, despite his ornamental language, is little more than a boaster, coward, and thief. The tavern revelers are now the opportunists of war, troublemakers such as are found in every army, engaging rascals deserving to be cudgeled by more honorable men.

Pistol gets his comeuppance from Captain Fluellen, who replaces Falstaff as the chief comic figure both in prominence (his role is second in length to that of Henry) and in proximity to the King. Fluellen is a Welshman, like Henry of Monmouth, and is proud of this kinship. Because Fluellen is loyal and valiant, he is a person worthy to be seen in Henry's company. Yet there is none of the brilliant duel of wits previously linking Henry and Falstaff. Fluellen is a humorous character, identified at once by such comically exaggerated features as his Welsh accent and mannerisms of speech, his old-fashioned and somewhat fanatical sense of military propriety, and his devotion to the ancient rules of military discipline. Fluellen is a caricature, subject to mild satirical laughter, and there is a note of condescension in Henry's habit of playing practical jokes on the captain. (Henry makes practical jokes at others' expense as well, such as the soldier named Williams with whom he exchanges gloves.) Unlike Falstaff, Fluellen lacks perspective on his own pomposity. He is a zealot for duty, and one feels Henry is taking unfair advantage to pick on one who is such an easy mark for laughter. We suspect that Henry is using people again, bolstering his public image as the king with the common touch, borrowing a little Welsh color for mythmaking purposes. At the same time, Fluellen is steadfast, upright, a credit to his countryman Henry. With his fellow captains from Scotland, Ireland, and England, he demonstrates that Britishers can fight together even if they do antagonize one another with their proud regional customs. Those customs are to be cherished as part of the British character; because Pistol offers gratuitous insult to the Welsh tradition of wearing a leek in the cap on St. Davy's Day, he must be thrashed.

As with the comic characters and Henry's political enemies, *Henry V* is rhetorically one-sided in its presentation of the French. Patriotism is a raw emotion, and Henry cannot appeal to it without awakening hostility toward the enemy. (Ironically enough, the great film version of *Henry V* by Laurence Olivier was created during World War II to arouse national feelings against the Germans rather than against the French, and with complete success. Any enemy will do in such patriotic moods.) The French are portrayed as haughty, vastly superior in numbers, envious of one another, contemptuous of their own leadership (especially the Dauphin), treacherous (attacking the boys with the luggage), and craven. Even their joking is characterized by an unattractively bestial kind of bawdry (3.7.48–68). The British—"we few, we happy few" (4.3.60)—are tired and outnumbered, but invincible and seemingly protected by God. Henry's order to kill the French prisoners and his description of the rapes and pillages his soldiers will commit if Harfleur fails to surrender (3.3.1–27), do, to be sure, raise serious questions about the morality of war under the best of kings; the play may be caustic toward the French nobility but does not necessarily exonerate the English. Even here, however, we are led to believe that, because the French are so execrably governed, France will suffer less under English rule. Henry takes care that his soldiers do not despoil the French countryside except under conditions of military "necessity." Only in Montjoy, the Duke of Burgundy, and Katharine of France does Shakespeare offer redeeming portraits of the French character, and in these instances the terms of hierarchical ascendancy seem clear: masculine English dominance, gentle French submissiveness. Katharine becomes "la belle France," depicted in Burgundy's eloquent peacemaking speech as being so much in need of competent management.

Henry woos Katharine with real flair, despite their unstated mutual recognition that their courtship is above all a matter of state in which they must play predetermined roles. The individual within Henry V gives way to the public personality, but he never loses his style. He manages always to be true to himself, as a wooer or as a soldier. We see him in disguise hobnobbing with common soldiers of his camp on the eve of battle, earnestly discussing with them the morality of war. We see him, with endearing human inconsistency, coveting all the glory of victory over the French and then adjuring his soldiers to give credit for that victory to God alone. Even if we are at times less attracted to this successful warrior and politician than to the carefree young man of *1 Henry IV,* we can still honor Henry's choice of responsible maturity and see that it is even compassionately self-denying. A king cannot be like other men, and Henry is willing to accept this price of leadership.

The Chorus presents *Henry V* to us as if it were epic as well as drama. Henry is an epic hero, defined in terms of mythic allusions and abstractions. He is compared to Mars, the god of war, with Famine, Sword, and Fire leashed at his heels, crouched and ready for employment. He is the "mirror of all Christian kings," and his followers are "English Mercurys" (2.0.6–7) with winged heels. Personified Expectation sits in the air, promising crowns and crownets to Henry and his followers. Henry's fleet of ships on the English Channel becomes "A city on th' inconstant billows dancing" (3.0.15). On the eve of battle, amidst his brothers, friends, and countrymen, Henry warms every heart with "cheerful semblance and sweet majesty" and with his "largess universal like the sun" (4.0.43). He forbids vainglorious pride and gives credit for his victory "Quite from himself to God" (5.0.22).

The action the Chorus describes is comparably epic, as it moves from England to France and back again, leaping over time, surveying all levels of society in the English nation, portraying famous military encounters seemingly more suited to epic narration (or to film) than to the stage. The stage's limitation forms indeed a major burden of the Chorus's argument. He apologizes to the spectators for the "flat unraisèd spirits" that have dared to bring forth so vast an object "On this unworthy scaffold," in this "cockpit" or "wooden O" (Prol.). The play confines "mighty men" "In little room," "Mangling by starts the full course of their glory" (Epil.).

This apology sounds like a becoming modesty on Shakespeare's part, in conceding the truth of Ben Jonson's objection that a few hired actors with rusty swords can scarcely do justice to England's great wars of the past. *Henry V* is not a Jonsonian neoclassical play. Paradoxically, however, Shakespeare's acknowledgment of the limited means at his disposal to create mimetic spectacle amounts to a defense of his own theater of the imagination. Through the Chorus's repeated urgings that we use our "imaginary forces" to supply what the actors and the theater necessarily lack, Shakespeare invites us as spectators and partners into his world of art. The play becomes a journey of thought, of making "imaginary puissance." When Shakespeare and his acting company talk of horses, we are to "see them / Printing their proud hoofs i' the receiving earth" (Prol.). This is not to minimize the importance of the theatrical experience, but indeed quite the opposite, since we are instructed to liberate ourselves through that theatrical experience and to recreate by means of Shakespeare's script an epic vision. Shakespeare's stage, bare of scenery, relying on good actors and the words they speak, becomes through its very flexibility more versatile in creating that vision than the most ornate and mechanically sophisticated illusionistic theater.

Henry V in Performance

No Shakespearean play is more aware of its own theatrical limits than *Henry V.* Repeatedly, the chorus apologizes for the theatrical medium that requires us to supplement the spectacle before us with our imagination. We are asked to carry kings here and there on the wings of thought, to jump over long passages of time, to see horses when the actors speak of them, to make "imaginary puissance" by dividing each soldier into a thousand men, to see shipboys climbing the tackle of full-rigged ships at Southampton pier, to follow as the invasion army approaches Harfleur, to behold a siege there, to "entertain conjecture" of an army camp on the night before the battle of Agincourt with King Henry himself walking from tent to tent, to bear the King hence to Calais and London (where he is triumphally received) and back to France—in short, to "eke" out the performance with our minds. The Chorus speaks self-deprecatorily on behalf of his acting company and his author; the play cannot hope to "cram / Within this wooden O the very casques / That did affright the air at Agincourt," and so the actors must content themselves with confining "mighty men" in "little room," "Mangling by starts [i.e., in fits and starts] the full course of their glory."

Paradoxically, however, we grow increasingly aware that the Chorus is proud, not ashamed, of his spectacle and that his exhortations to us are a defense of a theater of imagination. All theater depends on synecdoche, that is, the part standing for the whole; the very essence of theater is illusion, to which an audience brings its understanding of the conventions by which theatrical signs are to be interpreted. This Chorus, in spelling out the conventions of Shakespeare's theater, places the emphasis where it rightly belongs, on our active participation in the reenactment or re-creation of the events that are being staged.

The original production of *Henry V* must have been spectacular in its own way, if only because it may have been the opener in 1599 for the company's new Globe Theatre.

Contemporary witnesses credit the London theaters of Shakespeare's day with being strikingly handsome. The conventions of illusion were, however, not verisimilar in the way the nineteenth century conceived of them, as we shall see. The original stage directions give clear hints as to staging. As the Chorus finishes the prologue to Act 3, for example, the text specifies *"Alarum, and chambers go off,"* suggesting that the stage action is supposed to mingle with the Chorus's final words. Then, *"Enter the King, Exeter, Bedford, and Gloucester. Alarum,* [*with soldiers carrying*] *scaling ladders at Harfleur."* The *Alarums* are forays onstage of armed soldiers; the *chambers* are cannon firing backstage. Much of the theatrical impression of warfare is conveyed by the sound effect of drum rolls and trumpet calls that the audience can readily interpret as signals of attack or retreat. The smell of gunpowder is in the spectators' nostrils, the sounds of war are in their ears, and before their eyes the theater facade now represents (without scenery) the walls of Harfleur. Scaling ladders are leaned up against the facade and used in breaching Harfleur's defenses. Spatially the theater provides a plausible three-dimensional locale for a siege, with fortified walls towering above the ground in front of them. When the Governor and some citizens appear on the walls in Act 3, scene 3, they are presumably in the gallery above the main stage, looking down on King Henry *"and all his train"* massing *"before the gates."* Clearly the acting company enlists as many extras as possible for this siege effort; their numbers are nonetheless symbolic, as they must be, even in the most epic of staging. The *gates* of Harfleur are represented by a door in the facade backstage, through which King Henry and his invading army exit from the stage, bringing to a close the military sequence at Harfleur: *"Flourish, and enter the town"* (3.3.58). Throughout, the theatrical emphasis is not so much on the military engagement itself as on Henry's ringing oratory and on the attempts of the irascible Fluellen to drive the reluctant Nym, Bardolph, and Pistol on into battle.

The early stage history of the play remains incomplete, despite these indications in the play script itself of how it was intended to be played. In 1605 the play was performed at court, and it seems to have been regularly acted at the

Globe Theatre. After the Restoration, it was infrequently produced. The diarist Samuel Pepys saw Thomas Betterton play in a non-Shakespearean *Henry V* in 1667 at the theater in Lincoln's Inn Fields, and it was not until 1738 that Shakespeare's play returned as a staple of the dramatic repertory. The Theatre Royal, Covent Garden, performed the play that year, and then in thirty-two of the remaining years of the century. *Henry V* was usually performed without the Choruses (though in 1747 and 1748 at the Theatre Royal, Drury Lane, David Garrick acted the Chorus), without Henry's arrest of the traitors in Act 2, scene 2, and without the soldiers' skeptical questioning in Act 4, scene 1. Dennis Delane, Sacheveral Hale, and Spranger Barry were among the finer eighteenth-century Henrys; Charles Macklin, Richard Yates, and Edward Shuter had great successes as Fluellen. John Philip Kemble first acted Henry at Drury Lane in 1789 and continued in the part until 1811.

On the nineteenth-century stage *Henry V* was regularly played, achieving a kind of monumental and costly splendor. By taking too literally the Chorus's appeal for visual effects, however, actor-managers often merely substituted verisimilar spectacle for the audience's imaginative participation. Set design undertook to supply, as far as was theatrically possible, all that was invoked by Shakespeare's poetry. William Charles Macready's production at Covent Garden in 1839, for example, hit on the novelty of accompanying the Chorus (spoken by John Vandenhoff in the character of Time) with a succession of pictorial illustrations executed by the painter Clarkson Stanfield. Act 3 began with a diorama that moved while the Chorus spoke, showing the English fleet as it left Southampton and traversed the English Channel until it came within sight of Harfleur. The action began onstage before the completion of the diorama, so that the picture melted, as it were, into the actual siege. Some enraptured spectators had difficulty telling when the diorama ended and the "real" action commenced. Samuel Phelps produced the play at the Sadler's Wells Theatre in 1852, striving, like Macready, for accurate and realistic visual effects, and succeeding in recreating English history in a theatrical experience that was, according to the *Morning Post,* "among the best things that the modern European stage has produced."

Charles Kean's 1859 revival at the Princess's Theatre attempted to outdo Macready and Phelps, with the siege of Harfleur realized onstage as literally as possible. Guns and engines of war that discharged smoke and flying stones were pointed at the walls of the town. Amid the confusion and din of war, King Henry, followed by seemingly countless soldiers, dauntlessly led the attack until Harfleur was reduced to rubble. In a similarly literal vein, Kean provided tableaux for the French and English camps on the night before Agincourt while Mrs. Kean (Ellen Tree), in the character of Clio, the muse of history, recited the Chorus to Act 4. Kean interpolated a crowd scene portraying King Henry's triumphant entry into London to accompany the recitation of the Chorus to Act 5.

Not until the twentieth century did directors attempt to recapture the fluidity and stage magic of the original script. Among recent productions, one that succeeds particularly in evoking the paradox of stage illusion is Laurence Olivier's film version (1944). Olivier places Act 1 and part of Act 2 in a reconstructed Globe Theatre in order to emphasize the limits and devices of theatrical illusion. We are ushered backstage to see boy actors filling out their women's bodices with pieces of fruit, or to see Olivier nervously clearing his throat before going onstage to a round of applause. The film condescends a bit to Shakespeare's theatre—sound effects such as striking clocks are late and require the intervention of the prompter (Shakespeare himself), and rain turns the open stage into a mire of wet hay in Act 2—but the point is well established by closeup shots that the actors wear makeup and are stylized in their Elizabethan dress. Having shown the way in which theatrical illusion is fabricated, Olivier then uses the camera to do what the theater cannot do, that is, show us the breathtaking gallop of horses across a French countryside (the sequence, in fact, was filmed in Ireland) and a flight of arrows toward the approaching enemy. When, at the concluding wedding of King Henry and Katharine of France, we suddenly find ourselves back in the Globe Theatre, we realize with a shock that the illusion has been contrived and yet wholly convincing. We accept the conventions of theater, while realizing that Olivier has been cheating by showing what we were to imagine. He has recreated the spectacle of

Macready and Kean, but with a theatrical self-awareness that aligns itself with Shakespeare's art.

Along with examining matters of illusion, stage history offers insight into the interpretation of Henry's character. Olivier's Henry—indomitable, brave and good-humored, unmistakably heroic and unabashedly English—was just the kind of patriotic tonic that war-wearied England needed in 1944. It was also recognizably part of a long stage tradition. Macready's and Kean's idealization of Henry as an invincible warrior had continued on into the early twentieth century in Frank Benson's many performances between 1897 and 1916; to demonstrate his prowess and fearless leadership, Benson as Henry pole-vaulted in full armor onto the walls of Harfleur. Lewis Walker (1900), not to be outdone by this sort of tireless athleticism, pushed himself off from a backstage wall just before his cue and thus arrived onstage at full speed for virtually every scene. Olivier played a heroic if restrained Henry in 1937 at the Old Vic directed by Tyrone Guthrie. In 1951, Alec Clunes, under Glen Byam Shaw's direction at the Old Vic, and Richard Burton, at Stratford-upon-Avon in a production directed by Anthony Quayle, each gave to Henry an interpretation that confidently stressed the play's patriotism and extolling of regal virtues.

Many recent productions, on the other hand, have explored the patriotism of *Henry V* with skepticism and, at times, open defiance. When Christopher Plummer played Henry in 1956 at Stratford, Ontario, with an attractive modesty qualifying his heroic energy, the production's most interesting political effect was achieved by its casting. Michael Langham invited French-Canadian actors from the Théâtre de Nouveau Monde to play the French roles, and in the context of Canadian politics the defeat of the French was no longer a simple patriotic triumph. Similar political concerns have shaped most recent productions. Certainly through the 1960s, the Vietnam War agonizingly forced a reappraisal of the play's insights into heroism and patriotism. The Royal Shakespeare Company's production in 1964 at Stratford-upon-Avon, for example, directed by Peter Hall, John Barton, and Clifford Williams, was a skeptical exploration of the realities of war, not the least part of which was its grimly realistic rendition of the Battle of Agincourt. Ian

Holm as Henry led troops who were visibly fatigued, enfeebled, their gayness and gilt all besmirched (as indeed the text calls for, 4.3.110). Theirs was the dogged heroism of trench warfare, of attrition, as one observer noted, "of men following a leader, not because he is a king, but because he is as tired and as stubbornly determined as they are." No doubt influenced by the Royal Shakespeare Company's production, Michael Langham again directed the play in 1966 at Stratford, Ontario, similarly focusing on war's brutality. Douglas Rain's Henry was impassively purposeful, showing no sign of remorse or even recognition when Bardolph's hanged body was dumped at his feet. Michael Kahn's Brechtian direction of the play at Stratford, Connecticut, in 1969, stressed even more overtly the antiwar theme. Hawklike bishops were shown manipulating Henry into an inglorious, imperialistic war that was then legitimized with the hollow rhetoric of patriotism.

Free of the immediate anxieties and tensions aroused by the war in Vietnam, recent versions have been more balanced, though still for the most part taking a disillusioned, antiromantic view of warfare. Terry Hands's production at Stratford-upon-Avon in 1975 was, as Hands said, "full of doubt." Alan Howard was a Henry always aware of the human costs of the war he must fight; his performance sought out Henry's self-doubt and showed the strain of overcoming it. At New York's Delacorte Theater in 1976, Joseph Papp directed an energetic *Henry V* with soldiers running helter-skelter across the smoke-filled stage, suggesting a war out of the control of any individual. In the final act, Meryl Streep's Katharine seemed ruefully aware that the ensuing marriage served Henry's political ambitions more than his romantic ones. *Henry V* returned to the New York Shakespeare Festival at the Delacorte Theater in 1984, directed by Wilford Leach with Kevin Kline in the title role.

Adrian Noble's direction of *Henry V* at Stratford-upon-Avon in 1984 revealed with unusual clarity what the play can be on the modern stage. On a drab open set designed by Bob Crowley, the play eloquently balanced its patriotic appeal with a full acknowledgment of the tawdry realities of war and politics. King Henry (Kenneth Branagh) eagerly wooed Katharine in the final scene even as the political negotiations earnestly continued, while behind a gauze curtain candles flickered on the graves of the soldiers who had died at Agincourt. If the complexity of the modern world insists that *Henry V* can no longer be played as an uncritical celebration of England's greatest medieval hero, it need not be taken to the opposite extreme as a harsh satire on imperialistic ambition. Without either glamorizing war or debunking public values, the play onstage, as in Noble's moving production, can effectively reveal the power of the heroic image that the play offers at the same time that it explores the physical, moral, and psychological costs of achieving that image.

— HENRY V —

[*Dramatis Personae*

CHORUS

KING HENRY THE FIFTH

HUMPHREY, DUKE OF GLOUCESTER, } *the King's brothers*
JOHN, DUKE OF BEDFORD,
DUKE OF CLARENCE,

DUKE OF EXETER, *the King's uncle*
DUKE OF YORK, *the King's cousin*
EARL OF SALISBURY
EARL OF WESTMORLAND
EARL OF WARWICK
EARL OF HUNTINGDON

ARCHBISHOP OF CANTERBURY
BISHOP OF ELY

RICHARD, EARL OF CAMBRIDGE, } *conspirators against the King*
HENRY, LORD SCROOP OF MASHAM,
SIR THOMAS GREY,

SIR THOMAS ERPINGHAM, } *officers in the King's army*
CAPTAIN GOWER,
CAPTAIN FLUELLEN,
CAPTAIN MACMORRIS,
CAPTAIN JAMY,

JOHN BATES, } *soldiers in the King's army*
ALEXANDER COURT,
MICHAEL WILLIAMS,

An English HERALD

PISTOL, } *Falstaff's former tavern-mates*
NYM,
BARDOLPH,

BOY, *formerly Falstaff's page*
HOSTESS, *formerly Mistress Quickly, now married to Pistol*

DUKE OF BURGUNDY

FRENCH KING, *Charles the Sixth*
QUEEN ISABEL *of France*
DAUPHIN, *Lewis*
KATHARINE, *Princess of France*
ALICE, *a lady attending Katharine*
DUKE OF ORLEANS
DUKE OF BERRI
DUKE OF BOURBON
DUKE OF BRITTANY
CONSTABLE OF FRANCE
LORD RAMBURES
LORD GRANDPRÉ
GOVERNOR OF HARFLEUR
MONSIEUR LE FER, *a French soldier*
MONTJOY, *the French herald*
French AMBASSADORS *to England*

Lords, Ladies, Officers, Soldiers, Citizens, Messengers, and Attendants

SCENE: *England, afterwards France*]

Prologue *Enter [Chorus as] Prologue.*

CHORUS

O, for a Muse of fire, that would ascend 1
The brightest heaven of invention! 2
A kingdom for a stage, princes to act,
And monarchs to behold the swelling scene! 4
Then should the warlike Harry, like himself, 5
Assume the port of Mars; and at his heels, 6
Leashed in like hounds, should famine, sword, and fire
Crouch for employment. But pardon, gentles all, 8
The flat unraisèd spirits that hath dared 9
On this unworthy scaffold to bring forth 10
So great an object. Can this cockpit hold 11
The vasty fields of France? Or may we cram 12
Within this wooden O the very casques 13
That did affright the air at Agincourt?
O, pardon! Since a crooked figure may 15
Attest in little place a million; 16
And let us, ciphers to this great account, 17
On your imaginary forces work. 18
Suppose within the girdle of these walls
Are now confined two mighty monarchies,
Whose high uprearèd and abutting fronts 21
The perilous narrow ocean parts asunder. 22
Piece out our imperfections with your thoughts:
Into a thousand parts divide one man,
And make imaginary puissance. 25

Prologue.
1 Muse of fire (Of the four elements, earth, air, fire, and water, fire is the most sublime and mounting.) **2 invention** poetic imagination **4 swelling** splendid, magnificent **5 like himself** i.e., presented in a fashion worthy of so great a king **6 port** bearing **8 gentles** gentlemen and gentlewomen **9 flat unraisèd** uninspired, lifeless. **spirits** i.e., actors and playwright **10 scaffold** stage **11 cockpit** (Elizabethan theaters were shaped rather like arenas for animal fighting.) **12 vasty** vast, spacious **13 O** (Refers to a round theater such as the Globe; the play may have been performed at the Curtain Theater.) **casques** helmets **15 crooked figure** cipher or zero (which, added to a number, will multiply its value tenfold) **16 Attest** stand for **17 account** (1) sum total (continuing the metaphor of *crooked figure*) (2) story **18 imaginary forces** forces of imagination **21 abutting** touching, bordering. **fronts** frontiers, i.e., the cliffs of Dover and Calais **22 perilous . . . ocean** i.e., English Channel **25 puissance** armed might, army

Think, when we talk of horses, that you see them
Printing their proud hoofs i' the receiving earth.
For 'tis your thoughts that now must deck our kings,
Carry them here and there, jumping o'er times,
Turning th' accomplishment of many years
Into an hourglass—for the which supply,
Admit me Chorus to this history,
Who, Prologue-like, your humble patience pray,
Gently to hear, kindly to judge, our play. *Exit.*

28 deck dress, adorn **31 the which supply** which service

1.1 *Enter the two bishops,* [*the Archbishop*] *of Canterbury and* [*the Bishop of*] *Ely.*

CANTERBURY
My lord, I'll tell you. That self bill is urged 1
Which in th' eleventh year of the last king's reign
Was like, and had indeed against us passed, 3
But that the scambling and unquiet time 4
Did push it out of farther question. 5

ELY
But how, my lord, shall we resist it now?

CANTERBURY
It must be thought on. If it pass against us,
We lose the better half of our possession.
For all the temporal lands which men devout 9
By testament have given to the Church
Would they strip from us, being valued thus:
As much as would maintain, to the King's honor,
Full fifteen earls and fifteen hundred knights,
Six thousand and two hundred good esquires, 14
And, to relief of lazars and weak age 15
Of indigent faint souls past corporal toil, 16
A hundred almshouses right well supplied;
And to the coffers of the King besides
A thousand pounds by th' year. Thus runs the bill.

ELY This would drink deep.

CANTERBURY 'Twould drink the cup and all.

ELY But what prevention?

CANTERBURY
The King is full of grace and fair regard.

ELY
And a true lover of the holy Church.

CANTERBURY
The courses of his youth promised it not.
The breath no sooner left his father's body
But that his wildness, mortified in him, 27
Seemed to die too; yea, at that very moment

1.1. Location: England. The royal court.
1 self same **3 like** likely (to have passed) **4 scambling** unsettled
5 question consideration **9 temporal** used for secular purposes
14 esquires members of the gentry, ranking just below knights
15 lazars lepers **16 corporal** physical **27 mortified** killed

Consideration like an angel came
And whipped th' offending Adam out of him,
Leaving his body as a paradise
T' envelop and contain celestial spirits.
Never was such a sudden scholar made;
Never came reformation in a flood
With such a heady currance, scouring faults;
Nor never Hydra-headed willfulness
So soon did lose his seat, and all at once,
As in this king.

ELY
We are blessed in the change.

CANTERBURY
Hear him but reason in divinity,
And, all-admiring, with an inward wish
You would desire the King were made a prelate.
Hear him debate of commonwealth affairs,
You would say it hath been all in all his study.
List his discourse of war, and you shall hear
A fearful battle rendered you in music.
Turn him to any cause of policy,
The Gordian knot of it he will unloose,
Familiar as his garter, that, when he speaks,
The air, a chartered libertine, is still,
And the mute wonder lurketh in men's ears
To steal his sweet and honeyed sentences;
So that the art and practic part of life
Must be the mistress to this theoric.
Which is a wonder how His Grace should glean it,
Since his addiction was to courses vain,

29 Consideration meditation, reflection **30 offending Adam** original sin **35 heady currance** headlong current **36 Hydra-headed** i.e., many-headed. (Alludes to the Lernaean Hydra, a monster of many heads overcome by Hercules.) **37 his seat** its throne **39 divinity** theological matters **41 prelate** ecclesiastical dignitary **44 List** listen to **45 rendered . . . music** i.e., eloquently narrated **46 cause of policy** matter of statecraft **47 Gordian knot** (It was foretold that whoever should untie the Gordian knot would rule Asia. Alexander solved the problem by cutting the knot.) **48 Familiar** as offhandedly or routinely. **that** so that **49 chartered libertine** licensed freeman, able to roam at will **50 the . . . ears** i.e., wonder makes men silent, eagerly listening **51 To . . . sentences** i.e., to hear more of his sweetly profitable wise sayings **52–53 So . . . theoric** so that experience in practical life must have been the teacher by which he acquired his theoretical conception **55 addiction** inclination

His companies unlettered, rude, and shallow, 56
His hours filled up with riots, banquets, sports, 57
And never noted in him any study,
Any retirement, any sequestration
From open haunts and popularity. 60

ELY
The strawberry grows underneath the nettle,
And wholesome berries thrive and ripen best
Neighbored by fruit of baser quality;
And so the Prince obscured his contemplation
Under the veil of wildness, which, no doubt,
Grew like the summer grass, fastest by night,
Unseen, yet crescive in his faculty. 67

CANTERBURY
It must be so, for miracles are ceased. 68
And therefore we must needs admit the means 69
How things are perfected.

ELY
But, my good lord,
How now for mitigation of this bill
Urged by the Commons? Doth His Majesty
Incline to it, or no?

CANTERBURY
He seems indifferent, 73
Or rather swaying more upon our part
Than cherishing th' exhibiters against us; 75
For I have made an offer to His Majesty,
Upon our spiritual convocation 77
And in regard of causes now in hand, 78
Which I have opened to His Grace at large, 79
As touching France, to give a greater sum
Than ever at one time the clergy yet
Did to his predecessors part withal. 82

ELY
How did this offer seem received, my lord?

CANTERBURY
With good acceptance of His Majesty,

56 companies companions. **rude** coarse **57 sports** amusements
60 open . . . popularity places of public resort and low company
67 crescive . . . faculty naturally inclined to grow **68 miracles are ceased** (Protestants believed that no miracles occurred after the revelation of Christ.) **69 means** i.e., natural causes **73 indifferent** unbiased
75 exhibiters those who introduce bills in Parliament **77 Upon** on behalf of. **convocation** formal assembly of the clergy **78 in hand** under consideration **79 opened** expounded. **at large** in full **82 withal** with

Save that there was not time enough to hear,
As I perceived His Grace would fain have done,
The severals and unhidden passages
Of his true titles to some certain dukedoms,
And generally to the crown and seat of France,
Derived from Edward, his great-grandfather.

ELY
What was th' impediment that broke this off?

CANTERBURY
The French ambassador upon that instant
Craved audience; and the hour I think is come
To give him hearing. Is it four o'clock?

ELY It is.

CANTERBURY
Then go we in to know his embassy,
Which I could with a ready guess declare
Before the Frenchman speak a word of it.

ELY
I'll wait upon you, and I long to hear it. *Exeunt.*

✤

1.2

Enter the King, Humphrey [*Duke of Gloucester*], *Bedford, Clarence, Warwick, Westmorland, and Exeter* [*with attendants*].

KING
Where is my gracious lord of Canterbury?

EXETER
Not here in presence.

KING Send for him, good uncle.

WESTMORLAND
Shall we call in th' ambassador, my liege?

KING
Not yet, my cousin. We would be resolved,
Before we hear him, of some things of weight

86 fain gladly **87 severals** details. **unhidden passages** obvious lines of descent **89 seat** throne **90 Edward** i.e., Edward III **96 embassy** message

1.2. Location: England. The royal court.
4 cousin (Correct form of address from royal family to nobles.) **be resolved** come to a decision

That task our thoughts, concerning us and France. 6

Enter two bishops, [*the Archbishop of Canterbury and the Bishop of Ely*].

CANTERBURY

God and his angels guard your sacred throne,
And make you long become it!

KING

Sure we thank you. 8
My learnèd lord, we pray you to proceed,
And justly and religiously unfold
Why the law Salic that they have in France
Or should or should not bar us in our claim. 12
And God forbid, my dear and faithful lord,
That you should fashion, wrest, or bow your reading,
Or nicely charge your understanding soul 15
With opening titles miscreate, whose right 16
Suits not in native colors with the truth; 17
For God doth know how many now in health
Shall drop their blood in approbation 19
Of what your reverence shall incite us to.
Therefore take heed how you impawn our person, 21
How you awake our sleeping sword of war.
We charge you in the name of God take heed;
For never two such kingdoms did contend
Without much fall of blood, whose guiltless drops
Are every one a woe, a sore complaint 26
'Gainst him whose wrongs gives edge unto the swords 27
That makes such waste in brief mortality. 28
Under this conjuration speak, my lord; 29
For we will hear, note, and believe in heart
That what you speak is in your conscience washed
As pure as sin with baptism.

CANTERBURY

Then hear me, gracious sovereign, and you peers,
That owe yourselves, your lives, and services

6 task engage, occupy **8 become** adorn, grace **12 Or** either **15 nicely charge** subtly and foolishly burden **16 opening titles miscreate** expounding spurious claims **17 Suits . . . colors** i.e., does not naturally harmonize **19 approbation** support, proof **21 impawn** pledge **26 woe** grievance. **sore** severe, grievous **27 wrongs** wrongdoings **28 in brief mortality** i.e., among mortal, short-lived men **29 conjuration** solemn adjuration

To this imperial throne. There is no bar
To make against Your Highness' claim to France
But this, which they produce from Pharamond: 37
"In terram Salicam mulieres ne succedant,"
"No woman shall succeed in Salic land."
Which Salic land the French unjustly gloze 40
To be the realm of France, and Pharamond
The founder of this law and female bar.
Yet their own authors faithfully affirm
That the land Salic is in Germany,
Between the floods of Saale and of Elbe; 45
Where Charles the Great, having subdued the Saxons, 46
There left behind and settled certain French,
Who, holding in disdain the German women
For some dishonest manners of their life, 49
Established then this law: to wit, no female
Should be inheritrix in Salic land—
Which Salic, as I said, twixt Elbe and Saale,
Is at this day in Germany called Meissen.
Then doth it well appear the Salic law
Was not devisèd for the realm of France;
Nor did the French possess the Salic land
Until four hundred one-and-twenty years
After defunction of King Pharamond, 58
Idly supposed the founder of this law, 59
Who died within the year of our redemption
Four hundred twenty-six; and Charles the Great
Subdued the Saxons, and did seat the French
Beyond the River Saale, in the year
Eight hundred five. Besides, their writers say,
King Pepin, which deposèd Childeric, 65
Did, as heir general, being descended 66
Of Blithild, which was daughter to King Clothair,
Make claim and title to the crown of France.
Hugh Capet also, who usurped the crown
Of Charles the Duke of Lorraine, sole heir male
Of the true line and stock of Charles the Great,

37 Pharamond legendary Frankish king **40 gloze** deceptively explain away **45 floods** rivers **46 Charles the Great** Charlemagne
49 dishonest unchaste **58 defunction** death **59 Idly** foolishly
65 which who (as also in l. 67) **66 heir general** heir through male or female line

To find his title with some shows of truth, 72
Though, in pure truth, it was corrupt and naught,
Conveyed himself as th' heir to the Lady Lingard, 74
Daughter to Charlemagne, who was the son 75
To Lewis the Emperor, and Lewis the son
Of Charles the Great. Also King Lewis the Tenth, 77
Who was sole heir to the usurper Capet,
Could not keep quiet in his conscience,
Wearing the crown of France, till satisfied
That fair Queen Isabel, his grandmother,
Was lineal of the Lady Ermengard, 82
Daughter to Charles the foresaid Duke of Lorraine;
By the which marriage the line of Charles the Great
Was reunited to the crown of France.
So that, as clear as is the summer's sun,
King Pepin's title and Hugh Capet's claim,
King Lewis his satisfaction, all appear 88
To hold in right and title of the female;
So do the kings of France unto this day.
Howbeit they would hold up this Salic law 91
To bar Your Highness claiming from the female,
And rather choose to hide them in a nct 93
Than amply to imbar their crooked titles 94
Usurped from you and your progenitors.

KING
May I with right and conscience make this claim?

CANTERBURY
The sin upon my head, dread sovereign!
For in the Book of Numbers is it writ, 98
When the man dies, let the inheritance 99
Descend unto the daughter. Gracious lord, 100
Stand for your own; unwind your bloody flag! 101

72 find provide **74 Conveyed himself** passed himself off **75 Charlemagne** (Holinshed's and Hall's error, followed by Shakespeare, for Charles the Bold.) **77 Lewis the Tenth** (Actually, Louis IX; an error copied from Holinshed.) **82 lineal of** descended from **88 Lewis his satisfaction** Lewis's conviction **91 Howbeit** notwithstanding **93 hide . . . net** i.e., conceal the weakness of their case in a tangle of contradictions **94 amply to imbar** frankly to bar claim to **98 Numbers** (See Numbers 27:8.) **99–100 When . . . daughter** (This paraphrase leaves out an important phrase. Numbers reads, "When a man dies leaving no son, his patrimony shall pass to his daughter.") **101 unwind** unfurl

Look back into your mighty ancestors:
Go, my dread lord, to your great-grandsire's tomb, 103
From whom you claim! Invoke his warlike spirit,
And your great-uncle's, Edward the Black Prince,
Who on the French ground played a tragedy, 106
Making defeat on the full power of France, 107
Whiles his most mighty father on a hill
Stood smiling to behold his lion's whelp 109
Forage in blood of French nobility. 110
O noble English, that could entertain 111
With half their forces the full pride of France
And let another half stand laughing by,
All out of work and cold for action! 114

ELY
Awake remembrance of these valiant dead,
And with your puissant arm renew their feats!
You are their heir; you sit upon their throne;
The blood and courage that renownèd them 118
Runs in your veins; and my thrice-puissant liege
Is in the very May morn of his youth,
Ripe for exploits and mighty enterprises.

EXETER
Your brother kings and monarchs of the earth
Do all expect that you should rouse yourself
As did the former lions of your blood.

WESTMORLAND
They know Your Grace hath cause, and means, and
might;
So hath Your Highness! Never king of England 126
Had nobles richer and more loyal subjects,
Whose hearts have left their bodies here in England
And lie pavilioned in the fields of France. 129

CANTERBURY
O, let their bodies follow, my dear liege,
With blood, and sword, and fire to win your right!
In aid whereof we of the spiritualty 132

103 great-grandsire's i.e., Edward III's **106 tragedy** i.e., the Battle of Crécy, 1346, a major defeat for the French **107 power** army **109 whelp** offspring **110 Forage in** prey on **111 entertain** engage, encounter **114 for action** for want of action **118 renownèd** brought renown to **126 So** so indeed **129 pavilioned** tented, encamped **132 spiritualty** clergy

Will raise Your Highness such a mighty sum
As never did the clergy at one time
Bring in to any of your ancestors.

KING

We must not only arm t' invade the French,
But lay down our proportions to defend
Against the Scot, who will make road upon us
With all advantages.

CANTERBURY

They of those marches, gracious sovereign,
Shall be a wall sufficient to defend
Our inland from the pilfering borderers.

KING

We do not mean the coursing snatchers only,
But fear the main intendment of the Scot,
Who hath been still a giddy neighbor to us.
For you shall read that my great-grandfather
Never went with his forces into France
But that the Scot on his unfurnished kingdom
Camc pouring, like the tide into a breach,
With ample and brim fullness of his force,
Galling the gleanèd land with hot assays,
Girding with grievous siege castles and towns;
That England, being empty of defense,
Hath shook and trembled at th' ill neighborhood.

CANTERBURY

She hath been then more feared than harmed, my liege.
For hear her but exampled by herself:
When all her chivalry hath been in France
And she a mourning widow of her nobles,
She hath herself not only well defended

137 lay . . . proportions allocate our forces **138 road** inroad, raid **139 With all advantages** whenever a good opportunity presents itself **140 marches** borderlands (here, in the north) **143 coursing snatchers** mounted raiders **144 intendment** plan, hostile intent **145 still** always. **giddy** unstable, fickle **148 unfurnished** unprovided with defense **150 brim** absolute, complete **151 Galling . . . assays** worrying the land stripped of defenders with hot attacks **154 neighborhood** neighborliness **155 feared** frightened **156 hear . . . herself** i.e., only listen how she can be instructed by an example from her own history **157 chivalry** knights

But taken and impounded as a stray
The King of Scots, whom she did send to France
To fill King Edward's fame with prisoner kings
And make her chronicle as rich with praise
As is the ooze and bottom of the sea
With sunken wrack and sumless treasuries.

A LORD
But there's a saying very old and true:
"If that you will France win,
Then with Scotland first begin."
For once the eagle England being in prey,
To her unguarded nest the weasel Scot
Comes sneaking, and so sucks her princely eggs,
Playing the mouse in absence of the cat,
To 'tame and havoc more than she can eat.

EXETER
It follows then the cat must stay at home;
Yet that is but a crushed necessity,
Since we have locks to safeguard necessaries
And pretty traps to catch the petty thieves.
While that the armèd hand doth fight abroad,
Th' advisèd head defends itself at home;
For government, though high, and low, and lower,
Put into parts, doth keep in one consent,
Congreeing in a full and natural close,
Like music.

CANTERBURY Therefore doth heaven divide
The state of man in divers functions,
Setting endeavor in continual motion,
To which is fixèd, as an aim or butt,
Obedience; for so work the honeybees,
Creatures that by a rule in nature teach

160 impounded as a stray (David II of Scotland was captured and imprisoned in 1346 while Edward III was in France.) **161 to France** (Historically, David II was imprisoned in London, not sent to France.) **165 wrack** wreckage. **sumless** inestimable **169 in prey** absent in search of prey **173 'tame** attame, cut into. **havoc** ravage **175 crushed necessity** forced conclusion **177 pretty** ingenious **179 advisèd** wise, prudent **180 though . . . lower** i.e., though composed of three broad social ranks **181 Put into parts** separated into different functions. **one consent** mutual harmony **182 Congreeing** agreeing together. **close** musical cadence **184 divers** various **186 aim or butt** i.e., target

The act of order to a peopled kingdom.
They have a king, and officers of sorts, 190
Where some, like magistrates, correct at home; 191
Others, like merchants, venture trade abroad;
Others, like soldiers, armèd in their stings,
Make boot upon the summer's velvet buds, 194
Which pillage they with merry march bring home
To the tent royal of their emperor,
Who, busied in his majesty, surveys 197
The singing masons building roofs of gold,
The civil citizens kneading up the honey,
The poor mechanic porters crowding in 200
Their heavy burdens at his narrow gate,
The sad-eyed justice with his surly hum 202
Delivering o'er to executors pale 203
The lazy yawning drone. I this infer,
That many things, having full reference 205
To one consent, may work contrariously. 206
As many arrows loosèd several ways 207
Come to one mark, as many ways meet in one town, 208
As many fresh streams meet in one salt sea,
As many lines close in the dial's center, 210
So may a thousand actions once afoot
End in one purpose, and be all well borne 212
Without defeat. Therefore to France, my liege!
Divide your happy England into four,
Whereof take you one quarter into France,
And you withal shall make all Gallia shake. 216
If we with thrice such powers left at home
Cannot defend our own doors from the dog,
Let us be worried, and our nation lose 219
The name of hardiness and policy. 220

190 They . . . king (A common error of early natural history, derived from Aristotle.) **of sorts** of various kinds **191 correct** administer justice **194 Make boot** prey **197 majesty** royal office **200 mechanic** engaged in manual labor **202 sad-eyed** grave-eyed **203 executors** executioners **205–206 having . . . consent** i.e., united by a common understanding **207 loosèd several ways** shot from different directions **208 ways** roads **210 close** come together. **dial's** sundial's **212 borne** carried out, sustained **216 Gallia** France. (Latin name.) **219 worried** torn apart, as by dogs **220 hardiness and policy** bravery and statesmanship

KING
Call in the messengers sent from the Dauphin. 221
[*Exeunt some.*]
Now are we well resolved, and by God's help
And yours, the noble sinews of our power,
France being ours, we'll bend it to our awe, 224
Or break it all to pieces. Or there we'll sit, 225
Ruling in large and ample empery 226
O'er France and all her almost kingly dukedoms,
Or lay these bones in an unworthy urn,
Tombless, with no remembrance over them.
Either our history shall with full mouth
Speak freely of our acts, or else our grave,
Like Turkish mute, shall have a tongueless mouth,
Not worshiped with a waxen epitaph. 233

Enter Ambassadors of France.

Now are we well prepared to know the pleasure
Of our fair cousin Dauphin; for we hear
Your greeting is from him, not from the King.

FIRST AMBASSADOR
May 't please Your Majesty to give us leave
Freely to render what we have in charge,
Or shall we sparingly show you far off 239
The Dauphin's meaning and our embassy?

KING
We are no tyrant, but a Christian king,
Unto whose grace our passion is as subject
As is our wretches fettered in our prisons.
Therefore with frank and with uncurbèd plainness
Tell us the Dauphin's mind.

FIRST AMBASSADOR
Thus, then, in few:
Your Highness, lately sending into France,
Did claim some certain dukedoms, in the right
Of your great predecessor, King Edward the Third.
In answer of which claim, the Prince our master
Says that you savor too much of your youth,

221 Dauphin heir apparent to the French throne **224 ours** i.e., ours by right. **our awe** submission to us **225 Or there** either there **226 empery** dominion **233 Not . . . epitaph** i.e., with not even so much as a wax (as opposed to bronze) epitaph; one easily effaced **239 sparingly** delicately. **far off** i.e., in general terms

And bids you be advised there's naught in France
That can be with a nimble galliard won; 252
You cannot revel into dukedoms there.
He therefore sends you, meeter for your spirit, 254
This tun of treasure, and in lieu of this 255
Desires you let the dukedoms that you claim
Hear no more of you. This the Dauphin speaks.
[*A casket is presented;*
Exeter examines its contents.]

KING
What treasure, uncle?

EXETER
Tennis balls, my liege.

KING
We are glad the Dauphin is so pleasant with us.
His present and your pains we thank you for.
When we have matched our rackets to these balls,
We will, in France, by God's grace, play a set
Shall strike his father's crown into the hazard. 263
Tell him he hath made a match with such a wrangler 264
That all the courts of France will be disturbed 265
With chases. And we understand him well, 266
How he comes o'er us with our wilder days, 267
Not measuring what use we made of them.
We never valued this poor seat of England, 269
And therefore, living hence, did give ourself 270
To barbarous license—as 'tis ever common
That men are merriest when they are from home. 272
But tell the Dauphin I will keep my state, 273
Be like a king, and show my sail of greatness 274
When I do rouse me in my throne of France.
For that I have laid by my majesty 276
And plodded like a man for working days, 277

252 galliard a lively dance **254 meeter** more fitting **255 tun** cask **263 crown** (1) coin staked in a game (2) symbol of majesty. **hazard** (1) in tennis of that time, an opening in the wall; hitting the ball into it scored a point (2) jeopardy **264 wrangler** adversary **265 courts** (1) tennis courts (2) royal courts **266 chases** (1) double bounce in tennis, an unsuccessful return (2) pursuits **267 comes o'er us** taunts me. (*Us* is the royal plural.) **269 seat** throne **270 living hence** not frequenting the royal court **272 from** away from **273 keep my state** i.e., fulfill the role of king **274 sail** full swell. (Henry says he has not yet revealed his full majesty in laying claim to France.) **276 For that** i.e., for my French kingdom. **277 for** ready for

But I will rise there with so full a glory
That I will dazzle all the eyes of France,
Yea, strike the Dauphin blind to look on us.
And tell the pleasant Prince this mock of his
Hath turned his balls to gunstones, and his soul 282
Shall stand sore chargèd for the wasteful vengeance 283
That shall fly with them; for many a thousand widows
Shall this his mock mock out of their dear husbands,
Mock mothers from their sons, mock castles down,
And some are yet ungotten and unborn 287
That shall have cause to curse the Dauphin's scorn.
But this lies all within the will of God,
To whom I do appeal, and in whose name
Tell you the Dauphin I am coming on
To venge me as I may, and to put forth 292
My rightful hand in a well-hallowed cause.
So get you hence in peace; and tell the Dauphin
His jest will savor but of shallow wit
When thousands weep more than did laugh at it.—
Convey them with safe conduct.—Fare you well. 297

Exeunt Ambassadors.

EXETER This was a merry message.

KING

We hope to make the sender blush at it.
Therefore, my lords, omit no happy hour 300
That may give furtherance to our expedition;
For we have now no thought in us but France,
Save those to God, that run before our business.
Therefore let our proportions for these wars 304
Be soon collected, and all things thought upon
That may with reasonable swiftness add
More feathers to our wings; for, God before, 307
We'll chide this Dauphin at his father's door.
Therefore let every man now task his thought, 309
That this fair action may on foot be brought.

Flourish. Exeunt.

282 gunstones cannonballs **283 sore chargèd** sorely burdened with responsibility. **wasteful** destructive **287 yet ungotten** not yet conceived **292 venge** revenge **297 Convey** escort **300 omit . . . hour** lose no favorable opportunity **304 proportions** levies of men **307 God before** with God leading, helping **309 task** tax, exercise

2.0 *Enter Chorus.*

CHORUS

Now all the youth of England are on fire,
And silken dalliance in the wardrobe lies. 2
Now thrive the armorers, and honor's thought
Reigns solely in the breast of every man.
They sell the pasture now to buy the horse,
Following the mirror of all Christian kings,
With wingèd heels, as English Mercurys. 7
For now sits Expectation in the air,
And hides a sword from hilts unto the point 9
With crowns imperial, crowns and coronets, 10
Promised to Harry and his followers.
The French, advised by good intelligence 12
Of this most dreadful preparation,
Shake in their fear, and with pale policy 14
Seek to divert the English purposes.
O England! Model to thy inward greatness, 16
Like little body with a mighty heart,
What mightst thou do, that honor would thee do, 18
Were all thy children kind and natural?
But see, thy fault France hath in thee found out,
A nest of hollow bosoms, which he fills
With treacherous crowns; and three corrupted men, 22
One, Richard, Earl of Cambridge, and the second,
Henry, Lord Scroop of Masham, and the third,
Sir Thomas Grey, knight, of Northumberland,
Have, for the gilt of France—O guilt indeed!— 26
Confirmed conspiracy with fearful France, 27
And by their hands this grace of kings must die,
If hell and treason hold their promises,
Ere he take ship for France, and in Southampton.

2.0. Chorus.
2 silken . . . lies i.e., silken apparel and idle pleasure are packed away **7 Mercurys** (Mercury, classical messenger of the gods, always wears winged heels.) **9 hides a sword** i.e., holds up a sword completely impaled with the prizes of war **10 With . . . coronets** with the crowns of emperors, kings, and nobles **12 intelligence** espionage **14 pale policy** fear-inspired intrigue **16 Model to** small replica of **18 would** would have **22 crowns** coins, money (as a bribe) **26 gilt** gold **27 fearful** frightened

Linger your patience on, and we'll digest 31
Th' abuse of distance, force a play. 32
The sum is paid, the traitors are agreed,
The King is set from London, and the scene
Is now transported, gentles, to Southampton.
There is the playhouse now, there must you sit,
And thence to France shall we convey you safe,
And bring you back, charming the narrow seas
To give you gentle pass; for, if we may, 39
We'll not offend one stomach with our play. 40
But, till the King come forth, and not till then, 41
Unto Southampton do we shift our scene. *Exit.* 42

2.1 *Enter Corporal Nym and Lieutenant Bardolph.*

BARDOLPH Well met, Corporal Nym.
NYM Good morrow, Lieutenant Bardolph.
BARDOLPH What, are Ancient Pistol and you friends 3
yet?
NYM For my part, I care not. I say little; but when time
shall serve, there shall be smiles—but that shall be as
it may. I dare not fight, but I will wink and hold out 7
mine iron. It is a simple one, but what though? It will 8
toast cheese, and it will endure cold as another man's 9
sword will—and there's an end. 10
BARDOLPH I will bestow a breakfast to make you friends, and we'll be all three sworn brothers to France. Let 't be so, good Corporal Nym.
NYM Faith, I will live so long as I may, that's the certain

31–32 digest . . . distance overcome the difficulties of representing distance, change of place **32 force a play** fill out the actions of a play in spite of difficulties **39 pass** passage **40 offend one stomach** (1) offend anyone's taste in plays (2) make anyone seasick **41–42 But . . . scene** i.e., the scene will be shifted to Southampton after a scene in London. (These lines sound as though added as an afterthought, to accommodate the inclusion of the comic scene in 2.1.)

2.1. Location: London. A street.
3 Ancient ensign, standard-bearer **7 wink** shut the eyes **8 iron** sword. **though** of that **9 endure cold** i.e., doesn't mind being drawn from its sheath **10 there's an end** that's all there is to it

of it; and when I cannot live any longer, I will do as I
may. That is my rest; that is the rendezvous of it. 16

BARDOLPH It is certain, Corporal, that he is married to
Nell Quickly, and certainly she did you wrong, for you
were trothplight to her. 19

NYM I cannot tell. Things must be as they may. Men
may sleep, and they may have their throats about
them at that time, and some say knives have edges. It
must be as it may. Though Patience be a tired mare, 23
yet she will plod. There must be conclusions. Well, I 24
cannot tell.

Enter Pistol and [Hostess] Quickly.

BARDOLPH Here comes Ancient Pistol and his wife.
Good Corporal, be patient here.

NYM How now, mine host Pistol?

PISTOL
Base tike, call'st thou me host? 29
Now, by this hand, I swear, I scorn the term!
Nor shall my Nell keep lodgers.

HOSTESS No, by my troth, not long; for we cannot lodge
and board a dozen or fourteen gentlewomen that live
honestly by the prick of their needles, but it will be 34
thought we keep a bawdy house straight. [*Nym and
Pistol draw.*] O welladay, Lady! If he be not hewn 36
now, we shall see willful adultery and murder com- 37
mitted.

BARDOLPH Good Lieutenant! Good Corporal! Offer noth- 39
ing here. 40

NYM Pish!

PISTOL
Pish for thee, Iceland dog! 42
Thou prick-eared cur of Iceland!

16 rest last stake (in the gambling game of primero). **rendezvous** last resort **19 trothplight** betrothed **23–24 Though . . . plod** i.e., patient persistence will ultimately achieve its goal. (Nym hints, as he does elsewhere, at violence toward Pistol.) **24 conclusions** an end to matters (i.e., the end must come sometime) **29 tike** cur **34 prick** (with a bawdy double meaning, as also in *Pistol's cock,* l. 53) **36 welladay** wellaway, alas. **Lady** i.e., by Our Lady. (An oath.) **hewn** struck down **37 adultery** (Blunder for *battery*?) **39–40 Offer nothing** i.e., do not offer to fight **42 Iceland dog** a small, shaggy dog often kept as a house pet. (Pistol's humor is to use extravagant epithets, like this one, tags from current plays, and scraps of foreign languages.)

HOSTESS Good Corporal Nym, show thy valor, and put 44
up your sword. [*They sheathe their swords.*]

NYM Will you shog off? I would have you solus. 46

PISTOL
Solus, egregious dog? O viper vile!
The solus in thy most mervailous face! 48
The solus in thy teeth, and in thy throat,
And in thy hateful lungs, yea, in thy maw, pardie, 50
And, which is worse, within thy nasty mouth!
I do retort the solus in thy bowels;
For I can take, and Pistol's cock is up, 53
And flashing fire will follow.

NYM I am not Barbason; you cannot conjure me. I have 55
an humor to knock you indifferently well. If you grow
foul with me, Pistol, I will scour you with my rapier, 57
as I may, in fair terms. If you would walk off, I would
prick your guts a little, in good terms, as I may, and
that's the humor of it. 60

PISTOL
O braggart vile and damnèd furious wight! 61
The grave doth gape, and doting death is near.
Therefore exhale! [*They draw.*] 63

BARDOLPH Hear me, hear me what I say. He that strikes the first stroke, I'll run him up to the hilts, as I am a soldier. [*He draws.*]

PISTOL
An oath of mickle might, and fury shall abate. 67
[*Pistol and Nym sheathe their swords.*]
[*To Nym*] Give me thy fist, thy forefoot to me give.
Thy spirits are most tall. 69

NYM I will cut thy throat, one time or other, in fair terms. That is the humor of it.

PISTOL *Couple a gorge!* 72
That is the word. I thee defy again.

44 valor (She means "calm," "forbearance.") **46 shog off** move along. **solus** alone **48 mervailous** marvelous **50 maw** belly. **pardie** i.e., *par Dieu,* by God **53 take** strike **55 Barbason** (Presumably the name of a fiend. Pistol's preceding speech is a parody of the formula for exorcising spirits.) **57 foul** (1) foulmouthed (2) fouled from firing and in need of scouring **60 that's . . . it** that's my mood **61 wight** person **63 exhale** draw (sword) **67 mickle** great **69 tall** valiant **72 Couple a gorge** i.e., *couper la gorge,* cut the throat

O hound of Crete, think'st thou my spouse to get? 74
No, to the spital go, 75
And from the powdering tub of infamy 76
Fetch forth the lazar kite of Cressid's kind, 77
Doll Tearsheet she by name, and her espouse.
I have, and I will hold, the quondam Quickly 79
For the only she; and—*pauca!* There's enough.
Go to. 80

Enter the Boy.

BOY Mine host Pistol, you must come to my master,
and you, hostess. He is very sick and would to bed.
Good Bardolph, put thy face between his sheets and 84
do the office of a warming pan. Faith, he's very ill.

BARDOLPH Away, you rogue!

HOSTESS By my troth, he'll yield the crow a pudding 87
one of these days. The King has killed his heart. Good 88
husband, come home presently. *Exit* [*with Boy*]. 89

BARDOLPH Come, shall I make you two friends? We must to France together. Why the devil should we keep knives to cut one another's throats?

PISTOL
Let floods o'erswell, and fiends for food howl on!

NYM You'll pay me the eight shillings I won of you at betting?

PISTOL Base is the slave that pays.

NYM That now I will have. That's the humor of it.

PISTOL As manhood shall compound. Push home. 98

[*They*] *draw.*

BARDOLPH [*Drawing*] By this sword, he that makes the first thrust, I'll kill him! By this sword, I will.

74 hound of Crete (Parallel to *Iceland dog,* l. 42.) **75 spital** hospital **76 powdering tub** (Originally a tub used for salting beef; here, alluding to a method of curing venereal disease by sweating.) **77 lazar . . . kind** i.e., diseased, leprous whore (a *kite* is a bird of prey) like Cressida, the fallen woman, who, in Robert Henryson's *Testament of Cresseid,* is shown as being rejected by Diomede and infected with leprosy
79 quondam former **80 only she** i.e., only woman in the world. **pauca** i.e., in brief **84 face** (Bardolph's face is fiery with drinking.)
87 yield . . . pudding i.e., be hanged on the gallows and eaten by carrion birds **88 his** i.e., Falstaff's **89 presently** immediately **98 As . . . compound** as valor shall settle the matter (in fight)

PISTOL
Sword is an oath, and oaths must have their course.
[*He sheathes his sword.*]

BARDOLPH Corporal Nym, an thou wilt be friends, be friends; an thou wilt not, why, then, be enemies with me too. Prithee, put up.

NYM I shall have my eight shillings I won of you at betting?

PISTOL
A noble shalt thou have, and present pay;
And liquor likewise will I give to thee,
And friendship shall combine, and brotherhood.
I'll live by Nym, and Nym shall live by me.
Is not this just? For I shall sutler be
Unto the camp, and profits will accrue.
Give me thy hand. [*Nym sheathes his sword.*]

NYM I shall have my noble?

PISTOL In cash most justly paid.

NYM Well, then, that's the humor of 't.

Enter Hostess.

HOSTESS As ever you come of women, come in quickly to Sir John. Ah, poor heart, he is so shaked of a burning quotidian tertian that it is most lamentable to behold. Sweet men, come to him. [*Exit.*]

NYM The King hath run bad humors on the knight, that's the even of it.

PISTOL
Nym, thou hast spoke the right.
His heart is fracted and corroborate.

NYM The King is a good king, but it must be as it may; he passes some humors and careers.

101 Sword is an oath (Quibbling on *sword* as *'s word,* i.e., "God's word.") **102 an** if **104 put up** i.e., put up your sword **107 noble . . . pay** i.e., I'll settle for paying you 6 shillings 8 pence ready money **110 Nym** (Quibbles on *nim,* meaning "thief.") **111 sutler** seller of liquor and provisions to the soldiers **117 come of** were born of **119 quotidian tertian** (A *quotidian* fever was one that came daily; a *tertian* fever, one that came on alternate days, though some authorities believed that different fevers might mix and intensify their effects.) **121 run bad humors** i.e., vented his displeasure **122 even** level truth **124 fracted** broken. **corroborate** (Blunder for *broken to pieces* or *corrupted*? The word means "strengthened, confirmed.") **126 passes** lets pass. **careers** gallops, capers

PISTOL
Let us condole the knight, for, lambkins, we will live. 127
[*Exeunt*.]

✤

2.2 *Enter Exeter, Bedford, and Westmorland.*

BEDFORD
'Fore God, His Grace is bold to trust these traitors.

EXETER
They shall be apprehended by and by.

WESTMORLAND
How smooth and even they do bear themselves! 3
As if allegiance in their bosoms sat,
Crownèd with faith and constant loyalty.

BEDFORD
The King hath note of all that they intend,
By interception which they dream not of.

EXETER
Nay, but the man that was his bedfellow, 8
Whom he hath dulled and cloyed with gracious favors— 9
That he should, for a foreign purse, so sell
His sovereign's life to death and treachery!

Sound trumpets. Enter the King, Scroop, Cambridge, and Grey, [*and attendants*].

KING
Now sits the wind fair, and we will aboard. 12
My lord of Cambridge, and my kind lord of Masham,
And you, my gentle knight, give me your thoughts.
Think you not that the powers we bear with us 15
Will cut their passage through the force of France,
Doing the execution and the act
For which we have in head assembled them? 18

127 condole express our commiseration of or sympathy with. **lambkins** (A term of endearment.)

2.2. Location: Southampton, a seaport on England's southern coast.
3 smooth and even pleasant and calm **8 bedfellow** i.e., constant companion. (Refers to Scroop.) **9 dulled** tired **12 sits . . . fair** the wind blows from a favorable quarter **15 powers** armed forces **18 in head** as an army

SCROOP
No doubt, my liege, if each man do his best.

KING
I doubt not that, since we are well persuaded
We carry not a heart with us from hence
That grows not in a fair consent with ours,
Nor leave not one behind that doth not wish
Success and conquest to attend on us.

CAMBRIDGE
Never was monarch better feared and loved
Than is Your Majesty. There's not, I think, a subject
That sits in heart-grief and uneasiness
Under the sweet shade of your government.

GREY
True. Those that were your father's enemies
Have steeped their galls in honey, and do serve you
With hearts create of duty and of zeal.

KING
We therefore have great cause of thankfulness,
And shall forget the office of our hand
Sooner than quittance of desert and merit
According to the weight and worthiness.

SCROOP
So service shall with steelèd sinews toil,
And labor shall refresh itself with hope,
To do Your Grace incessant services.

KING
We judge no less. Uncle of Exeter,
Enlarge the man committed yesterday
That railed against our person. We consider
It was excess of wine that set him on,
And on his more advice we pardon him.

SCROOP
That's mercy, but too much security.
Let him be punished, sovereign, lest example
Breed, by his sufferance, more of such a kind.

KING O, let us yet be merciful.

22 grows . . . consent does not act in harmony **30 galls** i.e., resentment **31 create** composed **33 office** use, function **34 quittance** requital **40 Enlarge** set free **43 more advice** thinking better of it **44 security** overconfidence **46 sufferance** being pardoned

CAMBRIDGE
So may Your Highness, and yet punish too.
GREY Sir,
You show great mercy if you give him life
After the taste of much correction. 51
KING
Alas, your too much love and care of me
Are heavy orisons 'gainst this poor wretch! 53
If little faults proceeding on distemper 54
Shall not be winked at, how shall we stretch our eye 55
When capital crimes, chewed, swallowed, and digested, 56
Appear before us? We'll yet enlarge that man, 57
Though Cambridge, Scroop, and Grey, in their dear care
And tender preservation of our person,
Would have him punished. And now to our French
causes.
Who are the late commissioners? 61
CAMBRIDGE I one, my lord.
Your Highness bade me ask for it today. 63
SCROOP So did you me, my liege.
GREY And I, my royal sovereign.
KING [*Giving them papers*]
Then, Richard Earl of Cambridge, there is yours;
There yours, Lord Scroop of Masham; and sir knight,
Grey of Northumberland, this same is yours.
Read them, and know I know your worthiness.
My lord of Westmorland, and uncle Exeter,
We will aboard tonight.—Why, how now, gentlemen?
What see you in those papers, that you lose
So much complexion?—Look ye how they change! 73
Their cheeks are paper.—Why, what read you there 74
That have so cowarded and chased your blood
Out of appearance?
CAMBRIDGE I do confess my fault, 76
And do submit me to Your Highness' mercy.

51 correction punishment **53 heavy orisons** weighty prayers, pleas **54 proceeding on distemper** resulting from excessive drinking **55 stretch** open wide, not wink **56 capital** punishable by death. **chewed . . . digested** i.e., premeditated **57 yet** in spite of what you say **61 late** recently appointed (to serve while Henry is in France) **63 it** i.e., my commission **73 complexion** color **74 paper** i.e., white as paper **76 appearance** sight. (Presumably the traitors kneel at this point.)

GREY, SCROOP To which we all appeal.

KING

The mercy that was quick in us but late 79
By your own counsel is suppressed and killed.
You must not dare, for shame, to talk of mercy,
For your own reasons turn into your bosoms,
As dogs upon their masters, worrying you. 83
See you, my princes and my noble peers,
These English monsters! My lord of Cambridge here,
You know how apt our love was to accord 86
To furnish him with all appurtenants 87
Belonging to his honor; and this man
Hath for a few light crowns lightly conspired 89
And sworn unto the practices of France 90
To kill us here in Hampton. To the which
This knight, no less for bounty bound to us 92
Than Cambridge is, hath likewise sworn. But, O,
What shall I say to thee, Lord Scroop, thou cruel,
Ingrateful, savage, and inhuman creature?
Thou that didst bear the key of all my counsels,
That knew'st the very bottom of my soul,
That almost mightst have coined me into gold,
Wouldst thou have practiced on me for thy use? 99
May it be possible that foreign hire
Could out of thee extract one spark of evil
That might annoy my finger? 'Tis so strange 102
That though the truth of it stands off as gross 103
As black and white, my eye will scarcely see it.
Treason and murder ever kept together,
As two yoke-devils sworn to either's purpose, 106
Working so grossly in a natural cause 107
That admiration did not whoop at them. 108
But thou, 'gainst all proportion, didst bring in 109

79 quick alive **83 worrying** tearing **86 accord** consent
87 appurtenants appurtenances, accessories **89 light** insignificant.
lightly readily **90 practices** plots **92 This knight** i.e., Grey
99 practiced on plotted against. **use** profit (with play on the meaning "interest derived from usury"; Scroop had served as Lord Treasurer)
102 annoy injure **103 stands . . . gross** appears as obvious **106 yoke-devils** partners in a diabolical cause **107–108 Working . . . them** working together with such obvious fitness, and toward a purpose that suits them so naturally, that they provoked no outcry of wonder
109 proportion fitness of things

Wonder to wait on treason and on murder; 110
And whatsoever cunning fiend it was
That wrought upon thee so preposterously 112
Hath got the voice in hell for excellence. 113
All other devils that suggest by treasons 114
Do botch and bungle up damnation 115
With patches, colors, and with forms being fetched 116
From glistering semblances of piety; 117
But he that tempered thee bade thee stand up, 118
Gave thee no instance why thou shouldst do treason, 119
Unless to dub thee with the name of traitor.
If that same demon that hath gulled thee thus
Should with his lion gait walk the whole world, 122
He might return to vasty Tartar back 123
And tell the legions, "I can never win
A soul so easy as that Englishman's."
O, how hast thou with jealousy infected 126
The sweetness of affiance! Show men dutiful? 127
Why, so didst thou. Seem they grave and learnèd?
Why, so didst thou. Come they of noble family?
Why, so didst thou. Seem they religious?
Why, so didst thou. Or are they spare in diet, 131
Free from gross passion or of mirth or anger, 132
Constant in spirit, not swerving with the blood, 133
Garnished and decked in modest complement, 134
Not working with the eye without the ear, 135
And but in purgèd judgment trusting neither? 136
Such and so finely bolted didst thou seem. 137
And thus thy fall hath left a kind of blot

110 Wonder astonishment (that Scroop should be a murderer). **wait on** attend, accompany **112 wrought** worked. **preposterously** unnaturally **113 voice** vote **114 suggest** tempt **115–117 Do . . . piety** i.e., clumsily conceal their damnable temptation by tricking it out in attractive-looking semblances of virtue **118 tempered** directed (to evil). **bade** ordered. **stand up** volunteer **119 instance** reason
122 lion gait (The devil, according to 1 Peter 5:8, strides about the world like a roaring lion, "seeking whom he may devour.") **123 vasty** vast. **Tartar** Tartarus, the hell of classical mythology **126 jealousy** suspicion **127 affiance** trust. **Show** appear **131 spare** sparing, frugal **132 or of** either of **133 swerving with the blood** sinning through passion **134 decked . . . complement** wearing the look of modesty **135 Not . . . ear** i.e., trusting neither eye nor ear alone
136 but . . . judgment except on the basis of impartial judgment
137 bolted sifted, refined

To mark the full-fraught man and best endued 139
With some suspicion. I will weep for thee;
For this revolt of thine, methinks, is like
Another fall of man.—Their faults are open. 142
Arrest them to the answer of the law;
And God acquit them of their practices! 144

EXETER I arrest thee of high treason, by the name of Richard Earl of Cambridge.

I arrest thee of high treason, by the name of Henry Lord Scroop of Masham.

I arrest thee of high treason, by the name of Thomas Grey, knight, of Northumberland.

SCROOP
Our purposes God justly hath discovered, 151
And I repent my fault more than my death,
Which I beseech Your Highness to forgive,
Although my body pay the price of it.

CAMBRIDGE
For me, the gold of France did not seduce,
Although I did admit it as a motive 156
The sooner to effect what I intended. 157
But God be thankèd for prevention,
Which I in sufferance heartily will rejoice, 159
Beseeching God and you to pardon me.

GREY
Never did faithful subject more rejoice
At the discovery of most dangerous treason
Than I do at this hour joy o'er myself,
Prevented from a damnèd enterprise.
My fault, but not my body, pardon, sovereign.

KING
God quit you in his mercy! Hear your sentence. 166
You have conspired against our royal person,
Joined with an enemy proclaimed, and from his coffers

139 full-fraught richly laden (with excellent qualities). **endued** endowed **142 open** apparent, obvious **144 practices** plots
151 discovered revealed **156 did . . . motive** i.e., accepted money from France as a means **157 The . . . intended** (Cambridge's real motive, barely hinted at here, was to assist his brother-in-law Edmund Mortimer, fifth Earl of March, to the throne as the standard-bearer of the Yorkist claim against the Lancastrian Henry.) **159 sufferance** my suffering and patient endurance **166 quit** pardon

Received the golden earnest of our death; 169
Wherein you would have sold your king to slaughter,
His princes and his peers to servitude,
His subjects to oppression and contempt,
And his whole kingdom into desolation.
Touching our person seek we no revenge,
But we our kingdom's safety must so tender, 175
Whose ruin you have sought, that to her laws
We do deliver you. Get you therefore hence,
Poor miserable wretches, to your death,
The taste whereof God of his mercy give
You patience to endure, and true repentance
Of all your dear offenses!—Bear them hence. 181
Exeunt [*Cambridge, Scroop, and Grey, guarded*].
Now, lords, for France, the enterprise whereof
Shall be to you, as us, like glorious. 183
We doubt not of a fair and lucky war,
Since God so graciously hath brought to light
This dangerous treason lurking in our way
To hinder our beginnings. We doubt not now
But every rub is smoothèd on our way. 188
Then forth, dear countrymen! Let us deliver
Our puissance into the hand of God, 190
Putting it straight in expedition. 191
Cheerly to sea! The signs of war advance! 192
No king of England, if not king of France!
Flourish. [*Exeunt.*]

✤

2.3 *Enter Pistol, Nym, Bardolph, Boy, and Hostess.*

HOSTESS Prithee, honey-sweet husband, let me bring thee to Staines. 2

169 golden earnest advance payment **175 tender** regard, hold dear **181 dear** grievous **183 like** alike, equally **188 But** but that. **rub** obstacle. (A bowling term.) **190 puissance** army **191 straight in expedition** immediately in action **192 signs** ensigns, banners

2.3. London. A street.
2 Staines town on the road from London to Southampton

PISTOL No; for my manly heart doth earn. Bardolph, be blithe; Nym, rouse thy vaunting veins; Boy, bristle thy courage up; for Falstaff he is dead, and we must earn therefore.

BARDOLPH Would I were with him, wheresoe'er he is, either in heaven or in hell!

HOSTESS Nay, sure he's not in hell. He's in Arthur's bosom, if ever man went to Arthur's bosom. 'A made a finer end, and went away an it had been any christom child. 'A parted ev'n just between twelve and one, ev'n at the turning o' the tide. For after I saw him fumble with the sheets, and play with flowers, and smile upon his finger's end, I knew there was but one way; for his nose was as sharp as a pen, and 'a babbled of green fields. "How now, Sir John?" quoth I. "What, man? Be o' good cheer." So 'a cried out, "God, God, God!" three or four times. Now I, to comfort him, bid him 'a should not think of God; I hoped there was no need to trouble himself with any such thoughts yet. So 'a bade me lay more clothes on his feet. I put my hand into the bed and felt them, and they were as cold as any stone; then I felt to his knees, and so upward and upward, and all was as cold as any stone.

NYM They say he cried out of sack.

HOSTESS Ay, that 'a did.

BARDOLPH And of women.

HOSTESS Nay, that 'a did not.

BOY Yes, that 'a did, and said they were devils incarnate.

HOSTESS 'A could never abide carnation; 'twas a color he never liked.

BOY 'A said once the devil would have him about women.

HOSTESS 'A did in some sort, indeed, handle women;

3, 5 earn (1) grieve (2) find other employment **9–10 Arthur's bosom** (Malapropism for *Abraham's bosom;* see Luke 16:22.) **10 'A** he **11 an** as if **11–12 christom** newly christened **16–17 'a babbled of green fields** (This line contains Theobald's famous emendation. The Folio has *and a Table of greene fields*. Falstaff would seem to have been reciting the Twenty-third Psalm.) **26 of sack** against sack (a Spanish wine) **36 handle** discuss (though an unintended literal sense is also comically present)

but then he was rheumatic, and talked of the Whore of 37
Babylon.

BOY Do you not remember, 'a saw a flea stick upon Bardolph's nose, and 'a said it was a black soul burning in hell?

BARDOLPH Well, the fuel is gone that maintained that 42
fire. That's all the riches I got in his service.

NYM Shall we shog? The King will be gone from South- 44
ampton.

PISTOL
Come, let's away. My love, give me thy lips.
[*They kiss.*]
Look to my chattels and my movables. 47
Let senses rule. The word is "Pitch and pay." 48
Trust none,
For oaths are straws, men's faiths are wafer cakes, 50
And Holdfast is the only dog, my duck. 51
Therefore, *caveto* be thy counselor. 52
Go, clear thy crystals. Yokefellows in arms, 53
Let us to France, like horseleeches, my boys,
To suck, to suck, the very blood to suck!

BOY And that's but unwholesome food, they say.

PISTOL Touch her soft mouth, and march.

BARDOLPH Farewell, hostess. [*Kissing her.*]

NYM I cannot kiss, that is the humor of it; but adieu.

PISTOL
Let huswifery appear. Keep close, I thee command. 60

HOSTESS Farewell! Adieu! *Exeunt* [*separately*].

✣

37 rheumatic i.e., feverish, or perhaps an error for *lunatic.* (Pronounced "rome-atic," preparing for the allusion to the Whore of Babylon, i.e., the Church of Rome. See also Revelation 17:4–5.) **42 fuel** i.e., liquor, supplied by Falstaff, that has given Bardolph his red face **44 shog** be off **47 chattels . . . movables** personal property **48 Let . . . pay** i.e., keep your eyes and ears open, and let your motto as hostess be "cash down" **50 wafer cakes** i.e., easily broken **51 Holdfast** clamp, staple. (Compare the proverb "Brag is a good dog, but Holdfast is a better.") **52 caveto** be cautious. (From the Latin imperative of *caveo.*) **53 clear thy crystals** wipe your eyes. **Yokefellows** i.e., companions **60 Let . . . close** i.e., be a thrifty housekeeper, and stay at home

2.4

Flourish. Enter the French King, the Dauphin, the Dukes of Berri and Brittany, [*the Constable, and others*].

FRENCH KING
Thus comes the English with full power upon us,
And more than carefully it us concerns
To answer royally in our defenses.
Therefore the Dukes of Berri and of Brittany,
Of Brabant and of Orleans, shall make forth,
And you, Prince Dauphin, with all swift dispatch,
To line and new-repair our towns of war
With men of courage and with means defendant;
For England his approaches makes as fierce
As waters to the sucking of a gulf.
It fits us then to be as provident
As fear may teach us, out of late examples
Left by the fatal and neglected English
Upon our fields.

DAUPHIN My most redoubted Father,
It is most meet we arm us 'gainst the foe;
For peace itself should not so dull a kingdom,
Though war nor no known quarrel were in question,
But that defenses, musters, preparations,
Should be maintained, assembled, and collected
As were a war in expectation.
Therefore, I say 'tis meet we all go forth
To view the sick and feeble parts of France.
And let us do it with no show of fear—
No, with no more than if we heard that England
Were busied with a Whitsun morris dance.
For, my good liege, she is so idly kinged,
Her scepter so fantastically borne
By a vain, giddy, shallow, humorous youth,
That fear attends her not.

2.4. Location: France. The royal court.
7 line reinforce **8 defendant** defensive **10 gulf** whirlpool **12 late** recent **13 fatal and neglected** fatally underestimated **14 redoubted** respected **15 meet** appropriate **20 As were** as if there were
25 Whitsun morris dance folk dance often performed during Whitsuntide, in early summer, by persons in fancy costumes and decked with bells **26 idly** frivolously **28 humorous** capricious

CONSTABLE O, peace, Prince Dauphin!
You are too much mistaken in this king.
Question Your Grace the late ambassadors,
With what great state he heard their embassy, 32
How well supplied with noble counselors,
How modest in exception, and withal 34
How terrible in constant resolution, 35
And you shall find his vanities forespent 36
Were but the outside of the Roman Brutus, 37
Covering discretion with a coat of folly,
As gardeners do with ordure hide those roots 39
That shall first spring and be most delicate.

DAUPHIN
Well, 'tis not so, my Lord High Constable;
But though we think it so, it is no matter.
In cases of defense 'tis best to weigh
The enemy more mighty than he seems.
So the proportions of defense are filled, 45
Which of a weak and niggardly projection 46
Doth, like a miser, spoil his coat with scanting
A little cloth.

FRENCH KING Think we King Harry strong;
And, princes, look you strongly arm to meet him. 49
The kindred of him hath been fleshed upon us; 50
And he is bred out of that bloody strain
That haunted us in our familiar paths.
Witness our too-much-memorable shame
When Crécy battle fatally was struck, 54
And all our princes captived by the hand
Of that black name, Edward, Black Prince of Wales;
Whiles that his mountain sire, on mountain standing, 57

32 state dignity **34 exception** making objections. **withal** in addition **35 terrible** awesome, terrifying **36 vanities forespent** follies now a thing of the past **37 Brutus** i.e., the elder Brutus, Lucius Junius Brutus, who pretended to be stupid (*brutus*) as a ruse to allay the suspicions of the tyrant Tarquin until the time for overthrow was ripe **39 ordure** manure **45 So . . . filled** i.e., thus an adequate and full defense is provided **46 Which . . . projection** i.e., which defense, if it should be provided on a small and miserly scale **49 look** be sure **50 kindred** i.e., his great-grandfather Edward III and great-uncle Edward the Black Prince. **fleshed** initiated in the shedding of blood, with foretaste of further success **54 Crécy** French defeat in 1346. **struck** waged **57 mountain sire** i.e., Edward III, born in mountainous Wales, and of sturdy proportions

Up in the air, crowned with the golden sun,
Saw his heroical seed and smiled to see him
Mangle the work of nature and deface
The patterns that by God and by French fathers
Had twenty years been made. This is a stem
Of that victorious stock; and let us fear
The native mightiness and fate of him.

Enter a Messenger.

MESSENGER
Ambassadors from Harry King of England
Do crave admittance to Your Majesty.

FRENCH KING
We'll give them present audience. Go and bring them.
[*Exit Messenger.*]
You see this chase is hotly followed, friends.

DAUPHIN
Turn head and stop pursuit; for coward dogs
Most spend their mouths when what they seem to threaten
Runs far before them. Good my sovereign,
Take up the English short, and let them know
Of what a monarchy you are the head.
Self-love, my liege, is not so vile a sin
As self-neglecting.

Enter Exeter [*and other lords*].

FRENCH KING From our brother of England?

EXETER
From him, and thus he greets Your Majesty:
He wills you, in the name of God Almighty,
That you divest yourself and lay apart
The borrowed glories that by gift of heaven,
By law of nature and of nations, 'longs
To him and to his heirs, namely, the crown
And all wide-stretchèd honors that pertain

59 seed i.e., son **62 twenty years** (i.e., because the warriors thus mangled were born twenty years or so before) **64 fate** what he is destined to do **69 Turn head** stand at bay. (A hunting term.) **stop pursuit** i.e., put an end to their pursuit **70 Most . . . mouths** bay the loudest **72 Take . . . short** quickly dispose of the English **78 apart** aside **80 'longs** belongs **82 wide-stretchèd** accompanying, reaching over a broad span

By custom and the ordinance of times
Unto the crown of France. That you may know
'Tis no sinister nor no awkward claim,
Picked from the wormholes of long-vanished days,
Nor from the dust of old oblivion raked,
He sends you this most memorable line,
[*Giving a paper*]
In every branch truly demonstrative,
Willing you overlook this pedigree.
And when you find him evenly derived
From his most famed of famous ancestors,
Edward the Third, he bids you then resign
Your crown and kingdom, indirectly held
From him the native and true challenger.

FRENCH KING Or else what follows?

EXETER
Bloody constraint; for if you hide the crown
Even in your hearts, there will he rake for it.
Therefore in fierce tempest is he coming,
In thunder and in earthquake, like a Jove,
That if requiring fail, he will compel;
And bids you, in the bowels of the Lord,
Deliver up the crown, and to take mercy
On the poor souls for whom this hungry war
Opens his vasty jaws; and on your head
Turning the widows' tears, the orphans' cries,
The dead men's blood, the privy maidens' groans,
For husbands, fathers, and betrothèd lovers
That shall be swallowed in this controversy.
This is his claim, his threatening, and my message—
Unless the Dauphin be in presence here,
To whom expressly I bring greeting too.

FRENCH KING
For us, we will consider of this further.
Tomorrow shall you bear our full intent
Back to our brother of England.

83 ordinance of times decrees of tradition **85 sinister** illegitimate
88 line pedigree **90 Willing you overlook** desiring that you look over
91 evenly directly **94 indirectly** wrongfully **95 challenger** claimant
97 constraint coercion, compulsion **101 requiring** requesting
102 bowels mercy, or innermost being. (Cf. Philippians 1:8.) **107 privy maidens' groans** maidens' secret grievings

DAUPHIN For the Dauphin,
I stand here for him. What to him from England?

EXETER
Scorn and defiance, slight regard, contempt,
And anything that may not misbecome 118
The mighty sender, doth he prize you at. 119
Thus says my king: an if your father's Highness 120
Do not, in grant of all demands at large, 121
Sweeten the bitter mock you sent His Majesty,
He'll call you to so hot an answer of it 123
That caves and womby vaultages of France 124
Shall chide your trespass and return your mock
In second accent of his ordinance. 126

DAUPHIN
Say, if my father render fair return, 127
It is against my will; for I desire
Nothing but odds with England. To that end, 129
As matching to his youth and vanity,
I did present him with the Paris balls. 131

EXETER
He'll make your Paris Louvre shake for it, 132
Were it the mistress court of mighty Europe.
And be assured, you'll find a difference,
As we his subjects have in wonder found,
Between the promise of his greener days 136
And these he masters now. Now he weighs time
Even to the utmost grain. That you shall read 138
In your own losses, if he stay in France.

FRENCH KING
Tomorrow shall you know our mind at full. 140
Flourish.

EXETER
Dispatch us with all speed, lest that our king

118 misbecome be inappropriate for **119 prize** value, appraise **120 an if** if **121 in grant of** in assenting to. **at large** in full **123 of it** for it **124 womby vaultages** deep caverns **126 second accent** echo. **ordinance** ordnance, cannon **127 fair return** courteous reply **129 odds** strife **131 Paris balls** tennis balls **132 Louvre** the French royal palace **136 greener** younger **138 That . . . read** i.e., you will see this new seriousness manifested **140 s.d. Flourish** (This trumpet call is sounded as the French King arises from his throne, thereby dismissing the embassy, but Exeter boldly insists on speaking further.)

Come here himself to question our delay;
For he is footed in this land already.

FRENCH KING

You shall be soon dispatched with fair conditions.
A night is but small breath and little pause
To answer matters of this consequence.

Flourish. Exeunt.

✤

3.0 *Enter Chorus.*

CHORUS
Thus with imagined wing our swift scene flies 1
In motion of no less celerity 2
Than that of thought. Suppose that you have seen
The well-appointed King at Dover pier 4
Embark his royalty, and his brave fleet 5
With silken streamers the young Phoebus fanning. 6
Play with your fancies, and in them behold
Upon the hempen tackle shipboys climbing;
Hear the shrill whistle, which doth order give
To sounds confused; behold the threaden sails, 10
Borne with th' invisible and creeping wind,
Draw the huge bottoms through the furrowed sea, 12
Breasting the lofty surge. O, do but think 13
You stand upon the rivage and behold 14
A city on th' inconstant billows dancing;
For so appears this fleet majestical,
Holding due course to Harfleur. Follow, follow!
Grapple your minds to sternage of this navy, 18
And leave your England as dead midnight still,
Guarded with grandsires, babies, and old women,
Either past or not arrived to pith and puissance; 21
For who is he whose chin is but enriched
With one appearing hair that will not follow
These culled and choice-drawn cavaliers to France? 24
Work, work your thoughts, and therein see a siege;
Behold the ordnance on their carriages,
With fatal mouths gaping on girded Harfleur. 27
Suppose th' ambassador from the French comes back,
Tells Harry that the King doth offer him
Katharine his daughter, and with her, to dowry,
Some petty and unprofitable dukedoms.

3.0. Chorus.
1 imagined wing wings of imagination **2 celerity** speed **4 well-appointed** well-equipped. **Dover** (Seemingly an error for Hampton, i.e., Southampton.) **5 brave** handsome **6 the . . . fanning** i.e., fluttering against the rising sun **10 threaden** woven of thread **12 bottoms** hulls of ships **13 surge** swell of the sea **14 rivage** shore **18 Grapple** attach, hook. **to sternage** to the sterns **21 pith** strength **24 choice-drawn** carefully selected **27 fatal** deadly. **girded** besieged

The offer likes not; and the nimble gunner 32
With linstock now the devilish cannon touches, 33
Alarum, and chambers go off.
And down goes all before them. Still be kind,
And eke out our performance with your mind.
Exit.

3.1

Enter the King, Exeter, Bedford, and Gloucester. Alarum, [*with soldiers carrying*] *scaling ladders at Harfleur.*

KING
Once more unto the breach, dear friends, once more,
Or close the wall up with our English dead!
In peace there's nothing so becomes a man
As modest stillness and humility.
But when the blast of war blows in our ears,
Then imitate the action of the tiger:
Stiffen the sinews, conjure up the blood,
Disguise fair nature with hard-favored rage. 8
Then lend the eye a terrible aspect: 9
Let it pry through the portage of the head 10
Like the brass cannon; let the brow o'erwhelm it 11
As fearfully as doth a gallèd rock 12
O'erhang and jutty his confounded base, 13
Swilled with the wild and wasteful ocean. 14
Now set the teeth and stretch the nostril wide,
Hold hard the breath, and bend up every spirit
To his full height. On, on, you noblest English,
Whose blood is fet from fathers of war-proof! 18

32 likes pleases **33 linstock** staff holding a gunner's match **s.d. Alarum** call to arms. **chambers** small cannon (fired off backstage, or "within")

3.1. Location: France. Before Harfleur.
s.d. scaling ladders (Presumably these are set up against the facade of the tiring house, backstage, which is perceived to be the walls of Harfleur.) **8 hard-favored** unsightly, ugly **9 terrible aspect** terrifying appearance **10 portage** portholes, eyes **11 o'erwhelm** project over **12 fearfully** frighteningly. **gallèd** washed away, undermined **13 jutty** overhang. **his confounded** its ruined **14 Swilled** washed. **wasteful** destructive **18 fet** fetched, derived. **of war-proof** proved in war

Fathers that, like so many Alexanders, 19
Have in these parts from morn till even fought, 20
And sheathed their swords for lack of argument. 21
Dishonor not your mothers; now attest
That those whom you called fathers did beget you.
Be copy now to men of grosser blood, 24
And teach them how to war. And you, good yeomen,
Whose limbs were made in England, show us here
The mettle of your pasture. Let us swear 27
That you are worth your breeding, which I doubt not,
For there is none of you so mean and base
That hath not noble luster in your eyes.
I see you stand like greyhounds in the slips, 31
Straining upon the start. The game's afoot!
Follow your spirit, and upon this charge 33
Cry, "God for Harry! England and Saint George!" 34
Alarum, and chambers go off. [*Exeunt.*]

3.2 *Enter Nym, Bardolph, Pistol, and Boy.*

BARDOLPH On, on, on, on, on! To the breach, to the breach!

NYM Pray thee, Corporal, stay. The knocks are too hot,
and for mine own part I have not a case of lives. The 4
humor of it is too hot, that is the very plainsong of it. 5

PISTOL
"The plainsong" is most just, for humors do abound.
"Knocks go and come; God's vassals drop and die;
And sword and shield
In bloody field
Doth win immortal fame."

19 Alexanders (Alexander grieved that there were no new worlds for him to conquer.) **20 even** evening **21 argument** i.e., opposition **24 copy** models **27 mettle . . . pasture** quality of your breeding. (Literally, *pasture* means "feeding.") **31 slips** leashes **33 Follow your spirit** i.e., obey the impulse of your vital powers (as also in l. 16) **34 Saint George** patron saint of England

3.2. Location: Before Harfleur, as in the previous scene; the action is essentially continuous.
4 case set **5 plainsong** i.e., simple truth

BOY Would I were in an alehouse in London! I would give all my fame for a pot of ale and safety.

PISTOL And I:

"If wishes would prevail with me,
My purpose should not fail with me,
But thither would I hie." 16

BOY

"As duly, but not as truly,
As bird doth sing on bough."

Enter Fluellen.

FLUELLEN Up to the breach, you dogs! Avaunt, you cul- 19
lions! [*Driving them forward.*] 20

PISTOL

Be merciful, great duke, to men of mold. 21
Abate thy rage, abate thy manly rage,
Abate thy rage, great duke!
Good bawcock, bate thy rage! Use lenity, sweet chuck! 24

NYM These be good humors! Your honor runs bad hu- 25
mors. *Exit* [*with all but Boy*]. 26

BOY As young as I am, I have observed these three
swashers. I am boy to them all three, but all they three, 28
though they would serve me, could not be man to me; 29
for indeed three such antics do not amount to a man. 30
For Bardolph, he is white-livered and red-faced, by the 31
means whereof 'a faces it out but fights not. For Pistol, 32
he hath a killing tongue and a quiet sword, by the
means whereof 'a breaks words and keeps whole 34
weapons. For Nym, he hath heard that men of few
words are the best men, and therefore he scorns to say
his prayers, lest 'a should be thought a coward; but

16 hie hasten **19 Avaunt** begone **19–20 cullions** rascals. (Original meaning: "testicles.") **21 men of mold** mere mortals **24 bawcock** fine fellow. (French *beau coq*.) **chuck** (A term of endearment.)
25–26 Your . . . humors i.e., you are behaving very idiosyncratically, your honor. (Addressed to Fluellen, who is doubtless threatening or beating them to make them go forward.) **28 swashers** swashbucklers **29 man** (1) master (2) a manly, brave person **30 antics** buffoons, zanies **31 For** as for (also in ll. 32 and 35). **white-livered** i.e., cowardly. (In extreme fear the blood was thought to sink below the liver, leaving it bloodless.) **32 'a faces it out** i.e., he puts on a brave front **34 breaks words** (1) misuses language and fails to keep his word (2) uses words as weapons

his few bad words are matched with as few good
deeds, for 'a never broke any man's head but his own,
and that was against a post when he was drunk. They
will steal anything and call it purchase. Bardolph 41
stole a lute case, bore it twelve leagues, and sold it for
three halfpence. Nym and Bardolph are sworn brothers in filching, and in Calais they stole a fire shovel. I
knew by that piece of service the men would carry 45
coals. They would have me as familiar with men's 46
pockets as their gloves or their handkerchiefs, which
makes much against my manhood, if I should take 48
from another's pocket to put into mine, for it is plain
pocketing up of wrongs. I must leave them and seek 50
some better service. Their villainy goes against my 51
weak stomach, and therefore I must cast it up. *Exit.* 52

Enter Gower [*and Fluellen, meeting*].

GOWER Captain Fluellen, you must come presently to
the mines. The Duke of Gloucester would speak with 54
you.

FLUELLEN To the mines? Tell you the Duke it is not so
good to come to the mines; for look you, the mines is
not according to the disciplines of the war. The con- 58
cavities of it is not sufficient. For look you, th' athver- 59
sary, you may discuss unto the Duke, look you, is digt 60
himself four yard under the countermines. By Cheshu, 61
I think 'a will plow up all, if there is not better direc- 62
tions.

41 purchase (Thieves' cant for "stolen goods.") **45–46 carry coals** i.e., submit to insult or degradation **48 makes** i.e., goes **50 pocketing . . . wrongs** (1) putting up with insults (2) receiving stolen goods
51–52 goes . . . stomach (1) goes against my inclination (2) makes me sick **52 cast it up** (1) cast it aside (2) vomit it **s.d. Exit** (A scene break may occur here, though it is not marked as such in most editions. Possibly Fluellen did not leave the stage at l. 26.) **54 mines** undermining operation in a siege **58 disciplines of the war** science of warfare (about which there were many books from Greek and Roman times down to the Renaissance; Fluellen's humor involves an obsession with this study and a preference for traditional methods) **58–59 concavities** i.e., depth **59–60 athversary** (Fluellen's pronunciation of *adversary*.) **60 discuss** explain **60–61 is digt . . . countermines** has dug himself countermines four yards beneath our mines **61 Cheshu** Jesu, Jesus
62 plow blow. (In Fluellen's Welsh dialect, "p" is regularly substituted for "b" and "f" for "v.")

GOWER The Duke of Gloucester, to whom the order of the siege is given, is altogether directed by an Irishman, a very valiant gentleman, i' faith.

FLUELLEN It is Captain Macmorris, is it not?

GOWER I think it be.

FLUELLEN By Cheshu, he is an ass, as in the world! I will verify as much in his beard. He has no more directions in the true disciplines of the wars, look you, of the Roman disciplines, than is a puppy dog.

Enter Macmorris and Captain Jamy.

GOWER Here 'a comes, and the Scots captain, Captain Jamy, with him.

FLUELLEN Captain Jamy is a marvelous falorous gentleman, that is certain, and of great expedition and knowledge in th' aunchient wars, upon my particular knowledge of his directions. By Cheshu, he will maintain his argument as well as any military man in the world, in the disciplines of the pristine wars of the Romans.

JAMY I say gud day, Captain Fluellen.

FLUELLEN Good e'en to your worship, good Captain James.

GOWER How now, Captain Macmorris, have you quit the mines? Have the pioners given o'er?

MACMORRIS By Chrish, la, 'tish ill done! The work ish give over, the trompet sound the retreat. By my hand I swear, and my father's soul, the work ish ill done; it ish give over. I would have blowed up the town, so Chrish save me, la, in an hour. O, 'tish ill done, 'tish ill done! By my hand, 'tish ill done!

FLUELLEN Captain Macmorris, I beseech you now, will you voutsafe me, look you, a few disputations with you, as partly touching or concerning the disciplines of the war, the Roman wars, in the way of argument, look you, and friendly communication—partly to satisfy my opinion, and partly for the satisfaction, look you, of my mind, as touching the direction of the military discipline, that is the point.

70 in his beard i.e., to his face **76 expedition** readiness of argument, quickness of wit **80 pristine** ancient **83 Good e'en** good afternoon or evening **86 pioners** sappers, diggers **94 voutsafe** vouchsafe, permit

JAMY It sall be vary gud, gud feith, gud captens bath, and I sall quite you with gud leve, as I may pick occasion. That sall I, marry.

MACMORRIS It is no time to discourse, so Chrish save me! The day is hot, and the weather, and the wars, and the King, and the dukes. It is no time to discourse. The town is beseeched, and the trumpet call us to the breach, and we talk, and, be Chrish, do nothing. 'Tis shame for us all. So God sa' me, 'tis shame to stand still, it is shame, by my hand! And there is throats to be cut, and works to be done, and there ish nothing done, so Chrish sa' me, la!

JAMY By the Mess, ere theise eyes of mine take themselves to slomber, ay'll de gud service, or I'll lig i' the grund for it, ay, or go to death! And I'll pay 't as valorously as I may, that sall I suerly do, that is the breff and the long. Marry, I wad full fain heard some question 'tween you tway.

FLUELLEN Captain Macmorris, I think, look you, under your correction, there is not many of your nation—

MACMORRIS Of my nation? What ish my nation? Ish a villain, and a bastard, and a knave, and a rascal? What ish my nation? Who talks of my nation?

FLUELLEN Look you, if you take the matter otherwise than is meant, Captain Macmorris, peradventure I shall think you do not use me with that affability as in discretion you ought to use me, look you, being as good a man as yourself, both in the disciplines of war and in the derivation of my birth, and in other particularities.

MACMORRIS I do not know you so good a man as myself. So Chrish save me, I will cut off your head!

GOWER Gentlemen both, you will mistake each other.

101 bath both **102 quite** requite, answer. **with gud leve** with good leave, with your kind permission **103 marry** indeed. (Originally, *by the Virgin Mary.*) **107 beseeched** besieged **108 be** by **112 Chrish sa' me** Christ save me **113 Mess** Mass **114 ay'll de** I'll do. **lig** lie **116 breff** brief **117 wad full fain heard** would very willingly have heard **117–118 question** discussion **121 What ish** i.e., what about. **Ish** i.e., (anyone who says anything against my nationality) is **133 will mistake** (Two possible meanings: [1] insist on misunderstanding [2] are going to misunderstand.)

JAMY Ah, that's a foul fault! *A parley* [*is sounded*]. 134
GOWER The town sounds a parley.
FLUELLEN Captain Macmorris, when there is more better opportunity to be required, look you, I will be so 137
bold as to tell you I know the disciplines of war; and
there is an end. *Exit* [*with others*].

3.3

[*Enter the Governor and some citizens on the walls.*] *Enter the King* [*Henry*] *and all his train before the gates.*

KING
How yet resolves the Governor of the town?
This is the latest parle we will admit. 2
Therefore to our best mercy give yourselves,
Or, like to men proud of destruction, 4
Defy us to our worst; for as I am a soldier,
A name that in my thoughts becomes me best,
If I begin the battery once again, 7
I will not leave the half-achievèd Harfleur
Till in her ashes she lie burièd.
The gates of mercy shall be all shut up,
And the fleshed soldier, rough and hard of heart, 11
In liberty of bloody hand shall range
With conscience wide as hell, mowing like grass 13
Your fresh fair virgins and your flowering infants.
What is it then to me if impious war,
Arrayed in flames like to the prince of fiends,
Do with his smirched complexion all fell feats 17
Enlinked to waste and desolation?

134 s.d. parley trumpet summons to a negotiation **137 required** found

3.3. Location: Before the gates of Harfleur, as in the previous scene. The action is essentially continuous, as usually in battle sequences; possibly some of the captains in 3.2 do not need to exit here. The gates are represented by the tiring house facade. Those who appear *on the walls* are seen in the gallery backstage.
2 latest parle last parley **4 like . . . destruction** i.e., like men elated at the prospect of death and glorying in destruction **7 battery** attack
11 fleshed made fierce with the taste of blood **13 wide as hell** i.e., letting anything pass **17 smirched** discolored, covered with grime. **fell** savage

What is 't to me, when you yourselves are cause,
If your pure maidens fall into the hand
Of hot and forcing violation?
What rein can hold licentious wickedness
When down the hill he holds his fierce career? 23
We may as bootless spend our vain command 24
Upon th' enragèd soldiers in their spoil
As send precepts to the leviathan 26
To come ashore. Therefore, you men of Harfleur,
Take pity of your town and of your people
Whiles yet my soldiers are in my command,
Whiles yet the cool and temperate wind of grace 30
O'erblows the filthy and contagious clouds 31
Of heady murder, spoil, and villainy. 32
If not, why, in a moment look to see 33
The blind and bloody soldier with foul hand 34
Defile the locks of your shrill-shrieking daughters;
Your fathers taken by the silver beards
And their most reverend heads dashed to the walls;
Your naked infants spitted upon pikes,
Whiles the mad mothers with their howls confused
Do break the clouds, as did the wives of Jewry 40
At Herod's bloody-hunting slaughtermen. 41
What say you? Will you yield, and this avoid,
Or, guilty in defense, be thus destroyed? 43

GOVERNOR

Our expectation hath this day an end.
The Dauphin, whom of succors we entreated, 45
Returns us that his powers are yet not ready 46
To raise so great a siege. Therefore, great King,
We yield our town and lives to thy soft mercy.
Enter our gates, dispose of us and ours,
For we no longer are defensible. 50

23 he . . . career it makes its fierce gallop **24 bootless** fruitlessly **26 precepts** written summons. **leviathan** whale **30 grace** mercy **31 O'erblows** blows away. (Contagion was thought to reside in clouds and mists.) **32 heady** violent; headstrong **33 look** expect **34 blind** i.e., blinded with lust and rage **40 Jewry** Judaea **41 Herod's . . . slaughtermen** (For the account of Herod's slaughter of the innocent children in his attempt to murder the infant Jesus, see Matthew 2:16–18.) **43 in defense** i.e., by not surrendering **45 of succors** for help **46 Returns** replies to **50 defensible** able to defend ourselves

KING
Open your gates. [*Exit Governor.*] Come, uncle Exeter,
Go you and enter Harfleur; there remain,
And fortify it strongly 'gainst the French.
Use mercy to them all. For us, dear uncle,
The winter coming on and sickness growing
Upon our soldiers, we will retire to Calais.
Tonight in Harfleur will we be your guest;
Tomorrow for the march are we addressed.
Flourish, and enter the town.

✤

3.4 *Enter Katharine and* [*Alice,*] *an old gentlewoman.*

KATHARINE Alice, tu as été en Angleterre, et tu parles bien le langage.

ALICE Un peu, madame.

KATHARINE Je te prie, m'enseignez; il faut que j'apprenne à parler. Comment appelez-vous la main en anglais?

ALICE La main? Elle est appelée de hand.

KATHARINE De hand. Et les doigts?

ALICE Les doigts? Ma foi, j'oublie les doigts; mais je me souviendrai. Les doigts? Je pense qu'ils sont appelés de fingres; oui, de fingres.

KATHARINE La main, de hand; les doigts, de fingres. Je pense que je suis le bon écolier; j'ai gagné deux

54 For as for **58 addressed** prepared

3.4. Location: The French court at Rouen.
Translation:
KATHARINE Alice, you have been in England and speak the language well.
ALICE A little, my lady.
KATHARINE I pray you teach me; I have to learn to speak it. What do you call *la main* in English?
ALICE *La main?* It is called de hand.
KATHARINE De hand. And *les doigts*?
ALICE *Les doigts?* Dear me, I forget *les doigts;* but I shall remember. I think that they are called de fingres; yes, de fingres.
KATHARINE *La main,* de hand; *les doigts,* de fingres. I think that I am a clever scholar; I have learned two English words in no time. What do you call *les ongles*?

mots d'anglais vitement. Comment appelez-vous les ongles?

ALICE Les ongles? Nous les appelons de nailes.

KATHARINE De nailes. Écoutez, dites-moi si je parle bien: de hand, de fingres, et de nailes.

ALICE C'est bien dit, madame; il est fort bon anglais.

KATHARINE Dites-moi l'anglais pour le bras.

ALICE De arm, madame.

KATHARINE Et le coude?

ALICE D' elbow.

KATHARINE D' elbow. Je m'en fais la répétition de tous les mots que vous m'avez appris dès à présent.

ALICE Il est trop difficile, madame, comme je pense.

KATHARINE Excusez-moi, Alice; écoutez: d' hand, de fingre, de nailes, d' arma, de bilbow.

ALICE D' elbow, madame.

KATHARINE O Seigneur Dieu, je m'en oublie! D' elbow. Comment appelez-vous le col?

ALICE De nick, madame.

KATHARINE De nick. Et le menton?

ALICE De chin.

KATHARINE De sin. Le col, de nick; le menton, de sin.

ALICE Oui. Sauf votre honneur, en vérité, vous prononcez les mots aussi droit que les natifs d'Angleterre.

ALICE *Les ongles?* We call them de nailes.

KATHARINE De nailes. Listen; tell me whether or not I speak correctly: de hand, de fingres, and de nailes.

ALICE That is correct, my lady; it is very good English.

KATHARINE Tell me the English for *le bras*.

ALICE De arm, my lady.

KATHARINE And *le coude*?

ALICE D' elbow.

KATHARINE D' elbow. I am going to repeat all the words you have taught me so far.

ALICE It is too hard, my lady, I fear.

KATHARINE Pardon me, Alice; listen: d' hand, de fingre, de nailes, d' arma, de bilbow.

ALICE D' elbow, my lady.

KATHARINE O Lord, I can't remember! D' elbow. What do you call *le col*?

ALICE De nick, my lady.

KATHARINE De nick. And *le menton*?

ALICE De chin.

KATHARINE De sin. *Le col,* de nick; *le menton,* de sin.

ALICE Yes. If I may say so, really you pronounce the words just as correctly as native Englishmen.

KATHARINE Je ne doute point d'apprendre, par la grâce de Dieu, et en peu de temps.

ALICE N'avez-vous pas déjà oublié ce que je vous ai enseigné?

KATHARINE Non, je réciterai à vous promptement: d' hand, de fingre, de mailes—

ALICE De nailes, madame.

KATHARINE De nailes, de arm, de ilbow.

ALICE Sauf votre honneur, d' elbow.

KATHARINE Ainsi dis-je; d' elbow, de nick, et de sin. Comment appelez-vous le pied et la robe?

ALICE Le foot, madame, et le count.

KATHARINE Le foot et le count! O Seigneur Dieu! Ils sont les mots de son mauvais, corruptible, gros, et impudique, et non pour les dames d'honneur d'user. Je ne voudrais prononcer ces mots devant les seigneurs de France pour tout le monde. Foh! Le foot et le count! Néanmoins, je réciterai une autre fois ma leçon ensemble: d' hand, de fingre, de nailes, de arm, d' elbow, de nick, de sin, de foot, le count.

ALICE Excellent, madame!

KATHARINE C'est assez pour une fois. Allons-nous à dîner. *Exit* [*with Alice*].

KATHARINE I have no doubt that I shall learn, with God's help, in a very short time.

ALICE Haven't you already forgotten what I have taught you?

KATHARINE No. I shall recite to you at once: d' hand, de fingre, de mailes—

ALICE De nailes, my lady.

KATHARINE De nailes, de arm, de ilbow.

ALICE By your leave, d' elbow.

KATHARINE That's what I said; d' elbow, de nick, and de sin. What do you call *le pied* and *la robe*?

ALICE Le foot, my lady, and le count. [As she pronounces them, *foot* sounds to Katharine like *foutre,* fornicate, and *count* (for *gown*) sounds like French for the female sexual organ, *cunt* in English.]

KATHARINE Le foot and le count! O Lord! Those are naughty words, wicked, coarse, and immodest, and are not fit to be used by ladies. I wouldn't say those words before French gentlemen for the whole world. Bah! Le foot and le count! Nevertheless, I shall recite my whole lesson once more: d' hand, de fingre, de nailes, de arm, d' elbow, de nick, de sin, de foot, le count.

ALICE Excellent, my lady.

KATHARINE That's enough for one time. Let's go to dinner.

3.5

Enter the King of France, the Dauphin, [*the Duke of Brittany,*] *the Constable of France, and others.*

FRENCH KING
'Tis certain he hath passed the River Somme.

CONSTABLE
And if he be not fought withal, my lord,
Let us not live in France; let us quit all
And give our vineyards to a barbarous people.

DAUPHIN
O Dieu vivant! Shall a few sprays of us,
The emptying of our fathers' luxury,
Our scions, put in wild and savage stock,
Spirt up so suddenly into the clouds
And overlook their grafters?

BRITTANY
Normans, but bastard Normans, Norman bastards!
Mort de ma vie, if they march along
Unfought withal, but I will sell my dukedom
To buy a slobbery and a dirty farm
In that nook-shotten isle of Albion.

CONSTABLE
Dieu de batailles, where have they this mettle?
Is not their climate foggy, raw, and dull,
On whom as in despite the sun looks pale,
Killing their fruit with frowns? Can sodden water,
A drench for sur-reined jades, their barley broth,
Decoct their cold blood to such valiant heat?
And shall our quick blood, spirited with wine,
Seem frosty? O, for honor of our land,

3.5. Location: The French court at Rouen.
2 withal with (as also in l. 12) **5 Dieu vivant** living God. **sprays** offshoots, illegitimate stock **6 fathers' luxury** ancestors' lust **7 scions** grafts. **put in** grafted upon **8 Spirt** shoot, sprout **9 overlook** rise above. **grafters** trees from which scions are taken **11 Mort de ma vie** death of my life, i.e., may my life end **12 but I will** i.e., if I do not **13 slobbery** slovenly **14 nook-shotten** full of nooks and angles. (Refers to the coastline.) **isle of Albion** island of England, Scotland, and Wales **15 Dieu de batailles** God of battles. **where** from where **17 despite** contempt **18 sodden water** boiled water **19 drench . . . jades** medicinal drink for overridden horses. **barley broth** ale **20 Decoct** warm up **21 quick** lively

Let us not hang like roping icicles 23
Upon our houses' thatch, whiles a more frosty people
Sweat drops of gallant youth in our rich fields!
"Poor" may we call them in their native lords. 26

DAUPHIN By faith and honor,
Our madams mock at us and plainly say 28
Our mettle is bred out, and they will give 29
Their bodies to the lust of English youth
To new-store France with bastard warriors. 31

BRITTANY
They bid us to the English dancing schools 32
And teach lavoltas high and swift corantos, 33
Saying our grace is only in our heels 34
And that we are most lofty runaways. 35

FRENCH KING
Where is Montjoy the herald? Speed him hence. 36
Let him greet England with our sharp defiance.
Up, princes, and, with spirit of honor edged 38
More sharper than your swords, hie to the field! 39
Charles Delabreth, High Constable of France,
You Dukes of Orleans, Bourbon, and of Berri,
Alençon, Brabant, Bar, and Burgundy,
Jaques Chatillion, Rambures, Vaudemont,
Beaumont, Grandpré, Roussi, and Faulconbridge,
Foix, Lestrelles, Boucicault, and Charolais,
High dukes, great princes, barons, lords, and knights,
For your great seats now quit you of great shames. 47
Bar Harry England, that sweeps through our land 48
With pennons painted in the blood of Harfleur. 49
Rush on his host, as doth the melted snow 50
Upon the valleys, whose low vassal seat

23 roping hanging down like a rope **26 Poor . . . lords** i.e., our fields, though rich in themselves, may be called poor in that they are owned by a spiritless aristocracy. (*Them* refers to "our fields"; *in* means "in respect to.") **28 madams** wives, ladies **29 bred out** exhausted by breeding **31 new-store** newly supply **32 bid us** bid us go **33 lavoltas, corantos** fashionable dances **34 in our heels** (1) in dancing gracefully (2) in running away **35 lofty** (1) noble (2) leaping. **runaways** cowards (but referring also to the movements of the dances) **36 Montjoy** title of the chief herald of France **38 edged** given a sharp edge **39 hie** hasten **47 For** in the name of, in defense of. **seats** positions. **quit** rid, free **48 Bar** stop, bar the way of **49 pennons** banners, streamers **50 host** army

The Alps doth spit and void his rheum upon. 52
Go down upon him—you have power enough—
And in a captive chariot into Rouen
Bring him our prisoner.

CONSTABLE This becomes the great. 55
Sorry am I his numbers are so few,
His soldiers sick and famished in their march,
For I am sure, when he shall see our army,
He'll drop his heart into the sink of fear 59
And for achievement offer us his ransom. 60

FRENCH KING
Therefore, Lord Constable, haste on Montjoy, 61
And let him say to England that we send
To know what willing ransom he will give.
Prince Dauphin, you shall stay with us in Rouen.

DAUPHIN
Not so, I do beseech Your Majesty.

FRENCH KING
Be patient, for you shall remain with us.
Now forth, Lord Constable and princes all,
And quickly bring us word of England's fall. *Exeunt.*

✤

3.6 *Enter Captains, English and Welsh: Gower and Fluellen,* [*meeting*].

GOWER How now, Captain Fluellen? Come you from the bridge? 2

FLUELLEN I assure you there is very excellent services 3
committed at the bridge.

GOWER Is the Duke of Exeter safe?

FLUELLEN The Duke of Exeter is as magnanimous as
Agamemnon, and a man that I love and honor with 7

52 rheum i.e., waters **55 becomes the great** befits greatness **59 sink** pit **60 for achievement** instead of achieving victory, as his sole accomplishment **61 haste** prod, hurry

3.6. Location: The English camp in northern France.
2 bridge (According to Holinshed, the French were beaten in their attempt to break down the bridge over the Ternoise. The audience is not told this, however, and might assume the river to be the Somme, mentioned in 3.5.1.) **3 services** exploits (as also in l. 71) **7 Agamemnon** leader of the Greeks against Troy

my soul, and my heart, and my duty, and my live, 8
and my living, and my uttermost power. He is not—
God be praised and blessed!—any hurt in the world,
but keeps the bridge most valiantly, with excellent discipline. There is an aunchient lieutenant there at the 12
pridge, I think in my very conscience he is as valiant
a man as Mark Antony, and he is a man of no esti- 14
mation in the world, but I did see him do as gallant 15
service.

GOWER What do you call him?

FLUELLEN He is called Aunchient Pistol.

GOWER I know him not.

Enter Pistol.

FLUELLEN Here is the man.

PISTOL
Captain, I thee beseech to do me favors.
The Duke of Exeter doth love thee well.

FLUELLEN Ay, I praise God, and I have merited some love at his hands.

PISTOL
Bardolph, a soldier, firm and sound of heart,
And of buxom valor, hath, by cruel fate 26
And giddy Fortune's furious fickle wheel,
That goddess blind
That stands upon the rolling restless stone—

FLUELLEN By your patience, Aunchient Pistol. Fortune
is painted blind, with a muffler afore her eyes, to sig- 31
nify to you that Fortune is blind; and she is painted
also with a wheel, to signify to you, which is the moral
of it, that she is turning, and inconstant, and mutability, and variation; and her foot, look you, is fixed upon
a spherical stone, which rolls, and rolls, and rolls. In
good truth, the poet is make a most excellent descrip- 37
tion of it. Fortune is an excellent moral. 38

PISTOL
Fortune is Bardolph's foe, and frowns on him; 39

8 live life **12 aunchient lieutenant** (Pistol is elsewhere given the rank of ancient, or ensign.) **14–15 estimation** fame **26 buxom** (1) vigorous (2) compliant, meek **31 muffler** blindfold **37 is make** has made **38 moral** emblem **39 Fortune . . . foe** (Probably alludes to the ballad "Fortune, my foe!")

For he hath stolen a pax,
And hangèd must 'a be—a damnèd death!
Let gallows gape for dog; let man go free,
And let not hemp his windpipe suffocate.
But Exeter hath given the doom of death
For pax of little price.
Therefore, go speak—the Duke will hear thy voice—
And let not Bardolph's vital thread be cut
With edge of penny cord and vile reproach.
Speak, Captain, for his life, and I will thee requite.

FLUELLEN Aunchient Pistol, I do partly understand your meaning.

PISTOL Why then rejoice therefor.

FLUELLEN Certainly, Aunchient, it is not a thing to rejoice at. For if, look you, he were my brother, I would desire the Duke to use his good pleasure and put him to execution; for discipline ought to be used.

PISTOL
Die and be damned! And *figo* for thy friendship!

FLUELLEN It is well.

PISTOL The fig of Spain! *Exit.*

FLUELLEN Very good.

GOWER Why, this is an arrant counterfeit rascal! I remember him now; a bawd, a cutpurse.

FLUELLEN I'll assure you, 'a uttered as prave words at the pridge as you shall see in a summer's day. But it is very well. What he has spoke to me, that is well, I warrant you, when time is serve.

GOWER Why, 'tis a gull, a fool, a rogue, that now and then goes to the wars to grace himself at his return into London under the form of a soldier. And such fellows are perfect in the great commanders' names, and they will learn you by rote where services were done—at such and such a sconce, at such a breach, at such a convoy; who came off bravely, who was shot,

40 pax metal disk with a crucifix stamped on it, kissed by the priest during Mass. (But Holinshed describes an incident in which the object stolen is a *pyx,* the vessel containing the consecrated host.) **44 doom** judgment, sentence **48 cord** rope **49 requite** repay **57 figo** gesture of contempt made by thrusting the thumb between the index and middle fingers **67 gull** simpleton **70 are perfect in** i.e., can recite perfectly **71 learn** teach **72 sconce** fortification

who disgraced, what terms the enemy stood on—and this they con perfectly in the phrase of war, which they trick up with new-tuned oaths. And what a beard of the General's cut and a horrid suit of the camp will do among foaming bottles and ale-washed wits is wonderful to be thought on. But you must learn to know such slanders of the age, or else you may be marvelously mistook.

FLUELLEN I tell you what, Captain Gower, I do perceive he is not the man that he would gladly make show to the world he is. If I find a hole in his coat, I will tell him my mind. [*Drum heard.*] Hark you, the King is coming, and I must speak with him from the pridge.

Drum and colors. Enter the King and his poor soldiers [*and Gloucester*].

God pless Your Majesty!

KING How now, Fluellen, cam'st thou from the bridge?

FLUELLEN Ay, so please Your Majesty. The Duke of Exeter has very gallantly maintained the pridge. The French is gone off, look you, and there is gallant and most prave passages. Marry, th' athversary was have possession of the pridge, but he is enforced to retire, and the Duke of Exeter is master of the pridge. I can tell Your Majesty, the Duke is a prave man.

KING What men have you lost, Fluellen?

FLUELLEN The perdition of th' athversary hath been very great, reasonable great. Marry, for my part, I think the Duke hath lost never a man, but one that is like to be executed for robbing a church, one Bardolph, if Your Majesty know the man. His face is all bubukles, and whelks, and knobs, and flames o' fire, and his lips blows at his nose, and it is like a coal of fire, sometimes plue and

74 terms . . . stood on conditions the enemy insisted on **75 con** learn by heart **76 trick** dress. **new-tuned** i.e., of the latest fashion
77 horrid . . . camp fierce battle costume **80 slanders of the age** persons who are a disgrace to the times **81 mistook** mistaken, deluded
84 a hole . . . coat i.e., a weak spot in him. (Proverbial.) **86 from the pridge** with news concerning the bridge **93 passages** deeds of arms.
was did **98 perdition** losses **100 like** likely **102 bubukles** carbuncles. **whelks** boils, pimples

sometimes red; but his nose is executed, and his fire's
out.

KING We would have all such offenders so cut off. And we
give express charge that, in our marches through the
country, there be nothing compelled from the villages,
nothing taken but paid for, none of the French upbraided or abused in disdainful language; for when lenity and cruelty play for a kingdom, the gentler gamester 112
is the soonest winner. 113

Tucket. Enter Montjoy.

MONTJOY You know me by my habit. 114

KING Well then, I know thee. What shall I know of thee?

MONTJOY My master's mind.

KING Unfold it.

MONTJOY Thus says my king: "Say thou to Harry of England, though we seemed dead, we did but sleep. Ad- 119
vantage is a better soldier than rashness. Tell him we 120
could have rebuked him at Harfleur, but that we
thought not good to bruise an injury till it were full 122
ripe. Now we speak upon our cue, and our voice is
imperial. England shall repent his folly, see his weak- 124
ness, and admire our sufferance. Bid him therefore 125
consider of his ransom, which must proportion the 126
losses we have borne, the subjects we have lost, the
disgrace we have digested; which in weight to re- 128
answer, his pettiness would bow under. For our losses, 129
his exchequer is too poor; for th' effusion of our blood, 130
the muster of his kingdom too faint a number; and for 131
our disgrace, his own person kneeling at our feet but
a weak and worthless satisfaction. To this add defiance; and tell him, for conclusion, he hath betrayed his
followers, whose condemnation is pronounced." So far 135
my King and master; so much my office.

112 gamester player **113 s.d. Tucket** trumpet signal, fanfare
114 habit i.e., tabard, herald's coat **119–120 Advantage** favorable circumstance **122 bruise an injury** i.e., squeeze a boil or pimple
124 England i.e., King Henry **125 admire our sufferance** wonder at our patience **126 proportion** be proportional to **128–129 which . . . under** i.e., to compensate for which his means are too slender
130 exchequer treasury **131 muster** total population
135 condemnation death sentence

KING
What is thy name? I know thy quality.
MONTJOY Montjoy.
KING
Thou dost thy office fairly. Turn thee back,
And tell thy King I do not seek him now,
But could be willing to march on to Calais
Without impeachment. For, to say the sooth,
Though 'tis no wisdom to confess so much
Unto an enemy of craft and vantage,
My people are with sickness much enfeebled,
My numbers lessened, and those few I have
Almost no better than so many French,
Who when they were in health, I tell thee, herald,
I thought upon one pair of English legs
Did march three Frenchmen. Yet, forgive me, God,
That I do brag thus! This your air of France
Hath blown that vice in me. I must repent.
Go, therefore, tell thy master here I am;
My ransom is this frail and worthless trunk,
My army but a weak and sickly guard.
Yet, God before, tell him we will come on,
Though France himself and such another neighbor
Stand in our way. There's for thy labor, Montjoy.
[*He gives a purse.*]
Go bid thy master well advise himself.
If we may pass, we will; if we be hindered,
We shall your tawny ground with your red blood
Discolor. And so, Montjoy, fare you well.
The sum of all our answer is but this:
We would not seek a battle as we are,
Nor, as we are, we say we will not shun it.
So tell your master.
MONTJOY
I shall deliver so. Thanks to Your Highness. [*Exit.*]
GLOUCESTER
I hope they will not come upon us now.
KING
We are in God's hand, brother, not in theirs.

137 quality rank and profession **142 impeachment** impediment. **sooth** truth **144 vantage** superiority in resources **152 blown** brought to bloom **154 trunk** body **159 advise himself** consider

March to the bridge. It now draws toward night.
Beyond the river we'll encamp ourselves,
And on tomorrow bid them march away. *Exeunt.*

✤

3.7

Enter the Constable of France, the Lord Rambures, Orleans, Dauphin, with others.

CONSTABLE Tut, I have the best armor of the world. Would it were day!

ORLEANS You have an excellent armor; but let my horse have his due.

CONSTABLE It is the best horse of Europe.

ORLEANS Will it never be morning?

DAUPHIN My lord of Orleans and my Lord High Constable, you talk of horse and armor?

ORLEANS You are as well provided of both as any prince in the world.

DAUPHIN What a long night is this! I will not change my horse with any that treads but on four pasterns. *Ça,* ha! He bounds from the earth as if his entrails were hairs; *le cheval volant,* the Pegasus, *qui a les narines de feu*! When I bestride him, I soar, I am a hawk. He trots the air. The earth sings when he touches it. The basest horn of his hoof is more musical than the pipe of Hermes.

ORLEANS He's of the color of the nutmeg.

DAUPHIN And of the heat of the ginger. It is a beast for Perseus. He is pure air and fire; and the dull elements of earth and water never appear in him, but only in

172 bid . . . away i.e., bid our army march toward Calais

3.7. Location: The French camp, near Agincourt.
12 pasterns i.e., hooves. (The *pastern* literally is the part of the horse's leg between the fetlock and the hoof.) **13–14 as . . . hairs** i.e., as if he were a tennis ball. (Tennis balls were stuffed with hair.) **14–15 le cheval . . . feu** the flying horse, Pegasus, with nostrils breathing fire **17 basest horn** (1) lowest part (2) hoofbeat **18 pipe of Hermes** (Hermes, messenger of the gods, charmed Argus of the hundred eyes asleep with playing on his pipe.) **21 Perseus** (According to some Greek legends and to Ovid, Perseus rode Pegasus when he rescued Andromeda from the dragon.)

patient stillness while his rider mounts him. He is indeed a horse, and all other jades you may call beasts.

CONSTABLE Indeed, my lord, it is a most absolute and excellent horse.

DAUPHIN It is the prince of palfreys. His neigh is like the bidding of a monarch, and his countenance enforces homage.

ORLEANS No more, cousin.

DAUPHIN Nay, the man hath no wit that cannot, from the rising of the lark to the lodging of the lamb, vary deserved praise on my palfrey. It is a theme as fluent as the sea; turn the sands into eloquent tongues, and my horse is argument for them all. 'Tis a subject for a sovereign to reason on, and for a sovereign's sovereign to ride on; and for the world, familiar to us and unknown, to lay apart their particular functions and wonder at him. I once writ a sonnet in his praise, and began thus: "Wonder of nature"—

ORLEANS I have heard a sonnet begin so to one's mistress.

DAUPHIN Then did they imitate that which I composed to my courser, for my horse is my mistress.

ORLEANS Your mistress bears well.

DAUPHIN Me well, which is the prescript praise and perfection of a good and particular mistress.

CONSTABLE Nay, for methought yesterday your mistress shrewdly shook your back.

DAUPHIN So perhaps did yours.

CONSTABLE Mine was not bridled.

DAUPHIN O, then belike she was old and gentle, and you rode like a kern of Ireland, your French hose off, and in your strait strossers.

25 absolute perfect **27 palfreys** saddle horses **32 lodging** lying down. **vary** produce variations of **35 argument** subject **36 reason** discourse **37–39 for . . . him** for both the known and unknown worlds to put aside their differences and join in wondering at him (the horse) **44 horse is my mistress** (Here begins a series of bawdy double entendres involving human and animal sexuality: *bears, shook your back, rode, foul bogs, doing,* etc.) **46 prescript** prescribed **47 particular** acknowledging only one master **49 shrewdly** viciously **51 Mine . . . bridled** i.e., at least my mistress was not a horse **52 belike** probably **53 kern** Irish foot soldier. (Here used to mean "rustic" or "boor.") **French hose** wide breeches **54 strait strossers** tight trousers, i.e., barelegged

CONSTABLE You have good judgment in horsemanship.

DAUPHIN Be warned by me, then: they that ride so, and ride not warily, fall into foul bogs. I had rather have my horse to my mistress.

CONSTABLE I had as lief have my mistress a jade.

DAUPHIN I tell thee, Constable, my mistress wears his own hair.

CONSTABLE I could make as true a boast as that if I had a sow to my mistress.

DAUPHIN *"Le chien est retourné à son propre vomissement, et la truie lavée au bourbier."* Thou mak'st use of anything.

CONSTABLE Yet do I not use my horse for my mistress, or any such proverb so little kin to the purpose.

RAMBURES My Lord Constable, the armor that I saw in your tent tonight, are those stars or suns upon it?

CONSTABLE Stars, my lord.

DAUPHIN Some of them will fall tomorrow, I hope.

CONSTABLE And yet my sky shall not want.

DAUPHIN That may be, for you bear a many superfluously, and 'twere more honor some were away.

CONSTABLE Even as your horse bears your praises, who would trot as well were some of your brags dismounted.

DAUPHIN Would I were able to load him with his desert! Will it never be day? I will trot tomorrow a mile, and my way shall be paved with English faces.

CONSTABLE I will not say so, for fear I should be faced out of my way. But I would it were morning, for I would fain be about the ears of the English.

RAMBURES Who will go to hazard with me for twenty prisoners?

58 to as **59 lief** happily **60–61 wears . . . hair** i.e., is not artificially wigged, like an elegant court lady, and perhaps bald from syphilis **64–65 Le chien . . . bourbier** the dog is returned to his own vomit, and the washed sow to the mire. (See 2 Peter 2:22.) **68 kin** related **73 sky** i.e., sky of honor. **want** be lacking (in honor) **74 a many** i.e., many. (Parallel to "a few.") **75 'twere . . . away** i.e., it would be more honest and proper if some of your stars were done away with **82–83 faced . . . way** braved out of my way, put to shame **84 fain** gladly. **about the ears** buffeting the heads **85 go to hazard** bet, play at dice. (But the Constable replies in the sense of "encounter danger.")

CONSTABLE You must first go yourself to hazard ere you have them.

DAUPHIN 'Tis midnight; I'll go arm myself. *Exit.*

ORLEANS The Dauphin longs for morning.

RAMBURES He longs to eat the English.

CONSTABLE I think he will eat all he kills.

ORLEANS By the white hand of my lady, he's a gallant prince.

CONSTABLE Swear by her foot, that she may tread out the oath.

ORLEANS He is simply the most active gentleman of France.

CONSTABLE Doing is activity, and he will still be doing.

ORLEANS He never did harm, that I heard of.

CONSTABLE Nor will do none tomorrow. He will keep that good name still.

ORLEANS I know him to be valiant.

CONSTABLE I was told that by one that knows him better than you.

ORLEANS What's he?

CONSTABLE Marry, he told me so himself, and he said he cared not who knew it.

ORLEANS He needs not; it is no hidden virtue in him.

CONSTABLE By my faith, sir, but it is. Never anybody saw it but his lackey. 'Tis a hooded valor, and when it appears it will bate.

ORLEANS Ill will never said well.

CONSTABLE I will cap that proverb with "There is flattery in friendship."

ORLEANS And I will take up that with "Give the devil his due."

95–96 tread . . . oath (1) fulfill the oath by dancing (2) stamp on, spurn the oath **99 Doing** i.e., acting, pretending. **still** continually **100 did harm** i.e., offended. (But the Constable uses it to mean "hurt any enemy.") **109 He needs not** i.e., there is no need for him to proclaim it himself. **it** i.e., valor **110–111 Never . . . lackey** i.e., he shows "valor" only in beating his servant **111 hooded valor** (The hawk was kept hooded to prevent it from beating its wings, or "bating.") **112 bate** (1) beat its wings (2) abate, be downcast **116–117 Give . . . due** give even the devil his due, allow praise even to those who criticize. (But the Constable turns this proverb against the Dauphin by likening him to the devil.)

CONSTABLE Well placed. There stands your friend for 118
the devil. Have at the very eye of that proverb with 119
"A pox of the devil."

ORLEANS You are the better at proverbs by how much
"A fool's bolt is soon shot." 122

CONSTABLE You have shot over. 123

ORLEANS 'Tis not the first time you were overshot. 124

Enter a Messenger.

MESSENGER My Lord High Constable, the English lie within fifteen hundred paces of your tents.

CONSTABLE Who hath measured the ground?

MESSENGER The Lord Grandpré.

CONSTABLE A valiant and most expert gentleman. [*Exit Messenger.*] Would it were day! Alas, poor Harry of England! He longs not for the dawning as we do.

ORLEANS What a wretched and peevish fellow is this
King of England, to mope with his fat-brained follow- 133
ers so far out of his knowledge!

CONSTABLE If the English had any apprehension, they 135
would run away.

ORLEANS That they lack; for if their heads had any intellectual armor, they could never wear such heavy headpieces.

RAMBURES That island of England breeds very valiant creatures; their mastiffs are of unmatchable courage.

ORLEANS Foolish curs, that run winking into the mouth 142
of a Russian bear and have their heads crushed like
rotten apples. You may as well say "That's a valiant flea
that dare eat his breakfast on the lip of a lion."

CONSTABLE Just, just! And the men do sympathize with 146
the mastiffs in robustious and rough coming on, leav- 147
ing their wits with their wives; and then give them
great meals of beef, and iron and steel, they will eat like

118–119 There . . . devil i.e., you just called the Dauphin the devil.
119 Have . . . eye shoot straight at the mark. (A sporting term appropriate to this verbal contest of "capping proverbs.") **122 bolt** short, blunt arrow **123 shot over** i.e., shot over the mark **124 overshot** i.e., outshot, defeated **133 mope** (1) wander about (2) be downcast
135 apprehension (1) sense (2) sense of danger **142 winking** shutting their eyes **146 Just** exactly. **sympathize with** resemble
147 robustious violent, boisterous

wolves and fight like devils.
ORLEANS Ay, but these English are shrewdly out of 151
beef.
CONSTABLE Then shall we find tomorrow they have
only stomachs to eat and none to fight. Now is it time 154
to arm. Come, shall we about it?

ORLEANS
It is now two o'clock; but let me see, by ten
We shall have each a hundred Englishmen. *Exeunt.*

✤

151 shrewdly out of devilishly short of **154 stomachs** appetites

4.0 *[Enter] Chorus.*

CHORUS
Now entertain conjecture of a time
When creeping murmur and the poring dark
Fills the wide vessel of the universe.
From camp to camp, through the foul womb of night,
The hum of either army stilly sounds,
That the fixed sentinels almost receive
The secret whispers of each other's watch.
Fire answers fire, and through their paly flames
Each battle sees the other's umbered face.
Steed threatens steed, in high and boastful neighs
Piercing the night's dull ear; and from the tents
The armorers, accomplishing the knights,
With busy hammers closing rivets up,
Give dreadful note of preparation.
The country cocks do crow, the clocks do toll,
And the third hour of drowsy morning name.
Proud of their numbers and secure in soul,
The confident and overlusty French
Do the low-rated English play at dice,
And chide the cripple tardy-gaited night,
Who like a foul and ugly witch doth limp
So tediously away. The poor condemnèd English,
Like sacrifices, by their watchful fires
Sit patiently and inly ruminate
The morning's danger; and their gesture sad,
Investing lank-lean cheeks and war-worn coats,
Presenteth them unto the gazing moon
So many horrid ghosts. O, now, who will behold
The royal captain of this ruined band
Walking from watch to watch, from tent to tent,
Let him cry, "Praise and glory on his head!"
For forth he goes and visits all his host,

4.0. Chorus.
1 entertain conjecture of i.e., imagine **2 poring** in which one must strain the eyes to see **5 stilly** softly **8 paly** pale **9 battle** army. **umbered** shadowed **12 accomplishing** equipping **17 secure** overconfident **18 overlusty** overly merry **19 play** gamble for **24 inly** inwardly **25 gesture sad** serious bearing **26 Investing** clothing **32 host** army

Bids them good morrow with a modest smile,
And calls them brothers, friends, and countrymen.
Upon his royal face there is no note
How dread an army hath enrounded him.
Nor doth he dedicate one jot of color
Unto the weary and all-watchèd night,
But freshly looks and overbears attaint
With cheerful semblance and sweet majesty;
That every wretch, pining and pale before,
Beholding him, plucks comfort from his looks.
A largess universal like the sun
His liberal eye doth give to everyone,
Thawing cold fear, that mean and gentle all
Behold, as may unworthiness define,
A little touch of Harry in the night.
And so our scene must to the battle fly;
Where—O, for pity!—we shall much disgrace
With four or five most vile and ragged foils,
Right ill-disposed in brawl ridiculous,
The name of Agincourt. Yet sit and see,
Minding true things by what their mockeries be.

Exit.

4.1 *Enter the King, Bedford, and Gloucester.*

KING

Gloucester, 'tis true that we are in great danger;
The greater therefore should our courage be.
Good morrow, brother Bedford. God Almighty!
There is some soul of goodness in things evil,
Would men observingly distill it out;

36 enrounded surrounded **37 dedicate** yield up. **color** i.e., bright color of complexion **38 all-watchèd** spent entirely in wakefulness and waiting **39 overbears attaint** overcomes the effects of weariness and depression **45 mean and gentle** those of low and of high birth **46 as . . . define** as we can express to you only imperfectly **53 Minding** bearing in mind. **mockeries** inadequate imitations

4.1. Location: The English camp at Agincourt.
5 observingly observantly

For our bad neighbor makes us early stirrers,
Which is both healthful and good husbandry.
Besides, they are our outward consciences
And preachers to us all, admonishing
That we should dress us fairly for our end.
Thus may we gather honey from the weed
And make a moral of the devil himself.

Enter Erpingham.

Good morrow, old Sir Thomas Erpingham.
A good soft pillow for that good white head
Were better than a churlish turf of France.

ERPINGHAM
Not so, my liege. This lodging likes me better,
Since I may say, "Now lie I like a king."

KING
'Tis good for men to love their present pains
Upon example; so the spirit is eased.
And when the mind is quickened, out of doubt
The organs, though defunct and dead before,
Break up their drowsy grave and newly move
With casted slough and fresh legerity.
Lend me thy cloak, Sir Thomas. [*The King puts on*
Erpingham's cloak.] Brothers both,
Commend me to the princes in our camp;
Do my good morrow to them, and anon
Desire them all to my pavilion.

GLOUCESTER We shall, my liege.

ERPINGHAM Shall I attend Your Grace?

KING No, my good knight,
Go with my brothers to my lords of England.
I and my bosom must debate awhile,
And then I would no other company.

ERPINGHAM
The Lord in heaven bless thee, noble Harry!
Exeunt [*all but King*].

7 husbandry economy, thrift **10 dress us fairly** prepare ourselves well **15 churlish** rough, hard **16 likes** pleases **19 Upon example** i.e., following or considering the example of persons such as King Henry and Erpingham **22 Break . . . grave** i.e., break out of their lethargy **23 With casted slough** i.e., as though having cast off its old skin, like a snake. **legerity** nimbleness **24 Brothers both** i.e., Bedford and Gloucester

KING
God-a-mercy, old heart! Thou speak'st cheerfully.

Enter Pistol.

PISTOL *Che vous là?* 36
KING A friend.
PISTOL
Discuss unto me: art thou officer, 38
Or art thou base, common, and popular? 39
KING I am a gentleman of a company.
PISTOL Trail'st thou the puissant pike? 41
KING Even so. What are you?
PISTOL
As good a gentleman as the Emperor. 43
KING Then you are a better than the King.
PISTOL
The King's a bawcock and a heart of gold, 45
A lad of life, an imp of fame, 46
Of parents good, of fist most valiant.
I kiss his dirty shoe, and from heartstring
I love the lovely bully. What is thy name? 49
KING Harry le Roy.
PISTOL
Le Roy? A Cornish name. Art thou of Cornish crew?
KING No, I am a Welshman. 52
PISTOL Know'st thou Fluellen?
KING Yes.
PISTOL
Tell him I'll knock his leek about his pate 55
Upon Saint Davy's Day. 56
KING Do not you wear your dagger in your cap that day, lest he knock that about yours.
PISTOL Art thou his friend?

36 Che vous là i.e., *qui va là,* who goes there; or *qui vous là,* who are you there. (Pistol's imperfect French.) **38 Discuss** declare **39 popular** of low birth **41 Trail'st . . . pike** i.e., are you in the infantry
43 Emperor i.e., Holy Roman Emperor **45 bawcock** fine fellow. (From French *beau coq.*) **46 imp of fame** child or scion of renown **49 bully** (A term of endearment meaning "fine fellow.") **52 Welshman** (Henry was born at Monmouth, then considered part of Wales.) **55–56 leek . . . Day** (On Saint David's Day, March 1, the leek was worn in memory of a Welsh victory over the Saxons, since Saint David, the Welsh leader, had commanded his followers to wear leeks in their caps on that occasion.)

KING And his kinsman too.
PISTOL The *figo* for thee, then!
KING I thank you. God be with you!
PISTOL My name is Pistol called. *Exit.*
KING It sorts well with your fierceness.
Manet King [*standing apart*].

Enter Fluellen and Gower [*meeting*].

GOWER Captain Fluellen!

FLUELLEN So, in the name of Jesu Christ, speak fewer. It is the greatest admiration in the universal world, when the true and aunchient prerogatifes and laws of the wars is not kept. If you would take the pains but to examine the wars of Pompey the Great, you shall find, I warrant you, that there is no tiddle-taddle nor pibble-pabble in Pompey's camp. I warrant you, you shall find the ceremonies of the wars, and the cares of it, and the forms of it, and the sobriety of it, and the modesty of it, to be otherwise.

GOWER Why, the enemy is loud; you hear him all night.

FLUELLEN If the enemy is an ass and a fool and a prating coxcomb, is it meet, think you, that we should also, look you, be an ass and a fool and a prating coxcomb? In your own conscience, now?

GOWER I will speak lower.

FLUELLEN I pray you and beseech you that you will.
Exit [*with Gower*].

KING
Though it appear a little out of fashion,
There is much care and valor in this Welshman.

Enter three soldiers, John Bates, Alexander Court, and Michael Williams.

COURT Brother John Bates, is not that the morning which breaks yonder?

61 figo (A provoking gesture of contempt; see 3.6.57, note.) **64 sorts** fits, agrees **s.d. Manet King** the King remains **66 fewer** i.e., calmly, more quietly **67 admiration** wonder **70 Pompey the Great** Roman general defeated by Julius Caesar **71–72 tiddle-taddle nor pibble-pabble** tittle-tattle nor bibble-babble **74 sobriety** orderliness, decorum **75 modesty** propriety **78–79 prating coxcomb** chattering fool

BATES I think it be. But we have no great cause to desire the approach of day.

WILLIAMS We see yonder the beginning of the day, but I think we shall never see the end of it.—Who goes there?

KING A friend.

WILLIAMS Under what captain serve you?

KING Under Sir Thomas Erpingham.

WILLIAMS A good old commander and a most kind gentleman. I pray you, what thinks he of our estate?

KING Even as men wrecked upon a sand, that look to be washed off the next tide.

BATES He hath not told his thought to the King?

KING No, nor it is not meet he should. For, though I speak it to you, I think the King is but a man, as I am. The violet smells to him as it doth to me; the element shows to him as it doth to me; all his senses have but human conditions. His ceremonies laid by, in his nakedness he appears but a man; and though his affections are higher mounted than ours, yet when they stoop, they stoop with the like wing. Therefore when he sees reason of fears, as we do, his fears, out of doubt, be of the same relish as ours are. Yet, in reason, no man should possess him with any appearance of fear, lest he, by showing it, should dishearten his army.

BATES He may show what outward courage he will; but I believe, as cold a night as 'tis, he could wish himself in Thames up to the neck; and so I would he were, and I by him, at all adventures, so we were quit here.

KING By my troth, I will speak my conscience of the King: I think he would not wish himself anywhere but where he is.

BATES Then I would he were here alone. So should he

97 estate condition **98 wrecked** shipwrecked **101 meet** fitting **103–104 element shows** sky appears **105 conditions** qualities, i.e., limitations. **ceremonies** observances due royalty; royal robes **106–107 affections . . . mounted** desires soar higher. (A falconry metaphor continued in *stoop,* descend, swoop down, and *with the like wing,* similarly.) **110 relish** taste **111 possess him with** induce in him **117 at all adventures** at all events (since the Thames would be less risky under any circumstances than the impending battle). **quit here** out of this situation

be sure to be ransomed, and a many poor men's lives saved.

KING I dare say you love him not so ill to wish him here alone, howsoever you speak this to feel other men's minds. Methinks I could not die anywhere so contented as in the King's company, his cause being just and his quarrel honorable.

WILLIAMS That's more than we know.

BATES Ay, or more than we should seek after; for we know enough if we know we are the King's subjects. If his cause be wrong, our obedience to the King wipes the crime of it out of us.

WILLIAMS But if the cause be not good, the King himself hath a heavy reckoning to make, when all those
legs and arms and heads, chopped off in a battle, shall
join together at the Latter Day and cry all, "We died at 137
such a place"—some swearing, some crying for a sur-
geon, some upon their wives left poor behind them,
some upon the debts they owe, some upon their children rawly left. I am afeard there are few die well that 141
die in a battle; for how can they charitably dispose of
anything, when blood is their argument? Now, if
these men do not die well, it will be a black matter for
the King that led them to it; who to disobey were 145
against all proportion of subjection. 146

KING So, if a son that is by his father sent about mer-
chandise do sinfully miscarry upon the sea, the im- 148
putation of his wickedness, by your rule, should be 149
imposed upon his father that sent him; or if a servant,
under his master's command transporting a sum of
money, be assailed by robbers and die in many irrec- 152
onciled iniquities, you may call the business of the 153
master the author of the servant's damnation. But this
is not so. The King is not bound to answer the partic- 155
ular endings of his soldiers, the father of his son, nor
the master of his servant; for they purpose not their 157
deaths when they propose their services. Besides,

137 Latter Day last day, Day of Judgment **141 rawly** without provision **145 who** whom **146 proportion of subjection** proper duty of a subject **148 sinfully miscarry** die in his sins **148–149 imputation** charge, accusation **152–153 in . . . iniquities** with his wicked deeds unabsolved **155 answer** answer for **157 purpose** intend

there is no king, be his cause never so spotless, if it come to the arbitrament of swords, can try it out with all unspotted soldiers. Some, peradventure, have on them the guilt of premeditated and contrived murder; some, of beguiling virgins with the broken seals of perjury; some, making the wars their bulwark, that have before gored the gentle bosom of peace with pillage and robbery. Now, if these men have defeated the law and outrun native punishment, though they can outstrip men, they have no wings to fly from God. War is his beadle, war is his vengeance; so that here men are punished for before-breach of the King's laws in now the King's quarrel. Where they feared the death, they have borne life away; and where they would be safe, they perish. Then if they die unprovided, no more is the King guilty of their damnation than he was before guilty of those impieties for the which they are now visited. Every subject's duty is the King's; but every subject's soul is his own. Therefore should every soldier in the wars do as every sick man in his bed, wash every mote out of his conscience; and dying so, death is to him advantage, or not dying, the time was blessedly lost wherein such preparation was gained. And in him that escapes, it were not sin to think that, making God so free an offer, He let him outlive that day to see His greatness and to teach others how they should prepare.

WILLIAMS 'Tis certain, every man that dies ill, the ill upon his own head, the King is not to answer it.

BATES I do not desire he should answer for me, and yet I determine to fight lustily for him.

KING I myself heard the King say he would not be ransomed.

WILLIAMS Ay, he said so, to make us fight cheerfully;

160 arbitrament arbitration **161 unspotted** innocent **164 bulwark** refuge from punishment (for offenses committed) **166 defeated** broken **167 native** at home **169 beadle** parish officer responsible for punishing petty offenders **170 before-breach** prior violation
171–173 Where . . . perish i.e., whereas before they feared execution but escaped punishment, here where they look for safety they die in battle
173–174 unprovided spiritually unprepared **176 visited** i.e., by punishment **179 mote** small impurity **186 dies ill** dies in sin

but when our throats are cut, he may be ransomed
and we ne'er the wiser.

KING If I live to see it, I will never trust his word after.

WILLIAMS You pay him then! That's a perilous shot out 196
of an elder-gun, that a poor and a private displeasure 197
can do against a monarch. You may as well go about
to turn the sun to ice with fanning in his face with a
peacock's feather. You'll never trust his word after!
Come, 'tis a foolish saying.

KING Your reproof is something too round. I should be 202
angry with you, if the time were convenient.

WILLIAMS Let it be a quarrel between us, if you live.

KING I embrace it.

WILLIAMS How shall I know thee again?

KING Give me any gage of thine, and I will wear it in 207
my bonnet. Then if ever thou dar'st acknowledge it,
I will make it my quarrel.

WILLIAMS Here's my glove. Give me another of thine.

KING There. [*They exchange gloves.*]

WILLIAMS This will I also wear in my cap. If ever thou
come to me and say, after tomorrow, "This is my
glove," by this hand, I will take thee a box on the ear. 214

KING If ever I live to see it, I will challenge it.

WILLIAMS Thou dar'st as well be hanged.

KING Well, I will do it, though I take thee in the King's company.

WILLIAMS Keep thy word. Fare thee well.

BATES Be friends, you English fools, be friends. We
have French quarrels enough, if you could tell how to 221
reckon.

KING Indeed, the French may lay twenty French crowns 223
to one they will beat us, for they bear them on their
shoulders; but it is no English treason to cut French 225
crowns, and tomorrow the King himself will be a
clipper. *Exeunt soldiers.*

196 You pay him then i.e., that will really pay him back for his perfidy, won't it. (Said sarcastically.) **197 elder-gun** popgun made from a branch of elder with the pith hollowed out **202 round** direct, brusque **207 gage** pledge **214 take** give, strike **221 could tell** knew **223 crowns** (1) coins (2) heads **225 English treason** (It was a treasonable offense to clip or "cut" English coins; it obviously is no offense to slash French heads, and even King Henry will be such a "clipper.")

Upon the King! Let us our lives, our souls,
Our debts, our careful wives, 229
Our children, and our sins lay on the King!
We must bear all. O hard condition,
Twin-born with greatness, subject to the breath 232
Of every fool, whose sense no more can feel 233
But his own wringing! What infinite heartsease 234
Must kings neglect that private men enjoy!
And what have kings that privates have not too, 236
Save ceremony, save general ceremony?
And what art thou, thou idol ceremony?
What kind of god art thou, that suffer'st more
Of mortal griefs than do thy worshipers?
What are thy rents? What are thy comings-in? 241
O ceremony, show me but thy worth!
What is thy soul of adoration? 243
Art thou aught else but place, degree, and form, 244
Creating awe and fear in other men?
Wherein thou art less happy, being feared,
Than they in fearing.
What drink'st thou oft, instead of homage sweet,
But poisoned flattery? O, be sick, great greatness,
And bid thy ceremony give thee cure!
Thinks thou the fiery fever will go out 251
With titles blown from adulation? 252
Will it give place to flexure and low bending? 253
Canst thou, when thou command'st the beggar's knee,
Command the health of it? No, thou proud dream,
That play'st so subtly with a king's repose.
I am a king that find thee, and I know 257
'Tis not the balm, the scepter, and the ball, 258
The sword, the mace, the crown imperial, 259

229 careful full of cares **232–234 Twin-born . . . wringing** i.e., inseparable from the condition of being born of royal rank, a condition that makes one the subject of the idle gossip of every fool, even those whose sensibilities pay attention to nothing other than the rumbling of their own stomachs **236 privates** private men **241 comings-in** revenues **243 thy soul of adoration** the essential quality that makes you so much admired **244 place** rank **251–252 will . . . adulation** will be extinguished by speeches breathed by flatterers **253 it give place to flexure** it (a fever, illness) yield to bowing **257 find** expose **258 balm** consecrating oil used to anoint a king in his coronation **259 mace** ceremonial staff

The intertissued robe of gold and pearl, 260
The farcèd title running 'fore the king, 261
The throne he sits on, nor the tide of pomp
That beats upon the high shore of this world—
No, not all these, thrice-gorgeous ceremony,
Not all these, laid in bed majestical,
Can sleep so soundly as the wretched slave
Who, with a body filled and vacant mind,
Gets him to rest, crammed with distressful bread; 268
Never sees horrid night, the child of hell,
But like a lackey from the rise to set 270
Sweats in the eye of Phoebus, and all night 271
Sleeps in Elysium; next day after dawn 272
Doth rise and help Hyperion to his horse, 273
And follows so the ever-running year
With profitable labor to his grave.
And but for ceremony, such a wretch,
Winding up days with toil and nights with sleep,
Had the forehand and vantage of a king. 278
The slave, a member of the country's peace, 279
Enjoys it; but in gross brain little wots 280
What watch the King keeps to maintain the peace, 281
Whose hours the peasant best advantages. 282

Enter Erpingham.

ERPINGHAM
My lord, your nobles, jealous of your absence, 283
Seek through your camp to find you.

KING
Good old knight,
Collect them all together at my tent.
I'll be before thee.

ERPINGHAM
I shall do 't, my lord. *Exit.* 286

KING
O God of battles, steel my soldiers' hearts;

260 intertissued interwoven **261 farcèd** stuffed (with pompous phrases) **268 distressful** earned by hard work **270 lackey** constant attendant. **rise to set** sunrise to sunset **271 Phoebus** the sun god **272 Elysium** in Greek mythology, the abode of the blessed **273 Hyperion** the charioteer of the sun. (The peasant is up before the sun.) **278 Had** would have. **forehand** upper hand **279 member** sharer **280 it** i.e., peace. **wots** knows **281 watch** wakeful guard **282 the peasant best advantages** most benefit the peasant **283 jealous of** apprehensive because of **286 be** be there

Possess them not with fear! Take from them now
The sense of reckoning, ere th' opposèd numbers 289
Pluck their hearts from them. Not today, O Lord,
O, not today, think not upon the fault 291
My father made in compassing the crown! 292
I Richard's body have interrèd new, 293
And on it have bestowed more contrite tears
Than from it issued forcèd drops of blood.
Five hundred poor I have in yearly pay
Who twice a day their withered hands hold up
Toward heaven, to pardon blood; and I have built
Two chantries, where the sad and solemn priests 299
Sing still for Richard's soul. More will I do; 300
Though all that I can do is nothing worth,
Since that my penitence comes after all, 302
Imploring pardon.

Enter Gloucester.

GLOUCESTER My liege!
KING My brother Gloucester's voice? Ay;
I know thy errand. I will go with thee.
The day, my friends, and all things stay for me.

Exeunt.

✣

4.2 *Enter the Dauphin, Orleans, Rambures, and others.*

ORLEANS
The sun doth gild our armor. Up, my lords!
DAUPHIN *Monte cheval!* My horse! *Varlet! Lacquais!* Ha! 2
ORLEANS O brave spirit!

289 sense of reckoning ability to count (the enemy) **291 the fault** i.e., the deposition and murder of Richard II **292 compassing** obtaining **293 new** anew **299 chantries** chapels in which masses for the dead were celebrated. **sad** grave **300 still** continually **302 Since that** i.e., as shown by the fact that

4.2. Location: The French camp.
s.d. others (The Folio text mentions Lord Beaumont but does not give him a speaking part.) **2 Monte cheval** to horse

DAUPHIN *Via, les eaux et terre!* 4
ORLEANS *Rien puis? L'air et feu?* 5
DAUPHIN *Cieux,* cousin Orleans. 6

Enter Constable.

Now, my Lord Constable!

CONSTABLE
Hark, how our steeds for present service neigh! 8

DAUPHIN
Mount them and make incision in their hides, 9
That their hot blood may spin in English eyes 10
And dout them with superfluous courage. Ha! 11

RAMBURES
What, will you have them weep our horses' blood?
How shall we then behold their natural tears?

Enter Messenger.

MESSENGER
The English are embattled, you French peers. 14

CONSTABLE
To horse, you gallant princes, straight to horse!
Do but behold yond poor and starvèd band,
And your fair show shall suck away their souls, 17
Leaving them but the shales and husks of men. 18
There is not work enough for all our hands,
Scarce blood enough in all their sickly veins
To give each naked curtal ax a stain 21
That our French gallants shall today draw out
And sheathe for lack of sport. Let us but blow on them,
The vapor of our valor will o'erturn them.
'Tis positive against all exceptions, lords, 25
That our superfluous lackeys and our peasants,
Who in unnecessary action swarm

4 Via . . . terre begone, waters and earth. (The Dauphin imagines himself riding above rivers and solid ground.) **5 Rien . . . feu** nothing more? What about air and fire? (i.e., Why not soar above all four elements, not just water and earth?) **6 Cieux** the heavens. (The Dauphin carries the metaphor one step further to its ultimate height.) **8 service** action **9 incision** i.e., with spurs **10 spin** gush, spatter **11 And . . . courage** i.e., and put out the English eyes with the horses' superfluous blood, the proof of their excessive courage. **dout** put out **14 embattled** arranged in battle order **17 fair show** impressive appearance **18 shales** shells **21 curtal ax** cutlass, short sword **25 exceptions** objections

About our squares of battle, were enough
To purge this field of such a hilding foe,
Though we upon this mountain's basis by
Took stand for idle speculation—
But that our honors must not. What's to say?
A very little little let us do
And all is done. Then let the trumpets sound
The tucket sonance and the note to mount;
For our approach shall so much dare the field
That England shall couch down in fear and yield.

Enter Grandpré.

GRANDPRÉ
Why do you stay so long, my lords of France?
Yond island carrions, desperate of their bones,
Ill-favoredly become the morning field.
Their ragged curtains poorly are let loose,
And our air shakes them passing scornfully.
Big Mars seems bankrupt in their beggared host
And faintly through a rusty beaver peeps.
The horsemen sit like fixèd candlesticks,
With torch staves in their hand, and their poor jades
Lob down their heads, drooping the hides and hips,
The gum down-roping from their pale-dead eyes,
And in their pale dull mouths the gimmaled bit
Lies foul with chewed grass, still and motionless;
And their executors, the knavish crows,
Fly o'er them all impatient for their hour.
Description cannot suit itself in words
To demonstrate the life of such a battle
In life so lifeless as it shows itself.

28 squares of battle four-sided military formation **29 hilding** worthless, base **30 basis** foot. **by** nearby **31 speculation** looking on **32 But that** except for the fact that **35 tucket sonance** trumpet call **36 dare** (1) defy (2) stupify with fear **39 carrions** skeletons, cadavers. **desperate of** without hope of saving **40 Ill-favoredly become** i.e., are an eyesore to **41 curtains** colors, banners **42 passing** exceedingly **43 Mars** the god of war **44 beaver** visor **46 torch staves** i.e., tapers in place of lances. (The horsemen themselves look like carved candleholders.) **47 Lob down** hang down. **drooping** letting droop **48 gum** watery discharge. **down-roping** hanging down ropelike **49 gimmaled** jointed **51 executors** those who will dispose of what remains behind **54 battle** army

CONSTABLE
They have said their prayers, and they stay for death.
DAUPHIN
Shall we go send them dinners and fresh suits,
And give their fasting horses provender,
And after fight with them?
CONSTABLE
I stay but for my guard. On to the field!
I will the banner from a trumpet take
And use it for my haste. Come, come, away!
The sun is high, and we outwear the day. *Exeunt.*

✤

4.3

Enter Gloucester, Bedford, Exeter, Erpingham, with all his host, Salisbury, and Westmorland.

GLOUCESTER Where is the King?
BEDFORD
The King himself is rode to view their battle.
WESTMORLAND
Of fighting men they have full threescore thousand.
EXETER
There's five to one. Besides, they are all fresh.
SALISBURY
God's arm strike with us! 'Tis a fearful odds.
God b' wi' you, princes all; I'll to my charge.
If we no more meet till we meet in heaven,
Then joyfully, my noble lord of Bedford,
My dear lord Gloucester, and my good lord Exeter,
And my kind kinsman, warriors all, adieu!
BEDFORD
Farewell, good Salisbury, and good luck go with thee!
EXETER
Farewell, kind lord. Fight valiantly today!
And yet I do thee wrong to mind thee of it,

56 stay for await **58 provender** fodder **60 guard** (including a standard-bearer) **61 trumpet** trumpeter **63 outwear** waste

4.3. Location: The English camp.
2 battle army **6 charge** post, command **10 kinsman** i.e., Westmorland, whose son had married Salisbury's daughter **13 mind** remind

For thou art framed of the firm truth of valor. 14
[*Exit Salisbury.*]

BEDFORD

He is as full of valor as of kindness,
Princely in both.

Enter the King.

WESTMORLAND O, that we now had here
But one ten thousand of those men in England
That do no work today!

KING What's he that wishes so? 18
My cousin Westmorland? No, my fair cousin.
If we are marked to die, we are enough 20
To do our country loss; and if to live, 21
The fewer men, the greater share of honor.
God's will, I pray thee, wish not one man more.
By Jove, I am not covetous for gold,
Nor care I who doth feed upon my cost; 25
It yearns me not if men my garments wear; 26
Such outward things dwell not in my desires.
But if it be a sin to covet honor
I am the most offending soul alive.
No, faith, my coz, wish not a man from England. 30
God's peace, I would not lose so great an honor
As one man more, methinks, would share from me 32
For the best hope I have. O, do not wish one more!
Rather proclaim it, Westmorland, through my host 34
That he which hath no stomach to this fight, 35
Let him depart; his passport shall be made
And crowns for convoy put into his purse. 37
We would not die in that man's company
That fears his fellowship to die with us. 39
This day is called the Feast of Crispian. 40
He that outlives this day and comes safe home

14 framed made, built **18 What's** who is **20–21 enough . . . loss** enough loss for our country to suffer **25 upon my cost** at my expense **26 yearns** grieves **30 coz** cousin, kinsman **32 share from me** take from me as his share **34 host** army **35 stomach to** appetite for **37 crowns for convoy** travel money **39 That . . . us** that is afraid to risk his life in my company **40 Feast of Crispian** Saint Crispin's Day, October 25. (Cripinus and Crispianus were martyrs who fled from Rome in the third century; according to legend they disguised themselves as shoemakers, and afterward became the patron saints of that craft.)

Will stand a-tiptoe when this day is named
And rouse him at the name of Crispian.
He that shall see this day and live old age 44
Will yearly on the vigil feast his neighbors 45
And say, "Tomorrow is Saint Crispian."
Then will he strip his sleeve and show his scars,
And say, "These wounds I had on Crispin's Day."
Old men forget; yet all shall be forgot, 49
But he'll remember with advantages 50
What feats he did that day. Then shall our names,
Familiar in his mouth as household words—
Harry the King, Bedford and Exeter,
Warwick and Talbot, Salisbury and Gloucester—
Be in their flowing cups freshly remembered. 55
This story shall the good man teach his son;
And Crispin Crispian shall ne'er go by,
From this day to the ending of the world,
But we in it shall be rememberèd—
We few, we happy few, we band of brothers.
For he today that sheds his blood with me
Shall be my brother; be he ne'er so vile, 62
This day shall gentle his condition. 63
And gentlemen in England now abed
Shall think themselves accursed they were not here,
And hold their manhoods cheap whiles any speaks
That fought with us upon Saint Crispin's Day.

Enter Salisbury.

SALISBURY
My sovereign lord, bestow yourself with speed. 68
The French are bravely in their battles set 69
And will with all expedience charge on us. 70

KING
All things are ready, if our minds be so.

WESTMORLAND
Perish the man whose mind is backward now! 72

44 live live to see **45 vigil** evening before a feast day **49 yet** in time **50 advantages** additions of his own **55 flowing** overflowing **62 vile** lowly **63 gentle his condition** raise him to the rank of gentleman **68 bestow yourself** take up your battle position **69 bravely . . . set** finely arrayed in their battalions **70 expedience** speed **72 backward** reluctant

KING
Thou dost not wish more help from England, coz?
WESTMORLAND
God's will, my liege, would you and I alone,
Without more help, could fight this royal battle!
KING
Why, now thou hast unwished five thousand men,
Which likes me better than to wish us one.— 77
You know your places. God be with you all!

Tucket. Enter Montjoy.

MONTJOY
Once more I come to know of thee, King Harry,
If for thy ransom thou wilt now compound 80
Before thy most assurèd overthrow;
For certainly thou art so near the gulf 82
Thou needs must be englutted. Besides, in mercy 83
The Constable desires thee thou wilt mind 84
Thy followers of repentance, that their souls
May make a peaceful and a sweet retire 86
From off these fields where, wretches, their poor bodies
Must lie and fester.
KING Who hath sent thee now?
MONTJOY The Constable of France.
KING
I pray thee, bear my former answer back:
Bid them achieve me, and then sell my bones. 91
Good God, why should they mock poor fellows thus?
The man that once did sell the lion's skin
While the beast lived was killed with hunting him.
A many of our bodies shall no doubt 95
Find native graves, upon the which, I trust, 96
Shall witness live in brass of this day's work.
And those that leave their valiant bones in France,
Dying like men, though buried in your dunghills,
They shall be famed; for there the sun shall greet them
And draw their honors reeking up to heaven, 101

77 likes pleases **80 compound** make terms **82 gulf** whirlpool **83 englutted** swallowed up **84 mind** remind **86 retire** retreat **91 achieve** capture **95 A many** many. (The phrase is an exact parallel to "a few.") **96 native** in their own land (i.e., England) **101 reeking** (1) breathing (2) smelling

Leaving their earthly parts to choke your clime,
The smell whereof shall breed a plague in France.
Mark then abounding valor in our English, 104
That, being dead, like to the bullets crazing 105
Break out into a second course of mischief,
Killing in relapse of mortality. 107
Let me speak proudly. Tell the Constable
We are but warriors for the working day. 109
Our gayness and our gilt are all besmirched
With rainy marching in the painful field.
There's not a piece of feather in our host—
Good argument, I hope, we will not fly—
And time hath worn us into slovenry.
But, by the Mass, our hearts are in the trim!
And my poor soldiers tell me, yet ere night
They'll be in fresher robes, or they will pluck 117
The gay new coats o'er the French soldiers' heads
And turn them out of service. If they do this— 119
As, if God please, they shall—my ransom then
Will soon be levied. Herald, save thou thy labor. 121
Come thou no more for ransom, gentle herald. 122
They shall have none, I swear, but these my joints,
Which if they have as I will leave 'em them,
Shall yield them little, tell the Constable.

MONTJOY

I shall, King Harry. And so fare thee well.
Thou never shalt hear herald any more. *Exit.*

KING

I fear thou wilt once more come again for a ransom.

Enter York [*and kneels*].

YORK

My lord, most humbly on my knee I beg
The leading of the vaward. 130

104 abounding overflowing, abundant **105 crazing** shattering, with a suggestion also of *grazing,* ricocheting **107 Killing . . . mortality** killing (their foes) as they (the English) fall back (decompose) into their elements; also, like the bullet, with a deadly ricochet **109 for the working day** i.e., to do serious work, not take a holiday **117 in fresher robes** i.e., in heavenly garb. (Or perhaps the phrase *or they will* means "even if they have to.") **119 turn . . . service** i.e., send them away stripped of their finery, like dismissed servants stripped of their livery **121 levied** collected **122 gentle** noble **130 vaward** vanguard

KING
Take it, brave York. Now, soldiers, march away.
And how thou pleasest, God, dispose the day!
Exeunt.

✤

4.4 *Alarum. Excursions. Enter Pistol, French Soldier, [and] Boy.*

PISTOL Yield, cur!
FRENCH SOLDIER *Je pense que vous êtes le gentilhomme de bonne qualité.*
PISTOL
Qualtitie calmie custure me!
Art thou a gentleman? What is thy name? Discuss.
FRENCH SOLDIER *O Seigneur Dieu!*
PISTOL
O, Signieur Dew should be a gentleman.
Perpend my words, O Signieur Dew, and mark:
O Signieur Dew, thou diest on point of fox,
Except, O signieur, thou do give to me
Egregious ransom. [*He threatens him with his sword.*]
FRENCH SOLDIER *O, prenez miséricorde! Ayez pitié de moi!*
PISTOL
"Moy" shall not serve. I will have forty moys,
Or I will fetch thy rim out at thy throat
In drops of crimson blood.
FRENCH SOLDIER *Est-il impossible d'échapper la force de ton bras?*

4.4. Location: The field of battle.
s.d. Excursions sorties **2–3 Je . . . qualité** I think that you are a gentleman of high rank **4 calmie custure me** (These words are perhaps derived from the refrain of a popular song, supposed to be Irish, "Calen o custure me.") **5 Discuss** speak **6 O Seigneur Dieu** O Lord God **8 Perpend** attend to, consider **9 fox** sword **10 Except** unless **11 Egregious** huge **12–13 O . . . moi** Oh, have mercy! Take pity on me! **14 Moy** (Pistol, not understanding, takes *moi* for the name of a coin, or a sum of money.) **15 rim** midriff, diaphragm **17–18 Est-il . . . bras** is it impossible to escape the strength of your arm. (But Pistol takes *bras*, arm, for *brass*.)

PISTOL Brass, cur?
Thou damnèd and luxurious mountain goat, 20
Offer'st me brass?
FRENCH SOLDIER *O, pardonnez-moi!*
PISTOL
Sayst thou me so? Is that a ton of moys? 23
Come hither, boy. Ask me this slave in French
What is his name.
BOY *Écoutez: comment êtes-vous appelé?* 26
FRENCH SOLDIER *Monsieur le Fer.*
BOY He says his name is Master Fer.
PISTOL Master Fer? I'll fer him, and firk him, and ferret 29
him. Discuss the same in French unto him.
BOY I do not know the French for fer, and ferret, and
firk.
PISTOL
Bid him prepare, for I will cut his throat.
FRENCH SOLDIER *Que dit-il, monsieur?* 34
BOY *Il me commande à vous dire que vous faites vous* 35
prêt; car ce soldat ici est disposé tout à cette heure de 36
couper votre gorge. 37
PISTOL
Owy, cuppele gorge, permafoy, 38
Peasant, unless thou give me crowns, brave crowns,
Or mangled shalt thou be by this my sword.
FRENCH SOLDIER *O, je vous supplie, pour l'amour de* 41
Dieu, me pardonner! Je suis le gentilhomme de bonne 42
maison. Gardez ma vie, et je vous donnerai deux cents 43
écus. 44
PISTOL What are his words?
BOY He prays you to save his life. He is a gentleman of
a good house, and for his ransom he will give you two 47
hundred crowns.

20 luxurious lecherous **23 a ton of moys** (This is what Pistol phonetically makes out of *pardonnez-moi.*) **26 Écoutez . . . appelé** listen: what is your name **29 firk** trounce. **ferret** worry (like a ferret) **34–37 Que . . . gorge** What does he say, sir? BOY He bids me tell you that you must prepare yourself, because this soldier intends to cut your throat immediately **38 Owy** i.e., *oui,* yes. **permafoy** *per ma foi,* by my faith
41–44 O . . . écus Oh, I pray you, for the love of God, to pardon me. I am a gentleman of a good house; preserve my life, and I shall give you two hundred crowns **47 house** family

PISTOL
Tell him my fury shall abate, and I
The crowns will take.

FRENCH SOLDIER *Petit monsieur, que dit-il?*

BOY *Encore qu'il est contre son jurement de pardonner aucun prisonnier, néanmoins, pour les écus que vous l'avez promis, il est content à vous donner la liberté, le franchisement.*

FRENCH SOLDIER [*Kneeling*] *Sur mes genoux je vous donne mille remercîments; et je m'estime heureux que j'ai tombé entre les mains d'un chevalier, je pense, le plus brave, vaillant, et très-distingué seigneur d'Angleterre.*

PISTOL Expound unto me, boy.

BOY He gives you, upon his knees, a thousand thanks, and he esteems himself happy that he hath fallen into the hands of one, as he thinks, the most brave, valorous, and thrice-worthy seigneur of England.

PISTOL
As I suck blood, I will some mercy show.
Follow me!

BOY *Suivez-vous le grand capitaine.* [*Exeunt Pistol and French Soldier.*] I did never know so full a voice issue from so empty a heart! But the saying is true, "The empty vessel makes the greatest sound." Bardolph and Nym had ten times more valor than this roaring devil i' th' old play, that everyone may pare his nails with a wooden dagger, and they are both hanged; and so would this be, if he durst steal anything adventurously. I must stay with the lackeys, with the luggage of our camp. The French might have a good prey of us, if he knew of it, for there is none to guard it but boys. *Exit.*

51–55 Petit . . . franchisement What does he say, little sir? BOY Although it is against his oath to pardon any prisoner, nevertheless, for the sake of the crowns you have promised, he is willing to give you your liberty, your freedom **56–60 Sur . . . d'Angleterre** On my knees I give you a thousand thanks; and I consider myself happy that I have fallen into the hands of a knight, as I think, the bravest, most valiant, and very distinguished gentleman in England **68 Suivez-vous . . . capitaine** follow the great captain **72 roaring devil** i.e., the devil in the morality play, a comic figure paired with the Vice who traditionally had a wooden dagger **77 a good prey** i.e., easy pickings

4.5 *Enter Constable, Orleans, Bourbon, Dauphin, and Rambures.*

CONSTABLE *O diable!*
ORLEANS *O Seigneur! Le jour est perdu, tout est perdu!*
DAUPHIN
Mort de ma vie! All is confounded, all.
Reproach and everlasting shame
Sits mocking in our plumes. *A short alarum.*
O méchante fortune! Do not run away.
CONSTABLE Why, all our ranks are broke.
DAUPHIN
O perdurable shame! Let's stab ourselves.
Be these the wretches that we played at dice for?
ORLEANS
Is this the king we sent to for his ransom?
BOURBON
Shame and eternal shame, nothing but shame!
Let us die! In once more! Back again!
And he that will not follow Bourbon now,
Let him go hence, and with his cap in hand,
Like a base pander, hold the chamber door
Whilst by a slave, no gentler than my dog,
His fairest daughter is contaminated.
CONSTABLE
Disorder, that hath spoiled us, friend us now!
Let us on heaps go offer up our lives.
ORLEANS
We are enough yet living in the field
To smother up the English in our throngs,
If any order might be thought upon.
BOURBON
The devil take order now! I'll to the throng.
Let life be short, else shame will be too long.
Exeunt.

4.5. Location: The field of battle still.
1 O diable O the devil **2 O . . . perdu** O Lord, the day is lost, all is lost **3 Mort de ma vie** death of my life, i.e., may my life end. **confounded** lost **6 O méchante fortune** O malicious fortune **8 perdurable** everlasting **16 gentler** (1) more nobly born (2) tenderer **18 friend** befriend **19 on** in

4.6 *Alarum. Enter the King and his train, [Exeter, and others,] with prisoners.*

KING

Well have we done, thrice valiant countrymen!
But all's not done; yet keep the French the field.

EXETER

The Duke of York commends him to Your Majesty.

KING

Lives he, good uncle? Thrice within this hour
I saw him down, thrice up again and fighting.
From helmet to the spur all blood he was.

EXETER

In which array, brave soldier, doth he lie,
Larding the plain; and by his bloody side, 8
Yokefellow to his honor-owing wounds, 9
The noble Earl of Suffolk also lies.
Suffolk first died; and York, all haggled over, 11
Comes to him where in gore he lay insteeped 12
And takes him by the beard, kisses the gashes
That bloodily did yawn upon his face. 14
He cries aloud, "Tarry, my cousin Suffolk!
My soul shall thine keep company to heaven;
Tarry, sweet soul, for mine, then fly abreast,
As in this glorious and well-foughten field
We kept together in our chivalry!"
Upon these words I came and cheered him up.
He smiled me in the face, raught me his hand, 21
And, with a feeble grip, says, "Dear my lord,
Commend my service to my sovereign."
So did he turn, and over Suffolk's neck
He threw his wounded arm, and kissed his lips,
And so espoused to death, with blood he sealed
A testament of noble-ending love.
The pretty and sweet manner of it forced
Those waters from me which I would have stopped; 29

4.6. Location: The field of battle still.
8 Larding fattening, enriching (with his blood) **9 honor-owing** honor-owning, honorable **11 haggled over** mangled, hacked **12 insteeped** immersed **14 yawn** gape **21 me in the** i.e., in my. **raught** reached **29 Those waters** i.e., tears

But I had not so much of man in me,
And all my mother came into mine eyes 31
And gave me up to tears.

KING I blame you not;
For, hearing this, I must perforce compound 33
With mistful eyes, or they will issue too. *Alarum.* 34
But, hark, what new alarum is this same?
The French have reinforced their scattered men.
Then every soldier kill his prisoners! 37
Give the word through. *Exit* [*with others*].

4.7 *Enter Fluellen and Gower.*

FLUELLEN Kill the poys and the luggage! 'Tis expressly 1
against the law of arms. 'Tis as arrant a piece of knavery, mark you now, as can be offert; in your conscience, now, is it not?

GOWER 'Tis certain there's not a boy left alive; and the cowardly rascals that ran from the battle ha' done this slaughter. Besides, they have burned and carried away all that was in the King's tent, wherefore the King most worthily hath caused every soldier to cut his prisoner's throat. O, 'tis a gallant king!

FLUELLEN Ay, he was porn at Monmouth, Captain 11
Gower. What call you the town's name where Alexander the Pig was born?

GOWER Alexander the Great.

FLUELLEN Why, I pray you, is not "pig" great? The pig, or the great, or the mighty, or the huge, or the mag-

31 my mother i.e., the tenderer part of me **33 perforce** necessarily. **compound** come to terms **34 issue** i.e., issue forth tears **37 kill his prisoners** (This follows Holinshed, who says that Henry, alarmed by the outcry of the lackeys and boys of the camp, feared a new attack and ordered the prisoners killed as a means of precaution. Gower, 4.7.9–10, attributes the King's action to revenge.)

4.7. Location: The field of battle still.
1 luggage i.e., lackeys guarding the luggage **11 Monmouth** (i.e., in Wales)

nanimous, are all one reckonings, save the phrase is a 17
little variations.

GOWER I think Alexander the Great was born in Macedon. His father was called Philip of Macedon, as I take it.

FLUELLEN I think it is in Macedon where Alexander is porn. I tell you, Captain, if you look in the maps of the 'orld, I warrant you sall find, in the comparisons between Macedon and Monmouth, that the situations, look you, is both alike. There is a river in Macedon, and there is also moreover a river at Monmouth. It is called Wye at Monmouth, but it is out of my prains what is the name of the other river; but 'tis all one, 'tis alike as my fingers is to my fingers, and there is salmons in both. If you mark Alexander's life well, Harry
of Monmouth's life is come after it indifferent well, for 32
there is figures in all things. Alexander, God knows, 33
and you know, in his rages, and his furies, and his wraths, and his cholers, and his moods, and his displeasures, and his indignations, and also being a little
intoxicates in his prains, did, in his ales and his an- 37
gers, look you, kill his best friend, Cleitus. 38

GOWER Our King is not like him in that. He never killed any of his friends.

FLUELLEN It is not well done, mark you now, to take the tales out of my mouth ere it is made and finished. I speak but in the figures and comparisons of it. As Alexander killed his friend Cleitus, being in his ales and his cups, so also Harry Monmouth, being in his right wits and his good judgments, turned away the fat
knight with the great-belly doublet. He was full of 47
jests, and gipes, and knaveries, and mocks. I have for- 48
got his name.

GOWER Sir John Falstaff.

17 reckonings judgment, evaluation. **is** i.e., has undergone **32 is . . . well** resembles it fairly well **33 figures** comparisons, similes **37 in his ales** i.e., under the influence of ale **38 Cleitus** a general and close associate of Alexander, whom Alexander killed in a drinking bout **47 great-belly doublet** a man's close-fitting jacket in which the lower part was stuffed out with bombast or padding **48 gipes** jibes, jokes

FLUELLEN That is he. I'll tell you there is good men porn at Monmouth.

GOWER Here comes His Majesty.

Alarum. Enter King Harry, [*Warwick, Gloucester, Exeter, and others,*] *and Bourbon with* [*other*] *prisoners. Flourish.*

KING
I was not angry since I came to France
Until this instant. Take a trumpet, herald;
Ride thou unto the horsemen on yond hill.
If they will fight with us, bid them come down,
Or void the field. They do offend our sight.
If they'll do neither, we will come to them,
And make them skirr away as swift as stones
Enforcèd from the old Assyrian slings.
Besides, we'll cut the throats of those we have,
And not a man of them that we shall take
Shall taste our mercy. Go and tell them so.

Enter Montjoy.

EXETER
Here comes the herald of the French, my liege.

GLOUCESTER
His eyes are humbler than they used to be.

KING
How now, what means this, herald? Know'st thou not
That I have fined these bones of mine for ransom?
Com'st thou again for ransom?

MONTJOY No, great King.
I come to thee for charitable license,
That we may wander o'er this bloody field
To book our dead and then to bury them,
To sort our nobles from our common men.
For many of our princes—woe the while!—
Lie drowned and soaked in mercenary blood;
So do our vulgar drench their peasant limbs

55 trumpet trumpeter **58 void** leave **60 skirr** scurry **61 Enforcèd** discharged **68 fined . . . ransom** i.e., agreed to pay as a fine or ransom only these bones of mine and no more **72 book** record **75 mercenary** i.e., of common soldiers, who fought for pay **76 vulgar** commoners

In blood of princes; and the wounded steeds
Fret fetlock-deep in gore and with wild rage
Yerk out their armèd heels at their dead masters, 79
Killing them twice. O, give us leave, great King,
To view the field in safety, and dispose
Of their dead bodies!

KING I tell thee truly, herald,
I know not if the day be ours or no,
For yet a many of your horsemen peer 84
And gallop o'er the field.

MONTJOY The day is yours.

KING
Praised be God, and not our strength, for it!
What is this castle called that stands hard by?

MONTJOY They call it Agincourt.

KING
Then call we this the field of Agincourt,
Fought on the day of Crispin Crispianus.

FLUELLEN Your grandfather of famous memory, an 't 91
please Your Majesty, and your great-uncle Edward the
Plack Prince of Wales, as I have read in the chronicles,
fought a most prave pattle here in France.

KING They did, Fluellen.

FLUELLEN Your Majesty says very true. If Your Majesties
is remembered of it, the Welshmen did good service in
a garden where leeks did grow, wearing leeks in their
Monmouth caps, which, Your Majesty know, to this 99
hour is an honorable badge of the service; and I do
believe Your Majesty takes no scorn to wear the leek
upon Saint Tavy's Day.

KING
I wear it for a memorable honor,
For I am Welsh, you know, good countryman.

FLUELLEN All the water in Wye cannot wash Your Majesty's Welsh plood out of your pody, I can tell you that. God pless it and preserve it, as long as it pleases His Grace, and His Majesty too!

KING Thanks, good my countryman.

79 Yerk kick **84 peer** (1) look about anxiously (2) appear **91 grandfather** i.e., great-grandfather, Edward III. **an 't** if it **99 Monmouth caps** round and rimless caps with a tapering crown, commonly worn by the Welsh

FLUELLEN By Jeshu, I am Your Majesty's countryman, I care not who know it. I will confess it to all the 'orld. I need not to be ashamed of Your Majesty, praised be God, so long as Your Majesty is an honest man.

KING
God keep me so!

Enter Williams [*with a glove in his cap*].

Our heralds go with him.
Bring me just notice of the numbers dead
On both our parts.

[*Exeunt Heralds and Gower with Montjoy.*]

Call yonder fellow hither.

EXETER Soldier, you must come to the King.

KING Soldier, why wear'st thou that glove in thy cap?

WILLIAMS An 't please Your Majesty, 'tis the gage of one that I should fight withal, if he be alive.

KING An Englishman?

WILLIAMS An 't please Your Majesty, a rascal that swaggered with me last night, who, if 'a live and ever dare to challenge this glove, I have sworn to take him a box o' th' ear; or if I can see my glove in his cap, which he swore as he was a soldier he would wear if 'a lived, I will strike it out soundly.

KING What think you, Captain Fluellen, is it fit this soldier keep his oath?

FLUELLEN He is a craven and a villain else, an 't please Your Majesty, in my conscience.

KING It may be his enemy is a gentleman of great sort, quite from the answer of his degree.

FLUELLEN Though he be as good a gentleman as the devil is, as Lucifer and Beelzebub himself, it is necessary, look Your Grace, that he keep his vow and his oath. If he be perjured, see you now, his reputation is as arrant a villain and a Jack-sauce as ever his black shoe trod upon God's ground and His earth, in my conscience, la!

KING Then keep thy vow, sirrah, when thou meet'st the fellow.

115 just exact **130 craven** coward **132 sort** rank **133 quite . . . degree** i.e., too high in rank to answer the challenge of one so low **138 Jack-sauce** saucy knave

WILLIAMS So I will, my liege, as I live.

KING Who serv'st thou under?

WILLIAMS Under Captain Gower, my liege.

FLUELLEN Gower is a good captain, and is good knowledge and literatured in the wars.

KING Call him hither to me, soldier.

WILLIAMS I will, my liege. *Exit.*

KING Here, Fluellen, wear thou this favor for me and stick it in thy cap. [*He gives Fluellen Williams's glove.*] When Alençon and myself were down together, I plucked this glove from his helm. If any man challenge this, he is a friend to Alençon and an enemy to our person. If thou encounter any such, apprehend him, an thou dost me love.

FLUELLEN [*Putting the glove in his cap*] Your Grace doo's me as great honors as can be desired in the hearts of his subjects. I would fain see the man that has but two legs that shall find himself aggriefed at this glove, that is all. But I would fain see it once, an 't please God of his grace that I might see.

KING Know'st thou Gower?

FLUELLEN He is my dear friend, an 't please you.

KING Pray thee, go seek him and bring him to my tent.

FLUELLEN I will fetch him. *Exit.*

KING
My lord of Warwick, and my brother Gloucester,
Follow Fluellen closely at the heels.
The glove which I have given him for a favor
May haply purchase him a box o' th' ear.
It is the soldier's; I by bargain should
Wear it myself. Follow, good cousin Warwick.
If that the soldier strike him, as I judge
By his blunt bearing he will keep his word,
Some sudden mischief may arise of it;
For I do know Fluellen valiant
And touched with choler, hot as gunpowder,
And quickly will return an injury.

147 literatured well read **153 helm** helmet **156 an** if **157 doo's** does **159 fain** willingly **161 an 't** if it (also in l. 164) **170 haply** perhaps **177 touched with choler** hot-tempered **178 return** repay. **injury** insult

Follow, and see there be no harm between them.
Go you with me, uncle of Exeter. *Exeunt [separately].*

✤

4.8 *Enter Gower and Williams.*

WILLIAMS I warrant it is to knight you, Captain.

Enter Fluellen.

FLUELLEN God's will and his pleasure, Captain, I be-
seech you now, come apace to the King. There is more
good toward you, peradventure, than is in your knowl- 4
edge to dream of.
WILLIAMS Sir, know you this glove?
FLUELLEN Know the glove? I know the glove is a glove.
WILLIAMS I know this, and thus I challenge it.
Strikes him.
FLUELLEN 'Sblood, an arrant traitor as any 's in the uni- 9
versal world, or in France, or in England!
GOWER [*To Williams*] How now, sir? You villain!
WILLIAMS Do you think I'll be forsworn?
FLUELLEN Stand away, Captain Gower. I will give trea-
son his payment into plows, I warrant you. 14
WILLIAMS I am no traitor.
FLUELLEN That's a lie in thy throat. I charge you in His 16
Majesty's name, apprehend him. He's a friend of the
Duke Alençon's.

Enter Warwick and Gloucester.

WARWICK How now, how now, what's the matter?
FLUELLEN My lord of Warwick, here is—praised be
God for it!—a most contagious treason come to light, 21
look you, as you shall desire in a summer's day.—
Here is His Majesty.

4.8. Location: The English camp.
4 peradventure by chance **9 'Sblood** by His (Christ's) blood **14 his** its. **into plows** in blows **16 lie in thy throat** i.e., inexcusable lie
21 contagious noxious

Enter King [*Henry*] *and Exeter.*

KING How now, what's the matter?

FLUELLEN My liege, here is a villain and a traitor that, look Your Grace, has struck the glove which Your Majesty is take out of the helmet of Alençon.

WILLIAMS My liege, this was my glove; here is the fellow of it. [*Showing his other glove.*] And he that I gave it to in change promised to wear it in his cap. I promised to strike him if he did. I met this man with my glove in his cap, and I have been as good as my word.

FLUELLEN Your Majesty hear now, saving Your Majesty's manhood, what an arrant, rascally, beggarly, lousy knave it is. I hope Your Majesty is pear me testimony and witness, and will avouchment, that this is the glove of Alençon that Your Majesty is give me, in your conscience, now.

KING Give me thy glove, soldier. Look, here is the fellow of it. [*He shows his other glove.*]
'Twas I indeed thou promisèdst to strike,
And thou hast given me most bitter terms.

FLUELLEN An 't please Your Majesty, let his neck answer for it, if there is any martial law in the world.

KING
How canst thou make me satisfaction?

WILLIAMS All offenses, my lord, come from the heart. Never came any from mine that might offend Your Majesty.

KING It was ourself thou didst abuse.

WILLIAMS Your Majesty came not like yourself. You appeared to me but as a common man—witness the night, your garments, your lowliness. And what Your Highness suffered under that shape, I beseech you take it for your own fault and not mine; for had you been as I took you for, I made no offense. Therefore I beseech Your Highness pardon me.

KING
Here, uncle Exeter, fill this glove with crowns,
And give it to this fellow. Keep it, fellow,

30 change exchange **35 is pear** will bear **36 avouchment** avouch
42 terms words **43 An 't** if it (also in l. 117) **52 lowliness** humble mien

And wear it for an honor in thy cap
Till I do challenge it. Give him the crowns.
[*Exeter gives the glove and gold to Williams.*]
And Captain, you must needs be friends with him.

FLUELLEN By this day and this light, the fellow has mettle enough in his belly. Hold, there is twelvepence for you. [*He offers a coin.*] And I pray you to serve God, and keep you out of prawls, and prabbles, and quarrels, and dissensions, and I warrant you it is the better for you.

WILLIAMS I will none of your money.

FLUELLEN It is with a good will. I can tell you, it will serve you to mend your shoes. Come, wherefore should you be so pashful? Your shoes is not so good. 'Tis a good silling, I warrant you, or I will change it.

Enter [*an English*] *Herald.*

KING Now, herald, are the dead numbered?

HERALD [*Giving a paper*]
Here is the number of the slaughtered French.

KING
What prisoners of good sort are taken, uncle?

EXETER
Charles Duke of Orleans, nephew to the King;
John Duke of Bourbon, and Lord Boucicault;
Of other lords and barons, knights and squires,
Full fifteen hundred, besides common men.

KING
This note doth tell me of ten thousand French
That in the field lie slain. Of princes, in this number,
And nobles bearing banners, there lie dead
One hundred twenty-six; added to these,
Of knights, esquires, and gallant gentlemen,
Eight thousand and four hundred, of the which
Five hundred were but yesterday dubbed knights.
So that in these ten thousand they have lost
There are but sixteen hundred mercenaries;
The rest are princes, barons, lords, knights, squires,

65 prabbles i.e., brabbles, scuffles **75 good sort** high rank
76–112 Charles . . . thine (The catalogue of the captured and slain is from Holinshed.) **82 bearing banners** i.e., with coats of arms

And gentlemen of blood and quality.
The names of those their nobles that lie dead:
Charles Delabreth, High Constable of France;
Jaques of Chatillion, Admiral of France;
The Master of the Crossbows, Lord Rambures;
Great-Master of France, the brave Sir Guichard Dau-
phin;
John, Duke of Alençon; Anthony Duke of Brabant,
The brother to the Duke of Burgundy;
And Edward, Duke of Bar; of lusty earls,
Grandpré and Roussi, Faulconbridge and Foix,
Beaumont and Marle, Vaudemont and Lestrelles.
Here was a royal fellowship of death!
Where is the number of our English dead?
[*He is given another paper.*]
Edward the Duke of York, the Earl of Suffolk,
Sir Richard Keighley, Davy Gam, esquire;
None else of name, and of all other men
But five-and-twenty. O God, thy arm was here!
And not to us, but to thy arm alone,
Ascribe we all! When, without stratagem,
But in plain shock and even play of battle,
Was ever known so great and little loss
On one part and on th' other? Take it, God,
For it is none but thine!

EXETER 'Tis wonderful.

KING
Come, go we in procession to the village.
And be it death proclaimèd through our host
To boast of this or take that praise from God
Which is his only.

FLUELLEN Is it not lawful, an 't please Your Majesty, to tell how many is killed?

KING
Yes, Captain, but with this acknowledgment,
That God fought for us.

FLUELLEN Yes, in my conscience, he did us great good.

KING Do we all holy rites.

95 Great-Master grandmaster, i.e., the chief officer of the royal household **98 lusty** vigorous **105 name** rank, importance **109 shock** confrontation. **even** equal

Let there be sung *Non nobis* and *Te Deum,*
The dead with charity enclosed in clay;
And then to Calais, and to England then,
Where ne'er from France arrived more happy men.
Exeunt.

✤

123 Non nobis i.e., Psalm 115, beginning, "Not unto us, O Lord, not unto us, but unto thy name give glory." **Te Deum** a hymn of thanksgiving, beginning, "We praise thee O God" **126 happy** fortunate

5.0 *Enter Chorus.*

CHORUS
Vouchsafe to those that have not read the story
That I may prompt them; and of such as have,
I humbly pray them to admit th' excuse
Of time, of numbers, and due course of things,
Which cannot in their huge and proper life
Be here presented. Now we bear the King
Toward Calais. Grant him there. There seen,
Heave him away upon your wingèd thoughts
Athwart the sea. Behold, the English beach
Pales in the flood with men, wives, and boys,
Whose shouts and claps outvoice the deep-mouthed sea,
Which like a mighty whiffler 'fore the King
Seems to prepare his way. So let him land,
And solemnly see him set on to London.
So swift a pace hath thought that even now
You may imagine him upon Blackheath,
Where that his lords desire him to have borne
His bruisèd helmet and his bended sword
Before him through the city. He forbids it,
Being free from vainness and self-glorious pride,
Giving full trophy, signal, and ostent
Quite from himself to God. But now behold,
In the quick forge and working-house of thought,
How London doth pour out her citizens!
The Mayor and all his brethren in best sort,
Like to the senators of th' antique Rome
With the plebeians swarming at their heels,
Go forth and fetch their conquering Caesar in;

5.0. (Between Acts 4 and 5 there is historically an interval of about five years during which Henry made a second campaign in France that brought the French to terms in the Treaty of Troyes, with which the play ends.)
1 Vouchsafe permit it **3 admit th' excuse** excuse our handling **10 Pales in** hems in, surrounds. **flood** sea **12 whiffler** an usher heading the procession to clear the way **16 Blackheath** open area just outside London, to the southeast **17 Where that** where **21 signal** token (of victory). **ostent** external show **25 sort** array

As by a lower but loving likelihood,
Were now the General of our gracious Empress,
As in good time he may, from Ireland coming,
Bringing rebellion broachèd on his sword,
How many would the peaceful city quit
To welcome him! Much more, and much more cause,
Did they this Harry. Now in London place him;
As yet the lamentation of the French
Invites the King of England's stay at home;
The Emperor's coming in behalf of France,
To order peace between them . . . and omit
All the occurrences, whatever chanced,
Till Harry's back-return again to France.
There must we bring him; and myself have played
The interim, by remembering you 'tis past.
Then brook abridgment, and your eyes advance,
After your thoughts, straight back again to France.
Exit.

5.1

Enter Fluellen [*with a leek in his cap, and a cudgel*], *and Gower.*

GOWER Nay, that's right. But why wear you your leek today? Saint Davy's Day is past.

FLUELLEN There is occasions and causes why and wherefore in all things. I will tell you asse my friend,

29–34 As . . . him (Seemingly an allusion to the Earl of Essex, who left London on his Irish expedition on March 27, 1599, in an attempt to put down Tyrone's rebellion; he returned unsuccessful and under a cloud on September 28 of the same year. These lines, therefore, were probably written between the dates mentioned.) **29 a . . . likelihood** a less exalted comparison but one that shows much love **30 Empress** i.e., Elizabeth **32 broachèd** transfixed, spitted **36–37 As . . . home** i.e., the French are so dejected that Henry can stay in England without fear of loss in France **38 Emperor's coming** (The Holy Roman Emperor, Sigismund, came to England on behalf of France in May 1416.) **39 them . . . and omit** (Something appears to be left out here. Possibly it should read, "them, and the death / O' the Dauphin, leap we over, and omit . . .") **41 Harry's back-return** i.e., Henry's second campaign, commencing in 1417 **43 remembering** reminding **44 brook** tolerate, excuse

5.1. Location: France. The English camp.
4 asse as

Captain Gower. The rascally, scald, beggarly, lousy, pragging knave, Pistol, which you and yourself and all the world know to be no petter than a fellow, look you now, of no merits, he is come to me and prings me pread and salt yesterday, look you, and bid me eat my leek. It was in a place where I could not breed no contention with him; but I will be so bold as to wear it in my cap till I see him once again, and then I will tell him a little piece of my desires.

Enter Pistol.

GOWER Why, here he comes, swelling like a turkey-cock.

FLUELLEN 'Tis no matter for his swellings nor his turkey-cocks.—God pless you, Aunchient Pistol! You scurvy, lousy knave, God pless you!

PISTOL
Ha, art thou bedlam? Dost thou thirst, base Trojan,
To have me fold up Parca's fatal web?
Hence, I am qualmish at the smell of leek.

FLUELLEN I peseech you heartily, scurvy, lousy knave, at my desires, and my requests, and my petitions, to eat, look you, this leek. [*He offers the leek.*] Because, look you, you do not love it, nor your affections and your appetites and your disgestions doo's not agree with it, I would desire you to eat it.

PISTOL
Not for Cadwallader and all his goats.

FLUELLEN There is one goat for you. (*Strikes him.*) Will you be so good, scald knave, as eat it?

PISTOL Base Trojan, thou shalt die.

FLUELLEN You say very true, scald knave, when God's will is. I will desire you to live in the meantime and eat your victuals. Come, there is sauce for it. [*He strikes him.*] You called me yesterday mountain squire, but I

5 scald scurvy **19 bedlam** crazy. **Trojan** i.e., rascal **20 Parca's** (The Parcae, or Fates, spun, drew out, and cut the thread of destiny.) **21 qualmish** squeamish, nauseated **28 Cadwallader** last king of the Welsh. **goats** (Pistol makes the customary taunt that the Welsh were goatherds.) **35 mountain squire** i.e., a squire owning mountainous, poor land

will make you today a squire of low degree. I pray you, fall to. If you can mock a leek, you can eat a leek.

GOWER Enough, Captain, you have astonished him.

FLUELLEN By Jesu, I will make him eat some part of my leek, or I will peat his pate four days. Bite, I pray you; it is good for your green wound and your ploody coxcomb.

PISTOL Must I bite?

FLUELLEN Yes, certainly, and out of doubt and out of question too, and ambiguities.

PISTOL
By this leek, I will most horribly revenge—
[*Fluellen threatens him.*]
I eat and eat—I swear—

FLUELLEN Eat, I pray you. Will you have some more sauce to your leek? There is not enough leek to swear by.

PISTOL
Quiet thy cudgel; thou dost see I eat.

FLUELLEN Much good do you, scald knave, heartily. Nay, pray you, throw none away; the skin is good for your broken coxcomb. When you take occasions to see leeks hereafter, I pray you, mock at 'em, that is all.

PISTOL Good.

FLUELLEN Ay, leeks is good. Hold you, there is a groat to heal your pate. [*He offers a coin.*]

PISTOL Me, a groat?

FLUELLEN Yes, verily, and in truth you shall take it, or I have another leek in my pocket which you shall eat.

PISTOL
I take thy groat in earnest of revenge.

FLUELLEN If I owe you anything, I will pay you in cudgels. You shall be a woodmonger and buy nothing of me but cudgels. God b' wi' you, and keep you, and heal your pate. *Exit.*

PISTOL All hell shall stir for this.

36 squire of low degree (Allusion to a popular medieval romance, *The Squire of Low Degree*. Fluellen threatens to make Pistol into a lowly, contemptible figure, towered over by a mountain squire.) **38 astonished** dazed, terrified **40 pate** head **41 green** raw **41–42 coxcomb** fool's cap; here, the scalp **57 groat** fourpenny coin **62 in earnest of** as a down payment for

GOWER Go, go, you are a counterfeit cowardly knave. Will you mock at an ancient tradition, begun upon an honorable respect and worn as a memorable trophy of predeceased valor, and dare not avouch in your deeds any of your words? I have seen you gleeking and galling at this gentleman twice or thrice. You thought because he could not speak English in the native garb he could not therefore handle an English cudgel. You find it otherwise; and henceforth let a Welsh correction teach you a good English condition. Fare ye well. *Exit.*

PISTOL

Doth Fortune play the huswife with me now?
News have I that my Doll is dead
I' th' spital of a malady of France,
And there my rendezvous is quite cut off.
Old I do wax, and from my weary limbs
Honor is cudgeled. Well, bawd I'll turn,
And something lean to cutpurse of quick hand.
To England will I steal, and there I'll steal;
And patches will I get unto these cudgeled scars,
And swear I got them in the Gallia wars. *Exit.*

5.2

Enter, at one door, King Henry, Exeter, Bedford, [*Gloucester, Clarence,*] *Warwick,* [*Westmorland,*] *and other lords; at another, Queen Isabel, the* [*French*] *King, the Duke of Burgundy,* [*the Princess Katharine, Alice,*] *and other French.*

KING HENRY

Peace to this meeting, wherefor we are met!
Unto our brother France and to our sister,
Health and fair time of day; joy and good wishes

70 respect consideration **71 predeceased valor** valor of those now dead **72–73 gleeking and galling** mocking and scoffing **79 huswife** hussy, fickle one **80 Doll** (An error for *Nell;* may indicate an earlier version in which the speaker of these lines was Falstaff.) **81 spital** hospital. **malady of France** veneral disease **82 rendezvous** refuge **83 wax** grow **85 something lean to** incline somewhat to **88 Gallia** French

5.2. Location: The French court.

To our most fair and princely cousin Katharine;
And, as a branch and member of this royalty, 5
By whom this great assembly is contrived,
We do salute you, Duke of Burgundy;
And princes French, and peers, health to you all!

FRENCH KING

Right joyous are we to behold your face,
Most worthy brother England. Fairly met!
So are you, princes English, every one.

QUEEN ISABEL

So happy be the issue, brother England, 12
Of this good day and of this gracious meeting,
As we are now glad to behold your eyes—
Your eyes, which hitherto have borne in them
Against the French that met them in their bent 16
The fatal balls of murdering basilisks. 17
The venom of such looks, we fairly hope,
Have lost their quality, and that this day
Shall change all griefs and quarrels into love. 20

KING HENRY

To cry amen to that, thus we appear.

QUEEN ISABEL

You English princes all, I do salute you.

BURGUNDY

My duty to you both, on equal love,
Great Kings of France and England! That I have labored
With all my wits, my pains, and strong endeavors
To bring your most imperial Majesties
Unto this bar and royal interview, 27
Your mightiness on both parts best can witness.
Since then my office hath so far prevailed
That, face to face and royal eye to eye,
You have congreeted, let it not disgrace me 31
If I demand, before this royal view, 32
What rub or what impediment there is 33
Why that the naked, poor, and mangled Peace,

5 royalty royal family **12 issue** outcome **16 in their bent** (1) as they were directed (2) in their glance **17 fatal balls** (1) cannon balls (2) eyeballs. **basilisks** (1) large cannon (2) monsters supposed to kill with their gaze **20 griefs** grievances **27 bar** court **31 congreeted** greeted each other **32 demand** ask **33 rub** obstacle. (A term from bowls.)

Dear nurse of arts, plenties, and joyful births,
Should not in this best garden of the world,
Our fertile France, put up her lovely visage? 37
Alas, she hath from France too long been chased,
And all her husbandry doth lie on heaps, 39
Corrupting in its own fertility.
Her vine, the merry cheerer of the heart,
Unprunèd dies; her hedges even-pleachèd, 42
Like prisoners wildly overgrown with hair,
Put forth disordered twigs; her fallow leas 44
The darnel, hemlock, and rank fumitory 45
Doth root upon, while that the coulter rusts 46
That should deracinate such savagery. 47
The even mead, that erst brought sweetly forth 48
The freckled cowslip, burnet, and green clover, 49
Wanting the scythe, all uncorrected, rank, 50
Conceives by idleness, and nothing teems 51
But hateful docks, rough thistles, kecksies, burrs, 52
Losing both beauty and utility.
And all our vineyards, fallows, meads, and hedges, 54
Defective in their natures, grow to wildness. 55
Even so our houses and ourselves and children 56
Have lost, or do not learn for want of time,
The sciences that should become our country, 58
But grow like savages—as soldiers will
That nothing do but meditate on blood—
To swearing and stern looks, diffused attire, 61
And everything that seems unnatural.
Which to reduce into our former favor 63
You are assembled, and my speech entreats
That I may know the let why gentle Peace 65

37 put up show **39 husbandry** cultivated fields, agricultural produce **42 even-pleached** smoothly intertwined **44 fallow leas** uncultivated open fields **45 darnel . . . fumitory** i.e., weeds that grow in cultivated land **46 coulter** cutting blade in front of the plowshare **47 deracinate** root out **48 even mead** level meadow. **erst** formerly **49 burnet** a herb **50 Wanting** lacking **51 Conceives** gives birth (to weeds). **teems** flourishes **52 kecksies** dry-stemmed plants, possibly dried hemlock stalks **54 fallows** land plowed and left lying **55 Defective . . . natures** i.e., perverted from their natural function, which is to grow useful plants **56 houses** households **58 sciences** skills **61 diffused** disordered **63 reduce . . . favor** return to our former good appearance **65 let** hindrance

Should not expel these inconveniences
And bless us with her former qualities.

KING HENRY
If, Duke of Burgundy, you would the peace,
Whose want gives growth to th' imperfections
Which you have cited, you must buy that peace
With full accord to all our just demands,
Whose tenors and particular effects
You have enscheduled briefly in your hands.

BURGUNDY
The King hath heard them, to the which as yet
There is no answer made.

KING HENRY
Well then, the peace,
Which you before so urged, lies in his answer.

FRENCH KING
I have but with a cursitory eye
O'erglanced the articles. Pleaseth Your Grace
To appoint some of your council presently
To sit with us once more, with better heed
To re-survey them, we will suddenly
Pass our accept and peremptory answer.

KING HENRY
Brother, we shall. Go, uncle Exeter,
And brother Clarence, and you, brother Gloucester,
Warwick, and Huntingdon, go with the King,
And take with you free power to ratify,
Augment, or alter, as your wisdoms best
Shall see advantageable for our dignity,
Anything in or out of our demands,
And we'll consign thereto.—Will you, fair sister,
Go with the princes, or stay here with us?

QUEEN ISABEL
Our gracious brother, I will go with them.
Haply a woman's voice may do some good
When articles too nicely urged be stood on.

68 would wish **69 want** lack **72 tenors** general purport. **particular effects** specific details **73 enscheduled** drawn up in writing
77 cursitory cursory, hasty **78 Pleaseth** may it please **81 suddenly** speedily **82 Pass . . . answer** deliver an answer acceptable to us and final, decisive **88 advantageable** advantageous **90 consign** agree, subscribe **93 Haply** perhaps **94 nicely** punctiliously, with insistence on detail. **stood on** insisted on

KING HENRY
Yet leave our cousin Katharine here with us.
She is our capital demand, comprised 96
Within the fore-rank of our articles. 97

QUEEN ISABEL
She hath good leave.

Exeunt omnes. Manent King [*Henry*] *and Katharine* [*with Alice*].

KING HENRY Fair Katharine, and most fair, 98
Will you vouchsafe to teach a soldier terms
Such as will enter at a lady's ear
And plead his love suit to her gentle heart?

KATHARINE Your Majesty shall mock at me. I cannot speak your England.

KING HENRY O fair Katharine, if you will love me soundly with your French heart, I will be glad to hear you confess it brokenly with your English tongue. Do you like me, Kate?

KATHARINE *Pardonnez-moi,* I cannot tell wat is "like me."

KING HENRY An angel is like you, Kate, and you are like an angel.

KATHARINE [*To Alice*] *Que dit-il? Que je suis semblable* 112
à les anges? 113

ALICE *Oui, vraiment, sauf Votre Grâce, ainsi dit-il.* 114

KING HENRY I said so, dear Katharine; and I must not blush to affirm it.

KATHARINE *O bon Dieu! Les langues des hommes sont pleines de tromperies.*

KING HENRY What says she, fair one? That the tongues of men are full of deceits?

ALICE *Oui,* dat de tongues of de mans is be full of deceits. Dat is de Princess.

KING HENRY The Princess is the better Englishwoman. 123
I' faith, Kate, my wooing is fit for thy understanding. I am glad thou canst speak no better English, for if thou couldst, thou wouldst find me such a plain king

96 capital chief **97 fore-rank** first row **98 s.d. omnes** all. **Manent** they remain onstage **112–114 Que . . . ainsi dit-il** What does he say? That I am like the angels? ALICE Yes, truly, save Your Grace, he says so **123 the better Englishwoman** i.e., she has a true Englishwoman's modesty and mistrust of flattery

that thou wouldst think I had sold my farm to buy my crown. I know no ways to mince it in love, but directly to say, "I love you." Then if you urge me farther than to say, "Do you in faith?" I wear out my suit. Give me your answer, i' faith, do, and so clap hands and a bargain. How say you, lady?

KATHARINE *Sauf votre honneur,* me understand well.

KING HENRY Marry, if you would put me to verses or to dance for your sake, Kate, why, you undid me. For the one I have neither words nor measure, and for the other I have no strength in measure, yet a reasonable measure in strength. If I could win a lady at leapfrog, or by vaulting into my saddle with my armor on my back, under the correction of bragging be it spoken, I should quickly leap into a wife. Or if I might buffet for my love, or bound my horse for her favors, I could lay on like a butcher and sit like a jackanapes, never off. But before God, Kate, I cannot look greenly, nor gasp out my eloquence, nor I have no cunning in protestation—only downright oaths, which I never use till urged, nor never break for urging. If thou canst love a fellow of this temper, Kate, whose face is not worth sunburning, that never looks in his glass for love of anything he sees there, let thine eye be thy cook. I speak to thee plain soldier. If thou canst love me for this, take me. If not, to say to thee that I shall die is true; but for thy love, by the Lord, no. Yet I love thee too. And while thou liv'st, dear Kate, take a fellow of plain and uncoined constancy, for he perforce must do thee right, because he hath not the gift to woo in other places. For these fellows of infinite tongue that can rhyme themselves into ladies' favors, they do always reason themselves out again. What? A speaker is but a prater, a rhyme is but a ballad. A good leg will fall,

128 mince it speak coyly **130 wear out my suit** expend all my resources as a wooer **131 clap** clasp **136 measure** meter **137 measure** dance **138 measure** amount **141 buffet** box **142 bound** make prance **143 jackanapes** ape, monkey **144 greenly** like a lovesick youth **146 downright** straightforward **148–149 not worth sunburning** i.e., so ugly that the sun couldn't make it worse **150 cook** (She must dress him with fine qualities as a cook dresses meat.) **155 uncoined** not coined for circulation; also, unalloyed, therefore fixed, steady **160 fall** shrink, lose its shapeliness a straight back will stoop, a black beard will turn white, a curled pate will grow bald, a fair face will wither, a full eye will wax hollow; but a good heart, Kate, is the sun and the moon—or rather the sun and not the moon, for it shines bright and never changes, but keeps his course truly. If thou would have such a one, take me. And take me, take a soldier; take a soldier, take a king. And what sayst thou then to my love? Speak, my fair, and fairly, I pray thee.

KATHARINE Is it possible dat I sould love de *ennemi* of France?

KING HENRY No, it is not possible you should love the enemy of France, Kate; but in loving me you should love the friend of France, for I love France so well that I will not part with a village of it. I will have it all mine. And, Kate, when France is mine and I am yours, then yours is France and you are mine.

KATHARINE I cannot tell wat is dat.

KING HENRY No, Kate? I will tell thee in French, which I am sure will hang upon my tongue like a new-married wife about her husband's neck, hardly to be shook off. *Je quand sur le possession de France, et quand vous avez le possession de moi*—let me see, what then? Saint Denis be my speed!—*donc vôtre est France et vous êtes mienne*. It is as easy for me, Kate, to conquer the kingdom as to speak so much more French. I shall never move thee in French, unless it be to laugh at me.

KATHARINE *Sauf votre honneur, le français que vous parlez, il est meilleur que l'anglais lequel je parle.*

KING HENRY No, faith, is 't not, Kate. But thy speaking of my tongue, and I thine, most truly-falsely, must needs be granted to be much at one. But, Kate, dost thou understand thus much English: Canst thou love me?

KATHARINE I cannot tell.

KING HENRY Can any of your neighbors tell, Kate? I'll

182–185 Je . . . mienne (Henry haltingly translates the last sentence in his previous speech.) **184 Saint Denis** patron saint of France. **be my speed** help me **189–190 Sauf . . . parle** save your honor, the French that you speak is better than the English that I speak **192 truly-falsely** truthfully but incorrectly **193 at one** alike

ask them. Come, I know thou lovest me. And at night, when you come into your closet, you'll question this gentlewoman about me; and I know, Kate, you will to her dispraise those parts in me that you love with your heart. But, good Kate, mock me mercifully, the rather, gentle Princess, because I love thee cruelly. If ever thou beest mine, Kate, as I have a saving faith within me tells me thou shalt, I get thee with scambling, and thou must therefore needs prove a good soldier-breeder. Shall not thou and I, between Saint Denis and Saint George, compound a boy, half French, half English, that shall go to Constantinople and take the Turk by the beard? Shall we not? What sayst thou, my fair flower-de-luce?

KATHARINE I do not know dat.

KING HENRY No; 'tis hereafter to know, but now to promise. Do but now promise, Kate, you will endeavor for your French part of such a boy, and for my English moiety take the word of a king and a bachelor. How answer you, *la plus belle Katharine du monde, mon très cher et devin déesse?*

KATHARINE Your Majestee 'ave *fausse* French enough to deceive de most *sage demoiselle* dat is *en France*.

KING HENRY Now, fie upon my false French! By mine honor, in true English, I love thee, Kate; by which honor I dare not swear thou lovest me, yet my blood begins to flatter me that thou dost, notwithstanding the poor and untempering effect of my visage. Now beshrew my father's ambition! He was thinking of civil wars when he got me; therefore was I created with a stubborn outside, with an aspect of iron, that when I come to woo ladies I fright them. But in faith, Kate, the elder I wax the better I shall appear. My comfort is that old age, that ill layer-up of beauty, can do no more spoil upon my face. Thou hast me, if thou hast me, at the worst; and thou shalt wear me, if thou wear me, better and better. And therefore tell me,

199 closet private chamber **205 scambling** scrambling, struggling **211 flower-de-luce** fleur-de-lis, the emblem of France **217–218 la plus . . . déesse** the most beautiful Katharine in the world, my very dear and divine goddess **219 fausse** i.e., false (both "incorrect" and "deceptive") **225 untempering** unsoftening **228 aspect** appearance

most fair Katharine, will you have me? Put off your
maiden blushes; avouch the thoughts of your heart 236
with the looks of an empress; take me by the hand,
and say, "Harry of England, I am thine." Which word
thou shalt no sooner bless mine ear withal, but I will
tell thee aloud, "England is thine, Ireland is thine,
France is thine, and Henry Plantagenet is thine"—
who, though I speak it before his face, if he be not
fellow with the best king, thou shalt find the best king
of good fellows. Come, your answer in broken music! 244
For thy voice is music, and thy English broken. Therefore, queen of all, Katharine, break thy mind to me in 246
broken English. Wilt thou have me?

KATHARINE Dat is as it shall please de *roi mon père.* 248

KING HENRY Nay, it will please him well, Kate. It shall
please him, Kate.

KATHARINE Den it sall also content me.

KING HENRY Upon that I kiss your hand, and I call you
my queen. [*He attempts to kiss her hand.*]

KATHARINE *Laissez, mon seigneur, laissez, laissez! Ma* 254
foi, je ne veux point que vous abaissiez votre grandeur 255
en baisant la main d'une—Notre Seigneur!—indigne 256
serviteur. Excusez-moi, je vous supplie, mon très 257
puissant seigneur. 258

KING HENRY Then I will kiss your lips, Kate.

KATHARINE *Les dames et demoiselles pour être baisées* 260
devant leur noces, il n'est pas la coutume de France. 261

KING HENRY [*To Alice*] Madam my interpreter, what
says she?

ALICE Dat it is not be de fashion *pour les* ladies of
France—I cannot tell wat is *baiser en* Anglish.

KING HENRY To kiss.

ALICE Your Majestee *entendre* bettre *que moi.* 267

KING HENRY It is not a fashion for the maids in France
to kiss before they are married, would she say?

236 avouch guarantee **244 broken music** music in parts **246 break** open **248 de roi mon père** the King my father **254–258 Laissez . . . seigneur** don't, my lord, don't, don't; by my faith, I do not wish to lower your greatness by kissing the hand of an—Our dear Lord!—unworthy servant; excuse me, I beg you, my most powerful lord **260–261 Les dames . . . France** it is not customary in France for ladies and young girls to be kissed before their marriage **267 entendre . . . moi** understands better than I

ALICE *Oui, vraiment.* 270
KING HENRY O Kate, nice customs curtsy to great kings. 271
Dear Kate, you and I cannot be confined within the
weak list of a country's fashion. We are the makers of 273
manners, Kate; and the liberty that follows our places 274
stops the mouth of all find-faults, as I will do yours, for upholding the nice fashion of your country in denying me a kiss. Therefore, patiently and yielding. [*He kisses her.*] You have witchcraft in your lips, Kate. There is more eloquence in a sugar touch of them than in the tongues of the French council, and they should sooner persuade Harry of England than a general petition of monarchs.—Here comes your father.

Enter the French power and the English lords.

BURGUNDY God save Your Majesty! My royal cousin, teach you our princess English?

KING HENRY I would have her learn, my fair cousin, how perfectly I love her, and that is good English.

BURGUNDY Is she not apt?

KING HENRY Our tongue is rough, coz, and my condi- 288
tion is not smooth; so that, having neither the voice 289
nor the heart of flattery about me, I cannot so conjure up the spirit of love in her that he will appear in his true likeness.

BURGUNDY Pardon the frankness of my mirth, if I answer you for that. If you would conjure in her, you 294
must make a circle; if conjure up love in her in his true
likeness, he must appear naked and blind. Can you
blame her then, being a maid yet rosed over with the 297
virgin crimson of modesty, if she deny the appearance
of a naked blind boy in her naked seeing self? It were,
my lord, a hard condition for a maid to consign to. 300
KING HENRY Yet they do wink and yield, as love is 301
blind and enforces.

BURGUNDY They are then excused, my lord, when they see not what they do.

270 Oui, vraiment yes, truly **271 nice** fastidious **273 list** limit, barrier **274 follows our places** attends our (high) rank **288–289 condition** personality **294 conjure in her** (with bawdy double meaning, continued in *circle, hard,* etc.) **297 yet rosed over** still blushing **300 consign** agree **301 wink** close the eyes

KING HENRY Then, good my lord, teach your cousin to consent winking.

BURGUNDY I will wink on her to consent, my lord, if you will teach her to know my meaning; for maids, well summered and warm kept, are like flies at Bartholomew-tide: blind, though they have their eyes, and then they will endure handling, which before would not abide looking on.

KING HENRY This moral ties me over to time and a hot summer; and so I shall catch the fly, your cousin, in the latter end, and she must be blind too.

BURGUNDY As love is, my lord, before it loves.

KING HENRY It is so; and you may, some of you, thank love for my blindness, who cannot see many a fair French city for one fair French maid that stands in my way.

FRENCH KING Yes, my lord, you see them perspectively, the cities turned into a maid; for they are all girdled with maiden walls that war hath never entered.

KING HENRY Shall Kate be my wife?

FRENCH KING So please you.

KING HENRY I am content, so the maiden cities you talk of may wait on her. So the maid that stood in the way for my wish shall show me the way to my will.

FRENCH KING
We have consented to all terms of reason.

KING HENRY Is 't so, my lords of England?

WESTMORLAND
The King hath granted every article:
His daughter first, and then in sequel all,
According to their firm proposèd natures.

EXETER
Only he hath not yet subscribèd this:

309 summered nurtured **309–310 Bartholomew-tide** August 24 (when flies, bees, etc., are sluggish) **316 As . . . loves** (Love is blind before it loves because it cannot yet see the beloved, and because love has not yet opened the lover's eyes.) **318–320 who . . . my way** (i.e., Henry is willing to forgo several French cities in exchange for Katharine that he might otherwise take possession of in the negotiations.)
321 perspectively i.e., distorted by a perspective glass **323 maiden** unbreached **327 wait on her** attend her, go along with her (as part of her dowry) **333 According . . . natures** exactly as specified in the proposals **334 subscribèd** agreed to

Where Your Majesty demands that the King of France, having any occasion to write for matter of grant, shall 336
name Your Highness in this form and with this addi- 337
tion, in French, *Notre très cher fils Henri, Roi* 338
d'Angleterre, Héritier de France; and thus in Latin, 339
Praeclarissimus filius noster Henricus, Rex Angliae et Haeres Franciae.

FRENCH KING
Nor this I have not, brother, so denied 342
But your request shall make me let it pass. 343

KING HENRY
I pray you then, in love and dear alliance,
Let that one article rank with the rest,
And thereupon give me your daughter.

FRENCH KING
Take her, fair son, and from her blood raise up
Issue to me, that the contending kingdoms
Of France and England, whose very shores look pale
With envy of each other's happiness,
May cease their hatred, and this dear conjunction
Plant neighborhood and Christian-like accord
In their sweet bosoms, that never war advance
His bleeding sword twixt England and fair France.

LORDS Amen!

KING HENRY
Now, welcome, Kate; and bear me witness all,
That here I kiss her as my sovereign queen. [*Kiss.*]
Flourish.

QUEEN ISABEL
God, the best maker of all marriages,
Combine your hearts in one, your realms in one!
As man and wife, being two, are one in love,
So be there twixt your kingdoms such a spousal 361
That never may ill office, or fell jealousy, 362
Which troubles oft the bed of blessèd marriage,
Thrust in between the paction of these kingdoms 364
To make divorce of their incorporate league;

336 for . . . grant in official deeds granting title to land and the like **337–338 addition** title **338–339 Notre . . . France** our very dear son Henry, King of England, Heir of France **342 so** so firmly **343 But** but that **361 spousal** marriage **362 ill office** unfriendly dealings. **fell** cruel **364 paction** alliance, compact

That English may as French, French Englishmen,
Receive each other. God speak this "Amen"!

ALL Amen!

KING HENRY

Prepare we for our marriage, on which day,
My lord of Burgundy, we'll take your oath,
And all the peers', for surety of our leagues.
Then shall I swear to Kate, and you to me;
And may our oaths well kept and prosperous be!

Sennet. Exeunt.

Epilogue *Enter Chorus.*

CHORUS

Thus far, with rough and all-unable pen,
Our bending author hath pursued the story, 2
In little room confining mighty men,
Mangling by starts the full course of their glory. 4
Small time, but in that small most greatly lived 5
This star of England. Fortune made his sword,
By which the world's best garden he achieved, 7
And of it left his son imperial lord.
Henry the Sixth, in infant bands crowned King 9
Of France and England, did this king succeed;
Whose state so many had the managing
That they lost France and made his England bleed,
Which oft our stage hath shown; and, for their sake, 13
In your fair minds let this acceptance take. [*Exit.*] 14

Epilogue.
2 bending i.e., under the weight of his task **4 by starts** in fits and starts, in fragments **5 Small time** (Henry V ruled for only nine years, dying at the age of thirty-five.) **7 best garden** i.e., France **9 infant bands** swaddling clothes **13 Which . . . shown** (Refers to the three parts of *King Henry VI.*) **for their sake** i.e., since you liked them **14 this acceptance take** this play meet with your approval

Date and Text

An entry in the Stationers' Register, the official record book of the London Company of Stationers (booksellers and printers), for August 4, 1600, provides that "Henry the ffift" and three other plays belonging to the Lord Chamberlain's men (Shakespeare's acting company) are "to be staied" from publication until further permission is granted. Evidently the Chamberlain's men were anxious to prevent unauthorized publication. They did not succeed, however, in preventing the appearance of a pirated text of *Henry V*. An entry in the Stationers' Register for August 14 assigns to Thomas Pavier an already published work entitled "The historye of Henry the Vth with the battell of Agencourt." The quarto volume to which this entry refers is the following:

> THE CHRONICLE History of Henry the fift, With his battell fought at *Agin Court* in *France*. Togither with *Auntient Pistoll. As it hath bene sundry times playd by the Right honorable the Lord Chamberlaine his seruants.* LONDON Printed by *Thomas Creede,* for Tho. Millington, and Iohn Busby. And are to be sold at his house in Carter Lane, next the Powle head. 1600.

The text of this play is manifestly corrupt. It is considerably shorter than the First Folio version and completely omits the choruses and three entire scenes (1.1, 3.1, and 4.2). The remainder seems to have been put together by memorial reconstruction. This bad quarto served as the basis for a second quarto printed by Thomas Creed for Thomas Pavier in 1602 and a third printed by William Jaggard for Thomas Pavier in 1619 but fraudulently dated 1608. The Folio text was printed seemingly from an authorial manuscript, perhaps with occasional reference to the third quarto (which contains some potentially troublesome contamination). The Folio text is thus the most reliable version, though the first quarto is also an interesting witness, especially for visual effects recorded in its stage directions, for a few readings in the text, and for verse lineation of Pistol's speeches.

Francis Meres does not mention the play in 1598 in his

Palladis Tamia: Wit's Treasury (a slender volume on contemporary literature and art; valuable because it lists most of the plays of Shakespeare's that existed at that time), though he does mention *"Henry the IV."* The epilogue to *2 Henry IV* (written probably in 1597) promises that "our humble author will continue the story, with Sir John in it, and make you merry with fair Katharine of France"; and since the prediction is not really accurate regarding Falstaff, we can be reasonably certain that Shakespeare had not yet begun *Henry V* in 1597. An allusion in the chorus of Act 5 to "the General of our gracious Empress," who may in good time come home from Ireland with "rebellion broachèd on his sword," has been taken by virtually all editors to refer to the Earl of Essex, who left in March of 1599 to quell the Irish rebellion headed by Tyrone. Although Essex returned on September 28 of that same year having failed utterly in his assignment, the departure of such a charismatic figure could have inspired Shakespeare's praising remark. A minority view holds that the choruses (which do not appear in the bad quarto of 1600) could have been written later in 1601 for Essex's far more victorious successor, Lord Mountjoy (see Warren D. Smith's article on *Henry V* in *JEGP*, 1954). Still, Essex was more center stage during those exciting years, more likely to have been the subject of adulation. In any case the play itself must have been written before August of 1600, most probably in 1599. The reference to "this wooden O" in the Chorus of Act 1 is often thought to be Shakespeare's compliment to the company's new theater, the Globe, which was ready for their use probably in 1599; but the play may have been produced at the Curtain instead.

Textual Notes

These textual notes are not a historical collation, either of the early quartos and folios or of more recent editions; they are simply a record of departures in this edition from the copy text. The reading adopted in this edition appears in boldface, followed by the rejected reading from the copy text, i.e., the First Folio. Only major alterations in punctuation are noted. Changes in lineation are not indicated, nor are some minor and obvious typographical errors.

Abbreviations used:
F the First Folio
Q the quarto of 1600
s.d. stage direction
s.p. speech prefix

Copy text: the First Folio.

Prologue.1 s.p. Chorus [not in F; also in prologues to other acts]

1.2. 38 succedant succedaul **45 Elbe** Elue [also at l. 52] **115 s.p. Ely** Bish **131 blood** Bloods **163 her** their **166 s.p. A Lord** Bish. Ely **197 majesty** Maiesties **212 End** [Q] And **237 s.p. First Ambassador** Amb [also at l. 245] **310 s.d. Flourish** [at the beginning of 2.0 in F]

2.1. 23 mare [Q] name **28 s.p. Nym** [Q; not in F] **42, 43 Iceland** Island **73 thee defy** [Q] defie thee **80 enough** enough to **83 you** your **105–106** [Q; not in F] **betting** beating [Q] **116 that's** that

2.2. 29 s.p. Grey Kni **87 furnish him** furnish **107 a** an **108 whoop** hoope **114 All** And **139 mark the** make thee **147 Henry** [Q] Thomas **148 Masham** [Q] Marsham **159 Which I** Which **176 have sought** [Q] sought **181 s.d. Exeunt** Exit

2.3. 16 'a babbled a Table **24 upward** vp-peer'd **32 s.p. Hostess** Woman **48 word** world

2.4. 1 s.p. [and elsewhere] French King King **132 Louvre** Louer **146 s.d. Flourish** [at the beginning of 3.0 in F]

3.0. [here F has "Actus Secundus"] **6 fanning** fayning **35 eke** eech

3.1. 7 conjure commune **17 noblest** Noblish **24 men** me **32 Straining** Straying

3.2. 25 runs wins **67 s.p. [and elsewhere in scene] Fluellen** Welch **82 s.p. [and elsewhere in scene] Jamy** Scot **87 s.p. [and elsewhere in scene] Macmorris** Irish **102 quite** quit **112 Chrish** Christ

3.3. 32 heady headly **35 Defile** Desire **43** [here F has s.d. "Enter Gouernour"] **54 all. For** all for

3.4. 1–2 parles bien bien parlas [throughout the play, the French has been somewhat modernized, besides the emendations listed here] **8 Et les doigts** [assigned to Alice in F] **9 s.p. Alice** Kat **les doigts** e doyt **10 souviendrai**

souemeray **12 s.p. Katharine** Alice **13 j'ai** Kath. l'ay **16 Nous** [not in F] **40 pas déjà** y desia **42 Non** Nome **46 Sauf** Sans

3.5. 11 de du **26 "Poor" may** Poore **43 Vaudemont** Vandemont **45 Foix** Loys **46 knights** Kings

3.6. 31 her [Q] his **37 is make** [Q] makes **111–112 lenity** Leuitie

3.7. 12 pasterns postures **14 qui a** ches **59 lief** liue **65 et** est **truie** leuye

4.0. [here F has "Actus Tertius"] **16 name** nam'd **20 cripple** creeple **27 Presenteth** Presented

4.1. 3 Good God **95 Thomas** Iohn **158 deaths** [Q] death **propose** purpose **227 s.d. Exeunt** Exit [at l. 222 in F] **243 adoration** Odoration **289 ere** of **307 friends** friend

4.2. 4 eaux ewes **6 Cieux** cein **47 drooping** dropping **49 gimmaled** Iymold

4.3. 12 [placed after l. 14 in F] **48** [Q; not in F] **124 'em** vm

4.4. 2 êtes estes le **15 Or** for **36 à cette heure** asture **37 couper** couppes **54 l'avez** layt a **57 remercîments** remercious **58 j'ai tombé** Ie intombe **59 très-distingué** tres distinie **68 Suivez-vous** Saaue-vous

4.5. 2 perdu . . . perdu perdia . . . perdie **3 Mort de** Mor Dieu **16 by a** [Q] a base **24 s.d. Exeunt** Exit

4.6. 34 mistful mixtfull

4.7. [F has "Actus Quartus" here] **69 s.p. [and elsewhere in this scene] Montjoy** Her **77 the** with **109 countryman** Countrymen **114 God** Good **123 'a live** aliue [also in l. 126] **161 an 't** and

4.8. 100 Vaudemont Vandemont **113 we** me **121 in my** [Q] my

5.0. 29 but but by

5.1. 39 By Jesu [Q] I say **69 begun** began **88 swear** swore

5.2. 1 s.p. [and throughout scene] King Henry King **12 s.p. [and throughout scene] Queen Isabel** Quee **12 England** Ireland **21 s.p. [also elsewhere] King Henry** Eng **50 all** withall **61 diffused** defused **77 cursitory** curselarie **98 s.d. Manent** Manet **114 s.p. [and elsewhere] Alice** Lady **190 meilleur** melieus **265 baiser** buisse **323 hath never** hath **364 paction** Pation

Epilogue s.p. Chorus [not in F]

Shakespeare's Sources

Shakespeare's principal historical source for *Henry V*, as for *Richard II* and the *Henry IV* plays, was the 1587 edition of Raphael Holinshed's *Chronicles*. Holinshed's account of Henry V, however, had depended so heavily on Edward Hall's *The Union of the two Noble and Illustre Families of Lancaster and York* (1542) that we sometimes have difficulty knowing whether Shakespeare consulted Holinshed or Hall. He was certainly familiar with both. Shakespeare's sources all acclaim Henry V a hero-king. Samuel Daniel's *The First Four Books of the Civil Wars* (1595), which Shakespeare may have used for his account of the treasonous plot against Henry (2.2), also praises the King in encomiastic terms.

Shakespeare follows the order of events laid down in Holinshed and Hall: the personal rivalry between Henry and the French Dauphin, Henry's request for reassurance from the clergy as to the legitimacy of the war, the maneuvering of the clergy to forestall a bill in Parliament threatening to seize church land, the foiling of a plot against Henry's life, the siege of Harfleur, the glorious victory at Agincourt. Both Holinshed and Hall offer Shakespeare many particulars about the English claim to France: in both accounts, the Archbishop quotes the law—*In terram Salicam mulieres ne succedant*—and goes on at length about King Pharamond, the rivers Elbe and Saale, King Pepin, Hugh Capet, the Book of Numbers, and the rest. On the other hand, Shakespeare omits a three-year campaign that historically intervened between Agincourt and the peace treaty of Troyes. He passes over the Lollard controversy in England, with the execution of Sir John Oldcastle. And, of course, he adds unforgettable characters that we do not find in the chronicles—Welshmen, Irishmen, Scots, common soldiers, thieves—who show the unity of the British nation under King Henry's charismatic leadership.

For many of his additions to the chronicles, Shakespeare was indebted to the anonymous *The Famous Victories of Henry the Fifth* (c. 1588). This old play, not registered until 1594 and not printed until 1598, exists today only in a corrupt text; quite possibly Shakespeare knew a fuller and more authentic version that would have given him still more material. Other plays may have existed on the subject, for the Admiral's men (a rival acting company) acted a "harey the v" in 1595 and 1596 that may or may not have been *The Famous Victories*. In any event, the relationship between *Henry V* and *Famous Victories* is at times close. *Famous Victories* omits Henry's long campaign between Agincourt and the final peace treaty, as does Shakespeare's play. The Archbishop of *Famous Victories* discusses the French claim just before the arrival of the French Ambassador with the tennis balls. (In Holinshed, the tennis-ball incident occurs first, at Kenilworth, whereas the Archbishop's lecture occurs sometime later at a meeting of Parliament in Leicester.) Henry assures the French Ambassador that he has "free liberty and license to speak." To the Dauphin's insolent gift, taunting Henry about his wild youth, the King suavely replies that "My lord prince Dauphin is very pleasant with me," and promises to repay the insult with balls of brass and iron. (Holinshed mentions this apparently nonhistorical legend only briefly.) When the French noblemen assembled at the French court hear of Henry's arrival on their shores, they tremble with fear even though the Dauphin recklessly scoffs at so young and prodigal a king. Henry is accompanied to France by a ludicrous assortment of London artisans and thieves, such as John Cobbler, who bids farewell to his wife in a comic scene similar to Pistol's parting from the Hostess, and Derick, who turns the tables on a French soldier much as Pistol deals with Monsieur le Fer. When King Henry woos Katharine of France, he protests to her that he cannot speak flatteringly because he is a plain soldier. She asks in return: "How should I love him that hath dealt so hardly / With my father?" Despite these resemblances, however, Shakespeare's *Henry V* is incomparably superior to the old play and contains many original scenes and characters, such as King Henry's touring of his camp incognito, the quarrel between Henry and Williams, and above all the scenes involving Fluellen and his fellow-captains.

Other possible sources include the *Henrici Quinti Angliae Regis Gesta* written by a chaplain in Henry V's army, the *Vita et Gesta Henrici Quinti* erroneously ascribed to Thomas Elmham, the *Vita Henrici Quinti* by "Titus Livius," translated 1513 (in which the French brag about their horses and armor), a ballad called "The Battle of Agincourt" (c. 1530), and *The Annals of Cornelius Tacitus*, translated 1598 (in which Germanicus walks disguised through his camp at night "to sound the soldiers' mind" and hears his leadership praised).

The Third Volume of Chronicles (1587 edition)

Compiled by Raphael Holinshed

Henry the Fifth

Any departures from the original text are noted with an asterisk and appear at the bottom of the page in boldface; original readings are in roman.

[Holinshed begins with an account of Henry's birth, his reformation, his coronation, and his banishment of the "misruly mates of dissolute order and life" he had known before. The King orders that King Richard II's body and that of Anne, his first wife, be reinterred at Westminster with great ceremony.]

Whilst in the Lent season[1] the King lay[2] at Kenilworth,* there came to him from Charles, Dauphin of France, certain ambassadors, that brought with them a barrel of Paris balls,[3] which from their master they presented to him for a token that was taken in very ill part, as sent in scorn to signify that it was more meet for the King to pass the time with such childish exercise than to attempt any worthy exploit. Wherefore the King wrote to him that ere aught long he would toss him some London balls that perchance should shake the walls of the best court in France. . . .

In the second year of his reign, King Henry called his high court of Parliament, the last day of April,[4] in the town of Leicester, in which Parliament many profitable laws were concluded, and many petitions moved were for that time deferred. Amongst which one was that a bill exhibited in the Parliament holden at Westminster in the eleventh year of King Henry the Fourth (which, by reason the King was then troubled with civil discord, came to none effect) might now with good deliberation be pondered and brought to some good conclusion. The effect of which supplication was that the temporal lands devoutly given and disordinately[5] spent by religious and other spiritual persons should be seized into the King's hands, sith[6] the same might suffice to maintain, to the honor of the King and defense of the realm, fifteen earls, fifteen hundred knights, six thou-

***Kenilworth** Killingworth

1 Lent season (in early 1414) **2 lay** resided **3 Paris balls** tennis balls
4 April (in 1414) **5 disordinately** prodigally, inordinately **6 sith** since

sand and two hundred esquires, and a hundred almshouses for relief only of the poor, impotent, and needy persons, and the King to have clearly[7] to his coffers twenty thousand pounds, with many other provisions and values of religious houses which I pass over.

This bill was much noted and more feared among the religious sort, whom surely it touched very near, and therefore, to find remedy against it, they determined to assay all ways to put by and overthrow this bill; wherein they thought best to try if they might move the King's mood with some sharp invention, that he should not regard the importunate petitions of the commons. Whereupon, on a day in the Parliament, Henry Chichele, Archbishop of Canterbury, made a pithy oration wherein he declared how not only the duchies of Normandy and Aquitaine with the counties of Anjou and Maine and the country of Gascony were by undoubted title appertaining to the King, as to the lawful and only heir of the same, but also the whole realm of France, as heir to his great-grandfather, King Edward the Third.

Herein did he much inveigh against the surmised[8] and false feigned law Salic, which the Frenchmen allege ever against the kings of England in bar of their just title to the crown of France. The very words of that supposed law are these: *In terram Salicam mulieres ne succedant,* that is to say, "Into the Salic land let not women succeed." Which the French glossers expound to be the realm of France, and that this law was made by King Pharamond; whereas yet their own authors affirm that the land Salic is in Germany, between the rivers of Elbe and Saale, and that when Charles the Great had overcome the Saxons he placed there certain Frenchmen, which having in disdain the dishonest[9] manners of the German women, made a law that the females should not succeed to any inheritance within that land, which at this day is called Meissen. So that, if this be true, this law was not made for the realm of France, nor the Frenchmen possessed the land Salic till four hundred and one-and-twenty years after the death of Pharamond, the supposed maker of this Salic law; for this Pharamond deceased in the year 426, and Charles the Great subdued the

7 clearly entirely **8 surmised** devised falsely **9 dishonest** unchaste

Saxons and placed the Frenchmen in those parts beyond the river of Saale in the year 805.

Moreover, it appeareth by their own writers that King Pepin, which deposed Childeric, claimed the crown of France as heir general for that he was descended of Blithild, daughter to King Clothair the First. Hugh Capet also, who usurped the crown upon[10] Charles, Duke of Lorraine, the sole heir male of the line and stock of Charles the Great, to make his title seem true and appear good, though indeed it was stark naught, conveyed himself as heir to the Lady Lingard, daughter to King Charlemagne, son to Lewis the Emperor that was son to Charles the Great. King Lewis also, the Tenth,[11] otherwise called Saint Lewis, being very heir to the said usurper Hugh Capet, could never be satisfied in his conscience how he might justly keep and possess the crown of France till he was persuaded and fully instructed that Queen Isabel his grandmother was lineally descended of the Lady Ermengard, daughter and heir to the above-named Charles, Duke of Lorraine, by the which marriage the blood and line of Charles the Great was again united and restored to the crown and scepter of France; so that more clear than the sun it openly appeareth that the title of King Pepin, the claim of Hugh Capet, the possession of Lewis, yea, and the French kings to this day, are derived and conveyed from the heir female, though they would under the color of such a feigned law bar the kings and princes of this realm of England of their right and lawful inheritance.

The Archbishop further alleged out of the Book of Numbers this saying: "When a man dyeth without a son, let the inheritance descend to his daughter." At length, having said sufficiently for the proof of the King's just and lawful title to the crown of France, he exhorted him to advance forth his banner to fight for his right, to conquer his inheritance, to spare neither blood, sword, nor fire, sith his war was just, his cause good, and his claim true. And to the intent his loving chaplains and obedient subjects of the spirituality might show themselves willing and desirous to aid His Majesty for the recovery of his ancient right and true

10 upon from **11 Tenth** (Actually Ninth; an error in Holinshed which Shakespeare copies in 1.2.77.)

inheritance, the Archbishop declared that in their spiritual convocation they had granted to His Highness such a sum of money as never by no spiritual persons was to any prince before those days given or advanced.

When the Archbishop had ended his prepared tale, Ralph Neville, Earl of Westmorland and as then Lord Warden of the Marches against Scotland, understanding that the King, upon a courageous desire to recover his right in France, would surely take the wars in hand, thought good to move the King to begin first with Scotland, and thereupon declared how easy a matter it should be to make a conquest there and how greatly the same should further his wished purpose for the subduing of the Frenchmen, concluding the sum of his tale with this old saying, that "Whoso will France win, must with Scotland first begin." Many matters he touched, as well to show how necessary the conquest of Scotland should be as also to prove how just a cause the King had to attempt it, trusting to persuade the King and all other to be of his opinion.

But after he had made an end, the Duke of Exeter, uncle to the King, a man well learned and wise (who had been sent into Italy by his father, intending that he should have been a priest), replied against the Earl of Westmorland's oration, affirming rather that he which would Scotland win, he with France must first begin. For if the King might once compass the conquest of France, Scotland could not long resist; so that conquer France, and Scotland would soon obey. For where should the Scots learn policy and skill to defend themselves if they had not their bringing up and training in France? If the French pensions maintained not the Scottish nobility, in what case should they be? Then take away France and the Scots will soon be tamed, France being to Scotland the same that the sap is to the tree, which being taken away the tree must needs die and wither.

To be brief, the Duke of Exeter used such earnest and pithy persuasions to induce the King and the whole assembly of the Parliament to credit his words that immediately after he had made an end all the company began to cry, "War! War! France! France!" Hereby the bill for dissolving of religious houses was clearly set aside and nothing thought on but only the recovering of France, according as the Archbishop had moved.

[At this Parliament, continued at Westminster, the King makes his uncle John the Duke of Bedford, his brother Humphrey the Duke of Gloucester, and Thomas Beaufort, Marquess Dorset, the Duke of Exeter. Meantime English ambassadors present Henry's demands to the French King, offering a marriage between King Henry and Lady Katharine of France in return for the surrender of certain French territories claimed by the English. The English ambassadors return to England with no answer as yet from the French, and Henry determines to prepare an invasion. The French, led by the Dauphin because his father "was fallen into his old disease of frenzy," prepare to resist. They send an embassage meanwhile to Henry with counterproposals (including still the marriage of Lady Katharine and Henry), but the offer of territories is insufficient and is refused. Henry replies to the French ambassador, the Archbishop of Bourges, in ringing terms:]

"I little esteem your French brags and less set[12] by your power and strength; I know perfectly my right to my region, which you usurp; and except[13] you deny the apparent[14] truth, so do yourselves also.[15] If you neither do nor will know it, yet God and the world knoweth it. The power of your master you see, but my puissance ye have not yet tasted. If he have loving subjects, I am, I thank God, not unstored of the same;[16] and I say this unto you, that before one year pass, I trust to make the highest crown of your country to stoop and the proudest miter to learn his humiliatedo.[17] In the meantime tell this to the usurper your master, that within three months I will enter into France as into mine own true and lawful patrimony, appointing[18] to acquire the same not with brag of words but with deeds of men and dint of sword by the aid of God, in whom is my whole trust and confidence. Further matter at this present I impart not unto you, saving that with warrant you may depart surely and safely into your country, where I trust sooner to visit you than you shall have cause to bid me wel-

12 less set set even less store **13 except** unless **14 apparent** self-evident **15 so . . . also** i.e., you know it just as well as I do **16 not . . . same** i.e., not lacking in loving subjects of my own **17 his humiliatedo** its humiliation **18 appointing** preparing

come." With this answer the ambassadors, sore displeased in their minds although they were highly entertained and liberally rewarded, departed into their country, reporting to the Dauphin how they had sped.[19]

[The King makes preparations to defend England against the Scots during the French campaign. Leaving the realm under the governance of his stepmother, the Queen Mother, Henry proceeds to Southampton and dispatches one last embassy to the French.]

When King Henry had fully furnished his navy with men, munition, and other provisions, perceiving that his captains misliked nothing so much as delay, he* determined his soldiers to go[20] a-shipboard and away. But see the hap! The night before the day appointed for their departure, he was credibly informed that Richard, Earl of Cambridge, brother to Edward, Duke of York, and Henry, Lord Scroop of Masham, Lord Treasurer, with Thomas Grey, a knight of Northumberland, being confederate together, had conspired his death. Wherefore he caused them to be apprehended. The said Lord Scroop was in such favor with the King that he admitted him sometimes to be his bedfellow, in whose fidelity the King reposed such trust that when any private or public counsel was in hand, this lord had much in the determination of it. For he represented so great gravity in his countenance, such modesty in behavior, and so virtuous zeal to all godliness in his talk that whatsoever he said was thought for the most part necessary to be done and followed. Also the said Sir Thomas Grey, as some write, was of the King's Privy Council.

These prisoners, upon their examination, confessed that for a great sum of money which they had received of the French King, they intended verily either to have delivered the King alive into the hands of his enemies or else to have murdered him before he should arrive in the duchy of Normandy. When King Henry had heard all things opened[21] which he desired to know, he caused all his nobility to come before his presence, before whom he caused to be brought

***he** [not in 1587 ed.]

19 sped fared **20 determined . . . go** determined that his soldiers should go **21 opened** made manifest

the offenders also, and to them said: "Having thus conspired the death and destruction of me, which am the head of the realm and governor of the people, it may be, no doubt, but that you likewise have sworn the confusion of all that are here with me and also the desolation of your own country. To what horror (O Lord) for any true English heart to consider, that such an execrable iniquity should ever so bewrap you as, for pleasing of a foreign enemy, to imbrue your hands in your blood and to ruin your own native soil! Revenge herein touching my person though I seek not, yet for the safeguard of you, my dear friends, and for due preservation of all sorts,[22] I am by office to cause example to be showed. Get ye hence, therefore, ye poor miserable wretches, to the receiving of your just reward, wherein God's majesty give you grace of his mercy and repentance of your heinous offenses." And so immediately they were had[23] to execution.

This done, the King, calling his lords again afore him, said[24] in words few and with good grace. Of his enterprises he recounted the honor and glory whereof they with him were to be partakers; the great confidence he had in their noble minds, which could not but remember them of [25] the famous feats that their ancestors aforetime in France had achieved, whereof the due report forever recorded remained yet in register;[26] the great mercy of God that had so graciously revealed unto him the treason at hand, whereby the true hearts of those afore him made[27] so eminent and apparent in his eye as they might be right sure he would never forget it; the doubt[28] of danger to be nothing in respect of the certainty of honor that they should acquire, wherein himself (as they saw) in person would be lord and leader, through God's grace, to whose majesty, as chiefly was known the equity of his demand,[29] even so to His mercy did he only recommend the success of his travels.[30] When the King had said, all the noblemen kneeled down and promised faithfully to serve him, duly to obey him, and

22 sorts ranks **23 had** taken **24 said** spoke **25 remember them of** recall to their minds **26 in register** in recorded history **27 made** i.e., were made, or being made **28 doubt** fear **29 as chiefly . . . demand** i.e., just as to God alone was fully known the justice of Henry's claim to France **30 travels** (with the idea also of *travails,* labors)

rather to die than to suffer him to fall into the hands of his enemies.

This done, the King thought that surely all treason and conspiracy had been utterly extinct, not suspecting the fire which was newly kindled and ceased not to increase till at length it burst out into such a flame that, catching the beams of his house and family, his line and stock was clean consumed to ashes. Divers[31] write that Richard, Earl of Cambridge, did not conspire with the Lord Scroop and Thomas Grey for the murdering of King Henry to please the French King withal, but only to the intent to exalt to the crown his brother-in-law Edmund, Earl of March, as heir to Lionel, Duke of Clarence; after the death of which Earl of March, for divers secret impediments not able to have issue, the Earl of Cambridge was sure that the crown should come to him by his wife and to his children of her begotten. And therefore, as was thought, he rather confessed himself for need of money to be corrupted by the French King than he would declare his inward mind and open his very intent and secret purpose which, if it were espied, he saw plainly that the Earl of March should have tasted of the same cup that he had drunken, and what should have come to his own children he much doubted.[32] Therefore, destitute of comfort and in despair of life, to save his children he feigned that tale, desiring rather to save his succession than himself, which he did indeed, for his son Richard, Duke of York, not privily but openly claimed the crown, and Edward his son both claimed it and gained it, as after it shall appear. . . .

But now to proceed with King Henry's doings. After this, when the wind came about prosperous to his purpose, he caused the mariners to weigh up anchors and hoise up sails and to set forward with a thousand ships on the vigil of Our Lady Day the Assumption,[33] and took land at Caux, commonly called Kidcaux, where the river of Seine runneth into the sea, without resistance. At his first coming on land, he caused proclamation to be made that no person should be so hardy,[34] on pain of death, either to take anything out of any church that belonged to the same or to hurt or do any violence either to priests, women, or any such as should be

31 Divers various (authors) **32 doubted** feared **33 Our Lady Day the Assumption** 15 August **34 hardy** audacious

found without weapon or armor and not ready to make resistance; also that no man should renew any quarrel or strife whereby any fray might arise to the disquieting of the army.

The next day after his landing, he marched toward the town of Harfleur, standing on the river of Seine between two hills. He besieged it on every side. . . .

The French King, being advertised that King Henry was arrived on that coast, sent in all haste the Lord Delabreth, Constable of France, the Seneschal of France, the Lord Boucicault, Marshal of France, the Seneschal of Hainault, the Lord Ligny, with other, which fortified towns with men, victuals, and artillery on all those frontiers towards the sea. And hearing that Harfleur was besieged, they came to the castle of Caudebec, being not far from Harfleur, to the intent they might succor their friends which were besieged by some policy or means. But the Englishmen, notwithstanding all the damage that that Frenchmen could work against them, forayed the country, spoiled the villages, bringing many a rich prey to the camp before Harfleur. And daily was the town assaulted, for the Duke of Gloucester, to whom the order of the seige was committed, made three mines under the ground and, approaching to the walls with his engines and ordnance,[35] would not suffer them within to take any rest.

For although they with their countermining somewhat disappointed the Englishmen and came to fight with them hand to hand within the mines so that they went no further forward with that work, yet they were so enclosed on each side, as well by water as land, that succor they saw could none come to them. . . .

The captains within the town, perceiving that they were not able long to resist the continual assaults of the Englishmen, knowing that their walls were undermined and like to be overthrown . . . at the first requested a truce until Sunday next following the feast of Saint Michael,[36] in which meantime, if no succor came to remove the siege, they would undertake to deliver the town into the King's hands, their lives and goods saved.

35 mines . . . engines and ordnance tunnels . . . catapults and artillery
36 feast of Saint Michael 29 September

The King advertised hereof, sent them word that, except they would surrender the town to him the morrow next ensuing without any condition, they should spend no more time in talk about the matter. But yet at length, through the earnest suit of the French lords, the King was contented to grant them truce until nine of the clock the next Sunday, being the two-and-twentieth of September, with condition that if in the meantime no rescue came, they should yield the town at that hour with their bodies and goods to stand at the King's pleasure. And for assurance thereof they delivered into the King's hands thirty of their best captains and merchants within that town as pledges.

[Since the Dauphin is unable to relieve the English siege of Harfleur, the town yields and is sacked by the English. Henry leaves Harfleur under the command of his uncle, the Duke of Exeter, and the Duke's lieutenant, one Sir John Falstaff.]

King Henry, after the winning of Harfleur, determined to have proceeded further in the winning of other towns and fortresses; but because the dead time of the winter approached, it was determined by advice of his Council that he should in all convenient speed set forward and march through the country towards Calais by land, lest his return as then homewards should of slanderous tongues be named a running away. And yet that journey was adjudged perilous by reason that the number of his people was much minished[37] by the flux[38]* and other fevers which sore vexed and brought to death above fifteen hundred persons of the army; and this was the cause that his return was the sooner appointed and concluded.

[Henry deals mercifully with his French prisoners in Harfleur, rebuilds the town's fortifications, and heads for Calais. The French destroy crops in advance of Henry's army and harass him with skirmishes. Henry crosses the Somme.]

[He] determined to make haste towards Calais and not to

***flux** flix

37 minished diminished **38 flux** dysentery

seek for battle except he were thereto constrained, because that[39] his army by sickness was sore diminished, insomuch that he had but only two thousand horsemen and thirteen thousand archers, billmen,[40] and of all sorts of other footmen.

The Englishmen were brought into some distress in this journey by reason of their victuals in manner spent and no hope to get more, for the enemies had destroyed all the corn[41] before they came. Rest could they none take, for their enemies with alarms[42] did ever so infest them. Daily it rained and nightly it freezed; of fuel there was great scarcity, of fluxes plenty; money enough, but wares for their relief to bestow it on had they none. Yet in this great necessity the poor people of the country were not spoiled,[43] nor anything taken of them without payment nor any outrage or offense done by the Englishmen except one, which was that a soldier took a pyx[44] out of a church, for which he was apprehended, and the King not once removed till the box was restored and the offender strangled. The people of the countries thereabout, hearing of such zeal in him to the maintenance of justice, ministered to his army victuals and other necessaries, although by open proclamation so to do they were prohibited.

The French King being at Rouen, and hearing that King Henry was passed the river of Somme, was much displeased therewith and, assembling his council to the number of five-and-thirty, asked their advice what was to be done. There was amongst these five-and-thirty his son the Dauphin, calling himself King of Sicily, the Dukes of Berri and Brittany, the Earl of Pontrieux* (the King's youngest son), and other high estates.[45] At length thirty of them agreed that the Englishmen should not depart unfought withal, and five were of a contrary opinion; but the greater number ruled the matter. And so Montjoy, King-at-Arms,[46] was sent to the King of England to defy him as the enemy of

***Pontrieux** Pontieu

39 because that because **40 billmen** soldiers armed with halberds
41 corn grain **42 alarms** alarums, surprise attacks **43 spoiled** plundered **44 pyx** vessel containing the consecrated host in the Mass. (But see *Henry V*, 3.6.40 and note, where Bardolph is reported to have stolen a *pax*, or metal disk stamped with the crucifix, employed in the Mass.)
45 estates ranks **46 King-at-Arms** chief herald

France and to tell him that he should shortly have battle. King Henry advisedly answered: "Mine intent is to do as it pleaseth God. I will not seek your master at this time, but if he or his seek me, I will meet with them, God willing. If any of your nation attempt once to stop me in my journey now towards Calais, at their jeopardy be it; and yet wish I not any of you so unadvised as to be the occasion that I dye your tawny ground with your red blood."

When he had thus answered the herald, he gave him a princely reward and license to depart. Upon whose return with this answer, it was incontinently[47] on the French side proclaimed that all men-of-war should resort to the Constable to fight with the King of England. Whereupon all men apt for armor and desirous of honor drew them toward the field. The Dauphin sore desired to have been at the battle, but he was prohibited by his father.

[King Henry, "without all fear or trouble of mind," rides forth unaccompanied by his soldiers to view the French army. Returning to his troops "with cheerful countenance," he puts them in order of battle. The English are unfamiliar with the terrain.]

There was not one amongst them that knew any certain place whither to go in that unknown country, but by chance they happened upon a beaten way, white in sight,[48] by the which they were brought unto a little village where they were refreshed with meat and drink somewhat more plenteously than they had been divers days before. Order was taken by commandment from the King, after the army was first set in battle array, that no noise or clamor should be made in the host, so that in marching forth to this village every man kept himself quiet. But at their coming into the village, fires were made to give light on every side, as there likewise were in the French host, which was encamped not past two hundred and fifty paces distant from the English. The chief leaders of the French host were these: the Constable of France, the Marshal,[49] the Admiral,[50] the Lord Rambures, Master of the Crossbows, and other of the French

47 incontinently immediately **48 sight** appearance **49 the Marshal** i.e., Lord Boucicault **50 the Admiral** i.e., Lord Châtillon

nobility, which came and pitched down their standards and banners in the county of Saint Paul, within the territory of Agincourt, having in their army, as some write, to the number of threescore thousand horsemen, besides footmen, wagoners, and other.

They were lodged even in the way by the which the Englishmen must needs pass towards Calais; and all that night, after their coming thither, made great cheer and were very merry, pleasant, and full of game. The Englishmen also for their parts were of good comfort and nothing abashed of the matter, and yet they were both hungry, weary, sore traveled, and vexed with many cold diseases. Howbeit, reconciling themselves with God by housel and shrift,[51] requiring[52] assistance at his hands that is the only giver of victory, they determined rather to die than to yield or flee. The day following was the five-and-twentieth of October in the year 1415, being then Friday and the feast of Crispin and Crispinian, a day fair and fortunate to the English but most sorrowful and unlucky to the French.

[The French army is reckoned to outnumber the English army six to one. Both armies are deployed for battle by their leaders. King Henry assigns to Edward, Duke of York, the leading of the vanguard.]

Thus the King, having ordered his battles,[53] feared not the puissance of his enemies. But yet to provide that they should not with the multitude of horsemen break the order of his archers, in whom the force of his army consisted (for in those days the yeomen had their limbs at liberty, sith their hosen were then fastened with one point,[54] and their jacks[55] long and easy to shoot in, so that they might draw bows of great strength and shoot arrows of a yard long, beside the head), he caused stakes bound with iron sharp at both ends, of the length of five or six foot, to be pitched before the archers and of each side the footmen like an hedge,

51 housel and shrift the Mass and confession **52 requiring** begging
53 battles battalions, troops **54 point** tagged lace for attaching lower to upper garment **55 jacks** sleeveless long coats, often mailed

to the intent that if the barded[56] horses ran rashly upon them they might shortly be gored and destroyed. Certain persons also were appointed to remove the stakes, as by the moving of the archers occasion and time should require, so that the footmen were hedged about with stakes and the horsemen stood like a bulwark between them and their enemies without the stakes. . . .

King Henry, by reason of his small number of people to fill up his battles, placed his vanguard so on the right hand of the main battle, which himself led, that the distance betwixt them might scarce be perceived, and so in like case was the rearward[57] joined on the left hand, that the one might the more readily succor another in time of need. When he had thus ordered his battles he left a small company to keep his camp and carriage, which remained still in the village, and then, calling his captains and soldiers about him, he made to them a right grave oration, moving them to play the men whereby to obtain a glorious victory, as there was hope certain they should, the rather if they would but remember the just cause for which they fought and whom they should encounter—such fainthearted people as their ancestors had so often overcome. To conclude, many words of courage he uttered to stir them to do manfully, assuring them that England should never be charged with his ransom nor any Frenchman triumph over him as a captive, for either by famous death or glorious victory would he, by God's grace, win honor and fame.

It is said that, as he heard one of the host utter his wish to another thus, "I would to God there were with us now so many good soldiers as are at this hour within England!" the King answered: "I would not wish a man more here than I have. We are indeed in comparison to the enemies but a few, but if God of his clemency do favor us and our just cause, as I trust He will, we shall speed well enough. But let no man ascribe victory to our own strength and might, but only to God's assistance, to whom I have no doubt we shall worthily have cause to give thanks therefor. And if so be that for our offenses' sakes we shall be delivered into the hands

56 barded caparisoned, with ornamental cloths covering saddle or harness **57 rearward** rearguard

of our enemies, the less number we be, the less damage shall the realm of England sustain; but if we should fight in trust of multitude of men and so get the victory, our minds being prone to pride, we should thereupon peradventure ascribe the victory not so much to the gift of God as to our own puissance and thereby provoke his high indignation and displeasure against us; and if the enemy get the upper hand, then should our realm and country suffer more damage and stand in further danger. But be you of good comfort[58] and show yourselves valiant, God and our just quarrel[59] shall defend us and deliver these our proud adversaries with all the multitude of them which you see, or at the least the most of them, into our hands." Whilst the King was yet thus in speech, either army so maligned the other, being as then in open sight, that every man cried "Forward, forward!" The Dukes of Clarence, Gloucester, and York were of the same opinion, yet the King stayed a while lest any jeopardy were not foreseen or any hazard not prevented. The Frenchmen in the meanwhile, as though they had been sure of victory, made great triumph, for the captains had determined before how to divide the spoil, and the soldiers the night before had played[60] the Englishmen at dice. The noblemen had devised a chariot wherein they might triumphantly convey the King captive to the city of Paris, crying to their soldiers, "Haste you to the spoil,[61] glory, and honor!"—little weening[62] (God wot) how soon their brags should be blown away.

Here we may not forget how the French, thus in their jollity, sent an herald to King Henry to inquire what ransom he would offer. Whereunto he answered that within two or three hours he hoped it would so happen that the Frenchmen should be glad to commune[63] rather with the Englishmen for their ransoms than the English to take thought for their deliverance, promising for his own part that his dead carcass should rather be a prize to the Frenchmen than that his living body should pay any ransom. When the messenger was come back to the French host, the men-of-war put on their helmets and caused their trumpets to

58 But . . . comfort but if you take comfort (in the justice of the cause)
59 quarrel cause **60 played** gambled for **61 spoil** plundering
62 weening believing, imagining **63 commune** confer, communicate

blow to the battle. They thought themselves so sure of victory that divers of the noblemen made such haste towards the battle that they left many of their servants and men-of-war behind them, and some of them would not once stay for their standards; as, amongst other, the Duke of Brabant, when his standard was not come, caused a banner to be taken from a trumpet and fastened to a spear, the which he commanded to be borne before him instead of his standard.

[The armies face each other in full order of battle and join in combat. The English throw the French into serious confusion, first with their archery and then in hand-to-hand combat.]

The King that day showed himself a valiant knight, albeit almost felled by the Duke of Alençon; yet with plain strength he slew two of the Duke's company and felled the Duke himself, whom, when he would have yielded, the King's guard (contrary to his mind)[64] slew out of hand. In conclusion, the King, minding[65] to make an end of that day's journey,[66] caused his horsemen to fetch a compass about[67] and to join with him against the rearward of the Frenchmen, in the which was the greatest number of people. When the Frenchmen perceived his intent, they were suddenly amazed and ran away like sheep, without order or array. Which when the King perceived, he encouraged his men and followed so quickly upon the enemies that they ran hither and thither, casting away their armor; many on their knees desired to have their lives saved.

In the mean season, while the battle thus continued and that the Englishmen had taken a great number of prisoners, certain Frenchmen on horseback . . . to the number of six hundred horsemen, which were the first that fled, hearing that the English tents and pavilions were a good way distant from the army without any sufficient guard to defend the same, either upon a covetous meaning to gain by the spoil or upon a desire to be revenged, entered upon the King's

64 to his mind i.e., to the King's wishes **65 minding** intending
66 journey i.e., battle, day's work **67 fetch a compass about** reverse course

camp and there spoiled the hales,[68] robbed the tents, brake up chests and carried away caskets, and slew such servants as they found to make any resistance. For which treason and haskardy[69] in thus leaving their camp at the very point of fight, for winning of spoil where none to defend it, very many were after committed to prison and had lost their lives if the Dauphin had longer lived.

But when the outcry of the lackeys and boys, which ran away for fear of the Frenchmen thus spoiling the camp, came to the King's ears, he, doubting[70] lest his enemies should gather together again and begin a new field,[71] and mistrusting further that the prisoners would be an aid to his enemies or the very enemies to their takers indeed if they were suffered to live, contrary to his accustomed gentleness commanded by sound of trumpet that every man upon pain of death should incontinently[72] slay his prisoner. When this dolorous decree and pitiful proclamation was pronounced, pity it was to see how some Frenchmen were suddenly sticked with daggers, some were brained with poleaxes, some slain with mauls,[73] other had their throats cut, and some their bellies paunched,[74] so that in effect, having respect to the great number,[75] few prisoners were saved.

When this lamentable slaughter was ended, the Englishmen disposed themselves in order of battle, ready to abide a new field and also to invade and newly set on their enemies. With great force they assailed the Earls of Marle and Faulconbridge and the Lords of Lorraine* and of Thines,* with six hundred men-of-arms, who had all that day kept together but now slain and beaten down out of hand. Some write that the King, perceiving his enemies in one part[76] to assemble together as though they meant to give a new battle for preservation of the prisoners, sent to them an herald, commanding them either to depart out of his sight or else to come forward at once and give battle, promising herewith that if they did offer to fight again, not only those prisoners which his people already had taken but also so many

***Lorraine** Louraie ***Thines** Thine

68 spoiled the hales plundered the pavilions, temporary shelters
69 haskardy baseness **70 doubting** fearing **71 field** battle **72 incontinently** immediately **73 mauls** maces **74 paunched** stabbed **75 having . . . number** in relation to the large number there were **76 part** part of the field

of them as in this new conflict which they thus attempted should fall into his hands should die the death without redemption.

The Frenchmen, fearing the sentence of so terrible a decree, without further delay parted out of the field. And so, about four of the clock in the afternoon, the King, when he saw no appearance of enemies, caused the retreat[77] to be blown and, gathering his army together, gave thanks to almighty God for so happy a victory, causing his prelates and chaplains to sing this psalm: *"In exitu Israel de Aegypto,"*[78] and commanded every man to kneel down on the ground at this verse: *"Non nobis, Domine, non nobis, sed nomini tuo da gloriam."*[79] Which done, he caused *"Te Deum"*[80] with certain anthems to be sung, giving laud and praise to God without boasting of his own force or any human power. That night he and his people took rest and refreshed themselves with such victuals as they found in the French camp, but lodged in the same village where he lay the night before.

In the morning, Montjoy, King-at-Arms, and four other French heralds came to the King to know the number of prisoners and to desire burial for the dead. Before he made them answer, to understand what they would say he demanded of them why they made to him that request, considering that he knew not whether the victory was his or theirs. When Montjoy by true and just confession had cleared that doubt to the high praise of the King, he desired of Montjoy to understand the name of the castle near adjoining. When they had told him that it was called Agincourt, he said, "Then shall this conflict be called the Battle of Agincourt." He feasted the French officers-of-arms that day and granted them their request, which busily sought through the field for such as were slain. But the Englishmen suffered them not to go alone, for they searched with them and found many hurt but not in jeopardy of their lives, whom they took prisoners and brought them to their tents. When the King of England had well refreshed himself and

77 retreat signal to cease fighting (not to retreat before the enemy)
78 In exitu . . . Aegypto When Israel went out of Egypt. (Psalm 114.)
79 Non nobis . . . gloriam Not unto us, O Lord, not unto us, but unto thy name give glory. (Psalm 115.) **80 Te Deum** We thank thee O God. (A hymn of thanksgiving.)

his soldiers that had taken the spoil of such as were slain, he with his prisoners in good order returned to his town of Calais.

When tidings of this great victory was blown into England, solemn processions and other praisings to almighty God with bonfires and joyful triumphs were ordained in every town, city, and borough, and the Mayor and citizens of London went the morrow after the day of Saint Simon and Jude from the church of Saint Paul to the church of Saint Peter at Westminster in devout manner, rendering to God hearty thanks for such fortunate luck sent to the King and his army. The same Sunday that the King removed from the camp at Agincourt towards Calais, divers Frenchmen came to the field to view again the dead bodies . . . wherein [eventually] were buried by account five thousand and eight hundred persons, besides them that were carried away by their friends and servants and others which, being wounded, died in hospitals and other places.

After this their dolorous journey and pitiful slaughter, divers clerks of Paris made many a lamentable verse, complaining that the King reigned by will and that councillors were partial, affirming that the noblemen fled against nature and that the commons were destroyed by their prodigality, declaring also that the clergy were dumb and durst not say the truth and that the humble commons duly obeyed and yet ever suffered punishment, for which cause by divine persecution the less number vanquished the greater. Wherefore they concluded that all things went out of order, and yet was there no man that studied to bring the unruly to frame. It was no marvel though this battle was lamentable to the French nation, for in it were taken and slain the flower of all the nobility of France.

There were taken prisoners Charles, Duke of Orleans, nephew to the French King; John, Duke of Bourbon; the Lord Boucicault, one of the Marshals of France (he after died in England); with a number of other lords, knights, and esquires, at the least fifteen hundred, besides the common people. There were slain in all of the French part to the number of ten thousand men, whereof were princes and noblemen bearing banners one hundred twenty-and-six; to these, of knights, esquires, and gentlemen, so many as made up the number of eight thousand and four hundred (of the which five hundred were dubbed knights the night before the battle); so as of the meaner[81] sort, not past sixteen hundred. Amongst those of the nobility that were slain, these were the chiefest: Charles, Lord Delabreth, High Constable of France; Jacques of Châtillon, Lord of Dampierre, Admiral of France; the Lord Rambures, Master of the Crossbows; Sir Guichard Dauphin, Great Master of France; John, Duke of Alençon; Anthony, Duke of Brabant, brother to the Duke of Burgundy; Edward, Duke of Bar; the Earl of Nevers, another brother to the Duke of Burgundy; with the Earls of Marle, Vaudemont, Beaumont, Grandpré, Roussi, Faulconbridge, Foix, and Lestrale,* besides a great number of lords and barons of name.

Of Englishmen, there died at this battle Edward, Duke of York; the Earl of Suffolk; Sir Richard Ketly* and Davy Gam, Esquire; and of all other not above five-and-twenty persons, as some do report; but other writers of greater credit affirm that there were slain above five or six hundred persons. Titus Livius[82] saith that there were slain of Englishmen, besides the Duke of York and the Earl of Suffolk, an hundred persons at the first encounter. The Duke of Gloucester, the King's brother, was sore wounded about the hips and borne down to the ground so that he fell backwards, with his feet towards his enemies, whom the King bestrid and like a brother valiantly rescued from his enemies and, so saving his life, caused him to be conveyed out of the fight into a place of more safety. . . .

After that the King of England had refreshed himself and his people at Calais, and that such prisoners as he had left at Harfleur (as ye have heard) were come to Calais unto him, the sixth day of November he with all his prisoners took shipping. . . . The Mayor of London and the aldermen, appareled in orient-grained scarlet,[83] and four hundred commoners clad in beautiful murrey,[84] well mounted and trimly horsed, with rich collars and great chains, met the King on Blackheath, rejoicing at his return. And the clergy of London, with rich crosses, sumptuous copes, and massy cen-

***Faulcon-bridge, Foix, and Lestrale** Fauconberge, Fois and Lestrake ***Ketly** Kikelie

81 meaner of lower station **82 Titus Livius** author of the *Vita Henrici Quinti* (c. 1437), an early biography of Henry V **83 orient-grained scarlet** a lustrous dyed scarlet cloth **84 murrey** cloth of purple-red mulberry color

sers, received him at Saint Thomas of Waterings with solemn procession.

The King, like a grave and sober personage and as one remembering from whom all victories are sent, seemed little to regard such vain pomp and shows as were in triumphant sort devised for his welcoming home from so prosperous a journey, insomuch that he would not suffer his helmet to be carried with him, whereby might have appeared to the people the blows and dints that were to be seen in the same; neither would he suffer any ditties to be made and sung by minstrels of his glorious victory, for that he would wholly have the praise and thanks altogether given to God. The news of this bloody battle being reported to the French King as then sojourning at Rouen filled the court full of sorrow.

[The Dauphin dies soon after Agincourt, either of melancholy or of some sudden disease. In 1415 the English continue further their successful campaigning in France, meanwhile forging a league with the Emperor Sigismund and signing a truce with the Duke of Burgundy. In 1417 Henry again campaigns in France and takes Caen. The Scots are successfully repulsed in the north of England. In 1418 Henry captures Cherbourg and lays down a siege before Rouen, causing extreme suffering and hunger within the city. Early in 1419, the King, still at the seige of Rouen, agrees to receive a French delegation requesting a parley.]

One of them, seen[85] in the civil laws, was appointed to declare the message in all their names, who, showing himself more rash than wise, more arrogant than learned, first took upon him to show wherein the glory of victory consisted, advising the King not to show his manhood in famishing a multitude of poor, simple, and innocent people but rather suffer such miserable wretches as lay betwixt the walls of the city and the trenches of his siege to pass through the camp, that they might get their living in other places, and then, if he durst manfully assault the city and by force subdue it, he should win both worldly fame and merit great

85 seen well versed, learned

meed[86] at the hands of almighty God for having compassion of the poor, needy, and indigent people.

When this orator had said,[87] the King, who no request less suspected than that which was thus desired,[88] began awhile to muse; and after he had well considered the crafty cautel[89] of his enemies, with a fierce countenance and bold spirit he reproved them both for their subtle dealing with him and their malapert presumption in that they should seem to go about to teach him what belonged to the duty of a conqueror. And therefore since it appeared that the same was unknown unto them, he declared that the goddess of battle, called Bellona, had three handmaidens ever of necessity attending upon her, as blood, fire, and famine. And whereas it lay in his choice to use them all three—yea, two or one of them, at his pleasure—he had appointed only the meekest maid[90] of those three damsels to punish them of that city till they were brought to reason.

And whereas the gain of a captain attained by any of the said three handmaidens was both glorious, honorable, and worthy of triumph, yet of all the three, the youngest maid, which he meant to use at that time, was most profitable and commodious. And as for the poor people lying in the ditches, if they died through famine, the fault was theirs that like cruel tyrants had put them out of the town to the intent he should slay them; and yet he had saved their lives, so that if any lack of charity was, it rested in them and not in him. But to their cloaked request,[91] he meant not to gratify them within so much, but they should keep them still to help to spend their victuals.[92] And as to assault the town, he told them that he would they should know he was both able and willing thereto, as he should see occasion; but the choice was in his hand to tame them either with blood, fire, or famine, or with them all, whereof he would take the choice at his pleasure and not at theirs.

86 meed reward **87 said** finished speaking **88 who . . . desired** who would have expected just about any request sooner than this one **89 cautel** device **90 the meekest maid** i.e., famine **91 cloaked request** i.e., a cunning request cloaked as a seemingly innocent one **92 but they . . . victuals** i.e., Henry will insist on their keeping all the poor etc. who depend on the city to be fed in order that Rouen's supplies will be the more quickly exhausted

[Rouen surrenders. After further campaigning, the Duke of Burgundy sends letters and ambassadors to King Henry urging a meeting between him and Charles, the French King. A place is arranged for the negotiations.]

The place of interview and meeting was appointed to be beside Meulan on the river of Seine, where in a fair place every part was by commissioners appointed to their ground. When the day of appointment approached, which was the last day of May, the King of England, accompanied with the Dukes of Clarence and Gloucester, his brethren, the Duke of Exeter, his uncle, and Henry Beaufort, clerk,[93] his other uncle, which after was Bishop of Winchester and Cardinal, with the Earls of March, Salisbury, and others, to the number of a thousand men-of-war, entered into his ground, which was barred about and ported, wherein his tents were pight[94] in a princely manner.

Likewise for the French part came Isabel, the French Queen, because her husband was fallen into his old frantic disease, having in her company the Duke of Burgundy and the Earl of Saint Paul, and she had attending upon her the fair Lady Katharine her daughter, with six-and-twenty ladies and damosels; and had also for her furniture a thousand men-of-war. The said Lady Katharine was brought by her mother only to the intent that the King of England, beholding her excellent beauty, should be so inflamed and rapt in her love that he, to obtain her to his wife, should the sooner agree to a gentle peace and loving concord. But though many words were spent in this treaty and that they met at eight several times, yet no effect ensued, nor any conclusion was taken by this friendly consultation, so that both parties after a princely fashion took leave each of other and departed, the Englishmen to Mantes and the Frenchmen to Pontoise.

[The negotations appear to be making slight progress, "save only that a certain spark of burning love was kindled in the King's heart by the sight of the Lady Katharine." Negotiations break off, and before they can be resumed more

93 clerk cleric **94 ported . . . pight** gated . . . pitched

fighting takes place. Pontoise and Gisors fall to King Henry, then all of Burgundy. When the Duke of Burgundy is murdered by the Dauphin's followers, his son Philip takes up the cause of urging peace.]

Whilst these victorious exploits were thus happily achieved by the Englishmen, and that the King lay still at Rouen in giving thanks to almighty God for the same, there came to him eftsoons[95] ambassadors from the French King and the Duke of Burgundy to move him to peace. The King, minding[96] not to be reputed for a destroyer of the country which he coveted to preserve, or for a causer of Christian blood still to be spilt in his quarrel, began so to incline and give ear unto their suit and humble request that at length, after often sending to and fro, and that the Bishop of Arras and other men of honor had been with him, and likewise the Earl of Warwick and the Bishop of Rochester had been with the Duke of Burgundy, they both finally agreed upon certain articles, so[97] that the French King and his commons would thereto assent.

Now was the French King and the Queen with their daughter, Katharine, at Troyes in Champagne governed and ordered by them, which so much favored the Duke of Burgundy that they would not, for any earthly good, once hinder or pull back one jot of such articles as the same Duke should seek to prefer. And therefore what needeth many words? A truce tripartite was accorded between the two Kings and the Duke and their countries, and order taken that the King of England should send, in the company of the Duke of Burgundy, his ambassadors unto Troyes in Champagne, sufficiently authorized to treat and conclude of so great matter. The King of England, being in good hope that all his affairs should take good success as he could wish or desire, sent to the Duke of Burgundy his uncle, the Duke of Exeter, the Earl of Salisbury, the Bishop of Ely, the Lord Fanhope, the Lord Fitzhugh, Sir John Robsert, and Sir Philip Hall, with divers doctors[98] to the number of five hundred horse, which in the company of the Duke of Burgundy

95 eftsoons again **96 minding** wishing, intending **97 so** provided
98 doctors i.e., doctors of divinity and law

came to the city of Troyes the eleventh of March [1420]. The King, the Queen, and the Lady Katharine them received and heartily welcomed, showing great signs and tokens of love and amity.

After a few days they fell to council, in which at length it was concluded that King Henry of England should come to Troyes and marry the Lady Katharine, and the King her father after his death should make him heir of his realm, crown, and dignity. It was also agreed that King Henry, during his father-in-law's life, should in his stead have the whole government of the realm of France, as Regent thereof, with many other covenants and articles, as after shall appear. To the performance whereof it was accorded that all the nobles and estates of the realm of France, as well spiritual as temporal, and also the cities and commonalties, citizens, and burgesses of towns that were obeisant at that time to the French King, should take a corporal oath.[99] These articles were not at the first in all points brought to a perfect conclusion. But after the effect and meaning of them was agreed upon by the commissioners, the Englishmen departed towards the King their master and left Sir John Robsert behind to give his attendance on the Lady Katharine.

[King Henry agrees to the meeting at Troyes.]

The Duke of Burgundy, accompanied with many noblemen, received him two leagues without[100] the town and conveyed him to his lodging. All his army was lodged in small villages thereabout. And after that he had reposed himself a little, he went to visit the French King, the Queen, and the Lady Katharine, whom he found in Saint Peter's church, where was a very joyous meeting betwixt them (and this was on the twentieth day of May), and there the King of England and the Lady Katharine were affianced. After this the two Kings and their council assembled together divers days, wherein the first concluded agreement was in divers points altered and brought to a certainty according to the effect above mentioned.

99 obeisant . . . corporal oath obedient . . . oath ratified by touching a sacred object **100 without** outside of

[The marriage between King Henry and the Lady Katharine is solemnized on the third of June, 1420, and Henry is proclaimed heir and Regent of France. The articles of peace include the following:]

1. First, it is accorded between our father and us that forsomuch as by the bond of matrimony made for the good of the peace between us and our most dear beloved Katharine, daughter of our said father and of our most dear mother Isabel, his wife, the same Charles and Isabel been made[101] our father and mother, therefore them as our father and mother we shall have and worship, as it fitteth and seemeth so worthy a prince and princess to be worshiped, principally before all other temporal persons of the world. . . .
6. Also, that after the death of our said father aforesaid, and from thenceforward, the crown and the realm of France, with all the rights and appurtenances, shall remain and abide to us, and been of us and of our heirs forevermore.
7. And forsomuch as our said father is withholden with[102] divers sickness, in such manner as he may not intend[103] in his own person for to[104] dispose for the needs of the foresaid realm of France, therefore during the life of our foresaid father, the faculties and exercise of the governance and disposition of the public and common profit of the said realm of France, with Council and nobles and wise men of the same realm of France, shall be and abide to us. . . .
24. Also, that during our father's life we shall not call nor write us King of France; but verily we shall abstain us from that name as long as our father liveth.
25. Also, that our said father, during his life, shall name, call, and write us in French in this manner: *"Notre très cher fils, Henri, Roi d'Angleterre, Héritier de France,"* and in Latin in this manner: *Praeclarissimus filius noster Henricus, Rex Angliae et Haeres Franciae."* . . .
28. Also that thenceforward, perpetually, shall be still

101 been made have been made (by the marriage) **102 withholden with** i.e., kept from the performance of his duties by **103 intend** direct his attention, pay heed **104 for to** to rest,[105] and that in all manner of wise, dissensions, hates, rancors, envies, and wars between the same realms of France and England and the people of the same realms, drawing to accord of the same peace, may cease and be broken.

[King Henry subsequently dies on campaign in France in April 1422. Holinshed gives a view of his character.]

This Henry was a king, of life without spot; a prince whom all men loved and of none disdained; a captain against whom fortune never frowned nor mischance once spurned; whose people him, so severe a justicer, both loved and obeyed, and so humane withal that he left no offense unpunished nor friendship unrewarded;[106] a terror to rebels and suppressor of sedition; his virtues notable, his qualities most praiseworthy.

In strength and nimbleness of body from his youth few to him comparable, for in wrestling, leaping, and running no man well able to compare. In casting of great iron bars and heavy stones he excelled commonly all men, never shrinking at cold nor slothful for heat; and when he most labored, his head commonly uncovered; no more weary of harness[107] than a light cloak; very valiantly abiding at needs[108] both hunger and thirst; so manful of mind as never seen to qunich[109] at a wound or to smart at the pain, not to turn his nose from evil savor nor close his eyes from smoke or dust; no man more moderate in eating and drinking, with diet not delicate but rather more meet for men-of-war than for princes or tender stomachs. Every honest person was permitted to come to him, sitting at meal, where, either secretly or openly, to declare his mind. High and weighty causes, as well between men-of-war and other, he would gladly hear, and either determined them himself or else for end[110] committed them to others. He slept very little, but

105 still rest continual peace **106 whose people . . . unrewarded** i.e., whose people both obeyed and loved him, obeying the severe judge who left no offense unpunished and loving the humane man who left no friendship unrewarded **107 harness** armor **108 abiding at needs** enduring when necessary **109 quinch** flinch **110 for end** for a final determination

that very soundly, insomuch that when his soldiers sung at nights or minstrels played he then slept fastest; of courage invincible; of purpose unmutable; so wisehardy[111] always as[112] fear was banished from him; at every alarum he first in armor and foremost in ordering. In time of war such was his providence, bounty, and hap as[113] he had true intelligence not only what his enemies did but what they said and intended; of his devises and purposes few, before the thing was at the point to be done should be made privy.[114]

He had such knowledge in ordering and guiding an army, with such a gift to encourage his people, that the Frenchmen had constant opinion he could never be vanquished in battle. Such wit, such prudence, and such policy[115] withal that he never enterprised anything before he had fully debated and forecast all the main chances that might happen, which done, with all diligence and courage he set his purpose forward. What policy he had in finding present remedies for sudden mischiefs and what engines[116] in saving himself and his people in sharp distresses, were it not that by his acts they did plainly appear, hard were it by words to make them credible. Wantonness of life and thirst in avarice had he quite quenched in him; virtues indeed in such an estate of sovereignty, youth, and power, as very rare, so right commendable in the highest degree. So staid of mind and countenance besides that never jolly or triumphant for victory nor sad or damped for loss or misfortune. For bountifulness and liberality, no man more free, gentle, and frank[117] in bestowing rewards to all persons according to their deserts; for his saying was that he never desired money to keep but to give and spend.

Although that story[118] properly serves not for theme of praise or dispraise, yet what in brevity may well be remembered, in truth would not be forgotten by sloth,[119] were it but only to remain as a spectacle for magnanimity to have al-

111 wisehardy intelligently brave (the opposite of foolhardy) **112 as** that **113 providence, bounty, and hap as** foresight, warlike prowess, and good luck that **114 of his devices . . . privy** i.e., he was careful that plans were kept secret and known to few until the time was ready for those plans to be executed **115 policy** stratagem **116 engines** clever devices **117 frank** openhanded **118 Although that story** although history **119 yet what . . . sloth** yet whatever can be only briefly recorded here truly should not be slothfully forgotten

ways in eye and for encouragement to nobles in honorable enterprises. Known be it therefore, of person and form was this prince rightly representing his heroical affects:[120] of stature and proportion tall and manly, rather lean than gross, somewhat long-necked and black-haired, of countenance amiable. Eloquent and grave was his speech, and of great grace and power to persuade. For conclusion, a majesty was he that both lived and died a pattern in princehood, a lodestar[121] in honor, and mirror of magnificence; the more highly exalted in his life, the more deeply lamented at his death and famous to the world alway.

The second edition of Raphael Holinshed's *Chronicles* was published in 1587. This selection is based on that edition, Volume 3, Folios 545–583.

120 of person . . . affects the person and shape of this prince truly reflected his heroical disposition **121 lodestar** guiding star, especially the North Pole star

Further Reading

Beauman, Sally, ed. *The Royal Shakespeare Company's Production of "Henry V" for the Centenary Season at the Royal Shakespeare Theatre*. Oxford: Pergamon Press, 1976. Beauman provides a record of the development of the Royal Shakespeare Company's 1975 production of *Henry V*. The working script, an introduction by director Terry Hands, interviews with the cast, and selections from the London drama critics are combined in a volume that is at once a portrait of a production and an unusual and powerful piece of literary criticism.

Berman, Ronald, ed. *Twentieth Century Interpretations of "Henry V."* Englewood Cliffs, N.J.: Prentice-Hall, 1968. Berman offers a useful selection of extracts and critical essays on the play, including commentary by William Butler Yeats, A. C. Bradley, J. Dover Wilson, E. M. W. Tillyard, and A. P. Rossiter.

Berry, Ralph. *"Henry V." Changing Styles in Shakespeare*. London: George Allen and Unwin, 1981. Berry studies recent changes in the dramatic presentation of *Henry V* as they reflect significant shifts in the understanding of the play. Focusing on Laurence Olivier's film (1944), two Canadian productions by Michael Langham, and two Royal Shakespeare Company productions, Peter Hall's (1964) and Terry Hands's (1975), Berry shows how performance reflects "current social assumptions and preoccupations."

Calderwood, James L. "*Henry V:* The Art of Order." *Metadrama in Shakespeare's Henriad: "Richard II" to "Henry V."* Berkeley and Los Angeles: Univ. of California Press, 1979. Calderwood explores the principles of order that the play presents. National unity and artistic unity are seen as parallel achievements, each accomplished by parts being subordinated to the whole. The process is visible even in the character of the King, as Henry's personal life disappears, subordinated to the necessities of rule.

Campbell, Lily B. "The Victorious Acts of King Henry V." *Shakespeare's "Histories": Mirrors of Elizabethan Policy.*

San Marino, Calif.: Huntington Library, 1947. For Campbell, *Henry V* is an epic celebration of the English "achieving victory through the blessing of God." Shakespeare portrays Henry as an "ideal hero," whose thoughts and actions are seen by Campbell to be based on Elizabethan theories of warfare.

Dollimore, Jonathan, and Alan Sinfield. "History and Ideology: The Instance of *Henry V.*" In *Alternative Shakespeares*, ed. John Drakakis. London and New York: Methuen, 1985. Dollimore and Sinfield examine the play's representation of power in the context of "the struggles of its own historical moment." They see Henry's effort to conquer France "as a re-presentation of [Elizabeth's] attempt to conquer Ireland and the hoped-for unity of Britain," and focus on the social conflicts and contradictions that the play, a fantasy of national unity, would deny.

Goldman, Michael. "*Henry V:* The Strain of Rule." *Shakespeare and the Energies of Drama*. Princeton, N.J.: Princeton Univ. Press, 1972. Goldman explores the play's focus on "the effort of greatness," the strain under which Henry places himself and his hearers. The play recognizes both the "glory of the ruler" and "the price of his role," and yet "with all its ironies it remains great patriotic drama."

Goddard, Harold C. *"Henry V." The Meaning of Shakespeare*. Chicago: Univ. of Chicago Press, 1951. Goddard finds the play colored by a pervasive irony that disrupts the celebration of Henry's role. The Chorus, Goddard finds, voices the popular conception of England's famous hero-king, but in the action and the parodic subplot Shakespeare "tells the truth about him": he is a brutal "Machiavellian prince."

Hazlitt, William. *"Henry V." Characters of Shakespear's Plays*, 1817. Rpt., London: Oxford Univ. Press, 1966. Hazlitt offers the first influential attack on the character of Henry. Hazlitt finds him "careless, dissolute and ambitious," and he argues that "he seemed to have no idea of any rule of right or wrong, but brute force, glossed over with a little religious hypocrisy and archiepiscopal advice."

Jorgensen, Paul A. *Shakespeare's Military World*, pp. 71–97. Berkeley and Los Angeles: Univ. of California Press, 1956. Jorgensen discusses *Henry V* in the context of his study of Renaissance theories and practice of warfare. Shakespeare "conscientiously followed" Elizabethan military handbooks in his portrait of Henry as a "Christian conqueror," and other aspects of the play similarly reflect Shakespeare's knowledge of Elizabethan military matters.

Kastan, David Scott. "'The King is a Good King, But it Must Be as it May': History, Heroism, and *Henry V*." *Shakespeare and the Shapes of Time*. Hanover, N.H.: Univ. Press of New England, 1982. For Kastan the play at once acknowledges Henry's heroism as it shapes historical material into patriotic myth and simultaneously recognizes the "instability of the shape of this restructured history." We are made to see Henry as a hero, but we are forced to recognize that his heroism is animated only by his radical simplification of the moral environment of the play.

Kernan, Alvin B. "The Henriad: Shakespeare's Major History Plays." In *Modern Shakespearean Criticism: Essays on Style, Dramaturgy, and the Major Plays*, ed. Alvin B. Kernan. New York: Harcourt, Brace, and World, 1970. Kernan treats *Henry V* as the culmination of a four-part epic moving from Richard II's sacred conception of kingship to Henry's pragmatic understanding of the role. *Henry V*, for Kernan, portrays a successful king, living "in the full glare of public life," who succeeds only by subordinating his private self to his "political function."

Ornstein, Robert. *"Henry V." A Kingdom for a Stage: The Achievement of Shakespeare's History Plays*. Cambridge: Harvard Univ. Press, 1972. Ornstein focuses on Henry's "moral temper": the King is a successful ruler, but one whose "moral awareness is of the mind, not of the heart." Though the play celebrates the heroism of the English, it speaks "candidly of the human cost of their great adventure."

Quinn, Michael, ed. *Shakespeare, "Henry V": A Casebook*. London: Macmillan, 1969. Quinn provides a useful selection of essays, including extracts from early critics such as Samuel Johnson, August Wilhelm von Schlegel, William Hazlitt, and Algernon Swinburne, as well as longer pieces by Derek A. Traversi, Rose Zimbardo, and L. C. Knights.

Rabkin, Norman. "Either / Or: Responding to *Henry V.*" *Shakespeare and the Problem of Meaning*. Chicago: Univ. of Chicago Press, 1981. Rabkin finds *Henry V* to be a play that deliberately seeks the ambiguity reflected in the critical debate it has attracted. The play at once celebrates and undermines its hero, revealing "the simultaneity of our deepest hopes and fears about the world of political action."

Reese, M. M. *"Henry V." The Cease of Majesty: A Study of Shakespeare's History Plays.* London: Edward Arnold; New York: St. Martin's Press, 1961. For Reese, Henry is a hero whose undertaking of the French war is right and just and whose success reveals England's recovered strength. Reese argues that the ironies that critics have found are not present in performance; the play provides a "heartening picture of a society cured of its sickness and united under a prince whose own redemptive experience corresponded with that of his people."

Ribner, Irving. "Shakespeare's Second Tetralogy." *The English History Play in the Age of Shakespeare,* 1957. Rev. ed., enl., New York: Barnes and Noble, 1965. Shakespeare's history plays, according to Ribner, reflect the political interests of sixteenth-century historians. *Henry V* is Shakespeare's portrait of an ideal king who displays both the military virtues he had learned in *1 Henry IV* and the civil virtues he had learned in *2 Henry IV*.

Saccio, Peter. "Henry V: The King Victorious." *Shakespeare's English Kings: History, Chronicle, and Drama.* New York: Oxford Univ. Press, 1977. Saccio studies the historical background of Shakespeare's play, examining Henry's claim to the French throne and the "talents and training" that determined his success.

Schlegel, August Wilhelm von. *A Course of Lectures on Dramatic Art and Literature,* trans. John Black, 1846. Rpt., New York: AMS, 1965, pp. 271–367. The argument that Shakespeare's histories "form one great whole," a "heroic poem in the dramatic form," can be traced to Schlegel. Schlegel also argues that Henry "is manifestly Shakespeare's favourite hero in English history," and that the play demonstrates his political maneuverings and personal charm, endowing him "with every chivalrous and kingly virtue."

Traversi, Derek A. *"Henry V." Shakespeare from "Richard II" to "Henry V."* Stanford: Stanford Univ. Press, 1957. Traversi finds in the play "the presence of a subsistent irony" that qualifies the portrait of Henry's success. The effect of Shakespeare's play is "to bring out certain contradictions, moral and human, inherent in the notion of a successful king."

WILLIAM SHAKESPEARE was born in Stratford-upon-Avon in April, 1564, and his birth is traditionally celebrated on April 23. The facts of his life, known from surviving documents, are sparse. He was one of eight children born to John Shakespeare, a merchant of some standing in his community. William probably went to the King's New School in Stratford, but he had no university education. In November 1582, at the age of eighteen, he married Anne Hathaway, eight years his senior, who was pregnant with their first child, Susanna. She was born on May 26, 1583. Twins, a boy, Hamnet (who would die at age eleven), and a girl, Judith, were born in 1585. By 1592 Shakespeare had gone to London, working as an actor and already known as a playwright. A rival dramatist, Robert Greene, referred to him as "an upstart crow, beautified with our feathers." Shakespeare became a principal shareholder and playwright of the successful acting troupe the Lord Chamberlain's men (later, under James I, called the King's men). In 1599 the Lord Chamberlain's men built and occupied the Globe Theatre in Southwark near the Thames River. Here many of Shakespeare's plays were performed by the most famous actors of his time, including Richard Burbage, Will Kempe, and Robert Armin. In addition to his 37 plays, Shakespeare had a hand in others, including *Sir Thomas More* and *The Two Noble Kinsmen,* and he wrote poems, including *Venus and Adonis* and *The Rape of Lucrece*. His 154 sonnets were published, probably without his authorization, in 1609. In 1611 or 1612 he gave up his lodgings in London and devoted more and more of his time to retirement in Stratford, though he continued writing such plays as *The Tempest* and *Henry VIII* until about 1613. He died on April 23, 1616, and was buried in Holy Trinity Church, Stratford. No collected edition of his plays was published during his lifetime, but in 1623 two members of his acting company, John Heminges and Henry Condell, published the great collection now called the First Folio.

Contributors

DAVID BEVINGTON, Phyllis Fay Horton Professor of Humanities at the University of Chicago, is editor of *The Complete Works of Shakespeare* (Scott, Foresman, 1980) and of *Medieval Drama* (Houghton Mifflin, 1975). His latest critical study is *Action Is Eloquence: Shakespeare's Language of Gesture* (Harvard University Press, 1984).

DAVID SCOTT KASTAN, Professor of English and Comparative Literature at Columbia University, is the author of *Shakespeare and the Shapes of Time* (University Press of New England, 1982).

JAMES HAMMERSMITH, Associate Professor of English at Auburn University, has published essays on various facets of Renaissance drama, including literary criticism, textual criticism, and printing history.

ROBERT KEAN TURNER, Professor of English at the University of Wisconsin–Milwaukee, is a general editor of the New Variorum Shakespeare (Modern Language Association of America) and a contributing editor to *The Dramatic Works in the Beaumont and Fletcher Canon* (Cambridge University Press, 1966–).

JAMES SHAPIRO, who coedited the bibliographies with David Scott Kastan, is Assistant Professor of English at Columbia University.

✤

JOSEPH PAPP, one of the most important forces in theater today, is the founder and producer of the New York Shakespeare Festival, America's largest and most prolific theatrical institution. Since 1954 Mr. Papp has produced or directed all but one of Shakespeare's plays—in Central Park, in schools, off and on Broadway, and at the Festival's permanent home, The Public Theater. He has also produced such award-winning plays and musical works as *Hair, A Chorus Line, Plenty,* and *The Mystery of Edwin Drood,* among many others.

THE COMPLETE WORKS OF WILLIAM SHAKESPEARE

Volume I

Love's Labor's Lost
The Comedy of Errors
The Two Gentlemen of Verona
Henry VI, Parts One, Two, and Three
Richard III

Volume II

The Taming of the Shrew
The Merchant of Venice
Romeo and Juliet
King John
A Midsummer Night's Dream
Richard II
Much Ado about Nothing

Volume III

Henry IV, Part One
Henry IV, Part Two
The Merry Wives of Windsor
Hamlet
As You Like It
Henry V

Volume IV

Julius Caesar
Twelfth Night
Troilus and Cressida
All's Well that Ends Well
Measure for Measure
Othello

Volume V

King Lear
Macbeth
Antony and Cleopatra
Pericles
Cymbeline
Coriolanus

Volume VI

Timon of Athens
Titus Andronicus
The Tempest
The Winter's Tale
Henry VIII
The Complete Poems and Sonnets